Quattro® Pro for Windows Handbook

BORLAND BANTAM

Quattro® Pro for Windows Handbook

Mary Campbell

BANTAM BOOKS
NEW YORK • TORONTO • LONDON • SYDNEY • AUCKLAND

Quattro® Pro for Windows Handbook

A Bantam Book/December 1992

Produced by Pageworks, Old Saybrook, Connecticut

Borland and Quattro are registered trademarks of Borland International, Inc.

Throughout this book, tradenames and trademarks of some
companies and products have been used, and no such uses
are intended to convey endorsement of or other affiliations with the book.

ISBN 0-553-37045-6

Published simultaneously in the United States and Canada

Bantam Books are published by Bantam Books, a division of Bantam Doubleday Dell
Publishing Group, Inc. Its trademark, consisting of the words "Bantam Books" and the
portrayal of a rooster, is Registered in the U.S. Patent and Trademark Office and in other
countries. Marca Registrada, Bantam Books, 666 Fifth Avenue, New York, NY 10103.

PRINTED IN THE UNITED STATES OF AMERICA

0 9 8 7 6 5 4 3 2 1

Contents

Foreword

At Borland we are justifiably proud of the continuing success of our Quattro Pro product line. With each new release, Quattro Pro has leaped forward in both functionality and market share. More than one million users have experienced first-hand why Quattro Pro has earned an unprecedented 43 international awards for excellence and top ratings in all major spreadsheet reviews.

Quattro Pro has always been an innovative spreadsheet. It was the first spreadsheet to combine multipage consolidation technology and spreadsheet publishing. Its electronic slide show features and automatic font-building have added graphic presentation capabilities unequalled in any other PC spreadsheet.

Now, Quattro Pro for Windows brings a whole new generation of technology to that innovative tradition. Quattro Pro for Windows was developed from the ground up to take full advantage of the Windows environment, resulting in a radically simplified yet powerful spreadsheet. Using the intuitive new metaphor of Spreadsheet Notebooks, the powerful Object Inspector, and a complete set of user-interface tools, Quattro Pro for Windows combines ease of use with ease of development for sophisticated applications.

Beginning with the first version of this software application, author Mary Campbell has been widely recognized for her spreadsheet mastery and her keen ability to teach thousands of users how to use Quattro Pro easily and productively. With each version of the product, she has led a new and larger group of users to higher levels of spreadsheet skills.

So it is with great pleasure that we have worked with Mary on Quattro Pro for Windows and now endorse her latest book, *Quattro Pro for Windows Handbook*, as the official Borland guide to our powerful software package. Mary's credentials as an expert author in this industry are well-established, and this book from Bantam Electronic Publishing continues her high standards for readability, comprehensiveness, and clarity.

We know that the many detailed examples of usage, as well as the novice-oriented "Getting Started" sections, will help the beginning Quattro Pro user get up to speed and become productive immediately. For the more advanced user, the many tips and shortcuts she provides, and the complete reference summaries of commands, will be of great value.

We are extremely proud of Quattro Pro for Windows and Mary Campbell's *Quattro Pro for Windows Handbook*. Together they will help you achieve maximum spreadsheet productivity under Windows.

Philippe Kahn
CEO, Borland International

Acknowledgments

I would like to thank the following people who contributed so much to the quality of this book:

Gabrielle Lawrence for her work on the entire project. Her many bright ideas and her knowledge of Quattro Pro contributed so much.

Kenzi Sugihara, Steve Guty, Jeff Rian, and Maureen Drexel of Bantam Books for the in-house effort necessary to achieve a quality product.

Nan Borreson at Borland, who helped in many ways throughout the many beta releases.

Art Chavez of Borland, who provided an excellent technical review. Not only were Art's comments helpful, his knowledge of both the product and its users' needs made his advice invaluable.

Elizabeth Reinhardt for capturing and printing the book's figures.

Preface

Quattro Pro for Windows is an exciting spreadsheet product offered by Borland. Although Borland is somewhat of a newcomer to the spreadsheet market, Quattro Pro's features indicate they did the right research to offer a product containing exactly what the spreadsheet user needs, whether you are a novice or an established expert.

Quattro Pro provides a state-of-the-art software solution for users with a wide variety of hardware types. You can run Quattro Pro on any system that you can run Windows 3.0 on with 4MB of RAM and 10MB of free disk space (before installation). Windows as well as Quattro Pro for Windows can use any additional equipment you have installed on your computer, so the more equipment you have, the better Windows and Quattro Pro for Windows will run.

Quattro Pro for Windows features the user-friendly interface available with Windows products. Quattro Pro's features such as Menus on Demand, a new notebook structure for storing your data, SpeedBars for frequently used commands, sharing data between applications, and a Database Desktop make the spreadsheet package powerful as well as easy to use.

WHO SHOULD BUY THIS BOOK

This book is designed as a one-stop source for all the information you need to use Quattro Pro effectively, whether you are a novice or an experienced spreadsheet user. If you are using an earlier release you can use this book, since many of Quattro Pro's features are the same in both releases. Unless a specific release is mentioned, *Quattro Pro* in the book refers to all releases.

We provide plenty of examples to guide the new user through an uneventful transition to this time-saving new product. The experienced user will find that this book continues where others leave off by providing full coverage of more advanced topics and tips. Although the new user may elect to skip these advanced topics initially, he or she will be able to continue learning from this book as his or her experience level grows.

CONVENTIONS

A set of conventions was used throughout this book to offer consistency and make learning easier.

Throughout the book, file names are shown in all capital letters to distinguish them from the surrounding text. Page names are shown in proper case.

Special keys such as ENTER, ESC, and F1 are also shown in capital letters. The ones separated by a space are pressed sequentially: for END HOME, press the key labeled END and then the one labeled HOME. Key combinations separated by a hyphen should be pressed simultaneously: for ALT-F4, hold down the ALT key and press F4.

Each chapter has a Getting Started section to encourage you to try some of the features that the chapter introduces. Examples in the Getting Started sections and elsewhere where an entry is typed are shown in boldface, as in: Type **ABC Company**.

Menu commands are indicated by the underlined letter that you need to type to make a selection. Menu commands are described as commands belonging to specific menus. For example, to quit Quattro Pro for Windows, you can select Exit in the File menu.

Some of the data in the figures use a different font (typeface) or a different magnification level to make it easier to see. If you enter the same data in your own files, they may look different. Font changes are described in Chapter 3 in the discussion of how to change the settings assigned to your data entries. Changing the magnification level by changing a setting of the file is covered in Chapter 12.

ORGANIZATION OF THIS BOOK

This book consists of 14 chapters covering every aspect of Quattro Pro. The chapters proceed from the basics to more sophisticated topics, but you can skip to the advanced topics once you have mastered the preliminary material.

Chapter 1 provides an overview of the Quattro Pro environment and features. These topics include moving in a file, called a *notebook*, using the mouse and keyboard. In this chapter you will learn how to use the help system, the SpeedBar, and the menus and dialog boxes.

Chapter 2 covers basic entries and the rules you must follow for these entries. You will learn how to make corrections to any type of entry and how to build formulas with both pointing and typing methods.

Chapter 3 teaches you how to change the appearance of your entries in a spreadsheet notebook. By selecting a group of cells, called a block, and then using the Menus on Demand, you can change many settings that control how the entry appears. These include fonts, lines, shading, alignment, and data entry limitations.

Chapter 4 shows how you can use Quattro Pro commands to reorganize the entries you have in a notebook. You can use these commands to copy and move entries to adjust your notebooks to fit your changing needs.

Chapter 5 covers several Quattro Pro commands that enter data into your notebook for you. These timesaving commands can generate an evenly spaced series of numbers or can perform an analysis on the entries you already have made into a notebook.

Chapter 6 starts with the basic print features. You will first learn how to obtain a quick printed copy, but then you can master the advanced features such as adding headers and footers, previewing the printed spreadsheet, and custom printing settings that let you produce exactly the output you need.

Chapter 7 covers basic save and open procedures. It also covers the advanced file features like data, reading and writing other file formats, and importing and exporting data.

Chapter 8 covers each of the @functions by type. The chapter includes a brief description of the function types. Each of the functions has a short description and an example showing its use. Where functions are similar, the same example may illustrate several functions.

Chapter 9 covers the basics for creating graphs. Basic features such as setting up a graph, changing most of the settings, putting the graph on the notebook page with your spreadsheet data, and printing graphs are covered here.

Chapter 10 covers the more advanced graphics features. These include slide shows, using the light table, drawing on a graph, importing and exporting graphics, and the Graphs page that a notebook uses to store its graphs.

Chapter 11 covers data management concepts, including sorting, querying, form input, and database statistical functions. This chapter also covers Quattro Pro for Windows new Database Desktop that you can use for advanced data querying between larger databases.

Chapter 12 covers the full range of options for customizing Quattro Pro. You will learn how to change the hardware defaults, color and mouse options, the defaults at startup, and any other default changes that Quattro Pro supports. You will also learn about the User Interface Management System to customize how Quattro Pro appears to its users.

Chapter 13 covers Quattro Pro's shortcuts and keyboard alternative macros. Keyboard alternative macros let you capture Quattro Pro keystrokes and commands and then execute the macro to repeat the keystrokes and commands. A number of sample keyboard macros will help you master the required techniques. You will also learn about techniques for removing errors from macros and for adding SpeedButtons to your notebooks to make macros easy to execute.

Chapter 14 focuses on the automation possibilities offered by the macro command language. A short example showing how each macro command can be used is provided. You will also learn about creating your own dialog boxes and developing your own applications.

Six appendixes provide help on a variety of other features. Appendix A provides detailed instructions for installing Quattro Pro. Appendix B introduces some features of Windows that you will need to use if Quattro Pro for Windows is your first Windows application. Appendix C is a command reference that includes a description of each command. Its organizational structure derives from the Quattro

Pro menu and property selections. Next, Appendix D lists the menu command equivalents and Appendix E lists the menu equivalent commands that you will use as you start designing your own macros. Appendix F displays Quattro Pro menus and the chapter in which each command is discussed.

GETTING THE MOST FROM THIS BOOK

You must assess your current knowledge of Quattro Pro and other spreadsheet products to select the most productive path through this book. If you have little or no knowledge of Quattro Pro or of another spreadsheet, start at the beginning of the book and complete the first eight chapters before attempting to skip around.

If you have used the older release of Quattro Pro or know another spreadsheet product well you will want to take a look at Chapters 1 and 2, and then begin to browse through the other chapters for the features you use most frequently as well as new Quattro Pro options with which you are unfamiliar.

Quattro® Pro for Windows Handbook

1

Starting with Quattro Pro for Windows

Quattro Pro for Windows is a powerful spreadsheet product with features that meet the needs of almost every spreadsheet user. In fact, the many options are so diverse that the average user will not work with all of them unless he or she is designing applications for a large number of other users. To access any of these features you must understand the basics of the Quattro Pro environment.

This chapter takes you on a quick tour of a few of Quattro Pro's major features. It provides the basics you need to understand how to start using Quattro Pro. You will learn how to begin and end a Quattro Pro session as well as how to ask for help at any point. You will also learn about how Quattro Pro organizes its information and how you can move through the files you create with Quattro Pro. And you will learn about dialog boxes, which are how Quattro Pro gets information from you, telling it how to perform a command.

NEW QUATTRO PRO FOR WINDOWS FEATURES

Quattro Pro for Windows has several features that expand its power beyond what you might expect from a spreadsheet package. Quattro Pro is for storing and processing your data, so these features set *how* the data is stored and *how* it is presented.

One of the first features of Quattro Pro for Windows you will see involves how your data is stored. Quattro Pro puts the spreadsheet data into a file called a *notebook*. A notebook in Quattro Pro, like other types of notebooks, can contain many pages. You can rearrange these pages and put any type of data you want on

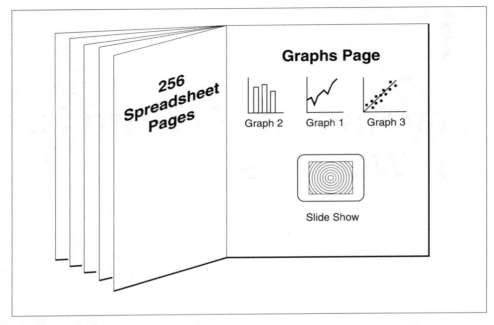

Figure 1.1   Structure of a Notebook

each page. Each of the pages has a name that you can alter. These page names appear as tabs along the bottom of the notebook. A notebook has 256 spreadsheet pages and one page called Graphs. Figure 1.1 shows how the pages in your notebook are stored. The spreadsheet pages are the ones that typically hold what you would think of as spreadsheet data. The Graphs page contains your graphs, slide shows, and dialog boxes. Each notebook is displayed in a window, and you can organize your open windows in any manner you want. Like other document windows in Windows, you can size these windows and position them where you want the data to appear. You can even have two separate windows that show the same notebook. You can have multiple notebooks open so you can see all the data you want at once.

One of Quattro Pro's features is the ease with which you can select what you want with the mouse. You can move and copy entries from one notebook location to another by dropping and dragging the entries with the mouse.

Quattro Pro for Windows has its most frequently needed commands in the SpeedBar. The SpeedBar buttons change depending on the task you are performing. For example, you have different SpeedBars depending on whether you are entering data into the spreadsheet or working on a graph. You can also add a second SpeedBar to the primary one to add even more features. Quattro Pro provides you with six extra SpeedBars now. Figure 1.2 shows the Ready mode SpeedBar with one of Quattro Pro's example SpeedBars, called Second.Bar.

Unlike Quattro Pro for DOS, most of the commands in Quattro Pro for Windows use *dialog boxes*. Dialog boxes prompt for the information the command needs in

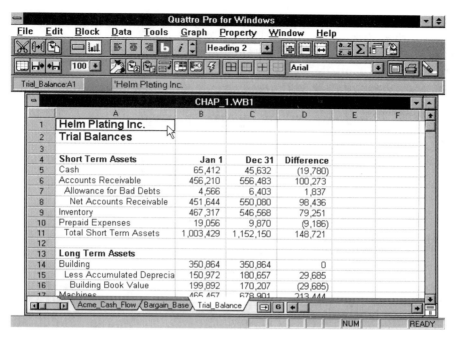

Figure 1.2   Extra SpeedBar Added to Quattro Pro

order to perform the action you want. In Figure 1.3, the Data Sort dialog box lets you tell Quattro Pro all the information needed to sort the data.

Like other Windows applications, Quattro Pro for Windows can use several of Windows' features. You can use Windows' Clipboard to share information between applications and between notebooks. Windows also lets you create DDE links between applications so you can reference data in a word processing document and know that it is always up to date. Also, you can create word processing documents that reference data in your Quattro Pro notebooks. Windows 3.1 also has OLE linking, which lets you put data from another application into the current one without changing its format. For example, you can put a Word for Windows document in your Quattro Pro spreadsheet page, or you can put a section of a Quattro Pro spreadsheet page in your Word for Windows document. In Chapter 7 you will learn about using DDE and OLE links, as well as the Clipboard, to share data.

The different items you work with in Quattro Pro for Windows are called *objects*. Just as you can describe items on your desk, the objects in Quattro Pro also have descriptive features called *properties*. You can look at these properties by inspecting them: Simply point to the object and *right-click* the mouse. Doing this presents the Object Inspector. Only the properties that apply to the selected object are shown. *Right-clicking* the mouse is pressing the right mouse button instead of the left (if you swap the mouse buttons with Windows' Control Panel, you will use the left mouse button). Most of the objects can also be inspected by pressing F12 (OBJECT INSPECTOR) or by selecting a menu command. Figure 1.4 shows the

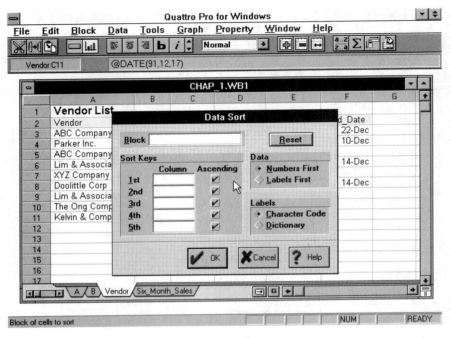

Figure 1.3 Data Sort Dialog Box

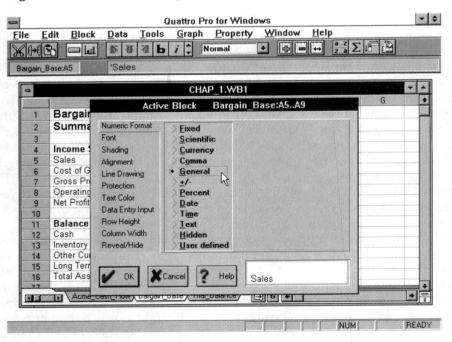

Figure 1.4 Menu on Demand for a Cell

dialog box that you will see when you inspect a cell on a page. In Chapter 3, you will learn about properties for cells and pages; in Chapter 9, you will learn about properties for graphs; and in Chapter 12, you will learn about properties for notebooks and applications.

If you are accustomed to Quattro Pro for DOS, the changeover to Quattro Pro for Windows is easier than you might think. You can change the application's property to display an alternative menu that matches the Quattro Pro for DOS menu. Quattro Pro for Windows also makes it easy to use data from other applications by directly opening and saving data in the most popular spreadsheet, database, and text formats. The ability to use other file formats also allows Quattro Pro to perform macros created with earlier releases of Quattro Pro and with Lotus 1-2-3 Version 2.x.

Besides using spreadsheet pages to hold text and numerical data, you can put graphs and SpeedButtons on a page. A graph on a page is called a *floating* graph. You can put a floating graph next to the data the graph illustrates. SpeedButtons put macros onto a page. When you select a SpeedButton, Quattro Pro performs the macro the SpeedButton is assigned to. Figure 1.5 shows a notebook page containing a floating graph and SpeedButtons. You will learn about floating graphs in Chapters 9 and 10 and SpeedButtons in Chapter 13.

One of the best graphics features of Quattro Pro for DOS is enhanced in Quattro

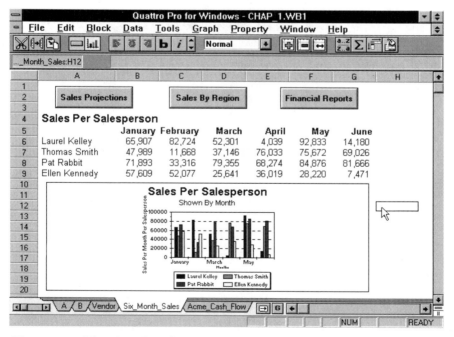

Figure 1.5   Floating Graph and SpeedButtons

Pro for Windows: Graph objects can include effects for filling in an area, such as putting a graphic inside a shape or adding shading to the object. You can import and export graphics into and out of Quattro Pro in many of the most popular formats. As in Quattro Pro for DOS, you can create slide shows, but Quattro Pro for Windows now has a Light Table to help you quickly create professional slide shows with special graphic capabilities.

Quattro Pro for Windows also has new data management features. The Database Desktop lets you create queries for a database using a query-by-example procedure. You can also use the Database Desktop to incorporate data stored on different tables. Figure 1.6 shows the Database Desktop in use. This makes it easy to find the data you want to work with in a database regardless of whether the database is in Quattro Pro, Paradox, or dBASE format. Chapter 11 will show you how Quattro Pro for Windows offers many of the features that you expect from database management applications.

Quattro Pro for Windows continues the customization options available in Quattro Pro for DOS. With the User Interface Management System, you can create SpeedBars, SpeedButtons, Menus, and dialog boxes to fit any application. You can also incorporate @functions and macro functions that are loaded with Quattro Pro to extend the more than 116 functions and many macro instructions Quattro Pro for Windows has.

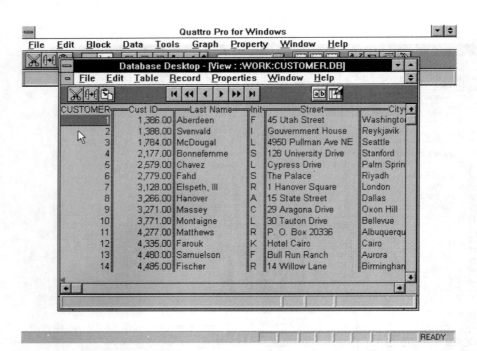

Figure 1.6   Using the Database Desktop to View a Database

HOW YOUR DATA IS ARRANGED IN QUATTRO PRO FOR WINDOWS

Quattro Pro is a spreadsheet product. As in other spreadsheet products, its basic features are to provide an electronic grid for the entry of numbers, labels, and formulas. The page, row, and column arrangement of the entries makes it easy to enter information.

Each Quattro Pro notebook is divided into pages. A notebook has 256 spreadsheet pages and one Graphs page. Every page in the notebook has a name. By default, the spreadsheet pages are named A . . . Z, AA . . . AZ, and so on until page IV. In Chapter 3, you will learn how you can change the name of a page. Naming the pages lets you quickly identify the page you want to use.

The spreadsheet pages are where you enter your data. A page is framed by vertical and horizontal bars showing the names of the rows and the columns. Quattro Pro's column names begin with A and continue to the right through Z, followed by AA to AZ, BA to BZ, and so on, finally ending with IA through IV, as shown by the spreadsheet overview in Figure 1.7. Quattro Pro's row numbers are labeled 1 through 8192. Unlike page names, you cannot change the name of a column or row.

Each entry in a Quattro Pro spreadsheet page is placed at the intersection of a row and a column, called a *cell*. Your entries can consist of labels, numbers, and formulas. In most cases, labels, which can be made up of any characters, describe the entries on the spreadsheet. Numbers represent a measure or a count of some type. Formulas, the real power of the product, allow you to make business, mathematical, and scientific computations. When you want to make an entry in a

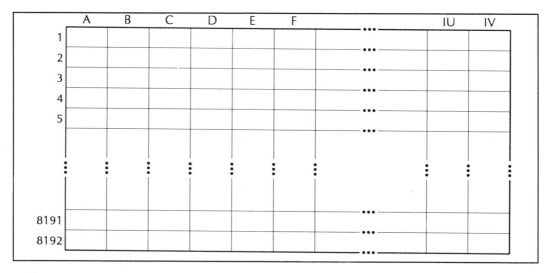

Figure 1.7 Spreadsheet Overview

spreadsheet, move the selector to the desired cell and type the entry. The *selector* is the rectangle that tells you where Quattro Pro will put an entry.

A spreadsheet enables you to update formula results as conditions change. When you change a cell entry that has an impact on a formula, Quattro Pro updates the result for the formula. Because Quattro Pro is aware of the impact of every change, the package is an ideal tool for tasks involving calculations that are updated frequently. Budget projections, profit analysis, aging receivables, and expense computations are tasks that are suited to a spreadsheet. Once you tell Quattro Pro how to perform the necessary calculations for each of these tasks, Quattro Pro can calculate them effortlessly each time a number changes.

In Chapter 2, you will begin to focus on making entries, and to build a set of model construction techniques that can apply to any business problem. Besides simply showing your entries in the spreadsheet, Quattro Pro can display the spreadsheet with many enhancements. This lets you give your calculations a professional appearance. In Chapter 3 you will learn the commands that let you alter the appearance of your spreadsheet data.

Quattro Pro also allows you to link notebooks. This makes it easy to create consolidated reports for several divisions of a company or to transfer forward totals to start the next period. Although this linkage is an advanced feature that will not be covered until Chapter 7, its presence tells you that Quattro Pro is a package that you will not outgrow. You can continue to build more and more sophisticated applications, and Quattro Pro will meet your needs.

STARTING QUATTRO PRO FOR WINDOWS

Starting Quattro Pro for Windows is like starting other Windows applications. After you start Windows, you must select the Quattro Pro for Windows group window in the Program Manager. To select this group window, or any other one, select Window and the group window name from the Window pull-down menu. You can also select the group window by double-clicking it. Next, select the Quattro Pro for Windows icon. You can select this icon by double-clicking it or by pressing the arrow keys until the text below the icon is highlighted and pressing ENTER. Once Quattro Pro is loaded, its application window appears (Figure 1.8). If Quattro Pro for Windows is the first Windows application you have used, you will want to read Appendix B, "Beginning with Windows." In this appendix you will learn basics such as starting applications, switching between applications, and changing the size and position of windows.

When you are finished with Quattro Pro for Windows, you will want to close its application window. Closing Quattro Pro for Windows makes the memory Quattro Pro used available for other applications. To close Quattro Pro for Windows, select Exit from the File menu, press ALT-F4, double-click the application's Control box, or select the application's Control box and Close. The application Control box is the box in the upper left corner, which you can select by clicking or pressing ALT-SPACEBAR.

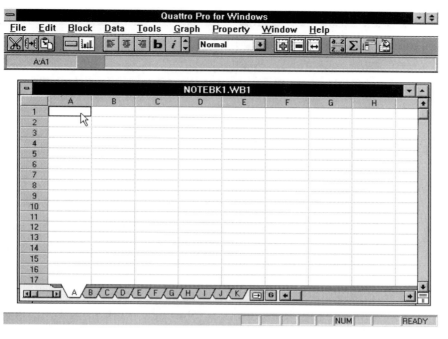

Figure 1.8 Initial Quattro Pro Window

THE QUATTRO PRO WINDOW

The main Quattro Pro window contains a notebook ready for you to start entering spreadsheet data. The Quattro Pro window is divided into several distinct areas: the menu bar, a SpeedBar, an input line, a spreadsheet area, and a status line. The initial window looks like Figure 1.8. The top line in the window contains the application Control box, the title bar containing the name of the application, and the minimize and maximize (or restore) buttons. All Windows applications have the same top line, so you can easily identify each application.

The Menu Bar

The second line in the window contains the menu bar. This line always appears even if you are in the middle of a task during which a menu selection is inappropriate. The bar will change as you switch to working on graphs or dialog boxes. To activate the menu, press ALT: File becomes highlighted to indicate that your selections will activate menu commands. Once you select an item from the menu bar, the menu item's pull-down menu will appear. If you are using a mouse, you can click a menu item in the menu bar, and the pull-down menu for that menu item will appear.

Table 1.1   SpeedBar Buttons

SpeedBar Button	Command or Effect
	Cuts selected data and stores it in the Clipboard
	Copies selected data to the Clipboard
	Pastes selected data from the Clipboard
	Adds a SpeedButton to a page
	Adds a floating graph to a page
	Left aligns selected cells
	Centers selected cells
	Right aligns selected cells
	Boldfaces selected cells
	Italicizes selected cells
	Increases the size of the characters in the selected cells to the next smaller or larger size
Normal	Assigns a style to the selected cells
	Inserts columns, rows, and pages to a notebook
	Deletes columns, rows, and pages from a notebook
	Resizes columns of selected cells to fit the width of the entries in the column
	Sorts the selected cells in ascending order or descending order, SpeedSort Button
	Adds @SUM functions to empty cells to total the values in adjoining cells, SpeedSum Button
	Fills a selected block with numbers based on the entry in the upper left of the block cell, SpeedFill Button
	Applies a predefined format that sets properties in various standard areas of the selected block, SpeedFormat Button

The SpeedBar

Immediately below the menu is the SpeedBar. This bar contains buttons that perform the most frequently used commands. To use one of these commands, you select the spreadsheet block or graph that the command will use and then click the button. These buttons can only be used with the mouse.

The buttons change depending on whether you are editing a cell, or working with a page, a graph, or a dialog box. The features these buttons perform are described in greater detail in later chapters with the commands that they represent. Table 1.1 lists the buttons for working with your spreadsheet data on a page, along with their associated commands.

The Input Line

Quattro Pro's input line is below the SpeedBar. While it usually uses one line, it can use more. It is not used with graphs and dialog boxes.

At a minimum, the input line displays the current cell address. If a cell contains an entry, its contents also display in this area, as shown in Figure 1.9. The input line also displays the contents of a cell when you are editing the cell. Since a cell can contain up to 1022 characters, Quattro Pro will expand the input line to

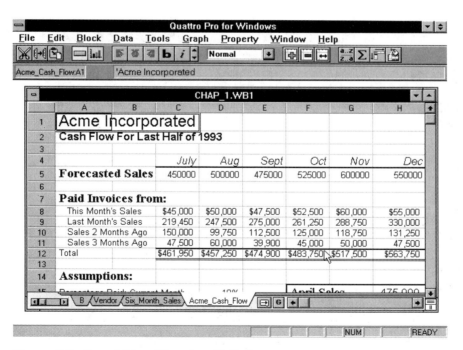

Figure 1.9   Input Line Showing Cell Contents

display the entire cell entry, as shown in Figure 1.10. Once an entry is finalized, Quattro Pro displays as much of the entry as it can fit in a single input line. While you are editing an entry, the input line also contains a ✓ button and an **X** button. The ✓ button finalizes the entry and the **X** button cancels the entry.

The Status Line

The status line, located at the bottom of the screen, contains general information about the current Quattro Pro session. The information that appears is determined by the mode that Quattro Pro is in.

When Quattro Pro is in the EDIT mode, because you pressed F2 (EDIT) or clicked the entry in the input line to modify the current cell's contents, the status line displays the cell contents that appeared previously in the input line. When you are entering an @function, a special type of formula you will learn about in Chapter 8, the status line displays the function syntax indicating the information you should enter. When the menu is activated, the status line contains descriptive information about the highlighted menu selection. Figure 1.11 shows the description Quattro Pro provides for the Paste command in the Edit menu. As the highlighted menu item changes, the information in the status line changes to correspond to the highlighted choice. The status line also displays a description about any SpeedBar button that your mouse is pointing at. In the remaining part of the status line, the

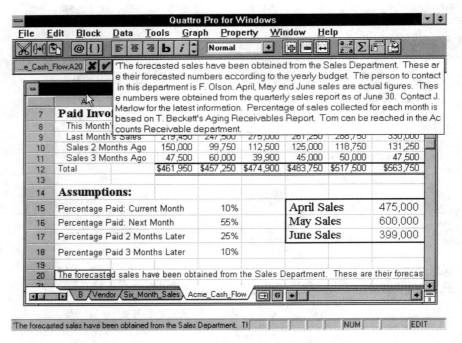

Figure 1.10   Input Line Expanded to Show Long Entry

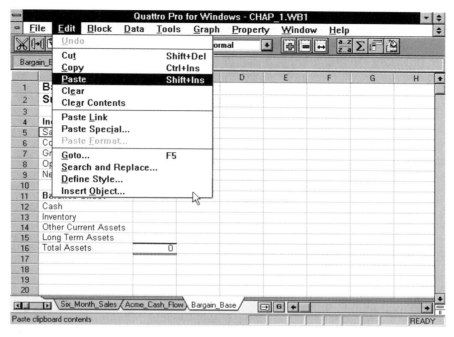

Figure 1.11   Status Line Displaying Information about a Command

status line provides two types of information. The status indicators and the mode indicator display in this area.

STATUS INDICATORS   The status indicator is designed to tell you about Quattro Pro's current state. Some of the indicators tell you that a particular key has been pressed. Others inform you of potential problems or macro activities. Table 1.2 provides a list of Quattro Pro's status indicators.

MODE INDICATORS   The mode indicator is in the last box of the status line. Like the status indicator, it tells you something about the package. The mode indicator is able to tell you exactly what task Quattro Pro is working on and its state of completion. It is a more comprehensive indicator than the status indicator, since it affects everything you attempt to do. Table 1.3 provides a list of Quattro Pro's mode indicators. When you want Quattro Pro to start a new task, the mode indicator must read READY before it can begin.

The Notebook Window Area

The notebook area is the major portion of the Quattro Pro window. It begins below the input line and continues to the status line. This area initially contains one notebook window. The top of the notebook window has its own title bar, Control

Table 1.2   Quattro Pro's Status Indicators

Status Indicator	Meaning
BKGD	Quattro Pro is performing calculations in the background.
CALC	Formulas in the notebook require recalculation. Do not print the spreadsheet with this indicator displayed.
CAP	The CAPS LOCK key is depressed. Pressing the alphabetic keys will result in uppercase letters.
CIRC	One or more spreadsheet formulas contain circular references.
DEBUG	The macro DEBUG feature is invoked. If you execute a macro the debug window appears at the bottom of the screen.
END	Quattro Pro is waiting for you to press an ARROW key, since the END key has been pressed.
EXT	SHIFT-F7 has been pressed to select a block. The next command you enter will use this block.
MACRO	Quattro Pro is executing a macro.
NUM	The NUM LOCK key has been pressed. Entries from a numeric keypad will generate numbers rather than movement commands.
OVR	Quattro Pro will type over characters in entries that you are editing. Overwrite mode is the opposite of insert mode.
REC	Quattro Pro is recording your keystrokes with the macro recorder.
SCR	The SCROLL LOCK key has been pressed. Pressing an arrow key scrolls the spreadsheet in the direction of the arrow.

box, and minimize and maximize (or restore) boxes. Most of the time, the notebook window will contain a spreadsheet page; in Chapter 10, you will learn about using the Graphs page to work with your graphs.

A page in a notebook window is framed by vertical and horizontal bars showing the names of the rows and the columns that are currently visible in the window. The page name appears along with the names of surrounding pages in page tabs at the bottom of the page in the window. At the corner of the row and column border is the Select-All button. When you click this button, you select the entire page. To the right of the page is the vertical scroll bar; below the page on the right side is the horizontal scroll bar. The scroll bar box on each scroll bar indicates the selector's position relative to the area of the page the entries use. Below the notebook window to the left of the page tabs is the Tab scroller. This scroll bar selects the page tabs in the notebook that are visible in the notebook window. To the right of the page tabs is the SpeedTab button; in Chapter 10 you will learn how you can use this button to quickly switch to the Graphs page. To the right of the SpeedTab button is the Group button; in

Table 1.3 Quattro Pro's Mode Indicators

Mode Indicator	Meaning
COPY	You are copying a block with the drag and drop method.
DATE	Quattro Pro processes your current entry as a date or time.
EDIT	You are editing the current cell.
FIND	You can only move to matching records that you ask for using the Query command in the Data menu.
FRMT	You are editing a line that determines how to divide text into smaller pieces.
INPUT	Selector movement is restricted to unprotected cells with the Restrict Input command in the Data menu.
LABEL	Quattro Pro processes your current entry as a label entry.
MOVE	You are moving a block with the drag and drop method.
NAMES	Quattro Pro is displaying block names that you can select.
POINT	Quattro Pro is expecting you to point to a cell or block address.
PREVIEW	You are looking at a preview of a printed document.
READY	Quattro Pro is waiting for you to make a new entry or request.
VALUE	Quattro Pro is processing your current entry as a value entry or a formula.
WAIT	Quattro Pro is busy processing your last request. New requests or entries will not be processed until it has completed this task.

Chapter 3 you will learn how to use it for changing the appearance of several pages while you make changes to a single page.

Quattro Pro displays your notebook data as it will appear when you print it. This is a WYSIWYG display. WYSIWYG stands for what-you-see-is-what-you-get. In several places in the book, the spreadsheet data will use larger fonts than Quattro Pro's defaults for legibility, so the figures may look different from your own Quattro Pro notebooks. The page that appears in the notebook window displays as many columns and rows as can fit in the notebook window. The exact number depends on the font you give to the text in the cells and the settings you use for column widths and row heights.

THE KEYBOARD

Quattro Pro makes effective use of the keyboard, using all the special keys to perform tasks quickly. The location of the special keys will depend on the computer you are using. Figure 1.12 shows an enhanced IBM keyboard. Many IBM-compatible machines have keyboards that are almost identical to this, although a few keys may be in different locations.

Keys for Typing Letters and Numbers

On all PC keyboards, the keys in the center are almost identical to those on a typewriter keyboard. These keys are used for typing letters and numbers into cells. Press any of the alphabetic keys for a lowercase letter. For uppercase letters, you can press the CAPS LOCK key, and note the CAP indicator in the status line. Each letter key pressed will result in a capital letter until you turn the feature off, by pressing the CAPS LOCK key again. Alternatively, press the SHIFT key while you press the letter that you want to see capitalized. To type special symbols such as {, ^, %, :, and #, press the SHIFT key while you press the key that has that special symbol at the top. The CAPS LOCK key will not generate the special symbols shown at the tops of keys, since it is only designed to capitalize letters.

To type numbers, you can use the number keys that are the top row of the main part of the keyboard, or a numeric keypad. The numbers on the numeric keypad are arranged in the same fashion as a 10-key adding machine to make entering numbers quicker. Some numeric keypads are dedicated solely to the entry of numbers. Others require that the NUM LOCK key be pressed to set these keys into their numeric mode. On these keypads, without NUM LOCK depressed, the keys function as *direction* keys (discussed shortly).

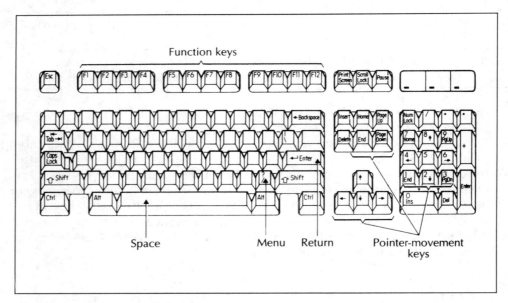

Figure 1.12 Enhanced IBM Keyboard

Function Keys

The function keys are labeled F1 through either F10 or F12 (that is, your keyboard may have 10 or 12 function keys). Quattro Pro has assigned tasks to F1 through F12. Quattro Pro provides a template, which will fit over your function keys, that serves as a quick reminder of what each key does.

Table 1.4 provides a list of the tasks assigned to the function keys. In some cases, one key may perform multiple tasks, depending on whether it is pressed by itself or in combination with the ALT, SHIFT, or CTRL key. For example, pressing F3 when Quattro Pro expects a cell or block address displays a list of the names that have been assigned to blocks of spreadsheet cells. Pressing F3 and the SHIFT key together displays a selection box of macro commands, pressing F3 and the CTRL key together lets you name cells just as you can name pages, and pressing F3 and the ALT key together displays the names of the @functions Quattro Pro provides. The tasks performed by the function keys will be discussed as each new feature is introduced.

One of these function keys helps you move to any spreadsheet cell you want. Press F5 (GOTO) when you want to quickly move to any spreadsheet cell. After you press F5 or select the Goto command in the Edit menu, you can type the cell you want to go to. This is usually the row and column address. You will need to include the page name and a colon, as in A:G10, if the cell you want is not on the current page. You may also need to include the name of the notebook in brackets, as in [NOTEBK1]A:G10, if the cell you want is in a different notebook.

Special Keys

In addition to the function keys, there are other keys on the keyboard whose purpose may not be obvious. Some of these keys affect entries you have typed, others allow you to move around the keyboard, and still others are used in combination with other keys.

DIRECTION KEYS When you first load Quattro Pro, the selector marks your position in cell A1 on page A. To make entries in other cells, you need to move the selector to other locations in the notebook. You can use an ARROW key to move one cell in the direction indicated by the arrow. Other keys also reposition the selector, and work much faster than repeatedly pressing the ARROW keys. Table 1.5 summarizes the effect of each of these keys.

Moving an entire screen at one time is easy. To move a screen to the right, use the CTRL and RIGHT ARROW keys in combination (or press the TAB key). Your view of the spreadsheet will scroll one screen to the right. The CTRL-LEFT ARROW (or SHIFT-TAB) combination scrolls one screen to the left. Moving an entire screen up or down requires only the PGUP or PGDN key. You can move between pages by pressing CTRL-PGUP and CTRL-PGDN.

Table 1.4   Function Key Assignments

Function Key	Action
F1	Help
F2	Edit
F3	Choices or Blocknames
F4	Abs
F5	Goto
F6	Pane
F7	Query
F8	Table
F9	Calc
F10	Menu
F11	Graph
F12	Object Inspector
ALT-F2	Run Macro
ALT-F3	@Functions List
ALT-F4	Quit Quattro Pro
ALT-F5	Group Mode
ALT-F6	Zoom
ALT-F7	Replace Text
ALT-F12	Application Inspector
SHIFT-F2	Debug
SHIFT-F3	Macro List
SHIFT-F5	Speed Tab
SHIFT-F7	Select Block
SHIFT-F12	Window Object Inspector
CTRL-F3	Name Block
CTRL-F4	Close Window
CTRL-F6	Next Window

Table 1.5   Direction Keys

Key Sequence	Action
LEFT ARROW	Moves one cell to the left.
RIGHT ARROW	Moves one cell to the right.
UP ARROW	Moves up one cell.
DOWN ARROW	Moves down one cell.
SHIFT-TAB or CTRL-LEFT ARROW	Moves one screen to the left.
TAB or CTRL-RIGHT ARROW	Moves one screen to the right.
PGUP	Moves up one screen.
PGDN	Moves down one screen.
HOME	Moves to A1.
END	Status indicator is set to END; Quattro Pro awaits pressing of an arrow key.
END HOME	Selector moves to the lower right cell in the non-blank part of notebook page.
END and ARROW	Moves to the next cell with an entry in the arrow's direction if the current cell is empty, or moves to the last entry in the arrow's direction before an empty cell if the current cell contains an entry.
CTRL-HOME	Moves to A1 in first page of active notebook.
CTRL-PGUP	Moves to the previous page.
CTRL-PGDN	Moves to the next page.

The END and HOME keys warrant special attention, since they can save considerable time in a large spreadsheet. Pressing the HOME key always returns the selector to A1 of the current page, which is known as the HOME position. Pressing the END key and then the HOME key positions the selector in the lower-rightmost cell in the area used on the spreadsheet. In a spreadsheet with the rightmost entry in K1 and the bottommost entry in A40, pressing END and then HOME places the selector in K40.

Unlike the HOME key, the END key is never used alone. If you press END, the END indicator is shown in the status line. Quattro Pro waits for you to press an ARROW key, and then it moves the selector in the direction indicated. The distance traveled depends on the contents of the current cell and other entries in the direction indicated. If you press the END key and then the DOWN ARROW key when the current cell contains an entry, Quattro Pro moves down to the next nonblank cell that is above an empty cell. If the current cell is blank, Quattro Pro moves to the next cell containing an entry in the direction indicated.

The direction keys assume different functions when used in EDIT mode or while using the menu. The actions of these keys in other modes will be explained in the next section.

EDITING KEYS   There are some special keys that operate only for editing entries, and some direction keys that take on new functions if used while you are editing. Editing entries means modifying cells in a spreadsheet or changing a setting in a text box (such as the information that you want printed at the beginning of a report). When you edit a cell, Quattro Pro places the cell's contents in the input line and uses an insertion point to indicate your position within the cell for editing purposes. An *insertion point* looks like an I within an entry. Moving the insertion point is different from moving the selector. Understanding the range of options for editing keys will make error correction easy. Several of these editing keys are listed in Table 1.6.

The BACKSPACE key performs the same function when you are editing as it does when you are typing an entry: It deletes the previous character. In EDIT mode, you can use BACKSPACE to remove a character anywhere in your entry if

Table 1.6   Editing Keys

Key Sequence	Action
BACKSPACE	Deletes the character to the left of the insertion point.
DEL	Deletes the character to the right of the insertion point.
HOME	Moves to the first character in the entry.
END	Moves to the last character in the entry.
INS	Switches between Insert (INS) and Overwrite (OVR) mode.
CTRL-BACKSPACE	Deletes the entire entry.
CTRL-\	Deletes all characters to the right of the insertion point.
TAB or CTRL-RIGHT ARROW	Moves five characters to the right.
SHIFT-TAB or CTRL-LEFT ARROW	Moves five characters to the left.

you first position the insertion point to the right of the character you want to remove.

The DEL key removes the character that is just above the insertion point. If you want to remove all characters in an entry, you can press CTRL-BACKSPACE. You can also remove part of an entry by moving the insertion point to the first character you want to remove and pressing CTRL-\ (backslash). This removes all characters from the insertion point's position to the end of the entry.

While you are in EDIT mode, the HOME key moves the insertion point to the first character in the entry. The END key moves the insertion point to a position immediately after the last character in the entry.

The INS key toggles between Insert and Overwrite. Initially when you enter EDIT mode, Quattro Pro is set to insert any new characters you type to the left of the insertion point. By moving the insertion point with the ARROW keys, you can add characters at any location within the entry. Pressing the INS key toggles to Overwrite mode, so that each character typed replaces a character in the current entry. The status line will display OVR, and the insertion point indicates where the character will be replaced. To begin inserting characters again, press the INS key to toggle to Insert mode. Whenever you complete an entry, Quattro Pro toggles to the Insert mode.

OTHER SPECIAL KEYS The remaining special keys Quattro Pro uses provide different features. Some change the meanings of keys, and others remove characters from an entry. Some of these keys are listed in Table 1.7.

There are three special keys that lock other keyboard keys to perform a specific task. These keys are NUM LOCK, SCROLL LOCK, and CAPS LOCK. NUM LOCK is used to lock the numbers on dual-function keys in place. With NUM LOCK on, these keys enter only numbers; with NUM LOCK off, these keys act as directional keys. SCROLL LOCK changes the way information scrolls off the screen. With SCROLL LOCK off, pressing the DOWN ARROW key does not scroll information off the screen until you are in the last row on the screen. With SCROLL LOCK on, each row you move down scrolls a row at the bottom of the screen. CAPS LOCK

Table 1.7   Special Keys

Key	Action
CAPS LOCK	Makes typed letters appear in uppercase.
NUM LOCK	Toggles the numeric keypad between numbers and directional keys.
SCROLL LOCK	Determines whether the page is scrolled when the selector moves.
SHIFT	Selects the cells you point to with the Arrow Keys or Mouse while holding down this key.

produces an uppercase letter when you press any alphabet key. CAPS LOCK does not result in entry of the special symbols at the tops of keys; you must use the SHIFT key to access these symbols.

USING A MOUSE WITH QUATTRO PRO

A mouse is a hand-held pointing device. Quattro Pro automatically knows if a mouse is installed on your system. For a mouse to be installed on your system, it must be physically attached, and the software that tells your operating system to use a mouse must be running. Installing Windows usually installs the mouse software as well.

A mouse points by moving across either a special surface called a mouse pad or any other flat surface such as a desk. (A trackball mouse has a ball that you move rather than moving the mouse.) As you move the mouse, Quattro Pro moves the pointer on the screen accordingly. Although a mouse may have up to three buttons, Quattro Pro uses only two. The default for the main button is the left button. Throughout this book, this button is referred to as the mouse button. When you press the mouse button, it selects whatever the pointer is on. This is called *clicking*. You will also use the right button for using the Object Inspector. This is called *right-clicking*. You can use the mouse to make menu selections, move to a position in the spreadsheet, or select a group of cells. Throughout this book, directions for using a mouse are included along with the directions for using the keyboard. In some cases, tasks can only be completed with a mouse because the feature does not have a keyboard equivalent. A mouse can take advantage of the SpeedBar, which appears above or to the right of the spreadsheet. The SpeedBar makes frequently used commands available by clicking a button.

With a mouse, you have other options for moving in a spreadsheet. When you see the cell you want, click it and that becomes the active cell. The arrows that appear at either end of the horizontal and vertical scroll bars move the screen one cell in the direction of the arrow. Clicking the scroll bar on either side of the scroll bar box shifts the page display one window's worth of rows or columns in the selected direction. You can also switch to another page by clicking the page tab of the page you want. If you do not see the page tab you want, click the Tab scroller to shift the page tab display forward or backward in the notebook. This scroller works much like the other scroll bars: You can click the arrows of the Tab scroller to shift the page tabs displayed one page at a time, or click either side of the box in the Tab scroller's scroll bar to shift the page tabs displayed several pages at a time.

When you are editing an entry, you can start the EDIT mode by clicking the entry in the input line as well as by pressing F2. You can move the insertion point in the entry with the mouse to select where you will add or remove characters. To move the insertion point, click where you want the insertion point positioned.

USING THE MENU

For most tasks other than entering data, you need to access the commands in Quattro Pro's menus. You can activate the menu by pressing ALT or by clicking the menu item in the menu bar you want. All of Quattro Pro's menus, except the Object Inspector, branch from the menu items in the menu bar. When you press ALT, the File menu item is highlighted. You can select this menu item or one of the other items. To select a menu item, use the LEFT or RIGHT ARROW to move to the item, and press ENTER. To select a menu item with the mouse, point to it and click. Another method is to type the underlined letter of the menu item you want. For example, if you want to see the Tools pull-down menu, type **T**. If you change your mind, press ESC until you are at the menu level you want or you have returned to the READY mode. As you can see, this book underlines the same letters as the menu so you can quickly see which letter to type to select the menu item you want. When you click a menu item in the menu bar, that menu item's pull-down menu displays just as if you used ALT and the underlined letter. For example, if you click Tools in the menu bar, Quattro Pro activates the Tools pull-down menu. If you want to leave a menu, you can either press ESC on the keyboard or click outside of the pull-down menu.

While the menu is active, the status line will display information about the highlighted menu selection. Once the menu is activated, you are ready to make selections from the pull-down menu and to use dialog boxes which vary by the command you select.

If you are accustomed to Quattro Pro for DOS, you can display an alternative menu to make menu selections using the commands you are already familiar with as described later in the chapter.

Menu Options

After a menu item from the menu bar is selected, Quattro Pro displays a pull-down menu box for the menu item. Figure 1.13 shows the File pull-down menu. If a command has a shortcut, such as using F5 for the Goto command in the Edit menu, it appears on the right side of the menu item. To select a menu item using the keyboard, press the UP or DOWN ARROW to move to the item you want, and press ENTER. You can also type the underlined letter. To use a mouse, click the menu item in the pull-down menu. For example, if you want to exit Quattro Pro, you can press ALT for the menu, type **F** for File, and **X** for Exit. You can also click File and Exit. You can press HOME or END to move to the first or last menu item in the pull-down menu box. If you decide that you want to see the pull-down menu for another menu item in the menu bar, you can use the LEFT or RIGHT ARROW key to switch pull-down menu boxes displayed, or click the desired menu item. If you change your mind, press ESC until you are at the menu level you want or until you have returned to the READY mode. If you want to leave the

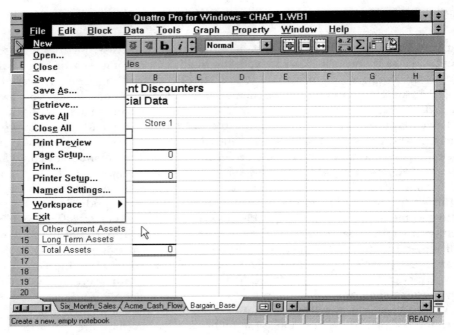

Figure 1.13   File Pull-Down Menu

menu system altogether, press CTRL-BREAK. You can also click outside of the menu area.

Throughout the book, each menu selection is described as a menu command in a pull-down menu command. For example, to open an existing notebook you would select Open in the File menu. You can use the mouse or the keyboard to make your selection. Since the results of making the menu selections are the same, use whichever method is most convenient.

Next to each of the items in the pull-down menu are characters that indicate what will happen when you select that menu item. For example, Exit in the File menu has nothing after it. If you select Exit in the File menu, Quattro Pro will immediately perform the command. The command Workspace in the File menu has a triangle after it. This triangle indicates that if you select Workspace, Quattro Pro will display a cascading menu that shows other menu selections. Figure 1.14 shows the cascading menu for Names in the Block menu. In this cascading menu, the Reset command will be performed as soon as you select it, but the other commands, like many of Quattro Pro's commands, have ellipses (three dots) that indicate that Quattro Pro will display a dialog box before the command is performed. Quattro Pro and other Windows applications use dialog boxes to provide the information the program needs. Finally, sometimes commands in a pull-down menu may appear in a different color. These commands are dimmed to indicate that you cannot select them at the current time.

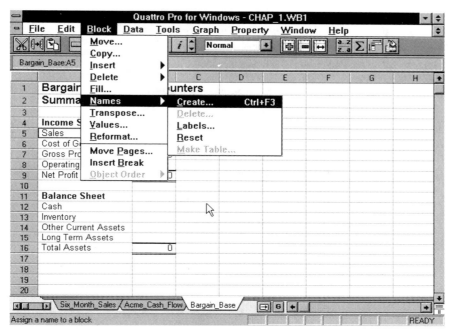

Figure 1.14 Cascading Menu next to a Pull-Down Menu

Using Dialog Boxes

A dialog box lets you give Quattro Pro the different pieces of information the program needs to perform a command. Each command has different requirements. For example, if you want to open a file, Quattro Pro needs to know the name of the file and where the file is located. When you sort a group of cells, you must tell Quattro Pro which cells to sort and how you want them sorted. While the type of information you will provide for a command is described as the command is introduced, the general way you will work with dialog boxes is outlined here.

The dialog boxes in Quattro Pro are like the dialog boxes you use in other Windows applications. A dialog box contains different components. These are illustrated in Figure 1.15. This sample dialog box does not belong to a specific Quattro Pro command but shows the different features you will find in dialog boxes. You can select the different components by clicking them or by pressing ALT and the underlined letter.

Text boxes let you type entries, which can be text, numbers, or selections of cells from a notebook. The information that you enter into the text box depends on what the command uses. The text before the text box describes the type of information you should enter. When the text box requires a selection of cells, you can press an arrow key or point to a cell in the notebook. Quattro Pro will shrink the

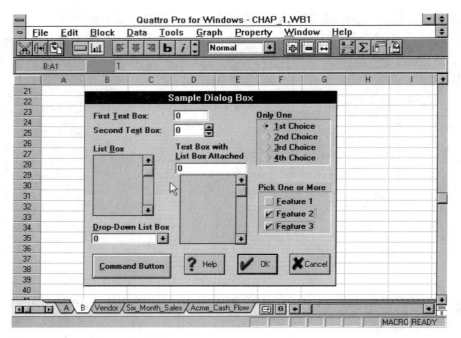

Figure 1.15   Sample Dialog Box

dialog box to make it easier to select the area of the notebook you want to use. When you release the mouse or press ENTER, the original dialog box with the selected block in the text box reappears.

Another special type of text box has arrows on the right side, as in the second text box shown in Figure 1.15. For the entry in this text box, usually a number, you have two options: You can either type the entry in the text box, or you can click the arrows to increase or decrease the amount entered in the text box.

Sometimes a text box has a list box attached. In this case, you can type the entry in the text box, or you can select an entry in the list box and that entry will be entered in the text box. List boxes without a text box only let you select an entry from the list. With some list boxes, double-clicking an item both selects the item in the list and finalizes the command. For example, to open a file, you can select (double-click) the file name in the list of files and Quattro Pro will close the dialog box and open the file for you. You can use the scroll bar on the side of the list box to change the portion of the list that appears in the box. The scroll bar only appears in the list box when you have more items in the list than can fit in the area assigned for the list box.

A special type of list box is a drop-down list box. This initially appears as a text box with a down arrow to the side of it as in the Drop-Down List Box in Figure 1.15. As with a text box with a list box attached, you can make your selection by typing an entry in the text box or by using the list box. To make the list box display, click the down arrow at the side of the text box or press ALT-DOWN ARROW. With any sort of list box, you can move through the list by typing the beginning characters of the list item you want.

Dialog boxes also have *radio buttons*, also called option buttons, which let you select one of several choices. In the dialog box in Figure 1.15, you can only select one of the four choices: 1st Choice, 2nd Choice, 3rd Choice, and 4th Choice. When you select one radio button within a group, you are *unselecting* the previously selected choice. Often radio buttons are put into groups just as these four are put in the group labeled Only One. A dialog box may have more than one group of radio buttons, but you can select only one radio button from *each* of the groups.

Another type of selection you can make in a dialog box is a check box. Feature 1, Feature 2, and Feature 3 are check boxes. A check box is an on/off switch for the feature described by its text. Unlike radio buttons, any number of check boxes in a group can be selected. When a check box is selected, the box is labeled with a ✓ and the feature the check box represents is turned on. When a check box is cleared, the box is empty and the check box's feature is turned off.

The last kind of option in a dialog box is a button or command button. These buttons perform some action. For example, when you are printing a notebook, you can select command buttons, so Quattro Pro shows the notebook on the screen as it will appear when printed. Other command buttons may display other dialog boxes. Most dialog boxes contain the Help, OK, and Cancel buttons that you see in Figure 1.15. The Help button displays help information for the dialog box you are using. Quattro Pro's Help system is described later in the chapter. The OK button finalizes the dialog box selections and performs the command. The Cancel button cancels the command and returns you to READY mode. Most of the time the OK button has a heavier outline than the other command buttons, as it does in Figure 1.15. This extra outline indicates that when you press ENTER while using the dialog box, Quattro Pro will select the OK button even if you are working on a different part of the dialog box.

The Quattro Pro for DOS

If you are accustomed to using Quattro Pro for DOS, you may want to make an alternative menu available. An alternative menu lets you perform Quattro Pro for Windows commands using the names of commands familiar to you from these programs. Initially Quattro Pro for Windows is set to activate the Quattro Pro for Windows menu bar when you type a / (slash), but you can change it to display a menu that looks more like the Quattro Pro for DOS. To make this change, select Application from the Property menu. This displays the application's Object Inspector. The dialog box contains the different properties you can select for the application. Press CTRL-PGDN three times or click Macro to select the Macro property. As you select different properties on the left side of the dialog box, the right side of the dialog box changes to match the types of selections you can make for the property. When Macro is selected, you can press ALT-S to select the Slash

Key drop-down list box, press the DOWN ARROW until Quattro Pro—DOS is selected, and press ENTER twice. Alternatively, you can click the down arrow next to the text box, then click Quattro Pro—DOS and the OK button. Figure 1.16 shows the Quattro Pro for DOS menu invoked with a / after making this change. Pressing ALT always activates Quattro Pro for Windows' menu system.

USING HELP

Quattro Pro's on-line help provides a quick source of information. At any time, you can press the F1 (HELP) key to see information pertaining to your current menu selection or another entry. Many of the dialog boxes also contain a Help button that you can select to to see information about the dialog box you are using. The Help window becomes the top window on your Windows desktop. You can switch back to Quattro Pro just as you would switch to any other Windows application. Since Windows only allows one help window open at a time, when you open the Help window from Quattro Pro, any other help window is closed. Figure 1.17 shows a sample Help window. Using Help for Quattro Pro in Windows is just like using Help in any other Windows application. Some of the Help window features depend on whether you are using Windows 3.0 or 3.1.

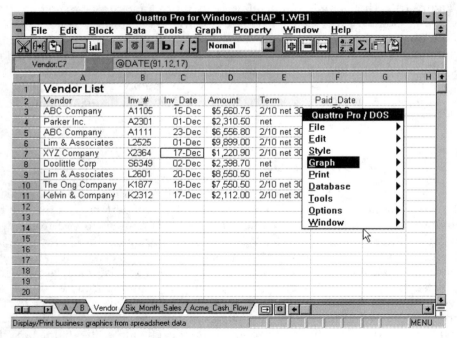

Figure 1.16   Quattro Pro for DOS Menu

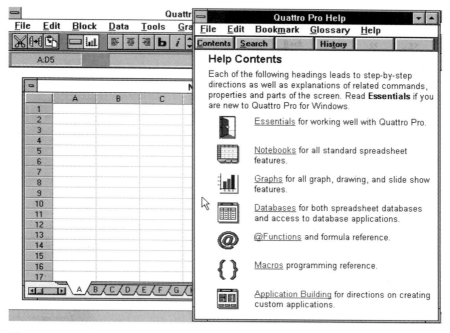

Figure 1.17 Sample Help Window

The selectable options on the Help screen are referred to as *topics*. Selecting any one of them changes the information in the Help window to the topic you selected. You can select a topic by clicking it, or by pressing TAB until the one you want is highlighted and then pressing ENTER. Some of the topics may use several windows that you can switch to by pressing PGUP and PGDN or clicking the scroll bar on the side. You can select buttons in a Help window by clicking them or typing the underlined letter. You can return to a prior Help screen by selecting the Back button. You can also select the Search button and then select one of the topics listed. You can type the name of the topic you want, to quickly move through the list. When you want to return to the basic help information for Quattro Pro, you can select the Contents button. If you want to switch between different help topics you have looked at before, you can select the History button and the help topic you want to display (even for a different application).

When you are finished using the help information, you can press ALT-F4, double-click its Control box, select Close from its Control box menu, or select Exit from the File menu. Since Quattro Pro for Windows and the help information are in different windows, you can leave the Help window open, but you may want to close it to prevent running out of system resources. The Help window will also close when you close Quattro Pro for Windows.

GETTING STARTED

All the chapters in this book end with a special hands-on section. These sections give you a set of short exercises for the material in the chapter. While the exercises do not cover all the Quattro Pro features covered in the chapter, they do provide a starting point from which you can try the more advanced features.

To try some of the keystrokes introduced in the chapter, follow these steps:

1. At the Program Manager, press ALT and type a **W** for Window and the number next to Quattro Pro for Windows (or the number next to the group in which you have placed Quattro Pro for Windows). If you can see the group window or its icon, click the window or double-click the group icon. This opens the Quattro Pro for Windows' program group, or the group in which you placed Quattro Pro for Windows. Next, either press the arrow keys until the Quattro Pro for Windows icon is selected and press ENTER, or double-click the Quattro Pro for Windows icon. Notice how the file name, in this case NOTEBK1.WB1, appears in the notebook window's title line. You may also notice that status indicators, such as CAP, NUM, or SCR if the CAPS LOCK, NUM LOCK, or SCROLL LOCK keys, have been pressed.

2. Press ALT to invoke the menu. Quattro Pro uses this area for menu item descriptions.

3. Type an **F** for File. Selecting a menu item from the menu bar displays the pull-down menu for the menu item.

4. Press the RIGHT ARROW to display the menu for Edit. You can use the LEFT ARROW and RIGHT ARROW to change the pull-down menu displayed.

5. Press the UP ARROW three times, and ENTER. When you press UP ARROW on the first menu item, the highlight wraps around to the bottom menu item. When you press ENTER, you are selecting the highlighted menu item.

6. Press F1 (HELP) to display the Edit | Search and Replace help information, which describes using this command to find data in your notebook.

7. Click the Help window's Control box and then click Close or press ALT-F4 to close the Help window. When you leave the Help screen, you return to the Quattro Pro window. When you switch to another application window, you leave the menu in Quattro Pro. If you are in a dialog box when you switch out of Quattro Pro to another application, the dialog box remains on the screen. Press ESC to leave the Search/Replace dialog box.

8. Click File and New or press ALT and type an **F** and an **N**. Quattro Pro adds another new notebook to your Quattro Pro application window. You can tell Quattro Pro will perform this command as soon as you select New because the File pull-down menu does not display any characters after New.

9. Click Edit and then Search and Replace or press ALT and type an **E** and an **S**. Quattro Pro shows the dialog box you must complete before Quattro Pro performs the Search and Replace command to find selected entries in your notebook. In this dialog box, you can see three text boxes, three radio buttons under Look In, three check boxes under Options, and seven command buttons (Next, Previous, Replace, Replace All, Reset, Close, and Help). Click the Close button or press ESC to leave this dialog box without performing the command.

10. Double-click the Control box in the Quattro Pro title bar or select Exit in the File menu to leave Quattro Pro. If you have made entries in the notebook, Quattro Pro will prompt you to see if you want to save your changes.

2

Basic Spreadsheet Entries

Mastering spreadsheet entries is the most important first step you can take with Quattro Pro. Every spreadsheet you create consists of the same types of entries. With these basic entries, you can create financial projections, supply the data needed for data-management features of the package, or complete the necessary entries on the spreadsheet for the creation of Quattro Pro graphs. Your time investment in mastering the basics of each type of Quattro Pro entry provides benefits in everything else you do with the package.

MAKING ENTRIES ON THE SPREADSHEET

In Chapter 1, you learned how Quattro Pro's spreadsheet is organized into pages, rows, and columns. Each intersection of a page, a row, and a column forms a unique location referred to as a cell. The location of every cell is uniquely identified by its cell address, consisting of the cell's page immediately followed by its column and row number (for example, A:A1, M:Z10, and IV:AX5000). If you tell anyone familiar with spreadsheets that an entry is stored in B:A10, they know to look at the intersection of column A and row 10 on page B to find the data. Initially most of your entries will be on the first page, page A. When you do not specify a page, Quattro Pro automatically assumes you want the current page.

Although you can make an entry in any cell on the Quattro Pro spreadsheet, you normally will want to organize your entries to make them easy to read and understand. Figure 2.1 displays product sales by month with the data neatly arranged to make it easy to find information quickly. Cell entries strewn about on the spreadsheet do not meet this objective, even though Quattro Pro does not prevent you from making entries that way.

Each entry you make on the spreadsheet uses some of the memory available in your system. Since all spreadsheet entries must be stored in memory, the number

33

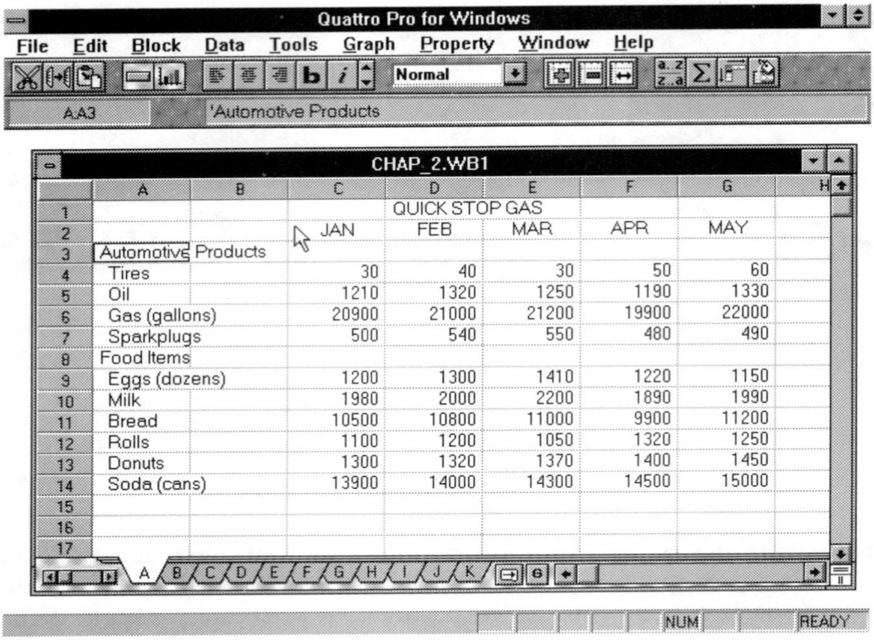

Figure 2.1 Spreadsheet Displaying Product Sales by Month

of cells that you are able to use on any spreadsheet depends on the average length of the entries you are making and the amount of memory in your system. The amount of memory your system has also affects the number of possible entries. Quattro Pro uses efficient memory-management techniques so that the location of your entries on the spreadsheet does not affect the amount of memory used. You do not have to put all of the information on the same page. Use the separate pages in a notebook to organize your data. Each of the pages can contain different types of data. Plan how you want to organize the data you place in a notebook ahead of time and you will save yourself frustration later by performing less reorganization, and also making it easier to find the data you want to use.

Before you can start a new spreadsheet entry, the mode indicator in the status line must read READY as shown in Figure 2.1. The READY mode indicates that Quattro Pro is ready to allow you to begin a new activity (for example, a cell entry). If the mode indicator displays another mode, you must take some action to return the indicator to READY mode before Quattro Pro allows you to make an entry. This action may be as simple as pressing ESC to back out of a menu or completing your specifications for an activity. Once you have started your entry, you can continue if the indicator shows EDIT, LABEL, or VALUE, since these indicator values are also acceptable after an entry has been started. In these modes, some of the buttons on the SpeedBar change to buttons that are more appropriate when you are creating and editing entries. For example, the SpeedBar contains buttons such as @ and { } to add functions and macro instructions to a cell entry. You will learn more about functions and macro instructions in cell entries in Chapters 8 and 13, respectively.

Entry Types

Quattro Pro supports two basic types of entries, label entries and value entries. John Smith, 34 North Ave., 216-89-6754, and AX-56-7890 are examples of label entries. In each case, the entry contains at least one text character, distinguishing it from a value entry. The entry 216-89-6754 consists of numbers and dashes, so Quattro Pro will not treat it as a label unless you take some special action. If it is entered as shown, Quattro Pro performs two subtraction operations and displays the result. To have Quattro Pro display the number as you entered it, you need to tell Quattro Pro to treat it as a label by entering **'216-89-6754**. The apostrophe at the beginning tells Quattro Pro that your entry must be treated as a label.

Value entries are numbers that are designed to be used in calculations. You can enter either numeric constants like **57, 89765,** or **-.0987865** or formulas like **+B2/B3** or **+D11*(B2+B3)** as Quattro Pro value entries. Dates and times are special types of number entries. You will learn more about them later in the chapter.

Quattro Pro assesses the type of data you intend to place in a cell by the first character you type. If the first character you type is a text character, Quattro Pro treats the cell as a label, and the mode indicator in the bottom right corner of the screen immediately changes to LABEL, as shown in Figure 2.2. When you finalize the entry, Quattro Pro will add a label indicator at the beginning of the cell. If the first character you type is a numeric character, Quattro Pro sets the mode indicator to VALUE. Once Quattro Pro has decided that the cell contains a value or a label, you have only two choices for changing it: (1) You can clear the cell and start your entry again, or (2) you can edit the cell and add or remove the label indicator.

You control the location at which you make an entry by positioning the selector before you begin typing. As you make an entry into a cell, Quattro Pro displays the characters you type in the input line at the top of the screen; the characters do not appear in the designated cell until you have finalized your entry. Figure 2.2 shows an entry being made in cell A2. You can verify where the entry will be stored by checking the location of the selector on the screen, or the cell address displayed in the input cell indicator to the left of the input line.

You can finalize the entry of a number or a label by pressing ENTER or any of the direction keys such as the arrow keys or PGUP and PGDN. You can also finalize the cell entry by clicking the ✓ in the input line. Another method of finalizing the entry is clicking another cell, which both finalizes the entry and moves to the cell you have selected. A formula can be finalized by pressing ENTER or clicking the ✓ in all situations. Depending on the formula and the method used for building it, you can finalize some formulas by pressing the arrow keys. Once finalized, the entry is displayed in the cell designated by the selector during entry. The input line also displays the contents of the cell. If you build your formulas by

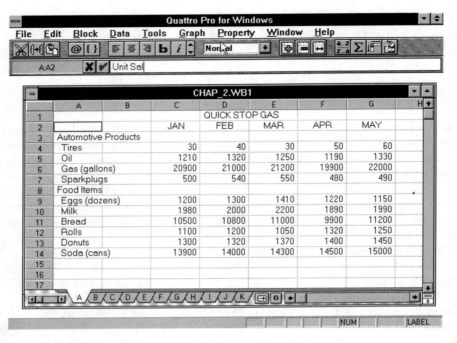

Figure 2.2   Quattro Pro Ready for Data Entry in Cell

pointing to cell addresses rather than typing them, you will not be able to finalize the formulas by moving with the arrow keys.

Making Corrections

Quattro Pro provides many different options for correcting data entry mistakes. The tactic you use depends on the length of the entry, the extent of the change, and whether the entry has been finalized. You can correct an entry that has not been finalized by pressing the BACKSPACE key to delete the previous character. If the mistake affects the entire entry, you can eliminate all the characters entered by pressing ESC, CTRL-BREAK, or CTRL-BACKSPACE. You can also click the X in the input line. The **X** is equivalent to pressing ESC or CTRL-BREAK.

To make a subtle change to an entry that has not been finalized, the BACK-SPACE key is too destructive. A better approach is to edit the cell by switching to EDIT mode. You can start EDIT mode by pressing F2 (EDIT). You can also enter the EDIT mode by selecting the cell, and clicking the cell entry in the input line. The EDIT mode allows you to use the LEFT and RIGHT ARROW keys to move within the entry. With a mouse, you can click the characters you want to edit to move the insertion point to that position. You can use the BACKSPACE more selectively by positioning the insertion point in the entry before pressing the

BACKSPACE key. You can also use other keys, such as the DEL key (which deletes the character at the insertion point), CTRL-\ (which removes all characters from the insertion point's position to the end of the line), the HOME key (which moves the insertion point to the front of the entry), the END key (which moves the insertion point to the end of the entry), and the INS key (which toggles between Insert and Overstrike).

Another option for editing a cell is to select characters and then subsequently to move or copy them. You can select characters by dragging the mouse over them in the input line. To remove these characters, click the Cut button in the SpeedBar or press DEL. You can also click the Copy button in the SpeedBar, so you have a copy of them ready to put in another location. When the insertion point is located where you want to insert the characters you have cut or copied, click the Paste button in the SpeedBar.

Figure 2.3 provides an example of the entry in A3 being edited to correct a spelling mistake. After starting EDIT mode by pressing F2 (EDIT) or clicking the entry in the input line, move the insertion point to just before the first d. Press DEL, type **t**, and then finalize the entry by clicking the ✓ or pressing ENTER.

Once an entry is finalized, you cannot use the BACKSPACE key to make corrections, since BACKSPACE does not have an effect on a finalized entry. You can type a new entry for a cell, replacing its current entry. You can use the edit technique just described to make a less extensive change to the cell entry. Or, you

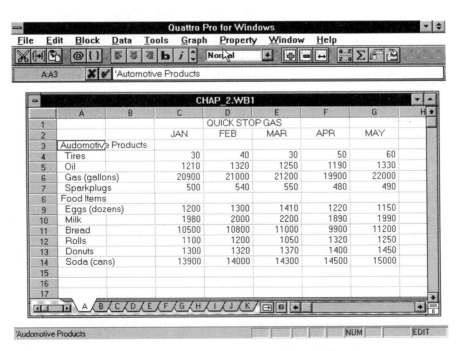

Figure 2.3 Cell Entry Edited to Correct Spelling Mistakes

can erase the current cell by pressing the DEL key or click the Cut button in the SpeedBar.

ENTERING LABELS

Label entries serve several purposes in Quattro Pro. You use them to add descriptive information to a spreadsheet. Without label entries, your numbers and formulas appear as a sea of value entries with no apparent meaning. By adding the account names, months of the year, or other descriptive information as labels, your colleagues can better understand your spreadsheet entries.

Label entries also supply character information when you use Quattro Pro's data-management features. A column of employee names, addresses, or social security numbers contains label entries.

The macro features of Quattro Pro allow you to record keystrokes and commands to automate Quattro Pro tasks using label entries. In Chapters 13 and 14, you will learn that label entries are required in all cells that are part of a Quattro Pro macro.

Following the Rules

Quattro Pro has a certain discipline that must be followed when entries are made on the spreadsheet. The rules that Quattro Pro follows for label entries are summarized in the box "Rules for Label Entries."

You can place your label entry anywhere on the spreadsheet. It is the first character, not the location, that causes Quattro Pro to recognize your entry as a

---

Rules for Label Entries

1. Label entries must begin with a label indicator, a space, an alphabetic character, or a special symbol other than @, ., $, +, −, (,), #, or /.

2. Label entries cannot exceed 1022 characters.

3. Labels wider than the current cell width borrow space from empty cells to the right for display purposes. If these labels are printed and the cells that they borrow space from are not included in the spreadsheet area to print, the printed labels are truncated.

4. The ' label indicator left-aligns the label entry, " right-aligns the entry, and ^ centers the entry.

5. An entry that starts with a label character or indicator is treated as a label even if it also contains numbers.

label. If your first character is anything other than the numeric digits 0 through 9 or one of several symbols, (., +, –, (,), $, #, @, /), Quattro Pro recognizes the character as the beginning of a label entry.

The default width for a spreadsheet cell is nine characters, but this does not restrict the length of your label entries. A label entry can contain as many as 1022 characters, even though they all cannot be displayed within the cell. If a cell contains more characters than can fit in the cell, the cell uses the space of the cells to the right to display the additional characters (provided that the adjacent cells are empty). The column width is measured in the average character width of the default font, so the number of characters you can actually fit varies according to the width of the characters in the entry.

LONG LABELS An entry that exceeds the current cell width borrows space from the cells immediately to the right if they are empty. Figure 2.4 shows a long label entered in C10; the long entry borrows space from cells D10 and E10 to complete the display. If these cells contain entries, the display of C10's contents is truncated to the number of characters that fit within the current cell. You do not need to be concerned with data loss, since Quattro Pro retains the entire entry in memory. If the current cell is widened or the cells to the right are erased, the entire entry may then be displayed.

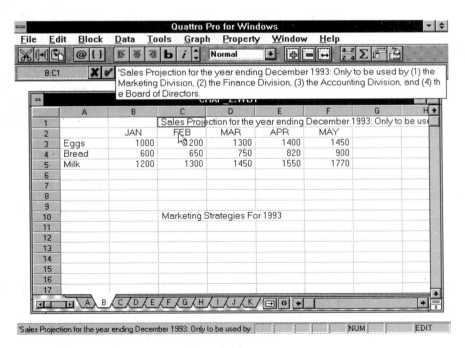

Figure 2.4 Entry Using Three Cells in Input Line

As you enter a label that fills the input line, Quattro Pro expands the box in the input line to display all of the cell's entry, as shown at the top of Figure 2.4. This expansion allows you to review a complete entry up to the maximum 1022 characters. While you are entering a long label, you cannot use the UP ARROW or DOWN ARROW to move to different lines of the entry. (In Chapter 12, you will learn how to set the key compatibility so you can use the UP ARROW and DOWN ARROW to switch between lines of a long entry.) When the selector is on a cell with a lengthy entry, Quattro Pro shows the entire entry in the input line using as many lines as necessary and overlapping the spreadsheet.

Since a long label entry resides completely in the cell where you make the entry, changes can only be made through this cell. To replace the entry, you move to this cell and type a new entry. To edit the entry, this cell must be the current cell when you switch to EDIT mode. If you try to change the entry by moving to other cells where space is borrowed for the display, the input line shows an empty cell even though information is displayed in these cells within the spreadsheet.

ALIGNMENT   When you enter a label, Quattro Pro generates a label indicator and places it at the beginning of your entry. The default label indicator on a new spreadsheet is an apostrophe (') that causes Quattro Pro to left-align your entry. Quattro Pro has other label alignment characters that can change how the label is aligned within the cell.

A quotation mark (") entered at the start of a label entry makes the label right-align within the current cell. This feature is useful if the cell is used at the top of a column that contains value entries (since value entries are initially right-aligned). Figure 2.5 presents a spreadsheet with right-aligned labels at the top of the Salary, Medical Benefits, and Disability Benefits columns.

You can center label entries by beginning your entry with a caret symbol (^). Frequently, the months of the year are centered at the tops of columns as they are entered across the spreadsheet. The months in row 2 of Figure 2.4 are centered using the ^ label prefix. For example, the entry in B2 is ^JAN. If you look at the input line when the selector is on one of these labels, you will see the caret symbol at the front of the entry for the current cell.

For now, you must type the appropriate label indicator if you want your labels to be centered or right-aligned. In Chapter 3, you will learn how to change the default label prefix that is generated automatically for all label entries. You will also learn how you can change the label prefix for existing entries without editing the cell or retyping the entire entry.

REPEATING LABELS   Quattro Pro provides a special label indicator that causes Quattro Pro to repeat the entry that follows until the current cell is filled with a repeated pattern of this entry. If the backslash (\) begins a label entry, the label repeats the designated character the required number of times to fill the cell regardless of its width. For example, entering * generates *'s to fill the cell, and entering \+− generates a series of +− entries to fill the cell. This feature is especially useful for creating dividing lines on the spreadsheet. The top and bottom lines for the box that contains

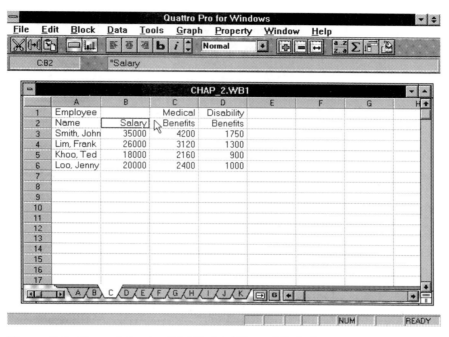

Figure 2.5 Spreadsheet with Right-Aligned Labels

the assumptions for the current spreadsheet are shown in Figure 2.6. They were generated with a series of \+ – entries in rows 1 and 8.

Labels That Contain Numbers

At times you may want to create label entries that begin with a numeric character. Since Quattro Pro automatically categorizes your entry as a label or a value based on the first character you type, you want to begin these entries with a label indicator. If you want to use the default (left-alignment), type **'34 North Avenue** to record the address 34 North Avenue.

Although it is not a common situation, you may sometimes want to create label entries that consist solely of numeric characters. This feature is useful if you are creating a spreadsheet in which a year appears at the top of each column. Since you do not want these year numbers to include any numeric formatting characters such as decimal points or dollar signs, you may wish to treat these entries as labels by entering a label prefix before you start your entry. Later, if you change how Quattro Pro displays numbers, the format for the years will not change.

Entries like phone numbers and social security numbers that have special characters like dashes or slashes to separate components of an entry are likely to cause problems for a new spreadsheet user. If you enter **213-46-1245** with the in-

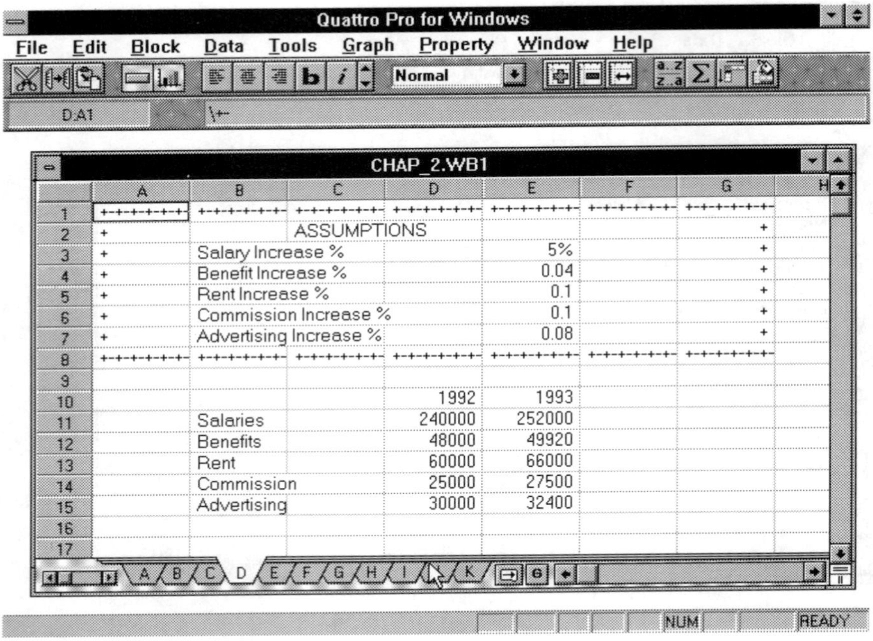

Figure 2.6   Backslash Used to Create a Repeating Label

tention of recording a social security number, you may be surprised to see that Quattro Pro displays your entry as –1078. The symbols you entered as dashes are interpreted as minus signs, and Quattro Pro performs two subtraction operations to arrive at the resulting negative number. Using the label indicator at the front of each entry produces a correct display such as the one in Figure 2.7.

ENTERING VALUES

Although label entries provide descriptive information on your spreadsheets, value entries form the backbone of any spreadsheet. These entries are used to record the current and projected numbers for your business operation and any calculations that you might want Quattro Pro to perform.

There are two basic types of value entries: numeric constants and formulas. Numeric constants are composed of the numeric digits from 0 through 9 with an optional + or – sign. Formulas offer a little more variety, since Quattro Pro supports arithmetic formulas, logical formulas, and string formulas. Each type of formula offers new possibilities for model creation, and each type is examined in depth in the sections that follow.

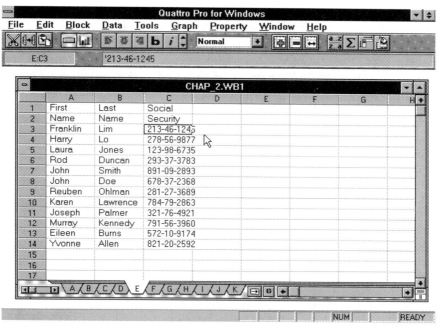

Figure 2.7 Storing Social Security Numbers as Labels

Entering Numeric Values

Entering a number in Quattro Pro is easy; the basic rules are summarized in the box "Rules for Numeric Entries." If you want to enter a positive number, the + sign is optional and is normally not used. All you do is enter the numeric digits, and finalize your entry. To enter a negative number, you must type a minus sign in front of the number. Entering **99** records a positive 99, and entering **–99** records a

---

Rules for Numeric Entries

1. Numbers cannot exceed 1022 characters.

2. If the first key you press is a digit or one of a few symbols (., +, –, (,), $, #, @), the entire entry is considered a numeric entry. Numeric entries are restricted to the following symbols: 0, 1, 2, 3, 4, 5, 6, 7, 8, 9, ., +, –, (,), $, #, @, E, ^, %, *, and /. However, the last five symbols (E, ^, %, *, /) cannot begin a numeric entry.

3. Spaces and commas can never be part of a numeric entry unless they are part of a formula.

negative 99. If you want to enter a percentage, you can enter the percent using the % sign like **15%** or you can type the decimal equivalent like **.15**.

LENGTH   Like labels, numbers can be up to 1022 characters in length. Quattro Pro can handle numbers as large as 1.7976931E+308 and as small as 1.7967931E–308 if, as in these two examples, scientific notation is used to record the entries as a power of ten, Quattro Pro retains 15 decimal digits of accuracy.

Numbers do not borrow space from cells to the right to continue the display if a cell is not wide enough. If the cell uses a General numeric format (the default until you set a different format), Quattro Pro displays any number that is too wide for the current cell width by using scientific notation. If the number is too wide for the cell in another format, the number appears as * 's that fill the cell width. The asterisks are sometimes generated when a number is entered but may also appear when an entry is reformatted with another display format that shows additional decimal places, adds commas, or adds other characters, such as $ or %. To eliminate the asterisks, you can reformat the affected cells with a display format that requires less space or widen the column to show more digits. Both techniques are covered in Chapter 3.

THE DEFAULT DISPLAY   The initial display format for numeric entries uses Quattro Pro's General format. The General format does not provide a consistent display for numeric entries since the magnitude of the number and the current cell width affect the display. Table 2.1 summarizes the types of entries you might see displayed with the default cell width of nine.

Using whole numbers that fit within the cell width causes the numbers to display exactly as you enter them. Extremely large or small numbers are displayed in scientific notation. Scientific notation displays a number times a power of 10. An

Table 2.1   Potential Cell Displays Using the Default Display

Number Entered	Quattro Pro's Display
15	15
1234567890	1.2E+09
6.022E27	6E+27
–.0000032	–3.2E-06
5.6E-200	5.6E-200
1.5%	0.015
.0000008	8E–07
.0001008	0.000101

E is used to precede the power that the number is being raised to (for example, 2.38E+05 tells Quattro Pro to multiply 2.38 by 10 to the fifth power—or 2.38 × 100,000).

Quattro Pro determines whether a number formatted with the General format is converted to scientific notation based on the magnitude of the number and the cell width (if a whole number entry is used). If you enter **–23456789**, Quattro Pro displays the entry as –2.3E+07 meaning that –2.3 is multiplied by 10 raised to the seventh power. Even though you do not see the other digits of the number, Quattro Pro remembers them and uses the full number in calculations.

The evaluation process is different for an entry consisting of a decimal fraction. If the first four digits after the decimal point are zeros, the number is converted to scientific notation regardless of the cell width. An entry of **.00008** is displayed as 8E-05 even if the current cell width is 40. If any of the first four digits is a number other than zero, the display is rounded to fit within the cell width (for example, an entry of **.123456789** is displayed as 0.123457 when the cell width is nine).

Decimal fractions have a zero added to the left of the decimal point of the entry in the General default display format. For example, entering **.9** causes Quattro Pro to display your entry as 0.9. Percentages in Quattro Pro are recorded as the equivalent decimal fraction. You can enter 10 percent as **10%** or **.1**. Quattro Pro displays your entry as 0.1 with either entry method. In Chapter 3, you will learn to use the format options to display the % symbol with your entry.

Negative numbers are displayed with a preceding minus sign when the General format is used. Typing **–99** in a cell causes Quattro Pro to display your entry exactly as you typed it. Quattro Pro has other options for displaying negative numbers, including enclosing them in parentheses and changing the color of the display. These options are covered in Chapter 3.

HANDLING ERRORS IN NUMERIC ENTRIES   Once Quattro Pro determines that you plan to enter a value in a spreadsheet cell, it checks your entry to ensure that every character entered is a value character. If you enter a character that is not a value character and attempt to finalize your entry, Quattro Pro displays an "Invalid reference" error message. When you select OK to continue, Quattro Pro places you in EDIT mode. This is Quattro Pro's way of telling you that you need to correct your entry before it can be finalized.

Once you are in EDIT mode, everything functions as if you had invoked the EDIT mode yourself. You can use the arrow keys to move within the entry. Your options are (1) delete the characters that are not value characters, or (2) insert a label indicator at the front of the entry, and finalize the entry.

ALIGNMENT OF NUMERIC ENTRIES   Numeric entries are normally right-aligned within a spreadsheet cell. A label indicator cannot change this alignment. If you enter a label indicator at the front of a number in an attempt to change its alignment, Quattro Pro uses the alignment you indicate with the label indicator, but the entry is a label (not a number). This prevents you from using the entry in any subsequent calculations. Figure 2.8 shows quantities that were entered as

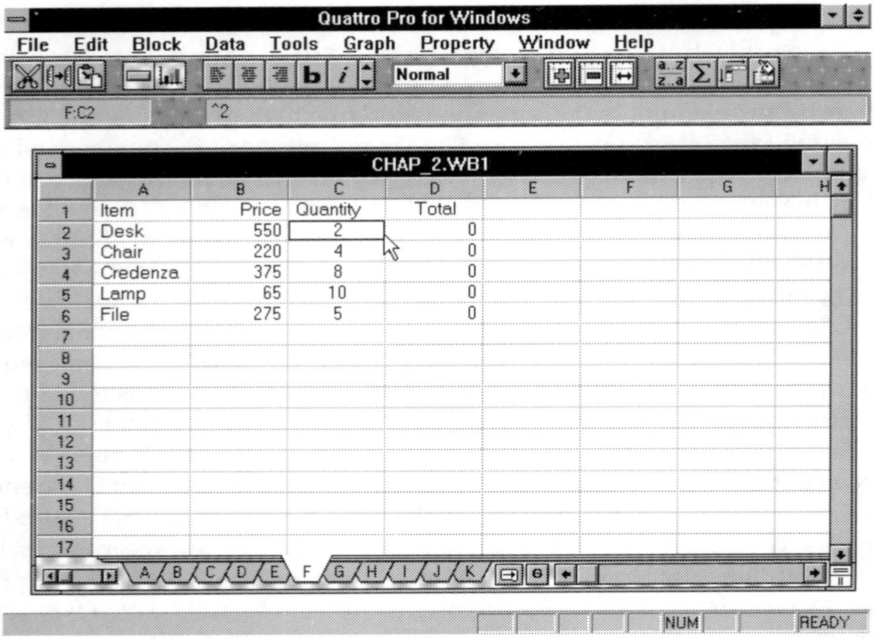

Figure 2.8   Formulas Computed Improperly Because Quantity is Stored as a Label

centered labels. When these entries are referenced in a formula, the labels are treated as 0, resulting in totals of 0. In Chapter 3, you will learn how you can change the alignment of numbers.

ENTERING FORMULAS

Quattro Pro's formulas are invaluable because they produce results that depend on the current contents of the spreadsheet cells referenced. You can use formulas to total a column of sales figures, forecast sales growth, calculate the federal withholding tax for a given level of earnings, or compute the monthly payment amount for a loan. Formulas can perform logical comparisons and combine character-string entries into one longer entry. Creating updated results for any of these calculations is as easy as placing a new entry in a spreadsheet cell referred to in the formula.

Many new users are a little intimidated at the prospect of entering formulas, but the thought process is exactly the same as the one used to enter the correct series of calculations with a hand-held calculator. In both cases, your results reflect the attention to detail and planning involved in the effort.

Formula Types

Quattro Pro supports three types of formulas: arithmetic, logical, and string formulas. Arithmetic formulas are used to perform mathematical calculations involving addition, subtraction, multiplication, division, and exponentiation. Also, you can use Quattro Pro's @functions in your arithmetic formulas to access higher-level mathematical features like random numbers, absolute values, and trigonometric functions. Many other categories of @functions exist and offer additional calculations, such as present value, internal rate of return, and depreciation calculations. These functions are covered in detail in Chapter 8.

Logical formulas are used in Quattro Pro to test a condition and ascertain if the condition is true or false. The result of a logical formula evaluated as true is displayed as a 1. The result of a logical formula evaluated as false is displayed as a 0. The ones and zeros resulting from these evaluations can influence other calculations on the spreadsheet.

A string formula can concatenate two or more strings. Once joined together with this process, the strings can be used as if they were one string. Concatenating two strings allows you to create a heading or other entry from two different pieces of spreadsheet information. String functions are especially useful when you transfer data to a Quattro Pro spreadsheet from another source and need to manipulate the information before it can be used.

Regardless of the type of formula you select, all cells that contain formulas display the results of calculations. The formula itself is still visible in the input line when you point to the cell, but it is not displayed within the cell unless you change the display format for the cell to Text, an option described in Chapter 3.

Quattro Pro uses different operators for each of the different types of formulas. Quattro Pro scans formulas from left to right, assessing the priority of each operator and evaluating the operators with the highest priority first. Each operator that is included in one of your entries is evaluated according to the priority sequence shown in Table 2.2.

Entering Arithmetic Formulas

Arithmetic formulas are constructed with numeric constants, cell references, and operators for addition (+), subtraction (−), multiplication (*), division (/), and exponentiation (^). Cell references are included in formulas by entering the cell address or the optional block names like Sales, Profit, or Benefits (Chapter 4 will explain how to assign these names to cells).

If you enter a formula that uses numeric constants, you can type these constants into the cell without any preparation (for example, 5*4), and Quattro Pro will compute and display the result of 20. Cell references used as variables in a formula make it easy to update the results of the formula. To use cell references, you must begin your entry with a value character rather than the first letter in a cell address. If you forget to begin a formula with a value character, Quattro Pro treats your entry as a label.

Table 2.2 Order of Calculation*

Operator	Action performed
( )	Parenthesis group operations to be performed
^	Exponentiation (raises the number on the left to the power on the right)
+ or −	Indicates a positive or negative number to the right of this operator
/ and *	Division and multiplication, respectively
+ and −	Addition and subtraction, respectively
=, <>, <, >, <=, >=	Logical operators (equals, not equals, less than, greater than, less than or equal to, and greater than or equal to)
#NOT#	Logical NOT
#AND#, #OR, &	Logical AND, Logical OR, and string combinator

*Quattro Pro evaluates mathematical calculations by using several rules. One rule is the order of calculation. This table lists each operator in the order it is evaluated within a formula. The higher on the list an operator is, the sooner it is evaluated within a formula. The other rule Quattro Pro uses when it finds multiple operators that should be evaluated at the same time is to evaluate the operators left to right.

If you enter **B2*C2** in a spreadsheet cell, Quattro Pro enters 'B2*C2 in the cell and displays the entry as a label as shown in Figure 2.9. If you enter **+B2*C2**, the + does not change the value of B2, but it causes Quattro Pro to treat the entry as a value and to process B2 and C2 as cell addresses. Using the current contents of these cells, Quattro Pro calculates the result of the formula and displays this result in cell D2 where the formula was entered. Parentheses are value characters and can be used, except they are needed at both ends of the entry, as in (A2*B3). The plus sign is a better choice, since one less keystroke is required for each formula entered. Figure 2.10 shows the edited formula in D2 that calculates the total cost for an order. The formula appears in the input line when the selector is on the cell, and the result appears in the cell.

You are not restricted to entering formulas with a single operator. With Quattro Pro, you can enter formulas as long as 1022 characters with as many operators as necessary. When you use more than one operator, Quattro Pro follows the order in Table 2.2 to determine which operation to perform first. For example, since multiplication has a higher priority than addition, the entry **6+2*4** yields 14, not 32. (Quattro Pro calculates $2 \times 4 = 8$, then $6 + 8 = 14$.) If more than one operation of the same level is in a single formula, the operation at the left is performed first, because Quattro Pro always moves from left to right when evaluating an expression.

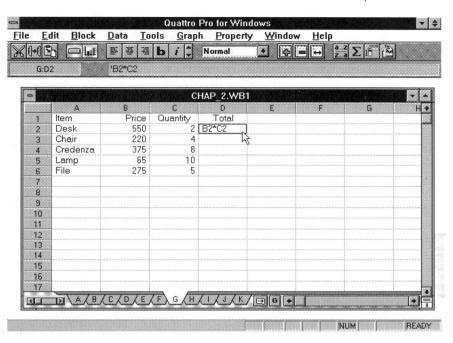

Figure 2.9 Formula Typed As a Label

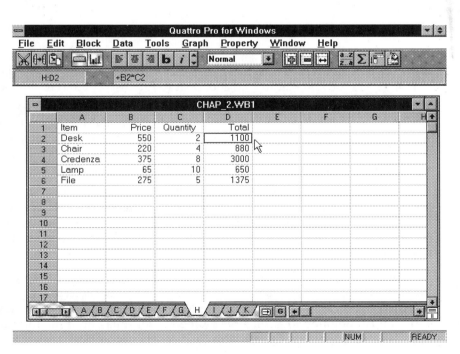

Figure 2.10 Formulas in Column D to Compute Totals

USING PARENTHESES   To override the natural priority sequence of operations, use parentheses. Enclosing an expression within parentheses causes Quattro Pro to evaluate the expression within parentheses before performing any other operations. Typing the previous expression as **(6+2)*4** produces a result of 32. Parentheses can also be nested, as in **((9+3)*(2+3))**, which causes Quattro Pro to perform the two addition operations before the multiplication, and produces 60 as a result for the expression.

BUILDING FORMULAS WITH THE POINTING INSTEAD OF TYPING METHOD   Most formulas you enter are built with cell references rather than numeric constants. This tactic allows you to change the results calculated by entering new numbers in spreadsheet cells rather than having to alter formulas to produce the new results. You can type any formula into the current cell by typing the arithmetic operators and the cell addresses, but the pointing method offers an alternative approach with an added advantage.

The advantage of the pointing method for formula construction is that pointing to each reference used in a formula causes you to visually verify that you are including the proper information in your calculation. This minimizes the possibility of including an incorrect cell reference in a calculation.

To build a formula with the pointing method, you type the arithmetic operators, parentheses, and numeric constants and point to the correct cell reference each time you want to include one in the formula. Before you decide that the steps involved seem to take more time than typing the formula, remember that the lower formula error rate actually saves time and improves the accuracy of your calculations. To enter +D4/F2 in the current cell the following steps are required:

1. Type a plus (+).
2. Move the selector to D4. As you move the selector, the mode indicator changes to POINT as shown in Figure 2.11, and Quattro Pro displays the cell address in the input line as part of the formula just as if you had typed it.
3. Type a /. The selector returns to the cell where the formula is being recorded when the operator is typed and can be moved to the next cell reference required.
4. Move the selector to F2.
5. Press ENTER. Pressing ENTER is your only option for finalizing the formula, since moving the selector to a new location changes the last reference in the formula. The exception to this rule is a formula that ends with a parenthesis or a numeric constant, since the arrow keys finalize these formulas.

As you are entering a formula in POINT mode, you may decide to abandon POINT mode and type the remainder of your formula. The mode indicator switches back to VALUE. You can switch back to POINT mode after you type the next operator. If you try pointing to a cell after typing the formula and if the formula does not end with an operator, Quattro Pro finalizes the formula.

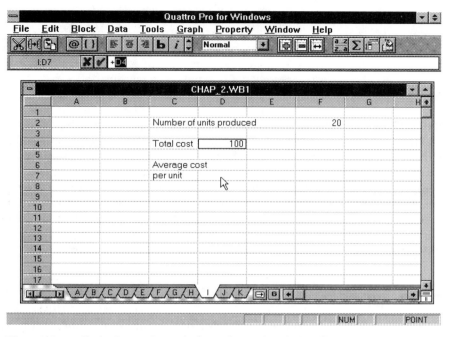

Figure 2.11   Pointing to Incorporate the Value for Cell D4 into a Formula

POINTING WITH A MOUSE   Pointing with a formula using a mouse is different from pointing using the keyboard directional keys. Quattro Pro does not use what the mouse is pointing to until you select it by pressing the mouse button. To build a formula with the pointing method using a mouse, you type the arithmetic operators, parentheses, and numeric constants and select the correct cell reference each time you want to include one in the formula. As in pointing with the keyboard directional keys, it may take longer to point to a cell with a mouse, but the time lost is balanced by the increased accuracy. Also, pointing with a mouse is quicker when the cells are farther apart or in different notebooks. To enter +D4/F2 in the current cell the following steps are required:

1. Type a plus (+).
2. Point to D4. The mode indicator does not change (as it does when you are using the keyboard directional keys).
3. Press the mouse button. Quattro Pro adds D4 to the cell's contents. If you selected the wrong cell, you can select a different cell by pointing to it and pressing the mouse button. Quattro Pro then replaces the previous cell with the more recently selected cell. For example, if you clicked D3 by mistake, you can click D4 to replace D3 with D4.
4. Type a /.

5. Click F2.

6. Click the ✓ in the input line. As when the keyboard directional keys are used, clicking the ✓ or pressing ENTER are your only options for finalizing the formula. If you select another cell instead, the last reference in the formula is changed.

@FUNCTIONS IN ARITHMETIC FORMULAS   Quattro Pro has additional computational capabilities beyond the simple arithmetic operators. These additional calculations are accessed through @functions so that you can round numbers, compute financial calculations, perform conditional computations, and many other additional sophisticated options. Each @function begins with the @ symbol and is followed by a keyword and your requirements for its specific use. Chapter 8 provides an in-depth look at the various categories of @functions that Quattro Pro offers. After you have mastered the basic formulas the package offers, Chapter 8 is a must-see chapter to add additional power to your spreadsheets.

Reference Types

Quattro Pro supports three types of cell references: relative, absolute, and mixed. Each formula discussed so far has used the default option of relative references. This style reference might look like A:A2, A:Z33, D:ST100, or IV:R94. An absolute reference has a $ in front of each portion of the address ($A:$A$4), and in a mixed reference style, half of the address is relative and the other half is absolute ($A:$A2 or A$2). When a page is relative, it is often dropped from the cell address.

All three reference styles produce the same results in the cell where the formula is entered initially. The difference in the three reference styles is not apparent until you copy the cell containing the formula. Relative references are adjusted as the formula is placed in another cell. Absolute references are not adjusted when they are copied. The updating of a mixed reference depends on which portion of the cell address is absolute and where the formula is moved to. This topic is covered in more detail in Chapter 4 in the section on copying formulas. For now it is only important to recognize the various types of cell addresses shown in the box "Cell Reference Types" and to realize that the type of reference you select can have far-reaching effects later in the model development process.

How Quattro Pro Recalculates Formulas

Early versions of spreadsheet packages recalculated the entire spreadsheet every time a single cell was changed. A more recent technique maintains a table of row and column dependencies so that only the rows and columns affected by a change are recalculated. However, even this slows you down; if you make a change that affects many cells, you must wait for Quattro Pro to finish recalculating the cells. Quattro Pro, therefore, provides background automatic recalculation. With background automatic recalculation, Quattro Pro recalculates the necessary formulas

Cell Reference Types

Quattro Pro has three types of cell references. These types of cell references do not affect the formula, but they do modify how the cell references change when a formula is copied.

Type	Examples
Relative Reference	A1, G13, AV1520
Absolute Reference	$A$1, $G$13, $AV$1520
Mixed Reference	A$1, $G13, $AV1520

only when you are not entering keystrokes. The BKGD indicator will appear in the status line while Quattro Pro has formulas that it needs to recalculate, but you can continue to enter data. If you are going to print the spreadsheet, you must wait until the BKGD indicator disappears before printing.

Formulas That Result in Special Values

Normally the formulas you enter produce either arithmetic results, string entries, or a logical 0 or 1 result. In error situations or other special circumstances, the result produced by a formula is not what you expect. If you enter a formula with a missing parenthesis, a missing operator, or an incorrectly spelled @function keyword, Quattro Pro displays an error message. When you select OK to continue, Quattro Pro places you in EDIT mode to make the correction. If you cannot find the source of the problem, you might want to convert the formula into a label temporarily by adding a label indicator at the front of the entry. This allows you to look at the formula later from a fresh perspective.

In other situations, a special value may display in the cell where you enter the formula. If you attempt an operation like dividing by zero or a label entry, Quattro Pro displays ERR in the cell. ERR also appears when you have provided an improper function argument for one of the @functions. Also, ERR appears when you reference a cell that contains a value that is an error. When a formula references a cell containing @NA or ERR, the formula returns @NA or @ERR.

The last special value that can appear is a row of *'s that fill the cell. Although these entries are not really values, they occur anytime a cell is not wide enough to display the current result of the formula in the current format. Changing the width of the column containing the formula or reformatting the cell with a different format, as described in Chapter 3, can solve the problem.

Using Logical Formulas

Logical formulas allow you to compare two values. Logical formulas add power to spreadsheet applications, since you can check the result of the comparison and use it to influence other operations on the spreadsheet. The results produced by the logical formulas are not the result of arithmetic calculations. Logical formulas always return either a 0 (representing a false result for the condition test) or a 1 (indicating that the condition tested as true).

You use logical operators when you build a logical formula. These operators are listed in Table 2.3. They test for equality (=), inequality (<>), greater than (>), greater than or equal to (>=), less than (<), or less than or equal to (<=). Quattro Pro has three others that operate on other logical comparisons: #AND#, #OR#, and #NOT#.

In Figure 2.12, a logical formula determines if a customer has met the minimum purchase amount for a discount. The logical formula +C8>C2 compares the amount of the purchase against the minimum purchase. If the condition tests true, the discount (C8*C9) is multiplied by one; if it tests false, the discount is multiplied by zero, effectively negating the discount calculation.

Logical operators all have the same priority level and are evaluated from left to right if more than one occurs in an expression. When logical operators are combined with arithmetic operators, the arithmetic operations are computed first, since they have a higher priority. The formula in C15, +(C8>C2)*C8*C9, provides an example of a formula that combines both logical and arithmetic operations.

Logical formulas can use text as the two quantities it compares. For example, +"Smith">"Jones" returns a 1, since it is true that Smith is after Jones in the

Table 2.3   Logical Operators

Operator	Result
=	Returns a 1 if the value on the left of the equal sign equals the value on the right; returns a 0 otherwise.
<>	Returns a 1 if the value on the left of this operator does not equal the value on the right; returns a 0 otherwise.
<	Returns a 1 if the value on the left of this operator is less than the value on the right; returns a 0 otherwise.
>	Returns a 1 if the value on the left of this operator is greater than the value on the right; returns a 0 otherwise.
<=	Returns a 1 if the value on the left of this operator is less than or equal to the value on the right; returns a 0 otherwise.
>=	Returns a 1 if the value on the left of this operator is greater than or equal to the value on the right; returns a 0 otherwise.
#AND#	Returns a 1 if the value on the left and the value on the right is true; returns a 0 otherwise.
#OR#	Returns a 1 if the value on the left or the value on the right is true; returns a 0 otherwise.
#NOT#	Returns a 1 if the value on the right is false; returns a 0 if the value on the left is true.

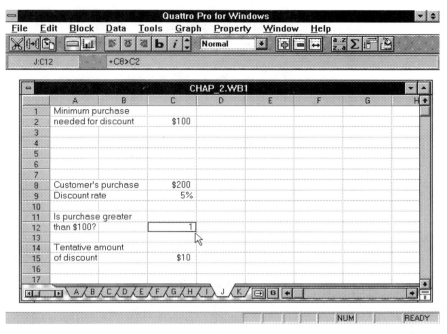

Figure 2.12   Logical Formula Used to Determine If Customer Is Eligible for a Discount

alphabet. When you use logical operators with strings, the comparisons are usually (1) whether one string is the same as the other or different, or (2) which string comes before the other.

Using String Formulas

String formulas are used to join or concatenate two strings or groups of characters into one longer string. The ampersand (&) is the only operator used in string formulas and must be used between any two strings that you wish to join. Because a string formula is a type of value entry, it must begin with a value character like the plus sign, as in the formula **+A2&D3** that joins the string entries in A2 and D3.

String constants can be incorporated into string formulas and are often used either to provide spaces between two string variables or to add a constant entry. Anytime a string is included directly in a formula it must be enclosed in quotation marks. Figure 2.13 shows a formula in D2 that has commas, spaces, and periods used as string constants. These commas, spaces, and periods are enclosed in the quotes. First names, middle initials, and last names are contained in columns A through C. By using the formula **+C2&", "&A2&" "&B2&"."**, the separate entries in row 2 are joined into one name entry with the appropriate spacing and punctuation, which appears in column D.

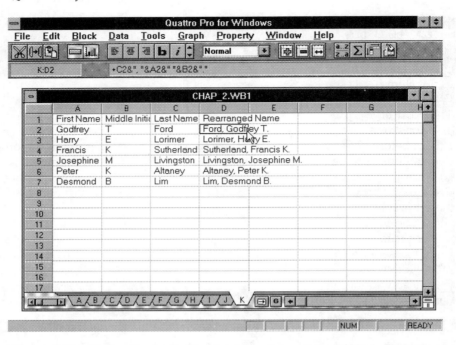

Figure 2.13   String Formula Used to Combine Several Strings into a Longer One

CREATING FORMULAS FROM DATA ON DIFFERENT PAGES   So far, the data and the formula that uses the data have been on the same page. You can have formulas that reference any page of the notebook. The data a formula uses can be on any page, so you do not have to clump all of your information on a single page. To use data from another page, you must tell Quattro Pro the page name as well as the column and row location.

You can enter a formula that uses data from a cell on another page by pointing to the cell or typing the cell reference. To point to a cell on another page, you may need to click the page name tab at the bottom of the notebook. You can also switch pages by pressing CTRL-PGDN or CTRL-PGUP. When you are typing the cell reference, type the page name, a : (colon), and the cell address.

As an example, suppose you want to include the name in D2 in Figure 2.13, which is on page K, in a formula in E5 on page N. First, from cell E5 on page N, type +. Then if you are using a mouse, click the K page tab and then click D2. To select this cell without the mouse, press CTRL-PGUP three times to go to sheet K and move the selector to D2. Finalize the entry by clicking the ✓ or pressing ENTER. Now your formula in E5 on page N is +K:D2. As the value in D2 on page K changes, so will the value in E5 on page N.

Testing Spreadsheet Formulas

Even though your formulas produce normal-looking results, you must test the results to ensure their accuracy. The potential problem with inaccurate results does not stem from any deficiencies in Quattro Pro's ability to calculate, but from the possibility of inadvertent errors on your part.

The most efficient testing is conducted in phases. If you plan to use a set of calculations to process periods of data, enter the formulas for the first period, and test them before copying the formulas for the other periods. Although the other periods still need to be verified, you minimize your total time investment.

Another part of the step-by-step approach is to increase the vigorousness of the test gradually. Your first test should be a reasonableness test. If sales are $100,000 and are the sole source of revenue for the company, it is totally unreasonable for profits to be $1,000,000. A quick check can tell you if the results produced by a model are reasonable.

The next set of data entered while testing should be easy-to-manage round numbers like 10, 100, or 1,000. It is easy to check the results of simple calculations in your head with this type of entry (multiplying 10 units by a selling price of $100 obviously yields a total of $1,000).

Once your model has passed both a reasonableness test and the entry of simple numbers, check the model with some real data. The best data to use is data from a previous period; you already have the manually calculated results and can check the results produced by the model quickly.

Once the accuracy of your model is verified, you do not need to check your model every time you use it. If you later modify the formulas in your model, you ought to repeat the testing process.

ENTERING DATES AND TIMES

Spreadsheet packages handle dates as date serial numbers to allow calculations that can determine if a loan is past due, the aging of your receivables, or the rental charge on a home-improvement product with a daily rental rate. Quattro Pro also stores times as time serial numbers, so you can use times in calculations such as calculating the time each person spent on a project. Most spreadsheet packages require you to use @functions to enter a date serial number that determines how many days a given date occurs after a past date. Quattro Pro makes the date-entry task easy, since a simple key sequence tells Quattro Pro that you are about to enter a date.

Quattro Pro's Date Features

To enter a date in Quattro Pro, you need to press CTRL-SHIFT-D and type a date in any of the formats shown in Table 2.4. Quattro Pro displays your entry with the

Table 2.4 Formats that CTRL-SHIFT-D Accepts as a Date

Format	Examples
DD-MMM-YY	25-Dec-92, 20-Aug-93
DD-MMM	25-Dec, 20-Aug (assumes current year)
MMM-YY	Dec-92, Aug-93 (assumes first day of the month)
Long International (initially set at MM/DD/YY)	12/25/92, 8/20/92, 08/20/93
Short International (initially set at MM/DD)	12/25, 8/20 (assumes current year)
Windows Long Date Format (set by the Control Panel)	Saturday, December 25, 1992 Thursday, August 20, 1993

date display format that is initially entered. Figure 2.14 displays a column of date entries entered with the CTRL-SHIFT-D option.

Although your date entry is displayed as a date, it is stored as a date serial

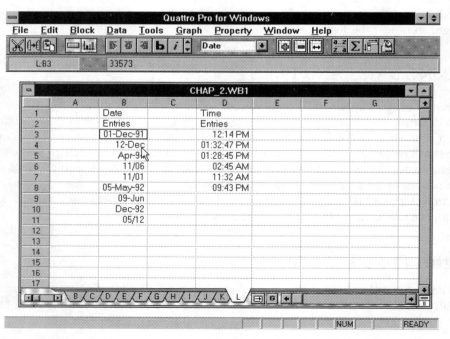

Figure 2.14 Dates and Times Entered with CTRL-SHIFT-D

number so you can perform date calculations. An entry of January 1, 1900 produces a date serial number entry of 2, since it is two days after December 30, 1899, which is the zero reference point for all Quattro Pro dates. An entry of July 7, 1993 produces a date serial number entry of 34157, since it is 34157 days after December 31, 1899. Although 1900 was not a leap year, other spreadsheet packages count February 29, 1900 as an actual date. To maintain compatibility over the vast range of useful dates, Quattro Pro uses December 30, 1899, rather than December 31, 1899, as a zero point. Negative numbers represent the number of days before December 30, 1899.

Performing Date Calculations

Once dates are recorded in a Quattro Pro spreadsheet, date calculations can be performed with the same operators used in other arithmetic calculations. Figure 2.15 shows dates representing invoice dates in column B. According to the terms of the invoice, payment should be made within 10 days of the invoice date. The payment due date is calculated by adding 10 days to the invoice date. The formula to perform this calculation is stored in column C. These entries have not been formatted as dates and appear as serial date numbers. You will learn how to set date serial numbers to appear as the dates they represent in Chapter 3.

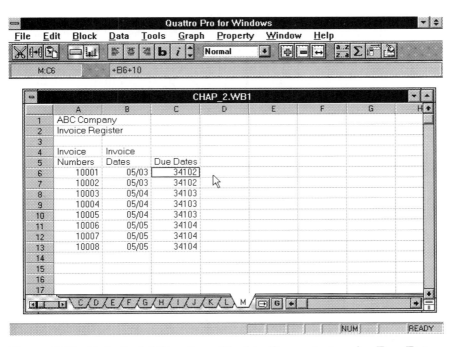

Figure 2.15   Date Serial Numbers Used to Compute Invoice Due Dates

Quattro Pro's Time Features

To enter a time in Quattro Pro, you must press CTRL-SHIFT-D and type a time in one of the acceptable time formats. These time formats are HH:MM:SS AM/PM, HH:MM AM/PM, HH:MM:SS, and HH:MM. The last two formats are the international time formats; so if you later change how the international time formats are displayed, the last two formats for directly entering dates change. Also, the international time formats use a 24-hour clock, which means that hours after noon are 12 plus the hour as in 18 for 6 PM. When you press CTRL-SHIFT-D and enter a time, Quattro Pro converts the time into a time serial number in the input line (which looks nothing like the time it represents) and displays the time using the time format you used. Times are represented as the portion of the day. For example, noon is .5, since it is half of the day. Once times are entered, you can use them in calculations. For example, if A1 and A2 contain times, you can calculate the difference between the times with the formula **+A1-A2**. When you format the result using one of the time formats described in Chapter 3, Quattro Pro will display the time difference in hours, minutes and seconds.

DOCUMENTING DATES, FORMULAS, AND NUMBERS

When you create models in your spreadsheet, the formulas and numbers you add will seem very clear to you. However, when you use the spreadsheet model later, you may forget why you entered certain dates, formulas, or numbers. You can add hidden comments to dates, formulas, and numbers. Quattro Pro uses a semicolon to separate the date, formula, or number part of a cell entry from the cell notation. After the semicolon, you can type the description of the cell's contents. The number of characters that you use in a comment is limited to 1022 for each cell entry. Figure 2.16 shows a cell containing a hidden comment. The comments only appear in the input line when the selector points to a cell containing a cell notation. If you want to show the comments, you must change the format to Text, as Chapter 3 will describe. You can also print comments by printing the cell formulas, as described in Chapter 6.

USING UNDO TO CORRECT MISTAKES

When you make a mistake in an entry, you can correct the mistake by editing the data or entering the entry again. However, you cannot correct a mistake this way if you accidentally use the wrong cells for the commands you will learn about in

---

▼ TIP: Converting Dates and Times

When you have a date or time entered as a label, you can convert it to a date or time serial number. Edit the cell, delete the label prefix, and then press CTRL-SHIFT-D to switch to DATE mode before pressing ENTER.

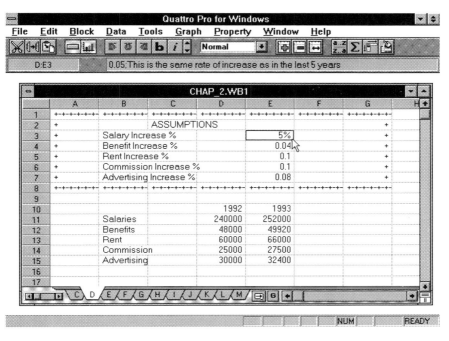

Figure 2.16 Cell Containing Cell Notation

subsequent chapters. Fortunately, Quattro Pro has an Undo feature that removes the effect of your most recent action. Quattro Pro remembers the differences in a spreadsheet from the time before you made a change so that you can undo the latest spreadsheet change. However, the Undo feature does not remove the effect of all changes. Some of the changes you cannot undo include: file actions such as saving a file; command settings such as the settings for the Edit Search & Replace command; format settings such as label alignment; and style changes such as fonts, line drawing, and shading. If using Undo has slowed your system too much, you can disable it by selecting Property, Application, Startup and Undo Enabled. While Undo is enabled, you can undo the effect of the last action (of the actions that Undo can remove) by selecting Undo from the Edit menu. When you display the Edit menu, Quattro Pro displays the action it will do after Undo. Once you have undone the last undo-able action, the first menu option in the Edit menu changes to Redo, which reapplies the change you have just undone.

GETTING STARTED

In this chapter, you learned how to make entries in spreadsheet cells. The options available for you include entering data, changing label alignment, and creating formulas to perform computations. You can practice these types of entries by creating an

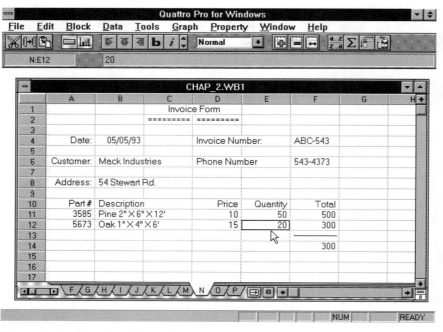

Figure 2.17 Invoice Form Created with Getting Started Section

invoice order form and entering the data for an invoice. Figure 2.17 shows the final spreadsheet. To create an invoice in the spreadsheet, follow these steps:

1. Move to C1. Type ten spaces and **Invoice Form**. The spaces at the beginning center the label in columns C and D.

2. Press the DOWN ARROW or click cell C2. Type \=, and move to cell D2 to create a dashed line in C2. Type \=, and finalize your entry by clicking the ✓ or pressing ENTER to create a dashed line in D2. You can use repeated labels to divide the spreadsheet and to create headings.

3. Make the following entries. For each cell, you must first position the selector to the cell address. Once the cell is selected, type the entry. To finish the entry, you can either (1) press ENTER, (2) click the ✓ in the input line, (3) press an arrow key, or (4) click another cell. Notice how some of the entries listed below have a quotation mark at the beginning so the label will be right-justified in the cell. You can use this feature for column headings for columns that will contain numbers.

A4: **"Date:**
D4: **Invoice Number:**
A6: **"Customer:**
D6: **Phone Number:**
A8: **"Address:**

A10: **"Part #**
B10: **Description**
D10: **"Price**
E10: **"Quantity**
F10: **"Total**

4. Move to F11 by using the arrow keys or by clicking the cell. This cell needs a formula that multiplies the value in the Price column with the value in the Quantity column. Type **+**. Press the LEFT ARROW twice or click D11. Type *****. Press the LEFT ARROW or click E11. Press ENTER or click the ✓ in the input line.

5. Move to F12 by using the arrow keys or by clicking the cell. This cell needs the same formula as F11. You will learn in the next chapter how to copy formulas, but now simply type the formula. Type **+D12*E12**. Since you did not enter this formula by pointing, you can use the DOWN ARROW or click F13.

6. Type **\-**, and press the DOWN ARROW or click F14 to create a repeating label of dashes. You can use the repeating labels to indicate that the value above or below the line is a summary figure.

7. The cell in F14 needs a formula that adds the value in F11 to the value in F12. Type **+**. Press the UP ARROW three times or click F11. Type **+**. Press the UP ARROW twice or click F12. Press ENTER or click the ✓ in the input line.

You have now completed the form and are ready to enter invoice data. To fill in the form you have just created, follow these steps:

1. Move to B4.

2. Enter the date by pressing CTRL-SHIFT-D and typing **5/15/93**. Press ENTER or click the ✓. Quattro Pro converts your entry in the input line to 34104, which is the integer value that represents May 15, 1993.

3. Move to F4 by pressing the RIGHT ARROW four times or by clicking F4. Type **ABC-543**. You can use ENTER or the ✓ in the input line to finalize the entry. Move to B6. Type **Mack Industries**. Either press the RIGHT ARROW key four times to move to F6 or click F6. This finalizes the entry in B6 and moves the selector to where you will be making your next entry.

4. Type **543-4373**, and press ENTER or click the ✓ in the input line. Since this entry starts with a number, Quattro Pro treats this entry as a value and displays –3830. As you can see in the input line, Quattro Pro stores this entry as you entered it. To change this entry so it is treated as a label, press F2 (EDIT) or click the cell's contents in the input line. Move to the 5, and type an apostrophe ('). Finalize the modified entry by pressing ENTER or clicking the ✓ in the input line.

5. Move to B8 by pressing the DOWN ARROW twice and the LEFT ARROW four times. If you are using a mouse, click B8. Type **54 Stewart Rd.**, and press ENTER or click ✓ in the input line. Since the first character is a number,

Quattro Pro tries to evaluate this entry as a value or formula. This is not a proper formula, so Quattro Pro displays an error message. Since you really want this entry treated as a label, you need to tell Quattro Pro to treat this entry as a label. After selecting OK, move to the beginning of the entry and type an apostrophe.

6. Move to A11 by pressing the DOWN ARROW three times and the LEFT ARROW once or by clicking A11. Type **3585** for the part number. Press the RIGHT ARROW or click B11 to finalize the entry in A10 and move the selector to where you want to make the next entry. Type **Pine 2" X 6" X 12'**. When you use apostrophes, quotation marks, and carets in a label entry for other than the first character, these characters will appear in the label. Press the RIGHT ARROW twice or click D11. Type **10**, and press the RIGHT ARROW or click E11 to finalize the first item's price. Type **50** to enter the first item's quantity. Press the DOWN ARROW to move to the row for the next item, and press END followed by the LEFT ARROW to move the cell selector to A12. With a mouse, click A12. Notice that as you entered the price and quantity, the formula in F11 automatically computed the total for the item, and the formula in F14 computed the total for the invoice.

7. Type **5673** for the part number. Press the RIGHT ARROW or click B12 and press the mouse button to finalize the entry in A12; move the selector to where you want to make the next entry. Type **Oak 1" X 4" X 6'**. Press the RIGHT ARROW twice or click D12. Type **15** and press the RIGHT ARROW or click E12 to enter the second item's price. Type **20** to enter the second item's quantity. Press ENTER or click the ✓ in the input line. Your screen now looks like Figure 2.17. The formulas in F11 and F12 automatically compute the totals for the items, and the formula in F14 computes the total for the invoice.

8. You can quickly save this spreadsheet by selecting Save from the File menu and typing a file name such as **INVOICE.** The first time you save a spreadsheet, Quattro Pro prompts you for the file name. If you select Save from the File menu a second time, Quattro Pro will save the file using the same file name. When the file name is entered, select OK.

3

Changing Cell and Page Properties

In the last chapter, you learned how you can enter labels, numbers, and formulas. These entries are the backbone of all your notebooks. To get the best use out of your entries, you need to present them well. Quattro Pro for Windows has many features that can change how your entries appear. These features are the *properties*. You can set properties for cells, pages, notebooks, and applications although, for now, you will focus on cells and pages. You can select cell properties such as the numeric formats of your value entries and the alignment of your value and label entries. Other cell properties offer desktop publishing features. These properties include setting the font and adding lines and shading. You can also select other properties for rows and columns such as their sizes and whether they are displayed or hidden. All of these changes affect how your entries look. These properties do not affect the cell entries themselves.

Page properties affect how an entire page appears. Some of the page properties you can change include renaming a page and changing the column widths of all columns in the page. These properties apply to an entire page rather than a specific block.

In this chapter, you will learn how to select blocks. Once you can select a block, you are ready to change the block's properties. Next, you will learn about creating and using named styles. Named styles let you work with a group of block properties at once. Once you learn how to change how individual cells look, you will learn how to change the properties of pages. Finally, you will learn about the GROUP mode, which makes changing the appearance of several pages at once more efficient.

SPECIFYING A BLOCK

A block is a rectangular section of your notebook. It can be as small as one cell or can include cells in many rows, columns, and pages. Blocks tell Quattro Pro the groups of cells you want to use for a feature or command. Figure 3.1 shows a block specified. All the highlighted cells are included in the block.

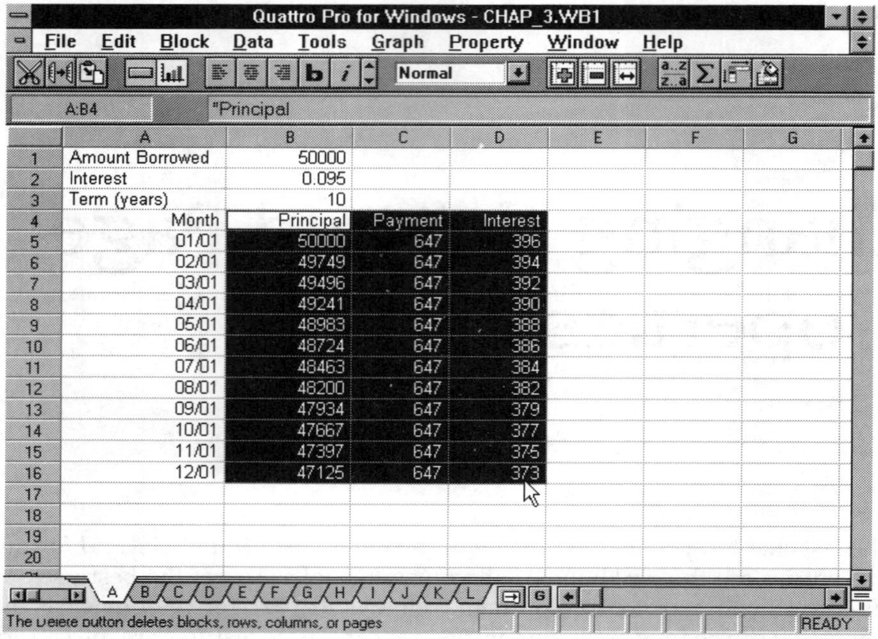

Figure 3.1   Page with Block Selected

Most of the blocks in Quattro Pro are in a contiguous rectangle. To describe a block to Quattro Pro, indicate two diagonally opposite corners of the block. Blocks are frequently specified by their upper left corner and lower right corner, but you can describe a block using any combination you wish. In Figure 3.1, the block is specified by the two block coordinates, B4 and D16 (the first cell selected as a block corner has a different color). Most of the time you can select the block before you select the command that uses the block. Some features like setting cell properties require that the block be selected before you use the feature. Other commands will prompt you for a block. You can also use blocks in formulas.

Blocks can contain multiple pages. These blocks have their pages indicated by the page names before the row and columns. Both A..B:B4..D16 and A:B4..B:D16 indicate the block shown in Figure 3.1 selected for pages A and B. The default method for indicating blocks on multiple pages is to put the page names separate from the row and column names, as in A..B:B4..D16.

Selecting a Block

You have three ways of selecting a block: You can drag your mouse to cover the cells you want in a block; you can select a block using the same directional keys you use to move to a cell; or you can type a block's specifications when a command prompts for a block or when you are typing a formula. The method you choose depends on what is convenient at the time. When you select a block, one of the corners is marked with an outline rather than being highlighted like the other cells. This cell is the *anchor point*.

The easiest method of selecting a block is with the mouse. To select a block with the mouse, drag the mouse from the first corner of the block to the opposite corner. If you want the block to include the same rows and columns from multiple pages, select the cells from the first page and then hold down the SHIFT key while you click the tag of the last page in the block. Another method of selecting a block with a mouse is to select the first cell of the block and hold down SHIFT before you select the opposite corner of the block. Quattro Pro highlights the block defined by the two selected cells. When you select a block with a mouse, you can select an entire row or column by clicking the row number or column letter in the row and column border. You can also select several rows or columns by dragging the mouse over the row numbers in the row border or column letters in the column border. You can select the entire page by clicking the Select-All button in the upper left corner of the row and column border. If you want to select a block with a mouse after you have already selected a command, you can click outside of the dialog box which shrinks the dialog box. After selecting the block, releasing the mouse button restores the dialog box to its original size. Another possibility is to click the dialog box's minimize box to shrink the dialog. When you shrink the dialog box this way, you must click the restore button to return to the dialog box.

Another method of selecting a block is to use the directional keys. To do so, move to one corner, and then hold down SHIFT while you use the directional keys to move to the diagonally opposite corner. For example, to select the block in Figure 3.1 with the keyboard, you would move to B4 and then hold down SHIFT while you pressed END, DOWN ARROW, END, and RIGHT ARROW. From this point, you can also hold down SHIFT while you press CTRL-PGDN and CTRL-PGUP to include additional pages in the block selection. When you use a command that prompts for a block, you can point to the block by pressing an arrow key to shrink the dialog box. Once the dialog box is reduced, you can select the block by pressing a period and using the directional keys. The only difference between selecting a block with the directional keys from a dialog box and selecting a block at other times is that you can type a period to anchor one of the corners rather than constantly pressing SHIFT. While you select a block this way, you can also type a period repeatedly to change the anchored corner of the block. When the block is selected, you can press ENTER or click the maximize button to return to the dialog box and use the block you have selected.

When you type a block selection, type the cell address of one corner, a period, and the cell address of the diagonally opposite corner. You only need to supply the page names if part of the block is not on the current page. You might want to type the block address if you have not selected a block before selecting the command that will use it, and you type faster than you use the directional keys.

Noncontiguous Blocks

A special type of block is a *noncontiguous* block. Like other blocks, a noncontiguous block selects a group of cells that you will use for a Quattro Pro feature or command. Unlike other blocks, a noncontiguous block is a combination of cells and blocks that do not necessarily adjoin, and do not form a single rectangle. Figure 3.2 shows a noncontiguous block. Selecting a noncontiguous block is just like selecting other cells and blocks except that you must hold down the CTRL key while you are selecting the blocks and cells that go into the noncontiguous block. As long as you are holding down the CTRL key, the cells and blocks you select are added to the noncontiguous block selection. For example, to select the noncontiguous block in Figure 3.2, you would select the block A1..A16, hold down CTRL, and then select the block B4..D4. As soon as you select a cell or block without pressing CTRL, that selected cell or block replaces the noncontiguous block as the current selection.

To type a noncontiguous block's coordinates, type the cell addresses and block coordinates for the cells and blocks that make up the noncontiguous block, separating the different parts with semicolons. For example, the noncontiguous block in Figure 3.2 can be described as A1..A16,B4..D4.

BLOCK PROPERTIES

Once you have selected a block, you can change the properties of the cells in the block. Changing these properties is called *inspecting* a block. You can inspect a

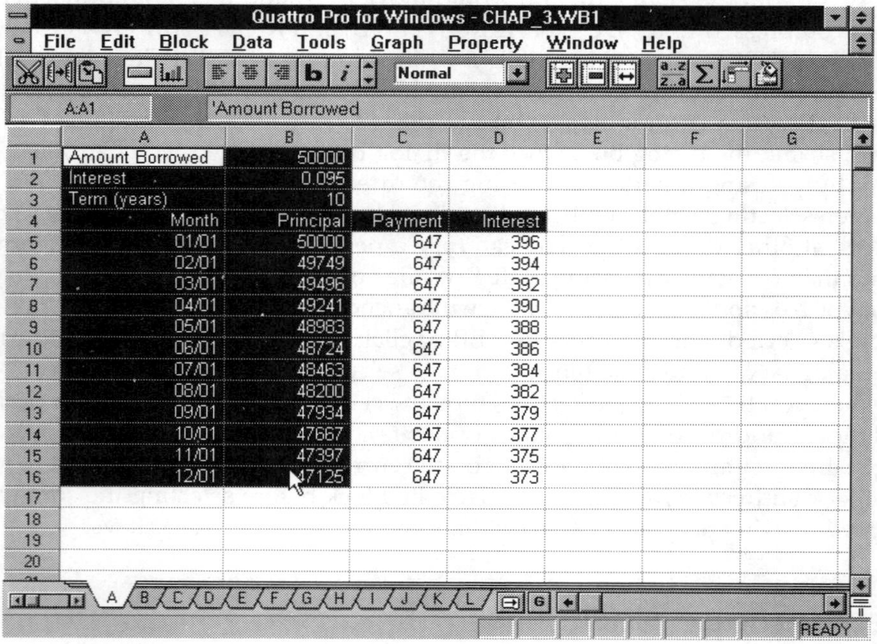

Figure 3.2   Page with Noncontiguous Block Highlighted

block by pointing to any cell in the selected block and pressing the right mouse button, or by selecting Current Object from the Property menu or pressing F12. When you inspect a block's properties, Quattro Pro displays the Object Inspector for the block in the Active Block dialog box, shown in Figure 3.3. On the left side of the dialog box are the properties you can select for the block. You can select the property you are changing by clicking the property name or pressing CTRL-PGUP and CTRL-PGDN until the property you want to change is displayed. The contents of the right side of the dialog box change to display the options available with the selected property.

Changing the Numeric Format

As discussed in Chapter 2, when you enter formulas and numbers in a cell, Quattro Pro displays as much of the entry that can fit in the current cell width. Using the default display format also results in scientific notation (e.g., 1.04E+26) for extremely large and small numbers. Decimal entries also are displayed with varying numbers of decimal digits. The default format display shows numbers inconsistently. Changing the display for value entries can make the data much easier to read and understand.

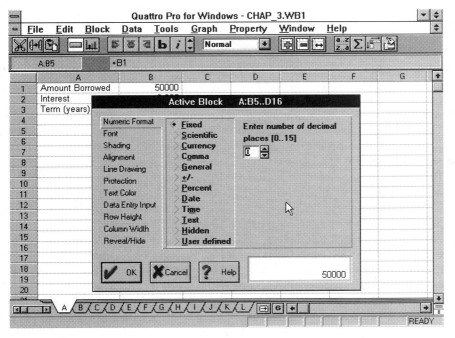

Figure 3.3 Active Block Properties Dialog Box

You can change how Quattro Pro displays numbers by *numerically formatting* them. Numerically formatting numbers and formulas does not change their value. The numeric format only changes the appearance of the entry. The contents of the cell that are used in calculations remain the same. Therefore, if you enter 3.333 and format the cell as a whole number, only 3 is displayed, but Quattro Pro uses 3.333 in all calculations that reference the cell.

To change how the numbers appear in the block, select the block and then inspect its properties. When you inspect the properties of a block, Quattro Pro displays the Active Block dialog box shown in Figure 3.3. With the Numeric Format property selected in the left column, you can select the numerical format you want to use for the selected block by choosing one of the radio buttons. If you select Fixed, Scientific, Currency, Comma, or Percent, you can enter the number of digits you want after the decimal point. For these numeric formats, type a number between 0 and 15 in the adjacent text box or click the up and down arrows on the right side of the text box to change its value. If you choose Date or Time, you need to refine your selection further by selecting from a second set of radio buttons to indicate the format of the date or time. The two international date and time formats are chosen by the International dialog box of Windows' Control Panel. A list and examples of the available numeric formats are given in Table 3.1. Later in the next section, you will learn how to create numeric format definitions for your own numeric formats. At this point, you can select OK to make the property changes you have selected or you can continue making other property changes by selecting another property in the left-hand column. When you change the numeric format, or other properties of the block, the lower right corner of the dialog box shows a sample of how a cell will look with the properties you have selected. Also, the properties you have changed will appear in a different color in the left side of the dialog box.

When you select OK, Quattro Pro formats the data in the selected block. The values stored in memory are not changed by numeric formatting even though their appearance may change. Quattro Pro performs the calculations using the numbers as stored in memory, not as displayed. If a cell is too narrow to fit its contents in the selected format, Quattro Pro displays asterisks in the cell. Changing the format or widening the column (described later in the chapter) eliminates the asterisks and returns the cell's contents to the display.

When you format a block of cells, the format you select applies to all the cells in the block. Cells in the block that contain values immediately change their appearance for the new format. Cells that are empty or contain labels retain the numeric format information in case they later contain values. The numeric format for the block overrides the default format. To change the default format, change the numeric format for the Normal style, as described later in the chapter.

Quattro Pro provides two unusual numeric formats. The Text numeric format displays formulas in the specified block instead of showing the formulas' results. Any cell comments also appear. This can be a good solution for documenting the contents of a notebook. You will probably need to widen the cells to see the formulas, as you will learn how to do later in the chapter. In Text numeric format,

Table 3.1   Choices for the Numeric Formats

Format	Effect on 9123.456	Effect on 195.4	Effect on .00987
Fixed (two decimals)	9123.46	-195.40	0.01
Scientific (two decimals)	9.12E+02	-1.95E+02	9.87E-03
Currency (two decimals)	$9,123.46	($195.40)	$0.01
Comma (two decimals)	9,123.46	(195.40)	0.01
General	9123.456	-195.4	0.00987
+/-	9123 +'s	195 -'s	0.00987
Percent (two decimals)	912345.60%	-19540.00%	0.99%
Date and Time	22-DEC-24	N/A	12:14:13AM
Text	9123.456	-195.4	0.00987
Hidden			

Note: N/A = not applicable; blanks appear in Hidden format because no numbers or characters appear on the screen when you choose that format.

unlike other numeric formats, if a cell is not wide enough to display the formula, only the part of the formula that fits in the cell is displayed. Unlike label entries, formulas formatted as text do not borrow adjoining cell display space.

The Hidden numeric format is the only numeric format that affects label entries as well as numbers and formulas. This numeric format hides the cell contents from the display. When the selector is on a cell with a Hidden format, the cell contents appear in the input line but do not appear in the cell. When you print a block that includes the hidden cells, the contents of these cells are not printed. This feature allows you to print a page containing salary data without printing the confidential salary information. While a cell is hidden, it can still be edited, changed, and referenced in calculations. To expose a hidden cell, select the block and change the numeric format property to another numeric format.

Figure 3.4 shows several cells that have had their properties changed to use other numeric formats. On this page, the date in D2 is formatted with the DD-MMM-YY date format. The values in C5..C8 are formatted with the comma format using no digits after the decimal point. The values in G5..G7 are formatted with the currency format using no digits after the decimal point. The percentage in C11 uses the percentage format with one digit after the decimal point.

CREATING YOUR OWN NUMERIC FORMATS   Besides choosing from the numeric formats listed in the Active Block dialog box, you can create your own.

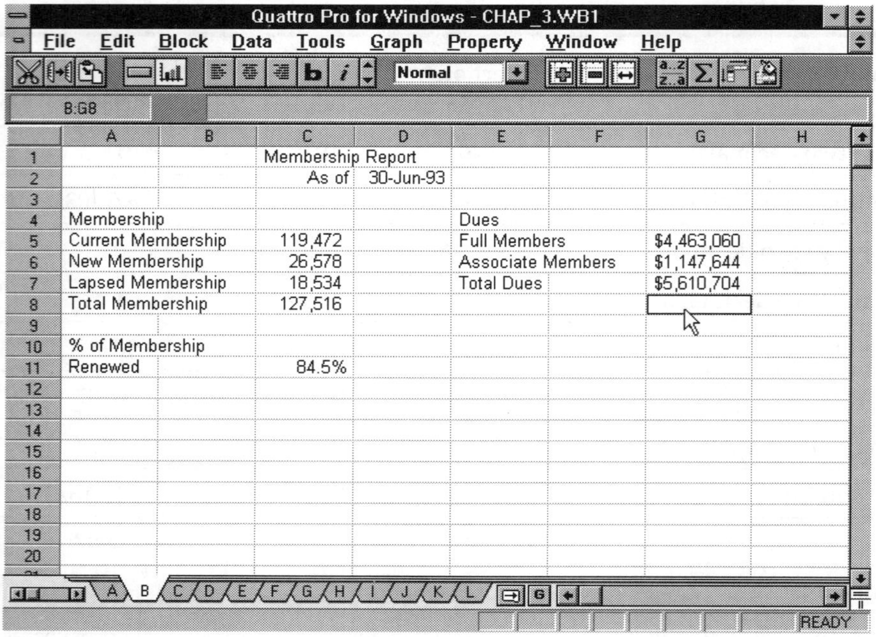

Figure 3.4 Example of Numeric Formats

You can create custom numeric formats that expand on the numeric formatting options. You can create custom formats that provide additional ways of displaying values, dates, and times. For example, you can create your own date formats to provide other options than the ones in the second set of date format radio buttons. Creating your own numeric formats is as simple as selecting the Under defined radio button and then entering the format code in the adjacent text box. Quattro Pro includes several User defined formats that you can use, or you can create your own from scratch. Once you enter the format code, it is available on any page in the active notebook or in any other notebooks that are open.

The first character of a format code is an N or a T to indicate whether the format applies to values (N) or dates or times (T), followed by format symbols that define the format. Table 3.2 lists characters you might use in a format code for values. You can also use other characters, such as ( ) for negative numbers. These characters are not listed because they are not codes. You can either enclose these characters in single quotes or let Quattro Pro do it for you.

For numbers, you can have one, two, or three formats as part of the same format code, separated by semicolons. When you use one format, as in *N $9999*, the format applies to all numbers, and negative numbers are indicated with a –. When you use two formats, as in *N$9999;N($9999)*, the first format applies to zero and positive numbers and the second format applies to negative numbers. When you

Table 3.2 Format Code Symbols for Value Entries

Character	Effect	Sample Format Code	Results on 5474.983	-3891.4852
N or n	Indicates that the following format code is for values	N999990.99	5474.98	-3891.49
0	Displays a digit in place of 0, substituting 0 where a digit is needed	N00000.00	05474.98	-03891.49
9	Displays digit in place of character, only if number has a digit in that place	N999999.99	5474.98	-3891.49
%	Displays a number as percentage	N999990.9%	547498.3%	-389148.5%
,	Inserts a comma separator	N999,999	5,475	-3,891
.	Inserts a decimal separator	N999,999.9	5,475.	-3,891.5
E- or e-	Displays a number using scientific notation with - or nothing after the E as appropriate	N9.99E-99	5.47E3	-3.89E3
E+ or e+	Displays a number using scientific notation using + or - after the E as appropriate	N9.99E+00	5.47E+03	-3.89E+03
\	Displays next character as it literally appears	N9999.99*	5474.98*	-3891.49*
*	Fills column not occupied with other characters with the character after the asterisk	N*-9999.0	- - - - 5474.0	-- - 3891.4
" "	Adds characters between quote to the entry	N"Price–"99.99	Price–5474.98	Price–3891.49

use three formats, as in *N$9999;N"Zero Balance";N($9999)*, the first format applies to positive numbers, the second format applies to zero values, and the third format applies to negative numbers.

For date or time formats, the first character is T. After the T are the codes for the parts of the date or time you want to display. The codes are case-sensitive: The case of the date and time codes controls the case of the text the codes display. For example, WEEKDAY for October 11, 1992 returns SUNDAY, but Weekday returns Sunday. Table 3.3 shows the format code characters for date entries, and Table 3.4 shows the format code characters for time entries. You can even combine the date and time with a User defined format. Quattro Pro includes the User defined format *TMM' 'DD' 'YY'   'HH':'MM':'SS' 'AMPM*: 3 PM on October 11, 1992 displays as 10 11 92 3:00:00 PM.

An example of User defined formats is shown in Figure 3.5. On this page, the date is formatted with a format code of *T Weekday Month D*. This format lets you include the weekday with the date, an option not possible with the other date and time formats. For phone numbers, the range B5..B17 is formatted with a format code of *N'('000')'000'-'0000*. Also, the range C5..C23 is formatted with a format code of N$9,999;N'New client';N'Incorrect Entry'. Sales of 0 as in C7 display "New client," and negative sales as in C11 display as "Incorrect Entry." In column F, the number of previous phone calls is formatted with the format code

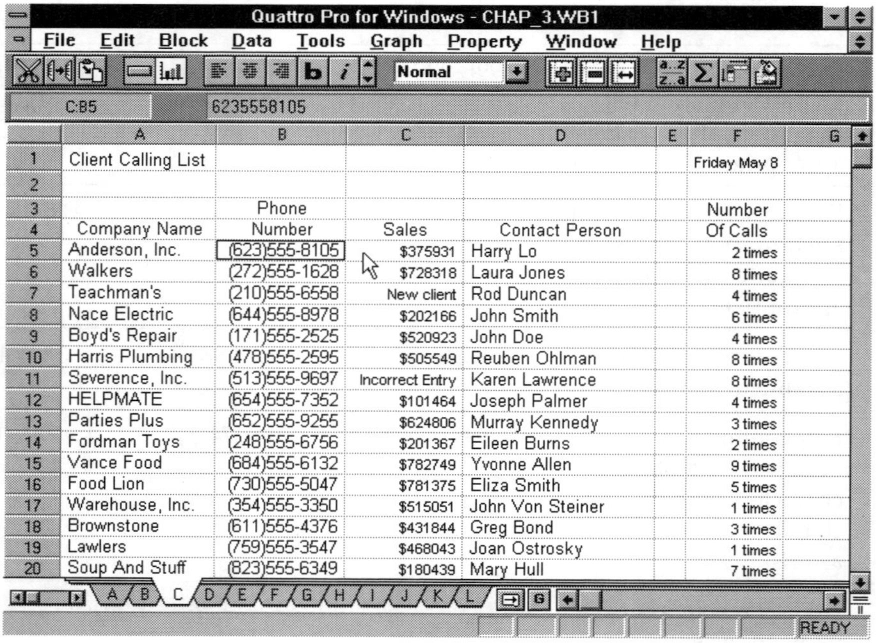

Figure 3.5   Page Using Custom Numeric Formats

Table 3.3   Format Code Symbols for Dates

Character	Effect	Sample Format Code	Results on May 5, 1992	December 12, 2010
T or t	Indicates that the format code is for a date or time	TMMO/DD/YY	05/05/92	12/12/2010
M or MO	Displays the month as a number between 1 and 12	TMo-D-YYYY	5-5-1992	12-12-2010
MM or MMO	Displays the month as a number between 01 and 12	TMMO/DD/YY	05/05/92	12/12/10
MON	Displays the month as a three-letter abbreviation	tMon d	May 5	Dec 12
MONTH	Displays the month spelled out	tMonth d	May 5	December 12
D	Displays the day as a number between 1 and 31	TMo-D-YYYY	5-5-1992	12-12-2010
DD	Displays the day as a number between 01 and 31	TMMO/DD/YY	05/05/92	12/12/10
WDAY	Displays the day as a three-letter abbreviation	tWday Mon d	Tue May 5	Sun Dec 12
WEEKDAY	Displays the weekday spelled out	tWeekday	Tuesday	Sunday
YY	Displays the last two digits of the year (00-99)	TMMO/DD/YY	05/05/92	12/12/10
YYYY	Displays four digits of the year (1900-2099)	TMo-D-YYYY	5-5-1992	12-12-2010

Table 3.4   Format Code Symbols for Time

Character	Effect	Sample Format Code	Results on 9:48:02 AM	3:09:12 PM
h	Displays the hour as a number between 1 and 12 if ampm or AMPM is used, or between 1 and 24 if ampm or AMPM is not used	Th:m:s AMPM	9:48:2 AM	3:9:12 PM
hh	Displays the hour as two digits between 01 and 12 if ampm or AMPM is used, or between 01 and 24 if ampm or AMPM is not used	Thh:mm:ss	09:48:02	15:09:12
M or MI	Displays the minute as a number between 1 and 60	Th:m:s AMPM	9:48:2 AM	3:9:12 PM
MM or MMI	Displays the minute as a number between 01 and 60	Thh:mm:ssAMPM	09:48:02AM	03:09:12PM
S	Displays the second as a number between 1 and 60	Th:m:s AMPM	9:48:2 AM	3:9:12 PM
SS	Displays the second as a number between 01 and 60	Thh:mm:ssAMPM	09:48:02AM	03:09:12PM
AMPM	Displays am or AM after times before noon, and pm or PM after times after noon	Thh:mm:ssAMPM	09:48:02AM	03:09:12PM

of *N99* 'time'. The format definitions let you create new formats that specifically meet your needs. Several of the columns are widened (as described later in the chapter) so the formatted entries do not appear as asterisks.

Using Different Fonts

Up to this point, your entries have used one font. A font is the typeface, size, style, and color in which the characters appear. Windows supports many different fonts that you can use for your data. You can use multiple fonts to create a professional-looking output. You can use any font in Quattro Pro for Windows that you have installed for Windows, including the fonts Windows provides, fonts available on your printer, and fonts you have installed through hardware and software. With Quattro Pro, you can change a block's properties to use a different font. As soon as you change the font, your data uses the new font. To change the font for your data, you must select the block, inspect the block's properties, and then select the font you want the block to use.

The fonts available in Quattro Pro for Windows are those that Windows makes available to the Windows applications. To have a font available, it must be installed with Windows. Since Windows 3.0 and 3.1 provide fonts with different names, the fonts you have available will vary with the release of Windows you are using. For example, in Windows 3.1 you have Arial and Times New Roman, while in Windows 3.0 you have Helvetica and Times Roman. You can also have more fonts by using font enhancement packages. Such products include the Adobe Typeface Manager and Bitstream Facelift. You may also have printer fonts that become available when you install the printer in Windows. With Windows 3.1, you will want to use the TrueType fonts (Arial, Times New Roman) or fonts available through a font enhancement package, since they look clearer. Chapter 12 covers more about installing fonts and printers in Windows.

SELECTING FONTS FOR A BLOCK   To select the font a block uses, select Font from the block's property dialog box. When you select Font, the dialog box changes to look like Figure 3.6. From the Typeface list box, you can select a font from the fonts installed in Windows. Figure 3.7 shows some of the typefaces you can select (depending on the fonts you have installed, your list may be different). From the Point Size drop-down list box, you can select from any of the available sizes. If you want a size that is not listed, you can type it in the text box. Some fonts are available in any size, while others can only be specific sizes. You can select check boxes for Bold, Italics, Underline and Strikeout, or clear the check boxes to turn those styles off. You can see in the box in the bottom right corner of the dialog box how your typeface, point size, and style selections will make your entries appear. At this point, you can continue selecting other properties for the block, or you can select OK to finish selecting properties and apply them to the cells.

The SpeedBar has a few buttons for applying font selections to cells. The **b** button boldfaces the currently selected block or removes the boldfacing from the already boldfaced entries in the selected block. The *i* button italicizes the currently selected block or removes the italics from the already italicized entries in the selected block. The ▲ and ▼ buttons change the point size of the selected cells to the next smaller or larger font size. The size of the increment may be one point or

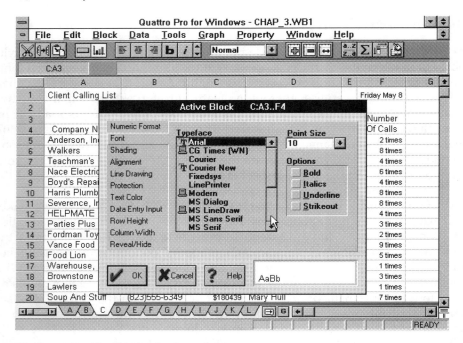

Figure 3.6   The Font Block Property

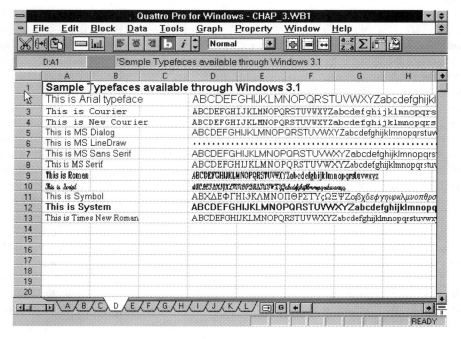

Figure 3.7   Sample of Windows 3.1 Fonts

some other amount, depending on the font. Using these buttons to change the block's font has the same effect as if you inspected and changed that block's properties.

Figure 3.8 shows a page that is enhanced using additional fonts. Different fonts are used to italicize and boldface text as well as for different typefaces. Unless you select another font, the cells use the font set with the Normal style. You will learn how to change this style later on in the chapter.

Adding Shading and Cell Colors

You can use shading and color to emphasize and customize your data. You can set the background color in a cell. To color cells, select the block to color and then inspect its properties. When you select the Shading property, you can select the two colors that are combined and how the two colors are blended. Quattro Pro takes your color selections and blend selection to create the shading and color that is displayed in the sample cell entry at the bottom of the dialog box. By selecting the first blend combination, you set the cell color to Color 1. By selecting the last blend combination, you set the cell color to Color 2. The other choices blend the two colors in varying amounts. At this point, you can select OK or continue changing other properties. When you select OK, all the cells in the block are

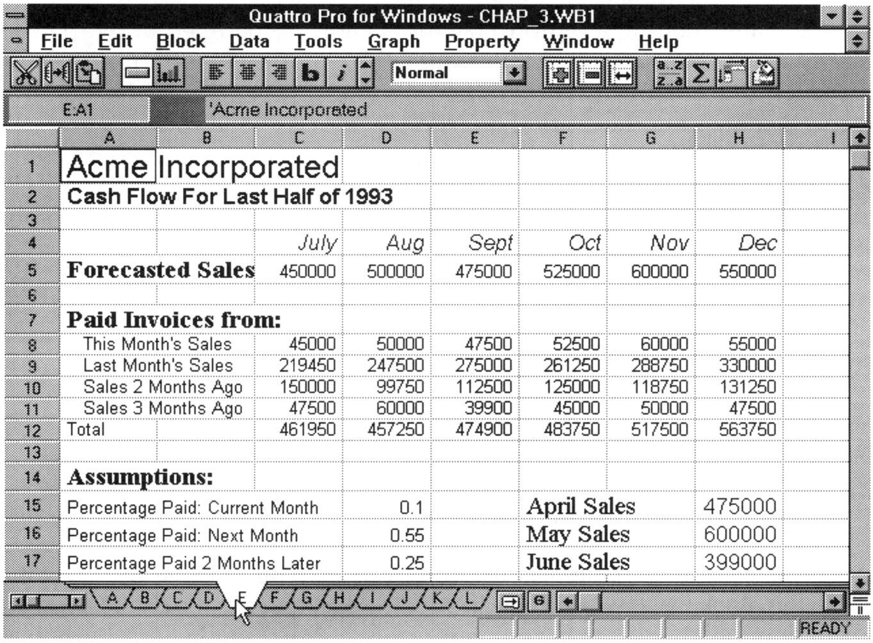

Figure 3.8 Page Enhanced by Using Additional Fonts

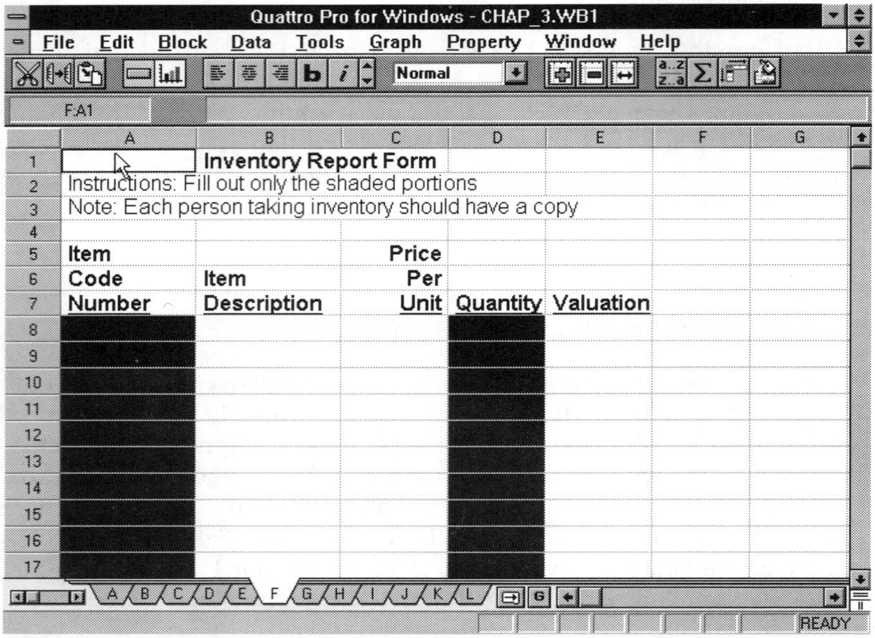

Figure 3.9   Page Using Shading to Emphasize Columns

shaded using the color and blending you have selected. Figure 3.9 shows a note-book page using shading to emphasize the sections to be filled in by the people taking inventory. When you print this data, the way the colors print depends on your printer. The shading carries to the cells that display the entries rather than just the cell containing the entry. For example, if you shade B1 in Figure 3.9 and B1 borrows space from C1, both B1 and C1 will be shaded. Any shading assigned to C1 only affects entries in C1.

If you want to remove shading, inspect the properties, and then set Color 2 to bright white and select the last selection under Blend.

Adding Color to the Text

Besides adding color to the background of a cell, you can also change the color of the text in a cell. To change the color of text, select the block entries to color and then inspect their properties. When you select the Text Color property, you can select the color of the text from the notebook's palette. In Chapter 12, you will learn how you can change the color palette for a notebook. At this point, you can select OK or continue changing other properties. When you select OK, all the entries in the block use the color you have selected. The way the colors print when you print your notebook depends on your printer. You can always return the text color to black to remove the color.

Text color belongs to an entry rather than to the cell's boundary. For example, if you change A2 in Figure 3.9 to have red text, the entry that appears in A2..D2 is red. The text color for B2, C2, or D2 only affects an entry that you make in B2, C2, or D2.

Changing Alignment

Chapter 2 discussed how labels are initially left-aligned unless you type a special label prefix as the first character, and numbers are initially right-aligned. If you have many labels to enter or want to change the alignment of existing labels, typing label prefixes is not an efficient solution. Also, you cannot use label prefixes on value entries.

You can change the alignment of existing entries by changing the alignment property for the cells. When you inspect a block's properties and select the Alignment property, you can choose from General, Left, Right, or Center alignment. At this point, you can select OK or continue changing other properties. When you select OK, Quattro Pro replaces the existing label prefixes in the selected block with the appropriate label prefix for the alignment that you have chosen. Also, if you select Left or Center, Quattro Pro changes the alignment of any numbers in the selected block. Quattro Pro has three buttons in the SpeedBar which also let you quickly change the alignment. If you select one of the Alignment buttons, which are the sixth through eighth buttons on the SpeedBar, Quattro Pro will left-, center-, or right-align the selected block.

Any labels that you subsequently enter in the selected block do *not* have the alignment that you have chosen by changing this property. These new entries use the page's label alignment setting. If you want to change the label alignment of empty cells, change the page's Label Alignment property as described later in the chapter. You can only change the default alignment of numbers by changing the Alignment property of the Normal style. The alignment setting of a block will affect both values already entered and any you enter in blank cells in the block. This means that if you apply an alignment to a block, any number you enter afterwards into the block will use the selected alignment.

Adding Lines and Boxes

Lines and boxes can be added to separate data and provide dividing lines between sections of data. To create a line or box, inspect the properties for the currently selected block, and select the Line Drawing property so the dialog box looks like Figure 3.10. This dialog box displays the different parts of the block you can add lines to under Line Segments, the types of lines you can add under Line Types, and buttons to add lines at preset locations. To change the lines of a block, select one of the line type boxes. If you want to remove lines, select the No Line box, which is the second line type. Next, click the lines in the Line Segments diagram

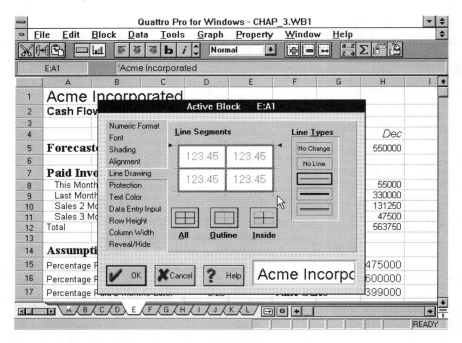

Figure 3.10   The Line Drawing Block Property

to indicate where you want the lines added or removed. By selecting different parts of the Line Segments diagram, you can add the selected line type to the different edges of the block and in between the cells in the block. You can also select Line Segments and then move through the different possibilities with the Arrow keys, pressing the SPACEBAR when you want to add a line at the location identified with the two black arrows. Initially, the lines in the Line Segments diagram are shaded to indicate that Quattro Pro will not change any lines that are drawn in that location. This is the same as selecting the No Change line type. Another option for adding lines is to select a line type and then one of the three preset location buttons. The All button adds lines around the block and between the cells in the block. The Outline button adds lines around the block without adding lines in between the cells in the block. The Inside button adds lines between the cells in the block without adding lines around the border of the block. As usual, you can select OK to apply the selected properties or you can continue changing other properties before you select OK. The line's color is initially black, but you will later learn how you can change that when you learn how to change page properties.

Figure 3.11 shows a page in a notepad that is enhanced with lines. The lines around A1..C1 are added by selecting the double line under Line Types and then the Outline preset button. The lines underneath C4..H4 are added by clicking the thick line under Line Types and the bottom line in the Line Segments diagram. The

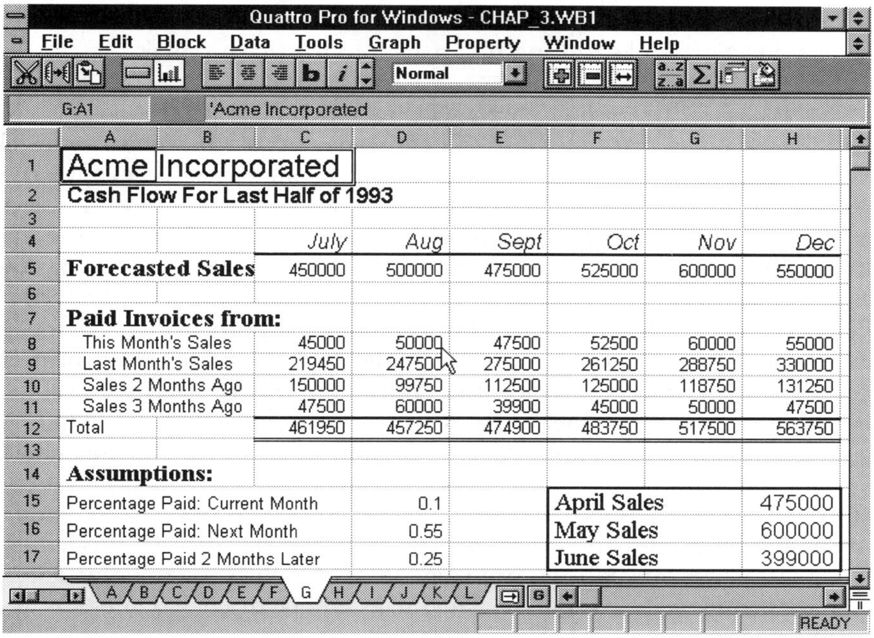

Figure 3.11   Spreadsheet Enhanced with Lines

lines above and below C12..H12 are added by selecting the thick line under Line Types and the top line in the Line Segments diagram and then selecting the double line under Line Types and the bottom line in the Line Segments diagram. To add the box around F15..H17, select the thick line under Line Types and the Outline button.

Using Protection

Protecting a page ensures that formulas and other entries you want to keep are not altered inadvertently. In Quattro Pro, protection is a two-step process. The first step is determining the protection status for a block of cells. The second step is enabling the protection features. You can tailor the protection features to your needs, since you can choose which portions of the notebook page are protected. Once you instruct Quattro Pro to protect the notebook page, you cannot modify any of the protected cells without disabling protection first. Each page uses protection independently of other pages. This means that you can have one page protected and other ones not.

You may want to think of protection as a plastic cover for the page in the notebook. Choosing which cells are not protected is like cutting holes in the plastic so you can make an entry on the underlying page. Selecting where you put the holes, or which cells are unprotected, has no effect until protection is enabled. Enabling protection is like putting that page into the plastic cover.

CHANGING THE PROTECTION STATUS   When page protection is enabled, Quattro Pro assumes that you want the entire page protected unless you tell it otherwise. Since you will normally only want to change specific cells, you must tell Quattro Pro which cells may be edited or have new entries made by unprotecting them. To unprotect a cell or block, choose the Protection property from the Active Block dialog box. Quattro Pro presents two radio buttons—Protect and Unprotect. Select Unprotect to make the cells in the block editable when the protection is enabled. Then select OK or continue making other property changes before you select OK. If you change your mind and want the unprotected cells to be protected, inspect the block's properties, select the Protection property, and then select the Protect radio button. In a typical page, you must unprotect each cell where data entry is required. You can unprotect cells even if protection is already enabled.

ENABLING PROTECTION   To use the protection status of the cells, you need to inspect the properties for the page. You can inspect a page's properties by pointing to its page name tab and pressing the right mouse button or by using the Active Page command in the Property menu, as will be discussed later. Once you inspect the page's properties, you can select the Protection property and Enable. Once protection is enabled, you cannot edit or make an entry in any protected cells. If you try to make an entry in a protected cell, Quattro Pro displays a Protected cell or block message. A protected cell cannot be edited, replaced, or deleted. However, you can move to a cell that is protected. When you want to disable the protection of an entire page, inspect the page's properties again, select the Protection property, and select the Disable radio button.

CREATING AN INPUT FORM FOR DATA ENTRY   One of Quattro Pro's features you can use with unprotected cells is limiting the movement of the selector to the unprotected cells only. You can restrict input to unprotected cells on the notebook page with the Restrict Input command in the Data menu. As the name suggests, the Restrict Input command in the Data menu restricts where you can make entries. This command allows you to enter data as if you were entering data in an entry form. This command restricts movement of the selector to unprotected cells in a block. All the other cells are visible but inaccessible to you. When you are

▼ TIP: Indicate which cells are protected.

When you use protection to limit entries to specific cells, add shading or color to indicate which cells are unprotected. This keeps another user from the frustration of trying to enter data into protected cells.

in Restrict Input mode, you cannot use the menu. You can only move between the cells that are unprotected and are specified by the block for this command. You can enter or edit data in any of these cells.

Before you use this command, you need to unprotect all the cells to which you would like to allow entries. You do not necessarily have to enable page protection. Next, before or after you select this command, you must select the block that you want visible on the screen as you move between the unprotected cells. When you select this command and select the OK button, the mode indicator changes from READY to INPUT. During INPUT mode, you can only move between cells that are unprotected. When you try moving to a protected cell, Quattro Pro moves you to the next unprotected cell in the selected direction. You can press ESC to exit from the INPUT mode, or you can press ENTER without making an entry. Either action returns you to READY mode in which you can access all cells.

As an example, suppose you want to change the sales forecast in C5..H5 of Figure 3.11. First, select the block C5..H5 and inspect the block's properties. Select the Protection property and the Unprotect radio button. Once this block is unprotected, activate the restricted input by selecting the block A1..H18. Next, select Restrict Input from the Data menu, then select OK to start this command. Since A1 is at the upper left corner of the block, it is the upper left cell Quattro Pro displays in the notebook window. While data entry is restricted, you can only move in the block C5..H5. When you press the DOWN ARROW in C5, Quattro Pro moves you to D5, which prevents you from accidentally typing an entry in other rows. When you are finished entering the new records, press ESC or ENTER to return to READY mode.

Restricting the Data Types

When you are entering a column of addresses or dates, you may find it inconvenient to remember to type the label prefix before typing an address or to press CTRL-SHIFT-D before typing a date. One of a block's properties you can set is the type of data it contains. You can set a block to contain only labels or only dates. You then do not have to remember to type the label prefix or press CTRL-SHIFT-D. Quattro Pro automatically translates your entries as labels or dates.

To control the type of entries made in a block, inspect the block's properties and then select the Data Entry Input property. The dialog box contains the General, Labels Only, and Dates Only radio buttons. (General is for resetting a cell's data type after selecting one of the other options.) After you have selected one of the radio buttons and then OK, Quattro Pro only accepts the type of entry you have indicated. If you selected Labels Only, any entry you make into the cell is a label with the label prefix automatically supplied. If you selected Dates Only, your entry in the cell is treated as if you had pressed CTRL-SHIFT-D. You must make a valid date entry, but you do not need to press CTRL-SHIFT-D.

Suppose you have to enter the data shown in Figure 3.12. You can quickly enter the social security numbers as labels by inspecting the block D3..D14 and changing

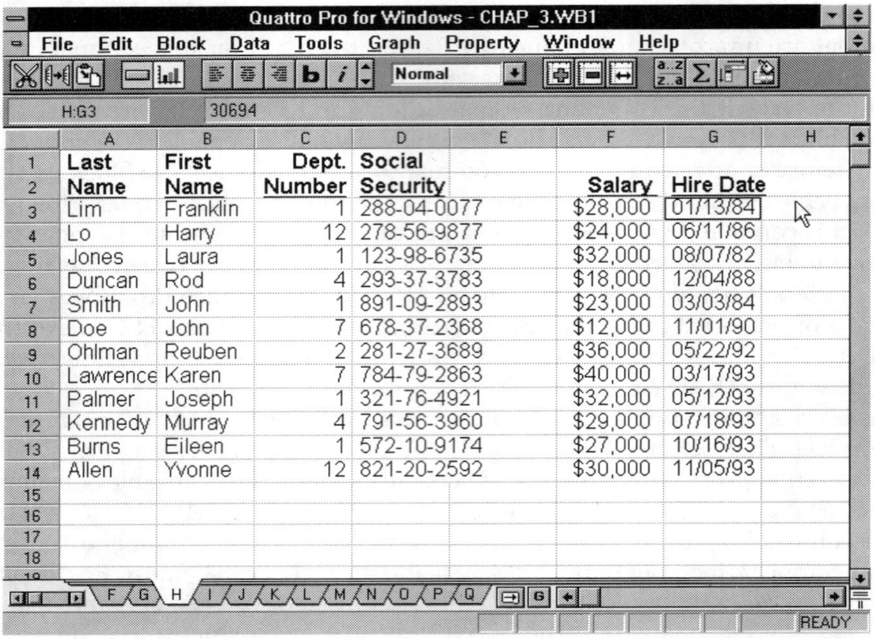

Figure 3.12   Data Entry Input Block Property Simplifies Data Entry

the Data Entry Input property to Labels Only. For the dates in column G, inspect the block G3..G14 and change the Data Entry Input property to Dates Only. When you enter the first social security number, you enter only **288-04-0077**; you do not have to include a label prefix, since Quattro Pro already knows that the entry is a label. For Franklin Lim's date of hire, you enter only **01/13/84**; you do not have to press CTRL-SHIFT-D, because Quattro Pro knows that the entry must be a date.

Setting the Row Height

You can set the row height of a block or have Quattro Pro automatically do it for you. When you changed the font of a cell, you may have noticed that Quattro Pro automatically adjusted the row height to fit the new text size. Quattro Pro's default is to set the row's height to the height of the tallest font in the row. You may want to use a different row height than the default, or return a modified row to the default. For example, you may have a block to print and you want it printed double spaced, which you can do by doubling the row height of the block of text.

When you change a row's height, you change the row height for all rows in the selected block, even in the columns that are not part of the selected block. To change the row height, inspect a block and select the Row Height property. Now the dialog box contains the Set Height and Reset Height radio buttons. If you select Reset Height, the row height returns to the row height most appropriate for the tallest font in the row. If you select Set Height, you can enter the row height in the Row Height text box. The number you enter must be the number of points, inches, or centimeters, according to which radio button is selected under Unit. A point is 1/72 of an inch. You will want a row height larger than the height of the text. If the row height is shorter than the text, the larger text is cut off at the top of the row. When you select OK to apply the block's modified properties, the rows in the block you selected automatically use the new height. Since row height affects an entire row, cells in that row that are not part of the selected block also use the new row height.

You can also change the height of a row or a block of rows using the mouse. First move the mouse to the line below the row whose height you want to change. In Figure 3.13, the mouse is positioned between the 1 and 2 to change row 1's height. Next, drag the mouse up or down to set the selected rows to the new height. The dashed line indicates where the new row height will be. When you release the mouse, the row height is adjusted. You can adjust the heights of several rows at once by selecting the rows you want to adjust and adjusting the height of one of them.

Changing Column Widths

For each page in a new notebook, the width of every column is set at the default width of nine characters. You may want to change the width of the columns to be either wider or narrower, depending on your data. Column width options include setting the column widths of a block, resetting the column widths of a block, and setting the column width of a block to fit the data. The default column width size is a property of the page, so you will learn how you can change the default column width later in the chapter.

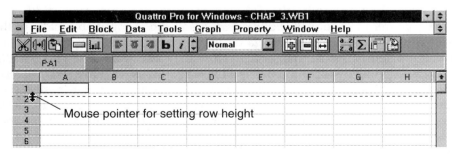

Figure 3.13 Mouse Changing a Row Height

CHANGING A COLUMN'S WIDTH   To change the width of the columns in a block, inspect the block's properties and select the Column Width property. Now the dialog box lets you enter the column width, whether you want the column width set, reset, or automatically set, the number of extra characters for automatically setting the column width, and how you want to measure the column width. If you want to enter the column width, you can type the new column width in the Column Width text box. The default measurement is the average width of characters using the default font. You can also measure columns by inches or centimeters by selecting another radio button under Unit. When you have entered the new column width, select OK or continue making property changes before you select OK. When you select OK, all of the columns in the block now use the new column width. Like the setting for row height, the new setting applies to the entire column not just to the part of the column in the block. Therefore, the block you select only has to contain one cell from each column you want to change.

When you change a column's width, if the new column width is too narrow to display any formatted numbers within the column, Quattro Pro displays them as asterisks instead of numbers. You can widen the column to change the asterisks into the formatted numbers.

An easier way to change the column's width is to drag the right edge of the column to a new location. You can point in the column border to the line between the column letters and the mouse will change to a black double-pointed arrow, as it does when you change row heights with the mouse. Then, drag the mouse to the left or right until the dotted line is where you want the new right edge of the column to be. When you release the mouse, the column's width is changed. Changing the column width with the mouse only changes the column that you explicitly narrow or widen. If a block that includes several columns is selected when you drag one column's border to a new location, only the column you have dragged is changed. If you want to change several columns at once with the mouse, you must select the columns by dragging the mouse over the column letters in the border.

RESETTING A COLUMN'S WIDTH   Once you change a column's width, that column continues to use that width regardless of the changes you make to the default width. If you change the default width, you may want to reset columns that you previously had set individually. You may also want to reset the width when you no longer want the column as wide or narrow as you have set it. To reset the column widths of a block, select that block, inspect its properties, select the Column Width property, and select the Reset Width radio button. The entry in the Column Width text box disappears, since it no longer affects the columns. Once you choose OK, Quattro Pro returns the width of the columns in the block to the page's current column width.

AUTOMATICALLY SETTING COLUMN WIDTHS A third option for column widths is to let Quattro Pro adjust each of the columns in the selected block to fit the data. You can have Quattro Pro automatically set columns to fit their contents by using the Fit button in the SpeedBar or by changing the block's properties. If the block contains only one row, Quattro Pro uses all of the column's entries to decide the new column width. If the block contains more than one row, Quattro Pro uses only those entries in the selected row to decide the new column width. For example, you can select A3..E3 in Figure 3.14 even though the block is empty. Next, either select the Fit button in the SpeedBar (the one containing the double-sided arrow) or inspect the block's properties, select the Column Width property, and select the Auto Width radio button before you select OK. Quattro Pro automatically adjusts the columns in the selected block to fit the longest entry in the selected block as shown in Figure 3.15.

By default, Quattro Pro assumes you want the columns one character wider than the longest entry. If you want to change the number of extra characters Quattro Pro leaves in each column, enter a new number in the Extra Characters text box after you select Auto Width when you inspect the block's properties.

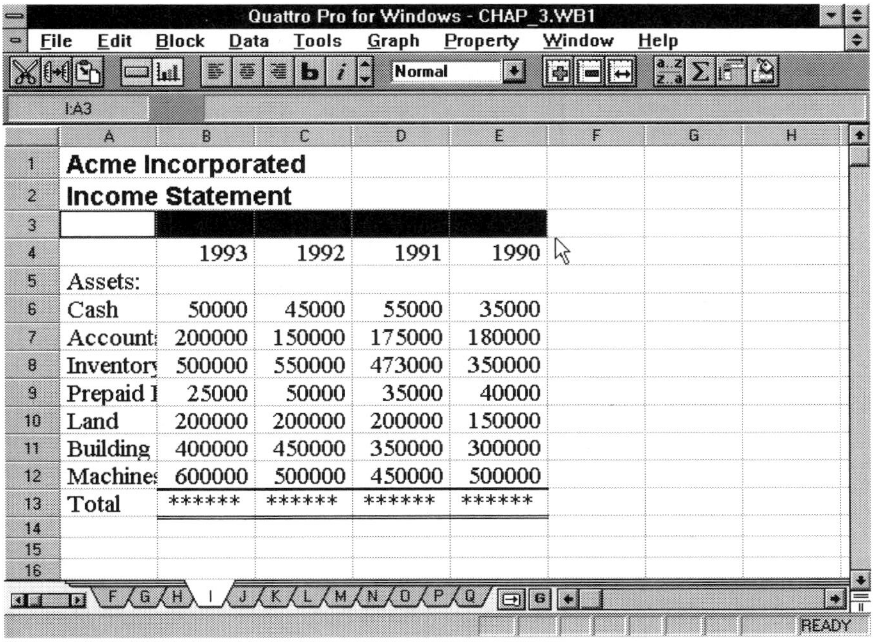

Figure 3.14   Page with Columns Needing to Be Widened

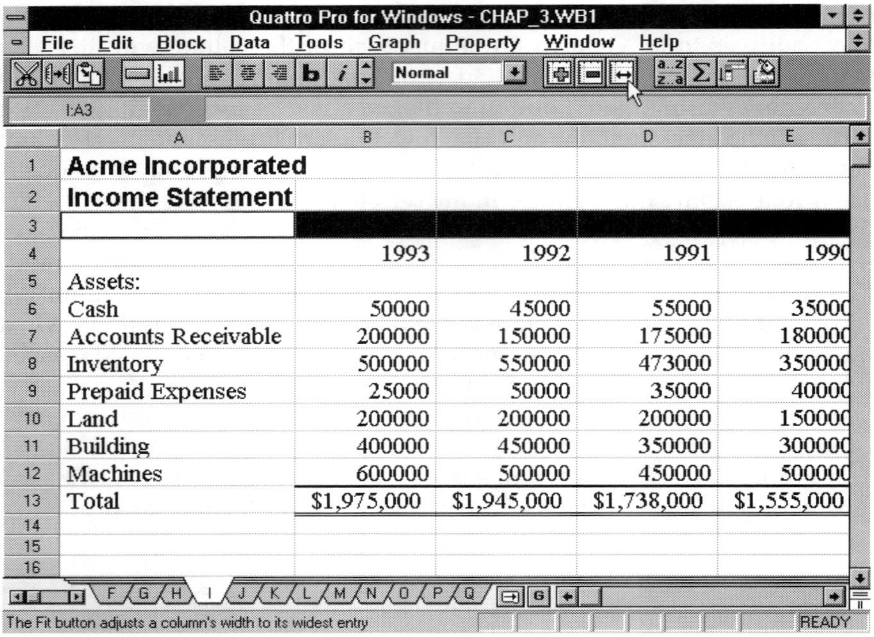

Figure 3.15   Page with Columns Automatically Widened

Hiding Columns and Rows

You can hide columns and rows from the display when you do not need to work with data in them. Columns and rows that are hidden from the display are also not printed, even if they are part of the block that you select to print. This feature is useful for hiding salary and other confidential information. It also can make it easier to work with a very wide or very long data page. If you have a notebook that tracks payroll costs for all the employees and this notebook contains columns of data that are not relevant to the current period, you may elect to hide some of these columns. If you are printing a lengthy report, you can hide most of the rows if you only want to show the column headings and totals for a summary report.

To hide columns or rows, select a block that contains at least one cell from each column or row you want to hide. Next, inspect the block's properties and select the Reveal/Hide property. Then, under Dimension, select Columns to hide the selected columns or Rows to hide the selected rows, and then select the Hide radio button under Operation. Like settings for column widths and row heights, settings for hiding columns or rows apply to entire columns or rows. When you have finished selecting properties for the block, select OK.

When Quattro Pro hides columns and rows, it adjusts the display of the rest of the columns and rows to the right of the hidden columns and below the hidden rows to display in the place of the hidden data. However, Quattro Pro does not re-letter the columns, as you can see in Figure 3.16, which has several hidden columns and rows.

The contents of the hidden columns and rows are still retained in memory. Any formulas that rely on hidden data are still accurate. Quattro Pro will display these hidden columns and rows during POINT mode when you are selecting a cell or block. When the hidden columns and rows are displayed, an asterisk appears next to their column letters and row numbers.

To make hidden columns and rows visible again, select a block that spans the hidden columns or rows. Inspect the block's properties and then select Reveal/Hide. Select Columns to display the hidden columns or Rows to display the hidden rows. Select the Reveal radio button. Select OK when you have finished selecting properties for the block. Now the hidden columns or rows reappear.

NAMED STYLES

Quattro Pro has named styles that let you assign a name to a group of block properties. Once a named style is created, you can assign the properties that the

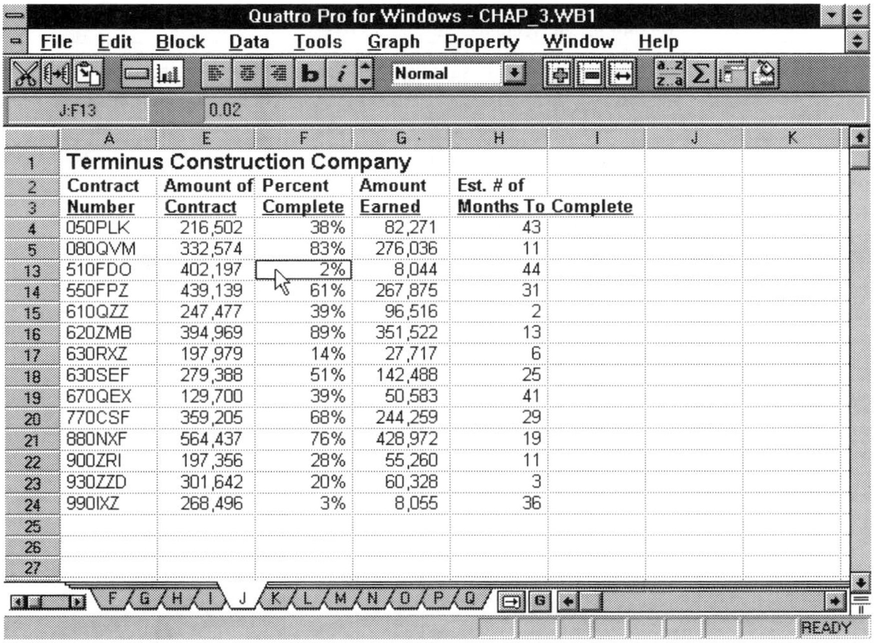

Figure 3.16   Page with Hidden Columns

named style represents by assigning the named style to blocks in your notebook. Named styles can include most of the block properties you have learned about previously.

Named styles make enhancing your notebook's appearance easier. You can create named styles for the different appearances you want the page to use. When you assign styles to blocks, you can change a style and all of the blocks that use the style are affected. For example, when you are developing a report, you can assign styles to blocks that you want to be treated identically, and then edit the styles until the report has the appearance you want. You can also share styles between pages and notebooks to give a consistent appearance to your data.

Creating a Named Style

Creating a named style is as simple as entering a command, supplying the name you want to use for the style, and selecting the properties the named style represents. To create a named style, select <u>D</u>efine Style from the <u>E</u>dit menu to display the dialog box shown in 3.17. Next, type the name for the named style in the <u>D</u>efine Style For drop-down list box. The bottom half of the dialog box contains the properties that you can select for the named style. When you select the

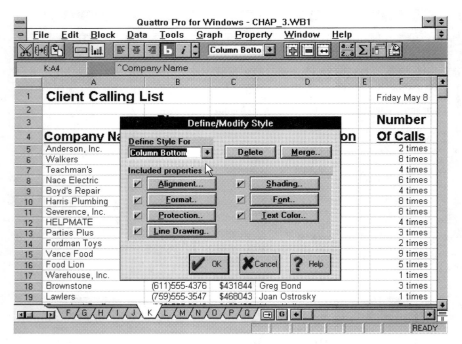

Figure 3.17   The Define/Modify Style Dialog Box

Alignment, Format, Protection, Shading, Font, and Text Color buttons, you see another dialog box containing the same selections as when you selected a block's properties. With Line Drawing, since styles apply to individual cells rather than blocks, several options are not present. You do not have the No Change line type or the All and Inside buttons, and the diagram of where you can add lines only includes the border of a single cell. When you finish changing a property, select OK to return to the Define/Modify Style dialog box. When you finish defining the properties represented by the named style, select OK to finalize the style. At this point you can apply the named style to any block. Besides the named styles you create, Quattro Pro for Windows also provides several predefined named styles.

If you later want to change a named style, use the Define Style command in the Edit menu again, and select the style name from the Define Style For drop-down list box. Then you can select from the buttons below the properties of the named style you want to change. When you select OK from the Define/Modify Style dialog box, the changes you make to the named styles are retained. Any notebook blocks that use the modified named style change to use the style changes you have made. If you want to change the default style of all cells, change the named style Normal, which is the style all cells automatically use unless they are assigned to another named style.

As an example, suppose you want a named style called Heading that centers its entries, boldfaces them with Arial 16-point font, and has a line at the bottom of the cell. You would select Define Style from the Edit menu and type **Heading** as a style name. Next, you would select Font and change the font, then select Line Drawing and add a line to the bottom of the cell. When you select OK from the Define/Modify Style dialog box, the Heading style is available to be assigned to any cell.

CREATING A NAMED STYLE USING A CELL'S CURRENT PROPERTIES If you already have a cell that uses the properties you want a named style to represent, you can use that cell to create the named style rather than selecting all of the same properties again. This lets you adopt a page to use styles that you have already formatted. Once you use the cells on that page to create the named styles, the other pages can use the same styles so all the pages in the notebook have the same appearance. To do this, select the cell that has the properties you want the named style to have. Next, select Define Style from the Edit menu, type the name for the named style in the Define Style For drop-down list box, and select the Merge button. From the Merge Style dialog box, select Cell. The Select Cell text box will already have the correct cell entered, since you selected the cell first. When you select OK to return to the Define/Modify Style dialog box, the named style in the Define Style For text box has all of the properties of the current cell. You can select OK to finish defining the style. Now, you have a named style based on the current cell that is available in the active notebook.

As an example, suppose you have an entry in a cell that is centered, boldfaced using Arial 16-point font, and has a line at the bottom of the cell. You want to use this as a named style called Heading. You would select Define Style from the Edit menu, type **Heading** in the Define Style For drop-down list box, select the Merge button, select Cell, and select OK twice to create this named style.

When you are in the Merge Style dialog box, you can also select the Style radio button and then select a named style from the Select Style drop-down list box. When you do this, the style you are defining in the Define/Modify Style dialog box adopts the properties of the named style you select in the Merge Style dialog box so you can subsequently modify it to be saved as a new style.

Using Named Styles

You can apply a named style to a block, using the Style List drop-down list box on the SpeedBar. The Style list is the only drop-down list box in the SpeedBar. You can click this box or press CTRL-SHIFT-S. To apply the style, select the block and select the style name from the drop-down Style List drop-down list box. When a style name is assigned to a cell, it appears in the Style List drop-down list box in the SpeedBar. When a style is applied, only the properties the style uses are changed. For example, if you apply the Heading named style, which does not affect the numeric format, any numeric format a cell had before applying the named style is retained by the cell. If you ever want to remove the effect of a named style, change the block's style to Normal.

Figure 3.18 shows a page after several named styles are created and applied. A1 uses the named style Heading, which sets the cells to use a 16-point boldfaced Arial font (MS Sans Serif in Windows 3.0). A3..F3 use the named style Column Top, which sets the cells to use a 14-point boldfaced Arial font. A4..F4 use the named style Column Bottom, which sets the cells to use a 16-point boldfaced and underlined Arial font. The numbers in columns B, C, and F and in F1 are named styles that include the user-defined formats you learned how to create earlier.

Removing Named Styles

While you can continue adding named styles to your notebook, you may also need to remove them. For example, you may no longer want a named style after you have assigned the blocks that use it to another named style. To remove a named style from a notebook, select the Define Style command in the Edit menu. Next, select the named style you want removed from the notebook from the Define Style For drop-down list box, and select the Delete button. When you remove a named style from a notebook, the blocks that used the named style return to the Normal style and lose their block properties. When you select a cell that used the deleted named style, the Style drop-down list box contains Normal. If you ever want to remove the properties originally set by the named style, select Normal from the Style List drop-down list box.

```
┌─────────────────────────────────────────────────────────────────────────┐
│ ═              Quattro Pro for Windows - CHAP_3.WB1              ▼ │ ▲     │
│ ═   File   Edit   Block   Data   Tools   Graph   Property   Window   Help  ▲│
├─────────────────────────────────────────────────────────────────────────┤
│ [✄][↔][▣]  [▭][▄]  [☰][☰][☰][b][i][↕]  [Column Top ▼]  [⊕][⊟][↔]  [a-z][Σ][▣][▣] │
├─────────────────────────────────────────────────────────────────────────┤
│   K:B3              ^Phone                                                  │
├─────────────────────────────────────────────────────────────────────────┤
│        A                 B          C            D              E    F      │
└─────────────────────────────────────────────────────────────────────────┘
```

	Company Name	Phone Number	Sales	Contact Person		Number Of Calls
1	Client Calling List					Friday May 8
2						
3		Phone				Number
4	Company Name	Number	Sales	Contact Person		Of Calls
5	Anderson, Inc.	(623)555-8105	$375931	Harry Lo		2 times
6	Walkers	(272)555-1628	$728318	Laura Jones		8 times
7	Teachman's	(210)555-6558	$849290	Rod Duncan		4 times
8	Nace Electric	(644)555-8978	$202166	John Smith		6 times
9	Boyd's Repair	(171)555-2525	$520923	John Doe		4 times
10	Harris Plumbing	(478)555-2595	$505549	Reuben Ohlman		8 times
11	Severence, Inc.	(513)555-9697	$754973	Karen Lawrence		8 times
12	HELPMATE	(654)555-7352	$101464	Joseph Palmer		4 times
13	Parties Plus	(652)555-9255	$624806	Murray Kennedy		3 times
14	Fordman Toys	(248)555-6756	$201367	Eileen Burns		2 times
15	Vance Food	(684)555-6132	$782749	Yvonne Allen		9 times
16	Food Lion	(730)555-5047	$781375	Eliza Smith		5 times
17	Warehouse, Inc.	(354)555-3350	New client	John Von Steiner		1 times
18	Brownstone	(611)555-4376	$431844	Greg Bond		3 times
19	Lawlers	(759)555-3547	$468043	Joan Ostrosky		1 times

```
┌─────────────────────────────────────────────────────────────────────────┐
│ [◄][ ][►] \A/B/C/D/E/F/G/H/I/J\K/L/ [⬇][G][◄]                    [►]      │
├─────────────────────────────────────────────────────────────────────────┤
│                                                              READY         │
└─────────────────────────────────────────────────────────────────────────┘
```

Figure 3.18   Page Enhanced with Defined Styles

SPEED FORMATTING

You can use named styles to apply formatting to cells in a block. However, each cell in the block has the same property settings. When formatting tables in your data, you will often want to format column and row headings or row or column totals differently from the body of the data. Quattro Pro for Windows makes this easier with the SpeedFormat button on the SpeedBar. You can use this button to apply formatting to a block of cells. If you used named styles, all the cells in the block would be formatted the same way. With the SpeedFormat, the cells within the block are formatted in different fashions, depending on where they are.

The SpeedFormat button, the last button to the right on the SpeedBar, opens the Speed Format dialog box, shown in Figure 3.19. The Formats list box lists Quattro Pro's predefined formats. The Example box shows how the formatting will appear in the spreadsheet, as you highlight each format in the Formats list box. The various check boxes at the bottom of the dialog box allow you to remove various properties used in the selected format before applying it to the selected block in your spreadsheet. You cannot specifically alter the setting of that property. You can either keep the property by leaving the check box selected, or revert the default for that property by clearing the check box. The four options in the last column of check boxes remove formatting from areas of the block. This does not

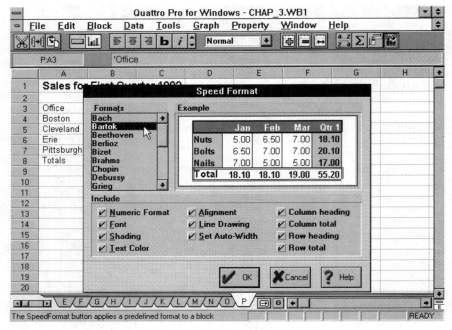

Figure 3.19   The Speed Format Dialog Box

reset all properties for those regions to the default, but causes those regions to have the same property settings as the body of the table.

To use the SpeedFormat feature, first select the block to which you want to apply the format. Then select the format from the Format list box, and change any format settings by clearing any of the check boxes in the lower part of the dialog box. Finally, select OK.

PAGE PROPERTIES

In addition to assigning properties to a block, you can set properties for a page. These properties include the page's name, protection status, line color, conditional colors to display values in a range, label alignment, display of zero values, default column width, borders, and gridlines. To inspect a page's properties, point to the page's tab and press the right mouse button. You can also inspect the page's properties by selecting Active Page from the Property menu. The initial dialog box for inspecting page properties looks like Figure 3.20. The page properties you select belong to the active page. This means that each page can have its own properties separate from the properties you select for other pages. As when you are selecting block properties, you can switch between page properties by clicking

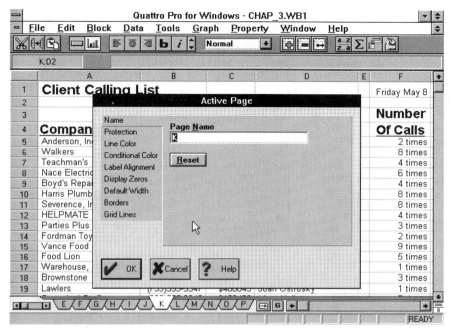

Figure 3.20 The Active Page Dialog Box

the desired property or pressing CTRL-PGUP and CTRL-PGDN. The selections in the dialog box change to match the property selected.

Setting the Page's Name

While page names of A through IV identify which page in the notebook your data is located, the page names do not tell you anything about the information stored on those pages. You can change the name of a page so that it describes the contents of the data in it. To name a page, inspect the page's properties. While the Name property is selected, enter up to 15 characters in the Page Name text box. You cannot use spaces in the page name. When you select OK to change the page's properties, the page uses the new name or use duplicate page numbers. Figure 3.21 shows a notebook with several pages renamed. You can easily see which page you will want to use. Also, the input line includes the new name of the page as part of the cell identifier in the input line. If you have formulas in other pages or other notebooks that refer to renamed pages (as you will learn about in Chapter 7), these formulas are updated to use the new page names. If you later decide to return to the default page name, you can inspect the page's properties and select the Reset button when the Name property is selected.

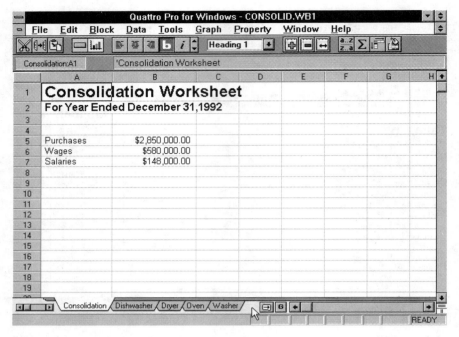

Figure 3.21   Notebook with Renamed Pages

▼ TIP: Use underscores in place of a space.

Since you cannot use spaces in page names, use an underscore (_) in place of
a space.

Enabling Protection

As you learned earlier, you can protect the pages in your notebook. For the
protection to be in force, you must enable the protection. To turn the protection
feature on, inspect the page's properties, select the Protection property, and select
the Enable radio button. While protection is enabled, you cannot edit or make an
entry in any protected cells. If you try to make an entry in a protected cell, Quattro
Pro displays a Protected cell or block message. When you want to disable the
protection of an entire page, inspect the page's properties again and select the
Disable radio button after selecting the Protection property. Each page has its
protection enabled separately so you can protect individual pages and leave
others available for use.

Setting the Color of Lines

Earlier, you learned how to add lines to your cells. These lines are black initially, but you can change them to another color by changing the color the page uses for lines. To change the color of lines on the page, inspect the page's properties, select the Line Color property and the color for the lines from the notebook's palette. In Chapter 12, you will learn how you can change the color palette for a notebook. When you select OK, all lines on the page, as well as any lines you subsequently add, use the color you have selected The way the colors print when you print your notebook depends on your printer.

Setting Conditional Colors

Besides setting the color of entries by changing a block's properties, you can also set the color of value entries that fall within different ranges. You can choose different colors for values less than a specified amount, values within a range, values above a specified value, and values that equal ERR. The conditional colors affect only value cell entries and emphasize values within certain limits. Changing the colors of the values applies to the entire page rather than to a block. To change the color of value entries, inspect the page's properties and then select the Conditional Color property. To use the conditional colors, select the Enable check box. In the Smallest Normal Value text box, enter the lowest value that is part of the normal range. For example, if normal values are 0 to 100000, you would enter **0** in this text box. In the Greatest Normal Value text box, enter the highest value that is part of the normal range. For example, if normal values are 0 to 100000, you would enter **100000** in this text box. Now, you can select the colors for values below the smallest normal value, values in the normal range, values above the highest value, and values equaling ERR. To set one of these colors, select the Below Normal Color, Normal Color, Above Normal Color, or ERR Color radio button and then select one of the colors from the color palette. When you select OK, all of the value entries use the new colors. The only value entries that do not are the ones that have had their color set separately by changing a block's properties.

As an example, Figure 3.22 uses conditional colors. On this page, the smallest normal value is 50000 and the greatest normal value is 75000. Values such as 16632 in B2 appear in red because that is the below normal color. Values such as 78893 in B4 appear in green because that is the above normal color. When you try printing this page, the way the conditional colors appear depends on your printer.

Setting the Page's Default Label Alignment

You can change the label alignment of all new entries by changing the page's label alignment. To change the page's label alignment, inspect the page's properties and select the Label Alignment property. Next, select between the Left, Right, and Center

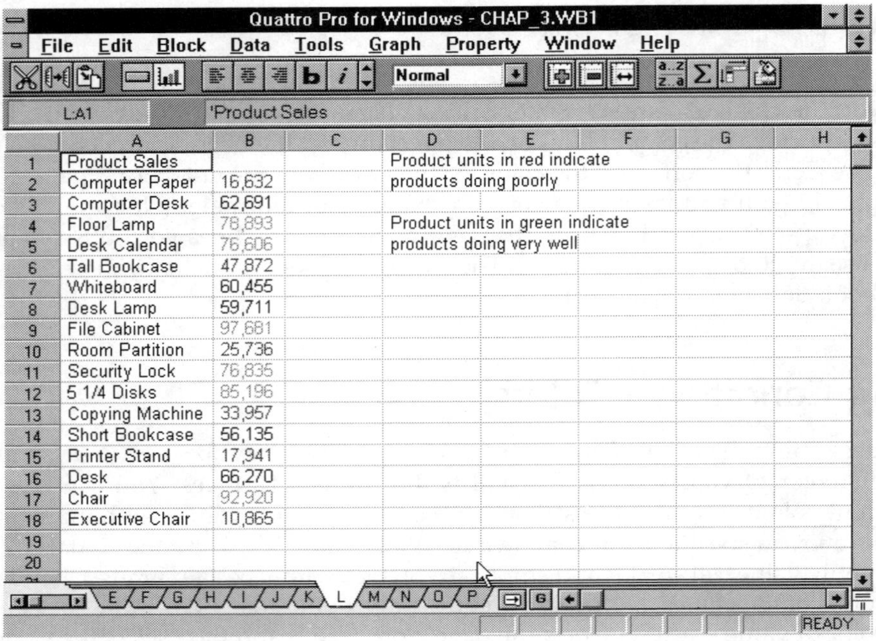

Figure 3.22   Page Using Conditional Colors

radio buttons. When you select OK, you have established the alignment for all new labels that are entered without a label prefix. This command does not affect existing label entries. The default alignment setting belongs to the active page and does not affect other pages in the notebook. This setting should be changed if you want most of the labels in a page to be right-aligned or centered.

Displaying or Hiding Zero Values

While you learned earlier how you can change how zero values display by using User defined formats, Quattro Pro has another method that applies to an entire page. You can select whether a page displays zero values or hides them. For example, Figure 3.23 shows several cells with zero values. The nonzero numbers in column E are the ones that require further analysis, and hiding the zero values emphasizes the remaining numbers. Figure 3.24 shows the same page with the zero values hidden. Hiding zero values is similar to using a hidden format for cells: The contents are still displayed on the input line when the selector is on the cell. To change whether a page displays zeros, inspect the page's properties and select the Display Zeros property. Next, select Yes to display hidden zero values or No to hide zero values. This command affects the entire page. If you want to hide zero values only within a block, create a User defined format. Also, remember that it is easy to accidentally type over hidden zeros, since they appear as blank cells.

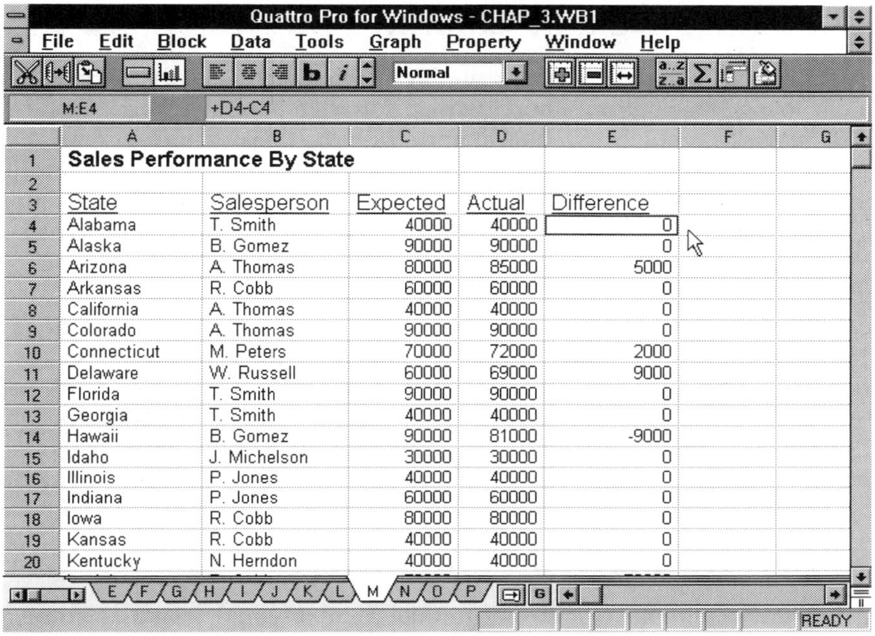

Figure 3.23   Page with Displayed Zeros

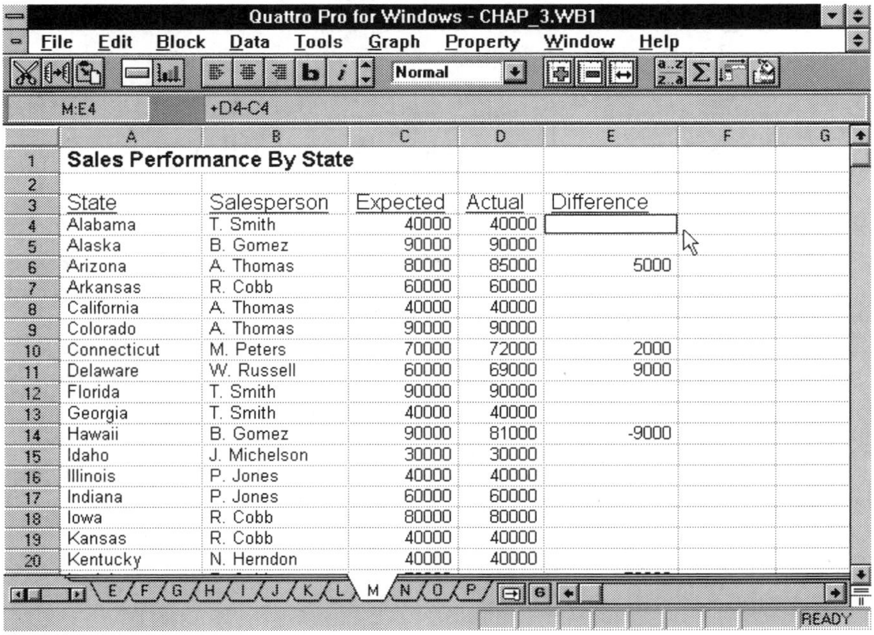

Figure 3.24   Page with Zeros Hidden

Setting a Page's Default Column Width

You can change the width of every column in a page by changing the page's column width. To change the page's column width, inspect the page's properties and select the Default Width property. In the Column Width text box, you can type the new column width. The default measurement of nine characters uses the average width of characters in the font set by the Normal named style. You can also measure columns by inches or centimeters by selecting another radio button under Unit. When you select OK to apply the page's new properties, all of the columns whose widths you have not set separately now use the new column width.

Since you are changing the widths of all columns, it does not matter which column you are in or block you select when you perform this command. Changing the default width of columns only affects the active page. Also, this command does not affect any columns that have had their widths changed by inspecting a block's properties or with the mouse. To use the default column width for columns that you have changed, you must reset the column width to the default setting.

Displaying Row and Column Borders

You may want to hide the row and column borders. If you do not look at the row numbers and column letters of a particular page to keep track of your position, you may prefer to remove them. This is especially true when you are entering data in a frequently used notebook where you keep track of your position by the surrounding entries. Custom designed entry forms often hide the row and column borders. To hide or display the row and column borders, inspect the page's properties and select the Borders property. Next, select Row Borders to display the row borders or Column Borders to display the column borders. You can clear one or both of these check boxes to remove the row and column borders from display. Figure 3.25 shows a notebook window hiding the row and column borders (the gridlines are also hidden, as described below).

Hiding and Displaying Cell Gridlines

Initially, a page has gridlines to indicate the boundaries of each cell. You can display or hide these lines. To change whether these gridlines appear, inspect the page's properties and select the Gridlines property. Next, select Horizontal to display the horizontal gridlines or Vertical to display the vertical gridlines. You can clear one or both of these check boxes to remove the horizontal and vertical gridlines from display. When these gridlines are hidden, the page looks like Figure 3.25 (which also has the row and column borders hidden).

GROUP MODE

Changing block properties normally affects only the current page. If you have several pages that you want to look identical, you will be annoyed at having to

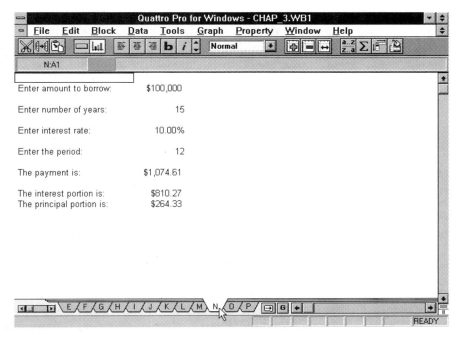

Figure 3.25 Page without Column and Row Borders or Gridlines

change the properties for blocks on each page or remembering to include the additional pages in the block you select. You can instead treat a group of pages as a group. When you work with a group of pages, making changes to any page in the group changes all of the pages. You can even make entries in one page and have them also be entered in other pages in the group. Pages that are not in the group are not affected by changes. Groups let you quickly format several pages to have the same format.

Starting a Group

Before you can use a group, you must select which pages in the notebook are part of the group. To select the pages that are in the group, select the Define Group command in the Tools menu. Next, in the Define/Modify Group dialog box, type the name for the group in the Group Name text box. Like page names, group names can have up to 15 characters, and may not include spaces. Then select the first and last pages by entering the page names in the First Page and Last Page text boxes. If you select a block containing multiple pages before you use this command, the page names are entered in the text box for you. The named pages and all of the pages between them are included in the group. Each page can belong to a separate group, but a page cannot belong to more than one group.

When you want to change the pages that are part of a group, select the Define Group command in the Tools menu, and then select the defined group from the

Defined Groups list box. Now the entries in the text boxes are filled with the name and pages of the selected group. Change the entries in the text boxes, then select OK to retain the modified group definition. You can also remove a defined group. When you want to delete a group, select the Define Group command in the Tools menu, and then select the defined group from the Defined Groups list box. Next, select the Delete button to remove the group.

Using a Group

Once a group is defined, you are ready to use it. To use a group, you activate the groups defined in the notebook by clicking the Group button, which is the button containing the G to the right of the notebook tabs. You can also activate groups by pressing ALT-F5 (GROUP). Quattro Pro puts a line connecting the pages that are part of the group, as shown in Figure 3.26. Now all of the changes you make in one page are automatically applied to the other pages.

As an example of a group, in Figure 3.26, the notebook has a group named Overall. While the group is activated, you can select A1 from the Consolidation page and select the Heading 1 style. Quattro Pro automatically applies the style change to every page in the group. This also applies to block and page property changes you make. The only change that you can make that does not apply to every page is making an entry.

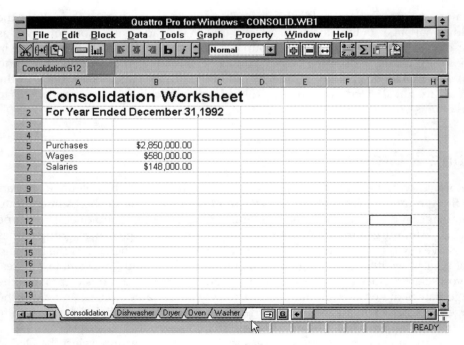

Figure 3.26 Notebook with a Group Selected

If you want an entry to be repeated in the same cell for each page in the group, you can repeat the entry in each page by drilling it through the group pages. This puts an entry on each page in the group. To do this, make the entry and then press CTRL-ENTER rather than ENTER to finalize the entry. For example, in Figure 3.26, the entry in A2 is repeated in each page of the Overall group by typing **For Year Ended December 31, 1992** and pressing CTRL-ENTER. You can also delete an entry on every page of a group by moving to that cell on one of the pages and pressing SHIFT-DEL.

When you no longer want to treat the pages in the group as a unit, you can deactivate the group by clicking the Group button or pressing ALT-F5 (GROUP) again. The line connecting the pages in the group disappears. Changes you subsequently make to one page are not reflected in the other pages. You may want to deactivate groups when you are copying entries or pointing to cells to build formula references. These operations select the data from all pages in the group, which may not be what you want.

▼ TIP: You can drill an existing entry to other pages in the group.

If you want an existing entry drilled through the other pages in the group, edit the cell by clicking the entry in the input line or pressing F2, and then press CTRL-ENTER.

GETTING STARTED

In this chapter, you learned how you can change the appearance of entries by changing block properties, changing page properties, applying named styles, and defining groups. You will want to try some of these features as you create the notebook page shown in Figure 3.27.

1. Create a group by selecting Define Group from the Tools menu. Type **Division_Sales** in the Group Name text box. Type **A** in the First Page text box and **C** in the Last Page text box. Select OK. Click the Group button or press ALT-F5 (GROUP) to turn the group on.

2. Make the following entries and press CTRL-ENTER to drill them to other pages in the group. If you press ENTER or click the ✓ accidentally, press F2 and CTRL-ENTER. You can use the sales report in Figure 3.27 as a guide or use the following cell references shown below:

    A1: **Division Sales**

    A3: **Sales**

Figure 3.27 Page Created in Getting Started Section

A4: **Cost of Goods Sold**

A5: **Gross Profit**

A6: **Operating Expenses**

A7: **Net Income**

3. Make the following entries but do not press CTRL-ENTER, so the entries only appear on the page where you enter them. You can either type the cell addresses or point to the cells. (If you are pointing to cells you may want to disable GROUP mode while you make the entries then activate GROUP mode when you are done.)

A:B3: **+B:B3+C:B3**

A:B4: **+B:B4+C:B4**

A:B5: **+B:B5+C:B5**

A:B6: **+B:B6+C:B6**

A:B7: **+B:B7+C:B7**

B:B3: **500000**

B:B4: **300000**

B:B5: **+B3-B4**

B:B6: **100000**

B:B7: **+B5–B6**

C:B3: **800000**

C:B4: **450000**

C:B5: **+B3-B4**

C:B6: **200000**

C:B7: **+B5–B6**

4. Edit B:A1 to be Division 1 and C:A1 to be Division 2. You will need to click the page tabs or press CTRL-PGDN to switch between pages. Return to page A when you are finished.

5. Apply the Heading 1 named style to A1. Select A1, then click the Style List drop-down list box or press CRTL-SHIFT-S to select Heading 1 from the Style List drop-down list box in the SpeedBar.

6. Change the numbers in column B to use the comma format. Select the block B3..B8 on page A and inspect its properties. With the Numeric Format property selected, choose the Comma radio button and type **0** in the text box. Select OK. Since this format makes the entries in B3..B8 wider than the column, you will need to change the column width.

7. Widen columns A and B so you can see the entire entries. Select a block such as A3..B3 for the block of columns you want to change. Either click the Fit button in the SpeedBar, or inspect the block's properties, select the Column Width property, select the Auto Width radio button, and select OK.

8. Rename the pages. Inspect page A's properties and with the Name property selected, type **Consolidation** in the Page Name text box, and select OK. Inspect page B's properties and with the Name property selected, type **Division_1** in the Page Name text box, and select OK. Inspect page C's properties and with the Name property selected, type **Division_2** in the Page Name text box, and select OK. Move to B3 on the Consolidation page. Notice how Quattro Pro automatically uses the updated page names in the formulas as you can see in Figure 3.27.

9. Save the notebook by selecting Save in the File menu. Next, type **DIVSALES** in the File Name text box and select OK.

4

Rearranging Cell Entries

As you become more proficient in making cell entries, you will find that your model does not have the appearance you want because you did not put the cell entries where you want them. Fortunately, Quattro Pro provides many commands that you can use to rearrange your entries in a notebook. These commands are a timesaving feature, since they enable you to quickly create the desired models.

In this chapter, you will learn to copy, move, and erase blocks of a notebook. Quattro Pro has several options for copying and moving your data. You can even change *how* Quattro Pro copies a section of your notebook by transposing the rows and columns, or by converting formulas into their string or numeric values.

Quattro Pro's commands that work with multiple cells are not limited to block activities; Quattro Pro also has commands that let you work with columns, rows, and pages. You can direct Quattro Pro to insert and remove columns, rows, and pages at specified locations. When you have text extending for many cells, you can direct Quattro Pro to reformat the text to fit different margins. And you can name blocks of cells so that you can use the name instead of the block address.

Quattro Pro lets you change how your window appears as you move around in your notebook, by creating rows and columns that are frozen on the screen. Finally, Quattro Pro lets you create windows to view two sections of your spreadsheet notebook at the same time. By the time you finish this chapter, you will have mastered a set of block commands that will provide speed features for your model-building activities.

COPYING

Copying is one of the most powerful features Quattro Pro provides. Copying lets you repeat entries anywhere you need them. Quattro Pro also updates formulas as you copy them—you can enter formulas for January and copy them for the other eleven months. Quattro Pro has several commands that copy data depending upon whether you want to use Windows' Clipboard to rearrange the entries, or you want to copy only a block's contents or properties. When you copy cell entries, you can copy both the cell's contents and the cell's properties. The cell properties include all properties you can inspect for a block except row and column features, which belong to the row and column.

Copying is extremely flexible and powerful. You can copy one cell to another cell, one cell to a larger block, or a block to another section of a notepad. When these copy options are combined with relative, absolute, and mixed addressing, the options for copying entries are extended even farther. Quattro Pro has other options for copying including copying only properties or contents, copying formula values instead of the formulas, and transposing rows and columns as Quattro Pro copies entries. You can copy cells by dragging them, using the Windows Clipboard, or by using some of the commands in the Edit and Block menus.

Copying Cells by Dragging and Dropping

One of the simplest ways to copy data on a page is to drag it to its new location. This method, called drag and drop, works for copying two or more cells to another location on the same notebook. If you have used Windows for a while before using Quattro Pro for Windows, you probably already know how to copy, since copying blocks is just like copying a program item in a Program Manager's group window or copying a file to the same disk in the File Manager. To copy cells, select the block containing the original data and then press CTRL while you drag the block to its new location.

As an example, suppose you have a column of entries for one project that you want to copy for another. Assume that these entries are in A3..B7 and you want a copy of them in D2..E6. To copy one block to another, follow these steps:

1. Select the block that you want to copy. In this example, it is A3..B7. The formula in B7 is +B3+B4+B5+B6.
2. Point to the block as if you want to change its properties.
3. Hold down CTRL as you drag the mouse to move the block's outline to where you want the block copied. In Figure 4.1, you can see the outline moved to cover D2..E6.
4. Release the mouse. Quattro Pro copies the block in the location of the block outline. Now the page contains a block of entries in A3..B7 and in D2..E6. The formula in E6 is now +E2+E3+E4+E5. Quattro Pro has adjusted this formula to match its new location. The page now looks like Figure 4.2 (the selector is moved to E6 to show the modified formula). The asterisks appear because column E is not wide enough to display the values using the chosen numeric format.

If the location you select in step 4 contains data, Quattro Pro will prompt you if you want to overwrite the existing entries. Select Yes to continue with the copying process and overwrite any entries or No to halt copying the block.

You can use the drag and drop method of copying entries when you have one block that you want to copy to one other location on the same page. If the block

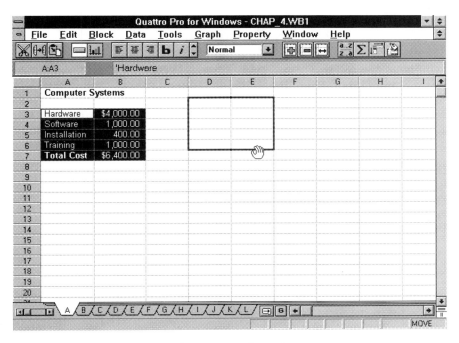

Figure 4.1   Entries Dragged to a New Location

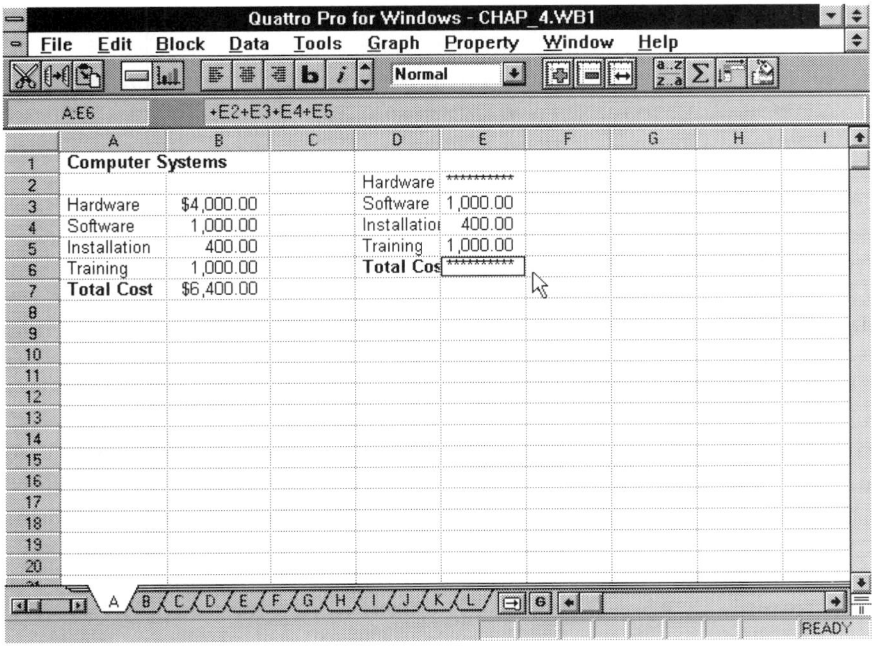

Figure 4.2   Entries Copied with Drag and Drop Method

> ## ▼ TIP: Dragging to Copy One Cell
>
> If you have one cell that you want to copy, you can still drag and drop it if you have a neighboring empty cell by including the empty cell in the block. For example, if you want to copy the cell A1 to A5, you can select A1..B1, then drag the two-cell block to A5, provided that B1 and B5 are empty.

contains any formulas, the formulas are adjusted as described below. If the outlined (destination) block contains any entries before you drop the copy into the notebook, you will be warned in a dialog box and asked to confirm that you want to copy the block, and replace the entries with the copied entries. The drag and drop method does not work with noncontiguous blocks.

Cell Reference Styles in Copied Formulas

When the formula in the previous section was copied, Quattro Pro adjusted all the cell addresses in the formula based on the new location of its data, because each cell reference is a *relative reference*. Quattro Pro always changes the relative cell references in copied formulas. Quattro Pro also supports absolute and mixed references to allow you to hold some or all references constant.

Adjusting cell addresses in formulas as you copy them allows you to create a formula in one cell, test that the formula produces the correct result, and copy it to other cells. By copying tested formulas rather than typing them, you reduce errors in your models. The method that Quattro Pro uses for changing the cell addresses in copied formulas applies whether you copy one or multiple cells. The adjustment Quattro Pro makes is also the same regardless of the method you use to copy the formulas.

RELATIVE ADDRESSES   A relative address is the default reference style in Quattro Pro. It consists of a column designation followed by a row designation, and may include a page name at the beginning. Relative addresses are the cell references used in all the examples to this point. When you use a relative address, Quattro Pro displays a cell address in the formula but does not really remember the cell addresses of all pertinent cells; rather, Quattro Pro remembers the distance and directions of the cells to use.

In Figure 4.3, cell A3 contains the formula **+A1+A2**. Since both of these are relative addresses, Quattro Pro stores its instructions for computing the formula in A3 as adding the value that is in the cell two rows above the formula to the value that is in the cell one row above the formula. This is referred to as a *relative* address, since the actual addresses used in the computation depends on the location of the cell where the formula is stored.

If the formula in A3 is copied to F5, Quattro Pro's relative addresses for the formula in F5 will be altered. The formula in F5 will still add the value of the cell

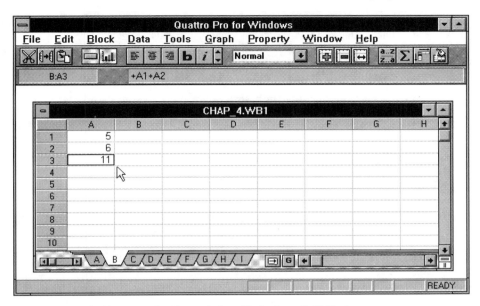

Figure 4.3 Cell Formula Containing Relative Cell References

two rows above the formula (F3) to the value of the cell one row above the formula (F4), as shown in Figure 4.4.

ABSOLUTE ADDRESSES Absolute cell addresses in copied formulas do not change. An absolute address allows you to make any cell references in a formula constant. To indicate that you want a cell reference to be absolute, you must put a dollar sign ($) in front of both the row and the column position of the address, as in $A$5 or $Z$1. You may also want to include the page name and a preceding $ sign. You can type these $ symbols. Or, if you are pointing to the cell or the insertion point is at a cell address in the input line, you can press F4 (ABS). Quattro Pro then inserts the $ symbols for you and will even add the page name for you. When you copy a cell containing a formula with absolute references, the new copy refers to the same cells as the original. For example, when you copy D5 to E5 in the notebook in Figure 4.5, the cell reference to D1 does not change even when the formula is copied to E5.

MIXED CELL ADDRESSES In a mixed address, there is a $ in front of only part of the cell address. You can type the $. Or you can press F4 (ABS) until the cell address has the $ in the correct places; each time you press F4 (ABS), the address cycles between the different combinations of absolute, mixed, and relative addressing. Mixed addresses combine the features of relative and absolute addresses. With a mixed address, the page, the row, or the column portion of the address is held constant, while other portions are allowed to change. Quattro Pro treats the

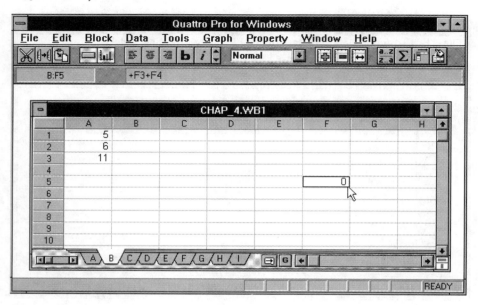

Figure 4.4   Formula Copied with Relative Addresses

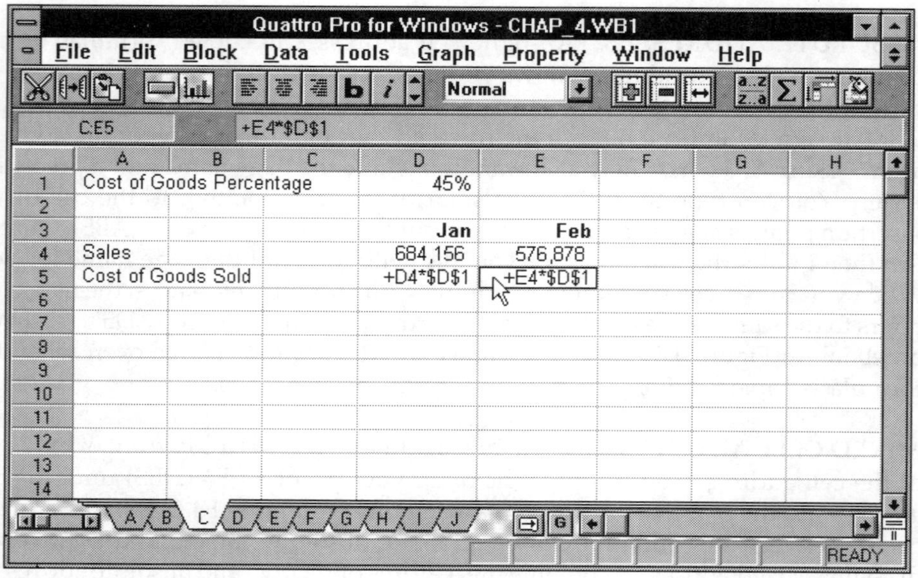

Figure 4.5   Cell Copied with Absolute Cell Address ($D$1)

part of the cell address that has the dollar sign in front of it as absolute and the part that does not have a dollar sign in front of it as relative. When a cell containing a formula using mixed addresses is copied, Quattro Pro adjusts the addresses in the formula of the new copy for the parts of the address that are relative and leaves the absolute parts of the address intact. For example, in Figure 4.6 the formula from A3 is copied to H3, H10, and A10 on the same page. The original formula adds the value that is in the same column as the formula in row 1 to the value that is in column A, one row above the cell with the formula. In H3, the formula still adds the value that is in the same column as the formula in row 1 to the value that is in column A, one row above the cell with the formula; but the column of the first cell reference has changed from A to H. In H10, the formula has changed the column from A to H for the first cell address, and changed the row number in the second cell address from row 2 to row 9. In A10, the formula has changed the row of the second cell address from 2 to 9. In each case, Quattro Pro treats the portion of the cell address without the dollar sign as relative and the portion with the dollar sign as absolute. If you copied these formulas to other pages, the formulas would have continued to refer to page D. If you want to let the formula reference adjust to different pages, do not include the page name in the cell reference, or make sure the page name does not have a $ in front of it.

A practical application of the mixed address is in the creation of pro forma reports. Figure 4.7 shows a page that projects different expenses. For this application, the absolute address may seem to be the best address type for referring to the expected percentage growth. But if you use an absolute address, you will have to

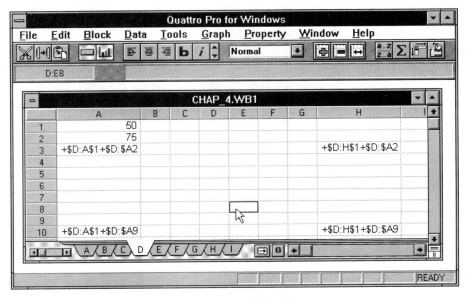

Figure 4.6 Cell Copied with Mixed Cell Addresses

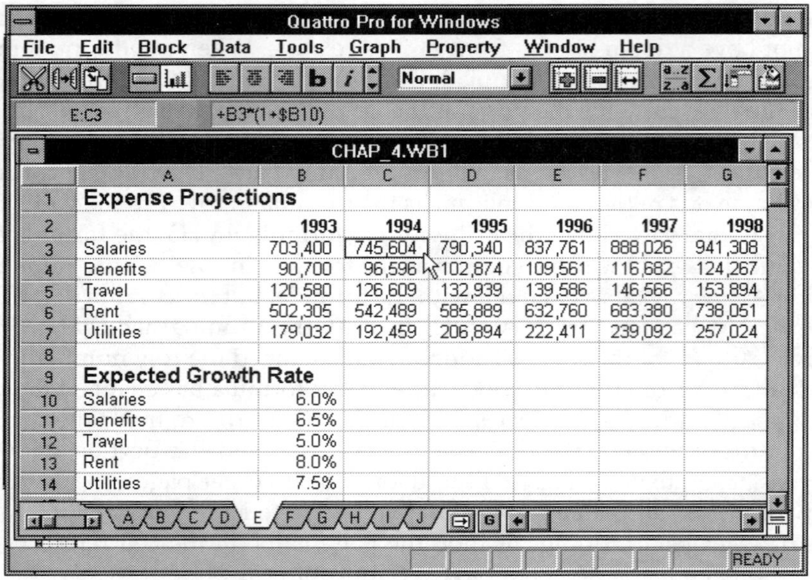

Figure 4.7   Using Mixed Addresses to Project Cost Growth

create a new formula for each different type of expense before copying the formulas to columns C through F. Using a mixed cell address when referencing the expected growth percentage is the best method for generating the formulas. If you use an absolute column reference then Quattro Pro will not adjust the column that the formula gets the percentage of growth from as it copies the formulas. By putting the formula +B3*(1+$B10) in C3 and copying it to the block C3..G7, you have typed only one formula and used it in 25 cells. Since the row portion of the mixed address for the growth percentage is relative, Quattro Pro adjusts the formula for each row so that each type of expense refers to the appropriate growth rate. Since the column portion of the mixed address is absolute, Quattro Pro does not adjust the column in the growth rate cell reference as the formula is copied across the columns.

Copying with the Clipboard

Windows has a Clipboard that can store information that you want to transfer between locations. You can use the Clipboard to copy data by copying data onto the Clipboard and then pasting it from the Clipboard to a notebook. You can use the Clipboard to copy one cell to another location, one cell to several locations, a block to another location (just like the drag and drop method described above), or a block to several locations. You can also copy noncontiguous blocks, just the properties or just the contents, formula or only values, transposed entries, and only cells with entries in them. The Clipboard can also be used for transferring data between applications, but you will learn more about this in Chapter 7.

COPYING ONE CELL TO ANOTHER You can copy a number, label, or formula entry in one cell to any other cell. Once you master this process, only a few modifications are required to expand the scope of the copy operation. To copy one cell to another, follow these steps:

1. Select the cell that you want to copy.
2. Click the Copy button, the second button on the SpeedBar, which shows two pages separated by an arrow. You can also select Copy from the Edit menu or press CTRL-INS.

At this point, you might think nothing has happened, but Quattro Pro just took a copy of that cell entry and put it on Windows' Clipboard. Now you are ready to paste the Clipboard's contents onto another cell.

3. Select the cell where you want the copy.
4. Click the Paste button, which is the third button on the SpeedBar and shows a clipboard and a page. You can also select Paste from the Edit menu or press SHIFT-INS. Quattro Pro copies the source entry to the address you chose in step 3. If the entry is a formula, the formula is adjusted depending on the types of references the cell addresses and block addresses in the formula use.

Figure 4.8 shows the selector on C8 after the formula **B6-B7** was copied from B8 to C8. This formula is adjusted because the formula uses relative references. In B8, the formula subtracted the value in the cell above it from the value two cells above it. When the formula is copied to C8, Quattro Pro changes the cell addresses in the formula so that the new formula subtracts the value in the cell above it (C7) from the value two cells above it (C6).

COPYING ONE CELL TO SEVERAL CELLS Once you enter the formulas to calculate the first month, year, or company totals, the difficult task of model construction is complete. Since all future periods and entries follow the same pattern for their calculations, the copy operation provides a quick solution for model completion. By copying formulas from one period to the subsequent periods, you can use the same formula for all twelve months.

An example of copying one cell to many is the trial balance shown in Figure 4.9. On this page, you need to copy the formula in D5 to the remaining accounts. This formula subtracts the January 1 balance in Column B from the December 31 balance in column C to compute the difference for the Cash account. Copying this formula for the other expense types reduces the typing, since you only have to put the formula in D5 and copy the formula for the remaining accounts.

To copy one cell to several cells, follow these steps:

1. Select the cell you want to copy. In Figure 4.9, this is D5.
2. Click the Copy button, select Copy from the Edit menu, or press CTRL-INS.

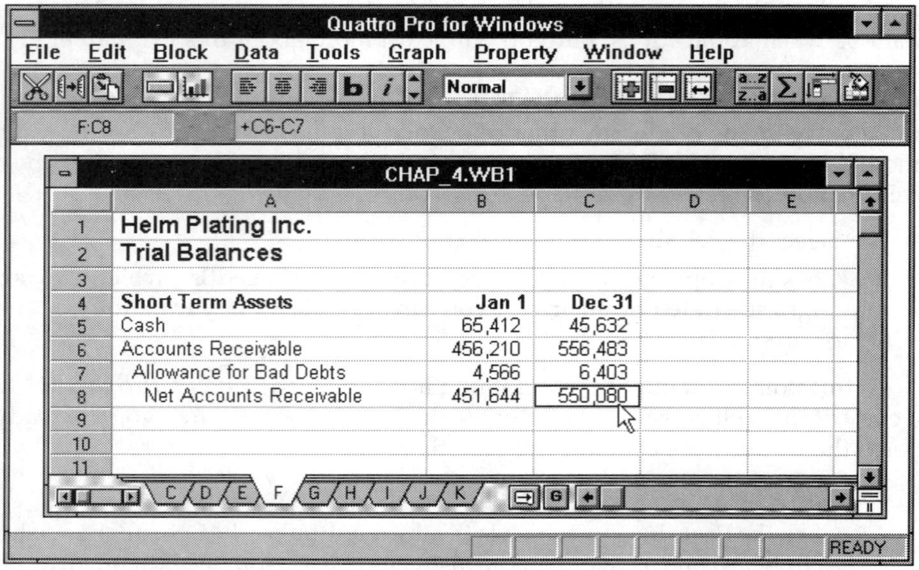

Figure 4.8   Cell Entry Copied to Another Location

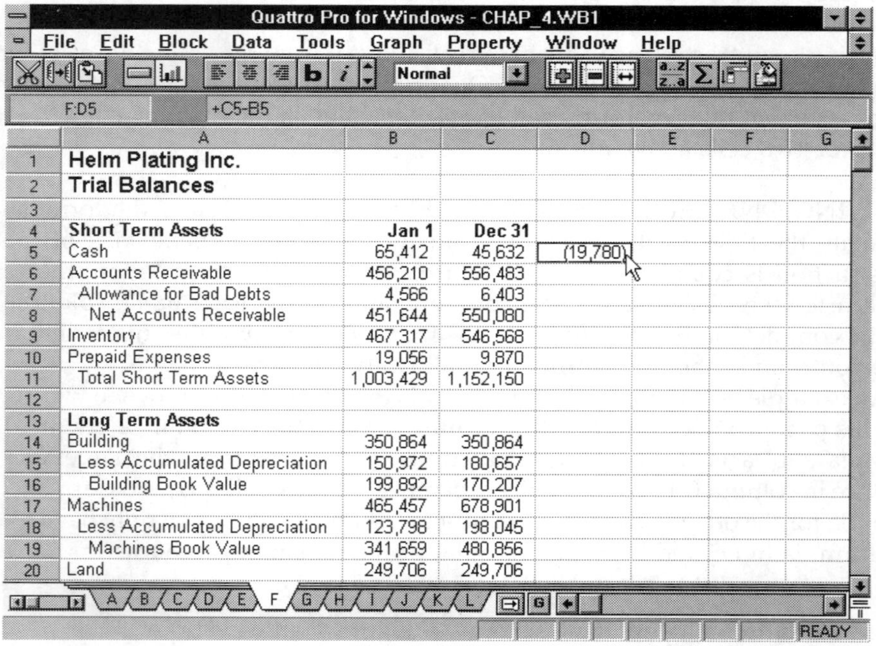

Figure 4.9   Spreadsheet before Copying Entry to a Block

3. Select the block where you want the original entry copied. In Figure 4.9, this is the block D6..D20.

4. Click the Paste button, select Paste from the Edit menu, or press SHIFT-INS.

The result of copying D5 in Figure 4.9 to D6..D20 is shown in Figure 4.10. For each of the copied formulas, Quattro Pro adjusts the cell references so that the new formulas refer to cells that are the same distance and direction as are the original formula's cell references. The formulas that are in D12 and D13 are meaningless and may be deleted. You may find it easiest to select the larger block and then remove the unnecessary entries. Another method of copying the formula is selecting the noncontiguous block D6..D11,D14..D20 in step 3 to omit the unnecessary formulas in D12 and D13.

COPYING ONE BLOCK TO ANOTHER   Copying one block to another location is a powerful tool, since it generates the same block in a different place. Copying one block to another location is the same as dragging and dropping to copy entries. As in the previous copy examples, if you copy formulas, Quattro Pro adjusts the relative and mixed cell references in the copied block. To copy one block to another, follow these steps:

1. Select the block you want to copy. For example, in Figure 4.11, the block to copy is A3..A16.

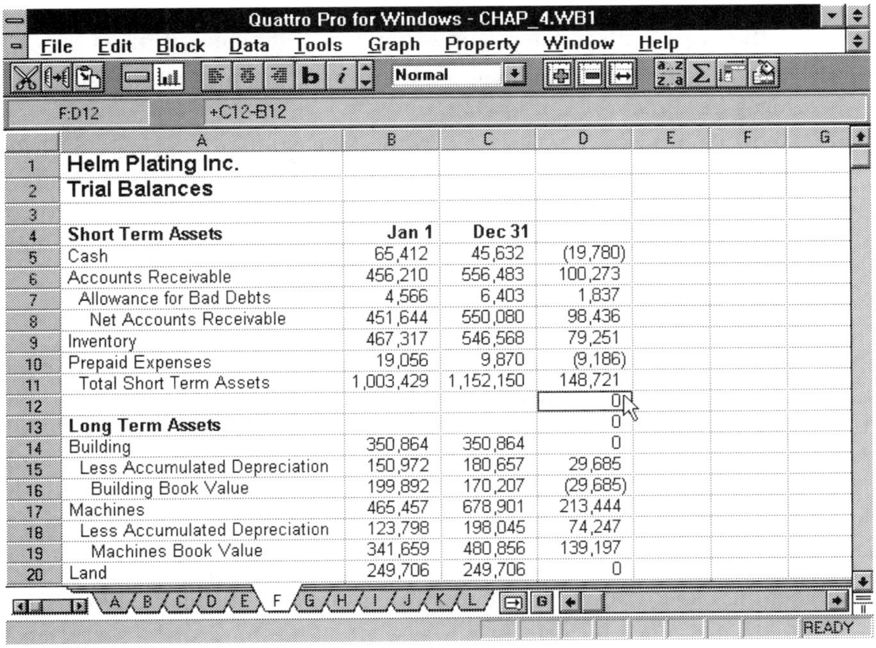

Figure 4.10   Spreadsheet after Single Cell Is Copied to a Block

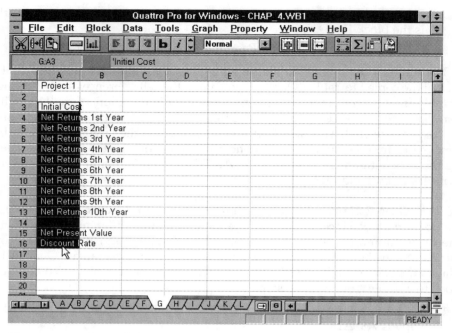

Figure 4.11   Spreadsheet with Block to Copy

2. Click the Copy button, select Copy from the Edit menu, or press CTRL-INS.

3. Select the cell where you want the copy of the block to begin. For the example in Figure 4.11, it is D3.

4. Click the Paste button, select Paste from the Edit menu, or press SHIFT-INS. Quattro Pro copies the block to the address selected in step 3. Even though you only specified one cell for the block's destination, Quattro Pro copies the entire block. Figure 4.12 shows the copied block after a new label is typed in D1. If there are any entries in the cells where you are putting the copy, these entries are replaced with the copied entries.

COPYING A BLOCK MORE THAN ONCE   Another model building tool is making multiple copies of a block. You may want to copy a block to several other locations. Copying a block multiple times is used frequently when you have a block consisting of a column or row of formulas that you want to copy across to several other columns or rows. An example is copying the formulas in column B in Figure 4.13 to columns C, D, E, and F. To copy a block multiple times, follow these steps:

1. Select the block you want to copy. In Figure 4.13, this is the block B4..B16.

2. Click the Copy button, select Copy from the Edit menu, or press CTRL-INS.

3. Select the first cell where you want each copy. Quattro Pro only needs to

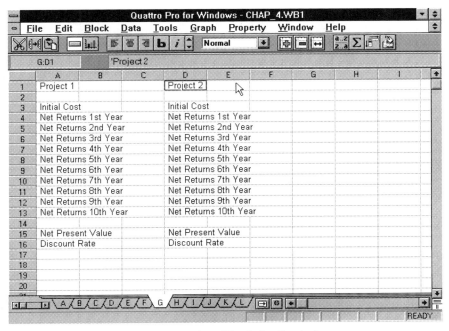

Figure 4.12 Notebook Page After Block Is Copied

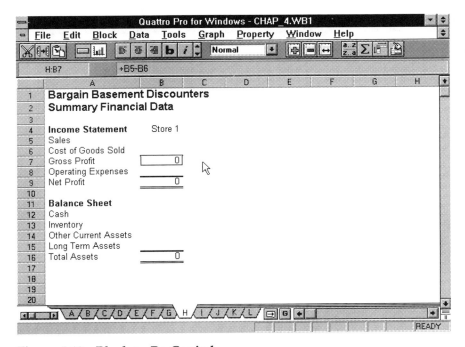

Figure 4.13 Block to Be Copied

know the first cell of each copy of the block, so you only need to provide it with the locations across row 4 where you want the column of entries in B4..B16 copied. Since you want the block copied multiple times, select C4..F4 to have the entries copied to these columns.

4. Click the Paste button, select Paste from the Edit menu, or press SHIFT-INS. Quattro Pro copies the block to the address selected in step 3. Since you specified several cells for the block's destination, Quattro Pro copies the entire block using each of the selected destination cells as the upper left corner of the copied block, as shown in Figure 4.14.

When copying a block multiple times, you are restricted to using a block that contains only one column or only one row. The exception is when you are copying the block to multiple pages. For example, to copy the block H:B4..B16 to pages I through L, you would copy H:B4..B16 to the Clipboard and paste it to I..L:B4.

MAKING MULTIPLE COPIES   The real advantage of copying using the Clipboard is that the data you have copied in the Clipboard remains there until you replace it with other data. You can continue copying the data to other locations by pasting the Clipboard's contents again. To copy the data you have put in the Clipboard a second time, follow these steps:

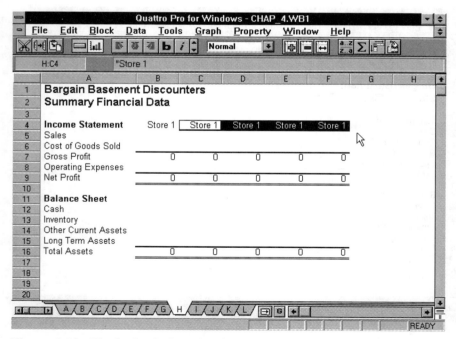

Figure 4.14   Block Copied Multiple Times

1. Select <u>N</u>ew from the <u>F</u>ile menu to open a new spreadsheet notebook.

2. Select where you want one or more copies placed. Since the cells you select tell Quattro Pro the starting location of each copy of the block, you only need select the first cell of each copy of the block. In this new notebook, you may want to select C2.

3. Click the Paste button, select <u>P</u>aste from the <u>E</u>dit menu, or press SHIFT-INS.

Quattro Pro copies the block to the address selected in step 2. Cells C2..C14 of your new notebook now contain the same entries as cells B4..B16 of Figure 4.13. You did not have to copy any data to the Clipboard because it still contains the entries you copied from the notebook in Figures 4.13 and 4.14.

You can use the Clipboard to copy between pages and notebooks. In Chapter 7, you will learn how you can use the Clipboard to copy between applications.

COPYING BETWEEN PAGES   The entries you have copied so far have all been on the same page. You can also copy blocks that include multiple pages and copy a block to multiple pages. The steps are the same as copying blocks on the same page. To try this yourself, follow these steps:

1. Type **ABC Company** in A1 on the new notebook and finalize the entry.

2. Click the Copy button, select <u>C</u>opy from the <u>E</u>dit menu, or press CTRL-INS to copy this cell to the Clipboard.

3. Select the block B..D:A1 so cell A1 is selected on pages B, C, and D.

4. Click the Paste button, select <u>P</u>aste from the <u>E</u>dit menu, or press SHIFT-INS.

5. Switch between pages B, C, and D to see how Quattro Pro copied the cell from A:A1 to cell A1 on the next three pages.

You can also copy a multipage block onto the Clipboard so that every time you paste the Clipboard's contents to a notebook, the multipage entries are copied starting at the entry you selected when you pasted the Clipboard's contents. Try it by following these steps:

1. Select the block A..D:A1 so cell A1 is selected on pages A through D.

2. Click the Copy button, select <u>C</u>opy from the <u>E</u>dit menu, or press CTRL-INS to copy this block to the Clipboard.

3. Select the cell A:B10.

4. Click the Paste button, select <u>P</u>aste from the <u>E</u>dit menu, or press SHIFT-INS.

5. Switch between pages B, C, and D to see how Quattro Pro copied the cell entries from A..D:A1 to A..D:B10.

COPYING NONCONTIGUOUS BLOCKS   Another special copying occasion you may have when copying data with the Clipboard is copying a noncontiguous block. You may remember from the last chapter that a noncontiguous block is a block that contains cells that are not in a single rectangle. When you copy a noncontiguous block, the cell that is on the first page, first column, and first row of the cells in the noncontiguous block is the corner of the block you are copying. Quattro Pro matches this corner cell with the cells you select to paste into when you paste the data from the Clipboard.

Suppose you have a noncontiguous block from Figure 4.15. To copy this noncontiguous block to a new notebook, follow these steps:

1. Select the block you want to copy. In Figure 4.16, this is the block B4..F4,A5,B7..F7.

2. Click the Copy button, select Copy from the Edit menu, or press CTRL-INS. The corner cell of this block is A4, since the first row of this noncontiguous block is row 4 and the first column of this noncontiguous block is column A—even though the contents of cell A4 are not to be copied.

3. Select New from the File menu to open a new spreadsheet notebook.

4. Select the cells where you want each copy to begin. Quattro Pro needs to know where the corner cell of each copy is. If you want the block copied once with Sales placed in A2, you must select A1.

5. Click the Paste button, select Paste from the Edit menu, or press SHIFT-INS. Quattro Pro copies the noncontiguous block to the new notebook. Now the copy of the block looks like Figure 4.17. Cells that are not part of the noncontiguous block are not affected, so if the new notebook already had an entry in A1, the entry would still be there after making the copy.

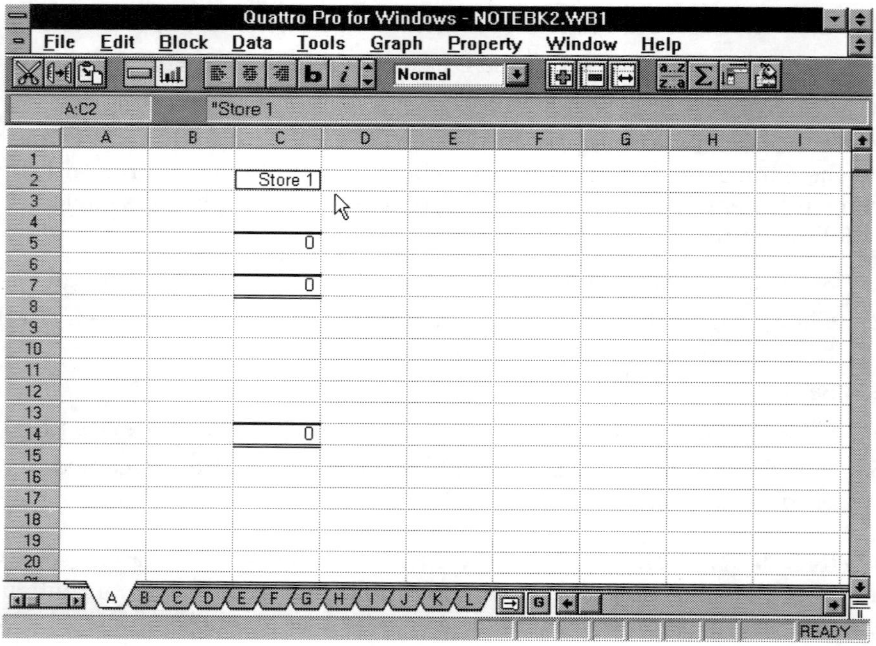

Figure 4.15   Block Copied to New Notebook

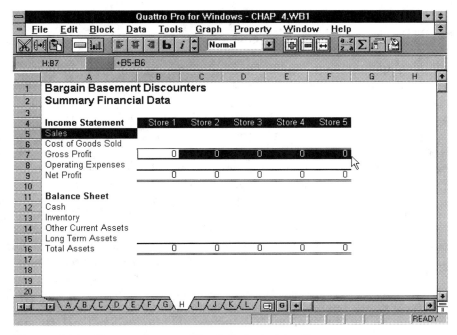

Figure 4.16   Noncontiguous Block Selected to Copy

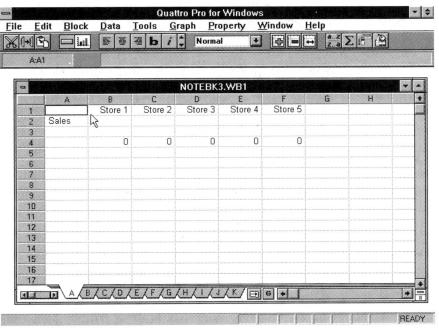

Figure 4.17   Copied Noncontiguous Block

▼ TIP: Selecting Noncontiguous Blocks

Selecting noncontiguous blocks is done by holding down the CTRL while selecting the next cell or block of cells.

SELECTIVELY COPYING A BLOCK   When you copy cell entries with the Clipboard or by dragging and dropping entries, you are copying both the cell entries and the properties you have assigned to the cells in the block. You can also copy either the cell entries or the properties. For example, after you have changed the properties of one block, you can apply the properties to another block so both sections have the same appearance. As when copying cells with the Clipboard, you can copy the contents or the properties of one cell to another, one cell to a block, a block to another location, or a block to several locations. The only difference is how you paste the contents of the Clipboard to the notebook. Instead of using the Paste SpeedBar button, the Paste command in the Edit menu, or SHIFT-INS, you use the Paste Special command in the Edit menu. You can use this command to give a notebook a consistent appearance by copying properties to other entries. You can also copy entries to a new location where you have already assigned the properties you want the entries to use.

When you use the Paste Special command in the Edit menu, you will see a dialog box that includes the Properties and Contents check boxes. To omit copying the properties or the cell contents, clear either box. When you select OK, only the properties or contents of the cell or block you selected before selecting the command from the two check boxes are copied.

Another special use of this command involves not copying empty cells. Earlier when you copied a block to several other locations to create the notebook page in Figure 4.14, if the notebook had contained entries in C5..F6, these entries would have been overwritten when you copied the formulas in columns B to columns C through F. One way around this problem that would leave the existing entries in C5..F6 is to select a noncontiguous block to copy. Another option is to use the Paste Special command in the Edit menu and to select the Avoid pasting blanks check box. When this option is selected, the entries in C5..F6 would remain because B5..B6 are empty. When you copy cells using this command and with this check box selected, empty cells do not overwrite existing entries in the area where you are copying.

CONVERTING FORMULAS WHEN YOU COPY   The same Paste Special command in the Edit menu that you used for copying properties or cell contents can also convert formulas into their results, effectively freezing the current value of the entry. You can use this command to freeze formulas that are no longer subject to variations. You can convert formulas to replace other cells with the results of the formulas. Also, you may want to compare the values produced by the formulas with those produced by the same formulas used with different assumptions. This command is useful when you are correcting data-entry errors. For example, the formulas in column E of Figure 4.18 construct a vendor identification (ID) number. Once the vendor numbers have been constructed from the detail entries, you can freeze the vendor numbers and eliminate the component entries if they are not required for other tasks. The Paste Special command in the Edit menu can take the current results from the formula entries that you have copied to the Clipboard and paste the values over the old entries or to a new location. All formulas are converted to their resulting numeric or string values.

To use this command, copy the entries in column E to the Clipboard. Next, since you want the formula results to replace the original formulas, select E2 as the location where you want to paste data. Select the Paste Special command in the Edit menu. Then select the Values only radio button under the Contents check box. (With the default, the Formulas radio button, this command will copy the formulas rather than their results when you copy the cell's contents.) When you select OK, Quattro Pro copies the *values* of the block to the new location. Any numeric formulas are converted to values, and string formulas are converted to labels.

TRANSPOSING ENTRIES   Another special type of copy operation is copying the data that is in columns so it is in rows and copying the data that is in rows so it is in columns. Quattro Pro can handle this restructuring change automatically with the Paste Special command in the Edit menu command. As with other Clipboard operations, you copy the data to the Clipboard; the only difference is how you paste it back onto the notebook.

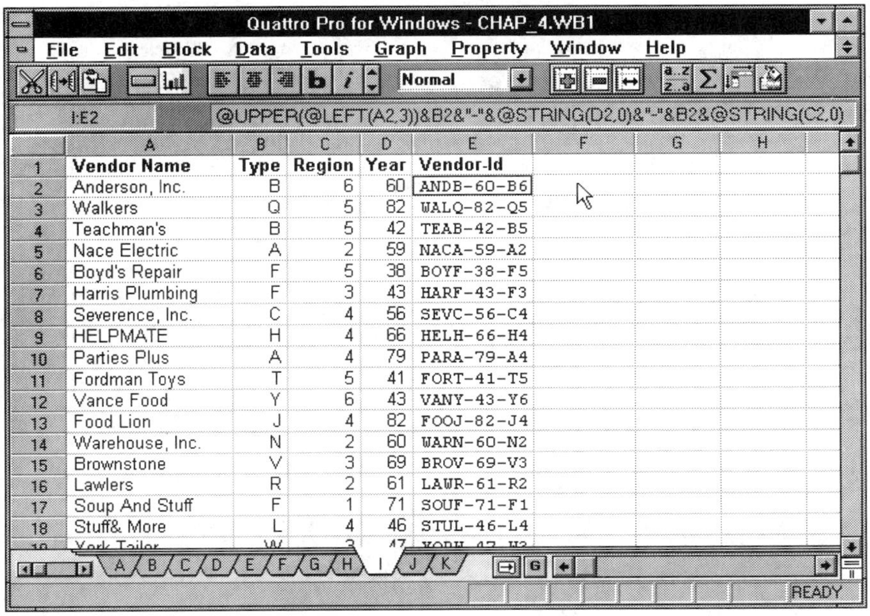

Figure 4.18   Copying the Values of Formulas

▼ TIP: Use Formula Conversion to Correct Data-Entry Errors

In Chapter 8, you will learn about functions you can use to rearrange your data and perform other types of conversions such as converting a label entry into uppercase. Once you use a function to convert an incorrect data entry to the proper format, you can use the Paste Special command in the Edit menu to replace the incorrect entry with the result of the function.

As an example, Figure 4.19 shows a table in a notebook that extends so far to the right that you can no longer see all the table's columns on the screen. Since the table is only a few rows in length, changing the orientation so that the sales personnel are in the top row and the months are in the left column provides a better table. To transpose this data, copy the block A2..M6 to the Clipboard and then move to A8, which is where you want to start copying the transposed data. Next, select the Paste Special command in the Edit menu. Select the Transpose rows and columns check box. When you select OK, the copied data is transposed as shown in Figure 4.20.

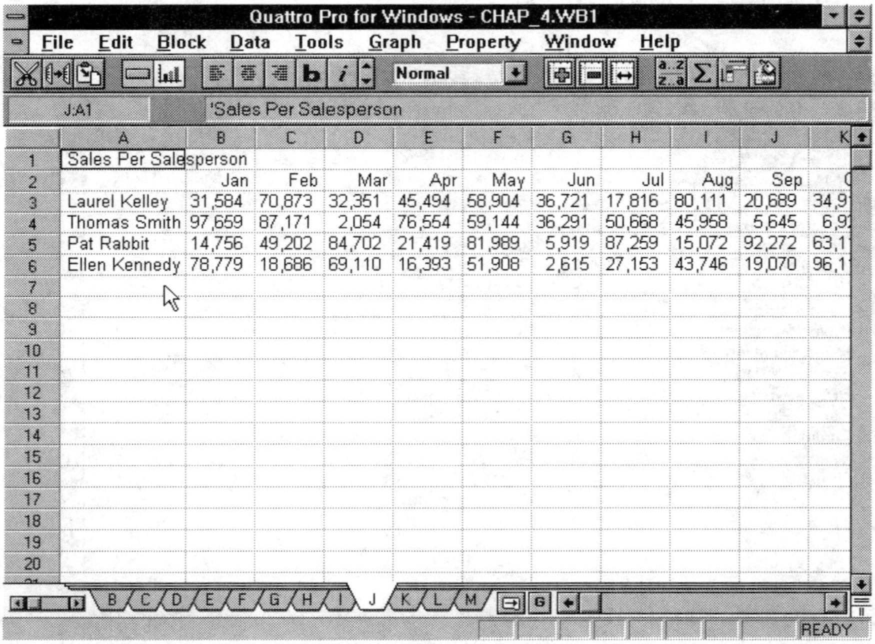

Figure 4.19   Entries before Transposition

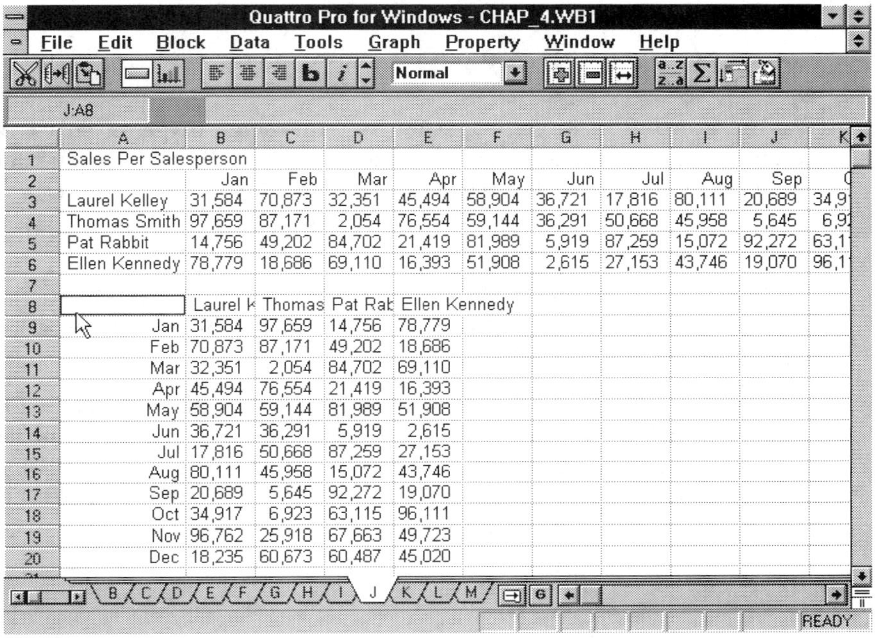

	A	B	C	D	E	F	G	H	I	J	K
1	Sales Per Salesperson										
2		Jan	Feb	Mar	Apr	May	Jun	Jul	Aug	Sep	(
3	Laurel Kelley	31,584	70,873	32,351	45,494	58,904	36,721	17,816	80,111	20,689	34,9
4	Thomas Smith	97,659	87,171	2,054	76,554	59,144	36,291	50,668	45,958	5,645	6,9
5	Pat Rabbit	14,756	49,202	84,702	21,419	81,989	5,919	87,259	15,072	92,272	63,1
6	Ellen Kennedy	78,779	18,686	69,110	16,393	51,908	2,615	27,153	43,746	19,070	96,1
7											
8		Laurel K	Thomas	Pat Rak	Ellen Kennedy						
9	Jan	31,584	97,659	14,756	78,779						
10	Feb	70,873	87,171	49,202	18,686						
11	Mar	32,351	2,054	84,702	69,110						
12	Apr	45,494	76,554	21,419	16,393						
13	May	58,904	59,144	81,989	51,908						
14	Jun	36,721	36,291	5,919	2,615						
15	Jul	17,816	50,668	87,259	27,153						
16	Aug	80,111	45,958	15,072	43,746						
17	Sep	20,689	5,645	92,272	19,070						
18	Oct	34,917	6,923	63,115	96,111						
19	Nov	96,762	25,918	67,663	49,723						
20	Dec	18,235	60,673	60,487	45,020						

Figure 4.20 Entries after Transposition

When the block you are copying contains formulas with relative cell references, you will want to also select the Values only radio button under Contents, since formulas do not convert properly when they are transposed.

REMOVING THE ORIGINAL ENTRIES So far, we have used the Clipboard to copy entries when we wanted more than one copy of the entries. You can also use the Clipboard to copy entries while removing them from the notebook. For example, you may want entries from B4..B10 put in D4..G10 and removed from B4..B10 at the same time. To do this with the Clipboard, you want to remove the entries from the notebook as you copy them to the Clipboard. Once the entries are on the Clipboard, you can paste them to another location even if the original entries are no longer in a notebook. The difference in copying entries this way is the way you put the information on the Clipboard. This method of putting the data on the Clipboard removes the original data from the notebook. To put data on the Clipboard *and* remove it from the notebook, select the Cut button on the SpeedBar, which is the button that has the pair of scissors, select Cut from the Edit menu, or press SHIFT-DEL. Once the data is on the Clipboard, you can paste it onto another location just as you can for other entries you are copying.

To use the Clipboard to delete the entries as it copies them, follow these steps:

1. Select the block you want to copy and remove. For example, in Figure 4.21, the block is B14..C14.

2. Click the Cut button, select Cut from the Edit menu, or press SHIFT-DEL. The entries that were in B14..C14 are now on the Clipboard even though they are removed from the notebook.

3. Select the cell where you want the copied data to start. For the example in Figure 4.21 it is B9.

4. Click the Paste button, select Paste from the Edit menu, or press SHIFT-INS. Quattro Pro copies the entries from the Clipboard to the block to the address selected in step 3.

Even though you only specified one cell for the block's destination, Quattro Pro copies the entire block as shown in Figure 4.22. If the page had any entries in B9..C9 before you pasted the data, they are replaced with the pasted entries. Any formulas in the block are adjusted just as if you copied the entries to the Clipboard and left the original entries intact on the notebook.

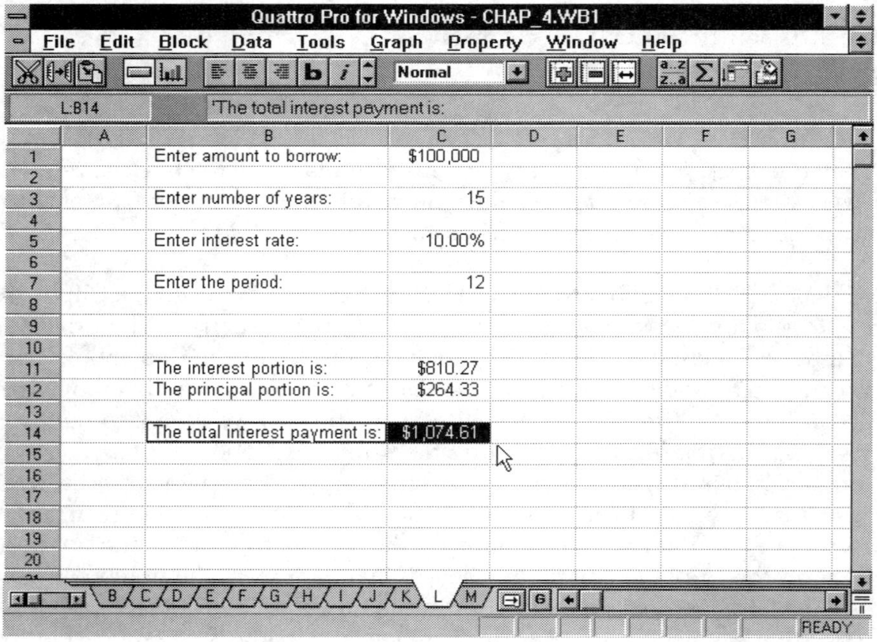

Figure 4.21   Entries to Be Copied to a New Location and Removed from the Original Location

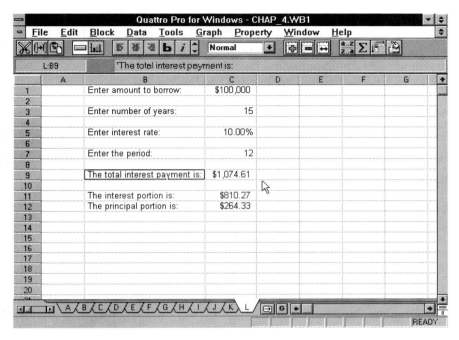

Figure 4.22 New Copy of Entry after Original Is Removed

Copying Cells with Commands in the Block Menu

Quattro Pro has several commands in the Block menu that copy data. These commands copy entries, copy formula or values, and transpose entries without the Clipboard. You do not have the options for copying only properties or only contents that you have with the Paste Special command in the Edit menu. Since the cells you are copying are not stored in a separate location like the Clipboard, the original location of the cells cannot overlap the location where you are putting the copies created using commands in the Block menu.

The commands in the Block menu to copy entries have a few advantages over using the Clipboard. When you name blocks, as you will learn how to do later in the chapter, you can select the block to copy or the location where the block is copied by entering the block name. Also, copying using the Block menu is faster than the Clipboard, a difference you will mostly notice with larger blocks. Copying with the Block menu does not overwrite the contents of the Clipboard, so if you want to copy cells without changing the Clipboard's contents, you can use the Block menu or the drag and drop method.

COPYING ENTRIES WITH THE BLOCK MENU   You can use the Copy command in the Block menu to copy data. This command is like the /Edit | Copy command used by Quattro Pro for DOS. As when copying with the Clipboard, you can copy one cell to another, one cell to a block, a block to another location, or a block to several locations. When you use this command Quattro Pro displays the Block Copy dialog box. In this dialog box, you can select the block to copy in the From text box. This text box will contain any block you have selected before selecting this command. In the To text box, you can select the starting location or locations for where you want the copies. When you use this command to copy one cell to a block, you can include the original cell in the destination block. For example, earlier, in Figure 4.7, the formula in C3 was copied to the block C3..G7. In this case, you can use C3 as the From block and C3..G7 as the To block. When you select OK, Quattro Pro copies the From block to the location selected by the To block.

One of the special features of the Copy command in the Block menu is the Model copy feature. Earlier, you learned that when you copy formulas, Quattro Pro does not adjust the absolute references. You can temporarily override this feature so that Quattro Pro will adjust absolute references. To adjust absolute references when you copy entries, use the Copy command in the Block menu and select the Model copy check box. When this check box is selected, the absolute references are adjusted. The absolute references are still absolute, so when you copy the cell later without this check box selected or without using this command, the addresses do *not* change. When this check box is cleared, absolute addresses do not change.

COPYING FORMULA VALUES WITH THE BLOCK MENU   You can use the Values command in the Block menu to copy the results of formulas to another location. This command is like copying with the Paste Special command in the Edit menu when the Values only radio button under Contents is selected. In the Block Values dialog box that this command displays, specify the block to copy in the From text box. This text box will contain any block you have selected before selecting this command. In the To text box, you can select the starting location or locations for where you want the copies. Unlike the Copy and Transpose commands in the Block menu, the Value command lets you use the same From and To block. When you select OK, Quattro Pro copies the values from the From block to the location selected by the To block.

TRANSPOSING ENTRIES WITH THE BLOCK MENU   You can use the Transpose command in the Block menu to transpose copied data. This command is like the Paste Special command in the Edit menu when the Transpose rows and columns check box is selected. From the Block Transpose dialog box that this command displays, select the block to copy in the From text box and where you want the transposition to start in the To text box. The From text box will contain any block you have selected before selecting this command.

Do not use this command to transpose formulas, since the formulas will not be properly adjusted.

MOVING

Good spreadsheet design makes your data easier to understand. When you are beginning to create your own spreadsheet notebooks, it takes time to achieve optimal designs. You may want to move existing entries to improve the appearance of your data. You may find yourself moving information around until you achieve an appearance that works best for your application. Quattro Pro's features for moving entries moves cells without changing their values. When you move cells, you move both the cells' contents and their properties, except for row and column features.

Move Cells by Dragging and Dropping

One of the simplest ways to move data on a notebook is to drag it to its new location. This drag and drop method works for moving two or more cells to another location on the same notebook. The drag and drop method is the same method you use in Windows to move a program item in a Program Manager's group window, or a file to another disk in the File Manager. To move cells, select the block containing the original data and then drag it to its new location. The drag and drop method does not work with noncontiguous blocks.

As an example, suppose you have the entries in A4..D16 in Figure 4.23 that you want to move to start in D1. To move the block to another location, follow these steps:

1. Select the block that you want to move. In this example, it is A4..D16.

2. Point to the block as if you want to change its properties.

3. Drag the mouse to move the block's outline to where you want the block moved. For the page shown in Figure 4.23, the outline of the block is dragged to cover D1..G13.

4. Release the mouse. Quattro Pro moves the block to the location of the block outline. Now the page contains a block of entries in A1..B3 and in D1..G13. The formulas in the moved block change to match the new locations of the data they reference. The page now looks like Figure 4.24.

> ## ▼ TIP: Dragging to Move One Cell
>
> If you have one cell that you want to move, you can still drag it if you have a neighboring empty cell by including the empty cell in the block. For example, if you want to move A1 to A5, you can select A1..B1, then drag the two-cell block to A5, provided that B1 and B5 are empty.

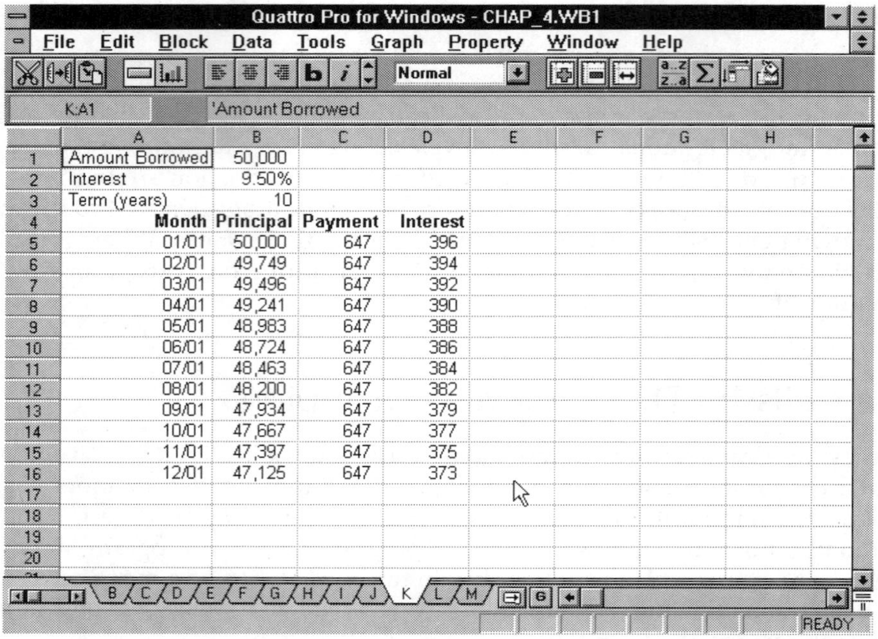

Figure 4.23   Entries to Move with the Drag and Drop Method

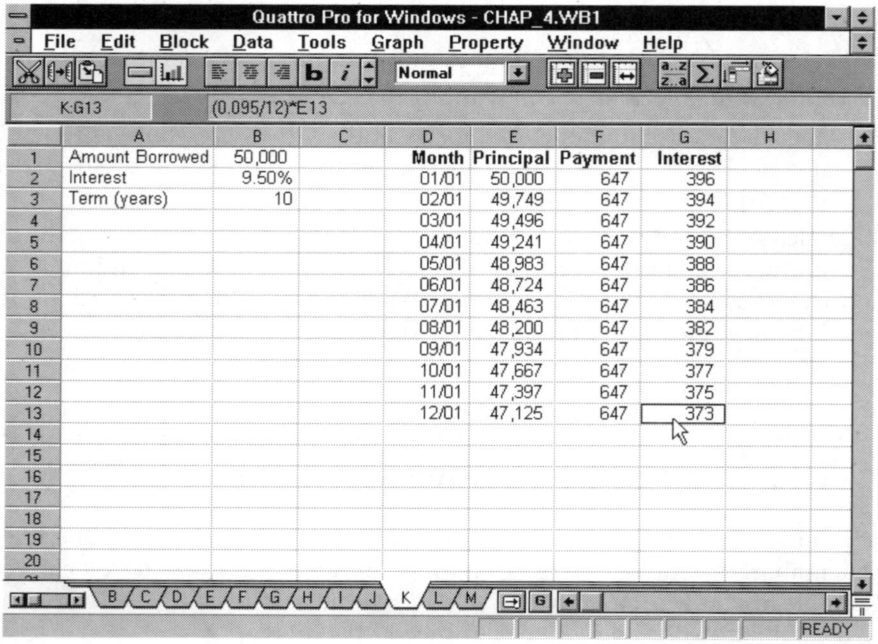

Figure 4.24   Entries Moved with the Drag and Drop Method

You can use the drag and drop method of moving entries when you have one block that you want to move to one other location on the same notebook. If the block contains any formulas, the formulas are adjusted as described below. If the outlined block contains any entries before you drop the moved entries into the notebook, you are warned that there are entries that will be replaced, and prompted to confirm that you do want to move the entries.

Adjusting Cell Addresses in Moved Formulas

When you move cells containing formulas, Quattro Pro modifies the cell addresses in the formulas to maintain the formula values. Therefore, moving a block does not change the results of the formulas in the block as copying cells does, because the cell addresses are modified to reflect the new location regardless of whether the cell references are relative, mixed, or absolute. Moving cells also differs from copying, since it changes formula references of cells that are not in the moved block but refers to cells in the moved block. Figures 4.25 and 4.26, which show a block before and after it is moved, illustrate how Quattro Pro changes the cell

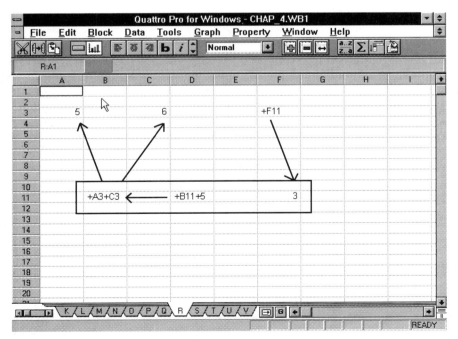

Figure 4.25   Block before It Is Moved

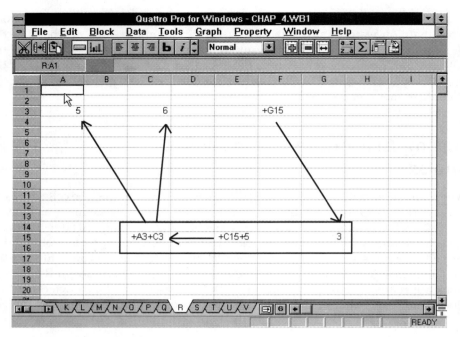

Figure 4.26 Block after It Is Moved

references. When a cell in a moved block references cells outside of that block, Quattro Pro does not change the formulas. For example, the formula that was moved from B11 to C15 (+A3+C3) did not change. When a cell in the moved block references cells inside the moved block, Quattro Pro changes the formulas to reflect the referenced cells' new positions. For example, a formula moved from D11 to E15 changes from +B11+5 to +C15+5. When a cell outside the moved block refers to cells inside the moved block, Quattro Pro changes the formula to reflect the referenced cell's new position. For example, since the entry in F11 moved to G15, Quattro Pro changes the formula in F3 from +F11 to +G15. This formula adjustment is the same regardless of the method you use to move the formulas, but it is not the same if you copy them.

Moving Cells with Commands in the Block Menu

You can use the Block menu to move as well as copy data. The Move command in the Block menu moves entries without the Clipboard. This command is like the /Edit Move command used by Quattro Pro for DOS. As when copying with Block menu commands, you can select block names to move. Moving data with the Move command in the Block menu will not change the current contents of the Clipboard. When you use the Move command in the Block menu, Quattro Pro displays the Block Move dialog box. In this dialog box, you can select the block to move in the From text box. In the To text box, you can select the starting location where you want the moved entries. To move a block, follow these steps:

1. Select the block that you want to move. Using the page in Figure 4.27, you select the block A4..G11.

2. Select Move from the Block menu to display the Block Move text box. The From text box contains the block you selected before selecting this command.

3. Select the first cell where you want the data moved for the To text box. Using the page in Figure 4.27, you would select A5.

4. Select OK.

Quattro Pro moves the block to the address you selected in step 3, as shown in Figure 4.28. Even though you only specified one cell for the block's destination, Quattro Pro moves the entire block using the selected destination cell as the upper left corner of the moved block. Any information that was in the section of the block's destination is replaced by the moved block.

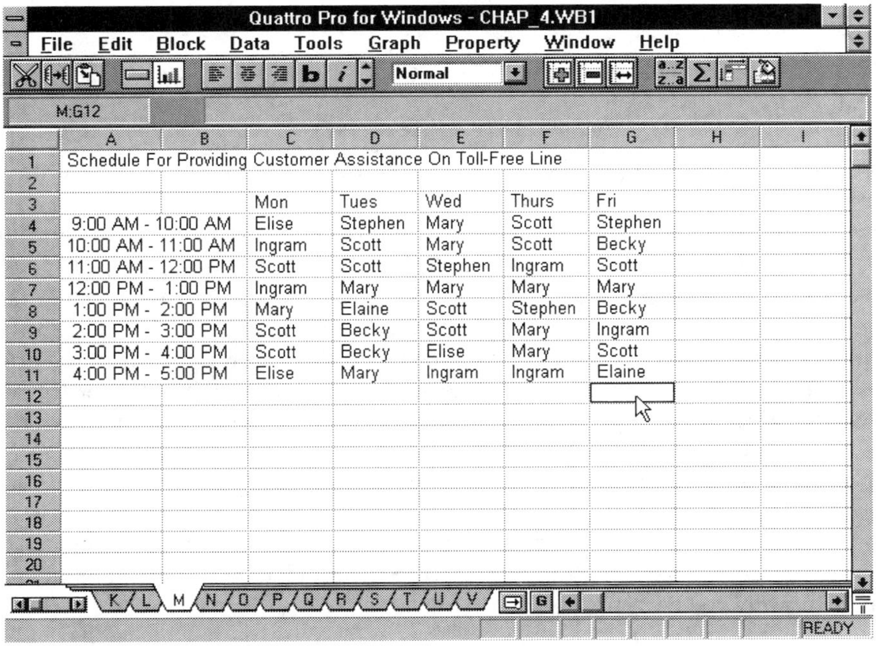

Figure 4.27 Page before Moving a Block

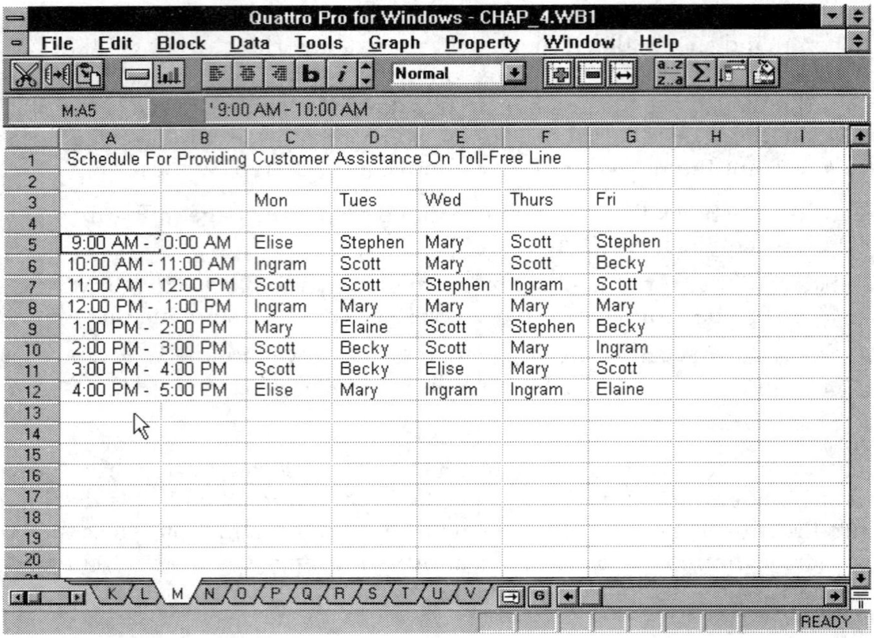

Figure 4.28   Page after Moving a Block

ERASING

As you add entries to a notebook, you may want to remove existing data. For example, if you are changing an income statement from January's figures to February's figures, you want to remove January's data before you type in February's data. Chapter 2 discussed how you delete individual cells or a selected block by pressing the DEL key. When you press this command, you are actually using the Clear Contents command in the Edit menu. The DEL key is a shortcut for this command. When you erase a block, any formulas that reference cells in the erased block remain intact, but the formula treats the empty cells as 0 in numeric formulas and empty labels in string formulas. If you want to protect some of your entries from being erased, use the page protection property, since Quattro Pro will not erase protected cells when protection is enabled. When you clear cells with the Clear Contents command you are clearing both their contents but not their properties. Another option for removing entries is removing the contents and the cells' properties. You can do this by selecting the block of cells and then using the Clear command in the Edit menu.

INSERTING AND DELETING

The commands you have worked with so far in the chapter have rearranged blocks of data. Quattro Pro has other commands for rearranging data by inserting and deleting columns, rows, and pages. You can also rearrange your notebook by moving pages.

Inserting Columns, Rows, and Pages

As you create a notebook, you may realize that you have forgotten to include a column or row of entries. You may also need to insert a page to the notebook that tracks your different sales divisions. Adding blank columns and rows can make the data easier to read. Quattro Pro makes it easy for you to enter blank columns, rows, and pages. Once inserted, you can leave them blank or make entries in them.

You can insert columns, rows, and pages anywhere on the notebook. The first step is selecting where you want the columns, rows, or pages inserted. Select a cell in the column, row, or page where you want the columns, rows, or pages inserted. Next, select how many columns, rows, and pages to insert. To do this, select a block starting from the cell you just selected that contains at least one cell from each of the columns, rows, or pages you want to add. For example, to insert three columns starting with column C, you might select C1..E1. To insert two rows starting at row 5, you might select A5..A6. If you want to insert two pages starting with page C, you might select C..D:A1. You only need to select one cell from each column, row, or page you want to add because inserting columns, rows, and pages applies to the entire column, row, or page.

Now that you have selected where and how many columns, rows, or pages to add to your notebook, click the Insert button on the SpeedBar, which is the button with the +. You can also select Insert from the Block menu. Then, select Columns, Rows, or Pages to indicate what you want to insert. Select OK and Quattro Pro will insert the number of columns, rows, or pages that you have selected. Quattro Pro also adjusts all the formulas accordingly, just as when moving entries. The notebook's formulas continue to refer to the appropriate cells after the new columns are inserted. For example, Figure 4.29 shows a page before two rows are inserted, and Figure 4.30 presents the same page after the new rows are inserted. The formulas in Figure 4.30 are adjusted after the blank rows are inserted. Each reference to a cell below the insertion is adjusted by one row for each row inserted. When Quattro Pro adjusts the formulas with cell references, it does not matter if the cell addresses are relative, mixed, or absolute. New columns and rows use the page's default settings such as label alignment, and column width, and the cells use the Normal named style.

A special feature of inserting columns, rows, and pages is that when you select *entire* columns, rows, or pages and *then* select the Insert button in the SpeedBar,

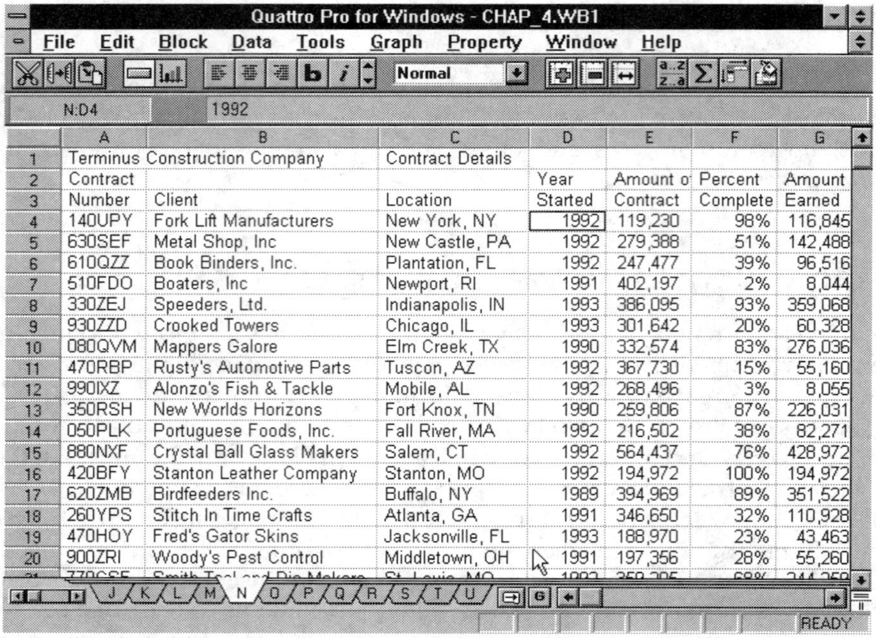

Figure 4.29   Page before Inserting Rows

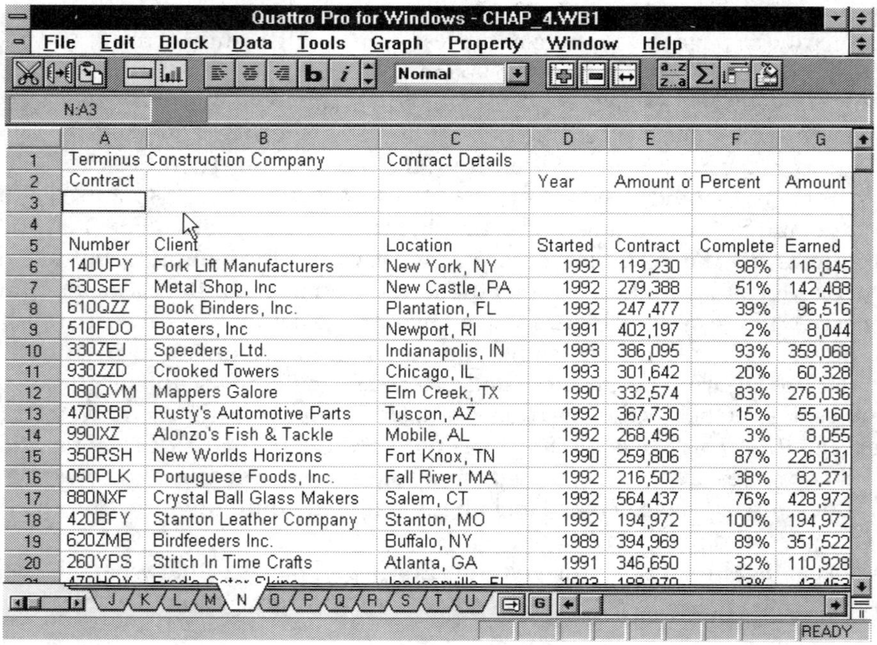

The spreadsheet before inserting rows contains the following data:

Row	A	B	C	D	E	F	G
1	Terminus Construction Company		Contract Details				
2	Contract			Year	Amount o	Percent	Amount
3	Number	Client	Location	Started	Contract	Complete	Earned
4	140UPY	Fork Lift Manufacturers	New York, NY	1992	119,230	98%	116,845
5	630SEF	Metal Shop, Inc	New Castle, PA	1992	279,388	51%	142,488
6	610QZZ	Book Binders, Inc.	Plantation, FL	1992	247,477	39%	96,516
7	510FDO	Boaters, Inc	Newport, RI	1991	402,197	2%	8,044
8	330ZEJ	Speeders, Ltd.	Indianapolis, IN	1993	386,095	93%	359,068
9	930ZZD	Crooked Towers	Chicago, IL	1993	301,642	20%	60,328
10	080QVM	Mappers Galore	Elm Creek, TX	1990	332,574	83%	276,036
11	470RBP	Rusty's Automotive Parts	Tuscon, AZ	1992	367,730	15%	55,160
12	990IXZ	Alonzo's Fish & Tackle	Mobile, AL	1992	268,496	3%	8,055
13	350RSH	New Worlds Horizons	Fort Knox, TN	1990	259,806	87%	226,031
14	050PLK	Portuguese Foods, Inc.	Fall River, MA	1992	216,502	38%	82,271
15	880NXF	Crystal Ball Glass Makers	Salem, CT	1992	564,437	76%	428,972
16	420BFY	Stanton Leather Company	Stanton, MO	1992	194,972	100%	194,972
17	620ZMB	Birdfeeders Inc.	Buffalo, NY	1989	394,969	89%	351,522
18	260YPS	Stitch In Time Crafts	Atlanta, GA	1991	346,650	32%	110,928
19	470HOY	Fred's Gator Skins	Jacksonville, FL	1993	188,970	23%	43,463
20	900ZRI	Woody's Pest Control	Middletown, OH	1991	197,356	28%	55,260

Figure 4.30   Page after Inserting Rows

The spreadsheet after inserting rows contains the following data:

Row	A	B	C	D	E	F	G
1	Terminus Construction Company		Contract Details				
2	Contract			Year	Amount o	Percent	Amount
3							
4							
5	Number	Client	Location	Started	Contract	Complete	Earned
6	140UPY	Fork Lift Manufacturers	New York, NY	1992	119,230	98%	116,845
7	630SEF	Metal Shop, Inc	New Castle, PA	1992	279,388	51%	142,488
8	610QZZ	Book Binders, Inc.	Plantation, FL	1992	247,477	39%	96,516
9	510FDO	Boaters, Inc	Newport, RI	1991	402,197	2%	8,044
10	330ZEJ	Speeders, Ltd.	Indianapolis, IN	1993	386,095	93%	359,068
11	930ZZD	Crooked Towers	Chicago, IL	1993	301,642	20%	60,328
12	080QVM	Mappers Galore	Elm Creek, TX	1990	332,574	83%	276,036
13	470RBP	Rusty's Automotive Parts	Tuscon, AZ	1992	367,730	15%	55,160
14	990IXZ	Alonzo's Fish & Tackle	Mobile, AL	1992	268,496	3%	8,055
15	350RSH	New Worlds Horizons	Fort Knox, TN	1990	259,806	87%	226,031
16	050PLK	Portuguese Foods, Inc.	Fall River, MA	1992	216,502	38%	82,271
17	880NXF	Crystal Ball Glass Makers	Salem, CT	1992	564,437	76%	428,972
18	420BFY	Stanton Leather Company	Stanton, MO	1992	194,972	100%	194,972
19	620ZMB	Birdfeeders Inc.	Buffalo, NY	1989	394,969	89%	351,522
20	260YPS	Stitch In Time Crafts	Atlanta, GA	1991	346,650	32%	110,928

you automatically insert the columns, rows, or pages without making additional selections. For example, to insert the two rows in Figure 4.29, you can easily use the mouse to select rows 2 and 3 and then click the Insert button in the SpeedBar to get the same results in Figure 4.30.

Quattro Pro will not allow you to insert another column, row, or page when you have data stored in the last possible column (column IV), row (row 8192), or page (page IV). You usually cannot insert columns and rows while protection is enabled because row 8192 and column IV are protected by default.

When you insert columns, rows, and pages in the middle of a block used by a formula, Quattro Pro stretches the block to include the inserted columns, rows, or pages. For example, if you have a formula that refers to the block E5..E10 in Figure 4.30 and you insert two rows starting at row 7, Quattro Pro changes the formula to refer to the block E5..E12. The additional two rows are automatically included. This means that as you add contracts to the notebook in Figure 4.30, any formulas that total columns on the page automatically include the new contracts. This is *not* the case when you insert the columns, rows, or pages at the beginning or the end of the block. If you added two rows to the notebook in Figure 4.30 starting at row 5 instead of row 7, the formula that referred to E5..E10 now refers to E7..E12.

Deleting Columns, Rows, and Pages

Columns, rows, and pages that are no longer needed can be removed from a notebook. As Quattro Pro makes this adjustment, it automatically moves the remaining information in place of the deleted columns, rows, and pages, then adjusts the formulas. For example, you may want to delete blank columns between a column of explanatory text and a column of numbers after widening the text column to contain the entire entries. You cannot delete columns, rows, and pages that are protected when page protection is enabled.

▼ TIP: Notebooks always Have 256 Columns, 8192 Rows, and 256 Pages.

Inserting and deleting columns, rows, and pages does not change the number of columns, rows, and pages a notebook has. When you insert columns, rows, and pages, Quattro Pro removes columns or rows from the end of the page in place of the ones you have added. When you insert pages, Quattro Pro removes pages from the end of the notebook in place of the ones you have added. Deleting columns, rows, and pages works the same way: Quattro Pro adds columns and rows to the end of the page, and pages to the end of the notebook, for the columns, rows, and pages you delete.

You can delete columns, rows, and pages anywhere on the notebook. The first step is selecting the columns, rows, or pages you want to delete. Select a block that includes at least one cell from each column, row, or page you want to delete. For example, to delete two columns starting with column C, you might select C1..D1. To delete three rows starting at row 10, you might select D10..D12. If you want to delete the active page, you might select any cell on that page. You only need to select one cell from each column, row, or page you want to remove because deleting columns, rows, and pages applies to the entire columns, rows, and pages.

Now that you have selected where and how many columns, rows, or pages to delete, click the Delete button on the SpeedBar, which has the –. You can also select Delete from the Block menu. Then, select from Columns, Rows, or Pages to indicate what you want to remove. Select OK, and Quattro Pro will delete the number of columns, rows, or pages that you have chosen. Quattro Pro adjusts all the formulas accordingly regardless of whether the addresses are relative, mixed, or absolute, just as when moving entries. The notebook's formulas continue to refer to the same entries after the columns are deleted. For example, if you delete columns C and D from Figure 4.30, the notebook looks like Figure 4.31. The formulas previously in column E and F are now in columns C and D.

Just as when inserting columns, rows, and pages, you can quickly delete columns, rows, or pages with the mouse. First, select the entire columns, rows, or pages (with the Select-All button), and then click the Delete button in the SpeedBar. For

	A	B	C	D	E	F	G	H
1	Terminus Construction Company							
2	Contract		Amount o	Percent	Amount	Est. # of		
3	Number	Client	Contract	Complete	Earned	Months To Complete		
4	140UPY	Fork Lift Manufacturers	119,230	98%	116,845	47		
5	630SEF	Metal Shop, Inc	279,388	51%	142,488	25		
6	610QZZ	Book Binders, Inc.	247,477	39%	96,516	2		
7	510FDO	Boaters, Inc	402,197	2%	8,044	44		
8	330ZEJ	Speeders, Ltd.	386,095	93%	359,068	36		
9	930ZZD	Crooked Towers	301,642	20%	60,328	3		
10	080QVM	Mappers Galore	332,574	83%	276,036	11		
11	470RBP	Rusty's Automotive Parts	367,730	15%	55,160	40		
12	990IXZ	Alonzo's Fish & Tackle	268,496	3%	8,055	36		
13	350RSH	New Worlds Horizons	259,806	87%	226,031	12		
14	050PLK	Portuguese Foods, Inc.	216,502	38%	82,271	43		
15	880NXF	Crystal Ball Glass Makers	564,437	76%	428,972	19		
16	420BFY	Stanton Leather Company	194,972	100%	194,972	15		
17	620ZMB	Birdfeeders Inc.	394,969	89%	351,522	13		
18	260YPS	Stitch In Time Crafts	346,650	32%	110,928	31		
19	470HOY	Fred's Gator Skins	188,970	23%	43,463	0		
20	900ZRI	Woody's Pest Control	197,356	28%	55,260	11		

Figure 4.31   Page after Deleting Columns

example, to remove the two columns in Figure 4.30, you can use the mouse to select columns C and D and then click the Delete button in the SpeedBar to get the same results in Figure 4.31.

When you delete columns, rows, and pages that contain cells that are referenced by formulas, Quattro Pro converts the references to deleted cells to ERR. When you delete columns, rows, and pages in the middle of a block used by a formula, Quattro Pro shrinks the block to reflect the removed columns, rows, or pages. For example, if you have a formula that refers to the block A1..G1 in Figure 4.30 and you delete columns C and D, Quattro Pro changes the formula to refer to the block A1..E1. This also means that when you remove a contract from the notebook in Figure 4.30 or 4.31 by deleting the row it is in, any formula that totals columns on the page automatically adjusts its cell references for the removed contract. The only exception is when you delete the column, row, or page at the beginning or ending cell of the block. This means that if you have a formula that refers to A1..G1 and you delete column G, row 1, or that page, the cell references in the formula change to ERR.

Inserting Blocks of Columns, Rows, and Pages

Another option for inserting columns, rows, and pages is to insert portions of them. This is similar to cutting a section of the notebook and shifting it right or down. You may want to think of it as an earthquake on your notebook, since only the columns, rows, or pages you select are affected while the remaining data stays in place. As an example of inserting a block of a column or row, look at Figure 4.32. In this notebook, the O..P:B1..C2 block is selected. Quattro Pro uses the selected block to indicate how many columns, rows, or pages to insert, as well as which columns, rows, and pages are affected. Just as when copying entire columns, rows, and blocks, you select the block, and click the Insert button in the SpeedBar or select Insert from the Block menu, and select between Columns, Rows, and Pages. The difference is that before you select OK, you select the Partial radio button. When you select OK, Quattro Pro takes your selection for inserting columns, rows, or pages with the block you have selected to determine which columns, rows, and pages are affected.

If you insert partial columns for the block in Figure 4.32, Quattro Pro inserts two new columns in rows 1 and 2 on both pages, but rows 3 through the rest of each page are not affected. If you insert partial rows for the block in Figure 4.32, Quattro Pro inserts two new rows in columns B and C on both pages, but columns A and D through the rest of each page are not affected. A third option would be to insert a partial page. If you insert partial pages for the block in Figure 4.32, Quattro Pro shifts B1..C2 on page O to page Q, B1..C2 on page P to page R, and so forth until the end of the notebook. Rows 3 through the end of the page and columns A and D through the end of the page of each page are not affected. Figure 4.33 shows the notebook after inserting two partial rows.

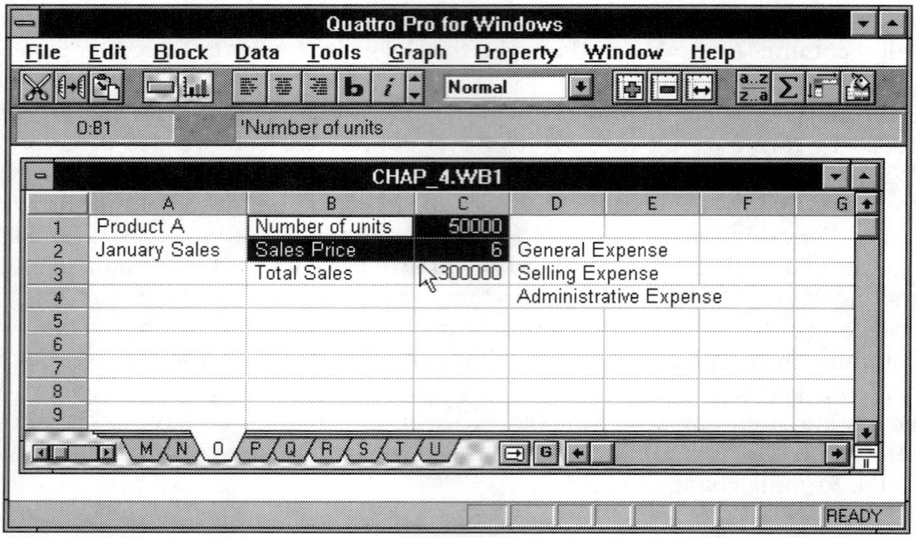

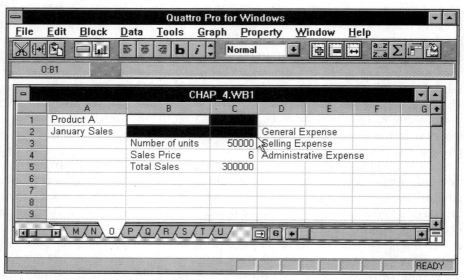

Figure 4.32   Before Inserting Partial Rows

Inserting partial columns, rows, and pages has the same restrictions as inserting complete columns, rows, and pages. Quattro Pro also adjusts formulas the same way as when you insert complete columns, rows, and pages.

Figure 4.33   After Inserting Partial Rows

Deleting Blocks of Columns, Rows, and Pages

You can also delete partial columns, rows, and pages. This lets you shift a section of a notebook up, to the left, or forward. For example, if you have many reports on a page and then delete one, you can shift up the remaining reports that use the same columns, or shift left reports using the same rows. Deleting partial columns, rows, or pages removes a block then shifts the remaining data into its place. For example, if you deleted the partial columns selected in Figure 4.32, the general and selling expenses would move from columns D and E to columns B and C. The block you select when deleting partial columns, rows, and pages specifies the columns, rows, or pages to delete, and determines the columns, rows, or pages that are affected by the deletion. To delete partial rows, select the block and then click the Delete button in the SpeedBar or select Delete from the Block menu, select between Columns, Rows, and Pages, and then select the Partial radio button.

As an example, consider what happens when you delete the partial block selected by O:B1..P:C2 in Figure 4.32. If you delete partial columns for the block in Figure 4.32, Quattro Pro deletes columns B and C in rows 1 and 2 on both pages and moves the contents of column D, rows 1 and 2 over to fill in the deleted cells. Row 3 does not change on either page. If you delete partial rows for the block in Figure 4.32, Quattro Pro deletes rows 1 and 2 in columns B and C on both pages and moves the contents of rows 3, 4, and 5, in columns B and C up to fill in the deleted spaces, but does not change the contents of columns A and D through the rest of each page. If you deleted partial pages, you would see B1..C2 from page Q on page O, B1..C2 from page R on page P, and so forth until the end of the notebook. On each page, rows 3 through the end of the page and columns A and D through the end of the page do not change.

Deleting partial columns, rows, and pages has the same restrictions as deleting complete columns, rows, and pages. Quattro Pro also adjusts formulas the same way as when you delete complete columns, rows, and pages.

Moving Pages

Besides using insertion and deletion features to add and remove pages from a notebook, you can also rearrange them. Moving a page is just like taking a piece of paper out of one location of a notebook and putting it into another. You can move one page at a time. Quattro Pro has two methods of moving pages.

The simplest method of moving a page is to pick the page's tab up and move it to a new location. To do this, point to the page tab as if you want to inspect the page's properties. Next, select it using the left mouse button, and drag the page tab down. When you do this, the page tab will look like it is separated from the page. Drag the page tab to be on top of where you want to place the page. This means that if you want to move page C to page A, drag the C page tab down and then on top of page A. When you release the page tab, the page is moved in place of the tab you have selected. The remaining pages are shifted back. If you move a page that is part of a selected block containing more than one page, the page you are dragging and the other pages that are part of a block are moved as well.

The other way of moving a page is to move it with the Move Pages command in the Block menu. Quattro Pro automatically fills in the Move page text box with the current page name. In the To before page text box, type the page name where you want the current page moved, then select OK.

REFORMATTING TEXT BLOCKS

When you create a spreadsheet notebook, you usually include text to describe your numeric entries and formulas. The text may be a short heading at the top of the data and one- or two-word descriptions for row and column headers. Other models demand more extensive documentation. For example, Figure 4.34 shows a notebook that contains lengthy notes in A21..A23. The descriptive information is lengthy, but only the portion that fits on the screen is displayed. The Reformat command in the Block menu can restructure lengthy text in a block to fit within the width of selected columns.

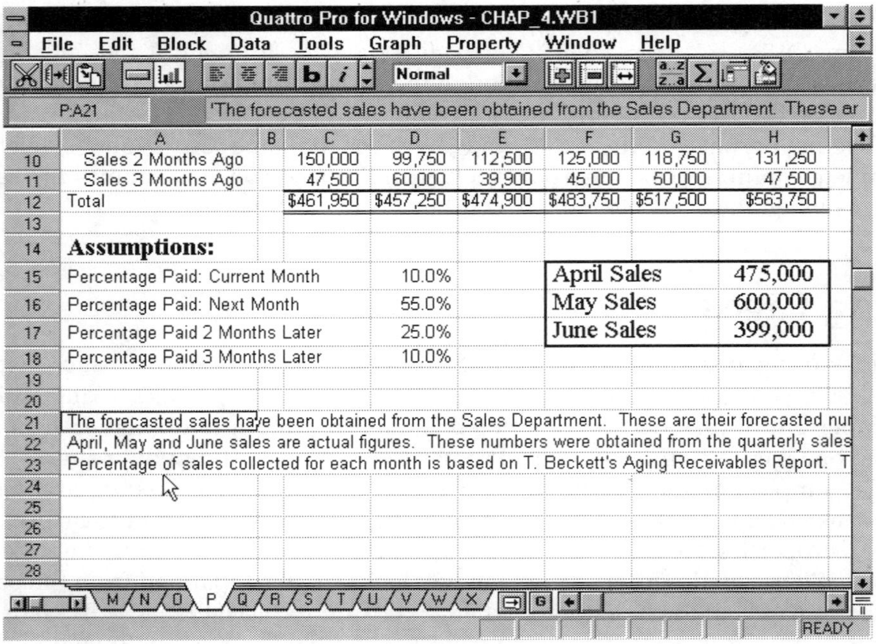

Figure 4.34   Labels That Extend beyond the Display

Before you use this command, select the block to reformat. You have two options. You can select one row and as many columns as you want the reformatted text to use. This type of block selection, such as A21..G21, lets Quattro Pro use as many rows as necessary. However, if the page has any entries below the text you are reformatting, they are adjusted upward or downward by how much Quattro Pro has adjusted the location of the text. The other option is to select the number of columns as well as the number of rows that Quattro Pro can use to reformat the entries. This specifies the columns Quattro Pro can distribute the entries across and the number of rows Quattro Pro can use. This type of block selection, such as A21..G27, only lets Quattro Pro use the rows you have selected. If you have any entries below the selected block, they are not shifted up or down.

After you select the block, you can select Reformat from the Block menu. When you select OK, Quattro Pro word-wraps the long-label entries, splitting the long labels between words to fit within the allotted space. The reformatted text using the block A21..G21 is shown in Figure 4.35. When Quattro Pro performs the reformatting command, it uses as many rows as necessary to store the restructured data. If you selected a block that does not contain enough rows, like A21..G25, Quattro Pro displays the message "Not enough room in reformat block." Like the original labels that were only stored in one cell but displayed across several columns, the reformatted labels are stored in the first column of the display area.

When there are entries below the area that you are reformatting, Quattro Pro

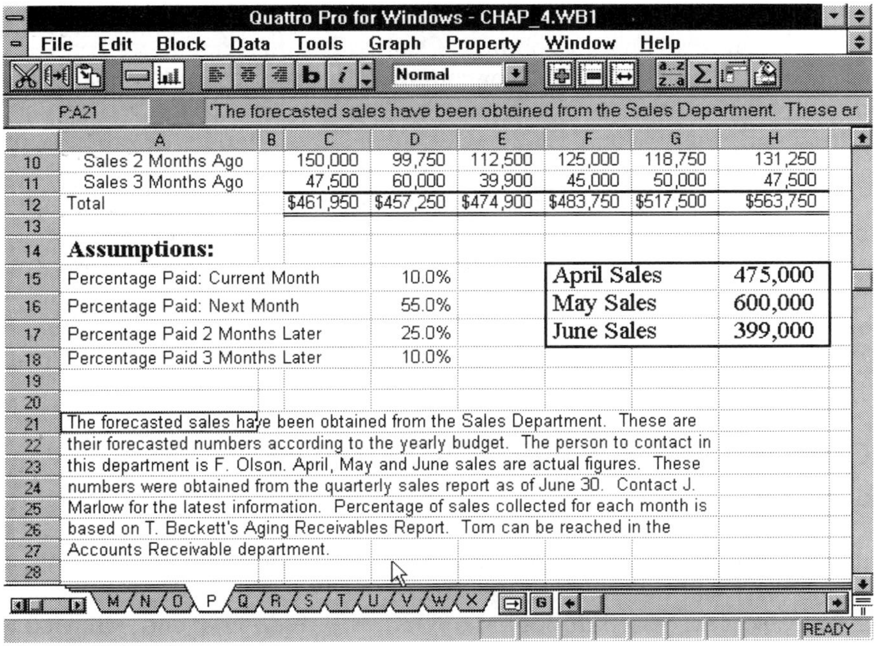

Figure 4.35   Labels Reformatted to Fit into the Display

inserts partial rows in the selected columns to provide sufficient space to reformat the labels. For example, if A25 in Figure 4.34 contains the entry Sales Summary and you reformat the block after selecting A21..G21, Quattro Pro inserts five partial rows in columns A through G starting at row 23 so the notebook has enough room to reformat the labels. The entry from A25 is now in A30.

TITLES

When your data stretches beyond one screen, it is difficult to remember what every row and column represents. Quattro Pro lets you freeze rows and/or columns in the page to keep labels at the top and left of the page. With rows and/or columns frozen, Quattro Pro uses the remaining portion of the window for other notebook information. Freezing columns and rows only applies to the active page.

To create titles, move the selector so the columns and/or rows you want always displayed on the screen are at the left and/or at the top of the window. Then move the selector to the row just below the title row, and/or to the column to the right of the title column. Next, select Locked Titles from the Window menu. Then choose Horizontal, Vertical, or Both. If you select Horizontal, every row above the selector is frozen in place. If you select Vertical, every column to the left of the selector is frozen in place. If you select Both, every row above the selector and every column to the left of the selector are frozen in place. Select OK to freeze the titles.

When you freeze titles, the selected rows and/or columns remain frozen on the screen. In Figure 4.36, rows 1 through 4 and columns A and B are frozen. When you have frozen rows and/or columns, Quattro Pro does not allow you to move the selector into the title rows and/or columns. The mouse pointer looks different when you point to this location, as you can see in Figure 4.36. However, you can move to the title area if you press F5 (GOTO) or select Goto in the Edit menu and type in the address of a cell in one of the title rows and/or columns. When you do this, you will temporarily see a duplicate of the title's contents. Any change that you make to this accessible copy of the title cells is reflected in the original. Moving out of the title area in any direction that causes the screen to scroll removes the second copy from the display.

To clear your titles, select Locked Titles from the Window menu and then select Clear. After this command, Quattro Pro no longer freezes any rows or columns.

WINDOW OPTIONS FOR YOUR SPREADSHEET NOTEBOOKS

Quattro Pro uses notebook windows to display spreadsheet notebooks. Quattro Pro has several features that change how it displays your notebook windows. These features are accessed through the Window pull-down menu. Many of these features can also be activated by using the mouse. You can split a single notebook

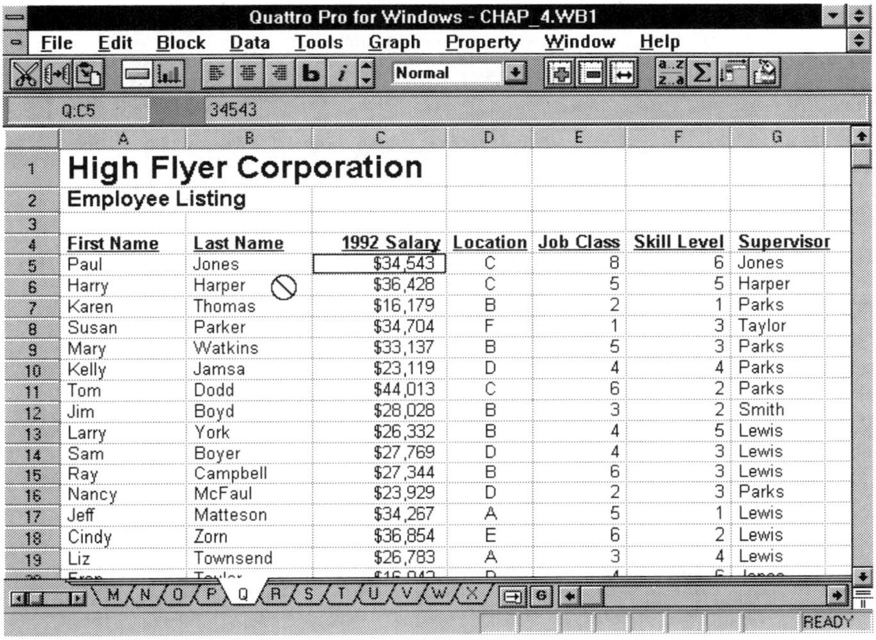

Figure 4.36 Page Using Titles to Freeze Columns and Rows

window into two panes (either vertically or horizontally) and look at two different portions of your notebook at once. You can also choose whether the panes move independently or together. You can create more than one window to look at the same notebook. You can hide windows to temporarily remove them from the desktop. When you have several windows available at once, you have additional options for displaying them. Additional options for notebook windows include having Quattro Pro arrange them automatically on the Quattro Pro window. Other features that control the appearance of a window, such as manually sizing it or dragging it to a new location are the same as in other Windows applications. These features are covered in Appendix B, "Windows Basics."

Creating Window Panes

Window panes are the result of splitting a window into two parts so that you can look at different sections of the same notebook window. To split the notebook window into two window panes, move the selector to the cell where you want the split to occur. Select Panes from the Window menu. Select Horizontal if you want to split your notebook horizontally as shown in Figure 4.37. Select Vertical if you want to split your notebook vertically as shown in Figure 4.38. When you select

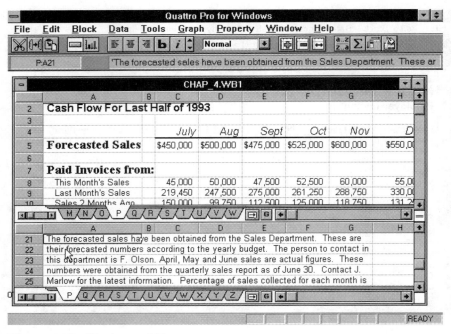

Figure 4.37   Horizontal Panes

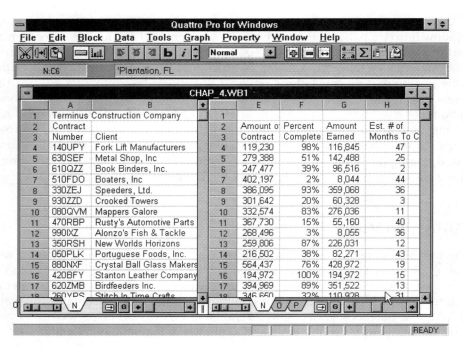

Figure 4.38   Vertical Panes

Horizontal, Quattro Pro puts all the rows above the selector into the first pane and all the remaining rows into the second pane. When you select Vertical, Quattro Pro puts all columns to the left of the selector into the first pane and the rest of the columns in the second pane.

You can also split a window into panes by dragging the *pane splitter*. The pane splitter is the symbol in the lower right corner of the window. You can drag the pane splitter up to create horizontal panes or to the left to create vertical panes. The advantage of using the pane splitter to split a window into panes is that you can subsequently adjust where a window splits into panes, which you cannot do with the Panes command in the Window menu.

While you are using panes, most of the block and page properties affect only the current pane. For example, you can hide columns, expose columns, make titles, clear titles, change column widths, and change the numeric format in one pane without affecting the other pane. Most of the commands, however, operate on both panes. Even though the display looks as if it is splitting the notebook into two, it is not. The panes do not split the notebook but provide two different views of the same notebook. To switch from one pane to another, press F6 (PANE) or click a cell in the other pane with the mouse. The selector is in the current pane at all times.

SYNCHRONIZING WINDOWS   The two panes can display information from different areas of the notebook. Your movement in one pane is, by default, synchronized with the other pane. For example, if your notebook with horizontal panes is synchronized, both panes display the same columns, but can show different rows or pages. Quattro Pro moves the inactive pane when you move the current pane to the left or right. If your notebook with vertical panes is synchronized, both panes display the same rows, but can show different columns or pages. Quattro Pro moves the inactive pane when you move the current pane up or down. If the panes of a notebook with either type of split are not synchronized, moving one pane around in the notebook has no effect on the other pane's position.

Quattro Pro normally has the panes move in synchronization. However, to make them unsynchronized, when you create the panes, clear the Synchronize check box. To make unsynchronized panes synchronous again, select the Panes command in the Window menu and select the Synchronize check box.

REMOVING A PANE   To return the two panes to a single notebook window, select the Panes command in the Window menu and select the Clear radio button. When you select OK, Quattro Pro removes the right or bottom pane. You can also close a pane by dragging the pane splitter back to the lower right corner of the window. Any changes that were made in an upper or left pane are retained when the notebook is returned to one view, but changes to the other pane are lost.

Creating a Second Window for a Notebook

Panes are one method of looking at a notebook in two different ways. You can also create more than one view into a notebook by opening more than one window that contains the same notebook. For example, if you want to look at page A and page N of the notebook shown in Figure 4.38, you could split the window into unsynchronous panes and then use each pane to display separate pages. Another option is to have two windows open for the notebook, with one window showing page A and another showing page N. Since both windows look into the same notebook, changes made in one window are also made in the other window.

To create a second window for the same notebook, select <u>N</u>ew View from the <u>W</u>indow menu. This displays a second window containing the same notebook. Figure 4.39 shows four windows opened to display the same notebook. Windows are not synchronized as panes are. Each window can be moved separately, and you can move to different locations in each window. When you make an entry in one window, you will not see the new entry in the other until you finalize the entry. When you want to close a window to the notebook, use the <u>C</u>lose command in the window's control menu box. You can select this by clicking the control menu box or pressing ALT-HYPHEN, then selecting <u>C</u>lose. You can also close the current notebook window by pressing CTRL-F4. When you use the <u>C</u>lose command in the <u>F</u>ile menu instead, you close *all* views of the notebook.

Moving Between Windows

When you have multiple windows open, whether they show the same notebook or different ones, you can easily switch between them. Quattro Pro has several

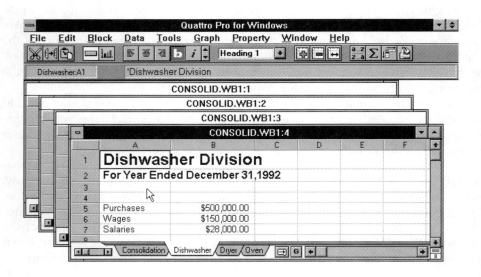

Figure 4.39 Multiple Windows of the Same Notebook

menu commands, keystroke combinations, and mouse selections you can use to switch between windows.

The easiest method of selecting a window, if you can see it in the Quattro Pro window, is to select it with the mouse. If you are using a mouse and part of the window you want is visible, you can always click the window to make it active.

At the bottom of the Window menu, you can select the active window. The bottom of the Window menu lists up to nine window names. Selecting the window name from the list makes that window active. If you have more than nine windows open, the Window menu also contains the More Windows command. When you select this command, Quattro Pro displays the Activate Window dialog box, which lists the window names of all the windows. When you pick a window from the list, Quattro Pro makes it current.

You can use the CTRL-F6 (NEXT WINDOW) key to switch between the windows. This key makes the next window current. The order of the windows used by CTRL-F6 (NEXT WINDOW) matches the order in which they are listed in the Activate Window dialog box.

Hiding Notebooks

In the last chapter you learned how you can hide columns and rows. You can also hide windows. You can hide windows when your Quattro Pro desktop is too cluttered or you do not want other people to see the spreadsheet notebooks you are using. Hidden windows do not appear on the desktop and are not listed in the Window menu.

To hide a window, activate the window and select Hide from the Window menu. Now, the previously active window no longer appears in the Quattro Pro desktop. It may seem like you have closed the window. The only time you will notice it is present is if you exit Quattro Pro and the notebook has unsaved changes. If you open a notebook that was hidden when saved last, the notebook remains hidden.

To make a hidden window visible again, select Show from the Window menu. The Show Window dialog box will list the hidden windows. When you select a window from the list by double-clicking it or selecting the window name and OK, the window will reappear just as if you had never hidden it.

Arranging Multiple Windows

Quattro Pro has other options for showing multiple windows on Quattro Pro's desktop. You can use these options to change how many windows appear and which ones appear. Each window is separate from the others, so you can move each one or change its size separately.

One simple method of showing the windows and their contents is to cascade the windows. This is like taking a pile of papers and staggering their placement so you can see the top line from each page. To cascade notebooks, use the Cascade command in the Window menu. When you use this command, Quattro Pro has a three-dimensional effect, and you can see the title bar of each window. Figure 4.39 shows several windows cascaded. Cascaded windows make it easy to select the window you want with the mouse, since you always have at least a corner of every window visible.

Another option for showing all the windows is to divide the Quattro Pro desktop among the nonminimized windows, so that each open window is about the same size. This is done by dividing up the screen into *tiles*. To divide the screen into tiles, select Tile from the Window menu. When you execute this command, Quattro Pro divides the Quattro Pro desktop among the open windows into small, equal-sized windows and displays as much as possible in each window. Figure 4.40 shows four tiled windows. As the number of windows increases, the amount of space allocated to each window decreases.

NAMING BLOCKS OF DATA

In the last chapter, you learned that you can assign meaningful names to pages rather than using the initial names of A to IV. You can also assign names to blocks so you can use a name to reference a block rather than using the block's address. Using block names instead of block addresses has several advantages. Most users

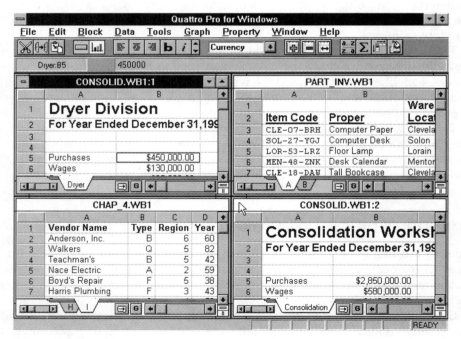

Figure 4.40   Multiple Windows Tiled

find that a block name is easier to remember than an address. Quattro Pro updates a block name's address automatically when the block is moved. The use of a block name in a formula makes the formula easier to comprehend. Also, a block name better describes the contents of a block than the block's address.

Block names can be used any place that a block address or cell address is used. Quattro Pro provides commands to create block names, delete block names, and make a table listing the block names and their addresses. Block names are easier to use for formula references to another notebook, a feature covered in Chapter 7. Block names are also useful in macros (see Chapters 13 and 14).

The use of block names is not any more difficult than the use of a cell address, as long as you are aware of potential problems. Misspelling a block name in a block command prevents the block command from executing. Misspelling a block name in a formula causes Quattro Pro not to accept the entry until the spelling error is corrected.

Creating a Block Name

Assigning a block name to a block address is as simple as telling Quattro Pro the name and the block address. Quattro Pro provides two methods of creating block names. The first method offers complete flexibility in the size of the block. The second method has limited applicability, since (1) the block name must be stored on the notebook already, and (2) it can only apply to a single cell.

CREATING ONE BLOCK NAME AT A TIME   The simplest method of creating a block name is using the Names command in the Block menu and then selecting Create. This command also has the shortcut of CTRL-F3. When you select this command, you can enter the block name and select the block that uses that name.

In the Create Name dialog box, you can enter up to 15 characters for the block name in the Name text box. The Names list box lists the existing block names. When you finalize the block name, Quattro Pro converts all letters to uppercase letters. Although you can use any character available on your keyboard, you should not use mathematical operators, since including such symbols in a block name that is used in a formula makes the formula difficult to understand. Also, you should use an underscore (_) instead of a space to separate words, since spaces, especially at the end of a block name, can be misinterpreted in a formula. In the Block(s) text box, you can enter the block address. If you have selected a block before the command, the block is listed in the Block(s) text box. When both the block name and the block address are correct, select OK to finalize the block name.

CREATING MULTIPLE BLOCK NAMES AT ONCE   If you have label entries already on the notebook that you want to use to name individual cells that are adjacent to the names, Quattro Pro has a special command you can use to name several cells at once. You can select the block containing the labels to use as the block names and then select Names from the Block menu and select Labels.

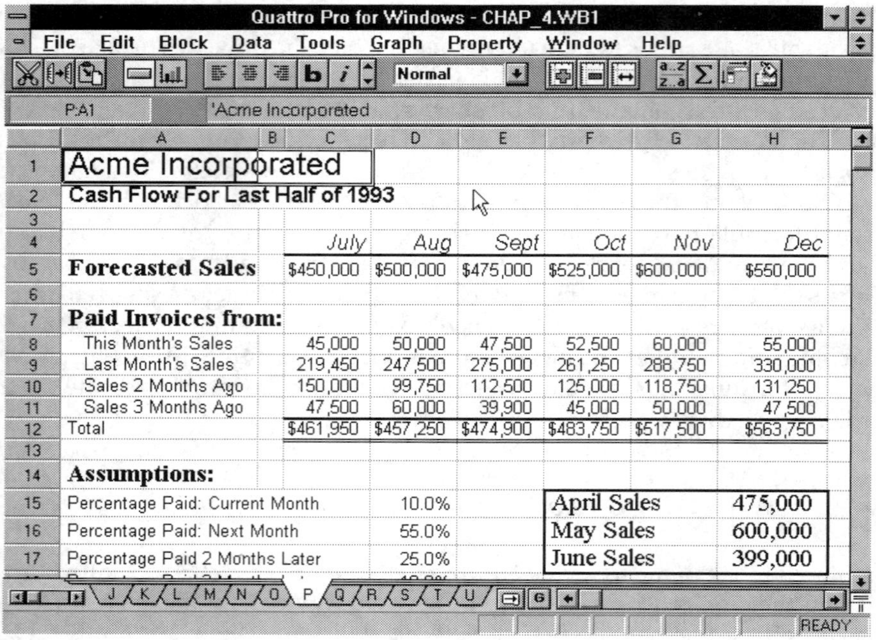

Figure 4.41   Page Computing Cash Flows from Sales

Figure 4.41 displays a notebook that computes the cash flows from sales for six months. The formulas in rows 8 through 11 each refer to a different month's sales (rows) to compute the portion of sales receipts that is expected to be collected. These formulas are not difficult, but they would be easier to understand if they used the month names rather than the cell references. By attaching block names to the cells containing each month's sales, you can use the month names in the formulas. To apply the block names to these cells, select C4..H4. This is the block containing the labels rather than the cells you want the labels to name. Next, select Names from the Block menu, then select Labels. The Create Names From Labels dialog box chooses whether the cells that you want to name are to the right of, left of, above, or below the labels that you have chosen. (If you want to you can change the selected block by changing the Blocks text box.) For the notebook in Figure 4.41, you should choose Down. Once you select OK to finalize the command, Quattro Pro creates block names for each month's sales entry.

If you look at the formulas in the cells that refer to the sales of July through December, Quattro Pro has changed the cell addresses to their block names. For example, the formula in C8 is +JULY*$D$15. This command is restricted in its application, but if you have the correct set of conditions, it can save a significant amount of time.

Using Block Names

Once you have created a block name, you can use it in formulas, functions, and commands. For example, with the commands in the Block menu that copy and move commands, you can type the block name instead of describing the coordinates. You can also use the block name in formulas and, as discussed in Chapter 8, @functions. Using block names instead of cell or block addresses creates formulas that are easier to understand.

When the selector is on a cell containing a formula that uses a block name, the block name appears in the input line instead of the actual cell or block reference. When you edit a cell with a block name in a formula, the formula appears in the input line using the block name. Quattro Pro continues to use the block names instead of the cell addresses when the cell formulas are displayed in the input line and when the cells use the Text format. When you enter block names in a formula, you achieve the same results as entering the address. You can create a block name that is handled as an absolute reference by adding a dollar sign ($) in front of the block name when you type it (as in $SALES). Another option for making the reference absolute is using F4 (ABS) to change the relative block name into an absolute block name. Block names do not use mixed addresses.

When you type in a formula with cell addresses, you can quickly add a block name to your formula by pressing F3 (CHOICES). Quattro Pro displays a list of the existing block names (as shown in Figure 4.42) as long as Quattro Pro is waiting for you to specify a block. If you press the + (PLUS) key, Quattro Pro widens the box and shows the cell addresses referenced by each of the block names. Pressing the – (MINUS) key reduces the box size to its original size that just lists the block names. If you press F3 (CHOICES) again while Quattro Pro is listing the block names, the box expands. To include a block name in the input line using F3 (CHOICES), highlight the desired block name, and press ENTER or click it. You can also use this key whenever you want to use a block name for a Quattro Pro command—for example, pressing F3 (CHOICES) when Quattro Pro prompts for a block to move.

Removing a Block Name

As you create names for blocks, you may want to remove some of them. For example, if you enter a name of a block incorrectly when you type it, you must delete the block name, and create it again. To remove a block name, select Names from the Block menu and then select Delete. In the Delete Name dialog box, select the named block from the Names list box. Quattro Pro fills in the block name in the Name text box and the block address in the Block(s) text box. You can also select which block to delete by typing the name in the Name text box. When you select OK, the selected block name is deleted. Since you are only deleting the name associated with a block address, the contents of the named block do not change. Formulas that reference the deleted block name will convert the block names to

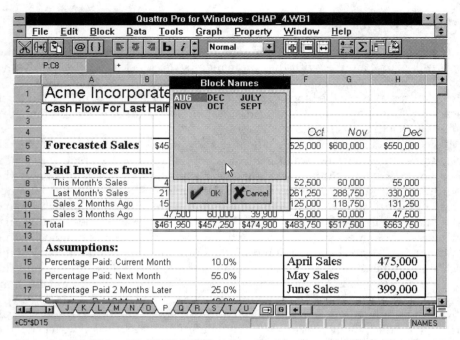

Figure 4.42   Using F3 (CHOICES) to List the Notebook's Block Names

the cell addresses. Once you have deleted a block name, you must re-create it if you want to use it again.

If you want to remove all block names, select Names from the Block menu and then select Reset. When you use this command, Quattro Pro displays a confirmation menu prompting you to confirm your request. Select Yes to delete all named blocks. If you delete one or all of the block names and then change your mind, you can only restore the block names if the Undo feature is enabled.

Changing a Block Name's Address

After you create a block name, Quattro Pro keeps track of the current location of your named block. If you move the block, Quattro Pro changes the block address referenced by the block name. In some instances, you may need to change the address Quattro Pro uses for a block name (if, for example, an original specification was incorrect or you wish to use that name elsewhere).

To change the address that Quattro Pro uses for a block name, select Names in the Block menu, select Create, and select the block name from the Names list box displaying the existing block names. When Quattro Pro enters the block name in the Name text box and the block address in the Block(s) text box, in the Block(s) text box enter the new address that you want Quattro Pro to use for the block name and select OK.

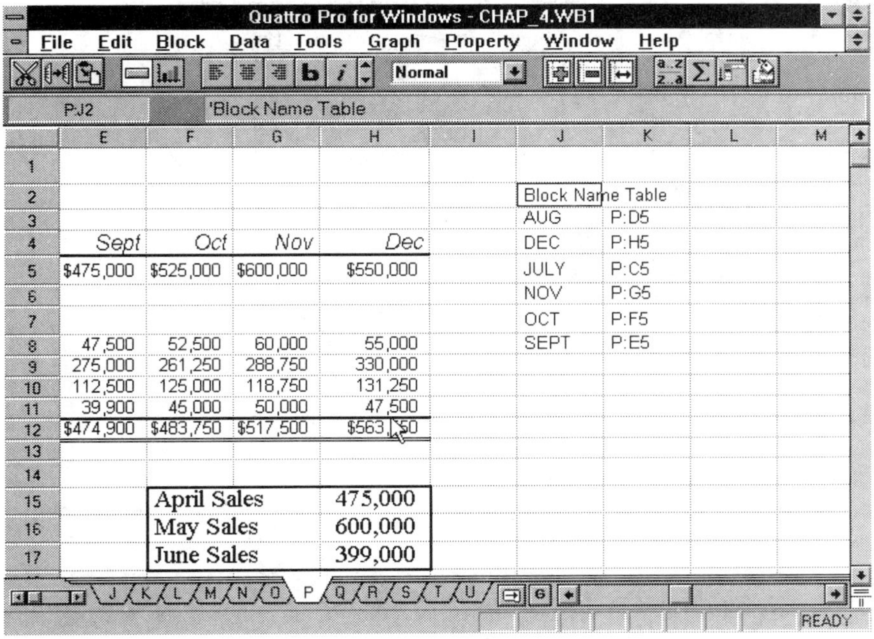

Figure 4.43   Table of Block Names and Addresses

Creating a Block Name Table

When you have many block names, it may be difficult to keep track of all the locations that the blocks represent. You can list the block addresses of block names by pressing the + key (as shown in Figure 4.42) after you have pressed F3 (CHOICES). To create a list of the existing block names and their addresses in the notebook, select a cell where you want the table you will create to start. Select an empty area of a page so that the table will not overwrite any important data. Next, select <u>N</u>ames from the <u>B</u>lock menu and then select <u>M</u>ake Table and OK. A sample table created with this command is shown in Figure 4.43. The table you create contains the notebook's block names and the cell or block address each block name represents.

GETTING STARTED

In this chapter, you learned how to use Quattro Pro commands that rearrange your entries in a notebook. With these commands, you learned how to copy, erase, move, and name cells. Other commands let you insert and delete rows or columns, and change how Quattro Pro displays notebooks by using titles and panes. You can try some of these commands by creating the sales projection notebook shown in Figure 4.44. To create this notebook, follow these steps:

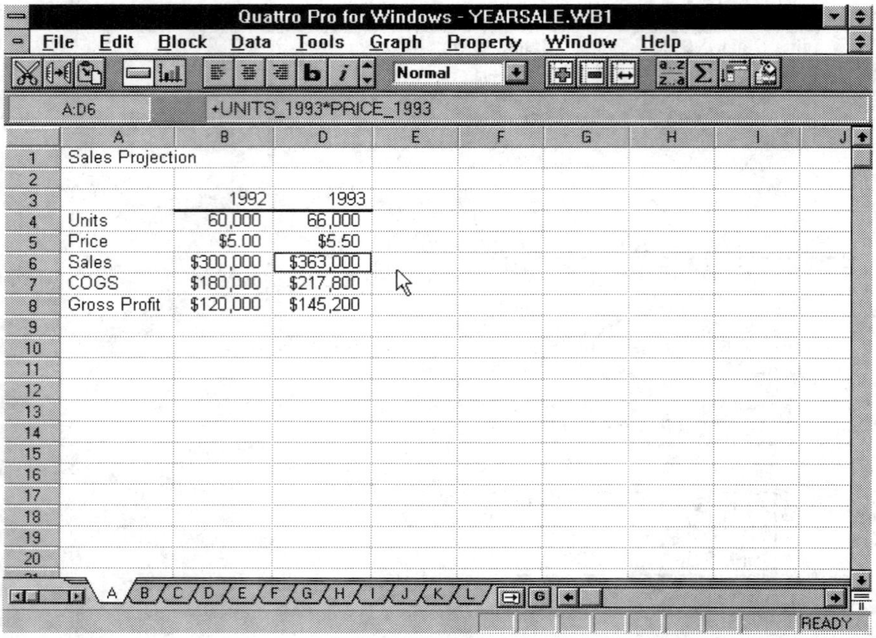

Figure 4.44   Notebook Used with Getting Started Section

1. Make the following entries. With a mouse, you can click the ✓ or another cell to finalize each entry. If you are not using a mouse, press ENTER or an arrow key to finalize the entry.

   A1: **Units**
   A2: **Price**
   A3: **Sales**
   A4: **COGS**
   A5: **Gross Profit**
   B1: **60000**
   B2: **5**

2. Enter the following formulas. You can either type the cell address or point to the cell as described in Chapter 2.

   B3: **+B1*B2**
   B4: **+B3*.6**
   B5: **+B3-B4**

3. Use the Clipboard to copy one value to another. Move to C1. Type **10%**, and press ENTER or click ✓ in the input line. Press CTRL-INS or click the Copy button in the SpeedBar to copy this entry to the Clipboard. Copy this entry to C2 by selecting that cell and then pressing SHIFT-INS or clicking the Paste button in the SpeedBar.

4. Use the Clipboard to copy a formula. Move to D1. Enter the formula **+B1*(1+C1)**. You can either point to the cells or type the cell addresses. Finalize the formula by pressing ENTER or clicking ✓ in the input line. Press CTRL-INS or click the Copy button in the SpeedBar to copy this formula to the Clipboard. Copy this formula to D2 by selecting that cell, and then pressing SHIFT-INS or clicking the Paste button in the SpeedBar.

5. Use the Clipboard to copy multiple formulas. Select B3..B5. Press CTRL-INS or click the Copy button in the SpeedBar to copy these formulas to the Clipboard. Copy these formulas to D3..D5 by selecting D3, and then pressing SHIFT-INS or clicking the Paste button in the SpeedBar.

6. Move the entries to have room for column headings. Select A1..D5. Drag these entries to A3..D7. You can also select <u>M</u>ove from the <u>B</u>lock menu, type A3 in the <u>T</u>o text box, and select OK to move the entries.

7. Make the following entries:

   A1: **Sales Projection**
   B2: **1992**
   C2: **% Increase**
   D2: **1993**

8. Change the block's properties so that the values use different numeric formats. The values need numeric formats so the numbers of units appear with commas separating the thousands, prices appear with two digits after the decimal point, the percentages appear as percents, and the remaining numbers appear using the currency format. Select the block B3..D3 and inspect its properties. With the Numeric Format property selected, choose C<u>o</u>mma, and type **0** in the text box. Select OK to format these three cells. For the prices, select the block B4..D4 and inspect its properties. With the Numeric Format property selected, choose <u>C</u>urrency and select OK. For the percentages, select the block C3..C4 and inspect its properties. With the Numeric Format property selected, choose <u>P</u>ercent, and type **0** in the text box. Select OK to format the two percentages. For the remaining numbers, format them as currency by selecting the block B5..D7, inspecting its properties, selecting the <u>C</u>urrency radio button, and typing **0** in the text box before selecting OK.

9. Expand the columns to fit the entries. Select A2..D7 and then either click the Fit button on the SpeedBar or inspect the block's properties, select the Column Width property, select the <u>A</u>uto Width radio button, and select OK.

10. Draw a line under the column headings. Select the block B2..D2 and inspect the block's properties. Select the Line Drawing property, the thick line under Line <u>T</u>ypes, and the bottom line in the <u>L</u>ine Segments diagram. Select OK so Quattro Pro draws a line below the cells.

11. You may want to add space between the report title and the report body. You can increase the spacing by inserting a row between the title in A1 and

the column headings in row 2. To insert a row, move to A2 and click the Insert button in the SpeedBar or select Insert from the Block menu. Select Rows and OK to insert a single row.

12. The formulas that you have created do not provide much information about why these calculations are being performed. A quick method of documenting this notebook is to name some of the cells. For each of the cells listed below, move to the cell, select Names from the Block menu and select Create, or press CTRL-F3 to name the cell. When Quattro Pro prompts for the block address of the cell, enter the address of the cell that you are naming.

B4 named **Units_1992**
B5 named **Price_1992**
B6 named **Sales_1992**
D4 named **Units_1993**
D5 named **Price_1993**
D6 named **Sales_1993**

13. Hide column C. To do this, select a cell in this column and inspect its properties. Select the Reveal/Hide property and the Columns and the Hide radio buttons. Select OK.

14. Save your data. Select Save from the File menu. Next, type **YEARSALE** in the File Name text box and select OK. Your notebook now looks like Figure 4.44.

5

Making Cell Entries with Commands

So far, you have learned how to create entries, change their appearance, and rearrange them. Quattro Pro also has commands that can create entries for you. These commands include entering a series of numbers, and analyzing other entries you have in your notebook. The entries are created by Quattro Pro once you tell Quattro Pro the types of entries you want to make. Once you use the commands, the entries these commands make are part of your notebook just like the entries you have typed yourself.

Some of these commands provide analytical features. These analytical commands cover a variety of techniques that can solve a wide range of problems. Some commands allow you to automate a what-if analysis by storing the results of spreadsheet calculations in a table on a page. The matrix features included in these commands allow you to simplify complicated mathematical operations. Other commands in this group can compute a frequency distribution or a regression analysis. The most advanced analytical features let you perform linear programming and have Quattro Pro find the value of one cell that produces the desired result in another. The one thing that all these commands have in common is the power to save you a significant amount of time.

GENERATING VALUES IN A BLOCK

Most data you enter into your notebooks is data you have typed. When you enter data, you may find that some entries, such as consecutive dates or numbers, are monotonous. Quattro Pro eliminates this monotonous data entry by generating a

163

series of values that are an equal distance apart. The following lines contain samples of series you can create:

1 2 3 4 5 6 7 8 9 10
01/07/90 01/14/90 01/21/90 01/28/90
100 60 20 -20 -60 -100
1000000 1100000 1210000 1331000 1464100 1610510

The Fill command in the Block menu generates a series of numbers in a block. Before Quattro Pro generates the numbers, you must tell Quattro Pro the block to fill, the number you want to start with, the increment between numbers, and the highest possible number. The numbers can be evenly spaced as in the first three examples, or can be a constant rate of increase as in the 10% growth of the last example. To generate a series of values, follow these steps:

1. Select the block to fill with the numbers. For example, if you want to fill A1..B10 with the numbers 0 through 190 in steps of 10, you would select the block A1..B10.

2. Select Fill from the Block menu to display the dialog box shown in Figure 5.1.

3. Enter a number in the Start text box. The start value is the first value Quattro Pro puts in the block. For the example of entering 0 through 190 in A1..B10, you would want to leave the default of 0. You can also enter other values such as a date or time or a formula or cell reference.

4. Enter a number in the Step text box. The step value is the amount each value generated by Quattro Pro increases or decreases. If the step value is posi-

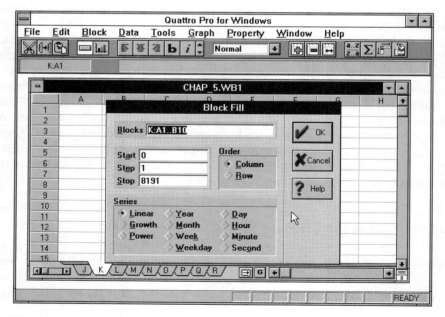

Figure 5.1   Block Fill Dialog Box

tive, the numbers generated by Quattro Pro increase. If the step value is negative, the numbers generated by Quattro Pro decrease. You can also enter other values such as a date or time, a formula or a cell reference. For the example of entering 0 through 190 in A1..B10, you would enter 10.

5. Enter a number in the Stop text box. The Stop value sets the highest number Quattro Pro will generate when it fills the series. Quattro Pro uses this number and the block size to determine when to stop generating numbers. Quattro Pro continues to generate numbers until it reaches the stop value or it has filled all the cells in the block.

6. Select the radio button for how Quattro Pro will generate the series. Table 5.1 shows the different options, with samples of the series that each Series radio button can generate. For the example of entering 0 through 190 in A1..B10, you would want to leave the default of Linear.

Table 5.1 Series Options for Generating a Series of Values

Series	Increments By	Sample Start	Sample Step	Sample Results
Linear	Adding step value	15	1	15, 16, 17
Growth	Multiplying by step value	100	1.5	100, 150, 225
Power	Raising by step value	2	2	2, 4, 16
Year	Years	06/14/93	2	06/14/93, 06/14/95, 06/14/97
Month	Months	06/14/93	1	06/14/93, 07/14/93, 08/14/93
Week	Weeks	06/21/93	1	06/21/93, 06/28/93, 07/05/93
Weekday	Weekdays	06/11/93	1	06/11/93, 06/14/93, 06/15/93
Day	Days	06/14/93	3	06/14/93, 06/17/93, 06/20/93
Hour	Hours	11:25 AM	2	11:25 AM, 1:25 PM 3:25 PM
Minute	Minutes	11:25 AM	15	11:25 AM, 11:40 AM 11:55 AM
Second	Seconds	8:43:00	25	8:43:00, 8:43:25, 8:43:50

7. Select whether you want the block filled by rows or columns. When you have a block that includes more than one column or row, the two radio buttons below Order select whether Quattro Pro will fill a row at a time or a column at a time. For the example of entering 0 through 190 in A1..B10, you would want to leave the default of Column.

8. Select OK. Quattro Pro fills the block and creates the block of numbers shown in Figure 5.2. Notice how Quattro Pro fills each column in the block before going on to the next.

Quattro Pro is very flexible with the values that you provide for the start, step, and stop values. You can use functions such as @DATE and @TIME to create date and time serial numbers. You can also use formulas for the start, step, and stop values.

Another method of quickly filling a block with a series of numbers is using the SpeedFill button in the SpeedBar that is the next to last button. When you click this button, Quattro Pro looks at the values already entered in the selected block and continues the pattern. This means that if you select the block A1..A10 and A1 has 0 and A2 has 10, selecting the SpeedFill button in the SpeedBar fills A1..A10 with 0, 10, 20, 30 through 90. Quattro Pro assumes each column or row is filled separately. To use the SpeedFill button, you must have the initial value in the first cell of the block. If you do not have subsequent values, Quattro Pro assumes you want to increment by one. SpeedFill also recognizes other patterns such as the names of days and months. You can use SpeedFill when the initial entry includes extra text to be repeated for each entry such as using Month 1 to be repeated through up to Month 12. If you use the SpeedFill button with a noncontiguous block, each block that is part of the block selection is treated separately. For example, the block address A1..F1;A5..A15 is treated as the block A1..F1 and the block A5..A15. This separate treatment of blocks means each block in the noncontiguous block address must have its own initial value.

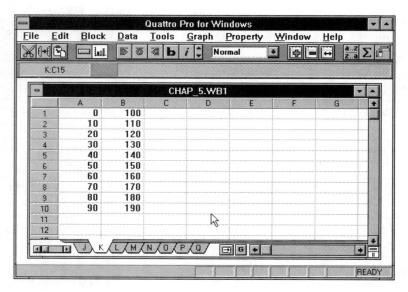

Figure 5.2   Numbers Generated with Fill in the Block Menu

Search and Replace

Quattro Pro has a special command that lets you find characters in a block and replace them with other characters. Instead of making new entries you can enhance the ones you already have. This command can locate all occurrences of a particular cell reference. One of its uses is to correct a misspelling that occurs repeatedly in a notebook.

To use Quattro Pro's search and replace feature, follow these steps:

1. Select the block you want to search. You can easily select the entire page by clicking the Select-All button in the corner of the row and column border.

2. Select Search and Replace from the Edit menu. Quattro Pro displays the Search/Replace dialog box shown in Figure 5.3. Quattro Pro already has your block selection in the Block(s) text box.

3. Type the characters you want to find in the Find text box. Your entry can be one or more numbers, letters, or both. When Quattro Pro searches for this entry, it looks at all the cells, whether they contain labels, numbers, or formulas. If you are searching for a cell reference, such as A1, Quattro Pro finds it even if it is buried in a formula. If you are looking for an absolute or mixed cell address, the search string must include the dollar signs in that address.

4. Type the characters you want to find in the Replace text box if you want to replace the entry in the Find text box with another where it appears in the

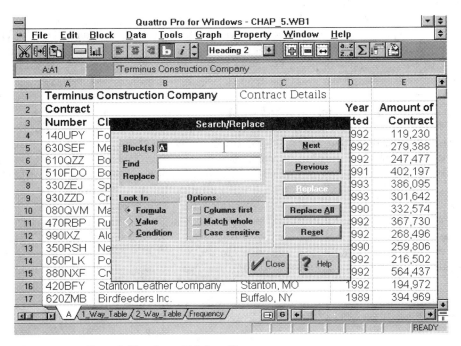

Figure 5.3 Search/Replace Dialog Box

notebook. This entry can be one or more numbers, letters, or both. If you only want to find occurrences of the entry in the Find text box but do not want to replace them, leave this text box empty.

5.   Select Next. Quattro Pro searches for the specified search string. If Quattro Pro does not find a match, it beeps and displays the error message "Not found." When Quattro Pro finds a match, you can select whether you want to replace the entry Quattro Pro has found with the entry in the Replace text box. You may want to shift the dialog box out of the way (by dragging its title bar) so you can better see the matching entry Quattro Pro has found. If you choose Replace, Quattro Pro replaces the Find entry with the Replace entry, and then searches for the next occurrence. If you choose Next again, Quattro Pro does not make the replacement, and looks for the next occurrence. Replace All replaces all occurrences of the Find text box entry in the specified block with the Replace entry. You can also select Previous to return to a prior occurrence of the Find entry in the selected block. When you choose Next, Replace, or Replace All, Quattro Pro continues to look for all occurrences of the Find entry. When Quattro Pro can no longer find a match, it displays the Not Found error message. Selecting Close returns to the notebook. Quattro Pro remembers all the settings that you used with this command except the block, making it easier to use the command again.

SEARCH AND REPLACE OPTIONS

Quattro Pro provides other options for finding cells containing the Find entry. The Search and Replace command in the Edit menu makes several assumptions that you can change. These options are listed in the bottom of the dialog box in Figure 5.3. You can change the order Quattro Pro uses to search the selected block for the Find entry. When the Columns first check box is selected, Quattro Pro will finish searching one column before searching the next. When it is cleared, Quattro Pro will finish searching a row before searching the next row for the Find text.

The radio buttons below Look In determine how Quattro Pro searches formulas. The default setting (Formula) searches the formulas themselves. Value searches the results that the formulas display. Condition searches the formulas' results and other cell entries to find cells whose values meet the condition provided by the Find entry. To select this option, the Find entry must be entered first. The Find entry is a logical condition. As an example, if you want to find cells with values greater than 400,000 for the notebook shown in Figure 5.4, you enter **?>400000**. The ? represents the current cell, so every cell in the search block is checked to see if it matches the condition. You can also enter the current cell by supplying the upper left cell in the selected block. When the Find entry is a condition, the cell address in the Find entry is always updated for the current cell position, so when you look at the Find entry at another time, the cell reference in the Find entry will be different.

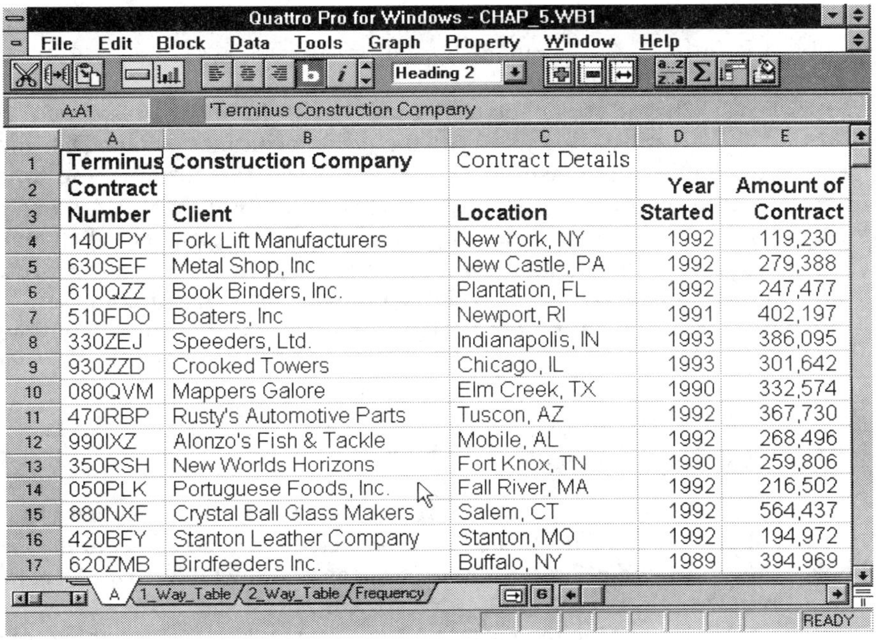

Figure 5.4 Notebook to Search for Entries

The Match whole check box determines whether the Find entry matches the entire cell entry, or only part of a cell entry. If Smith is the Find entry, it matches with Smithfield if the Match whole check box is cleared, but it does not match if it is selected.

The Case sensitive check box determines if the Find entry must have the same capitalization pattern as a cell entry. If this check box is cleared, Quattro Pro accepts a match with any capitalization pattern as long as the entry meets the other match criteria. If you select this check box, Quattro Pro considers it a match only if the capitalization pattern and other characteristics of the entry are exactly the same as the Find entry. You can return Search and Replace options to the default by selecting Reset. The default options check formulas, search by rows, find cells that contain at least the Find entry, and include matches that have a different capitalization pattern. Selecting Reset also removes the Find and Replace entries.

SENSITIVITY TABLES

Spreadsheet notebooks are designed for what-if analysis since changing a value in a cell causes the formulas relying on that cell to be updated immediately. Although these what-if features supply a quick answer when you want to look at the impact of one change, exploring a whole range of possibilities can still be quite time-consuming with this approach. Also, unless you print the results from each possibility, it is difficult to remember the impact of each change as you proceed through the range of options.

Quattro Pro's What-If command can provide a solution that is much more sophisticated, yet it is still easy to use. With the What-If command in the Data menu, you can create a table of the results from your analysis that permits you to view the impact of each option at a glance. The what-if analyses that can be accommodated with this feature can be as simple as monitoring the effect of change on a single formula or as complex as analyzing the effects of changing many formulas and calculations. To analyze your model, Quattro Pro's What-If command generates a table of results by varying the values for either one or two variables in the notebook.

Creating a 1 Way What-If Table

When you use Quattro Pro's What-If command for one variable, you need to store the values that you wish to substitute for the selected variable in a column on the notebook. This type of what-if table is referred to as a 1 Way table. In a 1 Way table, the values on the left side of the table contain the input values of the variable. The values on the right side of the table contain the results when the variable replaces another cell entry.

The procedure for creating a 1 Way table requires some setup work before the command can be executed. To set up the required entries for a 1 Way table, follow these steps:

1. Select a blank area of a notebook as the table location.

2. Enter the values you wish to substitute for another cell entry in the leftmost column of this table area.

3. Move one row above and one column to the right of the first variable value.

4. Across the top row of the table, enter the formulas you wish to evaluate for each new value of the variable.

The formulas can be an integral part of the model, requiring many preliminary results to be calculated before the effect is evaluated. Rather than reentering a formula that is already stored elsewhere in the notebook, you can reference it as in +B11, which references the formula currently stored in B11. With a 1 Way table, you can enter multiple formulas across the top row in the table, and the appropriate results are stored below each formula when the command is evaluated.

When the What-If command in the Data menu is executed for a 1 Way table, Quattro Pro fills the cells in the right columns with the results of the formulas at the top of each column. Quattro Pro evaluates each formula, one input value at a time, and places the evaluated results in the column beneath the formula and on the same row as the input value.

The what-if analysis has unlimited potential. For example, this command can compute a company's performance assuming different sales growth percentages.

Figure 5.5 displays a notebook that calculates different measurements of a company's performance, assuming a sales growth rate of 5%. To create the table area shown in Figure 5.6, the sales growth percentages are generated with the Fill command in the Block menu. The fill block is A10..A15. This command uses a Start value of 5%, a Step value of 1%, and a Stop value of 10%. The generated numbers are formatted as percentages. You can also use the SpeedFill button.

The first formula for this table is entered in B9 as +C4 to place the new sales figure next to the growth percentage. In C9, the formula +C7 is entered to place the new profit figure next to the sales figure for each sales growth percentage. These formulas use the text numeric format so that they can be documentation for the table. As shown in this example, Quattro Pro can fill in multiple values in a table for each of the growth rates. Figure 5.6 shows the completed setup work for the table with the two formulas at the top of the table formatted as text. Once the What-If command in the Data menu is invoked, this what-if analysis creates a table that shows performance measurements for different growth rates.

To create a 1 Way what-if table after performing the initial setup, follow these steps:

1. Select the block containing the table. The table's upper left corner is the cell above the first input value. The lower right corner is in the same row as the last input value and the same column as the last formula entered. In Figure 5.6, the table location is A9..C15.

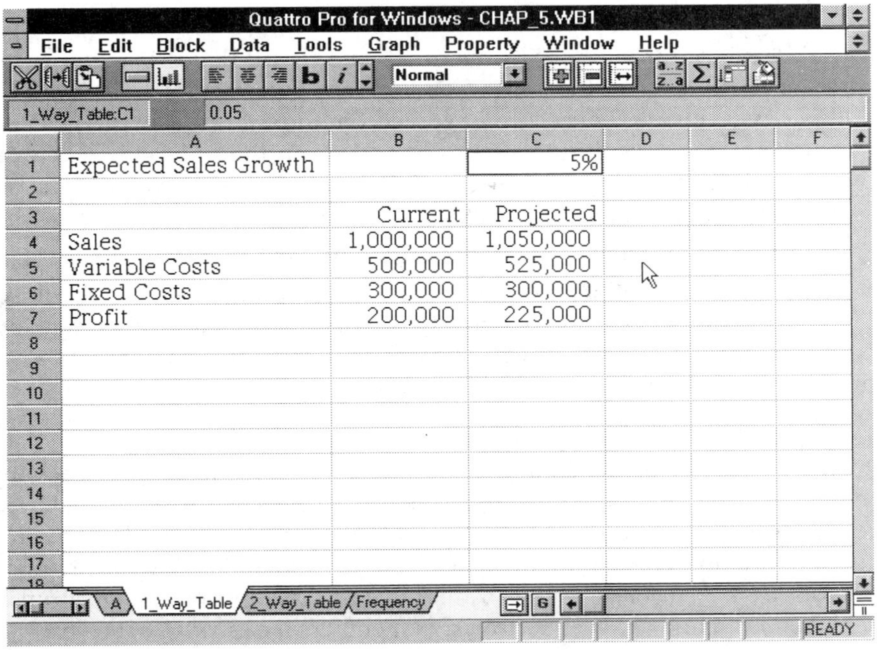

Figure 5.5 Page Computing Company Performance for a Projected Growth Rate (5%)

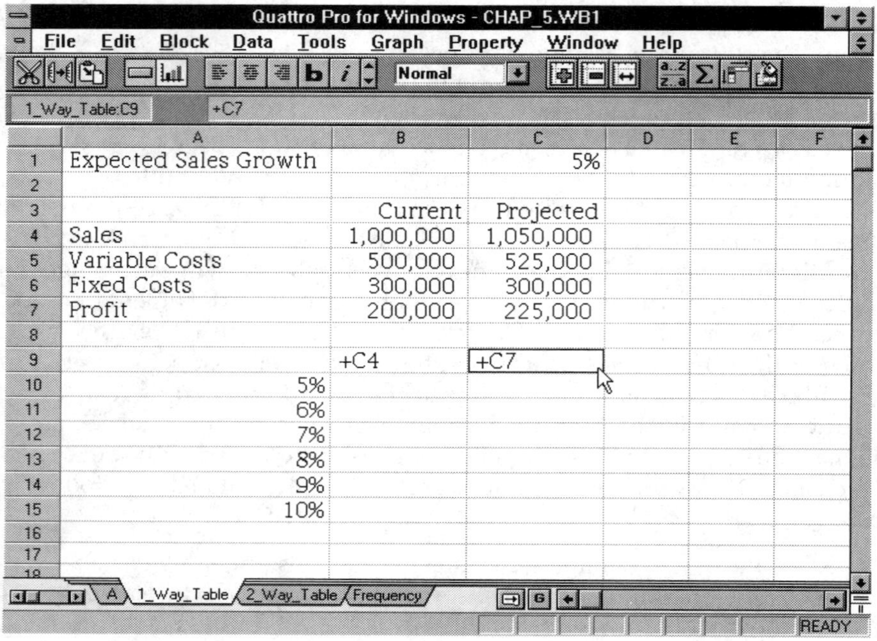

Figure 5.6   Table Set Up to Create a 1 Way Table

2. Select <u>W</u>hat-If from the <u>D</u>ata menu. In the What-If dialog box, you need to enter the address of the cell containing the value to be varied. Quattro Pro systematically places each input value from the data table in this cell before calculating the resulting value to be placed on the right side of the table under the two formulas. The <u>D</u>ata table text box already contains the block you selected before selecting this command.

3. Select the <u>O</u>ne free variable radio button to create a 1 Way What-If table.

4. Enter the input cell for the column of entries in the Input <u>c</u>ell text box. In Figure 5.6, this is C1. Initially, the input cell can be blank or filled with other information. If the input cell already contains data, its contents are left unchanged after this command executes.

5. Select <u>G</u>enerate and then Close.

Quattro Pro fills in the data table with the results for the formula as each input value is used as a replacement value in the input cell. The calculated entries are values. As such, modifications to the input values or to any cells used in the calculations are not reflected in the table's results. For example, if you change the fixed costs from 300,000 to 250,000, the table values do not change until you execute this command again. Quattro Pro remembers the settings of the last <u>W</u>hat-If command, which makes executing the command again quicker. You can also execute the command again by pressing F8 (TABLE), which performs the <u>W</u>hat-If command in the Data menu again using the same addresses for the data table and the input cell. Figure 5.7 shows the notebook after Quattro Pro fills in the table and the table's results have been formatted in the comma format.

If you need to execute the command with new settings, you first eliminate the existing settings. Entering the What-If command in the Data menu and then selecting Reset eliminates any settings used for creating a what-if table and makes it easier to specify a new table location.

Creating a 2 Way What-If Table

Quattro Pro's **2 Way** What-If command for two variables allows you to perform a what-if analysis while varying the values of two different variables. Since two variables are being evaluated, the command is only able to evaluate the effect on one formula. Just like the 1 Way What-if table, the 2 Way What-if table stores the results in a data table in the notebook.

With a 2 Way What-if table, values on the left side of the table are used for one variable, and values in the top row of the table are used to provide values for a second variable. When the What-If command is executed, Quattro Pro systematically substitutes one of the input values for the first variable and one of the input

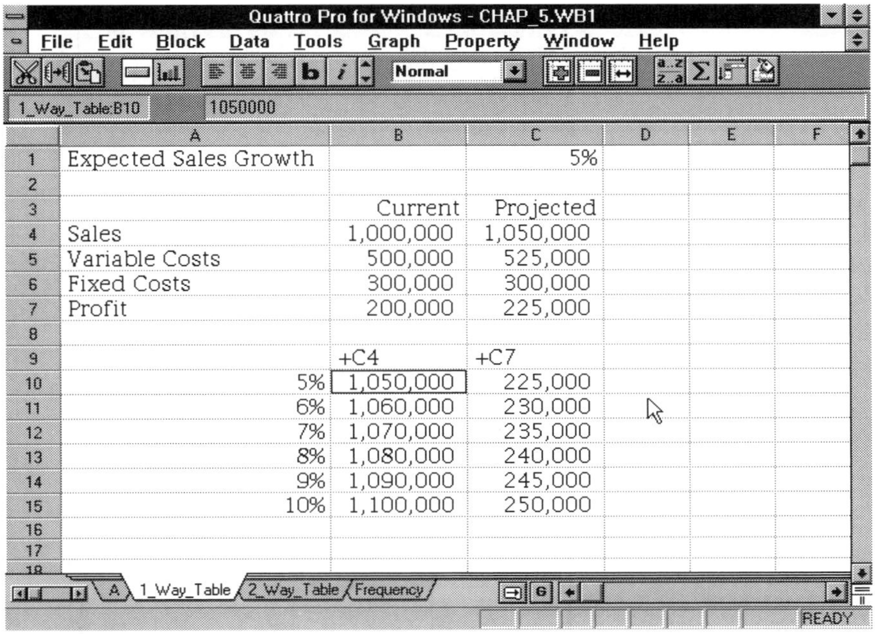

Figure 5.7   1 Way Table Filled in by What-If Command in the Data Menu

values for the second variable in place of their substitution cells and puts the formula's result at the row and column intersection of the two input values. You can determine the values of the variables used to produce any result value by looking to the left to obtain the variable value for variable 1 and looking across the top of the table to determine the value for variable 2.

As when using the <u>W</u>hat-If command in the <u>D</u>ata menu to create a 1 Way table, using this command to create a 2 Way table requires some setup work before it can be executed. What-if analysis saves time by mechanically performing many steps for you regardless of your application. One example of two-variable analysis is showing how different debt/equity ratios affect earnings per share at various income levels. As debt replaces stock in a company's capital structure, the interest expenses increase but the remaining profit is shared among fewer stockholders; therefore, the stock's value is increased. Figure 5.8 shows the shell for a table that computes the earnings per share (EPS) for different types of capital structure and different income levels. Variable costs are 50% of sales. Interest is 10% of the debt. Taxes are 40% of profit. The actual amount of debt is the debt-to-equity ratio multiplied by the 10 million dollars of total equity. The remaining equity is stock. The actual number of shares is the amount of stock divided by 1,000. A separate calculation is needed to compute the earnings per share for each income level. Quattro Pro's <u>W</u>hat-If command in the <u>D</u>ata menu can execute these computations automatically.

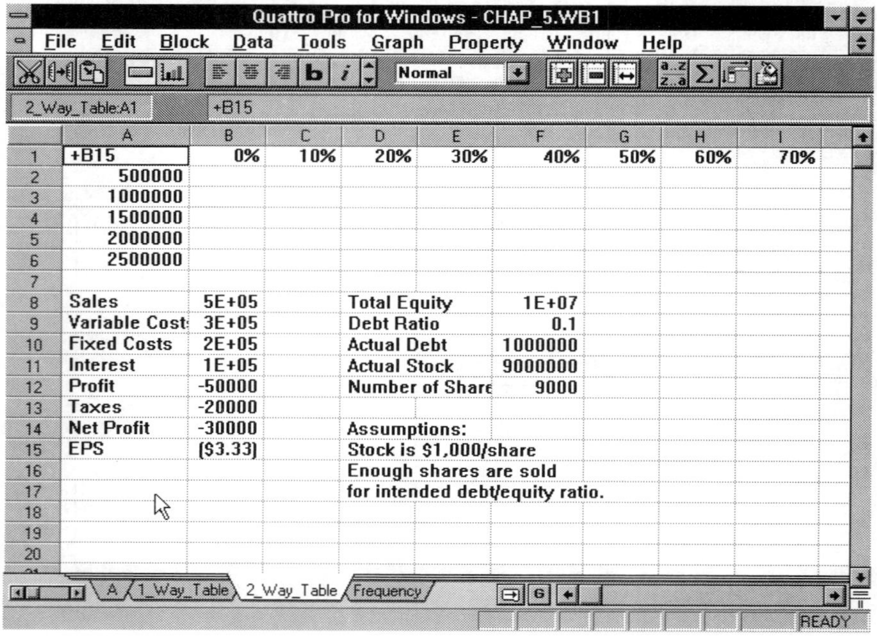

Figure 5.8   Table Set Up for 2 Way What-If Analysis for Computation of Earnings Per Share (EPS)

To create a 2 Way What-if table, follow these steps:

1. Move to a blank area of a notebook with sufficient space for the what-if table.

2. Enter the values for the first input variable in the leftmost column of the table. In this example, the values are generated with the Fill command in the Block menu with a fill block of **A2..A6**, a Start value of **500,000**, a Step value of **500,000**, and a Stop value of **2,500,000**. You can also use the SpeedFill button to generate these entries.

3. Move to the cell that is one cell above and one column to the right of the first input value generated in step 2. In Figure 5.8, this is B1.

4. Enter the values to be substituted for the second variable in the top row of the table. In this example, the values are generated with the Fill command in the Block menu with a fill block of **B1..I1**, a Start value of **0**, a Step value of **.1**, and a Stop value of **.70**. You can also generate these entries with the SpeedFill button.

5. Move to the intersection of this row and column of values. In Figure 5.8, the intersection is A1.

6. Enter the formula to be computed for each combination of variable values. In A1, the formula **+B15** is typed to place the new EPS for each combination of debt/equity ratio and income level at the intersection of the two variable entries and this formula is formatted as text.

7. Select the block containing the table. The table's upper left corner is the cell with the formula. The lower right corner is in the same row as the last value of the first variable and the same column as the last value of the second variable. In Figure 5.8, the table location is A1..I6.

8. Select What-If from the Data menu. In the What-If dialog box, you need to enter the two input cells where Quattro Pro systematically places each combination of first input and second input values from the data table before determining the result value to be placed at the intersection of the row and column input values. The Data table text box already contains the block you selected before selecting this command.

9. Select the Two free variables radio button to create a 2 Way What-If table.

10. Enter the input cell for the column of entries in the Column input cell text box. In Figure 5.8, this is A8.

11. Enter the input cell for the column of entries in the Row input cell text box. In Figure 5.8, this is F9.

12. Select Generate and then Close.

Quattro Pro fills the remainder of the data table with the results from the formula, as in Figure 5.9. The calculated table entries contain values. Therefore, modifications to the input values or to any other cells used in the calculations are not reflected in the table's results. For example, if you changed the last income level from 2,500,000 to 3,000,000, the table values do not change until you execute this command again or until you press F8 (TABLE), which performs this com-

```
┌──────────────────────────────────────────────────────────────────────┐
│  —          Quattro Pro for Windows - CHAP_5.WB1            ▼ ▲        │
│  ▭  File  Edit  Block  Data  Tools  Graph  Property  Window  Help   ▲  │
│ ┌──┬──┬──┐ ┌──┬──┐ ┌─┬─┬─┬──┬─┐ ┌─────────┬─┐ ┌──┬──┬──┐ ┌──┬─┬──┬─┐  │
│ │✂│⊞│▥│ │▭│▥│ │≣│≣│≣│b│i│≑│ │Normal   │▼│ │⊞│⊟│⊞│ │▦│Σ│▦│▨│  │
│ ┌──────────────┬────────┐                                              │
│ │ 2_Way_Table:A1│   +B15 │                                             │
│ ├──────────────┴────────┘                                            ▲ │
│ │   A      B       C        D        E        F        G       H      I│▾│
│ │1 +B15    0%     10%      20%      30%      40%      50%     60%    70%│
│ │2   500000 $3.00 ($3.33) ($11.25) ($21.43) ($35.00) ($54.00) ($82.50) ($130.0│
│ │3  1000000 $18.00 $13.33  $7.50    $0.00  ($10.00) ($24.00) ($45.00) ($80.0│
│ │4  1500000 $33.00 $30.00  $26.25   $21.43  $15.00   $6.00   ($7.50) ($30.0│
│ │5  2000000 $48.00 $46.67  $45.00   $42.86  $40.00   $36.00   $30.00  $20.0│
│ │6  2500000 $63.00 $63.33  $63.75   $64.29  $65.00   $66.00   $67.50  $70.0│
│ │7                                                                      │
│ │8  Sales        500000        Total Equity   1E+07                     │
│ │9  Variable Costs 250000      Debt Ratio      0.1                      │
│ │10 Fixed Costs   200000       Actual Debt    1E+06                     │
│ │11 Interest      100000       Actual Stock   9E+06                     │
│ │12 Profit        -50000       Number of Shares  9000                   │
│ │13 Taxes         -20000                                                │
│ │14 Net Profit    -30000       Assumptions:                             │
│ │15 EPS          ($3.33)       Stock is $1,000/share                    │
│ │16                            Enough shares are sold                   │
│ │17                            for intended debt/equity ratio.          │
│ │18                                                                     │
│ │19                                                                     │
│ │20                                                                    ▾│
│ ├──┬──┬──┬───────┬───────────┬────────────┬──────────┬─────────────────┤
│ │◄│ │►│ A / 1_Way_Table \ 2_Way_Table / Frequency /  ┌→│G│◄│         ►│▤│
│ └────────────────────────────────────────────────────────────┬──────┐ │
│                                                              │READY │ │
└──────────────────────────────────────────────────────────────────────┘
```

Figure 5.9 2 Way Table Filled In

mand using the same cell addresses for the table and the input cells. If you need
to update the table again, note that Quattro Pro remembers the settings of the last
<u>W</u>hat-If command in the <u>D</u>ata menu.

The examples so far have used a single page for all the table information. You
can use different pages for the different parts of the table. You can use separate
pages for the table and the input cells. While you can select a multiple page block
for the table's location, Quattro Pro adjusts the input cells for each page just as if
you are copying entries between pages. You would want to select a multiple page
block for a table when you have several pages set up for both the table and the
input cells. For example, if you copied page C in Figure 5.9 to pages D through F
and then used the different pages for different assumptions for other entries such
as variable or fixed costs, you would select C..F:A1..I6 as the table's location. Later
when you learn more about working with multiple files in Chapter 7, you can use
cells from other notebooks by including the notebook name in brackets before the
cell or block address.

FREQUENCY DISTRIBUTION

Obtaining the average for a set of data values provides one meaningful piece of
information about the entries. In Chapter 8, you will learn about @functions you
can use to return statistical analysis about a set of values. Knowing the average,

minimum, and maximum values provides a partial picture of the entries but does not provide any indication about the distribution of these values. With a large number of entries, you may be interested in categorizing these values to get a better feeling for their distribution within the range represented by the minimum and maximum values.

Knowing the distribution of the data entries tells you how many entries are in each category. Categories can be established to group numeric entries. A distribution may be useful for dividing the records in an employee database into two groups of approximately equal size in order to assign two individuals an equal number of records for verification.

For numeric information, a distribution is of interest, for example, when you have a series of products that are assigned product numbers 1 through 5 and you want to know how many records are in the database for each product type. A distribution quickly tells you the number of records for each product type.

The Frequency command in the Data menu operates by using *bin* entries that you create. Each bin represents an entry within your data or a range of possible entries. Quattro Pro analyzes the block that you specify and increments the frequency count for the appropriate bin as it processes each entry in the block.

To use this command, you first have to set up an area on a page to record the bin values. Since your data is analyzed against these bins with a count supplied for these bins, the column immediately to the right of the bin values should be blank. To account for entries that are larger than any of the bin values that you supply, the row beneath your last bin value should also be empty, since Quattro Pro supplies a count of entries exceeding the largest bin value at this location.

When you select bin values, the value you enter for each bin is the largest value to be included in the count for the bin. For example, if you are creating bin intervals of 1,000 and if the first bin value is 1,000, it includes the count of all entries equal to or less than 1,000. A second bin of 2,000 includes the count of all entries greater than 1,000 but less than or equal to 2,000. Cells equaling @NA are counted in the first bin and cells equaling @ERR are counted in the last bin.

A practical example of using frequency distribution is analyzing market survey data. For example, if you have computed that the average salary of the people who purchase your product is $35,000, you might want to know the distribution so that you can target your advertising. By knowing the distribution, you can learn whether your product appeals to people from many income groups or only from a few income groups close to the $35,000 average.

The steps to create a frequency distribution are shown below:

1. Select an empty area of a page or a separate page for the frequency distribution table. The area required for the frequency distribution table is determined by the number of categories you want to create. This area must have two columns with the number of rows for this area equal to the number of bins plus one.

2. Enter the highest value for each bin in each cell within the leftmost column of the table. Figure 5.10 shows the income values from respondents to a market survey. Bins are created to categorize this data, with each bin

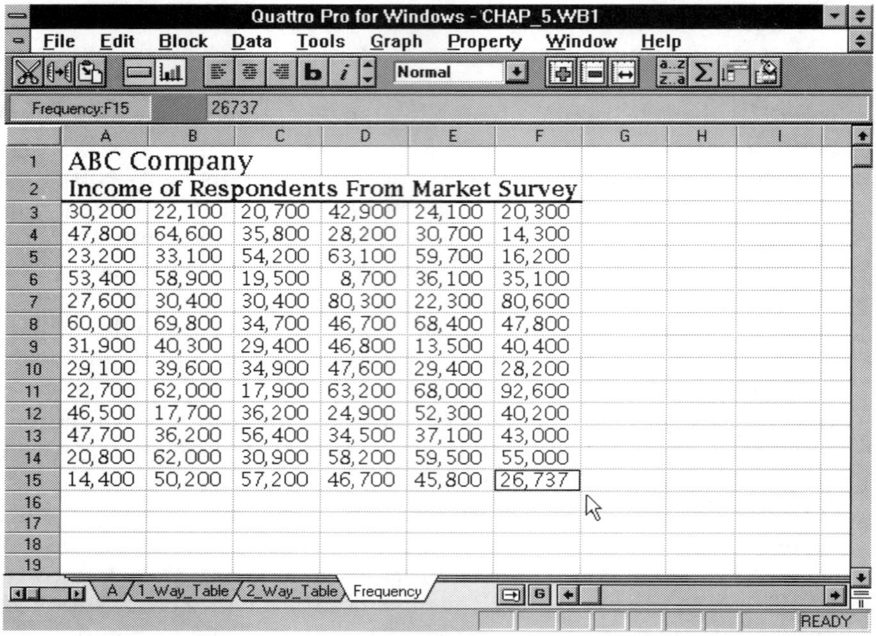

	A	B	C	D	E	F	G	H	I
1	ABC Company								
2	Income of Respondents From Market Survey								
3	30,200	22,100	20,700	42,900	24,100	20,300			
4	47,800	64,600	35,800	28,200	30,700	14,300			
5	23,200	33,100	54,200	63,100	59,700	16,200			
6	53,400	58,900	19,500	8,700	36,100	35,100			
7	27,600	30,400	30,400	80,300	22,300	80,600			
8	60,000	69,800	34,700	46,700	68,400	47,800			
9	31,900	40,300	29,400	46,800	13,500	40,400			
10	29,100	39,600	34,900	47,600	29,400	28,200			
11	22,700	62,000	17,900	63,200	68,000	92,600			
12	46,500	17,700	36,200	24,900	52,300	40,200			
13	47,700	36,200	56,400	34,500	37,100	43,000			
14	20,800	62,000	30,900	58,200	59,500	55,000			
15	14,400	50,200	57,200	46,700	45,800	26,737			
16									
17									
18									
19									

Figure 5.10 Data from Market Research

having the highest income for each group. If the last bin value is 70,000, anything that is above 70,000 is counted in the cell to the right and below the last bin. The bin values must be in ascending sequence from the top to the bottom of the column.

3. Select Frequency from the Data menu. Quattro Pro needs to know two blocks. The first block is the block that contains the values you want to measure the frequency. The second block is the block that contains the bins. If you have selected a block before selecting this command, it is entered in the Value Block(s) text box.
4. Select the block containing the values to measure in the Value Block(s) text box. In the notebook shown in Figure 5.10, the Values block is A3..F15.
5. Select the block containing the bin values in the Bin Block text box. For the notebook shown in Figure 5.10, the block to select is H2..H15.
6. Select OK.

Quattro Pro enters the frequency numbers in the column to the right of the bin numbers. The row immediately below the last bin is used to record the frequency number of the values that exceed the last bin value. For example, any salary above $70,000 is included in the last row of the table, as in Figure 5.11. The numbers in the table are values and are not updated as the values in the values block change unless you execute the Frequency command again. Once this table is generated, it can be used for other Quattro Pro features (such as graphs).

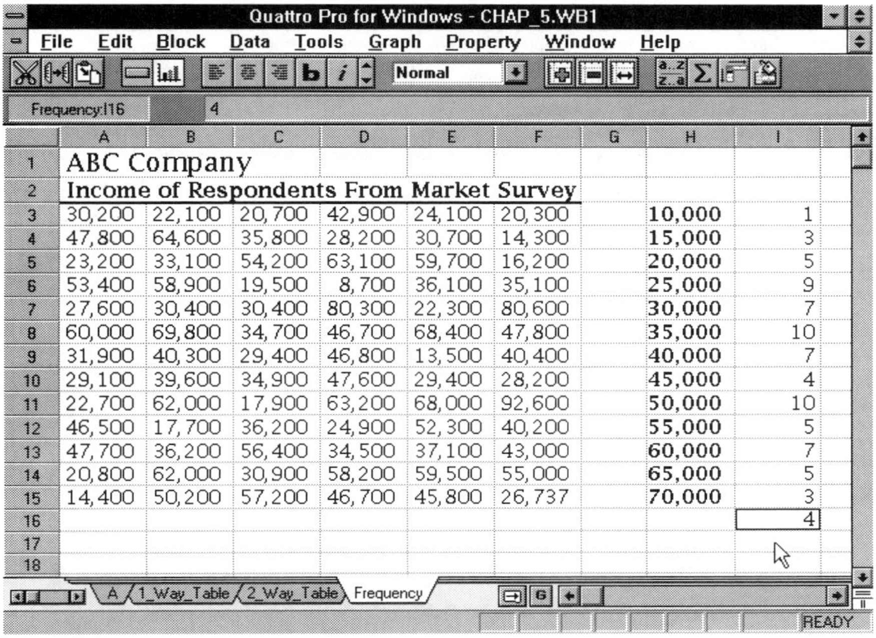

	A	B	C	D	E	F	G	H	I
1	ABC Company								
2	Income of Respondents From Market Survey								
3	30,200	22,100	20,700	42,900	24,100	20,300		10,000	1
4	47,800	64,600	35,800	28,200	30,700	14,300		15,000	3
5	23,200	33,100	54,200	63,100	59,700	16,200		20,000	5
6	53,400	58,900	19,500	8,700	36,100	35,100		25,000	9
7	27,600	30,400	30,400	80,300	22,300	80,600		30,000	7
8	60,000	69,800	34,700	46,700	68,400	47,800		35,000	10
9	31,900	40,300	29,400	46,800	13,500	40,400		40,000	7
10	29,100	39,600	34,900	47,600	29,400	28,200		45,000	4
11	22,700	62,000	17,900	63,200	68,000	92,600		50,000	10
12	46,500	17,700	36,200	24,900	52,300	40,200		55,000	5
13	47,700	36,200	56,400	34,500	37,100	43,000		60,000	7
14	20,800	62,000	30,900	58,200	59,500	55,000		65,000	5
15	14,400	50,200	57,200	46,700	45,800	26,737		70,000	3
16									4
17									
18									

Figure 5.11 Frequency Distribution of Incomes (Column H)

REGRESSION ANALYSIS

Regression analysis determines how an independent variable affects a dependent one and can be used to identify data that may have predictive ability. When you have market research results, you may want to measure the degree to which external factors cause your customers to buy your product. For example, advertising affects sales. Advertising is an independent variable and sales is a dependent variable. Regression analysis can help you determine how closely sales correlate with advertising to allow you to predict the likely sales growth from a given advertising expenditure. Quattro Pro's regression analysis determines several statistics that measure how much the independent variable affects the dependent one. Quattro Pro computes a regression line that predicts how much one value affects the other and how well one value predicts the other.

Like Quattro Pro's other analytical commands, the regression command requires a few preliminary steps. First, the dependent and independent data must be stored in columns in a notebook. This data must contain only numeric values. Also, these columns must have the same number of entries. A sample data area is shown in Figure 5.12. This notebook shows the direct labor hours, the material costs, and the total costs for each project that uses the Assembly Department. Each set of data for a different product is a different observation. Generating a regression equation helps predict future project costs.

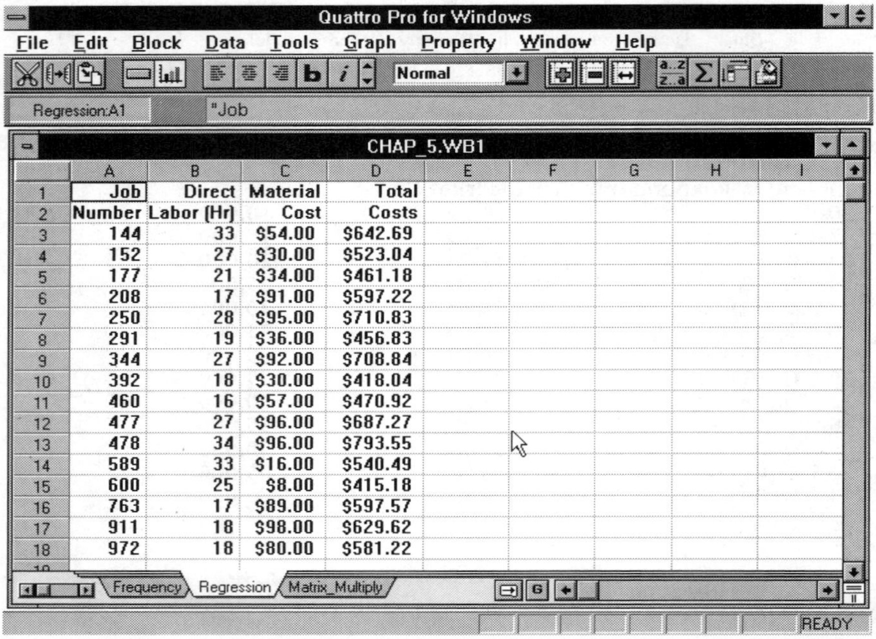

Job Number	Direct Labor (Hr)	Material Cost	Total Costs
144	33	$54.00	$642.69
152	27	$30.00	$523.04
177	21	$34.00	$461.18
208	17	$91.00	$597.22
250	28	$95.00	$710.83
291	19	$36.00	$456.83
344	27	$92.00	$708.84
392	18	$30.00	$418.04
460	16	$57.00	$470.92
477	27	$96.00	$687.27
478	34	$96.00	$793.55
589	33	$16.00	$540.49
600	25	$8.00	$415.18
763	17	$89.00	$597.57
911	18	$98.00	$629.62
972	18	$80.00	$581.22

Figure 5.12 Job-Costing Information

To create a regression analysis, follow these steps:

1. Create a data table that has the dependent and independent values for each observation. Figure 5.12 shows data entered for this example.
2. Select Advanced Math from the Tools menu and then select Regression to display the Linear Regression dialog box shown in Figure 5.13.
3. Select the block that contains the independent variable values in the Independent text box. If you select multiple columns, Quattro Pro computes the multiple regression for all variables selected. Otherwise, Quattro Pro computes the simple regression for the one variable chosen. The block you select can be noncontiguous if your independent variable values are not in adjacent columns. In the example in Figure 5.12, the independent variable block is B3..C18.
4. Select the dependent variable block containing the data that is influenced by the other variables in the Dependent text box. In the project-costing example, the dependent block is D3..D18.
5. Select the upper left cell where you want the regression output placed in the Output text box. In the example in Figure 5.12, the output block starts at E5. The regression table that Quattro Pro creates is nine rows deep and two columns wider than the number of independent variables. If you have any existing information in the output area, it is overwritten when you execute the command.

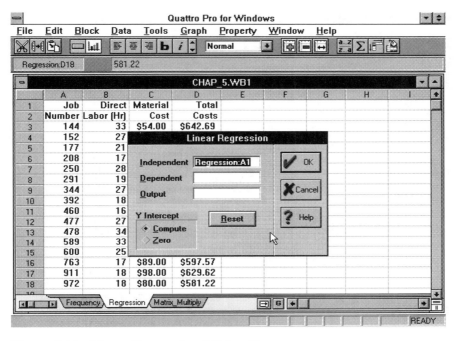

Figure 5.13   Linear Regression Dialog Box

6. Under Y Intercept, select the Compute or Zero radio button to select whether the regression equation should be created to have a y intercept. For some types of data, a y intercept is meaningless and is more appropriately set to zero instead of having Quattro Pro compute the intercept. For example, suppose you are attempting to determine a correlation between age and trips to the doctor. At age zero, anything other than zero trips is illogical; therefore, setting the intercept to zero is the best decision. In other situations, having Quattro Pro compute the y intercept provides a more useful equation. With many regression equations, the equation has a relevant range. For example, in a regression equation for predicting the total production costs based on the number of units, the equation may only be useful for predicting costs for production between 100,000 and 500,000. A practical reason for this relevant range is that the fixed costs may change for production below 100,000 and above 500,000. In this case, you want to compute an intercept, since the resulting equation produces better results for values between 100,000 and 500,000. For values outside of this range, you need to generate another equation.

7. Select OK. Quattro Pro performs the regression analysis as shown in Figure 5.14. While you are in the Linear Regression dialog box, you can select Reset if you want to remove the block settings in the text boxes and return the Y Intercept to Compute.

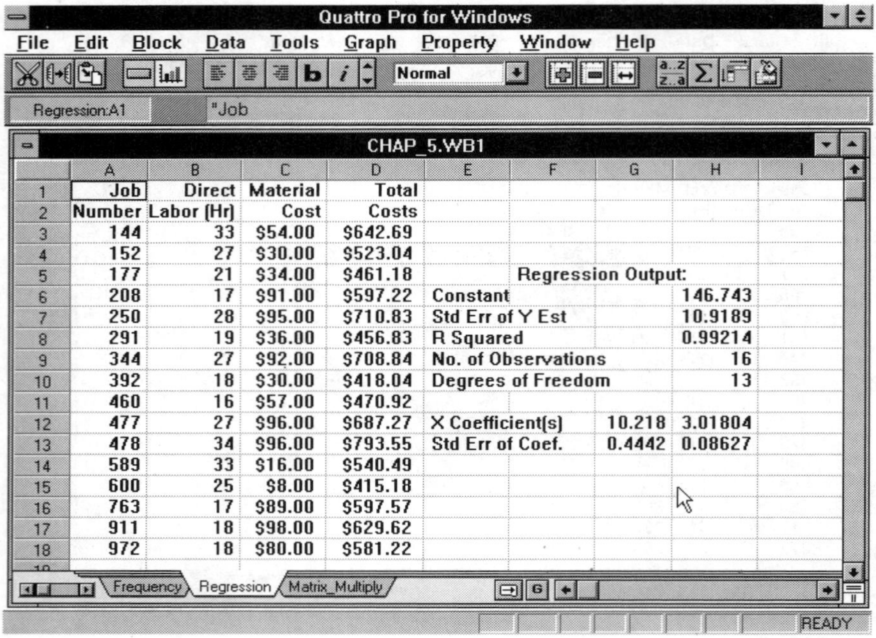

	A	B	C	D	E	F	G	H
1	Job	Direct	Material	Total				
2	Number	Labor (Hr)	Cost	Costs				
3	144	33	$54.00	$642.69				
4	152	27	$30.00	$523.04				
5	177	21	$34.00	$461.18		Regression Output:		
6	208	17	$91.00	$597.22	Constant			146.743
7	250	28	$95.00	$710.83	Std Err of Y Est			10.9189
8	291	19	$36.00	$456.83	R Squared			0.99214
9	344	27	$92.00	$708.84	No. of Observations			16
10	392	18	$30.00	$418.04	Degrees of Freedom			13
11	460	16	$57.00	$470.92				
12	477	27	$96.00	$687.27	X Coefficient(s)		10.218	3.01804
13	478	34	$96.00	$793.55	Std Err of Coef.		0.4442	0.08627
14	589	33	$16.00	$540.49				
15	600	25	$8.00	$415.18				
16	763	17	$89.00	$597.57				
17	911	18	$98.00	$629.62				
18	972	18	$80.00	$581.22				

Figure 5.14 Output from Regression Analysis

Applying the Results of Regression Analysis

Once you have the results of the regression analysis, you can use the information for different purposes. The X Coefficient(s) and Constant are the values for the regression equation. For example, the regression equation from Figure 5.14 is as follows:

$$(DIRECT\ HOURS \times 10.2183\ ) + (MATERIAL\ COST \times 3.018039) + 146.7428 = TOTAL\ COST$$

This equation can predict the costs of future jobs in that department. For example, if the department is about to perform a job that is expected to require 30 hours of labor and $90 of materials, this equation predicts that the job will cost 724.92. The Std Err of Coef. and the Std Err of Y Est describe how well the coefficients fit the data. The smaller the number, the better the coefficient describes the relationship between the independent variable and the dependent variable. The number of observations is the number of dependent variables that Quattro Pro counted and used in the equation. The Degrees of Freedom result is the number of observations minus the number of independent variables and 1 for the y intercept (if it is computed). R Squared represents the validity of the model. The closer to 1 this value is, the better the independent variables predict the dependent variable. You can examine the variables as a group and then examine each one individually to see which analysis produces the highest R-squared result. A value close to 0 means that the regression equation is not a useful predictor of the dependent variable.

MATRIX MATH

Matrices are tabular arrangements of data used in many higher-level math applications. Matrix operations are popular because they can be used to simplify calculations and avoid complicated formulas. Quattro Pro provides two commands that operate on matrices: matrix multiplication and matrix inversion. Although the rules for matrix operations may make them seem complex initially, they actually serve to simplify problem solutions and provide practical approaches to job-costing, linear programming, and econometric modeling problems.

Since Quattro Pro's matrix commands perform the matrix computations, you do not need to know the theory behind the required mathematics. Once you see how these operations can be used in problem solving, you can focus on how to set up the matrix operation to have Quattro Pro solve the problem.

Multiplying Matrices

Multiplying matrices can streamline formulas that require multiplying each of the values in one matrix by the values in a second matrix and adding the products of these operations together. One application for multiplying matrices is job costing. If you need to compute the labor cost for a multiphase project that requires several categories of labor, matrix multiplication can handle the tasks much more easily than a formula can. A formula to determine costs for each project phase requires that you multiply each labor rate by the number of hours required at that rate and then total each of the labor categories to obtain total labor costs. To solve the same problem with matrix multiplication, labor rates are stored in one matrix and the number of hours at each rate are stored in another matrix. The Advanced Math Multiply command in the Tools menu provides the total charges for each project phase without the need for a formula.

When Quattro Pro multiplies a matrix, Quattro Pro multiplies the first element of the first row in the first matrix with the first element of the first column of the second matrix. It does this also with the second and third elements and so on until the elements in the first row of the first matrix are multiplied with the first column of the second matrix. For example, if your matrices look like this:

First Matrix:	6	5	8		Second Matrix:	3	5
	9	18	4			12	4
						5	2

Quattro Pro multiplies 6 by 3, 5 by 12, and 8 by 5. Then Quattro Pro totals all the products for the first row and column. In this example, it is 118. Quattro Pro performs these computations for each row of the first matrix and column of the second matrix. Then Quattro Pro multiplies the elements in the first row of the first matrix by the second column of the second matrix and totals the products. Quattro Pro performs this for all columns in the second matrix. The resulting matrix has the same number of rows as the first matrix and the same number of columns as the second matrix. When Quattro Pro multiplies the matrices, it creates this resulting matrix:

(6*3)+(5*12)+(8*5)	(6*5)+(5*4)+(8*2)	or	118	66
(9*3)+(18*12)+(4*5)	(9*5)+(18*4)+(4*2)		263	125

RULES FOR MULTIPLYING MATRICES   Although matrix multiplication offers the potential for streamlining your calculations, you must be willing to follow a set of specific rules to obtain these benefits. If your matrices deviate from these rules, Quattro Pro cannot calculate usable results for you. The following rules are the ones you must adhere to:

- Each cell within either of the matrices you multiply must contain a value entry. Blanks are not equivalent to an entry of zero and must be replaced with zeros before attempting the operation.

- To multiply two matrices, you must look at the order of the matrices. Matrix order describes the size of a matrix as an x by y matrix, where x is the number of rows in the matrix and y is the number of columns. For example, a matrix with three rows and four columns is a 3 x 4 matrix. If the information in the 3 x 4 matrix is transposed, it becomes a 4 x 3 matrix. The two matrices are not interchangeable in a matrix-multiply operation. To multiply matrices, the number of columns in the first matrix must be exactly equal to the number of rows in the second matrix. Without this relationship, it is not possible to multiply the contents of two matrices. Since the order of matrices is critical to successful multiplication, the sequence in which you specify the two matrices to be multiplied is important. You can multiply a 5 x 7 matrix by a 7 x 1 matrix, but you cannot multiply a 7 x 1 matrix by a 5 x 7 matrix. To determine whether you can multiply two matrices, write the two matrix orders side by side, as in 2 x 3 and 3 x 2. When the two inside numbers are the same, you can multiply the matrices. The resulting matrix has the order of the two outside numbers, as in 2 x 2.

A MATRIX MULTIPLY EXAMPLE   A closer look at multiplying matrices may clarify the process for its use. This procedure is useful for project-costing solutions like defense contract costs, which are sometimes awarded on a cost-plus basis. This requires the contractor to properly attribute all costs to specific products. For each project, the product manufactured must be processed by different departments. Each department has its own direct labor and overhead costs.

Figure 5.15 shows a list of the hours required for each project by department and a list of the hourly cost for direct labor and overhead. To compute the hourly cost for each project for the labor and the overhead cost, you must multiply the number of hours by the cost per hour for each department. Rather than using a formula, you can use the <u>A</u>dvanced Math <u>M</u>ultiply command in the <u>T</u>ools menu to compute the values.

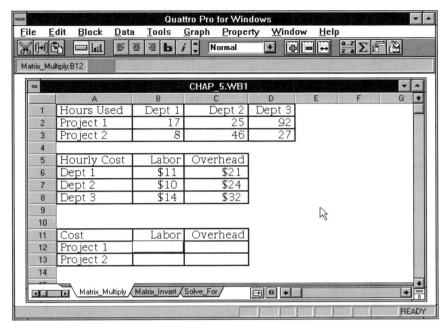

Figure 5.15   Matrices Containing Hourly Information for Two Projects

First, the data must be stored in the proper form within matrices that are compatible for multiplication purposes. After storing the data, select $\underline{A}$dvanced Math from the $\underline{T}$ools menu and then select $\underline{M}$ultiply. In the Matrix Multiply dialog box, you can enter the location of the two matrices and where you want the destination matrix placed. Using the data in Figure 5.15, the first matrix is B2..D3. The second matrix is B6..C8 in Figure 5.15. Next, select the destination of the resulting matrix, which can be indicated by supplying the upper left corner of the matrix. In Figure 5.15, B12 is specified as the location for the results. When you select OK, Quattro Pro multiplies the matrix and puts the result starting at B12 as Figure 5.16 shows. Like other commands, the matrices may be stored in separate notebooks, as long as you include the file name before the block address.

Inverting Matrices

Inverting matrices is the first step in solving linear equations. A practical application of linear equations is production planning, which assumes several projects are competing for limited resources and computes the best distribution among the projects. Special rules apply to matrices used in an inversion operation since they must be square matrices with the same number of rows as columns and cannot be larger than 90 x 90.

An example of using an inverted matrix to solve for the best distribution between projects is shown in Figure 5.17. In the figure, the different requirements

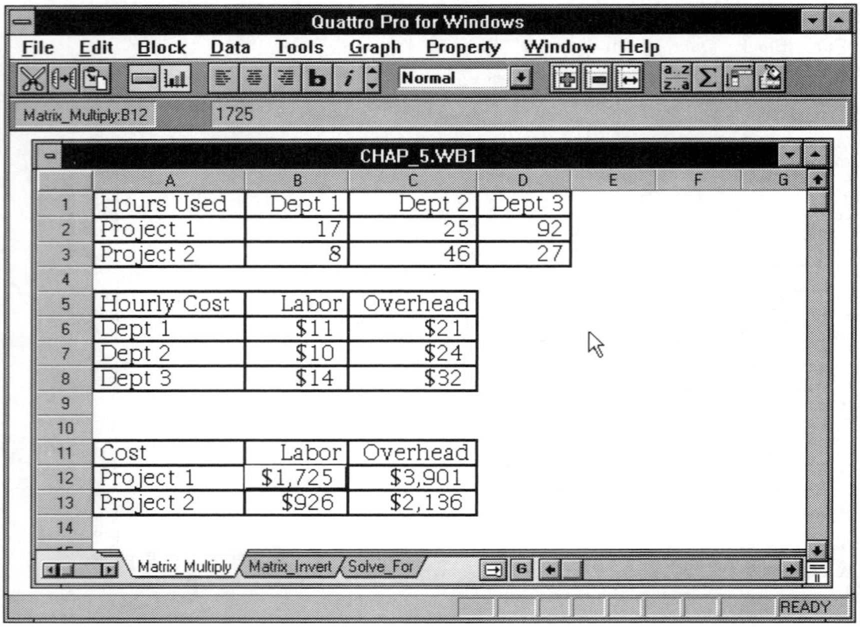

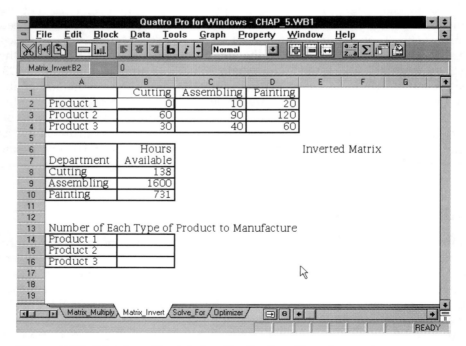

Figure 5.16 Multiplied Matrix Computing Total Labor and Overhead for Two Projects

Figure 5.17 Matrices Containing Production Requirements

for three processes are shown for three products. Just below this information is the number of hours available in each department. To compute the best distribution among these resources, follow these steps:

1. Set up a matrix with the different resource requirements for each product. In Figure 5.17, the matrix is the block B2..D4. Each row contains the resource requirements of each department for a product, and each column contains the resource requirements for each product of a department.

2. Set up a matrix with the resource limitations. In Figure 5.17, the matrix is the block B8..B10. Each row in the matrix represents the resource limitation of each column in the first matrix.

3. Select Advanced Math from the Tools menu and then select Invert. In the Matrix Invert dialog box, you can enter the location of the matrix in the Source text box and where you want the inverted matrix placed in the Destination text box.

4. Select the matrix to invert in the Source text box. For the example in Figure 5.17, select the matrix block B2..D4.

5. Select the destination for the inverted matrix, and press ENTER. The inverted matrix is the same size as the original matrix. E7 is selected for the destination of the inverted matrix in B2..D4. When you select OK, the matrix is inverted, as in Figure 5.18. The inverted matrix is used in determining the optimal production of the three products.

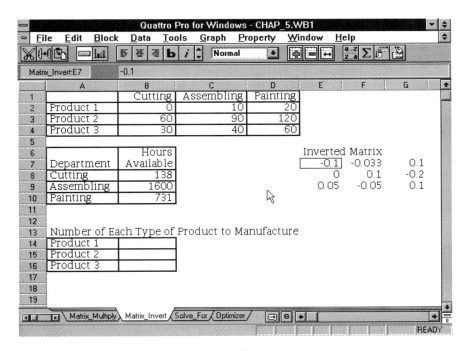

Figure 5.18   Result of Inverted Matrix

6. Select Advanced Math from the Tools menu and then select Multiply.

7. Select the first matrix to be multiplied in the Matrix 1 text box. This is the matrix that is created in step 5. In the example in Figure 5.18, it is the matrix E7..G9.

8. Select the second matrix to be multiplied in the Matrix 2 text box. This is the matrix created in step 2. In the example in Figure 5.18, it is the matrix B8..B10.

9. Select the destination block, and select OK. The destination block is specified by the upper left corner in which the multiplied matrix will be placed. In this example, it is B14. Figure 5.19 shows the notebook after the matrices have been multiplied. As the figure shows, producing approximately 6 units of product 1 and 14 units of product 2 uses up all available hours in the departments. When you use matrix inversion and multiplication, the equation is forced to use all resources. In many cases, you can find a better solution using the linear programming available with Optimizer in the Tools menu.

SOLVING FOR A VALUE

Quattro Pro can work through calculations backward to find the value of a cell that makes another cell return the result you desire. For example, if you are reviewing production costs, you may want to determine the break-even points for

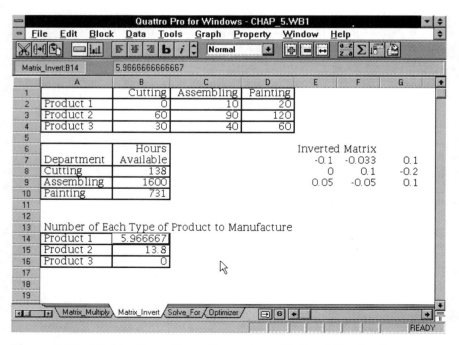

Figure 5.19   Matrix Operations Computing Optimal Production

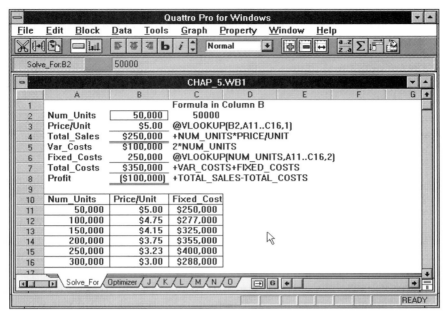

Figure 5.20   Problem to Use with Solve For in the Tools Menu

production. Figure 5.20 shows a worksheet that calculates the sales, total costs, and profits based on the number of units produced and sold. This model makes the assumption that the price and fixed costs vary at different quantities. When deciding how much to produce, you may want to find any break-even points, that is, where the profit equals zero.

Before you can use the Solve For command in the Tools menu, you must enter the formulas that the command will affect. For example, in Figure 5.20, you must enter the formulas in column B and the horizontal lookup table in B10..G12. The labels in column A and C are there for documentation, the lines are added for clarity, and the block names are added with the Names Labels command in the Block menu to make the formulas easier to understand. In this example, Quattro Pro will find the value of B2 that makes B8 equal zero.

To find any values that make another cell equal a desired value, use the Solve For command in the Tools menu. The Solve For dialog box this command displays includes text boxes for Formula Cell, Target Value, Variable Cell, Max Iterations, and Accuracy. The Formula Cell is the cell address or block name that contains a formula that you want to equal another value. For the example in Figure 5.20, it is B8. The Target Value selects the value that you want the Formula Cell to equal. In Figure 5.20, it is 0, but you can enter any value at the prompt. The Variable Cell is the cell or block name that contains a value that Quattro Pro can alter in order to make the Formula Cell equal the Target Value. In the example in Figure 5.20, it is B2, which is the number of units. As this number changes, the @HLOOKUP functions return different numbers based on the number of units and the formulas in B4, B6, B7, and B8 that use the new values. The value in the Variable Cell must affect the value of the Formula Cell. Before you try to solve for the value, you may want to change the parameters Quattro Pro uses. The Max Iterations is a number between 1 and 1000 that selects the number of attempts Quattro Pro performs to find an answer. The higher the number, the more attempts Quattro Pro makes and the longer it may take. Accuracy selects how close the values the result of the Formula Cell can be from the Target Value for Quattro Pro to assume that it has found an answer. For example, the default of .0005 means that Quattro Pro assumes that it has found an answer when the value of the Formula Cell is .0005 more or less than the Target Value.

When you are ready to find the answer, select OK. Figure 5.21 shows the result from Figure 5.20. Quattro Pro uses the initial value of the Variable Cell as a starting point for generating the solution. Since this example abruptly changes the fixed costs and price per unit, it can have more than one potential solution. While the example shows the results of 83333, by starting with other different initial guesses you can also have results of 100727, 151163, and 202857. If Quattro Pro cannot find an answer in the number of iterations set by Max Iterations in the Solve For dialog box, Quattro Pro displays an error message. You will want to enter a new guess or increase the maximum number of iterations. This will also occur when the problem does not have a feasible solution. Using the example of Figure 5.20, if you tried finding a solution where the profit would be a negative $50,000, Quattro Pro would not be able to find a solution because one does not exist.

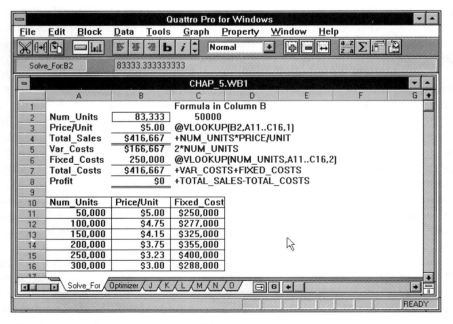

Figure 5.21   Answer Generated by Solve For

OPTIMIZING ENTRIES

In the previous section, you learned about how you can have Quattro Pro work backward through a problem to find the value in one cell that makes another cell equal a stated value. This Quattro Pro feature works if you are calculating the number of products to reach a predetermined profit. If you need to consider how changing several variables at once will change the final result, you cannot use the Solve For command, because it only varies one cell's value at a time. When you have a model that you want to try varying several values at once, you will want to use Quattro Pro's Optimizer instead. The types of problems you will want to use the Optimizer with are the ones that you are thinking to yourself "What if I changed this, and this, and ..." or "What combination of these several values gets me the best results?"

The Optimizer takes at its input the values it can change, the constraints it must meet, and the results you want and then finds combinations of values that provide the desired results. The constraints the Optimizer uses are the limitations that you place on the cell values. You can have many intermittent calculations between the values you tell Quattro Pro to change and the formula that calculates the final desired result. The Optimizer can solve many different types of equations. Some of the examples include linear and nonlinear programming problem solving. An example of linear problem solving is the problem that you used when you inverted and multiplied matrixes to find production quantities that would consume all the available resources and finding instead the product mix that maximizes profit. The company may be better off not using all of its resources and to concentrate production on the most valuable products instead. An example of a nonlinear problem is when you are calculating the change to overall sales volume with different prices when the change of price does not proportionally cause a change in volume.

Quattro Pro can solve problems like this through its Optimizer command in the Tools menu. Just as in the other analytical commands, you must set up data in a format the command can use. This includes selecting the values that Quattro Pro may change, the formulas you want calculated as Quattro Pro tries a different set of values for the problem, and the limitations placed on cell values.

Setting Up a Problem for the Optimizer

Before you can use the Optimizer, you must set up the model so Quattro Pro knows the values it will change and the formulas it will recalculate to find the solution to your problem. The values that Quattro Pro will change must be in an unprotected block. These values cannot be dates, formulas, or text. The cells that contain these values must be used by other formulas in the cell. They must be used to calculate the final formula that you want to optimize if you select a cell to optimize. The initial values in these cells can be important. Problems that you use with the Optimizer that are nonlinear (cannot be described in linear equations) may have more than one answer. The way to find the best answer for what you want is to put your best guess into these formulas. As an example, if you are using the model to plan future product mixes or sales, a good set of initial values would be the last period's production or sales.

The next type of information Quattro Pro needs to optimize a model is the constraints. These constraints limit values in other cells that are affected by the values you tell Quattro Pro to change. For example, if you are working with a model to decide how much of several products you will produce, the model will have as constraints the amount produced of each product not exceeding the capacity or being less than zero. To decide on the constraints, decide which cells have limits on their values, then put that the value of this cell must be less than or equal to, equal to, or greater than or equal to (or written down), so that you will have it ready to tell Quattro Pro.

The last step before you use Quattro Pro's Optimizer is to set up the formulas that you want Quattro Pro to calculate and any formula that you will use as a solution cell. The solution cell is the cell that you want to be the largest value possible, the smallest value possible, or equal to a specific value. For example, if you are working with different product mixes, you will use the cell that calculates the maximum sales or profit as the solution cell. If you are working with different expenses, you will minimize the cell that totals the expenses. You can omit using a solution cell as well. You would do this when you are only interested in finding a combination of values that will meet a set of constraints.

An example of a model set up for Quattro Pro's Optimizer is shown in Figure 5.22. The value in B2, 0, is the value you will tell Quattro Pro it can change. Many

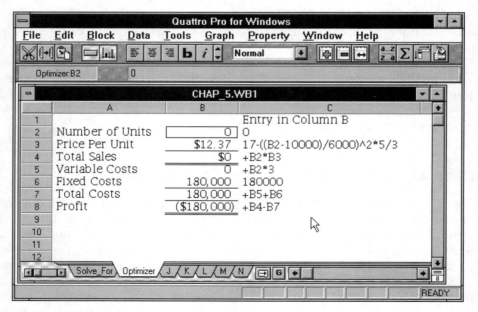

Figure 5.22   Problem Setup for the Optimizer

of the other formulas use B2's value in their own calculations. Your model may have different constraints depending on your production facilities. For example, one constraint is that the units sold cannot be less than zero. Other sample types of constraints might be that the units sold be more than sales commitments already made or less than the production capacity. You can also have constraints on other cells such as having a constraint that limits the total variable cost to a set amount.

Using Quattro Pro's Optimizer

When you have set up the model to use with the Optimizer, you are ready to to use the Optimizer. As an example of using the Optimizer, suppose you are thinking of changing a product's price to increase volume and you want to find the product price that will produce the maximum of profits. With all the data entered, follow these steps to tell Quattro Pro to find the optimal solution:

1. Select Optimizer from the Tools menu to display the dialog box shown in Figure 5.23.

2. Select the cell that contains the formula that you want to minimize, maximize, or make equal to a specific value in the Solution Cell text box if you want to use one. For the problem in Figure 5.22, the solution cell is B8, the profit.

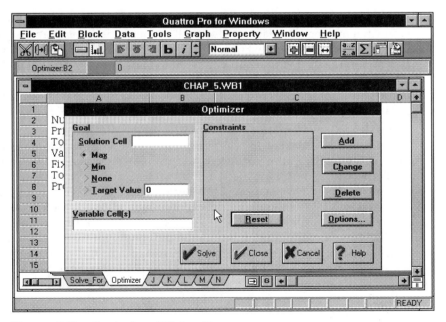

Figure 5.23   Optimizer Dialog Box

3. Select Ma<u>x</u> to maximize the result of the solution cell; <u>M</u>in to minimize the result of the solution cell; <u>T</u>arget Value to type the number you want the solution cell to equal; or <u>N</u>one if you do not want to use a solution cell in the problem.

4. Select the cells that contain the values Quattro Pro can change as it works through the problem in the <u>V</u>ariable Cell(s) text box. For the problem in Figure 5.22, the variable cell is B2, the number of units sold.

5. Select <u>A</u>dd to add the constraints for the problem. Then add a constraint in one of three ways:

   a. If you want one cell to have a value relative to another cell's value, select the cell in the <u>C</u>ell text box. Next, select between <=, =, >=, and <> (not equal) in the <u>O</u>perator drop-down list box for the relationship you want to have between the cell in the left text box and the right. Select the cell containing the value you want the first cell less than or equal to, greater than or equal to, or not equal to in the Co<u>n</u>stant text box. Select <u>A</u>dd to add the constraint.

   b. If you want one cell to be less than, greater than, or equal to another value, or not equal to another cell, select the cell in the <u>C</u>ell text box. Next, select between <=, =, >=, and <> (not equal) in the <u>O</u>perator drop-down list box for the relationship you want to have between the cell in the left text box and the right. Type the value you want the first cell less than or equal to, equal to, greater than or equal to, or not equal to in the Co<u>n</u>stant text box. Select <u>A</u>dd to add the constraint.

   c. If you want multiple cells to be less than, greater than, or equal to another value that may be stored in a cell, select the block containing the cells you want to limit in the <u>C</u>ell text box. Next, select between <=, =, >=, and <> (not equal) for the relationship you want to have between the cell in the left text box and the right. Select the cell containing the value or type the value you want the cells in the block to be less than or equal to, equal to, greater than or equal to, or not equal to in the Co<u>n</u>stant text box. Select <u>A</u>dd to add the constraint.

   This step must be repeated for each constraint you want to add. For the problem in Figure 5.23, after you select <u>A</u>dd from the Optimizer dialog box, you will select B2 in the <u>C</u>ell text box and >= in the <u>O</u>perator drop-down list box, then type **0** in the co<u>n</u>stant text box before selecting the <u>A</u>dd button to add the constraint. When you are finished adding constraints, select OK to return to the Optimizer dialog box. If you later change your mind about a constraint, you can select <u>C</u>onstraints, then the constraint that you want to modify in the list. Select C<u>h</u>ange. From the Change Constraints dialog box, you can modify the three different entries you have made for the constraint. Select OK to use the modified constraint and return to the Optimizer dialog box. You can also remove a constraint by highlighting it in the list of constraints and selecting <u>D</u>elete.

6. Select Options, and then select any of the options that you want to change as described later. You only need to perform this step if you want to change how Quattro Pro solves the problem you have created. You may only want to perform this step after you have tried solving the optimization problem once with the default settings.

7. Select Reporting from the Optimizer Options dialog box and choose a cell where you want the answer report to start if you want one in the Answer Report Block text box. For the sample problem, select J1.

8. Choose a cell where you want the detail report to start if you want one in the Detail Report Block text box. For the sample problem, select A30. Select the OK button twice to return to the Optimizer dialog box.

9. Select Solve and let Quattro Pro find the variables that will satisfy the constraints and optimize any solution cell you have selected and return to READY mode.

If you want to start over, you can select Reset in the Optimizer dialog box.

After you select Solve, Quattro Pro puts the best values for the variable cells in those cells. Now you can look at the answer and detail report. The answer report returns the values of the solution cell, variable cells, and constraint cells. An example of an answer report is shown at the top of Figure 5.24. Besides including information like cell addresses, starting and final values, and constraints, the

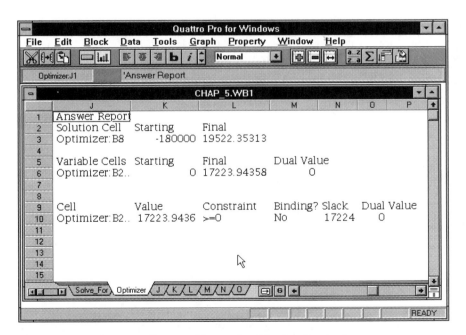

Figure 5.24   Answer Report Created with the Optimizer

answer report provides additional information. The Binding column tells you which of the constraints prevents the solution from equaling a higher or lower number. The Slack column indicates how much the constraint cell's value must change before the constraint causes the solution to change. The Dual Value for the constraints indicates how much additional resources are worth. For example, if you are trying different product mixes and one of your departments is a binding constraint, the dual value indicates the value of increasing the department's capacity since increasing the department's capacity by one unit will increase the solution cell's value by the amount of the dual value. This means that if the cost of increasing the department's capacity is less than the dual value (the amount the solution will increase by adding the one unit), you would be better off increasing capacity.

Figure 5.25 shows the detail report in A30..C37 created for the sample optimization problem. In this report Quattro Pro places the values of the variable cells and solution cell for each iteration Quattro Pro performs as it finds the solution. The number of columns this report uses is the number of variable cells and solution cell plus two, and the number of rows this report uses is the number of iterations plus three. You would use this report when you want to see some of the intermediate values made in the Optimizer's calculations.

If you have more than one optimization problem in a notebook, you need to store the solution cells, variable cells, constraints, option settings, and report

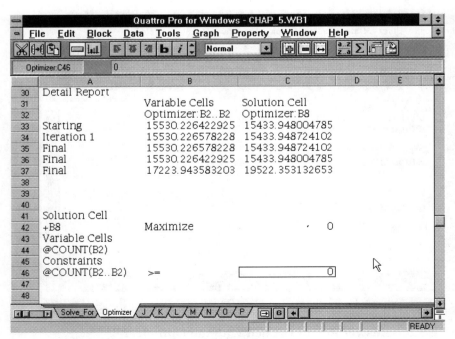

Figure 5.25   Detail Report and Optimizer Model Settings

locations separately. You can store the settings for an optimization problem in the notebook and then later when you want to use the same information for an optimization problem, you can tell Quattro Pro to use the information you have stored in a block. To put the existing optimization problem information in the notebook, select the Options button from the Optimizer dialog box and then select the Save Model button. Select a cell where you want the model information and select OK. The bottom of Figure 5.25 shows a model added to a notebook. When you want to use the optimization settings that are stored in a block, select the Options button from the Optimizer dialog box and then select the Load Model button. Select the beginning of the block where the model information is stored and select OK.

Optimizer Options

The Optimizer has several option settings you can change to affect how the Optimizer finds the best solution for your model. While you may not need to change these settings when you use the Optimizer, at other times you might so you will want to know about the settings you can change. These are the following options you can change after you select Options.

- Max. Time—This sets the maximum number of seconds the Optimizer can work on your problem. If the Optimizer does not find the solution within the time specified, Quattro Pro displays the message Maximum time exceeded. You can change the maximum time by typing a number between 1 and 1000 for the maximum number of seconds. The default is 100 seconds.
- Max. Iterations—This sets the maximum number of iterations the Optimizer can work on your problem. If the Optimizer does not find the solution within the number of iterations specified, Quattro Pro displays the message Maximum iterations reached. You can change the maximum number of iterations by typing a number between 1 and 1000. The default is 100 iterations.
- Precision—This sets how close a constraint cell value can be to its limit and still satisfy. For example, if a constraint limits a cell to being no more than 100 and precision is set to .5, then the number can be as high as 100.5 and still be within its limit. If the Optimizer does not find the solution that fulfills the constraints within the precision selected, Quattro Pro displays the message "Maximum iterations reached" or "No feasible solution can be found." You can change the precision from the default of .0005 to any number between 0 and 1.
- Assume Linear—This selects whether the problem you are solving should be solved by linear or nonlinear problem solving techniques. Linear problems are solved faster, but nonlinear approaches can solve more types of problems. You can try selecting this check box to speed up the Optimizer. If the problem is nonlinear, Quattro Pro will display the message "Linear model is not a valid assumption." If you get this message, clear this check box and solve the problem again.

- Show Iteration Results—This selects whether Quattro Pro pauses after each iteration so that you can see how each iteration changed each cell. When you select this check box and then solve a problem, Quattro Pro performs the first optimization iteration and then displays a menu box prompting Continue Solving, which you can select to continue with the next iteration, or select Keep current solution to stop the optimization. The default is to leave this check box cleared so that Quattro Pro does not pause between iterations.
- Estimates—This sets how the Optimizer finds the initial estimates of the variable cells. The default of Tangent uses linear extrapolation from a tangent vector. You may want to choose the other option, Quadratic, if you are working with highly nonlinear problems.
- Derivatives—This sets how the Optimizer calculates partial derivatives, which are used in solving the problem. Most of the time you will want to leave this setting at the default of Forward; but if you get the message "All remedies failed to find better point," then change this setting to Central and solve the problem again.
- Search—This sets the direction the Optimizer pursues as it determines the best values for the optimization problem. Most of the time you will want to leave this setting at the default of Newton; but if you get the message "Objective function changing too slowly," then change this setting to Conjugate.

As you modify these settings, you can also return all of them to the defaults by selecting Reset in the Optimizer dialog box, which also returns all of the Optimizer dialog box settings to the default.

GETTING STARTED

This chapter covered commands that you can use to add entries to your spreadsheet notebooks. These commands provide a wealth of analytical features. You should review the section for any feature covered in this chapter before using it for your own applications. You can try two of these features (a sensitivity analysis and a frequency distribution) by following these steps to create the spreadsheet notebook in Figure 5.26:

1. Make the following entries:

   B1: **"Last Year**
   C1: **"% Change**
   D1: **"Forecast**
   A2: **Sales**
   B2: **1000000**
   D2: **+B2*(1+C2)**
   A3: **COGS**
   B3: **600000**
   D3: **+B3*(1+C3)**

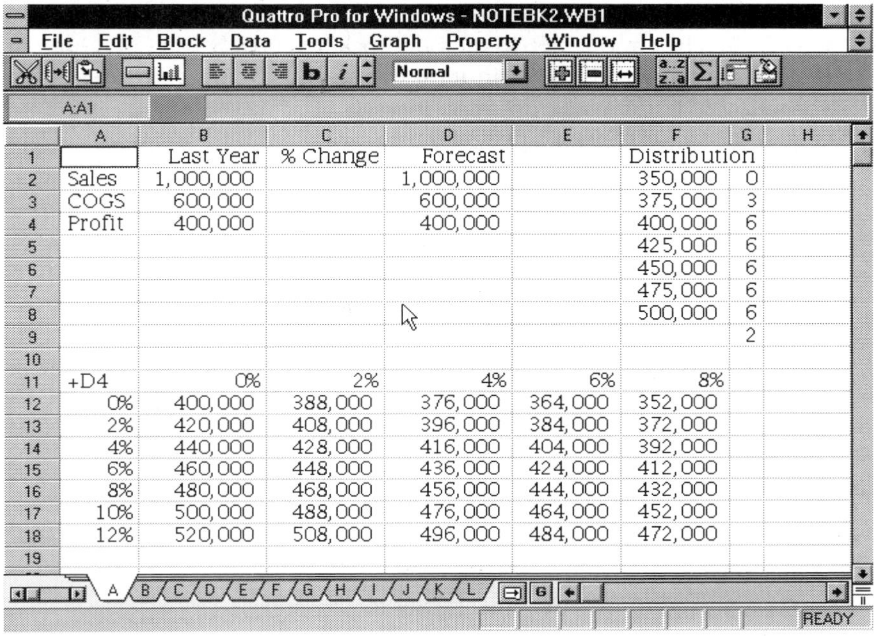

	A	B	C	D	E	F	G	H
1		Last Year	% Change	Forecast		Distribution		
2	Sales	1,000,000		1,000,000		350,000	0	
3	COGS	600,000		600,000		375,000	3	
4	Profit	400,000		400,000		400,000	6	
5						425,000	6	
6						450,000	6	
7						475,000	6	
8						500,000	6	
9							2	
10								
11	+D4	0%	2%	4%	6%	8%		
12	0%	400,000	388,000	376,000	364,000	352,000		
13	2%	420,000	408,000	396,000	384,000	372,000		
14	4%	440,000	428,000	416,000	404,000	392,000		
15	6%	460,000	448,000	436,000	424,000	412,000		
16	8%	480,000	468,000	456,000	444,000	432,000		
17	10%	500,000	488,000	476,000	464,000	452,000		
18	12%	520,000	508,000	496,000	484,000	472,000		
19								

Figure 5.26 Spreadsheet Notebook Created in Getting Started Section

A4: **Profit**
B4: **+B2-B3**
D4: **+D2-D3**

2. Create a shell for a 2 Way table that computes the profits for different rates of growth in sales and cost of goods sold. Move to A11. Type **+D4**, and move to A12. Select the block A12..A18 and then the Fill command in the Block menu. Type **.02** in the Step text box and then select OK to fill the block with 0 to .12 in .02 increments. Select the block B11..F11 and then the Fill command in the Block menu. Select OK to fill the block with 0 to .08 in .02 increments.
3. Fill the shell with the profits that would result from different growth rates for cost of goods sold and sales. Select A11..F18 for the block containing the table. Select What-If from the Data menu. Select the Two free variables radio button. Then, type **C2** or select C2 in the Column Input cell text box. Type **C3** or select C3 in the Row input cell text box. Select Generate and Close to create the 2 Way table.
4. Create a frequency table. Move to F1. Type **Distribution** and move to F2. Select the block F2..F8 and then the Fill command in the Block menu. Type **350000** in the Start text box, **25000** in the Step text box, and **500000** in the Stop text box. Select OK to fill the block with 350000 to 500000 in 25000

increments. Select Frequency in the Data menu. Select B12..F18 in the Value Block(s) text box and F2..F8 in the Bin Block text box. Select OK. Quattro Pro fills column G with the distribution of the values you generated with the two-variable table.

5. Format the cells. Select the block B2..F18 and inspect its properties. With the Numeric Format property selected, choose Comma, and type **0** in the text box. Select OK to format these cells. Select A11 and inspect its properties. With the Numeric Format property selected, choose Text and select OK. For the percentages, select the block A12..A18;B11..F11 and inspect its properties. With the Numeric Format property selected, choose Percent, and type **0** in the text box.

6. Widen the columns, since some of the cells appear as asterisks. Select the sheet with the Select–All button or select A1..G18. Either click the Fit button on the SpeedBar or inspect the block's properties, select the Column Width property, select the Auto Width radio button, and select OK. The spreadsheet now looks like Figure 5.26.

6

Printing Your Entries

Once you have created a notebook to hold your data, you will want to share the information it contains with others. Since a screen is not as portable as a piece of paper, printing the notebook affords you this opportunity. Quattro Pro provides many options to control the appearance of your printed output. Its default settings provide a quick method for printing your data without being bogged down in the specifics of the various print operations. Quattro Pro can also provide you complete control of the printed output, and has many features for printing your notebook.

This chapter covers the basic print procedure as well as the more advanced print options. You will be introduced to the terms to use for Quattro Pro's more advanced print features. Once you have covered the basics, you will be prepared to use as many of the special options as you need. As a final step, this chapter describes some changes you can make through Windows that affect how your output is presented.

THE BASIC PRINT PROCEDURE

Printing a Quattro Pro notebook is as simple as telling Quattro Pro which part of the notebook you want to print and starting the print process. Once you select the block to print, Quattro Pro uses all its default settings to determine the appearance of the printed page. In addition to understanding how to invoke printing, you need to understand the default settings completely so that you will know when and how to change them.

Printing a Notebook with the Default Settings

The first step of printing your notebook is defining a print block. This action informs Quattro Pro which part of the notebook you want to print. The process requires these steps:

1. Select the block you want to print.

2. Select Print from the File menu to display the dialog box shown in Figure 6.1.

3. Select the Print button. Quattro Pro will start printing your data.

If the block that you are printing exceeds the page in width or length, Quattro Pro prints the data on multiple pages, automatically breaking the pages at the appropriate location. When Quattro Pro finishes printing your data, the paper in the printer is automatically advanced to the next page. All of the settings you make for printing a notebook are saved when you save the notebook.

PRINTING IN WINDOWS   When you print with a Windows application, the Windows application only does half the work of printing your data. Windows applications are designed to tell Windows what data to print and how. Once it has that information, Windows handles putting in the printer codes to create the desired output. This feature puts all of the individual printer information in one place—in Windows. All of the Windows applications can share the printer information. Windows includes a Print Manager application that you can use to control how Windows prints each printing task, or *print job*.

Since each print job is performed separately, Windows handles advancing the paper in the printer to the next page when it is finished. You do not have to worry about advancing the paper so your next printing task starts at the top of the page. You can even have multiple print jobs ready to print at once. The print jobs you create are put into a queue and then sent to the printer one by one.

▼ TIP: Quattro Pro picks up the block of
                entries in a new notebook.

When you print a notebook for the first time and you have not selected a block to print ahead of time, Quattro Pro picks up the block that contains your entries from the current page. You can use this feature to quickly select the block to print a new notebook.

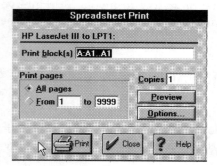

Figure 6.1   Spreadsheet Print Dialog Box

THE DEFAULT PAGE LAYOUT   When you print a spreadsheet notebook with the default settings in effect, Quattro Pro makes a number of decisions that affect the appearance of your data. You need to know the different options available before you can make changes to the default settings. The special terms that Quattro Pro uses to describe print options are illustrated in Figure 6.2. The definition and default settings for the terms are as follows:

- *Top Heading*—The top heading is one or more rows from the notebook that print above the data at the top of every page. Quattro Pro does not have a

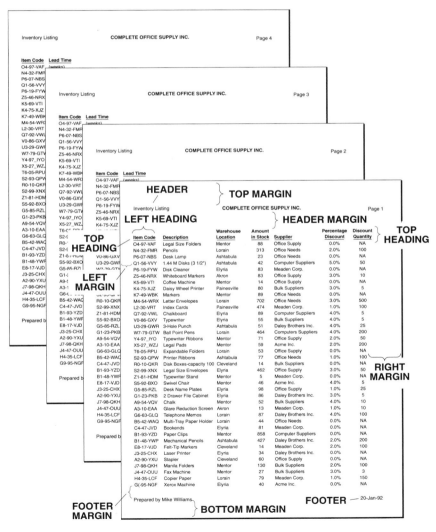

Figure 6.2   Printout Illustrating Different Printer Terms

default top heading, but you can specify one to create column headings on every page.

- *Left Heading*—The left heading is one or more columns from the notebook that print to the left of the data on every page. Quattro Pro does not have a default left heading, but you can specify one to create row headings for every page.

- *Format*—Quattro Pro defaults to print the data as it appears on the screen. You can change Quattro Pro's default to print the cell contents instead. Other printing options select whether the grid lines that divide the cells and the row and column borders are printed.

- *Header*—The header is the line at the top of every page. Quattro Pro's default settings leave this blank, but you can specify text to be placed in this line.

- *Footer*—The footer is the last line at the bottom of every page. Quattro Pro's default settings leave this blank, but you can specify text to be placed in this line.

- *Page Breaks*—Quattro Pro breaks the printed text into pages according to the page size setting. You can instruct Quattro Pro to put page breaks at any location on the notebook.

- *Margins*—The margin is the space between the edge of the paper and where Quattro Pro starts printing your data. Your page has a top, bottom, left, and right margin. Quattro Pro's default setting is 1/3 inch for the top and bottom and .4 inches for the left and right margins.

A CLOSER LOOK AT SELECTING A PRINT BLOCK   You have already looked at the basic steps for selecting a print block for a notebook, but Quattro Pro has a few specifics that you will want to know. When you select a block to print, you use the mouse or keyboard just as if you are selecting a block for a command or for inspecting a block's properties. When you select the Print command in the File menu, Quattro Pro displays the block it will print in the Print block(s) text box. You can enter a new block to print or modify the currently selected block in the Print block(s) text box. The block you select can contain as many notebook pages as you want.

Quattro Pro remembers the last block you have printed. When you choose Print from the File menu again, the Spreadsheet Print dialog box contains the same block address, unless you have selected a new multicell block before selecting the Print command. If you select this command when more than one cell is selected, the selected block replaces the previously selected block to print.

If the contents of a cell within the print block borrows display space from cells that are not part of your print block, the portion of these entries that uses the display space of other cells will *not* print. To print these entries, you can change the column width so that the entire cell's contents display in their own column, or expand the print block to include the cells where the long labels borrow display space.

The block you print can be a noncontiguous block. When you print a noncontiguous block, Quattro Pro prints separately each block within the selected noncontiguous block. This is different when you copy and move noncontiguous blocks, where Quattro Pro uses a corner cell as a reference point and then includes only the information in the noncontiguous block. Figure 6.3 shows the printout of a noncontiguous block. In the printed data, the block A8..B15,D8..F12 is selected. The row and column borders are included so that you can see how this information

---

▼ TIP: Naming the Print Block

If you have several blocks in a notebook that you want to print, you should name each block. Then, when you want to print one of the blocks, select Print in the File menu and press F3 (CHOICES) to select the named block to print.

▼ TIP: Expanding the Existing Print Block

When you want to expand or contract the last selected print block, select Print in the File menu and then modify the block using the arrows to expand or contract the selected block. You can also change which corner is the anchor corner by typing a period.

2_Way_Table	A	B
8	Sales	500000
9	Variable Costs	250000
10	Fixed Costs	200000
11	Interest	100000
12	Profit	−50000
13	Taxes	−20000
14	Net Profit	−30000
15	EPS	($3.33)

2_Way_Table	D	E	F
8	Total Equity		10000000
9	Debt Ratio		0.1
10	Actual Debt		1000000
11	Actual Stock		9000000
12	Number of Shares		9000

Figure 6.3   Printed Noncontiguous Block

is printed. You will learn how you can add row and column borders later in the chapter. When you want to print a noncontiguous block where all of the separate blocks are on the same page, you may want to hide the columns and/or rows in between the individual blocks you want to print so you can select a contiguous block to print. Any information that is hidden on the notebook is also hidden when you print a block from the page.

Selecting the Number of Copies to Print

Quattro Pro usually assumes that you want only one copy of your printed notebook data. Besides repeating the Print command for each copy you want, you can also print multiple copies of the selected block by entering a number between 1 and 1000 in the Copies text box. To prevent you from printing out extra copies of subsequent blocks, this setting always reverts to the default of 1 after you print.

Selecting the Pages to Print

When you print many pages at once, you may need to reprint one or more pages. Rather than printing the entire block again, you can print only the pages you select by choosing the From radio button in the Spreadsheet Print dialog box. To select the first page of a block to print, enter that page's number in the text box after From. To select the last page of a block to print, enter that page's number in the text box after to. When you select the Print button, Quattro Pro will divide the block into pages just as if printing every page, but then will only print the pages you have selected. This feature lets you selectively print pages. You would use this feature after you have fixed a spelling error or made a small change that only affects a few cells in the block you have previously printed. You can return to printing all the pages by selecting the All pages radio button.

Handling Print Problems

Once you define the block to print and tell Quattro Pro to begin printing your data, you expect the print output to be directed to your printer. Most of the time your expectations are met, but you also want to be prepared to handle problem situations. You can have two types of problems when you print. You may run into a problem when you have made settings that are incompatible so Quattro Pro is unsure of what you want to print. For example, if you type an invalid block address or name in the Print block(s) text box of the Spreadsheet Print dialog box, you will get a message that Quattro Pro cannot print your data. Another type of message is caused when Windows has a problem printing a print job. This type of problem occurs when your printer has run out of paper or you have not turned your printer on.

RESPONDING TO AN ERROR MESSAGE   You can have two types of error messages when you print. If Quattro Pro is unable to print your notebook, it displays an error message. When you select OK, you return to READY mode in the notebook so you can fix the error and then try the printing process again. Another type of error message occurs when Windows has a problem printing the Quattro Pro data. Figure 6.4 shows a sample message Windows 3.1 displays. This type of an error message can be caused by a printer that is either turned off, off-line, or out of paper. If you correct the problem and want to continue printing, choose Retry. You can also select Cancel to acknowledge the message and then continue with what you were doing when Windows displayed the message. Even when you select Cancel, the print job is still in Windows memory so it is ready to be printed as soon as you fix the problem and tell Windows to start printing again. To restart printing print jobs, activate the Print Manager, highlight the printer, and select Resume.

INTERRUPTING PRINT   Sometimes, you will want to interrupt printing before the entire block is printed. For example, you may want to abort printing if you change your mind about the block you are printing. Other reasons include incorrect page breaks and print settings. While Quattro Pro is sending the information to Windows to print, you can cancel the print job by selecting Cancel. Once Windows has the print job listed in its Print Manager, you can cancel the print job by displaying the Print Manager window, moving through the list to the print job to delete, and selecting the Delete button. When the Print Manager prompts for confirmation, select OK to confirm that you want to delete the print job.

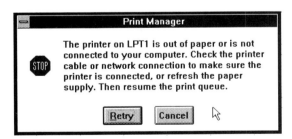

Figure 6.4 Windows 3.1 Message When Printer is Not Turned On

▼ TIP: Check that the printer is ready to print.

Most of the time when you cannot print, it is because of a simple error. When Windows displays a message that it cannot print, check that the printer is on, it has paper, and, if you are sharing the printer with other users, that the connection between your computer and the printer is attached. These problems are the simplest to fix and the cause of most printer problems.

PRINT OPTIONS FOR A PAGE

While printing your spreadsheet notebook can be as simple as defining a block to print, creating customized, professional-looking reports normally requires the use of Quattro Pro's special print features. Some of these special options set how Quattro Pro prints each page. The settings you make for printing a page in a notebook include setting the margins, adding a header or footer, and controlling page breaks. These print options that change the appearance of each page are set by selecting Page Setup in the File menu. This command displays the Spreadsheet Page Setup dialog box shown in Figure 6.5. The selections you make in this dialog box go into effect when you select OK. When you print the notebook using Print in the File menu or Print Preview in the File menu (as you will learn about later), Quattro Pro will print using all of the selections you have made in the Spreadsheet Page Setup dialog box.

Adding Headers and Footers

Quattro Pro can print headers and footers to the top and bottom of each page. Header and footer information is separate from the data you have in cells in the notebook. The header and footer stay constant for all pages with the exception of the page number. The header and footer are excellent locations for the name of your notebook, your name, the current date, and the page number.

To create a header, enter the text you want to use for the header in the Header text box in the Spreadsheet Page Setup dialog box. To create a footer, enter the text you want to use for the footer in the Footer text box in the Spreadsheet Page Setup dialog box. The header is printed before the notebook data is printed. If you add a top heading as described later in the chapter, the top heading prints after the header. The footer is printed below the notebook data.

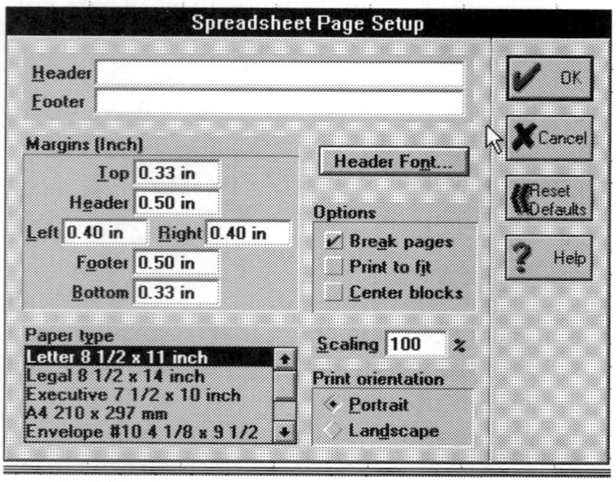

Figure 6.5   Spreadsheet Page Setup Dialog Box

SPECIAL HEADER AND FOOTER CHARACTERS   Quattro Pro provides many special characters that you can use in a header or footer. These special characters let you print the current date, time, and the appropriate page number, and they allow you to divide the header into several sections that are left-aligned, centered, or right-aligned. These special characters are listed in Table 6.1.

The | is often used to split a line in a header or footer into thirds. All of the text before the first | is left-aligned. If you add any text after the first |, the text is centered. To right-align text, enter the text after the second |. A sample header or footer may look like this:

Smith & Co. | Income Statement | Date: @D Page #p of #P

Table 6.1 Characters for Headers and Footers

Code	Effect of Code
|	Divides header text into text that is left-aligned, centered, and right-aligned.
#	Inserts the current page number.
@	Inserts the current date.
#d	Inserts the current date using Windows short international date format.
#D	Inserts the current date using Windows long international date format.
#ds	Inserts the current date using standard short date format (MMM-DD).
#Ds	Inserts the current date using standard long date format (MMM-DD-YY).
#t	Inserts the current time using Windows short international format.
#T	Inserts the current time using Windows long international format.
#ts	Inserts the current time using standard short format (HH:MM AM/PM).
#Ts	Inserts the current time using standard long format (HH:MM:SS AM/PM).
#p	Inserts the current page number.
#p+n	Inserts the value of the current page number plus the value of n.
#P	Inserts the total number of pages.
#P+n	Inserts the value of the total number of pages plus the value of n.
#f	Inserts the name of the notebook.
#F	Inserts the name of the notebook that includes the path information.
#n	Continues the header or footer text on the next line (can only be used once in a header or footer).

When this header is printed, Smith & Co. is left-aligned, Income Statement is centered in the middle of the line, and the date and the page number are right-aligned. When the header is printed, it looks like this:

Smith & Co.   Income Statement   Date: Friday, February 05, 1993 Page 1 of 4

You can also use the header and footer codes to create a header or footer using two lines. For example, you might have an entry in the Header text box that looks like this:

Acme Corporation| |Income Statement #nFor the Year Ended #D| |Page #p

When this header is printed, Acme Corporation is left-aligned on the first line, Income Statement is right-aligned on the first line, and the date and page information is on the second line. When the header is printed, it looks like this:

Acme Corporation   Income Statement
For the Year Ended December 31, 1992   Page 1

Another special character you can use in a header or footer is the backslash. When you use this character followed by a cell address or block name, Quattro Pro uses the contents of the selected cell. This special character cannot be combined with others. For example, Date: #d| |\A:A1 is unacceptable. If you want to use the special characters listed in Table 6.1 with the \ character in the header or footer, you must put the special characters in the cell that the \ character references, rather than in the text box with the backslash. For example, to create the previous example of a header, you could enter **Acme Corporation| |Income Statement #nFor the Year Ended #D| |Page #p** in A:A1 and then enter **\A:A1** in the Header text box.

SELECTING THE FONT FOR THE HEADER AND FOOTER   You can change the font that the header and footer use. However, you cannot inspect a header or footer's properties to change its appearance the way you can with cells. To select the font for the header and footer, select Header Font from the Spreadsheet Page

---

▼ TIP: Remember the page name when you use the \ special character in a header or footer.

When you use the \ special character in a header or footer, you need to include the page name if you supply a cell address. If you forget the page name, Quattro Pro uses the first page (page A by default). Since block names refer to specific pages, you do not need to include a page name for them.

▼ TIP: Putting Cell Entries in the Text Box
of a Dialog Box

Besides using the \ special character to put the contents of a cell into the Header or Footer text box, you can copy a cell entry or part of a cell entry to a text box. To put part of a cell's entry or all of a cell's entry in a text box, edit the cell, select the entry or part of the entry you want to put in the text box, and press CTRL-INS to copy the data to the Clipboard. Next, go to the text box in the dialog box where you want to repeat the entry and press SHIFT-INS.

Setup dialog box. The Select Font dialog box looks like the right side of the Active Block dialog box. You can select a font style from the Typeface list box; select a font size from the Point Size drop-down list box; and select attributes from the Bold, Italics, Underline, and Strikeout check boxes. When you select OK, your settings are used by the header and footer. Both the header and footer use the same font. When you do not select a font, the header and footer use the Normal style font.

Changing the Page's Margins

Quattro Pro allows you to change all the margins for printing your notebook. In the Spreadsheet Page Setup dialog box, Quattro Pro displays the measurements it will use for margins in the Margins section of the dialog box. Initially, Quattro Pro displays this information in inches. The unit of measurement is selected in the Measurement drop-down list box in the International dialog box of Windows' Control Panel. The values in the Left, Right, Top, and Bottom text boxes set the distance between the edge of the page and where data is printed. The top and bottom margins set the distance between the edge of the paper and where the header and footer appear, if they are used. The Header and Footer text boxes set the distance from the bottom of the header to where the notebook data starts and the bottom of the notebook data to where the footer starts. The left and right margins set the distance between the edge of the paper and where the notebook data will print. You can enter a new margin by typing a new measurement in the text box. If you want to enter a measurement in centimeters when Quattro Pro expects inches or vice versa, include a **cm** or **in** after the measurement to tell Quattro Pro the measurement system you are using.

Controlling Page Breaks

When you print more data than can fit on the page, Quattro Pro breaks the text into pages according to the margins and page size setting. You can instruct

Quattro Pro not to use page breaks except the ones you have created. Quattro Pro automatically adjusts the page breaks every time you print. However, Quattro Pro provides you with several options to insert page breaks at different locations. For example, if you have a notebook that contains several reports, creating your own page breaks can force each report to start on a new page.

ELIMINATING PAGE BREAKS   You can suppress Quattro Pro's page breaks by clearing the Break pages check box. When you print your file, Quattro Pro will not print headers or footers and will not insert automatic page breaks. Quattro Pro prints the top and left headings once at the beginning and again at each of the page breaks that you insert.

ADDING PAGE BREAKS   Quattro Pro provides two methods of manually inserting page breaks. You can either enter a page break directly into the notebook or use a menu command.

Adding a page break directly into your notebook is as simple as moving to a blank row and typing |:: (a vertical line and two colons) in the first column of the print block. If you do not have a blank row, you must insert one first. Entries in the same row as the page break are ignored. This method is quicker when you already have a blank row available. If you do not have a blank row, you will want to use the menu option.

Quattro Pro's menu command for adding a page break is Insert Break in the Block menu. When you execute this command, Quattro Pro inserts a blank row just above the selector and puts |:: (a vertical line and two colons) in the empty row. Any entries later inserted in the same row as the page break are not printed.

Expanding or Compressing the Printed Data

If you want to make the printed copy of your notebook smaller or larger, Quattro Pro has two options. With Quattro Pro, you can either decide how much you want the notebook expanded or compressed, or let Quattro Pro decide for you. Both sizing features are in the Spreadsheet Page Setup dialog box. If you select the Print to fit check box, Quattro Pro contracts your printed block to fit on one page or as few pages as possible. Quattro Pro makes the determination as to how much to compress the data so that the text is still readable based on the selected printer and the printer's resolution. This feature is most frequently useful when you have a large block to print that you want to fit on one page.

The other option, the Scaling text box, lets you select how much Quattro Pro expands or compresses the printed block. When you use this feature, enter a number between 1 and 1000 for the percentage of the original size you want to expand or compress the printed copy in the Scaling text box. Entering a number less than 100 prints the notebook smaller, and entering a number greater than 100 prints the notebook larger. Figure 6.6 shows several sheets printed with different

This text is scaled to 50%

This text is scaled to 100%

This text is scaled to 200%

Figure 6.6   Printing Using Different Scaling

scaling. When you use this feature, Quattro Pro divides the output into pages based on the amount of information that fits on each page. Quattro Pro will not reduce the point size of any font below 1 point or expand the point size of any text beyond 72 points. Both scaling methods use the page breaks you have added with the Insert Break command in the Block menu. Also, the margins remain the same. Print to fit has priority over Scaling, so if the Print to fit box is selected, Quattro Pro ignores the entry in the Scaling text box.

Centering Blocks

The data that you print is usually left-aligned according to the left margin you have set. When Quattro Pro does not use the full width of the page to print your data, you might want the block centered on the page. You can center the block on the page by selecting the Center blocks check box in the Spreadsheet Page Setup dialog box. When this check box is selected, Quattro Pro evenly divides the empty space on the right and left sides of the page. When this check box is cleared, the print block starts printing at the left margin.

▼ TIP: Do not include extra columns if you
are centering blocks.

You do not want to include additional columns on the right side of the block (for example, to ensure that you have all of your data) if you will be centering blocks. These extra columns prevent Quattro Pro from correctly centering blocks.

Changing the Page Size

You can change the page size for printing your data. This feature lets you select the size of the paper you will use to print your data. The available page sizes are listed in the Paper type list box. You can select any of the page sizes listed. When you print your notebook, Quattro Pro will use the selected page size and readjust the amount of data that will fit on each page. While Figure 6.5 shows the page sizes for the Hewlett-Packard LaserJet Series III, the actual page sizes you will see will depend on the selected printer.

Rotating the Printed Block

Quattro Pro is initially set to print the selected block from the top to the bottom of the page. If you are printing a wide block, it may be more convenient for you to print the data sideways. To print a notebook block sideways, select the Landscape radio button in the Spreadsheet Page Setup dialog box. When you print the block, the text will be rotated 90°. To return the orientation of the printing to the default, select the Portrait radio button.

Resetting Print Settings

When you need to change your print settings, it may be easier to undo the existing settings. You can reset all of the page setup settings at once. Resetting them does not affect other settings that affect printing. To reset the page setup settings, select the Reset Defaults command button. Resetting the page setup settings removes the header and footer, returns the margins to the defaults, selects the Break pages check box, clears the Print to fit and Center blocks check boxes, returns Scaling to 100%, selects the Portrait radio button, and returns the page size to the default.

SPREADSHEET PRINTING OPTIONS

Most of the page setup options are ones that would apply whether you are printing data from a spreadsheet or from another application. When you print your spreadsheet notebook, Quattro Pro has printing options that apply solely to spreadsheet data. These options include printing columns or rows that appear at the beginning of every page, printing cell formulas, printing grid lines, printing row and column borders, and dividing notebook pages or blocks within a noncontiguous block by lines or pages. These options are set by selecting Print from the File menu to display the Spreadsheet Print dialog box and then selecting the Options button. The Spreadsheet Print Options dialog box that includes these spreadsheet printing options is shown in Figure 6.7. When you select the OK

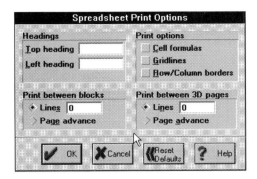

Figure 6.7   Spreadsheet Print Options Dialog Box

button, you will return to the Spreadsheet Print dialog box. The print settings you make in this dialog box are saved with the notebook.

If you want to return the spreadsheet printing options to the defaults, you can do so by selecting the Reset Defaults command button. Resetting the spreadsheet printing options removes the top and left headings, clears the check boxes, and sets Quattro Pro not to skip lines between blocks or pages that are part of the print block.

Adding Headings to a Page

When you print a notebook block that spans many pages, you may want to include identifying information for each row or column. For example, if your print block is very long, you will want column headings on each page to explain what the entries in each column represent. On the other hand, if your print block is very wide, adding row headings identifies the information in each row on every page of the report.

USING HEADINGS AT THE TOP   Creating a top heading allows you to include entries from multiple rows at the top of every page that you print. You can use this feature to repeat column headings when a block spans several pages When you choose a top heading, you do not have to specify the entire block that you want to use as a top heading; you only have to include one cell in a row for the entire row to be selected. Quattro Pro determines which columns of the selected rows are used according to which columns are in the print block.

To create a top heading, follow these steps:

1. Display the Spreadsheet Print Options dialog box.
2. Select a block that includes one cell from each row you want to use for top headings in the Top heading text box.
3. Select OK to return to the Spreadsheet Print dialog box.
4. Select Print to print the data with the top headings.

Terminus Construction Company				
Contract			**Est. # of Months**	
Number	**Client**		**to Complete**	
140UPY	Fork Lift Manufacturers		47	
630SEF	Metal Shop, Inc		25	

Terminus Construction Company		Contract Details				
Contract			**Year**	**Amount of**	**Percent**	**Amount**
Number	**Client**	**Location**	**Started**	**Contract**	**Complete**	**Earned**
140UPY	Fork Lift Manufacturers	New York, NY	1992	119,230	98%	116,845
630SEF	Metal Shop, Inc	New Castle, PA	1992	279,388	51%	142,488
610QZZ	Book Binders, Inc.	Plantation, FL	1992	247,477	39%	96,516
510FDO	Boaters, Inc	Newport, RI	1991	402,197	2%	8,044
330ZEJ	Speeders, Ltd.	Indianapolis, IN	1993	386,095	93%	359,068
930ZZD	Crooked Towers	Chicago, IL	1993	301,642	20%	60,328
080QVM	Mappers Galore	Elm Creek, TX	1990	332,574	83%	276,036
470RBP	Rusty's Automotive Parts	Tucson, AZ	1992	367,730	15%	55,160
990IXZ	Alonzo's Fish & Tackle	Mobile, AL	1992	268,496	3%	8,055
350RSH	New Worlds Horizons	Fort Knox, TN	1990	259,806	87%	226,031
050PLK	Portuguese Foods, Inc.	Fall River, MA	1992	216,502	38%	82,271
880NXF	Crystal Ball Glass Makers	Salem, CT	1992	564,437	76%	428,972
420BFY	Stanton Leather Company	Stanton, MO	1992	194,972	100%	194,972

Figure 6.8   Top and Left Headings on a Printed Notebook

Figure 6.8 shows pages printed with top headings. Rows 1 through 3 are used as column headings for every page. A block such as A1..A3 is selected in the Top heading text box. The block that is printed is C4..H65. Columns A and B appear on every page because they are selected as the left heading as described below. For the first page, Quattro Pro knows to include rows 1, 2, and 3 of columns A through G in the heading, since these are the notebook columns that are printed below it.

When you print your notebook, Quattro Pro uses the rows that you specify at the top of each page. The columns match the columns selected in the print block. To remove the top heading, remove the entry from the Top heading text box.

If you have a top heading, do not include the rows of the top heading as part of the print block. If you accidentally include the data in both places, the top heading is printed once as a top heading and a second time as part of the notebook data on the first page of the report.

USING INFORMATION AT THE SIDE   The addition of a left heading allows you to print a wide notebook block spanning several pages without losing track of what the data in each row represents. When you choose a left heading, you do not have to specify the entire block that you want to use as a left heading; you only have to include one cell in a column for the entire column to be selected. Quattro Pro determines which rows of the selected columns are used by which rows are in the print block.

To create a left heading, follow these steps:

1. Display the Spreadsheet Print Options dialog box.
2. Select a block that includes one cell from each column you want to use for left headings in the Left heading text box.
3. Select OK to return to the Spreadsheet Print dialog box.
4. Select Print to print the data with the left heading.

Figure 6.8 shows pages printed with left headings. Columns A and B are used as left headings for every page. A block such as A1..B1 is selected in the <u>L</u>eft heading text box. The block that is printed is C4..H65. Rows 1, 2, and 3 appear on every page because they are selected as the top heading.

When you print your notebook, Quattro Pro prints the entries in the columns that you specify at the left side of each page. The rows that Quattro Pro uses match the rows in the print block. To remove the left heading, remove the entry from the <u>L</u>eft heading text box.

If you have a left heading, do not include the columns in the print block. If you include the left heading columns in the print block, the information is printed once as a left heading and then again as part of the notebook data.

Printing Row and Column Borders

You may want to print the row and column borders. If you are printing a notebook page as documentation or you are creating a new model, you may want to see the row and column borders so that you can position your data. You can include the row and column borders in the printed copy by selecting the <u>R</u>ow/Column borders check box in the Spreadsheet Print Options dialog box. When this check box is selected and you print a block from the notebook, the printed copy includes the row and column borders. If you clear this check box, the printed block does not have the row and column borders. Figure 6.9 shows a notebook block printed with the row and column borders (it also has grid lines printed as described below). As you can see in the printed data, the corner of the row and column borders contains the page name.

C	A	B	C	D	E	F	G
1			Warehouse	Amount		Percentage	Discount
2	Item Code	Description	Location	in Stock	Supplier	Discount	Quantity
3	O4-97-VAF	Legal Size Folders	Mentor	88	Office Supply	0.0%	NA
4	N4-32-FMR	Pencils	Lorain	313	Office Needs	2.0%	100
5	P6-07-NBS	Desk Lamp	Ashtabula	23	Office Needs	0.0%	NA
6	Q1-56-VVY	1.44 M Disks (3 1/2")	Ashtabula	42	Computer Suppliers	5.0%	50
7	P6-19-FYW	Disk Cleaner	Elyria	83	Meaden Corp.	0.0%	NA
8	Z5-46-NRX	Whiteboard Markers	Akron	83	Office Supply	3.0%	10
9	K5-69-VTI	Coffee Machine	Mentor	14	Office Supply	0.0%	NA
10	K4-75-XJZ	Daisy Wheel Printer	Painesville	80	Bulk Suppliers	3.0%	5
11	K7-49-WBK	Markers	Mentor	89	Office Needs	0.0%	NA
12	M4-54-WRX	Letter Envelopes	Lorain	702	Office Needs	3.0%	500
13	L2-30-VRT	Index Cards	Painesville	474	Meaden Corp.	1.0%	100
14	Q7-92-VWL	Chalkboard	Elyria	89	Computer Suppliers	4.0%	5
15	V0-86-GXV	Typewriter	Elyria	55	Bulk Suppliers	4.0%	5

Figure 6.9   Printed Notebook with Printed Grid Lines and Borders

Hiding and Displaying Cell Grid Lines

By default, when you print a notebook, it does not contain the grid lines that you see on the screen. You can include these grid lines in the printed copy by selecting the Gridlines check box in the Spreadsheet Print Options dialog box. When this check box is selected and you print a block from the notebook, the grid lines are printed as well. If you clear this check box, the grid lines are omitted. Figure 6.9 shows a notebook block printed with the grid lines as well as the row and column borders described above.

Printing Cell Contents to Document the Worksheet

You can document your notebooks by printing your entries. Quattro Pro provides two methods for printing the information in notebook formulas. One method is to change the numeric format to Text so that Quattro Pro displays the formulas and then prints the resulting notebook. The other method changes the format of your printed data so that Quattro Pro prints a list of the cells and their contents. Although the second method may be used more often, the first method usually provides better results.

PRINTING THE NOTEBOOK WITH FORMULAS DISPLAYED   You can use Quattro Pro's numeric formats to show your entire notebook as text, numbers, and formulas. Once the notebook displays the formulas instead of the results, printing the notebook provides you with a hard copy of each cell's contents with the same row and column orientation that you are familiar with. You can also combine this method with printing the grid lines and the row and column borders as described above. Although this requires more steps, the resulting printout is easier to understand.

To print out your notebook's formulas, numbers, and labels, follow these steps:

1. Open the notebook containing formulas you want to print, such as the one in Figure 6.10.

2. Select Save As in the File menu, type a new name for the file, and select OK to save the file under a different name. If you save the notebook under another name, you can later save the modified version in case you want to return to it and any numeric formatting and column width changes you have made will not affect the original.

3. Press HOME then END-HOME to select the data area then inspect the block's properties. With the Numeric Format property selected, choose the Text radio button. Select the Column Width property and the Auto Width radio button. Select OK to use the new properties. Now, all the columns are wide enough and you can see the contents of the entries. Cells containing

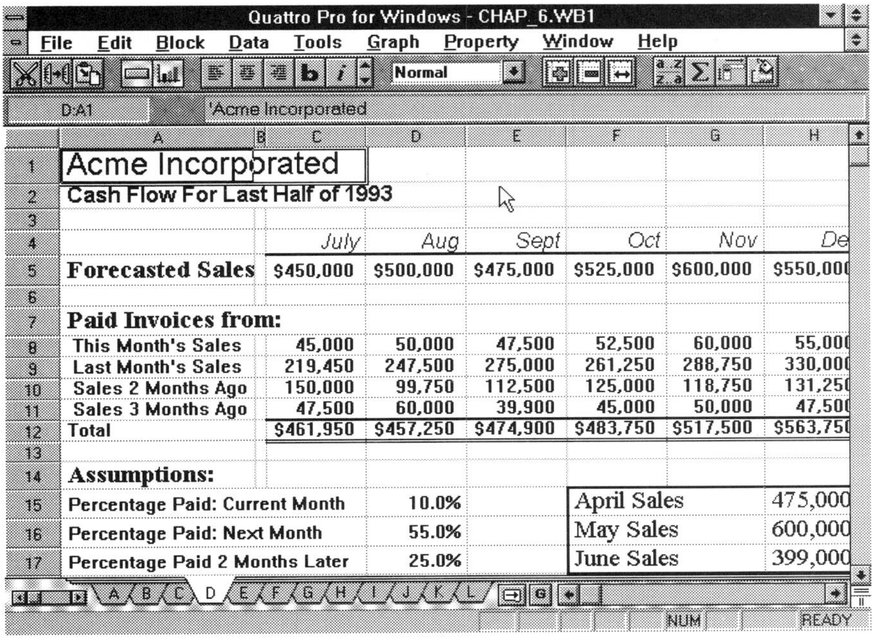

Figure 6.10   Notebook Using Text Numeric Format

formulas are displayed as formulas. Labels do not change. Numbers lose any numeric formatting. Any cells that have hidden comments show the comments.

4. Repeat step 3 for each page whose contents you want to print.

5. Select the block containing the entries you want to document.

6. Select Print from the File menu. Select Options, the Gridlines and Row/Column borders check boxes, and OK.

7. Choose Print. Quattro Pro then starts printing your notebook in the format that appears on the screen, as in Figure 6.11.

CHANGING THE PRINT FORMAT TO PRINT CELL CONTENTS   The Cell formulas check box in the Spreadsheet Print Options dialog box provides another method for printing formulas. This method is quicker, but the printout is not as easy to understand. This check box is normally cleared, but if you select this check box, Quattro Pro prints out the cell address and the contents (including any cell comments in a cell within the print block) for every cell with an entry in the print block. Figure 6.12 provides a look at some output produced with the Cell formulas check box selected. For each line in the output, you can see the cell's address and contents.

D	A	B	C	D	E
1	**ACME INCORPORATED**				
2	Cash Flow For Last Half of 1993				
3					
4			*July*	*Aug*	*Sept*
5	Forecasted Sales		450000	500000	475000
6					
7	Paid Invoices from:				
8	This Month's Sales		+ JULY*$D15	+ AUG*$D15	+ SEPT*$D15
9	Last Month's Sales		+ JUNE*$D16	+ JULY*$D16	+ AUG*$D16
10	Sales 2 Months Ago		+ MAY*$D17	+ JUNE*$D17	+ JULY*$D17
11	Sales 3 Months Ago		+ APR*$D18	+ MAY*$D18	+ JUNE*$D18
12	Total		+ C8 + C9 + C10 + C	+ D8 + D9 + D10 + D	+ E8 + E9 + E10 + E1
13					
14	Assumptions:				
15	Percentage Paid: Current Month			0.1	
16	Percentage Paid: Next Month			0.55	
17	Percentage Paid 2 Months Later			0.25	
18	Percentage Paid 3 Months Later			0.1	

Figure 6.11   Printed Notebook Showing Cell Entries in Cells

```
D:A1:    'Acme Incorporated
D:A2:    'Cash Flow For Last Half of 1993
D:C4:    "July
D:A5:    'Forecasted Sales
D:C5:    450000
D:A7:    'Paid Invoices from:
D:A8:    ' This Month's Sales
D:C8:    +JULY*$D15
D:A9:    ' Last Month's Sales
D:C9:    +JUNE*$D16
D:A10:   ' Sales 2 Months Ago
D:C10:   +MAY*$D17
D:A11:   ' Sales 3 Months Ago
D:C11:   +APR*$D18
D:A12:   'Total
D:C12:   +C8+C9+C10+C11
```

Figure 6.12   Printed Cell Formulas from a Notebook

Leaving Space between Blocks and Pages

When you print multiple pages or a noncontiguous block, you can select how the separate pages or blocks within the print block are printed. You can select whether Quattro Pro puts no separation between the pages or blocks, or separates them with empty lines or page breaks. To change how the blocks and pages within the print block are printed, select between the Lines and the Page advance radio buttons that appear under Print between blocks and Print between 3D pages. When the Lines or Lines radio button is selected, each block or notebook page is separated from the other by the number of lines in the adjoining text box. These lines use the row height appropriate for the Normal style. When the Page advance or Page advance button is selected, each block or notebook page is printed on a separate page. The default is to separate the blocks or pages with no lines—the Lines and Lines radio buttons are selected and 0 appears in the adjoining text boxes.

PREVIEWING THE PRINTED NOTEBOOK

After you print a notebook for the first time, you may find that you need to reprint it, because the output is missing information or includes lines and boxes that are inappropriately placed. Rather than checking that you have the correct output every time you print a notebook block, you can save time by viewing the notebook block on the screen before Quattro Pro prints it. This is Quattro Pro's previewer. When you preview a notebook, Quattro Pro displays the print block as it will be printed on paper.

To tell Quattro Pro that you want to preview a notebook, select Print Preview in the File menu. You can also preview the print block by selecting the Preview button from the Spreadsheet Print dialog box you see when you select Print from the File menu. Figure 6.13 shows Quattro Pro previewing the print block.

The white rectangle that represents the page Quattro Pro will print does not show the actual text well because it is reduced in size. If you want to look more closely at the page, point to the part of the page you want to look at more closely and click the left button on the mouse. You can also press the + key to increase the magnification. You can zoom the page up to 1600% so you can look closely at the entries on the page. Figure 6.14 shows the previewer displaying a potential print job at 800% magnification so you can easily see how the entries will appear on the page. When you want to return to a smaller magnification to see more of the page, press the right button on the mouse. This is also the same as pressing the – key. While you are looking closely at the page, you can shift the part of the page you are viewing using the scroll bars or arrow keys. When the block you are printing uses multiple pages, you can switch pages in the preview windows by clicking the Next and Previous buttons, which have the left and right arrows, or by pressing PGUP and PGDN. Another option is to type the page number you want to see in the text box adjacent to the Next and Previous buttons.

The remaining buttons in the window let you change the print settings you are using so you can dynamically modify how Quattro Pro will print the block. As you change the print settings with these buttons, their effects are immediately displayed on the screen. The first button after the zoom percentage is the Color button. You can click this button to switch between showing the printed output using colors and using shading. For example, if you have added a text color property to a block,

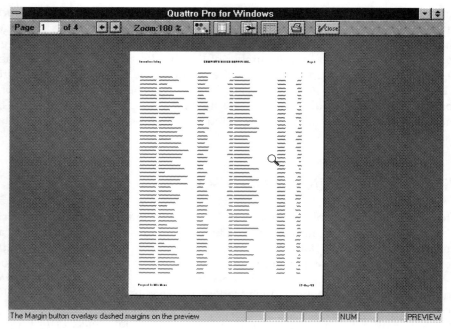

Figure 6.13   Previewed Notebook

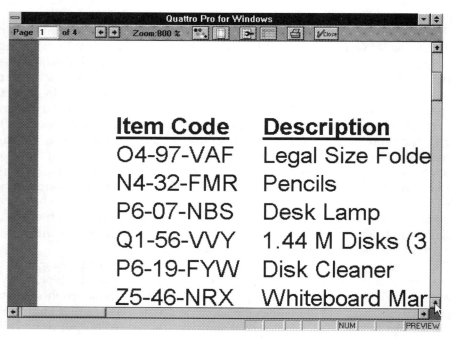

Figure 6.14   Closer Look at Previewed Notebook

clicking the Color button switches between showing the block with the selected color and with the shading as a black-and-white printer will print it. Since every printer is different, the way the color converts to a shade will vary by the printer you are using. With some printers, the colors will all appear as black. The next button, the Margin button, adds and removes the margin lines. The first time you click this button, Quattro Pro adds dashed lines to indicate the left, right, top, bottom, header, and footer margins as shown in Figure 6.15. These margin lines are never printed. When you select this button again, the margin lines are removed. You can drag and drop these margin lines with your mouse to change the margin settings.

The third button after the zoom percentage, the Setup button, displays the Spreadsheet Page Setup dialog box so that you can change the header, footer, margin, scaling, and page size options. The next button, the Options button, displays the Spreadsheet Print Options dialog box. This dialog box lets you add top and left headings, print grid lines and borders, and divide blocks and pages within the print block. With both of these dialog boxes, when you select OK, you return to the previewed output and the printing settings you change are incorporated into them. If the preview window shows the output you want, you can start printing by clicking the Print button. This is the same as selecting the Print button in the Spreadsheet Print dialog box. When you are finished looking at the previewed output and you want to return to the notebook window or the Spreadsheet Print dialog box, select the Close button, the last one, or press ESC.

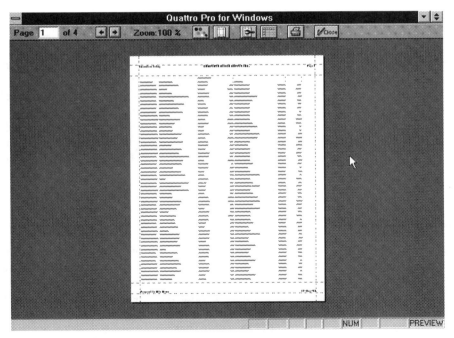

Figure 6.15 Previewed Notebook with Margins Added

ADVANCED PRINT OPTIONS

To print most of your spreadsheet notebooks, you will use the basic Quattro Pro print commands. However, Quattro Pro provides other features that help you customize the printed notebook's appearance. You can name print settings so you can quickly change from one set of printer settings to another. Or you can change the printer you will use and change that printer's settings. Other options let you send the output to a file, or hide columns or rows from the printed copy. While these options are not used every time you use Quattro Pro, they can help provide the output you want.

Named Print Settings

Using the same print settings for each of your printing tasks in a notebook does not get the best use out of Quattro Pro's printing features. You can have several sets of print settings in a notebook, and change the print settings you use to match the data you want to print. The print settings are saved with a print setting name that includes all of the print features you have learned about and the selected print block.

To create a named print setting, make all of the print setting selections and print block selections that you want the print setting name to represent. Next, select Named Settings from the File menu. In the Named Print Settings dialog box, select the Create button, type the name you want to use for the print settings, and select OK. When you finish naming the print settings, select OK or Close.

Once you have the print settings named, you can make the settings the current ones again by selecting Named Settings from the File menu, highlighting the print setting name in the Named Settings list box, and selecting OK.

When you want to change a named print setting, first make that named print setting current, then change the print settings to what you want. Next, select Named Settings in the File menu, highlight the print setting name, and select Update. If you want to remove a named print setting from the Named Print Settings dialog box, highlight the print setting name to delete, and select the Delete command button.

Specifying the Printer

You can have more than one printer installed in Windows. The Windows Control Panel and Windows installation let you select the printer you use as the default. This default printer is used unless you select another one. You can select any of the printers installed in Windows to print your data. To select which of the installed printers you will use, select Printer Setup in the File menu. Next, in the Printer and Port list box, select the installed printer that you want to use to print your output. When you select OK, subsequent printing in the notebook uses the selected printer.

> ▼ TIP: Use easily identifiable names for the
> print setting names.
>
> You may want to use a page name or report name for the print setting name
> so that you can easily remember which print setting name belongs with each
> print output you want to create.

Changing the Printer Setup

Besides the settings you make with the Page Setup and Print commands in the File menu, you can also make changes that affect your printouts by changing some of the Windows printer settings. These printer settings are the same printer settings that you can make through the Printer dialog box in the Windows Control Panel. The exact options you have depend on the printer you are using.

To change the Windows printer settings in Quattro Pro, select Printer Setup in the File menu. In the Printer Setup dialog box, you can select the printer you want to change the printer settings for in the Printer and Port list box. Next, select the Setup button. Quattro Pro displays a dialog box that contains selections for features that are specific for your printer. Figure 6.16 shows the dialog box Windows shows for the Hewlett-Packard LaserJet Series III. At this point, you can change the settings for your printer. When you select OK, you are returned to the Printer Setup dialog box. The printer setting changes you have made are just like changes to the printer settings made through the Windows Control Panel. These printer settings affect all Windows applications that use the printer.

Sending the Printout to a File

Besides printing your output, you can also "print" the output to a file. Directing the print output to a file instead of the printer offers new possibilities. You can print the file at a later time, or print it on a machine that does not have Windows or Quattro Pro for Windows. If you put the print output in a file, you can print the file with the DOS COPY command at a later time. When you print to a file, Quattro Pro sends all the headers and footers, headings, and other print settings to the file so the file contains the same information that is sent to the printer.

To print your notebook data to a file, make all the print setting changes you would if you were actually printing it immediately. Next, select Printer Setup in the File menu. From the Printer Setup dialog box, make sure the correct printer is selected in the Printer and Port list box. Select the check box below Redirect To File and type a file name into the adjoining text box. When you select OK, you can select Print in the File menu. When you select the Print button, the output is sent to the file instead of to the printer. To print the file later, return to DOS, and type **COPY** followed by the file name and the port the printer is attached to.

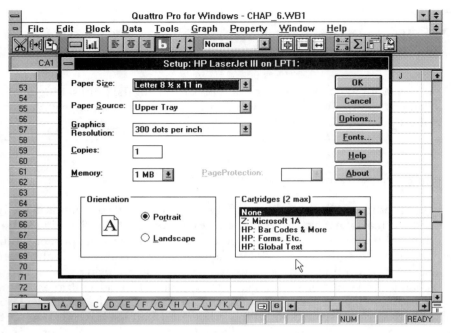

Figure 6.16   Setup Dialog Box for an Installed Printer

▼ TIP: Make sure the proper printer is selected before you print to a file

Since each printer has its own instructions that must be provided when you print, it is important that when you print your notebook data to a file, the proper printer is selected. If the wrong printer is selected, the file will not contain the appropriate printer instructions and you will be disappointed with the results.

▼ TIP: Creating an ASCII File

If you want to create a file with no coding that employs only text characters, select the Generic/Text Only printer and then print to a file. When you use this Windows printer driver, all the codes are stripped away from your data. You may need to use a text file to transfer your data to a non-Windows application.

1

Hiding Columns and Rows to Change the Print Output

When you print a block, Quattro Pro prints the information as it appears in the notebook window. You can hide columns and rows to omit information from printing. For example, suppose a page contains your inventory records and you want to print the item code, description, amount in stock, percentage discount, and discount quantity in columns A, B, D, F, and G. You can hide the warehouse and supplier in columns C and E. To hide these two columns, select cells in these columns, inspect the properties, select the Reveal/Hide property, Columns, and Hide, then select OK. After they are hidden, the columns disappear from the display and are not printed, even when the columns are included in the print block. Figure 6.17 shows a notebook printed with hidden columns (the printed row and column borders indicate which columns are hidden). Quattro Pro still keeps track of the hidden columns and, therefore, does not relabel the displayed columns. To display a hidden column, inspect the properties of the columns on either side of the hidden column, select the Reveal/Hide property, Columns, and Reveal, then select OK. You can also hide and reveal rows following the same steps. Data in a hidden column is still maintained and is also available for access by formulas in columns that are still displayed.

PRINTING IN WINDOWS

When you print with Quattro Pro for Windows, you may want to use two of Windows features. One of these is the Print Manager, which Windows uses to

C	A	B	D	F	G
1			Amount	Percentage	Discount
2	**Item Code**	**Description**	**in Stock**	**Discount**	**Quantity**
3	O4-97-VAF	Legal Size Folders	88	0.0%	NA
4	N4-32-FMR	Pencils	313	2.0%	100
5	P6-07-NBS	Desk Lamp	23	0.0%	NA
6	Q1-56-VVY	1.44 M Disks (3 1/2")	42	5.0%	50
7	P6-19-FYW	Disk Cleaner	83	0.0%	NA
8	Z5-46-NRX	Whiteboard Markers	83	3.0%	10
9	K5-69-VTI	Coffee Machine	14	0.0%	NA
10	K4-75-XJZ	Daisy Wheel Printer	80	3.0%	5
11	K7-49-WBK	Markers	89	0.0%	NA
12	M4-54-WRX	Letter Envelopes	702	3.0%	500
13	L2-30-VRT	Index Cards	474	1.0%	100
14	Q7-92-VWL	Chalkboard	89	4.0%	5
15	V0-86-GXV	Typewriter	55	4.0%	5

Figure 6.17   Printed Notebook with Hidden Columns

process taking print jobs from the Windows applications and sending them to the printer one at a time. The other Windows feature you may use with printing is the Printers dialog box in the Control Panel.

Using the Print Manager

The Print Manager in Windows handles storing all the information to send to the printer and sending the information to the printer as the printer is ready for more. Since Windows does this automatically in the background, you will only realize that the Print Manager is at work when you notice the minimized icon. The Print Manager is opened when you start to print in a Windows application. Unless you display its window instead of its icon, it automatically puts itself away when it is finished printing all the information. You can look at the contents of the Print Manager by opening it as a window. The Print Manager is opened as a window by selecting Print Manager in the Main group window of the Program Manager. If it appears on the screen as an icon, you can also open the Print Manager window by selecting Restore from its Control menu. When it is open, it displays all the print jobs it is processing. Figure 6.18 shows a Print Manager window with several print jobs in its queue. Your Quattro Pro print jobs show the notebook name you are printing, its size, and the time and date you printed it from Quattro Pro.

Most of the time, you will not need to look at the Print Manager window. Usually, the only time you do is when a printer has stalled printing, such as when a printer runs out of paper. When a printer is stalled, you can restart it by selecting the printer in the list and then selecting the Resume button. The other function of using the Print Manager is to remove a print job from the queue when you have decided you no longer want it. To do this, highlight the print job in the list and

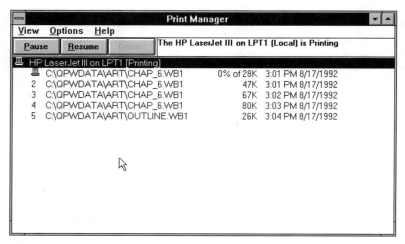

Figure 6.18   Print Manager Window Showing Print Jobs

press DEL or select the Delete button. You will have to select OK as confirmation that you want to delete the print job.

Printers in the Control Panel

Windows Control Panel sets how Windows and Windows applications operate. Use Printers in the Control Panel to select the printers and the printer settings that Windows and Windows applications use. You can look at the printer settings by opening the Printers dialog box in the Control Panel. The Control Panel is opened by selecting Control Panel in the Main group window of the Program Manager window. From the Control Panel window, you can select the Printers icon or select Printers from the Settings menu. This displays a dialog box like the one shown in Figure 6.19.

In the Printers dialog box, you can select the default printer by highlighting an installed printer in the Installed Printers list box and selecting the Set As Default Printer button. You can install another printer by selecting the Add button, the name of the printer to install from the List of Printers list box, and then the Install button. Windows may need to copy a printer driver from one of Windows' original disks to your system. You can also disable the Print Manager from the Printers dialog box by clearing the Use Print Manager check box.

The remaining buttons in the Printers dialog box let you control printer selections such as printer-defined fonts and the connection of the printer to your system. The Connect button lets you select how your printer is connected to your system and any settings the connection uses. The Setup button displays the same dialog box that you can see when you select the Setup button available in the Printer Setup dialog box displayed by the Printer Setup command in the File menu. You can change a variety of settings, depending on your printer's capabilities. The Remove button removes an installed printer. The Connect, Setup, and Remove buttons operate on the printer selected in the Installed Printers list box.

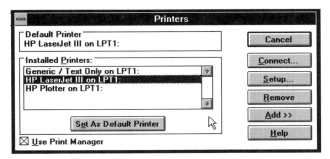

Figure 6.19 Printers Dialog Box for Changing a Printer (Windows 3.1)

GETTING STARTED

In this chapter you learned how to print your spreadsheet notebooks. With the options covered in this chapter, you learned how you can control your output's appearance. You can try some of these printing features by following these steps:

1. Make the following entries in a new notebook. You can use the inventory report in Figure 6.20 as a guide. This notebook is designed for you to try Quattro Pro's printing features.

   A2: **Inventory Report**
   A4: **Nails**
   A5: **Rivets**
   A6: **Screws**
   A7: **Tacks**
   A8: **Total**
   C4: **60000**
   C5: **50000**
   C6: **45000**
   C7: **90000**
   C8: **+C4+C5+C6+C7**

2. To change the appearance of the heading in A2, select A2 and then select the Heading 1 named style from the Style List drop-down list box in the SpeedBar. (Remember you can activate this drop-down list box by pressing CTRL-SHIFT-5.) Inspect this cell's properties and change the font so that it uses Arial 18 point bold (Helv in Windows 3.0). Add a line by selecting the block A2..C2 and inspecting its properties. Select the Line Drawing prop-

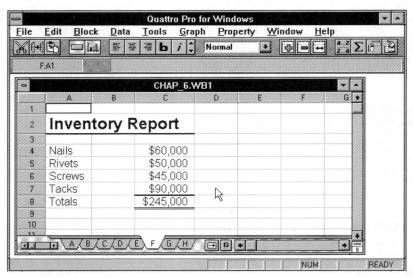

Figure 6.20   Inventory Report Used for Getting Started Section

erty and then select the thick line style under Line Types and the bottom of the block in the Line Segments diagram. Select OK.

3. To change the appearance of A4..C8, select the block A4..C8 and inspect its properties. With the Numeric Format property selected, select the Currency radio button and type **0** in the text box. Select the Font property and select the Arial typeface (Helv in Windows 3.0) and 12 point size. Select the Column Width property and the Auto Width radio button. Select OK.

4. To add lines to C8, select C8 and inspect its properties. Select the Line Drawing property, select the thick line style under Line Types and the top of the block in the Line Segments diagram. Select the double line style under Line Types and the bottom of the block in the Line Segments diagram. Select OK.

5. Select Print in the File menu. Notice how Quattro Pro already has entered A2..C8 as the print block because this is the first time you are printing the notebook and A2..C8 is the block on the current page that contains entries.

6. Select the Print button. This prints the spreadsheet using the default print settings as shown in Figure 6.21. You can try printing with several different settings to see how the different print options will make your notebook appear.

7. To print the notebook data with grid lines and row and column borders, select the block A1..C9. Select Print in the File menu and the Options button. Select the Gridlines and the Row/Column borders check boxes. Select OK and then Print to print with grid lines and row and column borders.

8. To center the notebook data and add a header, select Page Setup from the File menu. Select the Center blocks check box. Type **Acme Corporation | | Date:#d** in the Header text box. Select OK.

9. Select Print Preview in the File menu to see the preview of this printed data. Select the Options button (the third from the end) and clear the Gridlines and

Inventory Report

Nails	$60,000
Rivets	$50,000
Screws	$45,000
Tacks	$90,000
Totals	$245,000

Figure 6.21   Notebook Printed in Getting Started Section

the Row/Column borders check boxes. Select OK to return to the previewed notebook data. Select the Print button (next to last one) to print the data.

10. Select the End button or press ESC to leave the preview of the notebook data and return to the notebook.

7

Files

Spreadsheet notebooks created in the memory of your machine are lost if power to the machine goes off for even a brief instant. This loss occurs because random access memory (RAM) where your data is stored is a transient storage medium. Files, however, offer permanent storage for your spreadsheet notebooks.

Quattro Pro provides all the basic file handling commands and adds certain options for creating backups and protecting your files with passwords. Quattro Pro's file-handling features surpass those of other packages by translating data directly from the formats used by other popular packages into Quattro Pro's format and from Quattro Pro's format to the format required by other popular packages. Quattro Pro also lets you use more than one spreadsheet notebook at once. You can share data between spreadsheet notebooks by using Quattro Pro's commands and by using data from other spreadsheets in formulas.

This chapter covers the basic concepts of DOS as they relate to the storage of Quattro Pro files. You will learn how to save, open, and close files, and change the current directory. You will also learn how to share data between different notebook files. And you will learn how to take advantage of special features that allow you to share data between applications as well.

FILE BASICS

Disks are like file cabinets that provide an area for you to keep your information. Just as you can store printed information in a folder within a file cabinet, you can store your computer information in a file on a disk. However, unlike a file cabinet's contents, you do not see a file. Your operating system acts as an intermediary between you and your files. DOS is needed to work with files on a disk, but

Windows and Windows applications work with DOS so that you don't have to work with DOS directly. For DOS to store and retrieve your information, you must provide unique names for your files. To make it easier to find information on large-capacity disks, DOS supports the use of directories and subdirectories to organize your files.

Directories and Subdirectories

Directories and subdirectories contain information about the files that you store on your disk. The main directory on a disk is called the root directory. On a floppy disk, this may be the only directory, but a larger disk normally contains logical divisions called subdirectories. Subdirectories provide a method of logically organizing the information that you keep on your disks.

The file cabinet analogy also illustrates the concept of subdirectories. Most file cabinets contain several drawers, and typically each drawer is used for a different type of information. One drawer may contain financial information, and another may contain production information. Although subdirectories do not physically divide a disk the way drawers do a file cabinet, they provide a logical structure for recording information on a specific type of data. One subdirectory can be used for production information, and another subdirectory can be used for financial information. The disk contains both types of files but has separated the information into logical directories to help you locate the information more quickly.

Within each drawer of a file cabinet, the information can be further organized. For example, in the financial drawer, the information can be separated into inventory valuation, financial statements, and forecasting information. Likewise, the financial subdirectory on your disk can be divided into inventory valuation, financial statements, and forecasting information subdirectories. Any subdirectory can be broken into further levels of subdirectories. For example, the subdirectories can be established for the different years of financial statements.

Suppose you need to find last year's income statement. To find it in the file cabinet, you must first go to the financial drawer, locate the financial statements section, and then find the section for the financial statements for last year. Finally, you look for the specific folder you want. While it may seem to require a significant effort to choose a specific location before searching for the exact information that you need, it is much quicker than going through a pile of papers in random order. Accessing computer file information works the same way. Positioning yourself in a specific subdirectory locates the required file quickly.

Directories and subdirectories store information on your file and subdirectory entries. They are similiar to a piece of paper on top of a file cabinet that describes what each drawer contains; you can look at the piece of paper and know which drawer you want to use. On a disk, the initial or root directory lists all of its subdirectories. If all your files are stored in either the production or financial subdirectory, the root directory contains only the entries for the production and financial subdirectories and not the file entries for the contents of the subdirectories.

If you examine the financial's subdirectory entries, you may find that it has no direct file entries, only the entries for the subdirectories for inventory valuation, financial statements, and forecasting information. As you look down through each level, you will see entries for the files and subdirectories at each level. Figure 7.1 shows how the information stored in one file cabinet might be converted into computer directories.

Although subdirectories present the information on the disk in an orderly fashion, your disk does not store information in the order that it appears in the subdirectories. In other words, the operating system does not mark off an area of your disk to use for each subdirectory. If it assigned storage areas to each subdirectory, you would have to preset each directory's size and would not be able to expand beyond the preset limit. When you create a new file and add it at the level of the production subdirectory, the operating system stores the new file in the next free area. It puts the name and location of the new file in the production subdirectory, although you only see the name entry. When you ask for the file again, the operating system uses the location and finds the file. Your file's physical location on the disk is only important to the operating system. The subdirectory that contains the location information for a file is important in order to tell the operating system where to look for the information. The specification of the

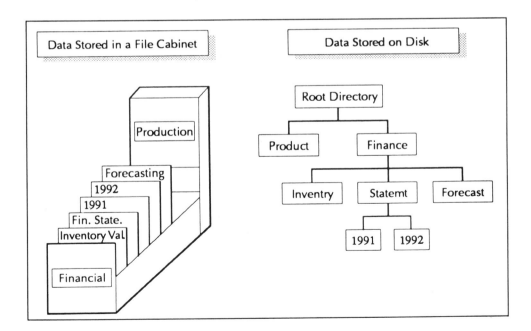

Figure 7.1 Directory Structures of File Cabinet and Computer Disk Information

correct directory for a file is known as the *path*. The path begins with the drive destination and includes each directory level off the root directory that is required to reach the correct subdirectory. For example, a file inventory valuation subdirectory that is under the financial subdirectory on drive C may have the path of C:\FINANCE\INVNTRY.

File-Naming Conventions

The operating system in your computer uses several conventions to describe files. To tell it which file you want to use, you must present your information in a manner that the operating system understands. Once you understand these file name conventions, you will want to develop a set of standards to name your files consistently. A standard naming convention helps you locate files readily and allows you to use the DOS * and ? wildcards to copy your files quickly.

RULES FOR FILE NAMES   DOS uses several rules for file names. You must follow the DOS rules for file names when you create files with Quattro Pro or any other program. If you want to store a file in a subdirectory, you must include the path. C:\QPW\FILENAME.EXT is an example of a usable file name.

The C: represents the disk drive that your operating system should refer to when looking for the file. Traditionally, drives A and B are floppy disk drives, and C is a hard disk. If you do not specify the disk, your operating system assumes it should use the one it is currently using. The \QPW\ represents the path that lists the subdirectories in which the operating system can find the file. Since the subdirectory list starts with a backslash (\), your operating system starts in the root directory. A backslash also separates the different subdirectories from one another and the last subdirectory from the file name. Each subdirectory consists of one to eight characters. If you need to use a lower-level subdirectory, you can create a path that leads the operating system to the subdirectory that contains your file. For example, if your file is in the subdirectory FINANCE located under the subdirectory QPW, which is a subdirectory of the root directory, your description of the path is \QPW\FINANCE\. If you do not specify a path, your operating system will use the current subdirectory. If you indicate the drive to use and do not specify a path, your operating system will use the current directory of the specified drive.

The FILENAME is the name of the file that you provide. It is from one to eight characters long and may include letters, numbers, and certain punctuation symbols, although no spaces. The EXT represents the file name's extension. While a file name extension is not necessary, it is frequently used to describe the format of the data in the file. A file's extension is normally provided by the program that you use to create a file. Unless you provide another, Quattro Pro provides a .WB1 extension. Later you will learn about other file extensions that you can use with the files you create in Quattro Pro.

The combination of the file name and extension must be unique within a directory. For example, you cannot have two files named SALES.WB1 on your

QPW subdirectory, since your operating system cannot distinguish the two files. Your operating system will let you have multiple files with the same name in different subdirectories; for example, you can have a SALES.WB1 file in the QUATTRO directory and a SALES.WB1 file in the QPW directory.

ESTABLISHING A WORKABLE NAMING STANDARD   A set of file-naming standards can help you remember what is in a file and can make it easier to copy a group of files. First, although DOS permits the use of several punctuation symbols, you should restrict yourself to the underscore (_). Use the underscore when you prefer to use a space, since spaces are not allowed in some operating systems and create problems with operating system commands in others. Second, use a name for your file that describes the information stored in it to help you remember what is in the different files. Also, use similar names for related files. For example, if you have two files that contain production information, give them similar names, like PROD_1 and PROD_2. Similar names help organize the information and make it easier to execute DOS commands on the files as a group. Also, when you have many files containing related information, create a subdirectory and move the files to the new subdirectory.

SAVING QUATTRO PRO NOTEBOOKS

Quattro Pro provides several options for saving your spreadsheet notebooks. You can password protect your notebook or change the directory where Quattro Pro saves your file. You can change the format that Quattro Pro uses to save your file, save only a portion of your file, or make a backup copy.

The Basic Save Operation

Until you save a copy of your notebook on disk, you are at risk of losing your time invested in building the model. A sudden loss of power erases the memory of your machine. When you reload Quattro Pro and Windows, you will have to start from the beginning and rebuild the model. But, if the model is available on your disk, you can retrieve it and continue. Even if you do not think that you will need a model, you should save it later, because you may find a mistake in spelling or in one of the numbers or formulas and need to reprint the model and also because a copy of the model on disk may serve as the basis for another model.

To save your file, follow these steps:

1. Select <u>S</u>ave from the <u>F</u>ile menu, opening the Save File dialog box shown in Figure 7.2.

2. Type the name you want to use for the file. You can provide up to eight characters for a file name consisting of letters, numbers, and the special

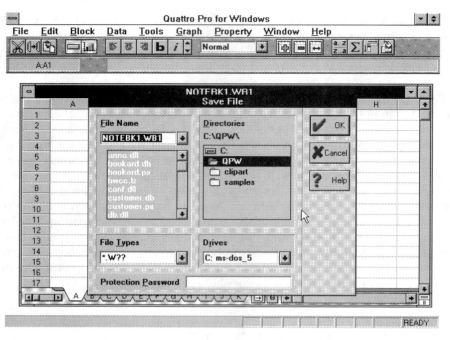

Figure 7.2   Save File Dialog Box

symbols that DOS accepts. You do not need to add an extension, since Quattro Pro automatically adds .WB1.

3. Select OK. Assuming you do not already have a file with that name in the selected directory, Quattro Pro saves your file.

Another option for saving the file is the Save As command in the File menu. Using this command to save a spreadsheet the first time is identical to using the Save command. The difference between the two commands occurs when you save a notebook you have already saved and named before. The Save As command in the File menu displays the same Save File dialog box every time you use the command. This dialog box lets you change the name, location, or format of the file you are saving. The Save command in the File menu only displays the Save File dialog box the first time you save a notebook. On subsequent saves, the Save command in the File menu saves the file without further prompting. However, even if you are saving the notebook to the same name, the Save As command in the File menu asks you whether you want to cancel your command, replace the existing file with the current spreadsheet, or backup the file before saving.

If Quattro Pro is unable to save your file, it displays an error message. Normally, this error is caused by a situation that is easily remedied, such as an open disk drive, a missing disk, an unformatted disk, or a full disk. If Quattro Pro is unable to save your notebook because the disk is unformatted, use Window's File Manager to format the disk, using the Format Disk command in the Disk menu. If

Quattro Pro is unable to save your notebook because the disk is full, replace the disk with another disk that has more room. You can also redirect Quattro Pro to save the file to another drive by saving the file again after selecting a new drive from the Drives drop-down list box. A third alternative is to remove files from the current diskette using Windows' File Manager. Once the problem is remedied, save your spreadsheet again.

Using Passwords

When you store information in a file cabinet, you can lock it to prevent unauthorized access. When you lock the cabinet, you then need the key the next time you need to look at that data. Quattro Pro provides passwords to offer the same type of protection for your spreadsheet notebooks. Just as you need a key to unlock the file cabinet, you need to use the password key to access password-protected Quattro Pro files. To save a spreadsheet with a password, type the password in the Protection Password text box. You can do this when you save a file for the first time with the Save command in the File menu or, when you subsequently save it, using the Save As command in the File menu. In the Protection Password text box, you can type a password up to 15 characters. For each character you type, Quattro Pro displays a # as shown in Figure 7.3. After you select OK, Quattro Pro asks you to verify the password by typing it and selecting OK again. If the two passwords are not identical, Quattro Pro displays an error message and returns to the Save File dialog box.

When you try to open a password-protected file, Quattro Pro asks for the password. If you do not enter the correct password, Quattro Pro does not open the file. Since Quattro Pro encrypts password-protected files, you cannot use the file in either Quattro Pro or any other program if you forget your password. Quattro Pro can retrieve 1-2-3 encrypted files when supplied with the correct password, although 1-2-3 cannot do the same with an encrypted Quattro Pro file. To save and

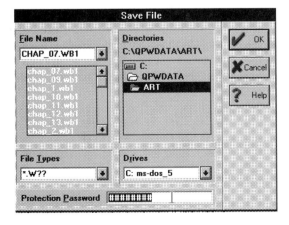

Figure 7.3   Entering a Password

encrypt a file to be used in 1-2-3, when you encrypt, it make sure to use the .WK1 extension.

To remove the password protection from your notebook, select Save <u>A</u>s from the <u>F</u>ile menu again. Remove the # characters from the Protection <u>P</u>assword text box. Then select OK to save the file, and <u>R</u>eplace to replace the file with a password with the file without a password. To change the password, simply enter the new password into the Protection <u>P</u>assword text box instead of deleting the old one. Quattro Pro will ask you to verify the new password just as it did the original password when you select OK to save the file.

Saving to a Different Directory

When you select Save <u>A</u>s in the <u>F</u>ile menu Quattro Pro suggests saving a spreadsheet notebook under its existing file name if it has been saved before. If you have not saved your spreadsheet notebook previously, Quattro Pro assumes that you want to save your file in the current directory. The current directory is either the subdirectory that Quattro Pro is in or the one specified by the <u>D</u>irectory text box for the Startup property in the Application dialog box invoked by selecting <u>A</u>pplication from the <u>P</u>roperty menu. When you first start Quattro Pro and no directory is set as an application property, Quattro Pro will use any directory set by the Working Directory in the Program Item Properties dialog box of the icon you use to start Quattro Pro for Windows.

You can change the location where your files are saved to another drive and directory. To save a notebook to a different directory, select a new drive or directory from the D<u>r</u>ives and <u>D</u>irectories list boxes in the Save File dialog box. For example, to save the current notebook as LOANS.WB1 in the FINANCE subdirectory on drive C, check that C: is selected in the D<u>r</u>ives drop-down list box. Then select Finance in the <u>D</u>irectories list box, and type **LOANS** into the <u>F</u>ile Name text box. When you select OK, this file is saved to this new location. In the <u>D</u>irectories list box, you can select a parent directory by double-clicking the directory name you want to switch to. The directory listing is hierarchical, so you may need to switch to a higher level directory to get to the one you want. For example, using the disk structure shown on the right in Figure 7.1, if the current directory is PRODUCT and you need to switch to FINANCE, you must first select C: before you will see FINANCE in the <u>D</u>irectories list box. The currently selected directory appears above the <u>D</u>irectories list box. The CAPITALIZED directory names in the list box show the current path. The directory names in lowercase indicate the directories within the currently selected directory.

When you change the directory where you are saving a file, you are also changing the current directory. When you change the drive and directory as you save a file, you are setting where subsequent files are saved as well. You can always change the location as you save your files.

You can also change the directory where a file is saved for that file only. For example, if you want to copy a single file to drive A so that you will have the file

---

▼ TIP: Saving Multipage Notebooks

When you save a notebook with any extension other than .WB1, or .WK3, only the first page is saved. If you want to save pages other than the first to a file format other than Quattro Pro for Windows or 1-2-3 Release 3.*x*, use the Extract command in the Tools menu described later in the chapter.

---

backed up, you can type **A:** as part of the file name in the File Name text box. Changing the directory this way only affects the single file you are saving.

Saving Data in Another Format

Many spreadsheet applications save their data in different formats. You can use Quattro Pro for Windows to open and save files in the different formats used by different applications. Quattro Pro changes the format it uses to save your notebook according to the file name extension that you enter as part of the file name in the Save File dialog box. Using an extension other than .WB1 changes the format in which the data is saved. To change the format for saving your data, select Save As from the File menu. Either enter the appropriate file extension after the file name in the File Name text box, or select a format from the File Types drop-down list box. For example, to translate your Quattro Pro for Windows notebook called TEMPLATE to a 1-2-3 spreadsheet, change the file extension to .WK1 (for 1-2-3 Releases 2.0 through 2.4). The file name extensions supported by Quattro Pro for Windows are listed in Table 7.1.

When you save your Quattro Pro notebook in another format, some information may be lost because that format does not support all of Quattro Pro for Windows features. For example, when you save your Quattro Pro notebook in another format that does not support multiple pages, only the contents of the first page are saved. If there are four pages with data A through D, in the notebook called TEMPLATE.WB1, when you save it into the 1-2-3 format as TEMPLATE.WK1, only page A is saved. The rest of the pages, B through D, are lost because they cannot be saved in the 1-2-3 format. 1-2-3 also cannot support some graph information, and converts absolute addresses in link formulas into relative addresses.

If you want to save the new spreadsheet notebooks you create in a different format, you may want to change the default extension. You can change the default extension used to save your notebooks by inspecting the application properties, selecting the Startup property, and entering the extension to use in the File Extension text box. This sets the file extension and the format that all new files you create with Quattro Pro will have unless you select a different one. While the current setting is .WB1 for Quattro Pro for Windows format, you can type another extension that is in Table 7.1 to save your new files in a different format.

Table 7.1 File Name Extensions for Saving and Opening Files

.WB1	Saves and opens Quattro Pro for Windows spreadsheets. This is normally the default setting. To save files in this format, you do not have to specify an extension.
.WQ1	Saves and opens Quattro Pro for DOS notebooks.
.WKQ	Saves and opens Quattro Pro spreadsheets.
.WKS	Saves and opens 1-2-3 Release 1A spreadsheets.
.WK1	Saves and opens 1-2-3 Release 2.0, 2.2, 2.3, and 2.4 spreadsheets.
.WK3	Saves and opens 1-2-3 Release 3.0 and 3.1 spreadsheets.
.WKE	Saves and opens 1-2-3 Educational spreadsheets.
.WRK	Saves and opens Symphony data files.
.WR1	Saves and opens Symphony version 2.0 spreadsheets.
.WKP	Saves and opens Surpass data files.
.XLS	Saves and opens Excel spreadsheets.
.DB	Saves and opens Paradox data files.
.DBF	Saves dBASE III data files and opens dBASE II, dBASE III, or dBASE IV data files.
.DB2	Saves and opens dBASE II files.
.DIF	Saves and opens Visicalc data files.
.RXD	Saves and opens Reflex data files.
.R2D	Saves and opens Reflex 2 data files.
.SLK	Saves and opens Multiplan data files.

EXPORTING QUATTRO PRO DATA TO dBASE OR PARADOX   Quattro Pro has extra prompts when you save the data in a dBASE or Paradox format. These formats let you save the data in the format of the most popular database management applications. Although exporting your Quattro Pro spreadsheet to dBASE is as simple as using a .DB2, or a .DBF file extension, or .DB for Paradox, Quattro Pro provides you with several options that are particular to a database. When Quattro Pro translates a notebook to a database file, Quattro Pro normally uses the first row of the first page as the field names for the database. For example, in the spreadsheet shown in Figure 7.4, Quattro Pro uses Warehouse, Item_Code, and other headings in the first row as field names (Quattro Pro converts spaces in the

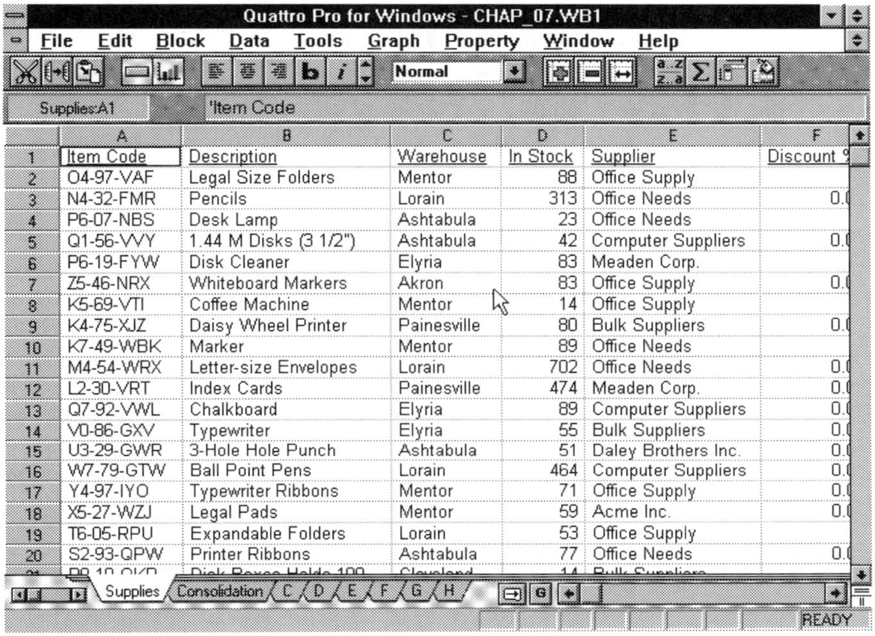

	A	B	C	D	E	F
1	Item Code	Description	Warehouse	In Stock	Supplier	Discount
2	O4-97-VAF	Legal Size Folders	Mentor	88	Office Supply	
3	N4-32-FMR	Pencils	Lorain	313	Office Needs	0.
4	P6-07-NBS	Desk Lamp	Ashtabula	23	Office Needs	
5	Q1-56-VVY	1.44 M Disks (3 1/2")	Ashtabula	42	Computer Suppliers	0.
6	P6-19-FYW	Disk Cleaner	Elyria	83	Meaden Corp.	
7	Z5-46-NRX	Whiteboard Markers	Akron	83	Office Supply	0.
8	K5-69-VTI	Coffee Machine	Mentor	14	Office Supply	
9	K4-75-XJZ	Daisy Wheel Printer	Painesville	80	Bulk Suppliers	0.
10	K7-49-WBK	Marker	Mentor	89	Office Needs	
11	M4-54-WRX	Letter-size Envelopes	Lorain	702	Office Needs	0.
12	L2-30-VRT	Index Cards	Painesville	474	Meaden Corp.	0.
13	Q7-92-VWL	Chalkboard	Elyria	89	Computer Suppliers	0.
14	V0-86-GXV	Typewriter	Elyria	55	Bulk Suppliers	0.
15	U3-29-GWR	3-Hole Hole Punch	Ashtabula	51	Daley Brothers Inc.	0.
16	W7-79-GTW	Ball Point Pens	Lorain	464	Computer Suppliers	0.
17	Y4-97-IYO	Typewriter Ribbons	Mentor	71	Office Supply	0.
18	X5-27-WZJ	Legal Pads	Mentor	59	Acme Inc.	0.
19	T6-05-RPU	Expandable Folders	Lorain	53	Office Supply	
20	S2-93-QPW	Printer Ribbons	Ashtabula	77	Office Needs	0.

Figure 7.4 Notebook Set Up as a Database

field name to underscores). When the first row contains a blank cell, a date, numbers, or a label that starts with a number, Quattro Pro uses the letter representing the column in place of the field names. Every row below the first row is a record in the database with each column representing a different field. Quattro Pro lets you change the field name and its characteristics before it translates it into a file. The database-type information in Figure 7.4 illustrates the process of converting your spreadsheet to a dBASE database and the different options available. For other database packages such as Paradox and Reflex, the steps are similar but the rules for field definitions follow the conventions of the particular database package. To convert this file to dBASE III or IV, follow these steps:

1. Select Save As from the File menu.
2. Type or select the file name. You can often change the name by deleting the WB1 in the File Name text box and typing **DBF** in its place.
3. Select OK to accept your file name. Quattro Pro then displays dBASE File Structure dialog box like the one shown in Figure 7.5.

   The dBASE File Structure dialog box shows the database structure as Quattro Pro plans to save it. You can select Write to immediately save the file or Cancel to abort the saving process. Usually you will want to review the field structure before you save it. As you select the different field names in

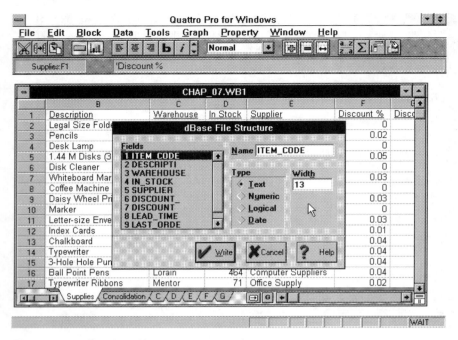

Figure 7.5   dBASE File Structure Dialog Box

the Fields list box, the dialog box changes on the right to show each field's current name, field type, and width, if applicable. As you can see in the figure, Quattro Pro uses the text from the first line of the data for the field names. For each column, Quattro Pro uses the first 10 characters of the first row and replaces any spaces with underscores (_). Quattro Pro determines the data type by looking at the information in the second row of the data. Quattro Pro uses the column width for each column as the field width.

4. Modify the structure to meet your needs. To change a field's characteristics, select the field from the Fields list box. When you change a field's characteristics, the rules of that database package apply. For example, dBASE field names can have up to 10 characters, may not start with a number, and must be unique. You can change the name by entering a new name in the Name text box. Select a new field type from one of the radio buttons below Type. You have a choice of Text, Numeric, Logical, and Date for the types of fields. (Quattro Pro does not save dBASE memo fields, which is also why .DBF is the extension for both dBASE III and dBASE IV databases, since only the format of their memo fields is different.) For date fields, Quattro Pro converts the dates in the column into the database's date format, regardless of how the dates appear in the notebook. When you make a column a logical field, Quattro Pro converts cells containing a 1 to T and cells containing a 0 to F. If you select a type of Text or Numeric, you need to enter a column

▼ TIP: Make sure that the first row contains valid entries for field names in a database.

If you are saving a file in a database format, make sure all of the field names are valid for the database package. Since Quattro Pro will pick up the field names for you if they are in a correct format, you will save yourself time by having the field names in acceptable format before you save the file.

width in the Width text box. For numbers, you can enter the number of digits to have after the decimal point in the Decimal pt. text box.

In this example, the sixth field was renamed to DSCNT_PCNT. IN_STOCK, DSCNT_PCNT, DISCOUNT, and LEAD_TIME have their widths modified to 5 with 0 decimals, 4 with 2 decimals, 4 with 0 decimals, and 2 with 0 decimals, respectively. Also, the DISCOUNT_A field is removed from the database by moving to this field and pressing the DEL key. To restore a field, press the DEL key again, which removes the asterisk that indicates which columns are omitted.

5. Select Write. Quattro Pro translates and stores your spreadsheet as a dBASE III or IV file. The file, when loaded into dBASE, looks like Figure 7.6.

This example shows how to convert a spreadsheet to a dBASE III or IV file; however, the process of converting the file to another database format is the same, except the extension in step 2 is different. When you convert a file to the dBASE II format, you have to rename it later to a .DBF extension. dBASE II, dBASE III, and dBASE IV use the same file extension.

Saving Part of a File

At times you may want to create subsidiary files with only part of the information in your current file, using the Extract command in the Tools menu. You can use this command when you want to save data in a format that does not support multiple pages, so that you can extract information from a selected page in your notebook. This command also allows you to create subsidiary notebooks, such as a salary notebook extracted from a notebook containing personnel information. Use this command to divide a large notebook into two. Extracting file data is useful when you want to create notebooks with selected information. You can create such notebooks to accompany reports, or to give to people who do not need the extra information.

When you extract data, you are creating a new file, just as if you were saving a separate notebook for the first time. You need to assign a file name, a directory,

```
┌─────────────────────── dBASE IV version 1.5 ────────────────── ▾│▴│
│ Records   Organize   Fields   Go To    Exit                       │
│ ITEM_CODE    │DESCRIPTI        │WAREHOUSE   │IN_STOCK│SUPPLIER       │
├──────────────┴─────────────────┴────────────┴────────┴───────────────┤
│ 04-97-UAP    Legal Size Folders    Mentor          88 Office Supply    │
│ N4-32-FMR    Pencils               Lorain         313 Office Needs     │
│ P6-07-NBS    Desk Lamp             Ashtabula       23 Office Needs     │
│ Q1-56-UUY    1.44 M Disks (3 1/2")  Ashtabula       42 Computer Supplier│
│ P6-19-FYW    Disk Cleaner          Elyria          83 Meaden Corp.     │
│ Z5-46-NRX    Whiteboard Markers    Akron           83 Office Supply    │
│ R5-69-UTI    Coffee Machine        Mentor          14 Office Supply    │
│ K4-75-XJZ    Daisy Wheel Printer   Painesville     80 Bulk Suppliers   │
│ K7-49-WBK    Marker                Mentor          89 Office Needs     │
│ M4-54-WRX    Letter-size Envelopes  Lorain         702 Office Needs     │
│ L2-30-URT    Index Cards           Painesville    474 Meaden Corp.     │
│ Q7-92-UWL    Chalkboard            Elyria          89 Computer Supplier │
│ U0-86-GXV    Typewriter            Elyria          55 Bulk Suppliers   │
│ U3-29-GWR    3-Hole Hole Punch     Ashtabula       51 Daley Brothers In │
│ W7-79-GTW    Ball Point Pens       Lorain         464 Computer Supplier │
│ Y4-97-IYO    Typewriter Ribbons    Mentor          71 Office Supply    │
│ X5-27-WZJ    Legal Pads            Mentor          59 Acme Inc.        │
├──────────────────────────────────────────────────────────────────────┤
│Browse  ║C:\SUPPLIES            ║Rec 1/58     ║File ║        ║   Num     │
└──────────────────────────────────────────────────────────────────────┘
```

14	U0-86-GXV	Typewriter	Elyria	55	Bulk Suppliers	0.
15	U3-29-GWR	3-Hole Hole Punch	Ashtabula	51	Daley Brothers Inc.	0.
16	W7-79-GTW	Ball Point Pens	Lorain	464	Computer Suppliers	0.
17	Y4-97-IYO	Typewriter Ribbons	Mentor	71	Office Supply	0.
18	X5-27-WZJ	Legal Pads	Mentor	59	Acme Inc.	0.
19	T6-05-RPU	Expandable Folders	Lorain	53	Office Supply	0.
20	S2-93-QPW	Printer Ribbons	Ashtabula	77	Office Needs	0.

Figure 7.6   Database Saved in a dBASE Format

and a file type. You can also assign a password to the new file to ensure security. You can also choose whether you are extracting formulas (which may refer to cells that are not being extracted, yielding errors) or values. When you extract values, each cell that contains a formula is extracted into the new file as a value, with the new value being the same as the current result of the formula. Finally, you need to determine the cells to extract in order to create the new file. You select blocks of data to be extracted.

To extract data from the current notebook to create a new file, select the Extract command from the Tools menu. This opens the File Extract dialog box, shown in Figure 7.7. Type a name for the new file in the File Name text box. You can change the location of the extracted file by making selections in the Directories list box and the Drives drop-down list box. If you do not want to save the extracted data in a Quattro Pro for Windows notebook format, select another format using the File Types drop-down list box or by typing the appropriate extension in the File Name text box. If you want to assign a password to the file, type the password into the Password Protection text box. In the Option section, you can choose to extract formulas as formulas or as values by selecting either the Formulas or Values radio button. In the Block(s) text box, you enter the blocks of data that you want to extract. Separate the addresses of different blocks of data with commas. You may prefer to select the block before you select the command; Quattro Pro will enter the selected block in the text box. Then select OK or press ENTER. If you elected to

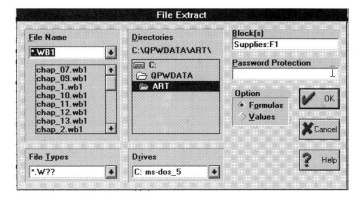

Figure 7.7 File Extract Dialog Box

enter a password, you are prompted to confirm the password before the file is saved.

As an example, suppose you extract the blocks A3..A19, F3..F19 in Figure 7.8. When you extract this noncontiguous block, the resulting notebook file will contain entries in columns A and F. The entries are placed in rows 1 through 17, since you did not extract row 1. If you extract the block as values, the entries in column F contain the values you see in Figure 7.8. For example, F2 in the extracted file

	A	B	C	D	E	F	G
1		1st	2nd	3rd	4th	Year End	
2		Quarter	Quarter	Quarter	Quarter	Totals	
3	Product 1						
4	Number of Units Sold	4,210	4,125	4,275	4,464	17,074	
5	Average Cost Per Unit	3	3	3	3	3	
6	Cost of Units Sold	13,430	12,416	12,697	14,240	52,783	
7	Price of Units Sold	17,514	15,469	16,117	18,302	67,402	
8							
9	Product 2						
10	Number of Units Sold	5,732	6,120	6,555	5,750	24,157	
11	Average Cost Per Unit	6	6	6	6	6	
12	Cost of Units Sold	35,023	39,719	40,510	33,350	148,602	
13	Price of Units Sold	39,322	47,002	53,685	46,978	186,987	
14							
15	Total for All Products						
16	Number of Units Sold	9,942	10,245	10,830	10,214	41,231	
17	Average Cost Per Unit	5	5	5	5	5	
18	Cost of Units Sold	48,452	52,135	53,207	47,590	201,384	
19	Price of Units Sold	56,835	62,470	69,802	65,280	254,387	
20							

Figure 7.8 Data to Extract into a New File

contains the value 17074. This may be exactly what you want in order to combine this notebook with other data to summarize the production. Extracting the values is just like copying the entries to the Clipboard and then using Paste Special in the Edit menu in a new notebook and selecting the Values only radio button to copy the formula values instead of the formulas. On the other hand, if you extract the block as formulas, the new notebook contains the formulas instead of the values. Extracting the formulas is just like copying the entries to a new notebook with the Clipboard using Copy and Paste. The resulting notebook will contain the formulas from the old notebook, adjusted for copying the extracted block to the first row of the notebook. For example, F2 in the extracted file would contain @SUM(B2..E2) rather than @SUM(B4..E4) or 17074. Since you did not copy the values the formula uses, the formula now equals 0. This may be exactly what you want, though, when you are setting up a notebook for 1993 production.

The extracted file has many of the same properties as the original file. The extract file has all the original file's block names, even though the block names are meaningless if they refer to cells that are not part of the extracted file. The extracted file has the original page and notebook properties for features such as numeric formats, column widths, and print settings.

Saving Files in Text Format

When you send data from Quattro Pro to another package, you are *exporting* data. Quattro Pro provides automatic translation features with the Save and Save As commands in the File menu for a number of packages such as 1-2-3, Reflex, Paradox, and dBASE. You can also use Windows' Clipboard to transfer data from Quattro Pro to other applications. You might not be able to use the Clipboard if the application for which you need the data is not a Windows application or is on another computer. When you need to send data to a package for which Quattro Pro does not provide automatic translation, or which you cannot use the Clipboard to copy into, you can capture the data in a text file.

One way to save a file in a text file format is to copy it from Quattro Pro into the Notepad accessory. The Notepad can create text files. To do this, select the data from the notebook and copy it to the Clipboard. Next, switch to the Notepad and use the Paste command in the Edit menu to put the data into the Notepad. When you save the Notepad file with the copied Quattro Pro data, you have just saved

---

▼ TIP: Extracting Floating Objects

When you extract a block of cells, you also extract any floating objects that appear over those cells. These include macro buttons, floating graphs, and OLE objects. These topics are discussed later in this book and in Chapters 10 and 13.

that data in a text file. Another method is to print the notebook data to a file using the Generic/Text Only printer selection.

RETRIEVING DATA

Opening a file is as simple as telling Quattro Pro what file you want to work with. Quattro Pro's support for multiple file formats makes it easy to work with data in many file formats. To open a file, select Open from the File menu. Quattro Pro displays the Open File dialog box. Like other commands that select files, it has the same File Name text box, Directories list box, File Types drop-down list box, and Drives drop-down list box that you used for saving a file. The File Name list box displays the files in the current directory with file extensions that begin with a W in alphabetical order, including the file extensions, so that you can tell which are saved in a Quattro Pro format. Other spreadsheet files with similar extensions, such as 1-2-3, are also displayed.

To select a file to open, select it in the File Name list box and select OK, or double-click on the file name with your mouse. You can also type the file name in the File Name text box. If the file that you want to open is not in the current directory, select the directory icons in the Directories list box until the proper one is opened. If you want to look for files other than spreadsheet files, such as dBASE or Paradox files, change the file extension in the File Name text box, or select a new file extension from the File Types drop-down list box.

If you want to reopen a file that you opened and closed recently, there is a shortcut available to you. In the File name text box in the Open File dialog box, press the DOWN ARROW. A box listing the last ten files, called a history list, opened appears under the text box as you can see in Figure 7.9. You can select the file from that list and reopen it quickly.

If Quattro Pro cannot open the file, it displays an error message. A disk drive that is not ready, a file being used by another application, or a file not on the specified drive can cause the error. An error also occurs when a file is renamed using an extension that is inappropriate for the data format the file contains.

Once Quattro Pro has found the file, it starts loading the file into memory. If the file is password protected, you will have to supply the correct password when Quattro Pro prompts for it. If the file is in a format that Quattro Pro can translate

---

▼ TIP: Spelling counts!

If you enter a file name and Quattro Pro cannot find it, check the spelling of the file name and entries that you have specified. Better yet, use the Directories list box and the File Name list box to select the file name rather than entering it.

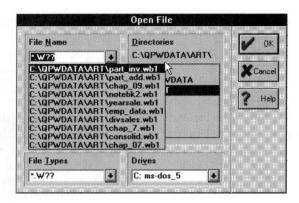

Figure 7.9 A Shortcut to Opening Files

to a Quattro Pro notebook, Quattro Pro will automatically translate the data when you retrieve the file.

Retrieving Data in a Different Format

Quattro Pro makes it easy to work with data in a variety of formats since it does not require a separate translation process. To open a file in a supported format, open it as you would a Quattro Pro file; you can select the file from the File Name list box or you can type the file name in the text box. You may want to type *.* in the File Name text box to view files with all extensions in the list box. Quattro Pro automatically translates the file as it opens it. For example, to use a 1-2-3 Release 2 file called SALES.WK1, enter or select the file name from the file list box. Quattro Pro automatically translates the file to Quattro Pro as it loads the spreadsheet. The list of file name extensions in Table 7.1 provides a summary of the various file types supported.

When you open a file, the File Name list box lists only files with extensions that start with W. To list other types of files in the File Name list box, type an asterisk (*), a period, the desired file extension, and then select OK. For example, to list all the dBASE files on your current directory, type **.DBF** and select OK.

If you are retrieving a 1-2-3 Release 2.2, 2.3, or 2.4 file, Quattro Pro converts file links (described later) into its own format. Addresses in link formulas are absolute in Quattro Pro even if they are mixed or relative in 1-2-3. If there is any spreadsheet formatting stored in an Allways, Impress, or WYSIWYG format file, Quattro Pro will prompt you if you want to load the formats with the spreadsheet. Most formatting is included although some features that do not have an equivalent in Quattro Pro are not. This includes graphs inserted into a spreadsheet that are actually stored in another file. Graphs inserted in the spreadsheet that are part of the spreadsheet file, as you will learn about in Chapter 9, are brought into the spreadsheet in Quattro Pro.

If you are retrieving a 1-2-3 file that uses the Lotus International Character Set (LICS) or the Lotus Multibyte Character Set (LMBCS) to create foreign and graphics characters, you may want to select the LIC<u>S</u> check box that appears as part of the International property when you inspect the application's properties. When this check box is selected, Quattro Pro uses LICS or LMBCS to convert the international characters between the 1-2-3 file and Quattro Pro. When this check box is not selected, the foreign and graphics characters will not appear correctly in Quattro Pro. This command is not needed if the 1-2-3 files are created with the ASCII No-LICS driver.

Retrieving a Notebook in Place of the Current One

You can use the <u>O</u>pen command in the <u>F</u>ile menu to open a file in addition to the ones already opened, or you can use the <u>R</u>etrieve command in the <u>F</u>ile menu to open a notebook in place of one already open. Retrieving a file is just like opening a file except that the file you select replaces the notebook in the active notebook window. Since any version of the notebook you have saved is still on disk, retrieving a file does not permanently remove all copies of the previously active notebook. To retrieve a notebook, select <u>R</u>etrieve in the <u>F</u>ile menu. If the active notebook has unsaved changes, Quattro Pro prompts if you want to lose your changes. You can select <u>Y</u>es to lose any unsaved changes and continue with the command or you can select <u>N</u>o to cancel the command. Next, select the notebook you want to open, just as if you had selected <u>O</u>pen in the <u>F</u>ile menu. The previous notebook is removed from the Quattro Pro application window to be replaced by the notebook you have selected.

Automatically Retrieving a File

Quattro Pro provides a feature that can automatically open the same notebook for you at the beginning of every Quattro Pro session. To do this, inspect the application properties by right-clicking the Quattro Pro title bar or by selecting <u>A</u>pplication from the <u>P</u>roperty menu. Select the Startup property and then type the name of the notebook file you want to automatically open in the <u>A</u>utoload File text box. By default it is QUATTRO.WB1, but you can enter another file or notebook name. Each time that you start Quattro Pro, Quattro Pro loads this file for you, assuming it is in the startup directory or you have provided directory information with the file name.

Another way to start Quattro Pro with a file already open in it is with the <u>R</u>un command in the <u>F</u>ile menu of the Program Manager. When you type the command for starting Quattro Pro (usually C:\QPW\QPW.EXE), add a space, and the full path and file name of the file that you want to open.

A third way to open Quattro Pro with a file already open in the application window is to create a program item for a notebook. You can do this two ways. You can enter the command to start Quattro Pro (usually C:\QPW\QPW.EXE), a space, and the full path and file name of the file that you want to open in the Command Line text box for the program item's properties. Another method is to associate the .WB1 extension with C:\QPW\QPW.EXE. To do this, start the File Manager application, select any .WB1 file in the window, and select the Associate command in the File menu. In the Associate dialog box, type **C:\QPW\QPW.EXE** in the Associate With text box. When you select OK, the icon that .WB1 files use in the File Manager changes because now Windows recognizes that files with a .WB1 extension belong to Quattro Pro. At this point, you can drag the .WB1 file to a group window in the Program Manager to add the notebook file to a group, or you can select a .WB1 file in the Command Line text box. You do not need the C:\QPW\QPW.EXE, since Windows automatically knows to use it.

CHANGING DIRECTORIES

When Quattro Pro saves and retrieves files, it uses the current disk drive and directory. This is the last drive and directory you used to open or save a file. When you start Quattro Pro, it uses the directory in the Directory text box for the Startup application property, or, if a directory is not provided, the working directory of the program item you used to start Quattro Pro for Windows. You are not restricted to that directory and can use several methods to change the directory, depending on whether you want the change to affect an individual file, the current session, or all future sessions.

Changing the Directory for a Single File

To change the directory for a single file, you will not want to make a permanent change to Quattro Pro's directory settings. You can change the directory for Quattro Pro's file commands (like Open and Save) by typing the directory

---

▼ TIP: Add your favorite Quattro Pro notebooks to a Program Manager group window.

After you associate .WB1 files with Quattro Pro for Windows, you may want to put your most frequently used notebooks into a group window. Then you can start Quattro Pro and the notebook you want to use simply by selecting the program item in the group window. You can even use the File Manager to add a notebook to a group window by dragging the file's icon from the File Manager window to the group window or group icon in the Program Manager to which you want the notebook added.

where you want a file opened or saved with the file name in the File Name text box.

Changing the Directory for the Current Session

When you are planning to use files in another directory for your current Quattro Pro session, you can change the directory for the entire session by using the Directories list box and the Drives drop-down list box to change the location of files listed in the Open File or Save File dialog boxes. For example, if you are planning to work with a group of Lotus 1-2-3 Release 2 files in your 123 subdirectory, changing the directory to C:\123 eliminates the extra typing required for each file operation. You will double-click the C: icon in the Directories list box and then double-click the 123 folder in the Directories list box. After you select the file to open or save, Quattro Pro uses the new directory for all subsequent file operations in the current session.

Making a Permanent Change to the Directory

Quattro Pro allows you to make a permanent change to the directory where it looks for files for each session. If you have a partitioned hard disk with a drive C and a drive D, you may want to use drive C for your programs and drive D for your data. You may also want to change the directory if you prefer to store your data on a floppy disk, reserving the hard disk space for additional programs.

To change the directory for your data permanently, inspect the application properties. Select the Startup property and enter the preferred directory in the Directory text box. Select the OK button to close the Application dialog box. Quattro Pro uses this directory setting until you select another drive or directory with a file command. The initial directory for each Quattro Pro session does not change until you change the entry in the Directory text box of the Startup application property.

USING MULTIPLE NOTEBOOKS

So far, the applications you have created in Quattro Pro have used only one notebook. Since a notebook has 256 pages, one notebook is usually enough. However, you may want to work with more than one notebook at a time. You can have multiple notebooks open in the Quattro Pro application window at any one time. You can move between these notebook windows as easily as you move between the pages of a single notebook. You can also share the data in one notebook with other notebooks.

The advantage to having multiple windows open is so that you can easily transfer data between notebooks. You can use the Clipboard commands from the Edit menu to move the data between the two notebooks the same way that you would copy information from one notebook page to another. Also, Quattro Pro has several features, discussed in the following sections, which you can use to access information stored in one notebook for use in another. Having both notebooks open makes it easier to specify the data you want. Not only can you see the data, so that you are sure of the addresses, but you can also use the point method to specify the data, and let Quattro Pro add the file names and other information it needs to know when it is accessing another file for information.

Opening Multiple Notebooks

Opening a second or third notebook is as simple as opening the first notebook. You can open existing notebooks or a new notebook. To open an existing notebook, simply select Open from the File menu and select the notebook that you want to open, as described earlier in this chapter. Select the file name from the File Name list box, or enter the name in the File Name text box, switching directories in the Directories list box as needed. You can select a different drive in the Drives drop-down list box. If the notebook was saved with a password, you are prompted for the password after you select OK in the File Open dialog box.

If you prefer to open a new notebook rather than a previously saved notebook, simply select New from the File menu instead. Each new notebook that you open is given the name NOTEBK#.WB1, with # representing the next unused number. Use this command when you want a notebook for new data that you want to enter. Figure 7.10 shows a new notebook window added as well as two other notebook windows that contain data you have already saved.

Once you have several notebooks open, you will want to save your changes. Rather than switching to each one and saving it individually, you can use the Save All command in the File menu. This command goes through each open notebook and performs the Save command in the File menu on each one. If a notebook has not been saved, you have the opportunity to name it.

Displaying Notebook Windows

When you open a second notebook, the notebook window appears in the application window. It may look as if your first notebook window disappeared, and was replaced with the one you just opened, but this is not the case. The new notebook's window is the same size as the notebook you have been working with, and may cover it completely. Quattro Pro has several options for presenting the information in a notebook. Most of these options were introduced in Chapter 4, "Rearranging Cell Entries." These window presentation commands and features

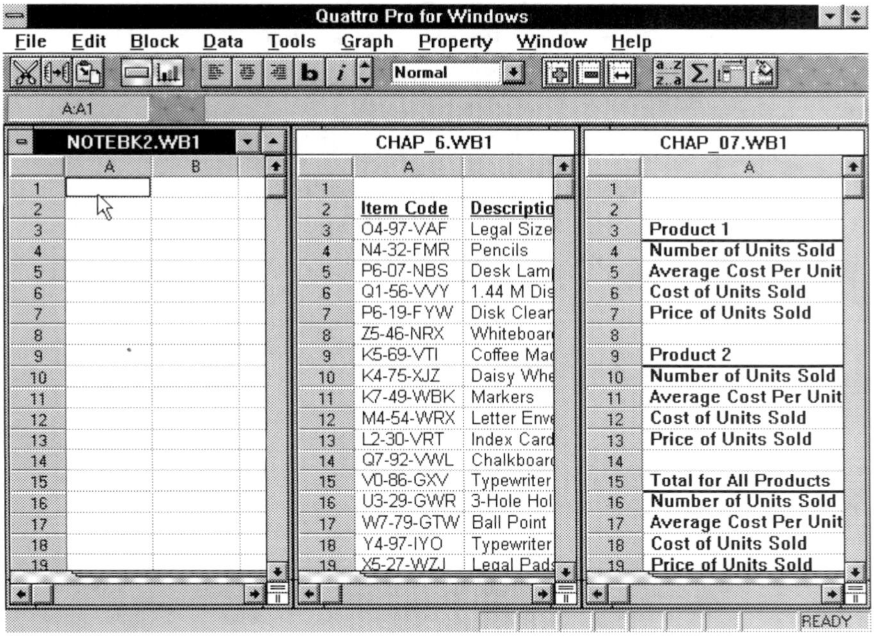

Figure 7.10 Multiple Views of a Single Notebook

are especially useful when you are working with multiple windows. The options include cascading windows, tiling windows, opening a second window to the same notebook, and panes. Of course, you also have the window moving and sizing techniques shared by all Windows windows. Moving and sizing windows are described in Appendix B.

As described in Chapter 4, you can size and arrange multiple notebook windows so that you can see all of them at once. By selecting Cascade from the Window menu, you arrange all the open notebook windows so that they are all the same size and arranged one on top of the other starting in the upper left corner, with the title bar of each document window visible. If you select Tile from the Window menu, Quattro Pro sizes and arranges the notebook windows like tiles on the floor, so that you can see a smaller part of each window. If you have minimized several notebooks as icons, you may want to use the Arrange Icons command in the Window menu to neatly place each icon in the bottom of the application window.

At times, you may find it necessary to open multiple windows of a single notebook. To open a second window on the same notebook, you can move to the window containing that notebook and select New View from the Window menu. When you have more than one window looking at the same notebook, each window into that notebook is distinguished by its title bar. If the first notebook window's title bar reads BUDGETS.WB1, after you open a second window onto

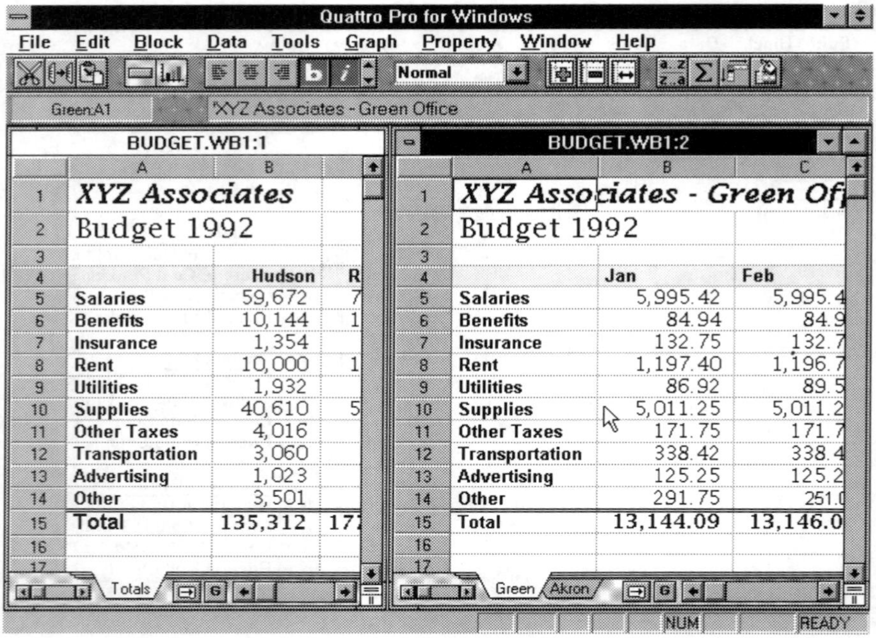

Figure 7.11   Panes Show Different Parts of a Single Notebook

that notebook, the original window reads BUDGETS.WB1:1 and the new window's title bar reads BUDGETS.WB1:2, as you can see in Figure 7.11. This continues for all the other windows into that notebook. Remember that these are all views into the same notebook, like looking through different windows of the same house. Any changes made are to the notebook itself, and are therefore displayed in all windows that access that notebook. If you make a change in BUDGETS.WB1:2, that change also appears in all other windows that display that notebook, such as the window titled BUDGETS.WB1:1.

Panes also let you look at two sections of the same notebook at once. You can have the two panes shift in the same direction or move independently. You can split a window into panes by dragging the page splitter (in the lower right corner of the notebook window) up or to the side to create horizontal or vertical windows. You can also create panes by moving the selector to where you want the break between the panes to occur, then selecting Panes from the Window menu and choosing either Horizontal or Vertical.

At times, you may want to have a notebook open, but to hide it from view. The most effective method of doing this is to use the hiding feature. To use this feature, select Hide from the Window menu. It hides the current window. The window is not deleted or lost; it just does not appear. To display a window you have hidden with this command, select Show from the Window menu, opening the Show Window dialog box. You select the hidden window you want to show from the Hidden Windows list box, and then select OK to show the window again.

Moving Between Windows

Moving from one notebook window to another is very easy. With a mouse, you can simply click on any exposed portion of the window to which you want to move. If you cannot see any part of the window to which you want to move, select Cascade or Tile from the Window menu, as described above, so that you will be able to see a portion of that window. Alternatively, you can move to the window directly from the Window menu. Up to the first nine windows are listed at the bottom of the Window menu. Simply select the correct window, and that window moves to the top of the other windows. If more than nine windows are open at one time, the last entry in the Window menu is More Windows. Select this command to open the Activate Windows dialog box. In this dialog box, you can select the window that you want to activate from the list box, and then select OK. Another way, if you are using the keyboard, is to press CTRL-F6. This will move you from one window to another, without changing the size or position of the window.

Closing a Window

When you are finished working with a particular notebook, you will want to close it. To close a notebook window, select Close from the File menu. Selecting Close closes the currently active notebook, the one that you are working with. If you want to close all of the notebook windows currently open, select Close All from the File menu. When you close a notebook window and the notebook has changed since the last time you saved it, you are prompted to save the notebook. If it has not been previously named, you must provide a name for the notebook file, just as if you were saving it using the Save command in the File menu. If it has been saved before, you are simply asked if you want to save it, and if you want to replace the previously saved version or create a backup. When you close all of the notebook windows at once, you may be prompted to save each one of them, if you have not recently saved each one. You can also close a notebook window by pressing CTRL-F4 or selecting Close from the window's Control menu box. The difference between closing a window this way and closing it with the Close command in the File menu is that if you have more than one window open to the same notebook, pressing CTRL-F4 or selecting Close from the Control menu box only closes the active window but leaves the other windows for the same notebook open.

SHARING DATA BETWEEN NOTEBOOKS

If you limit the data that your application can use to one notebook, you end up with notebooks that contain data duplicated in other notebooks. When notebooks contain duplicate data, you increase the number of changes that you must make, and the risk that one or more of the notebooks will not have the most current data. If you change the data in one notebook that appears in many notebooks, you have no guarantee that you changed the same numbers in the other appropriate notebooks. A better solution is to enter the data in one notebook, and have other notebooks reference the data in the original notebook. You can reference a single cell or a block of any size from another notebook. A block can only contain cells from one notebook, so if you want to use blocks from multiple notebooks, you must select the block from each notebook individually. Creating formulas that reference data in other notebooks creates *Hotlinks* between notebooks. The notebook that contains the formulas with references to other notebooks is the *primary notebook*. The notebooks that the formulas reference are the *supporting notebooks*. The supporting notebooks can be in any data format that Quattro Pro can read, but you must save the primary notebook in a format that supports linking.

If the primary spreadsheet has a .WK1 file extension, when you save it, Quattro Pro displays an extra prompt telling you that the spreadsheet contains links to other files and wants to know if it should remove them. If you select Yes to the prompt, Quattro Pro saves the file using the values of the links as the cell entries removing the links themselves. If you are saving the file with a .WK1 extension, Quattro Pro saves the simpler link formulas using the 1-2-3 Release 2.2 format and saves the more complex link formulas as their values. You can also select No to abort the command. 1-2-3 Releases 2.2, 2.3, and 2.4 have the requirement that a cell containing a link formula cannot perform other calculations, so using the Quattro Pro file format provides more flexibility. Also, the .WK1 link formulas expect that the supporting notebooks have .WK1 extensions as well.

Linking notebooks provides several advantages. First, it lets one notebook share the information it contains with other notebooks. Second, you can break a complex notebook into smaller and more manageable notebooks so that each notebook is easy to understand. Third, when an application is divided between many people, linking each person's notebook in a consolidating notebook allows each person to use his or her notebook without interfering with the other people's work. In this case, the overall notebook contains the most up-to-date information. Fourth, with large applications, a single notebook may be too small for all the data. Using multiple notebooks bypasses the memory limitations of your machine. Fifth, if the supporting data is not in a spreadsheet format, such as a Paradox format, file links allow you to access the portions of the data you want without converting it to a Quattro Pro format by loading the file into a notebook.

Referencing Other Notebook Cells in Formulas

Most formulas include a reference to other cells. These cell references tell Quattro Pro the data the formula uses to calculate its result. It is not necessary that the data be on the same page, or even in the same notebook, as the formula. You can create formulas in many notebooks that refer to a central notebook that contains data. If your formulas refer to that one file, you only need to change the data in that file when the information changes. This feature is especially useful when you have several notebooks that all have calculations using the same set of data. For example, you may have several notebooks that have formulas that reference a database stored in a separate notebook.

To create a reference, or link, to another notebook, you need to include the name of the notebook file encased in square brackets before the address of the cell in the notebook you want to access. For example, suppose you want a formula in the BUDGETS.WB1 notebook to access information from A:B6 in the EMPLOYEE.WB1 notebook. When you entered the address of the data in the formula, it would read [EMPLOYEE.WB1]A:B6. You can also use references to blocks in another notebook within formulas. If you attempt to reference a block of cells in another notebook in a formula when the formula expects a single cell, you will receive the message, "Cannot accept a block here."

The file name in the link provides Quattro Pro the information it needs to find the file. Quattro Pro assumes that the supporting notebook has a .WB1 extension and is in the same drive and directory as the primary notebook. If these assumptions are not correct, you must provide the information Quattro Pro needs to find the notebook. [SALES]TOTAL, [BUDGET.WK1]B3, [D:\QPW\FOCUS.WKQ]B3 are examples of links to cells in other notebooks. The address after the file name is the address of the cell or block that you want to use from the supporting notebook. You can have links to as many as 62 notebooks.

Formulas in a Quattro Pro format file can use other formula features besides the link to a supporting spreadsheet. The link to another spreadsheet can be by itself, or it can be part of a larger formula as in the following examples:

```
+[SALES]TOTAL
@PMT([LOANS]B3,[INT_RATE]SHORT_TERM,30)
@AVG([AREASALE]B2.B25)*.025
```

You can also create links to supporting notebooks by pointing to the cells, by typing the cells that you want, or by using two special "wild card"characters that will reference all open spreadsheets. Once the link references are established, you can change and delete them using Quattro Pro commands.

CREATING FORMULA LINKS BY POINTING You do not necessarily need to type in the reference to another notebook. You can also point to the cell or block you want in the other notebook. Just as you can point to a cell in the same

▼ TIP: Include the page name in link formulas.

When you have a link to another .WB1 notebook or a .WK3 file, you should include the page name. If you forget the page name in the link, Quattro Pro uses the first page. If you point to the cell or block, Quattro Pro will automatically include the page name for you.

notebook while creating a formula to include that cell name in the formula, you can also point to a cell or block in another notebook and include that file name and block address in your formula. The advantage of pointing to the entry is that you do not need to worry about spelling the file name correctly. Quattro Pro will add the file name reference as well as any other information needed to use the correct notebook. To point to the supporting notebook, you need to display both the primary and the supporting notebooks in windows. Since this is most easily done when you can see both notebooks, select <u>T</u>ile from the <u>W</u>indows menu. Begin creating the formula in the primary notebook. When you reach the point where you need to include the reference to the cells in the other notebook, move your mouse to that other notebook and select the appropriate block or cell. When you release the mouse button, the correct file name and address appear in the formula, just as if you typed them. You can also start POINT mode and then press CTRL-F6 until you switch to the correct notebook. After selecting the cells in the notebook, you can type the next operator or finalize the formula to complete the reference to the cell or block in the other notebook.

If BUDGETS.WB1 is not saved in the same directory as the file containing the reference to it, you would need to include the full path name before the file name, like this: [C:\PERSONEL\BUDGETS.WB1]A:B6. If Quattro Pro cannot find the file in the same directory as the primary file, it displays the File Not Found dialog box, asking you to locate the file for it. You find the file in the File Not Found dialog box in the same fashion that you find a file in the File Open dialog box. If you moved the file from the directory specified in the link, Quattro Pro will recognize that the file has moved, and will update the path name in the link.

For example, look at Figure 7.12. Suppose you want A:B8 in the TRIALBAL notebook to add the contents of A:B6 of the TRANSFER notebook and the block A:B3..B8 of the CHECKS notebook. First, you click B8 in the TRIALBAL notebook. Then, type **@SUM(** to begin the formula. To select the B6 cell from the TRANSFER notebook, you click B6 in the TRANSFER notebook. Quattro Pro automatically adds the file name reference. Then type **,** (a comma) to lock the reference to B6 in the TRANSFER notebook and select the next function argument. To select the block to add, click B3 in the CHECKS notebook, and drag the mouse as you move to B8. Then type **)** to finish the formula, and press ENTER to finalize the formula. The result is shown in Figure 7.13.

CREATING LINKS TO ALL OPEN FILES   Quattro Pro provides two "wild card" characters that can reference any open notebooks. When you use an asterisk or question mark in the file name of a link reference, it represents one or more

---

▼ TIP: Save Before Linking

If you are planning to use a new notebook in formulas in other notebooks, save the notebook before creating the formulas so Quattro Pro uses the correct file name in the formulas.

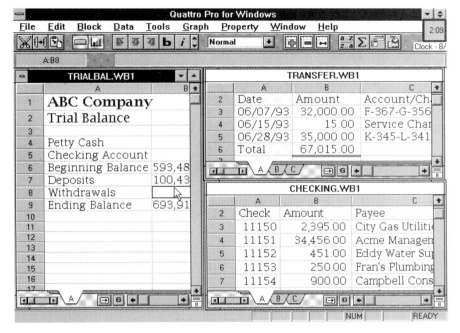

Figure 7.12   Files to Create Links With

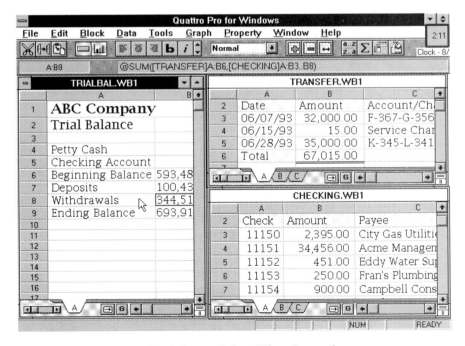

Figure 7.13   Files with Links to Other Files Created

characters. You can use these special characters to quickly consolidate all open files. The asterisk represents zero or more characters in a file name. The question mark represents one character in a file name. Some examples of these characters in file names are:

[*]   Represents all open notebooks, such as SALES_92, BUDGET

[SALES_*]   Represents all open notebooks with file names beginning with SALES_, such as SALES_92, SALES_93, SALES_IV

[SALES_9?]   Represents all open notebooks with file names that have the first seven characters of SALES_9 followed by a single character, such as SALES_91, SALES_92

[??????92]   Represents all open notebooks with file names of eight characters that end with 92, such as BUDGET92, SALES92, SALE1992

When you use these characters in the file name, they only apply to *open* notebooks. Since they apply to *all* open notebooks, you will want to check that only those files that you want to include are open. Once you enter the formula in a cell, Quattro Pro converts the formula to list all the files included in the formula. For example, if you enter **@SUM([*]A:B3)** to add B3 from the GAS, ELECTRIC, and COAL notebooks, Quattro Pro will convert the formula to @SUM([GAS]A:B3,[ELECTRIC]A:B3,[COAL]A:B3).

An example of a formula link reference that uses these special characters is the consolidation notebook shown in Figure 7.14. **@SUM([*]PURCHASES)** is

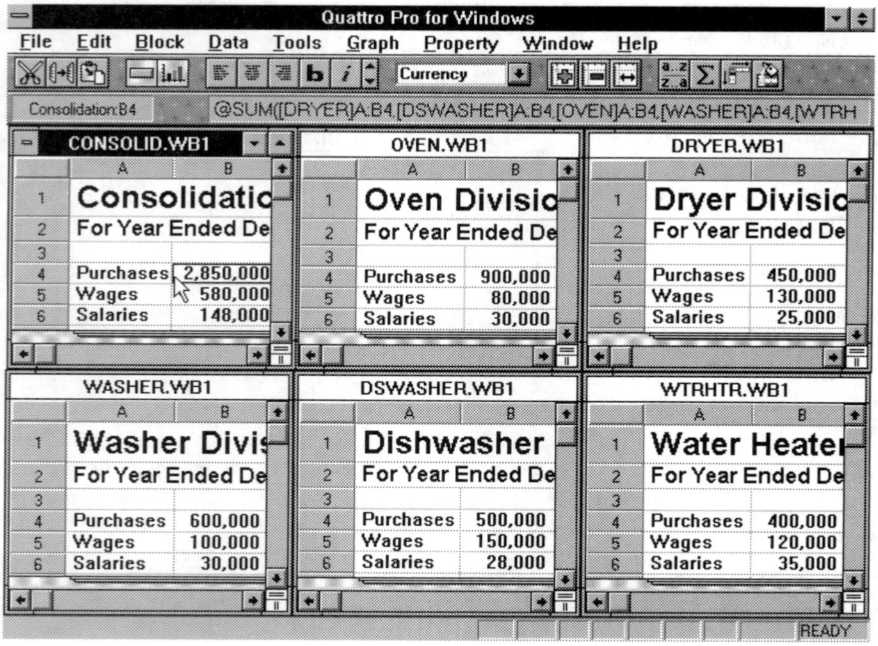

Figure 7.14   A Consolidation File Using Links

entered in B4. Each of the supporting notebooks contains data that the primary notebook combines. Since all of the supporting notebooks are in the same format, you can use a formula like **+@SUM([*]A:B4)** to add the purchases for all the divisions. However, a better alternative is to use block names. In each of the supporting notebooks, the cells containing the values to combine are labeled using the adjacent labels. As a result, the formula to combine purchases is **+@SUM([*]PURCHASES)**. If the PURCHASES cell in one of the notebooks is later moved, the formula will adjust for the cell's new location in one of the supporting notebooks.

Referencing Other Notebooks in Commands

Just as you can create a link to another notebook at any place in a formula that you can include a reference to another cell, you can also create links to other notebooks in many Quattro Pro commands. Many Quattro Pro commands reference a block of cells for information. For example, when you create a 2 Way table with the <u>W</u>hat-If command in the <u>D</u>ata menu, you can specify the block for the table and the two cells that this command systematically replaces with input values from the table. You can, if you want, have the block and the two cells in different notebooks. For example, you may want a table in one notebook to work through a model you already have in another. Suppose your central file has sales and budget data. In another notebook, you may want to create a what-if table showing the potential advantages of changing the pricing on a particular product, as shown in Figure 7.15.

Creating a link in a command is just like creating a link in a formula. Wherever you need to specify a block of cells, you specify a block of cells from another notebook. If you are typing, you can do this by typing the file name of the notebook enclosed in square brackets at the beginning of the reference to the block. If the supporting file is not in the same directory that the primary file is saved in, you may need to include the path name. If you are pointing to the data, make sure that both files are open on the screen when you start invoking the command. Simply point to the block in the other notebook, just as you would point in the same notebook. The complete file reference is automatically included.

OPENING A FILE WITH LINK REFERENCES   When you open a notebook that contains formulas with link references, Quattro Pro checks if the supporting notebooks are open, and displays the dialog box in Figure 7.16. If the supporting notebooks are not loaded, you must make one of three choices. The first option, <u>O</u>pen Supporting, opens any supporting notebooks that are not already open. If the supporting notebooks also have link references, Quattro Pro will display another selection box to select whether to open the supporting notebooks of the original supporting notebooks. This will continue until a selection is made from the dialog box shown in Figure 7.16 for all open notebooks that contain link references to unopened notebooks.

The second option, <u>U</u>pdate References, checks the current value of the cells in the

		Quattro Pro for Windows						
File	Edit	Block	Data	Tools	Graph	Property	Window	Help

AA3   'Period

	TABLE.WB1				CHAP_3.WB1	
	A	B	C			
1	Loan Tables			Enter amount to borrow:	$100,000
2		Principal	Interest		
3	Period	+[CHAP_3]N:B13	+[CHAP_3]N:B12	Enter number of years:	15
4	1	$241	$833		
5	2	$243	$831	Enter interest rate:	10.00%
6	3	$245	$829		
7	4	$247	$827	Enter the period:	12
8	5	$249	$825		
9	6	$251	$823	The payment is:	$1,074.61
10	7	$254	$821		
11	8	$256	$819	The interest portion is:	$810.27
12	9	$258	$817	The principal portion is:	$264.33
13	10	$260	$815		
14	11	$262	$812		
15	12	$264	$810		
16	13	$267	$808		
17	14	$269	$806		
18	15	$271	$804		
19	16	$273	$801		

A / B / C /   N / 0 /

NUM   READY

Figure 7.15   A What-If Table Based on Data in Another Notebook

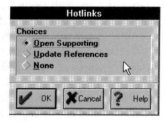

Figure 7.16   The Hotlinks Dialog Box

supporting notebooks and uses these values in the link references. These values can be rechecked by selecting Update Links in the Tools menu and then selecting Refresh Links. The actual notebooks can be opened later by selecting the Update Links command in the Tools menu and then selecting Open Links. This option works best when you do not have the memory to open the supporting notebooks and you know that the supporting notebooks contain the most current values.

The last option, None, temporarily substitutes the values of the link references with NA. This lets you know that the values of the link formulas have not been computed. Any formulas that reference formulas containing link references will also have the value NA. This option is best when you want to change cell entries that do not include link references. If you want to change the formulas to use the values in the link references, you can select Update Links from the Tools menu and then select Refresh to use the values from the supporting notebooks or Open to open the supporting notebooks and update the formulas in the primary notebooks.

RECALCULATION WITH LINK REFERENCES   Quattro Pro is designed to recalculate your notebook in the background and minimize the amount of recalculation. This does not affect linked notebooks, since it only applies to formulas that use the current and loaded notebooks. When a notebooks contains link references to an unloaded file, the values from the supporting notebook are only checked and updated when the primary file is loaded and Update References is chosen, or when you select Update Links in the Tools menu and then Refresh Links. If you use Quattro Pro on a network and other people may be using the supporting notebooks, you will want to update this command before printing the notebook to ensure that your notebook is using the most current values from the supporting notebook.

COPYING AND MOVING LINK REFERENCES   Quattro Pro lets you copy and move cells that contain link references. The results produced depend on whether you move formulas with link references in the same notebook or between different notebooks.

When you copy a formula containing a link reference to another area in the same notebook, Quattro Pro treats the formula just as if you were copying cells in one notebook without link references. When you copy formulas containing link references, Quattro Pro adjusts the formulas and the cells that the link reference refers to, depending on whether the original formulas contain absolute, mixed, or relative addresses. For example, suppose you want to copy the block A:A3..B5 to A:A8 in the RECEIVE notebook in Figure 7.17 to produce the results shown in Figure 7.18 (the formulas are formatted Text). Quattro Pro has adjusted the relative references in the formulas to refer to the same relative address as the original formula. The cells used by the link references are adjusted by the same number of rows and columns as the other data.

When you copy a block to another notebook, the file names in link references cells remain unchanged, although the cell or block address may change depending on the address type. As an example, Figure 7.19 shows the results of copying A:A3..B5 in the RECEIVE notebook shown in Figure 7.17 to A:A13 in the BALSHEET notebook. The cell addresses have been changed to reflect the new relative positions the copied formulas have in the BALSHEET notebook relative to the position the original has in the RECEIVE notebook. The file names in the link references are unchanged. The link references even remain when a link reference refers to itself.

When you move a block containing link references to another position in the same notebook unlike when you copy it, the link references do not change. When you move the block A:A3..B5 in Figure 7.17 to A:A8..B10, you obtain the results shown in Figure 7.20; Quattro Pro does not change the link references.

When you move entries between notebooks, link references can be changed, created, or deleted as Quattro Pro adjusts formulas so that they refer to the same data as they did before you moved the entries. Quattro Pro determines which cell

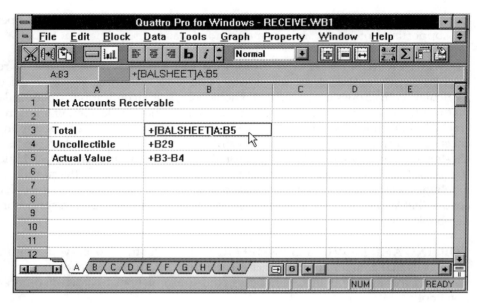

Figure 7.17   A Notebook with a Link to Another Notebook

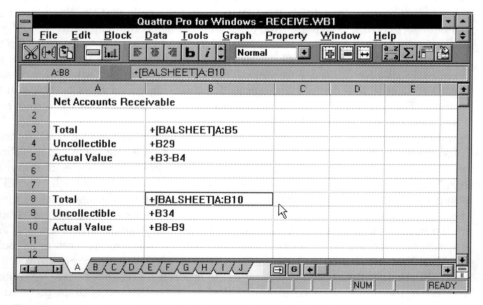

Figure 7.18   Copying a File Reference in a Notebook

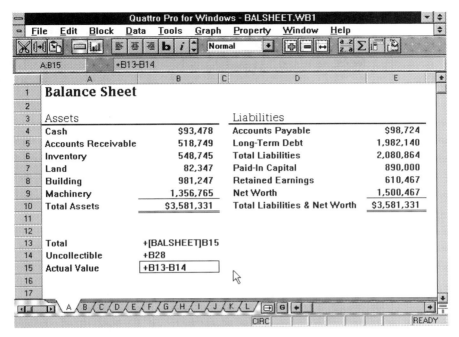

Figure 7.19   Copying a File Reference to Another Notebook

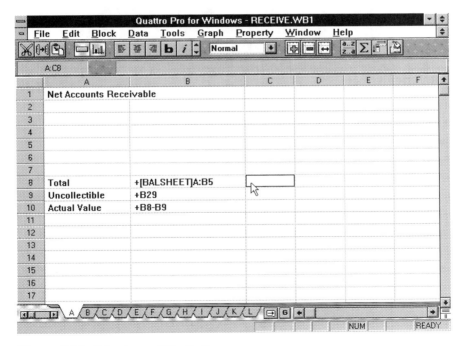

Figure 7.20   Moving a File Reference

and block addresses need to be changed. Quattro Pro also must determine which cell or block addresses become link references, which link references are no longer link references but simple cell or block addresses, and which file names in link references need to be changed. As an example of moving a block with link references, suppose that you move A:A3..B5 in the RECEIVE notebook shown in Figure 7.17 to A:A13 in the BALSHEET notebook. The result (Figure 7.21) shows how Quattro Pro adjusts link references. In A13, Quattro Pro removes a link reference, since the reference is moved to its own notebook. A link reference is created in A14, since the cell it references is in the RECEIVE notebook. The formula in B15 specifies the same relation to cells B13 and B14 as it did when it was in B5 referring to B3 and B4.

Creating Block Names for Supporting Files

By assigning a name to a block of cells, you can make referring to that block of cells much easier. You can assign a block name to a block of cells in another notebook, and use that name in the current notebook. You can use this block name in formulas and commands, just as you would use a block name referring to a set of cells in the same notebook. To use this block name in the primary notebook, you must create it while in the primary notebook, not in the supporting notebook.

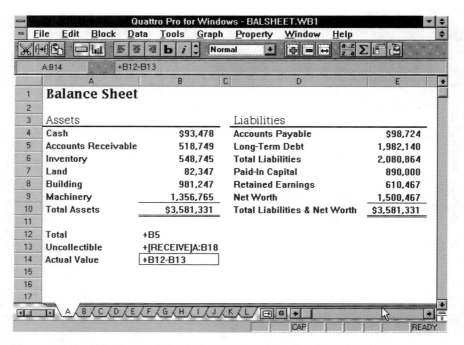

Figure 7.21   Moving a File Reference to Another Notebook

You create block names that refer to another notebook the same way that you create block names that refer to the same notebook. Select Names from the Block menu, and then select Create. Alternatively, you can press CTRL-F3. Type the name for the block in the Name text box. Move to the Block(s) text box. Specify the block either by typing it in or by pointing to it.

Using Block Names with Link References

When you create link references, it is preferable to use a block name rather than a cell or block address. Since the correct block name is easier to remember than the correct block address, using block names reduces initial entry mistakes. Also, using block names prevents mistakes later on if the cells containing the data are moved. Since a block name is adjusted when the cell is moved, any link references that use the block name automatically use the relocated cell. Quattro Pro also has other features that are available when you use block names for link addresses. You can create a block name that is actually a link reference to another notebook. You can also create a block name whose contents are a link reference and use the block name in place of the link reference without reentering the link reference. Finally, you can create a link reference library that is a spreadsheet notebook containing references to other notebooks.

USING A BLOCK NAME AS A LINK REFERENCE Chapter 4 introduced using block names to refer to one or more cells in a notebook. With link references, you can have a block name that refers to another notebook. You might use this feature instead of typing a link reference into a cell directly. For example, in a consolidating balance sheet, you may get the number for accounts receivable from the block TOTAL in the ACCT_REC notebook. Rather than entering **+[ACCT_REC]TOTAL** in the balance sheet notebook, you can select Names in the Edit menu, select Create, and type **ACCOUNT_RECEIVE** as the block name. For the block location, you can select the TOTAL block in the ACCT_REC notebook by typing the location or pointing to it. Then, when you want to use TOTAL in the ACCT_REC notebook, you can type + and press F3 (CHOICES). Quattro Pro will include ACCOUNT_RECEIVE in the list of block names even though the block address for this block name is in another notebook. Using this method is more convenient when you are entering formulas, since you do not have to enter a lengthy link reference and you can use the F3 (CHOICES) key to select the block.

ASSIGNING A BLOCK NAME TO A LINK REFERENCE When your notebook contains multiple link references to the same block, one way to simplify your work is to (1) create one link reference to the block, (2) name the cell containing the block reference, and (3) use the named block in other locations where you would use the link reference. For example, you may have a notebook that uses the monthly production, stored in a cell called MONTH_PROD from the MONTHLY notebook, several times. Rather than typing in a link reference every time you need the monthly production, you can enter a link reference once, name the cell containing the link reference, and use the named cell in place of the link reference in the other places in the notebook where you need the monthly production. In this example, you would enter +[MONTHLY]MONTH_PROD in a cell and select Names in the Edit menu and Create to name the cell. Then each time you needed the monthly production, you would press F3 (CHOICES) and select the name of the cell containing the link reference. As in the previous section, using this method is convenient for entering formulas, since you do not have to enter a lengthy link reference and you can use the F3 (CHOICES) key to select the block.

CREATING A LINK LIBRARY   Another problem with link references is remembering which notebook contains the data you want. One solution is to create a *link library*. A link library contains formulas that are link references to other notebooks. Instead of browsing through many notebooks to find the value you want, you can look at the link library and use the cell containing the link reference. The link library also has the advantage of letting you change the file reference in the link library; then, any notebook that uses the link library will automatically use the value from the replaced notebook.

As an example, suppose you want to combine the monthly totals of the production costs for each department. Each department has a notebook that looks something like Figure 7.22. Rather than create a consolidation notebook that adds

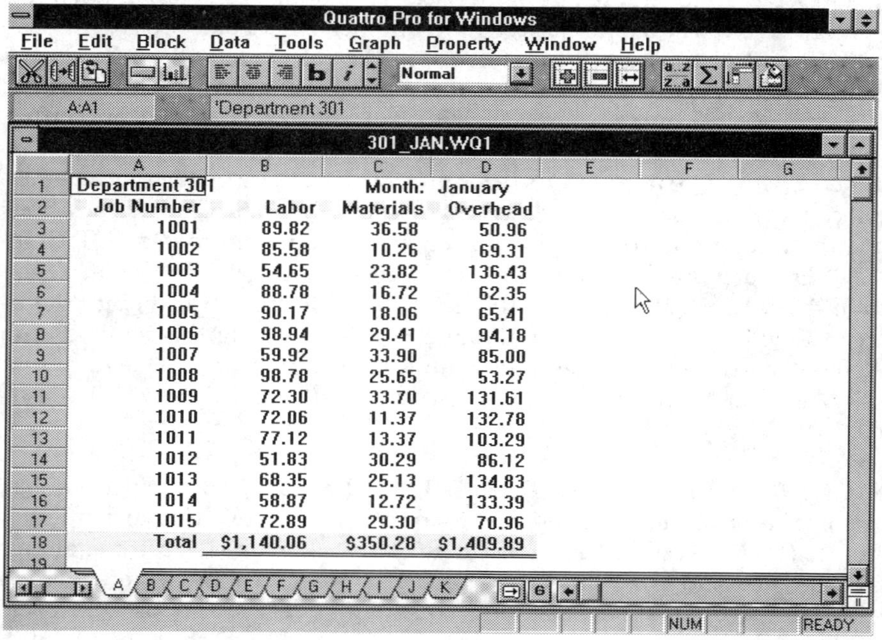

Figure 7.22   One Notebook Serves a Single Department

the total from each department and change the formulas each month, you can create a link library like the one on the right of Figure 7.23. Such a library stores all the file names and block names for each department. As the month changes, the file names in the link library change, and the consolidation notebook as shown on the left of Figure 7.23 is updated for the new values. The formulas in the consolidation file use the block names assigned to the link reference formulas in the LIBRARY notebook. For example, if you need to change the consolidation data shown in Figure 7.23 to February's data, you can use the Search and Replace command in the Edit menu to change the JAN file name to FEB. A link library has a greater advantage when multiple notebooks use the same link references, since changing the link reference in the link library notebook automatically changes the notebook that the other notebooks get their data from.

Updating Links

When both the primary and the supporting files are open on the screen at one time, Quattro Pro immediately updates the linked information. As soon as you make a change in a supporting file, the primary file immediately updates its link to that supporting file. However, both files are not always open when you make

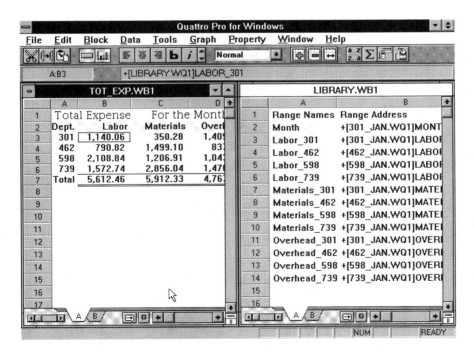

Figure 7.23 Link Libraries Make it Easier to Reference Multiple Notebooks

changes. You may want to update the links to closed files. When you update a link, you can open the linked files, refresh the information from those files, delete the connection to a supporting file, or change which file is the supporting file.

OPENING LINKED FILES   While you are working with a notebook containing links, you may find it helpful to be able to open the supporting notebooks. You may want to open them in order to verify that you have the correct information, or because you have data that you need to add to a supporting notebook rather than to the primary notebook. Remembering all the files that your notebook is linked to might be difficult. One way to quickly open the supporting files is to select Update Links from the Tools menu and then select Open Links. When you select this command, you are presented with an Open Links dialog box listing all of the supporting files to which the active notebook has links, as shown in Figure 7.24. Select the file you want to open and then select OK. The selected file is opened as if you used the Open command in the File menu.

REFRESHING LINKS   You may find it necessary to manually refresh the links to other notebooks. When you refresh a link, Quattro Pro goes into the supporting files and updates the values from the files that the current notebook uses. You need to refresh links whenever a change might have been made to a supporting

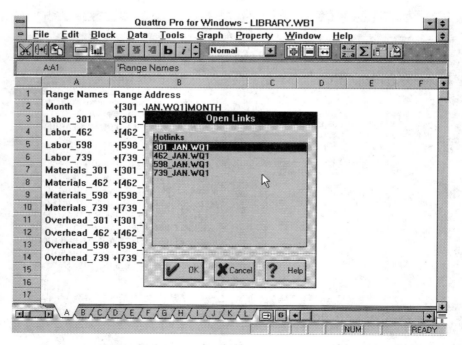

Figure 7.24   The Open Links Dialog Box

file that is not reflected in your primary notebook. Quattro Pro normally refreshes a link each time the supporting file is changed, if the supporting file is open, or each time you open the primary file. You may want to refresh the links manually, especially if you are working in a network environment. Someone may be editing the contents of your supporting file at the same time that you are working on the primary file. Quattro Pro does not refresh the links automatically under these circumstances. To refresh the links manually, select Refresh Links after selecting Update Links from the Tools menu. Then select one of the files to which you have links from the Hotlinks list box of the Update Links dialog box, and select OK. This updates all the links in the primary notebook to that specific supporting notebook. You will have to repeat this process for each supporting notebook. If you have no unopened links, you will receive a dialog box warning, since you do not need to refresh open links.

DELETING LINKS   You may find it necessary to delete links between the primary and supporting files. When a link is deleted, the reference to the other notebook is deleted from your formulas and commands. Your linked formulas will appear as ERR instead of showing the link to the file. For example, if you delete the link to 301_ JAN in the LIBRARY notebook shown in Figure 7.23, the formula in B2 changes from +[301_JAN]MONTH to +ERR. You might want to delete your links if you deleted one of the supporting files. To delete the links to one of the supporting files, select Update Links from the Tools menu and then select Delete Links. Select the supporting file that you wish to delete links from the Hotlinks list box. Select OK to delete the links to that file.

CHANGING LINKS   Changing a link changes the file a link uses but does not change other information about the link. If you rename a supporting file, you will want to change the linked formulas to use the new file name. Changing a link effectively substitutes one file for another as the supporting file in the link. For example, if you had your quarterly budget report prepared in one notebook, and all the raw data for the quarter in another notebook, you might have a problem when the quarter changed. You would have to change all of the links to the new quarter's notebook by retyping them. By changing the links using the Change Link, you replace all of the links to the first quarter's file with the file for the second quarter in one step. You simply select one command rather than reediting your entire report. While you can use the Search and Replace command in the Edit menu to substitute one file name for another, you can easily miss a link formula by not including the link formula in the block you search. Changing the link by using this command ensures that you do not forget any link formulas to a particular supporting file.

To change a link, select Update Links from the Tools menu and then select Change Link. In the Change Link From list box, select the supporting file you want to replace. In the To text box, enter the name of the file to which you want to change the link. If the file is not in the same directory as the primary file, include the path.

SHARING DATA WITH OTHER APPLICATIONS

Using Quattro Pro for Windows allows you to share data not only between notebooks or files created with other spreadsheet applications, but with other types of applications as well. The basic method of doing this is to use the Clipboard. You can copy information from an application to the Clipboard, and then paste the data into your Quattro Pro notebook, just as you might use the Clipboard to copy from one notebook or page to another. You can also copy data from Quattro Pro to the Clipboard and then copy it to another application. The problem with copying with the Clipboard is that the data is copied once, and then is left as is in the new location. When you change the data in the original file, you need to go through the entire process again. With Windows, however, you can create Dynamic Data Exchange (DDE) links. When you create a DDE link, you do not have to worry about copying your changes again. Instead, when you change the original data, the copies of the original data are updated as well. You might want to think of a DDE link as a formula link reference, except that the reference is to a file Quattro Pro does not necessarily accept for File commands.

With Windows 3.1, you have another option—Object Linking and Embedding (OLE). OLE expands your choices for integrating data created or prepared in different applications by allowing you to view and edit in the original application while you are in another application. It is like having a word processor in your Quattro Pro notebook or putting a Quattro Pro notebook in your favorite word processor.

Copying Data Between Applications

You have already learned to use the Windows Clipboard when copying and moving data within your Quattro Pro notebook. As you know, you can also use these commands to copy information between notebooks. Another use of the Clipboard is to copy information between applications. You can copy information between applications as easily as from one cell to another, using the Windows Clipboard.

While simply pasting information into your Quattro Pro notebook may not have the long-range utility of creating DDE and OLE links, it is often suitable for your needs. You may simply want a copy of certain information,without concerning yourself with the ability to edit or change it in the future. If so, simply copying the information and pasting it in without the more complex linking features will satisfy your needs.

To copy information from another application's document into Quattro Pro, you need to start that application and open the relevant document. Use the application's commands to copy that information from the application into the Clipboard. Usually, this means selecting the information in the application, and then selecting Copy from the Edit menu of that application. If you are not sure how to copy to the Clipboard in that application, or if you want to copy information from a non-Windows program into the Clipboard, check with the application's documentation or Windows' documentation for the full instructions.

When you have copied the information to the Clipboard, switch back to Quattro Pro. Move the selector to the cell where you want the information. Be aware that if you are copying information in a text format, the end of each line is the end of the row, and the next line will appear in the next row of the Quattro Pro notebook. If there is any previous information in the affected cells, the information is deleted when the new information is pasted in. Select Paste from the Edit menu, press SHIFT-INS, or click the Paste button in the SpeedBar. If you want the entire Clipboard contents pasted into one cell, you can do this by moving to a cell, pressing F2, pressing SHIFT-INS, and finalizing the entry.

When you want to put Quattro Pro information into another application, copy the Quattro Pro information to the Clipboard just as if you are using the Clipboard to copy information within Quattro Pro. Next, switch to the other application and use that application's command to paste the Clipboard's contents to the desired location. Most Windows applications have a Paste command in an Edit menu for this purpose.

Normally, when you paste the Clipboard's contents into Quattro Pro, the information is pasted in with a format that Quattro Pro can use. If you are pasting a graphic object, the pasted information appears in Quattro Pro as a floating object on top of the notebook page. If you are pasting text, the Clipboard contents are added as values or labels. However, if the application that you copied the information from is capable of providing information for a DDE link or an OLE object, the information may be pasted in as a link, or as an embedded OLE object, as described shortly.

If you want to control the format in which copied information is pasted into your notebook, use the Paste Format command from the Edit menu. From the Paste Format dialog box, the Paste special format list box lists the formats you can use for pasting the current contents of the Clipboard into Quattro Pro. For a graphic object, you might have the choice of importing the graphic as an embedded OLE object, a linked OLE object, a bitmap, or a metafile. The bitmap option pastes the Clipboard contents as a bitmapped drawing, which is the same format the Windows Paintbrush application uses. The OLE options are described below. The metafile option copies the graphic in the Clipboard in a metafile format. The choices provided depend both on the type of information you are copying and the Clipboard formats that the application you are copying from can support.

Creating and Using DDE Links

DDE links can be created between a Quattro Pro notebook and a file created with another Windows application. When you create a DDE link, one application is a server and the other is a client. The *server application* provides the original information to be used. The server application is like the supporting file for a formula link reference. The *client application* accepts the data. The client application is like the primary file for a formula link reference. Quattro Pro for Windows is capable of being both a server and a client. Some other programs can only be servers, others can only be clients.

You create a link in the client application. The link is to the file created by the server application, not to the application itself, just as in formula link references, where the link is to a file, not to Quattro Pro. You do not need to link the entire file's worth of data, only that part of it which you want to use. To link another application's file into a Quattro Pro notebook, you must start in the server application. Select the data that you want to link into your Quattro Pro notebook, and copy it to the Clipboard. Switch to the Quattro Pro notebook. Select the block of cells that you want to fill with the link. If the block of cells is too small, not all of the data will appear in Quattro Pro. Because of this, you might want to select a large block of cells in a section of the notebook that does not have much data.

When you have selected the block where you want the linked data to appear, select Paste Link from the Edit menu. The linked data appears as shown in Figure 7.25. The input line, instead of displaying the data itself, shows a function in that cell, the @DDELINK function. This function is the link to the original file. If you make any changes to the original file, the @DDELINK function refreshes the information that appears in Quattro Pro to match the changed data. This DDE link is a Hotlink, just like the notebook links you learned about in the last section. You

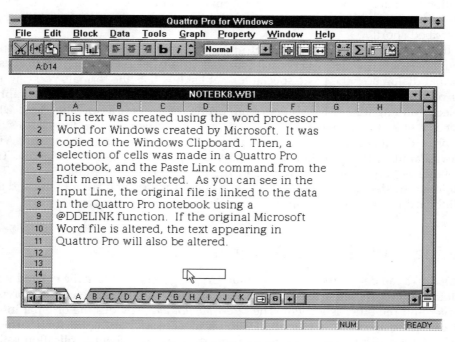

Figure 7.25   Data from a Notepad File Linked into Quattro Pro

can therefore use the Update Links command on the Tools menu to refresh, delete, and change the link. You can even open the linked document, by selecting Open Links from the Tools Update Links submenu and selecting that linked document from the Hotlinks list box in the Open Links dialog box. When you do this, Quattro Pro opens the other application, and opens the saved file into that application window.

Remember that a DDE link links your Quattro Pro notebook and the other application's file. If you change the name of the file, Quattro Pro does not know this, and will lose the connection to the file. If you copy information from an unsaved file and create a DDE link to that data in Quattro Pro, you are certain to lose the link when you save the file with a name. However, the data is not completely lost if the link breaks because you have saved the file under another name. The data originally copied into your Quattro Pro notebook with the link still appears in the Quattro Pro file, and the DDE link function still appears in the input line. You can change the link to the file using the same Update Links command in the Tools menu that you use with formula link references to other notebooks.

To create DDE links in which Quattro Pro is the server, copy the Quattro Pro information to the Clipboard. Then switch to the client application. Follow the directions given in the client application for creating DDE links. Usually, the application will have a command that lets you select the format for the data that you are pasting from the server application (Quattro Pro), or a command that pastes the Clipboard data in as a DDE link. For the exact steps, you must check the application's documentation.

Creating and Using OLE Objects

Object Linking and Embedding (OLE) is a new data sharing feature of Windows 3.1. With this feature you can link or embed data from various applications into a Quattro Pro notebook. OLE objects are inserted as *floating objects.* Floating objects are objects that appear above the notebook page, but not on it, as you can see in Figure 7.26. They are not confined to single cells. A floating object may appear either as an icon of the program that originated the object, or as a graphic image. You can double-click on these floating OLE objects in order to start and switch to the applications that created them. In those applications, you can edit, run, or view the contents of the OLE objects. The advantage of OLE objects is that you can include data in formats that Quattro Pro cannot import or edit, such as sound files, and both run and edit these files quickly from within Quattro Pro.

LINKED VERSUS EMBEDDED OLE OBJECTS   OLE objects can be either embedded or linked. When an OLE object is embedded, the data is actually stored with the Quattro Pro notebook. There is no connection to the original file. This means that there is no problem if the data originally came from an unnamed, unsaved file. The data is stored with the Quattro Pro notebook. When you edit an embedded object, the server application is opened, and the embedded object

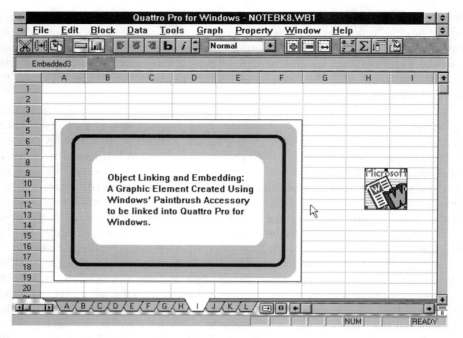

Figure 7.26   OLE Objects as Floating Objects

appears in a document window inside its application window. When you finish running or editing the embedded object, you exit and return to Quattro Pro. You cannot edit an embedded OLE object from outside of Quattro Pro, and any changes made to an embedded OLE object in a notebook are not made to other embedded objects that initially contained the same data. Since embedded objects are stored with your Quattro Pro notebook, they increase the size of the notebook's file.

A linked OLE object, such as DDE links, creates a link between a saved file and the objects that appear in Quattro Pro. Since the file is saved independently of Quattro Pro, your Quattro Pro notebook is not larger, and disk space memory is conserved. Also, you can edit the contents of the file separately from Quattro Pro. Multiple notebooks that have OLE objects linked to a single saved file can be updated at one time, just by editing that file. Linked OLE objects are different from DDE links, since DDE links require you to go through the steps to open the application and the file the link is connected to. With a linked OLE object, you double-click the OLE object in your notebook and Quattro Pro automatically opens the application and file for you.

CREATING OLE OBJECTS WITH THE CLIPBOARD   Creating an OLE object is as simple as copying and pasting using the Clipboard. First, copy the information from the server application to the Clipboard. Then, switch to Quattro Pro and select Paste Format in the Edit menu. In the Paste Format dialog box, the Paste special format list box lists all the formats in which you can paste the Clipboard's contents. Among the potential formats are Linked OLE and Embedded OLE. Depending on the server application, you may only be able to embed an OLE object. If the application from which you copied the data does not support OLE features, or supports them only as a client and not as a server, you will not have these options. Also, if the data you are copying is from an unnamed file, you cannot create a linked OLE object, since the link is to the file.

To create an embedded OLE object, simply select the Embedded OLE format, and select OK to paste it into your document. If you want a linked OLE object, select Linked OLE and select OK. OLE objects, whether linked or embedded, look the same. Depending on the server application, when you simply paste the data from the Clipboard, you may create a linked or embedded OLE object. Use the Paste Format command in the Edit menu to ensure that you have the correct format.

INSERTING OLE OBJECTS   You can create an embedded OLE object without ever leaving Quattro Pro. Simply select the Insert Object command from the Edit menu, opening the Insert New Object dialog box. In this dialog box, select the type of object that you want to insert from the Object Type list box. This list box lists all the various types of objects that can be created by the server-capable applications available on your computer system. When you select one of these object types and select OK, the application used to create that type of object is started in a window, as you can see in Figure 7.27 with Windows' Paintbrush accessory. You can then

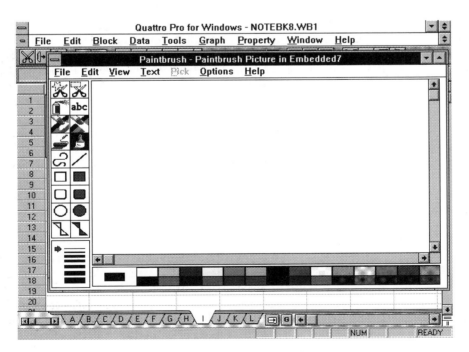

Figure 7.27   An Application Started with the Insert Object Command

create the object that you want, be it a graphic object created using Windows Paintbrush accessory, or a word processing document. When you are finished creating the contents of the object, you need to embed the object. To do this, activate the File menu of the server application. New choices are added to the server application's file menu: Update, and Exit and Return. Selecting Update updates the information in the OLE object created in your Quattro Pro notebook. This is the equivalent of saving, because it saves the contents of the application to the embedded OLE object. When you select this Exit and Return, you exit the server application and return immediately to Quattro Pro.

If you open a file into the server application while inserting an object, you break the link to the object. This means that you are no longer creating or editing the embedded OLE object, and anything that you now do will not become part of the contents of the embedded OLE object.

When you exit the server application and return to your Quattro Pro notebook, you will see a floating OLE object. This object is embedded and contains the contents that you created in the server application. Since the object is embedded and not linked, there is no file that you can edit or use in other applications. However, if you use the Save As command from the File menu of the server application (assuming that it has this option), you can save the contents of the embedded OLE object to a file. This does not make the object into a linked OLE object. You can only create embedded OLE objects using the Insert Object command.

USING OLE OBJECTS   When you want to see, edit, or run an OLE object's contents, you double-click the object. This activates the server application, and opens the OLE object's contents up into the application window. If the OLE object is linked rather than embedded, then the entire file appears in the application window, even if you only use a very small portion of it in your OLE object. If the object is embedded, only the contents of the object appear, and the document name indicates that this is an embedded object in Quattro Pro. In the server application, you can edit, run, or view the contents of your application. If the object was embedded, you can exit the server application and be returned to Quattro Pro. The Exit command may read Exit and Return to Quattro Pro rather than just Exit. The contents of the object are not saved in the edited form until you exit. If the object was linked rather than embedded, you may prefer to simply switch back to Quattro Pro. The Exit command is not changed, and you must save the file with the same name again before the changes to the object are saved.

SETTING OBJECT PROPERTIES   Just as cells, blocks, and the application have properties in Quattro Pro, so do the linked and embedded OLE objects. You can inspect and set these properties in the same way that you would inspect and set the properties of any other kind of object in Quattro Pro. Select the OLE object by clicking it. Then you can right-click the object, or select Current Object from the Property menu. The property menu contains Object Settings or Link Settings (depending on whether the OLE object is linked or embedded), Border Color, Box Type, and Object Name. Using this menu, you can change the width and color of the box surrounding the OLE object, the name of the object, and the settings affecting the link or embedding itself.

The Border Color and Box Type properties change the frame around the OLE object on the notebook. You can select Border Color and click the color you want or use the slider bars to select a new color. You will learn more about changing colors using this menu in Chapter 9, "Basic Graphs," since the information in your graphs can use the same color selections. To change the size of the lines around the OLE object, select Box Type from the menu. From the Box Type dialog box, you can select the None, Thin, Medium, and Thick radio buttons for the width of the line you want around the OLE object. You can also select the Drop Shadow check box to add a shadow to the box around the OLE object. Select OK from the Border Color or Box Type dialog boxes to use the new settings.

The last property, Object Name, lets you assign a more meaningful name to the floating graph object. Object names are used in macros, as you will learn in Chapter 14. You can enter a new name for the OLE object following the same rules as for block names, which can be up to fifteen characters without using spaces. After you rename the OLE object, you will notice that the object's new name appears in the input line when you select the object.

You can also alter the link or object settings of the OLE object. In the Object Settings dialog box, the name of the server application is displayed, along with information defining the object, such as size coordinates for a Paintbrush Picture. You can convert the object from an embedded object to a picture of the OLE object's contents by selecting Change to picture. Selecting this command button changes the OLE object just as if you had selected Bitmap for the format when you pasted it onto the notebook. If you want to edit the contents of the object, select the Edit command button to start the server application.

If the object is linked, you can select the Link Settings menu option. The Link Settings dialog box displays the name of the server application, the settings for the object, and the name of the document file to which the object is linked. You can also select the Update method. If you choose Automatic, the link updates each time that there are changes to the saved file, and each time that the Quattro Pro notebook is opened. If you select Manual, you must choose to update the link. If you do not choose to update a manually updated link, the information is not updated. If you select On save, then the link is refreshed each time you save the Quattro Pro notebook. To update the link manually, select the Update now command button. This refreshes the link immediately, going to the file and updating the information that appears in the object.

If you want to change the file the object is linked to, select the Change link command button, opening the Change Link dialog box. In this dialog box, use the list and text boxes to select the file you now wish to link to. This dialog box is just like the one for opening a file. You should make sure that the same data format appears in the linked file. If you want to delete the link, select the Unlink command button. This removes the link between the object and the file, making the linked OLE object into a static object. You will not be able to access the contents of that object again. If you want to edit the file, select the Edit button. This opens the server application with the linked file open, and enables you to edit that file. When you are finished editing it, save the file, which causes the link to update. You do not need to exit the server application when you are done; you can simply switch back to Quattro Pro as you can from other applications.

SETTING OBJECT LAYERS   When you add objects to a notebook page, they are layered in the order they are added. You can think of adding these layers on a notebook page as putting each object on a separate transparency. The spreadsheet data in the cells below are always the bottom layer, but you can rearrange the transparencies that contain the OLE objects. You will only want to use this feature when you have several OLE objects on a page and one of them overlaps another. When you change the layer of an object, the other objects are adjusted to reflect the changed object's layer. When you select an OLE object on a page that has more than one object, you can select Object Order from the Block menu. The cascade menu lets you move an object one layer forward or backward or to the top or bottom of the stack. To move the object to the top, select Bring to Front from the cascade menu. To move the object to the bottom, select Send to Back from the cascade menu. To move the object one layer forward, select Bring Forward from the cascade menu. To move the object one layer backward, select Send Backward from the cascade menu. Figure 7.28 shows several OLE objects added to a page.

Figure 7.28   Several Floating OLE Objects

By selecting the object with the mouse, Object Order from the Block menu, and Send to Front, we have ensured the order of the OLE objects on the page.

COMBINING NOTEBOOKS AND FILES

In addition to using Hotlinks, you can share data between notebooks by inserting other files into your notebook. When you do this, the inserted files take the place of pages in your notebook. In a more controlled version of inserting a file, you can combine files. When you combine files, you combine a saved file and the current notebook into one. You can choose what parts of the saved file you want to combine with the current notebook. You can also perform calculations when you combine files, such as adding values together, one from the saved file and one from the current notebook. You can bring data into Quattro Pro in different formats by importing a file. Importing a file into a Quattro Pro notebook is usually done to bring text data into the notebook. Once the data is in the notebook, you can use another command to *parse* (divide) the data into smaller pieces.

Inserting Files

With Quattro Pro, you can insert other files as pages in your notebook. Inserting a file is just like inserting a blank page except that you already have data in the inserted location. For example, you may have several spreadsheets created with Quattro Pro for DOS. Each file is the equivalent of one page in a Quattro Pro for Windows notebook. Now that you are using Quattro Pro for Windows, you may want to consolidate a number of these files into one notebook. You may also want to insert a spreadsheet file you have received from someone else into a Quattro Pro notebook you have already created.

Every file you insert must be in one of the formats that Quattro Pro can open. These are the same formats shown in Table 7.1 that Quattro Pro can automatically translate. Most of these formats do not support notebooks, but only single spreadsheet pages which, when inserted, they use only a single page of your notebook. Some other formats also support notebooks, and may have several pages worth of data.

To insert a file, move to the page where you want the file inserted. If you are inserting a file that has multiple pages already, be careful which page you select. You can only have 256 pages in a Quattro Pro notebook. When you insert a file, Quattro Pro counts the number of pages the inserted file has and inserts that many pages into your notebook. Since Quattro Pro will also delete the same number of pages from the back of your notebook, you want to have more empty pages at the end of the notebook than you are inserting. When Quattro Pro runs out of pages to delete, it will display an error message telling you that it ran out of notebook space in which to insert the file. Thus, not only the format of the file you are inserting, but also the page you select when you insert a file, can be important.

After you select the page where you will insert a file, select Insert from the Block menu. Then select File. This invokes the Insert File dialog box. Select the file that you want to insert into your current notebook, just as if you were selecting a file to open. Then select OK. The pages from the selected file are inserted starting on the page containing the selector. The page that previously contained the selector is moved farther back in the notebook by as many pages as the file you select used. For example, if you insert the Quattro Pro for DOS file RECEIVE.WQ1 into the current notebook starting at page B, the second sheet in the notebook is named RECEIVE. Any data that was on sheet B is now on sheet C. As this example shows, when the file you insert takes a single page, that page adopts the name of the file you have inserted. If you insert another notebook, the inserted pages will retain the page names originally assigned in the Quattro Pro notebook, if you have named the pages, or will use the default page name if you have not changed the page names.

Combining Files

Transferring totals from one report to another and producing consolidated reports by product line or division are tasks that must be handled by any business reporting package. Quattro Pro has another option for combining the data in notebooks. The Combine command in the Tools menu allows Quattro Pro to meet this challenge with commands that are easy to use and flexible enough to work in a variety of situations. You can combine several similar notebooks to produce a consolidated summary sheet of the information in each detailed notebook.

With the Combine command in the Tools menu, you can take two notebooks or two notebook blocks and combine them into one notebook. When you combine notebooks, Quattro Pro provides the options for copying, adding, subtracting, multiplying, and dividing. You can combine the contents of an entire file with the current notebook or, if you prefer to be more selective, you can select a block from the incoming file to combine with the current notebook. Regardless of whether you use the contents of a block or an entire file, the replacement of the cells in the current notebook begins at the location of the selector. The extent of the replacement is determined by the number of cells you are copying from the notebook file. Each cell from the notebook file that you select is combined with a cell from the current notebook.

When you combine files, one of the files must be the current notebook. The second or incoming file must be saved on a hard or floppy disk. You can choose to combine either the entire saved file or specific blocks from the saved file. When you combine rather than insert files, only cells in the file on disk that contain entries are included in the combination process. Blank cells in the saved file do not overwrite cells in the current notebook that contain data entries, nor are new pages, columns, or rows inserted.

You can carry out certain operations when you combine files or blocks from files. You can choose to add values of the two files together, subtract, multiply, or divide them. Alternatively, you can choose to simply copy the incoming file's entries into the current notebook. You might want to carry out operations when combining four notebooks containing the budget data for each quarter of the last year into one notebook containing data for the entire year—for example, instead of entering new numbers, adding all the values together to create the aggregate sums. However, you might just want to copy when combining headings from an old report with new data to create a new report.

To combine two files, position your selector in the cell of the current notebook that you want to be the upper left hand corner of where the files combine. Select Combine from the Tools menu, opening the Combine Files dialog box shown in Figure 7.29. Select the incoming saved file using the File Name text and list box, the Directories list box, and the File Types and Drives drop-down list boxes. The process is like selecting a file to open. In the Operation section, select the operation you would like to carry out. You can select Copy simply to copy the entries of the saved file into the current notebook, Add to add the value entries together, Subtract to subtract the saved file's value entries from the current notebook's values, Multiply to multiply them, or Divide to divide the values of the current file by those of the saved file. In the Source section, select Entire File to combine the

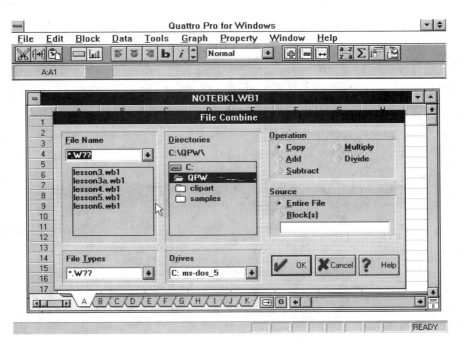

Figure 7.29   The File Combine Dialog Box

entire file or <u>B</u>lock(s) to combine only selected portions of the saved file. If you select <u>B</u>lock(s), you can type the block name or block address of the file on disk you are combining. You can specify more than one block, separating the different block specifications with commas.

As an example of combining files, Figure 7.30 shows two notebooks. One displays the production costs per unit for four products during the first half of the year. The second displays the total units produced for the same four product lines over the same time period. To produce a model containing the total production costs for the four products, follow these steps:

1. Open a new notebook in which to create the total production cost report by selecting <u>N</u>ew from the <u>F</u>ile menu.

2. Move to A1, which is where you want Quattro Pro to begin adding information. In this example, you are copying an entire file first, in order to provide you with both a template and the first data required to create your report.

3. Select <u>C</u>ombine from the <u>T</u>ools menu.

4. Select the name of the file to combine from the <u>F</u>ile Name list box. In this example, it is UNITS.

5. Select OK. You are using the defaults of a copy operation and combining the entire file.

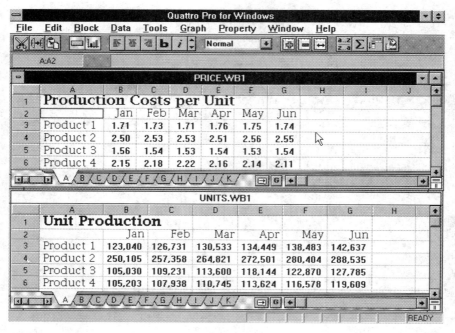

Figure 7.30   Two Files to Be Combined

6. Type **Total Production Costs** to replace the label in A1.

7. Move the selector to B3.

8. Select Combine from the Tools menu.

9. Select the file to combine in the File Name list box. In this example, it is PRICE.

10. Select the Block(s) radio button, and specify the block B3..G6 in the text box.

11. Select the Multiply radio button.

12. Select OK.

13. Select the block B3..G3 and the Fit button from the SpeedBar. The combined data looks like Figure 7.31.

The units cost values originally combined into the current notebook in steps 1 through 3 are multiplied by the units produced to provide the value for the Total Production Costs for each product during the first six months of the year.

When you copy to combine files, the results are just as if you copied the data from the notebook on disk to the active notebook using the Clipboard. With the other combine operations, the results are different. Whether Quattro Pro copies a block or an entire file, it leaves all formulas in the active (current) file intact. Quattro Pro changes any formulas in the incoming notebook into values. Any cells

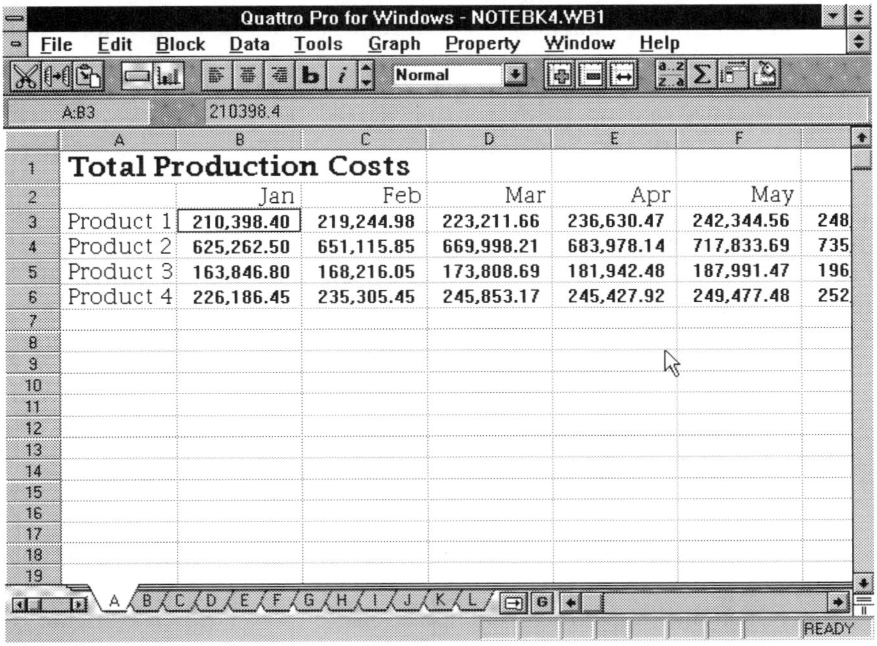

Figure 7.31 The Combined File

containing labels or values are not affected by this operation. Any labels or blank cells from the incoming file are assumed to have an entry of 0 for the purpose of the calculation. Also, any incoming values or formulas with a value of @NA or @ERR are changed to 0. Entries of @NA or @ERR in the current notebook are not changed. Also, Quattro Pro uses the cell formats of the current notebook.

When you combine two notebooks, you must make sure that the data you want to combine aligns. If, for example, the selector was in B5 when you combined the notebooks shown in Figure 7.30, your results would be meaningless because the values that you wanted to combine would not properly align so Quattro Pro would multiply the units for the wrong products with each product unit cost.

Importing Text Data

When you bring data from another package into Quattro Pro, you are *importing* data. Quattro Pro provides automatic translation features for importing data from packages like 1-2-3 and dBASE with the Open command in the File menu. For data in other formats, you have several options. One popular one is to bring in text files as labels. For this method of importing data, Quattro Pro has a command that breaks the imported long-label entries into individual cell entries—the Parse command in the Data menu explained below. While Quattro Pro cannot translate all file formats, you can almost always either save a file in a text format, or convert it to a text format by copying it into the Notepad accessory in Windows. Using the Import command in the Tools menu, you can import that text file into a Quattro Pro notebook.

A file simply consists of a bunch of letters and words. There is no coding or formatting in such a file. Quattro Pro has three options for importing a text file. First, you can import the file so that each line of text in the file is a separate entry in a column of the spreadsheet. This means if the first line of the file contains ABC Company and the second line contains XYZ Company, when you import this file starting at A1, A1 contains ABC Company and A2 contains XYZ Company. The other two options use delimiters to break the text on a line into separate fields. You can delimit the fields by commas, as in ABC Company, XYZ Company. When you import a line starting at A1 that contains ABC Company, XYZ Company, A1 contains ABC Company and B1 contains XYZ Company. You can also delimit the fields with commas for numbers, quotes and commas for text data. An example of this type of delimiting is "ABC Company",5761,"XYZ Company". When this example is imported starting at A1, ABC Company is put in A1, 5761 in B1, and XYZ Company in C1. The advantage of enclosing character data in quotes is that the character data can include commas, as in "LJM Partners, LTD". With either the comma or the comma and quotes, each line in the file is imported as a separate row in the notebook.

To import a text file into your current notebook, you select Import from the Tools menu, opening the Import File dialog box. Select the file you want to import using the list and text boxes on the left of the dialog box just as if you are selecting a file to open. Select the radio button from the Option section that tells Quattro Pro how the file is delimited. You have a choice of ASCII Text File, which imports the file without delimiters, Comma and " Delimited File, which imports the document using both commas and quotation marks as delimiters, and Only Commas, which uses only commas as delimiters. When you select OK, the file is imported starting at the selector's location. Figure 7.32 shows the beginning of a text file in the Notepad accessory and the beginning of the imported data in Quattro Pro.

Parsing Data

Parsing data is both a way to format imported text files and a way to correct data entry errors. Parsing is done to long label entries, breaking these entries down into smaller pieces of data. This can be useful if you are importing a database saved in a text file format, for example, because a text file does not mark which column the information is in. Each row of data is treated like a single label entry. You can use data parsing to break the label up into separate parts. Also, if you have a column of entries where both last and first names are entered in one column, you may find it necessary to break these entries into columns, one for first and the other for last names.

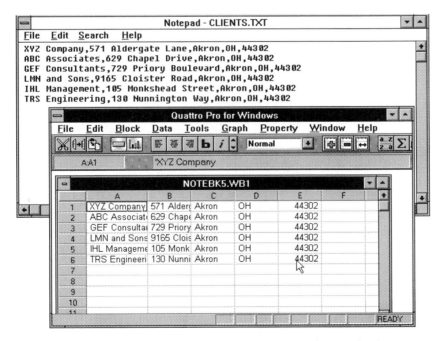

Figure 7.32 Data Imported from a Text File with Commas as Delimiters

When you parse data, you create a *format line*. Quattro Pro uses the format line as a guideline for how to break the labels. The symbols used in the format line indicate whether the new entry is a label or a value, and how many characters in from the beginning of the label the new entry starts and ends. To parse data, select the block containing the long labels you want to divide into smaller parts. Next, Parse from the Data menu, opening the Data Parse dialog box. The Input text box contains the block you have selected with the labels to break up. Specify the block of cells where you want the parsed data to start in the Output text box. If you select one cell in an empty area rather than a multicell block, this command will use only as much space as necessary. Then select the Create button. The data will be moved down by one row, and a format line will appear above the top row of the database.

The format line that is originally created is based on the first line of the input block. You may need to edit it to make it more applicable to the entire group of data. Each of the characters in the format line has a meaning as described in Table 7.2. The format line parses all of the entries in the input block. To edit the format line, select Edit from the Data Parse dialog box. This opens the Edit Parse Line dialog box (Figure 7.33). In this dialog box, you can edit the format line by moving to where you want to make a change and typing valid format line characters. The data in your input block appears beneath the line where you are editing the format block so that you can compare the format line to the data itself, which will help you create a more accurate format line. The data from the input block appears in a monospace font so you can see how the format line characters will align with the characters in the input block. In this dialog box, you can edit the format line just as you would edit a label entry in the input line, using the DEL and BACKSPACE keys to delete characters. If you want to add characters to the format line, you must press INS first. In the Format text box, you initially are in Overstrike

Table 7.2   Format Line Symbols for Parsing Data

|	Format line indicator, only appears in the input line.
V	Marks the beginning of a value entry.
L	Marks the beginning of a label entry.
T	Marks the beginning of a time value to be translated into a serial number.
D	Marks the beginning of a date value to be translated into a serial number.
>	Continues an entry one character.
*	Indicates a blank space that may be occupied by longer entries underneath the first one.
S	Tells Quattro Pro to ignore the character in this position.

Data Parse
Input C:A1
Output
Create
Edit
Reset
OK
Cancel
Help

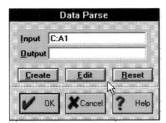

Figure 7.33 The Data Parse Dialog Box

mode, and each character you type in the format line replaces a character rather than adding a character. Select OK when the format line is complete.

When you are finished editing the format line, select OK from the Data Parse dialog box to begin the actual parsing. The parsed data will appear in the output area, as in Figure 7.34. The next time that you open the Data Parse dialog box, the settings you last specified during the current Quattro Pro session are still set in the text boxes. If you want to change all of them, select the Reset button, erasing all of the information that you have added so that you can reenter that data. Resetting this command's settings does not remove the format line from the notebook. If you need to use several format lines to break up the lengthy labels, you must select Parse in the Data menu for each group of labels you want to divide.

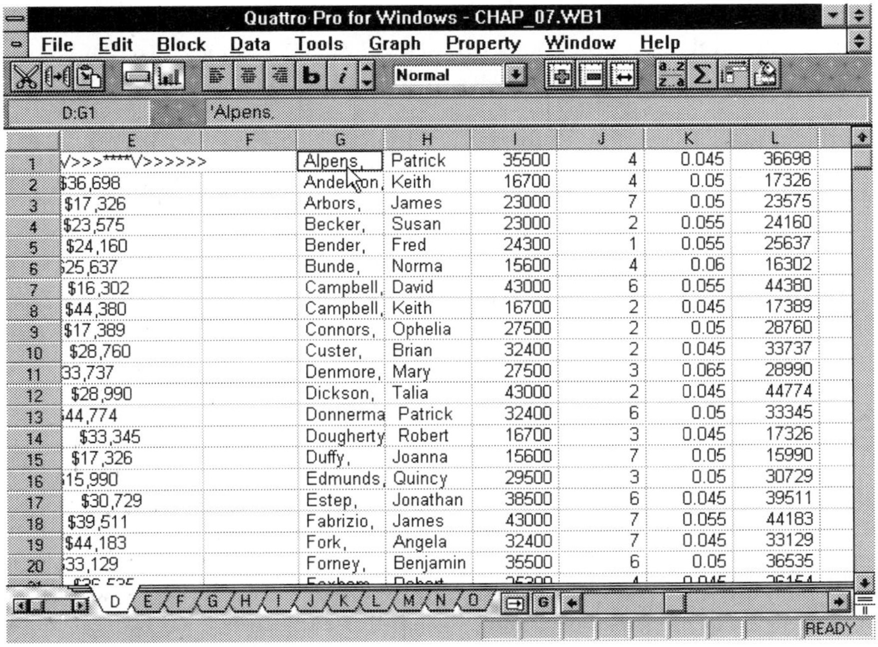

Quattro Pro for Windows - CHAP_07.WB1
File Edit Block Data Tools Graph Property Window Help
Normal
D:G1 'Alpens,
E F G H I J K L
1 V>>>****V>>>>>> Alpens, Patrick 35500 4 0.045 36698
2 $36,698 Anderson, Keith 16700 4 0.05 17326
3 $17,326 Arbors, James 23000 7 0.05 23575
4 $23,575 Becker, Susan 23000 2 0.055 24160
5 $24,160 Bender, Fred 24300 1 0.055 25637
6 $25,637 Bunde, Norma 15600 4 0.06 16302
7 $16,302 Campbell, David 43000 6 0.055 44380
8 $44,380 Campbell, Keith 16700 2 0.045 17389
9 $17,389 Connors, Ophelia 27500 2 0.05 28760
10 $28,760 Custer, Brian 32400 2 0.045 33737
11 33,737 Denmore, Mary 27500 3 0.065 28990
12 $28,990 Dickson, Talia 43000 2 0.045 44774
13 44,774 Donnerma Patrick 32400 6 0.05 33345
14 $33,345 Dougherty Robert 16700 3 0.045 17326
15 $17,326 Duffy, Joanna 15600 7 0.05 15990
16 15,990 Edmunds, Quincy 29500 3 0.05 30729
17 $30,729 Estep, Jonathan 38500 6 0.045 39511
18 $39,511 Fabrizio, James 43000 7 0.055 44183
19 $44,183 Fork, Angela 32400 7 0.045 33129
20 33,129 Forney, Benjamin 35500 6 0.05 36535
D E F G H I J K L M N O
READY

Figure 7.34 Data Parsed Using the Data Parse Command

CREATING WORKSPACES AND TEMPLATES

Quattro Pro has two special features that make working with its notebooks more productive—workspaces and templates. A *workspace* is a group of open windows and their contents. You can use workspaces to quickly bring up a set of notebooks. *Templates* let you create an empty notebook with your settings and formatting, to use for notebooks you subsequently create.

Creating Workspaces

When you are designing an application, you can carefully size and position the windows so that each one is where you want it. You may want to save the arrangement and files currently active so that you can quickly retrieve the entire group at once. The group of windows, their contents, and their positions are called a *workspace*. To save this workspace, select Workspace from the File menu, and then select Save. Quattro Pro opens the Save Workspace dialog box, which has the same list and text boxes as the Save File dialog box you learned about in the beginning of this chapter. Type the name for the workspace in the File Name text box. When you select OK, Quattro Pro automatically adds an extension of .WSP and saves the workspace. The workspace remembers the names of each open notebook window, its size, and its position. The workspace does not store notebook data. It only remembers which file is in each window and the size and position of the window. You can change data in a notebook spreadsheet saved with a workspace without using a workspace, and the workspace will use the updated contents when it's restored.

When you want to work with the same notebooks again, select Workspace from the File menu and then select Restore. From the Restore Workspace dialog box, which is just like the Open file dialog box, select the workspace file's name and select OK. Quattro Pro opens the notebooks in windows at the same location and size that you saved them when you saved the workspace. Using workspaces is more convenient than opening every file in a group.

Saving Notebook Templates

Another way to customize Quattro Pro to suit your needs is to create notebook templates. As you work with Quattro Pro, you are likely to find that you regularly use certain property settings, macros, or formats in your notebooks. If you find yourself regularly customizing your notebooks in the same fashion, you may prefer to set up a notebook template. A template has all the basic notebook features. Instead of entering and changing all these features each time you start a new notebook, you can simply use the template to start a notebook with the features already set. Another advantage of this is that you can standardize your notebooks, so that they all have similar appearances and formatting.

To create a template, simply create a notebook file with all the settings and formatting that you want to use in a standard notebook. These changes include the named styles available in the notebook and how the Normal style is defined. You can even use a notebook you have previously created with this formatting. First, make sure that the current version of the notebook is saved. Next, clear the contents of the notebook using the Clear Contents command from the Edit menu. This clears the contents of the notebook without removing your formatting changes. Then save the now cleared notebook under another name. Anytime you want to use the template, retrieve the template file, and then use Save As from the File menu to save the created notebook under another name.

You can have several different templates, for different purposes. Alternatively, if you use one template consistently, you can load the template every time you start Quattro Pro. To do this, inspect the application properties and select Startup. Enter the file name in the Autoload File text box. The template is opened every time you load Quattro Pro.

GETTING STARTED

In this chapter, you learned how you can store and use data in files. You also learned how you can open multiple windows and share data between files and applications. You can try some of the commands you learned in this chapter by following these steps:

1. Make the following entries. You can use the report in Figure 7.35 as a guide. This spreadsheet will be used as the model of a consolidation spreadsheet.

   A1: **Division A**
   A3: **Units Sold**
   A4: **Product A**
   A5: **Product B**
   A6: **Product C**
   A8: **Total**
   B4: **49523**
   B5: **12340**
   B6: **23480**
   B8: **@SUM(B4..B6)**

2. To expand column A so that the text in the column does not run into the numbers in column B, select any cell in column A. Either click the Fit button on the SpeedBar or inspect the block's properties, select the Column Width property, select the Auto Width radio button, and select OK.

3. Save this file as DIV_A by selecting Save from the File menu, and typing **DIV_A** in the File Name text box. Select OK to save the file.

4. Make the following entries replacing the entries you made in step 1.

   A1: **Division B**
   B4: **35702**

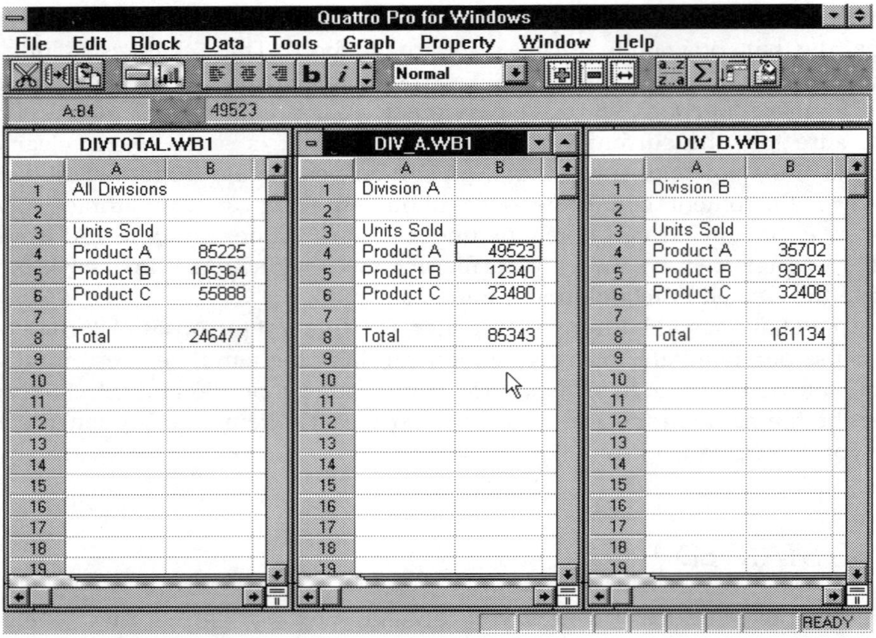

Figure 7.35   Files Created in Getting Started

B5: **93024**
B6: **32408**

5. Save this file as DIV_B. Select Save As from the File menu. You cannot use Save, because you want to save this file with a different name. Type **DIV_B** in the File Name text box and select OK.

6. Move to A1, and type **All Divisions** to replace Division B.

7. Save this file as DIVTOTAL. Select Save As from the File menu. Type **DIVTOTAL** in the File Name text box and select OK.

8. Open the files for Division A and Division B. Select Open from the File menu. Select DIV_A from the File Name list box and select OK. Repeat this command for the DIV_B notebook.

9. Select the DIVTOTAL notebook from the Window menu to make it the active window. Select Tile from the Window menu.

10. Make the following entries in the DIVTOTAL notebook replacing the entries you made in step 4.

    B4: **@SUM([*]B4)**
    B5: **@SUM([*]B5)**
    B6: **@SUM([*]B6)**

    Notice how Quattro Pro converts these formulas into **@SUM([DIV_A] A:B4,[DIV_B]A:B4);@SUM([DIV_A]A:B5,[DIV_B]A:B5)** and **@SUM([DIV_A]A:B6, [DIV_B]A:B6)**.

11. Select Save All from the File menu to save the three files.

12. Copy A1..B8 from DIVTOTAL to the Clipboard. Select the block A1..B8 and either click the Paste button in the SpeedBar or press CTRL-INS.

13. Start the Notepad. Press CTRL-ESC to display the Windows Task List. Select the Program Manager from the list. In the Program Manager, click the Accessories group window, double-click the Accessories group icon, or select the number next to Accessories in the Window menu. Double-click the Notepad icon or move to it with the arrow keys and press ENTER.

14. Paste the Clipboard's contents into the Notepad. Select Paste from the Edit menu to display your Quattro Pro data in the Notepad. Since the Notepad does not support the formatting you can use with Quattro Pro, your entries look plain in the Notepad. You can try pasting the Quattro Pro data into the different accessories and applications you have installed on your system to try out the Clipboard feature. Some applications will even let you create a link with the Quattro Pro data.

15. Close the Notepad without saving the data. Press ALT-F4 or double-click the Notepad's Control menu box to close this application window. When Windows prompts about saving the file, select No.

8

Functions

Quattro Pro provides functions to make calculations easier for you. Quattro Pro's functions are prerecorded formulas that you can access with a special keyword. Some of Quattro Pro's functions provide computations that are impossible to achieve without a function (like the generation of a random number). Other functions calculate results that could be entered with a formula (like the payment for a loan). Quattro Pro still offers an advantage in the latter example, because you do not have to remember the correct formula. Also, since Quattro Pro's functions have already been tested, you can rely on them for more accurate results.

Quattro Pro provides 116 different functions. These functions are organized into categories based on the type of calculations they perform. Quattro Pro's function categories are statistical, string, date and time, logical, financial, mathematical, cell and table, database aggregation, and system. The database aggregation functions are covered with Quattro Pro's other database features in Chapter 11. Once you have identified functions that are useful to you, take a look at other functions in the same category, since they probably will also apply to the Quattro Pro tasks you perform.

The functions in this chapter are organized into the same categories that Quattro Pro uses in the Help menu except that the miscellaneous functions are split into groups called Cell & Table and System. Each category includes functions that relate to the same types of feature. For example, this organization allows users working with financial calculations to review all financial functions quickly, without the need for sifting through functions that perform trigonometric calculations or other unrelated calculations. In this chapter, the material on each function includes a general description, the format of the function, and (in most cases) one or more examples that provide instant ideas for ways that you can use each function. Before looking at a specific group of functions, you need to master the basic function rules. These rules include those covering the syntax of functions and the types of arguments you can use for a function.

FUNCTION BASICS

Quattro Pro has a set of syntax rules that apply to all functions. Every Quattro Pro function starts with the commercial at sign (@). This character triggers Quattro Pro to treat the entry as a value, since all functions are considered formulas, even if the results they return are labels. Following the @ sign is a keyword that describes what the function does. Since function keywords are not case-sensitive, you may type them lowercase or uppercase. Although you have an option with regard to the case used for entry, you cannot modify the spelling of the function name in any way. Quattro Pro recognizes only one keyword for each of its functions.

When you enter a function, as soon as Quattro Pro knows which function you are entering, the status line includes the format of the function. For example, as soon as you type **@PMT**, the status line contains @PMT(principal,rate,term). Also, as you edit different parts of the function, the status line displays the part you are entering or editing in uppercase. This means when you type **@PMT(** and you are ready to enter the principal, the status line will contain @pmt(PRINCIPAL,rate,term). You can use this prompt as a reminder of the information you must tell Quattro Pro so that the function returns the correct result.

With a few exceptions, each function word is followed by a set of parentheses enclosing specific arguments for the function. When functions are nested, each function must have its own set of parentheses in order for Quattro Pro to determine where each function begins and ends.

The arguments for each function are enclosed within the parentheses. These arguments contain your specifications for the information the function uses when completing the computation. Each function requires a different number of arguments. Some functions like @INT require only one argument, while others like @PAYMT use up to six. Quattro Pro has a few functions like @NOW that do not require an argument. Multiple arguments are separated by commas (the comma can be changed to a semicolon or period by changing the International property of the application). You must specify each argument listed for a function and cannot enter the comma by itself as a placeholder except to indicate that you are not using an optional argument. Entering **@PMT(65000,,360)** results in ERR, since Quattro Pro does not know what interest rate to use in calculating a payment amount. Table 8.1 summarizes each function and the arguments required to use the function.

Function Arguments

Quattro Pro accepts several types of information for function arguments. Every function description in this chapter indicates the acceptable types of data for each function argument. Using a different type of argument results in ERR or in results other than what you expect. Quattro Pro's function arguments are numbers, integers, date/time serial numbers, strings, cell references, blocks, block names, or lists.

A *number* is any group of digits that you can type with the number keys on your keyboard. Unless the default punctuation settings are altered, the period separates

Table 8.1 Quattro Pro Functions and Their Arguments*

Function	Function with Arguments	Function Type
@ABS	@ABS(x)	Mathematical
@ACOS	@ACOS(x)	Mathematical
@ASIN	@ASIN(x)	Mathematical
@ATAN	@ATAN(x)	Mathematical
@ATAN2	@ATAN2(x,y)	Mathematical
@AVG	@AVG(list)	Statistical
@CELL	@CELL(attribute,block)	Cell & Table
@CELLINDEX	@CELLINDEX(attribute,block,column, row[,page])	Cell & Table
@CELLPOINTER	@CELLPOINTER(attribute)	Cell & Table
@CHAR	@CHAR(code)	String
@CHOOSE	@CHOOSE(number,list)	Cell & Table
@CLEAN	@CLEAN(string)	String
@CODE	@CODE(string)	String
@COLS	@COLS(block)	Cell & Table
@COMMAND	@COMMAND (command-string)	System
@COS	@COS(x)	Mathematical
@COUNT	@COUNT(list)	Statistical
@CTERM	@CTERM(rate,fv,pv)	Financial
@CURVALUE	@CURVALUE(general-action, specific-action)	System
@DATE	@DATE(yr,mo,day)	Date & Time
@DATEVALUE	@DATEVALUE(date-string)	Date & Time
@DAY	@DAY(date)	Date & Time
@DDB	@DDB(cost,salvage,life,period)	Financial
@DEGREES	@DEGREES(x)	Mathematical
@ERR	@ERR	Logical
@EXACT	@EXACT(string1,string2)	String
@EXP	@EXP(x)	Mathematical

*Optional arguments are shown in square brackets [ ].   *(continued)*

Table 8.1 Quattro Pro Functions and Their Arguments *(continued)*

Function	Function with Arguments	Function Type
@FALSE	@FALSE	Logical
@FILEEXISTS	@FILEEXISTS(filename)	Logical
@FIND	@FIND(substring,string,startnumber)	String
@FV	@FV(payment,rate,term)	Financial
@FVAL	@FVAL(rate,nper,pmt[,pv][,type])	Financial
@HEXTONUM	@HEXTONUM(string)	String
@HLOOKUP	@HLOOKUP(x,block,row)	Cell & Table
@HOUR	@HOUR(time)	Date & Time
@IF	@IF(cond,trueexpr,falseexpr)	Logical
@INDEX	@INDEX(block,column,row[,sheet])	Cell & Table
@INT	@INT(x)	Mathematical
@IPAYMT	@IPAYMT(rate,per,nper,pv[,fv][,type])	Financial
@IRATE	@IRATE(nper,payment,pv[,fv][,type])	Financial
@IRR	@IRR(guess,block)	Financial
@ISERR	@ISERR(x)	Logical
@ISNA	@ISNA(x)	Logical
@ISNUMBER	@ISNUMBER(x)	Logical
@ISSTRING	@ISSTRING(x)	Logical
@LEFT	@LEFT(string,num)	String
@LENGTH	@LENGTH(string)	String
@LN	@LN(x)	Mathematical
@LOG	@LOG(x)	Mathematical
@LOWER	@LOWER(string)	String
@MAX	@MAX(list)	Statistical
@MEMAVAIL	@MEMAVAIL	System
@MEMEMSAVAIL	@MEMEMSAVAIL	System
@MID	@MID(string,startnumber,num)	String

(continued)

Table 8.1 Quattro Pro Functions and Their Arguments *(continued)*

Function	Function with Arguments	Function Type
@MIN	@MIN(list)	Statistical
@MINUTE	@MINUTE(time)	Date & Time
@MOD	@MOD(x,y)	Mathematical
@MONTH	@MONTH(date)	Date & Time
@N	@N(block)	String
@NA	@NA	Logical
@NOW	@NOW	Date & Time
@NPER	@NPER(rate,payment,pv[,fv][,type])	Financial
@NPV	@NPV(rate,block[,type])	Financial
@NUMTOHEX	@NUMTOHEX(x)	String
@PAYMT	@PAYMT(rate,nper,pv[,fv][,type])	Financial
@PI	@PI	Mathematical
@PMT	@PMT(pv,rate,nper)	Financial
@PPAYMT	@PPAYMT(rate,per,nper,pv[,fv][,type])	Financial
@PROPER	@PROPER(string)	String
@PROPERTY	@PROPERTY(object.property)	Cell & Table
@PV	@PV(payment,rate,nper)	Financial
@PVAL	@PVAL(rate,nper,payment[,fv][,type])	Financial
@RADIANS	@RADIANS(x)	Mathematical
@RAND	@RAND	Mathematical
@RATE	@RATE(fv,pv,term)	Financial
@REPEAT	@REPEAT(string,num)	String
@REPLACE	@REPLACE(string,startnum,num, newstring)	String
@RIGHT	@RIGHT(string,num)	String
@ROUND	@ROUND(x,num)	Mathematical
@ROWS	@ROWS(block)	Cell & Table

(continued)

Table 8.1   Quattro Pro Functions and Their Arguments *(continued)*

Function	Function with Arguments	Function Type
@S	@S(block)	String
@SECOND	@SECOND(time)	Date & Time
@SHEETS	@SHEETS(block)	Cell & Table
@SIN	@SIN(x)	Mathematical
@SLN	@SLN(cost,salvage,life)	Financial
@SQRT	@SQRT(x)	Mathematical
@STD	@STD(list)	Statistical
@STDS	@STDS(list)	Statistical
@STRING	@STRING(num,decplaces)	String
@SUM	@SUM(list)	Statistical
@SUMPRODUCT	@SUMPRODUCT(block1,block2)	Statistical
@SYD	@SYD(cost,salvage,life,period)	Financial
@TAN	@TAN(x)	Mathematical
@TERM	@TERM(payment,rate,fv)	Financial
@TIME	@TIME(hr,min,sec)	Date & Time
@TIMEVALUE	@TIMEVALUE(time-string)	Date & Time
@TODAY	@TODAY	Date & Time
@TRIM	@TRIM(string)	String
@TRUE	@TRUE	Logical
@UPPER	@UPPER(string)	String
@VALUE	@VALUE(string)	String
@VAR	@VAR(list)	Statistical
@VARS	@VARS(list)	Statistical
@VERSION	@VERSION	System
@VLOOKUP	@VLOOKUP(x,block,column)	Cell & Table
@YEAR	@YEAR(date)	Date & Time
@@	@@(cell)	Cell & Table

the whole number from the decimal portion of the number. When a function uses a number, you can enter the number directly, enter a formula that returns a number, or use a cell address or block name to reference a cell containing the number to use in the formula. Some number function arguments use only intergers. An *integer* is in a subset of number entries since integers only include whole numbers. If you give Quattro Pro a number like 4.5 when it expects an integer, Quattro Pro truncates the number and uses the whole portion. In this example, Quattro Pro uses **4**. A *date/time serial number* is a special type of number that some functions use. It is a number that represents a date, time, or both.

A *string* is any combination of characters and special symbols. Quattro Pro cannot perform mathematical calculations on strings, but Quattro Pro does have a whole category of functions that operates exclusively on strings. When a function uses a string, you can enter the string directly by enclosing it in quotes, enter a formula that returns a string, or use a cell address or block name to reference a cell containing the label to use in the formula. When you use a string in place of a number in a function, Quattro Pro treats the string as a zero and uses the zero value in the function. In other categories of functions, the use of a string entry can cause an error condition. Examples of strings are shown below:

"Tom Jones"
"The total of the numbers is:"
"December 14, 1989"

A *cell reference* is a single cell address. Rather than typing in a number or string as a function argument, you may want to reference the cell that contains these entries. When a function has a cell reference as one of its arguments, the function uses the value from the cell reference in place of the cell reference. Cell references provide flexibility, since they let you change a value of a function's argument without changing the function. A cell reference can reference a cell in another spreadsheet notebook by including the file name in brackets ([ ]) before the cell address.

A *block reference* is a rectangular group of cells on a notebook. Rather than referring to one cell in your notebook, a block refers to multiple cells. A block is defined by referring to two diagonally opposite corners of the group of cells you wish to reference. Typically, the reference is to the upper left corner and the lower right corner of the area of cells. When you type the block reference, one period separates the two corners; Quattro Pro, however, displays it as two periods. To include all cells from row 1 to 10 in columns A through D, the block is A1..D10, A10..D1, D10..A1, or D1..A10. A block reference can reference a block in another spreadsheet notebook by including the file name in brackets ([ ]) before the block address (see linking in Chapter 7). Some functions that only operate on one cell entry will use the first cell in a block when given a block address.

You can also refer to a block or cell reference with a *block name*. A block name is a name that you assign to one or more cells. When you need to refer to the cells, you can use the block name instead of the cell references. Block names are discussed in Chapter 4. Block names provide an ideal solution when you need to reference blocks from other spreadsheet notebooks. When you move a named block, Quattro Pro adjusts the formulas that reference the block for the new address.

A *list* consists of either (1) a single block of cells, (2) a block of cells and several individual cells, or (3) several blocks of cells separated by commas. The cells in the list can refer to numbers or strings, although the statistical functions that support list entries expect values for most of the functions. A list allows you to combine several groups of information into one function. For example, @SUM, which uses a list as a function argument, allows you to total multiple areas of your notebook, numbers, multiple cell references, and cells from multiple notebooks—all within the same function. A list can also include other entries such as strings and values. A1..D10,E15,"Tom",15 is an example of a list. As you can see by this example, the different parts of the list are separated with commas.

Using the Functions Key

Quattro Pro provides a quick method of choosing a function. If you press ALT-F3 (FUNCTIONS), Quattro Pro displays a dialog box containing a list of all available functions. This is the same dialog box that Quattro Pro displays when you click the @ button on the SpeedBar in EDIT, POINT, VALUE, or LABEL mode. To choose one of these functions, highlight that function and select OK, or double-click the function. Using the function key or SpeedBar prevents spelling mistakes and saves typing time.

Nesting Functions

In most examples in this chapter, the functions are covered individually. Quattro Pro also supports *nested* functions, which means that one function can be used as the argument for another function as long as the result of the nested function supplies the proper type of argument. This additional level of sophistication allows you to combine the different features of Quattro Pro's functions to create formulas to fit your needs.

Using Added Functions

Besides the 116 functions available automatically with Quattro Pro, you can also add other functions to Quattro Pro. These functions are stored in add-in files. The add-in files let you add functions that expand Quattro Pro's features. To use one of these functions, you put the name of the add-in file and a period before the function name. After the function name is the parentheses and any arguments the function uses. This means that if you have a function called @TIMETOSTRING in the TIME add-in file that uses a time number as an argument, you would enter **@TIME.TIMETOSTRING(@NOW)**.

STATISTICAL FUNCTIONS

Quattro Pro provides several functions that perform basic quantitative or statistical measures. All these functions except @SUMPRODUCT perform their computations on a list of arguments. Just as with any function, when multiple arguments are provided as part of the list, they are separated by commas. These functions perform simple arithmetic calculations like adding, counting, and averaging.

In this category, Quattro Pro also provides four functions to measure dispersion. Dispersion is a measure of the degree to which data is distributed within a range. The higher the dispersion, the more the data is spread out within the range. Dispersion is measured as a deviation from the mean (that is, from the average). Another function in Quattro Pro, @SUMPRODUCT, computes the dot product of two blocks. All statistical functions except @SUMPRODUCT will use the notebook shown in Figure 8.1, which lists the expenses for a factory for the first six months of the year.

@MAX

The @MAX function returns the maximum value from the values provided in a list. The format of this function is @MAX(list). Although numeric values are

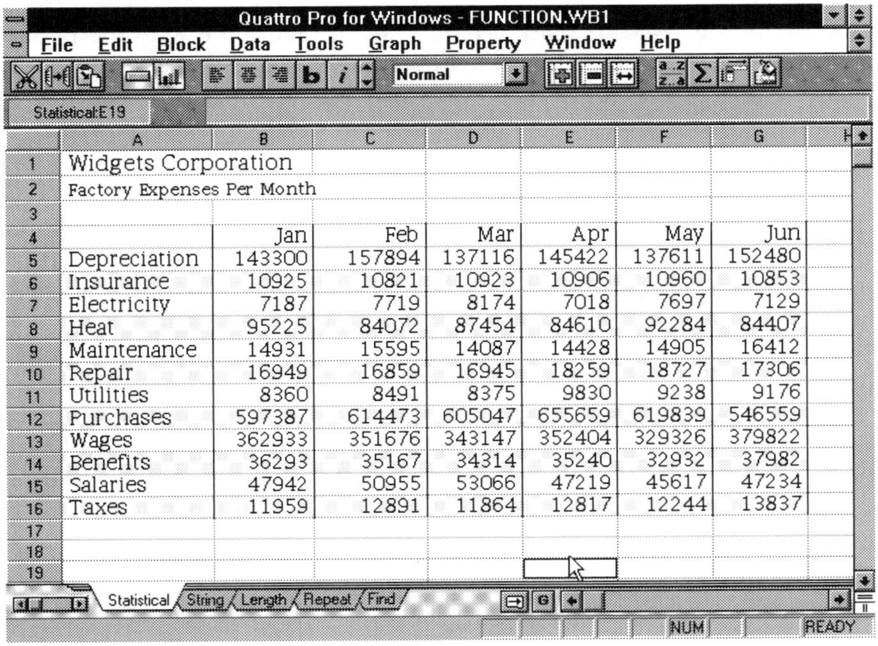

	A	Jan	Feb	Mar	Apr	May	Jun
1	Widgets Corporation						
2	Factory Expenses Per Month						
5	Depreciation	143300	157894	137116	145422	137611	152480
6	Insurance	10925	10821	10923	10906	10960	10853
7	Electricity	7187	7719	8174	7018	7697	7129
8	Heat	95225	84072	87454	84610	92284	84407
9	Maintenance	14931	15595	14087	14428	14905	16412
10	Repair	16949	16859	16945	18259	18727	17306
11	Utilities	8360	8491	8375	9830	9238	9176
12	Purchases	597387	614473	605047	655659	619839	546559
13	Wages	362933	351676	343147	352404	329326	379822
14	Benefits	36293	35167	34314	35240	32932	37982
15	Salaries	47942	50955	53066	47219	45617	47234
16	Taxes	11959	12891	11864	12817	12244	13837

Figure 8.1 Notebook Page Used to Illustrate Statistical Functions

normally referenced in the list, the inclusion of labels and character strings does not have an effect since they are treated as 0.

An example of the @MAX function using Figure 8.1 would be @MAX(B5..G5). Once this formula is entered in H5, you can copy it down the column for the other expenses. For each type of expense, the last column shows the highest expense. This information tells you the largest amount expended in each category for any one month. You can use this information to locate costs that should be reviewed for possible cost reductions.

The @MAX function can also be used for determining the best performance figure for sales personnel, the highest grade on an examination for creating a curve, or the largest budget deviation. The ease with which the entire column or rows of data can be selected with the combinations of the END key and various arrow keys makes it easy to specify a contiguous block as the list.

@MIN

The @MIN function returns the minimum value from the values provided in a list. The format of this function is @MIN(list). Since character strings and labels are given a numeric value of 0, including them in the list with other positive numbers causes the @MIN function to return 0.

An example of the @MIN function using Figure 8.1 would be @MIN(B5..G5). Once this formula is entered in H5, you can copy it down the column for the other expenses. For each type of expense, the last column shows the lowest expense. This information is used for variance analysis to determine why the minimum number varies from the average. @MIN quickly selects the lowest bid price for a contract, the lowest score on a test, or the lowest temperature reading.

@COUNT

The @COUNT function counts the number of nonzero cells in a list. This function counts both numbers and strings. The format of this function is @COUNT(list). If one or more arguments in the list are single-cell references, each single-cell reference is counted as a nonblank cell even if it is blank.

You can use an entry like @COUNT(B5..B16) in B20 for the expense notebook in Figure 8.1 to count the number of expenses. A quick check of the counts tells you whether an entry was missing in any column of entries. As described above, a single-cell reference changes the count even if the cell referenced is blank. For example, if the formula in B20 is **@COUNT(B5..B16,D2)**, the function returns 13, since it counts the number of nonblank entries in B5..B16 and then adds one for D2, even though D2 is blank.

@SUM

The @SUM function adds the values referenced in the list. The format of this function is @SUM(list). Since strings have a numeric value of zero, strings do not affect the result of this function.

Using the @SUM function in row 20 of Figure 8.1 as in @SUM(B5..B16) for B20 computes a total of each month's expenses. Using @SUM in column H totals the expenses for the first six months. This information is used for budget planning and variance analysis.

You can also easily add @SUM functions with the SpeedSum button in the SpeedBar. This is the button that contains the Σ. You can select a block that includes the values you want to total and the adjacent empty cells you want to contain the formulas. For example, you can select the block B5..H17 and click SpeedSum in the SpeedBar to sum the expenses for each month. Quattro Pro adds each of the rows in columns B through G and puts the @SUM formula that calculates the total in column H. Row 17 contains @SUM formulas that total expenses for each month. Since the cells in column H and row 17 are blank, Quattro Pro knows to put the formulas in these cells.

@AVG

The @AVG function averages the values in the list. The @AVG function is equal to the @SUM function divided by the @COUNT function for the same list. The format of this function is @AVG(list). As with the @COUNT function, if one or more arguments in the list are single-cell references, each single-cell reference is counted as 0 even if it is blank. Also, since strings have a value of 0, their inclusion affects the result returned by the function.

An example of the @AVG function using Figure 8.1 would be @AVG(B5..G5). Once this formula is entered in H5, you can copy it down the column for the other expenses. For each expense category, the column H averages the expenses for the first six months of the year. In this example, the result indicates the approximate amount that is spent on each of the expense categories per month. Management can use this information for budget planning and variance analysis.

As described above, a single-cell reference that is blank or is a string changes the result. For example, entering the formula **@AVG(A5..G5)** in H5 returns 124,832 instead of 145,637, since it adds the values (873,823) and divides that number by 7, which is the number of nonblank cells in the block.

@VAR

@VAR measures the degree to which the individual values in a group of data vary from the average of that group. The lower the variance, the less individual values vary from the average. The lower the variance, the more reliable the average is as a representation of the data. The format for the variance function is @VAR(list). Cells containing labels and single-cell references cause this function to return an erroneous result.

An example of the @VAR function using Figure 8.1 would be @VAR(B5..G5). Once this formula is entered in H5, you can copy it down the column for the other expenses to calculate the variance for each expense. The variance for Purchases is larger than the variance for Insurance, indicating that the monthly expense fluctuates more.

@VAR uses the n method (biased) for computing the variances, which is designed to compute the variance for an entire population. For example, the variance for Insurance is 2203, and the variance for Purchases is 1,056,031,029. When you are computing for a sample of a population, such as when you are evaluating question-naires, you should use the @VARS function instead. If you compute the sample variance of the expense categories, the variances become slightly higher.

The variance is frequently used to measure deviations in production runs for different machines or shifts. In this type of application, the differences are normally much smaller, making the variance a much smaller number.

@VARS

@VARS is a function added to Quattro Pro that measures the degree to which the individual values in a group of data vary from the average of the sample of a population. The lower the variance is, the less individual values vary from the average and the more reliable the average is as a representation of the data. The format for the variance function is @VARS(list). Cells containing labels and single-cell references cause this function to return an erroneous result.

An example of the @VARS function for Depreciation using Figure 8.1 would be @VARS(B5..G5), which would return 67918522. Once this formula is entered in H5, you can copy it down the column for the other expenses to calculate the sample variances for each expense. Since the expenses only include some of the months that the expenses are measured, the sample variance is more appropriate than the whole-population method. The variance for Purchases (1,267,237,235) is larger than the variance for Insurance (2,643).

@VARS uses the n-1 method (nonbiased) for computing the variances, which compensates for measuring the variance for a sample instead of the entire population.

The variance is frequently used to measure deviations in production runs for different machines or shifts. In this type of application, the differences are normally much smaller, making the variance a much smaller number.

@STD

@STD calculates the standard deviation of a group of data. The standard deviation measures the degree to which the individual values in the group vary from the average of that group. The standard deviation is the square root of the variance. The lower the standard deviation, the less individual values vary from the average and the more representative the average is. The format for the standard deviation function is @STD(list). Arguments are separated by commas. Cells containing labels and single-cell references are counted as 0 and cause this function to return an incorrect result.

An example of the @STD function for Depreciation using Figure 8.1 would be @STD(B5..G5), which would return 7523. Once this formula is entered in H5, you can copy it down the column for the other expenses to calculate the standard deviation for each expense. Like the variance computation, the standard deviation (32,497) for Purchases is larger than the standard deviation for Insurance (47).

The @STD function uses the n method (biased) for computing the standard deviation, which computes the standard deviation for an entire population. When you are computing the standard deviation for a population sample, such as evaluating questionnaires, you should use the @STDS function instead. When you compute the standard deviation for a sample instead of the standard deviation for an entire group, the standard deviations become slightly higher. For example, the sample standard deviation for Insurance becomes 51, and the sample standard deviation for Purchases is 35,598.

@STDS

@STDS calculates the standard deviation of a group of data. Unlike the @STD function, the @STDS is designed for measuring the standard deviation of a sample of the population. The standard deviation measures the degree to which the individual values in the group vary from the average of that group. The standard deviation is the square root of the variance. The lower the standard deviation, the less individual values vary from the average and the more representative the average is. The format for the standard deviation function is @STDS(list). Cells containing labels and single-cell references count as 0 and cause this function to return an incorrect result. The @STDS function uses the n-1 method (nonbiased) for computing the standard deviation for a sample. It compensates for not including the entire population in the standard deviation computation.

An example of the @STDS function for Depreciation using Figure 8.1 would be @STDS(B5..G5), which would return 8241. Once this formula is entered in H5, you can copy it down the column for the other expenses to calculate the sample standard deviation for each expense. Like the variance computation, the standard deviation (35,598) for Purchases is larger than the standard deviation for Insurance (51). It is also larger than the results for the @STD function, since the standard deviation for a sample compensates for not including the entire population. Use @STDS when you are using only a portion of the items you are measuring, such as when you measure the standard deviation of the rejection rate for 20 production runs instead of all production runs.

@SUMPRODUCT

The @SUMPRODUCT function computes the dot product of two vectors. Quattro Pro uses blocks of data for each vector. The format for this function is @SUMPRODUCT(block1,block2). The terms *block1* and *block2* represent block addresses or names that contain the same number of rows and columns. If the sizes of the blocks differ, Quattro Pro returns ERR.

While computing dot products of vectors may seem like a lot of math theory, the idea behind this function is simple. This function multiplies the first cell of the first block with the first cell of the second block. The function does this for the second cells of each block and so forth until the function has multiplied all the cells in both blocks. Then this function returns the total of the values from the multiplying operation. To illustrate how this function works, assume that you have to compute an invoice's subtotal before computing the sales tax. The invoice might look like this:

Item	Quantity	Item Price	Item Total
Disk drive cleaner	5	6.49	$ 32.45
3 1/2" disks	12	24.99	$299.88
Disk boxes	30	5.39	$161.70
Total			$494.03

This invoice computes the dot product of two vectors—one containing the quantity and the other containing the item price. In the last column, the invoice multiplies the quantity and the item price for each item. In the bottom row, the invoice totals the results of the multiplication. If you use the @SUMPRODUCT function to compute the invoice total, the cells containing the quantity are the first block and the cells containing the item prices are the second block. When you enter the formula, Quattro Pro returns 494.03 as the result. This function can also be used to check other formulas in the notebook.

STRING FUNCTIONS

Quattro Pro provides string functions to manipulate numbers and strings. Some of these functions change the capitalization of string entries and transform strings into uppercase, lowercase, or proper case. Other functions return part of a string. Most string functions operate on strings, although a few expect numbers as arguments. Most of the following discussions of string functions use the inventory listing shown in Figure 8.2.

@LENGTH

The @LENGTH function returns the length of the string reference by the argument. The format of this function is @LENGTH(string).

An example of the @LENGTH function is @LENGTH("Computer Paper"), which returns 14. In this case you can also use the formula @LENGTH(B3), since B3 contains the label Computer Paper. This function counts the number of actual characters rather than the character width a column needs to display the entry. The @LENGTH function is also combined with other string functions like @FIND and @MID to reverse name entries or perform other string manipulations.

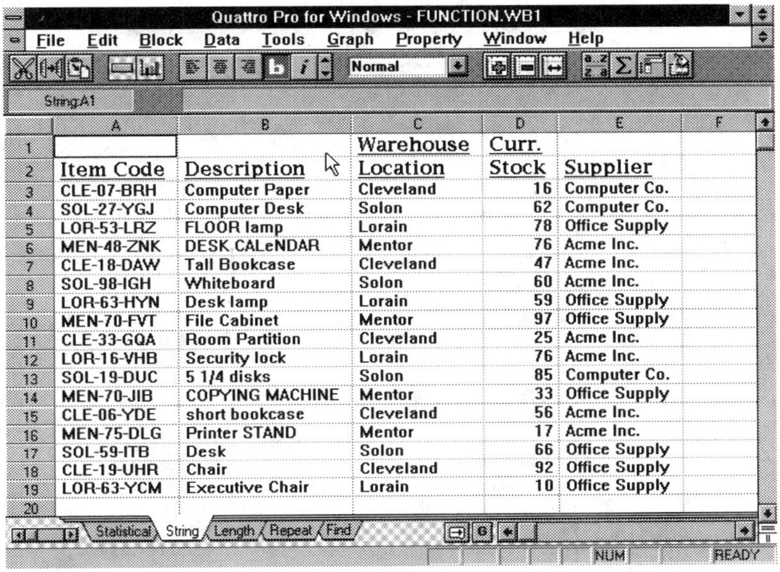

Quattro Pro for Windows - FUNCTION.WB1

	A	B	C	D	E
1			Warehouse	Curr.	
2	Item Code	Description	Location	Stock	Supplier
3	CLE-07-BRH	Computer Paper	Cleveland	16	Computer Co.
4	SOL-27-YGJ	Computer Desk	Solon	62	Computer Co.
5	LOR-53-LRZ	FLOOR lamp	Lorain	78	Office Supply
6	MEN-48-ZNK	DESK CALeNDAR	Mentor	76	Acme Inc.
7	CLE-18-DAW	Tall Bookcase	Cleveland	47	Acme Inc.
8	SOL-98-IGH	Whiteboard	Solon	60	Acme Inc.
9	LOR-63-HYN	Desk lamp	Lorain	59	Office Supply
10	MEN-70-FVT	File Cabinet	Mentor	97	Office Supply
11	CLE-33-GQA	Room Partition	Cleveland	25	Acme Inc.
12	LOR-16-VHB	Security lock	Lorain	76	Acme Inc.
13	SOL-19-DUC	5 1/4 disks	Solon	85	Computer Co.
14	MEN-70-JIB	COPYING MACHINE	Mentor	33	Office Supply
15	CLE-06-YDE	short bookcase	Cleveland	56	Acme Inc.
16	MEN-75-DLG	Printer STAND	Mentor	17	Acme Inc.
17	SOL-59-ITB	Desk	Solon	66	Office Supply
18	CLE-19-UHR	Chair	Cleveland	92	Office Supply
19	LOR-63-YCM	Executive Chair	Lorain	10	Office Supply
20					

Figure 8.2 Notebook Page Used to Illustrate String Function

@LOWER

The @LOWER function converts a string into lowercase letters. This function is often used to correct data entry inconsistencies by putting all entries into a consistent format. The syntax of the function is @LOWER(string).

The left pane of Figure 8.3 shows an example of item descriptions that have not been entered consistently in column B. In column F, the @LOWER function converts the item description into lowercase letters. Once the item descriptions are in lowercase, you can freeze the string functions at their current values. You can do this by copying to the Clipboard and then pasting back to the notebook with the Paste Special command in the Edit menu or using the Values command in the Block menu to copy the values without the Clipboard. You can copy the values in place of the functions or in place of the original entries.

@UPPER

The @UPPER function converts a string into uppercase letters. This function also is often used to put a group of data into a consistent format. The format of the function is @UPPER(string).

The left pane of Figure 8.3 provides an example of item descriptions that have not been entered consistently in column B. In column G, the @UPPER function converts the item description into all uppercase letters. Once the item descriptions

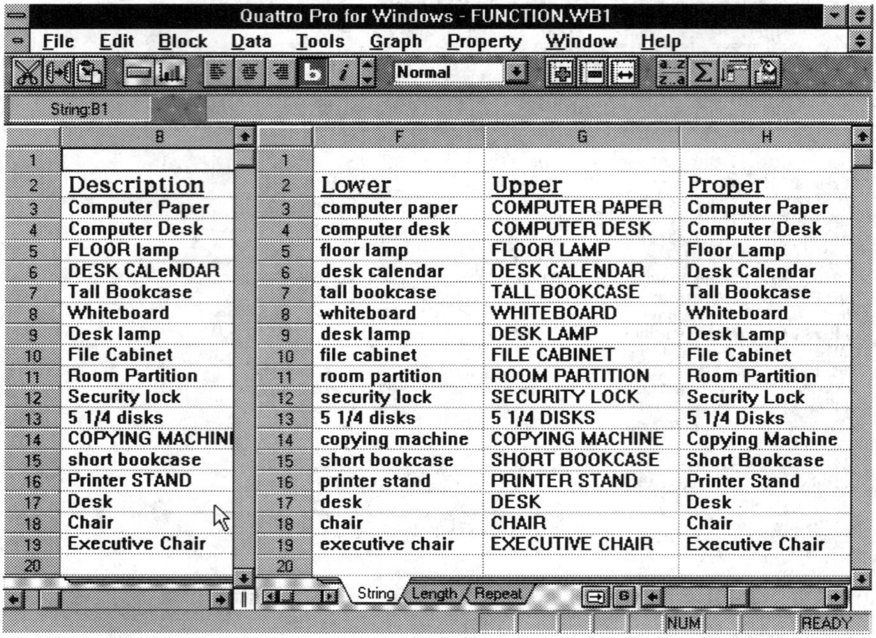

	B		F	G	H
1		1			
2	Description	2	Lower	Upper	Proper
3	Computer Paper	3	computer paper	COMPUTER PAPER	Computer Paper
4	Computer Desk	4	computer desk	COMPUTER DESK	Computer Desk
5	FLOOR lamp	5	floor lamp	FLOOR LAMP	Floor Lamp
6	DESK CALeNDAR	6	desk calendar	DESK CALENDAR	Desk Calendar
7	Tall Bookcase	7	tall bookcase	TALL BOOKCASE	Tall Bookcase
8	Whiteboard	8	whiteboard	WHITEBOARD	Whiteboard
9	Desk lamp	9	desk lamp	DESK LAMP	Desk Lamp
10	File Cabinet	10	file cabinet	FILE CABINET	File Cabinet
11	Room Partition	11	room partition	ROOM PARTITION	Room Partition
12	Security lock	12	security lock	SECURITY LOCK	Security Lock
13	5 1/4 disks	13	5 1/4 disks	5 1/4 DISKS	5 1/4 Disks
14	COPYING MACHINI	14	copying machine	COPYING MACHINE	Copying Machine
15	short bookcase	15	short bookcase	SHORT BOOKCASE	Short Bookcase
16	Printer STAND	16	printer stand	PRINTER STAND	Printer Stand
17	Desk	17	desk	DESK	Desk
18	Chair	18	chair	CHAIR	Chair
19	Executive Chair	19	executive chair	EXECUTIVE CHAIR	Executive Chair
20		20			

Figure 8.3 @LOWER, @UPPER, and @PROPER Used to Convert the Item Descriptions

are uppercase, you can freeze the values and transfer the uppercase descriptions to the Description column.

@PROPER

The @PROPER function converts a string into proper case (capitalization as used for proper nouns). This function also is often used to provide a consistent format to data entered with different capitalization styles. The syntax of the function is @PROPER(string).

The left pane of Figure 8.3 shows an example of item descriptions that are entered inconsistently in column B. In column H, the @PROPER function converts the letters in the item description to proper case. Once the item descriptions are in proper case, you can freeze the current results, and transfer the proper case descriptions to the Description column.

@CLEAN

The @CLEAN function removes special nonprintable characters from a string entry. These special characters can result from data that is imported from another application to share information with the notebook. The syntax of the function is @CLEAN(string). For example, you might have a cell that contains "ABC □Company" in A1. When you enter @CLEAN(A1), the function returns ABC Company.

@TRIM

The @TRIM function strips a string of its extra spaces. It eliminates spaces at the beginning of a string up to the first nonspace character, the extra spaces between characters in the string, and the spaces after the last nonspace character. The format of the @TRIM function is @TRIM(string).

The @TRIM function is often used for imported data. In Figure 8.4, the data illustrating most of the string functions was imported from a database file. Some columns (like Description) contain extra spaces from the original database file. The Description column is isolated from the rest of the data. Column A contains the original item descriptions. Column B shows that the length of the original strings are all 18. Column C contains the @TRIM function, which trims the appropriate description from column A. Once the original descriptions are trimmed, column D lists the lengths of the shortened description entries. If you look at row 12, you will notice that the @TRIM function took out the extra spaces between the 5 and

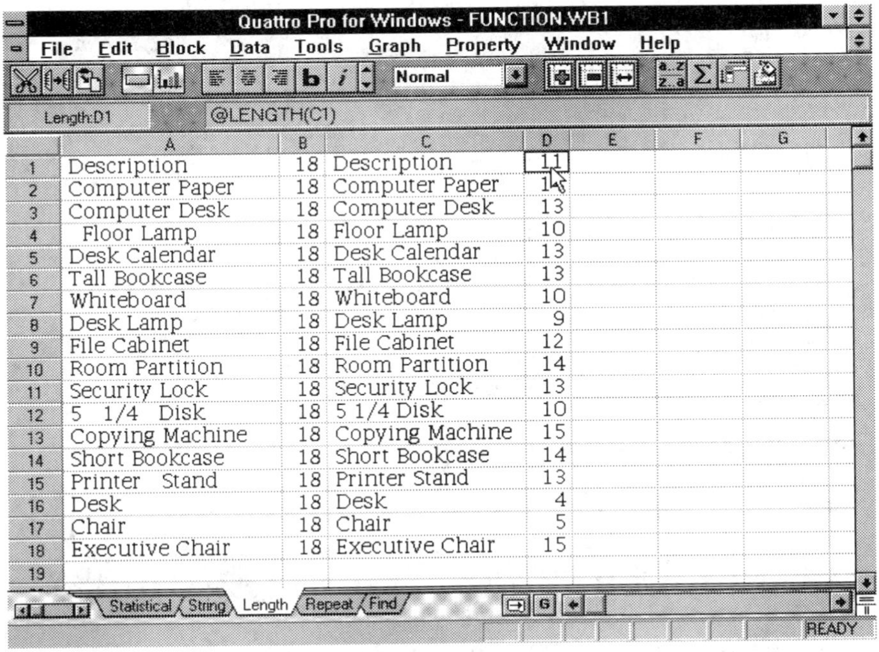

Figure 8.4 **@TRIM Used to Remove Extraneous Spaces**

the 1 and between the 4 and the D. Once the extra spaces are removed, you can freeze the results of the function, and return the new copies of the descriptions to their original locations.

@LEFT

The @LEFT function returns a specified number of characters from the left side of the string. The format for the function is @LEFT(string,num). The term *num* is the number of characters that the function takes from the string.

Column I in Figure 8.5 shows an example of the @LEFT function used to obtain the first three characters from the item code. This type of extraction is useful if the first three characters indicate storage requirements, the vendor, or a product abbreviation.

A shortened version of the item code allows you to hide the item code column and use the extra space to display additional information. The @LEFT function in column I takes the first three characters from the item code in column A. After the portion of the item code is extracted, you can hide the unabbreviated item code column and use the new column for other Quattro Pro features. Truncating the item codes narrows the width required, when you only need specific information.

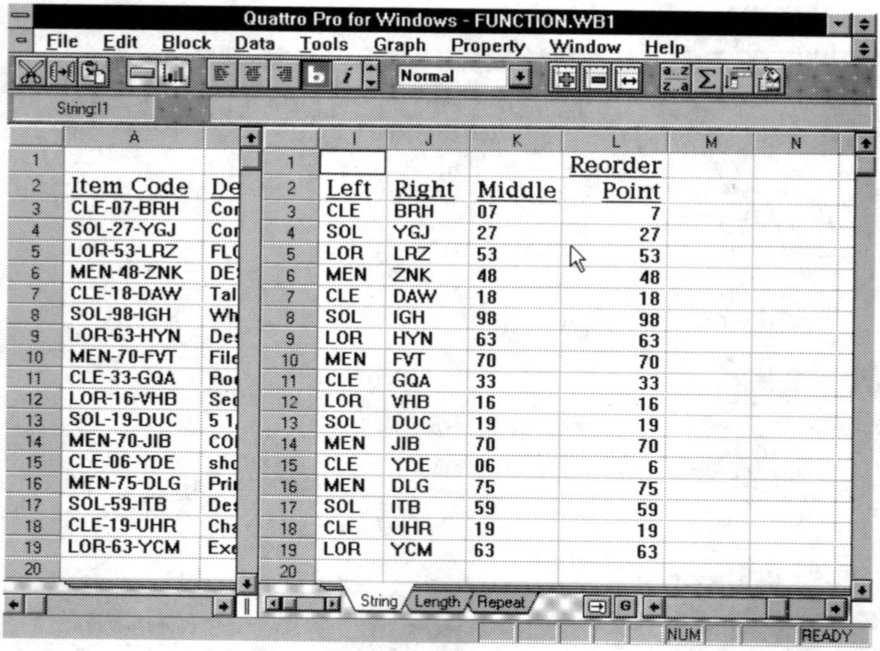

Figure 8.5   @LEFT, @RIGHT, and @MID Used to Create Abbreviations

@RIGHT

The @RIGHT function returns a specified number of characters from the right side of the string. The format for the function is @RIGHT(string,num). The term *num* is the number of characters that the function takes from the string.

Column J in Figure 8.5 provides an example of the @RIGHT function used to obtain the last three characters in the item code. In the item code, the last three characters are unique to each item. Having three alphabetical characters uniquely identifying each product allows up to 17,576 different items. The @RIGHT function in column J takes the last three characters from the item code in column A. After the unique portion of the item code is extracted, you can use this information with other Quattro Pro features, such as sorting.

@MID

The @MID function returns a specified number of characters from a given starting point in a string. The format for the function is @MID(string,startnumber,num). The term *startnumber* is the position in the string where the extraction begins. Quattro Pro considers the first character in the string to be in position 0, so you must make this mental adjustment when you specify the location to begin the extraction. Subtracting 1 from the character location you obtain when counting the characters provides the correct number to Quattro Pro. *Num* is the number of characters that the function extracts from the string. Startnumber or num may be numbers, formulas, or cell references to either.

Column K in Figure 8.5 shows an example of the @MID function used to obtain the reorder point for each of the items. The middle two characters in the Item Code contain the reorder point for each item. The @MID function in column K takes two characters from the Item Code, starting in position 4 (that is, the fifth character in the string). For example, the entry 07 in cell K3 and 06 in cell K15 are returned as strings. To transform the cells into values, you must use the @VALUE function.

If you are extracting characters from a string and wish to vary the position from which you take characters, you may need to start extracting characters based on the location of a specific character. For example, if you wanted the reorder quantity for the item code G-68-NHA, you could use the @FIND function to determine the location of the first hyphen. Since the reorder quantity is between two hyphens, you can use the @FIND function. For example, to find the reorder point for G-68-NHA, which is in A22, type **@MID(A22,@FIND("-",A22,0)+1,2)**. This formula accommodates an item code in which the location of the first hyphen varies.

@VALUE

The @VALUE function returns the numeric value of the string provided in the function argument. The format is @VALUE(string). The string must look like a number. The string can contain dollar signs ($32); commas (32,967,586); extra spaces (" 45.34"); or percent signs (16%). This function is often combined with the @LEFT, @RIGHT, or @MID function to extract a portion of text from a string before converting it to a value. If you try converting a string that does not convert to a number, the function returns ERR.

Column L of Figure 8.5 provides an example of the @VALUE function used to convert the labels in column K to numbers in column L. The entries in column K were extracted from the Item Code using the @MID function, which extracted the number between the two hyphens in the Item Code. For example, in K3, the @MID function extracted 07 from the Item Code. In L3, the @VALUE function converted the label 07 in K3 to the number 7. Once the reorder points are determined for each item, you can compare these numbers to the current stock using a logical formula to determine which items need to be reordered.

@STRING

The @STRING function transforms a number into a string. This function is frequently used to combine text and numbers. The format of this function is @STRING(num,decplaces). The term *num* represents a number. The term *decplaces* is the number of digits after the decimal point that the function includes in the string. If the original value has fewer digits after the decimal point than num, zeros are added. If the original value has more digits after the decimal point than num, the extra digits are truncated.

The @STRING function is used to combine strings and numbers. For example, in Figure 8.2, if you want to compute the total number of items currently in stock, you add the numbers in column D. If you want an explanatory label, you must guess how far to the left you must be for the entire label to display and type your entry. By using the @STRING function, you can combine the label and the total. For example, in B20, you might enter **+" Total number of items in stock is "&@STRING(@SUM(D3..D19),0)** to have the cell display "Total number of items in stock is 955". With the combination approach, you do not have to worry about the total obscuring the label. Also, as the number in stock changes, the total in B20 also changes.

@REPEAT

The @REPEAT function returns a specified string repeated the number of times specified. The format of the @REPEAT function is @REPEAT(string,num). The term *num* is the number of times the string is repeated by the function.

This function is often used instead of the backslash for emphasizing labels or separating sections of a notebook. The function is also used when you want to repeat a label a set number of times without worrying if the column is wide enough. For example, the page shown in Figure 8.6 repeats -> for each 10,000 of

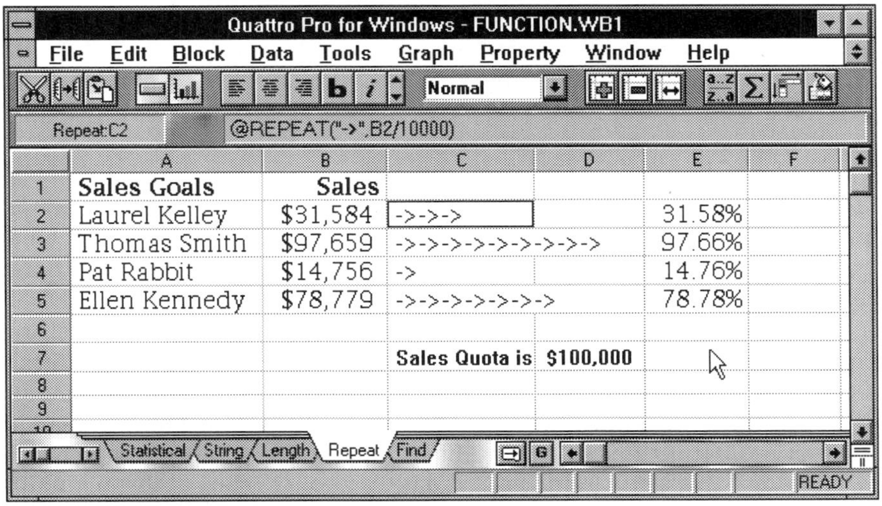

Figure 8.6   @REPEAT Used to Repeat Characters

sales. The formula in C2 is @REPEAT("->",B2/10000), which is copied for C3..C5. While you could enter the formula +B2/10000 in C2 and use the +/- format to repeat + for each 10,000 of sales or create your own user-defined format, you would have to widen column C to display the complete results. The string this function creates can use display space of adjoining cells just like other labels that you enter. C2..C5 uses the Symbol font so the -> has a better appearance.

@EXACT

The @EXACT function takes two strings and compares them. If they are identical, the function returns a 1. If they are not identical, it returns a 0. These values are identical to the values that Quattro Pro uses for @TRUE and @FALSE. The syntax of the function is @EXACT(string1,string2). *String1* and *string2* are the strings this function compares. Since this function is case-sensitive, the characters in the two strings must have identical capitalization.

The @EXACT function is frequently used in combination with the @IF function to check for errors. For example, by using the @MID function to return the fourth and seventh characters, you can use the @EXACT function to check that these characters are hyphens. A sample formula for testing the item code in A3 might be @IF(@EXACT("-",@MID(A3,3,1))#AND#@EXACT("-",@MID(A3,6,1)), " ","Item Code Error"). This function would return an empty string when the fourth and seventh characters are hyphens and would return the message Item Code Error when the fourth and seventh characters are not hyphens. With this formula in a cell such as M3, you can copy the formula down the column for the other item codes. Once the formulas are entered in the column, you can fix the incorrect item codes. Although this function screens for some errors, others are undetected.

@FIND

The @FIND function returns the position in a string where a specified string begins. This function is often used in combination with other functions. Quattro Pro begins counting position numbers for a string at 0, which is the first character of the string, and increments the count for each character to the right. If @FIND finds the string you are searching for in the second character in the string, it returns the starting position number of the string you want to find. The format of this function is @FIND(substring,string,startnumber). *Substring* represents the string that you are trying to find. *String* represents the string that you are searching. *Startnumber* represents the position number in the string where the search should begin. Although this last parameter is usually set to 0 to start at the beginning of the string, it can be any number less than the length of the string.

An example of the @FIND function used with another function is shown in Figure 8.7 which shows the same inventory listing with several errors introduced. The @FIND function is used with the @IF function to check that each item code's hyphens are in the correct position. In this example, #AND# joins two @FIND

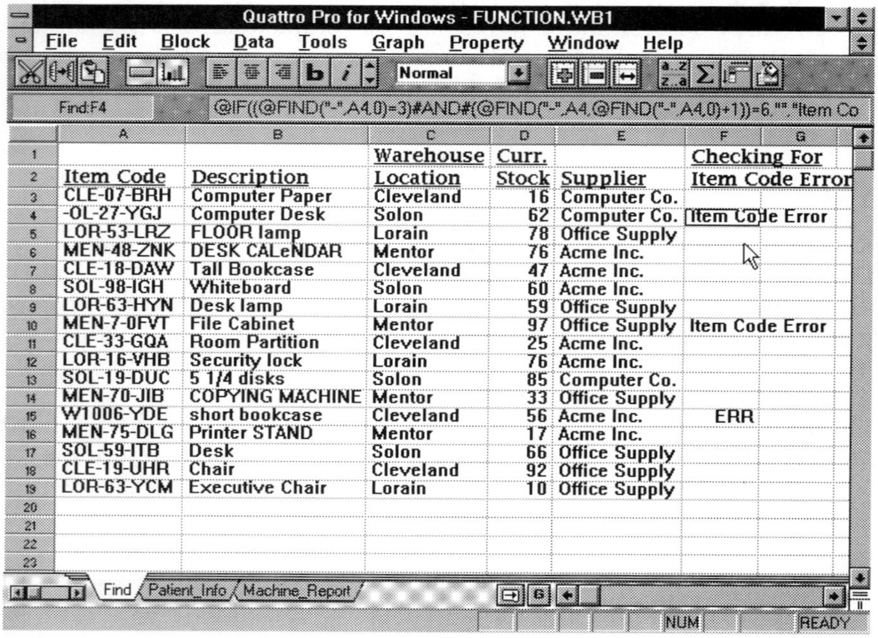

Figure 8.7   @FIND Used to Check for Item Code Errors

functions. The first finds the position of the first hyphen in the item code. The second @FIND function recalculates the position of the first hyphen, adds one to the position, and starts at that position to look for the second hyphen. If the result of the first @FIND function is 3, which is the fourth character, and the result of the second @FIND is 6, which is the seventh character, the @IF function puts an empty string into column F. If the item code does not match this pattern, the @IF function puts an error message in column F, as shown in F4 and F10. In F15, the formula returns ERR, since the @FIND function cannot find a second hyphen. These error codes inform you which item codes need correction.

@REPLACE

The @REPLACE function returns a string, replacing part of an original string with a new string at a specified position and removing a specified number of characters. This function also lets you insert text in the middle of a string without removing any characters. You can also remove characters from the middle of the string without making a replacement. The format of the function is @REPLACE(string,startnum,num,newstring). *String* is the string that the @REPLACE function operates on. *Startnum* is the position number where @REPLACE starts inserting and removing characters. The term *num* is the number of characters to be removed. The term *newstring* is a string that @REPLACE inserts into *string* at start.num's location. The number of characters removed does not have to be the same as the number of characters inserted. If any of the arguments are omitted, a syntax error results. Therefore, if you are not deleting any characters or you are not inserting any characters, the appropriate values for num and newstring are **0** or **""**, respectively.

The @REPLACE function is used frequently to change characters in an entry to characters stored in another cell. For example, if you want to replace the item codes in Figure 8.2 so that the first two letters of the supplier's name are used in place of the three letters of the warehouse, the @REPLACE function can perform this task. Your formula for A3 is @REPLACE(A3,0,3,@UPPER(@LEFT(E3,2))). The arguments indicate that the function starts at the beginning in position 0 (the function's second argument), deletes three characters (the function's third argument), and inserts the first two capitalized characters from the supplier in column E.

The @REPLACE function is also used to insert or remove characters from the middle of an entry without removing or replacing the inserted or deleted characters. If you want to include the supplier as part of the Item Code after the reorder point, the @REPLACE function is: **@REPLACE(A3,6,0,@UPPER(@LEFT(E3,2)))**. This @REPLACE function inserts the first two capitalized characters from column E after the reorder point for the item currently shown in position 6. The first item code becomes CLE-07CO-BRH after this @REPLACE function. The same function can also delete the reorder point from the Item Code. For example, if cell F3 contains **@REPLACE(A3,4,3,"")**, this @REPLACE function removes three characters starting at position 4 and does not insert anything in their place. For example, the first item code becomes CLE-BRH. Use of the double quotes (with nothing between them) prevents a syntax error.

@S

The @S function retrieves the string from the upper-left cell of a block. This function prevents errors in string functions occurring due to a number, @NA, and @ERR occurring in one of the string function's arguments. The format is @S(block). If you reference a single cell, Quattro Pro converts it to a block address. If the upper-left cell of the block contains a number, @ERR, or @NA, the function returns a blank string.

The @S function is often combined with other functions. For example, suppose you are combining two cells that you expect to contain labels. If either of the cells contains a value, the formula combining the string will return ERR. You can use @S in the formula that combines the strings in case one of the cells contains a value. A formula might look like this: **+@S(A9)&@S(A10).** In this example, if A9 or A10 contains a value, the @S function converts the value to a blank string for that portion of the formula.

@N

The @N function retrieves the numeric value from the upper-left cell of a block. This function prevents errors in formulas occurring in calculations due to a string entry for one of the formula's arguments. The format is @N(block). If you reference a single cell, Quattro Pro will change it to a block address.

The @N function is often used when one of the cells in a formula reference might contain a string. For example, if you need to add A1 and A2 and know that one of the two cells may contain a label, using the @N function around the two cell addresses prevents your formula from returning ERR. Therefore, your formula looks like this: **+@N(A1)+@N(A2).**

@CODE

The @CODE function returns the first ANSI code in a string. The format is @CODE(string). For example, @CODE("$^1/_4$") returns 188, which is the ANSI code number to generate the character $^1/_4$.

@CHAR

The @CHAR function returns the character specified by an ANSI code. The format of this function is @CHAR(code). The term *code* represents any number or formula that has a value from 1 to 255.

The @CHAR function can generate random characters when combined with the @RAND function. For example, if you want to add another item to the inventory listing, you need a unique item number. One method of generating a unique number is to combine the @CHAR and the @RAND functions. The @RAND function generates a number between 0 and 1. Since you need a number between 1 and 26, you must multiply the number by 27, one higher than you need. Once you have the random number between 1 and 26, you must add 64 if you want an uppercase letter and 96 if you want a lowercase letter. (Adding 64 or 96 converts the random number between 1 and 26 to a number that is in the ANSI code range for uppercase or lowercase letters, respectively.) The @CHAR function converts this random number into a random letter. The formula can be written as **@CHAR((@RAND*27)+64)**. In its current form, this formula generates a random uppercase letter. To generate a random item code, use this formula three times, and join the result with an ampersand as follows: **@CHAR((@RAND*27)+64) &@CHAR((@RAND*27)+64)&@CHAR ((@RAND*27)+64).** Sorting the inventory items by the unique item code lets you scan the entries to ensure that your newly created item code is unique.

@HEXTONUM

The @HEXTONUM function takes a hexadecimal value stored as a string and converts it into a decimal number. The format of this function is @HEXTONUM(string).

One purpose of this function is to convert imported numbers that are in a hexadecimal format into decimal values. Since Quattro Pro causes values with the letters A through F to generate errors, hexadecimal values must be stored as a string. If data you have imported contains hexadecimal values, convert them to strings with the Parse command in the Data menu, then use this function to convert them into decimal values.

@NUMTOHEX

The @NUMTOHEX function takes a decimal value and converts it into a hexadecimal number stored as a string. The format of this function is @NUMTOHEX(x). The *x* represents the decimal number to convert to a hexadecimal number. An example of this function is @NUMTHOHEX(198), which returns C6, the hexadecimal equivalent of 198.

DATE AND TIME FUNCTIONS

Quattro Pro provides a full complement of date and time functions. You can use these functions to create date and time serial numbers to work with the data in existing date and time entries. With these functions, you can perform all types of date and time calculations from computing an hourly payroll to aging your accounts receivable.

As you learned in Chapter 2, dates are represented as date serial numbers, or the number of days from December 30, 1899. Times are represented as time serial numbers, indicating the fraction of the day. In Chapter 3, you learned how you can change block properties to display date and time serial numbers as the dates and times they represent. You can use the date and time functions to create date and time serial numbers and to extract information out of date and time serial numbers.

Date and time functions provide several specialized features. For dates and times that are typed in as labels, Quattro Pro has two special features that transform the strings into date values. Quattro Pro also has two functions that produce the current date and time. Two other functions create date or time values from the numbers that you provide. Finally, several functions extract the number of years, months, days, hours, minutes, and seconds from a time and/or date serial number.

@NOW

The @NOW function returns a date and time serial number. This function is entered as @NOW with no function arguments. This number is recalculated whenever another part of the notebook is recalculated.

This function is often placed near the top of a page to date reports printed from the notebook. This feature enables you to identify the most recent copy of a page when you have several printed copies. If you put the @NOW function in B2 as shown in Figure 8.8 (the entry uses the user-defined format MM DD YY hh:mm:ss AMPM to display both the date and the time), the date and time are printed whenever this data is printed.

@TODAY

The @TODAY function returns a date serial number. This function is typed in as @TODAY with no function arguments. The @TODAY function is the integer value of @NOW. Therefore, @INT(@NOW) equals @TODAY.

This function is often used at the top of a page to date a report printed from the notebook. It is also used to show the day that a page is printed to help keep track of the latest printout. For example, if you put the @TODAY function in cell B2, format B2 with the DD-MMM-YY format, and include this entry in the print block, the print output displays the date on which the report was printed.

@DATE

The @DATE function accepts values for a year, month, and day and converts them into a date serial number. The format of the @DATE function is @DATE(yr,mo,day). The *yr* represents the year, with a range from -300 to 1299 for the number of years

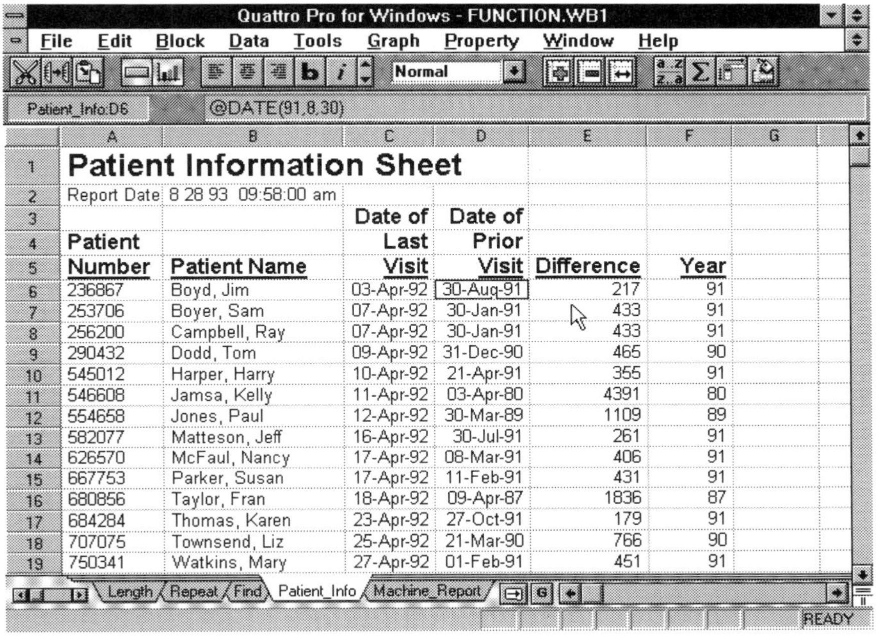

Quattro Pro for Windows - FUNCTION.WB1

File Edit Block Data Tools Graph Property Window Help

Patient_Info:D6 @DATE(91,8,30)

	A	B	C	D	E	F	G
1	**Patient Information Sheet**						
2	Report Date	8 28 93 09:58:00 am					
3			Date of	Date of			
4	Patient		Last	Prior			
5	Number	Patient Name	Visit	Visit	Difference	Year	
6	236867	Boyd, Jim	03-Apr-92	30-Aug-91	217	91	
7	253706	Boyer, Sam	07-Apr-92	30-Jan-91	433	91	
8	256200	Campbell, Ray	07-Apr-92	30-Jan-91	433	91	
9	290432	Dodd, Tom	09-Apr-92	31-Dec-90	465	90	
10	545012	Harper, Harry	10-Apr-92	21-Apr-91	355	91	
11	546608	Jamsa, Kelly	11-Apr-92	03-Apr-80	4391	80	
12	554658	Jones, Paul	12-Apr-92	30-Mar-89	1109	89	
13	582077	Matteson, Jeff	16-Apr-92	30-Jul-91	261	91	
14	626570	McFaul, Nancy	17-Apr-92	08-Mar-91	406	91	
15	667753	Parker, Susan	17-Apr-92	11-Feb-91	431	91	
16	680856	Taylor, Fran	18-Apr-92	09-Apr-87	1836	87	
17	684284	Thomas, Karen	23-Apr-92	27-Oct-91	179	91	
18	707075	Townsend, Liz	25-Apr-92	21-Mar-90	766	90	
19	750341	Watkins, Mary	27-Apr-92	01-Feb-91	451	91	

Length Repeat Find Patient_Info Machine_Report

READY

Figure 8.8 Using @NOW, @DATE, and @YEAR to Work with Dates

since 1900 (for example, 1989 is 89 and 2001 is 101); *mo* represents the number of the month and has an acceptable range from 1 for January to 12 for December; and *day* represents the number of the day in the month (1 to 31).

The number of days used as the function's argument must be consistent with the month and year. For example, if month is 2, day can be 29 when year is 92, since in 1992, February has 29 days. Day cannot be 29 when year is 93, since February 1993 has only 28 days. Since you can also enter dates with the CTRL-SHIFT-D key, this function is often used when one or more of the function's arguments are formulas or cell references.

An example of @DATE function is shown in Figure 8.8, which uses the @DATE function in column C and column D. For each of these dates, the @DATE function includes the year, month, and day. By using the date values, you can compute the number of days between dental visits. In this example, it is easier to use CTRL-SHIFT-D to enter the dates in columns C and D.

@YEAR

The @YEAR function returns the number of years in a date serial number. The format of the function is @YEAR(date).

One purpose of the @YEAR function is to determine the year of a date entered in another cell. Figure 8.8 shows the @YEAR function returning the year of the prior visit entered in column D. The @YEAR function is often used when you have entered dates with CTRL-SHIFT-D and you want just the year portion of the date.

@MONTH

The @MONTH function returns the month's portion of a serial date number. It does not return the total number of months, rather it returns the number of months of a date serial number in the current year. The formula of the function is @MONTH(date).

One use of the @MONTH function is to extract a month number to use in building another date. You can also use @MONTH to return the month portion of a date entered in another cell. For example, if you are analyzing the breakdown history, you might want to determine when the machine breaks down most often. In Figure 8.9, you can use the @MONTH function to return the month of each breakdown. Once you have this part extracted, you can use the Frequency command in the Data menu to analyze this function's results.

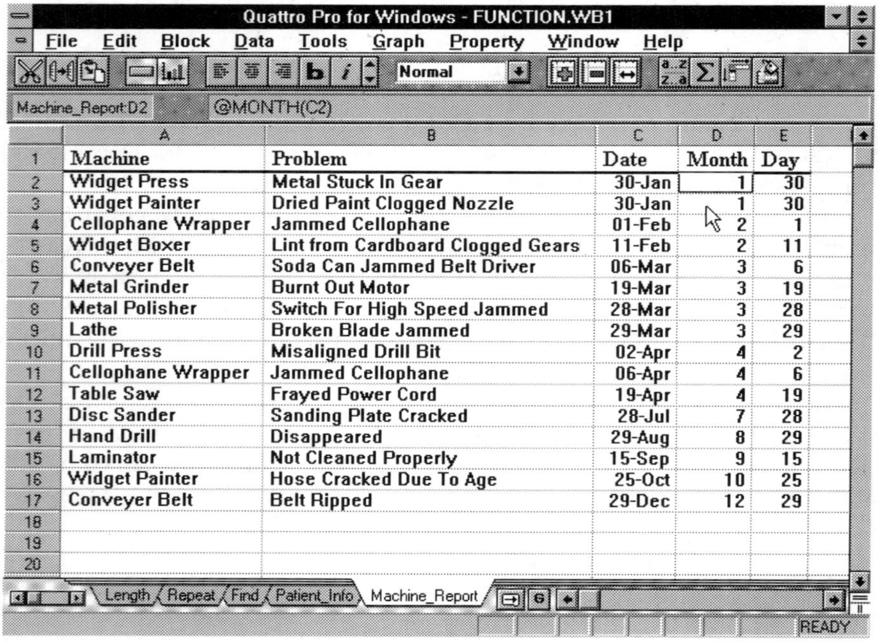

	Machine	Problem	Date	Month	Day
1	Machine	Problem	Date	Month	Day
2	Widget Press	Metal Stuck In Gear	30-Jan	1	30
3	Widget Painter	Dried Paint Clogged Nozzle	30-Jan	1	30
4	Cellophane Wrapper	Jammed Cellophane	01-Feb	2	1
5	Widget Boxer	Lint from Cardboard Clogged Gears	11-Feb	2	11
6	Conveyer Belt	Soda Can Jammed Belt Driver	06-Mar	3	6
7	Metal Grinder	Burnt Out Motor	19-Mar	3	19
8	Metal Polisher	Switch For High Speed Jammed	28-Mar	3	28
9	Lathe	Broken Blade Jammed	29-Mar	3	29
10	Drill Press	Misaligned Drill Bit	02-Apr	4	2
11	Cellophane Wrapper	Jammed Cellophane	06-Apr	4	6
12	Table Saw	Frayed Power Cord	19-Apr	4	19
13	Disc Sander	Sanding Plate Cracked	28-Jul	7	28
14	Hand Drill	Disappeared	29-Aug	8	29
15	Laminator	Not Cleaned Properly	15-Sep	9	15
16	Widget Painter	Hose Cracked Due To Age	25-Oct	10	25
17	Conveyer Belt	Belt Ripped	29-Dec	12	29

Figure 8.9 @MONTH and @DAY Used to Extract the Month and Day from a Date

@DAY

The @DAY function returns the day's portion of a date serial number. The formula of the function is @DAY(date).

The @DAY function can be used in the analysis of date entries. With dates representing machine breakdowns, employee absences, or delivery dates, you may be interested in the distribution of these dates by day of the month. Figure 8.9 provides a sample of entries representing machine breakdowns. The @DAY function is used to extract the day from the date of the problem occurrence. The records can be sorted by this field or these entries can be used with the Frequency command in the Data menu for a more rigorous analysis.

The @DAY function can also construct a set of dates for loan repayments that are exactly one month apart. If the original date is in A2, this formula calculates the date of the next payment:

@DATE(@IF(@MONTH(A2)=12,@YEAR(A2)+1,@YEAR(A2)),
@IF(@MONTH(A2)=12,1,@MONTH(A2)+1),@DAY(A2))

By copying this formula farther down the column, you can list every loan repayment date. This formula changes the year every time the month equals 12.

@TIME

The @TIME function takes three values for the hour, minute, and second and converts them into a time serial number. The format of the @TIME function is @TIME(hr,min,sec). The *hr* represents the hour that ranges from 0 to 23 for the hours of midnight to 11 P.M. (numbers greater than 12 represent the evening hours); *min* represents the number of minutes within the hour (this number ranges from 0 to 59); *sec* represents the number of the seconds within the minute (this number ranges from 0 to 59). Most of the time, you will use CTRL-SHIFT-D to enter times rather than this function.

An example of the @TIME function is in Figure 8.10, which uses the @TIME function in columns B and C. For each of these times, the @TIME function includes the hour, minute, and second. By using the time values, you can compute the time passed between when an employee clocks in and clocks out.

@HOUR

The @HOUR function returns the number of hours in the serial time number. The syntax of the function is @HOUR(time). The *time* is a serial time number provided as a number, a formula, or a numeric function, or as a cell reference.

One purpose of the @HOUR function is to determine the number of hours in a time. Figure 8.10 shows one way you can use the @HOUR function to return the hour of a time. For example, if you are planning a meeting, you want to know

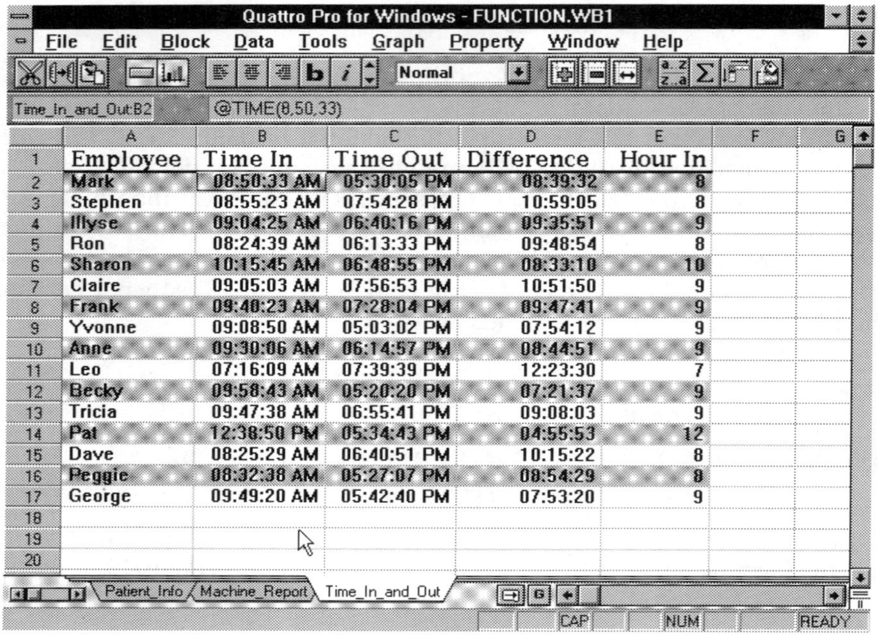

	A	B	C	D	E
1	Employee	Time In	Time Out	Difference	Hour In
2	Mark	08:50:33 AM	05:30:05 PM	08:39:32	8
3	Stephen	08:55:23 AM	07:54:28 PM	10:59:05	8
4	Illyse	09:04:25 AM	06:40:16 PM	09:35:51	9
5	Ron	08:24:39 AM	06:13:33 PM	09:48:54	8
6	Sharon	10:15:45 AM	06:48:55 PM	08:33:10	10
7	Claire	09:05:03 AM	07:56:53 PM	10:51:50	9
8	Frank	09:40:23 AM	07:28:04 PM	09:47:41	9
9	Yvonne	09:08:50 AM	05:03:02 PM	07:54:12	9
10	Anne	09:30:06 AM	06:14:57 PM	08:44:51	9
11	Leo	07:16:09 AM	07:39:39 PM	12:23:30	7
12	Becky	09:58:43 AM	05:20:20 PM	07:21:37	9
13	Tricia	09:47:38 AM	06:55:41 PM	09:08:03	9
14	Pat	12:38:50 PM	05:34:43 PM	04:55:53	12
15	Dave	08:25:29 AM	06:40:51 PM	10:15:22	8
16	Peggie	08:32:38 AM	05:27:07 PM	08:54:29	8
17	George	09:49:20 AM	05:42:40 PM	07:53:20	9

Figure 8.10 @TIME Used to Enter Times

when all of your employees will be in. By using the @HOUR function in Figure 8.10, you can return the hour that everyone arrives. For example, the formula in E2 is @HOUR(B2), which is copied down the column for the other employees. From this information, you know that scheduling a 1 PM meeting will allow everyone to be present.

@MINUTE

The @MINUTE function returns the minute's portion of a serial time number. It does not return the total number of minutes; rather it returns the number of minutes of a time serial number in the current hour. The syntax of the function is @MINUTE(time).

One purpose of the @MINUTE function is to determine the number of minutes in a time difference. You can use this function when you are recording the time a manufacturing process takes to be completed. In Figure 8.11, the formulas in column D subtract the times in column B from those in column C and then, from the resulting time differences, calculate the number of minutes. This comparison allows you to compare between different processes or machines. D4 contains the formula @MINUTE(C4-B4), which you can copy for the remaining machines.

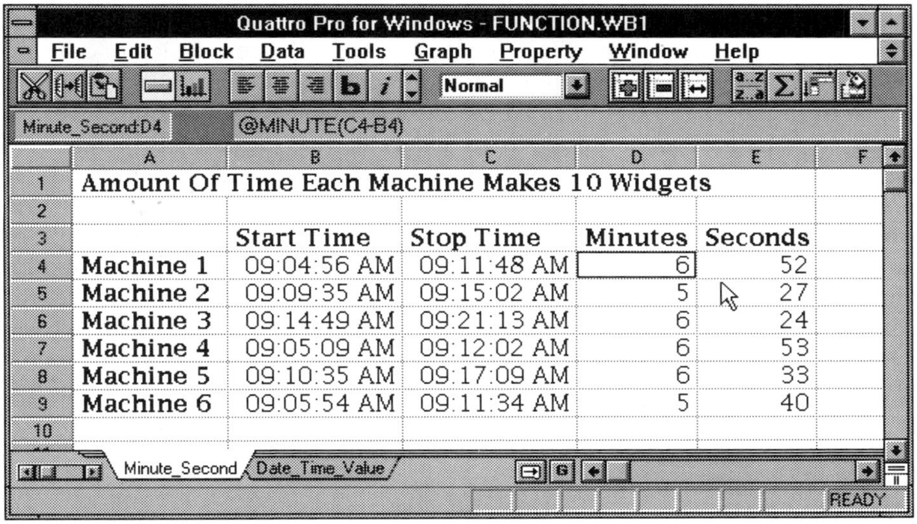

Figure 8.11 **@MINUTE and @SECOND Used to Compute Minute's and Second's Portion of the Difference Between Two Times**

@SECOND

The @SECOND function returns the second's portion of a time serial number. The formula of the function is @SECOND(time).

The @SECOND function is appropriately used where preciseness is important, as in monitoring the times for two production runs. For example, if you are deciding between several machines to perform a certain task, the time that each machine takes for each task is very important. You can use @SECOND to compute the amount of time for the different machines. In Figure 8.11, the start and stop times that each machine takes to produce 10 widgets is shown in columns B and C. The @MINUTE function in column D computes the minute's portion of the difference between the two times. In column E, @SECOND computes the second's portion of the difference between the two times. This information can be used to determine which machines can produce the required production levels in minimal time.

@DATEVALUE

@DATEVALUE accepts a string that is in the form of a date and converts it into a date serial number. Since you can directly enter dates by pressing the keystroke sequence, CTRL-SHIFT-D, it is more efficient to use the special key than to type date information in as labels. Still, you will want to be prepared to work with date labels entered by someone unaware of the importance of date serial numbers. The syntax of the function is @DATEVALUE(date-string). Here, *date-string* is a string that is in the format of a date. This function permits the conversion of date entries that are stored as labels and conversion of them into date serial numbers.

An example of the @DATEVALUE function is shown in Figure 8.12. In this example, all dates are entered in as labels in the format 'MM/DD/YY. The @DATEVALUE functions in column D transform the strings into date serial numbers so they can be used in computations. You can tell that the @DATEVALUE function has made the conversion because the strings in column B are by default left-aligned and the date serial numbers in column D are by default right-aligned. Once these labels are converted to date values, you can use the Paste Special command in the Edit menu or the Values command in the Block menu to copy the values returned by the @DATEVALUE functions in place of the labels. The results of the @DATEVALUE functions appear as dates because the block has had its properties changed to use a date numeric format.

@TIMEVALUE

@TIMEVALUE accepts a string that is in the form of a time and converts it into a time serial number. This function converts times that were originally entered as labels when there was no plan to use mathematical capabilities on time values. The format of the function is @TIMEVALUE(time-string). Here, *time-string* is a string which must be in the format of a time. This function is used frequently when you are updating a notebook where the time entries are stored as labels.

An example of the @TIMEVALUE function is shown in Figure 8.12. In this example, the times are entered in as labels in the format 'HH:MM:SS with a PM

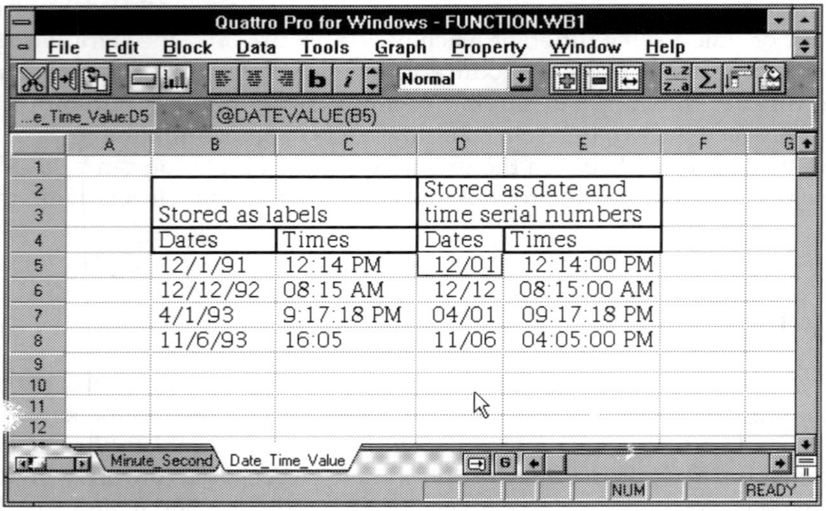

Figure 8.12   @DATEVALUE and @TIMEVALUE Used to Convert Labels

following the times that are in the afternoon, except for C8, which uses a 24-hour clock to distinguish between hours in the morning and in the afternoon. The @TIMEVALUE functions in column E transform the strings into time serial numbers. The results of the @TIMEVALUE functions appear as times because the block has had its properties changed to use a time numeric format.

LOGICAL FUNCTIONS

Quattro Pro's logical functions evaluate conditions to determine if the condition is true or false. Quattro Pro also provides several special logical functions that place special values in cells. Quattro Pro's logical functions that produce true and false values operate with Boolean logic. That is, the functions evaluate an expression and determine whether it is true or false. The logical functions that represent special values include the values Quattro Pro uses to store true and false and the values that Quattro Pro uses for data that is missing or contains an error.

@IF

The @IF function evaluates a condition as true or false and returns one value if the condition is true and another value if the condition is false. This function allows you to select an entry for a cell depending on other entries in the notebook. The syntax of this function is @IF(cond,trueexpr,falseexpr). The term *cond* represents the condition that the function evaluates. The condition must be a logical condition that Quattro Pro can evaluate as true or false. Examples are B6>5 and @SUM(A1..A15)<100. The first example is evaluated as true when B6 is greater than 5. The second one produces true as a result when the total of the values in the cells A1..A15 is less than 100. This function argument can contain strings, numbers, cell references, block references, and other formulas, as long as they are part of a logical formula.

@IF can have multiple conditions, since Quattro Pro allows the AND, OR, and NOT operators to be used within the condition expression. To use any of these conditions, you must precede and follow the operator with a number sign (#). If you use **#AND#** in a condition, the condition to the left and to the right of the #AND# must be true for the @IF function to use the function argument for a true value. If either part of the condition is false, the @IF function uses the function argument for a false value. If a condition uses an **#OR#** connector, the condition to the left and/or the condition to the right of the #OR# connector must be true for the function to use the function argument for a true value. If a condition uses the **#NOT#** operator, the condition to the right of the #NOT# operator must be false to yield a true value or must be true to yield a false value. None of these operators can override parentheses in establishing the order of operations.

The term *trueexpr* represents the value that the function returns when the condition is true (this can be a formula, a value, or a string); *falseexpr* represents the value the function returns when the condition is false (this can be a formula, a value, or a string).

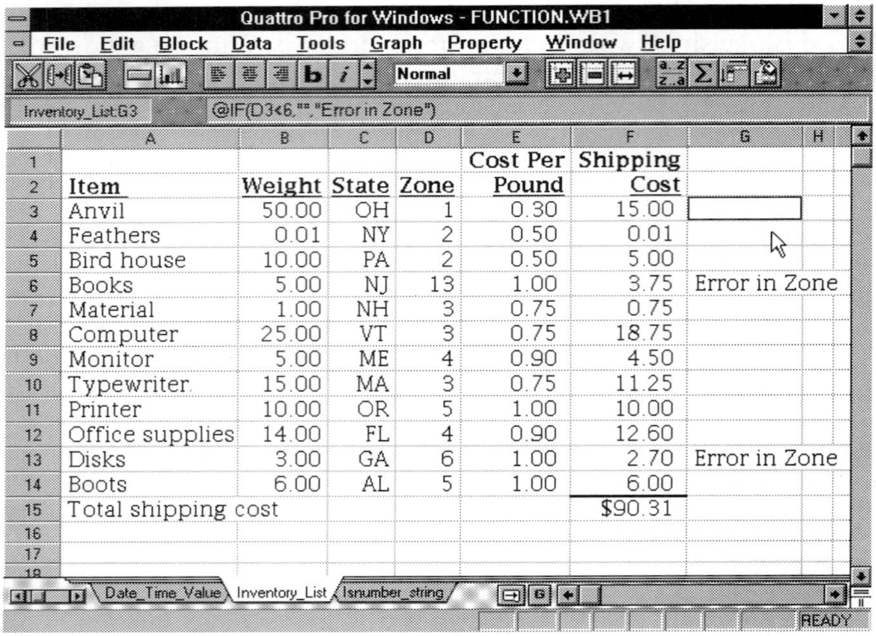

	A	B	C	D	E	F	G	H
1					Cost Per	Shipping		
2	Item	Weight	State	Zone	Pound	Cost		
3	Anvil	50.00	OH	1	0.30	15.00		
4	Feathers	0.01	NY	2	0.50	0.01		
5	Bird house	10.00	PA	2	0.50	5.00		
6	Books	5.00	NJ	13	1.00	3.75	Error in Zone	
7	Material	1.00	NH	3	0.75	0.75		
8	Computer	25.00	VT	3	0.75	18.75		
9	Monitor	5.00	ME	4	0.90	4.50		
10	Typewriter	15.00	MA	3	0.75	11.25		
11	Printer	10.00	OR	5	1.00	10.00		
12	Office supplies	14.00	FL	4	0.90	12.60		
13	Disks	3.00	GA	6	1.00	2.70	Error in Zone	
14	Boots	6.00	AL	5	1.00	6.00		
15	Total shipping cost					$90.31		
16								
17								

Figure 8.13 @IF Used to Check the Validity of the Zone Number

The @IF function often is used to check for errors. For example, in Figure 8.13, the Zone column may contain numbers that are too large. For each row, the @IF function in Column G takes the value in column D and compares it to six. If it is less than six, meaning that the zone number is within the acceptable range, it displays a blank label generated by the two double quotes after the first comma. If the value in column D is not less than six (any number that is six or higher), the function displays Error in Zone in column G. This technique provides a quick check for errors in zone entries since you only need to scan the column quickly for an error message display.

The @IF function can contain other @IF functions. This creates nested @IF functions that expand your choices from the two options provided in a single @IF function. When the true or false argument is expressed as another @IF function, the process proceeds normally with the first condition being evaluated and a true or false value selected for evaluation based on the outcome of the condition test. If the argument selected contains another @IF, Quattro Pro evaluates the second condition and determines whether to use the true or false argument of the second @IF function. An example of a nested @IF function is @IF(A1<100,@IF(B1>50,"A","B"),@IF(C1<=1,"C","D")). In this function, Quattro Pro first checks if A1 is less than 100. If A1 is less than 100, it then tests to see if the value in B1 is greater than 50. If B1 is greater than 50, the function returns A. If A1 is less than 100 and B1 is less than or equal to 50, this function returns B. If A1 is greater than or equal to 100, Quattro Pro checks if C1 is less than or equal to one. If C1 is less than or equal to one, this function returns C. If A1 is greater than or equal to 100 and C1 is greater than one, the function returns D.

A more complicated example using several levels of nested @IF functions can determine the proper cost per pound for shipping based upon the zone. In Figure 8.14, a series of nested @IF functions checks the zone and determines the correct cost per pound. The function first determines if the zone is equal to 1. If the zone is equal to 1, the function returns 0.3. If the zone is not equal to 1, the second @IF function checks if the zone is 2 and returns 0.5 if a true condition test results. If the function does not equal 1 or 2, a third @IF function determines if the zone equals 3 and returns 0.75 if the condition test is true. If the function does not equal 1, 2, or 3, the fourth function checks if the zone equals 4 and returns 0.9 for a true condition test. If the function does not equal 1, 2, 3, or 4, the fifth and final @IF function determines if the zone equals 5 and returns 1 if the test is true. If the zone does not equal 1, 2, 3, 4, or 5, the function returns the label Error. Since labels have a value of zero, this label causes an item with an incorrect zone to have a shipping cost of zero. To avoid this problem, you can either add an @IF to the shipping cost calculation or use @ERR for the false value in the fifth @IF statement.

You need to be careful with the number of nesting levels you use. A good rule of thumb for most users is not to exceed three levels. Other functions like @VLOOKUP and @INDEX offer alternatives for multiple levels of @IF statements.

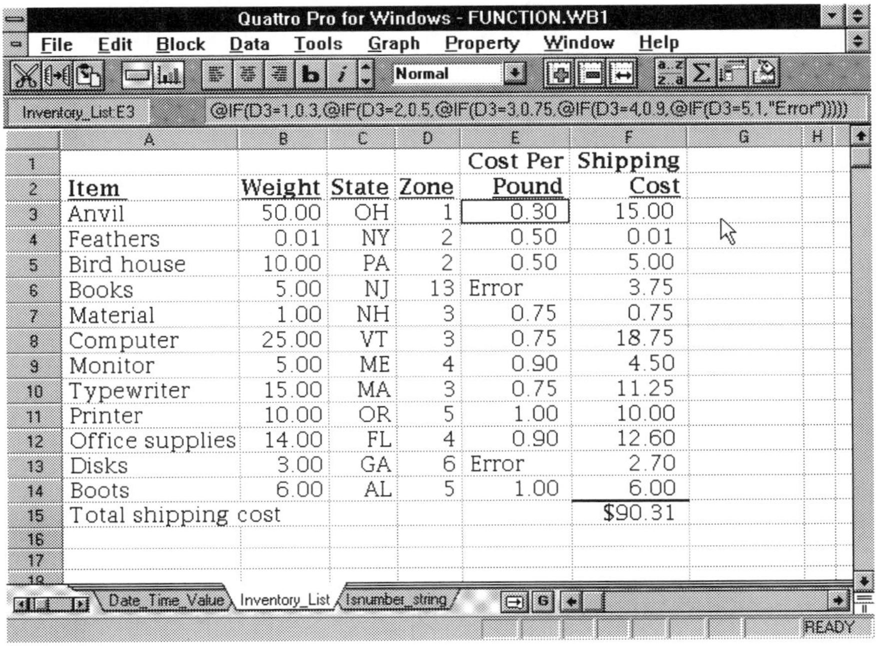

	A	B	C	D	E	F
1					Cost Per	Shipping
2	Item	Weight	State	Zone	Pound	Cost
3	Anvil	50.00	OH	1	0.30	15.00
4	Feathers	0.01	NY	2	0.50	0.01
5	Bird house	10.00	PA	2	0.50	5.00
6	Books	5.00	NJ	13	Error	3.75
7	Material	1.00	NH	3	0.75	0.75
8	Computer	25.00	VT	3	0.75	18.75
9	Monitor	5.00	ME	4	0.90	4.50
10	Typewriter	15.00	MA	3	0.75	11.25
11	Printer	10.00	OR	5	1.00	10.00
12	Office supplies	14.00	FL	4	0.90	12.60
13	Disks	3.00	GA	6	Error	2.70
14	Boots	6.00	AL	5	1.00	6.00
15	Total shipping cost					$90.31

Figure 8.14 Nested @IF to Determine Cost per Pound

@ISNUMBER

The @ISNUMBER checks the function's argument to determine if it is a number. This function returns a 1 if the argument is a number and a 0 if it is not. Quattro Pro evaluates numbers and numeric functions as numbers. The format of this function is @ISNUMBER(x).

The @ISNUMBER function is often used in combination with other functions to verify that an entry made in a cell is a number. For example, one type of data error that may occur in the calculations to determine the total shipping cost is that label entries are placed in the Zone column. Figure 8.15 shows the page in which the state abbreviation was mistakenly entered in two rows instead of a numeric zone. In column G, the @ISNUMBER determines whether the value in column D is a number. For example, G4 contains the formula @IF(@ISNUMBER(D3)," ","Zone Error"), which is copied for the other items. This function returns the true or false value that the @IF function uses to determine which argument to place in column G. For those rows that have a numeric value in column D, the function returns a blank string. For those rows that have a label in column D, the @ISNUMBER and @IF functions return the error message displayed in rows 4 and 8.

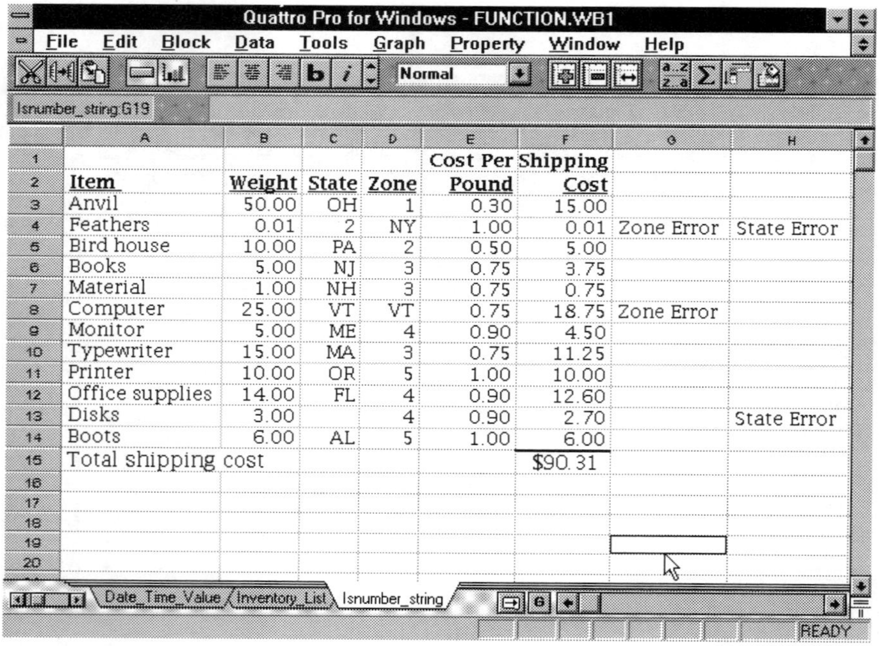

	A	B	C	D	E	F	G	H
1					Cost Per	Shipping		
2	Item	Weight	State	Zone	Pound	Cost		
3	Anvil	50.00	OH	1	0.30	15.00		
4	Feathers	0.01	2	NY	1.00	0.01	Zone Error	State Error
5	Bird house	10.00	PA	2	0.50	5.00		
6	Books	5.00	NJ	3	0.75	3.75		
7	Material	1.00	NH	3	0.75	0.75		
8	Computer	25.00	VT	VT	0.75	18.75	Zone Error	
9	Monitor	5.00	ME	4	0.90	4.50		
10	Typewriter	15.00	MA	3	0.75	11.25		
11	Printer	10.00	OR	5	1.00	10.00		
12	Office supplies	14.00	FL	4	0.90	12.60		
13	Disks	3.00		4	0.90	2.70		State Error
14	Boots	6.00	AL	5	1.00	6.00		
15	Total shipping cost					$90.31		
16								
17								
18								
19								
20								

Figure 8.15 @ISNUMBER and @ISSTRING Used to Check the Validity of Entries

@ISSTRING

The @ISSTRING checks the function's argument to determine if it is a string or label. This function returns a 1 if the argument is a string and a 0 if it is not. A string includes labels and strings in quotes. The format of this function is @ISSTRING(x).

The @ISSTRING function is often used in combination with other functions to verify that entries are labels. For example, one type of data error that may occur in the shipping cost listing is that the state is entered improperly. Figure 8.15 shows the page in which a few of the states and zones have incorrect information. In column H, the @ISSTRING determines whether the entry in column C is a string. For example, H4 contains the formula @IF(@ISSTRING(D3),"","State Error"), which is copied for the other items. This function returns the true or false value that the @IF function uses to determine which of its next two arguments it places in column G. For those rows that have a string value in column C, the function returns a blank string. For those rows that have a number in column C, the @ISSTRING and @IF combination returns the error message displayed in rows 4 and 13. This function cannot detect, however, the state entered as the zone in row 8.

@ISERR

The @ISERR checks the function's argument for ERR. This function returns a 1 if the argument equals ERR and a 0 if it does not. The format of this function is @ISERR(x). Here, x is a formula or cell reference.

The @ISERR function can be combined with @IF to remove @ERR from computations. Figure 8.16 shows an example of the @ERR function in B4, preventing a computation for the cumulative shipping cost. While one method of computing the total cost is to substitute a 0 for the @ERR in B4, it is not the correct approach since the correct value may not be substituted at a later time. Another possibility is to use column G to add the shipping costs that do not have a value of ERR. In column G, @ISERR is the condition for the @IF function. The @ISERR checks the value in column B to determine if it is ERR. If the value in column B is zero, the @IF function returns zero. If the value in column B does not equal ERR, the @IF function returns the shipping cost for that item. Therefore, you have the cumulative total shipping cost in column G, and a reminder in column F that information must be entered to make the calculations complete.

@ISNA

The @ISNA checks to determine if its argument contains NA. This function returns a 1 if the argument equals NA and a 0 if it does not. The format of this function is @ISNA(x), and x is either a formula or a cell reference.

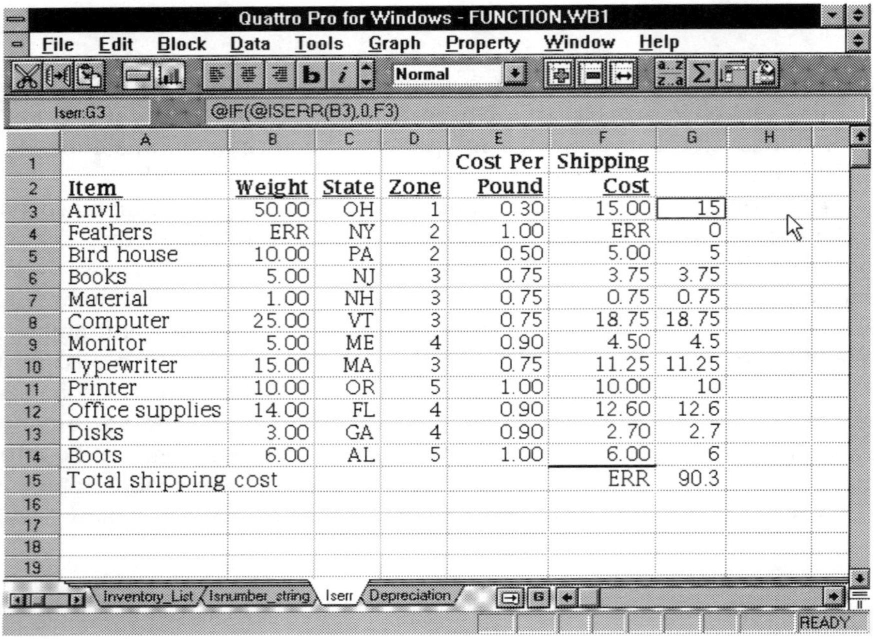

Quattro Pro for Windows - FUNCTION.WB1

File Edit Block Data Tools Graph Property Window Help

Iserr:G3 @IF(@ISERR(B3),0,F3)

	A	B	C	D	E	F	G	H
1					Cost Per	Shipping		
2	Item	Weight	State	Zone	Pound	Cost		
3	Anvil	50.00	OH	1	0.30	15.00	15	
4	Feathers	ERR	NY	2	1.00	ERR	0	
5	Bird house	10.00	PA	2	0.50	5.00	5	
6	Books	5.00	NJ	3	0.75	3.75	3.75	
7	Material	1.00	NH	3	0.75	0.75	0.75	
8	Computer	25.00	VT	3	0.75	18.75	18.75	
9	Monitor	5.00	ME	4	0.90	4.50	4.5	
10	Typewriter	15.00	MA	3	0.75	11.25	11.25	
11	Printer	10.00	OR	5	1.00	10.00	10	
12	Office supplies	14.00	FL	4	0.90	12.60	12.6	
13	Disks	3.00	GA	4	0.90	2.70	2.7	
14	Boots	6.00	AL	5	1.00	6.00	6	
15	Total shipping cost					ERR	90.3	
16								
17								
18								
19								

Figure 8.16 @IF and @ISERR Used to Substitute 0 for @ERR in Formula

The @ISNA function is often used in notebooks in which you expect data to be missing for some time. The @ISNA function can help make preliminary computations before all the data is in, without forcing some NA values to be removed. Figure 8.17 shows an example where the NA value in E3 has prevented the computation of the cumulative shipping cost. While replacing all NA entries with 0 produces this computation, it eliminates the reminder to complete the entries. In Figure 8.17, column G uses the @ISNA function and @IF function to create a temporary column that accepts the shipping cost if it does not equal NA and returns 0 if the shipping cost per pound is NA as returned by the @NA function. The @ISNA compares the value in column E to NA, the @IF function returns zero if the entry matches NA. If the value in column E does not equal NA, the @IF function returns the shipping cost from column F for that item in column G. Therefore, you have the cumulative total shipping cost in column G and a reminder in column F that more entries must be made to complete the shipping calculations.

@FILEEXISTS

@FILEEXISTS returns a 1 for a true value if the specified file exists and a 0 for a false value if the specified file does not exist. The format of the function is @FILEEXISTS(filename). The *filename* is the string containing the name of the file

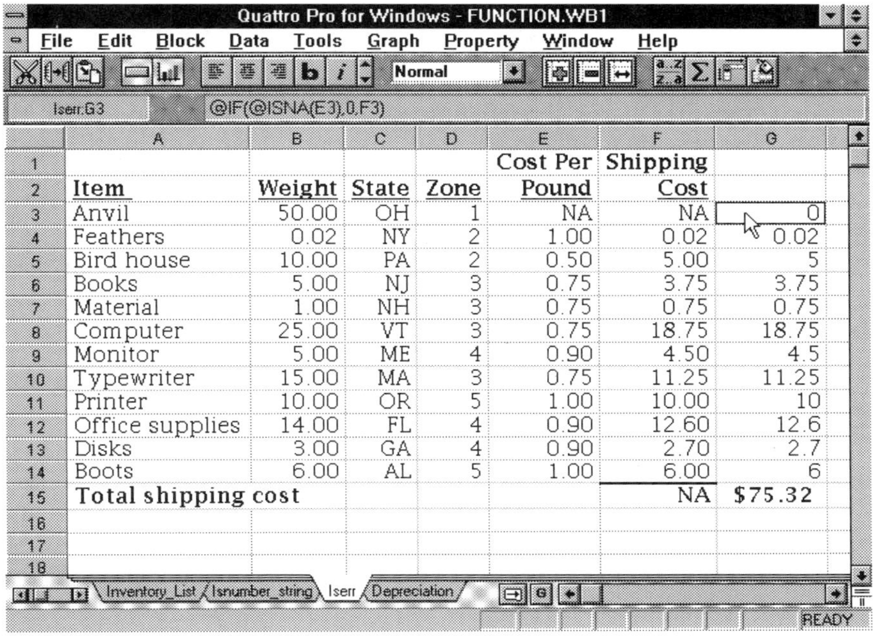

	A	B	C	D	E	F	G
1					Cost Per	Shipping	
2	Item	Weight	State	Zone	Pound	Cost	
3	Anvil	50.00	OH	1	NA	NA	0
4	Feathers	0.02	NY	2	1.00	0.02	0.02
5	Bird house	10.00	PA	2	0.50	5.00	5
6	Books	5.00	NJ	3	0.75	3.75	3.75
7	Material	1.00	NH	3	0.75	0.75	0.75
8	Computer	25.00	VT	3	0.75	18.75	18.75
9	Monitor	5.00	ME	4	0.90	4.50	4.5
10	Typewriter	15.00	MA	3	0.75	11.25	11.25
11	Printer	10.00	OR	5	1.00	10.00	10
12	Office supplies	14.00	FL	4	0.90	12.60	12.6
13	Disks	3.00	GA	4	0.90	2.70	2.7
14	Boots	6.00	AL	5	1.00	6.00	6
15	Total shipping cost					NA	$75.32
16							
17							
18							

Figure 8.17 @IF and @ISNA Used to Substitute 0 for @NA in Formula

that you want to check. The file name must include the file name extension and the path if the file is not in the current directory.

The following are some examples of the @FILEEXISTS function used to check if the file MODEL.WB1 in Quattro Pro's PICTURE subdirectory exists.

@FILEEXISTS("MODEL") = 0 No file extension specified
@FILEEXISTS("MODEL.WB1") = 0 Path not specified
@FILEEXISTS("C:\QPW\PICTURE\MODEL.WB1") = 1 Quattro Pro found the file

This function is used primarily with the {IF} macro command in macros to check that a file exists before performing other macro commands.

@TRUE

One of Quattro Pro's special logical functions is @TRUE. The @TRUE function has the same value that Quattro Pro uses when it evaluates a statement as true. Quattro Pro stores true and false values as 1 and 0, respectively. The @TRUE function is often used in place of a 1 since the @TRUE function provides documentation by its presence. The @TRUE function does not have parentheses or a function argument and is normally used with other functions. Often the @TRUE function is an argument in an @IF function. For example, you can use the @IF function to check if the weight is valid. If it is valid (that is, if it is a weight other than ERR), the @IF function can return the value 1 as @TRUE. If the cost per pound is less than 0 or greater than 1, the @IF function can return the value 1 as @FALSE. Figure 8.18 shows the @TRUE and @FALSE functions used with an @IF function to determine which weight entries are valid and which are not. For each item, if the cost per pound for shipping is valid, the @IF function returns the @TRUE function. This function returns the value 1. If the cost per pound is not valid, the @IF function returns the @FALSE function, which returns the value 0. By sorting the rows according to this column, you can group the ones that do not have a valid cost per pound.

@FALSE

Another Quattro Pro special logical function is @FALSE. The @FALSE has the same value that Quattro Pro stores when it evaluates a true or false statement. Quattro Pro stores true and false values as 1 and 0, respectively. The @FALSE function is often used in place of a 0 since the @FALSE function provides more

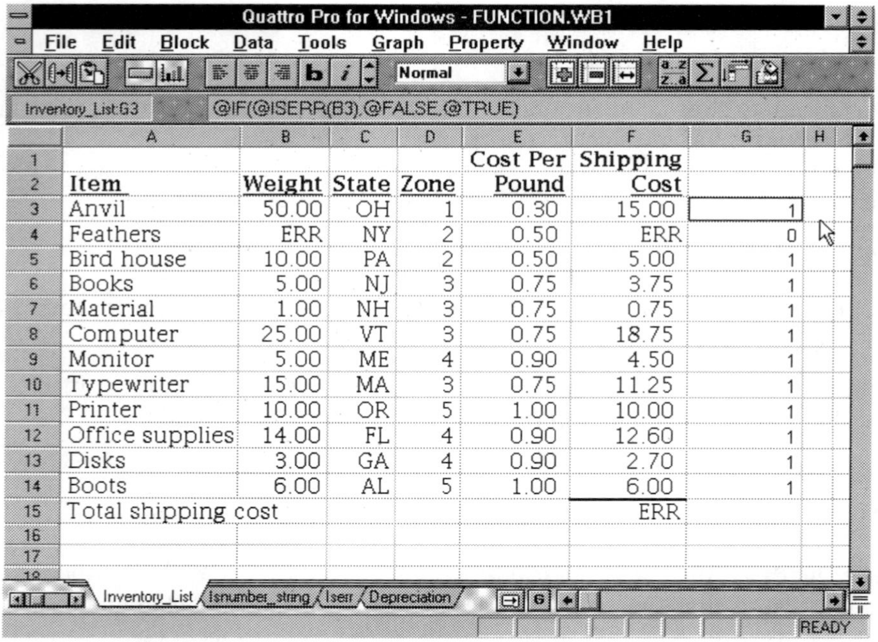

	A	B	C	D	E	F	G	H
1					Cost Per	Shipping		
2	Item	Weight	State	Zone	Pound	Cost		
3	Anvil	50.00	OH	1	0.30	15.00	1	
4	Feathers	ERR	NY	2	0.50	ERR	0	
5	Bird house	10.00	PA	2	0.50	5.00	1	
6	Books	5.00	NJ	3	0.75	3.75	1	
7	Material	1.00	NH	3	0.75	0.75	1	
8	Computer	25.00	VT	3	0.75	18.75	1	
9	Monitor	5.00	ME	4	0.90	4.50	1	
10	Typewriter	15.00	MA	3	0.75	11.25	1	
11	Printer	10.00	OR	5	1.00	10.00	1	
12	Office supplies	14.00	FL	4	0.90	12.60	1	
13	Disks	3.00	GA	4	0.90	2.70	1	
14	Boots	6.00	AL	5	1.00	6.00	1	
15	Total shipping cost					ERR		
16								
17								

Figure 8.18 @TRUE and @FALSE Used to Indicate the Results of Checking for @ERR

information by virtue of its presence than the 0 does. The @FALSE function does not have parentheses or a function argument. These true and false values are usually used with other functions. An example of this special function is shown with the @TRUE example (in Figure 8.18).

@ERR

Quattro Pro provides two special logical functions for data that contains an error or is unavailable. The @ERR function is used when the data contains an error. The @ERR returns the same value produced by the formulas or functions that contain an error. The @ERR function has a ripple effect. That is, every function that references a cell containing the @ERR function returns the ERR value. This prevents you from using the information from your notebook without being aware that some cells contain @ERR. The format of this function is @ERR. This function does not require parentheses or an argument. Often this function represents a piece of data that is incorrect.

An example of the @ERR function is in Figure 8.16. In this example, the weight for the feathers to be mailed was incorrect and @ERR was entered in the item's weight column instead of a weight. Since the @ERR function is part of the formula that determines the shipping cost, the ERR value ripples through that computation and is displayed as the item's shipping cost. Likewise, the ripple effect also makes the total shipping cost in F15 equal ERR. Therefore, you know that the error in the weight of the feathers must be corrected before you can know the correct total shipping cost.

@NA

The other special logical function for a data value is @NA. This function usually represents missing data or entries that are not applicable. Like the @ERR function, @NA has a ripple effect. That is, every function that references a cell containing the @NA function returns either NA or ERR. This prevents you from using the information from your notebook without being aware that some cells contain @NA. The @NA function does not require parentheses or a function argument.

An example of the @NA function is in Figure 8.17. In this example, the cost per pound for shipping to Ohio is unknown, so @NA has been entered in cell E3. Since the @NA function is part of the formula that determines the shipping cost, the NA value ripples through that computation and causes the item's shipping cost to equal NA. Likewise, the ripple effect also makes the total shipping cost in F15 equal NA. You must enter the cost per pound for the item before you know the total shipping cost.

FINANCIAL FUNCTIONS

Quattro Pro provides several built-in functions for financial calculations. Several financial functions compute depreciation, a dollar value for how much of an asset's capacity you are using. Other financial functions focus on the time value of money, the concept that a dollar today is worth more than a dollar tomorrow. Several financial functions that are new to Quattro Pro are enhancements of earlier financial functions that expand the applications for which you will use the functions.

The financial functions that use the time value of money concept use time periods and interest rates in the calculations. The interest rate must match the time period. If the time period is a year, you use an annual interest rate. When you use a different time period, you must use the applicable rate of interest. For example, if you are computing an annuity that is paid monthly, you must use the monthly interest rate. Converting from a year to months for an interest rate or time period is easy: You divide an annual interest rate by 12 to get the monthly interest rate, and multiply the number of years by 12 to get the total number of months in the time period. You can express interest rates in percentage terms, such as 10% or 15.5% or in decimal notation such as .1 or .155.

@SLN

@SLN computes the straight-line depreciation for an asset. Straight-line depreciation depreciates the same amount each year for the life of the asset. The formula for straight-line depreciation is:

$$\frac{Cost - salvage\ value}{life\ of\ asset}$$

The format of the @SLN function is @SLN(cost,salvage,life). Here, *cost* is the amount paid for the asset; *salvage* is the amount that you expect to receive when you dispose of the asset at the end of the asset's useful life; and *life* is the length of time that the asset is useful to you. Since you do not know the exact period for which the asset will continue to be useful, you must make an intelligent approximation. Each of these arguments can be a number, formula, or cell reference to either.

Figure 8.19 shows the depreciation calculations for different assets. In this example, the function uses the information in the Cost, Salvage Value, and Life columns to determine the depreciation and ignores the Period column. For example, the metal grinder, the last item on the list, originally cost $70,000; the company expects to recover $5,000 when they dispose of it; and it is expected to last 7 years. Therefore, straight-line depreciation is one-seventh of the difference between the cost and the salvage value ($65,000/7 = 9,286), as you can see in C19 that has the formula @SLN(D9,E9,F9).

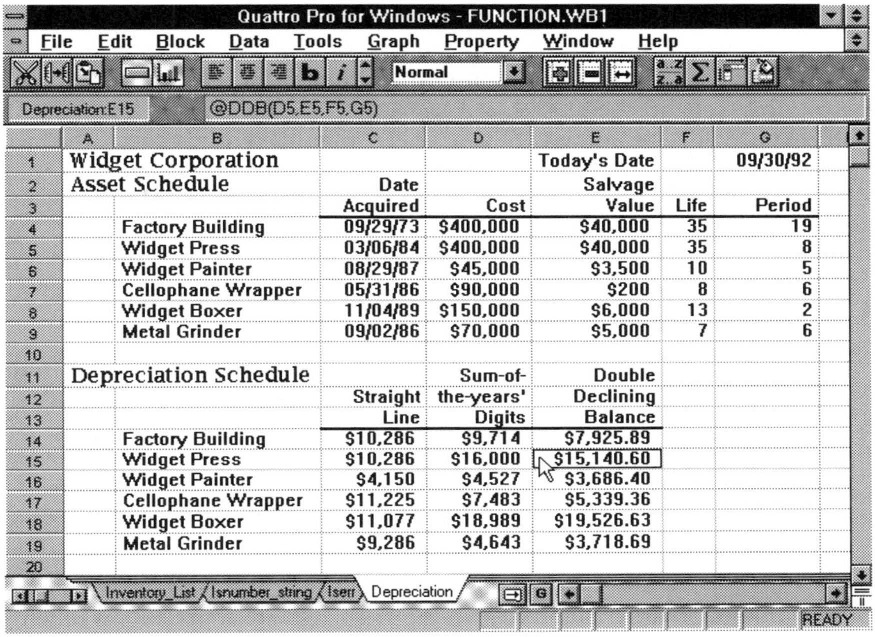

Figure 8.19 Computing Depreciation for Assets

@SYD

@SYD returns the depreciation computed by the sum-of-the-years' digits method. Sum-of-the-years' digits method depreciates a greater portion of the asset's value at the beginning of the asset's life. This depreciates the asset more quickly than the straight-line method, although not as quickly as the double-declining balance method (discussed next). The formula for sum-of-the-years' depreciation is:

$$\frac{(Cost - salvage\ value\ ) \times (life - period + 1\ )}{(asset\ life \times (asset\ life + 1))/2}$$

The format of this function is @SYD(cost,salvage,life,period). Here, *cost* is the initial price of the asset; *salvage* is the expected value when you sell the asset at the end of its useful life; *life* is the length of time that asset is expected to be used; and *period* is the year of the asset's life for which you are calculating the depreciation. The period must be supplied for the accelerated methods of depreciation, since more is depreciated at the beginning of the asset's life. Each of these arguments is a number, formula, or cell reference to either.

Figure 8.19 shows the sum-of-the-years' digits depreciation calculations for the same assets used in straight-line depreciation. This example uses the information in the Cost, Salvage Value, Life, and Period columns to determine the depreciation. The period is computed as the difference between the current date and the date the asset was acquired. The first and second assets illustrate accelerated depreciation. Both assets have the same cost, salvage value, and life. The formulas for these two assets are @SYD(D4,E4,F4,G4) in D14 and @SYD(D5,E5,F5,G5) in D15. Since the factory building is 11 years older than the widget press, the factory building has a lower depreciation. A larger percentage of the cost of the widget press is depreciated, since the period considered is closer to the beginning of the useful life of the widget press.

@DDB

@DDB computes an asset's double-declining balance depreciation. The double-declining balance method depreciates the asset most quickly by depreciating more in the beginning years of an asset's life than do the other two depreciation methods that Quattro Pro supports. The double-declining balance formula is

$$\frac{book\ value \times 2}{life\ of\ asset}$$

The book value of an asset is the cost of the asset less all depreciation taken.

The format is @DDB(cost,salvage,life,period). In this format, *cost* is the initial cost of the asset; *salvage* is the amount that you expect to receive when you dispose of the asset at the end of its life; *life* is the length of time that the asset is expected to be used; and *period* is the year of the asset's life that you are calculating the depreciation for. Each of these arguments is a number, formula, or cell reference to either.

Figure 8.19 shows the same assets used for the other depreciation functions using the double-declining balance method of depreciation. In this example, the function uses the information in the Cost, Salvage Value, Life, and Period columns to determine the depreciation. The first and second assets illustrate the effect of accelerated depreciation, since they have identical cost, salvage value, and life but were purchased almost 10 years apart. The formulas for these two assets are @DDB(D4,E4,F4,G4) in E14 and @DDB(D4,E4,F4,G4) in E15. The widget press has a higher depreciation than the factory building, since it is newer. Of the three depreciation methods described, double-declining balance produces the highest depreciation at the beginning of an asset's life and the lowest at the end of an asset's life.

@PMT

The @PMT function computes a payment based on the principal, an interest rate, and a number of periods. This function can compute loan and annuity payments. The format is @PMT(pv,rate,nper), where *pv* is the present value of the annuity or the loan principal; *rate* is the interest rate of the annuity or the loan per term; and *nper* is the number of periods that you are paying of the annuity or loan. Each of these arguments is a number, formula, or cell reference to either.

One application for the @PMT function is to determine the monthly payment for the house of your dreams. Figure 8.20 has the relevant information for six homes. For each home, make the assumption that the current home will be sold and the equity from it will be applied to the new home. Therefore, the amount borrowed is the difference between the cost of the new home and the equity of the old home. The mortgage rate and term are shown in annual terms. The basic formula in B7 is @PMT(B4-$D$1,B5,B6), which is then copied across the row. To compute the monthly payment, you must convert the rate and term to months. To convert the rate and term into the monthly interest rate and number of months for the loan, divide the annual rate by 12 and multiply the number of years by 12, respectively. For example, B8 contains the formula @PMT(B4-$D$1,B5/12,B6*12). By using the monthly rate and term, the @PMT function in row 8 computes the monthly payment. The monthly payment is not 1/12 of the yearly rate. For example, 1/12 of the yearly payment is 222.33. The difference is caused by the compounding interest rate effect. At the end of each period, the interest is computed based upon the balance at the end of the period. Since the balance declines more quickly when you pay monthly, the monthly payment is less.

@PAYMT

The @PAYMT function computes a payment based on the principal, its future value, an interest rate, a number of periods, and whether the payment is made at the beginning or end of the period. It can also compute annuity amounts. This

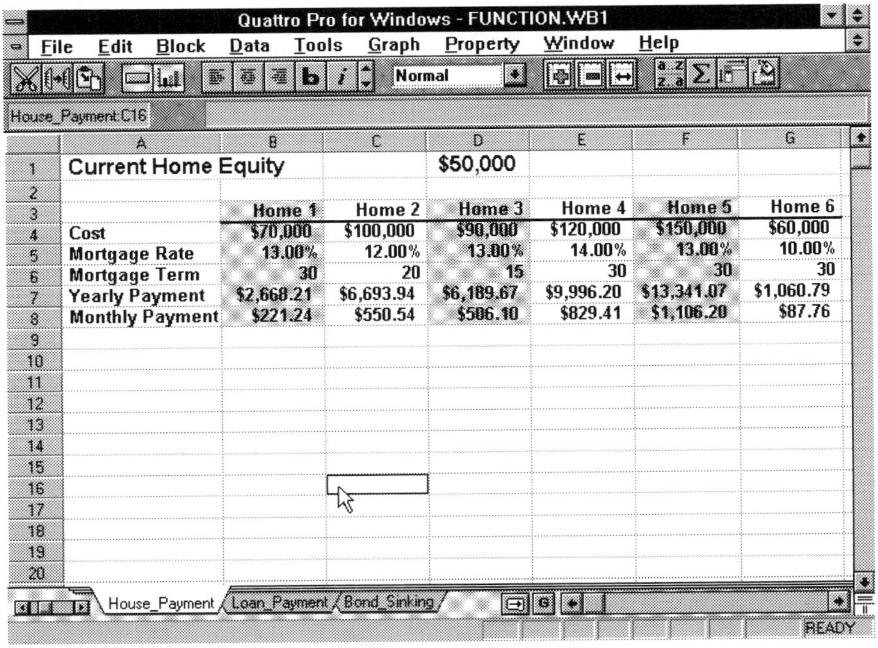

	A	B	C	D	E	F	G
1	Current Home Equity			$50,000			
2							
3		Home 1	Home 2	Home 3	Home 4	Home 5	Home 6
4	Cost	$70,000	$100,000	$90,000	$120,000	$150,000	$60,000
5	Mortgage Rate	13.00%	12.00%	13.00%	14.00%	13.00%	10.00%
6	Mortgage Term	30	20	15	30	30	30
7	Yearly Payment	$2,668.21	$6,693.94	$6,189.67	$9,996.20	$13,341.07	$1,060.79
8	Monthly Payment	$221.24	$550.54	$506.10	$829.41	$1,106.20	$87.76

Figure 8.20 @PMT Used to Compute Monthly and Annual Payments on Different Houses

function is an enhancement of the @PMT function. The format is @PAYMT(rate,nper,pv[,fv][,type]), where *rate* is the interest rate you are paying on the loan per term; *nper* is the number of periods that you are paying on the loan; *pv* is the principal of the loan; *fv* is the future value that is still due at the end of the loan; and *type* indicates whether the payment is made at the beginning of the period (1) or end of the period (0). If the fv or type arguments are omitted, Quattro Pro assumes they are 0—just as in the @PMT function. Each of these arguments is a number, formula, or cell reference to either.

This function is used instead of @PMT when the function uses one of the two optional arguments. As an example, if a fledgling business is borrowing $100,000 to buy a building, the lender may not want to offer a long-term loan. One option is to offer the loan for a shorter time period, such as five years. At the end of the loan period, some of the loan principal remains, so the borrower must take out another loan or sell the building to pay the remaining principal. The lender may also require that the loan payment is made at the beginning of the month. Figure 8.21 shows this example in a notebook page. This example assumes that the loan principal at the end of five years is $50,000. Since you are receiving $100,000 for the loan, this number, the present value, is positive. Since you will owe $50,000 at the end of the loan, the future value is negative. The function result of ($1,466.80) is the monthly payment the borrower will make for the next five years. It is negative since the borrower is paying this money instead of receiving it. At the end of five years, the borrower may seek another loan, the lender may offer to extend the loan, or the borrower may sell the building and pay the remaining principal.

Changing when the loan payment is made also changes the function's result. If the payment is made at the end of the month, the 1 in the formula in B5 is changed to a 0. The result of ($1,479.02) indicates how this payment amount is affected by when payment is made.

@IPAYMT

The @IPAYMT function computes the interest portion of a loan payment. The format is @IPAYMT(rate,per,nper,pv[,fv][,type]), where *rate* is the interest rate you are paying on the loan per term; *per* is the loan payment period for which you want to know the interest portion; *nper* is the number of periods that you are paying on the loan; *pv* is the principal of the loan; *fv* is the future value that is still due at the end of the loan; and *type* indicates whether the payment is made at the beginning of the period (1) or end of the period (0). If the fv or type arguments are omitted, Quattro Pro assumes they are 0. These arguments are a number, formula, or cell reference to either.

Using the example described above for the @PAYMT function, suppose you want to know how much interest you will pay in the first year. Column F in Figure 8.21 contains the formulas to compute the interest for the first year of the loan. The formula in F2 is @IPAYMT($B$1/12,E2,$B$2*12,$B$3,–$B$4,1). This formula is copied down the column for the remaining months. As the results show, the interest portion of the loan payment decreases in each period.

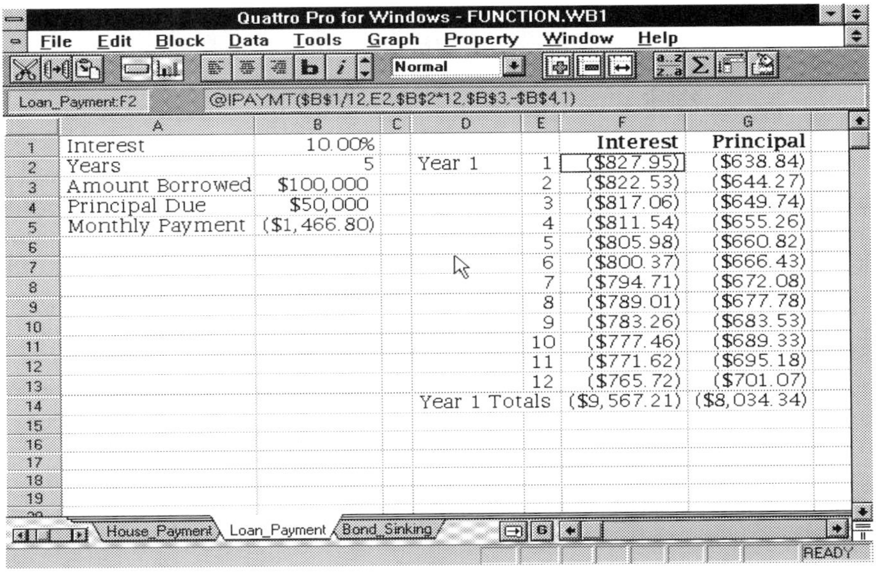

	A	B	C	D	E	F	G
1	Interest	10.00%				**Interest**	**Principal**
2	Years	5		Year 1	1	($827.95)	($638.84)
3	Amount Borrowed	$100,000			2	($822.53)	($644.27)
4	Principal Due	$50,000			3	($817.06)	($649.74)
5	Monthly Payment	($1,466.80)			4	($811.54)	($655.26)
6					5	($805.98)	($660.82)
7					6	($800.37)	($666.43)
8					7	($794.71)	($672.08)
9					8	($789.01)	($677.78)
10					9	($783.26)	($683.53)
11					10	($777.46)	($689.33)
12					11	($771.62)	($695.18)
13					12	($765.72)	($701.07)
14				Year 1 Totals		($9,567.21)	($8,034.34)

Figure 8.21 Financial Functions Calculating Loan Amounts

@PPAYMT

The @PPAYMT function computes the principal portion of a loan payment. The format is @PPAYMT(rate,per,nper,pv[,fv][,type]), where *rate* is the interest rate you are paying on the loan per period; *per* is the loan payment period for which you want to know the principal portion; *nper* is the number of periods that you are paying on the loan; *pv* is the principal of the loan; *fv* is the future value that is still due at the end of the loan; and *type* indicates whether the payment is made at the beginning of the period (1) or end of the period (0). If the fv or type arguments are omitted, Quattro Pro assumes they are 0. These arguments are a number, formula, or cell reference to either.

Using the example described above for the @PAYMT function, suppose you want to know how much principal you will pay in the first year. Column G in Figure 8.21 contains the formulas to compute the principal for the first year of the loan. The formula in G2 is @PPAYMT($B$1/12,E2,$B$2*12,$B$3,–$B$4,1). This formula is copied down the column for the remaining months. As the results show, the principal portion of the loan payment increases in each period. By adding the values in columns F and G, you will notice that the results of the @PPAYMT for each month is the result of @PAYMT less @IPAYMT.

@TERM

The @TERM function determines the number of periodic payments made each period at a specified rate of interest to accumulate a future value. The format is

@TERM(payment,rate,fv), where *payment* represents the present value that you have; *rate* represents the interest rate of the investment opportunity; and *fv* represents the future value you want to have.

When a company sells a bond issue, it must make provisions to repay the bonds when they become due either by redeeming them or by reissuing another series of bonds. When bonds are issued, the company can create a bond-sinking fund that accumulates until the bonds are due, by which point the contributions to the bond-sinking fund and the earnings equal the bond's face value. One way to accumulate earnings in the bond-sinking fund is to invest a fixed amount every month. For example, suppose you invest $5,000 every month for the next 10 years, earning 10% annual interest. At the end of 10 years, you will sell the investments and use the proceeds to redeem the bonds, then totaling $1,000,000. However, before you start this investment program and deposit the first $5,000, you need to check if your assumptions are correct. Figure 8.22 shows a page with the assumptions. The first assumption to be tested is if 10 years of investing $5,000 monthly is enough to reach your goal of $1,000,000. Cell D8 uses the @TERM function to determine the minimum number of years that you need to save. Because you are investing monthly, the function needs a monthly interest rate. Since you want the number of years and the function returns the number of months, the result of the function

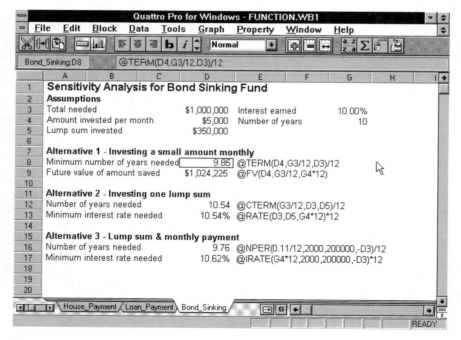

Figure 8.22 Financial Functions Used to Compute Minimum Rate to Reach Financial Goal

needs to be divided by twelve to convert the number of months to number of years. In D8, the @TERM function refers to the monthly saving of $5,000 entered in D4; the annual interest rate in G3 (which is divided by twelve to convert it to a monthly rate); and the targeted value of $1,000,000 entered in D3. By referring to the cell values instead of typing them directly into the formula, you can change your assumptions quickly without changing any formulas. The result of 9.85 years indicates that investing $5,000 a month for 10 years will earn enough to redeem the bonds in 10 years.

Another option for this example is to use annual figures by entering the invested amount as **D4*12** and not dividing the interest rate and the function's result by 12. The resulting answer of 10.29 is larger due to the compounding effects of investing annually instead of monthly; your investments accumulate more quickly if your interest is compounded monthly rather than annually.

@FV

The @FV function computes the future value of a series of equal cash flows, each earning interest. This function treats cash flows as it would treat an ordinary annuity. An ordinary annuity is an investment where you put in a fixed amount every period and at the end of a fixed number of periods, you receive the amount that you have saved plus the interest earned on all money invested.

The format is @FV(payment,rate,term), where *payment* represents the periodic fixed payment; *rate* represents the interest rate each payment earns per period; and *term* represents the number of periods the annuity covers. The function assumes that interest is compounded at the end of each period within the term.

In the example for @TERM, the minimum number of years it takes to invest enough for the bond-sinking fund is computed. Since you found that it takes less than the 10 years that you planned to invest, the investment proceeds will exceed your needs at the end of the 10 years. The @FV function can determine the final amount that is actually saved and earned if you continue to save for the full 10 years.

Although both the @FV and @TERM work with the same basic problem, their approach and solutions are different, since both functions work with different unknowns. @TERM computes the minimum number of years and @FV computes the future value of your investments as shown in Figure 8.22. As you can see in the formula in D9 which also appears in cell E9, the annual rate is divided by 12 to generate the monthly interest rate, and the term of 10 years in cell G4 is multiplied by 12 to compute the number of months of the annuity. The result of $1,024,225 indicates that you will have $24,225 more than needed by saving $5,000 per month for 10 years at 10% interest.

@CTERM

The @CTERM function computes the number of time periods required for a present value to reach a future value by earning a fixed interest rate. The format is @CTERM(rate,fv,pv), where *rate* is the interest rate per period; *fv* is the future value that you are trying to reach; and *pv* is the present value that you currently have.

Using the example of the bond-sinking fund, an alternative to investing a fixed sum monthly is investing a larger sum now. For example, if you invest $350,000 for 10 years earning 10% interest, the original amount will grow to a larger amount due to compounding interest. To determine if the future value is enough for your goal, use the @CTERM function in D12 to compute the number of years for which you need to earn interest on the lump sum to reach your goal. Like the examples for @TERM and @FV, this example also uses monthly compounding. The @CTERM function uses the interest rate in G3 divided by 12, the future value in D3, and the present value in D5. To modify this function to return the number of years instead of the number of months, the interest and the function's result must be divided by 12. From the result shown in Figure 8.22, investing $350,000 and earning 10% annual interest yields your goal in 10.54 years, or approximately $10^1/2$ years. Since this is longer than desired, if you want to invest a lump sum now for redeeming bonds in 10 years, you would have to invest more than $350,000 or earn more than 10% interest.

@RATE

The @RATE function returns the minimum interest rate required for a present value invested over a period of time to equal a future amount compounded each time period. The format is @RATE(fv,pv,term), where *fv* is the future value you want to earn; *pv* is the present value that you have; and *term* represents the number of periods for the investment.

Using a current lump-sum investment approach for the bond-sinking fund, you can use the @RATE function to determine the minimum interest rate that your lump-sum investment must earn to accumulate the $1,000,000 goal at the end of the 10 years. Figure 8.22 uses the @RATE function to determine the interest rate required to accumulate $1,000,000 from your initial $350,000 investment in 10 years. In B13, the @RATE function computes the minimum annual interest rate that must be earned. This function produces a monthly rate, since the number of years in G4 is multiplied by 12. The function's result then is converted to an annual figure by multiplying the result by 12. Therefore, 10.54% is the minimum annual interest rate you can earn on a lump sum of $350,000 to accumulate $1,000,000 in 10 years when the interest is compounded monthly. If the interest is compounded annually, you need at least 11.07% interest. The difference illustrates the benefit of having interest compounded more frequently.

@NPER

The @NPER function returns the number of periods required for a lump sum and/or a number of periodic payments invested over a period of time and compounded each time period to equal a future amount. The @NPER function combines the @TERM and @CTERM, since it can handle a single amount at the beginning of the period, a fixed amount every period, or both. The format is @NPER (rate,payment,pv[,fv][,type]), where *rate* represents the interest rate of the investment opportunity; *payment* represents the payment made at the beginning or end of each period; *pv* is the present value the investment starts with; *fv* is the future value that will be earned at the end of the last period (pv and fv have opposite signs—if you think of the money that you earn or receive as positive numbers and money you have to pay as negative numbers, you will remember to put the correct sign in front of the pmt, pv, and fv function arguments); and *type* is 1 if the payment is made at the beginning of the period, or 0 or omitted if the payment is made at the end of the period.

A third alternative to the bond-sinking fund example is investing $200,000 now and also $2,000 monthly. You can use the @NPER function to determine the minimum number of periods you must invest to accumulate the $1,000,000 goal. D16 in Figure 8.22 uses the @NPER function to determine the number of periods required to accumulate $1,000,000 from your initial $200,000 investment and the additional $2,000 monthly earning 10% interest (the $200,000 and $2,000 are in the formula that also appears as a label in E16). The function arguments are in a different order than for the @TERM or @CTERM function. Also, the fv argument has a minus sign, since you are paying it to the bondholders. In D16, the @NPER function computes the number of periods this investment must be maintained. The function's result is divided by 12 to convert the resulting number of months to the number of years. Therefore, you must pursue this investment for 9.76 years.

@IRATE

The @IRATE function returns the minimum interest rate required for a present value invested over a period of time to equal a future amount compounded each time period. Unlike the @RATE function, the @IRATE function has two additional arguments that let you enter a final investment value and whether the periodic amount is deposited or withdrawn at the beginning or end of the period. The format of this function is @IRATE(nper,payment,pv[,fv][,type]). Here, *nper* represents the number of periods for the investment and *payment* is the payment made at the beginning or end of the period. The *pv* is the present value the investment starts with, and *fv* is the future value that will be earned at the end of the last period. (The pv and the fv have opposite signs. If you think of the money that you earn or receive as positive numbers and money you have to pay as negative numbers, you will remember to put the correct sign in front of the pmt, pv, and fv function arguments.) The *type* is 1 if the payment is made at the beginning of the period, or 0 or omitted if the payment is made at the end of the period.

Using the combined lump sum and monthly payment approach for the bond-sinking fund, you can use the @IRATE function to determine the minimum interest rate that your lump sum investment must earn to accumulate the $1,000,000 goal at the end of the 10 years. D17 in Figure 8.22 uses the @IRATE function to determine the interest rate required to accumulate $1,000,000 from your initial $200,000 investment and the additional $2,000 monthly in 10 years (the 2000 and 200000 are in the formula that appears as a label in E17). The function arguments are in a different order than in D13 and E13 for the @RATE function. Also, the fv argument has a minus sign, since you are paying it to the bondholders at the end of 10 years. In D17, the @IRATE function computes the minimum annual interest rate that must be earned. This function produces a monthly rate, since the function uses the number of months for the nper argument. The function's result is converted to an annual figure by multiplying the result by 12. Therefore, 10.62% is the minimum annual interest rate you can earn on a lump sum of $200,000 and a monthly addition of $2,000 to accumulate $1,000,000 in 10 years when the interest is compounded monthly.

@PV

The @PV function computes the present value of an annuity, or series of equal cash flows, invested at a certain interest rate for a number of periods. The format is @PV(payment,rate,nper), where *payment* is the amount of a fixed payment that is made every period; *rate* represents the interest rate per period; and *nper* represents the number of periods that the investment covers. The function assumes that interest is compounded at the end of each period within the term.

Most state lotteries award their prizes as annuities. For example, if you win a lottery of $1,000,000, you often do not receive a check for $1,000,000. Usually you get a payment once a year for a percentage of your winnings. For example, assume that you have just won a $1,000,000 lottery that is to be paid out at $50,000 for the next 20 years. As an option, the group operating the lottery allows you to choose a lump sum payment of $500,000 immediately. To decide which has the greater present value, you use the @PV function to compute the present value of the 20-payment option. In Figure 8.23, the three assumptions are listed in rows 1 through 3. This example assumes that the interest is computed annually. The function in B5 computes the present value of your annuity (lottery prize winnings). As you can see from this example, the present value of the $500,000 immediately is worth more than that of taking $50,000 for the next 20 years since you can earn more by putting the money in an investment that earns at least 8% and withdrawing $50,000 per year from your investment. (These results do not include the effects of taxes, which may change your decision.)

@PVAL

The @PVAL function computes the present value of an annuity, or series of equal cash flows, and an end of the term payment invested at a certain interest rate for a number of periods. The format is @PVAL(rate,nper,payment[,fv][,type]), where *rate* represents the interest rate per period; *nper* represents the number of periods

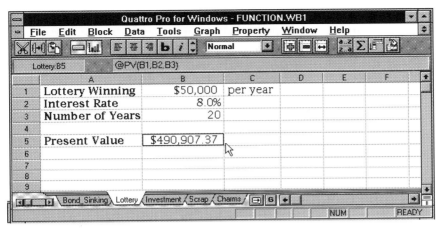

Figure 8.23 @PV Used to Compute the Present Value of Lottery Winnings

that the investment covers; *payment* is the amount of a fixed payment that is made every period; and *fv* is the future value of the investment at the end of the last period. If you think of the money that you earn or receive as positive numbers and money you have to pay as negative numbers, you will remember to put the correct sign in front of the pmt and fv function arguments. The *type* is 1 if the payment is made at the beginning of the period, or 0 or omitted if the payment is made at the end of the period.

One application of this function is deciding if a sales offer is a good price. For example, suppose you own a restaurant and someone offers $300,000 to buy it. You can use the @PVAL function to determine if the sales offer is high enough to make selling the restaurant worthwhile. Assume that if you did not sell it now, you could expect to earn $40,000 per year for the next 10 years and that after 10 years it would be worth $100,000. To evaluate whether to sell now, you can check whether the selling price is greater than the present value of your expected cash flows. To find the present value of the restaurant, you would enter this formula in a cell: **@PVAL(.1,10,40000,100000)**. The **.1** (10%) represents the interest you would earn on a similar investment. This is an annual rate. The **10** represents the number of years you would receive the yearly income. The **100000** represents the restaurant value at the end of the 10 years. The function returns −284337. Since this is less than the sales offer, it is worthwhile to sell the restaurant now.

@FVAL

The @FVAL function computes the future value of a present value and the value of an annuity, or series of equal cash flows invested at a certain interest rate for a number of periods. The format is @FVAL(rate,nper,payment[,pv][,type]), where *rate* represents the interest rate per period; *nper* represents the number of periods that the investment covers; *payment* is the amount of a fixed payment that is made every period; and *pv* is the present value of the investment. If you think of the money that you earn or receive as positive numbers and money you have to pay as negative numbers, you will remember to put the correct sign in front of the pmt and pv function arguments. The *type* is 1 if the payment is made at the beginning of the period, or 0 or omitted if the payment is made at the end of the period. Each of these arguments is a number, formula, or cell reference to either.

As an example, imagine that you are saving for a luxury vacation. So far, you have saved $500 and plan to put aside $50 per week in your bank account, which earns 5.25% interest. You can use the @FVAL function to learn how large your vacation budget is. To use the @FVAL function with this data, enter the following formula into a cell: **@FVAL(.0525/52,52,50,500)**. The number of periods is 52 for 52 weeks in one year, and the annual interest rate is divided by 52 to convert the annual rate to a weekly rate. The result of –3195.02 tells you how much you can spend on your vacation.

@NPV

The @NPV function computes the present value of a stream of future cash flows. The format is @NPV(rate,block[,type]). The *rate* is the interest rate for the period. This function assumes that the same interest rate applies for each period. The *block* represents the area on your notebook that contains the cash flows. This function assumes that cash flows occur on a regular basis in the order they appear in the block with blank cells representing periods with no cash flows. Positive numbers represent cash inflows, and negative numbers represent cash outflows. This function assumes the cash flows occur at the end of the period unless you enter 1 for the optional *type* argument. If the project's cash flows include an initial cost, use a 1 for the type argument. An alternative is to omit this cash outflow from the block for the @NPV function and subtract the initial cost from the result of the @NPV function. A cash flow at the beginning of a period is the same as a cash flow at the end of the previous period.

One use of the @NPV function is computing the net present value of investment opportunities. If you have several investment opportunities, the one with the highest net present value is the most valuable. Figure 8.24 shows four investment opportunities with different cash flows. The initial cost is in row 2, and the yearly cash flows are in rows 3 through 12. The formula in row 14 computes the net present value of each of the cash flows in rows 2 through 12 with a type argument indicating that the cash flows are made at the beginning of the period. In this example, B16 provides the discount or interest rate the @NPV function uses. Therefore, the investment opportunity D is the most valuable of the investment opportunities.

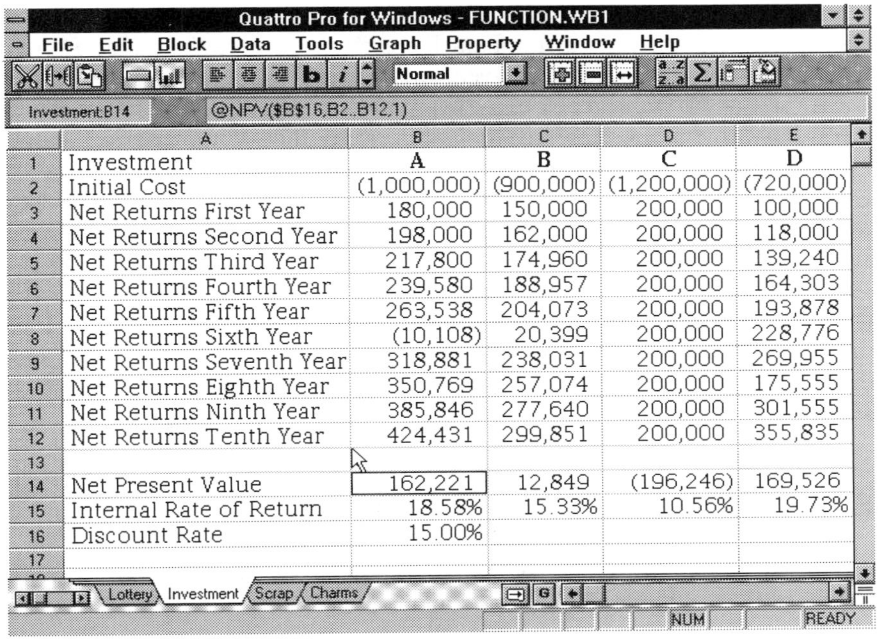

	A	B	C	D	E
1	Investment	A	B	C	D
2	Initial Cost	(1,000,000)	(900,000)	(1,200,000)	(720,000)
3	Net Returns First Year	180,000	150,000	200,000	100,000
4	Net Returns Second Year	198,000	162,000	200,000	118,000
5	Net Returns Third Year	217,800	174,960	200,000	139,240
6	Net Returns Fourth Year	239,580	188,957	200,000	164,303
7	Net Returns Fifth Year	263,538	204,073	200,000	193,878
8	Net Returns Sixth Year	(10,108)	20,399	200,000	228,776
9	Net Returns Seventh Year	318,881	238,031	200,000	269,955
10	Net Returns Eighth Year	350,769	257,074	200,000	175,555
11	Net Returns Ninth Year	385,846	277,640	200,000	301,555
12	Net Returns Tenth Year	424,431	299,851	200,000	355,835
13					
14	Net Present Value	162,221	12,849	(196,246)	169,526
15	Internal Rate of Return	18.58%	15.33%	10.56%	19.73%
16	Discount Rate	15.00%			
17					

Figure 8.24 @NPV and @IRR Used to Evaluate Investment Opportunities

@IRR

The @IRR function computes the internal rate of return for a series of cash flows. The internal rate of return is the rate of interest the cash flows must earn to have a net present value of 0. This internal rate of return is the minimum interest rate a project or asset should earn to be considered a viable option.

The format of the function is @IRR(guess,block). Here, *guess* is a number that is your approximation of the internal rate of return. While your guess is probably different from the result of the function, it should be reasonably close. By using a reasonable guess, you shorten the time the @IRR function takes to compute the internal rate of return and ensure a correct internal rate of return. Every time the cash flows alternate between positive and negative numbers, there is another possible internal rate of return. Since some of the internal rates of return are impractical, your guess indicates which one Quattro Pro should use. The *block* is the area of cells that contains the cash flows. The @IRR function assumes that the first cell in the block is the initial cash outflow for the investment opportunity and is a negative number. Quattro Pro also assumes that cash flows occur on a regular basis in the order they appear in the block with blank cells representing periods with no cash flows. Positive numbers represent cash inflows and negative numbers represent cash outflows.

The internal rate of return is frequently used to help decide which projects should be considered for your investment dollars. For example, companies have a minimum internal rate of return for projects; a project must have an internal rate of return higher than the company's minimum before the company invests in the project. For example, when you have several possible investment opportunities, you must decide among them. Figure 8.24 displays four investment opportunities to be evaluated. The @IRR can determine which is providing the best return on investment. Since @IRR assumes that the first cell is the initial cash outflow, rows 2 through 12 are included in the formula. In this example, if you expect a minimum of 15% from your investments (entered in cell B16), you are willing to acquire the investment opportunities A, B, and D. Investment opportunity D is again the best of the three, since it has the highest internal rate of return. @IRR and @NPV usually agree on which is the best of several investment opportunities. When they do not agree, it is often due to an inappropriate guess in the @IRR function.

MATHEMATICAL FUNCTIONS: INTRODUCTION

Quattro Pro has a separate category of mathematical functions that perform one of three types of tasks. One type includes functions that focus on basic mathematical capabilities (like deriving absolute values) and rounding and other functions that provide basic mathematical values (like random numbers). The second type focuses on the trigonometric functions that relate to the properties of angles and allow you to perform computations on geometric shapes. The third type is used in logarithmic computations.

MATHEMATICAL FUNCTIONS: BASIC

@ROUND

The @ROUND function rounds a number to a specified place to the left or right of the decimal point. The format is @ROUND(x,num). Here, *x* is the value to be rounded; *num* is the number of places before or after the decimal at which the rounding should take place whose value ranges from –15 to 15. A positive value causes rounding to the right of the decimal. For example, if this argument equals 2, an entry of **2.5672** would be rounded to 2.57. A negative value causes rounding to the left of the decimal point. For example, if this argument equals -3, then **34,285.2** would be rounded to 34,000. A value of 0 causes the function to round the number to an integer. Rounding a value differs from truncating the value, since truncating a value ignores the numbers to the right of the point you are truncating from, and rounding a number uses the value to the right of the point that you are rounding to determine whether the number should be rounded up or rounded down. For example, **25.68** would be truncated to 25.6 but rounded to 25.7. Quattro Pro follows the convention of rounding to the next higher digit if the number to the right of num is 5 or greater. Rounding changes the internal storage of the value to match the displayed value, unlike changing the numeric format property of a block, which changes the number's appearance but does not change how the number is stored. For example, if 1.00797 is stored in a cell, changing the format to Fixed with 2 decimal places does not affect the value of the cell. On the other hand, if the cell contains @ROUND(1.00797,2), the value is stored as 1.01 and used as that value in all subsequent computations.

One practical application of the @ROUND function is combining several measurements that have a different number of places of decimal accuracy. For example, if you are combining the weights of steel scrap from a process and each scrap was measured on one of three scales, the three different scales may provide different accuracy measurements, as in the example shown in Figure 8.25. Each piece of scrap is listed in column A. One of the scales measured to the nearest pound, another measured to the nearest tenth of a pound, and the third measured to the nearest hundredth of a pound. Since the accounting for scrap only requires accuracy to the nearest pound, it is not important to maintain the weight of the scraps to the nearest tenth and hundredth of a pound. In column C, each of the columns is rounded to the nearest whole number by using @ROUND with a 0 for the second function argument. By rounding the pieces of scrap to the nearest pound, you create a cleaner display without excessive detail. The @ROUND function is often

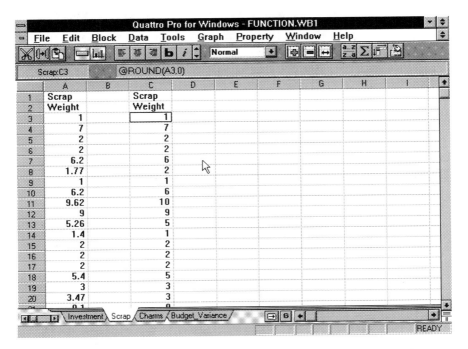

Figure 8.25 @ROUND Used to Convert Numbers to a Consistent Format

used to control the accuracy of the results produced by other functions and formulas, as the example for the @RAND function later in the chapter illustrates.

@INT

@INT returns the integer portion of a number. Any digits after the decimal point are truncated. The format is @INT(x), where x is the number to be truncated. @INT differs from @ROUND with the second function's argument equaling 0 in that @INT ignores the numbers to the right of the decimal point while @ROUND uses the numbers to the right of the decimal point to round the value to the next higher or lower value. Like the @ROUND function, the @INT function changes the way the value is stored. Both @ROUND and @INT differ from changing the numeric format property of a block, which changes the number's appearance but does not change the way the number is stored. For example, if 6.022 is stored in a cell, changing the cell's format to Fixed with 0 decimal places does not affect the value of the cell. On the other hand, if the cell contains @INT(6.022), the value is stored as 6 and used as that value in all subsequent computations.

Figure 8.26 shows a schedule listing each piece of silver used for pressing charms. In this process, a press uses 0.75 ounces for each charm and presses as many as may fit on each piece of the silver sheet. Column B computes the number

	A	B	C	D	E	F	G
2	Sheet (18 gauge)	Pressed from	Remaining				
3	(ounces)	Each Sheet	(ounces)				
4	2	2	0.5				
5	1	1	0.25				
6	4	5	0.25				
7	7	9	0.25				
8	14	18	0.5				
9	4	5	0.25				
10	9	12	0				
11	15	20	0				
12	4	5	0.25				
13	15	20	0				
14	5	6	0.5				
15	7	9	0.25				
16	3	4	0				
17	2	2	0.5				
18	7	9	0.25				
19	2	2	0.5				
20	12	16	0				
21							

Figure 8.26   Using @INT and @MOD to Compute Production and Scrap

of 0.75-ounce pieces that are in each sheet by putting the formula @INT(A4/.75) in B4 and copying it down the column. Since you cannot press only a portion of a charm from the piece of silver, the number of charms pressed from each piece is the integer portion of the calculation. You cannot use the @ROUND function since you do not want any of the calculations rounded to the next highest number.

@MOD

@MOD returns the modulo of two numbers. A modulo is the remainder when a number is divided by a divisor. For example, the modulo of seven divided by three is one since three goes into seven twice with a remainder of 1. The format is @MOD(x,y), where x is the number to be divided and y is the number being divided into x. The second argument must not equal 0.

Using the data from the @INT example, you can use the @MOD function to determine the remainder of each sheet of silver. As shown in Figure 8.26, once you know the leftover silver from each sheet, you can determine the weight of the silver sheet you can create by melting the scraps into one sheet. In column C, the remaining silver from each sheet is computed by putting the formula @MOD(A4,.75) in C4 and copying it down the column. If you add the scraps from each sheet by using the @SUM function, you find that you can create a 4.25-ounce sheet by melting the scraps into one sheet.

@ABS

@ABS returns the absolute value of a number. The absolute value is a number's absolute distance from zero whether the number is positive or negative. This function returns a positive number equal to the function's argument if the argument is positive or a positive number equal to –1 times the function's argument if the argument is a negative value. The format is @ABS(x), where x is the number for which you want the absolute value. This function is often used to process another function's argument before the other function uses the value, such as the @SQRT and the logarithmic functions described later in the chapter.

In some applications, you need to know the absolute value of a result. For example, when you compare a budget versus an actual spending plan, several differences appear. Since it is not worthwhile to check every variance, you can set a criterion, such as checking out all variances that exceed 10% of the budgeted expense. In Figure 8.27, the @IF function in column E determines which expense variances exceed 10% (0.1) of its budget. Since you want to know all variances that are over or under by 10%, you must use the absolute value of the variances. If you do not use the @ABS function, you miss checking the variances for utilities and wages since their negative variances are much more than 10% of their budget.

The @ABS function is also used within other functions to ensure that a value used in or produced by a function is positive. For example, if you want the square root of a formula's result, you may take the absolute value of a formula's result to ensure that a positive value is used by the @SQRT function (described next).

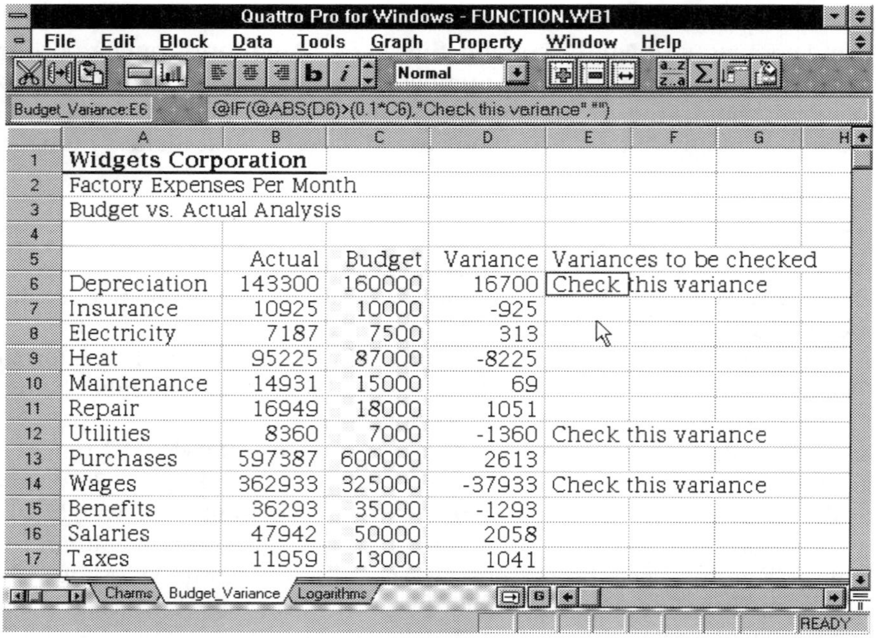

Figure 8.27 @ABS Used to Measure the Absolute Amount of the Variances

@SQRT

The @SQRT function returns the square root of a number. The square root of a number is another number that, if multiplied by itself, produces the original number (for example, the square root of 9 is 3, because $3 \times 3 = 9$). The syntax of the function is @SQRT(x), where *x* is the number of which you want the square root. Quattro Pro can only determine the square roots of positive numbers. You can also compute the square root by raising the number to the 0.5 power.

Various applications use the square root function, such as the Pythagorean theorem and the economic order quantity. The Pythagorean theorem states that, in a right angle triangle (one in which one of the angles is 90°), the square of the longest side is equal to the sum of the squares of the other two sides. For example, if you have a triangle that has a height of 4 units and a base of 3 units with a 90° angle between the base and the height, you can use the Pythagorean theorem to compute the third side with this formula: **@SQRT(3^2+4^2)**. This formula squares 3 and 4, resulting in 9 and 16, respectively; then it adds them together for a result of 25, and computes the square root of 25, which is 5. While you can compute a square root of a value by raising it to its one-half root, the @SQRT function is quicker and easier to understand for someone who does not know that the two formulas are equivalent.

Generating a value's square root by raising a number to the inverse of the root that you want is usually not done for square roots; however, this formula can generate third and fourth roots for numbers. For example, to compute the cube (3rd) root of the value in A1, use this formula: **+A1^(1/3)**. For example, if A1 is 125, this formula returns 5 (5×5×5=125). This same formula works for the fourth root if you replace the **3** with a **4**.

@PI

The @PI function returns the value of pi (π), which equals approximately 3.14159. This function is primarily used in other formulas and functions. This function has no argument or parentheses.

The @PI function is often used for calculations involving circles. For example, suppose you had to purchase chairs for a large round table. You know that each chair requires approximately 3 feet, including some extra space for the comfort of the individual sitting in the chair. If you know that the diameter of the table is 10 feet, determining the perimeter is easy (perimeter = $\pi \times 10$). Therefore to compute the perimeter of the table using Quattro Pro, enter the formula **10*@PI**. To compute how many chairs you can comfortably fit at the table, use this formula: **@PI*10/3**. This formula calculates that you can put 10.47 chairs around the table. Since you can only order chairs in whole numbers, you can order 10 and be assured that each person has at least 3 feet of space.

@RAND

The @RAND function generates a random number between 0 and 1. By combining this function with other arithmetic operators, you can use this function to generate random numbers for any range. The function does not use parentheses or arguments.

To generate a group of numbers within a range, determine the range for the numbers you plan to generate and subtract the start of the range from the end of the range. Multiply this number by @RAND. For example, entering **@RAND*40** generates a random number between 0 and 40. If you want the random numbers to start at a different point than 0, add the starting point of the range to the number generated by @RAND. For example, if you want to generate integers between –20 and 20, the formula is: **@ROUND(@RAND*40,0)–20**. In this formula, the @RAND function generates a number that is multiplied by 40 to have the range spread over 40 integers. After this, the number is rounded to 0 decimal places to convert the number into an integer. Finally, this number has 20 subtracted from it to make the numbers start at –20 and extend to 20. An example of using @RAND to generate random alphabetic letters is demonstrated with the @CHAR function in an earlier section.

MATHEMATICAL FUNCTIONS: TRIGONOMETRIC

Trigonometric functions involve the relationships of the sides and angles of triangles. They provide information about a part of a triangle if you provide information about another part of the triangle.

Quattro Pro has nine trigonometric functions. The first two convert degrees to radians and radians to degrees. The next three are the basic functions for sine, cosine, and tangent. The last four are inverse functions. This means that these functions accept an appropriate ratio as an argument and return an angle rather than accepting an angle and returning a ratio. Each of these trigonometric functions is based on ratios that measure angles and are useful in applications that involve calculations with angles. The secant, cosecant, and cotangent are computed by using the basic trigonometric functions. Although you can use tables to determine the values for the trigonometric functions for various angles, Quattro Pro automatically calculates these ratios for you.

The trigonometric angle ratios can be understood by inscribing an angle in one of the four quadrants of a circle as shown in Figure 8.28. The angle in this circle that is the focus of trigonometric function examples is angle YXZ (an angle is described by listing the letters representing the points on the two lines that create the angle; the center letter is the pivot point for the two lines that form the angle). Angle YXZ is created by the rotation of the line XY to point Z on the circle's circumference.

By dropping a perpendicular line from the horizontal axis to Z, you create a right triangle, since the angle created by the line to the horizontal axis is 90°. This

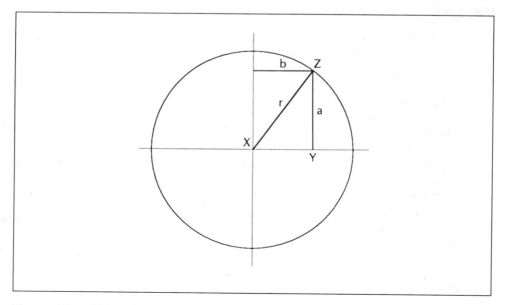

Figure 8.28   Triangle Illustrating Trigonometric Functions

triangle has several key measurements used in trigonometric calculations. The hypotenuse is the distance from Z to X and is labeled *r*. This is the longest side of the triangle. The distance from Z to the vertical axis is *b* and is the same whether it is measured from Z to the vertical line or from X to the point where the dropped line meets the horizontal axis. The distance from the horizontal axis to Z is *a*. By comparing these three sides to one another, you create ratios that depend on the size of the triangle's angles. These ratios remain the same as the triangle is enlarged or contracted as long as the triangle's angles remain the same.

In any right triangle, if you know the length of any two sides, you can determine the length of the third side using the Pythagorean theorem. The Pythagorean theorem is $a^2 + b^2 = r^2$ (letters as in the triangle in Figure 8.28).

Angles are normally measured in one of two ways. An angle measured in degrees uses a circle divided up into 360°. In advanced mathematical calculations, the radian is used frequently as the unit of measure. One revolution around the circle is approximately two radians. A revolution through one quadrant of the circle is approximately 0.5 radians. One radian equals approximately 57.296°. For both methods of measuring angles, a positive angle is one that is measured counterclockwise starting from the positive X axis. A negative angle is measured clockwise from the positive X axis.

@DEGREES

The @DEGREES function converts radians to degrees. The format of this function is @DEGREES(x), where *x* is a number that equals an angle's radians. Since Quattro Pro uses radians in its trigonometric functions, this function converts the output of other trigonometric functions into degrees. Quattro Pro converts radians to degrees by multiplying the radians by 180/@PI.

The following are some examples using the @DEGREES function:

@DEGREES(0.5) = 28.64789
@DEGREES(1.0471975) = 60
@DEGREES(1) = 57.29578
@DEGREES(2) = 114.5916
@DEGREES(0.456456) = 26.153

@RADIANS

The @RADIANS function converts degrees to radians. The format of this function is @RADIANS(x), where *x* is a number, formula, or cell reference to a value that equals an angle's degrees. Since Quattro Pro uses radians in its trigonometric functions, this function converts angles measured in degrees to radians that are directly usable in the trigonometric functions. Quattro Pro computes radians by multiplying the degrees by @PI/180.

The following are some examples using the @RADIANS function:

@RADIANS(30) = 0.523599
@RADIANS(45) = 0.785398
@RADIANS(60) = 1.047198
@RADIANS(90) = 1.570796
@RADIANS(135) = 2.356194
@RADIANS(180) = 3.141593
@RADIANS(270) = 4.712389
@RADIANS(–30) = –0.523599

@SIN

The @SIN function returns the sine of an angle in a right triangle. The sine is the ratio of the side opposite the angle you are trying to compute to the hypotenuse. For example, in Figure 8.28 the sine of YXZ is a/r. The format of this function is @SIN(x), where *x* is the number of an angle, measured in radians.

The @SIN function can be illustrated by using Figure 8.28 and a few assumptions. The first assumption is that the triangle XYZ is a property on which you are constructing a building for lease. A potential lessee wants to know how much storefront is available if he leases the side r. Another assumption is that angle YXZ is 60°. The last assumption is that side a is 2,000 feet. To compute the length of r, you must first convert the degree measurement into radians by using the @RADI-ANS function. From earlier examples, 60° is 1.047198 radians. Then you must compute the sine of the angle (0.866025). Since the sine of the angle must equal a/r, r must equal a/(sine(YXZ)). Therefore, you divide 2,000 by 0.866025, which equals 2,309.4022. Combining all of these steps into one formula looks like this: **2000/@SIN(@RADIANS(60))**, which returns 2309.4022. Putting this formula into a cell quickly computes the result.

@COS

@COS returns the cosine of a given angle in a right triangle. The cosine is the ratio of the adjacent side of the angle you are trying to compute to the hypotenuse. For example, in the triangle in Figure 8.28, the cosine of the angle XZY is a/r. The format is @COS(x), where *x* is the number of the angle, measured in radians.

Using the same assumptions described in the @SIN function, suppose you have another potential lessee who is interested in the smallest storefront area (side b). To compute the length of b, you must first convert the degree measurement into radians using the @RADIANS function. As in the earlier example, 60° is 1.047198 radians. Then you must compute the cosine of the angle, which is 0.5 in this example. Since the cosine of the angle must equal b/r, b must equal r *cosine(YXZ). Therefore, you multiply 2309.4022 by 0.5, which returns 1154.7011. Combining all these steps into one formula looks like this: **2309.4022*@COS(@RADIANS(60))**.

@TAN

@TAN determines the tangent of an angle in a right triangle. The tangent is the ratio of the side opposite the angle you are measuring to the side adjacent to the angle you are measuring. The tangent is equal to the sine divided by the cosine. The format is @TAN(x), where *x* is the number of the angle measured in radians.

Using the same assumptions described in the @SIN function, the @TAN function can calculate the length of b in the Figure 8.28 triangle, also used in the @SIN and @COS examples. First, you must convert angle YXZ's 60° into radians with the @RADIANS function which returns 1.047198. Second, you must compute the tangent of this angle, which is 1.732051 in this example. Since the tangent of the angle must equal a/b, b must equal tangent (YXZ)/a. Therefore, you divide 2,000 by 1.732051, which equals 1154.701. Combining all these steps into one formula produces this entry: **2000/@TAN(@RADIANS(60))**. Putting this formula into a cell computes the same value that this illustration has provided in a step-by-step approach.

@ASIN

@ASIN returns the angle that has a sine of the specified ratio. This function returns the arc sine for a ratio. The format is @ASIN(x), where *x* is the sine of an angle in a right triangle and is a number that must be between –1 and 1. The sine of an angle is always in this range since the absolute value of the ratio of the side opposite the angle to the hypotenuse is always less than or equal to one. The result is the angle measured in radians.

All examples for the inverse trigonometric functions use different assumptions than used for @SIN, @COS, and @TAN. However, the examples of inverse trigonometric functions can use the same triangle (Figure 8.28). The inverse functions use the following assumptions. Side a represents a 40-foot telephone pole. Side b represents 26 feet on the ground. Side r represents a 47.7-foot guy wire holding the pole upright. The angle between the pole and the ground is 90 degrees, but the sizes of the other two angles are not known. You can calculate the angles by knowing the distances of each side of the triangle and by using the inverse trigonometric functions.

To use the @ASIN function to determine the angle YXZ, you must compute the ratio of the side opposite to the hypotenuse. In this example, it is 40/47.7 or 0.851064. Using this number as the input for the @ASIN function, the function returns 1.018008 radians. To convert this number to degrees, use the @DEGREES function on the output from the @ASIN function. Combining all the steps produces a formula like this: **@DEGREES(@ASIN(40/47.7))**. This function returns approximately 57 degrees as the angle YXZ.

@ACOS

@ACOS returns the angle that has a cosine of the specified ratio. This function returns the arc cosine for a ratio. The format is @ACOS(x), where *x* is the cosine of an angle in a right triangle and is a number that must be between –1 and 1. The cosine of an angle is always in this range since the absolute value of the ratio of the side opposite the angle to the hypotenuse is always less than or equal to one. The result is the angle measured in radians.

Using the assumptions described in the @ASIN function, you can confirm the result. To use the @ACOS function to determine the angle YXZ, you must compute the ratio of the opposite side to the hypotenuse. In this example, it is 40/47.7 or 0.851064. Using this number as the input for the @ACOS function, the function returns 0.552788 radians. To convert this number to degrees, use the @DEGREES function on the output from the @ACOS function. Combining all the steps produces a formula like this: **@DEGREES(@ACOS(40/47.7))**. This function returns approximately 33° as the angle YXZ. Since the angle opposite the hypotenuse is 90°, 90 plus 33 is 123, and 180 minus 123 equals 57 as the third angle, which confirms the results of the @ASIN function.

@ATAN

@ATAN returns the arc tangent of a ratio. The arc tangent of a ratio is the angle that has a tangent of the specified ratio. The format is @ATAN(x), where *x* is the tangent of an angle. The result is an angle between 90° and –90°. All angles between 90° and 180° produce an @ATAN result between 0 and –90. All angles between 180 and 270 produce a result between 90° and 0°.

To illustrate @ATAN, use the assumptions described in the @ASIN function, with one exception. Since most wires stretch and sag to accommodate external pressures on the pole, assume that you do not know the distance between points Z and Y and cannot use the @ACOS or @ASIN function to determine the angle YXZ. To use the @ATAN function to determine the angle YXZ, you must compute the ratio of the opposite side to the adjacent side. In this example, it is 40/26 or 1.538462. Using this number as the input for the @ATAN function, the function returns 1.538462 radians. To convert this number to degrees, use the @DEGREES function on the output from the @ATAN function. Combining all these steps produces a formula like this: **@DEGREES(@ATAN(40/26))**. This function returns approximately 57° as the angle YXZ. Since you are certain that the two sides are correct, using the @ATAN function removes any problems caused by a loose wire.

@ATAN2

@ATAN2 is similar to @ATAN since it calculates an arc tangent, but @ATAN2 differentiates between angles larger than 90°. All angles start from the positive x axis (see Figure 8.29); negative angles are measured clockwise, and positive angles are measured counterclockwise.

The format for @ATAN2 is @ATAN2(x,y) where *x* is the x coordinate of the angle and *y* is the y coordinate of the angle. If x and/or y is negative, the negative sign must be entered, since a missing sign changes the result by 90° or 180°.

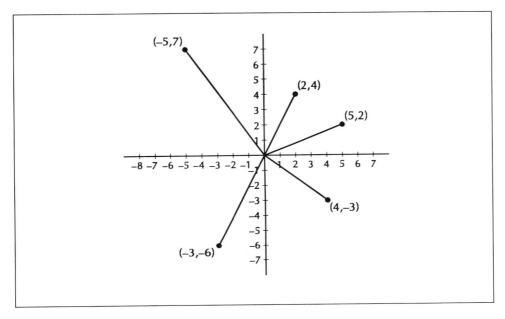

Figure 8.29   Inscribed Points

Figure 8.29 shows an x,y coordinate system that has several points marked in the different quadrants. For each point, a line is drawn to the origin of the x,y coordinate system. To determine the angle of each line, the @ATAN2 uses the x and y coordinates of each point. The following functions compute the angle for each point:

@ATAN2(5,2) = 0.380506 = approximately 38°
@ATAN2(2,4) = 1.107149 = approximately 63.4°
@ATAN2(–5,7) = 2.191046 = approximately 125.5°
@ATAN2(–3,-6) = –2.03444 = approximately –153.4°
@ATAN2(4,–3) = –0.643501 = approximately –36.9°

MATHEMATICAL FUNCTIONS: LOGARITHMIC

The logarithmic functions are useful in problems involving compound growth, such as population studies, and computations in which very large numbers are multiplied and divided by very small numbers, as in scientific or engineering applications and in chemistry problems. A logarithm is defined as the power to which a number, called the base, must be raised to result in a specified number. The mathematical expression for a logarithm is $\log_b y = x$, which is read "the logarithm of y to the base b is x." This formula is expressed as $b_x = y$, which is read "b raised to the power of x is y." This formula expresses the same relationship as an exponential relationship.

The base b is any number greater than zero with the exception of the number one. The most widely used bases are base 10 and base e. The number represented by e is a real number approximated by 2.7182818285. When a base 10 is used, the logarithm is called a common logarithm or base 10 logarithm. When a base is not specified (for example, log 100 = 2), then the base is assumed to be 10. If a base of e is used, the logarithm is called a natural logarithm.

@LOG

The @LOG function determines the base 10 log of a number. The format for this function is @LOG(x), where *x* is a positive number. To change a logarithm value to a decimal value, raise 10 to the power of the logarithm.

Logarithms can perform calculations on very large numbers and very small numbers without exceeding the computer's storage capacity for large numbers. Use of the @LOG function in Einstein's $E = mc^2$ equation illustrates this advantage. Figure 8.30 shows the computations necessary to compute the value of the energy in one atom of hydrogen. Column B shows the calculation using actual values, column C shows the calculation using logarithms, and column D shows the formulas in column C. In cell C3, the logarithm of the speed of light squared is calculated by multiplying the logarithm of the speed of light by two. Multiplying a logarithm by a number is equivalent to raising the actual number of the logarithm to the power of the number. The weight of a single hydrogen atom is

	A	B	C	D	E
	Quattro Pro for Windows - FUNCTION.WB1				
	File Edit Block Data Tools Graph Property Window Help				
	Logarithms:C2 @LOG(B2)				
1	Base 10 Logarithms	Actual Values	Logarithms	Formula in Column C	
2	Speed of light	1.86E+05	5.27E+00	@LOG(B2)	
3	Speed of light squared	3.47E+10	1.05E+01	+C2*2	
4	Avogadro's number	6.02E+23	2.38E+01	@LOG(B4)	
5	Weight of hydrogen	1.01E+00	3.45E-03	@LOG(B5)	
6	Weight of 1 hydrogen atom	1.67E-24	-2.38E+01	+C5-C4	
7	E=mc^2	5.81E-14	-1.32E+01	+C6+C3	
8	Double check		5.81E-14	10^C7	
9					
10	Natural Logarithms	Actual Values	Logarithms	Formula in Column C	
11	Speed of light	1.86E+05	1.21E+01	@LN(B11)	
12	Speed of light squared	3.47E+10	2.43E+01	+C11*2	
13	Avogadro's number	6.02E+23	5.48E+01	@LN(B13)	
14	Weight of hydrogen	1.01E+00	7.94E-03	@LN(B14)	
15	Weight of 1 hydrogen atom	1.67E-24	-5.47E+01	+C14-C13	
16	E=mc^2	5.81E-14	-3.05E+01	+C15+C12	
17	Double check		5.81E-14	@EXP(1)^C16	
18					
19					
20					

Figure 8.30 @LOG and @LN Used to Compute the Energy in a Hydrogen Atom

determined by dividing the weight of a mole in row 5 by the number of atoms in a mole (Avogadro's number) in row 4. To divide values using their logarithms, you subtract their logarithms as done in C6. C7 multiplies the values of the weight of one hydrogen atom by the speed of light squared by adding their logarithms together. The final result in C7 is the value of the energy in one hydrogen atom. In C8, C7 is raised to the power of 10 to confirm that the value obtained by using logarithms is the same as if actual numbers had been used. Since most of these numbers are too wide to fit into the columns with the regular default setting, the numeric display format setting is changed to Scientific with 2 decimal places.

@EXP

The result of the @EXP function is the value e, approximated by 2.718281828, raised to a specified power. The format is @EXP(x), where x is the number of the power to which e is raised. To generate the value of e, use the formula, @EXP(1). To convert a natural logarithm to its actual value, use the natural logarithm as this function's argument.

The @EXP function can be used to compute continuous compounding. Continuous compounding is often used for savings accounts and other investment opportunities. For example, if you are putting $50,000 into savings at an 11% continuous compounding rate for the next 10 years, use the @EXP function in a formula to compute the value of your investment at the end of the investment's term. To compute the value of your investment at the end of 10 years, use this formula: **+50000*@EXP(.11*10)**. Putting this formula into a cell computes the value of this investment at the end of 10 years as 150208.3.

@LN

The natural logarithm is written as either $\log_e y = x$ or $\ln y = x$. The format for the natural log function is @LN(x), where x is the number for which you want to determine the natural log (x must be a value greater than zero). If x is an invalid value, the function returns @ERR. The x can be a number, a formula, or a cell reference.

Natural logarithms can be used to perform calculations on very large and very small numbers without exceeding the computer's storage capacity for large numbers, just as you can with base 10 logarithms. This example uses the same information provided in the @LOG example. The bottom half of Figure 8.30 shows the computations necessary to compute the amount of energy in one atom of hydrogen by using the natural logarithm. The calculations are identical to the calculations used in the @LOG example. The only difference is the method used for double checking the computation by comparing it with the actual values. In the @LOG example, 10 was raised to the logarithm result. In this example, e, computed as @EXP(1) in C17, is raised to the power of the result in C16. The two logarithms are different due to the different base used.

CELL AND TABLE FUNCTIONS

Quattro Pro's cell and table functions provide advanced features, such as looking up values in tables and returning information about the attributes of a block in your notebook. Quattro Pro has four functions that provide you with specific attributes for the current or a specified cell. Three functions tell you the number of rows, columns, and pages in a block to describe the block's size. These cell and table functions are used in macros to add decision-making features. These functions also increase the logic features of your models by letting current values determine the next calculation or value used.

@@

The @@ function returns the value of a cell referenced by the function's argument. The @@ function uses indirect addressing, since the @@ function assumes that the argument is a cell address containing another cell address whose value the @@ function returns. If the function's argument is enclosed in quotes, this function returns the value of the cell referenced in the quotes. The format of the @@ function is @@(cell). The *cell* is either a cell name, a cell name enclosed in quotes, a block name, or a formula that produces a cell address. Examples of the four types of entries are: cell name, A1; cell name in quotes, "A1"; block name, "START" (where START is a predefined block beginning at cell A1); and a formula that produces a cell address as "A"&"1".

This function is normally used as an argument for other functions. Figure 8.31 shows an example of the @@ function that helps in determining the budget for labor cost. Since the labor cost varies for each type of job and each shift, a table is created to list the hourly cost for each job and shift. By using the @@ function in column C, this model is created so that you only have to type in the number of hours for each department that you expect to use and the shift that you are making this budget for. The @@ function in column C takes the shift number and converts it to A, B, or C to correspond to the three different shifts by adding 64 to the shift number so that it generates an ASCII code number equal to A, B, or C. The ASCII code is transformed into a letter and appended after an A. Next, the row number is added to the cell reference. Since this cell reference is a string rather than directly entered, the @@ function takes the value of the cell for which you have created a cell reference. Once you have the value, you can multiply it by the number of hours in column B. Using the table and the formulas reduces the number of characters to type and so helps prevent mistakes.

@CELL

The @CELL function returns the requested attribute of the upper-left cell of a block. The format of the @CELL function is @CELL(attribute,block). The *attribute* can be a string containing any of a number of words discussed in the next section. For all attributes except rwidth, @CELL uses only the upper-left cell in the block. The @CELL function is often used in macros to check a cell's attributes or to store

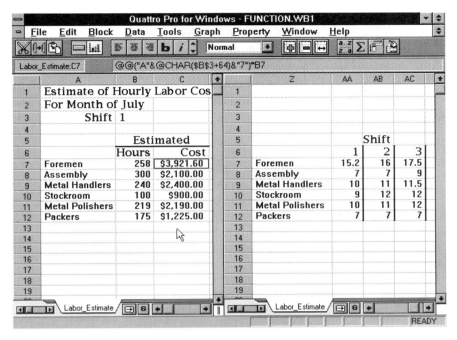

Figure 8.31 @@ Used to Reference a Table

an attribute to be used later in the macro. The possible attributes that may be checked are as follows:

- address—returns the absolute cell address with dollar signs preceding the row and column
- row—returns the row number
- col—returns the column number, which may range from 1 to 256 for the columns A through IV
- sheet—returns the sheet number which may range from 1 to 256 for the pages in the notebook
- NotebookName—returns the name of the active notebook without any extension
- NotebookPath—returns the name of the active notebook that includes the extension and path
- TwoDAddress—returns the cell and row of the current cell as an absolute address
- ThreeDAddress—returns the page, cell and row of the current cell as an absolute address
- FullAddress—returns the notebook name, page, cell and row of the current cell as an absolute address
- contents—returns the cell's value or label
- type—returns a b for a blank cell, a v for a cell that contains a value or formula, or an l for a cell that contains a label

- prefix—returns the label prefix: returns an apostrophe (') for a left-aligned label, a double quote (") for a right-aligned label, a caret (^) for a centered label, a backslash (\) for a repeating label, an empty string for a number, formula, or blank cell
- protect—returns 1 if protected and 0 if not
- width—returns the column width truncated to an integer
- rwidth—returns the sum of the width of all the columns in the block truncated to an integer
- format—returns letters or numbers to represent the numeric format; the following symbols returned indicating the different formats:
    Fn—Fixed with n representing the number of decimal places
    Sn—Scientific with n representing the number of decimal places
    Cn—Currency with n representing the number of decimal places
    ,n—Comma with n representing the number of decimal places
    G—General such as for unformatted cells, cells that have had their format reset, and labels
    +—+/—format
    Pn—Percent with n representing the number of decimal places
    Dn—Date or time; the number representing the format of the date or time:
        1 DD-MMM-YY
        2 DD-MMM
        3 MMM-YY
        4 Long Date Intl.
        5 Short Date Intl.
        6 HH:MM:SS AM/PM
        7 HH:MM AM/PM
        8 Long Time Intl.
        9 Short Time Intl.
    T—Text, which displays a cell's formula rather than the formula's result
    H—Hidden, which prevents cell entries from appearing
    U—User-defined which displays the cell's contents according to the selected format code

Figure 8.32 provides an example of the @CELL function used to check the format of the cells in column E. The attribute checked is in cell G2; therefore, the cell reference in the formula is absolute. To change the attribute you are determining, type the new attribute in cell G2. If you want to change the cells that the function uses, you must modify the formula.

@CELLPOINTER

The @CELLPOINTER function returns a specified attribute of the current cell. The current cell is the cell that the selector is on. Quattro Pro only updates this function when you press F9 (CALC) or edit a cell.

The format is @CELLPOINTER(attribute), where *attribute* is a string containing

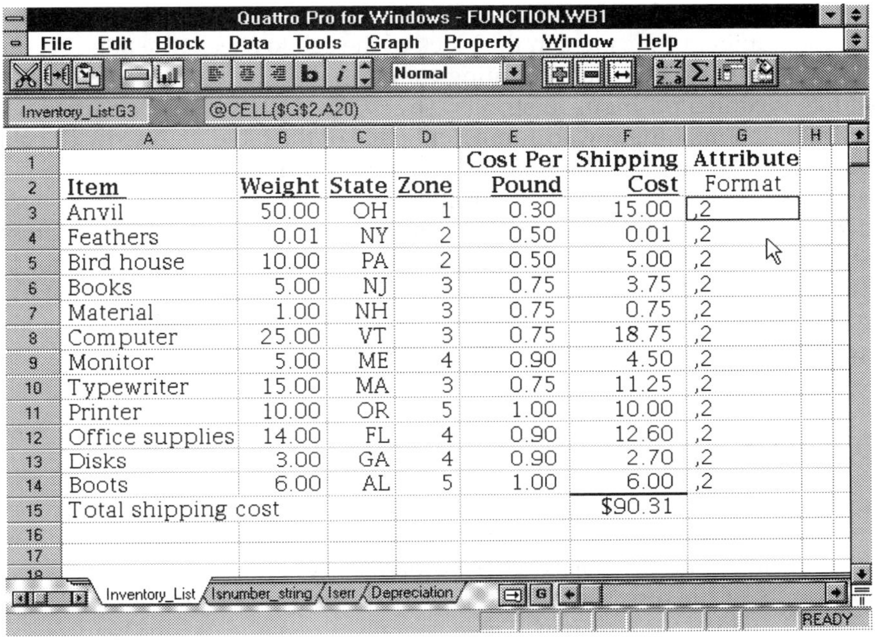

	A	B	C	D	E	F	G
1					Cost Per	Shipping	Attribute
2	Item	Weight	State	Zone	Pound	Cost	Format
3	Anvil	50.00	OH	1	0.30	15.00	,2
4	Feathers	0.01	NY	2	0.50	0.01	,2
5	Bird house	10.00	PA	2	0.50	5.00	,2
6	Books	5.00	NJ	3	0.75	3.75	,2
7	Material	1.00	NH	3	0.75	0.75	,2
8	Computer	25.00	VT	3	0.75	18.75	,2
9	Monitor	5.00	ME	4	0.90	4.50	,2
10	Typewriter	15.00	MA	3	0.75	11.25	,2
11	Printer	10.00	OR	5	1.00	10.00	,2
12	Office supplies	14.00	FL	4	0.90	12.60	,2
13	Disks	3.00	GA	4	0.90	2.70	,2
14	Boots	6.00	AL	5	1.00	6.00	,2
15	Total shipping cost					$90.31	

Figure 8.32 @CELL Used to Check That the Cost per Pound is Formatted Consistently

one of the words described for the @CELL function. The attribute must be enclosed in quotes unless it is placed in a cell.

You can use the @CELLPOINTER function on the page shown in Figure 8.32 to learn about the entry in F15. If you enter **@CELLPOINTER(H15)** in G15, you can try different attributes by typing the attribute in H15, moving to F15, and pressing F9 (CALC). For example, you can use this formula on cell F15 with address in H15 to return $F$15, with row in H15 to return 15, with col in H15 to return 6, with contents in H15 to return 90.31, with type in H15 to return v, with protect in H15 to return 1, with width in H15 to return 9, and with format in H15 to return C2. While this example only uses F15 to determine @CELLPOINTER's results, you can also try the function with other cells to return the attributes for the currently selected cell.

@CELLINDEX

The @CELLINDEX function returns a specified attribute of a cell in a block as specified by the row and column number provided. This function differs from @CELL since @CELLINDEX lets you choose the cell in the block that you wish to examine.

The format is @CELLINDEX(attribute,block,column,row[,page]). The *attribute* is one of the words described for the @CELL function. The *column* is the number of the column in the block that you want the attribute from, the *row* is the number of the row in the block that you want to use to determine the cell's attribute, and *page* is the number of the page in the block of the cell to check (the page argument is optional). Quattro Pro starts counting columns, rows, and pages in a block with 0 just like it counts positions in strings. The @CELLINDEX function uses the cell at the intersection of the row, column, and page of the table. If the row or column number exceeds the block's limits, the function returns ERR.

In Figure 8.33, the @CELLINDEX function returns the format of the cells in row 3. H3..H8 contains the numbers that correspond to the column in the block address the @CELLINDEX function uses. These numbers correspond to columns A through F in the block $A$3..$F$3. The function uses the first row and page of the block which has the row and page number of 0. When you do not include the page argument, Quattro Pro uses 0 as a default. The attribute this function checks is in G2.

@PROPERTY

The @PROPERTY function returns the value of a selected property for a specific object. You can use this function to return information about a block, page, notebook, application, or any object whose properties you can select.

The format of the function is @PROPERTY(object.property). The *object.property* is a string in which the first half, *object*, contains the name of the Quattro Pro for

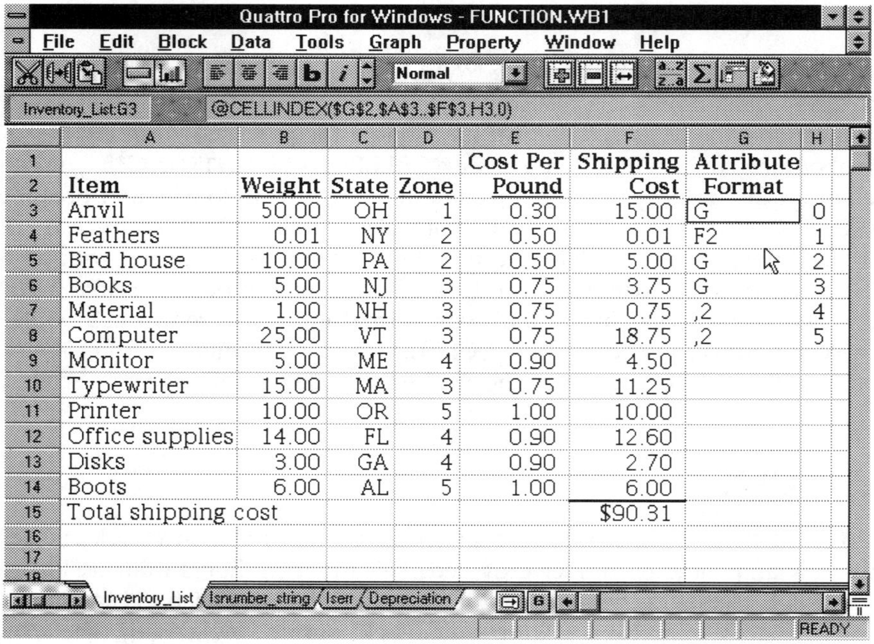

	A	B	C	D	E	F	G	H
1					Cost Per	Shipping	Attribute	
2	Item	Weight	State	Zone	Pound	Cost	Format	
3	Anvil	50.00	OH	1	0.30	15.00	G	0
4	Feathers	0.01	NY	2	0.50	0.01	F2	1
5	Bird house	10.00	PA	2	0.50	5.00	G	2
6	Books	5.00	NJ	3	0.75	3.75	G	3
7	Material	1.00	NH	3	0.75	0.75	,2	4
8	Computer	25.00	VT	3	0.75	18.75	,2	5
9	Monitor	5.00	ME	4	0.90	4.50		
10	Typewriter	15.00	MA	3	0.75	11.25		
11	Printer	10.00	OR	5	1.00	10.00		
12	Office supplies	14.00	FL	4	0.90	12.60		
13	Disks	3.00	GA	4	0.90	2.70		
14	Boots	6.00	AL	5	1.00	6.00		
15	Total shipping cost					$90.31		
16								
17								
18								

Figure 8.33 @CELLINDEX Used to Check the Format of Row 3

Windows object for which you want to know the value of a property. You may want to think of this as the text that appears at the top of a dialog box when you inspect an object's properties. Some examples include Active Block and Active Page. The second half, *property*, is the name of the property that you want the value of. It must be a valid property of the object. You may want to think of this as the text that appears in the left side of the dialog box when you inspect an object's properties.

Figure 8.34 shows several examples of the @PROPERTY function. The functions are entered in column F and the formula is entered as a label in column A. When the object is the active block, the function is recalculated every time the values in the notebook are. As you learn about more objects that you can select properties for, such as the graphs that you will learn about in the next chapter, you can try this function to return the values of those object properties.

Using Quattro Pro's Table Features

Quattro Pro provides several useful functions for working with tables. A table is a block of information that contains information that you can access with Quattro Pro's table functions. You can retrieve information from a table based on one or

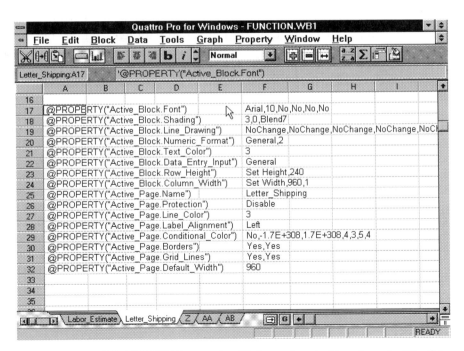

Figure 8.34 @PROPERTY Returning Values about a Page's and a Block's Properties

more criteria. To use one of the table retrieval functions, you must have a table in a notebook. A table is a block created by using columns and rows in the same way that you create a table on paper. You can create a vertical or horizontal table. The appearance of the table does not necessarily determine if the table is a horizontal or vertical table. The difference in the two types of tables is the function used to access the table entries. When the table is constructed vertically, the @VLOOKUP function searches the first column of entries in the table. With the @HLOOKUP function, the table is expected to have horizontal entries with the search conducted against the entries in the top row of the table.

@VLOOKUP

The @VLOOKUP function returns a value in a table in a notebook based on the function arguments. @VLOOKUP can look up both strings and numbers.

The format of the function is @VLOOKUP(x,block,column). The x is the value that the command looks for in the first column of the block. If x is a number, the @VLOOKUP command stops when it reaches a value equal or higher than the value of the function argument. Because the search is for the highest value that is not greater than the value you are searching for, the numbers in the first column of the @VLOOKUP table must be in ascending sequence. If x is a string, the sequence of the entries in the first column of the table is not important since this function searches for an exact match. The *block* must include the index column (the column that contains the values the function will look for), the columns that contain the values to be returned, and all columns in between. The *column* is the number of columns to the right of the index column that the @VLOOKUP function uses to obtain the return values. The column number must be greater than or equal to 0. If the column number is zero, the function returns the value from the index column.

When the entry you are searching for is a number, Quattro Pro returns the value determined by searching the index column for the largest value not greater than the search value. If the column number is negative or refers to a column that is beyond the block's limits, the function returns ERR. If the function is looking for a string and does not find it, the function returns ERR.

The @VLOOKUP function can determine shipping costs when the shipping rates are determined by a zone code assigned by state. Figure 8.35 shows the @VLOOKUP function in column D. The @VLOOKUP function determines the proper zone for each state by looking for the state in column AA. Since the last function argument is 1, the function takes the value in the cell one column to the right of the index column in the row where the state code is located. If the function does not find a match for the state, it returns ERR. This error message alerts you that your list of states and their appropriate zones is incomplete.

@HLOOKUP

The @HLOOKUP function returns a value in a table in a notebook based on two function arguments. @HLOOKUP can look up both strings and numbers. The difference between the @HLOOKUP and the @VLOOKUP functions is that the

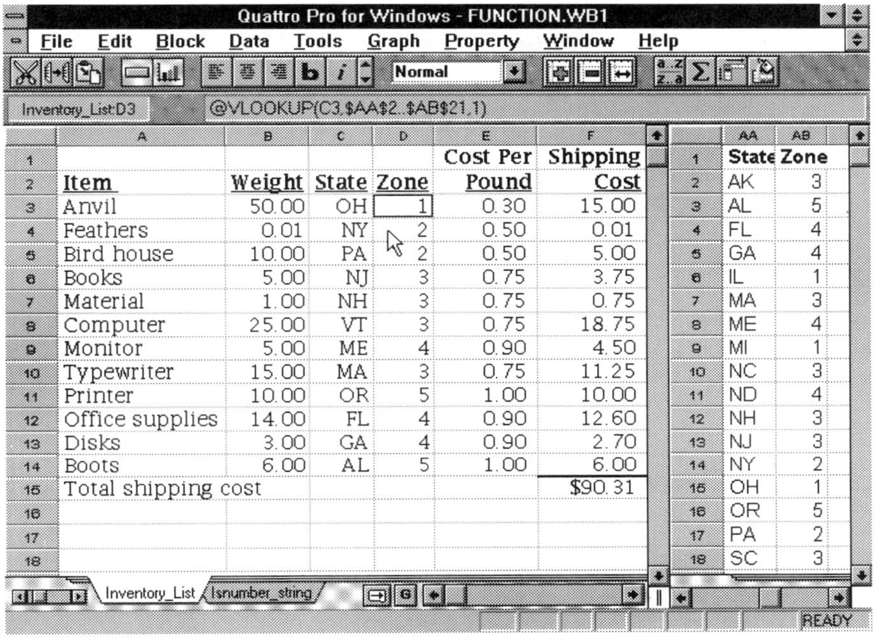

Figure 8.35 @VLOOKUP Used to Determine the Zone for Each State

entries that @HLOOKUP searches for are in the top row rather than in the left column in the table.

The format of the function is @HLOOKUP(x,block,row). The x is the value that @HLOOKUP searches for. It is a number, a string in quotes, or a cell reference to a number or string. When you use the @HLOOKUP function, the formula looks for the value of x in the table. It starts from the left corner of the table and looks for the value of x along the top row of the table, the index row. If x is a number, the search is conducted looking for the highest value that does not exceed x. If x is a string, Quattro Pro looks for an exact match between the value of x and the labels in the index row. The *block* must include the index row, the row that contains the values that the function will retrieve and all rows in between. The *row* is the number of rows below the index row that @HLOOKUP gets the return value from. The row number must be greater than or equal to 0. If the row number is zero, the function returns the value from the index row.

If @HLOOKUP cannot find the value and it is a number, it returns the value associated with the largest entry that does not exceed the value you are searching for. When @HLOOKUP is searching for a number, the numbers in the first row of the table must be in ascending sequence. If the value the function is looking for is a string and the function cannot find it, the function returns ERR. The function also returns ERR when the row number is negative or refers to a row beyond the specified block of the function.

Figure 8.36 shows the @HLOOKUP function used to retrieve the proper cost per pound for each zone from the table shown at the bottom of the figure. The

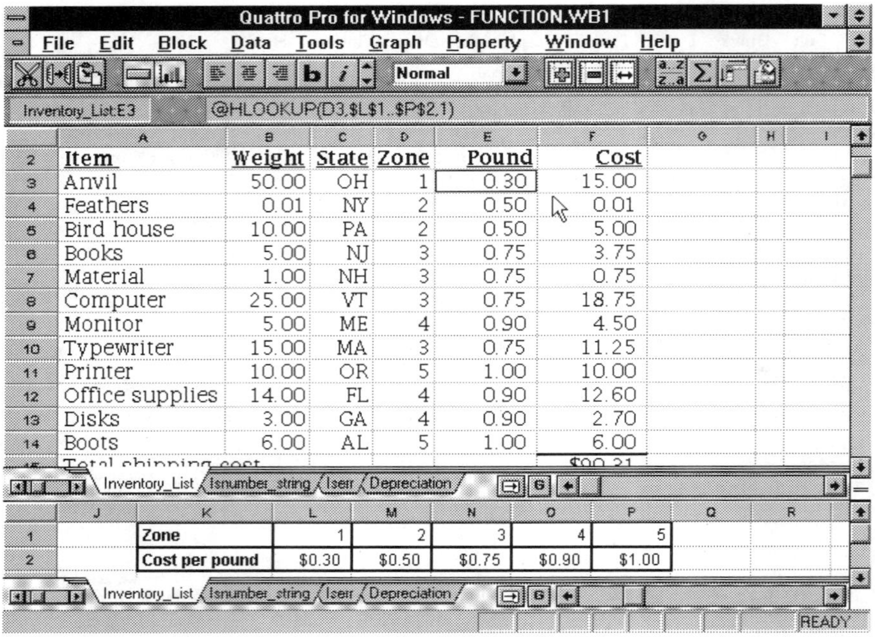

Figure 8.36   @HLOOKUP Used to Determine the Cost per Pound for Each Zone

@HLOOKUP function looks for the Zone in the table's first row and then takes the number right below it, since the row number is 1. Using the @HLOOKUP table instead of typing the numbers in yourself reduces mistakes. Also, having the table with a different cost per pound for each zone makes it easier to change the cost per pound. Making a change in the table immediately reflects these new values in all the calculations.

@CHOOSE

The @CHOOSE function returns one argument from a list of choices, based on a specification of a choice number. The @CHOOSE function is different from the table lookup functions since the entries are all contained within the function rather than in an external table. Another difference between @CHOOSE and the table lookup functions is that the @CHOOSE function uses consecutive integers to determine the function's results. The format of the function is @CHOOSE(number,list). The *number* is the number of the list entry that the function returns. If it exceeds the number of choices available or is a negative value, the function returns ERR. The *list* represents the different choices that the @CHOOSE function has available. The first entry is choice 0. Thus, to select the second entry in the list, the number must be 1. While the number of choices are unlimited, the entire formula is limited to 1022 characters. Each choice may be a number, string, formula, or cell reference. The different entries do not have to be the same type of entry. One entry can be a label, another a formula, and a third a number. To omit one of the choices, enter two double quotes in place of the entry you want to omit. For example, suppose A1 contains this function: **@CHOOSE(A31, B3*4,"","Marketing Strategy",16)**. Quattro Pro first takes the value from A3 and subtracts one so that it is reduced by 1 to match the way @CHOOSE numbers its choices. If A3 equals one, A1 equals the value of B3 times four. If A3 equals two, A1 equals a blank cell. If A3 equals three, A1 equals "Marketing Strategy." If A3 equals four, A1 equals 16. If A3 equals five, A1 equals ERR.

The @CHOOSE function can sometimes replace an @VLOOKUP or @HLOOKUP function. @CHOOSE is suitable for determining the cost per pound since there are a limited number of consecutive zone numbers. For example, if you wanted to use the @CHOOSE function in place of the @HLOOKUP function shown in Figure 8.36, you would enter the formula **@CHOOSE(D3-1,0.3,0.5,0.75,0.9,1)** in E3, then copy the formula to E4..E15. Since all choices are integers ranging from one to five, the @CHOOSE function is a good alternative. For each item, the function takes the zone, subtracts one and uses the result to pick the correct cost per pound for shipping. This function is not optimal if there are many choices. A table is a clearer presentation of the different options and is easier to update than the list in the @CHOOSE function. Also, @CHOOSE is limited to choices indicated by numeric entries and cannot work with strings as @VLOOKUP and @HLOOKUP can.

@INDEX

The @INDEX returns a value from a specified row, column, and page in a table of information. @INDEX differs from @HLOOKUP and @VLOOKUP, since it does not search for a matching entry but selects information with a row, column, and page designation.

The format is @INDEX(block,column,row[,sheet]). The *block* is the location of the table. The *column* is the number of the column from the left column of the table from which you want the function to retrieve the value, the *row* is the number of the row from the table from which you want the function to retrieve the value, and the *sheet* is the number of the page from the table from which you want the function to retrieve the value. If you omit the optional page argument, the function uses the default of 0. Quattro Pro starts counting the column, row, and page numbers of a table from 0. For example, the top row is row 0 and the fourth row of the table is row 3. The @INDEX function returns the value at the intersection of the row, column, and page of the table. If the value refers to a column, row, or page that is not included in the block or is a negative number, the function returns ERR.

Many shipping companies provide different types of services for transporting packages. For each package, the cost per pound is determined by the distance the package has to travel and the type of service that you are paying for. The bottom of Figure 8.37 contains a table for the different zones and service types. At the top

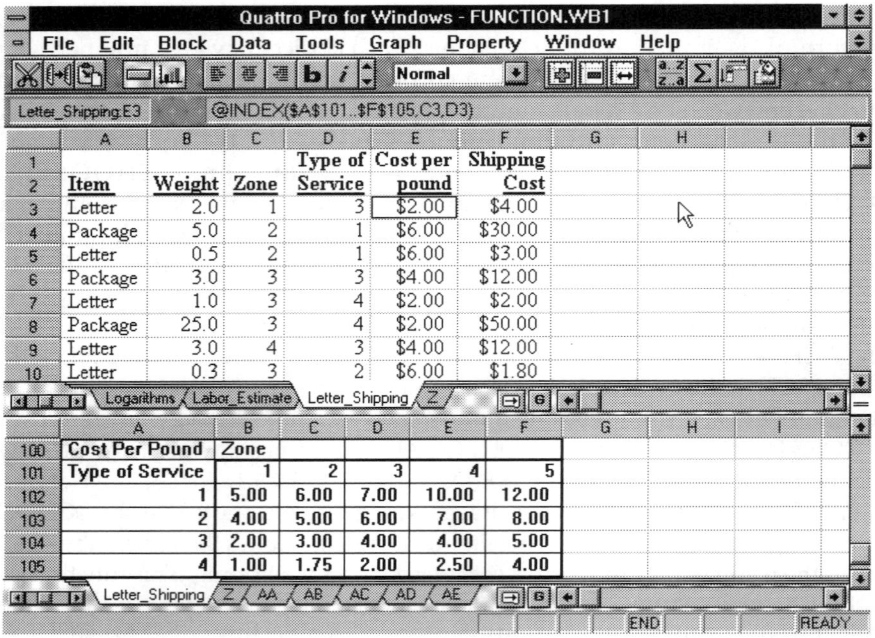

Figure 8.37 @INDEX Used to Find the Cost Per Pound for Different Types of Service

of the figure, the shipping costs for various packages are computed. The block of the function's argument includes the zone row and the service types columns. By including this row and column, you do not have to subtract one from the zone and service type to determine the proper row and column for the @INDEX function.

@ROWS

The @ROWS function determines the number of rows in a block. The format of the @ROWS function is @ROWS(block), where *block* is the block that the function uses to count the number of rows.

The @ROWS command can number the items in a block better than the Fill command in the Block menu, since one formula can handle the entire task. In Figure 8.38, the function @ROWS counts the number of rows between the absolute reference to B1 and the current row. Column A is not used for the computation since it creates a circular reference, which means the formula is referring to its own cell. Two is subtracted from this result to compensate for the two lines of titles at the beginning. This function is better than using the Fill command in the Block menu, since the function recalculates the numbers when a row is deleted. Also, as new items are added, the function takes them into account although you will need to copy the formula for the new items to have an item number assigned.

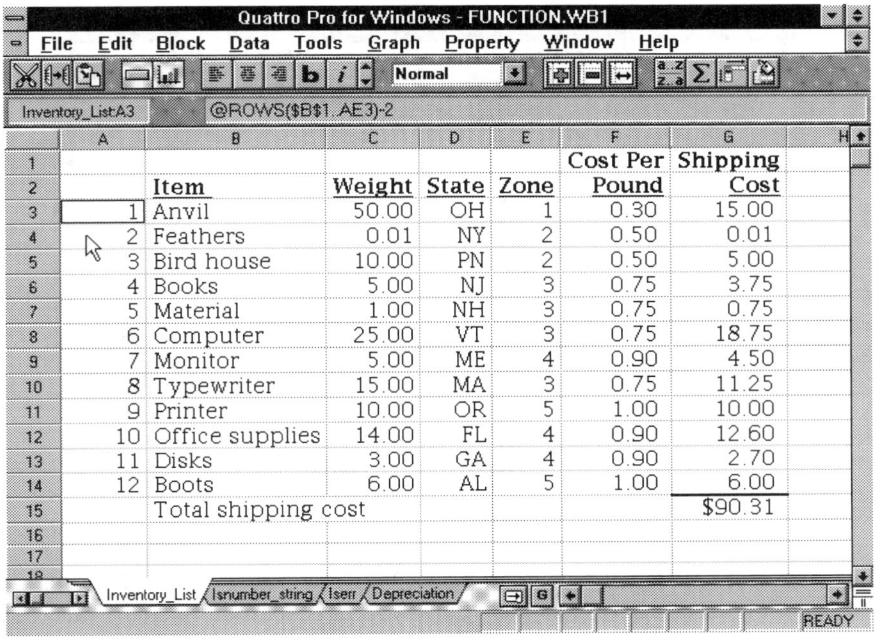

Figure 8.38 @ROWS Used to Number Items

@COLS

The @COLS function returns the number of columns in a block. The format is @COLS(block), where *block* is the block that the function uses to count the number of columns.

The @COLS command can number columns by using the @COLS function to count the number of columns between the current column and another column with an absolute address. In Figure 8.39, each zone is in a different column. The @COLS function counts the number of columns between the absolute reference to L2 and the current column. Therefore, if zones are added or removed, the @COLS function renumbers the columns for you.

@SHEETS

The @SHEETS function returns the number of pages in a block. The format of the @SHEETS function is @SHEETS(block), where *block* is the block that the function uses to count the number of pages.

The @SHEETS command can tell you how many pages a block has. This can be especially useful to return the number of pages in a block name or in a block where you have renamed pages. For example, you may want to know how many pages are used between the first page (page Statistical) and the page shown in Figure 8.39 (page

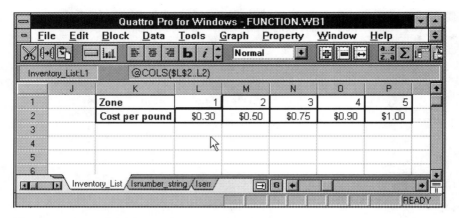

Figure 8.39   @COLS Used to Number Columns

Inventory_List). You can find this out by entering @SHEETS(Statistical:..Inventory_List:) in a cell. The result of 11 is for the nine pages between Statistical and Inventory_List and the first and last page of the block. Once you have learned to create macros and you have a macro that prints a page at a time, you can use this function to decide how many pages are in a block.

SYSTEM FUNCTIONS

Quattro Pro provides several system functions that are not available in other spreadsheet packages. These functions are primarily used in macros.

@COMMAND

The @COMMAND function returns the current value of a Quattro Pro for Windows menu command. The format is @COMMAND (command-string), where *command-string* is a string containing a Quattro Pro for Windows menu comand equivalent. These can be listed when you are entering the function by pressing SHIFT-F3 (MACROS) or clicking the { } button in the SpeedBar and selecting Command Equivalents. The function returns ERR when Quattro Pro cannot determine what you want. The function returns an empty string when the menu command that you specify does not have a setting. The commands equivalent are listed in Appendix D.

Here are a few examples of the function: **@COMMAND("Print.Block")** returns Statistical:A1..G16 if A1..G16 on page Statistical was the last page to print; **@COMMAND("BlockFill.Stop")** returns 8191 if you have not changed the Stop value setting for the Fill command in the Block menu.

@CURVALUE

The @CURVALUE function returns the current value of a menu-equivalent command setting. The format of the function is @CURVALUE(general-action, specific-action), where *general-action* is a string containing the general menu category, and *specific-action* is the string containing the specific menu action for which you want to know the setting. The function arguments must use the menu-equivalent commands. While some of the menu-equivalent commands are the same as Quattro Pro for DOS's menu commands, most of them are different. The function returns @ERR when Quattro Pro cannot determine what you want. The function returns an empty string when the menu command that you specify does not have a setting. These can be listed when you are entering the function by pressing SHIFT-F3 (MACROS) or clicking the {} button in the SpeedBar and selecting /Commands. The menu-equivalent commands are listed in Appendix E.

Here are a few examples of the function: **@CURVALUE("file","directory")** returns "C:\QPW" if Quattro Pro is in the subdirectory QPW on disk C. **@CURVALUE("print","format")** returns "As Displayed" if you have not changed this setting to print cell formulas. **@CURVALUE("intnl","currency")** returns Windows Default if the currency symbol is set to use Windows' default, which can be changed by changing the International application property.

@MEMAVAIL

This function returns the amount of conventional memory available in your computer. This information can determine when you need to split a spreadsheet notebook in two. The format of this function is @MEMAVAIL. It uses no arguments and no parentheses. If you are planning a major expansion for your spreadsheet notebook, use this function first to determine if you have sufficient memory for the expansion. If the available memory is limited, split the notebook into smaller ones.

@MEMEMSAVAIL

This function returns the amount of expanded memory available in your computer. The format of this function is @MEMEMSAVAIL. It uses no arguments and no parentheses. Since the @MEMAVAIL function includes all of your memory available in Windows, this function always returns NA. This function is present to maintain compatibility with Quattro Pro for DOS.

@VERSION

This function returns the version of Quattro Pro you are using. The function has the format @VERSION. For Quattro Pro for Windows, this function returns 101. The function is for use in macros so that, as different versions are used, you can test the version of Quattro Pro in use as a macro runs and change the macro commands performed accordingly. For example, you might have two macro instructions like this: **{IF @VERSION=101}{BRANCH Q_Pro_Instruct}** and **{BRANCH Other_Instruct}**. In these macro instructions, Quattro Pro performs the macro instructions starting at the cell named Q_Pro_Instruct if you are executing this macro with Quattro Pro for Windows. If you are executing this macro using a different version of Quattro Pro, the macro would perform the macro instructions starting at the cell named Other_Instruct. Chapter 14 has more information on how you might use these macro commands.

GETTING STARTED

In this chapter, you learned the functions available in Quattro Pro. As you use Quattro Pro you will develop your skills learning the different functions as you need them. Use the following steps to create the notebook in Figure 8.40 and try a few of these functions:

1. Make the following entries into an empty spreadsheet notebook. Do not worry about not seeing all of the entries since you will widen the columns later.

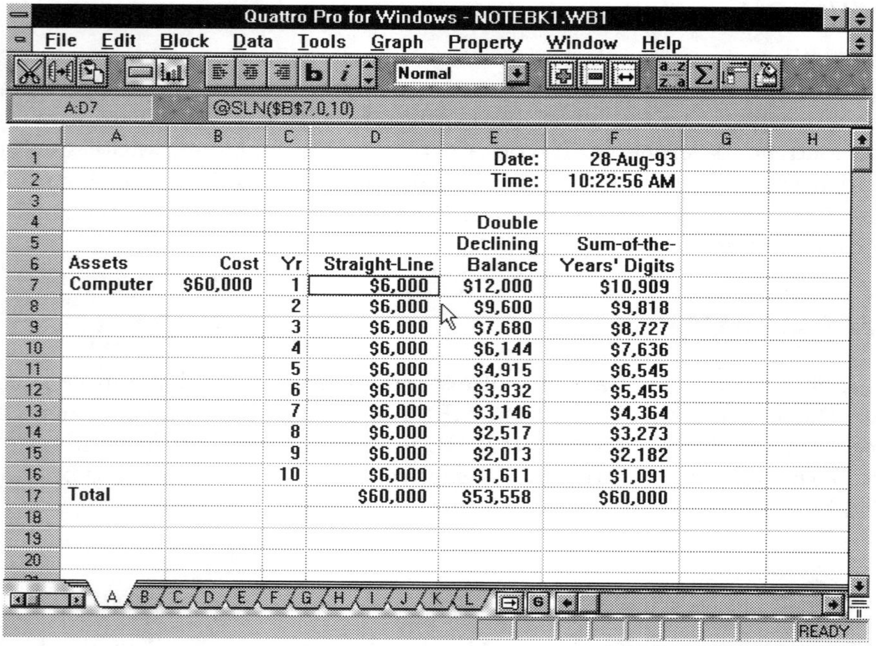

	A	B	C	D	E	F
1					Date:	28-Aug-93
2					Time:	10:22:56 AM
3						
4					Double	
5					Declining	Sum-of-the-
6	Assets	Cost	Yr	Straight-Line	Balance	Years' Digits
7	Computer	$60,000	1	$6,000	$12,000	$10,909
8			2	$6,000	$9,600	$9,818
9			3	$6,000	$7,680	$8,727
10			4	$6,000	$6,144	$7,636
11			5	$6,000	$4,915	$6,545
12			6	$6,000	$3,932	$5,455
13			7	$6,000	$3,146	$4,364
14			8	$6,000	$2,517	$3,273
15			9	$6,000	$2,013	$2,182
16			10	$6,000	$1,611	$1,091
17	Total			$60,000	$53,558	$60,000

Figure 8.40 Spreadsheet Created in Getting Started Section

E1: **Date:**
E2: **Time:**
A6: **Assets**
B6: **Cost**
C6: **Yr**
D6: **Straight-Line**
E4: **Double**
E5: **Declining**
E6: **Balance**
F5: **Sum-of-the**
F6: **Years' Digits**
A7: **Computer**
B7: **60000**
A17: **Total**

2. Add the date and time so that you can tell at a quick glance when the page was created or printed. Move to F1, and type **@TODAY**. Either press the DOWN ARROW or click F2. Type **@NOW**, and either press ENTER or click ✓ in the input line. While these values do not look like dates and times, you will format them later so that they will look like dates and times.

3. Add the years in column C. First, move to C7. Type **@ROWS($B$7..B7)** and press ENTER or click the ✓. Copy this function for the remaining years. Press CTRL-INS or click the Copy button in the SpeedBar to copy this entry to the Clipboard. Copy this entry to C8..C16 by selecting that block, and then pressing SHIFT-INS or clicking the Paste button in the SpeedBar. This fills C7..C16 with the years 1 through 10.

4. Enter the following formulas either by pressing ENTER or by clicking ✓ on the input line to finalize the entry. For each of the formulas, you can type the cell address or point to the cell as described in Chapter 2. These formulas compute the year's depreciation for the computer (assuming no salvage value) using the straight-line, double-declining balance, and sum-of-the-years' digits methods.

D7: **@SLN($B$7,0,10)**
E7: **@DDB($B$7,0,10,C7)**
F7: **@SYD($B$7,0,10,C7)**

5. Copy the formulas entered in step 4 for the other years of the asset's life. Select D7..F7. Press CTRL-INS or click the Copy button in the SpeedBar to copy these formulas to the Clipboard. Copy these entries to D8..F16 by selecting D8..D16, and then pressing SHIFT-INS or clicking the Paste button in the SpeedBar.

6. Add the depreciation calculated with each method. With a mouse, select the block D7..F17 so that you have the depreciation formulas and an empty row below. Next select the Σ button in the SpeedBar. To enter these same formulas without using the mouse, move to D17, type **@SUM(D7..D16)**, press

ENTER, press CTRL-INS, select E17..F17, and press SHIFT-INS. At this point you have the actual values entered in, but you need to improve the page's appearance.

7. Most of these cells need formatting. The original price in B6 and the depreciation is measured in dollars, so the entries need the Currency format. Select the noncontiguous block B7,D7..F17 and inspect its properties. With the Numeric Format property selected, choose Currency, and type **0** in the text box. Select OK to format these cells.

8. Move to F1. Inspect its properties and with the Numeric Format property chosen, select Date and DD-MMM-YY. Select OK to format this cell. Select cell F2 and inspect its properties. Select the Time numeric format and HH:MM:SS AM/PM. Select OK to format this cell as a time.

9. The column widths need to be changed. Although you currently cannot see all of the labels and some numbers appear as asterisks, these values and labels are still in the cells. Select A1..F17 and then either click the Fit button on the SpeedBar or inspect the block's properties, select the Column Width property, select the Auto Width radio button, and select OK.

10. The last change to the spreadsheet is the alignment of some of the labels. Select B1..F6 and then either click the Right Alignment button on the SpeedBar or inspect the block's properties, select the Alignment property, select the Right radio button, and select OK. Your spreadsheet now looks like the one in Figure 8.40.

9

Basic Graphic Features

Graphs provide a visual picture of the information in your notebook. Graphs can show trends, patterns, and relationships between elements of data. Rather than emphasizing the actual values, graphs emphasize the essence of the data. A graph enhances the information in your spreadsheet by displaying a visual representation of your notebook entries.

Graphing with Quattro Pro is easy, since Quattro Pro uses the data that are already in a notebook. This reduces the number of steps that you must perform to create a graph. Since Quattro Pro's graphics capabilities are an integral part of the program, you do not have to transfer data between programs or use another program to print your graph. Also, Quattro Pro provides a what-if graphic feature by using the most up-to-date information for a graph and referring to the current values in a notebook. Quattro Pro's graphics commands use the same Quattro Pro interface mastered for other commands. Quattro Pro's graphs provide many customization features that allow you to tailor a graph to convey your message. Since Quattro Pro keeps the current graph settings in memory, you can change any of the settings and Quattro Pro immediately incorporates the change into the graph. You can view the graph as you create it. You can even include a graph in a notebook page.

This chapter covers all the options for creating a graph. First, you will look at the basics of graphics, including terminology, graph types, and ways to create a simple graph. Once the basics are covered, you will learn to customize your graph with all the features that Quattro Pro provides. Once the graph is complete, you will learn how to print a graph. In the next chapter you will learn about more advanced graphics features such as slide shows, graph buttons, and sharing graphics between applications.

CREATING BASIC GRAPHS

Creating a graph with Quattro Pro is easy, since you only have to tell Quattro Pro what data to use and what kind of a graph you want. Quattro Pro provides several graph types to choose from. The best type to use depends on the data and your specific presentation requirements.

Terminology

Because graphs are different from spreadsheets, you need to learn some new terms that describe features of the graph. The terms discussed below are also illustrated in Figure 9.1.

- Axis—The axis is the vertical or horizontal line to the left, right, or bottom. The x-axis is the horizontal line at the bottom of the graph, and the y-axis is the vertical line at the left or right of the graph. A graph can have two y-axes, so you can graph data measured in more than one way. Most graph types have both an x-axis and a y-axis. In Figure 9.1, the x-axis is divided into the different months, and the y-axis is scaled from 0 to 600. Axes are not used in pie charts or column and text graphs.

- Border—Most of the items in a graph have a border that indicates the

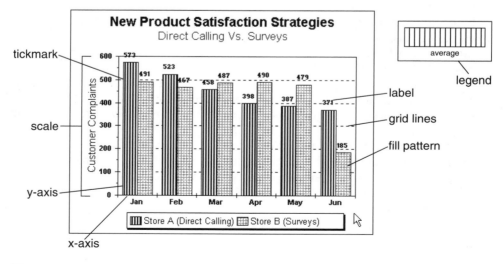

Figure 9.1 Sample Graph Illustrating Graph Terms

object's boundaries. Quattro Pro has several options for an object's border separate from the object itself.

- Data Point—A data point is a spreadsheet value displayed in a graph. Data points are grouped into series. Quattro Pro has a variety of options for displaying data points: They can be pie wedges, or bars in a column (as in Figure 9.1), or they can be marked with a symbol, a line, or both.

- Graph Objects—Every item in a graph that can be selected separately is an object. A graph contains many different objects. Objects are like blocks and pages that you can select and customize by inspecting their properties. In Figure 9.1, the graph objects include the legend, the axes, the titles, and the series.

- Graph Pane—This is the area where the data points are charted in the graph. Many graphs have a box that indicates the boundaries of the graph pane. You have many options for this area, such as making it a different color or making the area invisible.

- Grid lines—The grid lines are the lines that connect to the tick marks stretching across the graph; they make the values easier to estimate by providing comparison points to the y-axis and/or x-axis. In Figure 9.1, the grid lines are the dotted lines from the numbers on the y-axis. For most graph types, the grid lines extend from the y-axis. Grid lines are not used in pie charts or column and text graphs.

- Label—In a graph, labels are text or numbers from the spreadsheet that describe the different points in the graph. In Figure 9.1, 573, 490, and 371 are three labels.

- Legend—The legend is the box in a graph that describes the color, fill style, and marker indicating each series of values. For example, the legend in Figure 9.1 labels the fill pattern for the two stores.

- Scale—The scale is a numeric range divided into regular intervals along an axis. Quattro Pro uses the scale to determine the position of points and lengths of bars in the graphs. For example, Figure 9.1 has a scale on the y-axis that determines the height of each of the bars.

- Series—A series is a group of related data points. Figure 9.1 has a series with five data points. You can have many series of data in a graph.

- Tick Marks—Tick marks are the small lines that divide the scale into regular intervals. In Figure 9.1, the x-axis has tick marks that divide it for the bars.

Graph Types

Quattro Pro provides ten different basic graph types. The selection of a graph type depends on the data and the objective that you are attempting to achieve with your presentation. Unless you specify otherwise, Quattro Pro uses a stacked bar graph. You can quickly change from one type of graph to another. A variety of graph types are shown in Figures 9.2A through 9.2I and are described below:

- Line—A line graph (Figure 9.2A) consists of a line that connects the points for each series of data on the graph. Each series value is plotted against the y-axis. This graph effectively shows trends in sales, expenses, or profit projections.

- Bar—A bar graph has horizontal bars whose heights are determined by the value of the data points in the series measured against the y-axis scale. Figure 9.1 shows a bar graph. Bar graphs effectively compare and contrast values like profit contributions from several product lines or expense categories over time. Quattro Pro also has special types of bar graphs such as variance and step bar graphs. A variance graph shows the amount each data point is above or below a specific value (usually 0). A step bar puts each of the bars for a series next to each other.

- Column—A column graph (Figure 9.2B) stacks bars representing each data point in a series to create a column. Each column section size is determined by the data point's percentage of the total. This is like a pie chart except the

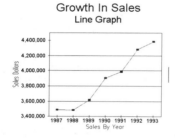

A

B

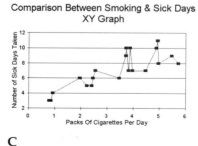

C

D

Figure 9.2   Different Graph Types

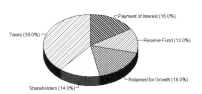

E

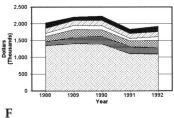

F

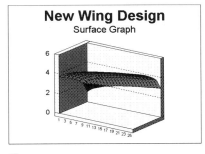

G

H

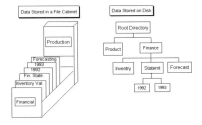

I

Figure 9.2   Different Graph Types *(continued)*

data points are represented by column sections instead of pie wedges. A column graph leaves more room for data labels and other text. You can use a column graph when you want to show the contributions several numbers have to the total, such as division sales relative to company sales.

- XY—An XY graph (Figure 9.2C) plots the values in one series against the values in a second series. You can use an XY graph to plot years of education against salary, age against sick days, or snow drift depth against wind velocity. This graph effectively shows series of data that are not divided into the same unit of measure.

- Stacked Bar—The stacked bar graph (Figure 9.2D) places each value of a series on top of the values from other series for each point on the x-axis. This graph effectively shows the total for different points on the x-axis as well as showing the individual series components. The profit contribution of various company units or the composition of expenses by quarter can be effectively shown with a stacked bar graph.

- Pie—A pie graph (Figure 9.2E) shows one series of values. Each value in the series is represented as a wedge in the pie. The size of each wedge is proportionate to the percentage that each value represents of the total (100%) of all values in the series. This type of graph is used to illustrate the proportions between numbers in the first series. The composition of company expenses can be shown effectively with a pie chart.

- Area—The area graph (Figure 9.2F) places a line graph for each series on top of another series matching each point in the x-axis. Instead of using bars as does the stacked bar graph, the area graph fills the entire area between the line. This graph effectively shows the total for different points on the x-axis as well as showing the individual components.

- Surface—A surface graph (Figure 9.2G) is like a line graph in which each series is behind the other and a sheet is draped across the lines. You can also think of a surface graph as an area graph that has several rows of x-axes. A surface graph can show amounts for the data points in each series.

- High-Low—A high-low graph (or high-low-open-close graph, Figure 9.2H) plots statistical data showing the high, low, open, and close values for each point on the x-axis. The first series contains the high values, the second series contains the low values, the third series contains the values at the opening of the day or period, and the fourth series contains the values at the close of the day or period. Quattro Pro draws a line from the high value to the low value then draws a horizontal line on the left side for the opening value and a horizontal line on the right side for the closing value. This graph type is used primarily for plotting financial commodities and statistical data.

- Text—A text graph (Figure 9.2I) provides a screen that you can fill with data. This graph does not use the spreadsheet. It is used for creating drawings and text.

These basic graph types are only the beginning of the graph type selections you can make. Quattro Pro can combine these basic graph types with other features, allowing you to rotate the axes, put multiple graphs in a single graph window, and add a variety of three-dimensional effects. Quattro Pro can also combine two graph types into one graph to emphasize one series of data. The combination options can be selected from line, bar, and XY graphs.

Choosing a Graph's Data Values

Creating a graph with Quattro Pro is easy. All you need to do is tell Quattro Pro which data to use. You have two options. You can select the data to graph and the name you want to use for the graph when you create a graph in a graph window. Another option is to create a graph and put it on a notebook page. This creates a *floating graph*. The steps for creating the graph in Figure 9.5 use the spreadsheet shown in Figure 9.3.

CREATING A GRAPH IN A WINDOW   You can create a graph that appears in its own separate window. This is just like a window you use to display the spreadsheet data in a notebook. To create a graph in a window, follow these steps:

1. Select the data from the notebook you want in the graph. For the data in Figure 9.3, the block is A3..G6.

2. Select New from the Graph menu. Quattro Pro displays the Graph New dialog box shown in Figure 9.4.

3. Type the name you want to use for the graph in the Graph Name text box. The graph name must follow the same rules as a block name. Quattro Pro supplies a default name of Graph#, where # represents the next unused number. You will want to enter a name that fits the data you are graphing. In the next chapter, you will learn how you can change the names assigned to different graphs.

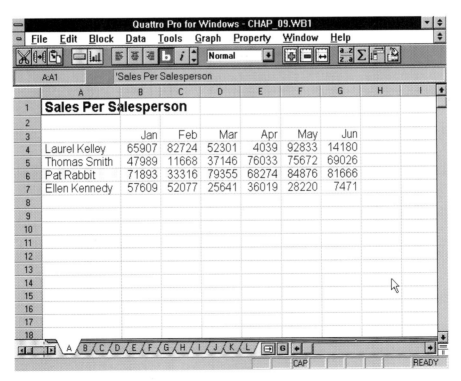

Figure 9.3   Sample Spreadsheet

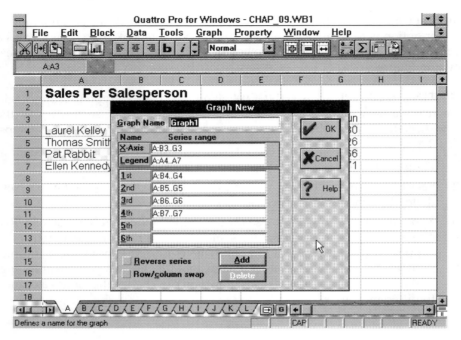

Figure 9.4   Graph New Dialog Box

The middle section of the dialog box contains the block addresses of the notebook data to include in the graph. The X-Axis text box contains the block that the graph uses as the entries for the bottom of the x-axis. The Legend text box selects the block containing the entries to use to identify each series in the graph. The remaining text boxes select the series that are charted in the graph. These series are sequentially numbered.

4.   Select or review the block selections for the different parts of the graph you are using. The step you perform depends on whether you have selected a block before selecting the New command in the Graph menu.

If you have a block selected when you use the New command in the Graph menu, Quattro Pro divides the selected block by rows or columns and puts the individual block addresses in the text boxes. Quattro Pro assumes you would rather have more data points with fewer series than the opposite way. Quattro Pro counts the number of columns and rows in the block to decide whether to divide the block by columns or rows. If you have more columns than rows, Quattro Pro divides the block by rows. If you have more rows than columns, Quattro Pro divides the block by columns. When the block has the same number of columns and rows, Quattro Pro also divides the block by columns. If you want to change the arrangement so Quattro Pro divides by columns instead of rows or vice versa, select the

Row/column swap check box. If you select a noncontiguous block before selecting the command, Quattro Pro looks at the first contiguous block to decide whether to divide the block by rows or columns. If the first row or column contains labels, that row or column is used for the x-axis. If the first row or column contains values, Quattro Pro starts using the first row or column as the first series. When the first entry in every row or column is a label, Quattro Pro uses the block containing the first entries for the legend.

If you do not have a block selected when you use the New command in the Graph menu, or you want to change the blocks the graph uses, you can select new blocks in the text boxes. In the X-Axis and Legend text boxes, you can enter the blocks containing the entries to use for the x-axis and legend. To add a block for the series, select the Add button and then in the next empty box, select the block the series will use. If you later decide you want to remove a series, select the series in the list and select the Delete button. You can select data from any open notebook to include as part of the graph. When you press an arrow key or click the dialog box's minimize box, you can switch to another open notebook by pressing CTRL-F6. You can also type the address, as in **[NotebookName]Page:Block**, which also allows you to select data from notebooks that are not opened.

For the data in Figure 9.3, the blocks should be correctly entered for you already because you selected A3..G6 in step 1. The dialog box picks up B3..G3 as the x-axis block, A3..A7 as the Legend block, B4..G4 for the first series, B5..G5 for the second series, B6..G6 for the third series, and B7..G7 for the fourth series.

5. Select the OK button to accept the block selections and create a graph with the data you have just selected. Quattro Pro opens a graph window and puts the graph you have just created in this window. The graph using the data in Figure 9.3 looks like Figure 9.5. When you follow these steps, each series uses a different color, shown in this book as a different shade or fill style. The graph currently is a very basic bar graph. From this point, you can change the graph's type as described in the next section.

Later, if you want to change the series the graph uses, you can switch to the graph window and use the Series command in the Graph menu. The Graph Series dialog box is just like the Graph New dialog box, except that you cannot change the graph's name. When you select OK, any changes you make to the graph's blocks are reflected in the graph.

ADDING A NEW GRAPH TO A SPREADSHEET PAGE   Another option for creating a graph and selecting the values the graph displays is to create the graph on your notebook. One of the advantages of having a graph on a notebook page is that if you include the block containing the graph in the block you print, the graph is included in the printed output. Also, you can show the graph next to the data it represents.

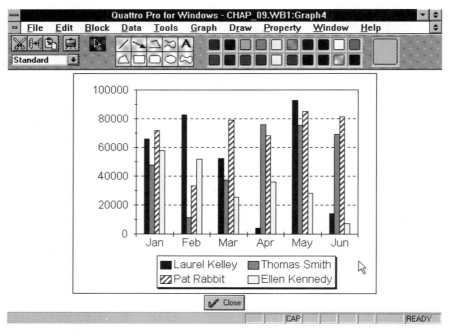

Figure 9.5   New Graph in a Graph Window

1.   Select the data from the notebook you want in the graph. For the data in Figure 9.3, the block is A3..G7.

2.   Select the Graph button in the SpeedBar, which looks like a miniature bar graph. While you point at the spreadsheet page, the pointer is a small cross with the outline of the SpeedBar's Graph button attached to it.

3.   Select the location on the page where you want the graph placed. Since the graph is a floating graph that lies above the data on the page, you do not select cells but rather a rectangular area on the page where the graph will

---

▼ TIP: Put a graph in a window if you are still rearranging your notebook page.

Since you can add a graph to a notebook after you create it in a graph window, you may want to postpone adding a graph to a notebook page if you are in the process of rearranging it. Waiting until later to add a graph to the notebook page prevents the graph from getting in the way of the data you are moving.

appear. Any data below this block is still in the notebook but it is hidden by the graph. You can think of the data below the graph as using the hidden numeric format. For the page in Figure 9.3, select an area that includes the block A8..G7.

4. Release the mouse by dragging the mouse across this block. You can also click a cell to place the graph on the page. If you click instead of drag to put a graph on a notebook, the graph is the default size starting at the cell you select.

Quattro Pro creates a graph using the default graph settings and the data you have just selected. This graph you have just created uses the default name of Graph#, where # represents the next unused number. Just as above, Quattro Pro has divided the block by rows or columns and has used the first row and first column for legends and x-axis labels, if they contain labels. If you want to change how the data is divided, or you want to add or remove series, select the Series command in the Graph menu to display the Graph Series dialog box and change how Quattro Pro uses the spreadsheet data. You will learn how you can rename graphs in the next chapter.

The graph using the data in Figure 9.3 looks like Figure 9.6. At this point, this floating graph is still the selected object. You can tell because it has *handles* on it. These handles are the little boxes at the sides of the graph that you can see in Figure 9.6. You can use other commands in the Graph menu to change the graph's

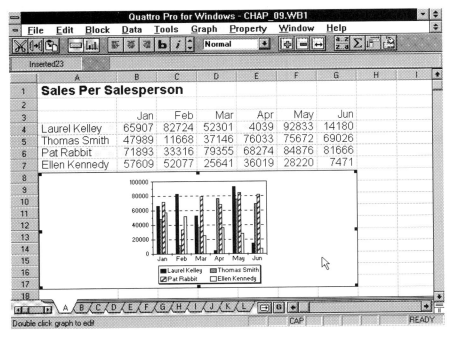

Figure 9.6 New Graph on a Notebook Page

▼ TIP: Creating a Text Graph.

To make a text graph which does not use spreadsheet data, select <u>N</u>ew from the <u>G</u>raph menu, type the name for the graph, and select OK. You can also do this by selecting the Graph button on the SpeedBar without a block selected and selecting an area for the empty text graph. You do not have to select a graph type — since no data is selected for this command, Quattro Pro automatically makes the graph a text graph.

---

data, type, and text. You can also move and size a graph on a page just like you can move and size a notebook window within Quattro Pro. To move a floating graph, point to an area within the graph and drag it to a new location. The pointer will look like a hand while you are moving the graph. To size a floating graph, point to one of the handles so the pointer changes its shape to a cross. Next, drag it to its new size. The graph will resize itself to fit the new area.

Selecting a Graph Type

Once you have the graph window open or the graph on the page selected, you can select the graph's type. To select the graph type, use the <u>T</u>ype command in the <u>G</u>raph menu. The Graph Types dialog box (shown in Figure 9.7) has divided the different graph type combinations into five groups. The <u>2</u>-D group contains the simplest versions of most of the graph types. The <u>3</u>-D group contains several of the graph types using a variety of effects to give the graph a three-dimensional appearance. The <u>R</u>otate group offers some of the graph types with the axes rotated so the x-axis is on the left side and the y-axis is on the top or bottom. The <u>C</u>ombo group combines graph types by offering a graph type that combines two graphs, as in a line and a bar, or a graph type that contains more than one of a single graph type, as in four pies or columns in a single graph. The <u>T</u>ext group makes the graph a text graph. A text graph ignores the spreadsheet data you may have selected. After you select one of the first four groups, you can make another selection of the graph type you want from that group. The right side of the dialog box contains sample diagrams of the graph type each button represents. When you select a button from the right and then select OK, the current graph changes to use the new graph type.

Besides looking at the graph in the window, you can expand the graph so it occupies the entire screen. To do this, press F11. This is the same as the <u>V</u>iew command in the <u>G</u>raph menu. When you use this keystroke or command, Quattro Pro displays the graph so it fills the screen. To return to the previous display, press a key or click the mouse. Sometimes as you are creating graphs, the information is too congested in the window, but you can use the full screen to see the effects of changes you make.

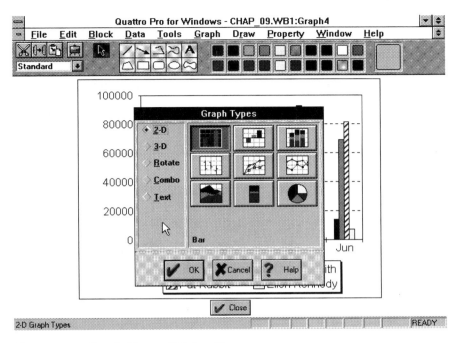

Figure 9.7   Graph Types Dialog Box

▼ TIP: Try different graph types to find the best one.

No graph type will be the best graph type for every occasion. You should try out several graph types when you are creating a graph. You will want to try different types, such as an area or bar graph instead of just a line graph. You will also want to try some of the enhanced types for the basic graph, such as a rotated option or some of the three-dimensional effects.

Adding Text to a Graph

In the previous examples, the graph showed several series. However, it is not possible to determine which data the graph represents, since the graph is missing information that describes its contents. Adding titles to a graph provides two lines at the top of a graph and an x-axis and y-axis title. These are essential first steps in adding descriptive information to a graph. You can also add legends which will identify how each series is represented in the graph.

ADDING TITLES To add titles, select Titles from the Graph menu. From the Graph Titles dialog box, enter the text you want to appear for the titles in the appropriate text box. Type the graph's title (like New Product Satisfaction Strategies for the graph in Figure 9.1) in the Main Title text box. Type the graph's secondary title (like Direct Calling Vs. Surveys in Figure 9.1) in the Subtitle text box. The subtitle normally continues or explains the first title. Type the title for the x-axis in the X-Axis Title text box. Type the title for the y-axis in the Y1-Axis Title text box. Later you will learn about adding data to a second y-axis. You can label this y-axis by typing the text for the title in the Y2-Axis Title text box. When you select OK, the graph uses the modified text. Using the graph created in Figure 9.5, the same graph with titles might look like Figure 9.8.

To use a cell's contents as a title, type a backslash followed by the cell address in place of the text for the title such as \B:A2 (which uses the contents of B:A2 as a title). To remove a title, remove the entry from the Graph Titles dialog box. When you want to modify an existing graph title, you can select Titles in the Graph menu. From the Graph Titles dialog box, modify the text box entries and select OK. A special option for modifying the title or subtitle is to click the title or subtitle. This lets you modify the title just as if you are modifying a cell entry. If either the title or subtitle is the contents of a cell, clicking the title or subtitle converts the title entry into the backslash and the cell's address.

ADDING A LEGEND The graph in Figure 9.8 displays several series of data in one graph that the legend identifies. If the first row or column in the block does not contain labels when you are dividing the block by columns or rows, your graph will not have a legend. You will want to include one when you have several series so you can see how each series is indicated in the graph. If you did not select a block containing the legend when you created the graph, you can select legend text while editing the graph. To add or modify a legend for a series, select a data point for the series and inspect its properties by right-clicking the data point or pressing F12. With the Series Option property selected, enter the text for that series legend in the Legend text box. This must be done separately for each series. When you select OK, Quattro Pro adds the legend to the graph.

Another option for adding a legend is to reference a legend entry in a spreadsheet cell rather than typing the legend. When prompted for the legend, type a backslash (\) and the address of the cell containing the legend. For example, using the data that created Figure 9.8, you can enter the legend for the first series by typing \A3.

Although Quattro Pro puts the legends at the bottom of the graph, you can change the graph so that the legends appear at the bottom of the graph, or so they do not appear at all. To do this, inspect the legend's properties by right-clicking on the legend, or by selecting Legend from the Property menu. Then select one of the Legend Position buttons. You can remove a legend or place one in on the right or bottom of the graph. For the Legend Position property, select one of the potential legend locations. You can also select the first legend position to remove the legend.

The appearance of the symbol next to the legend text that shows how a series is presented depends on the graph type selected. It might include the series'

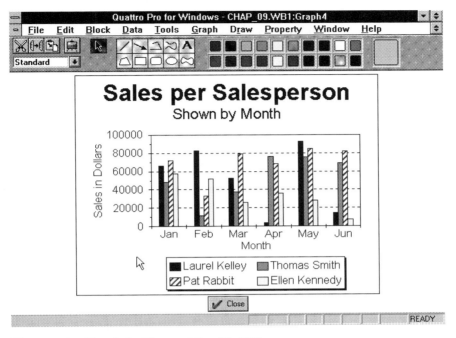

Figure 9.8   Graph in Figure 9.5 with Titles

symbol, line style, or pattern. A legend can have other properties such as text type and color and the appearance of the box. Other graph objects use these properties, and so they are described below in "Changing Graph Properties."

Editing the Graph

Once you create a named graph, the graph is available at any time while you are working in the notebook. You can display a named graph in a graph window by selecting Edit from the Graph menu and then selecting the graph name from the Graph Edit dialog box. This opens a graph window containing the selected named graph. If you want to display a floating graph in a graph window, double-click it. The advantage of editing a graph in a window is that you have the use of the graph window SpeedBar, the ObjectInspectors for inspecting different graph object properties, and menu selections that apply specifically to graphs. When the graph is displayed in a graph window, all of the changes you make affect that graph only. If you want to make changes to another graph that is not the active one, you must make it the active graph and then make the changes. As with other windows in Quattro Pro, you can change the graph window's size and position as well as closing or minimizing it. Each graph window open is listed in the Window menu as the notebook name followed by the name of the graph. You cannot use Close in the File menu to close the window. To close a graph window, use CTRL-F4, the graph window's Control menu box, or the Close button at the bottom of the window. When you close the notebook that includes graphs shown in graph windows, those graph windows are closed as well. When you open the notebook back up, the graph windows are *not* opened as well.

INSERTING A GRAPH TO A NOTEBOOK PAGE

Besides adding a graph to a notebook page when you create the graph, you can also add a graph you have already created to a notebook page. When you add it to the spreadsheet, you select the graph and its desired location within the current spreadsheet.

To add a graph to the spreadsheet, select Insert from the Graph menu. Quattro Pro lists and prompts you for a graph name. Select a named graph to add to the page. Once a graph is selected, you can use the mouse to select the block that you want the graph to fill. You will notice that the pointer now looks like it does after you select the Graph button in the SpeedBar. When the block is selected, Quattro Pro creates as large a graph as can fit into the selected block, adjusting the height-to-width ratio as necessary. As you change the data the graph uses, Quattro Pro updates the graph on the page just as it does for the graph in the graph window. You can even have more than one copy of a graph on notebook pages.

Once you add the graph, you may want to change its position or size. To move a graph, select the graph, then drag it to its new location. This is just like moving one block to another location using the drag and drop method. To change a graph's size, select the pane, then point to one of the corner handles. Now the pointer changes to a cross. You can drag this corner to a new location until the outline is the size you want the graph. When you release the mouse, the graph is resized to fit the outline.

If you want to remove an inserted graph, select the graph and then press DEL, click the Cut button on the SpeedBar, or use the Cut command in the Edit menu. Quattro Pro removes the graph from the page so you can see any underlying data. You have not deleted the graph itself, only its location on the page.

CHANGING GRAPH PROPERTIES

The remainder of the chapter focuses on different properties for a graph that you can change. Some properties, like text appearance and border appearance, can apply to multiple graph objects. Other properties, such as legend position and axis settings, only apply to a few or to a single graph object. The properties are divided into the following categories: Changing the Appearance of Text, Changing the Appearance of Filled Shapes, Legends, Rearranging Graph Objects, Adding Data Point Labels, Enhancing the Three-Dimensional Effect, Using Two Graph Types, Using Two Y-Axes, Changing the Axes, Overall Graph Changes, and Special Properties of Graph Types.

To change the graph's property, select the object to change and inspect its properties.

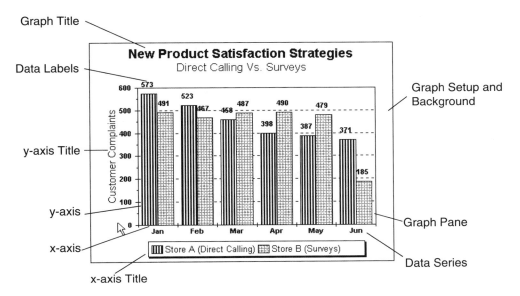

Figure 9.9   Different Parts of the Graph That You Can Inspect

Select a graph object by clicking it. Figure 9.9 shows the different parts of the graph for which you can inspect the properties. Each graph series, pie slice, and column section has its own properties, and can be selected and given a customized appearance. Some of these object properties can be inspected by selecting Graph Window, Graph Setup, Graph Pane, Legend, X Axis, or Y Axis in the Property menu. The properties and the objects that use the properties are listed in Table 9.1.

Several of the graph properties are also set with Graph menu commands. You can change the spreadsheet data used for a series or x-axis by inspecting the series or X-Axis; then for the X-Axis Series or Series Options property, change the selected block in the Select range or Data series text box. You can also inspect the X-Axis Title and Y-Axis Title and then, with the Title property selected, modify the text in the text box below Enter text to change the x- or y-axis property instead of using the Titles command in the Graph menu. You can change the graph type by inspecting the Graph Setup properties and changing the Graph Type property. The Graph Setup and Background properties dialog box also has a setting called Graph Button, which will be covered in the next chapter.

Changing the Appearance of Text

A graph can have text in its titles, in its legend, and along its axes. You can add text to the values in a series, slices in a pie graph, and sections in a column graph. You can also add text in other locations as described in the next chapter. There are more

Table 9.1   Properties and the Graph Objects That Use Them

Property	Graph Object
3D Options	Graph Setup
3D View	Graph Setup
Aspect Ratio	Graph Window
Bar Options	Graph Series
Bkg Color	Graph Pane, Graph Series, Graph Setup, Graph Title Box, Legend, Pie Graph
Border Color	Column Graph, Graph Pane, Graph Series, Graph Setup, Graph Title Box, Legend, Pie Graph
Border Options	Graph Pane
Border Style	Column Graph, Graph Pane, Graph Series, Pie Graph
Box Type	Graph Setup, Graph Title Box, Legend
Explode Slice	Pie Graph
Fill Color	Graph Pane, Graph Series, Graph Setup, Graph Title Box, Legend, Pie Graph
Fill Style	Graph Pane, Graph Series, Graph Setup, Graph Title Box, Legend, Pie Graph
Format	Series Label
Graph Button	Graph Setup
Graph Type	Graph Setup
Grid	Graph Window
Label Alignment	Series Label
Label Options	Column Graph, Pie Graph
Legend Position	Graph Setup, Legend
Line Color	Graph Series
Line Style	Graph Series
Major Grid Style	X-Axis, Y-Axis
Marker Style	Graph Series
Minor Grid Style	Y-Axis

Table 9.1 Properties and the Graph Objects That Use Them *(continued)*

Property	Graph Object
Numeric Format	Y-Axis
Scale	Y-Axis
Series Options	Graph Series
Subtitle Bkg Color	Graph Subtitle
Subtitle Color	Graph Subtitle
Subtitle Font	Graph Subtitle
Subtitle Style	Graph Subtitle
Text Bkg Color	Column Graph, Graph Title, Legend, Pie Graph, Series Label, X-Axis, X-Axis Title, Y-Axis, Y-Axis Title
Text Color	Column Graph, Graph Title, Legend, Pie Graph, Series Label, X-Axis, X-Axis Title, Y-Axis, Y-Axis Title
Text Font	Column Graph, Graph Title, Legend, Pie Graph, Series Label, X-Axis, X-Axis Title, Y-Axis, Y-Axis Title
Text Style	Column Graph, Graph Title, Legend, Pie Graph, Series Label, X-Axis, X-Axis Title, Y-Axis, Y-Axis Title
Tick Options	X-Axis, Y-Axis
Title	X-Axis Title, Y-Axis Title
X-Axis Series	X-Axis

text enhancement features for text in graphs than for text in cells. You can select the style, size, color, and background color for text. Also, most text in a graph has a box around it that you can set to show how the box looks so the text is separated from the surrounding objects or blends in with them. When you inspect a graph object containing text, you can inspect the properties of the text or the properties of the box around the text. The appearance of the pointer indicates whether you are inspecting the text's or the box's properties. When the pointer appears as an I beam, you are inspecting the text's properties. When the pointer appears as an arrow while the text object is selected, you are inspecting the properties of the box around the text. If the text does not use a box, you are inspecting the text's properties. The properties for the box around text are the same as for other borders and boxes, and are described with filling shapes below. The graph objects for which you can change the properties of the text include Graph Subtitle, Column Graph (for the text labeling the column segments), Graph Title, Legend, Pie Graph (for the text identifying the pie slices), Series Label (if the series uses labels), X-Axis (for the text along the x-axis), X-Axis Title, Y-Axis (for the text along the y-axis), and Y-Axis Title. With some of the text items that are part of a group, changing the text properties changes them for every item in the group.

For text properties, you can select the font, color, and background color properties. All the graph objects that let you customize text have Text Bkg Color, Text Color, Text Font, and Text Style properties except for the subtitle, which uses Subtitle in place of Text. Text Font is the same as the Font property for cells. Text Color is similar to setting the Text Color property for cells. The Text Bkg Color sets a second color the text can use when you are using some of the special text appearance features for graphs.

Selecting colors in a graph is slightly different from selecting colors for notebook cells. When you select the Text Color or Text Bkg Color property, you can select from one of the available colors in the palette. Figure 9.10 shows the dialog box for changing the text color. Another option is creating a custom color by changing the sliding scales. Quattro Pro for Windows can create colors using three color models. You select the radio button for the model you want to use. HSB combines hue, saturation, and brightness to create colors. RBG combines red, blue, and green to create colors. CMY combines cyan, magenta, and yellow to create colors. You can change the color model and the sliding scales to create the text color or background color you want to use.

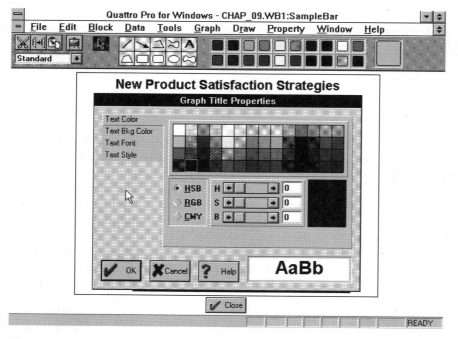

Figure 9.10   Dialog Box to Change Colors

The Text Style property adds features to your graph's text that are not available for notebook cells. By default Quattro Pro assumes you want to fill the text with the solid color chosen with the Text Color property. You can add a shadow effect by selecting the S<u>h</u>adow check box to use the background color as a shadow for the graph's text. If you select the <u>W</u>ash radio button, the text makes a transition effect between the text color and the text background color based on the wash pattern selected above the radio buttons. You can also select <u>B</u>itmap and supply the name of a bitmap file whose contents you want to use to fill the text. Figure 9.11 shows several examples of these different text features applied to a graph.

Changing the Appearance of Filled Shapes

Any graph you create has many filled-in shapes. These shapes include boxes around text and the pie slices, column segments and bars that represent each series. You can change the appearance of these shapes by changing how they are filled and the border around them. Later, in the next chapter, you will learn how you can add many different types of shapes as if you are using a graphics program like Paintbrush. These items have the same properties. You can change the properties of the filled-in appearance and the borders for graph objects including the Graph Pane (the area where the data values are charted), Graph Series (if the series

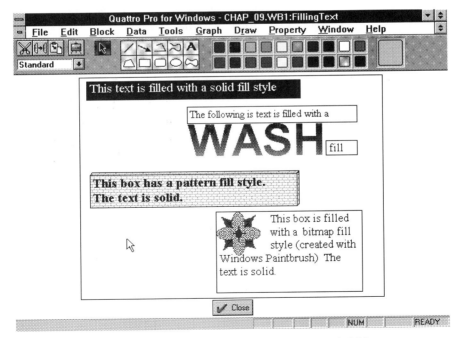

Figure 9.11   Different Fill Effects for Text and Filled Objects

uses bars or column segments), Graph Setup (the graph's background), Graph Title Box (around the title and subtitle), Legend, and Pie Graph. Some of these objects do not have all the border and fill properties.

For most of these properties, you can select the color an item is filled with, any background color it uses, and the style of how the object is filled in. As when selecting the color and background color for text, you can select one of the displayed colors in the palette or create one of your own using the sliding bars and the HSB, RBG, and CMY radio buttons. The Fill Style property selects how the object is filled in. You have the same Solid, Wash, and Pattern radio buttons as when filling text. You also have Pattern and None. Pattern combines the color and background color in one of the patterns you select from the buttons above. Choose None to use the color of whatever is behind the object. You can also select Bitmap and supply the name of the bitmapped file to fill the object with the contents of a graphic file.

For the border, you can select the color of the line and either the style of the line or the style of the box. The Border Color property lets you choose the color of the line from one of the current palette colors or by selecting your own. The objects that have borders have either the Box Type or Border Style property. The Box Type property selects the style of the box. Figure 9.12 shows several different box styles in a graph. The Border Style selects the style of the line of the border. The Graph Pane also has a Border Options property that allows you to select which sides of the graph pane have a border by selecting or clearing the Left border, Top border,

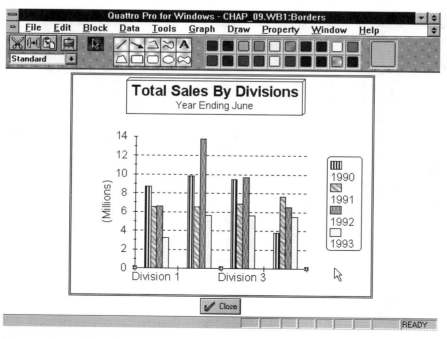

Figure 9.12   Graph with Different Border Types

▼ TIP: Changing Colors Using the Color Palette in the SpeedBar

Besides changing colors by inspecting properties, you can also change the color of a selected object by selecting the object, selecting the color from the color palette in the SpeedBar, and then selecting the object again. This feature works for the Column Graph (segments, not text), Graph Pane, Graph Series, Graph Title Box, Legend (box, not text), and Pie Graph (slices, not text) properties.

<u>R</u>ight border, and <u>B</u>ottom border. For example, in Figure 9.12, the top and right borders of the graph pane are removed.

Legends

Legends on a graph let you know how each series is represented. Most of the time Quattro Pro automatically takes care of sizing the legend and adjusting it for changes in the legend text and how the series are represented. You can inspect the legend if you want to change how the text appears, how the box around the legend appears, and where the legend is positioned. The text appearance is altered just as for other text objects. The box's appearance is controlled by the same Bkg Color, Border Color, Border Options, Fill Color, and Fill Style properties that you use to change other filled objects as described above. You can use the Legend Position property to change the legend location between predefined locations. You can change the Legend Position property by inspecting the legend or by inspecting Graph Setup. When the Legend Position property is selected, the three buttons hide the legend, display the legend below the graph, or display the legend to the right of the graph. Another option for moving the legend is to drag it to a new location yourself. To move the legend by dragging, point to the legend, then drag it to its new location. In Figure 9.13, the graph has the legend moved to the top of the graph pane. In this graph, the pane is also enlarged so it fills the area the legend would otherwise occupy. While you can always put the legend inside the graph pane, you will want to be sure that it does not obscure the data points.

A legend has several limitations. You can change the legend text appearance so more or less data will fit within the legend, but you cannot rearrange the contents of the legend box, and you cannot change the size of the legend. If you are not happy with the legend size, you probably will need to change the legend text size to make it smaller or larger depending on whether you want to increase or decrease the box's size.

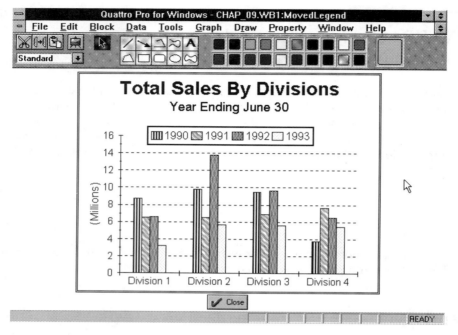

Figure 9.13   Legend Moved by Dragging

Rearranging Graph Objects

You can move other parts of the graph besides the legend. You can move the graph pane and the title as well as other objects you will learn how to add in the next chapter. To move a graph object, point to it, then drag it to its new location. You can see when you will be able to move an object because if you hold down the mouse button while pointing to the object, the pointer will change to a hand and an outline will appear around the object's border if it is an object you can move. You can change the size of the graph pane, as well as that of other objects you will learn how to add in the next chapter. Change a pane's size by selecting the pane. Then, when you point to one of the corner handles, the pointer changes to a cross. Now you can drag this corner to a new location until the outline is the size you want the pane. When you release the mouse, the pane is resized to fit the outline.

Adding Data Point Labels

The graph in Figure 9.8 shows multiple series of data plotted in one graph, but the graph does not show the exact values for each point. You can approximate each point's value by its relation to the y-axis. If you need more exact information, you can instruct Quattro Pro to display the values of each point in a graph. Displaying the data point labels can be done for all graph types except pie, column, and text.

To add data point labels to a series, select the series, inspect its properties, and then for the Series Options property, select the block containing the entries for the data point labels in the Label Series text box. This must be repeated for each series to which you want to add labels. The data used for the labels is usually the same used for the data points, but you can also display other information, such as department numbers, or years, as the data point labels. After you select OK, Quattro Pro adds the labels as shown in Figure 9.14. You can also choose where the data point labels are placed in relation to the data points. To change the position of the data point labels, inspect the data point labels properties. Select the radio button representing your selected location for the labels in relation to the data points for the Label Alignment Property in the Series Label Properties. If you plan to display the data point labels in place of the data points, select Center. You may also want to select the Format property and choose a numeric format for the values of the data point labels. When you select OK, Quattro Pro places the data labels in the selected position and numeric format. Figure 9.15 shows the same line graph with the data labels displayed in place of the data points. For this graph, the label alignment is Center, and the marker weight is 0.

Certain graph types select the location for data point labels, regardless of the choices that you make for the Label Alignment property. In 3-D graphs, the labels are always above the data points. In stacked bars, only the labels of the last series are shown at the top of the bars; the labels of other series are not shown. You can

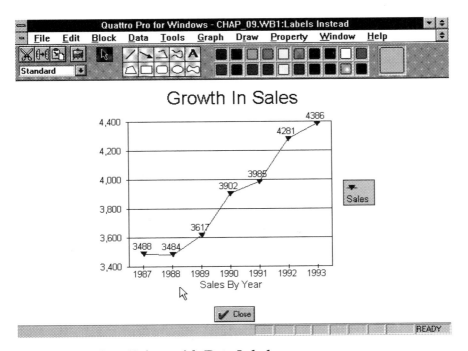

Figure 9.14   Data Points with Data Labels

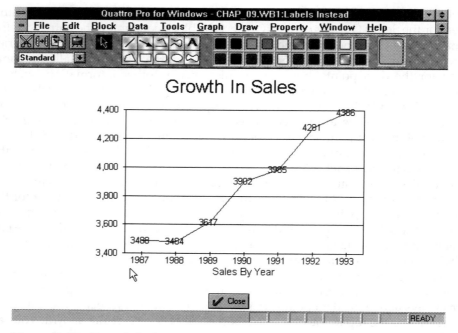

Figure 9.15   Data Labels without Data Points

change the appearance of the data labels by changing their text properties (Text Bkg Color, Text Color, Text Font, and Text Style) just as you would for other graph objects.

Enhancing the Three-Dimensional Effect

You already know that you can use three-dimensional enhancements to many of the graph types by selecting a 3-D graph type for the graph's graph type property. You can also change how that three-dimensional look appears. The graph has two properties to change the three-dimensional appearance. These options do not apply for three-dimensional pie and column graphs. To change the appearance of a 3-D graph, inspect the Graph Setup's properties or select Graph Setup in the Property menu.

The 3D View property changes the angles from which you are viewing the three-dimensional image of the graph. Imagine that you are holding the shape of the graph in your hand. When you hold an object in your hand, you can adjust the angle that you are looking at it by twisting your hand. You add the same effect to your graph. The dialog box, when the 3D View property is selected, shows a sample graph so you can see how the graph's appearance will change as you modify the settings. You can also apply the current settings to the graph by selecting Apply. If you change your mind, you can always return to the default settings for the 3D View property by selecting the Reset button. You can use either slider bars or text boxes to make the changes to the 3D View settings, since most of the features use both. The Rotation setting changes how much the graph is turned to the right or left. When it is 0, the graph appears as if you are looking at it from the front. When it is 90, the graph appears as if you are looking at it from its right side. Usually you want to be somewhere in between these two values so the graph looks as if you are looking at it obliquely. The Elevation setting changes how much the graph is turned up or down. When it is 0, the graph appears as if you are looking at it at eye level. When it is 90, the graph appears as if you are above the graph looking straight down at it.

You can also change how the graph's shape fits into the graph pane area. When you look at an object, you will notice that the part closest to you looks bigger than the part that is further away. This is called perspective. You can add perspective to your three-dimensional graphs by selecting the Perspective check box. When you select this check box, you can also select the degree to which the perspective is shown. The higher the number in the text box, the more noticeable the perspective is. You can select how deep the box that contains the graphed data is by modifying the Depth value. The higher the number, the deeper the box appears. Also, changing the depth changes the shapes of the bars in three-dimensional bar graphs. When the number is 100, the bars are square; at other numbers, the bars are rectangular. The remaining selection, Height, sets how tall the box appears. Changing the height does not change the graph pane size, but rather the ratio between the height and width of the graph. Figure 9.16 shows a graph that has several changes made to the 3D View property. In this graph, rotation is set to 54 and elevation is set to 28.

The other change you can make to a three-dimensional graph is to the walls that appear around the graphed data. You can omit some or all of them and you can also select whether the walls appear thick or thin. To make these changes, select the 3D Options property. You can add or remove the left, back or base (the floor of the graphed data) by selecting or clearing the Show left wall, Show back wall, and Show base check boxes. You can also make the walls thick by selecting the Thick walls check box. Figure 9.16 shows a graph that has the walls removed by changing the 3D Options property.

Using Two Graph Types

For bar, line, variance and high-low graphs, Quattro Pro can combine two types of graphs into a single graph. You can combine different graph types in a single graph to display types of information that need to be graphed differently but have a relationship to each other. For example, you may graph defective products with product sales to illustrate how sales increase as defective products decrease. In this case, you may show the defective products in an area graph and the sales in a line

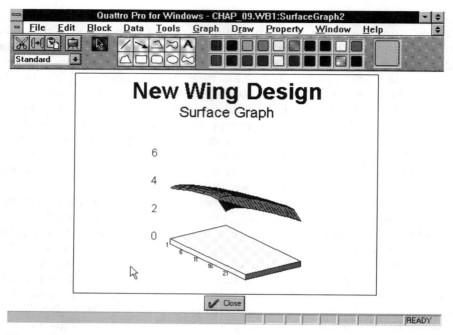

Figure 9.16   Altering the Look of a 3-D Graph

graph. To create a graph with combined graph types, first select the basic graph type as bar, line, or variance high-low. To select the second graph type, select the series and inspect its properties to change the type of graph used to display that series. With the Series Options property selected, choose the second graph type from the Override type radio buttons: Bar, Line, Area, and Default (which returns the series' graph type back to the overall graph type).

Figure 9.17 shows a graph that combines two graph types. In this graph, the profits are shown as a bar graph and the sales are shown as a line graph. Since the number of sales dollars is so much larger than the number of profit dollars, the two data series are pushed to the extreme top and bottom of the graph. By creating two y-axes, as discussed in the next section, you can display the data better. To change the customization settings of the second graph type, you must temporarily change the default graph type to the overriding graph type and customize the second graph type. After changing the settings of the second graph type, return the graph type to the original graph type.

Using Two Y-Axes

When you combine graphs, the data you are displaying often are not measured by units of the same size. For example, in the data graphed in Figure 9.17, the sales are in millions while the profits are in the thousands. Since the data values are so

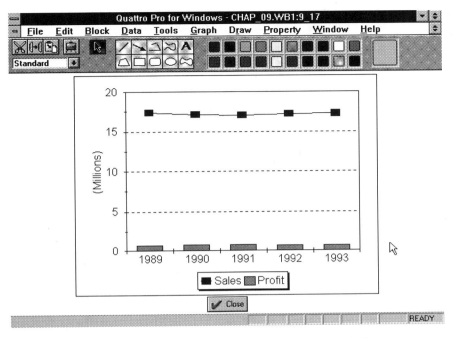

Figure 9.17 Data Point Labels Above the Data Point Markers

different, the graphed data appear skewed, with the sales squeezed at the top of the graph and the profits squeezed at the bottom. Another alternative is to have two axes. The sales data of Figure 9.17 can be assigned to the first y-axis, and the profit data can be assigned to the second y-axis. When you assign data to a second y-axis, Quattro Pro automatically creates it for you making the same assumptions Quattro Pro uses to create the first y-axis. The second y-axis appears to the right of the graph. Only bar, line, and high-low (for series beyond the first four) graphs can have a second y-axis. To assign a series to the second y-axis, inspect a series' properties and, with the Series Options property selected, select the Secondary radio button below Y-Axis. If you change your mind, you can inspect the series' properties again and select the Primary radio button with the Series Options property selected. Figure 9.18 shows a graph with two axes. In this graph, the sales uses the second y-axis, which is measured in thousands of dollars. By adjusting the axis using customization options for the axes (covered later in the chapter), you can control how Quattro Pro places the data values on the graph.

Changing the Axes

The axes have several properties you can change. These changes include the scaling, the appearance of the tick marks, and grid lines. To select an axis, select

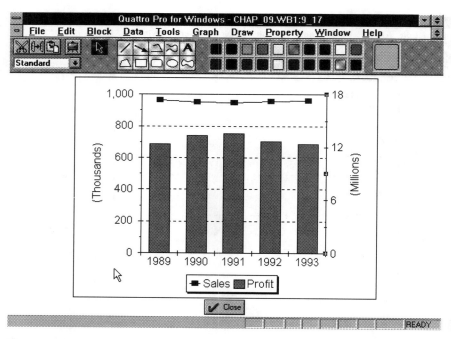

Figure 9.18 Data Point Labels Instead of Data Point Markers

any area of the axis other than the title. You can also modify the x- or y-axis by selecting X Axis or Y Axis from the Property menu. The properties you have for an axis depends on whether the axis contains values or labels. The two y-axes always have values, but the x-axis can have either values or labels. When the x-axis has values, the axis has the same properties as the y-axes. When the x-axis has labels, the properties are slightly different.

SETTING THE SCALING   In most graphs, the y-axis is automatically scaled to fit the data points. In XY graphs, the x-axis is automatically scaled. Quattro Pro creates the scale so that the graph has extra space on the top not used by the data points, and usually starts the graph at zero. You can reset the scale to any consistent format that you want. For example, if you are graphing the change in your company's gross margin profit percentage, you want to readjust the scale to show the small changes in the gross profit margin, since a small change can drastically change the company's profit. In this example, you may want to show only the range from 40% to 60%. Changing the scale requires these steps:

1.   Inspect the x-axis or y-axis, depending on the axis you want to change. If you have two y-axes, you can make setting changes for each one independent of the other. For the Scale property, the Automatic check box tells Quattro Pro that it will create the axes scale. You can clear this box if you want to enter your own scale settings, although as soon as you make an entry in the

Basic Graphic Features 413

High, Low, or Increment text boxes, Quattro Pro will automatically clear the Automatic check box for you. Later when you want to revert back to using the scale Quattro Pro creates for you, you can select the Automatic check box again.

2. Type the highest number that you want on the scale in the High text box. The number you type should be as large as or larger than the largest number in the series. In the gross profit margin example, you would enter **.6** or **60%**.

3. Type the lowest number you want on the scale in the Low text box. The number you provide should be as small as or smaller than the lowest number in the series. If you are graphing negative numbers, make sure that this number has a minus sign before it. In the gross profit margin example, you would enter **.4** or **40%**.

4. Type the number representing the interval between tick marks in the Increment text box. If this number is too small, the grid lines and tick marks become indistinguishable. In the gross profit margin example, the entry is **.02** or **2%**.

5. Type the number of minor tick marks you want between major ticks in the No. of minors text box. Major tick marks are the markings along the axis that have values next to them. Minor tick marks are the axis markings that are not identified. Entering a number greater than 0 adds minor tick marks between the major ones. When a scale has small intervals, the numeric labels become jammed together, making it difficult to read the graph. Since the tick marks appear at regular intervals, removing some tick mark labels makes the remaining values legible and makes it easier to determine the values on the graph. Figure 9.19 contains a graph that combines minor and major ticks on the y-axis.

6. Select the Show units check box if you want to allow Quattro Pro to divide the axis values by thousands or a similar number and include the scaling information below the y-axis title. When this check box is cleared, the units along the axis appear unchanged and the axis does not include a scaling indicator.

7. Check which Scale Type radio button is selected. When you are graphing data, Quattro Pro initially uses a normal scale. A normal scale means the increments are the same between all tick marks. Quattro Pro also has a logarithmic scale. In a logarithmic scale, the difference between tick marks increases by a power of 10. For example, if the first tick mark is 1, the second tick mark is 10, and the third tick mark is 100. To change the tick mark scaling to logarithmic, select the Log radio button. To return the axis to the normal scaling, select the Normal radio button. Figure 9.20 (a and b) shows two versions of a graph, one scaled with a standard scale and one with a logarithmic scale.

When you select OK, Quattro Pro uses the scale settings you have selected. For the gross profit margin example, the rescaled graph looks like Figure 9.19. You may want to select the Numeric Format property for the y-axis and select a numeric percent format to apply to the values along the axis.

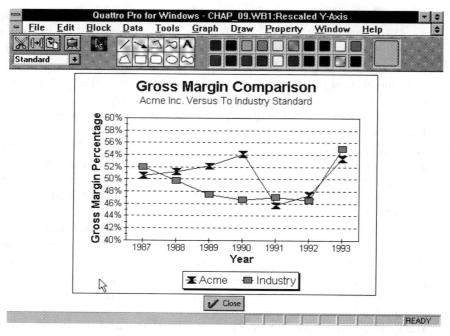

Figure 9.19   Graph Combining Major and Minor Ticks on the Y-Axis

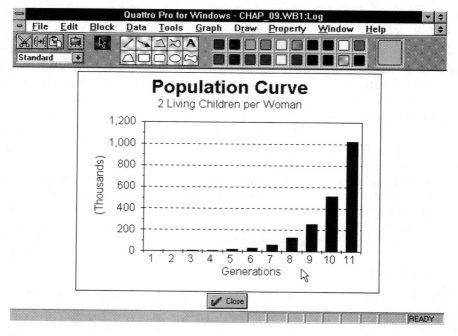

Figure 9.20(a)   Normal Axis Scale

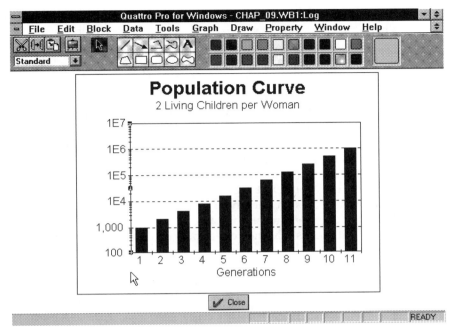

Figure 9.20(b) **Logarithmic Axis Scale**

CHANGING THE TICK MARKS When you create a graph, Quattro Pro uses default settings for the tick marks, but these can be changed. You can change the appearance of the tick marks, set limitations on how the values next to the tick marks are displayed, or make other changes to the tick mark settings. Quattro Pro initially creates tick marks that evenly divide the axis. You can instruct Quattro Pro to place them at different intervals. For the x-axis you can alternate the placement of labels on two lines next to the tick marks to prevent overlapping labels (for all graph types except XY graphs).

To make changes to the tick marks, follow these steps:

1. Inspect the axis whose tick marks you want to change.
2. Select the Tick Options property.
3. Select the radio button under Tick Style that selects the side of the axis line where you want the tick marks to appear. You can select None to remove the tick marks.
4. Select whether you want the labels to appear by selecting or clearing the Display labels check box. When this check box is selected, (the default), the axis displays the labels. When this check box is cleared, the labels do not appear and the remaining options of the Tick Options property disappear.

5. Select any length limitation on the labels by selecting the Length limit check box. When this check box is selected, the axis labels (which can be either values or labels) are abbreviated to the number of characters that you select or type in the text box that appears. When the check box is cleared, the labels appear on the graph with as many characters as needed. This option is often used when the x-axis contains lengthy labels.

6. Make any changes to how the x-axis labels appear if the axis does not have enough room by modifying the remaining settings below Labels. The Number of Rows radio buttons select how many rows the axis uses to display the labels. The default is 1 to put all the labels on the same row, but you can select 2 or 3 to use two or three rows to display x-axis labels. The axis uses the number of rows you select regardless of whether it has enough room to display all of the labels on one line. Figure 9.21 shows a graph with the x-axis labels split over two lines. You can also select whether all of the labels appear even if it means that they overlap. When the No overlapping labels check box is selected, the graph only contains the labels that can fit on the graph without the labels overlapping one another. When this check box is cleared, the graph contains every label, which may also mean that the text of one label overlaps another. You can also skip labels by selecting or typing a number in the Skip text box. When the number in this box is greater than

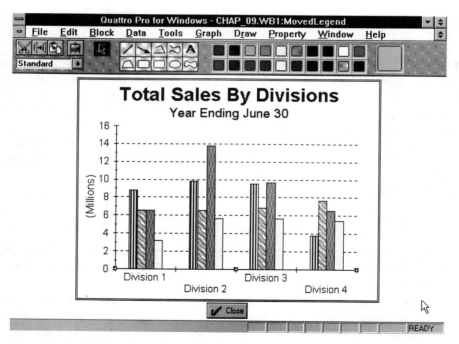

Figure 9.21   Using Two Lines for X-Axis Labels

0, the graph displays the first label and skips the number of labels in this text box before displaying the next label.

When you select OK to apply the property changes, the axis uses the tick marks at the selected locations and adds any restrictions to the axis display that you have added.

ADDING GRID LINES TO A GRAPH The grid marks that Quattro Pro initially puts on a graph for the y-axis are designed to make it easier to estimate the exact values for data in a series. Quattro Pro provides different settings that let you change the appearance of the grid. Quattro Pro initially displays dotted grid lines starting from the major tick marks on the y-axis. Major and minor grid line properties can be set for each axis.

To set the major and minor grid line properties, inspect the properties of the axis and select the Major Grid Style or Minor Grid Style property. For either property, you can select the grid line's color and style. With the Color radio button selected, you can select the grid line's color from the available choices or by creating your own with the sliding bars and text boxes. This is just like selecting a color for text or a box. With the Line style radio button selected, you can select the style of the line that starts from the major or minor tick mark and continues to the opposite side of the graph pane. If you do not want a line from the major or minor tick mark on the axis, select the top left button, which removes any line selection. When you select OK, the axis adopts the line style and color for the major or minor tick marks that you have selected.

Overall Graph Changes

A Graph has two properties that affect every graph type, including text graphs: the aspect ratio, which selects how any graph appears in a graph window, and the grid, which adds or removes a graph grid that is separate from any grid in the graph pane. Neither of these properties affect how a graph appears when you put it on a spreadsheet page, when you print it, or when you include it in a slide show as described in the next chapter. The aspect ratio selects the area of a graph window the graph occupies. Changing the aspect ratio changes the graph's height-to-width ratio. When you change the aspect ratio, you may notice that text that was overlapping no longer does, or that text that fit before now overlaps adjoining graph objects. When you change this property by inspecting the graph window, you can select between Floating Graph, Screen Slide, 35mm Slide, Printer Preview, and Full Extent. Floating Graph displays the graph in the graph window using the same height-to-width ratio as for the graph as it appears on a spreadsheet page. If you change the graph size on the notebook page, the graph in the graph window also changes. Screen Slide shows the graph using the same height-to-width ratio as your screen, since when you run a slide show, the graphs in the slide show fill up the screen. 35mm Slide shows the graph using the same height-to-width ratio as 35mm screens. Printer Preview shows the graph in the window as it will appear when it prints the graph. This is similar to previewing printed data except that you can continue to modify the graph. Since this aspect ratio takes printer settings into account, you may want to use the Page Setup command in the File menu to change the page setup settings just as you changed them for printing spreadsheet data on your notebook pages. Finally, Full Extent displays the graph in the graph window so that it fills the entire window. Figure 9.22 (a through e) shows a sample graph at the different aspect ratios.

The other property you can change is a grid that covers the entire graph. A grid on the graph helps you align objects. You will find this feature especially helpful as you add additional objects as described in the next chapter. You can both display the grid and select whether all objects you move must start at a grid position. To add the grid, inspect the graph window and select the Grid property, and select the Display Grid check box. You can also change its size by adjusting the slider bar or typing a new number in the adjoining text box. This number is the percentage of the graph size. The default of 4% means that there is a grid point at 4% of the width and height and grid points continue over 4% of the graph's size in both directions. If you want all objects you move to start at a grid point, select the Snap to Grid check box. When this check box is selected, when you move an object, it will leap from grid point to grid point, since grid points are the only place it can start. You can clear this box when you no longer want to position objects according to grid points. You can also clear the Display Grid check box when you no longer want the grid points to appear. The grid is for helping you position items on the screen. It never appears anywhere except in a graph window.

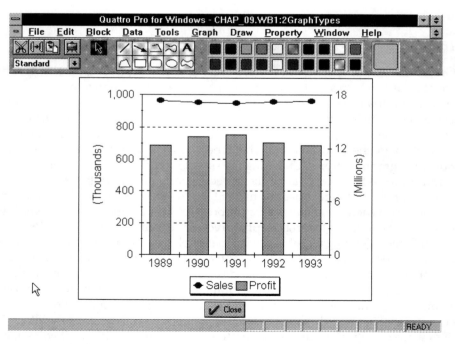

Figure 9.22(a)   One Graph Using Floating Graph Aspect Ratio

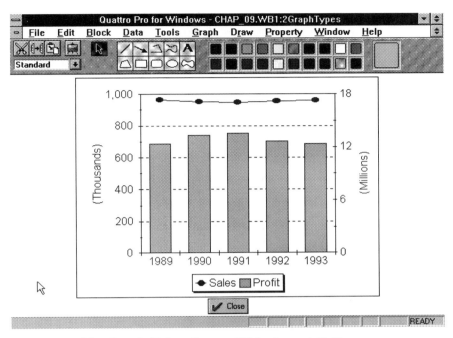

Figure 9.22(b)   Graph Using Screen Slide Aspect Ratio

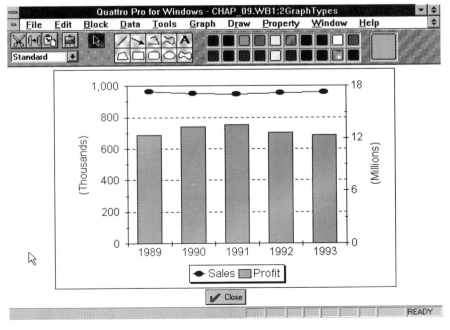

Figure 9.22(c)   Graph Using 35mm Slide Aspect Ratio

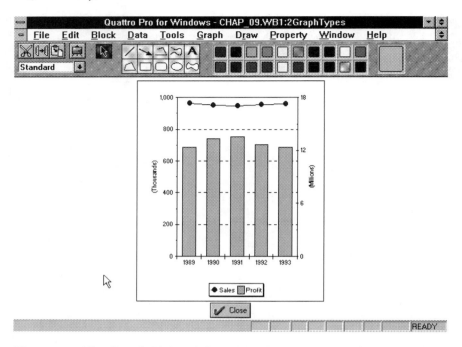

Figure 9.22(d)   Graph Using Printer Preview Aspect Ratio

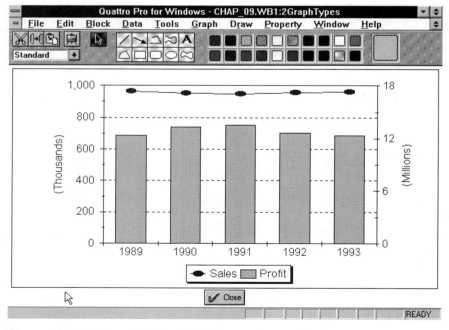

Figure 9.22(e)   Graph Using Full Extent Aspect Ratio

Special Properties of Graph Types

Some of the properties only affect certain graph types. For example, in a line or XY graph, you can select the markers that indicate each data point. Bar graphs, pie and column graphs, and high-low graphs have several features that are specific to those graph types.

LINE AND XY GRAPHS For line and XY graphs, Quattro Pro assigns each series a different marker and connects the markers with a solid line. You can change the symbol and line that represent the data points for each series. To change the markers and lines, use the Line Style, Line Color, and Marker Style properties. To change the appearance of the lines, choose one of the buttons after selecting the Line Style property. If you do not want to connect the data points in a series with a line, select the first line style button. You can set the color for the line by selecting the Line Color property and one of the colors shown, or create your own colors using the radio buttons and slide bars as described for text colors. To change the marker for a series, select a marker's button after selecting the Marker Style property. You can set the size of the markers by entering a new weight in the text box or using the sliding bar next to Weight. The higher the number, the larger the marker. If you do not want to mark the data points with a marker, set the Weight to 0%.

BAR GRAPHS In bar and stacked bar graphs, Quattro Pro uses part of the x-axis for the bars and the remaining part for blank areas between bars. The bars are all the same width. You can change the bar size and how much the bars of one series overlap those of another. These bar graph changes apply to all of the bars in a graph, so you only need to change the Bar Options property for one series and the change will affect the entire graph. Some of these options are not available for all bar graphs, so you may see them dimmed if the current graph type does not use the Bar Option setting.

Quattro Pro initially uses 55% of the x-axis for the bars and 0% of the x-axis for the margins. The margins are the distance between the left and right sides of the graph pane and where the graphed data starts in the pane. You can change the percentage that Quattro Pro uses for the bars and margins by changing the Bar width percentage and Bar margin percentage. To increase the bar width or margins, use the slider bars to change the current percentage or enter the percentage in the adjoining text box.

Another graph property specific to bar graphs is bar overlap. In Figure 9.23, the bars are set to partially overlap by selecting the Partial radio button under Bar overlap options. The default is None, but you can also select Full when you want bars placed one behind the other. Full is usually used when you are using a three-dimensional bar graph.

SPECIAL PIE AND COLUMN GRAPH OPTIONS Many of the graph properties do not affect pie charts or column graphs. Pie and column graphs are very different from line and bar graphs: Only one series of data is graphed by using a

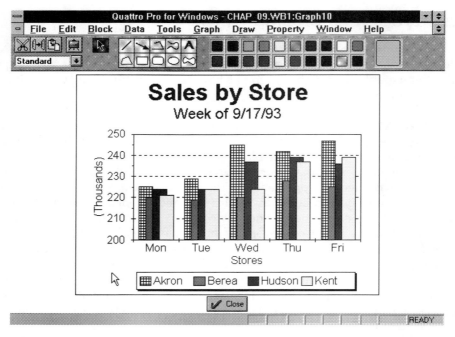

Figure 9.23   Bar Graph with Partially Overlapping Bars

circle or column instead of axes. If you select a multiple column or pie graph type, each series (up to four) has its own column or pie. Also, the x-axis contains the labels that identify each section or slice. If you select a multiple column or pie graph type, each column or pie uses the same values for labeling the sections and slices.

Pie and column graphs have several properties that are unique to these two graph types. They use different properties to select the numeric format of their labels. Also, each value in a pie or column can have its own border and fill properties. You can select the column section or pie slice, inspect its properties, then change the Bkg Color, Border Color, Border Style, Fill Color, and Fill Style properties as described previously. If you select a multiple column or pie graph type, each related section or slice from each column or pie uses the same border and fill properties. Quattro Pro also lets you explode slices of the pie to focus attention on a particular data point.

Formatting Labels   When you first create a pie graph or column graph, Quattro Pro divides the pie into slices or the column into sections. Each slice of the pie or each section of the column represents a value in the series in proportion to the total. Quattro Pro displays the proportion next to the pie slice or column section as a percentage. You can change the format of the proportion by inspecting any column section or pie slice, then selecting the Label Options property. Under Data label, you can then select <u>V</u>alue to show the values as they appear on the spreadsheet; <u>P</u>ercent to show the values as a percentage of the total; <u>C</u>urrency to show the values with a preceding dollar sign and commas inserted; or <u>N</u>one to omit displaying the proportion. The same text properties that change other text in the graph (Text Bkg Color, Text Color, Text Font, and Text Style) will change how the labels and X-axis values appear. While you are inspecting a column or pie graph's Label Options property, you can also alter or select the spreadsheet data to use as the section or slice labels in the <u>L</u>abel Series text box.

Displaying and Hiding Tick Marks   The pie slices and column sections initially have tick marks that connect the labels to the slices or sections. You can remove them. To remove the tick marks, clear the <u>S</u>how Tick check box for the Label Options property. If you decide you want to add them at a later time, select this check box.

Exploding Pie Slices   QuattroPro allows you to explode pieces from a pie, effectively pulling slices out from the rest of the pie graph. This option is not available for column graphs. Exploding a pie slice emphasizes the particular piece. You can explode a pie slice by selecting the slice, inspecting its properties, and with the Explode Slice property selected, select the E<u>x</u>plode check box. Figure 9.24 shows a pie graph with a slice exploded. When you want to return the pie slice to the pie, modify the Explode Slice property and clear the check box. You can also change how far the slice is from the center of the pie with the E<u>x</u>plode distance slider bar and text box. By increasing the value (with the slider bar or by typing a percentage in the text box) you increase the amount all exploded slices are removed from the pie.

HIGH-LOW GRAPHS   A high-low graph is specifically designed for graphing financial commodities. As such it presents its data differently and expects that it is given data in a specific order. A high-low graph assumes the first series contains the high values, and the second series contains the low values. This graph type connects these two data points for each point along the x-axis. If you only provide

---

▼ TIP: Using a Second Series in Pie and Column Graphs from Quattro Pro for DOS

If you are using a graph from a Quattro Pro for DOS spreadsheet, the pie or column graph will continue to use the second series of data as codes setting the pie slice and column section colors and patterns. As soon as you inspect a slice or section in the graph, the graph stops using the second series for colors and patterns.

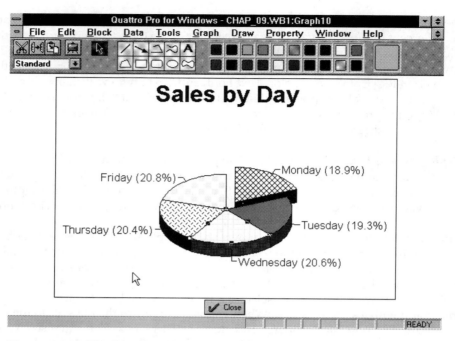

Figure 9.24   Pie Graph with Monday Slice Exploded

three series, the third series should contain the closing values. If you provide four series, the third series should contain opening values and the fourth series should contain closing values. Other series are graphed as line graphs. These additional series are often used to chart volume. You can also override the graph type if you want to display additional series as areas or bars. When you combine high, low, close, and open data with other information in a graph, you usually must adjust the axes so the data does not obscure the first four series. You may also want to assign the series, other than the first four, to the secondary y-axis.

A high-low graph also has a property that applies specifically to this graph type. You can make changes in it by selecting any one of the first four series and inspecting its properties. When you select the Hi-Lo Bar Style property, you can select how the graph connects the high values to the low values for each point along the x-axis. The default of Line draws a plain line from the high to the low value. I-Beam is similar to Line except that it puts horizontal lines at the high and low values so the lines for the high and low values look like a large I. Marker is also like line except that it marks the high, low, open, and close with different markers. Bar draws a bar from the high to low points with lines indicating the open and close values. The bars use the background color only when the close value is higher than the open, and use a diagonally striped fill style when the open value is higher than the close. Figure 9.25 shows a High-Low graph that uses the different colored error bars.

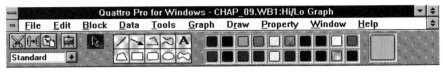

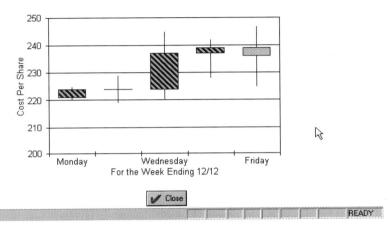

Figure 9.25   A High-Low Graph with Bars and Error Colors

▼ TIP: Changing the Marker Appearance

To change the appearance of markers in a high-low graph, temporarily change the graph type to a line graph, inspect the series property, change the Line Series property to use the marker you want, and then change the graph type back to high-low.

PRINTING A GRAPH

Once you have created a graph, you will want to print it. Printing a graph is as easy as printing spreadsheet data on the pages in your notebooks, because you are using the same commands. Most of the commands you learned about in Chapter 6 to print notebooks also print graphs. You can print graphs independently or as part of a notebook.

When you print a graph independently of a page, you use the same Print command in the File menu to print the graph in the current graph window. You will notice that the Graph Print dialog box is much emptier than the Spreadsheet Print dialog box. It is missing the Options button, the block selection text block, and the selections for choosing which pages to print. From the Graph Print dialog box, you can select Print to print the graph or select P̲review to preview the printed graph. This preview is just like Print Preview from the F̲ile menu. When you preview a graph, you do not have the Options button in the SpeedBar, since the Options button is for printing options that belong specifically to spreadsheet data.

When you have a floating graph in the block you are printing, Quattro Pro automatically prints the graph along with the other notebook data. This means that printing a floating graph is identical to printing a notebook page without a floating graph. You have all of the options available in Chapter 6. Figure 9.26 shows a notebook printed with a floating graph.

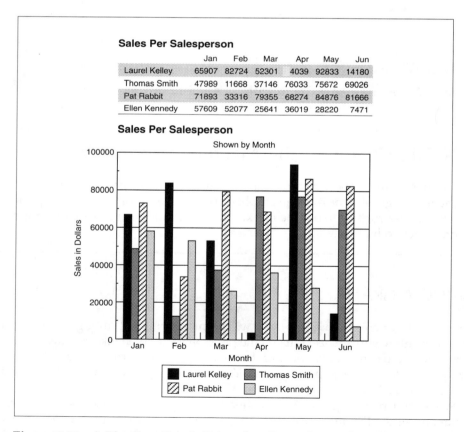

Sales Per Salesperson

	Jan	Feb	Mar	Apr	May	Jun
Laurel Kelley	65907	82724	52301	4039	92833	14180
Thomas Smith	47989	11668	37146	76033	75672	69026
Pat Rabbit	71893	33316	79355	68274	84876	81666
Ellen Kennedy	57609	52077	25641	36019	28220	7471

Figure 9.26　A Floating Graph Printed as Part of a Notebook

GETTING STARTED

In this chapter, you learned how you can create graphs. With the customization options, you learned how you can tailor the graph's appearance. You can try some of your graphic skills by following these steps to create the graph in Figure 9.27.

1. Enter the following data in a new spreadsheet. Notice that years are entered as right justified labels.

   A1: **VaporWrite is Becoming the Market Leader**
   A3: **Units Sold**
   B3: **"1991**
   C3: **"1992**
   D3: **"1993**
   A4: **VaporWrite Products**
   B4: **60000**
   C4: **175000**
   D4: **450000**
   A5: **Leading Competitor**
   B5: **300000**
   C5: **350000**
   D5: **400000**

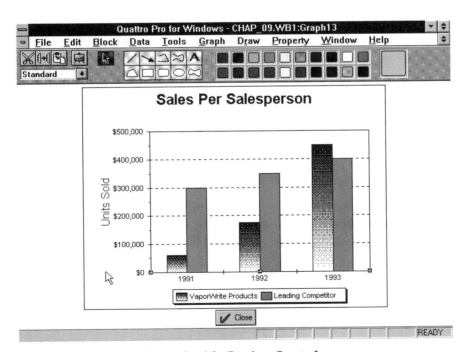

Figure 9.27   Graph Created with Getting Started

2. Expand column A so the text in column A is not clipped. Move to A3. Click the Fit button or inspect this cell's properties, select the Column Width property, select the Auto Width radio button, and select OK.

3. Make a graph with this data. Select the block A3..D5. Select the Graph button and then select the block A6..D18 for the location of the graph. Double-click the graph so that you can change its properties. If you do not want to use a mouse, select the block A3..D5, then select New in the Graph menu, and select OK. Since the block uses more columns (four) than rows (three), Quattro Pro divides the data according to rows. Since row 3 contains the years entered as labels, the years entered as labels becomes the x-axis data. Since column A contains labels, A4 and A5 become the legend text. Quattro Pro divides the remainder of the block into the first and second series according to rows. The graph uses the remaining default graph settings.

4. Add titles to the graph. Select Titles in the Graph menu. Type \A:A1 in the Main Title text box and **Units Sold** in the Y1-Axis Title text box. Select OK to add the titles.

5. Select the legend and inspect its properties. Select the Text Font property and change the point size from 18 to 12. Select OK.

6. Select the main title and inspect its text properties (the pointer looks like an I beam). Select the Text Font property and change the point size from 36 to 24. Select OK.

7. Select the first series (the blue) and inspect its properties. Select the Fill Style property, the Wash radio button, and the fourth wash style button.

8. Select the y-axis and inspect its properties by right clicking the 300000 in the axis. Select the Numeric Format property and the Currency radio button and type **0** in the adjoining text box. Select the Text Font property and change the point size from 18 to 12. Select OK.

9. Select the x-axis and inspect its properties by right clicking the 1992 in the axis. Select the Text Font property and change the point size from 18 to 12. Select OK. Your graph looks like Figure 9.27.

10. Select Window and the number next to the notebook window to return to the notebook window that contains the graph's data and has the graph as a floating graph.

11. Select A1..D18 and then select Print from the File menu. Select the Print button to print the graph.

10

Advanced Graphics

Most of the time when you create graphs for your notebook data, you will use the features you learned about in the last chapter. But Quattro Pro has even more graph features. Several of these features provide graphics capabilities that you would expect from a full featured graphics program rather than from the same package you use for its number processing features. You can draw on a graph to add lines, shapes, and freeform text. You can import and export graphics with Quattro Pro to share the graphs with other applications. You can take the graphs you have created in Quattro Pro and put them into slide shows. Quattro Pro has a light table that simplifies organizing a slide show. You can add transition effects for a professional look when going from one graph to another.

In this chapter, you will learn more about floating graphs. You will also learn about the Graphs page that Quattro Pro uses to store the graphs, slide shows, and dialog boxes that you have in a notebook. Using the Graphs page makes tasks such as renaming, copying, and deleting graphs easy. Besides using the Clipboard to share data with applications, you will also learn about importing and exporting graphics. You will learn how to add graph objects such as lines, shapes, and text, and a special type of text object, a graph button, that can change what Quattro Pro does when you select different parts of the graph. Finally, you will learn about creating slide shows using the wonderful transition effects that Quattro Pro provides.

WORKING WITH FLOATING GRAPHS

In the last chapter, you learned how you can add a graph to a notebook page by adding a floating graph. A floating graph has properties just as cells and graph objects do. You can change the floating graph's properties to change the graph displayed on the floating graph, the border of the floating graph, and the name this object has. Just as when changing other objects in a notebook, you can change

429

the floating graph's properties by right-clicking it. When you inspect the floating graph's properties, the property menu looks like Figure 10.1. If you select Source Graph, you can select an existing graph from the list of available graphs to appear on the floating graph. A floating graph does not belong to a specific graph, so you can freely change the graph displayed on a floating graph without changing the graphs in the notebook. Even when a graph no longer appears on a floating graph, it is still in the notebook, so you can display it using the Edit command in the Graph menu or by using the Graphs page as described later in this chapter.

▼ TIP: The input line tells you how much you are resizing a floating graph.

When you resize a floating graph, you can look in the input line to see how much in each direction the graph is resized. The input line starts with 100% x 100% to represent that the graph is 100% of its original width and height. As you change the floating graph's size, Quattro Pro will change the percentages to match the percentage of the original graph's size.

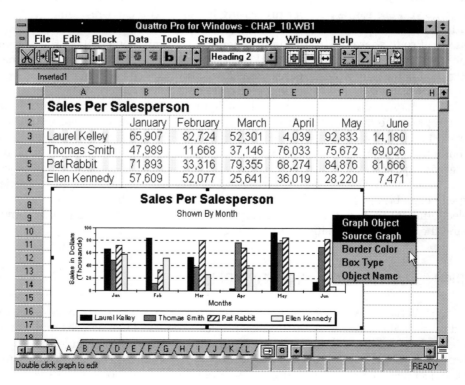

Figure 10.1   Properties for a Floating Graph

The Border Color and Box Type properties let you change the color of the border of the object and the box style of the border. The choices for the border color are the same as for colors of other graph objects. The choices for the box type are the same as those for legends and other objects that can have a frame.

The last property, Object Name, lets you assign a more meaningful name to the floating graph object. Just as graphs have default names, so do floating graphs and other objects you can add to the notebooks. The default name for a floating graph is Inserted#, where # is the next smallest unused number. Floating graph names follow the same rules as block names—they can be up to fifteen characters and cannot contain spaces. After you rename a floating graph, you will notice that its new name appears in the input line when you select the floating graph. You can use floating graph names in macros, as you will learn in Chapter 14.

THE GRAPHS PAGE

In Chapter 1, you learned that every Quattro Pro notebook has a last page called Graphs. This page stores the graphs, slide shows, and dialog boxes that are part of a notebook. You can use this page to organize your graphs, slide shows, and dialog boxes. You can also use this page to select the graphs you want to display in a graph window, to rename graphs, to delete graphs, to copy graphs, and to work with slide shows.

You can go to the Graphs page using the SpeedTab button. The SpeedTab button is the one with the right arrow located to the right of the page name tabs. When you click this button, or press its keyboard equivalent, SHIFT-F5, you switch to the Graphs page. Figure 10.2 shows a sample Graphs page. On this page, every graph, slide show, and custom dialog box in the notebook appears as an icon. If you want to organize the icons on this page, you can drag them to new locations. You can also select Arrange Icons from the Window menu to have Quattro Pro neatly organize them.

You will also notice that the SpeedBar has changed. The Graphs page SpeedBar is different from the one for notebook spreadsheet pages. Besides the three Clipboard buttons that are the same as for spreadsheet pages, the Graphs page SpeedBar also has buttons for creating a new slide show, creating a new graph, creating a dialog box, creating a SpeedBar, rearranging graphs in a slide show, and displaying a slide show. The Graph SpeedBar button that looks just like the Graph button on the Notebook SpeedBar displays the Graph New dialog box that you already know how to use from the previous chapter.

▼ TIP: Display a graph from the Graphs page.

You can display a graph window containing any graph whose icon appears on the Graphs page by double-clicking it. Double-clicking the icon on the Graphs page is the same as choosing the Edit command in the Graph menu.

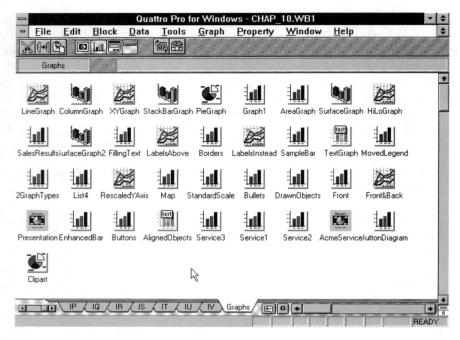

Figure 10.2   Graphs Page

Renaming a Graph

One of the tasks you will perform in the Graphs page is renaming the graphs. For many of the graphs you have created, you probably originally used the default graph name. To rename any graph on the Graphs page, right-click the graph. The only graph property you can change is its name. In the text box below Enter text, type the name for the graph and select OK. Again, graph names follow the same rules as block names—up to fifteen characters with no spaces. You can only rename graphs on the Graphs page.

Deleting a Graph

All of the graphs you create in a notebook remain part of the notebook unless you delete them. Deleting a graph is different from closing its graph window or removing it from a floating graph on a page. Closing a graph window or deleting the floating graph a graph appears on only changes where the graph is displayed. The graph continues to be part of the notebook even if you do not see it. You can delete a graph using the Delete command in the Graph menu or by deleting it on the Graphs page using the Clipboard. When you delete a graph, you are only deleting the graph settings and objects you have added to the graph. Deleting a graph does not change the data the graph uses.

To delete a graph with the <u>D</u>elete command in the <u>G</u>raph menu, select this command and then select the graph name of the graph you want to delete. If the graph appears on a floating graph, the floating graph disappears. If the graph appears in a graph window, the graph window closes. On the Graphs page, the icon for the graph disappears. You can delete a graph this way from any location.

To delete a graph using the Clipboard, you must be on the Graphs page. Then, select the graph icon on the Graphs page and select Cut or Clear from the <u>E</u>dit menu. You can also click the Cut button on the Graphs page SpeedBar. Any graph window or floating graph that displayed the graph also disappears.

COPYING GRAPHS

You will want to use some of the graphs you create as the basis for other graphs. You can copy a graph and then use the copy as the basis for a new graph. You can copy a graph to another graph in the same notebook or to a graph in another notebook. You can also copy parts of graphs to share the same style or data between the graphs.

Copying a Graph to the Same Notebook

When you copy a graph to the same notebook, you can select the parts of the graph you copy to a new graph. You can also copy a graph to another existing graph and have some of the graph's features be replaced by the graph features of the graph you are copying. If you want to copy an entire graph, you may prefer to use the Clipboard instead.

To copy a graph, select the <u>C</u>opy command in the <u>G</u>raph menu. In the <u>F</u>rom list box, select the existing graph you want to copy. If you are in a graph window, pointing to a graph in the Graphs page, or have selected a floating graph, that graph is initially chosen. In the <u>T</u>o drop-down list box, you can either type the name of the graph to copy the selected graph to or display the list box and select one of the existing graphs. You will usually type the destination graph's name when you are creating a new graph with the copy, and select the destination graph from the drop-down list box when the destination graph is an existing graph. The check boxes under Copy choose the parts of the graph that are copied. When <u>S</u>tyle is selected, the graph's properties (which you learned how to change in the last chapter) are copied. The copied information includes the graph type, text fonts, how filled objects are colored, and any series overrides. When <u>D</u>ata is selected, the data referenced as data points for each series, x-axis labels, legend text, legend label overrides, data point labels, axis titles, and graph titles are copied. Since you are copying the reference to the data and not the data itself, the data remains in the same location. When <u>A</u>nnotate objects is selected, the drawn objects are copied. The drawn objects include lines, texts, and shapes you have added to the graph as described later in the chapter. When the two graphs and the check boxes you want are selected, select OK to copy the graph.

Suppose you have the text graph shown in Figure 10.3. When you are presenting this graph as part of a slide show, you may want the four agenda items added one by one so the graph changes to match your discussion. To do this, you would create the final graph, like the one shown in Figure 10.3. Then you would make as many copies of the graph as you have points in the list. Then you would delete an increasing number of items from preceding lists. This means that if you have the graphs LIST1, LIST2, LIST3, and LIST4, LIST1 has only one bulleted item, LIST2 has two bulleted items (with the two subpoints below the second), LIST3 has three bulleted items, and LIST4 has four bulleted items. When you put the graphs into a slide show, the bulleted items are added one at a time.

Copying a Graph with the Clipboard

You can copy a graph with the Clipboard just as you use it to copy other sorts of data. When you copy a graph to the Clipboard, you can paste it to another location in the same notebook, another notebook, or another application.

To copy a graph to the Clipboard, you must first select the graph. If the graph readily appears as a floating graph or as an icon on the Graphs page, you can select it by clicking it. If the graph appears in a graph window, you have the option of selecting just the graph without any drawn objects or selecting drawn objects as

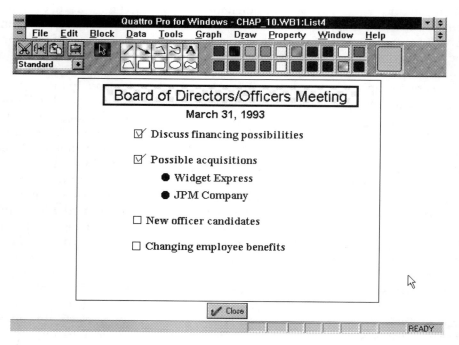

Figure 10.3   Bulleted List Text Graph

▼ TIP: Copy a graph's style and annotation when you want several graphs to have the same style.

You can use a graph's style as a template for other graphs in a notebook. To apply one graph's style to other graphs, copy the graph to the other existing graphs with the Data check box cleared. The destination graph will continue to use the same data as before, but the style will match the graph style of the graph you have copied.

well as the graph to be copied. To select just the graph without any drawn objects, hold down the CTRL key while you click the graph's background. If you want to add any drawn objects as well, release the CTRL key and hold down SHIFT while you click each of the drawn objects you want to add to the selection. The selected drawn objects are marked with handles.

Once the graph you want to copy is selected, you can select Copy in the Edit menu or click the Copy button in the SpeedBar. With the graph on the Clipboard, you can switch to the location where you want the graph copied. Usually you will switch to the Graphs page of the notebook where you want the graph copied or go to the page where you want the graph pasted in a floating graph. Next, select Paste in the Edit menu or click the Paste button in the SpeedBar. The graph you have just copied has the graph name of the source file followed by a number. For example, if the source graph was **Test**, the copy created has the name **Test1**. The copy of the graph refers to the same notebook data as the original graph. If you copy a graph to another notebook, the copy of the graph continues to refer to the original graph's data. You may thus need to change the data the graph uses after you copy it.

COPYING A GRAPH TO ANOTHER APPLICATION Copying a graph to another application is just like copying a graph to another notebook. First, you put the graph on the Clipboard and then switch to the application where you want the graph. Then, assuming the application can accept graphical information from the Clipboard, select Paste from the application's Edit menu. Some applications can accept the Quattro Pro graph in more than one format, so if your application has a command such as Paste Special in the Edit menu, you can try the different formats in which the application can use the Clipboard information. Usually, when you copy a graph from the Clipboard to another application, the data is a picture of the image rather than a link to the graph; if the graph changes, you must again copy the graph to the application's data file. Figure 10.4 shows a Quattro Pro graph copied to a Windows' Cardfile document using the Clipboard. This graph is created using the grid, so you are sure you are drawing straight lines.

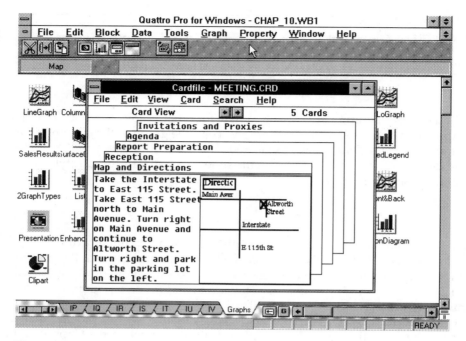

Figure 10.4   Quattro Pro Graph Put in Another Application

DRAWING ON THE GRAPH

Most of the basic graph features are provided automatically based on the selected graph type. You can add drawn objects to any of your graphs as in Figure 10.5, or use drawn objects to create the entire graph as in the map in Figure 10.4. Drawing on a graph is free-form graphics manipulation, so you can draw and reposition any object in a graph. An object can be text, a shape, a line, or an image stored in a file. Drawing on a graph provides the ultimate in graphics manipulation, since there are few restrictions on what you add to the graph or where you put it. Text graphs often use drawn objects, since they provide an empty screen that you can fill with drawn objects. Unlike Quattro Pro for DOS, Quattro Pro for Windows makes drawing on a graph immediately available. You add drawn objects using the buttons in the graph window SpeedBar.

Drawing on a graph is different from drawing in packages like Windows' Paintbrush. In Windows' Paintbrush, everything is stored as a collection of dots. In Quattro Pro, drawings are remembered as objects. This means you can easily resize objects in Quattro Pro and put one object on top of another without losing the information behind the object in front. The drawn objects in a graph are layered on top of one another. For example, if you add text in the middle of a graph, that text is on top of whatever else is in that location. When you select an object, Quattro Pro moves the object to the top, just as selecting a window places that window on top of other windows.

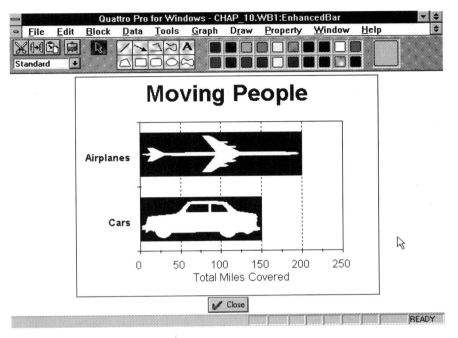

Figure 10.5 Bar Graph Enhanced with Drawn Objects

▼ TIP: Set the aspect ratio before you start drawing on the graph.

Since a drawn object can change as you change the aspect ratio, select the aspect ratio appropriate for what you want to do with the graph before drawing. For example, if you will be using the graph in a floating graph, use the floating graph aspect ratio; if you are using the graph in a slide show, use the slide show aspect ratio, and if you will print the graph from the graph window, select the print preview aspect ratio. Remember, the aspect ratio is changed by inspecting the graph window's properties (right click the area around the graph or select Graph Window from the Property menu). If you wait until after drawing on the graph to change the aspect ratio, you may need to modify many of the objects you have drawn.

Adding Drawn Objects to a Graph

Each of the drawn object types that you can add to a graph appears in one of the SpeedBar buttons that you can select to draw it. These Quattro Pro objects, shown in Figure 10.6, are the following:

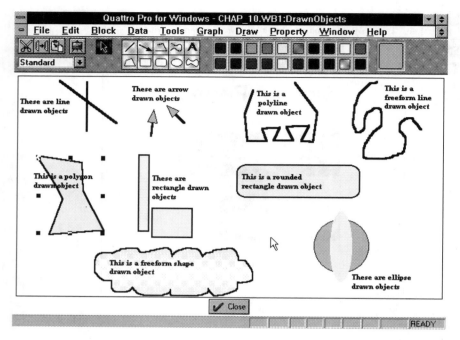

Figure 10.6   Sample Objects You Can Draw

- Line—A line object adds a straight line in any direction with any thickness. You can use lines to connect objects in a graph as well as to separate portions of the graph. You can control the color and style of the line.

- Arrow—An arrow object is a line with an arrowhead on one end. Arrows emphasize other objects in a graph. You can customize the arrow's line appearance and how the arrowhead is filled.

- Polyline—A polyline object consists of several connected lines. Use polyline objects for drawing lines that connect without breaks. You can change the color or style of the line.

- Freeform Line—A freeform line object draws a line wherever you drag the mouse across the graph. Use freeform lines to draw curved lines and lines that are in unusual shapes. You can change the color and style of the line.

- Text—A text object contains text surrounded by an optional box. A text object is used for adding text to describe and explain the graph. In a text graph, it can be used to create opening slides, flow charts, or organization charts. Text objects have the same customization options as other graph objects containing text, such as graph titles. You can also use a text object as a graph button that will display another graph or perform a macro when selected.

- Polygon—A polygon object is a closed shape created by connecting lines. When you draw a polygon, you select each endpoint of the shape you are creating. You can select the line style of the shape's border and how the shape is filled.

- Rectangle—Use a rectangle object to create a rectangle or square by selecting two opposite corners. A square is a special type of rectangle, since its height and width are the same. You can add rectangles to frame other drawn objects. You can select the line style and color of the rectangle's border as well as how the rectangle is filled.

- Rounded Rectangle—A rounded rectangle object is identical to a rectangle object except that the corners are curved. You create a rounded rectangle like a rectangle, by selecting two opposite corners. You can customize its border color, style, and how it is filled.

- Ellipse—An ellipse object creates a circle or ellipse by the selection of two opposite corners that create a box for the ellipse or circle to fill. A circle is a special type of ellipse, since a circle's height and width are the same. Use an ellipse object to draw a circle or ellipse that is part of a drawing (such as a logo) or an area in which you can add text. You can select the ellipse's border color and line style, as well as how the ellipse is filled.

- Freeform Shape—A freeform shape object draws a closed shape wherever you drag the mouse across the graph surface. Use freeform shapes to draw shapes that you cannot draw with the other tools. You can change the color and style of the shape's border as well as how the shape is filled.

- Clip art—Clip art is a collection of different graphic objects stored in files. Clip art provides ready-made images in popular shapes. When you need a drawing of something, using clip art instead of drawing it yourself is a great timesaver. Quattro Pro provides several pieces of clip art, such as several business people, a truck, a snowflake, and a computer. Since you bring in clip art by importing it, you will learn about using clip art with importing graphics later in this chapter. Clip art has the same customization options as other drawn objects.

▼ TIP: Use a grid to draw vertical and horizontal lines as well as circles and ellipses.

You can make drawing straight lines easier by displaying the graph's underlying grid. Add the grid by changing the graph window's properties and selecting the <u>D</u>isplay Grid check box with the Grid property selected. You may also want to select the <u>S</u>nap to Grid check box so that as you draw objects, they always start at the nearest grid point.

ADDING AN OBJECT   To add an object, select the SpeedBar button for the object you want to add, set the object's color, then tell Quattro where you want to put the object in the graph. When adding text, you also must supply the text you want to add. To add objects, follow these steps:

1.   Click the SpeedBar button for the object type you want to add.
2.   Click the color you want the object to be from the color palette.
3.   Point to where you want the object to begin in the drawing area.
4.   Draw the object. The process for drawing an object depends on the object you are drawing:

   - Line—Drag the pointer from the beginning point of the line to the end.
   - Arrow—Drag the pointer from the beginning point of the line to the end.
   - Polyline—Click the beginning point of the line and then click the subsequent end points of each part of the polyline. When you are ready to select the last point of the polyline, double-click it.
   - Freeform Line—Drag the pointer to indicate where you want the line drawn. Release the mouse when you are finished drawing the line.
   - Text—You have two choices. You can click where you want the text to start and type the text to let Quattro Pro handle selecting the size of the box that contains this text object. You can also drag the pointer from where you want the text object to start to where you want it to end and *then* type the text. This second alternative sets the box for the text to the size you select. You can later change the size of the text's box regardless of the method you choose. Press ENTER when you want to force the text to start on a new line.
   - Polygon—Click each corner of each line that creates the shape. When you have selected the last corner of the polygon, double-click the mouse. Quattro Pro handles drawing a line from the first point you have selected to the last.
   - Rectangle—Drag the pointer from one corner of the rectangle to the opposite corner.
   - Rounded Rectangle—Drag the pointer from one corner of the rectangle to the opposite corner.
   - Ellipse—Drag the pointer from one corner of a rectangle to the opposite corner. The ellipse will fill the selected rectangle.
   - Freeform Shape—Drag the pointer to indicate where you want the border of the shape. When you release the mouse, Quattro Pro draws a line from the beginning of the line you have drawn to the end to close the line into a shape.

5.   Add more of the same types of objects by repeating steps 3 and 4. You can change the color by selecting another color in the palette or change the object you are adding by selecting another SpeedBar button.

Special Text Object Features   Text objects have two special features that do not apply to other graphs. You can add bullets to text as in Figure 10.3. You can also change the alignment and word wrapping of the text within its box. As with the

---

▼ TIP: Use the Clipboard to copy different parts of a graph.

Another method of adding a drawn object of a type you have already produced is to select one of the objects you have added and copy it to the Clipboard. When you subsequently paste it back to the graph, the copy is placed in the upper left corner and is the currently selected object. You can also use the Clipboard to copy drawn objects from one graph to another or between graphs on different notebooks.

---

objects containing text that you learned about in the last chapter, you can inspect the text or its box's properties separately. A special feature of adding text objects allows you to inspect the text's button in the SpeedBar to change both the text and the text box's properties at once. These property changes apply to all text objects in the graph you subsequently add.

You can add bullet characters to text objects in your graphs for emphasis as shown in Figure 10.3. To add a bullet character to a text object, enter **\bullet #\,** where the # symbol is a number between 0 and 8. Each number represents a different bullet character as shown in Figure 10.7. When you type **\bullet #**, you

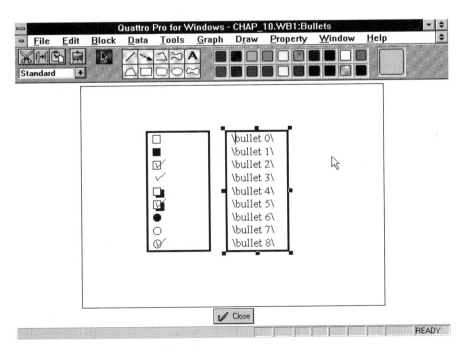

Figure 10.7   Sample Bullet Characters

will not initially see the bullet character. As soon as the text object is no longer selected, the \bullet #\ is replaced by the bullet character. Bullet characters are often used in text graphs to create bulleted lists like the one shown in Figure 10.3.

Text alignment changes are made to the Alignment property for the text object's box (not the text). Text objects can be left-aligned, centered, or right-aligned in their boxes just as cell entries can be left-aligned, centered, or right-aligned in their cells. With the Alignment property selected, you can select the button to left-align, center, or right-align the text in the box. You will also notice that the Wordwrap check box is selected. When this box is selected, the text that does not fit in the box's current width advances to the next line and the text object expands downward. If you want to control what text appears on each line, clear this box and create line breaks by pressing ENTER at the end of each text line. As you add text to a text object that has this check box cleared, the text box will expand to the right instead of downward. Of course, the box will also continue to expand downward if you keep pressing ENTER. Finally, for text objects, you can select the distance between tab stops. The default is .5", but you can enter a different number in the Tab stops every text box.

You can right-click the text button in the SpeedBar and set the text object's properties before you add the text object to the graph. When you right-click the text button in the SpeedBar, the dialog box contains the properties for both the text and the box around the text. The properties you select continue to apply to the text objects you subsequently add to the graph.

Changing Drawn Objects in a Graph

Although adding objects lets you create graphs with unlimited possibilities, you probably do not always draw the objects the way you want the first time. You may want to change their color, position, or size, or remove them altogether.

▼ TIP: Use the Clipboard to add text to a text object.

If you have text in a Quattro Pro cell that you want to use as the text in the text object, you can copy the text using the Clipboard. First, copy the cell or the section of its contents that you want to use to the Clipboard. Next, switch to the graph, select the text object, move the insertion point to where you want the text added, and press SHIFT-INS or click the Paste button in the SpeedBar. If the text is from another application, select the text to use from the application and copy it onto the Clipboard using the command the application has for that feature.

CHANGING AN OBJECT'S ATTRIBUTES   The drawn objects have properties just as other graph objects do. You may not remember to set the properties for an object before you create it, or you may change your mind and want different properties. You can right-click the graph object or select the graph object, and use the Current Object command in the Property menu. When the dialog box for the object's properties appears, you can make changes. These are the same properties that you learned how to change for other types of graph objects in the last chapter. Text objects contain the same properties as graph titles. Lines, polylines, freeform lines, and arrows can have the style and color of the line changed. Rectangle, rounded rectangles, ellipses, polygons, and freeform shapes can have their border style and color style changed. These objects also have the same fill options described for other filled shapes in the last chapter. Text boxes also have an Alignment property described earlier, and a Graph Button property described later in this chapter.

   If you want to change the attributes for more than one object, you must select the objects you want to use. To select additional objects, hold down SHIFT while you click the additional objects you want to select. Later, you will learn how to create groups of objects. The properties of a group of objects include only those properties that all the objects in the group have in common.

MOVING AN OBJECT   Moving a drawn object is just like moving any object in a graph. To move an object, select it, then drag the object to where you want it moved. If you select several objects to move, you can drag one of the selected objects and all of the selected objects are moved to the new location.

REMOVING AN OBJECT   If the drawn object you added is not what you want, you can remove it. To remove an object, select it and use the Cut or Clear command in the Edit menu or click the Cut button on the SpeedBar. You will not delete the graph, because only the single object is selected; you cannot delete a graph from a graph window this way.

RESIZING AN OBJECT   When you rearrange a graph, you may want to change the size of objects. To change the size of an object, select the object and then point to one of the handles so the pointer looks like a cross. Now, drag the handle to a

---

▼ TIP: Use resizing to flip an object.

If you want to make a mirror image of an object, resize it so the corner you are dragging is on the opposite side of the shape. For example, if you want to flip a polygon and you are using the object's lower right handle, drag the handle so it is left of the object's lower left handle. When you release the mouse, the object is flipped. This feature does not work for text.

new location. The object's outline will change as you move the handle. If you have several objects selected, you can resize one of the selected objects and all of the selected objects are proportionally resized. Since one corner of the object remains in the same position, resizing multiple objects changes their relative distance from each other. Changing the size of a text object only changes the size of the box that the text is placed in. To change the text size, you must inspect its properties. When you change the size of a polyline, freehand polyline, polygon, or freehand polygon, you are changing the overall size rather than the individual points of the polyline, freehand polyline, polygon or freehand polygon.

ALIGNING OBJECTS   Besides moving an object by dragging it, you can also have Quattro Pro move the object for you when you want to align it with other objects. To align objects with each other, select the different objects you want aligned. Next, select <u>A</u>lign in the D<u>r</u>aw menu and select the menu choice that describes how you want the objects aligned. Figure 10.8 shows the different alignment options applied to groups of text objects and to groups of two circles.

CHANGING THE LAYER OF AN OBJECT   When you add objects to a graph, they are layered in the order they are added. You can think of layers in a graph as transparencies, each holding a graph object. By putting the transparencies on top of one another, you create the overall graph. You can change the layer of an object,

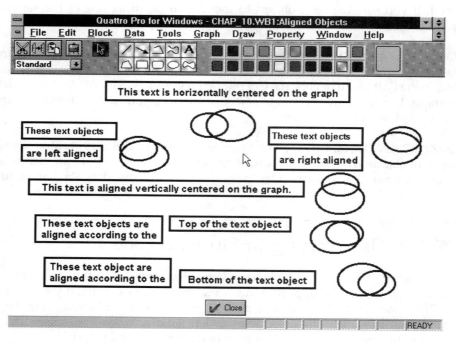

Figure 10.8   Different Alignment Options

or a set of objects, which is like rearranging the pile of transparencies on the graph. When you move objects to the top or bottom, the other objects are adjusted to reflect the changed object's layer. To move objects to the top, select the objects, then select Bring to Front from the Draw menu. You may want to do this when one object is blocking the display of another object, as in Figure 10.9. If you select the object and select Bring to Front from the Draw menu, the display looks like Figure 10.10. If you only want to move an object by one layer, you can select Bring Forward from the Draw menu.

You can also move objects to a previous layer. To move objects to the bottom layer, select the objects then select Send to Back from the Draw menu. The objects become the bottom layers of the graph, and the remaining objects are placed above them. If you only want to move an object backward by one layer, you can select Send Backward from the Draw menu. You will want to move an object to the back when you are using it as a backdrop for other objects.

PUTTING AN OBJECT IN A GROUP   The objects that you put on a graph can be treated as a group. Once graph objects are put into a group, they are moved and sized as a unit, and property changes are made to all group objects at once. Putting objects in a group when a graph has many drawn objects prevents you from modifying the wrong object. To put objects in a group, select all of the objects you

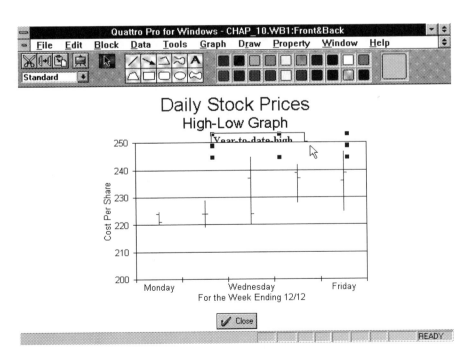

Figure 10.9   Graph with an Object behind Another

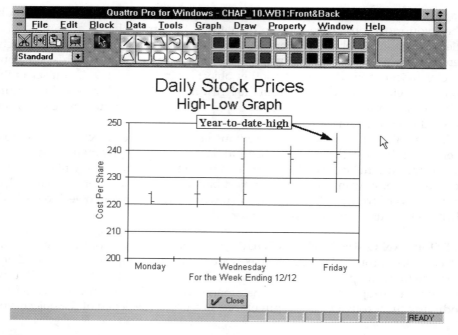

Figure 10.10   Graph after Moving Object to the Top

want as part of the group by clicking each one as you hold down the SHIFT key. Next, select Group from the Draw menu. Now, when you select any object in the group, you are selecting the entire group. You will notice how instead of each object in the group having its own handles, the group has the handles. When you move or resize the group, the objects are moved or resized as a unit. When you inspect the group's properties, you can change only the properties that are common to all objects in the group. The "year-to-date-high" box and arrow in Figure 10.10 are an example of a group. You can move the box and arrow together as the data point they refer to changes.

When you want to work with the individual objects within a group, you must ungroup the grouped objects. To ungroup a group of objects, select the group and then select Ungroup from the Draw menu. Now instead of the group having one set of handles, each object within the group has its own set of handles. At this point, the objects in the group are individually selectable.

You can have one group within another. This means that you can put the group containing the arrow and box from Figure 10.10 in a group with other objects. To create this larger group, the text box and arrow can only be selected as part of the larger group. After this larger group is created, when you ungroup the larger group, the group containing the text and arrow are still in a group, since you must ungroup these grouped objects separately.

THE GRAPH COLOR PALETTE

The graphs you create can use many colors. The right half of the graph window SpeedBar contains the graph's palette. You can use this palette to change the color of the objects in your graph by selecting them and then selecting the color you want for them in the palette. When you change the color of an object with the palette, you change the fill style, fill color, background color, border style, and border color. You are not limited to the twenty colors displayed in one palette. You can change between the nine color palettes Quattro Pro supplies, or you can create your own pallette. You can change the color of a graph object whenever you wish by inspecting its properties. The advantage of using the palette is that you have a set of colors that looks good next to each other. You also ensure that different objects have the same color without having to remember the values you used for the slider bars when you set the objects' colors by inspecting their properties.

To change the current color palette to one of the predefined color palettes, select the palette drop-down list box, which is the drop-down list box below the three buttons for the Clipboard. When you select one of the palette names from the list, the colors in the palette change, but the colors already selected in the graphs do not.

To create a color palette, you can start by selecting the predefined palette closest to providing the colors you want. Next, for each color you want to change, right-click the color as if you are inspecting the properties of a drawn object. For each color in the palette, you can select the fill style, fill color, background color, border style, and border color. As soon as you change the first color in the palette, you will notice that the palette name in the palette drop-down list box has changed to *new*, the name of the palette until you give it a new name. When you have changed all of the colors you want and you are ready to give a better name to this palette, select <Edit> from the palette drop-down list box. In the Edit Palettes dialog box, you can replace the *new* with a more descriptive name and then select New to assign a name to the palette you have just created. Later, when you have a palette you want to delete, select <Edit> from the palette drop-down list box, the name of the palette from the list box, and Delete. If you later make changes to a palette, you can update the palette by selecting <Edit> from the palette drop-down list box, the name of the palette from the list box, and Replace. When you change a custom palette, Quattro Pro changes the name of the palette to *new* again, so you need to reselect the previous name under which you saved the palette in the list box.

Importing and Exporting Graphics

Quattro Pro lets you store the image of a graph in a file. You can use this graphics file in different graphs or in different applications. You may have a company logo that you want to appear at the top of many graphs. If you store the logo, you only have to draw it once and it is then available for use in any graph as well as in other applications that can use the graphics file. In addition, Quattro Pro can use graphics files created by itself or other applications in its graphs.

Exporting a Graph

When you export a graph, you are putting the image of how the graph looks at that moment into a file. You can store the graph's image into one of six different graphic file formats. If you are exporting a graph that you will want to include in other graphs, such as a logo or drawing, you want the objects in the graph to remain in the same relative position on the graph when they are imported, usually in the upper left corner. You can use the graphics file you create to incorporate Quattro Pro graphs into documents in other applications, such as your favorite word processor.

To export a graph into a graphics file, select Export from the Draw menu. The Export graphics file dialog box lets you enter the name of the file and select where the file will be stored. Under File Types, you select the extension, which determines the format the file is stored in. You have the choices of .BMP for Windows Bitmap, .CGM for Computer Graphics Metafile, .EPS for PostScript's encapsulated file format, .GIF for Compuserve's picture format, .PCX for Windows Paintbrush, and .TIF for TIFF (Tagged Image Format File). If you select .BMP for the file type, you can also select the Bitmap gray scale check box if you want the colors in the graph converted to gray scales. Select this check box when you will print the graphic file in another application that does not convert the colors into gray scales. If you select .TIF for the file type, you can select None or PackBits, for how the TIF file is compressed. If the application you will use the graphics file in can use PackBits compression for TIFF data, select the PackBits radio button. Otherwise, select None, which causes the TIF files to be larger. When you have entered the file name and location, as well as its file type, you can select OK to store the graph in a graphics file. Once the graph is exported into a graphics file, any application that accepts the selected file type can import the graph. Figure 10.11 shows the graph in a TIFF format file added to a Word for Windows document.

▼ TIP: Use the Clipboard to copy a graph between Windows applications.

Most of the time, when you want to put a graph from Quattro Pro into another Windows application, you can use the Clipboard to copy it to its location instead. You can copy the graph to the Clipboard, switch applications, and paste the graph from the Clipboard to the application. This is usually quicker and provides better results than importing and exporting graphics.

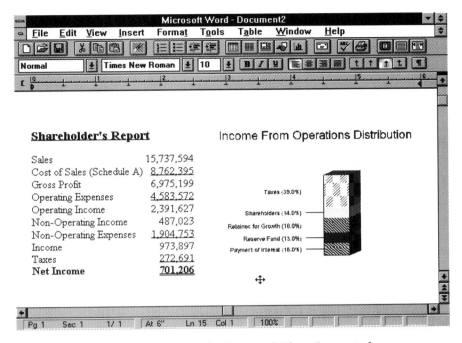

Figure 10.11   Quattro Pro Graph Exported Then Imported

Importing a Graphics File

Just as you can take a graph and put it into a graphics file, you can take a graphics file and put it into a graph. Depending on the format of the graphics file, you are either importing a group that contains the drawn graph objects, adding a large box that is filled with the contents of the graphics file and which can be modified like other drawn objects, or a large box containing the contents of the graphics file, which cannot be modified in any way. Some formats that you can import provide different options for editing the graphics file you import.

To import a graphics file into a graph, select Import from the Draw menu or select the Import button on the SpeedBar, which is the one that looks like the painting on the easel. The Import graphics file dialog box lets you select the file to import by selecting its location and type. Under File Types, you can see the different file formats that you can import. You have the choices of .BMP for Windows Bitmap, .CGM for Computer Graphics Metafile, .CLP for Quattro Pro for DOS art, .EPS for PostScript's encapsulated file format, .GIF for Compuserve's picture format, .PCX for Windows Paintbrush, .PIC for Lotus's graph files, and .TIF for TIFF (Tagged Image Format File). When you select the file to import and OK, the selected graphics file is imported.

A graphics file is imported in three ways. One method is to add a large rectangle with the contents of the graphics file as the fill style. This is often used when you want to use the graphic as a backdrop to another graph. BMP, GIF, EPS, PCX, and TIF files are imported this way. When a graphics file is imported this way, you cannot ungroup its elements. If you want to change the graphic, you must modify the original graphic that you used to create the graphics file you imported. If you inspect the rectangle's properties, you will notice that the fill style property has Bitmap selected with the name of the imported file in the File name text box. This is just like filling in any box with a bitmapped graphic, as you learned about in the last chapter. You may want to try the two radio buttons at the top of the dialog box. When Crop to fit is selected, only the part of the graphic that naturally fits in the box displays. Use this radio button when you want only the part of the graphic file that is in the upper left corner to appear. Changing the rectangle's size when the Crop to fit radio button is selected changes how much of the graphics file appears in the rectangle. You cannot change the size of the graphic within the rectangle. The other option is to select the Shrink to fit radio button. This radio button tells Quattro Pro to expand or contract the graphic in the graphics file to fit the rectangle's size. Use this radio button when you want to see all of the graphic image in the file. As you change the size of the rectangle the graphic appears in, you are also changing the size of the graphic in the rectangle.

The second way a graphics file can be imported is as a group of drawn objects. When a graphics file is imported this way, you can modify the drawn objects in the graphic. CGM and CLP files are imported this way. You can ungroup the objects in the imported file and then subsequently modify the objects in the group. Since the different parts of the graphic are separate objects, you can select each one and modify its properties. Text objects are split into separate objects for each word in the group. Quattro Pro provides several clip art images that you can incorporate into your graphs. Figure 10.12 shows a graph using some of Quattro Pro's clip art.

The final way a graphic file can be imported into Quattro Pro is as an unmodifiable object. This object is part of a rectangle. You can move and size the object but you cannot change its properties. PIC files work this way.

▼ TIP: Try different graphic file formats when you share graphics between applications.

When the graphic you want to put into a Quattro Pro graph can be saved in several formats, try the different formats the two applications share in common. Trying the different formats as well as the Crop to fit and Shrink to fit radio buttons lets you find the combination of graph formats and fill formats that work best for the graphics.

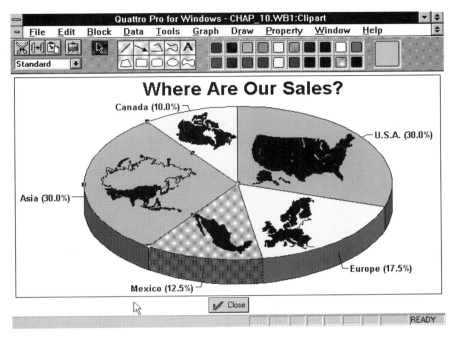

Figure 10.12   Graph Using Quattro Pro Clip Art

SLIDE SHOWS

One wonderful feature of Quattro Pro allows you to create slide shows out of the graphs you have created. Slide shows show each graph you select for a limited time or until you press a key. Quattro Pro has many transition effects so you can make your slide show look as if it was done by a professional. These slide shows make Quattro Pro's graphics features resemble more expensive graphics programs.

A slide show is created by adding an empty slide show to your Graphs page and then adding the graphs that you want to be part of the slide show. Once the graphs are added, you can rearrange them in the slide show and add transition effects. You can run your easily designed slide show and see it appear as if you had hired a professional to create it for you. Creating graphs requires a mouse, although you can run a slide show without one.

Creating a Slide Show

Quattro Pro makes creating a slide show so easy you can do it without even remembering how. Creating a slide show is as easy as going to the Graphs page, selecting the Create Slide Show button in the SpeedBar, typing a name, and

▼ TIP: You can create and run a temporary
           slide show.

If you want to create a temporary slide show, you can select the graphs you
want to see in order. (Hold down SHIFT while you select the graphs after the
first one). Then, select View from the Graph menu or press F11. This displays
the graphs in the order you selected them and displays each one until you
press a key or click the mouse.

selecting OK. (The Create Slide Show button is the fourth button and looks like a
pie graph on a 35 mm slide.) The slide show name that you enter must follow the
rules of block names and graph names—up to fifteen characters with no spaces. As
soon as you select OK, Quattro Pro adds a slide show icon to your Graphs page.
Now, you are ready to add the graphs that you want to be in your slide show.

ADDING GRAPHS TO A SLIDE SHOW   Once you have a slide show, you can
start adding graphs to it. To add a graph to a slide show, select the graph you want
to add on the Graphs page. Next, drag the icon for the graph to be on top of the
icon for the slide show. When you do this, the slide show icon changes color as if
it is selected. When the slide show icon is highlighted, you can release the graph
icon and the graph is added to the slide show. You can repeat this for each graph
you want to add to a slide show. Another method is to select several graphs by
holding down SHIFT while you select the graphs. Then drag and drop one of the
selected graph icons to the slide show icon and all of the selected graphs will be
added to the slide show. The graphs will initially display in the slide show in the
order you added them. If you are selecting many graphs to add to the slide show,
you can select them in the order they will appear.

PREPARING THE SLIDE SHOW   Once you create the slide show and add the
graphs that will appear in it, you can arrange how the slide show is presented. You

▼ TIP: Drag a box around all of the graphs
           you want to add.

A quick method of selecting several graphs on a Graphs page is to drag a box
to cover the graphs you want selected. All of the graphs in the box you draw
are selected. If you use this method to select graphs to add to a slide show,
they are ordered by the sequence in which they appear on the Graphs page.
You can always rearrange them by displaying the slide show's light table.

can change the order of the graphs in the slide show, add transition effects, and set how long a graph appears. This arrangement process is done on a *light table*. To display the light table for a slide show, double-click the slide show icon. You can also display the slide show's light table by selecting the slide show and selecting the Edit Slide Show button on the SpeedBar, which is the eighth button. Figure 10.13 shows an example of a light table. In the main part of the window are small versions of the graphs in the slide show. In the bottom of the window are the selections for adding transition effects and speeds.

Initially, the graphs in the slide show appear in the order you added them. To change where a graph appears in the slide show, click the graph to select it and then drag it to where you want it. When you release the mouse, the slides are rearranged. If you have a slide you accidentally included or want to remove, select the slide and then press DEL.

The remaining features about the graphs in a slide show, time of display and transition effect, are assigned for each graph individually. As you select the different graphs in the top of the light table, the time display and transition effects will change to match the settings you have made for the selected graphs. Initially all of the graphs have 0 in the Display time text box. The Display time text box sets how long each graph displays as part of the slide show. When the display time is 0, the graph displays until you press a key or click the mouse. You can enter the number of seconds (from 1 to 3600) for how long you want the graph to appear.

The remaining options in the light table set how the slide show makes the

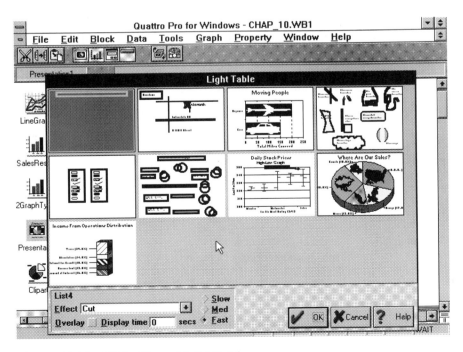

Figure 10.13   Slide Show Light Table

transition from one slide to another. The default setting is to cut quickly from one slide to the next. Quattro Pro has 30 transition effects. These effects and a brief description are listed in Table 10.1. Some of the transitions can be done at different speeds. You can set how quickly these transition effects take place by selecting the Slow, Med, or Fast radio buttons. The difference in speed between these buttons depends on the transition effect selected. Some video adapters cannot use all of Quattro Pro's transition effects.

The last transition effect you can change is whether the replacement graph appears on top of the graph you are switching from. When the Overlay check box is selected, the graph you are changing is put on top of the previously displayed graph. When this check box is cleared, the previous graph is completely removed from the screen as the new one is displayed. Most of the time you will want the check box cleared. An example of when you want this check box selected is when displaying a bulleted list. Figure 10.14 shows a bulleted list after all of the graphs that are part of the slide show are displayed. The overlapping graphs allow you to display each subsequent item in the bulleted list in a different color as it is introduced. You can do this when you are discussing the items one at a time and you want the one you are presenting to have a different appearance.

Table 10.1   Quattro Pro Transition Effects

Transition Effect	Description
Cut	Switch instantaneously to the next graph
Fade out/fade in	Fade old graph out to black, then fade new one in
Wipe right	Wipe new graph on and old one off from left to right
Wipe left	Wipe new graph on and old one off from right to left
Wipe down	Replace new graph from the top to the bottom
Wipe up	Replace new graph from the bottom to the top
Sides to center	Replace old graph with new one starting from the left and right sides and working to the vertical center
Center to sides	Replace old graph with new one starting from the vertical center and working to the left and right sides
Double edge vertical in	Replace old graph with new one starting from the top and bottom and working to the horizontal center
Double edge vertical out	Replace old graph with new one starting from the top and bottom and working to the horizontal center
Square edges in	Replace old graph with new one starting from the outside and working to the center

Table 10.1   Quattro Pro Transition Effects *(continued)*

Square edges out	Replace old graph with new one starting from the center and working to the outside
Tilt down	Slide old graph down and replace with new one sliding down from the top
Tilt up	Slide old graph up and replace with new one sliding up from the bottom
Single vertical stripes	Replace old graph with new one in small vertical stripes working from left to right
Double vertical stripes	Replace every other vertical line with the new graph from left to right and then replace remaining vertical lines with new graph from right to left
Spiral	Replace old graph with new one starting from the center and working a block at a time from the center in a counterclockwise circle
Dissolve: 1 by 2 pixels	Replace old graph with new one by 2x1 rectangles
Dissolve: 2 by 2 pixels	Replace old graph with new one by 2x2 squares
Dissolve: 4 by 4 pixels	Replace old graph with new one by 4x4 squares
Dissolve: 8 by 8 pixels	Replace old graph with new one by 8x8 squares
Dissolve: 16 by 16 pixels	Replace old graph with new one by 16x16 squares
Dissolve: 32 by 32 pixels	Replace old graph with new one by 32x32 squares
Dissolve: 64 by 64 pixels	Replace old graph with new one by 64x64 squares
Curtain down	Slide new graph on top of the old starting from the top and working down
Curtain up	Slide old graph up to reveal new graph underneath from the bottom and working up
Diamond in	Replace new graph with old in a diamond shape from the outside of the graph to the inside
Diamond out	Replace new graph with old in a diamond shape from the inside of the graph to the outside
Square corners in	Replace new graph with old starting from the corners and working to the inside in square shapes
Square corners out	Replace new graph with old starting from the center and working to the outside in square shapes

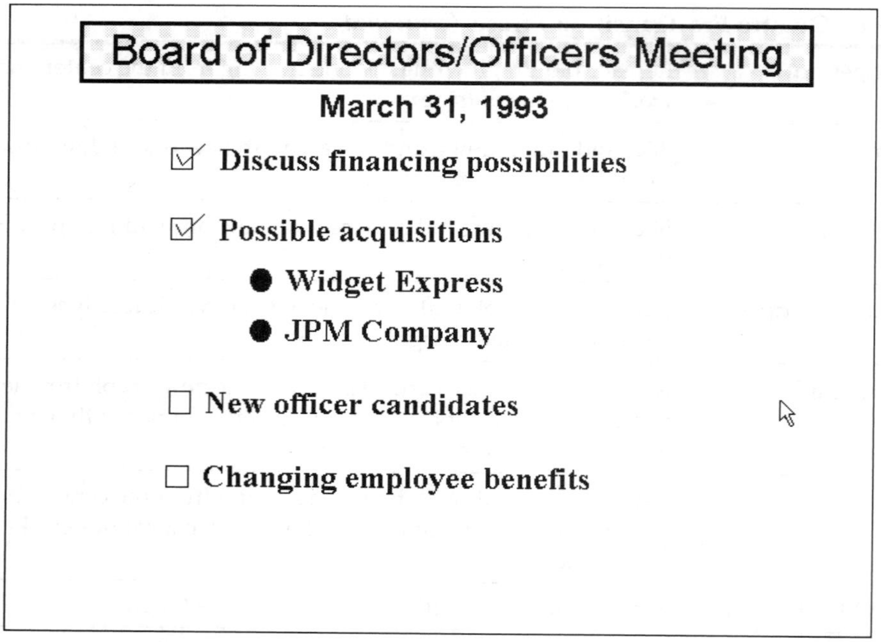

Figure 10.14   Graph Created by Overlapping Other Graphs

The slide show has its own properties that you can change outside of the light table, by right-clicking its icon on the Graphs page. You can rename the slide show, as you can graphs, although you must select Name first. You can also set the default transition setting for all of the graphs in a slide show that are not set separately in the light table. When you select Default Effect, you can enter the display time, select the transition effect, set the transition speed, and select whether the graph overlays the previous one just as if you are setting these properties for a graph in a slide show. Finally, you can select whether the mouse appears when you run a slide show. The default setting for Show Pointer is Yes, so when you run the slide show, as soon as you move the mouse, the mouse pointer appears on the slide. You may want to select No when you are using the mouse solely to advance from one slide to another and you never want to see the mouse pointer on the screen.

▼ TIP: Be careful about using too many transition effects.

You will only want to use a few transition effects in a slide show. If you use too many, your audience will spend its time watching the pretty graphics rather than focusing on the information you are presenting in the graphs.

▼ TIP: Create your own slide show to try
out the different features.

Create a dummy slide show to try rearranging graphs and using the different
transition effects. Once you try the sample slide show, you will be more
comfortable creating slide shows when one is needed. And by trying the
transition effects on dummy slide shows, you are ready to carefully select the
transition effects that are appropriate for your presentation.

Running a Slide Show

When you have completed a slide show, you can run it. To run a slide show, select
Slide Show from the Graph menu, select the name of the slide show from the list,
and select OK. If you use this command on the Graphs page with a slide show
selected, you do not have to select a slide show or OK. You can also start a slide
show from the Graphs page by selecting the slide show and selecting the Run Slide
Show button, which is the last button on the Graphs page SpeedBar The slide
show starts with the first graph and displays each named graph for the number of
seconds specified. The mouse does not appear on the graph until you move it,
assuming the Show Pointer property of the slide show is set to Yes. You can press
a key or click the mouse to go to the next slide when the display time is set to 0.
You can also return to a previous slide by right clicking the mouse or pressing the
BACKSPACE key. Press ESC when you want to quit the slide show.

Creating a Slide Show with Graph Buttons

You can also add graph buttons to your graphs. A graph button is a text object that
displays another graph or performs a macro instruction when it is selected. You
can also make the underlying graphic a graph button for when you select anything
on the graph that is not a text graph button. You can use graph buttons to create
a slide show or to change the order that the graphs are presented. You can also use
graph buttons as part of a macro (which are discussed further in Chapters 13 and
14) to display a fancy opening screen from which the user can make selections.
Using text objects or the graph background as a button does not have any effect on
the graph except when you display the graph as part of a slide show or display it
with View in the Graph menu or by pressing F11.
    To create a graph button, create the text object you want to use as a graph
button. Then select the box for the text object or select the graph's background and
inspect its properties. Select the Graph Button property. Now the dialog box
includes the Select Graph and the Execute Macro check boxes. If you select the

Select Graph check box for the Graph Button property, you then select a graph that is to be displayed when the object which is a graph button is selected. When the Select Graph check box is selected, the middle part of the dialog box changes. From the list box you can select the name of the graph to display when the graph button is selected. You also have the same Effect drop-down list box, Display time text box, Overlay check box, and transition speed radio buttons you have when you change the display time and transition effect of a graph in a slide show. The Display time text box affects how long the chosen graph is displayed. When the Execute Macro check box is selected for the Graph Button property, you can enter macro instructions to perform when the graph button is selected. You can select any of the macro instructions you would use for macros or you can enter the name of a macro to perform. You will learn more about macro commands in Chapters 13 and 14. You can select both check boxes so that macro instructions are performed in the background as you make selections from the graphs that you select. When you select OK, the underlying graph or the selected text object is a graph button. You will want to display the box around a text object so the graph users can see the boundaries of the graph buttons they can select.

When the graph is displayed on the full screen by selecting View in the Graph menu or by pressing F11, you can select the graph button by clicking any part of the text object with the mouse or by typing the first letter of the graph button. With this last method of selecting a graph button, it is important that the text of all graph buttons in a graph start with a different letter. If you click another part of the graph or type a letter that does not start one of the graph buttons, you select the graph background button. If the graph is not set to be a background button, Quattro Pro removes the graph and displays the next graph. When you use graph buttons in a slide show, they override the order of graphs in a slide show. A diagram in

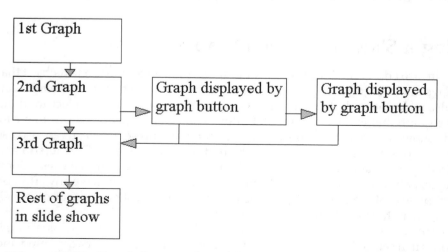

Figure 10.15   Graph Buttons Overriding Slide Show Order

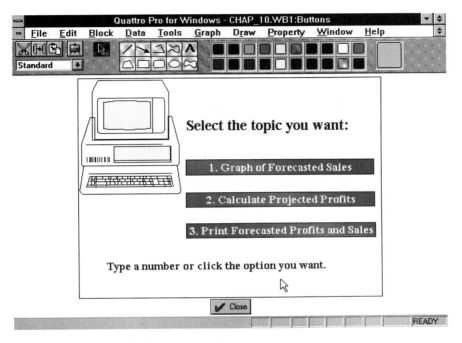

Figure 10.16   Graph Containing Graph Buttons

Figure 10.15 shows how this would work. Figure 10.16 shows a graph with several graph buttons added. In this graph, you can select any one of the text objects to display another graph or to perform a macro.

GETTING STARTED

In this chapter, you learned about many of the more advanced graphics features Quattro Pro for Windows provides. These advanced features include using the Graphs page, drawing objects on a graph, and creating slide shows. You can try some of these features by following these steps:

1. To create the Front graph shown in Figure 10.17, select New from the Graph menu. Type **Front** in the Graph Name text box and select OK. Inspect the properties of the text tool in the SpeedBar. Select the Alignment property, clear the Wordwrap check box, and select OK. Then add the two text objects, Acme Corporation and Let Us Serve You Better. For the Acme Corporation text object, set the fill style to None, the box type to the empty one, and the font's point size to 24, and add bold. For the Let Us Serve You Better text object, set the fill style to None, the box type to the empty one, and the

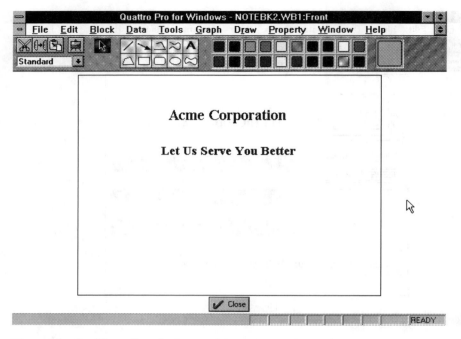

Figure 10.17   First Graph Created in Getting Started

       font's point size to 20, and add bold. Select both text objects, then select
       Align in the Draw menu and Vertical Center.

2.   Create the Service graph shown in Figure 10.18, select New from the Graph
       menu. Type **Service_3** in the Graph Name text box and select OK. Then add
       the three text objects, Industry Customer Service Winner, Fast Delivery, and
       Deliver Anywhere (press ENTER between Customer and Service). For the
       three text objects, set the fill style to None, the box style to the empty one,
       and the font's point size to 18, and add bold. Select the three text objects,
       then select Align in the Draw menu and Left. Next, use the Import button
       in the SpeedBar or the Import command in the Draw menu to import
       LOVINCUP.CGM. Change the directory to C:\QPW\CLIPART (on the
       directory where Quattro Pro clip art is stored), select *.CGM in the File
       Types dialog box, select LOVINCUP.CGM in the File Name list box, and
       select OK. Resize the clip art and position it as shown in Figure 10.18. Use
       the Import button in the SpeedBar or the Import command in the Draw menu
       again to import VAXPHONE.CGM following the same steps. Resize the
       image and position it as shown in Figure 10.18. Use the Import button in the
       SpeedBar or the Import command in the Draw menu to import
       TRUCK3.CGM. Resize the truck and position it as shown in Figure 10.18.

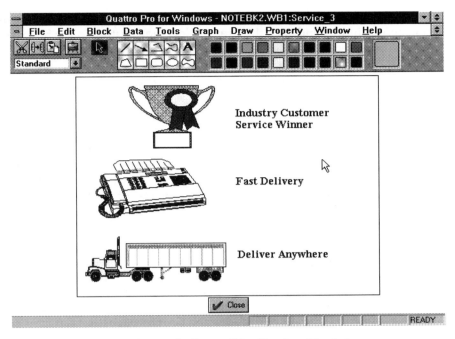

Figure 10.18   Second Graph Created in Getting Started

3. To create two copies of the Service_3 graph, switch to the Graphs page in the notebook window. Select Service_3 on the Graphs page, then click the Copy button in the SpeedBar or select Copy in the Edit menu to create a copy of this graph in the Clipboard. Make the two copies by clicking the Paste button on the SpeedBar or selecting Paste in the Edit menu twice. The two copies of the graph use the graph name and the next number, Service_4 and Service_5.

4. Rename the two new graphs: Right-click Service_4 on the Graphs page, type **Service_1** and select OK. Right-click Service_5 on the Graphs page, type **Service_2** and select OK.

5. Modify the Service_2 graph. Double-click Service_2 on the Graphs page. Then hold down SHIFT while you click the Deliver Anywhere text object as well as the truck clip art object. Click the Cut button in the SpeedBar or select Cut or Clear from the Edit menu to remove the selected objects.

6. Modify the Service_1 graph, switch to the Graphs page in the notebook window and double-click Service_1. Then hold down SHIFT while you click the Fast Delivery and Deliver Anywhere text objects as well as the truck and faxphone clip art objects. Click the Cut button in the SpeedBar or select Cut or Clear from the Edit menu to remove the selected objects.

7. Create a slide show for your graphs. Switch to the Graphs page in the notebook window and click the Create Slide Show button in the SpeedBar. When prompted for a slide show name, type **Acme_Service** and select OK.

8. To add graphs to the slide show, drag the graphs Front, Service_1, Service_2, and Service_3 to the Acme_Service slide show icon.

9. Add transition effects to your slide show. Double-click the Acme_Service slide show. For the Front graph, select Fade out/fade in for the transition Effect, Slow for the speed, and 5 for the Display time. For the Service_1 graph, select Fade out/fade in for the transition Effect, Slow for the Speed, and 5 for the Display Time. For the Service_2 graph, select Dissolve: 2 by 2 pixels for the transition Effect, Fast for the Speed, and 5 for the Display Time. For the Service_3 graph, select Dissolve: 2 by 2 pixels for the transition Effect, Fast for the Speed, and 10 for the Display Time. Select OK to finish using the light table.

10. Run the Acme_Service slide show you have created. Either click the Run Slide Show button in the SpeedBar or select Slide Show from the Graph menu. You only need to select Acme_Service as the name of the slide show you want to run when you use the Slide Show command in the Graph menu without a slide show selected on the Graphs page first. When the slide show is finished, you are returned to the Graphs page.

11

Data Management

Quattro Pro's data-management features can be used to supplement the spreadsheet techniques covered in earlier chapters. Data-management features can also be used alone to create a database of information on the spreadsheet that does not require any of the calculations of the spreadsheet environment. As a supplement to the spreadsheet features, the database commands can be used to resequence detail entries in a spreadsheet (as long as sorting these entries does not jeopardize the integrity of the formulas). The database features can also be used to produce an exception report from the calculations produced by spreadsheet formulas. An exception report can help you focus your attention on important issues rather than on the details.

In the more traditional sense, Quattro Pro's data-management features can be used to maintain data for employees within your department, vendors that you contact on a regular basis, or the inventory codes and prices for merchandise items that you stock. This data may be stored as label and/or number entries without any formulas. The emphasis in these applications may be strictly on the storage and retrieval features of the package.

Quattro Pro has features that parallel those found in traditional database-management systems: its abilities to present data in any sequence desired and to selectively present information from the database. Quattro Pro differs from other systems in that the capacity of the database is limited to the capacity provided by the memory available on your machine. With Quattro Pro's and Windows memory management features, database size is only an issue with very large databases.

In addition Quattro Pro can work with other database formats. In Chapter 7, you saw how you could save and open database files. You can also work directly with these database files as part of Quattro Pro's data management features. Quattro Pro also has a Database Desktop that you can use to directly display information from Paradox and dBASE databases. These data management features provide many of the features of database management packages while still using the familiar Quattro Pro interface.

DATA MANAGEMENT CONCEPTS IN QUATTRO PRO

Before you begin to learn the database functions and commands that Quattro Pro provides, it is essential to first learn a few essential data-management terms. This section will introduce the basic concepts of database, record, and field.

A *database* is simply a collection of related information. The list of people and their telephone numbers found in a phone directory is an example of a database. Figure 11.1 is another example of a database. From its database, you can easily determine the vendor's name, as well as the invoice number, date, amount, and terms. Also, you can quickly check whether an invoice has been paid.

A *record* consists of all the information about one thing in the database. In Figure 11.1, a record consists of all the information about one vendor. The data contained in each row compose a record pertaining to a particular vendor.

Each individual piece of information is a *field*. Referring again to Figure 11.1, the fields are the vendor name, the invoice number, the invoice date, the invoice

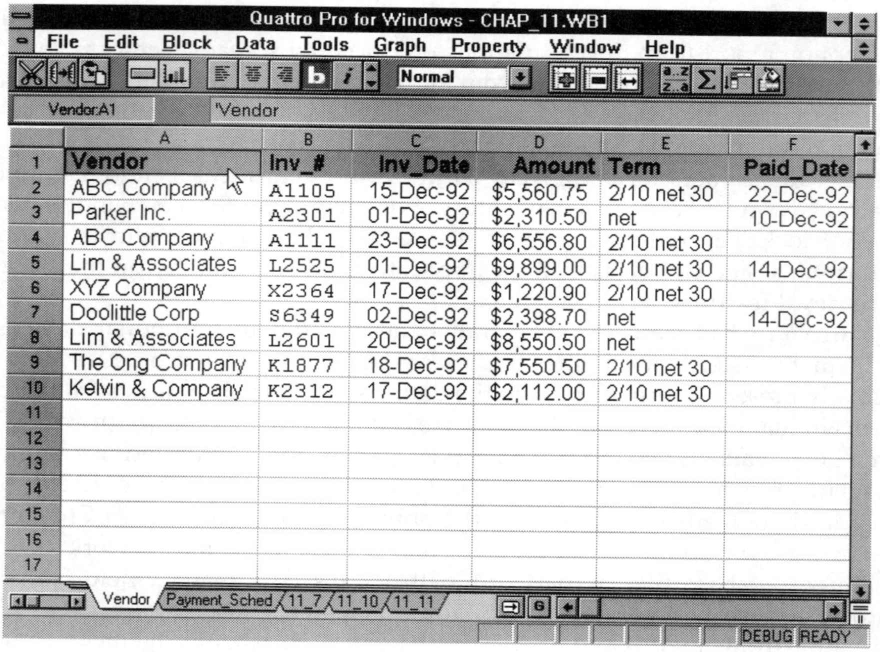

	A	B	C	D	E	F
1	Vendor	Inv_#	Inv_Date	Amount	Term	Paid_Date
2	ABC Company	A1105	15-Dec-92	$5,560.75	2/10 net 30	22-Dec-92
3	Parker Inc.	A2301	01-Dec-92	$2,310.50	net	10-Dec-92
4	ABC Company	A1111	23-Dec-92	$6,556.80	2/10 net 30	
5	Lim & Associates	L2525	01-Dec-92	$9,899.00	2/10 net 30	14-Dec-92
6	XYZ Company	X2364	17-Dec-92	$1,220.90	2/10 net 30	
7	Doolittle Corp	S6349	02-Dec-92	$2,398.70	net	14-Dec-92
8	Lim & Associates	L2601	20-Dec-92	$8,550.50	net	
9	The Ong Company	K1877	18-Dec-92	$7,550.50	2/10 net 30	
10	Kelvin & Company	K2312	17-Dec-92	$2,112.00	2/10 net 30	

Figure 11.1 Quattro Pro Page Containing Invoice Database

amount, the invoice terms, and the date of payment. The collection of one entry for each of these fields makes a record, and the collection of all the records makes a database.

CREATING A QUATTRO PRO DATABASE

A Quattro Pro database is a block of cells on the spreadsheet that follows the row and column organization needed to effectively use the database commands. The top row in the database consists of as many as 256 fields. Beneath these fields the record entries are stored. As many as 8,191 records can be entered, although memory constraints may preclude a database with both the maximum number of records and the maximum number of fields.

You can choose any location in a notebook to start the database. Since you can share data between notebooks and pages, the best location for your database is on its own page. When you want to use a Quattro Pro database, it can be in the notebook you are working in, another open notebook, or a notebook that is not opened. If a database is sharing the same page with calculations, the area immediately below and to the right of the calculations is best so that you can insert both rows and columns in the database without jeopardizing the integrity of your formulas.

Once you have selected an area for your database, you can place the field names across the top row of the database. Observing the tips in the "Rules for Field Names" box helps ensure success for your first Quattro Pro database effort. The field names are in the first row of the database, like the ones shown in Figure 11.1.

Rules for Field Names

1. A field name entry should be restricted to one cell immediately above the first field entry.
2. Do not place a dividing line between the field names and the first field entry. If you want a line, add it with the Line Drawing block property.
3. Select meaningful names, since they will be used in both the criteria table and output area.
4. Be especially careful not to include trailing spaces at the end of field names, since it will not be apparent that they are there, yet Quattro will require these spaces in other entries for the same field name.
5. Enter the field names in the same order in which they appear on the source document.
6. Use the underscore (_) instead of a space to separate words in the field name.

> ## ▼ TIP: Inspect properties to add a line under the field names.
>
> If you want a line between the field names and the field values, edit the properties of the block containing the field names and use the Line Drawing property to add lines to the cell. You can also add underlining by changing the Font property and selecting the Underline text box.

Quattro Pro does not impose limitations on the field names as some database packages do. If the field names follow Quattro Pro's rules for block names, you can name the fields, which lets you refer to the fields in the database by the field name instead of by cell address. For this reason, you may want to replace spaces in the field names with underscores (_) so using the field names in formulas does not create confusion.

ENTERING AND EDITING DATA

Making entries in a Quattro Pro database is the same as entering data into any other spreadsheet cell. You should place your first field entry in the cell directly beneath the first field name and move to the right to make the other entries for the first record. After completing the first record, move the selector to the next row to enter record 2.

Error corrections can be made by using the same methods used in a normal cell entry. If you realize a mistake immediately after typing a character, the BACKSPACE key can be used to eliminate the problem. If you have already finalized an entry, you need to retype the cell entry or edit the cell to make your corrections. Records can be inserted anywhere in the database by selecting Insert from the Block menu or clicking the Insert button on the SpeedBar and then selecting Rows and OK. Records can be deleted by selecting Delete from the Block menu or clicking the Delete button on the SpeedBar and then selecting Rows and OK. You can add database fields by selecting Insert from the Block menu or clicking the Insert button on the SpeedBar and then selecting Columns and OK. You can remove database fields by selecting Delete from the Block menu or clicking the Delete button on the SpeedBar and then selecting Columns and OK.

SORTING A DATABASE

As your database grows larger, finding entries may be difficult if the records are stored in their random entry sequence. Sorting the data may enable you to present the information in a more manageable sequence. For example, you may need a list

> ## ▼ TIP: Hide the field names to improve the appearance of your database.
>
> If you want to use headings that do not fit Quattro Pro's rules for field names, enter those headings above the row of field names. Then when you want to display the database with the new headings instead of the field names, inspect the properties of the block containing the field names, and use the Reveal/Hide property to hide them. The headings will appear to be just above the database entries, and yet you can use the field names to refer to the fields. You must make sure that you include the field names rather than the column headings when you select the location of the database.

of customer names in alphabetical order or a list of customer account balances in descending order (highest to lowest). Quattro Pro provides an easy method to perform these sort features.

Specifying the Records to Sort

Quattro Pro provides you with the capability to sort all the records or just a portion of them. Whether you sort all the records or just a few, you should always make certain that you sort all the fields.

To sort database records in Quattro Pro, you must follow a sequence of steps as summarized in the "Sort Steps" box. First, you need to specify the block to be sorted. Select the block containing all of the fields of the database records you want to sort. Next, select Sort from the Data menu to display the Data Sort dialog box. It is important to ensure that the field names are not included in the specified block as shown in Figure 11.2. Otherwise Quattro Pro treats your field names as a record and sorts them. If you are sorting spreadsheet data that is not part of a database, make sure the block to sort includes all the data in the rows or columns you want to sort.

Selecting from One to Five Sort Keys

You are able to specify up to five sort keys. A *sort key* selects a column or row of entries that you will use to determine the order of the rows or columns. The first, or primary, sort key always controls the sequence of the records. Even when you specify a second sort key, Quattro Pro ignores it unless there are duplicate entries of the first sort key. If this is the case, the second sort key determines the sequence of those records. If more than one record has the same values for the first and second sort keys, Quattro Pro uses the value of the third sort key to order those

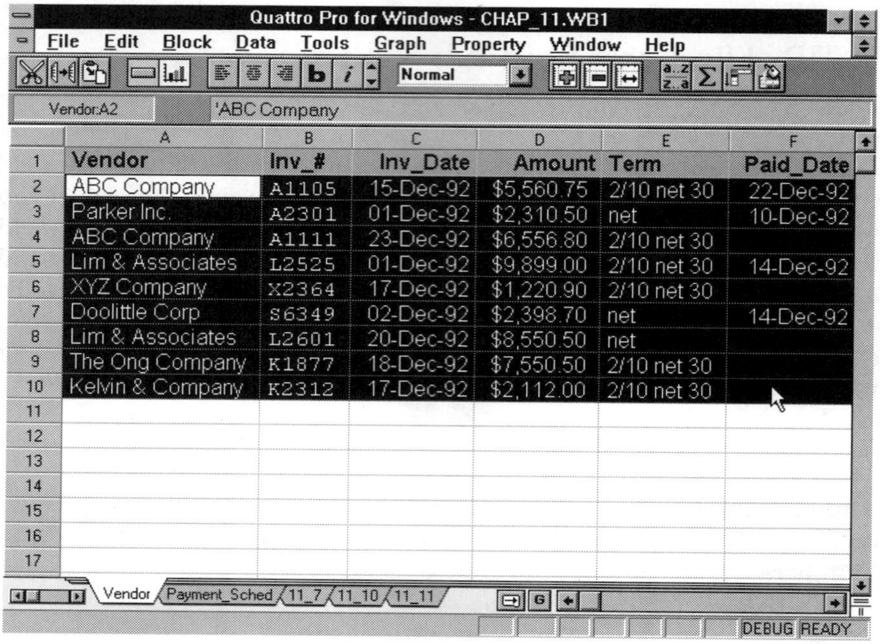

Figure 11.2 Selecting a Sort Block

records. Quattro Pro continues to use the next sort key when multiple records have the same values for the preceding sort keys.

CHOOSING A PRIMARY KEY You choose the sort keys using the Data Sort dialog box, shown in Figure 11.3, which is invoked by selecting Sort from the Data menu. You select a cell from the column containing the field by which you want to sort in the 1st text box. That cell selects the column of entries to use as the primary sort key. You can specify the sort key several ways. You can type a cell address or point to a cell in the

---

Sort Steps

1. Select the block containing the values in all rows and columns which you want to sort.
2. Select Sort in the Data menu.
3. Select a cell from the column whose values you want the rows sorted by in the 1st text box.
4. Select the second through fifth sort keys if you want to establish multiple criteria.
5. Select OK.

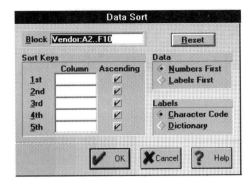

Figure 11.3 Data Sort Dialog Box

correct column. This cell must be in the block you are sorting. If you assigned field names from the Data Query dialog box, as described later, you can enter the field's name, either by typing it or by selecting the field name after pressing F3 (CHOICES). For example, with the data in Figure 11.2, you might want to sort according to the vendor. You can enter a cell address such as A2, or the field name (assuming you have named the fields) such as Vendor. After specifying the sort key, you need to determine the sort order. When the check box to the right of the sort key text box is selected, the field is sorted in ascending order, from lowest to highest (8,9,10 or A,B,C). If the check box is cleared, then the field is sorted in descending order, from highest to lowest (10, 9, 8 or Z, Y, X).

CHOOSING ADDITIONAL SORT KEYS   You can add four more sort keys that Quattro Pro may use to sort the database. If you want to use a second sort key, simply select the cell for the sort key in the 2nd text box. As mentioned previously, the second sort key is used as a tie-breaker to determine which data should be sorted first when the first sort key contains duplicates. The same procedure is followed for selecting sort keys three through five. With the sort block and keys selected, select OK to sort the database.

▼ TIP: Sort Blocks Using the SpeedSort Buttons

Besides sorting a block with the Sort command in the Data menu, you can also use the Upper and Lower SpeedSort buttons. These are on the button labeled a..z and z..a. After selecting a block, hold down CTRL and SHIFT then click cells in the columns in the order you want them used as sort keys. If you do not select sort keys, Quattro Pro uses the first column's entries as the first sort key, Then select the Upper SpeedSort button (the half labeled a..z) to sort the block in ascending order or select the Lower SpeedSort button (the half labeled z..a) to sort the block in descending order. For example, you can select the block A2..F10 in Figure 11.3 to sort the invoices by vendor name.

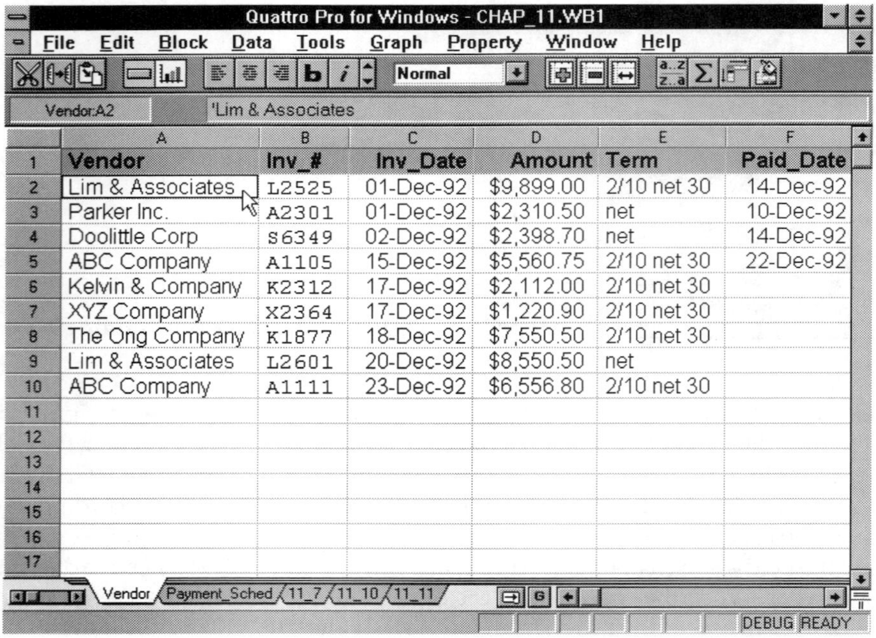

Figure 11.4   Records Sorted by Vendor Within Invoice Date

Figure 11.4 provides an example in which a primary and a secondary key are used to sort the data. The primary key is the Inv_Date field shown in column C, and the secondary key is the Vendor field shown in column A. Ascending order was specified for both of these keys. Note that the invoice dates are sorted from the earliest to the latest date. Also note that the secondary key comes into play only when sorting by the primary key results in a tie. Referring back to the example in Figure 11.4, notice that Lim & Associates is listed before Parker Inc. even though both records have an invoice date of December 1, 1992; the secondary sort key resulted in alphabetizing those two names. For the same reason, Kelvin & Company is listed before XYZ Company even though their invoice dates are the same.

Changing the Sort Order

Quattro Pro provides two different sort order options. You can choose to sort numbers before labels, and can change the order of labels from a strict dictionary sequence to a character code sequence that distinguishes between uppercase and lowercase entries.

The default sort order uses the following sequence when you choose Ascending:

Blank cells

Labels beginning with spaces

Labels beginning with numbers

Labels in alphabetical sequence

Labels beginning with special characters in their character code sequence

Value entries in numeric order

Formulas are sorted with the labels or values according to the formulas' results. To change the sort order, you can select options from the Data Sort dialog box shown in Figure 11.3. Under Data, you select Numbers First to sort the numbers before the labels, or Labels First to sort the labels before the numbers. These radio buttons only affect labels and how labels containing numbers as well as characters are sorted. Under Labels, you can select Dictionary, to sort uppercase and lowercase letters together, or Character Code, in which uppercase and lowercase letters are sorted independently, according to the character code for each letter.

If you are using international characters (ones not used in the English language), you may need to change how Quattro Pro sorts characters, so that it incorporates the international characters in the alphabetical order appropriate for that language. Windows has a language setting that is chosen by displaying the International dialog box from Windows' Control Panel. Quattro Pro uses this language setting unless you want to use a different one. To select a different country's language to sort by, inspect the application properties. You inspect the application properties by clicking the right mouse button on the application title bar, or selecting Application from the Property menu. Select the International property, the Language radio button, and the Quattro Pro/Windows radio button. Choose a language from the list box. When you sort your database, the international characters are included as appropriate for the alphabet of that language.

Ensuring Data Integrity During Sorting

While using the database sort commands, you must maintain data integrity. If your data contains relative cell references to cells outside the row in your database, the sort commands scramble your data. One example can show you how destructive a sort can be when you have relative cell references. Figure 11.5 is a loan amortization schedule with cell references to B1 (as seen in the input line), B2, and B3. These cell references are outside the database block. Figure 11.6 captures the spreadsheet after Quattro Pro sorts the database in descending order with a primary sort key of the Month field. The entries in the Principal and Interest columns are now totally different from the entries shown in Figure 11.5. Also, the lines around the entries are moved. Integrity of the database is not maintained if the sort command is used when the database contains relative references to cells outside the database. Saving the file before performing a sort is one good way to prevent this problem, since you can always retrieve the file if a problem is found after sorting.

ACCEPTABLE FORMULA REFERENCES Although the sort command is easy to use, you must still be very cautious when you perform the sort process involv-

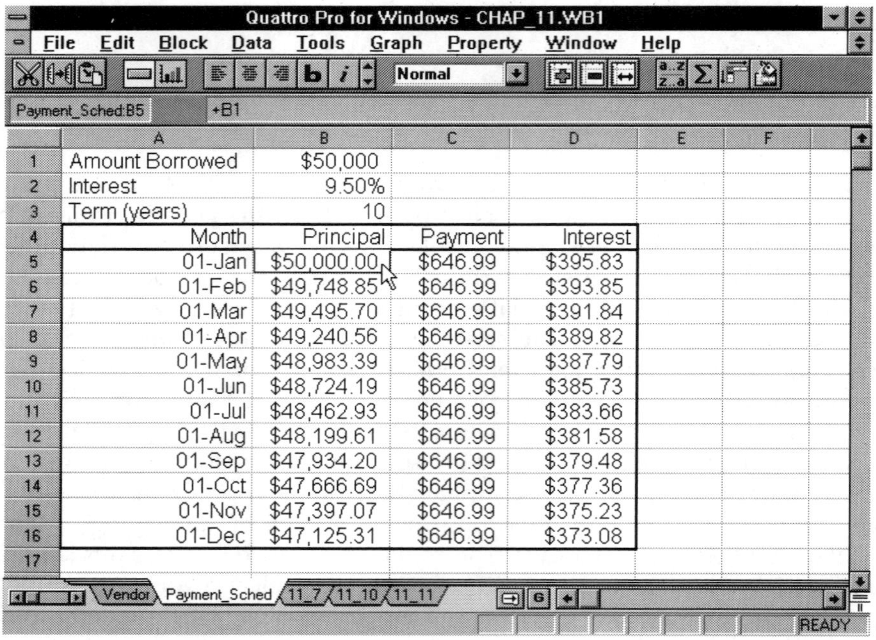

Figure 11.5   An Amortization Table

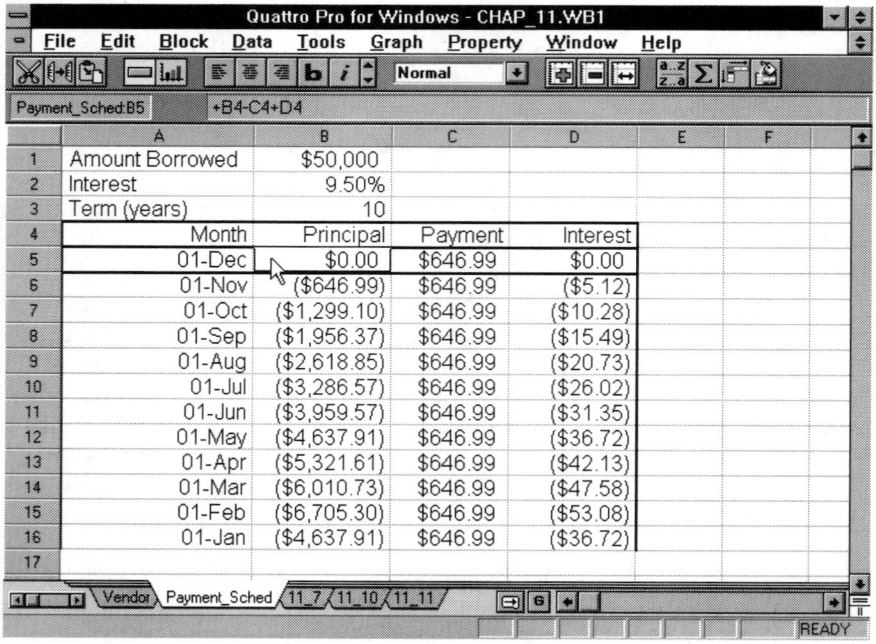

Figure 11.6   The Effect of a Sort on the Amortization Table Shown in Figure 11.5

ing formula references. Failure to use caution can cause the sort command to change the entries in your database and make your database useless.

You must remember that if you use relative formula references within the same row of data in your database and if the fields that contain the formulas are sorted simultaneously with the fields that these formulas reference, then the sort command does not change the data entries in your database. For example, if D4 has the formula +C4*.1, when the data is sorted, the formula might change to +C11*.1 if the entries on row 4 move to row 11. The formula still refers to the same data, so your formulas have not been damaged.

If your data entries contain formula references to cells outside your database, you should make sure that these cell references are absolute before you use the sort command. This includes formulas that refer to data in another notebook or page. This ensures that the sorting process does not affect the data entries in the cells. You can make cell references absolute by inserting $ signs in the cell addresses. For example, if you have a reference to cell A1, you can enter **$A$1** instead of just **A1**; Quattro Pro knows the dollar signs indicate absolute cell references. Furthermore, you cannot have absolute cell references between data entries within your database. If you do, the sort process changes your data entries and makes your database useless.

FORGETTING TO SORT ALL THE FIELDS   Quattro Pro only sorts the fields in the block you select for the <u>S</u>ort command in the <u>D</u>ata menu. If you forget to specify a field, Quattro Pro ignores this field when sorting, and some fields are lost in each record. For example, if you forget to include the salary field when sorting by employee name in an employee database, only the employee names are sorted. Therefore, the salary amounts are not properly matched with employee names after the sort. The database can no longer supply valid salary data. You should always check the fields included in the sort block before proceeding.

It is especially important to recheck the sort block if you have added fields to the database. Otherwise, Quattro Pro assumes that it should use its previous sort block, and the excluded fields remain stationary while the other fields are sorted.

SEARCHING FOR QUICK ANSWERS

When your database is large, searching for a specific record can be a time-consuming and tedious problem. Fortunately, Quattro Pro provides query features that can eliminate this problem. For example, you may want to search for records pertaining to the vendor Lim & Associates in the vendor database shown in Figure 11.4. These database features also provide you with an exception-reporting capability. Information that does not conform to expectations can easily be brought to your attention using the query features. You also can use these features to remove unwanted records from your database or to prepare reports in response to requests.

Just as several steps are required for sorting your data, a special sequence of steps is required before you can use the query features. These steps are summarized in the "Query Steps" box.

Query Steps

1. Enter the table criteria in the notebook from READY mode.
2. Select Query from the Data menu and specify the database block, including field names, in the Database Block text box.
3. Select Field Names to apply the names in the first row of the database to the fields in the first database record.
4. Specify the block containing the criteria table in the Criteria Table text box.
5. To highlight matching records, select Locate.
6. To extract matching records, you must first enter the field names of the data you wish to extract from the database in a row of a notebook page. Specify the block where you want the output to appear, including these field names, in the Output Block text box.
7. Select Extract or Extract Unique to copy data from matching records to the output block.

Completing the Preliminary Cell Entries

Quattro Pro's query features are available through the Data Query dialog box opened by selecting Query from the Data menu. Before you use this command, you have several steps you must perform. In the Data Query dialog box, you tell Quattro Pro the specific location of database records and a table of your specifications for matching records. These entries must be on the spreadsheet notebook when the command is invoked. Some of the query options also require an output area to which Quattro Pro copies the records that match the criteria. The entries for the output area must also be completed before you use this command.

At a minimum, you should complete the entry of all database records and criteria before invoking the Data Query dialog box. You already know the rules to follow in creating database entries, but entering criteria offers a few more variations. Criteria are stored in another part of the notebook and contain exact match criteria or formula criteria. Exact match criteria can match specific entries, like all invoices from ABC Company or all invoice dates of December 23, 1992. Formula criteria allow you to establish logical formulas for comparisons against the database field values, such as formulas for invoices that exceed $5,000.

If you want Quattro Pro to find matching entries, you are ready to proceed to the menu. If you plan for Quattro Pro to extract records that match your specifications, you must lay out at the top of the output area the fields for which data is to be extracted. You can select as many fields as you want and can place the fields in any order across a row in an empty area of the spreadsheet. You should be certain that you select an area for the output fields that allows adequate blank rows beneath it for Quattro Pro to use when it copies the matching records to the extract area. You can also use a separate page for the output area. For example, the page OUTPUT can be your output area, and you can use the resulting records for a report by adding the remaining information the report needs.

Defining the Block to Search

After preparing the database, table criteria, and output block entries, you are ready to make selections from the Data Query dialog box. The first step is defining the block of records to be searched. To specify this block, select the block containing the database in the Database Block text box. The field names must also be included in the specified block. For the database shown in Figure 11.7, you would select A1..F10. If you have assigned a block name to the block, you can enter the block name in the Database Block text box, using F3 (CHOICES) if it is convenient. While you do not need to include the entire database, you must ensure that you select all the fields specified in the criteria table or the output table. If the database is in a different notebook, you must enter the file name in brackets ([ ]) before entering the block address. You can also use CTRL-F6 (NEXT WINDOW) or the mouse to point to a block in another open notebook. If the drive or directory is different from Quattro Pro's defaults, you must supply this information in the brackets. If the extension is not .WB1, you must also supply this information in the brackets.

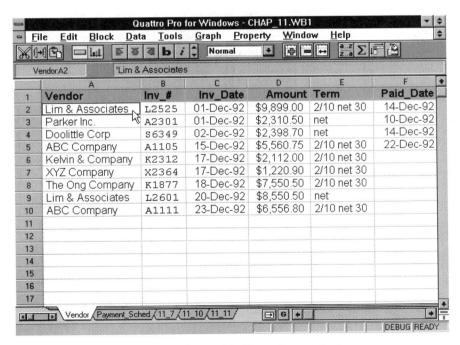

Figure 11.7   Database to Select with Data Query features

The notebook does not have to be open to use the Extract and Extract Unique query features discussed later in the chapter. The notebook must be open to use the Locate and Delete query options discussed later in the chapter.

When you use separate notebooks for the different blocks to be used by the Query command in the Data menu, the settings for the blocks in the different notebooks are saved only with the notebook that is active when you initially selected the Query command in the Data menu. Quattro Pro uses the database, criteria, and output blocks defined in the Data Query dialog box of the notebook in which the selector is located at the time that a Query command in the Data menu is performed. For example, with the data in Figure 11.8 and the selector in the OUTPUT notebook, the block [INVOICES]A1..F10 is entered in the Database Block text box, which is saved as one of the settings of the OUTPUT notebook. The INVOICES notebook may have its own settings in the Data Query dialog box.

Assigning Names to Fields

The Field Names option of the Data Query dialog box allows you to assign block names to the first entry of each field. This is not a required step. However, this option makes entering search criteria much easier. You can reference fields by

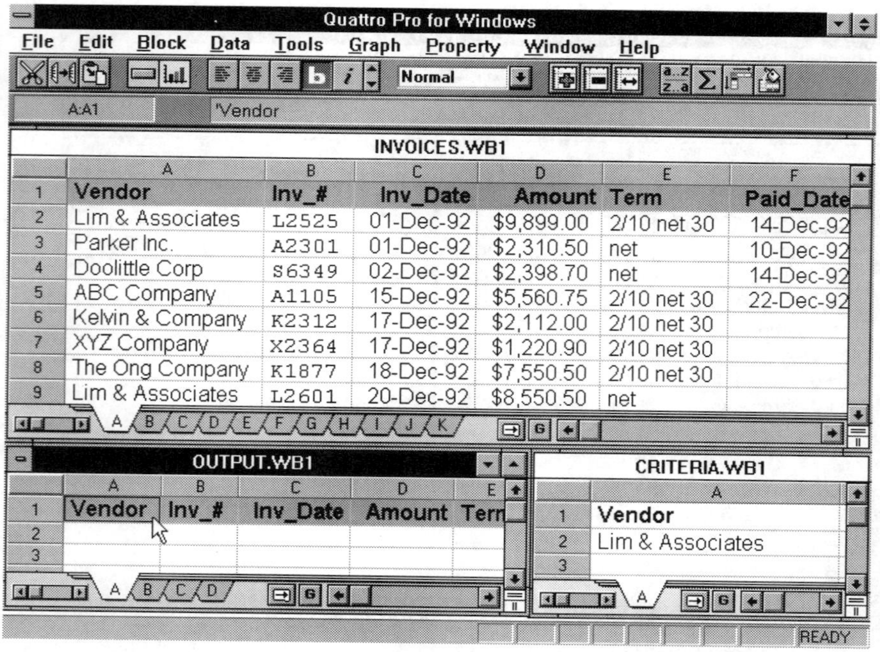

Figure 11.8 Using Separate Notebooks for Database, Criteria, and Output Blocks

name instead of having to specify a cell address. When you create criteria that compare the values in a database, you must select which fields you want to compare. For example, if you want to find invoice amounts greater than $5,000, you must tell Quattro Pro to use the fields in the column labeled Amount. One method is telling Quattro Pro the first cell containing an amount value; Quattro Pro then automatically compares all values in the Amount column using a formula like +D2>5000. Unfortunately, you cannot tell from looking at the formula which field it uses. Quattro Pro offers a better solution with the Field Names button in the Data Query dialog box. When you select Field Names, Quattro Pro names the cells below the field names for each column in the block specified in the Database Block text box. After this command, you can enter formulas like **+AMOUNT>5000** and know exactly which fields this formula uses.

The Field Names button is different from selecting Block Names Labels Down. Once you assign names with the Field Names button in the Data Query dialog box, the field names always apply to the cells below the field names. With Block Names Labels Down, the block names initially apply to the cells below the field names. As rows are inserted and deleted or the data is sorted, the position of the cells named with Block Names Labels Down changes. This does not happen with cells named with the Data Query dialog box. Since Quattro Pro treats cells named this way as block names, you can use other Quattro Pro features that apply to block names, such as pressing F3 (CHOICES) when Quattro Pro prompts for a block address, cell address, or sort key.

Specifying the Criteria

After defining and assigning names to your database, you need to specify the criteria. This allows Quattro Pro to match the specified criteria with the records from your database. The other buttons in the Data Query dialog box use the criteria to determine which records the command will use. The criteria use a table-type orientation with the field names in the top row and the values or formulas that the database records must match in the subsequent rows. The CRITERIA notebook in Figure 11.8 shows a tabular format in which Vendor is the field name and Lim & Associates is the value criterion for this field for which you want to search; thus, Quattro Pro searches for the records in which Lim & Associates is the vendor name field.

CHOOSING A LOCATION FOR CRITERIA   Although the actual positioning of the criteria is not significant, you should position the criteria in an area that will not hinder the addition of records to your database. If the criteria are in the same page as the database, you should position your criteria to the right of your database so that you can add additional records without having to move the criteria entries. You may even want to leave a few columns between your database and criteria so that you can add additional fields to your database in the future. However, you should try not to place your criteria too far from your database, since that may make it inconvenient to access.

You can also put the criteria table on a separate notebook or page; this prevents the database from interfering with the criteria. As an example, the data in Figure 11.8 can be in the notebook INVOICES, and the criteria could consist of Vendor in A1 and Lim & Associates in A2 of the CRITERIA notebook. The notebook containing the criteria must be open when the data queries are performed.

To create criteria, simply enter the field names of the desired data followed by the desired data below the field names, as shown in the CRITERIA notebook in Figure 11.8. Another option is to copy the field names from the database to the criteria table. Copying the field names ensures that the field names in the database and the criteria table are identical. The field names indicate to Quattro Pro the fields that the criteria should use. Below the field names, you put the exact match and/or formula criteria.

You define the criteria table by specifying the block for its location in the Criteria Table text box in the Data Query dialog box. Be sure that you do not include any blank rows when you specify the criteria table. A blank row serves as an ultimate wild card, matching everything in the database. Including a blank row in the criteria table block causes Quattro Pro to locate every record in the database as matching the criteria. You can, however, include extra columns in the criteria table, since Quattro Pro simply ignores them. For the same reason, if the criteria table includes fields with no formulas or exact matches below them, Quattro Pro will ignore those columns. A page can contain more than one criteria, letting you change which records you are using by changing the block defining the criteria. Before you proceed with selecting the criteria, be sure to look at the criteria you can provide and the options you have for exact match criteria and/or formula criteria.

EXACT MATCH CRITERIA   Criteria can be specified to exactly match the entries in your database. Quattro Pro searches for the data in specific database fields that exactly match the specified criteria. Exact match criteria consist of a field name and a specific value or label that you want to search for in the field beneath the field names. For example, if you are searching the database shown in INVOICES in Figure 11.8, you can specify your criteria so that Quattro Pro will search for records with a vendor name of Lim & Associates. The criteria would have Vendor in the first row and Lim & Associates in the second row. You can also do exact matches with values, such as finding invoices with an invoice amount equal to $5,000. The criteria will have Amount in the first row and 5000 in the second row. Quattro Pro does not care that the format of the number is different from the format of the numbers in the database. When entries in the database table are the results of formulas, Quattro Pro uses the formula results to determine if the records match the criteria. For example, using the criteria to find invoices with amounts equaling $5,000, the criteria would match a record with an invoice amount of +4700+300.

With exact match label entries, Quattro Pro does not distinguish between uppercase and lowercase labels. For example, Lim & Associates shown in the CRITERIA notebook in Figure 11.8 can also be entered as LIM & ASSOCIATES or lim

& associates with equivalent results. Exact match criteria for labels can also include the question mark and asterisk wild card characters, which increase the number of labels that match the criteria.

Wild Card Criteria for Label Fields   Quattro Pro provides wild card characters that can be useful in specifying criteria for fields that contain label entries. Special wild card characters can save typing time and provide flexible matching options. These wild card characters are *, ?, and ~.

The asterisk (*) tells Quattro Pro to accept any database record that matches the specified part of the criteria. For example, if you specify a search criteria as **Sm***, Quattro Pro searches for all records that begin with **Sm**. Entries such as Smith, Smyth, Smithsonian, and Smith & Company would match. Figure 11.9 shows a criterion that uses the asterisk wild card. The specified criterion Lim* is matched by Lim & Associates in the first and eighth records (rows 2 and 9) shown in Figure 11.8. You can also include the asterisk at the beginning of the criteria; for example, the entry ***Company** matches with ABC Company, XYZ Company, and Kelvin & Company.

The question mark (?) is used to replace any one character in an entry. When you use the question mark as a wild card entry, you are telling Quattro Pro to accept any character in place of the ? and to search for any entry that matches exactly the other characters in your specified criteria. Use the ? when you do not

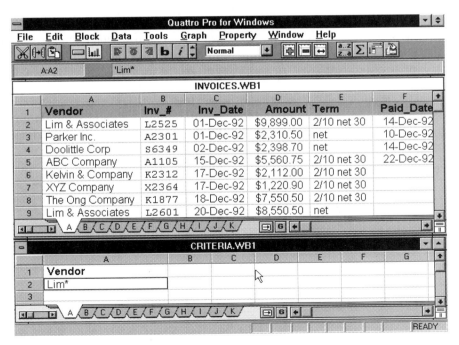

Figure 11.9   Using a Wild Card Character with Label Criteria

care what character is located in a specific position in an entry. Therefore, the criterion **L?m** would be matched by Lim, Lam, Lem, Lom, but not by Liming or Lin.

The ? wild card can be used several times in your specification. For example, if your specified criterion is **?????field**, Quattro Pro matches it with Smithfield, Mellefield, and Bellefield. If your specified criterion is **?lf?rd**, Quattro Pro finds such matches as Alford, Elford, and Alferd.

The tilde (~) is used whenever you want to negate an entry. For example, you might want to locate entries with last names other than Jones. You would then enter **~Jones** under the Last Name field in your criteria table. In this case, Quattro Pro matches the criterion with all entries whose last name is not Jones.

FORMULA CRITERIA   Formula criteria provide additional options for specifying your requirements to Quattro Pro. This option also allows you to search for records that contain numeric and label characters. Formula criteria use the logical operators shown in Table 11.1, since all formula criteria are expressed as logical formulas. When you use formula criteria, Quattro Pro analyzes the record to see if the values in the record make the formula in the formula criteria true (1) or false (0). If the formula evaluates to true for the record, the record matches that part of the criteria table. However, the criteria table may have other criteria the record must also match.

When the formula for formula criteria references a value from the database table, the formula references the first record in the database. After using the Field Names button in the Data Query dialog box, you can use the field names instead. For example, you can enter either **+D2>9000** or **+Amount>9000**. Quattro Pro interprets both these logical conditions in a similar manner. The formula criteria will display in the criteria table as 0 or 1 unless you set the format of the cells containing the formula criteria to text. In the examples below, the formula criteria are formatted as text. This is a good habit to develop, since it provides documentation.

If the database is in a separate notebook from the criteria, the formula criteria must reference the notebook containing the database. For example, if the database

Table 11.1 The Logical Operators

Operator	Meaning
=	Equal to
>	Greater than
<	Less than
>=	Greater than or equal to
<=	Less than or equal to
<>	Not equal to

is in the INVOICES spreadsheet, the criterion in a different spreadsheet to find the invoice amounts greater than $9,000 is **+[INVOICES]AMOUNT>9000**. If you use a cell address in the formula criteria, you must also include the page name and a colon before the block or cell address if the database and criteria are on separate pages.

Creating Criteria as Logical Formulas for Values and Labels   When you use formula criteria, you include the formula below the first row of the criteria table. The field name above the formula provides documentation about the formula. You can use cell references or blocks to build formula criteria by using the same entries as those in tables. The input line of Figure 11.10 shows the formula entered as **+AMOUNT>5000**. In this example, Quattro Pro locates all the records with invoice amounts greater than $5,000. The **+AMOUNT** entered as part of the formula represents the invoice amount field. If you do not use the Field Names button in the Data Query dialog box, you must use the cell address of the first entry in the field—for example, +D2>5000.

You can use formula criteria for fields that contain label entries. Any label included within the formula must be enclosed in quotation marks, as in **+VENDOR>"L"** (which finds all database records with vendors that start with the letter L through Z). Text in formulas that are used for comparison (like the L in the example) must be in quotes.

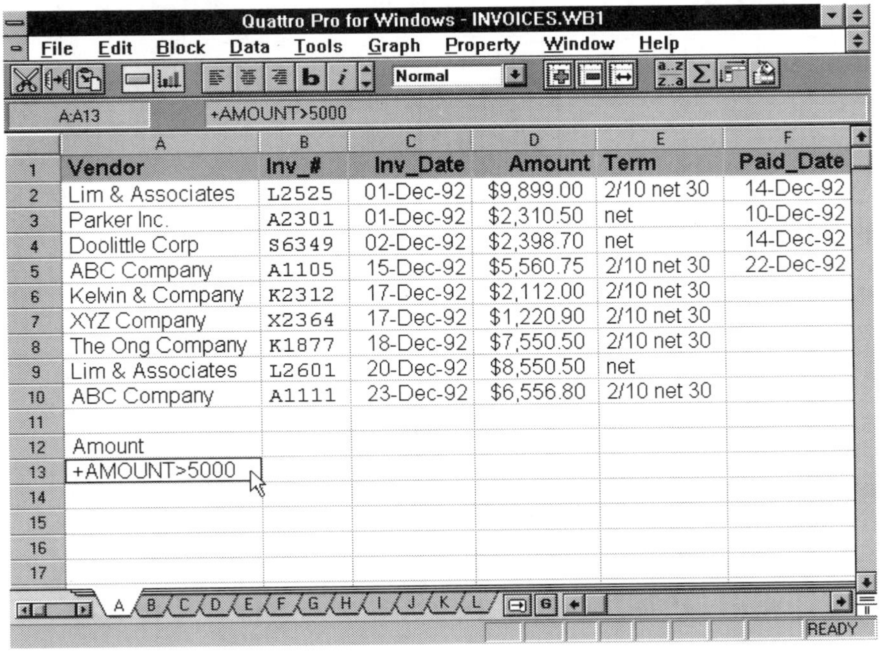

Figure 11.10   Entering Simple Formula Criteria

Formula Criteria Versus Quattro Pro Formulas   The formulas used for formula criteria follow the same rules as other Quattro Pro formulas. You can use @ functions just
as if you are building a logical function for another type of database entry. For
example, you can use the @TODAY function to create a formula to find out which
invoices are 30 days overdue: **+INV_DATE+30<@TODAY**. You may want to use
the @EXACT function if you want to compare labels and you want the match to be
sensitive to the uppercase or lowercase of the entries. For example, to find ABC
Company and not Abc Company, enter the formula criterion of
@EXACT(VENDOR,"ABC Company").

The only two differences are that in formula criteria, cell references to the
database fields use the cell address of the first entry below the field name or the
field name itself, and cell addresses that reference outside the database must be
absolute addresses. When Quattro Pro checks each record to see if it matches the
criteria, Quattro Pro makes imaginary copies down the column of the formula
criteria. These are imaginary copies because the actual entries below the formula
criteria do not change. Quattro Pro uses each of these imaginary copies to determine
which records match the criteria. This is also why you must reference the first
entry below the field name in formula criteria, since the imaginary copies have the
formula references adjusted. These imaginary copies are also why cell addresses
outside the database must be absolute addresses. For example, with the database
and criteria shown in Figure 11.11, Quattro Pro makes imaginary copies of the

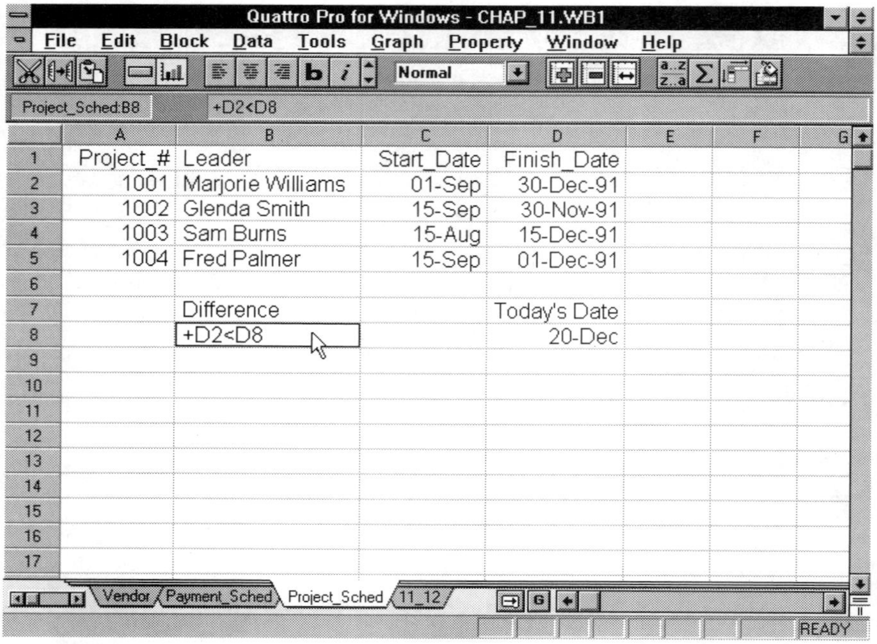

Figure 11.11   Formula Criteria that Reference Other Cells

formula criteria in B8 to B9..B11. The formulas in these imaginary copies are **+D3>D9**, **+D4>D10**, and **+D5<D11**. Since the cell address to D8 is not absolute, the formula criterion is only correct for the first record. The correct formula criterion in this case is +D2<$D$8.

COMPOUND CRITERIA Quattro Pro has two ways of building compound criteria. You can use compound criteria to find records that meet one of several criteria or records that meet multiple criteria. You can create compound criteria in a single formula criteria by using the #AND#, #OR#, and #NOT# logical operators. You also have the option of creating compound criteria by putting the criteria on one or more rows in the criteria table. Compound criteria can combine exact match and formula criteria.

The #AND#, #OR#, and #NOT# operators can all be used in formula criteria. These operators are the same ones you use to build logical functions for applications not related to a database, as well as to create the conditions that an @IF function tests. When you use the #AND# logical operator, Quattro Pro selects database records only if these records satisfy all the conditions specified by your search criteria. For example, if you specify your search criteria as **+Age=25#AND#Sex="Male"** in an employee database, Quattro Pro finds those employees who are both 25 years old AND male. If you want to search for employees who are 25 through 40 years old, the criteria formula can be entered as **+Age>=25#AND#Age<=40**. In this instance, an age entry must match both criteria.

If you specify your search criteria using the #OR# logical operator, Quattro Pro searches for any record that contains either of the specified criteria. Referring back to the employee example, any employee who is 25 years old or male will be matched if the criteria are entered as **+Age=25#OR#Sex="Male"**. Figure 11.12 contains another example of specified criteria using the #OR# logical operator. In this case, the formula criteria matches all records with amounts below 4000 and above 9000. If you want to look at records for employees under 25 as well as those employees over 40, you can use this formula criteria entry: **+Age<25#OR#Age>40**. The #OR# operator is perfect since it is not possible for one record to meet both conditions.

The #NOT# logical operator is used to match records that do not meet a set of criteria. For example, if your criterion is entered as **#NOT#Age= 25**, Quattro Pro finds employees whose ages are not equal to 25. (The same criterion can be specified by using the <> operator.) You can also use the #NOT# logical operator to negate multiple formula criteria, and it is more practical in this situation. For example, if you enter **+Age=25#OR##NOT#Sex="Female"**, Quattro Pro finds employees whose ages are equal to 25 OR whose sex is not female. The #NOT# logical operator can be used in another multiple criteria situation. For example, you can specify search criteria: **#NOT#(Vendor="ABCCompany" #AND#Amount=5560.75)**. Using the #NOT# logical operator in this manner alters the #AND# logical operator to an #OR# logical operator. In this particular example, Quattro Pro matches any record in which the vendor is not ABC Company OR the invoice amount is not equal to $5,560.75.

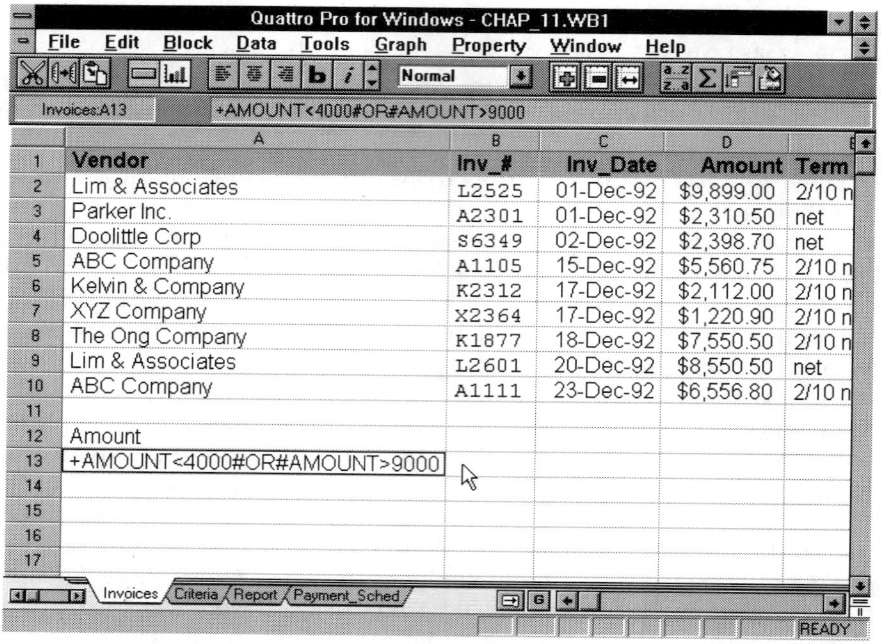

Figure 11.12   Formula Criteria Using Complex Logical Operators

You can also create compound criteria by selecting the row in the criteria table in which you want to place the exact match entries or formula criteria. Quattro Pro interprets the relationship between data entered on the same horizontal line as having an "AND" relationship. This means that a record must satisfy both criteria before it can be located. For example, to create criteria that find unpaid invoices with payment terms of 2/10 net 30 (2% reduction if paid within 10 days or the full sum paid within 30 days), you can have **Term** and **Paid_Date** in the first row of the criteria table and **'2/10 net 30** and **@CELL("type",PAID_DATE)="b"** as the entries below these field names on the second row (the @CELL function returns a "b" when the cell it references is blank, which indicates an unpaid invoice).

When entries are on separate lines, Quattro Pro interprets these entries as having an "OR" relationship. This means that a record is matched if it meets either of the specified criteria. For example, to create criteria that find unpaid invoices or invoices greater than $8,000, you can enter **Amount** and **Paid_Date** in the first row of the criteria table, **+AMOUNT>8000** one row below the Amount field name, and **@CELL("type",PAID_DATE)="b"** in two rows below the Paid_Date field name.

Locating Matching Records

Once you specify your criteria, you can locate all the records that match your specifications. To have Quattro Pro highlight the first matching record, choose

Locate from the Data Query dialog box. Quattro Pro searches only the block specified by the Block option. When a matching record is located, Quattro Pro highlights only the fields within the block. Figure 11.13 provides an example of a record highlighted with Locate. Notice the FIND mode indicator in the status line.

To view the next record, press the DOWN ARROW key. When you get to the last record, Quattro Pro does not allow you to go down any farther. It beeps whenever you try to do so. Similarly, Quattro Pro does not allow you to move above the first matching record. You can move to previous matching records with the UP ARROW key. Two other keys that can be used are the END and the HOME keys. The END key is used if you want to go to the last record matching your criteria, and the HOME key takes you back to the first record meeting your specifications. You can also move to a matching record by clicking it with the mouse. Quattro Pro beeps when you click a record that does not match the criteria.

You can edit the entry for any field when Quattro Pro locates the desired database record. You can use the LEFT and RIGHT ARROW keys to move the selector to the cell within the record that you wish to edit. Next, press F2 (EDIT) or click the entry in the input line to invoke the EDIT mode and make your changes, and then press ENTER to finalize the changes. You can move to other cells of the matching records to edit their entries. Instead of using the EDIT mode to change the cell entries, you can make the changes by typing in the entries. To exit from FIND mode, press ESC or ENTER, and Quattro Pro will return you to the Data Query dialog box.

	A	B	C	D	E	F
1	**Vendor**	**Inv_#**	**Inv_Date**	**Amount**	**Term**	**Paid_Date**
2	Lim & Associates	L2525	01-Dec-92	$9,899.00	2/10 net 30	14-Dec-92
3	Parker Inc.	A2301	01-Dec-92	$2,310.50	net	10-Dec-92
4	Doolittle Corp	S6349	02-Dec-92	$2,398.70	net	14-Dec-92
5	ABC Company	A1105	15-Dec-92	$5,560.75	2/10 net 30	22-Dec-92
6	Kelvin & Company	K2312	17-Dec-92	$2,112.00	2/10 net 30	
7	XYZ Company	X2364	17-Dec-92	$1,220.90	2/10 net 30	
8	The Ong Company	K1877	18-Dec-92	$7,550.50	2/10 net 30	
9	Lim & Associates	L2601	20-Dec-92	$8,550.50	net	
10	ABC Company	A1111	23-Dec-92	$6,556.80	2/10 net 30	
11						
12	Amount					
13	+AMOUNT<4000#C					

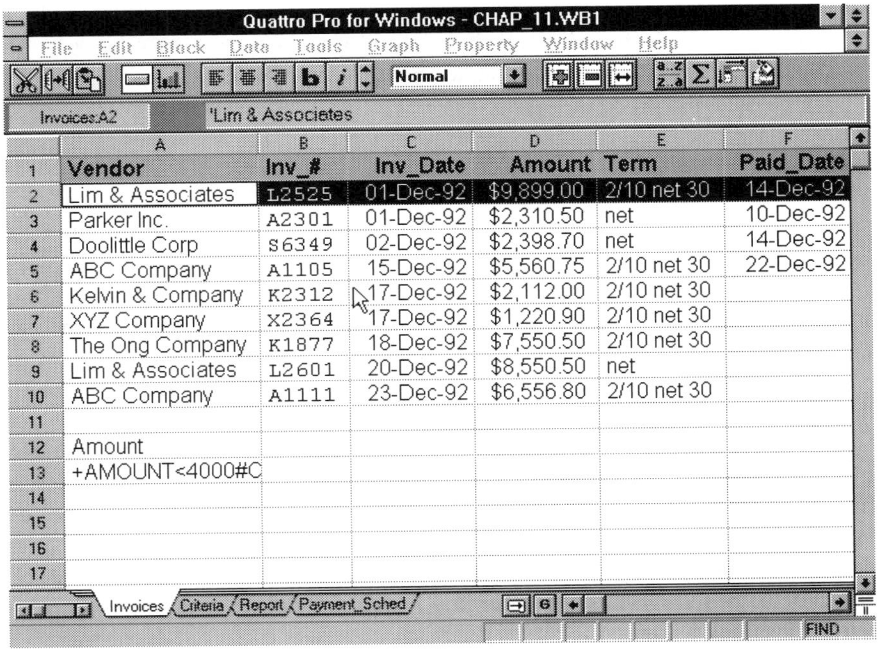

Figure 11.13 Matching Record Highlighted

If you want to quickly perform the same data query operation from the Data Query dialog box while you are in the READY mode, press F7 (QUERY). You can use this key when you return to the READY mode, change the criteria in the criteria table, and want to see the effect of the new criteria. You can use this for the Locate button in the Data Query dialog box as well as the Delete, Extract, and Extract Unique button covered later in the chapter.

BUILDING EXCEPTION REPORTS WITH QUATTRO PRO'S EXTRACT FEATURES

The Locate feature provides a quick answer for questions you might have about the data in your database. You can think of Locate as an ideal solution for handling telephone inquiries concerning data in your records. Sometimes you might want printed reports of records that meet your specifications. For example, you may need a report of all vendor invoice amounts over $7,000 to focus attention on the suppliers of large orders, or you may need to prepare a report of all invoices from a particular vendor. In these instances, the Locate feature in Quattro Pro cannot serve your objectives efficiently, since you only can look at one matching record at a time. Quattro Pro can handle this new task through Extract from the Data Query dialog box. This dialog box also has Extract Unique, which finds unique records for you, and Delete, which removes records from the database that meet the criteria.

Before invoking Extract, you need to create an output area and define its location to Quattro Pro. In other respects, Extract follows the same procedures as Locate and accepts either table or formula criteria for your specifications.

Creating an Output Area

You must create an output area in READY mode before you can define its location to Quattro Pro. Selecting an appropriate location will make it easier to work with your data-management application. If you want the output on the same page as your database, the area beneath the database is frequently selected for the output area. If you choose this location, you should leave a number of blank rows after your database to allow for expansion. Alternatively, you can use an area to the right of your database.

Another possibility is to use a separate notebook page or another notebook for the output area so that your database and output do not interfere with each other as the database and output areas expand. When you use a separate page for the output block, you reference that page with the page name and a colon before the block address, as you learned in Chapter 2. If you are using a separate notebook for the output block, you must enter the notebook name in brackets ([ ]) before entering the block address. If the drive or directory is different from those of the current notebook, you must supply this information in the brackets. If the extension is not .WB1, the notebook name in the brackets must include the extension. If you point to the block, Quattro Pro will add the notebook name and the page name for you.

The notebook with the output block must be open to use the Extract and Extract Unique query features. As an example, the database in Figure 11.14 is on the INVOICES page, the criterion is on the CRITERIA page, and the output block is on the REPORT page.

After you choose a location for your output area, type in the field names you wish to extract from the records or copy the field names you used above your database records. The fields need not be in the same sequence as the fields in your database, and you do not need to include every field. However, correct spelling is essential, since Quattro Pro matches these field names with the ones in your database. If you are including heading information above the field names in the output area for the report you are creating with the results of extracting records, you can hide the field names with the Hidden numeric format. When you print the report, the hidden field names appear in the report as a blank line. You can also hide the row with the field names by inspecting the properties of one of the cells and changing the Hide/Reveal property to hide the row.

After typing or copying the field names to the top of the output area, you must define the output area to Quattro Pro. Specify the output area in the Output Block text box in the Data Query dialog box. You select the block using any of the

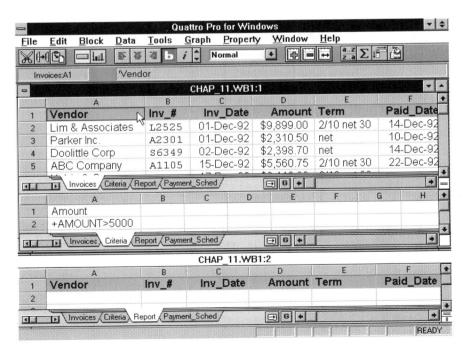

Figure 11.14   Locating an Output Area on a Separate Page

methods that you learned about in Chapter 2. In Figure 11.14, the selected output block is A1..F1. If you point to a block on another page or notebook, Quattro Pro will add the page and notebook information for you.

The size of the output block you select affects the results of the extract operation. If you specify a block that consists of only the field names, Quattro Pro interprets the output block to extend from the field names you selected as the output area to the bottom of the spreadsheet. Any previous data located in this area are lost, since Quattro Pro erases the entire output area before copying new records to it. If you have data stored below the output block, you must select the output area carefully to ensure that any previous data is not lost. For the example in Figure 11.14, this is the method used, since only Report:A1..F1 is selected.

Another option for the output block is including as many rows as you want the output block to fill. When Quattro Pro copies records to the output block, it copies only as many records as it can fit in the block. If you specify an output block that is too small for the extracted data, Quattro Pro stops copying records when the output block is full and displays an error message informing you that the output block is too small to contain all the desired data. To correct this situation, you need to expand the size of the output area and execute Extract or Extract Unique again. An example of this type of selection is choosing A1..F5 in Figure 11.14. If the data query operation has more than four records to copy, Quattro Pro will fill this block, then display an error message.

Extracting Matching Information

After you have set up the criteria table and defined the output block, select the Extract option from the Query menu. Quattro Pro extracts the data from your database that meet your criteria and places them in your specified output block. At this point, you may want to select OK to return to your data while saving the data query settings. Figure 11.15 shows the extracted data for invoice amounts above $5,000. Any formulas in the database are converted into numbers in the output area.

Extracting Unique Records

Your database may contain information in some fields in one record that exactly matches the contents of the same fields in another record within the database. This duplicate data may indicate duplicate records or specific fields with repeating entries. If you use the Extract feature, Quattro Pro extracts all records that meet your specification and may produce a list that includes the duplicate data. These duplicate entries may be what you are looking for; however, in some cases, you may prefer to have a listing of each unique entry that meets your specifications. One such situation occurs when the output block does not include all the fields from the database. For example, if you are compiling a list of your customers to create a mailing list, you will want a list of all the unique names in the Vendor

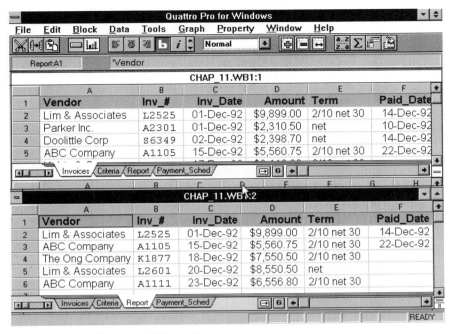

Figure 11.15   Extracted Records

field. Using the Extract command button creates a list of all the vendors, but many of them will be listed more than once.

Quattro Pro's Extract Unique option lists only those records that are different from records already in the extract area. If two records have a different entry in any field that is copied to the output block, the records are considered unique. Quattro Pro extracts the data from these records as separate and unique records. In this case, the two records are not unique. The Unique_Vendors page in Figure 11.16 shows a list of company names, with each listed one time by use of the Extract Unique option. The criteria table consists of Vendor with a blank cell below it to purposefully match with every record in the database. Note that Lim & Associates appears twice in the invoice database but is only listed once in the output area.

Deleting Matching Records

Quattro Pro's Query features allow you to delete database records that match your criteria. This feature is useful, for example, if your database includes obsolete inventory items. Instead of searching through the database to delete one item at a time, you can use Delete from the Data Query dialog box to delete them all at once based on the criteria set up in a criteria table.

To delete the matching records you must select a database block and criteria when you select Delete from the Data Query dialog box; Quattro Pro prompts you to

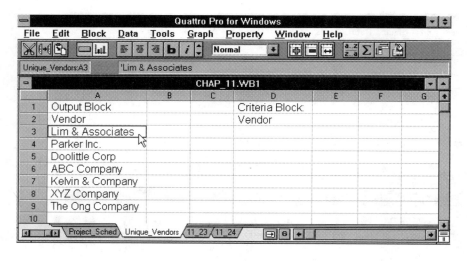

Figure 11.16   A List of Unique Vendor Names

confirm your decision by selecting Yes. A word of caution is necessary at this stage. You can purge outdated records in one easy step; however, if your criteria are not correct, you may lose some records that you want to retain. You should test your criteria with the Extract or Locate option before electing to delete them. You can also delete database records by deleting the row containing the record, but you should only use this method if the page does not contain non-database information that might be erased by deleting the row and if you are not deleting the last record, which destroys the block address selected in the Database Block text box.

USING AN EXTERNAL DATABASE

While Quattro Pro provides excellent database features, you also may need to use databases that are stored in different formats. For example, if you have your employee database applications developed for dBASE or Paradox, you may not want to switch the data files to Quattro Pro's spreadsheet notebook format to edit the data in Quattro Pro. One option is to retrieve the file and let Quattro Pro automatically translate the database into a spreadsheet notebook. When you are finished editing, you can let Quattro Pro automatically translate the notebook containing your database to a file in the format you want. When you are performing queries on existing databases, you may not feel like translating all the files you want to use. Instead, Quattro Pro can perform queries on the file without translating the database file. There are so few differences between querying an external database and querying a database stored in another notebook that you will find Quattro Pro's advanced feature easy to use. When you query an external database, you can use the Extract and Extract Unique options. Since the database already has field names assigned, you do not need to use the Field Names button in the Data Query dialog box. You will want to use an external database when you want to extract data from it and use Quattro Pro's spreadsheet features to present the extracted information. You also have other options for working with external databases using the Database Desktop.

The most distinctive feature of using an external database is how you tell Quattro Pro which file to use. When you select the database location in the Database Block text box, you must type the database file name and extension enclosed in square brackets followed by a block address. For example, if you want to use the EMPLOY dBASE IV database, type **[EMPLOY.DBF]A1..A2** as the block. The block address that follows the file name has no meaning but prevents Quattro Pro from rejecting the external file name because of a syntax error. You can select any block address that contains at least two rows. If the file is in a drive or directory other than the default, you must supply the appropriate drive and path name. The file extension is required, since it is not Quattro Pro's default of .WB1.

The other distinctive feature of using an external database is that you must include the file name and extension just as if you were using a database in a separate notebook. For example, if you are querying the EMPLOY database partially shown in Figure 11.17 to list the employees hired after January 1, 1989, you would enter **+[EMPLOY.DBF]HIRE_DATE>@DATE(89,1,1)** in a line in the table criteria.

The file that contains the information for the external database, the criteria, and the output area to use must be saved as a Quattro Pro .WB1 file. The other file formats are not designed to store the information to link to the external database. When you later retrieve this spreadsheet, Quattro Pro prompts you to indicate whether you want to load the supporting files, update the references, or neither. Since the criteria are evaluated when a query is performed, you can select **None** (= neither). Even though the criteria are displayed as N/A, the criteria still work when you query the database.

THE DATABASE DESKTOP

Quattro Pro for Windows has a Database Desktop which you can use to work with data stored in dBASE, Paradox, and some SQL formats. The advantage of using the Database Desktop over putting the database's data directly opening the database in Quattro Pro is that you can create a new database that combines the results of the several databases into one. For example, you can combine your supplier address database with your inventory database to create another database with information from both databases.

In the Database Desktop, each dBASE, Paradox and database file is called a table. SQL data is already stored in tables. To combine the data from multiple

```
 Records      Fields      Go To      Exit                        5:46:04 pm
┌─────────────┬──────────────┬───────────┬────────────┬──────────────────┬────────────┬────┐
│SSN          │LAST_NAME     │M_INITIAL  │FIRST_NAME  │ADDRESS           │CITY        │ST  │
├─────────────┼──────────────┼───────────┼────────────┼──────────────────┼────────────┼────┤
│215-90-8761  │Jenkins       │M          │Mary        │11 North St.      │Cleveland   │OH  │
│675-98-1239  │Foster        │G          │Charles     │67 Green Rd.      │Chicago     │IL  │
│654-11-9087  │Garrison      │G          │Henry       │56 Chesaco Lane   │Baltimore   │MD  │
│888-99-7654  │Larson        │J          │Karen       │45 York Rd.       │Cleveland   │OH  │
│555-66-7777  │Walker        │P          │Paula       │123 Lucy Lane     │Chicago     │IL  │
│555-66-7777  │York          │J          │Sally       │1119 Oak Way      │Baltimore   │MD  │
│111-55-1111  │Stilman       │J          │Mary        │1124 York Rd.     │Baltimore   │MD  │
│900-11-1111  │Smith         │J          │Talon       │                  │            │    │
│900-22-2222  │St. John      │           │Anne        │                  │            │    │
└─────────────┴──────────────┴───────────┴────────────┴──────────────────┴────────────┴────┘
 Browse    F:\q2\EMPLOY              Rec 1/9           File                    Num
```

Figure 11.17   dBASE IV Database Containing Employee Records

tables, you create a query. The query selects how you join the tables and which records of the combined tables you want. The query's results are stored in an answer table.

Opening the Database Desktop

Opening the Database Desktop opens the Database Desktop application, which is a separate application from Quattro Pro. To open the Database Desktop, select Database Desktop from the Data menu. Once the Database Desktop is loaded, it looks like Figure 11.18. The area in this window is called a *desktop*, where you can place tables and queries. When you open the Database Desktop on subsequent times, the desktop will contain the tables and queries left on the desktop when you closed the Database Desktop. You can also start the Database Desktop by selecting the Database Desktop icon in the Program Manager. Once the Database Desktop is open, you can return to Quattro Pro by switching to that application just as you switch between other applications. When you are finished using the Database Desktop, you can close it using the same commands, mouse selections, or keystroke combinations you use to close Quattro Pro for Windows.

When you open the Database Desktop the first time you may want to tell the Database Desktop where your files are stored. To do this, select Working Directory from the File menu. In the Working Directory text box, type the location where your data files are stored. This is also the directory where the Database Desktop

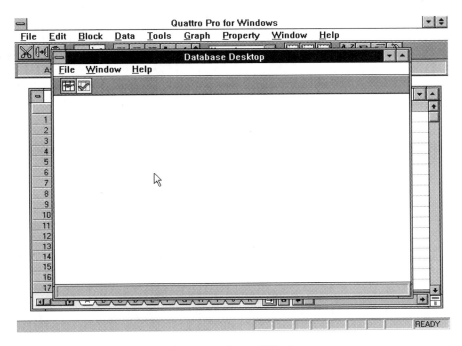

Figure 11.18   Initial Database Desktop Window

will put your queries, which are stored in separate QBE files. You also have the option of selecting an alias. An alias in the Database Desktop is a name that represents a path. For example, if you have a path called C:\QPW\DATA \PARADOX for the directory that contains the Paradox files you are using in Quattro Pro, you may want to create an alias called PARADOX that represents this path. To create an alias, select Aliases from the File menu and then select the New button. In the Database Alias drop-down list box, type the name you want to use for the alias. In the Path text box, type the path that the alias represents. Select Keep New and then the Save to disk button. Select OK to confirm the change. Once you create an alias, you can use the alias as the working directory by selecting it from the Aliases drop-down list box when you select Working Directory from the File menu. When you select an alias in the Database Desktop, you will notice that the Database Desktop has placed colons on either side. Another alias you will see is the *priv alias*. This is automatically set to the C:\QPW subdirectory that will store the answer tables for the queries you create. You can change it to another directory using the Private Directory command in the File menu.

Adding Tables to the Database Desktop

The Database Desktop contains a collection of related tables and the queries that use them. You can add tables to the Database Desktop to view the data in the table. To add tables to the Database Desktop, select Open from the File menu then select

Table. You can also click the Open Table button in the SpeedBar, which is the first button in the SpeedBar shown in Figure 11.18. The Database Desktop displays the Open a Table dialog box. From this dialog box, you can select a file to add as a table to the desktop. You can change the location of files listed by selecting an alias from the Path drop-down list box. Another option for selecting a file is to select the Browse button and browse through the files to select the one you want. You can open more than one table by holding SHIFT down while you select adjoining tables. You can select non-adjacent tables by holding down CTRL and clicking the files you want to open as tables on the desktop. Once you select OK, the table appears in a window like the one in Figure 11.19.

Once a table is added to the desktop, you can look at and edit the contents of the table. Figure 11.19 shows a table opened in a window in the Database Desktop. From this window, you can move to the data you want. The first three buttons in the SpeedBar are the same buttons for copying and pasting data between the Database Desktop and other applications. The next six buttons in the SpeedBar are for quickly moving between records. These buttons move you to the first record, up a window, to the previous record, to the next record, down a window, and to the last record, left to right. These six buttons also have keystroke equivalents of CTRL-F11, SHIFT-F11, F11, F12, SHIFT-F12, and CTRL-F12. You can also use the commands in the Record menu to move through the records in the table. You can

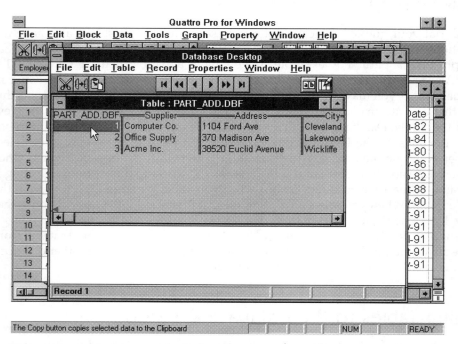

Figure 11.19   Table Added to Database Desktop

also use the keys that move you through the database the way they move you through a database on a notebook page.

While you display the table's data in a window, you can edit it. Move to the data you want to change. To tell the Database Desktop you want to edit the data, choose <u>E</u>dit Data from the <u>T</u>able menu, press F9, or click the Edit Data button (the last one in the SpeedBar). Now, the status line includes Edit to indicate that you can change the data displayed. You can then either type a new entry to replace the current entry or you can press F2 or click the part of the entry you want to change just as if you are editing a cell. You can add records by pressing INS or selecting <u>I</u>nsert from the <u>R</u>ecord menu. You can delete records by pressing CTRL-DEL or selecting <u>D</u>elete from the <u>R</u>ecord menu. When you are finished editing the data, choose <u>E</u>nd Edit from the <u>T</u>able menu, press F9 again, or click the Edit Data button again. When Edit does not appear in the status line, you cannot change the data, add records, or remove records.

Creating a Query

To effectively use the Database Desktop, you need to select the data you want to see. This selection process is called a *query*. A query includes selecting the fields from the tables you want to see and excluding data from the tables you do not want. To create a query, select <u>N</u>ew Query from the <u>F</u>ile menu. You can also create a query by selecting the New Query button from the SpeedBar shown in Figure 11.18. (The New Query button is the second one.)

The first step in creating a query is selecting the tables containing the data you want the query to use. From the dialog box presented, you can select the table or tables to add to the query. To select multiple adjoining tables, select one table then hold down SHIFT while you click the last table you want to add. If you want to add multiple non-adjoining tables, select the first one in the list then hold down CTRL while you click the remaining tables you want to add to the query. When you select OK, a table frame for each selected table is added to the query window as shown in Figure 11.20. You can later add tables to a query by selecting <u>A</u>dd Table from the <u>Q</u>uery menu or by clicking the Add Table button on the SpeedBar (the one with a plus sign on it). If you want to remove one of the tables from a query, select <u>R</u>emove Table from the <u>Q</u>uery menu or click the Remove Table button on the SpeedBar (the one with a minus sign on it).

The check boxes below the field names select which fields from the tables are included in the query. An empty check box means the field will not appear in the query; click it so that it contains a check mark to include the field in the query. You can also select the entire table by clicking the check box below the table's name. If you want to remove a field from the query's result, click the check box next to the field and that selects an empty check box from the drop-down list box.

There is another important step of a query: When you have more than one table, you must tell the Database Desktop how the tables are related. For example, when you have your supplier database and your inventory database in a query, you

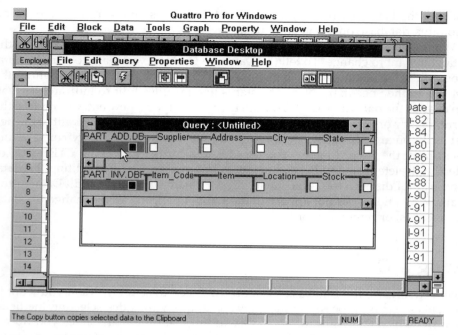

Figure 11.20   Query Design in the Database Desktop

want the suppliers in the supplier database to be matched to the inventory items that the suppliers provide. Usually the tables have one or more fields in common. To tell the Database Desktop which field from a table matches the contents of the field in another table, you need to place an example variable in the fields of each table. To create and add an example variable, select the Join Tables button in the SpeedBar. The status line now contains Performing join and Join. Next, click the field from one table that matches the values of a field in the other table. Quattro Pro adds EG01 or, if it is already used in the query, EG followed by the next lowest unused number. For example, in the tables shown in Figure 11.20, you would select Supplier in both the PART_ADD.DBF and PART_INV.DBF table frames. In this example the field names are the same, but they do not have to be. When you add an example variable, the Database Desktop matches the records in one table with the records in the second table using these matching fields to join the tables.

The final step of preparing the query is adding the criteria that select which records from the combined tables the query displays. The criteria you add in the Database Desktop are just like the criteria you add when you query a database in Quattro Pro. For example, to list the parts and supplier information for inventory items with fewer than 20 items, you will type **<20** under Stock.

Once you have the tables added to the query, the example variables added to join the records in the tables, and the criteria to select which records you want, you are ready to run the query. You can run the query by clicking the Run Query SpeedBar button (the fourth one on the SpeedBar), selecting Run from the Query menu, or pressing F8. The Database Desktop adds another window that contains a table of the query's results as shown in Figure 11.21. The query's results are stored in a table called ANSWER.DB, on your private directory (which is usually the directory containing Quattro Pro). Changes you make to the data in this query table are also updated in the table that contains the original data. This means that if you change the part number in the query's result table in Figure 11.21, it is also changed in the PART_INV.DBF table.

The query you have created can be put into a QBE file. This file is saved by switching to the window that you used to design the query and selecting Save from the File menu and typing a name for the query. You are also prompted to save the query when you close the window containing the query or close the Database Desktop application. When you save a query it is put into a file with a .QBE extension in the working directory. The query is a QBE format that Paradox can also use.

PUTTING QUERY RESULTS INTO A QUATTRO PRO NOTEBOOK The table from the query you have created provides you the information you need, but usually you will need to put the results of the query's table into Quattro Pro. You

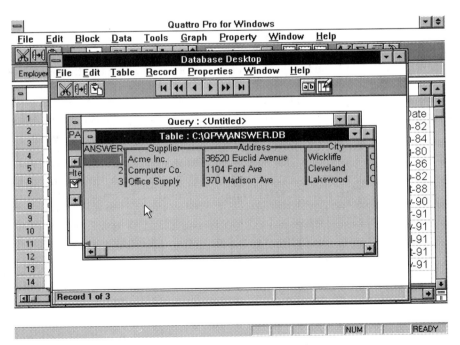

Figure 11.21 Query Table in the Database Desktop

have two methods to put the query's information into Quattro Pro: You can either use the Clipboard, or run the query from Quattro Pro.

Use the Clipboard to copy the data from the query's answer table to Quattro Pro just as you use it to copy the data between applications. First, in the answer table window in the Database Desktop, choose Select All from the Edit menu to select the entire answer table. Next, select Copy from the Edit menu to put the answer table on the Clipboard. Finally, switch to Quattro Pro for Windows and move to where you want the table placed. Select Paste from the Edit menu and the Clipboard contents are put into the current notebook.

The second method you have of putting the query's results into Quattro Pro is running the query from Quattro Pro. To run a Database Desktop query from Quattro Pro for Windows, select Table Query from the Data menu in Quattro Pro. In the Table Query dialog box, enter the name of the QBE file you have created in the Database Desktop or Paradox in the QBE file text box. You can also select the Browse button and select a file to add to the QBE file text box. Next, select where you want the answer table placed in the Destination text box. When you select OK, the query is performed and the answer table's contents are placed in the Quattro Pro block. If you have inserted a Paradox or Database Desktop query onto a notebook, you can also select to use the query stored in the block by selecting the Query in Block radio button in the Table Query dialog box and selecting the block containing the query in the QBE block text box.

CREATING QUERIES UPDATED WITH QUATTRO PRO DATA Besides entering the criteria for a query in the Database Desktop underneath a field name in the query window, you can create a query that uses data stored in a Quattro Pro notebook. For example, you can have a criterion that you store in Quattro Pro that is also used in a query in the Database Desktop. Figure 11.22 shows one of these queries. In the notebook, the entry in M:A1 of the C:\QPW\DATA\CHAP11 notebook contains the supplier name that you want to find in the combined PART_INV.DBF and PART_ADD.DBF tables in the Database Desktop. This Quattro Pro cell entry is copied to the Clipboard with Copy in the Edit menu. Next, you switch to the field in the table frame of the Query window of the Database Desktop where you want to use the data from Quattro Pro for the query's criterion. Select Paste Link from the Edit menu. In the query design in Figure 11.22, the Database Desktop has added the formula @DDE:QPW!C:\QPW\DATA\CHAP11.WB1!$M:$A$2..$A$2!@ as the criterion. This DDE formula tells the Database Desktop to use the data from the Quattro Pro notebook for that criterion entry. Every time you run the query in the Database Desktop, the Database Desktop uses the most current value of M:A2. You may also want to select Wait for DDE from the Query menu. When this command has a check mark next to it, every time you change the Quattro Pro cell entry the link uses, Database Desktop reperforms the query to include this updated entry. When this command does not have a check mark next to it, the Database Desktop only updates the query when you explicitly tell it to by running the query from the Database Desktop.

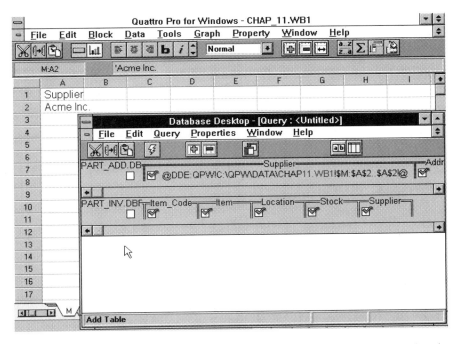

Figure 11.22 Query That Uses Criterion from a Quattro Pro Notebook

DATABASE STATISTICAL FUNCTIONS

The database statistical functions combine the power of the statistical functions with the flexibility of the database features. You can selectively include the values in database records within these calculations by using criteria specifications like the ones used for the Query operations.

▼ TIP: Creating a Macro to Use the Database Desktop

If you frequently are using the Database Desktop and then putting the query back into Quattro Pro, you may want to use the DDE commands you will learn about in Chapter 14. The DDE commands let you run applications, such as the Database Desktop, from within Quattro Pro.

The database statistical functions can be used to perform quick computations. They can also be used with the sensitivity analysis features you learned about in Chapter 5 to exhaustively perform computations for each unique field entry. A complete report composed of nothing but database statistical functions provides a quick solution for a management summary report.

For example, you can use these functions to calculate the average salary paid to employees in a specific location or job code using the employee data in Figure 11.23. With a quick change in a function you can calculate the total amount of salaries paid employees whose records meet an established set of criteria.

Syntax of the Database Functions

The arguments for the statistical functions follow the same basic format as other arguments previously described. They begin with an @ followed by the keyword for the function and an open parenthesis. The three arguments for any of these functions select the input records, the offset column in the database, and the criteria location.

The *block* argument is the location of your database. The input records include the field names and all the database records. You can specify a block by a block address or you can assign a name to the block and specify the input records using

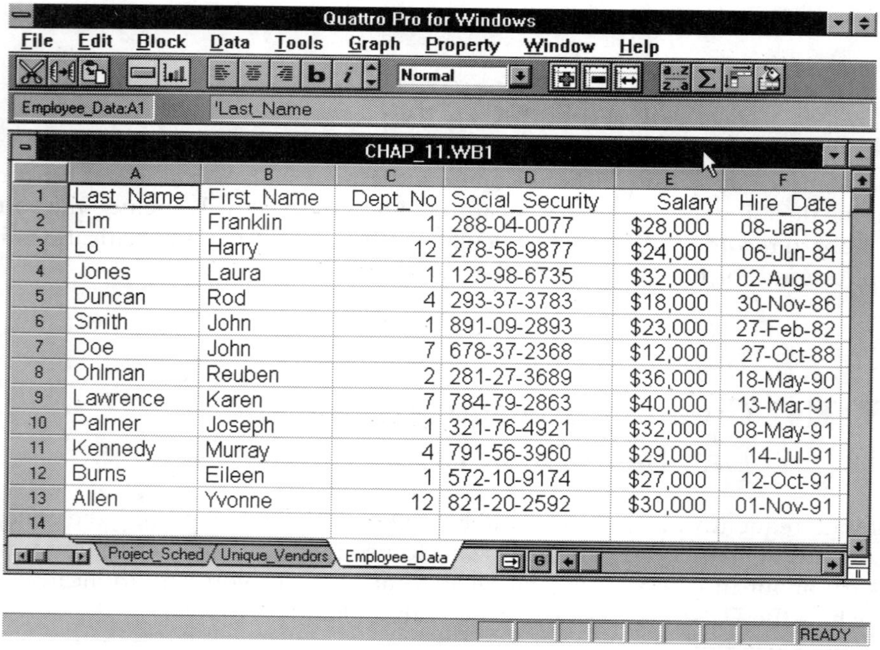

	A	B	C	D	E	F
1	Last Name	First_Name	Dept_No	Social_Security	Salary	Hire_Date
2	Lim	Franklin	1	288-04-0077	$28,000	08-Jan-82
3	Lo	Harry	12	278-56-9877	$24,000	06-Jun-84
4	Jones	Laura	1	123-98-6735	$32,000	02-Aug-80
5	Duncan	Rod	4	293-37-3783	$18,000	30-Nov-86
6	Smith	John	1	891-09-2893	$23,000	27-Feb-82
7	Doe	John	7	678-37-2368	$12,000	27-Oct-88
8	Ohlman	Reuben	2	281-27-3689	$36,000	18-May-90
9	Lawrence	Karen	7	784-79-2863	$40,000	13-Mar-91
10	Palmer	Joseph	1	321-76-4921	$32,000	08-May-91
11	Kennedy	Murray	4	791-56-3960	$29,000	14-Jul-91
12	Burns	Eileen	1	572-10-9174	$27,000	12-Oct-91
13	Allen	Yvonne	12	821-20-2592	$30,000	01-Nov-91
14						

Figure 11.23   Employee Database

the assigned name. You can also refer to a particular section of your database; however, the block must include all fields that are included in the criteria block and the column of the database that you want to use in the database statistical function. If the database is in a different spreadsheet, the block address or name must be preceded by the file name in brackets ([ ]). If you provide a block address for a database on a different page, make sure to include the page name and a colon as part of the block address.

The *column* refers to the position number of the field used for the computations. To specify the column of the field, remember that the first column in your database is column 0, and the second column is column 1 according to Quattro Pro's numbering scheme. The field that you select should contain numeric entries, except for @DCOUNT, which counts label entries as well as numeric entries. If the column the function uses contains label entries other than the field name, the labels are treated as zeros for the computations (which distorts the results of functions like @DAVG, @DSTD, @DSTDS, @DVAR, and @DVARS).

The *criteria* argument is the location of your criteria table on the spreadsheet. You can specify the location of your criteria by referring to a block of cells or by referring to an assigned name. Remember to include the field names that appear at the top of your criteria when selecting the location.

@DAVG   The @DAVG command allows you to compute the average of a set of values in a field within a selected group of records. @DAVG(block,column,criteria) is the syntax for this command. The function arguments are the ones defined in the previous section.

You can use @DAVG to obtain the average salary for all employees who work in department 1. The input line in Figure 11.24 shows the syntax and results of the @DAVG formula. The result of this computation is shown in cell D15. The block is located in **A1..F13**. This is the location of your database. Notice that the field names are included as part of your block. The column number is **4** since Salary is the fifth column. Quattro Pro averages the values for the Salary field of the records that meet the criteria. The criteria argument is **A16..A17**. In this example, you have instructed Quattro Pro to compute the average salary of all employees who are employed in department 1; that average salary is $28,400.

@DCOUNT   The @DCOUNT command allows you to count the number of nonblank entries in a field within database records, which match your criteria. @DCOUNT(block,column,criteria) is the syntax for this command. The column argument for @DCOUNT differs from the other database statistical function arguments in that the offset can reference a field that contains label entries. Since the nonblank entities are counted and not involved in arithmetic computations, it is not necessary for them to contain values.

You can use the @DCOUNT function with the data in Figure 11.24 to obtain the total number of employees in department 1 by using the formula **@DCOUNT(A1..F13,0,A16..A17).** The offset number is 0 for this example to reference the Last Name field. In this case, Quattro Pro has been instructed to count

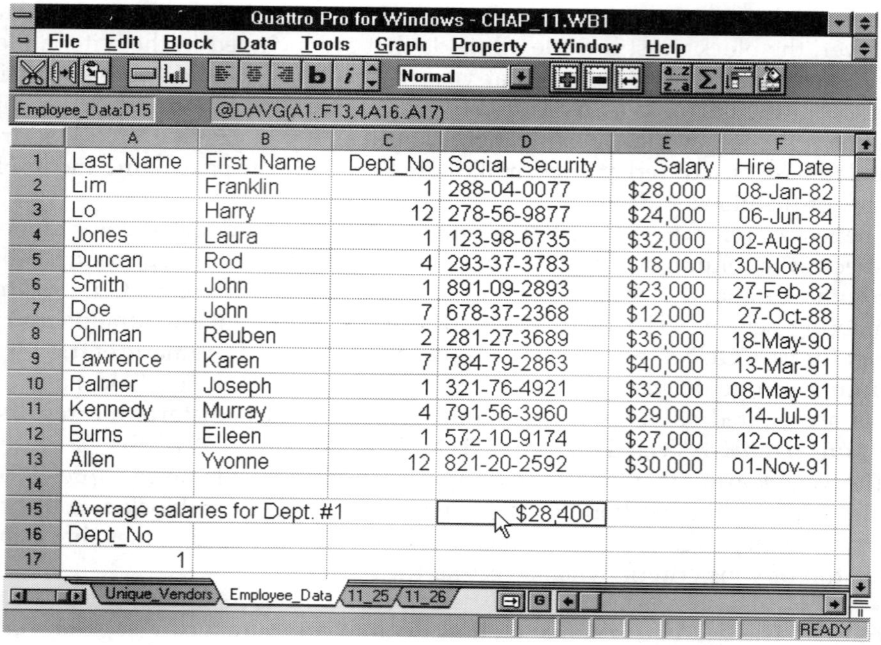

Figure 11.24   @DAVG Used to Find the Average Employee Salary for Department 1

the number of records in department 1 with a nonblank entry in the Last Name field, and it returns a 5.

@DMAX   The @DMAX command allows you to locate the maximum value in a field within a selected group of database records. @DMAX(block,column,criteria) is the syntax for this command. @DMAX uses the same function arguments defined earlier. You can use the @DMAX function in place of @DAVG in Figure 11.24 to find the highest salary paid to an employee in Department 1 with the formula **@DMAX(A1..F13,4,A16..A17)**. The block is **A1..F13** and includes the field names. The offset number is 4 to work with the Salary field. The criteria argument is **A16..A17**, which directs Quattro Pro to select records in department 1. Using the employee database, Quattro Pro computes the maximum salary of the employees in department 1 as $32,000.

@DMIN The @DMIN command allows you to locate the minimum value in a field within a selected group of database records. @DMIN(block,column,criteria) is the syntax for this command. @DMIN uses the same function arguments defined earlier. You can use the @DMIN function in place of @DAVG to find the lowest salary paid to an employee in Department 1. This @DMIN formula is **@DMIN(A1..F13,4,A16..17)**. The block is **A1..F13** and includes the field names.

The offset number is **4** to work with the Salary field. The criteria argument is **A16..A17**, which directs Quattro Pro to select records in department 1. For the employee database, Quattro Pro computes the minimum salary of the employees in department 1 to be $23,000.

@DSUM The @DSUM command allows you to selectively sum the values in a field within a group of records. @DSUM(block,column,criteria) is the syntax for this command.

For example, you can obtain the total salary for all the employees in department 1 as shown in Figure 11.25. The syntax for using the @DSUM function is shown in the input line. The block is **A1..F13**, and the field names are included as part of the block. The column number (**4**) tells Quattro Pro that the field you want to use for your calculations is the Salary field. The criteria argument is described in **A16..A17**. In this case, the $142,000 shown in cell D15 is the result of the @SUM computation.

@DSTD The @DSTD command allows you to compute the standard deviation of values in a field within a selected group of database records. This function uses the assumption that the database contains the records for all possible cases. If the database does not contain all records, use the @DSTDS function instead. The standard deviation measurement is very useful because it allows you to determine the amount of variation between a set of individual values and their mean. For

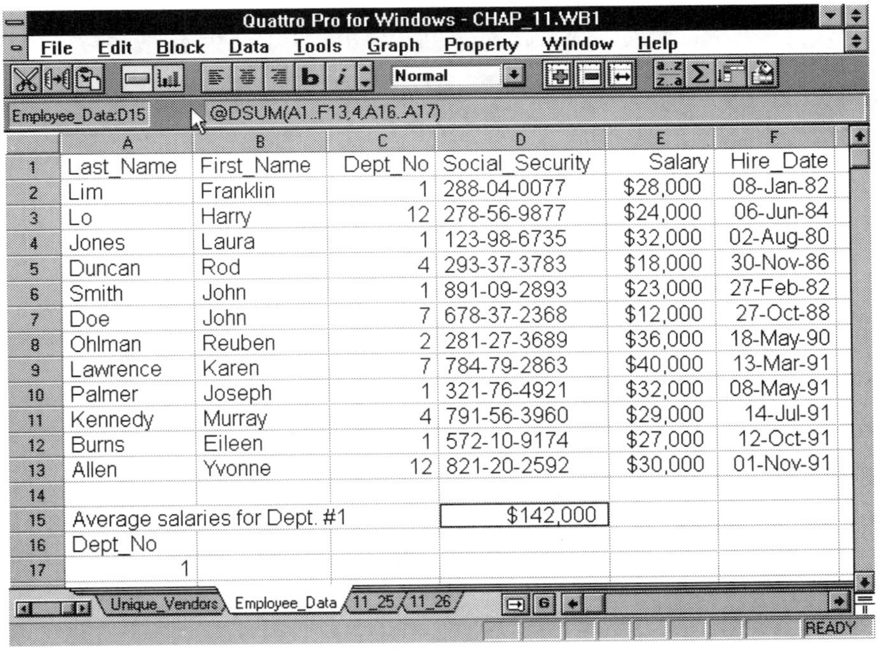

	A	B	C	D	E	F
1	Last_Name	First_Name	Dept_No	Social_Security	Salary	Hire_Date
2	Lim	Franklin	1	288-04-0077	$28,000	08-Jan-82
3	Lo	Harry	12	278-56-9877	$24,000	06-Jun-84
4	Jones	Laura	1	123-98-6735	$32,000	02-Aug-80
5	Duncan	Rod	4	293-37-3783	$18,000	30-Nov-86
6	Smith	John	1	891-09-2893	$23,000	27-Feb-82
7	Doe	John	7	678-37-2368	$12,000	27-Oct-88
8	Ohlman	Reuben	2	281-27-3689	$36,000	18-May-90
9	Lawrence	Karen	7	784-79-2863	$40,000	13-Mar-91
10	Palmer	Joseph	1	321-76-4921	$32,000	08-May-91
11	Kennedy	Murray	4	791-56-3960	$29,000	14-Jul-91
12	Burns	Eileen	1	572-10-9174	$27,000	12-Oct-91
13	Allen	Yvonne	12	821-20-2592	$30,000	01-Nov-91
14						
15	Average salaries for Dept. #1			$142,000		
16	Dept_No					
17	1					

Figure 11.25 @DSUM Used to Total Salaries for Department 1

example, the average time to complete a production run in department 1 is 3 hours. The range of completion times may be 1–5 hours, or it may be 2.5–3.5 hours. The standard deviation of the latter case is probably smaller than that of the former because of the smaller variance from the mean. This measurement is useful in this case because, if the standard deviation is large, it implies that there are many production runs that vary significantly from the average, indicating that potential problems exist in these runs. The standard deviation is the square root of the variance. The units for the standard measurement are the same as those of the field used to calculate this measurement. @DSTD(block, column, criteria) is the syntax for this command. The arguments for @DSTD are identical to those of the other database statistical function arguments.

You can use @DSTD to calculate the standard deviation of the completion time of product 1 as shown in Figure 11.26. The syntax for using the @DSTD function is shown in the input line and references the block in **A1..B13**. An offset of **1** is used to reference the Completion Time field. Quattro Pro calculates the standard deviation of the completion time for product 1 as 1.019804.

@DSTDS   The @DSTDS command allows you to compute the standard deviation of values in a field within a selected group of database records. This function assumes that the database does not include all records that apply. @DSTDS(block, column, criteria) is the syntax for this command. The arguments for @DSTDS are identical to the other database statistical function arguments.

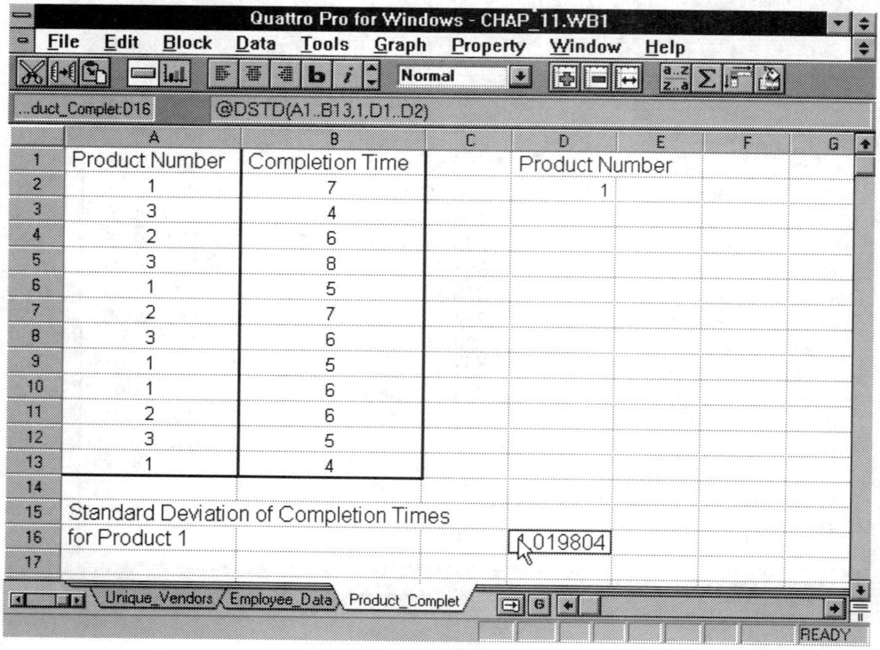

Figure 11.26   @DSTD Used to Calculate a Selective Standard Deviation

You can use @DSTDS to calculate the standard deviation of the completion time of product 1, if you are assuming the database does not contain all records for product 1. The formula is **@DSTDS(A1..B13,1,D1..D2)**. Quattro Pro calculates the standard deviation of the completion time for product 1 as 1.140175. The difference between the standard deviation with @DSTD and @DSTDS is due to changing the assumption about whether the database includes all possible records for product 1.

@DVAR   The @DVAR command allows you to compute the variance of a set of values in a field within a selected group of database records. The variance is the square of the standard deviation. It also measures the amount of variation between a set of individual items about its mean. This function uses the assumption that the database contains the records for all possible cases. If the database does not contain all of the records, use the @DVARS function instead. @DVAR(block,column,criteria) is the syntax for this command. The arguments for @DVAR are identical to the arguments for the other database statistical functions.

You can use @DVAR to calculate the variance of the completion time of product 1 as shown in Figure 11.27. The syntax for using the @DVAR function is shown in the input line. The database is in **A1..B13**; an offset of **1** references the Completion Time field. Quattro Pro calculates the variance to be 1.04.

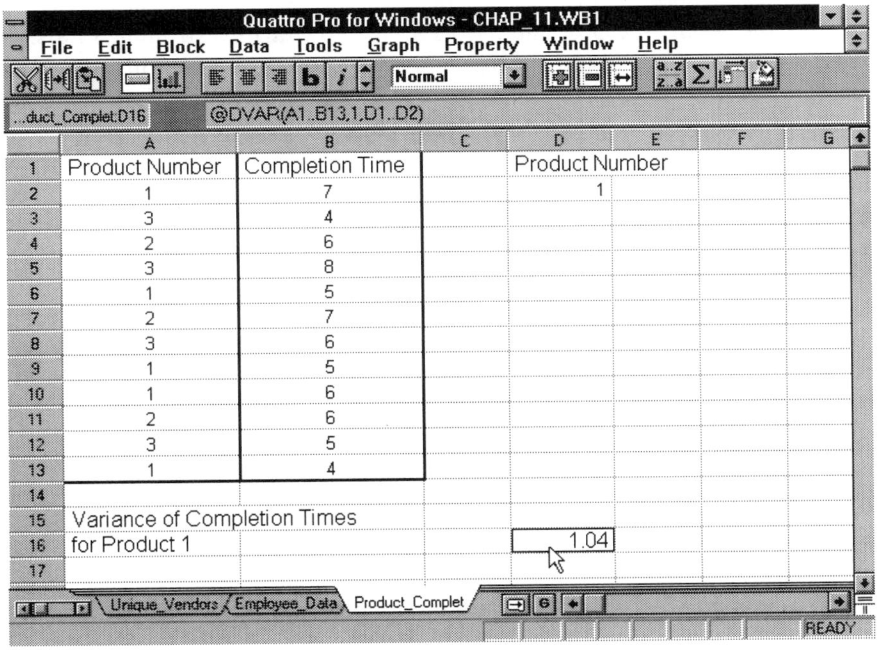

Figure 11.27   @DVAR Used to Calculate a Selective Variance

@DVARS   The @DVARS command allows you to compute the variance of values in a field within a selected group of database records. This function assumes that the database does not include all records that apply. The syntax for this command is @DVARS(block, column, criteria). The arguments for @DVARS are identical to the arguments for other database statistical functions.

You can use @DVARS to calculate the variance of the completion time of product 1, if you are assuming the database does not contain all records for product 1. The @DVARS formula for this example is **@DVARS(A1..B13,1,D1..D2)**. Quattro Pro calculates the variance of the completion time for product 1 as 1.3. The difference between the variance with @DVAR and @DVARS is due to changing the assumption about whether the database includes all possible records.

Building a Management Summary Report with Database Statistical Functions

The database statistical functions can be used to provide a simple total or average at the bottom of the database, but they also can be used to create an entire summary report. For databases that consist of large numbers of detailed transactions, the database statistical functions can help clarify the meaning of the data. You can use these functions to prepare a summary report consisting of totals and averages by product, sales region, or any other feature of the database. Use the database statistical commands described earlier to perform these computations.

Figure 11.28 provides an example from a management summary report that assimilates the detail in 2,500 database records into a few succinct totals. This report was prepared using only those database statistical functions already described. The entries in column D are the @DSUM functions that reference a database stored in Region Sales: A1..G2500. This database contains detailed sales transactions for the current quarter by region and product. A series of criteria entries on the spreadsheet reference the appropriate records. The criteria used in the formula displayed in D5 select records for June 1992 for the sales of computers in region 1. The offset of 1 references the sales column, totaling only the records that match the criteria.

Although it takes a little effort to create all the criteria areas required for this type of report, your efforts will be rewarded month after month. If you name the database area with a block name, the formulas produce the correct results as the database size expands and contracts from month to month.

Combining the What-If Analysis with the Database Statistical Functions

The what-if analysis features discussed in Chapter 5 can be combined with the database statistical functions to provide statistics on the entries of a Quattro Pro database quickly. The values stored in the columns and rows of the table can be

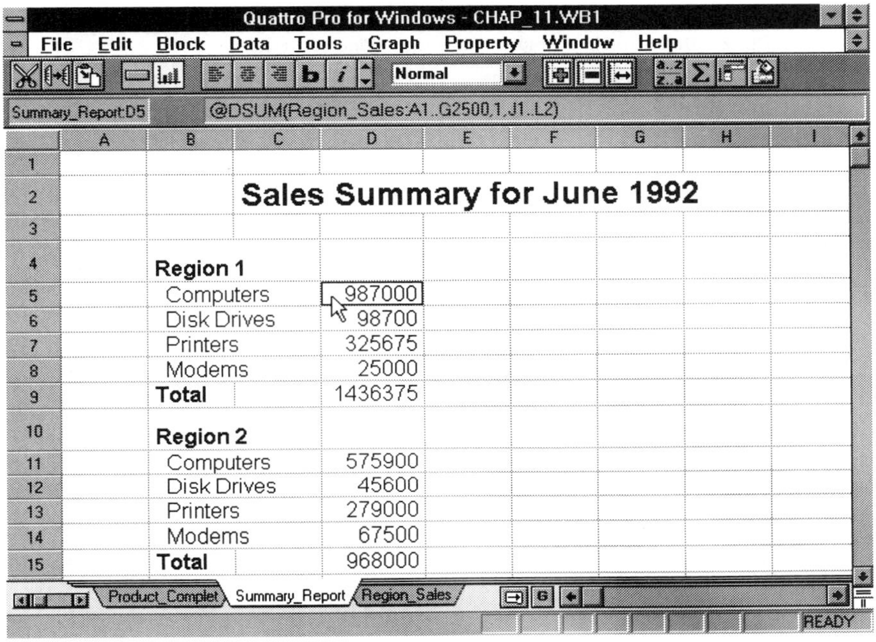

Figure 11.28 A Portion of a Summary Report Created with Database Statistical Functions

used to replace criteria values, and the table's formula can be one of the database statistical functions that references these criteria entries.

Figure 11.29 shows a 2 Way what-if table that uses a database statistical function. The table's formula adds the selling cost of the automobiles, depending on the salesperson and the type of automobile. The what-if analysis computes the total sales of each type of automobile sold by each salesperson.

After placing the input values in the rows and columns of the table, the database statistical function @DSUM is entered in E7 and a hidden format is selected. Select the What-If command from the Data menu to open the What-If dialog box. Select the Two free variables radio button, type F2 as the first input cell in the Column input cell text box, and G2 as the second input variable in the Row input cell text box. Both the input cells are criteria entries for the database function. Select Generate and the Close button. The information in this table can be used for commission computations and sales reports.

Unlike using the database statistical functions directly, combining these functions with the what-if table features does not recalculate the values in the table automatically if the values in the database change. However, combining the database statistical functions with the what-if features provides a quick approach for performing the same calculation with multiple criteria values.

When you are creating the table to be combined with a database statistical function, the input values that you are going to use as the criteria must all be

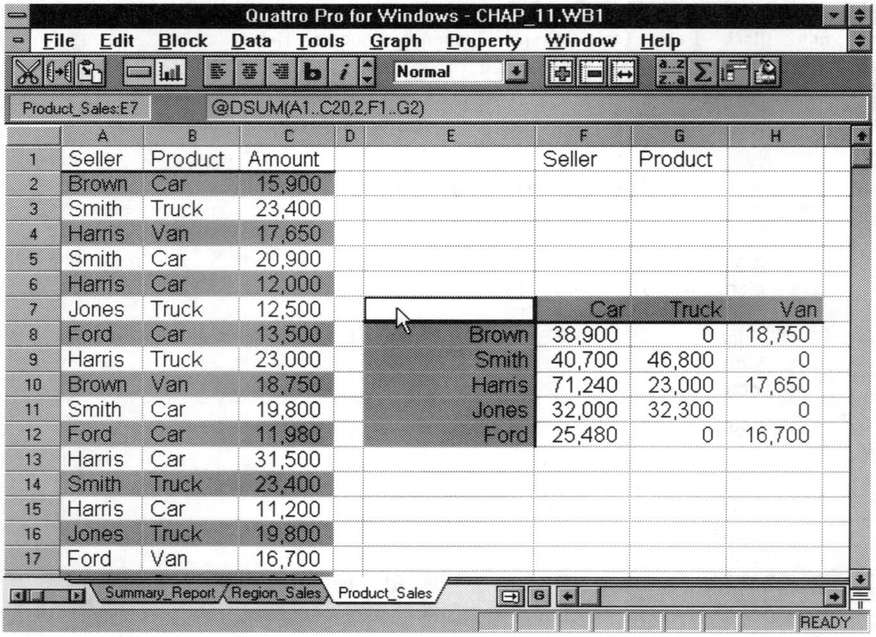

Figure 11.29 2 Way Table Combined with a Database Statistical Function

acceptable criteria values. For example, if one of the criteria that the input value replaces uses dates, all values for the input row or column must be valid date serial numbers. You can always generate a list of the unique entries in a database field by using the Extract Unique command. You can subsequently use the query's output for row or column input values.

GETTING STARTED

In this chapter, you learned how to create databases and how to use the information stored in the databases to answer queries and create reports. You can try some of these skills by following these steps:

1. Set column A to accept only dates since the first field in this database contains date information. Select the block A4..A20 and inspect its properties. Select the Data Entry Input property, the Dates Only radio button, and OK. Although you will not use all the cells in this column, you select a block with more rows than necessary so that your database can expand without your entering this command again. A1 through A3 is omitted so

you can enter a title for your spreadsheet and a column heading for the date field.

2. Make the following entries to create a database. Since you have set A4..A20 to accept only dates, you can type them as they appear.

A1: **Petty Cash Register**
A3: ^**Date**
B3: "**Amount**
C3: **Explanation**
A4: **9/20/92**
B4: **14.87**
C4: **Sugar for coffee**
A5: **9/18/92**
B5: **3.99**
C5: **Coffee filters**
A6: **9/15/92**
B6: **30**
C6: **Stamps**
A7: **9/21/92**
B7: **25.36**
C7: **Computer screen cleaner**

3. Set the amounts in column B to currency with two digits. Select the block B4..B20 and inspect its properties. With the Numeric Format property selected, select the Currency radio button, and OK.

4. Find the records that are used for coffee supplies. Select the cell C3. Press CTRL-INS or click Copy in the SpeedBar to copy the field name to the Clipboard. Select G1 and press SHIFT-INS or click Paste in the SpeedBar to copy the entry from C3 to G1. You will make fewer mistakes if you copy the field names to the criteria table instead of retyping them. Type ***Coffee*** in G2 and finalize the entry. Select Query in the Data menu. Select the block A3..C7 in the Database Block text box. Select Field Names so that you can use the field names instead of the addresses. Select the block G1..G2 in the Criteria Table text box. Select Locate. Quattro Pro highlights the record in row 4. Since the search is not case sensitive, Quattro Pro finds coffee whether the letters are uppercase or lowercase. Press ESC, and select Close to return to the READY mode.

5. Sort the records you entered in step 1. Select the block A4..C7, then select Sort from the Data menu. The dialog box already has the correct block entered in the Block text box. In the 1st text box, press F3 (CHOICES), and select DATE. Select the adjoining check box in the Ascending column. Select OK to sort the records according to their dates. Your entries should now be in the same sequence as those in Figure 11.30.

6. Change the criteria to a formula criteria that can find all amounts greater than or equal to $25.00. Move to G1. Type "**Amount**, and press the DOWN

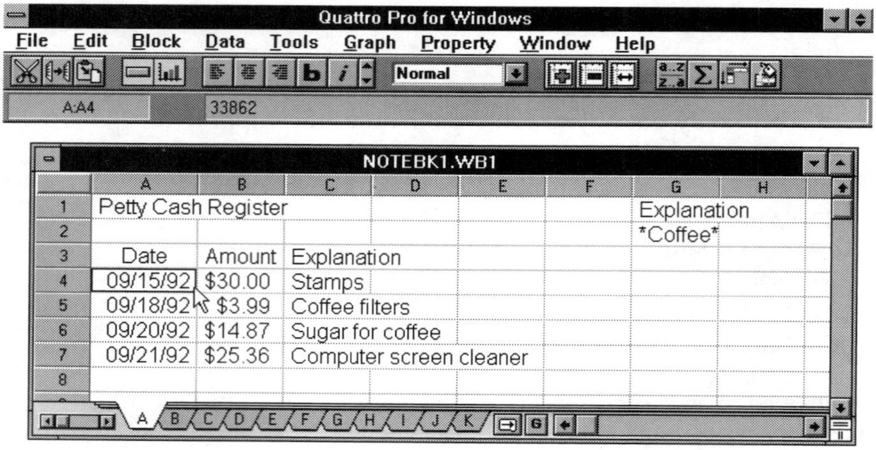

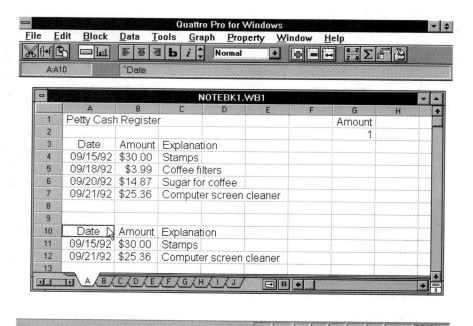

Figure 11.30   Database Created in Getting Started Section

ARROW or click G2. Since the field name is short, typing may be a shorter method, even if you have to correct typing mistakes. Type **+**. Press F3 (CHOICES), and select AMOUNT. Type **>=25** and press ENTER or click ✓ in the input line.

Figure 11.31   Extracted Records from Getting Started Section

7. Create an output block that you can use as the basis for a report. Select the block A3..C3. Press CTRL-INS or click Copy in the SpeedBar to copy the field names to the Clipboard. Select A10 and press SHIFT-INS or click Paste in the SpeedBar to copy the field names to A10..C10. Select Query from the Data menu and select the block A10..C10 in the Output Block text box.

8. Select Extract and Close. This copies two of the records to the output block as shown in Figure 11.31. You may use this output block as the basis for determining which petty cash payments you want to check to confirm that the petty cash fund is being used correctly.

12
Customizing Quattro Pro

Once you have mastered Quattro Pro's basic features, you can consider customizing some of Quattro Pro's settings. Customizing Quattro Pro's settings increases your performance with Quattro Pro by eliminating some of the changes that you make for each session and by allowing you to set up the menus, which offer the package's features, to meet your specific needs.

Several of the customization commands were covered in earlier chapters along with the specific features they affect. These customization options include properties for blocks, pages, and graphs and the objects in the graphs. This chapter summarizes the notebook and application properties covered earlier and includes others that have not been discussed, thus providing a one-stop reference for customizing Quattro Pro. It also provides information on the different parts of Windows' Control Panel that control how Quattro Pro operates, including some of the settings Quattro Pro can borrow as well as the fonts and the printers Quattro Pro uses. Finally, this chapter covers creating SpeedBars and dialog boxes. You can create SpeedBars to supplement Quattro Pro's primary SpeedBar or to replace it. You can create dialog boxes to combine with the macros that you will learn about in the next chapter.

APPLICATION PROPERTIES

Application properties affect how Quattro Pro performs. These options include which parts of the window are displayed; how dates, currency values, and times are formatted; the location where Quattro Pro looks for files; how Quattro Pro runs macros; and whether you are using a secondary SpeedBar. These options are available by inspecting the application's properties. To inspect the application's properties, right click the title bar, press ALT-F12, or select Application from the Property menu. Quattro Pro displays a dialog box like the one shown in

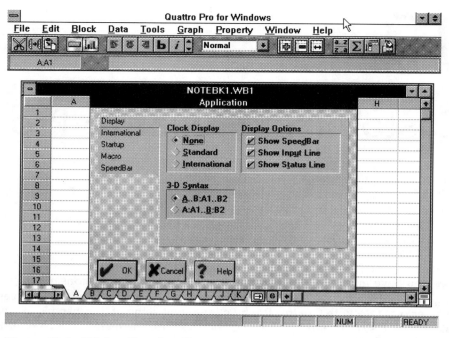

Figure 12.1   Dialog Box for Changing Application Properties

Figure 12.1. Changes made to these properties are automatically saved for future Quattro Pro sessions.

Changing the Application Window Display

The Display property contains several features that change how the Quattro Pro application window appears. These changes include displaying a clock in the status line, setting how three-dimensional blocks are indicated, and displaying the status line, SpeedBar, and input line.

Quattro Pro uses the status line to display information about the current session. You can use the status line to display the date and time. Quattro Pro displays the date and time on the left side of the status line if you select Standard or International for the Display application property. If you select Standard, the date is shown in the DD-MMM-YY format and the time is shown in the HH:MM AM/PM format. If you select International, the date uses the long format and the time uses the short format of the date and time formats set by the International application property. If you select None, the date and time disappear from the status line.

If the date or time is incorrect, activate the Control Panel from the Program Manager's Main group window. Then select the Date/Time icon or Date/Time from the Settings menu. In the Date & Time dialog box, type the new numbers for the different components of the date and time or use the arrows to increase or decrease the current values. When you select OK, the date and time in Quattro Pro's status line, as well as other Windows applications that use the date and time, are updated.

If you need more room in the application window for notebook and graph windows, you can increase the space for them by removing the status line, input line, and SpeedBar. To remove any one of these items, clear the Show SpeedBar, Show Input Line, or Show Status Line check box. You only need to clear the boxes for the parts of the screen you want to remove. Figure 12.2 shows a Quattro Pro window after the status line, input line, and SpeedBar are removed. When you want to add one or more parts of the application window back, select the Display application property and then select the Show SpeedBar, Show Input Line, or Show Status Line check boxes. When you hide the SpeedBar, you are hiding it in all situations it appears including as you work on graphs and dialog boxes.

When a block refers to two or more pages, it is a three-dimensional block. This is just like comparing one loose-leaf page as a two-dimensional block instead of a full notebook, which has depth as well as width and height. The three-dimensional block addresses in Quattro Pro can appear in formulas and commands two ways: with the first and last pages before the column and row information as in A..C:D10..H50, or with the first page name before the first column and row and the

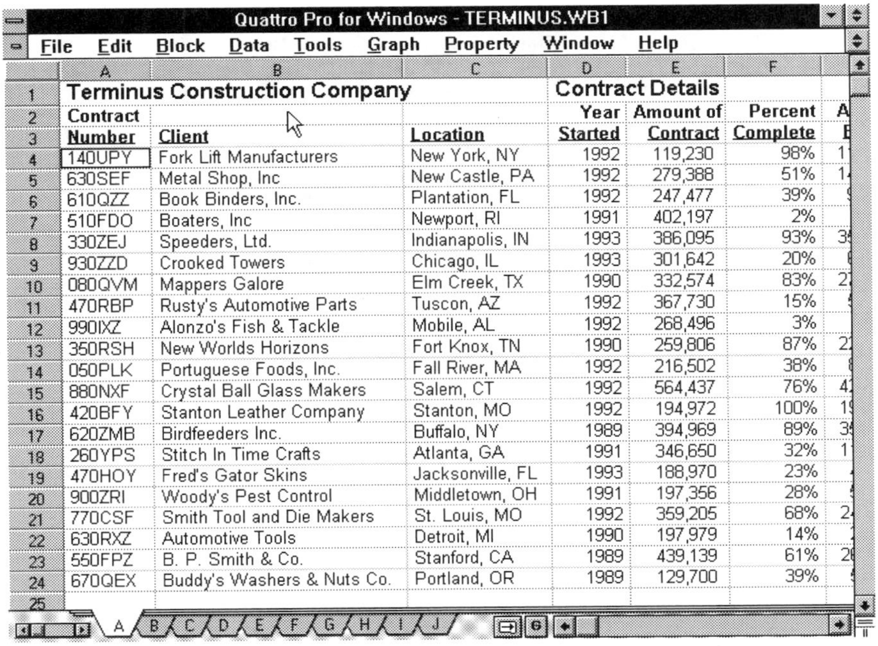

	A	B	C	D	E	F
1	Terminus Construction Company			Contract Details		
2	Contract			Year	Amount of	Percent	A
3	Number	Client	Location	Started	Contract	Complete	
4	140UPY	Fork Lift Manufacturers	New York, NY	1992	119,230	98%	1
5	630SEF	Metal Shop, Inc	New Castle, PA	1992	279,388	51%	1
6	610QZZ	Book Binders, Inc.	Plantation, FL	1992	247,477	39%	
7	510FDO	Boaters, Inc	Newport, RI	1991	402,197	2%	
8	330ZEJ	Speeders, Ltd.	Indianapolis, IN	1993	386,095	93%	3
9	930ZZD	Crooked Towers	Chicago, IL	1993	301,642	20%	
10	080QVM	Mappers Galore	Elm Creek, TX	1990	332,574	83%	2
11	470RBP	Rusty's Automotive Parts	Tuscon, AZ	1992	367,730	15%	
12	990IXZ	Alonzo's Fish & Tackle	Mobile, AL	1992	268,496	3%	
13	350RSH	New Worlds Horizons	Fort Knox, TN	1990	259,806	87%	2
14	050PLK	Portuguese Foods, Inc.	Fall River, MA	1992	216,502	38%	
15	880NXF	Crystal Ball Glass Makers	Salem, CT	1992	564,437	76%	4
16	420BFY	Stanton Leather Company	Stanton, MO	1992	194,972	100%	1
17	620ZMB	Birdfeeders Inc.	Buffalo, NY	1989	394,969	89%	3
18	260YPS	Stitch In Time Crafts	Atlanta, GA	1991	346,650	32%	1
19	470HOY	Fred's Gator Skins	Jacksonville, FL	1993	188,970	23%	
20	900ZRI	Woody's Pest Control	Middletown, OH	1991	197,356	28%	
21	770CSF	Smith Tool and Die Makers	St. Louis, MO	1992	359,205	68%	2
22	630RXZ	Automotive Tools	Detroit, MI	1990	197,979	14%	
23	550FPZ	B. P. Smith & Co.	Stanford, CA	1989	439,139	61%	2
24	670QEX	Buddy's Washers & Nuts Co.	Portland, OR	1989	129,700	39%	
25							

Quattro Pro for Windows - TERMINUS.WB1

File   Edit   Block   Data   Tools   Graph   Property   Window   Help

Figure 12.2   Hiding the Status Line, Input Line, and SpeedBar

last page name before the last column and row, as in A:D10..C:H50. The first method is similar to Excel and the second method is similar to 1-2-3. You can display multi-page blocks by either method, so choose the one that is the most comfortable. To select the first method, select the A..B:A1..B2 radio button. To select the second method, select the A:A1..B:B2 radio button. The change in how multi-page blocks appear only changes their appearance, not how they are identified. You can continue entering them using either method, since both are valid ways of indicating a block. The difference is that the block you enter using the method you did not select is converted to display using the method you did select.

Changing International Settings

Quattro Pro has several settings that set how currency, dates, times, sort order, and punctuation appear. Initially, these are set to match the usage in the United States. You can change these settings to match another country. Changing the International application property changes how currency values, dates, and times appear as well as usage of the appropriate punctuation and the correct language for sorting. You can also change how extended characters are transferred between 1-2-3 files and Quattro Pro files. When you display the International application property, Quattro Pro changes the Application dialog box to look like Figure 12.3.

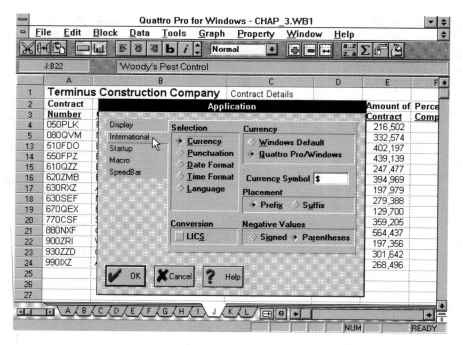

Figure 12.3   Changing the International Application Property

When you select a radio button under Selection, the selections you can make on the right side change to match the selected radio button. This means you can select Date Format to change the format of dates, then select Time Format to change the format of times, all from the same dialog box.

CHANGING THE CURRENCY DISPLAY   Selecting Currency allows you to change the default of the dollar ($) to another currency symbol, its position, and how negative numbers are indicated. For example, you may want to prepare financial statements in pounds (£). In the Currency Symbol text box, you can type the desired symbol. Type the new currency symbol and press ENTER. If the desired symbol cannot be found on the regular keyboard, you can create an ANSI character by holding down the ALT key and typing in the appropriate ANSI code on the numeric keypad. You can also select the location of the currency symbol in relation to the value by choosing the Prefix radio button if you want the currency symbol placed at the beginning of numbers or the Suffix radio button if you want the currency symbol to be placed at the end of numbers. To change how the comma and currency formats indicate negative numbers, under Negative Values, select either Parentheses to display negative numbers enclosed in parentheses or Signed to display negative numbers preceded by a minus sign.

Alternatively, you can select Windows Default. Windows Default sets the currency symbol, placement, and how negative values are displayed from the International dialog box in the Control Panel. When you open the Control Panel from the Program Manager's Main group window and then select the International icon or select International from the Settings menu, you can select Currency Format. This displays the International—Currency Format dialog box with Symbol Placement, Negative, Symbol, and Decimal Digits. This last option sets the default of how many digits are displayed after the decimal point for applications that do not have their own decimal digits settings. Symbol Placement, Negative, and Symbol let you make the same types of changes (to the symbol placement, how negative values are indicated, and the currency symbol used) as you can make in Quattro Pro. When you install Quattro Pro, it picks up the current currency settings from Windows to use as the initial settings for Quattro Pro for Windows.

CHANGING THE PUNCTUATION   Quattro Pro allows you to change the punctuation style that it uses to conform to the standards used in different countries. The choice of punctuation also affects how function and macro arguments are separated. When you select Punctuation, Quattro Pro displays the different selections for punctuation. The initial setting is 1,234.56 (a1,a2). Quattro Pro shows how the thousands are separated as the character between the 1 and the 2, the decimal point as the character between the 4 and the 5, and the function and macro argument separator as the character between a1 and a2. When you change the punctuation, Quattro Pro adjusts all existing functions and display formats for the new punctuation. Quattro Pro does not automatically change the macro argument separators.

▼ TIP: Change all macro instructions if you change punctuation.

If you change the punctuation used, use the Search and Replace command in the Edit menu to change the punctuation in the macro instructions.

If you select <u>W</u>indows Default, Quattro Pro uses the thousands separator, decimal indicator, and argument indicator that were set with the International dialog box in the Control Panel. When you open the Control Panel from the Program Manager's Main group window and then select the International icon or select <u>I</u>nternational from the <u>S</u>ettings menu, you can select <u>N</u>umber Format. This displays the International—Number Format dialog box, which displays the options 1000 <u>S</u>eparator, <u>D</u>ecimal Separator, D<u>e</u>cimal Digits, and <u>L</u>eading Zero. D<u>e</u>cimal Digits sets the default of how many digits are displayed after the decimal point for applications that do not have their own decimal digits settings. <u>L</u>eading Zero sets the default for whether a 0 is placed before a number that does not have any digits to the left of the decimal point in some applications. The 1000 <u>S</u>eparator and <u>D</u>ecimal Separator text boxes let you enter the characters to use to separate thousands and the decimal digits.

CHANGING THE DATE FORMAT   Selecting <u>D</u>ate Format for the International application property allows you to change the international date formats. The international formats for dates set the fourth and fifth date formats, which are available when you change a block's Numeric Format property. Quattro Pro has five date formats to choose from. The date formats except for the Windows Default are:

Long Form	Short Form
MM/DD/YY	MM/DD
DD/MM/YY	DD/MM
DD.MM.YY	DD.MM
YY-MM-DD	MM-DD

The long form of the international date format is the fourth selection of available date numeric formats. The short form of the international date format is the fifth selection of available date formats. Changing the international date format changes only the entries that use the fourth and fifth date format. Initially, Quattro Pro has the initial international date formats set to MM/DD/YY and MM/DD.

If you select <u>W</u>indows Default, Quattro Pro uses the date format set by the International dialog box in the Control Panel. When you open the Control Panel from the Program Manager's Main group window and then select the International icon or select <u>I</u>nternational from the <u>S</u>ettings menu, you can select <u>D</u>ate Format. From the International–Date Format dialog box, you can select the format for the short and long date format Quattro Pro and other Windows applications can use as

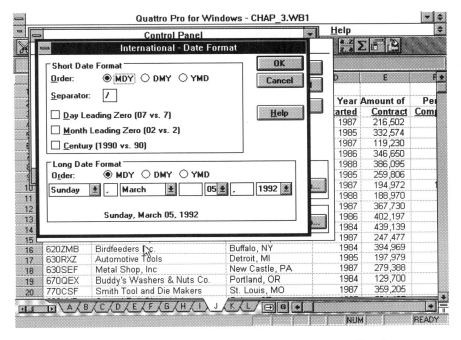

Figure 12.4   Setting the Date Format for Windows Applications

shown in Figure 12.4. For the short date format, you can select the order of the components, the character that separates the parts of the date, and whether single digits have a preceding 0. For the long date format, you can select the order, and then for each part of the date, you can select one of the options available from a drop-down list box, or type a character to use in a text box. When you close this dialog box and the International dialog box, Quattro Pro and other Windows applications can use the selected date format you have chosen.

CHANGING THE TIME FORMAT   Selecting Time Format for the International application property allows you to change the international time formats. The international time formats are the third and fourth time format when you change a block's Numeric Format property. Quattro Pro has five time formats to choose from. The time formats, except the Windows Default, are:

Long Form	Short Form
HH:MM:SS	HH:MM
HH.MM.SS	HH.MM
HH,MM,SS	HH,MM
HHhMMmSSs	HHhMMm

The long form of the international time format is the third selection of available time formats. The short form of the international time format is the fourth selection of available time formats. Changing the international time format changes only the entries that use the third and fourth time format. Initially, Quattro Pro has the initial formats set to HH:MM:SS and HH:MM.

If you select Windows Default, Quattro Pro uses the time format set by the International dialog box in the Control Panel. When you open the Control Panel from the Program Manager's Main group window and then select the International icon or select International from the Settings menu, you can select Time Format. From the International–Time Format dialog box, you can select whether 12 or 24 hours is used to represent the day. If you use 12, you can enter the characters you want to represent the morning and evening hours in place of AM and PM. You can also enter the character that separates the parts of the times. Finally, you can select whether single digits have a preceding 0. The time format you change with the Control Panel will affect other Windows applications that use the time and time format set by the Control Panel.

The international time formats use a 24-hour clock except for the Windows Default, which can use 12 or 24 hours. A 24-hour clock does not use A.M. or P.M. to designate whether a time is before noon or after noon. Instead, a 24-hour clock shows time before noon without any special designation. Times after noon have 12 added to the hour. For example, 9:00 A.M. is displayed as 9:00, and 9:00 P.M. is displayed as 21:00 (9 + 12 = 21).

CHANGING THE SORT ORDER　If you are using foreign characters in a block that you are sorting, you will want to change the order of the alphabet that Quattro Pro uses during sorting to include the foreign characters in their proper sequence. You can do this by selecting Language from the International application property. This changes the alphabet Quattro Pro uses to place data in alphabetical order. It can also affect the @UPPER, @LOWER, and @PROPER function to convert letters between upper- and lowercase. You can either select Windows Default or Quattro Pro/Windows. If you select Quattro Pro/Windows, you can also select the country from the list box below.

If you select Windows Default, Quattro Pro uses the language set by the International dialog box in the Control Panel. When you open the Control Panel from the Program Manager's Main group window and then select the International icon or select International from the Settings menu, you can select Language. From the drop-down list box, you can select the language you want to use in Quattro Pro as well as other Windows applications.

CHANGING CONVERSION OF LICS CHARACTERS　If you are using Quattro Pro with 1-2-3 files that include foreign characters and other characters for which the @CHAR function returns a number greater that 127, you will need to select the LICS check box. When this check box is selected, Quattro Pro retrieves LICS or LMBCS characters and converts them to their ANSI equivalents. When the file is saved, Quattro Pro saves all characters using the LICS or LMBCS character set that 1-2-3 uses (depending on the release). When this check box is not selected, Quattro Pro retrieves 1-2-3 files and treats the character numbers as ANSI character numbers so no conversion is performed.

Changing Startup Settings

Quattro Pro's startup settings provide information that Quattro Pro looks for each time the application is loaded. This information includes loading a designated spreadsheet, starting a macro, setting the default file extension, enabling undo, hearing the beep, and using keys compatible with Quattro Pro for DOS. All these startup options are part of the Startup property, which displays the dialog box shown in Figure 12.5.

SETTING THE STARTUP DIRECTORY   Every time you use a command that uses an external data file, such as saving or opening a file, Quattro Pro uses the current directory. This is usually the default directory selected with <u>D</u>irectory in the Startup application property but you can change it. Initially, the startup directory and drive are those containing the Quattro Pro application files. You can enter a new directory Quattro Pro should use by entering a new path in the <u>D</u>irectory text box for the Startup application property. The path must include the drive and directories, as in **C:\QPW\DATA**. Quattro Pro continues to use this directory until you change the directory using a command that opens and saves files. For example, if you save a file to another location, that other location becomes the current directory overriding the startup directory.

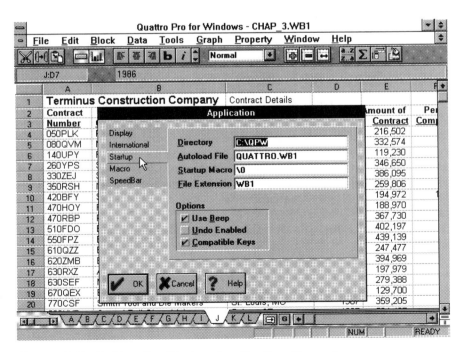

Figure 12.5   Setting the Startup Application Property

If no directory is put in the Directory text box, Quattro Pro uses the directory set by the program item in the Program Manager that starts Quattro Pro for Windows. A program item has the Working Directory property, which you can use to set the directory the application uses. Even when a working directory is set from the Program Manager, the startup directory set by Quattro Pro has priority. Quattro Pro only uses the Working Directory property of the program item when a startup directory is not selected.

AUTOMATICALLY LOADING A NOTEBOOK   You can automatically open a particular notebook each time you load Quattro Pro. When you enter a notebook name in the Autoload File text box of the Startup application property, Quattro Pro tries to open that notebook every time you start Quattro Pro. The file must be in the startup directory or you must supply the path as part of the notebook name. A practical use for this feature is when you use Quattro Pro primarily for one purpose and want to automatically load the notebook for that purpose every time you load Quattro Pro. This file name is initially set to QUATTRO.WB1, but you can change it to any file that Quattro Pro can load with the Retrieve or Open command in the File menu. If you remove the file name, Quattro Pro does not try to retrieve any file when you load Quattro Pro. Also, if you start Quattro Pro with QPW followed by a notebook's file name when you start Quattro Pro with the Run command in the File menu of the Program Manager, Quattro Pro loads the file name you enter after the QPW instead of the Autoload file.

AUTOMATICALLY STARTING A MACRO   If you use macros to automate using your notebooks, you may want a macro to take control of a particular spreadsheet immediately. This prevents a user from making any changes to the notebook that are not done under the control of the macro. For example, in a notebook with a macro that prompts for the monthly sales figures and creates graphs using the cumulative sales information, having a macro control the notebook as soon as it is opened immediately reduces potential errors.

You can specify the name of the macro that is automatically executed when a file containing a macro with that name is loaded. This autoload macro, initially called \0, can be changed to another valid macro name by entering the macro name in the Startup Macro text box for the Startup application property. Every time you open a notebook, Quattro Pro checks if the notebook has a macro with the selected name. If Quattro Pro finds a macro with the selected name, it executes the macro. If Quattro Pro does not find a macro with the selected name, it does nothing.

CHANGING THE DEFAULT EXTENSION   Quattro Pro allows you to specify the default file extension. Quattro Pro initially assumes that you are working with Quattro Pro notebooks and uses the default extension of .WB1. To change the default extension, enter a new extension without a period in the File Extension text box for the Startup application property. Change the default extension if you are using Quattro Pro primarily for non-Quattro data files such as 1-2-3, dBASE III, or

Paradox, since it will permit you to read and write these file types without supplying the file name extension each time.

SETTING THE ERROR BEEPS   Quattro Pro beeps when you make a mistake, such as trying to move beyond the edge of a spreadsheet. Although these beeps are informative, you may find them annoying. Quattro Pro allows you to turn off the beep that sounds whenever you make an error by clearing the Use Beep check box for the Startup application property. You can reinstate the beeping sound for errors by selecting this check box again.

The setting only affects beeping in Quattro Pro when the beeping is enabled for Windows. Windows controls the master switch that controls whether all Windows applications can beep. The Use Beep check box in Quattro Pro is the local switch for the application. To turn on or off beeping for all Windows applications, open the Control Panel from the Program Manager's Main group window and then select the Sound icon or select Sound from the Settings menu. Next, select the Enable System Sounds (Windows 3.1) or the Warning Beep (Windows 3.0) check box to allow Windows applications to beep to alert you to different messages. With Windows 3.1, you can also select different sounds to use for different occasions when you have a sound card installed.

SETTING UNDO   Quattro Pro's Undo feature, when it is enabled, allows you to remove the effect of a command you performed. To enable Undo, select the Undo Enabled check box. Once Undo is enabled, you can use Undo in the Edit menu to remove the effect of the last command.

Even when Undo is enabled, there are only some changes Quattro Pro can undo. Undo in the Edit menu undoes the effect of the last operation that can be affected by Undo. If you make several changes that Quattro Pro cannot undo and then select Undo in the Edit menu, Quattro Pro undoes the effect of the last change that Undo *can* change. When you display the Edit menu after selecting Undo, the Undo changes to Redo, which restores the change removed by selecting Undo the last time. Each time you select Undo in the Edit menu, Quattro Pro toggles between the spreadsheet before and after the operation that Undo is changing. Next to Undo and Redo is a brief description of the action this command will remove or restore the effect of.

When Undo is enabled, Quattro Pro runs slower, since it must spend some of your computer's computing power storing the effect of the changes you make. Undo also uses your computer's memory. Sometimes you cannot undo an action if Quattro Pro is short of memory. If you want to disable Undo, display the application properties, select Startup, and clear the Undo Enable check box.

SETTING COMPATIBLE KEYS   Depending on whether you have used Quattro Pro for DOS and other spreadsheet products before, you may want to set some of the keys to behave differently. Quattro Pro for Windows includes a Compatible Keys check box as part of the Startup application properties. This check box selects whether certain keys behave identically to other Windows applications or behave like they do in Quattro Pro for DOS. When this check box is selected (the default), the UP ARROW and DOWN ARROW keys move you from one entry to another, CTRL-LEFT ARROW and CTRL-RIGHT ARROW in EDIT mode move you five characters at a time in either direction, and, after pressing ALT-F3 (FUNCTIONS) to add a function, typing a letter adds the function that starts with the letter you have typed. If you are not accustomed to Quattro Pro with DOS, or you want to take advantage of Windows features, you will want to clear the Compatible Keys check box. When the check box is cleared, the UP ARROW and DOWN ARROW keys will move you between lines when you are editing a long entry, CTRL-LEFT ARROW and CTRL-RIGHT ARROW in EDIT mode will move you one word at a time, and, after pressing ALT-F3 (FUNCTIONS) to add a function, typing a letter highlights the function that starts with the letter you have typed without selecting it.

Setting Macro Options

Quattro Pro has several application properties that control how macros run. You will learn more about macros in the next two chapters, but you will want to know about these application properties to learn how to change how your macros and macros created for you work.

Quattro Pro performs macro instructions very quickly, much more quickly than you can enter the keystrokes. Quattro Pro must spend part of the computer's capacity updating the screen to reflect the most current changes. The updating process is called *redrawing the screen*. The macro can perform more quickly if Quattro Pro does not constantly redraw the screen. To set when Quattro Pro redraws the screen, select the Macro application property. You can select Both to suppress redrawing the entire Quattro Pro window while Quattro Pro performs the macro; Panel to suppress redrawing the menu bar, input line, status line, menus, and dialog boxes; Window to suppress redrawing the notebook windows; and None to remove suppression. You should remove redrawing suppression when you are checking your macros for errors. Once the macro performs as expected, you can suppress the redrawing so the macro performs quickly. If part or all of the screen is not redrawn when you perform a macro, Quattro Pro redraws the entire Quattro Pro window when the macro is finished.

If you are running a macro created for the 1-2-3 menu, you can easily run the macro in Quattro Pro for Windows. You will want to select the Key Reader check box. When this check box is selected, Quattro Pro assumes that the macro will use / followed by letters to select menu commands. Most of the time you want to clear the Key Reader check box. You do not need to make any change to run Quattro Pro for DOS macros in Quattro Pro for Windows, because Quattro Pro for Windows can correctly and automatically use the menu equivalent commands present in Quattro Pro for DOS commands. If you want to see a Quattro Pro for DOS macro execute as Quattro Pro for Windows executes it, select the Slash Key drop-down list box and Quattro Pro—DOS.

The Slash Key drop-down list box makes different menus available when you type a /. You can select which menu appears when you type a / by choosing between Menu Bar and Quattro Pro—DOS. The Quattro Pro—DOS choice imitates the Quattro Pro 3 for DOS menu. With the Quattro Pro—DOS menu, some commands are dimmed, since they do not apply to Quattro Pro for Windows. You can switch between using / to make menu commands from the alternate menu and using F10 or the mouse for Quattro Pro for Window's menu bar. If you are switching between packages, you may find that having the two menus available makes the transition easier.

Adding a Secondary SpeedBar

Besides the initial SpeedBar, you can have a second one. The second one is added below the first as in Figure 12.6. To add a second SpeedBar, select the SpeedBar application property. In the Secondary SpeedBar text box, you can type the name of the SpeedBar you wish to use. Another alternative is to select the Browse button and select a SpeedBar file. When you select OK from the Application dialog box, Quattro Pro adds the second SpeedBar as shown in Figure 12.6. If you only want to see and use the second SpeedBar, add the SpeedBar as described here and then select the Display application property and clear the Show SpeedBar check box. When you want to remove the secondary SpeedBar, select the SpeedBar application property, select the Reset button, and select OK.

Quattro Pro includes seven sample SpeedBars. Figure 12.6 shows the SECOND.BAR SpeedBar. You can also create your own SpeedBar. SpeedBars apply to the Quattro Pro application rather than a notebook. The steps involved in creating a SpeedBar are described later in the chapter.

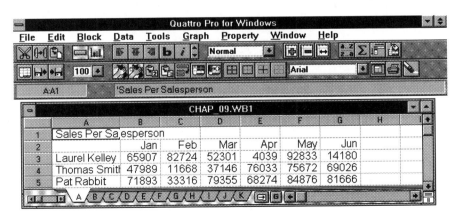

Figure 12.6 Secondary SpeedBar Added

NOTEBOOK PROPERTIES

Notebook properties apply to a specific notebook file. These properties include recalculation settings, notebook magnification, the colors in the notebook palette, information at the sides of a notebook window, and whether a notebook is a macro library. These options are available by inspecting the notebook's properties. To inspect the notebook's properties, right click the notebook's title bar if the notebook is not maximized to fill the Quattro Pro window, press SHIFT-F12, or select Active <u>N</u>otebook from the <u>P</u>roperty menu. Quattro Pro displays a dialog box like the one shown in Figure 12.7. The changes made to the notebook properties are saved with the notebook. If you have more than one copy of the notebook open by using <u>N</u>ew View in the <u>W</u>indow menu, the notebook properties of the copy of the notebook window that you save are kept.

Recalculation Settings

Initially Quattro Pro keeps the notebook up to date through automatic recalculation. Quattro Pro assesses the impact of every change on the spreadsheet and recalculates only those entries that are affected by the change. This process of assessing the need for recalculating a cell is referred to as *minimal recalculation*. It can save a

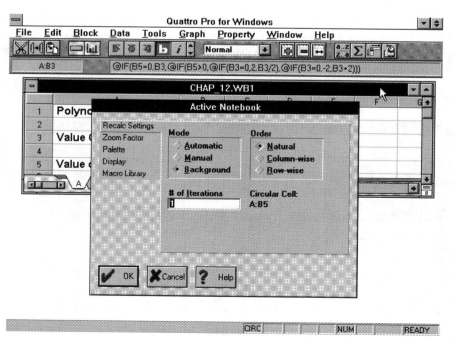

Figure 12.7   Dialog Box for Changing Notebook Properties

significant amount of time if most of your changes affect only a small percentage of spreadsheet cells. Since Quattro Pro does this in the background in between your entries, you do not have to wait for Quattro Pro to finish recalculating before you make the next entry.

Quattro Pro can monitor the need for recalculation through a table it maintains to track all cells that are referenced by another cell. When a cell's contents change, Quattro Pro refers to the table and determines which formulas need to be recalculated. This procedure may seem complex; but in situations where most cells are unaffected by a change, the overhead of table maintenance is more than offset by the quick recalculation that is possible due to Quattro Pro's selective recalculation.

While minimal recalculation is an integral part of Quattro Pro that does not require any effort on your part, Quattro Pro has other settings that affect how the recalculations are performed. You can disable the automatic recalculation. You can change the order in which Quattro Pro recalculates the spreadsheet. You can change the number of iterations that Quattro Pro performs for circular calculations. All of these options are part of the RecalcSettings notebook property.

SPECIFYING MANUAL OR AUTOMATIC CALCULATION   Although Quattro Pro uses minimal and background recalculation to reduce the amount of time needed to recalculate the notebook, it has other recalculation options. For instance, you can change Quattro Pro to recalculate only when you press F9 (CALC) by selecting the RecalcSettings notebook property and <u>M</u>anual. Once the spreadsheet is set to recalculate manually, Quattro Pro only calculates formulas that are entered or edited. The formulas that reference the changed cells are not recalculated. To recalculate formulas that have not been reevaluated, press F9 (CALC). Since Quattro Pro must still keep track of the formulas that need to be recalculated, you should press F9 (CALC) whenever Quattro Pro's performance slows. Quattro Pro displays CALC in the status line to remind you that the spreadsheet needs to be recalculated.

Another option is to recalculate the spreadsheet automatically but in the foreground so the user must pause until Quattro Pro has finished recalculating the necessary entries. You can use this automatic, but not background, recalculation by selecting the RecalcSettings notebook property and <u>A</u>utomatic. When you want to return to the default of background and automatic recalculation, select the RecalcSettings notebook property and <u>B</u>ackground. When you change to automatic or background recalculation, Quattro Pro begins the new method of recalculation whenever you press F9 (CALC) or edit a cell.

▼ TIP: Check for the CALC indicator before printing.

Before printing data, check that the CALC indicator does not appear in the status line so you are printing the most up-to-date values.

CHANGING THE ORDER OF SPREADSHEET CALCULATION   Quattro Pro recalculates a spreadsheet based on the dependencies within the formulas. This means that Quattro Pro determines that cells need to be calculated first in order for their results to be available for subsequent calculations. This is referred to as the natural order of calculation. As an example, when Quattro Pro recalculates cell B3 in Figure 12.8, Quattro Pro first checks if the formula in B7 or in G7 needs to be recalculated before computing a result for B3. If cells B7 or G7 contain formulas that refer to other cells, Quattro Pro continues this checking process. In summary, Quattro Pro intelligently chooses the order in which it evaluates the spreadsheet so that all formulas that are affected by a change are properly evaluated.

Quattro Pro provides two alternative orders for calculation: Column-wise and Row-wise. A spreadsheet calculated with the column-wise order has every cell in column A calculated before calculations are performed in column B and so on for all of the notebook columns. Using Figure 12.8 as an example, this means Quattro Pro recalculates B3 before recalculating G3. A spreadsheet calculated with the row-wise order has every cell in row 1 calculated before calculations are performed in row 2 and so on for all of the notebook rows. Using Figure 12.8 as an example, this means Quattro Pro recalculates B3 before recalculating B7. Column-wise and row-wise calculations were solely used in earlier spreadsheet packages. Now, they are only used in large notebooks where the recalculation time slows down macro execution. You can change the order by selecting the RecalcSettings notebook property and then selecting Column-wise or Row-wise. Except for large macros, you will want to leave the recalculation order set to the default of Natural.

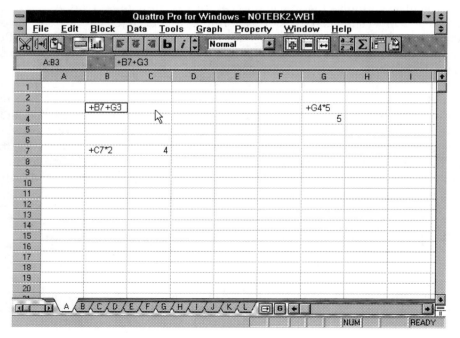

Figure 12.8   Formulas Illustrating Different Recalculation Methods

CHANGING THE NUMBER OF ITERATIONS The iteration count is the number of times Quattro Pro recalculates formulas in a circular reference. The iteration count is also the number of times Quattro Pro goes through a notebook to recalculate formulas when you are using a column-wise or row-wise recalculation order. The iteration count should be increased when you have purposely created a circular reference or you are using a column-wise or row-wise recalculation order. For example, Figure 12.9 displays a spreadsheet designed to solve a polynomial equation (that is, finding a value of x that makes the equation equal to 0). The formula in B5 evaluates the polynomial using the value in B3 as x. The formula in B3 is @IF(B5=0,B3,@IF(B5>0,@IF(B3=0,2,B3/2),@IF(B3=0,-2,B3+2))). This formula compares the results of the polynomial to zero and adjusts B3 if B5 does not equal 0. When the value in B5 is 0, the first @IF function stops any further adjustments to B3. If the iteration count is 1, you must press F9 (CALC) repeatedly until the formula is evaluated a sufficient number of times to reach the correct value. By increasing the iteration count, Quattro Pro reevaluates B3 the number of times specified by the iteration count or until B5 equals 0, whichever is less. To change the iteration count, type the new number of iterations in the Iteration text box (up to 255) after selecting the RecalcSettings notebook property.

When a spreadsheet contains a circular reference, Quattro Pro displays CIRC in the status line. Quattro Pro also displays the first cell in the circular reference in the dialog box for the RecalcSettings property, as shown in Figure 12.7. This cell reference informs you where to begin searching for a circular reference.

Changing the Display Magnification

You can expand or contract the notebook that appears in a Window. This feature lets you look at a notebook more closely by increasing magnification; by decreasing the magnification, you can see more information on the screen at once. To

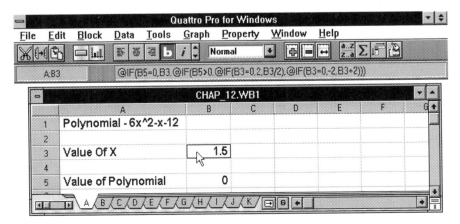

Figure 12.9 Iterative Formula Used to Solve Polynomial

change how much the notebook display is expanded or compressed, select the Zoom Factor notebook property and either type a number in the text box or use the Zoom Percentage drop-down list box to select one of the listed magnifications. Numbers below 100 display the notebook smaller than it will print and numbers above 100 display the notebook larger than it will print. Several of the notebooks in this book use different magnification levels to make them easier to read. If you have several views of the notebook open, changing the zoom factor only changes the zoom percentage of the current notebook window. Figure 12.10 shows a notebook expanded to 75%, 100%, and 150% of its original size. When you want to remove the effect of the magnification, return the zoom percentage setting to 100%.

▼ TIP: The zoom factor is different than print scaling.

The magnification set as the zoom factor for the notebook has no effect on the printed output. Conversely, changing the scaling percentage when you print the document does not affect how large the notebook appears in the notebook window.

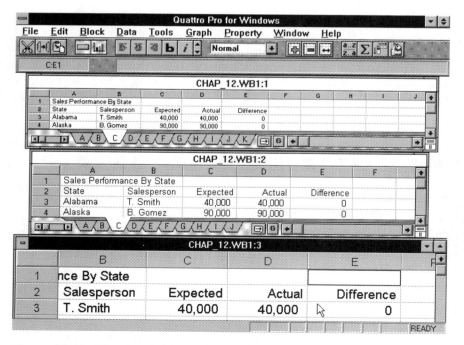

Figure 12.10   Notebook Magnified to Different Levels

Changing the Notebook Colors

In Chapter 3, you learned how you can change the colors of spreadsheet cells or the entries in the cells. You can change the color of the characters in an entry or the background to any one of the 16 colors in the notebook's palette. You can also select which 16 colors appear in the palette. The notebook palette sets the colors available for spreadsheet cells. Changes you make to the notebook palette have no effect on graphs, since their palette is separate from the spreadsheet cells in the notebook.

To change the colors of the notebook's palette, select the Palette notebook property. The right side of the dialog box shows the 16 colors the notebook currently uses. To change one of these colors, select the color from the palette you want to change and then select the Edit Color button. This displays the Edit Palette Color dialog box, which is the same one you have used for changing colors in graphs. As when selecting colors in a graph, you can select one of the displayed colors in the palette on top, or create one of your own. To use a color from the top, select the color and OK. To use a different color, select the color from the top that is closest to the color you want and then use the sliding bars and the HSB, RBG, and CMY radio buttons to modify the colors. Select the radio button for the scale you want to use. HSB combines hue, saturation, and brightness to create colors. RBG combines red, blue, and green to create colors. CMY combines cyan, magenta, and yellow to create colors. Then you can use the slider bars to further modify the color until it is the color you want. When you have the color you want, select OK. This puts the color you have just created into the palette in place of the color you selected. You will want to do this for each of the colors you want to change. When you have finished making the changes to the colors you want to change, select OK from the Notebook dialog box. At this point, any cell entries or backgrounds that used a color you have changed now use the new color you have selected in its place in the notebook palette. This means if you have selected A1..G1 to have a yellow background and then you change the yellow in the palette to orange, A1..G1 now have an orange background. If you ever want to return the palette to the original palette you started with, you can select the Palette notebook property and then select Reset Defaults.

Changing the Notebook Window Display

The Display property contains several features that change how the Quattro Pro application window appears. These changes include displaying the horizontal and vertical scroll bar and displaying the page tabs. You can add or remove this information. By removing the horizontal scroll bar, vertical scroll bar, and page tabs, you can see more of the notebook in the window. To remove any one of these items, select the Display notebook property and clear the Vertical Scroll Bar, Horizontal Scroll Bar, or Page Tabs check box. You only need to clear the boxes for the parts of the notebook window you want to remove. Figure 12.11 shows a

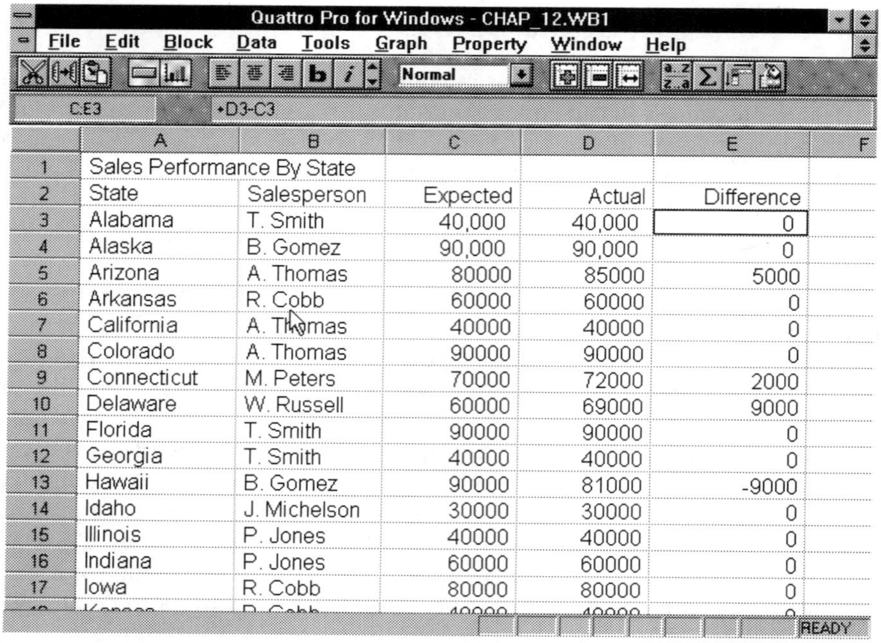

	A	B	C	D	E
1	Sales Performance By State				
2	State	Salesperson	Expected	Actual	Difference
3	Alabama	T. Smith	40,000	40,000	0
4	Alaska	B. Gomez	90,000	90,000	0
5	Arizona	A. Thomas	80000	85000	5000
6	Arkansas	R. Cobb	60000	60000	0
7	California	A. Thomas	40000	40000	0
8	Colorado	A. Thomas	90000	90000	0
9	Connecticut	M. Peters	70000	72000	2000
10	Delaware	W. Russell	60000	69000	9000
11	Florida	T. Smith	90000	90000	0
12	Georgia	T. Smith	40000	40000	0
13	Hawaii	B. Gomez	90000	81000	-9000
14	Idaho	J. Michelson	30000	30000	0
15	Illinois	P. Jones	40000	40000	0
16	Indiana	P. Jones	60000	60000	0
17	Iowa	R. Cobb	80000	80000	0

Figure 12.11 Notebook Without Scroll Bars and Page Tabs

notebook window after the scroll bars and page tabs are removed. When you clear the page tabs, you also remove the page scroll bar, the SpeedTab button, and the Group button. You can still switch between pages using CTRL-PGUP and CTRL-PGDN, use SHIFT-F5 (SPEEDTAB) to go to the Graphs page, and use ALT-F5 (GROUP) to activate group mode. When the page tabs are hidden, you cannot rearrange pages by pulling out a page tab and dragging it to a new location. When you want to add one or more parts of the notebook window back, select the Display notebook property and then select the Vertical Scroll Bar, Horizontal Scroll Bar, and Page Tabs check boxes.

Creating a Macro Library

When you execute a macro, Quattro Pro first checks the current notebook to see if the notebook has a macro with that name. If the notebook does not have a macro with that name, Quattro Pro goes though all open notebooks, even hidden ones, that are marked as macro libraries to find the specified macro to execute. The Macro Library notebook property tells Quattro Pro whether the current notebook is one of these notebooks that Quattro Pro should search for macros to execute. When you select Yes for the Macro Library property, the current notebook is marked as a macro library notebook. When you select No for the Macro Library property, Quattro Pro no longer treats the current notebook as a macro library notebook. A macro library notebook looks like any other notebook. The only difference is that Quattro Pro knows to look in a macro library notebook for a macro when it cannot find one in the notebook that is active when you run a macro.

Usually, you only want one macro library notebook open at a time. The reason is that you will otherwise not know the order Quattro Pro searches open macro library notebooks for the macro you want to execute. If more than one macro library notebook has a macro with the same name, you will not know which one Quattro Pro will execute. The best system is to put the macros you want to use in multiple notebooks into one notebook, and make that notebook a macro library.

USING NOTEBOOK TEMPLATES

Another way to customize Quattro Pro to suit your needs is to create notebook templates. A notebook template is a notebook where you already have the block, page, and notebook properties that you want for all notebooks. Instead of entering and changing the notebook's features each time you start a new notebook, you can simply use the template to start a notebook with the features already set. Using notebook templates gives all of your notebooks a standardized appearance.

To create a template, simply create a notebook file with all the block, page, notebook, and graph settings that you want to use in a standard notebook. You will also want to review the definitions of the named styles. The Normal style sets the default block properties of all cells that are not otherwise modified. If you have a notebook you have already created, you can use it as a template by selecting all of the entries in the notebook and selecting the Clear Contents command from the Edit menu, which clears the contents of the notebook without removing any formatting. Then save the now cleared notebook under another name. When you want to use the template, retrieve the template notebook, and then use Save As from the File menu to save the created notebook under another name. You may want to name the template notebook QUATTRO.WB1 so the template notebook is automatically opened every time you start Quattro Pro.

CUSTOMIZING QUATTRO PRO WITH THE CONTROL PANEL

Windows has a Control Panel that controls many features of how Windows and Windows applications operate. Already, you have learned about some of the features of the Control Panel that affect Quattro Pro features. The Control Panel has other features that you will want to review as you are using Quattro Pro. These Control Panel settings includes colors, fonts, and printers.

Windows Colors in Quattro Pro

Some of the colors you see in the Quattro Pro window are set by Quattro Pro for Windows, and other colors are set by Windows. You can change the color set used by Windows to use another color set or create your own. You can open the Control Panel from the Program Manager's Main group window and then select the Color icon or select Color from the Settings menu to display the current color set used. The Color dialog box displays a model Windows application window with the current color settings displayed. You can select another set of colors from the Color Schemes drop-down list box. You can also select Color Palette and create your own set of colors by clicking the part of the sample window you want to change and then the color you want to use. When you select OK, the colors in Windows and all Windows applications adopt the colors you have selected. Figure 12.12 shows the parts of the Quattro Pro window that use colors selected by the

Figure 12.12   Quattro Pro Window Parts with Colors Set by Windows

Windows' Control Panel. Many of the remaining parts of the Quattro Pro window cannot have their colors changed. The cells in a notebook can be changed by changing their Shading property.

Windows Fonts

Non-Windows applications must use the fonts that your printer supplies, or must supply their own additional fonts. For example, if you used Quattro Pro for DOS, you may remember that it included several Bitstream fonts to enhance the font selections available. Windows applications work differently. You can install a font once in Windows and then all the Windows applications can use the newly installed font. To add fonts to Windows, you can open the Control Panel from the Program Manager's Main group window and then select the Fonts icon or select Fonts from the Settings menu. The Fonts dialog box displays a list of the currently installed fonts. You can select the Add button, then select from the Drives drop-down list box and the Directories list box to select the location of the fonts you want to add. Select the fonts to add from the list and then select OK. Once the fonts are added to Windows, you can use them as you change the Font properties of blocks and graph objects in a notebook.

Windows Printers

Printers work like fonts with Windows applications. Once you install the printer for Windows, all Windows applications can start printing to that location. To install a printer for Windows, open the Control Panel from the Program Manager's Main group window and select the Printers icon or select Printers from the Settings menu. The Printers dialog box displays a list of the currently installed printers. You can select the Add button to expand the Printers dialog box to include a List of Printers list box and an Install button. Next, select the printer you want to install from the List of Printers list box and select the Install button. You may need to insert a Windows disk into the disk drive so Windows can copy a file from the disk to your hard drive. When the installation is complete, the selected printer is added to the list of installed printers. To make a different printer the default one, select the printer from the Installed Printers list box and then the Set As Default Printer button (select the Active radio button under Status in Windows 3.0). When you select OK, the installed printers are available in Quattro Pro as well as other Windows applications, and these applications will print using the selected default printer unless you select another one.

CREATING SPEEDBARS AND DIALOG BOXES

Earlier you learned how you can add a SpeedBar to Quattro Pro. Besides using the SpeedBar that comes with Quattro Pro, you can create your own. You can also create dialog boxes. The dialog boxes you create are used with macros. However, the steps for creating SpeedBars and dialog boxes are the same. In either case, you create an empty SpeedBar or dialog box, fill it with objects, called *controls*, change the control properties, and then assign the tasks you want each control to perform when selected. To create a dialog box or SpeedBar, you must have a mouse. As always, to use a dialog box, a mouse is not necessary, but one is necessary to use the SpeedBar.

SpeedBars and dialog boxes have several differences. SpeedBars appear only at the top—usually below the primary SpeedBar, or below the menu bar if you hide the primary SpeedBar by changing the Display application property. Dialog boxes appear wherever you want them. Dialog boxes have titles just like the Open File title you see when you select Open from the File menu, while SpeedBars do not have title bars. SpeedBars are saved in separate files, while dialog boxes are saved in a notebook. SpeedBars are continuously available. They stay in the window when you add them by changing the SpeedBar application property and only disappear when you remove them by changing the SpeedBar application property. Dialog boxes appear, are used, then disappear. They are displayed using a macro command called {DODIALOG} and disappear when the user selects one of the buttons in the dialog box designed to leave the dialog box.

Starting a Dialog Box or SpeedBar

The first step in creating a dialog box or SpeedBar is to create an empty one that you can subsequently fill. To create a dialog box, you can select UI Builder from the Tools menu. You can also create a dialog box by going to the Graphs page with the SpeedTab button or SHIFT-F5 (SPEEDTAB) and clicking the New Dialog button, which is the sixth button on the SpeedBar on the Graphs page. To create a SpeedBar, you can select UI Builder from the Tools menu to add an empty dialog box, then select New SpeedBar from the Dialog menu. You can also create a SpeedBar by going to the Graphs page with the SpeedTab button or SHIFT-F5 (SPEEDTAB) and clicking the New SpeedBar button, which is the seventh button on the SpeedBar on the Graphs page. Figure 12.13 shows a Quattro Pro window after a SpeedBar and a dialog box are added. You can see that the dialog box and SpeedBar look different than the Quattro Pro dialog boxes and SpeedBars you have used before. The dialog box has a title that includes the notebook name and the default dialog box name. The SpeedBar has a title bar, which you have not seen on other SpeedBars. Also, the dialog box and the SpeedBar have minimize and maximize buttons and a border that indicates it can be resized. When you use a dialog box in an application or add the SpeedBar to the Quattro Pro window, the dialog box uses a different title and the SpeedBar uses no title bar. Also, the dialog box and SpeedBar will not include the minimize and maximize buttons and will have a border indicating that you cannot change the dialog box's or SpeedBar's size.

Once you have the dialog box or SpeedBar in the window, you are using the dialog window. In the dialog window, the menu and primary SpeedBar change. The menu now has a Dialog pull-down menu containing commands specific to creating dialog boxes and SpeedBars. The primary SpeedBar has also changed. While you recognize

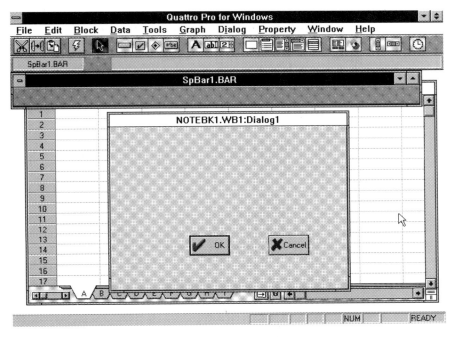

Figure 12.13   Empty Dialog Box and SpeedBar

the first three buttons as belonging to the Clipboard, the other ones are unique. These SpeedBar buttons are shown and described in Table 12.1.

A dialog box is saved with a specific notebook. When you save the notebook you are also saving any dialog boxes you create in that notebook. After you have created the dialog box, you will notice that the Graphs page has an icon for the dialog box. You can later edit the dialog box by going to the Graphs page and double-clicking the dialog box icon.

A SpeedBar is saved separately from any notebook. When you are finished creating a SpeedBar, you want to save it. The SpeedBar is saved by selecting Save SpeedBar or Save SpeedBar As from the Dialog menu. Saving a SpeedBar is just like saving a notebook file except that the SpeedBar uses a .BAR extension. When you save a SpeedBar with Save SpeedBar in the Dialog menu, you are never prompted for a file name since this command uses the default SpeedBar file name

---

▼ TIP: Make SpeedBars short.

SpeedBars can only be 56 pixels high. If you make the SpeedBar too tall, you cannot load it. Later when you learn how to change the properties of dialog boxes and SpeedBars as well as their components, you will want to check the SpeedBar's Dimension property and make sure that its height is 56 or less.

Table 12.1   SpeedBar Buttons for Dialog Boxes and SpeedBars

SpeedBar	Name	Effect
	Test	Tests the dialog box or SpeedBar to check how it behaves when you run the dialog box in a notebook or the SpeedBar in the Quattro Pro window.
	Pointer	Selects controls in a dialog box or SpeedBar. With a control selected, you can use the mouse to move, resize, delete, or change the properties of the selected control.
	Push Button	Creates a push button just like the Next, Previous, Replace, Replace All, and Reset buttons for the Search and Replace command in the Edit menu. These buttons are for performing a command or displaying another dialog box (remember to add the three periods to the push button's name if it will display another dialog box).
	Check Box	Creates a check box just like the Bold, Italics, Underline, and Strikeout check boxes when you inspect a block's Font property. Check boxes are for creating options that are turned on or off.
	Radio Button	Creates a radio button just like the different numeric formats when you inspect a block's Numeric Format property. Radio buttons are for selecting from a group of mutually exclusive choices.
	Bitmap Button	Creates a push button that contains a graphic instead of text. OK, Cancel, Help, and most of the selections in a SpeedBar are bitmap buttons. Use bitmap buttons for adding a push button that includes graphics as well as text.
	Label	Adds a label like Look In and Options in the Search/Replace dialog box. Use labels for text that is not necessarily part of another control.
	Edit Field	Adds text boxes like the Block(s), Find, and Replace text boxes in the Search/Replace dialog box. Use an edit field for the user to enter a block address or a string.

(continued)

Table 12.1   SpeedBar Buttons for Dialog Boxes and SpeedBars *(continued)*

SpeedBar	Name	Effect
	Spin Control	Adds text boxes with arrows next to them that let you change the value by typing a new number in the text box or clicking the up or down arrow. A spin control is like the box for the number of decimal places when you inspect a block's Numeric Format property. Use a spin control when you want the user to enter a value or be able to change the value with the mouse.
	Rectangle	Adds a rectangle like the ones around the Block(s), Find, and Replace text boxes in the Search/Replace dialog box. Use a rectangle to group related items.
	Group Box	Adds a box that contains other controls such as radio buttons or check boxes. An example of a group box is the group box in the Search/Replace dialog box that contains Look In as a title with the Formula, Value, and Condition radio buttons. Use group boxes to put radio buttons and check boxes in a group.
	List Box	Adds a list box like the list of fonts you can select when you inspect a block's font property. Use list boxes when you want the user to select an item from a predefined list.
	Combo Box	Creates a drop-down list box like the File Types and the Drives list boxes for file commands such as Open in the File menu. Use a combo box when you want the user to have the choice between selecting an item from the list or typing the entry.
	Pick List Button	Creates a bar that contains the current selection. You can drag the mouse from this selection to another one to change the pick list's setting.
	File Control	Adds the controls for the File Name text box and list box, the Directories list box, the File Types and the Drives list boxes for file commands such as Save As in the File menu.

(continued)

Table 12.1   SpeedBar Buttons for Dialog Boxes and SpeedBars *(continued)*

SpeedBar	Name	Effect
	Color Control	Adds the color settings that match how you set colors for the notebook palette by changing the notebook's Palette property. Use a color control to let the user change the color.
	Vertical Scroll Bar	Adds a vertical scroll bar like the one at the right side of the notebook window. Use a vertical scroll bar to let the user see information above or below or pick from a group of selections that appear in a vertical list.
	Horizontal Scroll Bar	Adds a horizontal scroll bar like the one at the lower right of the notebook window. Use a horizontal scroll bar to let the user see information to the right or left or pick from a group of selections that appear in a horizontal list.
	Time Control	Displays the time or performs a command at specific times or intervals.

if you are saving the SpeedBar for the first time. Later, you can return the SpeedBar to the screen for editing using the Open Speed**B**ar command in the D**i**alog menu and selecting the name of the SpeedBar. When you are finished working on the SpeedBar, you can select Clos**e** SpeedBar from the D**i**alog menu.

Adding Controls to Dialog Boxes and SpeedBars

When you have an empty dialog box or SpeedBar, it is like having a canvas ready for the artist. At this point, you can add the controls to either. Most of the controls can be added by clicking the tool on the primary SpeedBar, and clicking the position in the dialog box or SpeedBar where you want the control to start. Next, since the control is probably not the size you want it, move to the lower right corner and drag the bottom corner to a new position. When you add a control to a dialog box or SpeedBar, the tool button to add the control is unselected as the Pointer tool becomes selected. With controls that have text, you can change the text by double-clicking it. The control's text should include a & before the letter you want underlined. You can also move the control by dragging it to a new

---

▼ TIP: Order dialog box controls in the
order you expect the user to enter
the information.

By organizing the controls in the dialog box so the information the user adds
first is at the beginning, you make the dialog box easier to use. If you are
creating a dialog box to enter information, use a sample entry form to make
sure that you remember all of the components and that you have the order
laid out for you.

---

location. You can delete the control by pressing DEL. You can also use the Clipboard to make copies of the same control. Usually you want to add the controls in
the order you will use them. However, you can change the order later. You can
also use the Dialog menu to help you align controls in a dialog box or SpeedBar.

ALIGNING CONTROLS WITH THE DIALOG MENU   When you first add
controls to a dialog box or SpeedBar, you probably will want controls to be aligned
horizontally or vertically. Rather than aligning controls in a dialog box or SpeedBar,
you can have Quattro Pro do it for you. Figure 12.14 shows a SpeedBar just after
the different controls have been added and moved to their initial locations. While
this SpeedBar has multiple OK buttons, these will be changed later for other
features such as the three buttons for the Clipboard. To align the controls in Figure
12.14, first, select the controls you want to align. Clicking works for selecting the
first control, but you must hold down SHIFT while you click the other controls.
For example, to align the Open, Save, and Close buttons, select the Open button,
then hold down SHIFT while you click the Save and Close buttons. Next, select
Align from the Dialog menu. Next, select how you want the controls aligned.
Besides the easy ones like left, right, top, and bottom, this command has selections
that align controls according to the horizontal center of each control or the vertical
center of the dialog box or SpeedBar. For the Open, Save, and Close buttons in
Figure 12.14, you want to select Left. Also, the three combo controls and the push
buttons below them can be made the same size by selecting the control you want
to use as the basis for the size of the other controls and then selecting the other
controls you want to be the same size. When you select Align from the Dialog menu
and Resize to Same, all of the selected controls adopt the same size as the first
control selected. Figure 12.15 shows the SpeedBar after alignment changes are
made. Now the dialog box looks neater.

Another useful feature of the Align command in the Dialog menu is selecting
Horizontal Space or Vertical Space. With either option, Quattro Pro prompts for
the number of pixels you want between the selected controls. For example, the

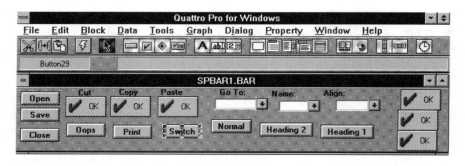

Figure 12.14　SpeedBar after Adding Controls

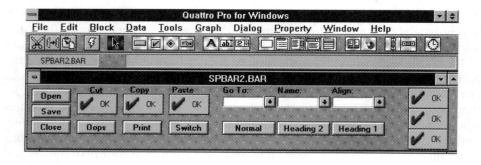

Figure 12.15　SpeedBar after Aligning Controls

Open, Save, and Close buttons are evenly spaced by putting three pixels between them. The OK buttons below Cut, Copy, and Paste are evenly spaced by putting eight pixels between them. This feature also reorders the controls to determine the order a user can move from one to another.

GROUPING CONTROLS You can put controls from a dialog box or SpeedBar into a group. Once objects are in a group, when you move or size the group, you change all of the objects within the group. Most groups are created by creating a rectangle and putting the controls that are part of the group into that rectangle. For example, in Figure 12.16, the Name, Address, City, State, and ZIP Code are all in one group, and the educational information is another. These groups are created by moving the text boxes and the labels identifying them into the rectangle. After a group is created, when you move or size the group, all of the objects in the group are moved or, in most cases, proportionally sized. Some controls have defined sizes. For example, when you size controls containing text, their height will not change. Grouping controls can also be used in SpeedBars, but since SpeedBars usually do not have groups of controls, it is primarily used in dialog boxes.

When you have many controls in a dialog box or SpeedBar, some controls may overlap one another. Suppose you do not want the educational information in a group, but you want the box around it. You can add the rectangle *after* adding the controls for the educational information. When you do this, the box covers the controls for the educational information. You can put this rectangle back one level or

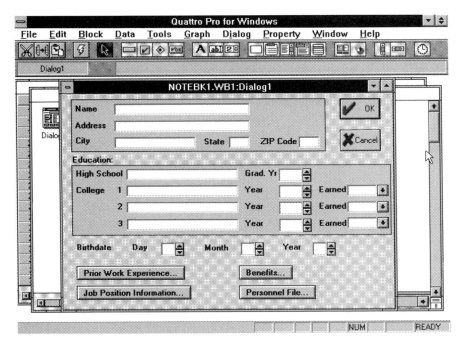

Figure 12.16 Dialog Box Containing Groups

all the way to the back. Another alternative is to put the other objects one level forward or all the way to the front. To take a selected object and move it by a layer, select Order from the Dialog menu. Quattro Pro presents the same Bring Forward, Send Backward, Send to Front, and Send to Back that move a floating object or a graph one layer back, one layer forward, all the way to the front, or all the way to the back.

ORDERING CONTROLS   With controls like the ones in dialog boxes you have used so far, the order of entries matters because the order of the controls in the dialog box determines where you will move when you press TAB. For example, in the Search/Replace dialog box, you start in the Block(s) text box, and then as you press TAB three times, you move to the Find text box, the Replace text box, and the Formula radio button. Knowing that each time you press TAB you move to the next item visually in the dialog box makes dialog boxes more comfortable to use. You want this same characteristic to apply to the dialog boxes you create. For example, when you press TAB four times starting from the Name text box in Figure 12.16, you want to move to the Address text box, the City text box, the State text box, and the ZIP Code text box. Initially, the controls in the dialog box are put in an order that matches the physical order in which you added them to the dialog box. Since no one makes the perfect dialog box on their first try, you will want to change the TAB order of the controls in the dialog box. You can see the current order of the controls by testing the dialog box and pressing TAB.

To change the TAB order of controls in the dialog box, you need to select them in the order you want to move from one control to another with the TAB key. For example, in Figure 12.16, you would select the Name text box, then hold down SHIFT while you select the Address text box, the City text box, the State text box, and so on for the remaining text boxes, combination boxes, spin controls, and push buttons. (When you select controls, you are not selecting the labels such as Name and Address that identify the adjoining text boxes.) Then when all of the controls are selected in the order you want to move to them, select Order from the Dialog menu and then select Order Tab Control. The other option, Order Tab From, inserts a few fields in the TAB key order. For example, with the dialog box in Figure 12.16, if you added the spin controls for the birthdate after adding the other controls, you can insert the three spin controls in between the controls in the Education box and the Prior Work Experience push button. To do this, select the control that you want the additional controls to follow and then select the additional controls. In Figure 12.16, this means selecting the last Earned spin control in the Education box and then the Day spin control, the Month spin control, and the Year spin control. When the controls are selected, select Order from the Dialog menu and then select Order Tab From. This feature of ordering controls also applies to SpeedBars, but since you use the mouse with the SpeedBar, it is not as important.

Testing the Dialog Box or SpeedBar

As you work on the dialog box or SpeedBar, you will want to test it to check that the controls in the dialog box or SpeedBar are functioning properly and that you like the

> ▼ TIP: Shortcut for Creating Radio Buttons
>   in a Dialog Box
>
> You can quickly create radio buttons in a group box within a dialog box if
> you have the text to use in notebook cells. First, copy the entries from the
> notebook cells to the Clipboard. Next, select the group box in the dialog box
> and paste the contents from the Clipboard to the Group box. Each cell entry
> becomes a different radio button. Any previous radio buttons in the group
> box disappear.

look of it. You should test the dialog box or SpeedBar at several points along the way.
To test a dialog box or SpeedBar you are creating, click the Test button in the primary
SpeedBar (the fourth one which has a lightning bolt). You can also select Test from the
dialog box's or SpeedBar's control menu. The dialog box's title bar is replaced with the
text that will appear, when the user uses it, followed by Test Mode. The SpeedBar's
title bar has Test Mode added to its name. At this point, the dialog box or SpeedBar
behaves exactly as it will when the user uses it. When you are finished testing the
dialog box or SpeedBar, press ESC. You can also select any Cancel or OK buttons. Any
actions you have assigned to these buttons are performed when you select them.

Setting the Properties of Dialog Box and SpeedBar Controls

Dialog box and SpeedBar controls have properties just like other objects you create
in Quattro Pro. As for other Quattro Pro objects, you can change the properties of
dialog box and SpeedBar controls by right clicking the controls, by selecting
Current Object from the Property menu, or by pressing F12. The properties and
the features they provide are listed below:

Add Down Button	Sets whether the combo box displays a down arrow on the right side that you can click to select from the list below. Even when this property is set to No, you can still press the DOWN ARROW to show the list box part of this control. The default of Yes displays this arrow.
Alarm On	Turns the alarm on or off. The default of No does not have the alarm activated. When you select Yes, the alarm is activated at the time set by Alarm Time. The dialog box or SpeedBar that uses an alarm must be open when the alarm time passes for the alarm to be activated.
Alarm Time	Sets the time the alarm is set. Use the alarm to have an event occur at a specific time.

Allow Point Mode	Sets whether you can start POINT mode to select a block for an edit field when the field type is set to Block. Select Yes to allow you to select a block by pointing to it from the edit field's text box, or No to prevent you from entering Point mode.
Attach Child	Selects whether a spin control, rectangle, group box, list box, combo box, pick list, file control, or timer control can be a parent object to another. When the default of Yes is selected, another object can become a child object. When a control is a parent control, the position and location of its child objects depend on the parent. You can select No to prevent another control from becoming a child of the selected control.
Bitmap	Selects the graphic that appears on the left side of a bitmap button. From the System Bitmaps list box, you can select from one of Quattro Pro's predefined bitmapped graphics. You can also select Browse and select a .BMP file. Another method of changing a bitmap's graphic is to copy the graphic to the Clipboard, select the bitmap button in the dialog box, and paste the Clipboard's graphic onto the button.
Button Type	Switches the button type of push button, check box, radio button, and bitmap button controls. You can select between Push Button, Radio Button, Check Box, OK Exit Button, and Cancel Exit Button. The last two make the currently selected control switch into a push button that will close the dialog box when selected.
Convert Text	Sets whether you can enter \t for a tab and \n to start text on the next line in an edit field. This feature is used for edit fields that are large enough to contain several lines. Selecting Yes interprets \t for a tab and \n for a new line. Selecting No treats these character combinations no differently than others.
Current Time	Displays the current time by showing the number of hours, minutes, and seconds. You can also set the time with the Control Panel.
Default Button	Selects whether the currently selected push button or bitmap button is the button selected by default. For example, in most dialog boxes, the OK button usually has a thicker outline indicating it is selected if you press ENTER. Select Yes to make the current button the default or No (the default setting) to make the button no longer the default. Since only one button in a dialog box can be the default, selecting one button as a default deselects any other button as a default button.

Default	Sets the default value of a spin control or an edit field when the field type is set to Integer. You can enter the number that is the most appropriate value for the spin control's or edit field's purpose.
Depend On	Sets which Quattro Pro windows the control appears in. Select or clear the Desktop, Notebook, Graph, Dialog, Input Line, and Graphs Page check boxes to include or hide the control in the selected window. You can set the Depend On property for all controls except group boxes and color controls.
Dimension	Sets the position and size of any control. All controls have a Dimension property. You can set the position of the object's upper left corner by entering the number of pixels in the X pos and Y pos text boxes. You can set the size of the object by entering the number of pixels in the Width and Height text boxes. You can also move controls by dragging them to a new location and size them by dragging a corner to a new location.
Disabled	Sets whether a control is selectable. For example, the Formulas and Values only radio buttons cannot be selected when you clear the Contents check box in the Paste Special dialog box. This feature is usually combined with Grayed to indicate which controls you cannot select. The default of No allows the control to be selected. You can select Yes to make the control unselectable. You can set Disabled for all controls except timer controls.
Draw to Right	Sets whether the text for a check box or radio button appears on the left or right side of the check box or radio button. Select Yes to put the text on the right of the check box or radio button or select No to put the text on the left of the check box or radio button.
Edit Disabled	Sets whether you can type an entry in the text box portion of a combo box. The default of No lets you make a selection in the combo box by typing an entry in the text box or selecting an item from the list box. Selecting Yes for Edit Disabled prevents you from making a selection by typing an entry.
Edit Length	Sets the maximum number of characters you can enter into an edit field, spin control, and combo box.
Field Type	Sets the type of data you can use in an edit field. You can select Integer (no digits after a decimal point), String, Real (includes formulas and numbers with digits after a decimal point), Block, or Hidden (same as string but displays entries as # signs, like when you enter a password).

Fill Color	Sets the interior color of the rectangle. Select a color the same way you set one of the colors in the notebook palette or the color of one of the objects in a graph.
Frame Color	Sets the color of the frame when the Rectangle Style is set to Framed. Select a color the same way you set one of the colors in the notebook palette or the color of one of the objects in a graph.
Grayed	Sets whether a control is grayed (as the Formulas and Values only radio buttons become when you clear the Contents check box in the Paste Special dialog box). This feature is usually combined with Disabled to indicate which controls you cannot select. The default of No does not gray the selected control. You can select Yes to make the control grayed. You can set this property for all controls except rectangles, group boxes, and timer controls.
Group Text	Sets the text that appears at the top of a group box. This is the same as double-clicking the current text and typing new text.
Help Line	Sets the text that appears on the status line when you have selected the control in a dialog box or you have moved the mouse pointer over the control in the SpeedBar. Type the text you want to appear in the status line. You can set the help line for all controls except labels, rectangles, group boxes, and timer controls.
Hidden	Sets whether a control is hidden. For example, when you set the international currency application property and you select the Windows default radio button instead of Quattro Pro, the other controls below the radio buttons in the dialog box become hidden. You can select Yes to hide the control or No, the default, to have the control displayed.
History List	Sets whether Quattro Pro remembers the last selections you have made using the combo box control. This feature is just like opening a file, where you can press the down arrow from the File Name text box to display the last ten files opened. The default of No does not remember the history list. If you select Yes, Quattro Pro maintains a history list.
Interval in Units	Sets how frequently Quattro Pro checks whether the timer or its alarm is activated. It is used in combination with the Units in Milliseconds. Quattro Pro checks the timer controls as frequently as the number for the Interval in Units multiplied by the number for the Units in Milliseconds. The default of 1 for Interval in Units and 1000 for Units in Milliseconds means Quattro Pro checks the timer once every second.

Label Font	Sets the text that appears in a label. You have the same choices as for selecting fonts for a cell.
Label Text	Sets the text that appears in a label, in a button, next to a check box, next to a radio button, and to the right of the graphic in a bitmap button. This is the same as double-clicking the current text and typing new text.
List Length	Sets the number of past selections made from a combo box when the history list property is set to Yes. The default is 10, but you can enter another number to change the number of selections from the combo box Quattro Pro remembers.
List	Sets the items that are in the list box or combo box. You can type a block name or address if the block contains the entries you want to appear, or you can select one of the predefined lists from the list box. You can also add entries to a list box by selecting the entries and copying them to the Clipboard. Then, select the list box or combo box in the dialog box and paste the entries from the Clipboard.
Maximum	Sets the maximum value of a spin control or an edit field when the edit field is set to an integer field type. You can enter the largest number that is appropriate for the value the spin control or edit field represents.
Minimum	Sets the minimum value of a spin control or an edit field when the edit field is set to an integer field type. The default is 0, but you can enter another number that is appropriate for the value the spin control or edit field represents.
Name	Sets the label that identifies each object in the dialog box. By default, a control uses the name of the control type followed by the object ID. You can enter another label that follows the rules for block names (15 characters with no spaces) to identify the object.
Number of Columns	Sets the number of columns that Quattro Pro divides the items in the list to appear in a list box. The default is 1, but you can enter a higher number to have the list split into two or more columns.
Object ID	Sets the number that identifies each object in the dialog box. Each item you add to the dialog box is sequentially numbered but you can enter another number to use instead.
Ordered	Sets whether Quattro Pro orders the items in the list of a list box or combo box in ascending order or leaves them in the order they appeared the last time you used the control. The default is Yes.
Parameters	Sets the value of the scroll bar that depends on how much

you have moved though the scroll bar. When the scroll bar is at the top or extreme left, it has a value of <u>M</u>in, which has a default of 0. When the scroll bar is at the bottom or extreme right, it has a value of Ma<u>x</u>, which has a default of 32. The value of Li<u>n</u>e (default is 1) sets how much the value of the scroll box changes as you click the arrows at the end of the scroll bar. The value of P<u>a</u>ge (default is 8) sets how much the value of the scroll bar changes when you click either side of the scroll bar to change the information displayed one section at a time. The Tim<u>e</u> text box lets you type the number of milliseconds between when you click a part of the scroll bar and when the scroll bar moves in the selected direction.

Position Adjust
Sets how Quattro Pro resizes and moves a child control when its parent control is sized and moved. This property applies to all controls. The <u>D</u>epend on parent check box selects whether the control will move and be sized as the parent control is moved and sized. When this check box is selected, the child and parent control are both moved and resized. The remaining check boxes select the sides of the child control that retain the same relative position to the parent object. The <u>T</u>op relative, <u>R</u>ight relative, <u>B</u>ottom relative, and <u>L</u>eft relative select the side of the child control that retains the same position with the parent control. You can also select Center <u>h</u>orizontally and Center <u>v</u>ertically to center the child control within the parent control.

Process Value
Sets whether Quattro Pro checks for an initial value of the control when the dialog box or SpeedBar is activated. When the default of Yes is selected, Quattro Pro checks for an initial value of the control when the dialog box or SpeedBar is activated. You can select No to disable this initial value check. You can set this property for all controls except bitmap buttons and rectangles.

Rectangle Style
Sets the style of the border of a rectangle. You can select from Plain, Framed, Beveled Out, Beveled In, or Transparent.

Resize
Sets whether the size of the pick list control is resized as different options are chosen from the pick list so the pick list size matches the size of the item chosen. The default is No, which does not adjust the pick list control's size as different options are chosen from the pick list, but you can select Yes to have the size adjusted to match the size of the selected option.

Selected
Selects which radio button in a group box, which item in a list, or which item in a pick list is initially selected. The default is 0, which selects the first possibility, but you can

	enter a larger number to make another radio button or item in the list selected.
Selection Text	Enters the text of the item in the list box that is initially selected.
Show Frame	Sets whether the text box of an edit field or spin control has a frame. Select Yes, the default, to include this frame or No to omit it.
Show Time	Sets whether a timer control displays as the current time. When you select Yes, the timer appears as the current time. When you select No, the current time does not appear.
Tab Stop	Sets whether you can move to the control by pressing TAB. The default is Yes to allow you to move to the control by pressing TAB. Select No to prevent moving to a control by pressing TAB. This property is not used by labels, rectangles, group boxes, and timer controls.
Terminate Dialog	Sets whether you select the default button when you press ENTER on this control. This property is used by edit fields and combo boxes. Usually, since the OK button is the default button, pressing ENTER finishes and closes the dialog box. You can select No so that when you use the dialog box and make an entry in the edit field or combo box, pressing ENTER will not select the default button.
Text Draw Flags	Sets how the label text for label, push button, check box, radio button, and bitmap button controls appear. You can select the Apply check box to use the other Text Draw Flags settings. When the Single line check box is selected, Quattro Pro does not split the control's label text into multiple lines. When the check box is cleared, the label text is split if necessary to fit it within the control's size. The text is also split between words when the Word break check box is selected. The radio buttons below Vertical position and below Horizontal position select the position of the label text relative to the size of the control.
Timer On	Turns the timer on or off. The default of No has the time off, but you can turn the timer on by selecting Yes.
Title	Selects the title that appears as the default setting in a pick list control. You can enter any selection. If you copy items to the pick list (to put the entries that appear as part of the pick list) the first one is used as a title.
Units in Milliseconds	Sets the number of milliseconds in each unit. With the default of 1000, each unit equals one second, but you can enter a different number.

Initializing the Controls

Most of the controls in a dialog box or SpeedBar can be initialized to set its initial starting point. Each of the controls are initialized a different way. Sometimes you provide an initial value by assigning it a value from a notebook block. Also, in the next section, you will learn how to assign initial values using link commands. The order Quattro Pro expects to receive initial values from can be important when you are initializing controls from a notebook block. This is the case when you use the {DODIALOG} command to start a dialog box.

When a control in a dialog box has its Process Value property set to Yes, the control looks at a block in a notebook for the values that the dialog box should start with. The dialog box controls expect the initial values in the block to be in a specific order to match the dialog box controls. You can change the order of the controls that Quattro Pro uses to assign values in the block to initialize the dialog box controls. Changing the control order for initial values is just like changing the order for moving between controls with the TAB key. To change the order of controls for which Quattro Pro initializes the value, you need to select the controls that get their initial values from a block in the order you want to assign values to them. Then when all of the controls are selected in the order you want, select Order from the Dialog menu and then select Order Controls. The other option, Order From, inserts a few fields in the order that controls are assigned values. To do this, select the control that you want the additional controls to follow and then select the additional controls. When the controls are selected, select Order from the Dialog menu and then select Order From. Since SpeedBars do not often get their initial values from a block, this feature is primarily used with dialog boxes.

A dialog box is displayed with the {DODIALOG} macro command. This macro command has the format {DODIALOG DialogName,OKExit?,Arguments, MacUse?}. *Dialog Name* is the text entered for the Name property for the dialog box. *OKExit?* tells Quattro Pro to put a 1 in the cell if the user exits the dialog box by selecting OK or a 0 if the user exits the dialog box by selecting the Cancel button. Arguments tells Quattro Pro the notebook block that contains the initial values for the controls in the dialog box. MacUse? tells Quattro Pro whether the macro that uses the {DODIALOG} command controls the macro or the macro's user controls the dialog box. For example, to show the dialog box in Figure 12.17, you can use the command {DODIALOG Sample_Dialog,A:B10,A:B1..A:B8}. You will learn more about macro commands such as {DODIALOG} in Chapter 14. The different controls you can initialize as part of the Arguments block for {DODIALOG} are as follows:

Check Box	Sets whether the check box is selected. A Yes indicates that the check box is initially selected, and an empty cell or No clears the check box. For example, Yes in B4 in Figure 12.18 selects the check box that appears in Figure 12.17.
Color Control	The value of this control is three numbers separated by semicolons for the values of the initial color using the RGB scale. For example, in Figure 12.18, the initial value for the Color Control in Figure 12.17 is 0;255;255.

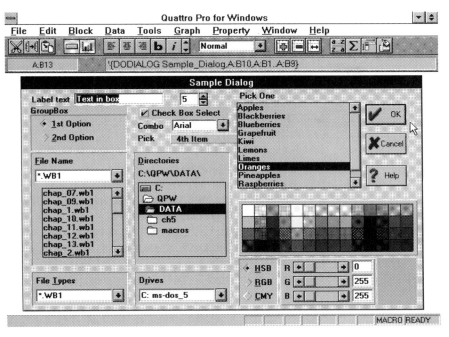

Figure 12.17   Dialog Box Activated with {DODIALOG}

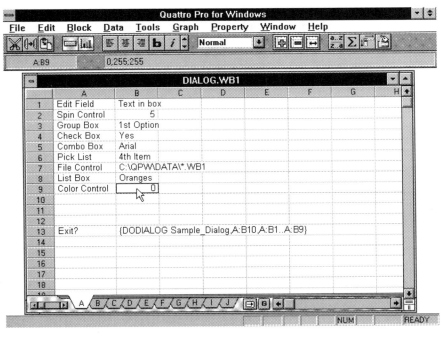

Figure 12.18   Block Providing Initial Values for Dialog Box

Combo box	The items in the list of the Combo box can be added just like the items are added to a list box. To select which of the combo box's items is selected, include the name of the item in the block the dialog box uses for the dialog box's initial value. An example of this is the Oranges in B8 of Figure 12.18 to select Oranges in Figure 12.17.
Edit Field	Sets the text that initially appears in the edit field. For example, the entry Text in box, in B1 of Figure 12.18, sets the text that initially appears in the text box in Figure 12.17.
File Control	The value of the File Control tells Quattro Pro the drive, directory, file name, and file type for the combo box, directory list box, and the File Types and Drives combo boxes. An example is C:\QPW\DATA*.WB1, which tells Quattro Pro to set the initial value of the Drives combo box to C:, the directory in the Directories list box to \QPW\DATA\, the file name in the File Name text box to *.WB1, and the File Types drop down list box to *.WB1.
List box	You can put a group of entries into the list box with the Clipboard. You can copy the entries into the Clipboard then paste them to the list box's List property. The other option, which you can use when the entries you want to appear in the list box also appear in a block in a notebook, is to select the List property for the list box control and enter the block address or name. To pick which of the entries in the list box is initially selected, include the name of the entry in the block the dialog box uses for the dialog box's initial values. An example of this is the Oranges in B8 of Figure 12.18 to select Oranges in Figure 12.17.
Pick List	The items in a pick list can be added just like the items in a list box control. To set which item in the pick list is the default, you can include the name of the item in the block the dialog box uses for the dialog box's initial value. An example of this is the 4th Item in B6 of Figure 12.18 to select 4th Item in Figure 12.17.
Radio button	Which radio button in a group is selected can be determined two ways. One way, when the radio buttons in the group are in a group window, is by altering the Selected property for the group box. The number you enter for the selected property indicates which radio button is selected, with the first radio button in the group being 0 and continuing from there for the remaining group buttons. For example, in Figure 12.18, to select the 1st Option radio button, the value of the Selected property for the group box is 0. The other

way is to enter the name of the radio button as the initial value of the group box control in the Arguments block used for the dialog box's initial values. An example of this is the 1st Option in B3 of Figure 12.18 to select the 1st Option radio button in Figure 12.17.

Scroll Bars | The value of this control is the position of the scroll box in the scroll bar.

Spin Control | You can set the initial value for this control two ways. One is by selecting the control while editing the dialog box or SpeedBar and changing its Default property. This method is usually used in SpeedBars. The other method is by including the value in the value block. For example, the 5 in B2 of Figure 12.18 sets the spin control in Figure 12.17 to use the initial value of 5.

Linking Controls to Actions

When you have all of the dialog box and SpeedBar controls, you are ready to add actions to the controls. This sets what happens when a control is selected. You have two choices. You can connect a control to a cell so that as the control's value changes so does the cell's. Another option is to develop link commands for the control that perform some action when the control is used. When you have the controls in place with their initial values and the actions they perform set, you have your dialog box or SpeedBar ready to use.

CONNECTING CONTROLS TO CELL ENTRIES   When you have a dialog box such as the one in Figure 12.16, you usually want the control values in the dialog box placed in other cells. You can do this by connecting a cell with the control. This feature is often used for edit fields, spin controls, list boxes, combo boxes, and pick lists. To create this link, select the control and then select Connect in the Dialog menu. In the Source text box is the name of the currently selected control. In the Target text box, enter the block name or cell address where you want the value of the control placed. For example, for the dialog box shown in Figure 12.16 that uses the block initializing the dialog box shown in Figure 12.19, you can use B:B1 as the target for the connection to the Name control.

You can also set when the value of the control updates the value of a cell. You can update the target's value as the change is made to the control's value, or when you finish the dialog box (usually by selecting OK). When the Dynamic Connection check box is selected, Quattro Pro updates the target's value as the change is made to the control's value. When the check box is cleared, Quattro Pro updates the target's value when you finish the dialog box. If you later select Connect in the Dialog menu again, you will notice that your previous entries do not appear. They are still present. Quattro Pro has taken your entries and converted them to link

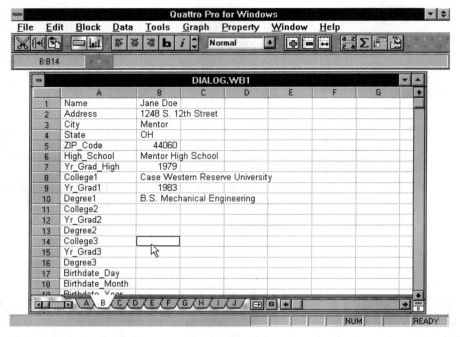

Figure 12.19   Cells Connected to Dialog Box in Figure 12.16

commands. The previous selections now appear in a list of link commands that you can see when you select Links from the Dialog menu.

CREATING LINK COMMANDS FOR CONTROLS   You can create link commands that Quattro Pro performs as you make different types of changes to controls in the dialog box or SpeedBar. Link commands can perform all of the types of actions you have come to expect from the dialog boxes and SpeedBar buttons you have used up to this point.

To create a link command for a selected control, select Links from the Dialog menu. The dialog box is empty except for the seven buttons. At this point, the control does not have any link commands. To add one, select Add. Quattro Pro adds a link command to the control like the link command shown in Figure 12.20. A link command is made up of several parts. The first part tells Quattro Pro when you want to perform a link command by selecting an event that invokes the link command. Table 12.2 lists the different events and when they occur as you are using a dialog box or SpeedBar buttons. The event part of the link command, like the other parts of the link command, is a pick list. This means you can point to Dynamic, hold the mouse down, drag the mouse up or down through the list, and when your selection in the pick list is highlighted, release the mouse to replace the current selection. To the right of the event, select the link command

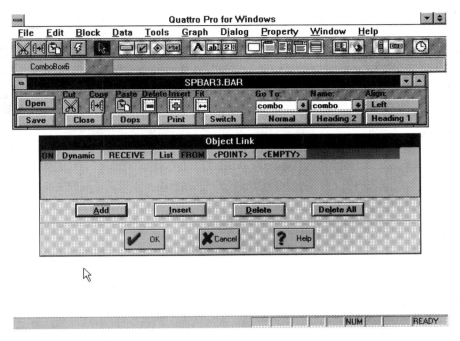

Figure 12.20   Adding a Link Command to a Control

you want performed when the event occurs. These link commands are listed in Table 12.3.

The RECEIVE, SEND, and SET commands change properties of objects. The SET command prompts for an entry for the new object property, but the RECEIVE and SEND commands use a property of the control (usually its value) for the new object property. For the RECEIVE, SEND, and SET link commands, you must select the object you want to change and its property. This appears after the FROM or TO displayed. You can use the pick list to select one of the listed objects. You can also select <POINT> and then point to the object if it appears on the screen. Another option is to select <ENTER> and then type the name of the object, which may also be a cell address. For the third pick list of the link command, you can select the property to receive or change. The options in the pick list change to match the property. Some of the properties include properties you have not seen elsewhere, such as Value, Title, Dimensions, Position_Adjust, Grid_Options, Name, and Disabled.

A control can have many link commands, since you may want Quattro Pro to perform several actions at once or perform different actions at different times. You can continue to add new commands by selecting Add, or add link commands in between others by selecting Insert. You can also delete the selected link command by selecting Delete or remove all of them by selecting Delete All.

Table 12.2 Events That Trigger a Link Command

Event	When it occurs
Activate	When user has selected the control to change
Alarm	When the time set by the timer control's Alarm Time property is reached (assuming that the Alarm On property for the time control is set to yes)
CancelExit	When user selects Cancel
Clicked	When user clicks control
Deactivate	When user has selected another control so the current control is unselected
Doubleclick	When user double-clicks control
Dynamic	During the process when user changes a value
Edit dynamic	When user inserts or deletes characters in a combo box's edit field
Enter	When user presses ENTER while editing an edit field
Init	Just before displaying a dialog box
Init_Complete	Immediately after all Init link commands
key:*keystroke*	When user presses the key *keystroke* (after you select this event while creating the link, press the key that you want to use for the keystroke)
Left_bdown	When user holds down mouse button over control (when mouse button is released, event becomes Clicked)
Linedown	When user clicks the down or right scroll arrow
Lineup	When user clicks the up or left scroll arrow
OkExit	When user selects OK
Pagedown	When user clicks below or to the right of the scroll bar control's scroll box
Pageup	When user clicks above or to the left of the scroll bar control's scroll box
Right_bdown	When user right clicks control
Thumb	When user drags the scroll bar control's scroll box
Timer	When the time indicated by the timer control's Timer Interval property has elapsed
Trigger	When another control uses TRIGGER as its link command
Valuechanged	When user presses ENTER or releases the mouse button (for scroll bars) after changing a control's value

Table 12.3 Actions for Link Commands

Command	Action
SEND	Sends the control value to another location
RECEIVE	Receives a value from another location to initialize the control value
DOMACRO	Performs a macro instruction or macro stored on a notebook
EXECUTE	Performs an action on another dialog box or dialog box control
SET	Sends a specific value to another location. The value is not set by the control's value
TRIGGER	Initiates any control links activated by the Trigger event

GETTING STARTED

In this chapter you learned how to make changes to Quattro Pro's settings and to other settings in the spreadsheet notebook. You can try some of these features by following these steps to create the spreadsheet in Figure 12.21.

1. Close any open notebooks by selecting Close All from the File menu. Open a new one by selecting New from the File menu.

2. Have two copies of this notebook visible by selecting New View from the Window menu. Next, select Tile from the Window menu. Click the B page tab or press CTRL-PGDN so one window shows page A and the other shows page B.

3. Make the following entries:

   A:A1: **50000**
   B:A1: **100000**
   B:A2: **@SUM(A..B:A1)**

4. Make some changes to the active notebook's properties. Right click the left window's title bar or select Active Notebook from the Property menu. Select the Zoom Factor property and select 150 from the drop-down list box or type **150**. Select the Display property and clear the Vertical Scroll Bar, Horizontal Scroll Bar, and Page Tabs check boxes. Select OK to apply these property changes. The property changes only affect the current copy of the notebook window. The version of the notebook you save chooses which notebook properties are saved. Other properties such as block and page properties are not affected.

5. Make some changes to the application's properties. Right click the Quattro Pro title bar or select Application from the Property menu. With the Display property selected, select the International radio button, clear the Show SpeedBar check box, and select the A:A1..B:B2 radio button. Select the Macro

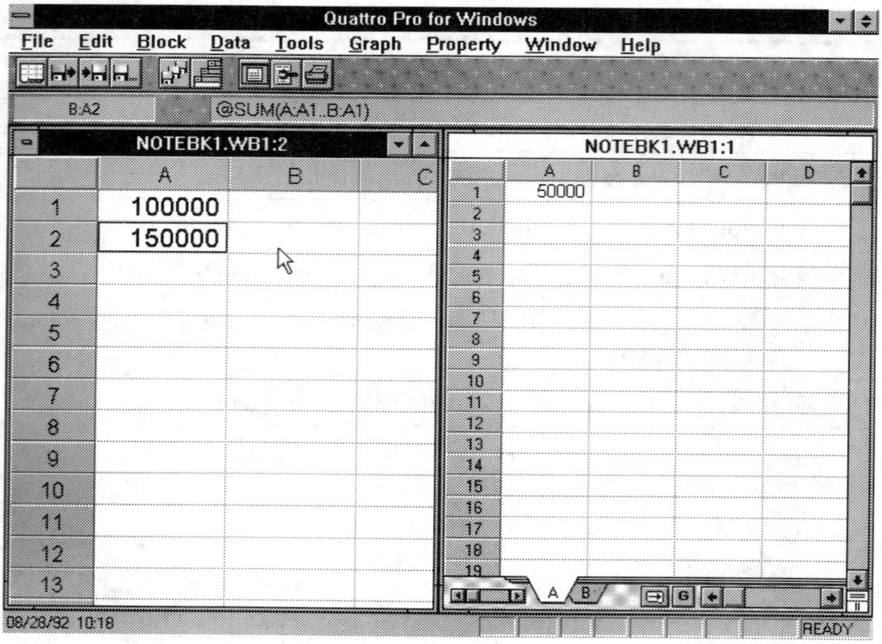

Figure 12.21　Notebook Created in Getting Started Section

property and select Quattro Pro—DOS from the Slash Key drop-down list box. Select the SpeedBar property and the Browse button, then select the PICASSO.BAR SpeedBar stored in the QPW\SAMPLES or QPW directory and select OK. Select OK in the Application dialog box to apply these property changes. Now, the formula in B:A2 is @SUM(A:A1..B:A1) as shown in Figure 12.21.

6. Type / to invoke the Quattro Pro—DOS menu. If you have used Quattro Pro for DOS before, this menu will look familiar, since it is organized the same way as Quattro Pro for DOS. Press ESC.

7. Close the current notebook by selecting Close from the File menu. Select No when Quattro Pro prompts if you want to save the notebook.

8. Return the application's properties to their previous settings. Right click the Quattro Pro title bar or select Application from the Property menu. With the Display property selected, select the None radio button, the Show SpeedBar check box, and the A..B:A1..B2 radio button. Select the Macro property and select Menu Bar from the Slash Key drop-down list box. Select the SpeedBar property and the Reset button. Select OK in the Application dialog box to apply these property changes.

13

Automating Quattro Pro Tasks

Macros can save you time by recording frequently needed tasks for repeated use. You will find much that is familiar in macros but will also need to master new terminology and concepts. This chapter focuses on the simplest type of macro— the keyboard alternative. You will learn all the basics of macro creation in this chapter. In addition, you will learn about many macro features that make macros a more productive tool as you use Quattro Pro. These features include finding errors in a macro, running Quattro Pro for DOS and 1-2-3 macros in Quattro Pro for Windows, SpeedButtons that perform a macro when selected, macro buttons, and menu commands that change how Quattro Pro performs the macros you run.

MACRO BASICS

A *macro* is a recording of Quattro Pro commands that can be executed at a later time. This recording of commands is stored as ordinary labels. The labels do not perform any function until you execute them. When you execute a macro, Quattro Pro performs each step in the macro exactly as it would if you were typing each command from the keyboard.

Figure 13.1 displays a macro. When this macro is executed, Quattro Pro performs the commands represented in each cell in column I. Quattro Pro continues executing the requests represented by these labels until it encounters a blank cell or a cell containing a value.

A macro is stored with the spreadsheet in which you created it. This allows each spreadsheet to have unique macros. You can share macros between spreadsheets, since Quattro Pro executes a macro on the current spreadsheet regardless of which open spreadsheet contains the macro.

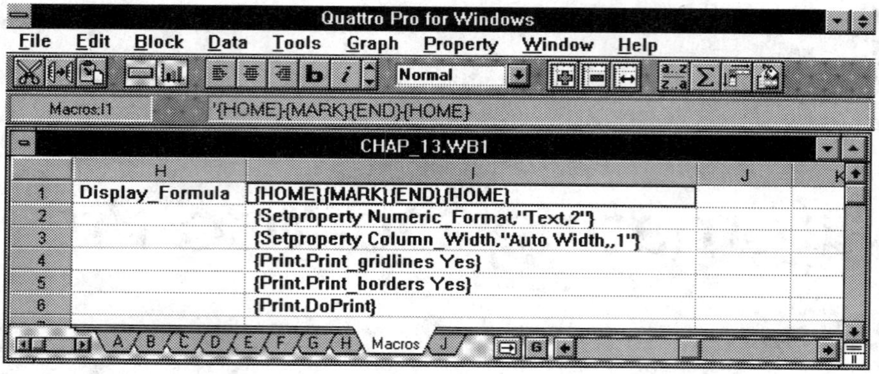

Figure 13.1   Macro in Column I

Types of Macros

Quattro Pro has two types of macros. One type is a keyboard macro. Keyboard macros are nothing more than a set of keystrokes. When you execute one of these macros, it is as if you are typing yourself. A keyboard macro provides efficiency for repetitive tasks and reduces errors. Once you have created and tested a macro, you do not have to worry about typing mistakes.

Quattro Pro's other type of macro is more advanced and uses macro commands. Macro commands perform functions unavailable from Quattro Pro's menu like repetitive processing, condition checking, and specialized file input and output options. The macro commands provide programming features that you would expect in a programming language within Quattro Pro's easy-to-use framework. These are covered in Chapter 14.

Picking a Location for a Macro

Before creating a macro, you need to select a location on the notebook. If a macro is in a good location, it will not affect the notebook's other entries and it will be protected from changes in other spreadsheet entries. Since Quattro Pro has efficient memory management, you do not have to consider memory allocation in your decision of where you place the macro.

If the macro is in the same page as other spreadsheet data, the location selected should allow room for data or macro expansion. For example, if your data is likely to expand to the right but not downward, you may want to put the macros below the data. Grouping the macros within one area is a good idea to make location of any macro easy. If your page has rows or columns that you expect to delete, do not put macros in those rows or columns. Protecting a macro after you have tested it eliminates accidental deletion later. Reserving a blank column to the left and right of the macro is useful for documenting the macro. You must have a blank cell or use the macro command {QUIT} to end each macro.

Another possible location for macros in a notebook is on their own page. For example, in Figure 13.1, the macro is stored on the page called Macros. This macro can be performed on any page in the notebook. When the macros are on their own page, you do not have to worry about accidentally changing the data in the notebook as you rearrange the macros.

You can place a macro in a notebook outside the notebook of the data on which the macro is used. Quattro Pro uses the current notebook when it executes a macro even if the macro is in a separate notebook. You can use this feature to create notebooks that contain only macros. You can also use this feature to create macros for use with data files that are not stored in a spreadsheet format. For example, you can create macros in a spreadsheet that use the data in a dBASE III database.

Another approach for macro organization is to create a macro notebook. A macro notebook contains the macros that you use most frequently and is sometimes referred to as a macro library.

Recording a Macro

Since macros are a column of labels containing instructions, you must convert the Quattro Pro task requests into labels. When you want the macro to type text, you type the text into the macro labels. For example, to enter ABC Company into a cell, the macro instruction is ABC Company.

Some special keys like ESC and ENTER require a different approach. Quattro Pro uses key-equivalent commands to represent these special keys. These key-equivalent commands are displayed in Table 13.1 and can be included in a macro exactly as shown there. For many of the macro instructions that represent direction keys, you can put a number in them to indicate the number of times the key should be performed as in {DOWN 10}. With {NEXTPANE}, you can include a 1 to tell Quattro Pro that the selector should be in the same cell when Quattro Pro switches between panes, or a 0 (the default) to indicate that the selector should be in the cell it was in last time it was in the pane Quattro Pro is switching to.

▼ TIP: Add a page called Macros to store the macros you have in a notebook

If you have these macros on a separate page, you do not have to worry that you will accidentally overwrite your data or that the macros will get in the way of the other notebook data. Also, once the macros on the page are complete and debugged, protect that page so you cannot accidentally overwrite the macros. Since only that page is protected, your other pages are not affected.

Table 13.1   Special Key Equivalents Used in Macros

Special Key	Key Equivalent Command
F1 (HELP)	{HELP}
F2 (EDIT)	{EDIT}
F3 (CHOICES)	{NAME}
F4 (ABSOLUTE)	{ABS}
F5 (GOTO)	{QGOTO} or {GoTo}
F6 (PANE)	{NEXTPANE}
F7 (QUERY)	{QUERY}
F8 (TABLE)	{TABLE}
F9 (CALC)	{CALC}
F10 (MENU)	{MENU}
F11 (GRAPH)	{GRAPH}
F12 (INSPECT)	{INSPECT}
SHIFT-F2 (DEBUG)	{STEP}
SHIFT-F3 (MACROS)	{MACROS}
SHIFT-F5 (GRAPHS PAGE)	{GRAPHPAGE GOTO}
SHIFT-F6	{NEXTTOPWIN}
SHIFT-F7 (MARK)	{MARK}
CTRL-F6 (NEXT WINDOW)	{NEXTWIN}
ALT-F3 (FUNCTIONS)	{FUNCTIONS}
UP ARROW	{UP} or {U}
DOWN ARROW	{DOWN} or {D}
RIGHT ARROW	{RIGHT} or {R}
LEFT ARROW	{LEFT} or {L}
CTRL-RIGHT ARROW or TAB	{BIGRIGHT} or {TAB}
CTRL-BREAK	{BREAK}
CTRL-LEFT ARROW or SHIFT-TAB	{BIGLEFT} or {BACKTAB}
PGUP	{PGUP}

Table 13.1   Special Key Equivalents Used in Macros *(continued)*

Special Key	Key Equivalent Command
PGDN	{PGDN}
HOME	{HOME}
END	{END}
ENTER	{CR} or ~
ESC	{ESC} or {ESCAPE}
INS	{INS}, {INSERT}, {INSOFF}, or {INSON}
DEL	{DEL} or {DELETE}
BACKSPACE	{BS} or {BACKSPACE}
CTRL-BACKSPACE	{CLEAR}
CTRL-\	{DELEOL}
CTRL-D	{DATE}
NUM LOCK	{NUMON} or {NUMOFF}
CAPS LOCK	{CAPON} or {CAPOFF}
SCROLL LOCK	{SCROLLON} or {SCROLLOFF}

Quattro Pro has four macro instructions that look just like the special key equivalents. In {WINDOW#}, # is a number between 1 and 9 representing the number of the window you want to make active. When you omit a number as in {WINDOW}, the macro instruction is equivalent to pressing F6 (PANE). {CHOOSE} displays a list of open windows from which you can select which window you want to make active. {UNDO} represents the Undo command in the Edit menu. {ZOOM} expands the active window to fill the Quattro Pro window just as if you selected Maximize from the window's Control menu. Many of the remaining keyboard combinations are shortcuts for menu commands so a macro uses the macro instruction for the menu command rather than having a separate special key equivalent for the shortcut.

Quattro Pro provides a different way to record menu commands. The default in Quattro Pro for Windows is to store menu commands as command equivalents. Command equivalents are easy to understand, since they look like the commands they represent. Command equivalents are listed in Appendix C. Quattro Pro can also use the menu-equivalent commands that Quattro Pro for DOS uses. These menu-equivalent commands are designed for the Quattro Pro for DOS menu. Quattro Pro for Windows can also accept menu commands that use keystrokes.

▼ TIP: Set the slash key menu to the menu
system you want the macro to use.

If you are creating a macro that you will use with Quattro Pro for DOS,
change the slash key menu (part of the Macro application property) to
display the Quattro Pro—DOS menu when the slash key is selected. Then
you can use the menu the macro is designed for as you are creating the
macro.

For example, {MENU}BC will select Copy from the Block menu. Most of the time,
you will not use keystrokes to select menu commands. While remembering the
command equivalent, menu-equivalent command, or the keystrokes to select the
menu command may be more difficult than remembering the special key
equivalents, you can record the macro and have Quattro Pro put the menu selections
on the notebook for you.

USING QUATTRO PRO'S RECORD MODE   Quattro Pro has a RECORD mode
that allows you to make your menu selections and record on your notebook. Quattro
Pro records every key you type and stores it in a block. To use this recording feature,
follow these steps:

1. Move to where you want the macro instructions recorded.

2. Select Macro from the Tools menu.

3. Select Record. Quattro Pro prompts for where you want the macro instructions recorded on your notebook. Since you have moved the selector
   ahead of time, select OK to start recording the macro. Quattro Pro returns
   to READY mode and displays REC in the status line.

4. Enter the keystrokes and commands you want to record. You can use the
   mouse as well, since Quattro Pro converts the selections you make with the
   mouse to macro instructions.

5. Select Macro from the Tools menu and Stop Record. REC in the status line
   disappears, since Quattro Pro is no longer recording macro instructions.

6. Move to the first cell of the macro instructions.

7. Select Names from the Block menu and Create, or press CTRL-F3 (NAME
   CREATE).

8. Type the name for the macro in the Name text box and select OK. Macro
   names are the same as block names you have for other purposes in a
   notebook. They can be up to fifteen characters without spaces. You can also

use \ and a letter for the macro name to create a macro that you can execute by pressing CTRL and the letter after the backslash.

The keystrokes, mouse actions, and commands you have used in step 4 are converted to macro instructions. By default, selected cells are represented by their specific cell address rather than the keys you press to select them. Quattro Pro records the cell selection with the {SELECTBLOCK block} command, where *block* is the block or cell address you are selecting. Also, entries made into cells are recorded with the {PUTCELL} command, where the entry after PUTCELL is the entry for the current cell. When you change the property of an object, Quattro Pro records the property change with the {SETPROPERTY} command. This command uses the format of {SETPROPERTY property,setting}, where *property* is the name of the property that appears on the left side of the dialog box with an underscore replacing spaces, and *setting* is a string in quotes containing the values for the settings in the right half of the dialog box. Usually, the settings use the selected text for text boxes, list boxes, drop-down list boxes, and radio buttons; Yes or No for check boxes; and the drive, path, and file name for the group of file settings.

When you record a macro with Quattro Pro's RECORD mode, Quattro Pro stores all the menu commands by their command equivalents. However, Quattro Pro records a macro by using the keystrokes if you select Macro from the Tools menu, Options, the Keystroke radio button and OK. When you record a macro using the keystrokes, mouse actions are ignored. You must use / or F10 (MENU) to invoke the menu. Also, selections are recorded literally as the keys you press rather than as command equivalents of the selections the keystrokes make. Macros recorded as keystrokes are not as efficient, so when you are creating a macro for Quattro Pro for Windows, you want to select Macro from the Tools menu, Options, the Logical radio button, and OK.

RECORDING A MACRO BY TYPING THE TEXT You can also record a macro by typing the macro instructions as label entries. To enter a macro by typing the text, follow these steps:

1. Plan the tasks that the macro should perform. For each task, you must consider all the steps that Quattro Pro must perform. This includes the menu command the macro will use, the special keys the macro will have to select, and other information that the commands and functions will need. If the macro consists of several tasks, divide the tasks into steps. With small steps, both creation of the macro and subsequent error corrections are simpler. A macro entered by typing the instructions into the macro block is more likely to have errors due to typing mistakes or an omitted character. A missing or incorrect character can cause the entire macro to be incorrect.

2. Move the selector to the cell where the macro should begin.

3. Type an apostrophe to insure that the subsequent characters are treated as a label.

4. Type the instructions for the step.

5. Move to the next cell where you want the next macro instruction placed. Store each step of the macro in a different cell in the column. Do not skip any cells between macro instructions, since Quattro Pro terminates the macro's execution when it encounters a blank cell or a value cell.

6. Repeat steps 3 through 5 for each step of the macro.

7. Move to the cell with the first macro instruction and select <u>N</u>ames from the <u>B</u>lock menu and <u>C</u>reate or press CTRL-F3 (NAME CREATE).

8. Type the name for the macro in the <u>N</u>ame text box and select OK. Macro names have the same format as names of blocks you have for other purposes in a notebook. They can be up to fifteen characters without spaces. You can also use \ and a letter for the macro name to create a macro that you can execute by pressing CTRL and the letter after the backslash.

When you enter the macro instructions as labels, you can use SHIFT-F3 (MACROS), or click the {} button in the EDIT mode SpeedBar to list the possible macro instructions. You can select <u>K</u>eyboard to add one of the macro instructions shown in Table 13.1. You can select Command <u>E</u>quivalents to add a command equivalent for a menu command by selecting one of the command equivalents from the list. Finally, if you select / Commands, you can select a general action and then a specific command to add a menu-equivalent command to a macro. The remaining options are for the macro commands you will learn about in the next chapter.

When you create a macro by typing the macro instructions into cells, you must follow the rules Quattro Pro has for cell entries. For example, each cell can contain up to 1,022 characters. While storing the maximum number of characters in each cell may seem quicker, it makes the macro difficult to understand, since you can only see a small portion of the macro's instructions on the screen.

Naming a Macro

The name that you assign to a macro determines how you can execute it. Quattro Pro has three types of names that you can assign to a macro. All three types of

---

▼ TIP: Consider where the selector is when you start executing the macro

If the macro instructions should be performed on specific cells, include the instructions in the macro to position the selector before the macro instructions that are performed on those specific cells. Other macros are designed to be performed wherever the selector is when you execute the macro. These macros do not need instructions to move the selector before performing additional instructions.

macro names are assigned as a block name to the top cell in the macro. You only need to name the top cell of the macro, because Quattro Pro continues executing macro instructions in a column of entries until it finds a non-label cell or the {QUIT} macro command.

The first type is an auto-execute macro. This type of macro is executed immediately when the file containing the macro is opened. Initially, Quattro Pro expects this type of a macro to be named \0. This macro name can be changed to another macro name by changing Startup Macro for the Startup application property. You can only have one auto-execute macro in each notebook.

The second type of macro name is an instant macro. Instant macro names have a single letter preceded by a backslash. These macros are executed by holding the CTRL key and pressing the letter of their name. The macros that you frequently use should be named as instant macros. With this approach, Quattro Pro supports 26 instant macros.

The third type of macro name can have up to 15 characters. The additional character limit allows you to provide a short description relating to the task the macro performs. Since Quattro Pro treats these macro names as block names, they must be unique from existing block names.

Several of Quattro Pro's features for named blocks have useful applications for macros. For example, to display the block address of all the macros, you can press the GRAY PLUS key when you press F3 (CHOICES) to list all named blocks and macros. When you select Names from the Block menu and Make Table, the resulting table lists all the macros and named blocks and their addresses.

To name the macros, you can use Create or Labels after selecting Names from the Block menu. The difference between using the two commands is whether the cell next to the first macro instruction contains the name of the macro. For example, in Figure 13.1, H1 contains Display_Formula, so you can use Labels after selecting Names from the Block menu to use the label in H1 to name the cell in I1. You can use either command to create the same results.

Executing a Macro

Quattro Pro provides several methods for executing a macro. The method you use to execute a specific macro depends on the name type. For example, Quattro Pro can execute an instant macro automatically when you press the CTRL key and the appropriate letter key.

EXECUTING A MACRO AUTOMATICALLY As Chapter 12 describes, you can direct Quattro Pro to execute a macro after it has loaded a notebook containing a macro of a specific name. The Startup Macro for the Startup application property lets you specify the name of the macro that Quattro Pro should execute once a file is opened. When the file is opened, if it has a macro with the specified name, the macro is executed immediately. Quattro Pro initially has the default startup macro set to \0. This default setting can be changed to any macro name, including the names that do not qualify as instant macros.

EXECUTING AN INSTANT MACRO   Quattro Pro can have up to 26 instant macros. The names of instant macros are each composed of a single letter preceded by a backslash. These macros are executed by holding down the CTRL key and pressing their single letter name. Using the CTRL key to execute a macro also executes the macros from Quattro Pro for DOS that you ran by pressing the ALT key.

EXECUTING A MACRO USING THE TOOLS MACRO EXECUTE COMMAND   Selecting Macro from the Tools menu and Execute lets you execute a macro. When you use this command, Quattro Pro prompts for the macro name or cell address containing the first macro instruction to perform, as shown in Figure 13.2. You can select a macro from the macro names listed in the Macros list box. If you want to run a macro in an open macro library, you can select the macro library from the Macro Library drop-down list box to have the macro names from the macro library listed in the Macros/Namedblocks list box. You can also start POINT mode to select the starting location of the macro instructions. This also works if you want to point to another notebook or page that contains the macro to run. Another option for executing a macro in another notebook is to include the file name in square brackets before the macro name. Once you select a macro and select OK, Quattro Pro begins executing the selected macro.

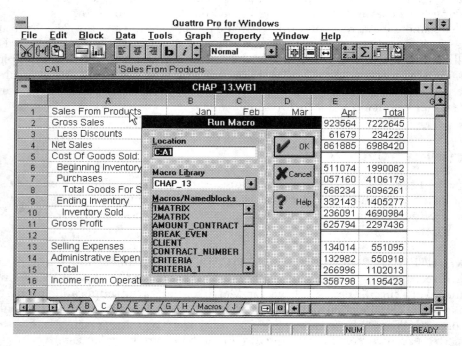

Figure 13.2   Dialog Box for Executing a Macro

RUNNING QUATTRO PRO FOR DOS MACROS Quattro Pro for Windows can automatically run your Quattro Pro for DOS macros when the macros use menu-equivalent commands to execute menu commands. If your Quattro Pro for DOS macros use keystrokes to perform menu commands, you will want to change the slash key menu to Quattro Pro—DOS. You will also want to do this and clear the Key Reader check box described below if you want the Quattro Pro for DOS macro to display the same prompts that the macro displays when performed in Quattro Pro for DOS.

RUNNING RECORDER MACROS Windows has its own macro capabilities. The Recorder accessory in Windows records keystrokes and plays them back. You can create a macro that starts Quattro Pro for Windows and also runs the application. The macros that you create with the Recorder do not have as extensive capabilities as those created in Quattro Pro for Windows since you cannot edit or view those macros. While you can use Windows' Recorder to open and start specific applications, once the Recorder puts you in Quattro Pro, you will want to use Quattro Pro's macro features to control the Quattro Pro environment. Windows' Recorder has the capability to work between applications, which not all Windows applications have, but Quattro Pro for Windows has DDE macro commands, which you will learn about in the next chapter, that let you control other applications from Quattro Pro macros.

Executing a 1-2-3 Macro in Quattro Pro

If you are running a macro that uses the 1-2-3 menu and you are using the Quattro Pro menu, you can easily run the macro. Selecting the Key Reader check box for the Macro application property sets whether Quattro Pro checks if a running macro uses 1-2-3 menus. When this check box is selected, Quattro Pro interprets all keystrokes for menu commands as applying to the 1-2-3 menu. When this check box is cleared, Quattro Pro interprets all keystrokes for menu commands as applying to the currently selected menu tree. You will want to select this check box when you are using macros in 1-2-3 worksheet files.

Changing a Macro

When you want to change the tasks a macro performs, you edit the cells that contain the macro instructions. A macro may need to be changed if it is not performing properly. Also, you may want to alter the task a macro performs. If you are building a long macro in steps, you may want to enter the next set of steps after testing and error checking the first set of instructions.

Quattro Pro provides a debugger that assists the editing process. You can use the debugger described later in the chapter to learn which macro instruction you want to change when a macro contains an error. To edit a macro instruction, move to the macro instruction that you want to change and press F2 (EDIT) or click the entry in the input line. This action places you in EDIT mode. You can use the same techniques used for editing any spreadsheet cell. After you make your changes, press ENTER or click the ✓.

When you edit a macro, you must follow the rules for macros. This includes using the special key equivalents. If you use the command equivalents or the menu-equivalent commands, you must make sure to include the proper command arguments. For example, to use the <u>M</u>ove command in the <u>B</u>lock menu in a macro, you use the command equivalent {BlockMove} that includes two arguments (block to move and where it is moved) separated by commas. A {BlockMove} command might look like {BlockMove A:I9..I14,A:I18..I23}. You can press SHIFT-F3 (MAC-ROS) or click the {} button in the EDIT mode SpeedBar and select Command <u>E</u>quivalents to select a command equivalent from a list.

Documenting a Macro

Documentation records descriptive information that helps you remember the reasons for your actions. When you document a macro, you record text next to the macro that describes how the macro works. Although you know the macro's name and function when you create it, you may not remember it when you have to change it a month later. Documenting a macro provides explanatory text that can describe the macro's name and an explanation of the different steps.

The style that you use to document your macros is something you can decide with time and practice. However, a few simple rules can get you started. A good method of documenting macros is to put the macro name to the left of the first macro cell and the description of each macro step to the right of the step. Figure 13.3 shows an example of a well-documented macro. On that figure, you can see clearly the macro's name and the various steps that it performs. If you are typing the macro name next to the macro, you can select <u>N</u>ames from the <u>B</u>lock menu and

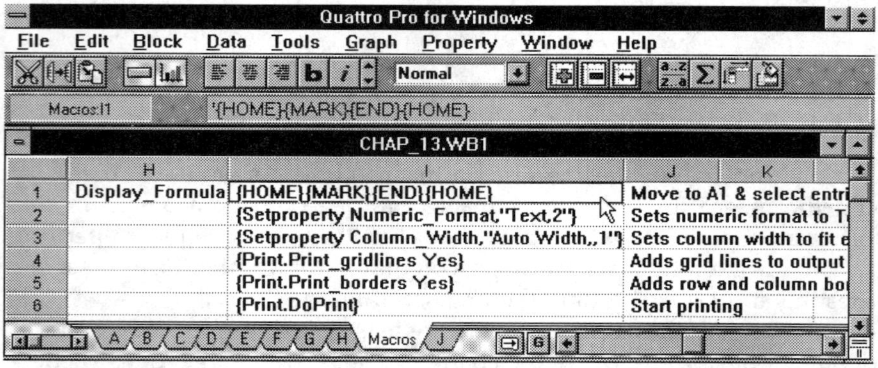

Figure 13.3   Documented Macro

then select Labels to name the macro so that you do not have to type the macro name a second time.

Deleting a Macro

Deleting a macro is an easy process that should be performed when the macro is no longer needed in the notebook. Since a macro is a named block, the process for deleting a macro is the same as deleting a named block. Selecting Names from the Block menu and then Delete removes a macro name without destroying its contents. When you execute the command, Quattro Pro lists all named blocks and prompts for the one that you want to delete. After you select one and select OK, Quattro Pro removes the macro name from the notebook and leaves the macro's contents intact. These macro instructions remain on the notebook until the cells are erased.

To remove an auto-execute macro, you have several options. You can erase the cells containing the macro instructions. You can erase the macro name by selecting Names from the Block menu and then Delete. You can change the auto-execute macro name by entering another macro name in the Startup Macro text box for the Startup application property.

MACRO FEATURES

Quattro Pro has several macro features that extend Quattro Pro's features. These macro features include macro libraries, relative addresses, macro debugging, macro buttons, self-modifying macros, letting the macro user modify dialog boxes in the middle of a macro, and limiting the part of the screen that Quattro Pro redraws.

Macro Libraries

Since Quattro Pro can perform a macro from a notebook in any open notebook, you can reduce the size of your notebooks by consolidating the macros for the individual notebooks into one notebook. This notebook that contains the macros designed for other notebooks is a macro library. You can benefit from macro libraries when the macros stored in a macro library are used in more than one notebook. A macro library also provides a storage area for your macros that cannot interfere with other spreadsheet data. To tell Quattro Pro that you want to use a notebook as a macro library, select the Macro Library notebook property and select Yes. The next time you enter a macro name to execute, Quattro Pro first looks in the active notebook, then it looks in the open macro libraries. Quattro Pro will still find the macro in the macro library even if you have hidden the notebook with Hide in the Window menu. Hiding the macro library notebook prevents anyone from unintentionally modifying the macros in the library. If you decide that you do not want to use a notebook as a macro library, select the Macro Library notebook property and select <u>N</u>o.

Relative References in Macro Commands

As you record a macro in Quattro Pro for Windows, you will notice that Quattro Pro remembers the specific cell and block addresses of the cells that the macro uses. While for some macros you want these cell and block references to be fixed, you may have other macros in which you want the cell references to be adjustable. For example, when the macro shown in Figure 13.3 was initially recorded, the instructions in I1 were {SelectBlock Macros:A1..J16}. Since we want this macro to use all of the entries on the current page, we needed to change the {SelectBlock} command to select all of the entries on the page. This is done by changing {SelectBlock Macros:A1..J16} to {HOME}{MARK}{END}{HOME}. Replacing the selection commands with arrow keys to select a block is one way to adjust the cells a macro uses. Another option is using relative addresses in macro commands.

Using relative addresses in macro commands is like using relative addressing when you copy formulas. Relative addresses in macro commands remember the position of pages, columns, and rows you are working with relative to the current cell. Quattro Pro judges which cells it selects based upon the current cell. The current cell has the relative address P(0):C(0)R(0). You can also use a relative address in a block address, as in P(0):C(0)R(0)..P(0):C(0)R(0). You do not need the page portion of the relative address if you are working with cells on a single page. By using positive or negative values in place of the zeros, you can select a cell that is a specified number of pages, columns, and rows away from the current cell. When the number in the parentheses is positive, you are selecting the number of pages forward, columns to the right, or rows down. For example, if you select the block C(0)R(0)..C(1)R(10), you are selecting a block that starts from the current cell and continues downward for another ten rows and one column to the right. You can also use a negative value to indicate the number of pages up, columns to the left, or rows up from the current cell. An example is C(0)R(-1), which selects the cell above the current cell. Another possibility is to select entire pages, columns, or rows by omitting the C or R. For example R(0)..R(3) selects the current row and the next three rows to the right.

To record macro instructions using relative addresses, select <u>M</u>acro from the <u>T</u>ools menu and select <u>O</u>ptions. In the Macro Options dialog box, select the <u>R</u>elative radio button. Macros made with this type of addressing are more useful in changing applications, but are not as easy to understand as those with absolute addresses. Later if you decide you do not want to use the relative addresses, select <u>M</u>acro from the <u>T</u>ools menu, <u>O</u>ptions, and the <u>A</u>bsolute radio button.

BLOCK NAMES IN MACROS   When you run a macro in one notebook that is stored in another, Quattro Pro has two choices about where the blocks the macro uses are located. Sometimes you want a block referenced in a macro to refer to the same notebook as the macro. You might be using one of the macro's notebook cells to store temporary information the macro will use later. Another possible location for referenced blocks is the macro that is active when you run the macro. When you have a macro that is formatting entries, you want the macro to operate on the current notebook.

Most of the blocks in a macro refer to the notebook that is active when you run the macro. When you run the macros it will seem that the active notebook contains a temporary copy of the macro. An exception is when a block address or block name is part of a macro command's argument. When you reference a block as a macro command's argument, Quattro Pro assumes that the block is in the same notebook as the one running the macro. Arguments for command equivalents are not included, so Quattro Pro assumes that the active notebook when the macro is run contains the referenced blocks.

You can override this choice of location where blocks referenced in a macro are stored. To indicate that a block reference belongs to the same notebook as the one that contains the macro, include the macro name in brackets just as you do for references to other notebooks in formulas. You can override using the macro's notebook as the location for a block by including macro instructions to put the active notebook's name in a cell in the same notebook as the macro. Then include that notebook name in the macro instruction as part of a formula. Later in this chapter, you will see several examples of using a formula in a macro instruction so the macro instruction changes to include an entry in another cell.

Finding Errors in Macros

Ideally every macro you create will be perfect, but that seldom happens. Rather than guessing where a macro contains an error, you can use Quattro Pro's debugger to slowly run through a macro to test it. Since a macro performs much more quickly than you can see, you can run the macro one instruction at a time and use breakpoint options to slow down the macro's execution. Trace options help you follow the values of cells as a macro executes. These debugging features are available by pressing SHIFT-F2 (DEBUG). You can also activate the DEBUG mode by selecting Macro from the Tools menu and Debugger. When you activate the DEBUG mode, Quattro Pro displays DEBUG in the status line. Any macro that is executed afterward uses Quattro Pro's debugger.

USING DEBUG MODE   When you execute a macro with DEBUG in the status line, the macro executes in *single step mode*. In single step mode, Quattro Pro executes the macro one keystroke at a time, waiting until you press the SPACEBAR or click the mouse before executing the next macro keystroke. Also, as it performs the macro, Quattro Pro displays a Macro Debugger window like the one shown in Figure 13.4. In the top half of the window, Quattro Pro displays two or three lines of the macro. The top line contains the previous macro instruction. The middle line contains the macro instruction that Quattro Pro is currently executing; the highlight is on the next step or keystroke that Quattro Pro will perform. The third line

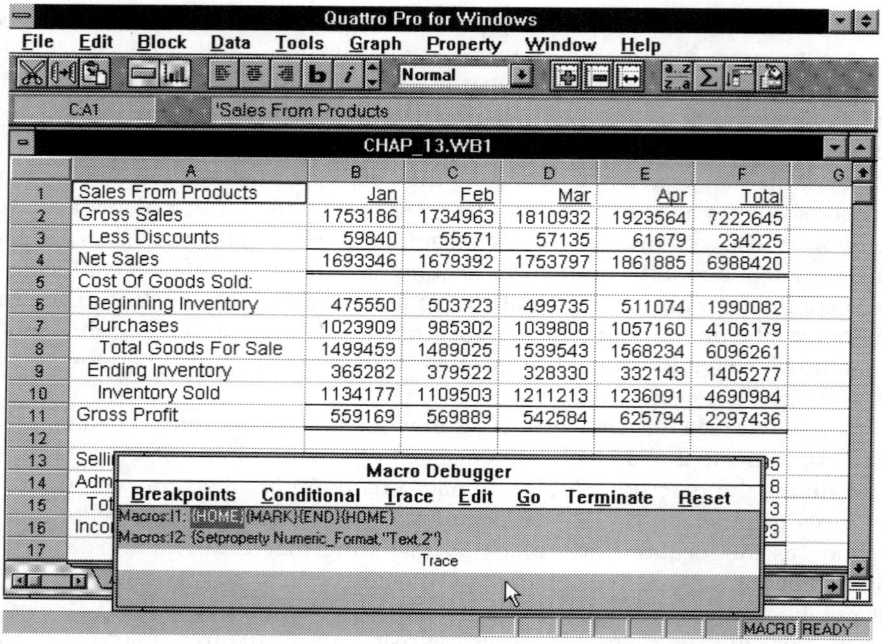

Figure 13.4   Macro Debugger Window

is the cell below. Quattro Pro uses the bottom half of the Macro Debugger window for trace cells, which are discussed later in the chapter.

While the DEBUG mode is on, you instruct Quattro Pro to perform the next step or keystroke by pressing the SPACEBAR or clicking on the mouse anywhere in the Macro Debugger window. Pressing ENTER returns the macro's execution speed to normal until either the macro ends or Quattro Pro reaches a breakpoint created with the debugger (discussed in the next section). The Macro Debugger window has its own menu that you can invoke by typing a / or the ALT-letter combination. The debugger window cannot be activated by the ALT key alone.

SETTING BREAKPOINTS   With long macros, you do not want to go through the entire macro one instruction at a time. Once you narrow the location of a problem in a macro to a specific area, you can use breakpoints to limit the single step mode to the area of the problem. Quattro Pro has two types of breakpoints. The first type, a standard breakpoint, sets the macro's execution speed to single step mode when Quattro Pro reaches a designated macro instruction. The second type, a conditional breakpoint, changes the macro's execution speed when a cell containing a logical formula is true.

Using a Standard Breakpoint   When a macro contains standard breakpoints, you can execute portions of the macro at normal speed and other portions in single step mode. When Quattro Pro reaches a breakpoint, Quattro Pro changes the macro's execution speed to single step mode. If you want to execute the macro's instructions until the next breakpoint at normal speed, press ENTER. To execute the macro in single step mode, continue to press the SPACEBAR or click the mouse. To set a breakpoint, select Breakpoints from the Macro Debugger window. The Breakpoints menu contains 1st Breakpoint, 2nd Breakpoint, 3rd Breakpoint, and 4th Breakpoint for the four standard breakpoints you can add to a macro. When you have selected one of the breakpoints, Quattro Pro displays the Break Point dialog box that lets you enter a location and the pass count. In the Location text box, Quattro Pro prompts you for a cell that will be a breakpoint. You can either point to the cell or type the address or block name directly. Once the cell is selected, you can set select OK to close the dialog box and continue running the macro in single step mode. You can continue using the Breakpoint menu to add as many as four breakpoints. When you press ENTER, Quattro Pro executes the macro at full speed until the macro reaches the next breakpoint, when the macro starts executing commands in single step mode. You can press the SPACEBAR or click the mouse to continue one macro instruction at a time or press ENTER to return to full macro execution speed. Each time you press ENTER, Quattro Pro continues executing the macro at normal speed until the next breakpoint or the end of the macro.

In macros that contain loops, a particular section may not be a problem the first time it is executed. On subsequent executions, the same macro can result in an error. The number in the Pass count text box in the Break Point dialog box sets how many times that Quattro Pro passes by the macro instruction before treating it as a breakpoint. For example, if you type 2 in the Pass count text box, the macro starts performing in single step mode every other time the macro reaches the designated breakpoint.

Using a Conditional Breakpoint   When a macro contains conditional breakpoints, you can alter its execution speed depending on a cell's value. A conditional breakpoint sets the macro execution to single step mode when a cell that contains a logical formula is true. For example, if you have a macro that is returning information that you know is incorrect, using a conditional breakpoint can help locate the macro instruction that is causing the problem. Once the logical formula checking for invalid entries is true, the breakpoint is in effect and Quattro Pro changes the macro's execution speed to single step mode. To return the macro's execution speed to normal, press ENTER. To continue to execute the macro in single step mode, continue to press the SPACEBAR or click the mouse.

To set a conditional breakpoint, select the Conditional menu. Select between 1st Cell, 2nd Cell, 3rd Cell, and 4th Cell to select which conditional breakpoint you will add. You can have up to four conditional breakpoints in your macro. When you have selected the conditional breakpoints, Quattro Pro prompts you for the cell with the logical formula. Indicate the cell with the logical formula by typing the cell address or name, or by pointing to the cell and then selecting OK. Once the cell is selected, you can select OK to return to the Macro Debugger window.

USING TRACE CELLS   The top half of the Macro Debugger window monitors the macro instructions as Quattro Pro performs them. The bottom half can monitor cell contents as Quattro Pro executes the macro. The cells monitored in the Macro Debugger window are called trace cells. Quattro Pro allows up to four trace cells. To set a trace cell, select the Trace menu and the number of the trace cell (1 to 4) that you want to select. Quattro Pro prompts for the cell address to be traced during the macro's execution. You can type the cell name or address, or you can point to the cell. The trace cell can be in the current notebook or in another one. Once the trace cell is selected, you can select OK to return to the Macro Debugger window. After you add the trace cell, Quattro Pro displays the cell address and its value as it appears in the cell. As the macro instructions change the value of the trace cells, Quattro Pro updates the values displayed in the lower half of the Macro Debugger window—even when the macro does not update the notebook windows. Figure 13.5 shows a Macro Debugger window with trace cells. Since the default window size does not show all four trace cells, the window can be enlarged by dragging the window up then dragging the border of the window to its new size.

REMOVING BREAKPOINTS AND TRACE CELLS   As you edit your macro, you may need to specify new breakpoints and trace cells or remove them altogether. To remove breakpoints and trace cells while in the Debug Window, select the Reset menu.

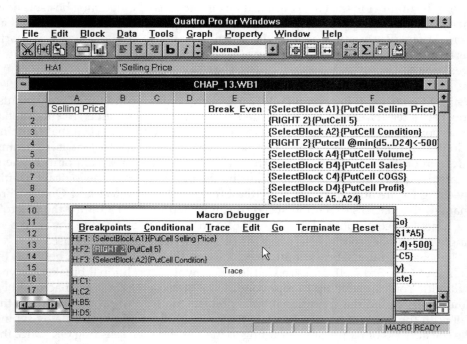

Figure 13.5   Macro Debugger Window with Trace Cells

EDITING A CELL USING QUATTRO PRO'S DEBUGGER While you are executing a macro within the Macro Debugger window, you may realize that a macro instruction needs to be edited before Quattro Pro executes it. Rather than aborting the macro, you can edit the cell while executing the macro from the Macro Debugger window. You can also use this editing feature to change other cells that are not part of the macro. To edit a cell's contents from the Debug Window, select the Edit menu. When you use this command, Quattro Pro updates the screen and prompts for the cell and contents that you want to edit. You can point to the cell or type the cell address or name. When you have specified the cell, Quattro Pro displays its contents in the Content text box. When you have finished editing the cell, select OK to return to the Macro Debugger window and execute the macro. If you are editing a macro instruction, Quattro Pro uses the edited macro instruction if it comes after the current macro instruction. For example, Figure 13.6 shows a macro in the middle of execution. The macro instruction in F18 contains a mistake ("Comma" is missing an m). By selecting Edit, editing F18, inserting a second m, and selecting OK, the macro instruction is corrected. When Quattro Pro continues executing the macro, it uses the corrected version of F18.

STOPPING THE MACRO'S EXECUTION While you are executing a macro, you may decide that you want to stop. To stop a macro from the Macro Debugger window, select Terminate from the menu bar. This terminates the macro just as if

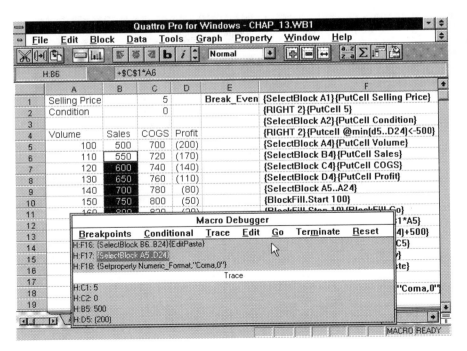

Figure 13.6 Macro with Mistake in the Middle of Execution

you pressed CTRL-BREAK. Selecting Terminate works even when the {BREAKOFF} macro command that you will learn about in the next chapter has disabled the CTRL-BREAK sequence.

LEAVING QUATTRO PRO'S DEBUGGER To remove Quattro Pro's debugger from the READY mode, press SHIFT-F2 (DEBUG). You can also deactivate the DEBUG mode by selecting Macro from the Tools menu and Disable Debugger. Any macros that are executed afterward are executed at the normal speed. If you are executing a macro when you press SHIFT-F2, the Debug Window disappears and the macro is executed at its normal speed. You can temporarily disable the Debugger by pressing ENTER instead of the SPACEBAR to continue performing the macro at normal speed until the next breakpoint.

SpeedButtons

SpeedButtons are buttons that perform tasks just like the buttons in the SpeedBar, except that they are on the notebook page rather than in the SpeedBar. SpeedButtons let you make a macro available for easy execution. This feature is especially useful for notebooks you are designing for novice users. Figure 13.7 shows a page that has five SpeedButtons. On this page, you can run the five macros represented by

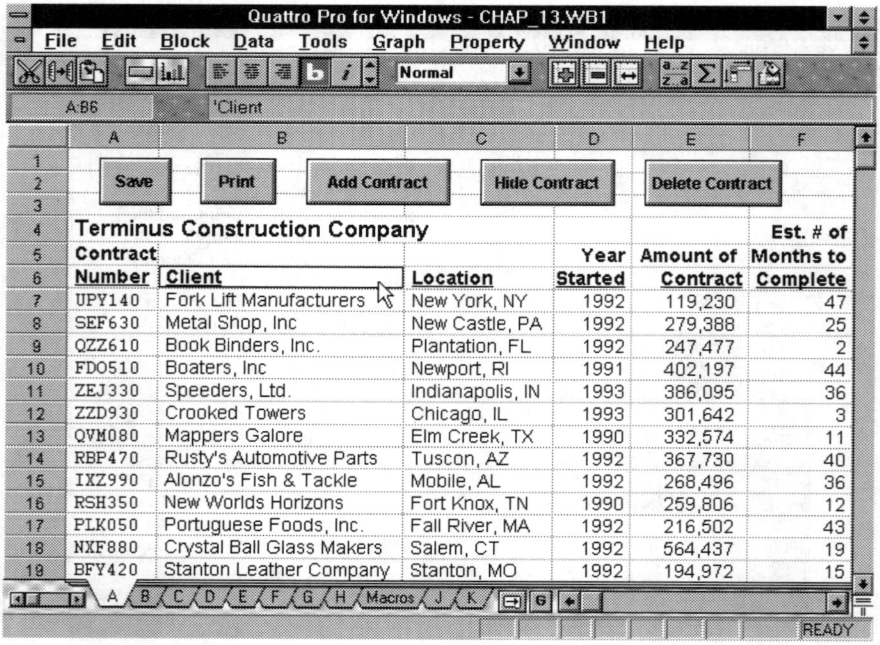

Contract Number	Client	Location	Year Started	Amount of Contract	Est. # of Months to Complete
UPY140	Fork Lift Manufacturers	New York, NY	1992	119,230	47
SEF630	Metal Shop, Inc	New Castle, PA	1992	279,388	25
QZZ610	Book Binders, Inc.	Plantation, FL	1992	247,477	2
FDO510	Boaters, Inc	Newport, RI	1991	402,197	44
ZEJ330	Speeders, Ltd.	Indianapolis, IN	1993	386,095	36
ZZD930	Crooked Towers	Chicago, IL	1993	301,642	3
QVM080	Mappers Galore	Elm Creek, TX	1990	332,574	11
RBP470	Rusty's Automotive Parts	Tuscon, AZ	1992	367,730	40
IXZ990	Alonzo's Fish & Tackle	Mobile, AL	1992	268,496	36
RSH350	New Worlds Horizons	Fort Knox, TN	1990	259,806	12
PLK050	Portuguese Foods, Inc.	Fall River, MA	1992	216,502	43
NXF880	Crystal Ball Glass Makers	Salem, CT	1992	564,437	19
BFY420	Stanton Leather Company	Stanton, MO	1992	194,972	15

Figure 13.7 Notebook with SpeedButtons

the buttons by clicking them. For each SpeedButton, you can enter the text that appears on the face of the button, the macro instructions the button performs, the name for the button, and the color and shape of the border around the button.

CREATING A SPEEDBUTTON   To create a SpeedButton, click the SpeedButton in the SpeedBar, which is the button to the right of the Paste button. The mouse pointer changes to a cross with an attached miniature button. At this point, you are selecting the size and position of the SpeedButton. You can point to where on the page you want the upper left corner of the button and click. Another possibility is to point to where you want the upper left corner of the button and drag the mouse to cover where you want the button. When you release the mouse, the button fills the area you have selected. You can move a SpeedButton after you create it by dragging it to a new location. You can size a SpeedButton after creating it by selecting it and then dragging one of the button's handles to a new location. When you want to select a SpeedButton after you have added macro instructions to the macro, you may want to right click the button first so you select the SpeedButton without performing its macro instructions first.

The SpeedButtons are on top of the spreadsheet data you have on a page. SpeedButtons are like graphs added to the notebook page that float on top of the page. Adding SpeedButtons does not affect the data underneath the buttons.

MODIFYING SPEEDBUTTONS   After you add the button to the page, you have a floating SpeedButton labeled Button#, where # is the next unused number that does not perform any macro instructions. You can change how this button is labeled and add macro instructions to perform when you click the SpeedButton. These changes are made by changing the SpeedButton's properties. Like other objects, you inspect its properties by right clicking it, pressing F12 (INSPECT), or selecting Current Object in the Property menu.

While initially a SpeedButton has default text that appears on the face of the button, you can change it to any other text you want. To change the text that appears on the face of the SpeedButton, inspect the button's properties and select Label Text. You can replace the default button name shown in the dialog box with other text. Since the text that appears on the face of the macro is not used for other purposes, you have few restraints on the text you use. You can also change the button's name that macro instructions (such as the positioning macro commands you will learn about in the next chapter) use to refer to the SpeedButton. To change the SpeedButton's name, select the macro, inspect its properties, and select Object Name. The SpeedButton name must follow the same rules as block names, with as many as fifteen characters with no spaces.

Another change you can make to a SpeedButton's appearance is the box around the button and its color. The box's appearance is set by the Box Type property. You can remove the line around the button or change the width of the line by selecting one of the line thicknesses from the Box Type dialog box. You can also select the Drop Shadow text box to add a drop shadow. This check box is initially cleared so a drop shadow does not appear initially for the SpeedButton. Figure 13.8 shows

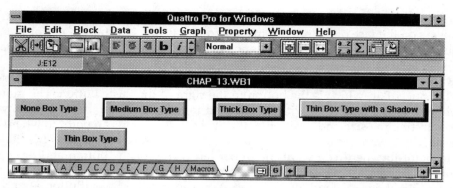

Figure 13.8   Different Box Type Styles Added to SpeedButtons

different box types added to several SpeedButtons. The color of the line around the border is set by the Border Color SpeedButton property. When you select Border Color, you have the same color selection box you have for selecting colors in the notebook palette or colors of an object in a graph.

The most important property you can set for a SpeedButton is the set of macro instructions Quattro Pro performs when you click the SpeedButton. These macro instructions are added three ways using the SpeedButton's Macro property. The first way is when you select the Macro property, by typing the macro instructions directly into the Enter Macro text box as shown for {File Save} in Figure 13.9. The second way is by entering the name of the macro in the notebook to perform in curly braces in the Enter Macro text box. For example, Figure 13.10 shows the macro instructions for the T_Print macro. The entry in the Enter Macro text box (like the one shown in Figure 13.9) for the Print SpeedButton is {T_Print}. The T_Add macro is used the same way but it is combined with other macro instructions. The third way is for when you want to run a dialog box when you click a SpeedButton. For example, the Add Contract SpeedButton in Figure 13.9 displays the dialog box shown in Figure 13.11. You can easily add the macro instructions that display the dialog box by selecting the Execute Dialog button in the Macro Text dialog box. From the next dialog box, you can select from the Activate Dialog list box the dialog box to activate when the SpeedButton is selected. In the Result Cell text box, you can enter the cell address or block name in which Quattro Pro stores a 1 or 0 to indicate whether you select OK or Cancel to leave the dialog box. In the Values Range text box, you can enter the cell address or block name that contains the initial values for the controls in the dialog box as described in Chapter 12. When you select OK, Quattro Pro converts the information you have entered to the {DODIALOG} command that invokes the dialog box for the text that appears in the Enter Macro text box. Once this macro instruction is added, you can subsequently modify it. For example, the macro instruction for the Add Contract SpeedButton is {BLANK New_Record}{DoDialog Dialog1, Macros:B46,Macros:B40..B45}{T_Add}, which clears the previous entries, activates the dialog box, then performs the remaining macro instructions stored in the T_Add macro. {BLANK} is a macro command you will learn about in the next chapter that empties the contents of a block without selecting the block first.

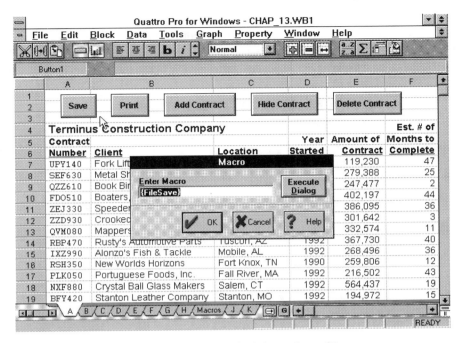

Figure 13.9   Macro Instructions Added for a SpeedButton

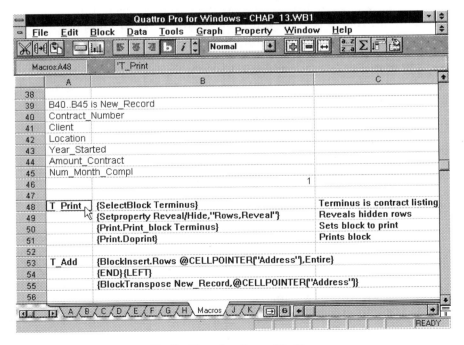

Figure 13.10   Macros To Be Run by SpeedButtons

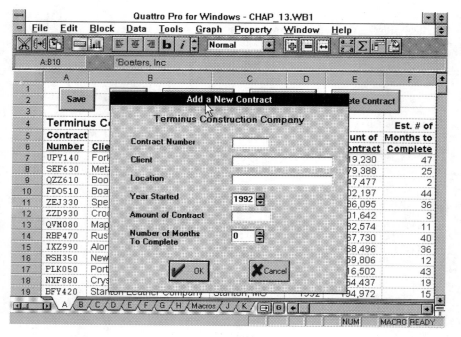

Figure 13.11   Dialog Box Run by Add Information Macro Button

Once you assign macro instructions to a SpeedButton, every time you click the SpeedButton, the macro runs. If you want to alter a SpeedButton, you can right click it to select it without performing the assigned macro instructions.

USING SPEEDBUTTONS   When you have the SpeedButtons created and properties assigned, you are ready to use the SpeedButtons. To run the macro assigned to a button, click the button. Quattro Pro performs the macro instructions assigned

---

▼ TIP: Entering macro instructions for using a dialog box and performing other actions

If you have a SpeedButtons that displays a dialog box, then performs several additional instructions, use two steps to add the SpeedButton's macro text. First, inspect the SpeedButton's macro text and select the Execute Dialog button to add the macro instructions that activate the dialog box. Next, inspect the SpeedButton's macro text again and go to the end of the {DODIALOG} command to add the additional macro instructions you want the SpeedButton to perform.

to the SpeedButton the same way as if you ran a macro by executing it with ALT-F2 (RUN MACRO) or by selecting <u>M</u>acro in the <u>T</u>ools menu and <u>E</u>xecute. If DE-BUG appears in the status line, the macro instructions assigned to a SpeedButton are run one step at a time in the Macro Debugger window.

Suppose you want to run the SpeedButtons shown in Figure 13.7. If you select the Save SpeedButton, Quattro Pro performs {FileSave}, which is the entry for the SpeedButton's macro text property. If you select the Print SpeedButton, Quattro Pro performs the T_Print macro, the entry for the SpeedButton's macro text property. If you select the Add Contract SpeedButton, Quattro Pro performs the macro instructions {BLANK New_Record}, {DoDialog Dialog1,Macros:B46, Macros:B40..B45}, and {T_Add}. T_Add is another macro, so Quattro Pro continues by executing the macro instructions in this other macro. If you select the Hide Contract SpeedButton, Quattro Pro performs {Setproperty Reveal/Hide, "Rows,Hide"}, which is the entry for the SpeedButton's macro text property to hide the current row. If you select the Delete Contract SpeedButton, Quattro Pro performs {BlockDelete.Rows @CELLPOINTER("Address"),Entire}, which is the entry for the SpeedButton's macro text property to delete the current row.

Self-Modifying Macros

Sometimes you need to adjust the instructions a macro performs as you execute the macro. In the next chapter, you will learn about macro commands you can add to a macro that change the flow of macro instruction execution. Another method when you only need one of the macro instructions to change depending on the situation is to create a self-modifying macro. A macro like this has macro instructions that are actually formulas or that contain macro instructions that modify instructions later performed in the macro.

The first type of self-modifying macro is one in which a macro instruction is actually a formula that returns a string that Quattro Pro can use as a macro instruction. For example, in the P_Name macro in Figure 13.12, the macro expects the current cell to contain a block name to print after displaying any hidden columns or rows and resetting the column widths in the block to fit the entries. The macro instruction in B61 and B65 needs to incorporate the block name into the {SelectBlock} and the {Print.Block} macro commands. The formula in B61 is +"{SelectBlock "&@CELLPOINTER("Contents")&"}" and the formula in B65 is +"{Print.Block "&@CHAR(34)&@CELLPOINTER("Contents")&@CHAR (34)&"}". The @CHAR(34) adds the parentheses around the block name in B65. Since Quattro Pro performs the macro instruction that is the cell's value, you can use the formula in these cells to modify the block that the macro uses. Macro commands like the ones covered in the next chapter will use formulas for macro instructions to adjust the macro instructions stored in a cell.

The second type of self-modifying macro is one in which a macro instruction changes the value of another macro instruction. An example of this type of macro is shown in Figure 13.13. This macro takes three label entries in a row and combines them as shown for the four names in the top of Figure 13.13. The {CALC} command

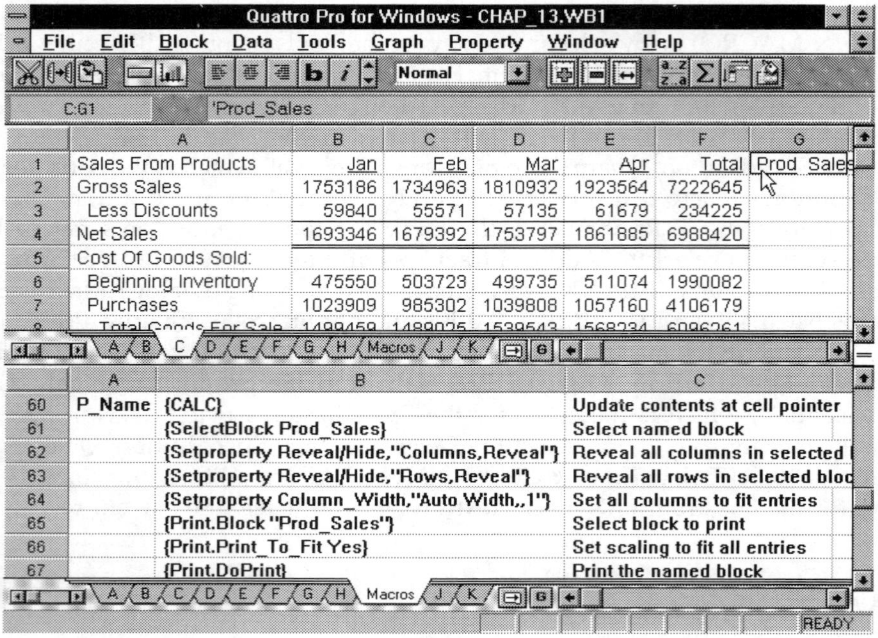

Quattro Pro for Windows - CHAP_13.WB1

File　Edit　Block　Data　Tools　Graph　Property　Window　Help

| | | Normal | | | | | |

C:G1　　'Prod_Sales

	A	B	C	D	E	F	G
1	Sales From Products	Jan	Feb	Mar	Apr	Total	Prod Sales
2	Gross Sales	1753186	1734963	1810932	1923564	7222645	
3	Less Discounts	59840	55571	57135	61679	234225	
4	Net Sales	1693346	1679392	1753797	1861885	6988420	
5	Cost Of Goods Sold:						
6	Beginning Inventory	475550	503723	499735	511074	1990082	
7	Purchases	1023909	985302	1039808	1057160	4106179	
8	Total Goods For Sale	1499459	1489025	1539543	1568234	6096261	

\A\B\C\D\E\F\G\H\Macros\J\K\

	A	B	C
60	P_Name	{CALC}	Update contents at cell pointer
61		{SelectBlock Prod_Sales}	Select named block
62		{Setproperty Reveal/Hide,"Columns,Reveal"}	Reveal all columns in selected
63		{Setproperty Reveal/Hide,"Rows,Reveal"}	Reveal all rows in selected bloc
64		{Setproperty Column_Width,"Auto Width,,1"}	Set all columns to fit entries
65		{Print.Block "Prod_Sales"}	Select block to print
66		{Print.Print_To_Fit Yes}	Set scaling to fit all entries
67		{Print.DoPrint}	Print the named block

\A\B\C\D\E\F\G\H\Macros\J\K\

READY

Figure 13.12　Macro Using a Formula to Change Macro Instructions

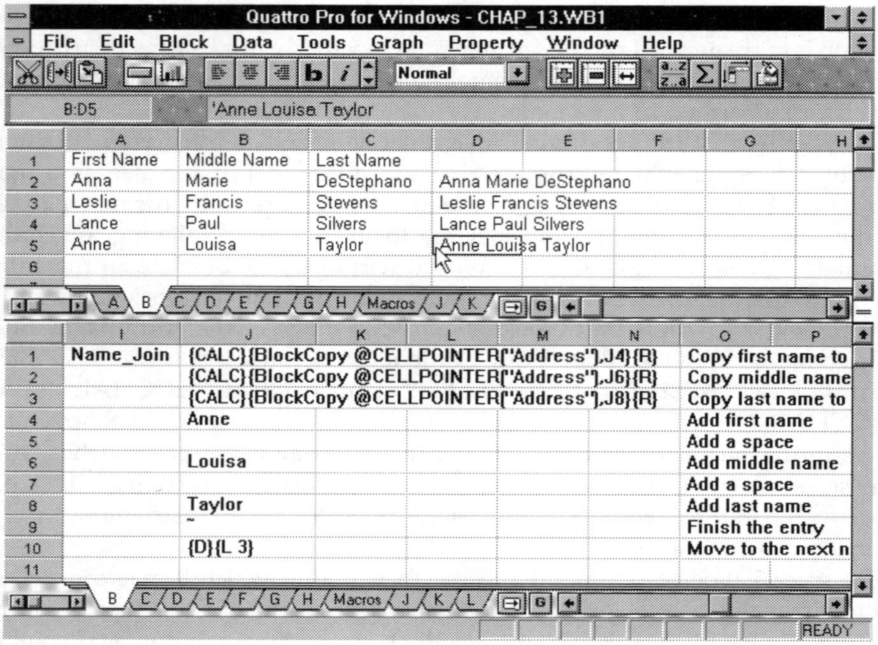

Quattro Pro for Windows - CHAP_13.WB1

File　Edit　Block　Data　Tools　Graph　Property　Window　Help

| | | Normal | | | | | |

B:D5　　'Anne Louisa Taylor

	A	B	C	D	E	F	G	H
1	First Name	Middle Name	Last Name					
2	Anna	Marie	DeStephano	Anna Marie DeStephano				
3	Leslie	Francis	Stevens	Leslie Francis Stevens				
4	Lance	Paul	Silvers	Lance Paul Silvers				
5	Anne	Louisa	Taylor	Anne Louisa Taylor				
6								

\A\B\C\D\E\F\G\H\Macros\J\K\

	I	J	K	L	M	N	O	P
1	Name_Join	{CALC}{BlockCopy @CELLPOINTER("Address"),J4}{R}					Copy first name to	
2		{CALC}{BlockCopy @CELLPOINTER("Address"),J6}{R}					Copy middle name	
3		{CALC}{BlockCopy @CELLPOINTER("Address"),J8}{R}					Copy last name to	
4		Anne					Add first name	
5							Add a space	
6		Louisa					Add middle name	
7							Add a space	
8		Taylor					Add last name	
9		~					Finish the entry	
10		{D}{L 3}					Move to the next n	
11								

\B\C\D\E\F\G\H\Macros\J\K\L\

READY

Figure 13.13　Macro That Adds Its Own Macro Instructions

updates the value of @CELLPOINTER before the {BlockCopy} command equivalents copy the current selector's contents to J4, J6, or J8. When the three {BlockCopy} commands copy the labels to column J, the labels are incorporated into the macro. When Quattro Pro performs the macro instruction in J4, Quattro Pro adds the first label in the current cell. The remaining macro instructions add spaces and the remaining parts of the name. Once all three parts of the name are added, the macro finishes the entry and moves to the beginning of the next name.

Changing Dialog Boxes in a Macro

When you use command equivalents in a macro you usually do not see the dialog boxes, since the command equivalents supply the information a dialog box needs as the information that appears between the command equivalent and the closing brace. You can create macros that manipulate dialog boxes so you see the dialog box on the screen. You can also choose whether the macro makes changes to the dialog box or lets the macro's user make the changes.

Whether you let the macro control the dialog box or the user make the changes to the dialog box, you enter the command equivalent the same way but change only one character. Either method requires that you enter the command equivalent without the additional information. If you want the macro to control the dialog box, type a ! immediately after the command equivalent. If you want the user to manipulate the dialog box, type ? immediately after the command equivalent. An example is {FileOpen!} or {FileOpen?}. When the macro controls the dialog box, the next macro instructions select the dialog box features. For example, you might have a cell in a macro containing {FileOpen!}{ALT-R}V, which opens the Open File dialog box and selects drive A.

An example of when you might use this feature is for adding another instruction to the Display_Formula macro described earlier. The modified macro might look like Figure 13.14. The {FileOpen?} macro instruction displays the Open File dialog box and lets you select which notebook you will use to perform the remaining macro instructions. In the next chapter, you will learn about the {PAUSEMACRO} command, which is often used to switch between letting a macro control a dialog box and letting the user control a dialog box.

Redrawing the Notebook Window

Quattro Pro performs the macro instructions as quickly as possible. Usually, updating the window to show every change the macro makes slows down how quickly Quattro Pro performs a macro. To make macros perform faster, Quattro Pro does not update the Quattro Pro window until it is completely finished. Not redrawing the Quattro Pro window means that once you start a macro you do not notice the change until the macro is finished performing. If you want, you can change when Quattro Pro updates the screen by changing the Macro Suppress-Redraw part of the Macro application property. When you select the Macro

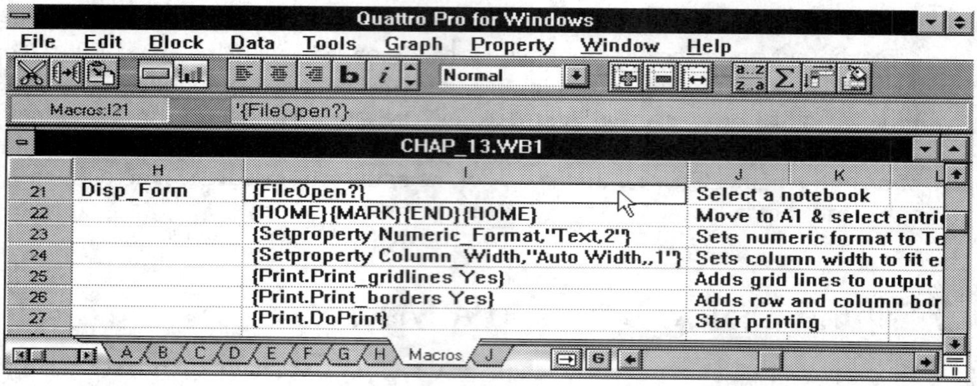

Figure 13.14   Macro Letting User Make Selections

application property, you can select the Bo*th* radio button to suppress redrawing the entire Quattro Pro window while Quattro performs the macro; the *P*anel radio button to suppress redrawing the menu bar, input line, status line, menus, and dialog boxes; the *W*indow radio button to suppress redrawing the notebook windows; or the *N*one radio button to remove suppression. You should select *N*one when you are checking your macros for errors. Once the macro performs as expected, you can suppress the redrawing so the macro performs faster. If part or all of the screen is not redrawn when you perform a macro, Quattro redraws the entire Quattro Pro window when the macro is finished. In the next chapter, you will learn about the {PANELON}, {PANELOFF}, {WINDOWON}, and {WINDOWOFF} commands that can control when the Quattro Pro window is redrawn in the middle of a macro.

▼ TIP: Name the macro library so it is always available

If you are using only one macro library, name the file the same name as the notebook in the *A*utoload File text box for the Startup application property. Quattro Pro will open this notebook for you every time you start Quattro Pro.

▼ TIP: Only one macro library should be open at any one time

Only have one macro library open at a time; Quattro will provide inconsistent results if you execute a macro in both macro libraries when both macro libraries are open.

SAMPLE KEYBOARD MACROS

The following section presents sample macros for you to use. Each of the macros has been tested and performs a specific task. Each macro has a description of the macro instructions and directions for its use. Since your notebook is probably designed differently from these examples, you need to modify the macros before adapting them to your own use. Each macro includes suggestions for customizing it to your use. Once you have adapted the macros for your own use, you can broaden the macro's application to perform other tasks for you.

The macros follow several conventions. Instead of using cell and block addresses, the macros use block names. The cells referenced by the block names are stated in the accompanying text or in the macro's documentation. The macro is documented in the style described earlier in this chapter (the macro name is at the left of the macro, and the macro documentation is at the right). The macros use command equivalents instead of keystrokes for menu selections. Appendix D contains a full list of the command equivalents. The command equivalents and block names are in proper case. Special key equivalents are shown in uppercase.

Macro for Copying a Block

Although copying cells from one location to another is already a simple operation, creating a macro to perform this task saves time if you are copying the same block repeatedly. For example, if a notebook is tracking the progress of several contracts, the notebook may look like Figure 13.15. Every time a new contract is added, the formulas that total the costs incurred to date and compute the percentage of completion and the percentage of profit earned must be copied to the column for the new contract. Since a construction company may have many projects at once, a notebook like this uses many columns. It is cumbersome to move the selector to the column with the blank formulas every time a new contract is entered. The macro copies the formulas to the column highlighted at the time that the macro is executed. When the dummy column is copied, it also erases any numbers that were in the column previously. Thus, this macro can remove the data for a contract when the contract is completed. In this macro, the selector must be in row 1 so the copied formulas are in the proper row. With a macro like this, you may want to hide column B to display more contracts on the screen. The block name Dummy_Contract is copied to the current location whenever you press CTRL-Z, press ALT-F2 (RUN MACRO) and select \Z, or select Macro from the Tools menu, Execute, and \Z.

SUGGESTIONS FOR CUSTOMIZATION   This macro can be modified for copying blocks of any size. This macro only makes one copy at a time but can be modified to create multiple copies. In the example using the construction company contracts, a mixture of absolute, relative, and mixed references may be the best solution to insure that Quattro Pro uses the correct rows. For example, if you are in row 2 when you use this macro, all formulas are one column below the other

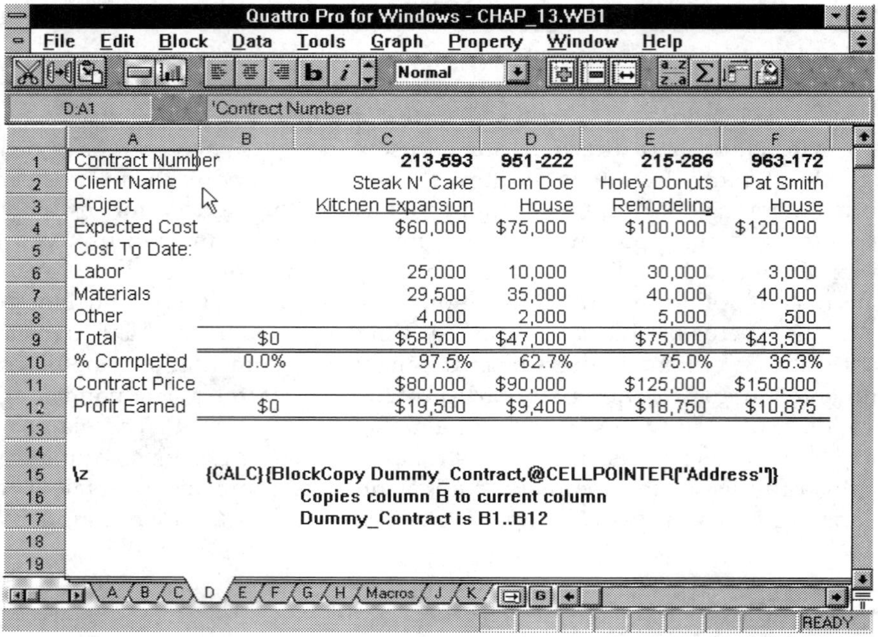

	A	B	C	D	E	F
1	Contract Number		**213-593**	**951-222**	**215-286**	**963-172**
2	Client Name		Steak N' Cake	Tom Doe	Holey Donuts	Pat Smith
3	Project		Kitchen Expansion	House	Remodeling	House
4	Expected Cost		$60,000	$75,000	$100,000	$120,000
5	Cost To Date:					
6	Labor		25,000	10,000	30,000	3,000
7	Materials		29,500	35,000	40,000	40,000
8	Other		4,000	2,000	5,000	500
9	Total	$0	$58,500	$47,000	$75,000	$43,500
10	% Completed	0.0%	97.5%	62.7%	75.0%	36.3%
11	Contract Price		$80,000	$90,000	$125,000	$150,000
12	Profit Earned	$0	$19,500	$9,400	$18,750	$10,875
15	\z	{CALC}{BlockCopy Dummy_Contract,@CELLPOINTER("Address")}				
16		Copies column B to current column				
17		Dummy_Contract is B1..B12				

Figure 13.15 Notebook Displaying Contracts

contracts. Depending on your notebook, the END-UP ARROW key sequence may be sufficient. You can also modify the macro to be on a different page so you can modify the contract information without affecting the macro. In the above example, you could also add a second macro to set the column widths to fit the project descriptions in rows 2 and 3.

Macro for Displaying and Printing Formulas

The process of displaying formulas and printing a notebook page with the formulas displayed requires many steps. If you frequently modify a notebook page to display the formulas, using the macro shown in Figure 13.16 can make the task simpler. This macro sets the default display format to Text. Once the new default format is set, the macro sets all the columns to be wider than the contents of the column. Once the formatting is complete, the macro prints the entire page with grid lines and the row and column borders.

SUGGESTIONS FOR CUSTOMIZATION You can use this macro with just about any notebook page. You may want to add commands that close the notebook without saving it so you will not have the original formatted version of the notebook overwritten by the version that has the numeric format set to Text. You may also want to include a {FileOpen?} command at the beginning of the macro

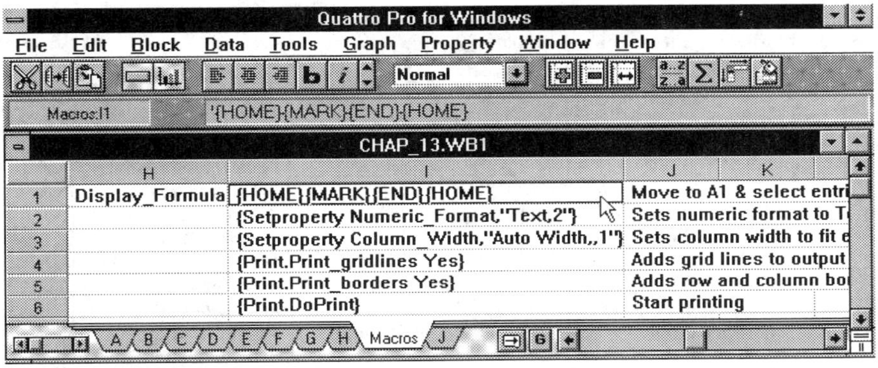

Figure 13.16 Macro That Displays and Prints Formulas

as in Figure 13.14, so that you can select which notebook you want to use for this macro.You may also want to change other print settings (such as margins and header). You can place this type of a macro in a macro library, since this macro is not specific to a particular notebook.

Macro for Printing Files

When a notebook contains several reports, it can be troublesome to modify the settings to print each report. Rather than repeat the print commands for each report, you can use a macro to set the print settings and start the print operation. Figure 13.17 shows three print macros. Each macro prints a different portion of the notebook with a different header and footer. To use these macros, the three blocks Income, Balance, and Aging must be named blocks in the notebook. Also, the block names Heading_Inc, Heading_Bal, and Heading_Age must be assigned as they are in Figure 13.17, to O16, O17, and O18.

SUGGESTIONS FOR CUSTOMIZATION   You can use macros to further customize the print selections. Each macro can have commands added that change the page layout or the headings. Another possible addition to a print macro is the choice of printer. While you can change the printer with the PrinterSetup command equivalent, many of the changes to the printer such as resolution are made through the Control Panel and there are no command equivalents.

Macro for Combining Notebooks

Combining notebooks allows you to summarize the results of several files. However, this process requires many steps. The macro in Figure 13.18 copies values from four other notebooks. Since this macro is named \0, the macro is executed

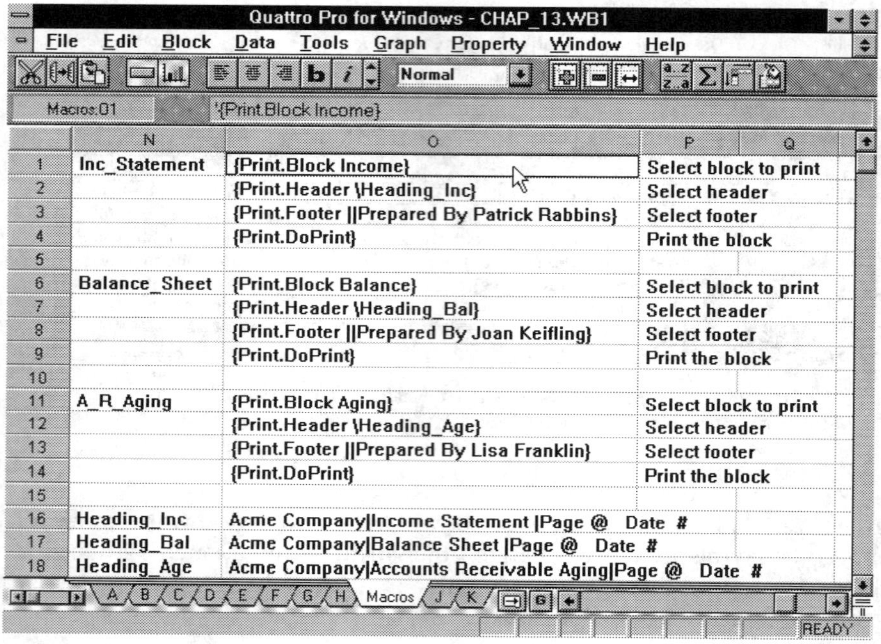

Figure 13.17   Print Macros

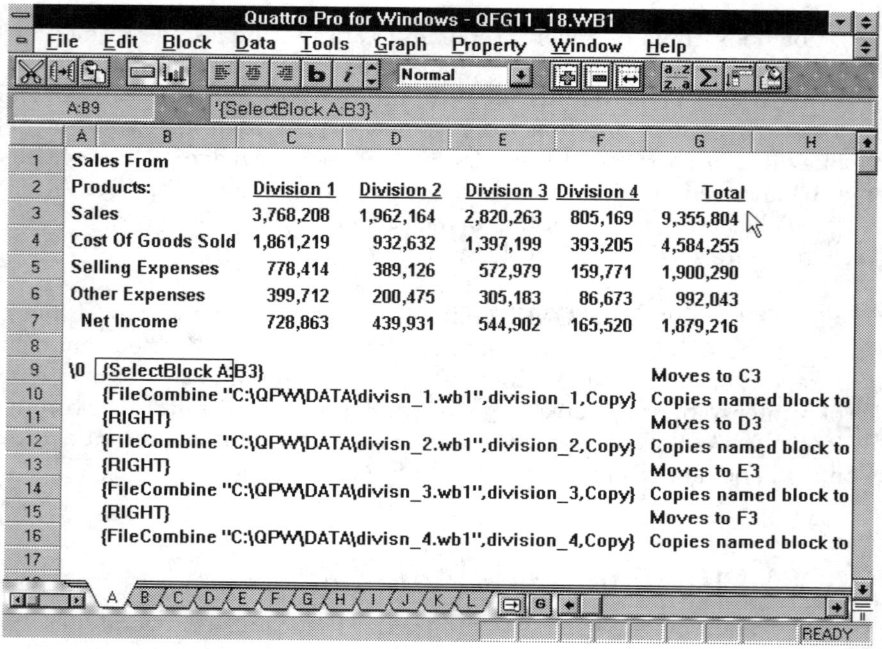

Figure 13.18   Macro That Combines Notebooks

whenever the file is opened. Making the macro an auto-execute macro insures that the spreadsheet always has the most up-to-date information. This macro copies data from the DIVISN_1, DIVISN_2, DIVISN_3, and DIVISN_4 spreadsheet files. This macro presumes that in each of the division's subsidiary spreadsheets, the summary information is a named block called Division_1, Division_2, Division_3, or Division_4. Using the block names prevents potential errors (for example, if the block containing the values you want to copy into this file is moved, its address may change, but its name remains the same).

SUGGESTIONS FOR CUSTOMIZATION   When you are using this macro for your own notebooks, you must modify the block names and file names to correspond to your application.

Although this example copies only four numbers from four spreadsheets, the macro can be expanded to provide additional consolidation information. For example, this macro can be expanded to consolidate information for several product lines or for all stores in a chain. The macro can also be changed to copy multiple blocks from each notebook. For example, you can design the macro to copy one block containing income information and another block containing balance sheet information.

A Macro for Product Costing

Chapter 5 described using the Advanced Math command in the Tools menu to work with matrices such as for computing product costs. The disadvantage of Quattro Pro's advanced math commands is that the results are not updated as the numbers change. Figure 13.19 contains the same notebook used in Chapter 5 to illustrate Quattro Pro's matrix multiply features. This notebook has a macro added that multiplies matrices by using the command equivalent for selecting Advanced Math in the Tools menu and Multiply. In this spreadsheet, the matrices are the block names Matrix1 (B2..D3) and Matrix2 (B6..C8). The resulting matrix is stored in the Output named block (B12..C13). The results of the multiplied matrices are recalculated whenever ALT-F2 (RUNMACRO) is pressed and MULT_MTRMTRX is selected from the Macros/Nameblocks list box. You can also select Macro from the Tools menu, Execute, and MULT_MTRMTRX or B15.

SUGGESTIONS FOR CUSTOMIZATION   This macro for multiplying matrices can be quickly modified to solve linear equations. Figure 13.20 shows a macro that solves the linear equations for the capacity-requirement problem that illustrated inserting matrices when you select Advanced Math in the Tools menu and Invert as described in Chapter 5. In this example, the macro first inverts the first matrix and then multiplies the inverted matrix by the second matrix. The macro for the multiplication of these two matrices follows the same steps as the macro shown in Figure 13.19, except that the address and name for the first matrix multiplied belongs to the inverted matrix rather than the original one. In this spreadsheet, InvertMatrix represents E7..G9, Matrix1 represents B2..D4, Matrix2 represents B8..B10, and Output represents B13..B15.

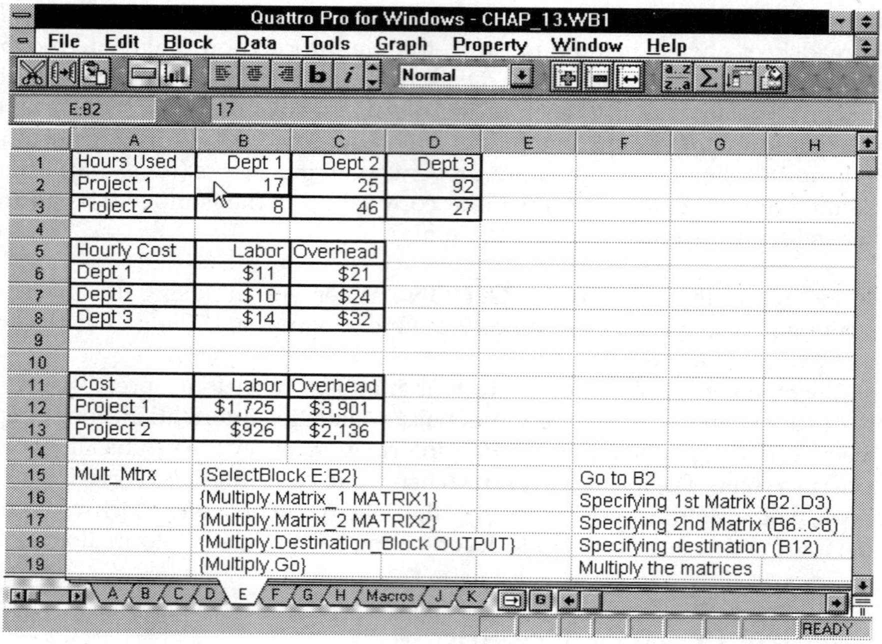

Figure 13.19   Macro That Performs Matrix Multiplication

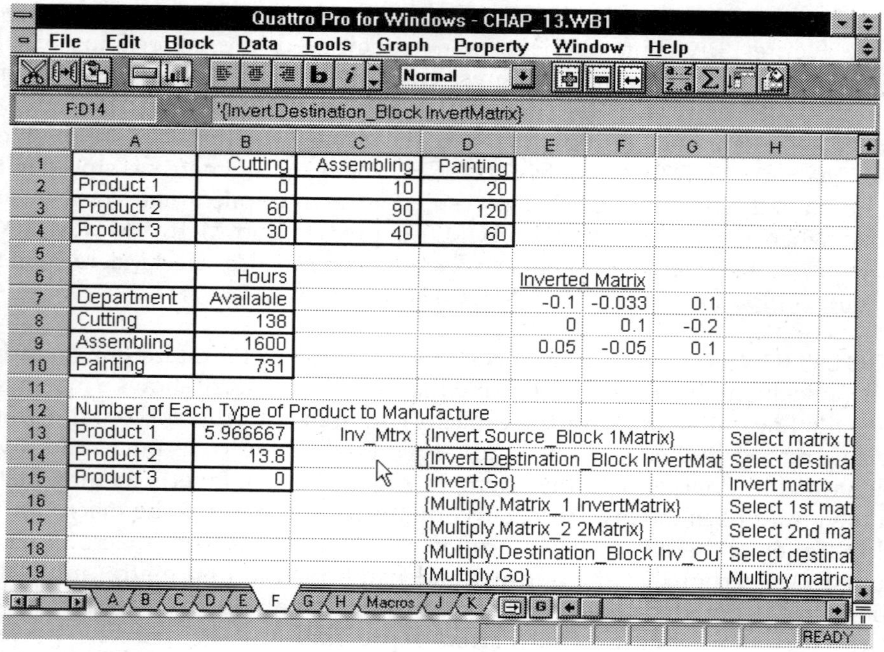

Figure 13.20   Macro That Performs Matrix Inversion and Multiplication

Macro for Creating a What-If Analysis

Like the matrix operations, several other advanced analytical features create blocks of numbers that are not updated if you change the numbers that they rely on. Updating what-if analysis tables is another application for a macro. Figure 13.21 shows a company's schedule of short-term investments. For each of the investments, the schedule shows the type of investment, the company, the maturity date, the amount, and the rate. Although you can sort the investments in order of their maturity dates and rates of interest, using the database statistical functions with the two-variable what-if table provides important information like the amount of securities for each interest rate and term. Figure 13.22 shows a macro that creates a two-way table and the table that it produces. The hidden formula in I7 is **@DSUM($Invest,3,$Criteria)**, which computes the investment in securities for each possible interest rate and maturity date. The block name **Mat_date** used in the macro is I2, representing the input cell for the table's column data. The block name **Inv_rate** used in the macro is J2, representing the input cell for the table's row data. The block name Table is assigned to the block I7..O17. The block name Criteria is assigned to I1..J2. The Invest block name is assigned to the block containing the investments partially shown in Figure 13.21.

SUGGESTIONS FOR CUSTOMIZATION The macro for creating a two-variable table can be modified to accept additional interest rates and maturity dates.

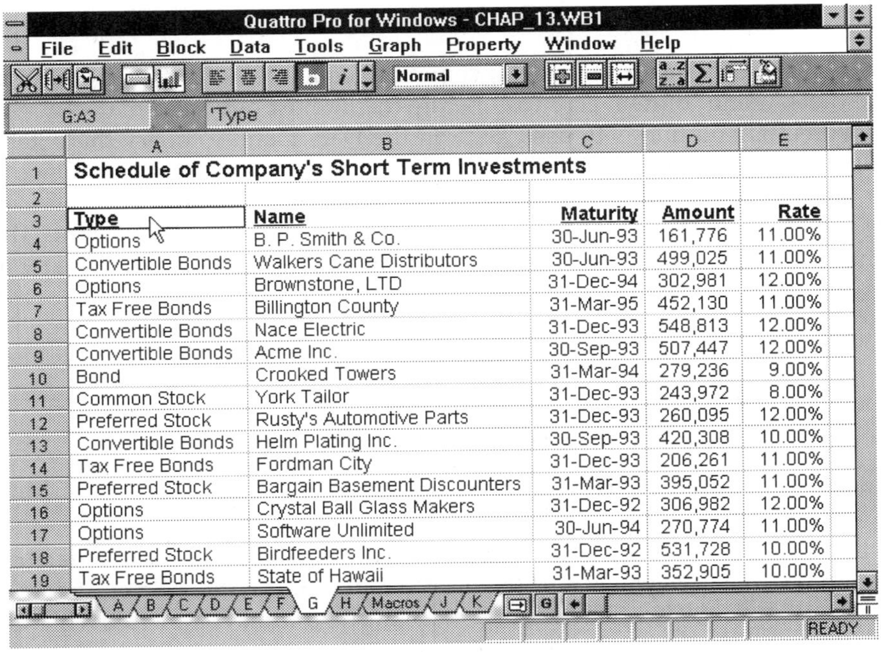
Quattro Pro for Windows - CHAP_13.WB1

File Edit Block Data Tools Graph Property Window Help

Normal

G:A3 'Type

	A	B	C	D	E
1	Schedule of Company's Short Term Investments				
2					
3	Type	Name	Maturity	Amount	Rate
4	Options	B. P. Smith & Co.	30-Jun-93	161,776	11.00%
5	Convertible Bonds	Walkers Cane Distributors	30-Jun-93	499,025	11.00%
6	Options	Brownstone, LTD	31-Dec-94	302,981	12.00%
7	Tax Free Bonds	Billington County	31-Mar-95	452,130	11.00%
8	Convertible Bonds	Nace Electric	31-Dec-93	548,813	12.00%
9	Convertible Bonds	Acme Inc.	30-Sep-93	507,447	12.00%
10	Bond	Crooked Towers	31-Mar-94	279,236	9.00%
11	Common Stock	York Tailor	31-Dec-93	243,972	8.00%
12	Preferred Stock	Rusty's Automotive Parts	31-Dec-93	260,095	12.00%
13	Convertible Bonds	Helm Plating Inc.	30-Sep-93	420,308	10.00%
14	Tax Free Bonds	Fordman City	31-Dec-93	206,261	11.00%
15	Preferred Stock	Bargain Basement Discounters	31-Mar-93	395,052	11.00%
16	Options	Crystal Ball Glass Makers	31-Dec-92	306,982	12.00%
17	Options	Software Unlimited	30-Jun-94	270,774	11.00%
18	Preferred Stock	Birdfeeders Inc.	31-Dec-92	531,728	10.00%
19	Tax Free Bonds	State of Hawaii	31-Mar-93	352,905	10.00%

A B C D E F G H Macros J K

READY

Figure 13.21 Notebook Showing Short-Term Investments

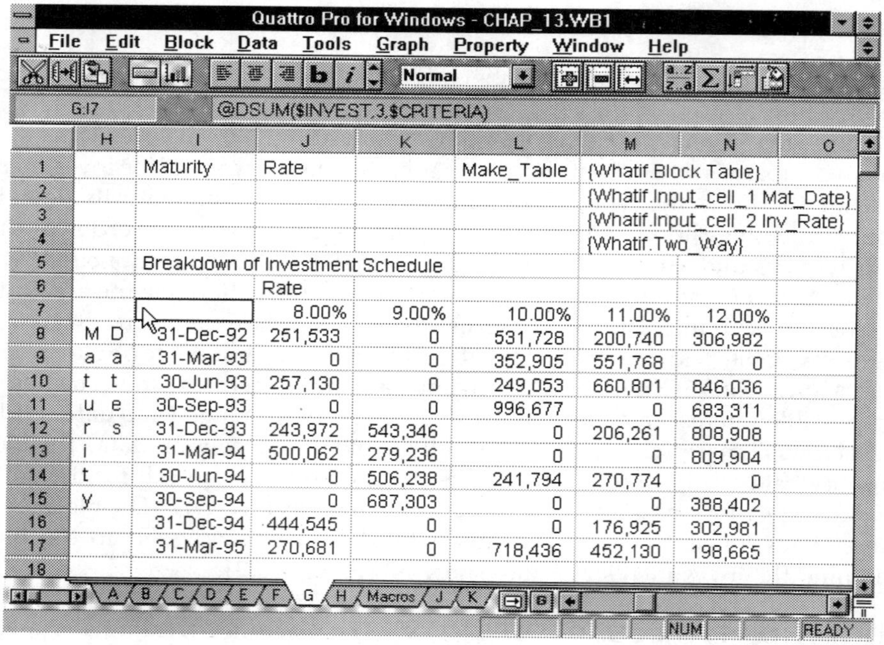

Figure 13.22   Macro That Generates Two-Variable Analysis

For example, you can add {BlockFill} command equivalents for the Fill command in the Block menu to the macro to generate the interest rates and maturity dates. An even better solution is to use Query in the Data menu to query the database and list all the unique maturity dates and interest rates in the schedule. Once you have the unique maturity dates and interest rates, you can sort them and copy them to the table with the Copy and Transpose commands in the Block menu. These enhancements insure that you have all of the most up-to-date maturity dates and rates.

▼ TIP: Record macros that will use user input with sample data

When you are recording a macro that uses user input, enter sample data as you record it where you expect the user to input information. Later, you can go back to the recorded macro and replace the data entry commands with the commands to pause the macro to accept user input.

GETTING STARTED

In this chapter, you learned how you can create macros that perform a variety of tasks. You can use these features to create the macro in Figure 13.23, which hides the row and column borders, waits for data entries, and prints the spreadsheet. To create this macro, follow these steps:

1. Make the following entries:

   A1: **Yearly Sales**
   A2: **Division A**
   A3: **Division B**
   A4: **Division C**

2. Change the default format. Select Define Style from the Edit menu. With Normal in the Define Style For drop-down list box, select the Format button and then select the Currency radio button. In the text box, enter **0** for the number of decimal digits, and select OK twice.

3. Unprotect and widen the cells in which you will enter values for the yearly sales of the different divisions. Select the block B2..B4 and inspect its properties. Select the Protection property and the Unprotect radio button. Select the column width property, type **12** in the Column Width text box, and select OK.

4. Start recording a macro. Select Macro from the Tools menu, and Record to start recording your keystrokes. You will use these keystrokes as the basis for the macro. When Quattro Pro prompts for where you want the macro instructions stored, type **B:B1** and select OK. By putting the macro instructions on a separate page, you can protect page A without worrying about Quattro Pro recording macro entries on a protected page.

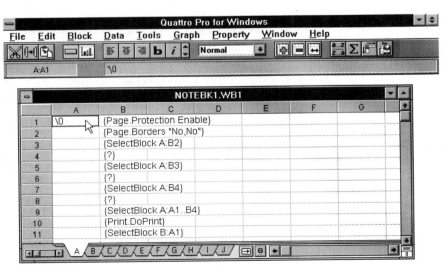

Figure 13.23 Macro Created in Getting Started Section

5. Hide the column and row borders and enable protection. Right click page A's tab or select Active Page from the Property menu. Select the Protection property and the Enable radio button to enable protection. Select the Borders property and clear the Row Borders and the Column Borders check box. Select OK to return to the notebook.

6. Select B2 as where you want the selector and make the following entries:

   B2: **650000**
   B3: **800000**
   B4: **450000**

7. Print the notebook. Select the block A1..B4. Select Print from the File menu and the Print button.

8. Finish recording the macro. Select Macro from the Tools menu, and Stop Record to stop recording your keystrokes.

9. Make some changes to the macro. Click page B's tab or press CTRL-PGDN to see the macro you have recorded. You will want to change your macro so it looks like the one in Figure 13.23. You will need to replace the {PutCell} macro instructions in G4, G6, and G8 with the {?} macro instruction so the macro waits for the user to input the sales for the divisions. Also, enter '**\0** in B:A1 to label the macro. If you made any typing mistakes, remove from the macro both the instructions containing the mistakes and the keystrokes you used to fix the mistakes.

10. Name the macro. You can either move to B:B1 and select Names from the Block menu and Create or press CTRL-F3 (NAME CREATE), then type \0 and select OK. Another possibility is to move to B:A1 and select Names from the Block menu, Labels, the Right radio button, and OK.

11. Save this macro by selecting Save from the File menu. Type **MACRO** as the file name, and select OK.

12. Close the notebook by double-clicking the notebook's control menu box or by pressing CTRL-F4 (CLOSE WINDOW).

13. Open this notebook so your startup macro will execute the commands. Select Open from the File menu. Type **MACRO** as the file name or select MACRO.WB1 from the list of files, and select OK. The \0 macro will start executing the commands. If it does not, press ALT-F2 (RUN MACRO), type **B:B1**, and select OK.

14. When the macro stops executing commands, it is waiting for you to enter the sales for Division A. Type **700000**, and either press ENTER or click ✓ in the input line. When the macro stops again and waits for your entry, type **350000**, and either press ENTER or click ✓ in the input line. When the macro stops a third time, type **600000**, and either press ENTER or click ✓ in the input line. The printed output from your macro shows the new data.

14

Advanced Macro Options

In Chapter 13 you were introduced to macro basics. Although there are some timesaving applications that can be developed with the exclusive use of these techniques, Quattro Pro offers much more. Quattro Pro's macro command language provides a full-fledged programming language for the Quattro Pro user who wants to develop customized applications. Whether you want to develop full-scale custom applications with menus and security features or just want to add a little sophistication to basic keyboard alternative macros, you will find the instructions you need within Quattro Pro's command set. You can build custom menus that perform separate macros allowing a user to select an option from a custom menu to accomplish a complete series of actions. The complete set of command language instructions is covered in this chapter.

Quattro Pro's command language instructions are used in the same manner as macro command equivalents except that Quattro Pro cannot automatically record them as you try out a new application. You can intersperse menu abbreviations, special key representations, menu-equivalent commands, and command equivalents with Quattro Pro's command language instructions. Most of Quattro Pro's macro command instructions are enclosed in a set of braces ({ }).

Most of the macro language commands that are not command equivalents allow you to add iterative processing and condition checking to a macro. Others let you display a prompt on the screen and accept appropriate information from the keyboard. Still others allow you to read information stored in a disk file or to write information to a disk file. You can create macros that create objects such as graphs and OLE objects. Other commands let you run other Windows applications from within Quattro Pro. You can also create and remove menu items from the menu bar and create the dialog boxes that different menu commands present.

ADVANCED MACRO FEATURES

Quattro Pro's advanced macro features require a little planning and attention to detail for successful application. Because they afford you all the opportunities of a programming language, you should invest some time planning the best solution for your problem before you begin coding these instructions. This planning parallels the process used by a programmer with any programming language.

Entering Menu Instructions as Labels

Once you have determined the set of macro instructions that are required to solve your problem, you can enter these instructions in the spreadsheet as labels. You must follow the unique syntax requirements for the particular command as you make these entries since most command language instructions use arguments in a manner similar to @ functions. Just as you can list the functions by pressing ALT-F3 (FUNCTIONS) or clicking @ in the EDIT mode SpeedBar, you can list the macro commands by pressing SHIFT-F3 (MACROS) or clicking { } in the EDIT SpeedBar. When you press SHIFT-F3 (MACROS) or click { } in the EDIT SpeedBar, Quattro Pro displays a selection box from which you can choose the type of macro command from Keyboard, Screen, Interactive, Program flow, Cell, File, / Commands, Command Equivalents, DDE, UI Building, Object, and Miscellaneous. Once the general type is selected, you can select the specific macro command from the list. / Commands lets you select menu-equivalent commands for Quattro Pro for DOS, and Command Equivalents lets you select command equivalents for the Quattro Pro for Windows menu.

Incorporating Macro Commands

Since command language instructions can add logic for iterative processing or condition checking, they are often useful in a macro that consists of command equivalent instructions. The best strategy to use for constructing these combination macros is to record the menu selections with Quattro Pro's recorder and to add the other instructions after testing the recorded macro.

Figure 14.1 shows a macro called Formatting that widens column A to 12 and formats the first 25 entries in the column as currency with 0 decimal places. The addition of a few block names and one or two instructions changes this macro into one that can make the same change to 10 consecutive columns. The Formatting2 macro in Figure 14.1 shows the macro with the addition of the command language instruction FOR, along with other changes required to ensure a successful application. Some of these changes include naming blocks Loop and Counter.

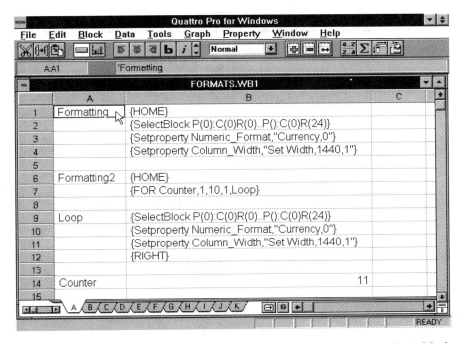

Figure 14.1   Keyboard Alternative Macro with Macro Commands Added

COMMAND LANGUAGE OPTIONS

The macro instructions in the sections that follow are grouped according to the categories that Quattro Pro's documentation uses. (These categories and their commands are shown in Table 14.1.) In addition to a description of each command language instruction, an example of its use is provided. The macro arguments that are optional are enclosed in brackets (<>). As you duplicate these examples, remember to assign block names to the appropriate fields so that the macros function properly. These names appear in proper case to make it easy to distinguish them from command language instructions, which appear in uppercase. The /X commands are only for compatibility with early versions of 1-2-3, so you will want to use the equivalent macro commands instead. Also, the {PLAY} command from Quattro Pro for DOS will not prevent a macro from executing, although the command is ignored in Quattro Pro for Windows.

Cell Contents Commands

The cell contents macro commands change the contents of spreadsheet cells. These commands can delete a group of cells, assign values to cells, and recalculate cells.

Table 14.1 Macro Commands by Category

Cell Contents

{BLANK}
{CONTENTS}
{GETDIRECTORYCONTENTS}
{GETWINDOWLIST}
{LET}
{PUT}
{PUTBLOCK}
{PUTCELL}
{RECALC}
{RECALCCOL}
{SPEEDFILL}
{SPEEDFORMAT}
{SPEEDSUM}

Program Flow

{BRANCH}
{DEFINE}
{DISPATCH}
{FOR}
{FORBREAK}
{IF}
{ONERROR}
{QUIT}
{RESTART}
{RETURN}
{Subroutine}

Interactive

{?}
{ACTIVATE}
{BREAKOFF}
{BREAKON}
{DODIALOG}

{BREAKON}
{GET}
{GETLABEL}
{GETNUMBER}
{GRAPHCHAR}
{IFKEY}
{LOOK}
{MENUBRANCH}
{MENUCALL}
{MESSAGE}
{PAUSEMACRO}
{STEPOFF}
{STEPON}
{WAIT}

File

{ANSIREAD}
{ANSIREADLN}
{ANSIWRITE}
{ANSIWRITELN}
{CLOSE}
{FILESIZE}
{GETPOS}
{OPEN}
{READ}
{READLN}
{SETPOS}
{WRITE}
{WRITELN}

Screen

{BEEP}
{INDICATE}
{PANELOFF}
{PANELON}

Table 14.1   Macro Commands by Category *(continued)*

{WINDOWSOFF}	{ROWCOLSHOW}
{WINDOWSON}	{ROWHEIGHT}
DDE	{SELECTBLOCK}
	{SELECTFLOAT}
{EXEC}	{SELECTOBJECT}
{EXECUTE}	{SETGRAPHATTR}
{INITIATE}	{SETOBJECTPROPERTY}
{POKE}	{SETPROPERTY}
{REQUEST}	**Miscellaneous**
{TERMINATE}	
	{}
UI Building	{;}
{ADDMENU}	{HLINE}
{ADDMENUITEM}	{HPAGE}
{DELETEMENU}	{VLINE}
{DELETEMENUITEM}	{VPAGE}
{SETMENUBAR}	
	/X for Compatibility with 1-2-3
Object	
	/XC={Subroutine}
{COLUMNWIDTH}	/XG={BRANCH}
{CREATEOBJECT}	/XI={IF}
{FLOATCREATE}	/XL={GETLABEL}
{FLOATMOVE}	/XM={MENUBRANCH}
{FLOATSIZE}	/XN={GETNUMBER}
{GETOBJECTPROPERTY}	/XQ={QUIT}
{GETPROPERTY}	/XR={RETURN}
{MOVETO}	
{RESIZE}	

{BLANK}   The {BLANK} command deletes the contents of the cell or block that you specify. This command is equivalent to using the DEL key or using the Clear command in the Edit menu.

Format   {BLANK Location} is the format of the {BLANK} command.
Location is the cell address, block address, or block name whose contents are to be deleted.

Use   The {BLANK} command can replace an {EditClear} command equivalent or the {DEL} special-key equivalent in a macro to erase one or more cells. Unlike the Clear command in the Edit menu, Quattro Pro can execute this command while in the middle of another command.

Example   Figure 14.2 shows a macro that uses the {BLANK} command. This macro gives the user the option of including notes with the budget. If the user wants to include notes, the macro lets the user type them and then prints the budget and the notes. If the user does not want notes, the macro prints only the budget. The {BLANK} command at the beginning of the macro removes the contents of the block named Notes (which is B16..H20) to prevent notes from a prior budget from appearing with the notes for the new budget.

{CONTENTS}   The {CONTENTS} command copies the contents from one location to another. If the original location contains a numeric value, you can specify a format and width to store the value as a string.

Format   {CONTENTS Destination,Source<,Width<,Format>>} is the format for the {CONTENTS} command.

Destination is the location in which you want to store the Source value as a left-aligned label. It is a block name or cell address.

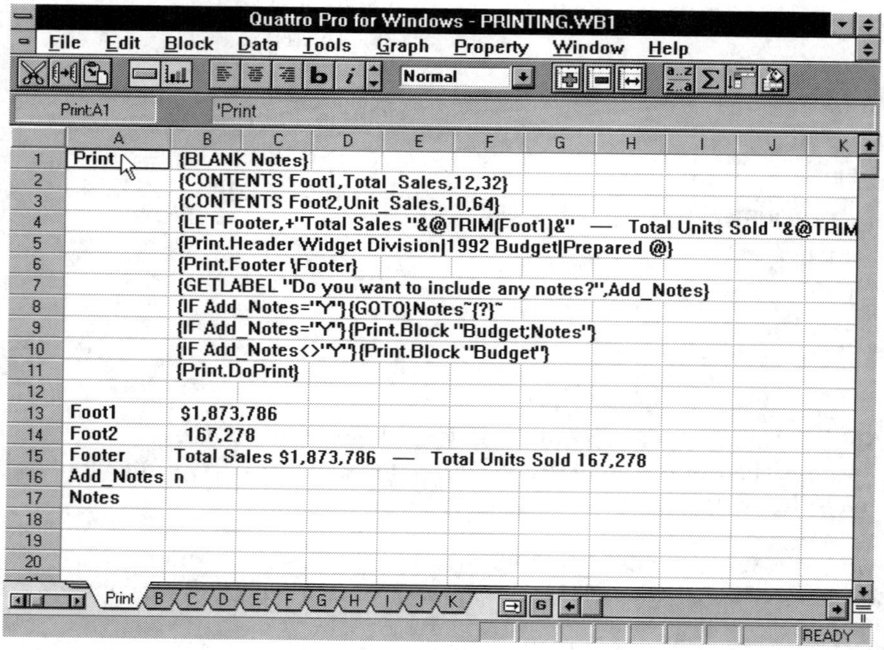

Figure 14.2   Macro Using {BLANK} and {CONTENTS} Commands

Source is the location of the entry you want copied to the destination. It is specified as a cell address or block name.

Width is the number of characters of the left-aligned label used when the value of the source is a number. It must be a number between 1 and 1023. This argument is optional, but if you use the Format argument, you must use this argument. If the width is missing, Quattro Pro uses the width of the source column. This command does not change the column width. This command puts the value of Source into Destination as the number would appear in a column of the specified width. For example, if the column width is 5 for a number that needs a width of at least 7, Quattro Pro stores the label '***** in the Destination. If the width is greater than the number needs, Quattro Pro adds spaces to the beginning so the length of the resulting label is the same as the width.

Format is a number corresponding to the format used in the Destination. Table 14.2 lists the numbers you can use as the Format argument. Like the Width

Table 14.2   Format Codes for the {CONTENTS} Macro Command

Code	Numeric Format
0-15	Fixed with 0-15 decimals
16-31	Scientific with 0-15 decimals
32-47	Currency with 0-15 decimals
48-63	Percentage with 0-15 decimals
64-79	Comma with 0-15 decimals
112	Plus/Minus
113	General
114	Date Format 1 = DD-MMM-YY
115	Date Format 2 = DD-MMM
116	Date Format 3 = MMM-YY
117	Text
118	Hidden
119	Time Format 1 = HH:MM:SS AM/PM
120	Time Format 2 = HH:MM AM/PM
121	Date Format 4 = Long International
122	Date Format 5 = Short International
123	Time Format 3 = Long International
124	Time Format 4 = Short International
127	Default set with Normal style

argument, this argument is optional. If the Format argument is missing, Quattro Pro uses the format of the Source cell.

Use   This command changes the spacing and format of cells. For writing to files that are in a structured format, this command changes the appearance so the information lines up with the information in other records of the file.

Example   Figure 14.2 shows the Print macro that prints the budget. Since the footer includes values that are in the notebook, the {CONTENTS} command stores the values the footer uses in named cells in a specific format. The first {CON-TENTS} command puts the value of Total_Sales in Foot1 as it appears in a cell that fits twelve characters, and using the currency format with no digits after the decimal point. The second {CONTENTS} command puts the value of Total_Units in Foot2 as it appears in a cell that fits ten characters, and using the comma format with no digits after the decimal point. Once these entries are stored as labels in Foot1 and Foot2, the {LET} command can combine the numbers to create the entry to use for the footer. The {Print.Footer \Footer} command equivalent sets the contents of the cell named Footer to be used as the budget's printed footer.

{GETDIRECTORYCONTENTS}   The {GETDIRECTORYCONTENTS} command fills a block with the files in a specific directory. You can use this command to learn which files are in a directory.

Format   {GETDIRECTORYCONTENTS Block<,Path>} is the format for the {GETDIRECTORYCONTENTS} command.

   Block is the location where this macro command places the contents of the selected directory. If the block is one cell, Quattro Pro uses this cell as the starting location and continues downward, overwriting any existing entries. If the block is more than one cell, Quattro Pro only uses the cell in the specified block to contain the directory entries.

   Path is the location on the disk and designates which files you want this macro command to return. When this optional argument is omitted, this macro command returns all of the files from the current directory. When you include the path argument, you must include the file specification, even if you use *.* to include all files. A sample of a file specification is *.WB1 to find all Quattro Pro notebook files. You can also include the drive and directory as in C:\QPW\DATA*.* to list all files from the C:\QPW\DATA directory. Usually this arguement is enclosed in quotes but you can also use a block name when the block name contains the entry that you want to use as the Path argument.

Use   Use this command to list files in a directory in a block in a notebook.

Example   If you want a macro that returns the names of the sample notebook files included with Quattro Pro for Windows, you will enter a macro command like {GETDIRECTORYCONTENTS A3,"C:\QPW\SAMPLES*.WB1"}. When you ex-ecute this macro instruction, Quattro Pro puts the names of all the notebook files in the C:\QPW\SAMPLES*.WB1 directory starting in A3. You will see entries such as business.wb1, drive.wb1, and loanpmt.wb1.

{GETWINDOWLIST}   The {GETWINDOWLIST} command fills a block with the names of all open windows. These are the same open window names that appear at the bottom of the Window pull-down menu.

Format   {GETWINDOWLIST Block} is the format for the {GETWINDOWLIST} command.
   Block is the location where this macro command places the names of the open windows. If the block is one cell, Quattro Pro uses this cell as the starting location and continues downward, overwriting any existing entries. If the block is more than one cell, Quattro Pro only uses the cell in the specified block to contain the window names.

Use   Use this command to list the open windows.

Example   You can create a macro that lists the open windows then uses the open window list to determine the window name that you can later use with the {ACTIVATE} command. For example, if you have an empty notebook, the CHAP_10 notebook and its Stack_Bar_Graph graph, the DIALOG notebook and its Sample_Dialog dialog box open, using the macro command {GETWINDOWLIST A3} will result in a list like this:

   NOTEBK1.WB1
   CHAP_10.WB1
   CHAP_10.WB1:Stack_Bar_Graph
   DIALOG.WB1
   DIALOG.WB1:Sample_Dialog

   Once you have this list, you can use the cell entries in {ACTIVATE} commands to select which menu is active. You can see from this example that the list of open windows look just like the window names that appear at the bottom of the Window pull-down menu. Any hidden windows are not included in the list.

{LET}   The {LET} command allows you to enter value or string entries in a cell during macro execution without having to move the selector to the location of the cell.

Format   {LET Location,Value<:Type>} is the format of the {LET} command.
   Location is the address or name of the cell or block in which the Value is to be stored.
   Value is the numeric or string entry you want stored in the cell or block specified by Location. This is a cell address or block name, a formula, a string enclosed in quotes, or a value.
   Type is either string or value. Using string stores the argument Value as a left-aligned label. If Value contains a formula, a type of string stores the formula as a

left-justified label. A type of value stores the Value argument as the value entered. If you omit this optional argument, Quattro Pro attempts to store Value as a numeric value. If Quattro Pro is unsuccessful, Quattro Pro stores Value as string.

Use   This command is very flexible, since you can specify either string or value entries. It is very useful in a loop that executes a section of code. You can use this command to increment a counter. Some examples follow:

{LET C1,12} This stores the value 12 in C1.
{LET C1,+C1+5} This increases C1 by 5.
{LET C1,+C1+5:string} This stores the label '+C1+5 in C1.

Example   Figure 14.3 shows a macro using several {LET} commands. This macro lists all possible account numbers. Using the file instead of typing the numbers directly into the notebook reduces the number of typing errors. Table is the block name for G5..G41, the location where the {PUT} command places the account numbers that are read from a file. The {LET} command in B3 stores the value of Size divided by 12 in Records. The {LET} command in B4 stores a value in Counter. The {LET} command in B8 increments the value of Counter by 1. This macro uses the {LET} command to change cell entries without the need for positioning the selector on the cell to be changed.

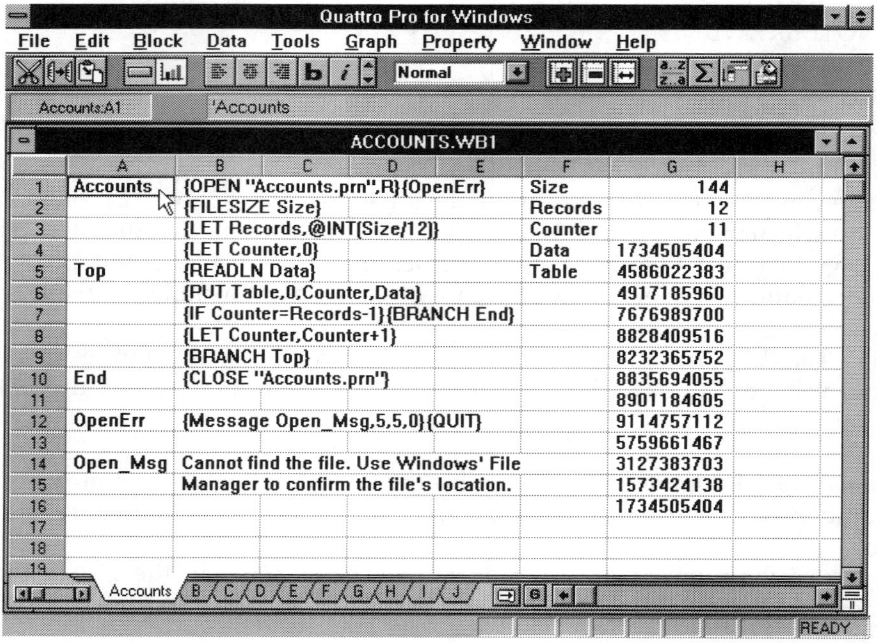

Figure 14.3   Macro Using {LET} and {PUT} Commands

{PUT}   Like the {LET} command, the {PUT} command allows you to copy a value or string from a specified cell to another cell. Instead of specifying a cell address or block name to which the value is to be copied, you need to specify the destination as the block name and the offset in the block. The offset is the number of columns to the right and number of rows down from the upper-left corner of the block. The {PUT} command creates an array of data in a block.

Format   {PUT Location,Column#,Row#,Value<:Type>} is the format for the {PUT} command.

Location is a block in which the command stores the value. This block must contain all the columns and rows that the {PUT} command uses. This argument is either a block address or block name.

Column# is the number of columns to the right of the first column of the block where Quattro Pro stores the value. This argument is a number, cell address, block name containing a value, or a formula that returns a value. Quattro Pro starts counting the columns with 0. The first column of a block has a Column# of 0, and the second column of a block has a Column# of 1. The identifying number is always one less than the number of columns in the block.

Row# is the number of rows below the top row of the location block where Quattro Pro stores the Value. This argument is a number, cell address, or block name containing either a value or a formula that returns a value. Quattro Pro starts counting the rows with 0. The first row of a block has a Row# of 0 and the second row of a block has a Row# of 1. This identifying number is always one less than the number of rows in the block.

Value is the value that Quattro Pro places in the cell specified by the column and row offset of the block. It is a string, numeric value, formula, cell address, or block name.

Type is string or value. If Type is string, Quattro Pro stores Value as a label. If Value is a block name or formula, the name or formula is stored in the specified location as a left-aligned label. If this argument is a value, Quattro Pro determines the value of Value before storing the value in the specified location. This argument is optional. If this argument is omitted, Quattro Pro attempts to store Value as a numeric value. If Quattro Pro is unsuccessful, Quattro Pro stores Value as a string.

Use   This command stores values in spreadsheet cells. Unlike the {LET} command, the {PUT} command uses an offset to determine the location. The argument Value is placed a specified number of rows and columns into the block. If the Column# or Row# argument is too high the macro aborts, since this is not an error that {ONERROR} can trap.

Example   Figure 14.3 provides an example of the {PUT} command. This macro lists all possible account numbers. Using the file instead of typing the numbers directly into the block reduces the number of typing errors. Table is the block name for G5..G41, the location where the {PUT} command places the account numbers that are read from a file. The macro reads one line at a time and stores the information in Data, G4. The {PUT} command copies this information from Data to the next blank row in Table. The {PUT} command uses the value of Counter in G3 for Row#. Since 0 is the Column#, the {PUT} command copies the data into column G.

{PUTBLOCK}   The {PUTBLOCK} command enters the same entry in a block of cells. This command works as if you put the value in the first cell in the block and copied it to the other cells in the block.

Format   {PUTBLOCK Value<,Block>} is the format for the {PUTBLOCK} command.

Value is the entry you want placed in each cell in the block. It can be a number, formula, or string in quotes.

Block is the location you want filled with the Value argument. It is a block address or block name. If you omit this optional argument, this macro command uses the currently selected block.

Use   This command is for putting the same entry in many cells at once. Use it where you want a block filled with a specific label or value or you want the same formula copied to each cell in the block.

Example   Figure 14.4 shows a macro that uses the {PUTBLOCK} command to enter the same formula. After the {PUTCELL} command enters the current date in A5, the {PUTBLOCK} command puts the formula +A5+1 in A6 and copies the formula to the other cells in the block. As a result, all of the date serial numbers in A6..A11 are incremented by 1. When you use {PUTBLOCK} with a formula, the formula is adjusted as shown in Figure 14.4. When you use {PUTBLOCK} with a

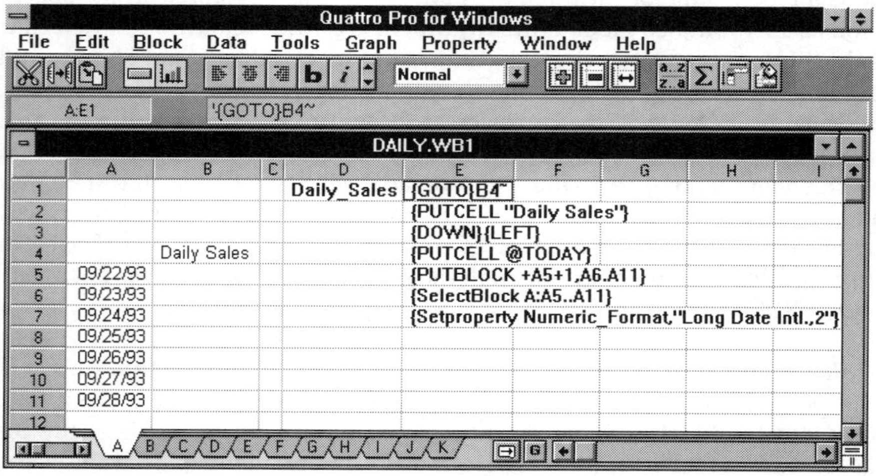

Figure 14.4   Macro Using {PUTBLOCK} and {PUTCELL} Commands

number or string, the value does not change. For example, to fill A5..A11 with 1992, you would enter {PUTBLOCK 1992,A6..A11}.

{PUTCELL} The {PUTCELL} command puts an entry into the current cell. You can use this command in place of typing the entries in the macro.

Format {PUTCELL Data} is the format for the {PUTCELL} command.
   Data is the entry you want placed in the current cell. It is a formula, number, or string enclosed in quotes.

Use Use this command in place of directly typing the entry in the macro.

Example Figure 14.4 shows a macro that uses the {PUTCELL} command to enter a date and a label. The {PUTCELL} command in E2 enters Daily Sales as a label in the current cell. Since the {GOTO} command in E1 puts the selector in B4, this is where the entry is placed. Next, the macro instructions in E3 move the selector to A5. The second {PUTCELL} command places the formula @TODAY in the cell. The first {PUTCELL} command can also be performed by entering Daily Sales~ in E2. The second {PUTCELL} command can also be performed by entering '@TO-DAY~ in E4. Once the {PUTCELL} commands make their entries, other macro instructions, such as the {PUTBLOCK} command in E5 can use the values the {PUTCELL} command enters. The advantage of using {PUTCELL} in place of directly entering the cell entries in the macro is that if the macro has a mistake, you will get fewer problems with the {PUTCELL} command, since it can *only* make a cell entry, while directly entering the instructions can perform anything that the entries are permitted to do.

{RECALC} The {RECALC} command recalculates a specified block of the notebook. Quattro Pro recalculates row by row within the block.

Format {RECALC Location<,Condition<,Iteration#>>} is the format for the {RECALC} command.
   Location is the block of cells you want recalculated.
   Condition is an optional argument that halts the recalculation process when the condition this argument represents is true. The recalculation process continues as long as this condition is false.
   Iteration# is also an optional argument. This argument is used in conjunction with the condition. It allows you to specify the maximum number of times Quattro Pro recalculates the formulas within the block while the condition is false.

Use The {RECALC} command recalculates an area of a notebook while leaving the remainder of the notebook uncalculated. This command speeds up macro execution by limiting the area in which Quattro Pro calculates the formulas. If the cells that the formulas in Location reference are not above or to the left of the formulas and in the Location block, you should use either {RECALCCOL} or

{CALC}. You may want to increase the iteration count to confirm that the cells in Location have been correctly computed. The number of iterations can be increased by using @FALSE for the condition and a number of iterations as parameters for the macro command.

Example   Figure 14.5 provides an example of the {RECALC} command. The projected figures in column E are formulas that use current figures increased by a specified sales growth rate. The block D2..E5 is named Forecast. The sales growth rate in E7 is named Growth. When the macro begins, Quattro Pro prompts you for the sales growth rate. The formula in E7 (which is +E15) duplicates the value in E7. After entering the rate, the {Notebook.Recalc_Settings "Manual,Natural,1"} command switches the recalculation mode from automatic to manual to reduce the macro execution time. When Quattro Pro executes the {RECALC} command, Quattro Pro recalculates the formulas in the block Forecast. In this example, the growth rate is 20%. Unless the recalculation mode is set to manual, Quattro Pro automatically recalculates the notebook, which makes the {RECALC} command unnecessary. Since recalculation is set to manual, Quattro Pro only recalculates the selected block when Quattro Pro executes the {RECALC} command. This macro instruction is primarily used for long macros and for macros that use large spreadsheet notebooks containing many formulas.

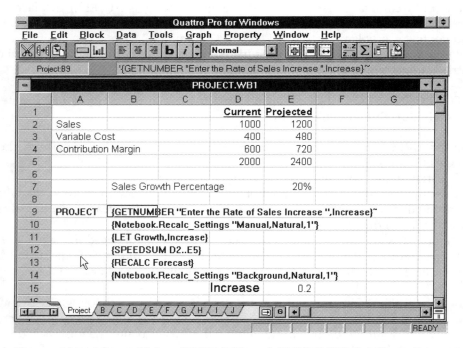

Figure 14.5   Macro Using {RECALC} and {SPEEDSUM} Macro Commands

{RECALCCOL} The {RECALCCOL} command recalculates the specified block column by column.

Format {RECALCCOL Location,<Condition<,Iteration#>>} is the format for the {RECALCCOL} command.

Location is the specified block of cells that you want recalculated.

Condition is a logical condition that stops the recalculation process when the condition is true. As long as the condition is false, the recalculation takes place. This argument is optional. If the command uses the Iteration# argument, Condition is a required argument.

Iteration# is the maximum number of times the formulas are recalculated in the block while the condition remains false. As long as the condition is false, Quattro Pro recalculates the block the number of times specified by Iteration#. However, when the condition is true, recalculation stops even though Quattro Pro has not recalculated the formulas the number of times specified by Iteration#.

Use The {RECALCCOL} command is used when the area to be recalculated is to the right of and above the cells that the formulas in this area reference. This command speeds up macro execution by limiting the area in which Quattro Pro calculates the formulas. If the area that the formulas reference are to the left of and below the block, you should use either {RECALC} or {CALC}. If the block contains several formulas that refer to values within the block, the formulas should be recalculated at least twice to insure that the formulas reflect the current values. The number of iterations is increased by including @FALSE for the condition and the number of iterations as parameters for the macro command.

Example An example of the {RECALCCOL} command is replacing the {RECALC Forecast} command in B13 of Figure 14.5 with {RECALCCOL Forecast}. As described for the {RECALC} command, the notebook recalculation is set to manual to speed macro execution. Next, the {GETNUMBER} command gets a new growth percentage from the user that replaces the entries in Increase. The {LET} command puts this value in Growth (E7). To recalculate the formulas, including the @SUM functions added by the {SPEEDSUM} command, the {RECALCCOL} command can tell Quattro Pro to recalculate the Forecast block (D2..E5). Since none of the calculations in column D change as this command recalculates column E, you only need one iteration.

{SPEEDFILL} The {SPEEDFILL} command fills a block with values just as if you selected the block and clicked the SpeedFill button in the SpeedBar.

Format {SPEEDFILL} is the format for the {SPEEDFILL} command.
The command has no arguments.

Use This command quickly fills in a block with the next logical entries based on the entries you have made in the beginning of the block.

Example   You can use the {SPEEDFILL} macro command after a {SELECTBLOCK} macro command to fill the block selected by the {SELECTBLOCK} macro command with a series of entries. For example, suppose you have the macro instructions {LET A1,1}, {SELECTBLOCK A1..A10}, and {SPEEDFILL}. When you perform these macro instructions, the block A1..A10 is filled with the numbers 1 through 10.

{SPEEDFORMAT}   The {SPEEDFORMAT} command applies a predefined format to a preselected block. This macro command performs the same action as when you select a block and use the SpeedFormat button in the SpeedBar.

Format   {SPEEDFORMAT FmtName, NumFmt?, Font?, Shading?, TextColor?, Align?, LineDraw?, AutoWidth?, ColHead?, ColTotal?, RowHead?, RowTotal?} is the format for the {SPEEDFORMAT} command.

FmtName is the format name you select from the Formats list box in the Speed Format dialog box.

NumFmt?, Font?, Shading?, TextColor?, Align?, LineDraw?, AutoWidth?, ColHead?, ColTotal?, RowHead?, RowTotal? represent the Numeric Format, Font, Shading, Text Color, Alignment, Line Drawing, Set Auto-Width, Column heading, Column total, Row heading, and Row total check boxes. For each of these arguments, you either supply a 1 to indicate that you want that part of the format applied or 0 to indicate that you want to omit that part of the format. These arguments are required. If you do not include enough 1 and 0 arguments separated by commas, Quattro Pro will display an error message.

Use   This command quickly applies formatting to a block you have already selected. This command is often preceded by a {SELECTBLOCK} command to select the block you want to apply the formatting.

Example   {SPEEDFORMAT "Puccini",1,1,1,1,1,1,1,0,0,0,0} applies the Puccini SpeedFormat style to the currently selected block. Now the selected block will have its text boldfaced with a cyan background and the columns separated by lines.

{SPEEDSUM}   The {SPEEDSUM} command totals the values in a block just as if you selected the block and clicked the SpeedSum button in the SpeedBar.

Format   {SPEEDSUM Block} is the format for the {SPEEDSUM} command.

Block is the block address or block name containing the values to sum plus the empty adjacent cells where the sums are placed.

Use   This command quickly totals entries you have made with other macro commands.

Example   Figure 14.5 shows the {SPEEDSUM} command that totals the entries in columns D and E. Assuming D5..E5 is empty when this macro is executed, the command {SPEEDSUM D2..E5} enters the formula @SUM(D2..D4) in D5 and

@SUM(E2..E4) in E5. The next macro instruction, the {RECALC} command, updates the formulas in columns D and E to use the new growth rate.

Program Flow Commands

Quattro Pro has several commands that allow you to change the macro instructions that Quattro Pro performs as the macro executes. Quattro Pro has several other commands that create loops; this allows you to repeat a group of macro instructions. Yet another set of commands lets you redirect Quattro Pro to another group of macro instructions. Quattro Pro can branch to a second group of instructions, thereby changing the execution flow of the macro. A macro that branches does not return to the first area of the macro after completing the instructions in the area where the macro instruction branches. However, Quattro Pro can treat a group of instructions as a subroutine. When a subroutine is used, Quattro Pro returns to the original macro location and continues with the next instruction after completing the subroutine.

Some of the program flow commands change the ending point of a macro or subroutine. These let you omit a group of instructions. One of the more important program flow commands is the {IF} command, which allows you to execute another set of instructions if a condition is true.

{BRANCH} The {BRANCH} macro command switches to a series of macro commands that begin in another location. When Quattro Pro alters the execution flow to the new location, Quattro Pro does not return to the original set of macro instructions. If the original set has additional instructions, the additional instructions will not be executed unless another branch instruction returns to them.

Format {BRANCH Location} is the format of the {BRANCH} command.

Location can be a block name or a cell address containing the first macro instruction that Quattro Pro performs after executing the {BRANCH} command. If Location is a block name, Quattro Pro starts with the macro instruction commands in the upper-left cell. If Location is in another notebook, the notebook name must be included in square brackets before the cell address or block name. From the new location, Quattro Pro continues performing macro instructions until Quattro Pro reaches a non-label cell, a {QUIT} command, or another command that redirects control to another macro.

Use The {BRANCH} command is often the macro instruction following an {IF} command. If the condition in a {IF} command is true, you may want macro execution to continue at another location. If the condition is false, the macro execution continues with the instruction in the cell below.

Example Figure 14.6 shows two examples of the {BRANCH} command. In B7, when the value of Counter reaches the value of Records less one, the macro branches execution to the End macro. In this case, the {BRANCH} command only

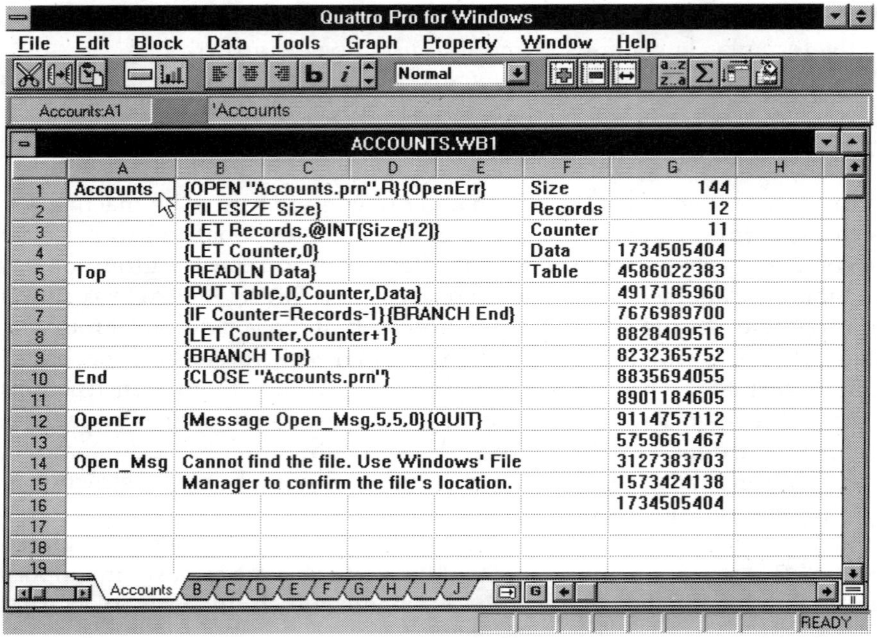

	Quattro Pro for Windows						

File   Edit   Block   Data   Tools   Graph   Property   Window   Help

	A	B	C	D	E	F	G	H
				Normal				

Accounts:A1   'Accounts

ACCOUNTS.WB1

	A	B	C	D	E	F	G	H
1	Accounts	{OPEN "Accounts.prn",R}{OpenErr}				Size	144	
2		{FILESIZE Size}				Records	12	
3		{LET Records,@INT(Size/12)}				Counter	11	
4		{LET Counter,0}				Data	1734505404	
5	Top	{READLN Data}				Table	4586022383	
6		{PUT Table,0,Counter,Data}					4917185960	
7		{IF Counter=Records-1}{BRANCH End}					7676989700	
8		{LET Counter,Counter+1}					8828409516	
9		{BRANCH Top}					8232365752	
10	End	{CLOSE "Accounts.prn"}					8835694055	
11							8901184605	
12	OpenErr	{Message Open_Msg,5,5,0}{QUIT}					9114757112	
13							5759661467	
14	Open_Msg	Cannot find the file. Use Windows' File					3127383703	
15		Manager to confirm the file's location.					1573424138	
16							1734505404	
17								
18								
19								

Accounts \ B \ C \ D \ E \ F \ G \ H \ I \ J

READY

Figure 14.6   Macro Using {BRANCH} Command

executes when the value of the condition in the {IF} command is true. The {BRANCH} command in B9 behaves differently. This macro instruction always branches macro execution back to the Top macro. This {BRANCH} command is always executed when the macro execution reaches this cell.

{DEFINE}   The {DEFINE} command defines all arguments that a macro passes to a subroutine. This command must be the first macro instruction in a subroutine that uses arguments.

Format   {DEFINE Location1<:Type1>,Location2<:Type2>,...LocationN<:TypeN>} is the format of the {DEFINE} function.

   Location1 through LocationN are the locations from which Quattro Pro copies arguments. These can be block names or cell addresses. This command defines the arguments sequentially. For example, Location1 and Type1 define the first argument.

   Type1 through TypeN are the data types for the different arguments. The types may be either value or string. Value stores the value of a formula or block name passed to a subroutine. String treats the argument as a literal string and stores the string in the specified location. This argument is optional. If this argument is omitted, Quattro Pro assumes that the argument is a literal string.

Use This command defines the location and types of variables. This command stores the values used by one macro separate from the values used by other macros.

If the number of arguments exceeds the number of locations, the subroutine ignores the extra arguments. If the number of locations exceeds the number of arguments, Quattro Pro aborts the macro and displays an error message.

Example Figure 14.7 shows the second and third macros that operate inventory information. As described in the {Subroutine} command, control passes to the Invent macro when the user types a **Y** in response to the first question in the Run_Inv macro. From this macro, Invent, control passes to the Add, Remove, or Change macro or returns to the initial macro, depending on the letter provided for the {GETLABEL} command in B14. If the user types **A**, control passes to the Add macro starting in B20. This {Subroutine} command passes the part number as an argument. The first macro instruction defines the location in which Quattro Pro should place a copy of the value of Part_No and the type. The type value evaluates the argument passed to the macro and places the value of Part_No into Part_Add. If the type is string, Quattro Pro places the left-aligned label "Part_No" in the block Part_Add. This {DEFINE} statement is required; otherwise, Quattro Pro terminates the macro and displays an error message.

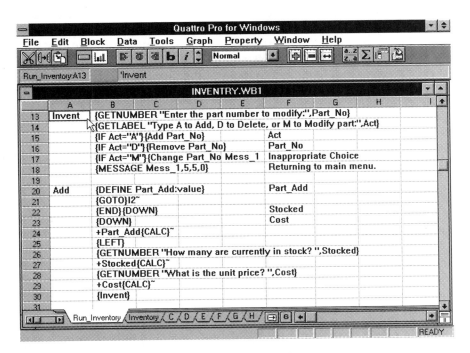

Figure 14.7 Macro Using {DEFINE} Command

{DISPATCH}   The {DISPATCH} macro command switches macro execution to a series of macro commands stored in another location. Unlike the {BRANCH} command, by which you specify the location of the first macro instruction, the {DISPATCH} command specifies a location of a cell containing the address of the branch location. The {DISPATCH} command indirectly references the new macro's location while the {BRANCH} command directly references it. When Quattro Pro switches execution flow to the new location, Quattro Pro does not return to the original set of macro instructions.

Format   {DISPATCH Location} is the format of the {DISPATCH} command.

Location can be a block name or a cell address that contains the address or block name of the first macro instruction that Quattro Pro performs after executing the {DISPATCH} command. Quattro Pro continues executing macro instructions starting from the location specified in the Location argument until Quattro Pro reaches a non-label cell, a {QUIT} command, or another command that redirects control to another macro.

Use   The {DISPATCH} command is used when you want the macro to branch to different macros depending on criteria that you have established elsewhere in the macro. You can create criteria to control the address placed in the location argument.

Example   Figure 14.8 shows an example of the {DISPATCH} command. This macro creates a form letter to inform subscribers when their subscription is about to expire. The formula in G1 converts the number of months until the subscription expires into one of several form letter names. When Quattro Pro executes the {DISPATCH} command, Quattro Pro looks at the block name stored in the block Form_Letter (which is G1). In the example shown in the figure, Quattro Pro uses the block name Letter_1 and begins executing the macro starting at B7. This macro prepares the form letter. Since the form letter depends on the number of months until a subscription lapses, the macro executes different subroutines for the subscribers in the database. The macros that create the form letters use the information from the subscription database to personalize the form letters sent.

{FOR}   The {FOR} command establishes a loop, which causes a set of instructions to be executed repeatedly. You can control the number of instructions executed as well as the number of iterations.

Format   {FOR Counter,Start#,Stop#,Step#,StartLocation} is the format of the {FOR} command.

The Counter argument is a cell address or block name used to count the number of iterations. The {FOR} command initializes this location with the value specified in the Start# argument.

The Start# argument is the initial value for the Counter that is either a value or a cell address or block name referencing a value.

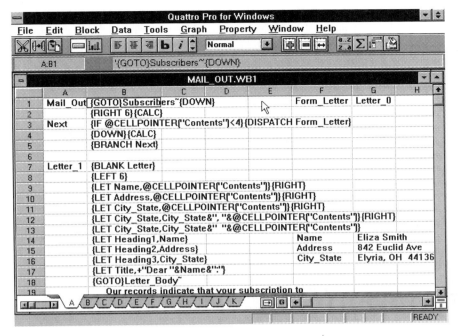

Figure 14.8   Macro Using {DISPATCH} Command

The Stop# argument ends the execution of the {FOR} command when the value of Counter exceeds this value. It is either a value or a cell address or block name referencing a value.

The Step# argument is the number that Quattro Pro adds to the value in Counter each time Quattro Pro executes the loop. It is either a value or a cell address or block name referencing a value.

The StartLocation is a cell address or a block name that contains the first instruction of the subroutine to be executed repeatedly.

If you alter the Counter or Step# arguments while the {FOR} command is executing, you change how many times Quattro Pro repeats the subroutine starting in StartLocation.

Use   The {FOR} loop performs repetitive tasks efficiently. Quattro Pro carries out the subroutine a specified number of times without the need to activate the routine each time.

Example   Figure 14.9 provides an example of the {FOR} command. This macro updates a text file containing inventory information to reduce the number of parts in stock for the number of pumps produced. After the \Y macro opens the text file and puts the size of the file in the block named Size_Out, the {FOR} command is

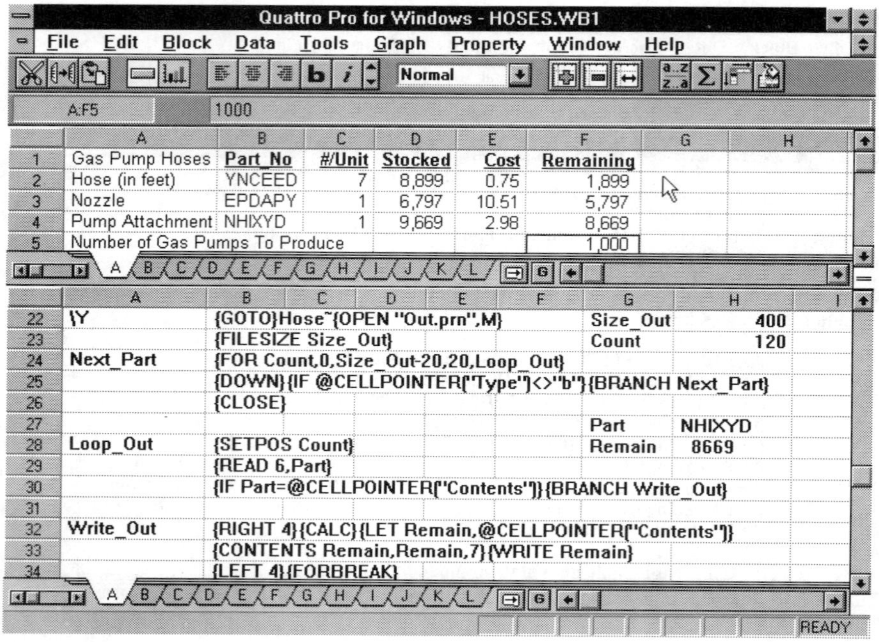

Figure 14.9   Macro Using {FOR} and {FORBREAK} Commands

repeated until the macro instructions find a matching part or the macro reaches the end of the file. For each iteration of the loop the {FOR} command creates, the {FOR} command performs the Loop_Out subroutine. This {FOR} command uses the block named Count as a counter, 0 as the start value, the value of Size_Out less 20 as the stop value, and 20 as the step number. The value of Count starts at 0 and increments by 20 each time Quattro Pro performs the Loop_Out subroutine. When Count equals 380, which is the value of Size_Out less 20, the {FOR} command ends. The {FOR} command can also end when the macro performs the {FORBREAK} command in B34.

{FORBREAK}   The {FORBREAK} command stops the execution of a {FOR} loop before Quattro Pro reaches the stop value specified in the {FOR} loop.

Format   {FORBREAK} is the format of the {FORBREAK} command.
   This command has no arguments.

Use   This command is often combined with an {IF} command to check for a specific condition. If the condition is true, a {FORBREAK} instruction can be used to stop the {FOR} loop from further execution. For example, you may want to use the {FORBREAK} command to stop a {FOR} loop from further execution when a variable (like inventory), is depleted. When Quattro Pro executes the {FORBREAK} command, the next command Quattro Pro performs is the command below the {FOR} command that the {FORBREAK} command is breaking.

Example Figure 14.9 shows a template designed for costing the production of gas pump hoses and the macro that updates the amount in stock in the inventory file after producing the gas pump hoses. The \Y macro opens the inventory file and the {FOR} command repeats the Loop_Out subroutine. The Loop_Out macro searches for the information for each part. Once the information for each part is located, the Write_Out macro moves the selector to the Remaining column for the part number. The {LET} command transfers the contents to the cell Remain in H28. The {CONTENTS} command converts the number to a label with a width of 7. The {WRITE} command in B33 replaces the old inventory quantity with the new quantity. The macro leaves the part number and price information intact. Since the {FOR} command does not need to search the rest of the inventory file after finding the part's data and writing the new inventory amount, the {FORBREAK} command ends the {FOR} command and execution continues at B25. Quattro Pro next performs the {DOWN} macro instruction in B25.

{IF} The {IF} command evaluates a condition and executes the macro instructions following the {IF} command in the same cell if the condition is true. The {IF} command operates as the @IF function does.

Format {IF Condition} is the format of the {IF} command.
Condition is a statement that Quattro Pro can evaluate as either true or false. A true condition has a value of 1 and a false condition has a value of 0. Conditions can include functions, block names, cell addresses, strings, values, and operators. When the {IF} command compares strings, the comparison does not consider case differences. {IF @CELLPOINTER("Contents")=9999} and {IF PASSWORD=OK} are sample {IF} commands.

Use The {IF} command performs a condition test within a macro. The {IF} command is often combined with the {BRANCH} command. The macro can perform one set of macro instructions if a condition is true and another set if the condition is false. The {IF} command can also be combined with {QUIT} to provide criteria for when the macro should be ended. Unlike the @IF function, {IF} commands cannot be nested, nor can the condition include other macro commands. If the macro instructions that follow the {IF} command do not branch the macro to another location, the macro proceeds with the macro instruction in the cell below the {IF} command.

Example Figure 14.10 shows a table listing names, departments, and phone numbers and the macro that uses the {IF} command to determine when the user is finished with data input into this table. When Quattro Pro executes this macro, the macro moves to the first blank line at the bottom of the table and accepts the information for another person by using the {?} command. After the name is

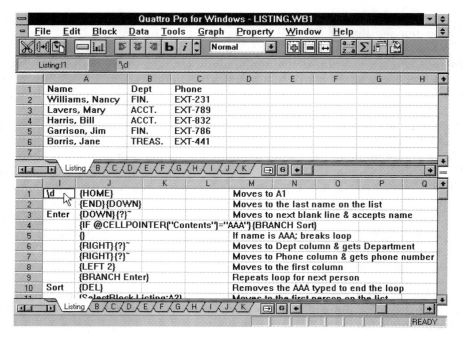

Figure 14.10   Table Listing Names, Departments, and Phone Numbers

entered, the {IF} command compares the entry to AAA to determine if the user has finished making entries. As long as the name does not equal AAA, the condition for the {IF} command is false and the macro does not execute the {BRANCH} command after the {IF} command. After the user enters each type of information, the macro finalizes the entry and moves to the next column. When all entries for a person are complete, the macro moves to the beginning of the next blank line. After all entries are made, the user types AAA to indicate that the user has finished entering information. The AAA in the current cell makes the condition in the {IF} command true, and the macro branches to Sort, causing the macro to sort the data in alphabetical order after deleting the AAA.

{ONERROR}   The {ONERROR} command redirects macro execution when Quattro Pro encounters an error. This command can store the error message in a cell that Quattro Pro would display.

Format   {ONERROR BranchLocation<,MessageLocation<,ErrorLocation>>} is the format of the {ONERROR} command.

BranchLocation is the location of the next macro instruction that Quattro Pro performs when Quattro Pro encounters an error. The location should be either a cell address or a block name.

The optional MessageLocation is the location where you want the error message placed. If MessageLocation is provided, Quattro Pro stores the message otherwise displayed in the cell. Like the BranchLocation, the MessageLocation is a cell address or block name.

The optional ErrorLocation is the location where you want Quattro Pro to place the address of the cell containing the macro instruction that includes the error. Like the BranchLocation, the ErrorLocation is a cell address or block name.

Use When a macro performs an {ONERROR} command, the command remains in effect until either Quattro Pro reaches another {ONERROR} command or the macro ends. The exception is when a {ONERROR} is to the right of another command that prevents {ONERROR} from executing unless a condition is met. For example, if {OPEN} or {CLOSE} in the same cell precedes {ONERROR}, the {ONERROR} command is only evaluated if the file cannot be opened or closed.

An evaluated {ONERROR} command is used once. Once Quattro Pro performs the macro instructions at the branch location, Quattro Pro treats the macro as if the macro does not contain {ONERROR} commands until another one is executed.

The {ONERROR} command applies only to certain errors. For example, the {ONERROR} command executes when there are disk read and write errors, when you press CTRL-BREAK, or when you try editing a protected cell. {ONERROR} also executes when you select Cancel from a dialog box displayed by the macro. The {ONERROR} command is not executed for other errors, such as a macro command that has incorrect arguments. If Quattro Pro encounters an error from the second group, the macro aborts or continues with the next macro instruction depending on the type of error.

Example Figure 14.11 shows a macro that positions the selector in the cell where the user should make data entries. Once the user has made the entries, the macro prints and saves the file before closing the notebook. When a macro uses {?} to get user entries, the user has control until ENTER is pressed. In this example, the user can move the selector to another cell before making an entry. To protect the page against this possibility, the page has protection enabled (only the cells in B3, B4, and B6 are unprotected). The macro contains the {ONERROR} command that displays an error message and then starts the macro over. If the user tries to enter data in a protected cell or presses CTRL-BREAK, the message in F18..H20 appears. The macro starts over as soon as the user presses a key.

{QUIT} The {QUIT} command ends the macro's execution and returns to the READY mode. If Quattro Pro is executing a subroutine, Quattro Pro does not return to the macro that called it.

Format {QUIT} is the format of the {QUIT} command.
This command does not have any arguments.

Use The {QUIT} macro command can end a macro before the last macro instruction. It is used in subroutines and within loops.

```
 ──                    Quattro Pro for Windows - VARIANCE.WB1         ▼ ▲
  ─    File   Edit   Block   Data   Tools   Graph   Property   Window   Help      ▲
  ✂ ▦▦  ▭▦   ▦▦▦ b i ▦  Normal      ▼  ▦▦▦  ▦Σ▦▦

      A:B3              98475

            A       B       C       D       E        F        G        H        I    ▲
   1   1992 Budget                          Open_Msg  Enter each actual number and
   2           Actual  Planned  Variance              press ENTER after each one.
   3   Sales   98,475  100,000   1,525                Press a key to continue.
   4   COGS    49,580   50,000     420
   5   Gross   48,895   50,000   1,105      \0        {MESSAGE Open_Msg,5,5,0}
   6   Expenses 23,896  25,000   1,104                {ONERROR Err_Occur}
   7   Net     24,999   25,000       1                {SelectBlock Variance:B3}{?}~
   8                                                  {SelectBlock Variance:B4}{?}~
   9                                                  {SelectBlock Variance:B6}{?}~
  10                                                  {Print.Block Variance:A1..D7}
  11                                                  {Print.DoPrint}
  12                                                  {FileSave}
  13                                                  {WindowClose}
  14
  15                                        Err_Occur {MESSAGE Err_Msg,5,5,0}
  16                                                  {\0}
  17
  18                                        Err_Msg   You have entered data in a
  19                                                  protected cell. Try entering
  20                                                  the data again.
  ◄▌ ▐►  \ A ⟨ B ⟨ C ⟨ D ⟨ E ⟨ F ⟨ G ⟨ H ⟨ I ⟨ J ⟨ K ⟨ L /  ▦ 6 ◄      ►  ▼
                                                                        READY
```

Figure 14.11   Macro Using {ONERROR} Command

Example   Figure 14.12 is an example of the {QUIT} command. This macro displays an opening message and then displays several previously created graphs. The user can quit at any time by typing Q while a graph is on screen. The {IF} commands in I13, I16, and I19 determine if the key the user pressed is either Q or q. If the user typed either Q or q, Quattro Pro executes the macro instruction {QUIT} to the right of the {IF} command. This stops the macro's execution.

{RESTART}   The {RESTART} command terminates the macro execution when Quattro Pro executes the last macro instruction in the current subroutine. Quattro Pro does not return control to the macro that called the subroutine and returns to READY mode. This command causes Quattro Pro to treat the subroutine as if the subroutine is the initial macro that Quattro Pro executes.

Format   {RESTART} is the format of this command.
   This command does not use any arguments.

Use   This command is for error handling.

Example   Figure 14.13 displays a group of macros that modify an employee database. In this example, the macro prompts for the person's name that you want to modify. Once the macro has the name, Quattro Pro executes the Find_Name

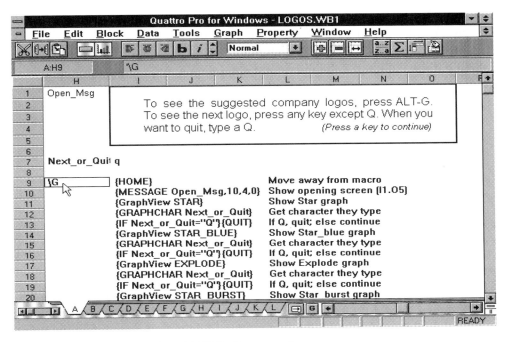

Figure 14.12   Macro Using {QUIT} Command

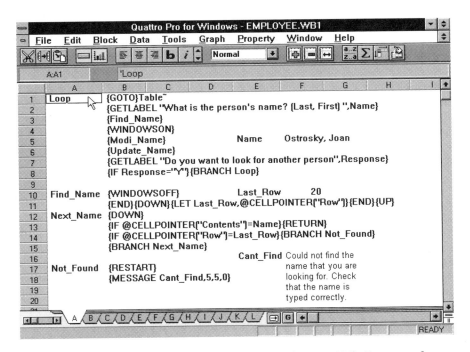

Figure 14.13   Macro Using {RESTART} and {RETURN} Commands

subroutine to search for the name. If Quattro Pro cannot find the name, Quattro Pro executes the subroutine Not_Found. In this subroutine, with the execution of the {RESTART} command, the flow of execution is changed so that when the subroutine is finished, Quattro Pro returns to the READY mode.

{RETURN}   The {RETURN} command returns the macro execution to the macro that called the subroutine.

Format   {RETURN} is the format of this command.
   This command does not use any arguments.

Use   This command ends a subroutine's execution at a location different from that of its last macro command. Since Quattro Pro automatically returns to a macro that calls a subroutine when Quattro Pro finishes executing the subroutine, a {RETURN} at the end of a subroutine is optional and shows that the instructions are a subroutine. This command often follows an {IF} command to return to the initial macro when a condition is true.

Example   The Find_Name subroutine in Figure 14.13 has a {RETURN} command to return the flow of the macro execution to the Loop macro once the macro instructions find the record in the database that matches the label stored in Name. Quattro Pro moves through the database, comparing the names with the label stored in Name. When Quattro Pro finds a match and the condition for the {IF} command in B13 is true, Quattro Pro executes the {RETURN} command. The next macro instruction Quattro Pro performs is the {WINDOWSON} command in B4. Quattro Pro executes this command next, because it is the command after the {Find_Name} subroutine command.

{Subroutine}   The {Subroutine} command transfers the macro's execution to a second macro. Once Quattro Pro completes the second macro, Quattro Pro returns execution to the first macro (starting with the macro instruction after the {Subroutine} command).

Format   {Subroutine <ArgumentList>} is the format of this command.
   Subroutine is a valid macro name. The upper-left corner of the named block contains the first macro instruction of the subroutine. The subroutine name must follow the rules of macro names. If Subroutine is in another notebook, the notebook name must be included in square braces before the cell address or block name.
   ArgumentList is a list of arguments that Quattro Pro passes to the subroutine. These arguments are optional, but if they are included, the first macro instruction in the subroutine must be the {DEFINE} command. The arguments must be separated by commas or semicolons.

Use   The {Subroutine} command allows the macro to execute another macro before competing the current macro. Subroutines are used for macro instructions that are executed repeatedly through a macro. Subroutines are also used when you want Quattro Pro to perform multiple macro instructions when the condition in an {IF} command is true.

A subroutine may contain other subroutines. Quattro Pro treats each subroutine as a level. Quattro Pro can accept up to 32 levels.

When a subroutine is called, Quattro Pro continues executing the subroutine until Quattro Pro reaches a non-label cell, {RETURN}, or {QUIT}. If Quattro Pro reaches a non-label cell or {RETURN}, Quattro Pro executes the next macro instruction after the {Subroutine} command. If Quattro Pro executes a {QUIT} command, the macro is terminated and Quattro Pro returns to READY mode. If Quattro Pro executes a {RESTART} command, Quattro Pro does not return to the macro containing the {Subroutine} command.

Quattro Pro allows a macro to call itself and refers to the macro as a recursive macro. Recursive macros are not recommended, since they are more complicated to debug.

Example   Figure 14.14 shows two of the macros that operate inventory information. The Run_Inv macro prompts the user with several questions to determine the next macro to execute. One of these selections executes the Invent macro. When Quattro Pro executes the Invent macro, it prompts for a part number and then prompts for the user to type **A**, **D**, or **M** to indicate which macro to perform next. Depending on the user's entry, the macro performs the Add, Change, or Remove

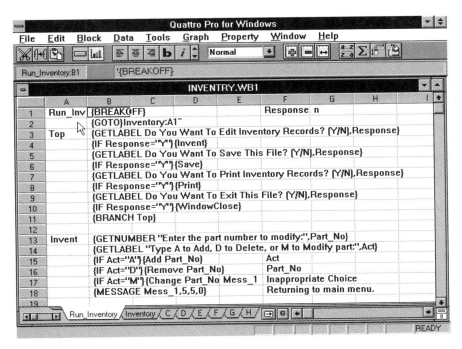

Figure 14.14   Macro Using {Subroutine} Command

▼ TIP: Use \ and a letter to call an instant
macro for a subroutine.

To call an instant macro (a macro that executes by pressing CTRL and a
letter) as a subroutine, use the backslash and letter in braces (for example,
{\A} for a CTRL-A macro and {\0} for an automatic macro).

---

macro. If the user types an inappropriate character, the Invent macro displays a
message and when the user presses a key to continue, the macro execution returns
to the macro that called the Invent macro. For the Add, Change, or Remove
macros, Quattro Pro passes the part number to the macro. In the Add, Change, and
Remove macros, the macro starts with a {DEFINE} command to define the argument. With the Add, Change, and Remove macros, Quattro Pro continues executing the macros until it either reaches a {RETURN} or executes the last macro
instruction. When Quattro Pro finishes executing one of these macros, Quattro Pro
returns to the Invent macro.

Interactive Commands

Quattro Pro's interactive macro commands take information from sources outside
of the macro. These commands prompt the user for different types of input. You
can even run a dialog box from a macro using an interactive macro command.
Other interactive macro commands prevent a macro from being prematurely
terminated or force macro execution to temporarily stop. Another group of interactive macro commands temporarily switch control to a custom menu. Finally,
Quattro Pro has program flow commands that activate and deactivate the Debug
mode from within a macro.

{?}   The {?} command returns control of Quattro Pro to the user temporarily until
the ENTER key is pressed.

Format   {?} is the format of this command.
   This command does not use any arguments.

Use   This command accepts input from the keyboard. Like the {GET} command,
this command does not display a prompt. Also, this command can accept numbers
as well as labels. Unlike the {GET} command, the {?} accepts multiple characters.
Also, the {?} command does not store the keyboard input in a cell. The keyboard
input functions exactly as if the macro was typing the keys in. The user can use any
keys except ENTER. The keys perform the same function that they provide when
the macro is not running. For example, the user can either access Quattro Pro's

menu or move to another cell. The {?} macro command cannot be used in graph buttons, the SpeedBar, or menu trees.

The {?} command is often followed by a tilde (~), since the ENTER key that the user types to end this command does not finalize the entry. When the user presses ENTER, the user relinquishes control to the macro.

Example   Figure 14.15 shows a table listing names, departments, and phone numbers and the macro that uses the {?} command to input data into a table. When this macro is executed, the macro moves to the first blank line at the bottom of the table and accepts the information for another person using the {?} command. The {?} commands in J3, J6, and J7 are followed by tildes, since the user does not finalize the entry by pressing ENTER. Pressing ENTER merely transfers control to the macro, and the tilde characters are needed to finalize the entries. After the user enters each type of information, the macro finalizes the entry and moves to the next column. When all entries for one person have been completed, the macro moves to the beginning of the next blank line. After all entries are made, typing AAA indicates that the user has finished entering information. The AAA in the current cell makes the condition in the {IF} command true and the macro branches to Sort.

{ACTIVATE}   The {ACTIVATE} command makes a selected window open as if you selected the window from the bottom of the Window pull-down menu.

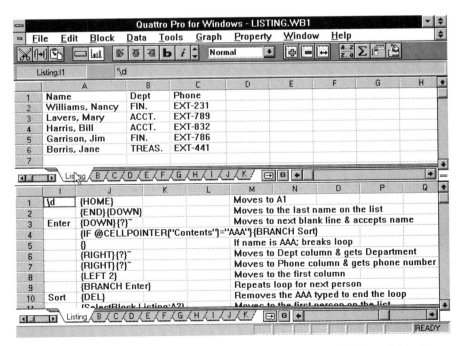

Figure 14.15   Table Listing Names, Departments, and Phone Numbers

Format {ACTIVATE WindowName} is the format for the {ACTIVATE} command.

WindowName is the name of the window you want to activate. It is the same name that appears in the window's title bar and also in the <u>W</u>indow pull-down menu. WindowName is either the name of the window in quotes or a reference to a cell containing the window name.

Use This command selects which window is the active window. Use this macro command to switch between windows.

Example You can use the {ACTIVATE} macro command to select an open window. If you have used the {GETWINDOWLIST} macro command, you can use this macro command to activate the windows listed in the notebook. For example, to activate each of the windows returned by the {GETWINDOWLIST} example, the {ACTIVATE} macro instructions are {ACTIVATE "NOTEBK1.WB1"}, {ACTIVATE "CHAP_10.WB1"}, {ACTIVATE "CHAP_10.WB1:Stack_Bar_Graph"}, {ACTIVATE "DIALOG.WB1"}, and {ACTIVATE "DIALOG.WB1:Sample_Dialog"}.

{BREAKOFF} The {BREAKOFF} command disables CTRL-BREAK. If CTRL-BREAK is disabled, the only way to terminate a macro before the macro is finished is by rebooting the computer (turning it off and on). (With Windows 3.1, you may be able to boot just Quattro Pro for Windows with CTRL-ALT-DEL.) CTRL-BREAK is enabled with the {BREAKON} command. The {BREAKOFF} command only affects the current macro. Any macros that are executed subsequently are not affected by this command.

Format {BREAKOFF} is the format of the {BREAKOFF} command.
This command does not use any arguments.

Use This command prevents a user from prematurely terminating a macro. For example, a macro may use {BREAKOFF} in a macro that reads and writes to files to prevent the file from being corrupted if the file is not properly closed.

Example Figure 14.16 shows a macro that uses the {BREAKOFF} command to prevent the user from accidentally or intentionally terminating the macro. After Quattro Pro performs this command, Quattro Pro executes the {MENUBRANCH} command and displays the custom menu defined starting in row 4. As Quattro Pro executes the macro instructions for the menu items selected, the CTRL-BREAK is disabled until either the macro ends or Quattro Pro executes the {BREAKON} command.

{BREAKON} The {BREAKON} command enables the CTRL-BREAK key that has been disabled with the {BREAKOFF} command. This allows a macro to be terminated by pressing CTRL-BREAK.

Format {BREAKON} is the format of the {BREAKON} command.
This command does not use any arguments.

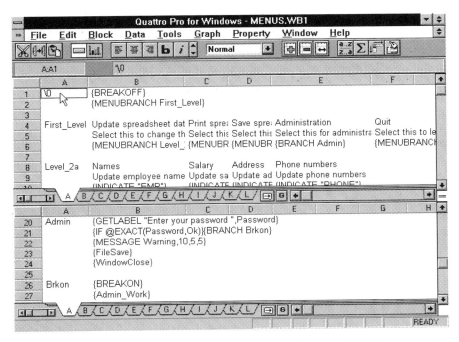

Figure 14.16 **Macro Using {BREAKOFF} and {BREAKON} Commands**

▼ TIP: Test the macro before including {BREAKOFF}.

Do not include {BREAKOFF} in a macro until the macro runs correctly. This avoids the need for rebooting the computer if it is locked by the macro.

Use This command allows a user to terminate a macro with CTRL-BREAK before the macro is finished.

Example Figure 14.16 shows the Brkon macro that uses the {BREAKON} command to allow the user to terminate the macro after a correct password is provided. At the beginning of the macro in Figure 14.16, Quattro Pro executes a {BREAKOFF} command to ensure that the user does not terminate the macro. After this command, Quattro Pro executes the {MENUBRANCH} command and displays the custom menu defined starting in row 4. If the menu item Administration (defined in column E) is selected, Quattro Pro branches to the Admin macro. After the password prompt and a user-typed entry, Quattro Pro compares the entry in Password with the entry stored in the block Ok. If the two labels are not the same, Quattro Pro saves the file and closes the notebook. If the two labels are the same,

Quattro Pro executes the macro instructions at Brkon, which is at B26. At Brkon, CTRL-BREAK is restored with the {BREAKON} command and the macro transfers control to Admin_Work. Before the break feature is restored, the only method available to stop the macro's execution is to restart Quattro Pro.

{DODIALOG}   The {DODIALOG} command activates a dialog box that the macro or the macro's user can change. The selections made in the dialog box are placed in a block when you leave the dialog box so you can create one dialog box in place of a series of other macro commands. Creating dialog boxes is covered at the end of Chapter 12.

Format   {DODIALOG DialogName,OKExit?,Arguments,MacUse?} is the format for the {DODIALOG} command.

DialogName is the name of the dialog box you have already created. If the macro you are running is in a different notebook than the active one the macro is operating on, the notebook name in braces must precede the dialog box name.

OKExit? is the block name or cell where you want this command to store how the dialog box is closed. After this command is performed, the OKExit? cell will contain a 0 if the dialog box is closed by selecting Cancel or 1 if the dialog box is closed by selecting OK.

Arguments is the block name or block address containing the initial settings of the dialog box. All of the dialog box elements that have their Process Value property set to Yes expect an initial value in the block for the arguments.

MacUse? selects how the dialog box is changed. When this command uses 1, the macro's user can change the dialog box. When this command uses 0, the macro controls the dialog box. You can override the macro's control of the dialog box by including a {PAUSEMACRO} command where you want the user to be able to make changes in the dialog box.

Use   This command is for using a dialog box you have created. You can use dialog boxes to get all sorts of information that the macro can use for other purposes. You can create dialog boxes to use as entry forms or to let the user make selections during the macro's execution.

Example   Figure 14.17 shows the beginning of a macro that displays a dialog box that has previously been created, as described in Chapter 12. The {DODIALOG} command displays the Add_Subscriber dialog box and lets the user make selections from it because 1 is used as the MacUse? argument. This Add_Subscriber dialog box is shown in the middle of Figure 14.17. The dialog box items pick up initial values from the block R21..R28. If you select OK to leave the dialog box, this macro command places a 1 in U21, and if you select Cancel or press ESC to leave the dialog box, this macro command places a 0 in U21. Once the dialog box is completed, other macro instructions take the entries made in the dialog box and put them at the end of the subscriber list.

{GET}   The {GET} command halts the macro's execution until a key is typed. The first character typed is stored in a cell.

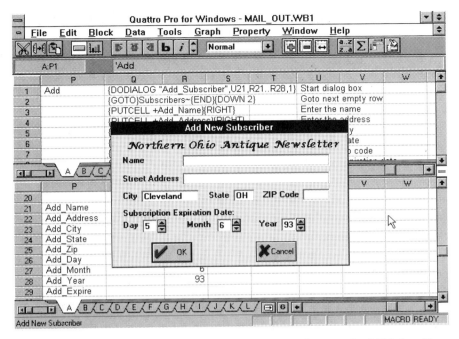

Figure 14.17   Macro Invoking Dialog Box and the Invoked Dialog Box

Format   {GET Location} is the format of the {GET} command.

Location is the cell address or block name where Quattro Pro stores the key pressed.

Use   The {GET} command captures the first character typed after Quattro Pro executes this command. If the character typed is a character that Quattro Pro represents with keyword equivalents, such as {DOWN} or {DEL}, the keystroke equivalent is stored in Location. This command does not provide a prompt as do the {GETLABEL} and {GETNUMBER} commands. This command is often used when the information on the screen directs the user to press a key. This command limits the input to one character; that character may be any key on the keyboard except for F10, F12, SHIFT-F2, PAUSE, CAPS LOCK, NUM LOCK, and SCROLL LOCK. If you press CTRL-BREAK as a response to the {GET} command, the macro ends. If the macro has executed a {BREAKOFF} command, the {GET} command will ignore CTRL-BREAK and wait for you to press another key.

Example   One use of the {GET} command is the creation of full-screen menus. Although {MENUBRANCH} and {MENUCALL} are for menus, the {GET} command may be preferable when the menu has more selections than {MENUBRANCH} or {MENUCALL} can display. Figure 14.18 shows a menu that has more selections than the {MENUBRANCH} or {MENUCALL} commands can display. In this menu, the text is on the notebook. The macro that uses this menu

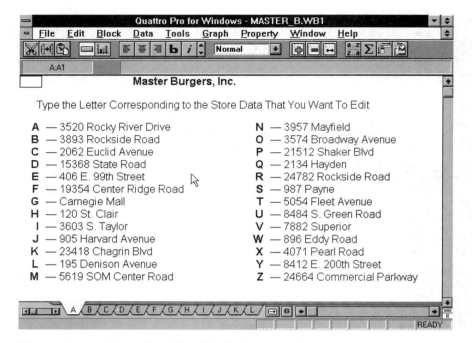

Figure 14.18   Menu Used by {GET} Command

is displayed in Figure 14.19. Using the key typed for the {GET} command, the macro determines the location to which to move in the notebook. The macro is created to move the user to the data to be manipulated since the notebook is so large. The {LOOK} command (discussed later) is not appropriate since the user may type keys accidentally or intentionally that do not reflect the intended response for the menu.

{GETLABEL}   The {GETLABEL} command prompts the user to enter information and accepts a string of characters from the keyboard. Unlike the {GET} command, the {GETLABEL} command cannot accept nonprintable characters as input. {GETLABEL} updates the panel even if {PANELOFF} is used.

Format   {GETLABEL Prompt,Location} is the format for this command.

The Prompt argument allows you to display instructions on the screen to guide the user to enter the desired data. When the macro is executed, Quattro Pro displays the first 70 characters of the Prompt in the input line. The string may be enclosed in double quotes; these are optional unless the string includes any punctuation. If the Prompt is stored in another cell, it must be followed by a colon and a v, which tell Quattro Pro to use the value of the cell referenced by the block name or cell address as shown in the example for {GETNUMBER}.

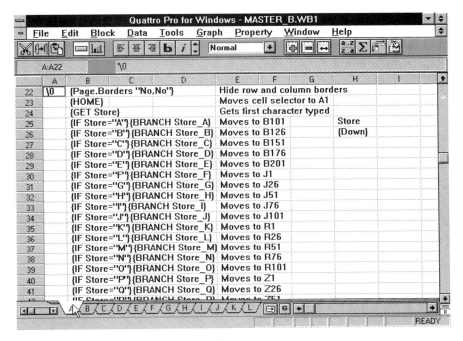

Figure 14.19   Macro Using {GET} Command for Use with Figure 14.18.

The Location argument is the address of a cell or block or the name of a block into which Quattro Pro places the typed input as a left-aligned label. Whenever you specify a block of cells as the Location argument, Quattro Pro stores the typed entries in the upper-left corner of the block. A maximum of 160 characters can be stored.

Use   Since this command stores your entry as a left-justified label, you can use it to store numeric values that need to be placed at the left edge of the cell for use as macro keystrokes.

Example   Figure 14.20 displays a macro that uses the {GETLABEL} command extensively. The macro instructions prompt the user for information pertaining to the specified person and store the information in the respective named block specified as the Location argument. In a macro like this, you can use a dialog box instead of using multiple {GETLABEL} commands.

{GETNUMBER}   The {GETNUMBER} command allows you to enter numeric entries in a specified cell in response to a prompt instruction.

Format   {GETNUMBER Prompt,Location} is the format for the {GETNUMBER} command.

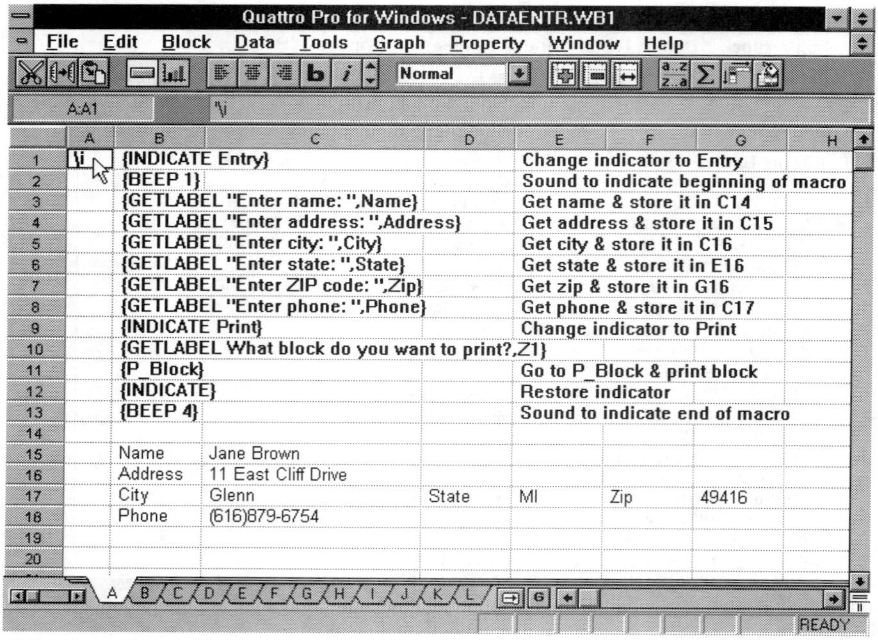

Figure 14.20   Macro Using {GETLABEL} Command

The Prompt argument allows you to display instructions on the screen to guide the user to enter the desired data. When the macro is executed, Quattro Pro displays the first 70 characters of the Prompt in the input line. The string may be enclosed in double quotes; these are optional unless the string includes punctuation. If the Prompt is stored in another cell, it must be followed by a colon and a v, which tell Quattro Pro to use the value of the cell referenced by the block name or cell address.

The Location argument is the address of a cell or a block address or the name of a block into which the numbers entered through the keyboard are stored. You can specify a formula, a value, or a block name as the Location argument.

Use   The {GETNUMBER} command is useful whenever you want a numeric value stored in a particular cell or block of cells. For example, you might want to store the price of a product or the salary of an employee in a specified location for further computations. Since this macro command expects a number or formula as input, Quattro Pro stores ERR in the cell specified by Location if you enter a string.

Example   Figure 14.21 shows a macro that uses the {GETNUMBER} command. In this example, the macro instructions in B9 and B10 prompt the user to enter the amount that the user wants to borrow and the number of years of the loan. Quattro Pro stores these values in B17 and B18. The {GETNUMBER} commands use prompts

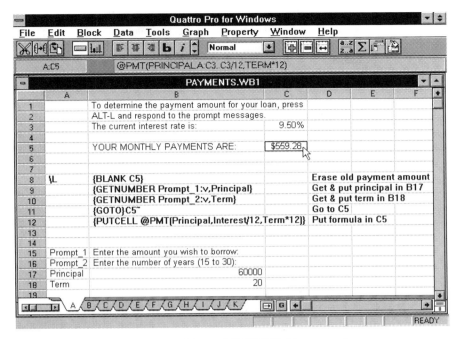

Figure 14.21   Macro Using {GETNUMBER} Command

stored in the named cells Prompt_1 and Prompt_2. Quattro Pro knows to use the contents of these named cells since the {GETNUMBER} command includes :v.

{GRAPHCHAR}   The {GRAPHCHAR} command halts the macro's execution until a key is typed to remove a graph or message from the screen. The first character typed is stored in a cell.

Format   GRAPHCHAR Location} is the format of the {GRAPHCHAR} command.
   Location is the location where Quattro Pro stores the key typed. It can be a cell address or a block name.

Use   The {GRAPHCHAR} command captures the first character typed after a macro displays a graph or message. This command does not provide a prompt as do the {GETLABEL} and {GETNUMBER} commands. This command is an alternative to {GET} and lets the users indicate that they have finished using the graph or viewing the message. You can use the entry stored in Location in place of a graph button where the character typed selects one of the topics described in a graph. In this case, you would follow the {GRAPHCHAR} command with {IF} commands to process the character stored in Location.

Example   The \G macro in Figure 14.22 shows how you can use {GRAPHCHAR}. The macro displays a graph and then waits until the user presses a key to continue.

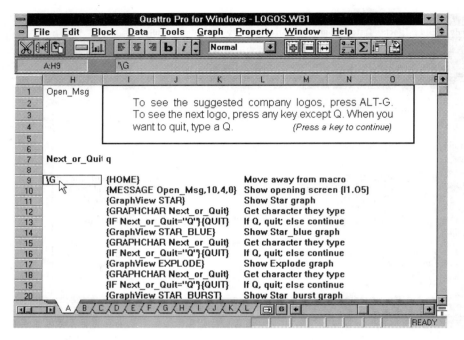

Figure 14.22   Macro Using {GRAPHCHAR} Command

If the user types **Q**, the macro stops; otherwise, the macro continues to show the next graph. The macro stores the key pressed by the user in the cell named Next_or_Quit. An alternative to the {GRAPHCHAR} command in this application is the use of macro commands to run a slide show or adding graph buttons to the graphs the \G macro displays.

IFKEY   The {IFKEY} command performs macro commands if it is given a valid macro key name as an argument. This command is for checking if a user has pressed a key such as a function key or an arrow key. If {IFKEY} does not accept the entry as a valid macro key name, it skips the macro instructions in the rest of the cell and continues executing macro instruction in the cell below.

Format   {IFKEY String} is the format of the {IFKEY} command. String is the text that you want {IFKEY} to determine if it is a valid macro key name. This must be the literal key name as in HOME. {IFKEY} cannot use the key name with braces as in {IFKEY {HOME}}, nor can it accept a block name that contains the key name. If the key name you want to test is in a block name, make the cell containing the {IFKEY} command a string formula that combines {IFKEY}, the key name, and the remaining macro instructions.

Use   The {IFKEY} command is used for testing if a macro has pressed a key such as a function key or a directional key.

Example In Figure 14.23, the Intro macro uses the {IFKEY} command to test if the user has pressed a key to indicate that they want help information. The macro first displays the information stored at Open_Screen. This opening screen might include information such as pressing HOME for assistance or pressing the SPACEBAR to continue. After waiting 20 seconds, the {GET} command puts their entry in the block named Answer. The {GET} command is useful for this purpose, since it captures keystrokes like function keys that other interactive macro commands ignore. The tilde calculates the formula in No_Braces, which removes the braces from the key stored in Answer. The formula that is entered in B4, +"{IFKEY "&No_Braces&"}{MESSAGE Help,5,5,0}" displays a help screen if the user has pressed a key like one of the function keys, which the text shown in Open_Screen may direct them to press if they require more help. If the user has not pressed a valid macro key, Quattro Pro ignores the {MESSAGE} command and branches to Main_Routine.

{LOOK} The {LOOK} command checks the first character from the keyboard buffer and stores the character in a spreadsheet cell. This command is similar to {GET}, except that the {LOOK} command does not remove the keystroke from the keyboard buffer so the keystroke is available for other macro commands or to affect the current notebook when the macro ends.

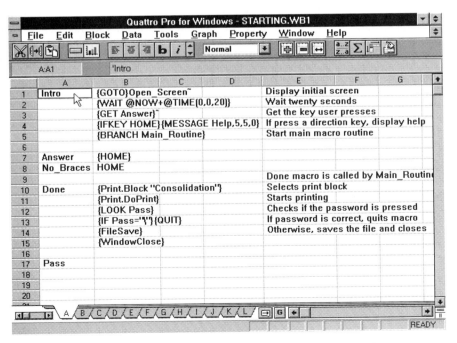

Figure 14.23 Macro Using {IFKEY} and {LOOK} Commands

Format   LOOK Location} is the format of the {LOOK} command.

Location is the cell address or block name where Quattro Pro stores the first keystroke in the keyboard buffer when Quattro Pro executes this command.

Use   This command uses the keyboard buffer. When you type keystrokes that Quattro Pro does not immediately use because it is executing another command, Quattro Pro stores the keystrokes in a keyboard buffer. Normally, when Quattro Pro finishes the task that caused the keystroke be stored in the buffer, Quattro Pro types that keystroke as if you were typing the character. This allows you to type ahead. The {LOOK} command takes the first keystroke and places the keystroke in the location that you have specified.

Example   The {LOOK} command can be used for a password that determines whether a particular user is authorized to update the notebook. For example, in a macro that controls the user's access to the spreadsheet data, the user can only perform certain steps. However, the person who wrote the macro may need to modify the macro. One method of allowing the macro to be edited is the addition of a special password. By using a password that the user is not aware of, the security of the system is further enhanced. This secret password could be an undocumented feature that the macro's author would use. Even a person who uses the notebook frequently may be unaware of this password. Figure 14.23 shows a portion of a larger macro that has this type of a password. When the user is finished, the initial macro sends control to the Done macro. This macro prints, saves, and closes the notebook. However, if the macro needs to be modified, typing a backslash (\) while the macro prints part of the spreadsheet data allows the user to edit the file by exiting the macro at that point. The {LOOK} command in B12 takes the first character typed and stores the character in the block Pass. The {IF} command in B4 compares this character to the backslash. If the characters are not the same, the macro saves and then closes the notebook.

Since this feature would not be known by the person who uses the notebook to produce the consolidated information, the macro would not be inappropriately terminated. The initial macro that uses the Done macro would also use the {BREAKOFF} command. This type of password protection is only effective if the user does not see the macro instructions that perform the tasks.

{MENUBRANCH}   The {MENUBRANCH} command displays a custom menu that you have previously created and lets you select one of the menu items. The menu item that you select determines the next macro instruction that Quattro Pro performs. The {MENUBRANCH} command is different from the {MENUCALL} macro command, since the {MENUBRANCH} command permanently alters the execution flow of the macro.

Format   {MENUBRANCH Location} is the format of the {MENUBRANCH} command.

Location is the first cell that defines the custom menu. It is either a cell address or a block name.

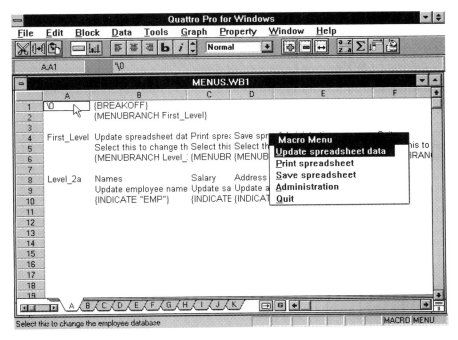

Figure 14.24 Macro Using {MENUBRANCH} Command

The custom menu that this macro creates must be defined before the macro is executed. The custom menu has the different menu choices on the first line, as in row 4 in Figure 14.24. The custom menu called First_Level has five choices. Each of these choices is in a different cell in row 4. Your menus can have up to 256 menu items. A menu created with the {MENUBRANCH} command behaves like Quattro Pro's pull-down menus. The only difference is if the macro user presses ESC, the macro execution continues with the macro instructions after the {MENUBRANCH} command.

Since Quattro Pro uses as much room as needed to display the menu items, the column width of the cells that display the menu item text is not important.

Underneath each menu choice is the description that is displayed in the status line when the highlight is on the menu choice. This feature allows you to create menu descriptions that are identical to Quattro Pro's menu. You can put a brief description of the menu item's function for the menu item text and a more detailed description for the custom menu item description. The description is limited to what can fit in the status line. Since Quattro Pro displays the entire cell contents of the descriptions in the status line, the column width of the custom menu columns are not important.

The row below each of the descriptions contains the macro instructions that Quattro Pro performs when a menu item is selected. Quattro Pro does not limit the number of macro instructions that you can put below each of the menu items. If you have many instructions, you may want to place them in another location and

---

▼ TIP: Start each menu choice with a unique first letter.

Make all menu choices start with a unique first letter so that the user can make a menu selection by typing the first letter. Quattro Pro automatically underlines the first letter in each menu selection for you.

▼ TIP: Include a Quit (or Exit) option.

Include a Quit or Exit option so the user knows how to leave the macro when desired for a more user-friendly interface.

---

have the macro instruction below the menu item's description branch to the additional instructions. For many macros using {MENUBRANCH}, the macro commands below the description are other {MENUBRANCH} commands to display a submenu of more specific options.

Use   The {MENUBRANCH} command creates custom menus that look and function as Quattro Pro menus do. Instead of offering Quattro Pro features, these menus can be designed to meet the needs of specific business applications.

Example   Figure 14.24 shows a macro that displays the custom menu that starts at First_Level. Figure 14.24 shows this custom menu. As the menu box displays, the menu items are described in different cells in row 4 starting with B4. The text for each of the menu items is below the appropriate menu item in row 5. When one menu item is selected, the next macro instruction that is performed is the macro instruction for the appropriate menu item in row 6. For each menu item, the macro branches to another menu. For example, if you select Update from the menu box, Quattro Pro executes the macro command in B6 and displays the menu located at Level_2a as shown in Figure 14.25. When one menu item is selected, Quattro Pro executes the appropriate macro command in row 10.

{MENUCALL}   The {MENUCALL} command displays a custom menu and performs the tasks related to the selected menu item. This command differs from {MENUBRANCH} in that this command returns control to the instruction following the {MENUCALL} command after executing the menu instructions. In essence, this command treats the menu as a subroutine and returns to the main macro routine once a menu item is selected and the macro commands below the appropriate menu item's description are executed. The {MENUBRANCH} command

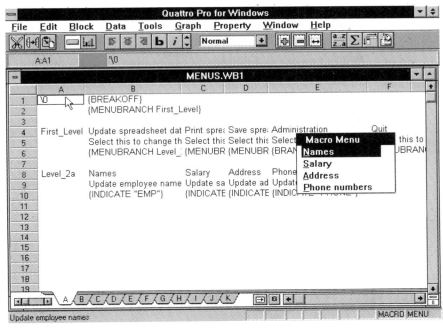

Figure 14.25 {MENUBRANCH} Command Generation of a Submenu of the Menu in Figure 14.24.

does not return to the macro containing the {MENUBRANCH} command unless the user presses ESC.

Format   {MENUCALL Location} is the format of the {MENUCALL} command.
   Location is the location of the first cell of a block containing a custom menu. It can be a block name or cell address. The custom menu that this macro command expects is identical to the menu defined for the {MENUBRANCH} command. See the instructions for how to create a menu in the {MENUBRANCH} instruction for further detail.

Use   This command creates custom menus. Since this command returns to the original macro, you can have many {MENUCALL} instructions in a macro and still maintain a logical flow within the macro.

Example   One use of the {MENUCALL} command is to have the user make selections from predefined choices. An example is a macro printing several reports. To print one report, several choices must be made. Chapter 13 contains a group of ready-made macros that allows you to select the report that you want to print by using the macro name. The macros do not provide you with the ability to change the name of the person preparing the report. Figure 14.26 shows a macro that prints any of the three

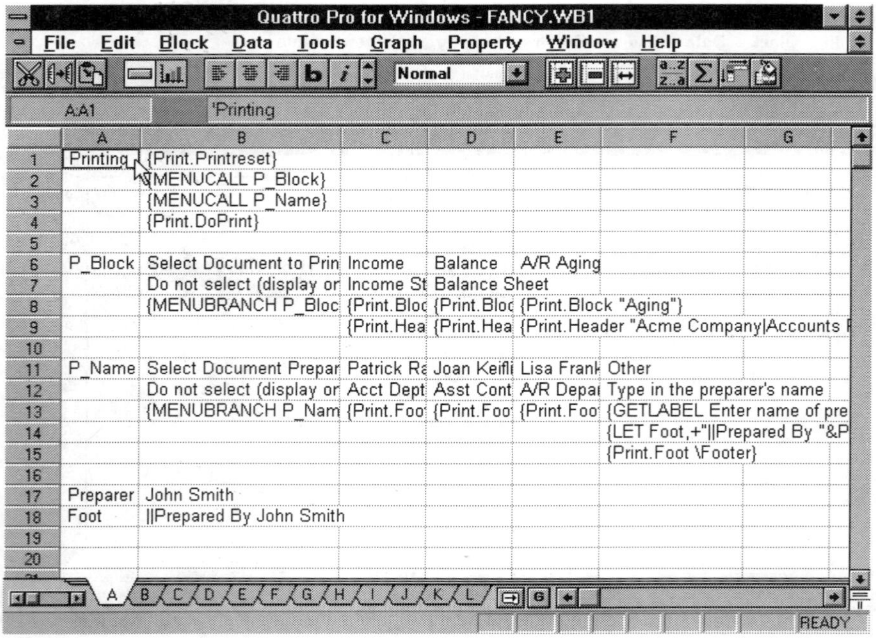

Figure 14.26 Macro Using {MENUCALL} Command

reports, with unlimited options for the preparer's name. This macro uses two {MENUCALL} commands. The first one creates a menu containing Select Document to Print, Income, Balance, and A/R Aging. This menu is identical to the ones you can create with the {MENUBRANCH} command. This menu prompts for the report to be printed. The macro instructions listed below each menu item's description define the appropriate print block and header. The second {MENUCALL} command displays a menu containing Select Document Preparer, Patrick Rabbins, Joan Keifling, Lisa Franklin, and Other, which prompts for the name of the preparer. As the entries in row 12 indicate, the descriptions display the position of the person's name that is highlighted. The last selection (Other) allows the user to provide a name that is not one of the menu selections. The macro instructions below the menu item description define the footer for each name selected. As the Other menu item indicates, the different menu selections can have various amounts of macro instructions. Once a menu item is selected from the second menu, the selected menu item adds a footer; then Quattro Pro performs the instruction in B4; which is the cell below the second {MENUCALL} command.

{MESSAGE}   The {MESSAGE} command displays a block in a box on the screen either for a specified time or until the user presses a key.

Format   {MESSAGE Block,Left,Top,Time} is the format of the {MESSAGE} command.

Block represents the block address or name containing the information you want in the message box. Since Quattro Pro uses the block size to determine the message box size, you must include the cells from which labels borrow display space. The message adopts all of the cell formatting of the block, so you can change the location's block properties to change how the message appears.

Left represents the first column of the message box on the screen. The default is 0, which displays the box in the leftmost column. This number must be low enough so Quattro Pro has room to display the block.

Top represents the first row of the message box on the screen. The default is 0, which displays the box in the top row (the same as the menu bar row). The row number must be low enough to display the block.

Time represents at which time the message box disappears from the screen. The default of 0 indicates that the message box remains on the screen until the user presses a key. Time can either be the number of seconds, such as 5, or the time the message box should disappear, such as @NOW+@TIME(0,0,5).

Use The {MESSAGE} command displays a message in the middle of a macro. A macro can use the message box to display any kind of message. This is unlike the {GETLABEL} and {GETNUMBER} commands, which prompt for information. This command can be used to tell the user an error has occurred, display an opening screen, or display a message telling the user the macro is performing a task (especially when the macro takes a long time to execute a command). This command's message appears over all other Quattro Pro windows including graphs.

You can also combine the {GRAPHCHAR} command with the {MESSAGE} command to display a message and then capture the keystroke. Combining the {GRAPHCHAR} and {MESSAGE} commands this way lets you display the prompt to press a key in a customized box and then use {GRAPHCHAR} to store the keystroke used to remove the message box. You must use {GRAPHCHAR} instead of the {GET} command, because the {MESSAGE} command without a Time argument assumes that the first key you press is the one to remove the message. The {GRAPHCHAR} captures this keystroke while {GET} will capture the second keystroke after the message is displayed.

Example In the example for the {GRAPHCHAR} command, shown in Figure 14.22, the macro includes the command {MESSAGE Open_Msg,10,4,0}. This macro command displays the Open_Msg block (I1..O5) on the screen as shown in Figure 14.27. Since the {MESSAGE} command uses 0 for the time argument, this message continues to appear until you press a key to remove it.

{PAUSEMACRO} The {PAUSEMACRO} command postpones macro execution until the macro user has completed a dialog box. This macro command is combined with the {DODIALOG} macro command and with command equivalents that use ! to invoke a dialog box.

Format {PAUSEMACRO} is the format for the {PAUSEMACRO} command. This command does not have any arguments.

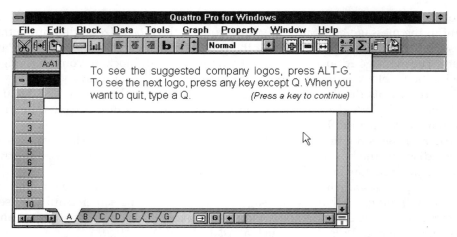

Figure 14.27   Message Displayed With {MESSAGE} Commands

Use   This command is for sharing control of a dialog box between the user and the macro. Usually, the macro displays the dialog box and makes any desired changes. Then this command lets the macro user continue making selections in the dialog box. Once the macro user selects OK, the macro resumes control.

Example   Figure 14.28 shows an example of the {PAUSEMACRO} command. The \S macro copies the values from the block labeled Current_Sales to the selector's position when the macro is executed. The PasteSpecial command equivalent displays the Paste Special dialog box and selects the Values only radio button. Since the user may want to transpose the values as well as copy them, the {PAUSEMACRO} command halts the macro's execution. When Quattro Pro performs the {PAUSEMACRO} command, it returns control over the application to the macro user. When the user selects OK to finish the Paste Special dialog box, Quattro Pro continues executing the remaining macro instructions.

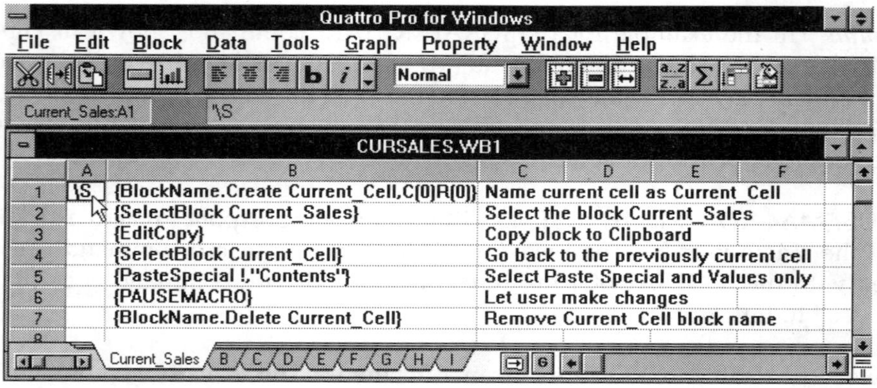

Figure 14.28   Macro Using {PAUSEMACRO}

{STEPOFF} The {STEPOFF} command returns the macro execution speed to normal and removes the Macro Debugger window from the screen. This macro command works the same as pressing SHIFT-F2 when the DEBUG indicator is on the screen. If Quattro Pro executes this command when the DEBUG indicator does not appear on the status line, Quattro Pro ignores this command.

Format {STEPOFF} is the format for this command.
This command does not have any arguments.

Use This command is a debugging tool to remove the effects of the {STEPON} command.

Example Once you isolate the general area of an error in a macro, you should observe this area of the macro closely. It is inefficient to execute the other parts of the macro in Single Step mode. Figure 14.29 shows a macro with the second and third arguments for the PUT command reversed. Since the error occurs in the loop, the {STEPON} command is the last command executed before the loop starts and the {STEPOFF} command is the first command after the loop.

{STEPON} The {STEPON} command changes the macro execution speed to Single Step mode. The effect of this macro command is the same as pressing SHIFT-F2 to activate DEBUG mode. The macro execution speed is returned to normal in the

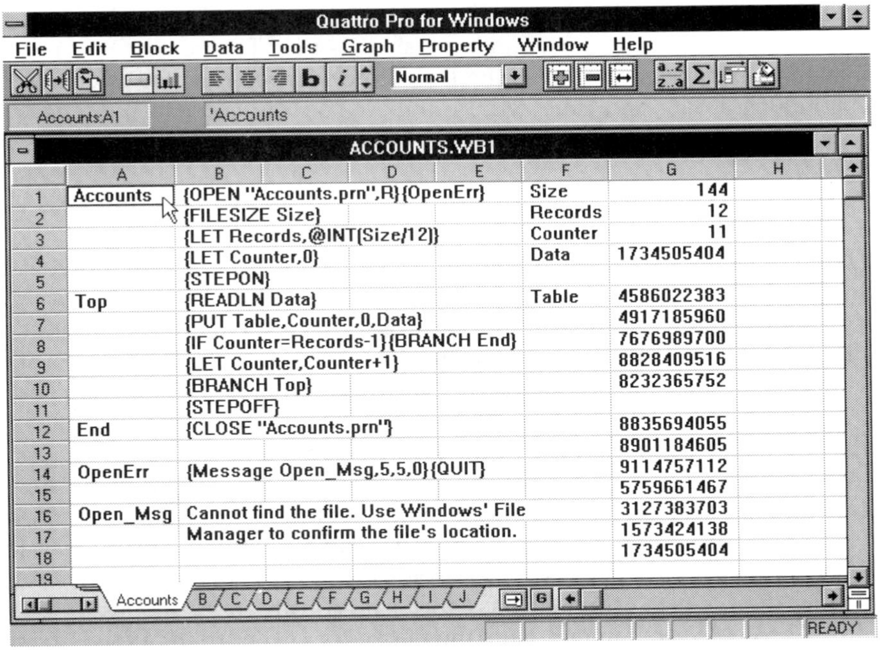

Figure 14.29   Macro Using {STEPON} and {STEPOFF} Commands

DEBUG mode either with the {STEPOFF} command or by pressing ENTER instead of the SPACEBAR. Since this command is equivalent to pressing SHIFT-F2, once Quattro Pro executes this command, all macros executed after the current one also execute in Single Step mode until Quattro Pro executes a {STEPOFF} command or until the user presses either SHIFT-F2 or ENTER.

Format   {STEPON} is the format for this command.
  This command does not have any arguments.

Use   This command is a debugging tool. When Quattro Pro executes this command, Quattro Pro displays the Macro Debugger window. All other options available through the Macro Debugger window are available with the {STEPON} command.

Example   Figure 14.29 shows a macro with the second and third arguments for the PUT command in B7 reversed. Since the error occurs in the loop, the {STEPON} command is the last command executed before the loop starts. Single Step mode continues until Quattro Pro executes the {STEPOFF} command. Since this command starts Quattro Pro's debugger, you can specify trace cells once the Macro Debugger window appears.

{WAIT}   The {WAIT} command halts the macro execution for a specific date and time serial number.

Format   {WAIT DateTimeNumber} is the format of the {WAIT} command.
  DateTimeNumber is the date and time serial number at which the macro execution continues. You can use functions such as @DATE and @NOW to specify the date and time serial numbers. The DateTimeNumber can also refer to a cell, which contains a date and time serial number. You can create a fixed delay by using the @NOW and @TIME function with this macro.

Use   The {WAIT} command temporarily halts a macro's execution. This command often provides the user sufficient time to view a screen display. While the {WAIT} command is in effect, Quattro Pro does not process anything. While Quattro Pro is postponing the macro's execution, Quattro Pro displays a WAIT indicator, or the indicator set with the {INDICATE} command (see later section). Also, the pointer for the mouse's location will appear as an hourglass. If the DateTimeNumber has already passed, Quattro Pro ignores this command.

Example   The most common use of the {WAIT} command is freezing the screen for a time so that the user has a chance to read the screen. Figure 14.30 shows a macro with this command. A {MENUBRANCH} command in another macro will transfer to the Admin macro when Administration is selected. If Administration is selected, the macro prompts for a password. If the password is incorrect, the macro puts the message "Invalid password" in Warning and moves to the cell Warning. The {WAIT} command halts the macro for a 0.0001th of a day (approximately ten seconds) from the current time before the notebook is saved and closed.

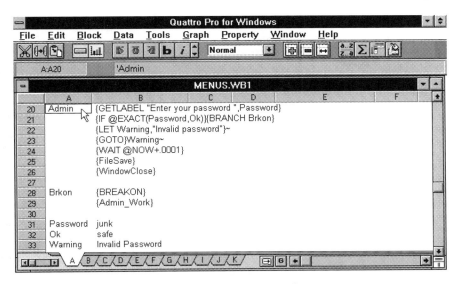

Figure 14.30 Macro Using {WAIT} Command

File Commands

Quattro Pro has several macro commands that can manipulate text files. These commands can open and close files, write to them, and read from them. Quattro Pro allows only one text file open at a time. These commands operate on a file in sequential order. While Quattro Pro's file macro commands can operate on any file, the commands work best with ASCII and ANSI text files. The {READ}, {READLN}, {WRITE}, and {WRITELN} commands work with ASCII text files. The {ANSIREAD}, {ANSIREADLN}, {ANSIWRITE}, and {ANSIWRITELN} commands work with ANSI text files. These two sets of commands perform the same features with the exception of the different character sets each command expects the data to use. The format and use of the {ANSIREAD}, {ANSIREADLN}, {ANSIWRITE}, and {ANSIWRITELN} commands are identical to the {READ}, {READLN}, {WRITE}, and {WRITELN} commands. An example of this type of file is the file you create when you print to a file or create a file with the Notepad accessary. Other file types may store their data in a format that is impossible to understand. Until a file is opened with the {OPEN} command, no other file macro command operates as designed. Once a file is opened, Quattro Pro monitors its position within the file with a file pointer.

FILE POINTERS Quattro Pro uses file pointers to mark its position in the file. A file pointer is the number of bytes from the beginning of the file. When the file pointer is at the beginning of a file, the file pointer's value is 0 (not 1). A byte equals one letter, number, space, or symbol (the exception is a carriage return which consists of two bytes). An example of how Quattro Pro counts bytes is illustrated by the phrase "A stitch in time saves nine." This phrase consists of 30 bytes—22 letters, 5 spaces, 1 symbol (the period), and a carriage return (2 bytes).

When you open a file, Quattro Pro puts the file pointer at position 0. For example, when the ASCII text file shown in Figure 14.31 is opened, the pointer is just before the first 4 in 42124. The file pointer is increased every time you read or write information by the number of characters read or written. For example, if you read six characters from the beginning of the file shown in Figure 14.31, the file pointer points to the S in Smith after reading the characters (remember, start counting at 0). You can also change the file pointer's position with the {SETPOS} command (explained later). At any point in time, you can assign a spreadsheet's cell value to the file pointer position with the {GETPOS} command (explained later). When you append to a file, the file pointer is positioned at the end instead of the beginning so you can quickly add data.

Within a text file like the one in Figure 14.31, moving the file pointer is simple since each line or record has the same number of characters. To move from one record to the next, change the file pointer by the same number of characters. Also, each type of data or field is the same number of characters away from the beginning of a line. For example, the names are all six characters from the start of the line. Most macros that use the file macro commands use files that have their data arranged in a fixed format like this because it is easier to find specific pieces of information.

{CLOSE}   The {CLOSE} command closes a file opened with the {OPEN} command. It allows another text file to be opened since Quattro Pro only permits one open text file at a time. This command adds an end-of-file character to the open file

```
┌─────────────────────────────────────────────────────────────────────┐
│ ▬                     Notepad - TEXTFILE.TXT                    ▼  ▲  │
├─────────────────────────────────────────────────────────────────────┤
│ File   Edit   Search   Help                                           │
├─────────────────────────────────────────────────────────────────────┤
│ 42124 Smith, Eliza        Mutual Insurance       500   04/28/93  08:30 AM ▲ │
│ 25939 Von Steiner, John   Healthcare Systems     500   02/24/93  08:40 AM   │
│ 42141 Bond, Greg          Blue Cross             500   05/04/93  08:50 AM   │
│ 58631 Ostrosky, Joan      Blue Shield            200   01/09/93  09:00 AM   │
│ 22621 Hull, Mary          Acme Inc. Trust Fund   250   02/01/93  09:10 AM   │
│ 99512 Larson, Karen       Blue Shield            250   10/11/92  09:20 AM   │
│ 15338 Doe, Dave           Monumental Life        100   10/23/92  09:30 AM   │
│ 23835 Winchester, Sue     USF&G                  500   12/23/92  09:40 AM   │
│ 91189 Campbell, Keith     Blue Cross             500   12/01/92  09:50 AM   │
│ 74466 Grant, Frank        Travelers Insurance    100   11/05/92  10:00 AM   │
│ 15982 Petrowski, Heather  Monumental Life        500   01/16/93  10:10 AM   │
│ 89350 Demoura, Liza       Mutual Insurance       500   01/23/93  10:20 AM   │
│ 63158 Lawrence, Mike      Maryland Casualty      500   02/23/93  10:30 AM   │
│ 44871 Martin, Amy         USF&G                   50   06/14/92  10:40 AM   │
│ 82423 Ventzke, Blair      Blue Cross             200   03/10/93  10:50 AM   │
│ 28627 Watts, Peg          Prudential Insurance   250   10/16/92  11:00 AM   │
│ 41263 Medici, George      Blue Cross             200   11/20/92  11:10 AM   │
│ 56464 Perez, Steve        USF&G                  200   03/15/93  11:20 AM   │
│ 58810 Stevens, Melissa    Healthcare Systems     100   03/08/93  11:30 AM   │
│ 63678 George, Charles     Blue Shield            100   11/11/92  11:40 AM ▼ │
├─────────────────────────────────────────────────────────────────────┤
│ ◄ │                                                               │ ► │
└─────────────────────────────────────────────────────────────────────┘
```

Figure 14.31   Text File

▼ TIP: Use {ONERROR} with file Macro commands.

Always include an {ONERROR} command after file macro commands so you are notified if they do not execute as expected. Remember that the macro does continue executing even if a file macro command does not perform as expected.

and updates the disk directory to include the date and time that the file is closed and saved, as well as the new size of this file. If the computer is turned off before the {CLOSE} command is executed, data may be lost. If there are no open files when Quattro Pro reaches this command, the command is ignored.

Format   {CLOSE} is the format of the {CLOSE} command.
   This command does not have any arguments. If you are opening and closing many files, you should put the file name in quotes between CLOSE and the right brace.

Use   This command closes an open file. It is necessary to use {CLOSE} to finalize changes made to a file. If Quattro Pro executes this command successfully, Quattro Pro executes the macro instruction in the line below the {CLOSE} command. If Quattro Pro cannot execute this command, Quattro Pro performs the macro instructions following the {CLOSE} command in the same cell, allowing you to use the {ONERROR} command in case the command fails. The usual cause of the command's failure is removal of the disk with the data file on a floppy disk.

Example   Figure 14.32 shows a macro that lists all accounts from the ACCOUNTS.PRN file. The first macro instruction opens the file. The macro instruction in B10 closes this file. As a reminder of which file is being closed, the {CLOSE} command includes the file name in quotes. Quattro Pro ignores anything between CLOSE and the right closing brace.

{FILESIZE}   The {FILESIZE} command determines the number of bytes in the file that is open and stores the number in a spreadsheet cell. If a file is not open when the command is reached, the command is ignored.

Format   {FILESIZE Location} is the format of the {FILESIZE} command.
   Location is a cell address or block name in which Quattro Pro stores the file size information.

Use   This command determines the size of a file. It is often combined with the {SETPOS} command (covered later). This command is used with the {FOR} command to determine the number of times a loop should be repeated.

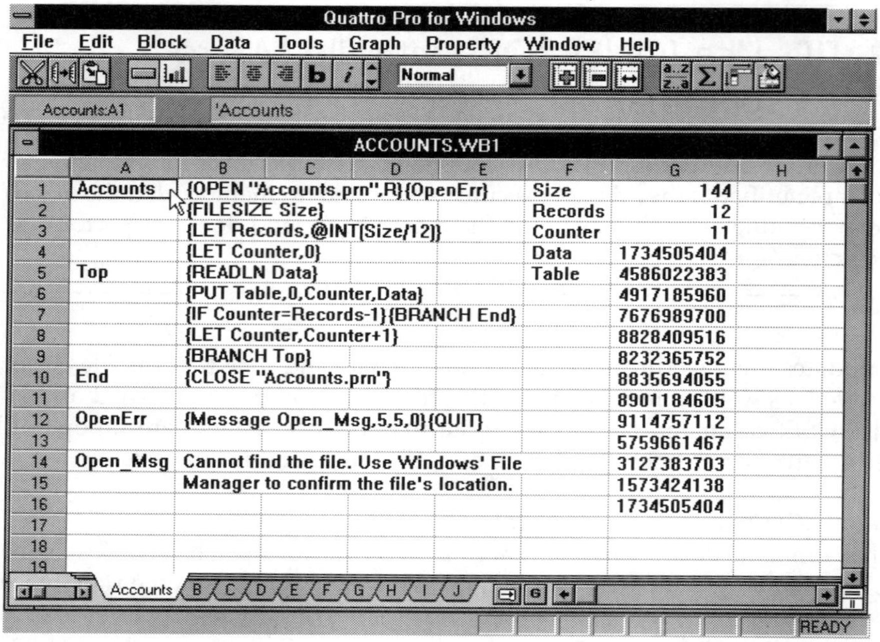

Figure 14.32   Macro Using {CLOSE} and {FILESIZE} Commands

Example   Figure 14.32 shows a macro that lists all possible account numbers in the block named Table. The {FILESIZE} command in B2 puts the number of bytes in the block Size (which is the cell G1). The {LET} command in B3 uses this number to determine the number of records in the file. This macro assumes that each record contains 10 characters and a carriage return. In B7, the macro uses the value of Records to determine when the macro should break out of the loop.

{GETPOS}   The {GETPOS} command determines the file pointer location and stores this value in a cell.

Format   GETPOS Location} is the format of the {GETPOS} command.
    Location is a cell address or block name in which Quattro Pro stores the value of the file pointer.

Use   This command is primarily used to determine the position of the file pointer before reading from or writing to a file. Quattro Pro ignores this command if a file is not open. Macros frequently use this command when the macros use files that have a different number of characters per line.

Example   Figure 14.33 shows a macro that reads the first twenty records of a file and stores the data and the length of each record in the block Output. The Loop_1

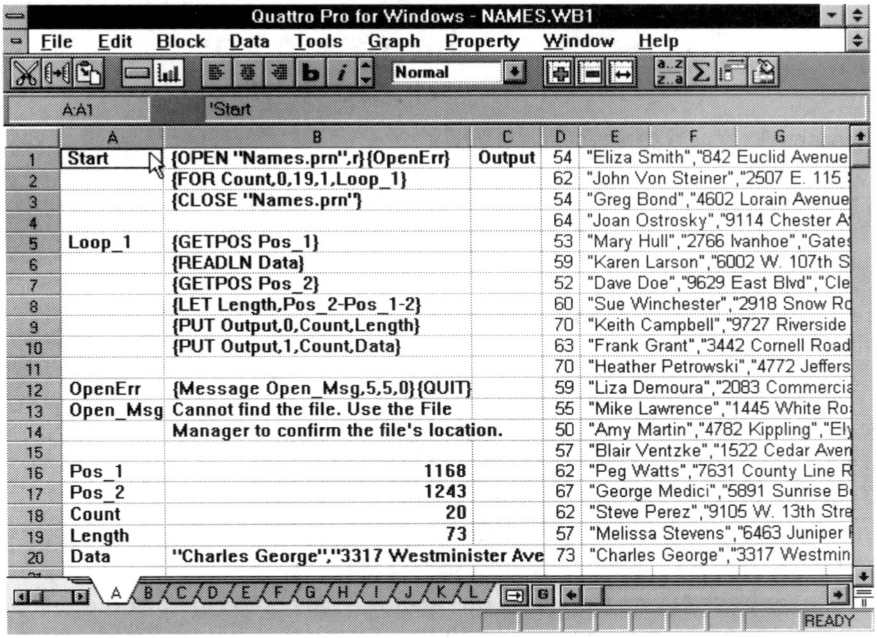

Quattro Pro for Windows - NAMES.WB1

File Edit Block Data Tools Graph Property Window Help

A:A1 | 'Start

	A	B	C	D	E ... G
1	Start	{OPEN "Names.prn",r}{OpenErr}	Output	54	"Eliza Smith","842 Euclid Avenue
2		{FOR Count,0,19,1,Loop_1}		62	"John Von Steiner","2507 E. 115
3		{CLOSE "Names.prn"}		54	"Greg Bond","4602 Lorain Avenue
4				64	"Joan Ostrosky","9114 Chester A
5	Loop_1	{GETPOS Pos_1}		53	"Mary Hull","2766 Ivanhoe","Gates
6		{READLN Data}		59	"Karen Larson","6002 W. 107th S
7		{GETPOS Pos_2}		52	"Dave Doe","9629 East Blvd","Cle
8		{LET Length,Pos_2-Pos_1-2}		60	"Sue Winchester","2918 Snow Rd
9		{PUT Output,0,Count,Length}		70	"Keith Campbell","9727 Riverside
10		{PUT Output,1,Count,Data}		63	"Frank Grant","3442 Cornell Road
11				70	"Heather Petrowski","4772 Jeffers
12	OpenErr	{Message Open_Msg,5,5,0}{QUIT}		59	"Liza Demoura","2083 Commercia
13	Open_Msg	Cannot find the file. Use the File		55	"Mike Lawrence","1445 White Ro
14		Manager to confirm the file's location.		50	"Amy Martin","4782 Kippling","Ely
15				57	"Blair Ventzke","1522 Cedar Aven
16	Pos_1	1168		62	"Peg Watts","7631 County Line R
17	Pos_2	1243		67	"George Medici","5891 Sunrise B
18	Count	20		62	"Steve Perez","9105 W. 13th Stre
19	Length	73		57	"Melissa Stevens","6463 Juniper
20	Data	"Charles George","3317 Westminister Ave		73	"Charles George","3317 Westmin

READY

Figure 14.33 Macro Using {GETPOS} Command

macro uses the {GETPOS} macro command before and after each {READLN} command. By subtracting the two values and subtracting two more for the end-of-line characters, the macro computes the length of each line. The macro shown in this example could be used as part of a larger macro that further processes the data in the Output block.

{OPEN} The {OPEN} command opens a file for reading, writing, appending, or modifying data and places the file pointer at the beginning of the file. A macro with this command should also have a {CLOSE} command.

Format {OPEN Filename,AccessMode} is the format of the {OPEN} command.

The Filename is either a string enclosed in quotes or a cell address or block name that contains the file name. The file name must include the file name extension. The directory must be included if the directory is not the current directory.

The AccessMode is a single-letter description of the actions to be performed on the file. The letter can be uppercase or lowercase and is not enclosed in quotes. Quattro Pro has four options for the AccessMode argument:

A—Append lets you modify an existing file. The difference between this and the other access modes is that Append positions the file pointer at the end of the file instead of at the beginning.

▼ TIP: **Macro file commands are not appropriate for editing spreadsheet or program files.**

Do not use the macro file commands to edit spreadsheet or program files, since these files contain information in a specialized format that you cannot use.

R—Read only does not permit you to change the file. The {WRITE} and {WRITELN} commands (see later sections) are invalid if the file is opened with this AccessMode.

M—Modify permits changes to be made to an existing file. All file macro commands can be used on a file opened with this AccessMode.

W—Write only creates and opens a file with the name specified as the Filename argument. If a file already exists with that name, that file is erased before the new file is created. While all file macro commands operate on a file opened with this AccessMode, the {READ} and {READLN} commands (see next two sections) cannot be used until data is written to the file.

Use The {OPEN} command provides access to data in a file. When Quattro Pro executes this command successfully, Quattro Pro performs the next macro instruction in the line below the {OPEN} command. If Quattro Pro cannot open the file, Quattro Pro performs the macro instructions following the {OPEN} command in the same cell, allowing you to use the {BRANCH} or {ONERROR} command to adjust the macro's execution if the {OPEN} command fails. Quattro Pro only allows one open file at a time.

Example Figure 14.32 displays a macro that retrieves and lists all the accounts. This information is kept in the file ACCOUNTS.PRN. This file is in the current directory. The first macro instruction opens the file as a read-only file. The {OpenErr} after the {OPEN} switches the control of the macro to OpenErr if Quattro Pro cannot open the file.

{READ} The {READ} command reads information from a file starting at the current file pointer position.

Format {READ #Bytes,Location} is the format of the {READ} command.
#Bytes is the number of characters to be read.
Location is the location in which Quattro Pro stores the information that Quattro Pro reads from the file. This may be specified as a cell address or a block name.

Use This command retrieves information from a file. When this command is executed, Quattro Pro starts at the file pointer's current location.

Two aspects of this command are different from {READLN} (see next section). {READLN} removes the two-byte carriage return at the end of a line. If you read a carriage return with the {READ} command, Quattro Pro displays two squares to represent these two bytes. Also, {READLN} reads characters until the command reaches a carriage return. The {READ} command reads only the number of characters specified. {READ} is used more frequently when the file is well structured. {READLN} is used more often when the file has a varying format. For example, the {READ} command can read different types of information stored in one line. If you used {READLN}, you would have to use Quattro Pro's string functions or the Parse command in the Data menu to extract the data contained within a line. On the other hand, if you do not know the position of the data that you are looking for, you should use the {READLN} command.

After this command is executed, the file pointer points to the character following the last character read. After this command is executed, Quattro Pro executes the next macro instruction in the cell below the {READ} command. If Quattro Pro cannot perform the command, Quattro Pro performs the macro instructions following the {READ} command in the same cell, allowing you to use the {ONERROR} command to adjust the macro's execution if the command fails.

Example Figure 14.34 shows a template that determines the production cost of gas pump hoses. The \Z macro retrieves the quantity and price information. The macro

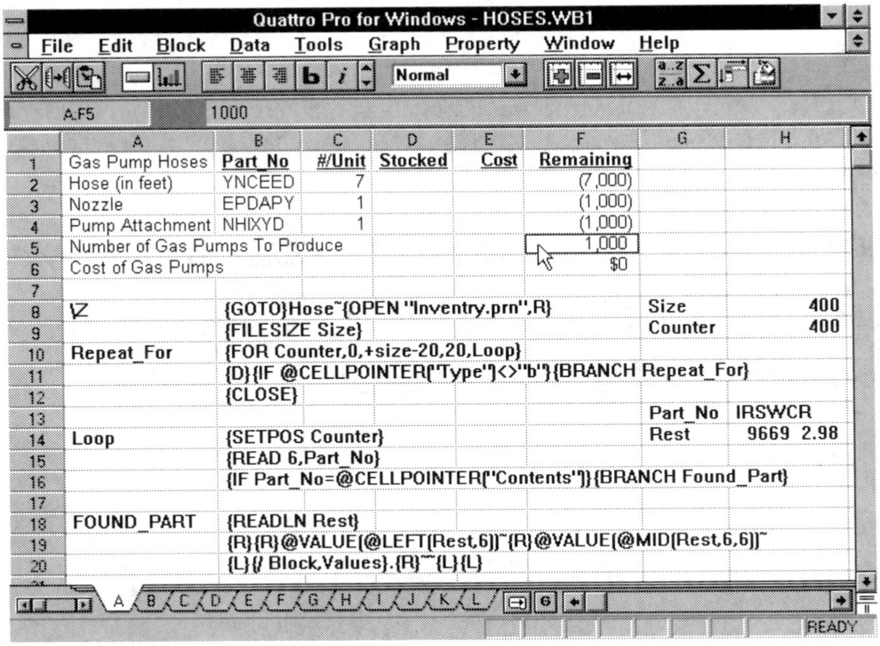

Figure 14.34 Macros Using {READ}, {READLN}, and {SETPOS} Commands

determines the inventory quantity and price for each part required to make a gas pump hose. For each component that makes up a gas pump hose, you have more than one part that you can use. For example, if you were making gas pump hoses for leaded gas, you would use a nozzle with a wide spout to prevent someone from putting leaded gas into a car that uses unleaded. Each component has a unique part number. Before you use this macro, you must provide the part number of the components to be used, the quantity of each component required for each gas pump hose, and the number of gas pump hoses that you are assembling, as shown at the top of Figure 14.34. The macro \Z moves to the first part number and opens the file INVENTRY.PRN, which contains all available inventory parts and their quantity and price information. Once the file is opened, the {FOR} loop starts the Loop branch, which moves the file pointer to the part number that the macro is looking for. In Loop, the {SETPOS} command moves the file pointer to every twentieth place, since 20 is the length of each record. The {READ} command in B15 reads the first six characters of every line. If the part number read by the {READ} command agrees with the current part number, the macro switches to Found_Part. If the part numbers do not agree, the macro moves the file pointer to the beginning of the next record and reads that part number. When the macro branches to Found_Part after finding the correct part number, the macro reads the remaining information and stores the information in Rest. The next two macro instructions direct Quattro Pro to put the value of the first six characters of Rest into the Stocked column and the value of the last six characters in the Cost column. After the macro provides this information for a part number, the macro moves to the cell below the current part number. The {IF} command in B11 repeats the {FOR} command if this cell is not blank. If this cell is blank, as cell B5 is, the macro closes the file and stops. Figure 14.35 shows the template after the macros have been executed.

{READLN} The {READLN} command reads characters from an input file until the command reaches the end-of-line character. The characters read by this command are stored in a spreadsheet cell.

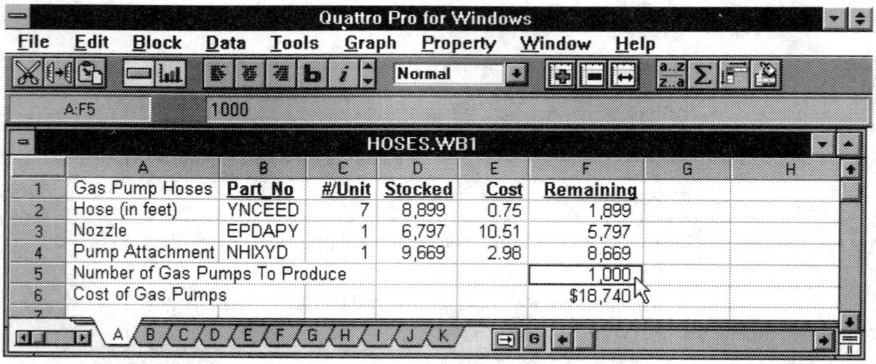

	A	B	C	D	E	F	G	H
1	Gas Pump Hoses	Part_No	#/Unit	Stocked	Cost	Remaining		
2	Hose (in feet)	YNCEED	7	8,899	0.75	1,899		
3	Nozzle	EPDAPY	1	6,797	10.51	5,797		
4	Pump Attachment	NHIXYD	1	9,669	2.98	8,669		
5	Number of Gas Pumps To Produce					1,000		
6	Cost of Gas Pumps					$18,740		

Figure 14.35 Template After Executing \Z Macros

Format {READLN Location} is the format of the {READLN} command.

Location is the storage area in which Quattro Pro places the characters that have been read. This may be a cell address or block name.

Use This command retrieves information from a file. When Quattro Pro executes the {READLN} command, Quattro Pro starts at the current file pointer's location and reads characters until the end-of-line character is reached. Quattro Pro stores the information in a spreadsheet cell specified by the command's argument and removes the end-of-line character from the string stored in the cell. Once Quattro Pro executes this command, the file pointer is at the beginning of the next line. When this command has been executed successfully, Quattro Pro moves to the next macro instruction in the line below the {READLN} command. If Quattro Pro cannot read the line, it executes the macro instructions following the {READLN} command in the same cell, so that you can use the {ONERROR} or {BRANCH} command to adjust the macro's execution if the {READLN} command fails.

Example Figure 14.34 shows a template that determines the production cost of gas pump hoses and also shows the \Z macro that retrieves the quantity and price information. The macros provide the inventory quantity and price for each part required to make a gas pump hose. For each component that makes up a gas pump hose, there are different parts that can be used. For example, if you are making gas pump hoses for leaded gas, you would use a nozzle with a wide spout to prevent someone from putting leaded gas into a car that uses unleaded gas. Each part has a unique part number. To use this macro, you must provide the part number of the components that you are using, the number of each component required for each gas pump hose, and the number of gas pump hoses that you are assembling, as shown in Figure 14.34. The macro \Z moves to the first part number and opens the file INVENTRY.PRN, which contains all available inventory parts and their quantity and price information. Once the file is opened, the {FOR} loop starts the Loop branch, which moves the file pointer to the part number that the macro is looking for. In Loop, the {SETPOS} command moves the file pointer to every twentieth place (each record contains 20 characters). The {READ} command in B15 reads the first six characters of every line. If the part number read by the {READ} command agrees with the current part number, the macro switches to Found_Part. If the part numbers do not agree, the macro moves the file pointer to the beginning of the next record and reads that part number. When the macro branches to Found_Part, the macro uses {READLN} to read the remaining information and to store the information in Rest. The next two macro instructions direct Quattro Pro to put the value of the first six characters of Rest into the Stocked column and the value of the last six characters in the Cost column. After Quattro Pro has found this information for a part number, the macro moves to the cell below the current part number. The {IF} command in B11 checks if the next cell is blank. If this cell contains a part number, the macro branches to Repeat_For. If this cell is blank, the macro closes the file and quits. Figure 14.35 shows the macros and template after the macros have been executed.

{SETPOS} The {SETPOS} command specifies the location for the file pointer.

Format   {SETPOS FilePosition} is the format of the {SETPOS} command.

FilePosition is a value between 0 and the number of bytes in the file. This can either be a number, or it can be a cell address or block name that refers to a number.

Use   This command positions the file pointer before reading from or writing to a file. If the value specified for the FilePosition is larger than the file size, Quattro Pro moves the file pointer to the end of the file. If Quattro Pro can move the file pointer to the position specified, the macro instruction in the next cell is executed and any macro instructions that follow the {SETPOS} command in its cell are ignored. If a file is not open when Quattro Pro tries executing this command, Quattro Pro executes the macro instructions following the {SETPOS} command in its cell. This allows you to trap errors with the {BRANCH} or {ONERROR} command.

Example   Figure 14.34 shows a template that determines the production cost of gas pump hoses and also shows the macros that retrieve the quantity and price information. The macros provide the inventory quantity and price for each part required to make a gas pump hose. For each component in a gas pump hose, you can choose from more than one part. For example, you may use a different type of hose depending on the chemical that the hose contains. Each part has a unique part number. Before using this macro, you must provide the part number of the components you want, the number of each component required for each gas pump hose, and the number of gas pump hoses that you are assembling, as shown in rows 1 through 4 of Figure 14.34. The macro \Z moves to the first part number and opens the file INVENTRY.PRN, which contains all available inventory parts and their quantity and price information. Once the file is opened, the {FOR} loop performs the Loop branch, which moves the file pointer to the part number that the macro is looking for. In Loop, the {SETPOS} command moves the file pointer to every twentieth place (each record contains 20 characters). The {READ} command in B15 reads the first six characters of every line. If the part number read by the {READ} command agrees with the current part number, the macro switches to Found_Part, which enters the data from the file into the template on top. If the part number read from the file does not agree with the current part number, the Loop branch repeats because of the {FOR} command, and the {SETPOS} command uses the value of Counter from the {FOR} command to read the next part number from the file.

{WRITE} The {WRITE} command writes information to a file starting at the current file pointer position.

Format   {WRITE String} is the format of the {WRITE} command.

String is the characters to be written as a single line. This information may be a string enclosed in quotes, a cell address, a block name, or a formula. You can combine strings by separating them by commas.

Use This command appends and replaces information in a file. When this command is executed, Quattro Pro starts at the file pointer's current location. If the file already has data stored at this location, the {WRITE} command replaces the information. If the file pointer is at the end of the file, the information is added to the end of the file. After this command is executed, the file pointer points to the character following the last character written. When Quattro Pro executes this command, Quattro Pro executes the next macro instruction in the cell below the {WRITE} command. If Quattro Pro cannot perform the command (for example, if there is a disk error), Quattro Pro performs the macro instructions following the {WRITE} command in the same cell, which allows you to use the {ONERROR} command to adjust the macro's execution if the command fails.

Example Figure 14.36 shows a macro that prompts for various types of information and converts the entered information into delimited format that other programs can import easily. This macro moves to the end of a text file and adds the data that you provide through the {GETLABEL} commands. The {WRITE} commands in B7 and B8 write the sections of the data that the macro adds. Since the data file is delimited with commas and double quotes, the macro instructions in B7, B8, and B9 use both the double quote stored in Quote and also the double quote, comma, and double quote combination stored in Delim. Rather than entering the characters directly, the macro uses these named cells to make the macro easier to read.

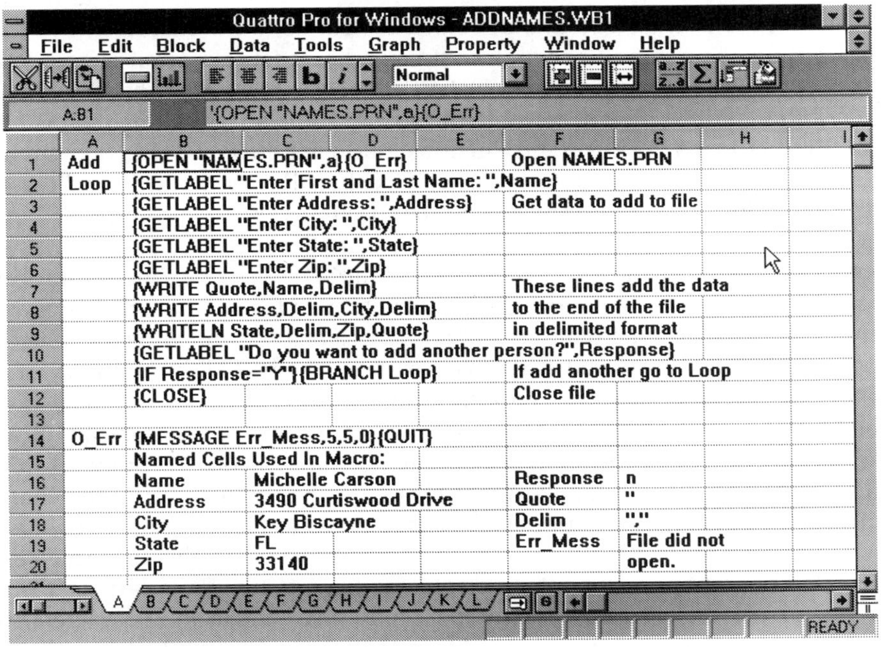

Figure 14.36   Macro Using {WRITE} and {WRITELN} Commands

Double quotes must be added by using a named block (as in this example) or by using @CHAR(34) (when you enter a double quote, Quattro Pro assumes it is the beginning or end of a string). In order to omit the end-of-line characters, the {WRITE} command is used in B7 and B8 instead of {WRITELN}. When the last information for a record is entered, the {WRITELN} command ends the line as it adds the state and zip code to the file.

{WRITELN}   The {WRITELN} command writes information to a file and adds end-of-line characters. The information is written at the current file pointer position.

Format   {WRITELN String} is the format of the {WRITELN} command.
    String is the characters to be written as a single line. This information may be a string enclosed in quotes, or it may be a cell address, a block name, or a formula. You can combine strings in the {WRITELN} command by separating the strings by commas. If the string " " is specified, Quattro Pro writes an end-of-line character. This puts a blank line in the file or ends a line started with the {WRITE} command.

Use   This command appends and replaces information in a file. When the {WRITELN} command is executed, Quattro Pro starts at the current file pointer location. If the file has information at the current location, the information is written over. If the file pointer is at the end of the file, the information is added to the end of the file. After this command has written the characters in the specified string, this command writes the two-byte character for the end-of-line marker. After this command is executed, the file pointer points to the character following the end-of-line character. When this command has been executed successfully, Quattro Pro moves to the next macro instruction in the line below the {WRITELN} command. If Quattro Pro cannot write the string (for example, if the disk is full), Quattro Pro performs the macro instructions following the {WRITELN} command in its cell, which allows you to use the {ONERROR} command to adjust the macro's execution if the {WRITELN} command fails.

Example   Figure 14.36 shows a macro that prompts for various types of information and converts the entered information into delimited format that other programs can import easily. This macro moves to the end of a text file and adds the data that you provide through the {GETLABEL} commands. The {WRITE} commands in B7 and B8 write the sections of the data that the macro adds. Since the data file is delimited with commas and double quotes, the macro instructions in B7, B8, and B9 use both the double quote stored in Quote and also the double quote, comma, and double quote combination stored in Delim. Rather than entering the characters directly, the macro uses these named cells to make the macro easier to read. Double quotes must be added by using a named block as in this example or by using @CHAR(34) (when you enter a double quote, Quattro Pro assumes it is the beginning or end of a string). In order to omit the end-of-line characters, the {WRITE} command is used in B7 and B8 instead of {WRITELN}. When the last information for a record is entered, the {WRITELN} command ends the line as it adds the state and zip code to the file.

Screen Commands

Quattro Pro's screen macro commands customize the screen's appearance during macro execution and ring the computer's bell. During a macro's execution, Quattro Pro displays all menu boxes, confirmation boxes, and prompts as if you were performing the steps yourself. The screen macro commands let you change the display of these features. While these features provide information about the macro's progress, the features can cause the screen to flicker as Quattro Pro performs the macro steps faster than the screen can update the display.

{BEEP} The {BEEP} command sounds the computer bell.

Format {BEEP Number} is the format for this command.

The Number argument can have any value from 1 to 10, with a default setting of 1. The argument number selected affects the tone of your computer's bell: 1 represents the lowest pitch, and 10 represents the highest pitch.

Use The {BEEP} command can alert the user to an error that has occurred, prompt the user to provide input, give the user some assurance that a long-running macro is still functioning while running, and inform the user that a step has been finished.

Example Figure 14.37 shows a set of macro instructions that use the {BEEP} command. The purpose of the macro instructions is to prompt the user to input his/her age, first and last name, and salary level. When the macro is executed, the first line of the macro changes the mode indicator to Entry. The {BEEP 1} command on the second line causes the computer to make a low-pitched beeping sound. The user is then prompted to enter several pieces of information. At the end of the macro, the {BEEP 4} command creates a higher-pitched beep to indicate that the macro is complete.

{INDICATE} The {INDICATE} command allows you to change the mode indicator (which appears in the status line) to some specified string.

Format {INDICATE String} is the format for this command.

String is any string of characters. However, only the first few characters that fit in the box for the mode indicator are shown. You can use an empty string {INDICATE ""} to remove the indicator from the status line. If you want spaces in the mode indicator string, enclose the string in quotes. The command {INDICATE} by itself returns the indicator to Quattro Pro's default.

Use You can use the {INDICATE} command in several situations. When you have a menu selection in a set of macro instructions, you can use this command to indicate which type of menu item the user has selected. You can also use this command to test macro shells. A subroutine within a macro can be represented initially by just an {INDICATE} command with an appropriate string of characters to check the flow of the macro.

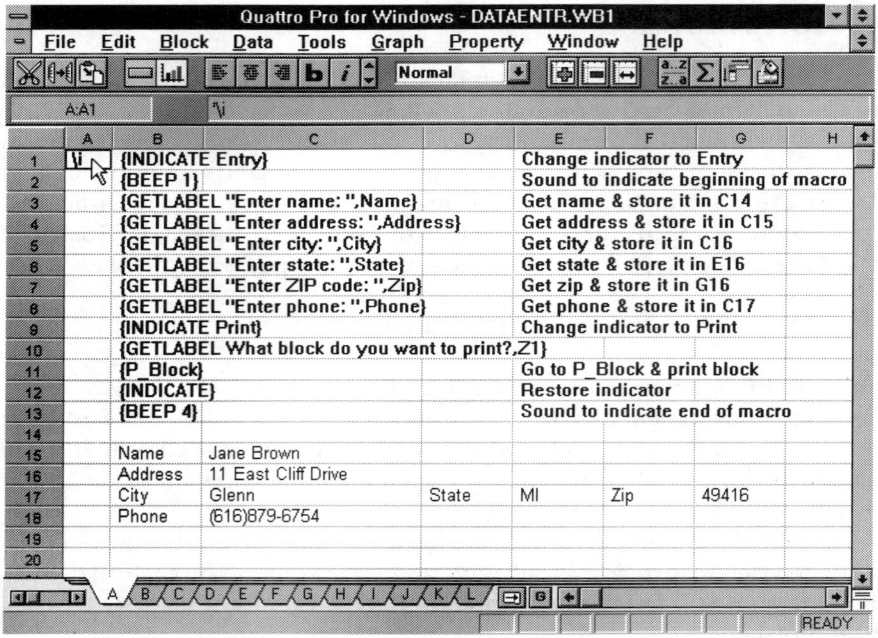

Figure 14.37   Macro Using {INDICATE} and {BEEP} Commands

Example   Figure 14.37 provides an example of the {INDICATE} command. The first line of the macro (B1) changes the mode descriptor at the lower right corner of the screen from READY to ENTRY. The second {INDICATE} command (B9) changes the mode descriptor from ENTRY to PRINT. Finally, the next to last line of the macro (B12) returns the mode descriptor to READY.

{PANELOFF}   The {PANELOFF} command disables the display of the menu and prompts during menu execution. The menu and prompts are restored when the {PANELON} command is used (see next section) or when Quattro Pro has finished executing the macro. Omitting the menu and prompt updating with the {PANELOFF} command is the same as selecting Panel or Both for the Macro Suppress-Redraw feature of the application's Macro property.

Format   {PANELOFF} is the format for the {PANELOFF} command.
    This command has no arguments.

Use   This command hides the display of Quattro Pro's menus and prompts. During macro execution, the menus change so quickly that they cannot be read. Also, since Quattro Pro must update the screen for every new menu and prompt, disabling their display speeds up macro execution.

Example Figure 14.38 provides an example of the {PANELOFF} command. The {PANELOFF} command in the first line of the macro (F1) instructs Quattro Pro not to update the control panel during the macro execution. The {PANELON} command in F10 enables the menu's display for the font change made with the macro instructions in F12..F13.

{PANELON} The {PANELON} command restores the menus and prompts that have been hidden with the {PANELOFF} command. {PANELON} cannot perform any action without a prior {PANELOFF}, so using this command without a prior {PANELOFF} has no effect.

Format {PANELON} is the format of the {PANELON} command.
This command has no arguments.

Use This command is used when you have hidden the menus and prompts with the {PANELOFF} command. Quattro Pro automatically performs {PANELON} when it reaches the end of a macro.

Example Figure 14.38 provides an example of the {PANELON} command. The {PANELOFF} command in F1 instructs Quattro Pro not to display the menus and prompts during the macro execution. The {PANELON} command in F10 restores the menus and prompts to display so that the font-selection macro instructions in F12..F13 display the menu boxes and prompts.

{WINDOWSOFF} The {WINDOWSOFF} command disables the automatic updating of the window display. The display is automatically updated when the

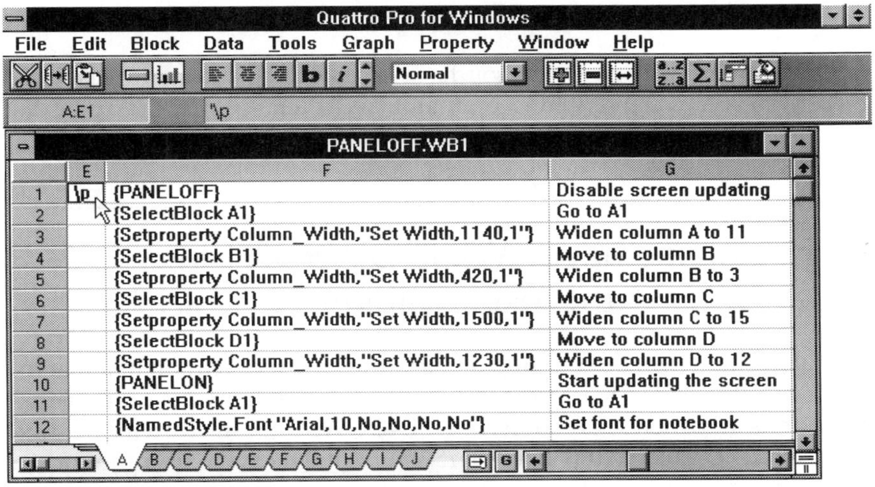
Quattro Pro for Windows
File Edit Block Data Tools Graph Property Window Help
Normal
A:E1
'\p
PANELOFF.WB1
E F G
1 \p {PANELOFF} Disable screen updating
2 {SelectBlock A1} Go to A1
3 {Setproperty Column_Width,"Set Width,1140,1"} Widen column A to 11
4 {SelectBlock B1} Move to column B
5 {Setproperty Column_Width,"Set Width,420,1"} Widen column B to 3
6 {SelectBlock C1} Move to column C
7 {Setproperty Column_Width,"Set Width,1500,1"} Widen column C to 15
8 {SelectBlock D1} Move to column D
9 {Setproperty Column_Width,"Set Width,1230,1"} Widen column D to 12
10 {PANELON} Start updating the screen
11 {SelectBlock A1} Go to A1
12 {NamedStyle.Font "Arial,10,No,No,No,No"} Set font for notebook
A B C D E F G H I J

Figure 14.38 Macro Using {PANELOFF} and {PANELON} Commands

{WINDOWSON} command is used (see next section) or when the macro execution is finished. Omitting the screen updating with the {WINDOWSOFF} command is the same as selecting Window or Both for the Macro Suppress-Redraw feature of the application's Macro property.

Format {WINDOWSOFF} is the format for the {WINDOWSOFF} command. This command has no arguments.

Use This command is used when you want to speed up the macro execution. Since Quattro Pro automatically updates the screen as changes are made, the amount of time consumed by the updating can slow down a macro significantly. Disabling window updating reduces the flickering that appears on the screen. Also, it is useful when you do not want the operator to see the execution of each instruction or be aware of each activity that takes place. This command does not affect the value of trace cells.

Example Figure 14.39 provides an example of the {WINDOWSOFF} command. The {WINDOWSOFF} command in the Find_Name macro (B10) instructs Quattro Pro not to update the display until Quattro Pro reaches the {WINDOWSON} command after it has found the name. The {WINDOWSOFF} and {WINDOWSON} commands hide the steps the Find_Name macro performs to find the name.

{WINDOWSON} The {WINDOWSON} command re-enables the updating of the window display. Since {WINDOWSON} does not perform any action without a prior {WINDOWSOFF}, using this command without a prior {WINDOWSOFF} does not have any effect.

Format {WINDOWSON} is the format of the {WINDOWSON} command. This command has no arguments.

Use This command is used when you have disabled the automatic display updating with the {WINDOWSOFF} command and then want the display to be updated.

▼ TIP: Do not have {WINDOWSOFF} in effect if the user will select a block.

If the macro's user will be selecting a block during the execution of a macro, such as for a {DODIALOG} command or a command equivalent that uses ? in place of its arguments, do not have {WINDOWSOFF} in effect at the time the user selects the block. If {WINDOWSOFF} is in effect, the user cannot see the block he or she is selecting.

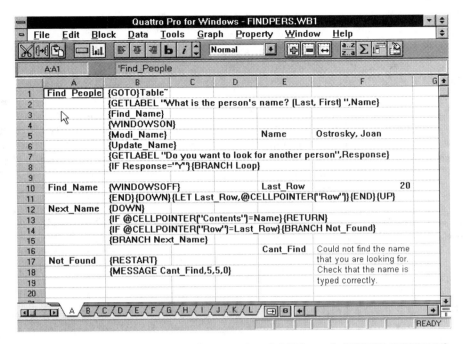

	A	B	C	D	E	F	G
	Find People	{GOTO}Table˜					
1	Find People	{GOTO}Table˜					
2		{GETLABEL "What is the person's name? (Last, First) ",Name}					
3		{Find_Name}					
4		{WINDOWSON}					
5		{Modi_Name}			Name	Ostrosky, Joan	
6		{Update_Name}					
7		{GETLABEL "Do you want to look for another person",Response}					
8		{IF Response="Y"}{BRANCH Loop}					
9							
10	Find_Name	{WINDOWSOFF}			Last_Row		20
11		{END}{DOWN}{LET Last_Row,@CELLPOINTER("Row")}{END}{UP}					
12	Next_Name	{DOWN}					
13		{IF @CELLPOINTER("Contents")=Name}{RETURN}					
14		{IF @CELLPOINTER("Row")=Last_Row}{BRANCH Not_Found}					
15		{BRANCH Next_Name}					
16					Cant_Find	Could not find the name	
17	Not_Found	{RESTART}				that you are looking for.	
18		{MESSAGE Cant_Find,5,5,0}				Check that the name is	
19						typed correctly.	
20							

Figure 14.39 Macro Using {WINDOWSOFF} and {WINDOWSON} Commands

Example Figure 14.39 provides an example of the {WINDOWSON} command. The {WINDOWSON} command after the {Find_Name} macro instruction directs Quattro Pro to refresh the display that was disabled with the {WINDOWSOFF} command. The {WINDOWSOFF} and {WINDOWSON} commands hide the steps the Find_Name macro performs to find the name.

DDE Commands

In Chapter 7, you learned how you can share data between Quattro Pro and other Windows applications with Dynamic Data Exchange (DDE). You can also use DDE to use one application to control another. Quattro Pro's DDE macro commands let you operate other applications and share data between Quattro Pro notebooks and documents for other applications. You can create Quattro Pro macros that start, run, and finish using another Windows application. With any Windows application that supports DDE, you can create macros that control Quattro Pro, although the steps you perform to do so must follow the rules for the other application.

{EXEC} The {EXEC} starts another Windows application so you can use other DDE macro commands to control the application from the Quattro Pro macro. You can also use this command to perform a DOS command.

Format   {EXEC AppName, WindowSize<,Result>} is the format for the {EXEC} command.

AppName is the name of the Windows application to execute. It is entered as if you are entering it in the Command Line text box of the Run command in the File menu of the Program Manager. It is a string in quotes or a reference to another cell containing the label.

WindowSize is the value for the size of the window the application will run in. 1 is the normal size, 2 is minimized as an icon, 3 is maximized to fill the screen.

Result is the cell where this macro will put the application ID for the operation. When the command is unsuccessful, this macro instruction returns a number less than 32. If you use this argument, you need to specify the cell address or block name where this instruction puts the result.

Use   This command is the command you use in a Quattro Pro macro to start another application. You can also use this command to perform a DOS command. {EXEC} is usually the first command used in a macro using DDE macro instructions unless you know that the application the {EXEC} command would otherwise open is already open.

Example   Figure 14.40 shows a macro that takes data from named cells and puts them into a Word for Windows document. It is used by other macros after they

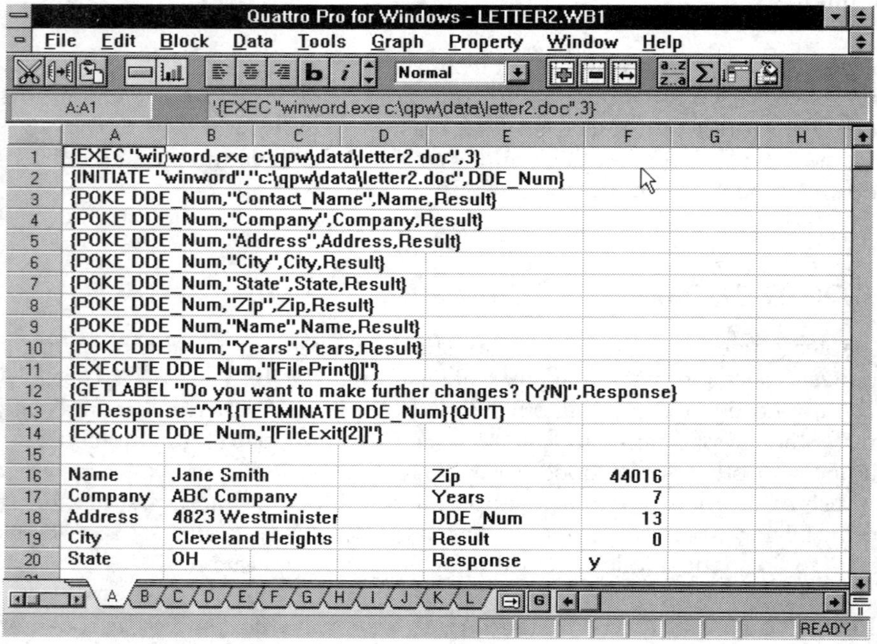

Figure 14.40   Macro Illustrating DDE Macro Commands

have put entries into the named cells. This macro starts Word for Windows with a specific document, then uses the {POKE} command to insert entries into pre-defined bookmarks. After the form letter is filled, it is printed and closed without saving. The macro uses the {EXEC} command to start Word for Windows. AppName is "winword.exe c:\qpw\data\letter2.doc", so Word for Windows is opened with the LETTER2.DOC document opened. The 3 tells Windows to open Word for Windows in a full-screen window. Once this command is performed, the remaining DDE commands can perform Word for Windows menu commands from Quattro Pro.

{EXECUTE} The {EXECUTE} command performs a DDE command in another application. The command it performs must be in a format the other application accepts. You can only use this command after using an {INITIATE} command.

Format {EXECUTE DDEChannel,MacroString<,Result>} is the format for the {EXECUTE} command.

DDEChannel is the number assigned to the DDE connection that the {INITIATE} command returns. It is a block name or cell address.

MacroString is the string in quotes containing the DDE instructions to perform in the selected application. It must be in a format the application accepts. This is not necessarily the format Quattro Pro for Windows uses.

Result is a block or cell where this macro instruction puts the result of the operation. This is either a block name or cell address. When this macro instruction returns a number less than 32, the {EXECUTE} command did not perform properly.

Use This command is for performing a command in an application from within Quattro Pro. Use the {EXECUTE} command to control another application from within Quattro Pro.

Example Figure 14.40 shows a macro that takes data put into named cells and puts them into a Word for Windows document. Other macros use this macro after

---

▼ TIP: You can use {EXEC} to run a DOS command within Quattro Pro.

To run a DOS command using the {EXEC} command, use C:\COMMAND.COM (or the path where COMMAND.COM is stored) followed by the DOS command to perform as the AppName argument. An example is "C:\COMMAND.COM DIR *.WB1 >NOTEBOOK.PRN", which creates a text file called NOTEBOOK.PRN that lists the notebook files in the current directory.

they have put entries into the named cells. This macro uses {EXEC} to start Word for Windows with the LETTER2 document then uses the {POKE} command to insert entries into predefined bookmarks. After the form letter is filled, this macro uses two {EXECUTE} commands to print the document and to exit the document and application. The first {EXECUTE} command performs the [FilePrint()] command that prints the current document. The second {EXECUTE} command closes Word for Windows. The document is not saved because the 2 in the [FileExit(2)] command tells Word for Windows to close the application without saving the documents. These two instructions apply to Word for Windows. If you created a macro in Word for Windows that opened and put data into the notebook, the instructions would be different because Quattro Pro expects different macro instructions.

{INITIATE}   The {INITIATE} command creates a channel of communication between Quattro Pro and another application. Once this channel is established, you can use the {EXECUTE}, {POKE}, {REQUEST}, and {TERMINATE} commands to control the other application. The {INITIATE} command is the first command in a series of DDE macro commands when the application is already open. Use {INITIATE} as the second command after {EXEC} when the application is not already open.

Format   {INITIATE AppName,ProjectName,DDEChannel} is the format for the {INITIATE} command.

AppName is the name of the Windows application to create a channel of communication. It is entered as a string in quotes. Usually you do not need to include as much information as in the AppName you use for the {EXEC} command because this macro command knows to check only the running applications. It is a string in quotes or a reference to a cell containing the label.

ProjectName is the name of the file in the application you want to work with. It is usually also the name of the document window within the application window you are manipulating. It is a string in quotes or a reference to a cell containing a label to use. Use "System" as the ProjectName when you do not want to work with a single file in the application.

DDEChannel is a block or cell where this macro instruction puts the number of the DDEChannel that the {EXECUTE}, {POKE}, {REQUEST}, and {TERMINATE} commands use. It is a cell address or a block name.

Use   This command enables the {EXECUTE}, {POKE}, {REQUEST}, and {TERMINATE} commands to work. Once this command is executed, you can use the other commands to control the other application.

Example   Figure 14.40 shows a macro that takes data from named cells and puts them into a Word for Windows document. This macro is used by other macros after they have put entries into the named cells. It starts Word for Windows with a specific document, then uses the {POKE} command to insert entries into predefined bookmarks. After the form letter is filled, it is printed and closed without saving. The macro uses the {INITIATE} command to create the bridge of communication between Quattro Pro and Word for Windows. The AppName tells Quattro Pro to connect with the Winword application, which represents Word for Windows. The ProjectName tells Quattro Pro that you want to use the LETTER2.DOC file in this application. The third argument, DDE_Num, tells Quattro Pro to put the number of the communication channel this command creates in the cell named DDE_Num (F18). Once this command is performed, the remaining DDE commands can perform commands on Word for Windows from Quattro Pro.

{POKE}   The {POKE} command enters data into another application. This command requires that the channel of communication be established with the application you are entering data into using the {INITIATE} command.

Format   {POKE DDEChannel,Destination,DataToSend<,Result>} is the format for the {POKE} command.

DDEChannel is the number assigned to the DDE connection that the {INITIATE} command returns. It is a block name or cell address.

Destination is the name of the location where you want the DataToSend placed in the other application. It must be a named location in the other application such as a bookmark name in a word processor or a cell location for another spreadsheet application. The destination is a string in quotes.

DataToSend is the Quattro Pro cell or block containing the data you want placed in another application.

Result is a block or cell where this macro instruction puts the result of the operation. This is either a block name or cell address. When this macro instruction returns a number less than 32, the {POKE} command did not perform properly.

Use   This command enters data into the other application, often as if you are entering it yourself. Use the {POKE} command to enter data in the other application and the {EXECUTE} command to perform other steps in the other application.

Example   Figure 14.40 shows a macro that takes data from named cells and puts them into a Word for Windows document. Other macros use this macro after they have put entries into the named cells. This macro uses {EXEC} to start Word for Windows with the LETTER2 document then uses the {INITIATE} command to establish the connection between Quattro Pro and Word for Windows in the LETTER2.DOC document. Once this connection is established, the {POKE} commands take the entries in B16..B20,F16..F17 and place them into the Word for Windows document. The entries of Contact_Name, Company, Address, City, State, Zip, Name, and Years represent bookmark names that are already in place in LETTER2.DOC. The Word for Windows document also uses more than one bookmark name for the same piece of data (Name), so the letter has two separate locations where the contents of Quattro Pro's named block, Name, are placed. All of the {POKE} commands use the DDEChannel number stored in DDE_Num and put the result this macro instruction returns in the cell named Result.

▼ TIP: Use the Result argument of the DDE
commands when you are debugging
the macro.

When you have a macro containing DDE instructions that are not behaving
correctly, use the Result argument of the {EXECUTE}, {POKE}, and {RE-
QUEST} commands to learn the status of each individual DDE command.
You will want to use different cells for each DDE command's Result function.
You can also do this using the same cell when you run the macro using the
debugger and you select the Result cell as one of the trace cells.

{REQUEST}   The {REQUEST} command returns information about the other
application that you have established communication with using the {INITIATE}
command.

Format   {REQUEST DDEChannel,DataToReceive,DestBlock<,Result>} is the
format for the {REQUEST} command.

DDEChannel is the number assigned to the DDE connection that the
{INITIATE} command returns. It is a block name or cell address.

DataToReceive is the name of the information you want from the other application. This is entered as a string in quotes. Some of the most frequently used
names used when System is the ProjectName argument of the {INITIATE} command are:

Formats—Returns the Clipboard formats in which the other application can accept
data from the Clipboard.

Selection—Returns the contents of the items selected in the other application. You
must select the items in the other application first.

Status—Returns the status of the other application. For example, if you use this on
another spreadsheet application, the command returns READY when the other
application is ready for your next request.

SysItems—Returns a list of the strings you can use for DataToReceive arguments.
The results depend on the application.

Topics—Returns a list of the open projects in the application.

DestBlock is the cell address or block address where you want to store the
information returned by this command.

Result is a block or cell where this macro instruction puts the result of the
operation. This is either a block name or cell address. When this macro instruction
returns a number less than 32, the {REQUEST} command did not perform properly.

Use   This command returns information about the application you are running in a macro with DDE commands. You can use this command to retrieve the available Clipboard formats so that you can choose the one you want. You can also use this function to return information about the selected application.

Example   You can use this command within an application to return information about the application you are operating with other DDE macro commands. For example, the command {REQUEST DDE_Num,"Formats",E22,Result}, used when the other application is Word for Windows, returns Rich Text Format, TEXT, METAFILEPICT, DIB, BITMAP, and Link. If the command is {REQUEST DDE_Num,"Sysitems",H25,Result} , the command returns SYSITEMS, TOPICS, and FORMATS. If the command is {REQUEST DDE_Num,"Topics",I26,Result}, the command returns System and C:\WINWORD\LETTER2.DOC assuming you have the document LETTER2.DOC open in Word for Windows.

{TERMINATE}   The {TERMINATE} command stops the macro from controlling the other application. This command leaves the application open with any data files in the application still open. After using this macro command, the communication channel to that application and project name is closed so further DDE macro commands directed to the communication channel cause an error, which you can trap with the {ONERROR} command.

Format   {TERMINATE DDEChannel} is the format for the {TERMINATE} command.
   DDEChannel is the number assigned to the DDE connection that the {INITIATE} command returns. It is a block name or cell address.

Use   This command is for breaking the DDE communication channel so that further DDE macro commands will not affect the application.

Example   Figure 14.40 shows a macro that takes data from named cells and puts them into a Word for Windows document. Other macros use this macro after they have put entries into the named cells. This macro uses {EXEC} to start Word for Windows with the LETTER2 document, then uses the {INITIATE} command to establish the connection between Quattro Pro and Word for Windows in the LETTER2.DOC document. Once this connection is established, the {POKE} commands take the entries in B16..B20;F16..F17 and place them into the Word for Windows document. In A12, the {GETLABEL} command prompts users if they want to make further changes to the document. If a user responds with a **Y**, the {TERMINATE} command breaks the connection between Quattro Pro and Word for Windows. The {QUIT} command leaves macro users in Word for Windows so they can make further changes. If you did not include {QUIT}, Quattro Pro for Windows will continue to perform Quattro Pro macro instructions but they are performed within Quattro Pro. Usually, you use {TERMINATE} when you want the other application to remain open. You use the {EXECUTE} command to pass the command to close the application when you want the application closed by the macro. Closing an application using an {EXECUTE} command also closes the communication channel to the closed application.

UI Building Commands

UI building commands let you create a custom user interface. You can design menus that perform commands or other macro instructions. You can use the UI commands to create a complete application that uses a different menu structure than Quattro Pro's default. You can create a menu structure for novices so only the commands they need are readily available. You can also use UI building commands to add commands so all of the macros you created for an application can be run by selecting an item from one of the pull-down items.

{ADDMENU} The {ADDMENU} command adds a menu with its own commands to the Quattro Pro menu. Use this macro command to create your own menu structure.

Format {ADDMENU MenuPath,MenuData} is the format for the {ADDMENU} command.

MenuPath is the string describing where the new command is placed in the menu. It contains the name of the menu path for the command the new menu item is placed before, with each part of the menu selection starting with a slash. For example, to create a menu item that appears between Regression and Invert in the cascade menu you see when you select Advanced Math from the Tools menu, use "/Tools/Advanced Math/Invert" for the MenuPath string. Use <- and -> (hyphen following less than or followed by greater than sign) to put a menu item at the top or bottom of the menu. For example, to create a menu item that appears above Regression in the cascade menu you see when you select Advanced Math from the Tools menu, use "/Tools/Advanced Math/<-" for the MenuPath string.

MenuData is the block name or address that contains the definition for the menu this command creates. Unlike the block for menu definitions of the {MENUBRANCH} and {MENUCALL} macro controls, this block address must include the entire menu definition rather than merely the first cell of the menu definition. Figure 14.41 shows a menu definition in B10..G18. In the first row is MENU followed by the name of the menu. The several rows define the menu items in the menu. In the first column below the menu name are the names of the menu items. As in the menu title, an ampersand (&) is used to the left of the character to underline. The second column contains the link instruction telling Quattro Pro wwhat to do when the menu item is selected. This is the same as the link instructions dialog boxes use. Menu items use Clicked, Init, Activate, and Deactivate after ON and then often DOMACRO followed by macro instructions or MACRO and the macro name. In the third column is the text that appears in the status line when the menu item is highlighted. The fourth column lists any short-

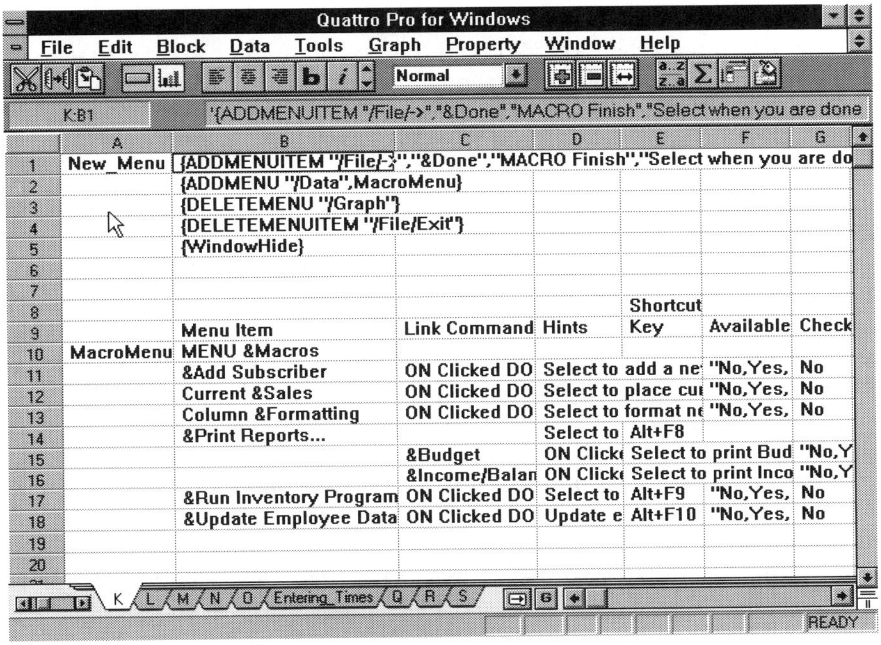

Figure 14.41 Macro Making Changes to the Quattro Pro Menu

cut keys you can press in place of making the menu selections. The fifth column contains Yes or No, followed by a comma to indicate whether the command is available in each of six environments: the desktop, notebook, graph window, dialog or SpeedBar window, input line and Graph's page. If you omit this information, Quattro Pro assumes the menu item is always available. The set of Yesses and Nos that you supply must be in quotes as in "No, Yes, Yes, No, Yes, Yes ". You will also need to include a separate label prefix so that Quattro Pro does not use the first quote to right-align the cell's contents. The last column contains a Yes if the menu item should have a check next to it or contains a No or is blank if the menu item should not have a checkmark next to it. The checkmark is just like the check mark next to the currently active window name in the <u>W</u>indow menu. You can change the menu item's properties even after you create them with this command. The entries in row 8 and 9 in Figure 14.41 are not necessary but are present to help you remember what each column of information is for. When a menu item like <u>P</u>rint Reports in Figure 14.41 displays a cascading menu with additional menu items, the additional menu items are placed one column to the right.

Use This command adds pull-down menus and commands for the pull-down menus to the current Quattro Pro menu. You can use this command rather than {ADDMENUITEM} when you want to add more than one item to the menu structure. Use this command to create a cascading menu that offers additional choices.

Example Figure 14.41 shows a macro that makes several changes to the current menu. The macro uses the {ADDMENU} macro command to add a Macros pull-down menu. The menu is placed to the left of the Data pull-down menu because /Data is the MenuPath argument. The actual menu definition is in B10..G18. In the first row, MENU &Macros identifies the name of the menu. The next rows, until another MENU followed by a menu name, describe the menu items in the Macros pull-down menu. The menu has six menu items—Add Subscriber, Current Sales, Column Formatting, Print Reports..., Run Inventory Program, and Update Employee Data. The ampersand indicates the underlined letters. In the next column, are the instructions Quattro Pro performs when each menu item is selected. Next is the text that appears in the status line when the menu item is highlighted. Some of the menu items have shortcut keys you can press in place of making the menu selections as you can see in the fourth column. The fifth column indicates the environments in which you can select each menu item. The last column selects whether the item has a check next to it. The Print Reports... menu item does not have an instruction in the second column because this menu item displays its own cascade menu. This cascade menu's menu items follow the same format as the pull-down menu items except that the menu items are shifted one column to the right. After this macro is performed, the Macros menu looks like Figure 14.42.

{ADDMENUITEM} The {ADDMENUITEM} command creates a single menu selection in the Quattro Pro menu structure.

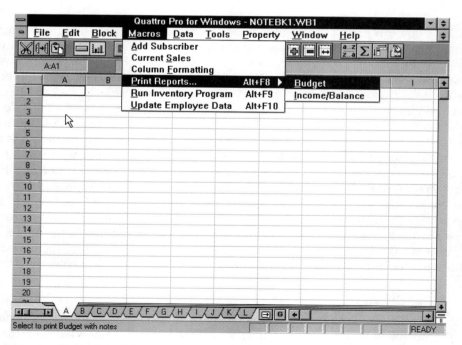

Figure 14.42 Modified Quattro Pro Menu

▼ TIP: Menu changes only apply to the current session

Menu items added and removed with the UI macro commands only affect the current session. When you exit Quattro Pro for Windows and then restart it, the menu commands altered with the UI commands do not appear or have not changed. If you want the menu changes to apply to all Quattro Pro for Windows sessions, save the macro that makes the menu changes in the autoload notebook and name the macro \0.

Format {ADDMENUITEM MenuPath,Command} is the format for the {ADDMENUITEM} command.

MenuPath is the string describing where the new command is placed in the menu. It contains the name of the menu path for the command the new menu item is placed before, with each part of the menu selection starting with a slash. For example, to create a menu item that appears between Regression and Invert in the cascade menu you see when you select Advanced Math from the Tools menu, use "/Tools/Advanced Math/Invert" for the MenuPath string. Use <- and -> (hyphen following a less than or followed by a greater than symbol) to put a menu item at the top or bottom of the menu. For example, to create a menu item that appears above Regression in the cascade menu you see when you select Advanced Math from the Tools menu, use "/Tools/Advanced Math/<-" for the MenuPath string.

Command is the menu item information for the menu item. This argument is actually made up of several arguments that are usually strings in quotes. You can provide the name, the instruction to perform for the menu item, the description, the shortcut key, when the menu item is available, and whether it is marked with a check. This is the same information provided in the six columns of a menu definition as described for the {ADDMENU} macro command.

Use This command adds individual menu items to the existing menu structure. If you want to add a group of menu commands, you should use {ADDMENU} instead.

Example Figure 14.41 shows a macro that makes several changes to the current menu. This macro uses the {ADDMENUITEM} macro command to add a Done menu item to the File menu. The full entry in B1 for the {ADDMENUITEM} command is {ADDMENUITEM "/File/->","&Done","MACRO Finish","Select when you are done","ALT+F4"}. This macro instruction adds a menu item called Done at the bottom of the File menu with the D underlined. When selected, this menu item performs the macro Finish. It also displays "Select when you are done" in the status line when you highlight Done without selecting it. This menu item uses the ALT-F4 key combination. Done is used instead of Exit to leave Quattro Pro, so {DELETEMENUITEM} is used to remove Exit from the File menu.

{DELETEMENU} The {DELETEMENU} command removes a pull-down menu from the Quattro Pro menu structure. The menu you remove can be one you have created or one that is part of Quattro Pro's default menu. Use this macro command to rearrange the menu structure.

Format {DELETEMENU MenuPath} is the format for the {DELETEMENU} command.

MenuPath is the string describing the location of the command to remove from the menu. It contains the name of the menu path for the command, with each part of the menu selection separated with a slash. For example, to remove the Pages menu item from the cascade menu you see when you select Delete in the Block menu, use "/Block/Delete/Pages" for the MenuPath string. Use <- and -> (hyphen following a less than or followed by a greater than symbol) for a menu item at the top or bottom of the menu. For example, to remove Insert Object from the Edit menu, use "/Edit/->" for the MenuPath string.

Use This command removes menus created by Quattro Pro or by the {ADDMENU} macro command. Use this command rather than {DELETEMENUITEM} when you want to remove a menu rather than a single menu item.

Example Figure 14.41 shows a macro that makes several changes to the current menu. This macro uses the {DELETEMENU} macro command to remove the Graph pull-down menu. The {DELETEMENU "/Graph"} removes the entire Graph menu. If you only wanted to remove one of the Graph menu items, you would use {DELETEMENUITEM} instead. You can see from the macro's results shown in Figure 14.42 how this command has removed Graph from the menu bar. This macro removes one of the menu items so the menu bar has room for the Macros menu. You do not want too many menu items, since they clutter the menu bar.

{DELETEMENUITEM} The {DELETEMENUITEM} command removes a single menu selection in the Quattro Pro menu structure.

Format {DELETEMENUITEM MenuPath} is the format for the {DELETE MENUITEM} command.

MenuPath is the string describing the location of the command to remove from the menu. It contains the name of the menu path for the command, with each part of the menu selection separated with a slash. For example, to remove the Pages menu item from the cascade menu you see when you select Delete in the Block menu, use "/Block/Delete/Pages" for the MenuPath string. Use <- and -> (hyphen following a less than or followed by a greater than symbol) for a menu item at the top or bottom of the menu. For example, to remove Insert Object from the Edit menu, use "/Edit/->" for the MenuPath string.

Use This command removes individual menu items from the existing menu structure. The menu item you remove can be one you have created or one that is part of Quattro Pro's default menu. If you want to remove a group of menu commands, you should use {DELETEMENU} instead.

Example Figure 14.41 shows a macro that makes several changes to the current menu. This macro uses the {DELETEMENUITEM} macro command to remove the Exit command from the File menu. Since an {ADDMENUITEM} command in B1 added a Done command in the File menu to take the place of this command, the {DELETEMENUITEM} command in B4 removes the extra command. Now, when you display the File menu, the last item in the menu is Done and the menu does not have an Exit menu item.

{SETMENUBAR} The {SETMENUBAR} command changes the current menu tree to the menu definition stored in a block. This command is also used to change the menu back to Quattro Pro's default menu.

Format {SETMENUBAR <MenuDefinition>} is the format for the {SETMENU BAR} command.

MenuDefinition is the block name or address that contains the definitions for the menus. The block menus must include the full menu definitions rather than merely the first cell. The different columns and their contents you use for a menu definition are described for the {ADDMENU} command; the only difference here is that several menu definitions are given one after another. For example, if you want part of a menu definition to appear after the Macros menu described in Figure 14.41, B19 will contain MENU followed by the name of the next menu. The menu items for a pull-down menu are the ones from one MENU command to the next in the MenuDefinition block. Each of the definitions appears on the menu bar in the order it is defined in the MenuDefinition block. If you want to reset the menu definition to return to Quattro Pro's default menu structure, omit the MenuDefinition argument.

Use This command substitutes the current menu with a menu definition you have stored in a block. Use this command to make many menu changes all at once rather than using several {ADDMENU} and {ADDMENU} commands.

Example As an example of the {SETMENUBAR} command, you can change the menu bar in Quattro Pro for Windows to only contain the Macros pull-down menu with the command {SETMENUBAR MacroMenu}. This command will remove all of the other menus as Quattro Pro places the Macros menu on the menu bar. Usually this command is used when the menu definition block is larger to create a complete menu that provides all of the commands you want to use for an application. When you want to return to Quattro Pro's default menu, execute the macro command {SETMENUBAR}.

Object Commands

The object macro commands create objects and make changes to them. You can use these commands to create drawings, floating objects on the notebook, dialog boxes, and graphs. Once you create these objects, you can continue using other object macro commands to change the properties and other features of the objects.

{COLUMNWIDTH}   The {COLUMNWIDTH} command changes the column width of a block of cells.

Format   {COLUMNWIDTH Block,FirstPane?,Set/Reset/Auto,Size} is the format for the {COLUMNWIDTH} command.
Block is the block reference that includes the columns you want to resize.
FirstPane? contains a 1 if the upper or left pane contains the columns to resize or a 0 if the lower or right pane contains the columns to resize. If the window is not split into panes, you can enter either number for this argument.
Set/Reset/Auto contains a 0 if you are using this macro instruction to set the column width, a 1 if you are using this macro instruction to reset the column width, or a 2 if you are using this macro instruction to automatically size the columns acording to their contents.
Size contains the size of the columns if Set/Reset/Auto contains a 0, is empty if Set/Reset/Auto contains a 1, or contains the optionally specified number of extra characters if Set/Reset/Auto contains a 2. When Size is the size of the columns, enter the column width as the number of twips where each twip is 1/1440 of an inch.

Use   Use this command to change column widths. Use this macro command rather than using {SETPROPERTY} to change the block's column width property when the block you want resized is not currently selected.

Example   You can use the {COLUMNWIDTH} command anytime you need to resize columns. If you have a block named Report_Ouput that you want to resize to fit its entries, you can include the macro instruction {COLUMNWIDTH Report_Output,0,2,1}. This macro instruction resizes all of the columns in the block Report_Output to be as wide as the entries with one extra space. The other way you can perform the same command is to have the macro instructions {SELECTBLOCK Report_Output} and {SETPROPERTY Column_Width,"Auto Width,1740,1"}.

{CREATEOBJECT}   The {CREATEOBJECT} command creates objects normally added by using one of the SpeedBar buttons. You can use this command for manipulating dialog boxes and graphs.

Format   {CREATEOBJECT ObjectName,x1,y1x2,y2<,x3,y3,...>} is the format for the {CREATEOBJECT} command.

ObjectName is the name of the object you want to create. When you use this command to add an object to the graph, ObjectName is a string that contains Line, Arrow, Rectangle, Ellipse, Rounded Rectangle, Text, Polyline, Polygon, Freehand Polyline, or Freehand Polygon. When you use this command to add an object to a dialog box, ObjectName is a string that contains Button, CheckBox, RadioButton, BitmapButton, Label, EditField, SpinCtrl, GroupBox, RangeBox, ComboBox, PickList, FielCtrl, ColCtrl, ScrollBar, HScrollBar, or TimeCtrl.

x1, y1, x2, y2, x3, y3,... are the coordinates of the object you are creating. X1 and Y1 indicate the object's starting point. The subsequent sets of coordinates select each end point of the object. Many of the objects only use two sets of coordinates to mark the opposite sides of the shape, but other objects that have multiple points use several more coordinates. The coordinates are measured from the top left corner of the graph or dialog box.

Use   This command creates drawn objects in a graph and creates dialog box components. Use this command to have a macro add a drawing to your graph or modify an application's dialog box as the application changes.

Example   Figure 14.43 shows a macro that puts the identical lines and text on any graph. This macro uses the {CREATEOBJECT} command to add lines and text objects to the graph. You can see these objects in the inserted graph on the right

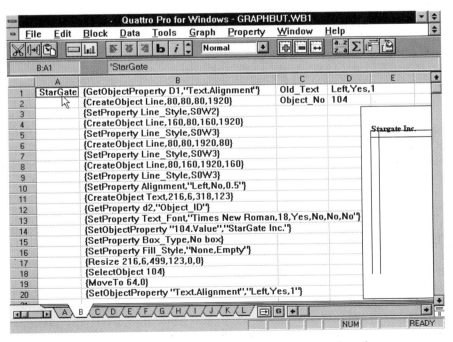

Figure 14.43   Macro for Adding Lines and Text to a Graph

of the notebook window. In B2, B4, B6, and B8, the {CREATEOBJECT} command draws a line. The lines start at different coordinates. For example, the first line is drawn from 80,80 to 80,1920. As each of the lines are drawn, their properties are changed with the {SETPROPERTY} command. In B11, another {CREATEOBJECT} command adds a text object from 216,6 to 318,123. This text object does not have any entry until the {SETOBJECTPROPERTY} command in B14 changes the object's values.

{FLOATCREATE}   The {FLOATCREATE} command creates a floating graph or SpeedButton.

Format   {FLOATCREATE Type,UpperCell,xoffset,yoffset,LowerCell,xoffset2, yoffset2,Text} is the format for the {FLOATCREATE} command.

Type is a string containing the type of object you want to add. It is either Graph to add a floating graph or Button to add a SpeedButton.

UpperCell is the cell address or block name where you want the object to start.

Xoffset is the horizontal distance between the left side of the cell selected by UpperCell and the left side of the floating graph or SpeedButton.

Yoffset is the vertical distance between the top of the cell selected by UpperCell and the top of the floating graph or SpeedButton.

LowerCell is the cell address or block name where you want the object to end.

Xoffset2 is the horizontal distance between the left side of the cell selected by LowerCell and the right side of the floating graph or SpeedButton.

Yoffsets is the vertical distance between the top of the cell selected by LowerCell and the bottom of the floating graph or SpeedButton.

Text is the text to appear on the SpeedButton's face when the Type argument is Button.

Use   This command creates and sets the size of floating graphs and SpeedButtons.

Example   Figure 14.44 shows the Add_Save macro that creates a SpeedButton on the current notebook to save the current notebook. In this macro, the {LET} command puts the address of the current cell in the named block This_Cell so other macro instructions can incorporate the current cell's address in their macro instructions. The macro instructions in B4 and B7 are actually string formulas that incorporate the cell address stored in This_Cell into their macro instructions. The {FLOATCREATE} command in B4 creates a SpeedButton starting at the current cell. This SpeedButton fills the current cell and the cell next to it. The SpeedButton's upper left corner is the upper left corner of the current cell and the SpeedButton's lower right corner is the upper left corner of the cell two columns to the right and one column down. This SpeedButton uses the text Save in place of the default of Button#. The SpeedButton does not actually perform any instructions until the {SETPROPERTY} command in B6 sets the button's Macro property to {FileSave}. Once the button is created, the last macro instruction in Add_Save selects the cell with the address stored in This_Cell.

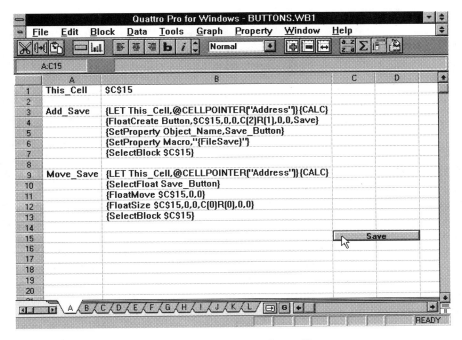

Figure 14.44   Macro for Adding a Save Macro Button

▼ TIP: To fill a cell, select one cell farther away from the corner.

If you want a floating graph or SpeedButton to fill all of a cell, select the cell that is one cell below and one cell to the right. Since the offset measurements for floating graphs and SpeedButtons use the upper left corner of the cell, if you select the cell that is one below and one to the right of the cell you want to use, and use 0 as the second horizontal and vertical offsets, the floating graph or SpeedButton will fill the cell you want.

{FLOATMOVE}   The {FLOATMOVE} command moves a floating graph or SpeedButton you have already created to another location. The floating graph or SpeedButton must be selected before you use this command to move it.

Format   {FLOATMOVE UpperCell,xoffset,yoffset} is the format for the {FLOATMOVE} command.

UpperCell is the cell address or block name where you want the moved object to start.

Xoffset is the new horizontal distance between the left side of the cell selected by UpperCell and the left side of the floating graph or SpeedButton.

Yoffset is the new vertical distance between the top of the cell selected by UpperCell and the top of the floating graph or SpeedButton.

Use   This command is for changing the position of a floating graph or SpeedButton that you have created with other commands.

Example   Figure 14.44 shows the Move_Save macro that moves the Save_Button SpeedButton the Add_Save macro added on the current notebook at the current cell. In this macro, the {LET} command puts the address of the current cell in the named block This_Cell so other macro instructions can incorporate the current cell's address in their macro instructions. The macro instructions in B11..B13 are string formulas that incorporate the cell address stored in This_Cell into their macro instructions. After the {SELECTFLOAT} command selects the Save_Button SpeedButton, the {FLOATMOVE} command can move it from its previous location to start at the current cell. After the SpeedButton is moved with the {FLOATMOVE} command, the {FLOATSIZE} command can readjust its size to match the column widths and row heights of the current cell and the cell to its right. Finally, the last macro instruction selects the current cell.

{FLOATSIZE}   The {FLOATSIZE} command changes the size of a floating graph or SpeedButton you have already created. The floating graph or SpeedButton must be selected before you use this command to move it.

Format   {FLOATSIZE UpperCell,xoffset,yoffset,LowerCell,xoffset2,yoffset2} is the format for the {FLOATSIZE} command.

UpperCell is the cell address or block name where you want the object to start.

Xoffset is the horizontal distance between the left side of the cell selected by UpperCell and the left side of the floating graph or SpeedButton.

Yoffset is the vertical distance between the top of the cell selected by UpperCell and the top of the floating graph or SpeedButton.

LowerCell is the cell address or block name where you want the object to end.

Xoffset2 is the horizontal distance between the left side of the cell selected by LowerCell and the right side of the floating graph or SpeedButton.

Yoffsets is the vertical distance between the top of the cell selected by LowerCell and the bottom of the floating graph or SpeedButton.

Use   This command changes the size of a floating graph or SpeedButton. Use this command to rearrange the floating graph or SpeedButton within an application.

Example   Figure 14.44 shows the Move_Save macro that moves the Save_Button SpeedButton the Add_Save macro added on the current notebook and resizes it to fit the current cell and the cell to its right. In this macro, the {LET} command puts the address of the current cell in the named block This_Cell so other macro instructions can incorporate the current cell's address in their macro instructions.

The macro instructions in B11..B13 are string formulas that incorporate the cell address stored in This_Cell into their macro instructions. After the {SELECTFLOAT} command selects the Save_Button SpeedButton, the {FLOATMOVE} command moves the SpeedButton from its previous position to start at the current cell. After this {FLOATMOVE} command is performed, the SpeedButton is readjusted to start in the upper left corner of the current cell and to end in the upper left corner of the cell two columns to the right and one row down to fill the two cells.

{GETOBJECTPROPERTY}   The {GETOBJECTPROPERTY} command puts the current setting of one of an object's properties into a cell.

Format   {GETOBJECTPROPERTY Cell,Object.Property} is the format for the {GETOBJECTPROPERTY} command.

Cell is the cell address or block name where you want to store the value of the object's property as a label.

Object is the string describing the object whose property you want to return information about.

Property is the name of the property you want the value of. It must be an applicable property for the object. The object and property are usually enclosed in quotes with a period separating them. Property is usually the name of the property in a dialog box or menu when you inspect the object's properties.

Use   This command is for any time the macro needs to know the current value of an object's properties. You may want to use this command to store an object's properties at the beginning of a macro so later you can return it to its previous setting.

Example   Figure 14.43 shows a macro that puts the lines and text on a graph, as you can partially see from the floating graph in the notebook page. At the beginning of the macro, the {GETOBJECTPROPERTY} command takes the value of the Alignment property for text objects in a graph and stores them in D1. In B10, the {SETPROPERTY} command changes the Alignment property for text drawn objects so wordwrapping is turned off. After the objects are created, the {SET OBJECTPROPERTY} command in B20 uses the entry in D1 to return the setting of the Text Alignment property to the previous setting.

{GETPROPERTY}   The {GETPROPERTY} puts the value of a property for the currently selected object into a cell. This command is just like {GETOBJECTPROPERTY} except that you do not identify the object, since it uses the currently selected object.

Format   {GETPROPERTY Property,Cell} is the format for the {GETPROPERTY} command.

Property is the string containing the name of the property you want the value of. It must be an applicable property for the currently selected object. Property is usually the name of the property in a dialog box or menu when you inspect the object's properties.

Cell is the cell address or block name where you want to store the value of the object's property as a label.

Use   This command is often used to return the name or identification information of an object that later will be modified by other object macro commands.

Example   Figure 14.43 shows a macro that draws the same set of lines and text on the currently displayed graph. The floating graph shows the beginning of the text and lines this macro creates. After the {CREATEOBJECT} command adds the lines and text objects, the macro has several commands that change how the text object appears. This macro uses the {GETPROPERTY} command in B12 to return the object's identification number. Every drawn object on a graph has one. The property this macro command uses is Object_ID and the information is placed in Object_No (D2). For example, for the graph displayed the last time this macro was used, the object identification number of the text object is 104. Once this information is in the cell, other macro instructions, like the ones in B14 and B18, use this information to modify the object. The macro instructions in B14, B18, and B20 are string formulas. B14 contains the formula +"{SETOBJECTPROPERTY "&@CHAR(34)&D2&".Value" &&@CHAR(34)&","&@CHAR(34)&"StarGate Inc."&@CHAR(34)&"}". B18 contains the formula +"{SELECTOBJECT "&D2&"}". B20 contains the formula +"{SETOBJECTPROPERTY "&@CHAR(34)&"Text.Alignment"&@CHAR(34)&"," &&@CHAR(34)&D1&@CHAR(34)&"}".

{MOVETO}   The {MOVETO} command moves objects in a graph or dialog box to another location. An object you are moving must be selected before you use this command to move it. If you have several objects selected, they are all moved as a unit as if you are moving a single object.

Format   {MOVETO x,y} is the format for the {MOVETO} command.
   X is the new horizontal position from the upper left corner of the graph or dialog box where the selected object is moved.
   Y is the new vertical distance from the upper left corner of the graph or dialog box where the selected object is moved.

Use   This command is for changing the position of an object in a graph or in a dialog box that you have created with other commands.

Example   Figure 14.43 shows a macro that draws the same set of lines and text on the currently displayed graph and a floating graph that shows the beginning of the text and lines this macro creates. After the {CREATEOBJECT} commands create the lines and the text object and other commands change their properties, the {MOVETO} command moves the text object to another location. The new location starts at the x,y coordinates of 64,0.

{RESIZE}   The {RESIZE} command changes the size of a graph object or a dialog box component you have already created. A graph object or dialog box object must be selected before you use this command to move it. If you have several objects selected, they are proportionally resized as if you are resizing a single object.

Format {RESIZE x,y,NewWidth,NewHeight<,VertFlip?<,HorizFlip?>>} is the format for the {RESIZE} command.

X is the new horizontal position from the upper left corner of the graph or dialog box where the selected object begins. It is a number or a cell reference to one.

Y is the new vertical distance from the upper left corner of the graph or dialog box where the selected object begins. It is a number or a cell reference to one.

NewWidth is the number of the width of the selected object you are resizing.

NewHeight is the number of the height of the selected object you are resizing.

VertFlip? is a 1 to flip it vertically so the object's top becomes its bottom and vice versa.

HorizFlip? is a 1 to flip it horizontally so the object's left side becomes its right side and vice versa.

Use This command changes the size and position of a graph or dialog box object. Use this command to rearrange a graph you are drawing or a dialog box a macro has created.

Example Figure 14.43 shows a macro that puts the same set of lines and text on a graph. This macro uses the {CREATEOBJECT} command to add lines and text objects to the graph. You can see these objects in the inserted graph on the right of the notebook window. The text object is initially added using a default size, but it needs to be enlarged to fit the larger text. The {RESIZE} command in B17 changes the size of the object so its upper left coordinates are 216,6 and its new size is 499 wide by 123 high. The object is not flipped.

{ROWCOLSHOW} The {ROWCOLSHOW} command hides or displays columns or rows in a block.

Format {ROWCOLSHOW Block,Show?,Row or Col,FirstPane?} is the format for the {ROWCOLSHOW} command.

Block is the block reference that includes the columns or rows you want to hide or display.

Show? contains a 0 if you are using this macro instruction to hide columns or rows, or a 1 if you are using this macro instruction to display columns or rows.

Row or Col contains a 0 if you are using this macro instruction to hide or display columns or a 1 if you are using this macro instruction to hide or display rows.

FirstPane? contains a 1 if the upper or left pane contains the columns to resize or an 0 if the lower or right pane contains the columns to resize. If the window is split into panes, you can enter either number for this argument.

Use Use this command to hide or display columns or rows. Use this macro command rather than using {SETPROPERTY} to hide or display columns or rows when the block you want to change is not currently selected.

Example   You can use the {ROWCOLSHOW} command any time you need to hide or display columns or rows. If you have a block named Report_Ouput that you want a macro to print, you may want to include a macro instruction that insures none of the data in this block is hidden. To display all of the columns, you can include the macro instruction {ROWCOLSHOW Report_Output,1,0,1}. To display all of the rows, you can include the macro instruction {ROWCOLSHOW Report_Output,1,1,1}. These two macro instructions display all of the columns and rows in the block Report_Output. The other way you can perform the same function is to have the macro instructions {SELECTBLOCK Report_Output}, {SETPROPERTY Reveal/Hide,"Rows,Reveal"}, and {SETPROPERTY Reveal/Hide,"Columns,Reveal"}.

{ROWHEIGHT}   The {ROWHEIGHT} command changes the row height of a block of cells.

Format   {ROWHEIGHT Block,FirstPane?,Set/Reset,Size} is the format for the {ROWHEIGHT} command.

Block is the block reference that includes the rows you want to resize.

FirstPane? contains a 1 if the upper or left pane contains the rows to resize, or a 0 if the lower or right pane contains the rows to resize. If the window is not split into panes, you can enter either number for this argument.

Set/Reset contains a 0 if you are using this macro instruction to set the row height, or a 1 if you are using this macro instruction to reset the row height.

Size contains the size of the rows if Set/Reset contains a 0, or is empty if Set/Reset contains a 1. When Size is the size of the rows, enter the row height as the number of twips where each twip is 1/1440 of an inch.

Use   Use this command to change row heights. Use this macro command rather than using {SETPROPERTY} to change the block's row height property when the block you want resized is not currently selected.

Example   You can use the {ROWHEIGHT} command any time you need to resize rows. If you have a block named Report_Ouput you want to resize to fit its entries, you can include the macro instruction {ROWHEIGHT Report_Output,0,1,1}. This macro instruction resizes all of the rows in the block Report_Output to be as tall as the tallest entry in the row. The other way you can perform the same command is to have the macro instructions {SELECTBLOCK Report_Output} and {SETPROPERTY Row_Height,"Reset Height,240"}.

{SELECTBLOCK}   The {SELECTBLOCK} command selects a block of cells in the notebook.

Format   {SELECTBLOCK Block} is the format for the {SELECTBLOCK} command.

Block is the cell address, block address, or block name you want to select.

Use This command is for quickly selecting a block in a notebook. Also, this command is for selecting a notebook block after you have selected a floating object.

Example In Figure 14.44, both the Add_Save and the Move_Save macros use the {SELECTBLOCK} command to select a notebook cell. In both macros, a floating SpeedButton is selected—while either creating the SpeedButton or moving it. After the SpeedButton is created or moved, the macro needs to select a notebook cell so the macro's user can return to the task they were performing before the macro added or moved the SpeedButton. In both B7 and B13, the macro instruction is created with the formula +"{SelectBlock "&This_Cell&"}". This string formula incorporates the cell address placed in This_Cell (B1) into the SelectBlock command.

{SELECTFLOAT} The {SELECTFLOAT} command selects a floating graph or SpeedButton on a notebook page.

Format {SELECTFLOAT ObjectID#<,ObjectID#...>} is the format for the {SELECTFLOAT} command.
   ObjectID# is the string containing the name of the object you want to select. You can find this name using the {GETPROPERTY} command. You can select more than one object by separating the object names with commas.

Use This command is for selecting a floating graph or SpeedButton in a notebook. Once the floating graph or SpeedButton is selected, you can use other commands to make changes to the floating graph or SpeedButton.

Example In Figure 14.44, the Move_Save macro repositions the Save_Button SpeedButton to start at the current cell. Before you can use the {FLOATMOVE} and {FLOATSIZE} commands to move and resize the SpeedButton, you need to select it. The {SELECTFLOAT} command in B10 selects this SpeedButton. In this example, you did not have to use a {GETPROPERTY} command to learn the SpeedButton's name. This is because the Add_Save macro gave it a name; you can easily supply the name of the SpeedButton in the {SELECTFLOAT} command.

{SELECTOBJECT} The {SELECTOBJECT} command selects graph or dialog box objects.

Format {SELECTOBJECT ObjectID#<,ObjectID#...>} is the format for the {SELECTOBJECT} command.
   ObjectID# is the string containing the name of the graph or dialog box object you want to select. You can find this name using the {GETPROPERTY} command. You can select more than one object by separating the object names with commas.

Use This command is for selecting objects in a graph or dialog box. Once the graph or dialog box objects are selected, you can use other commands to make changes to them. If you select more than one object with this command, the objects are treated as a unit when you move them, size them, or change their properties.

Example   Figure 14.43 shows a macro that draws the same set of lines and text on the currently displayed graph and a floating graph that shows the beginning of the text and lines this macro creates. The {CREATEOBJECT} command creates the lines and text objects and other commands changes their properties. The {SELECTOBJECT 104} command in B18 selects the object with the object ID of 104. The {GETPROPERTY} command in B12 has put the name of the text object in D2. Using the {SELECTOBJECT} command makes sure the text object is the object you move. You could also use the {SELECTOBJECT} command on the lines to select all of the lines at once and then change their properties at the same time.

{SETGRAPHATTR}   The {SETGRAPHATTR} command changes the property of the currently selected objects in a graph.

Format   {SETGRAPHATTR FillColor,BkgColor,FillStyle,BorderColor,BoxType} is the format for the {SETGRAPHATTR} command.
    FillColor is the string containing the RGB values for the fill color of the selected objects. The string contains the amount of red, green, and blue used to create the desired color.
    BkgColor is the string containing the RGB values for the background color of the selected objects. The string contains the amount of red, green, and blue used to create the desired color.
    FillStyle is a string containing one of the available fill styles. Examples are Solid, None, and Wash.
    BorderColor is the string containing the RGB values for the background color of the selected objects. The string contains the amount of red, green, and blue used to create the desired color.
    BoxType is a description for one of the available box types. It is S followed by a number representing the style number then W followed by a number representing the width.

Use   This command is for changing the properties of the currently selected graph objects. Use this command in place of {SETPROPERTY} when you want to change the Fill Color, Background Color, Fill Style, Border Color, and Box Type properties using a single macro command.

Example   If you have a macro that selects several drawn graph objects, you can use the {SETGRAPHATTR} macro command to change the appearance of selected graph objects. An example is {SETGRAPHATTR "255,255,255","0,0,0","Wash",,S5W1} to set the Fill Style. This makes all of the selected objects have a fill color of white, a background color of black, a wash fill style, and an invisible border.

{SETOBJECTPROPERTY}   The {SETOBJECTPROPERTY} command changes the property of an object. You can change the properties of graph objects, dialog box elements, menu items, block, pages, notebooks, and applications. This command makes Quattro Pro's Object Inspector feature available to macros.

Format {SETOBJECTPROPERTY Object.Property,Setting} is the format for the {SETOBJECTPROPERTY} command.

Object is the name of the object with the property you want to change. Property is the name of the property you want to set. It must be an applicable property for the object. Property is usually the name of the property in a dialog box or menu when you inspect the object's properties.

Setting is the string containing the setting you are changing the selected object property to. The value must match the information Quattro Pro expects for the property. You can set the object's properties to match the properties of another object (of the same type) by supplying an object name, period, and property in quotes.

Use This command is for setting the properties of the currently selected objects. Use this command in place of {SETPROPERTY} when the object you want to change is already selected.

Example The StarGate macro in Figure 14.43 uses the {SETOBJECTPROPERTY} command to return the text object properties to their previous setting. In B1, the {GETOBJECTPROPERTY} command puts the settings for the text object in D1. The {SETOBJECTPROPERTY} command takes the entry in this cell and uses it to restore the text object's settings. The macro needs this command because the {SETPROPERTY} command in B13 changed the settings so text did not word wrap. The SETOBJECTPROPERTY command is also used in B14 to set the text that is in the text object. 104 is the object number and Value is the name of the text object property that sets the text that appears in the text object. The graph name is not included because this macro is run in a graph window and the command operates on the current graph.

{SETPROPERTY} The {SETPROPERTY} command changes the property of the currently selected object. You can change the properties of graph objects, dialog box elements, menu items, block, pages, notebooks, and applications. This command makes Quattro Pro's Object Inspector feature available to macros.

Format {SETPROPERTY Property,Setting} is the format for the {SETPROPERTY} command.

Property is the string containing the name of the property you want the value of. It must be an applicable property for the currently selected object. Property is usually the name of the property in a dialog box or menu when you inspect the object's properties.

Setting is the string containing the new value for the property you are changing.

Use This command is often used to return the name or identification information of an object that later will be modified by other object macro commands.

Example   Figure 14.44 shows the Add_Save macro that creates a SpeedButton on the current notebook that saves the current notebook. After the {FLOATCREATE} command creates the initial SpeedButton, the macro uses two {SETPROPERTY} commands to change properties of the SpeedButton. Both instructions use {SETPROPERTY} instead of {SETOBJECTPROPERTY} because the SpeedButton is selected as the {FLOATCREATE} command creates it. The first {SETPROPERTY} command changes the name of the object to Save_Button. The second {SETPROPERTY} command assigns the macro instructions Quattro Pro performs when the button is selected.

Miscellaneous Commands

Quattro Pro has several miscellaneous commands. Two of these commands do not perform actions but are designed for documenting and editing a macro. Other commands are for shifting the contents of the notebook window within the windows. The remaining miscellaneous macro commands are for running slide shows.

{}   The {} command performs no actions but acts as a connector between the macro instruction in the line above and the macro instruction in the line below.

Format   {} is the format of this function.
    This function does not use any arguments.

Use   This macro often appears within other macros to provide additional rows for the documentation. You may want to use this macro command if you have deleted a macro instruction in a cell, but you want the macro execution flow to continue to the macro instructions below the deleted macro instruction.

Example   Many of the macros in this chapter have not included the macro's documentation to the right of the macro instructions due to screen width limitations. Figure 14.45 shows a macro with this spacing problem. For the macro instruction in J4, the display does not have enough space for the user to see the documentation. Therefore, the row below the {IF} command has the {} command (J5). This blank macro instruction provides the room in the documentation column to document the {IF} command without disrupting the macro's flow.

{;}   The {;} command causes Quattro Pro to ignore the text between the semicolon and the right brace. When Quattro Pro reaches this command, it continues to the next instruction.

Format   {;String} is the format of this function.
    String is any set of characters. This information may be a string enclosed in quotes, a cell address, a block name, or a formula.

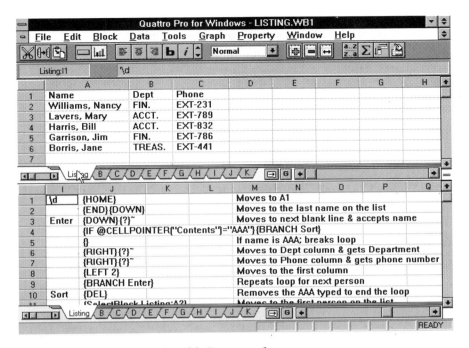

Figure 14.45 Macro Using { } Command

Use This macro command often appears in a macro to document the macro. During macro debugging, other macro instructions are converted to this macro instruction by entering a semicolon after the opening brace to temporarily disable a macro instruction. For example, if you place a semicolon in a {WRITELN} command, Quattro Pro ignores the {;WRITELN} command and performs the next macro instruction.

Example Figure 14.46 shows a macro that uses the {;} command to document the macro and to temporarily disable a {BRANCH} command. When this macro is executed, Quattro Pro skips over the documentation comment in B7. When the {IF} command in B12 is reached, Quattro Pro executes the macro instruction below the {IF} whether the {IF} command's condition is true or not (the macro instruction to be performed if the condition is true is a {;} command).

{HLINE} The {HLINE} command shifts the display in the notebook window one or more columns to the right or left.

Format {HLINE Distance} is the format for the {HLINE} command.

Distance is a number representing the number of columns you want the page in the notebook window shifted. If the value of distance is negative, the notebook page display is shifted that many columns to the left. If it is positive, the display is shifted to the right.

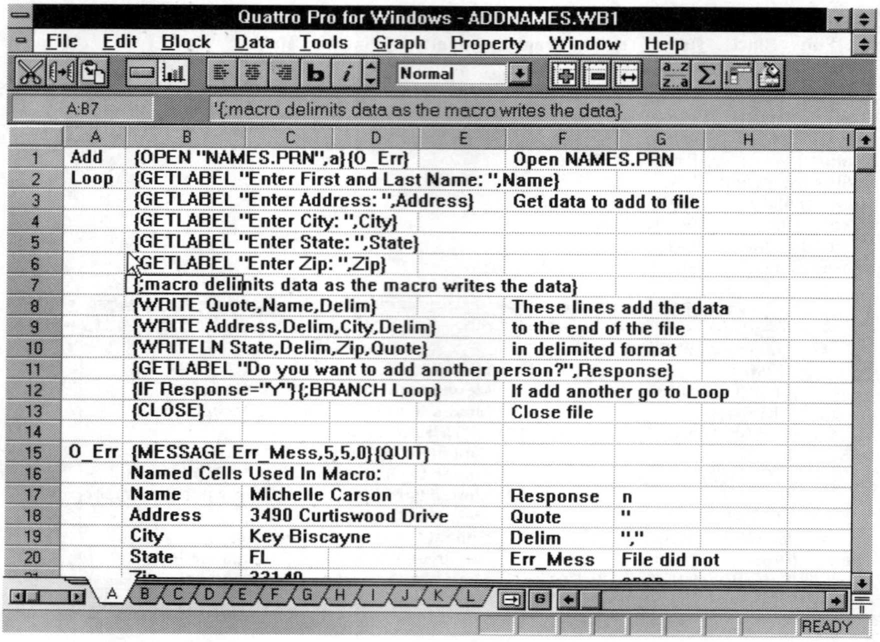

Figure 14.46   Macro Using {;} Command

Use   This command is for changing the part of the notebook that appears in a window. The command only scrolls the display–the selector's position does not change.

Example   If you use {HLINE 5} on the database shown in Figure 14.47, the columns shown will be F through L.

{HPAGE}   The {HPAGE} command shifts the display in the notebook window one or more screens to the right or left.

Format   {HPAGE Distance} is the format for the {HPAGE} command.
Distance is the number of screens you want the page in the notebook window shifted. If the value of distance is negative, the notebook page display shifts that many screens to the left; if it is positive, the display shifts to the right.

Use   This command is for changing the part of the notebook that appears in a window. The command only scrolls the display–the selector's position does not change.

Example   If you use {HPAGE 2} on the database shown in Figure 14.47, the columns shown will be N through V.

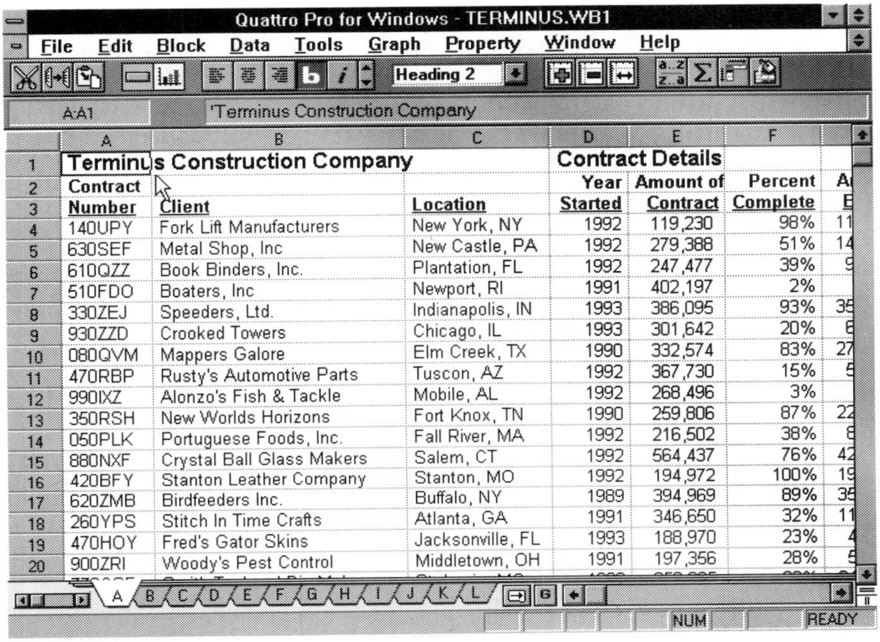

Figure 14.47   Notebook to Illustrate {HLINE}, {HPAGE}, {VLINE}, and {VPAGE} Commands

{VLINE}   The {VLINE} command shifts the display in the notebook window one or more rows up or down.

Format   {VLINE Distance} is the format for the {VLINE} command.

Distance is a number representing the number of rows you want the page in the notebook window shifted. If the value of Distance is negative, the notebook page display is shifted that many rows up;if it is positive, the display is shifted down.

Use   This command is for changing the part of the notebook that appears in a window. It only scrolls the display–the selector's position does not change.

Example   If you use {VLINE 25} on the database shown in Figure 14.47, the next rows shown are 25 through 44.

{VPAGE}   The {VPAGE} command shifts the display in the notebook window up or down by one or more screens.

Format   {VPAGE Distance} is the format for the {VPAGE} command.

Distance is the number of screens you want the page in the notebook window shifted. If the value of Distance is negative, the notebook page display shifts that many screens up; if it is positive, the display shifts that many screens down.

Use   This command is for changing the part of the notebook that appears in a window. It only scrolls the display–the selector's position does not change.

Example   If you use {VPAGE 4} on the database shown in Figure 14.47, the next rows shown are 81 through 100.

GETTING STARTED

In this chapter, you learned how you can create macros using macro command instructions to provide advanced programming features that you might expect more in a programming language than in a spreadsheet. You can use these features to create the macro in Figure 14.58, which formats columns of numbers to currency with 0 decimals. To create this macro, follow these steps:

1.   Make the following entries to enter the steps that the macro will perform. You can make these entries using uppercase or lowercase.

   A1: **Format**
   A4: **Col_Form**
   A8: **Counter**
   A9: **Num_Col**
   B1: **{GETNUMBER How many columns do you want to format?;Num_Col}**
   B2: **{FOR Counter,1,Num_Col,1,Col_Form}**
   B4: **{MARK}{END}{DOWN}**
   B5: **{SETPROPERTY Numeric_Format,"Currency,0"}**
   B6: **{ESC}{RIGHT}**

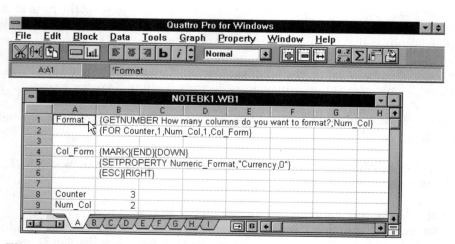

Figure 14.48   Macros Created in Getting Started Section

2. Name the cells used in the macro. Since the labels for the named blocks are all in column A, you can use the labels to name the blocks. Select the block A1..A9. You can select a larger block such as A1..A20, since the command you use to label the cells ignores empty cells. Next, select <u>N</u>ames from the <u>B</u>lock menu and then select <u>L</u>abels, <u>R</u>ight, and OK. Entering this command names B1 as Format, B4 as Col_Form, B8 as Counter, and B9 as Num_Col.

3. Press CTRL-PGDN to move to B:A1.

4. Make the following entries:

   A1: **Yearly Sales**
   A2: **Division A**
   A3: **Division B**
   A4: **Division C**
   B1: **1991**
   B2: **65000**
   B3: **80000**
   B4: **45000**
   C1: **1992**
   C2: **70000**
   C3: **35000**
   C4: **60000**

5. Execute the macro you have created. Move to B:B2. Press ALT-F2 (MACRO) to display the Run Macro dialog box. When Quattro Pro prompts for a macro name, select Format from the <u>M</u>acros/Namedblocks list box and select OK. When the {GETNUMBER} command prompts you for the number of columns you want to format, type **2** and select OK. This macro first formats B2..B4, then formats C2..C4. You can use this macro to format a varying number of columns of values, since the {FOR} command only repeats the macro commands in Col_Form the number of times you enter with the {GETNUMBER} command.

Appendix A

Installing Quattro Pro

Installing Quattro Pro is a simple process. Quattro Pro has an installation application that performs most of the installation for you. The installation application copies the program files from the disks to your hard drive. After Quattro Pro is installed, you are ready to use Quattro Pro.

THE INSTALLATION PROCEDURE

When you install Quattro Pro, you run an installation application. The installation process creates a directory for your Quattro Pro program files. Next, it copies the program files from the disks. Finally, the installation application prompts for several settings.

To install Quattro Pro to your hard disk, follow these steps:

1. Insert Disk 1 of the Quattro Pro disks in a floppy disk drive, and close the door (if any).

2. Run the installation program. If the first disk is in drive A, select Run from the File menu in the Program Manager, enter **A:INSTALL** in the Command Line text box and select OK.

3. Enter the registration information in the first screen of the Quattro Pro installation application. Enter your name, your company name, and your serial number, switching between the text boxes by pressing TAB. Enter the drive that contains the floppy disks you are installing from and the pathname of the directory to which you want Quattro Pro installed. The default installation directory is C:\QPW.

   Select from the three check boxes to decide which parts of Quattro Pro for Windows you want to install. Select the Quattro Pro for Windows check box to install Quattro Pro and its necessary components, the Database Desktop check box to install the Database Desktop, which allows you to access and query external databases, or the Sample and Clip Art Files check box to install the sample and clip art files that you can use with Quattro Pro. You can change how Quattro Pro is installed by selecting the Installation Options button that opens the Installation Options dialog box. The Create Program Manager Group check box is selected so the installation process adds a Quattro Pro for Windows group to the Program Manager. The Modify AUTOEXEC.BAT file check box is selected so the installation program will modify your AUTOEXEC.BAT file to include statements that make running Quattro Pro easier. You can also select the Network Installation button if you want to install Quattro Pro so that it can be used on a network. If you are installing the Database Desktop and you do not want the database driver files the Desktop uses placed in C:\WINDOWS\SYSTEM, you can select the ODAPI Directory button and provide another location for these files. When you are finished making selections in the Installation Options dialog box, select OK to return to the main installation dialog box.

4. When you are finished making your installation option choices and have entered the registration information, select Install. The installation application starts to read the files on the disk and writes them to the hard drive. The speedometer lets you monitor the progress.

5. Each time the installation application displays a message prompting for the next disk, remove the current disk and insert the next disk in the same drive, or enter the drive containing the next disk in the text box. Once the disk is inserted and any door or latch is closed, select OK to start reading and writing the files.

When Quattro Pro has finished, it displays a message that the installation is completed. Select OK to leave this box. As a default, you are then shown the README file containing release information about Quattro Pro. You can close the README file by selecting ESC. This also exits the installation application.

If you do not have the DOS program SHARE.EXE loaded, when you leave the installation program you will be prompted to add this to the path statement in your AUTOEXEC.BAT or CONFIG.SYS file. This program is needed to run the Database Desktop correctly.

Appendix B

Windows Basics

If Quattro Pro for Windows is your first Windows application, you will want to know a few basics about Windows to efficiently use Quattro Pro for Windows. Windows is a Graphical User Interface (GUI) designed to make it easier for you to use your computer's abilities. With Windows, instead of typing complex command codes, the tasks you can do are presented in a more visual and intuitive fashion. Precise coding becomes less important because Windows asks you for the required information to complete commands, rather than waiting for you to remember or find the correct format with which to enter a command.

Most programs designed for Windows, commonly called applications, have a similar feel, or interface to them. Most of the components are similar, if not identical, to other applications. The advantage of this similarity between applications is that once you have learned how to use one Window's application, you have a good idea how to work with many of the other applications. You still need to learn about the features of the specific application and the most efficient methods of using it, but the basic methods for accessing commands apply to all applications.

In this appendix, you will learn the basics of Windows. First, you will learn about the visual components of Windows. After that, you will learn how to use a mouse or a keyboard to make selections in Windows. You will learn elementary techniques for controlling the display on your screen and how to manipulate Windows components. You will also learn a little about three applications of Windows: the Program Manager, File Manager, and the Print Manager. This appendix assumes Windows is already installed on your machine. If not, you need to install Windows by following the directions that accompany the package.

STARTING WINDOWS

To start Windows, turn on your computer system. After it runs diagnostic tests, you will see the DOS prompt. Since you are using a computer system with a hard drive, the prompt is probably C>. At this prompt, type **WIN** and press ENTER. Win is the command you enter to start Windows. Since installing Windows modifies your AUTOEXEC.BAT file, you can start from any directory.

VISUAL COMPONENTS OF WINDOWS

Windows uses graphical features to make using your computer easy. Knowing the graphics that Windows uses makes using Windows and Windows applications easier. You can carry out complex commands, with the greatest of ease. The graphics Windows displays are either contained in windows or represented as icons.

Windows

The Windows display consists of windows for each application you run. These windows are the frame within which applications and documents appear. All windows have certain features in common which help you control them and the information within them. In this section you will learn about the basic components of the windows.

An application can have two types of windows: application windows and document windows. Applications windows run applications, while documents contain the data the application uses. Figure B.1 shows two document windows open inside an application window. Application windows that can only use one set of data at a time often do not use document windows. Most Windows applications that display document windows let you have several documents open in the application window at the same time. When you close an application window, you are exiting the application that is running within that window. If you close a document window, you are removing the document from the application. Document windows appear within the application window they belong to. Unless you save a document in a file before you close the window, you will lose the document that you created in that window. In Quattro Pro, the application window contains Quattro Pro for Windows and any document windows that contain the data you use in Quattro Pro. Sometimes you can enlarge a document window so it fills the application window.

A document or application window can be active or inactive. The difference is which window is immediately affected by your selections. For example, in Figure B.1, the 93SALES.WB1 document window is active because it is on the top. When you make selections and entries, they affect this window rather than the INVOICES.WB1 window. Also, since the Quattro Pro for Windows window is active, when you make a selection from a menu bar, you are selecting from the Quattro Pro menu rather than the Program Manager or another application window you have open at the time.

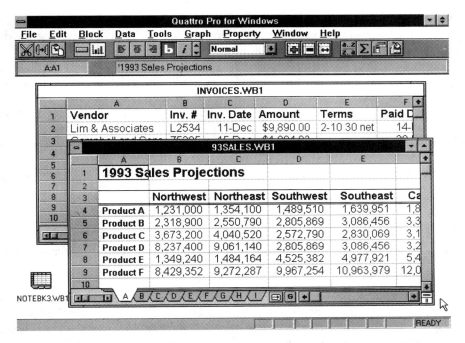

Figure B.1 An Application Window Containing Document Windows

TITLE BAR All windows have title bars that tell you the contents of the window. If the window is an application window, the title bar displays the name of the application as in Quattro Pro for Windows. If the window is a document window, then the title bar either displays the file name of the document or a temporary name, to be replaced when you first save the document to a file. In Quattro Pro, document names are the names of notebooks into which data is organized. If you enlarge the document window to fill the Quattro Pro application window, the notebook name will appear in the application title bar. Title bars come in two colors. The darker one in Figure B.1, 93SALES.WBI, indicates the active window. The lighter one in Figure B.1, INVOICES.WBI, indicates an inactive window. Both document and application windows use different colors to indicate which is active.

CONTROL MENU BOX The control menu box appears on the left edge of the title bar, and is the box filled with the long hyphen. When this button is selected it displays a menu that offers you selections of commands used for controlling the window. Using the options on this menu, you can size or move the window, close it, or switch to another window. Later in this appendix, you will learn how to use the control menu box.

SIZING BUTTONS   The sizing buttons appear on the right end of the title bar. These buttons provide shortcuts for changing the size of the window. The inside button with the down arrow is the minimize button. When you select this button, the window reduces to a small icon. The exact icon that a window reduces is controlled by the application that appears in the window or by the document that appears in the window. The single up arrow is the maximize button. When you select this button, the window grows to its maximum size. If you maximize an application window, the window fills your entire screen. If you maximize a document window, the window fills the application window. When a window is maximized, the maximize button has two arrows, pointing both down and up. It is now the restore button. When you select the restore button, the window changes back to its intermediate size.

MENU BAR   The menu bar appears immediately under the title bar in application windows. Each word on the menu bar is the title of a specific menu. When you select a menu title, as described later in this appendix, a menu is displayed. The menu presents you with various commands that you can select.

SCROLL BARS   Scroll bars appear at the right or bottom of document or application windows. They have three parts: the arrows at either end of the bar; the scroll bar itself, which is the long bar between the arrows; and the scroll box, which is the box displayed along the scroll bar. Scroll bars are used when there is more information than can be displayed at the current window size. They allow you to move to sections of the window that cannot be displayed. For example, if you have a lot of data entered in Quattro Pro, you cannot see all of the model in one window and still read it. In this case, you can use the scroll bars to move through the document.

ICONS   Icons are small graphic images. Some icons are used to represent minimized windows. These icons are individualized to indicate the minimized application. Other icons can represent the document window you have minimized. For example, you can minimize notebooks to show the notebooks as icons instead of windows. Quattro Pro and Windows use different icons for other objects you can see. These icons are small pictures of the objects they represent.

SELECTING IN WINDOWS

As you can tell from the discussion of windows, selecting is how choices are made and commands are executed in Windows. Because Windows shows you most of what you need, you simply have to select from the offered choices. When you know how to select menu options, buttons, and other items, you are halfway to knowing how to use Windows. Selecting can be done with either the mouse or the keyboard. Usually, the mouse is easier.

Using Your Mouse

A mouse has two parts. One is the small tracking device that you hold in your hand. This part of the mouse is the physical object that you move. The second part is the mouse pointer which appears on the screen. Your mouse can either be a true mouse, which is a small hand-held device that you move across a flat surface, or some other type of tracking device such as a pen-and-stylus, a trackball, or a joystick. The mouse or tracking object usually has two buttons, the left and right mouse button. If your mouse or tracking device has three buttons, you will find that the middle one is generally ignored. As you move the external mouse, the mouse pointer moves on the screen. The mouse pointer can change shapes, depending on what windows components it is pointing to, but it always has the same purpose. The position of the mouse pointer tells you which Windows component you are going to affect when you make a selection.

You can carry out several actions with a mouse. The easiest action is to point to an object. This simply means to move the mouse until the mouse pointer is pointing at an object on the screen. Sometimes, when you move your mouse to some objects, you will see the mouse pointer change its shape to match the action that you now use the mouse to do.

You can also drag a mouse. When you drag a mouse, you point the mouse at an object at the screen and then press the left mouse button. Without releasing the left mouse button, move the mouse to another position on the screen. Then release the mouse button. When you do this, you are dragging and releasing the object with the mouse. You can drag objects to change their size or place. In Quattro Pro, you can even use dragging to copy or move data. In some cases, when you drag a mouse, you are drawing a dashed rectangle that selects everything in the rectangle.

One of the most important things you can do with a mouse is to click it on an object. When you click on an object, you point the mouse at an object and click a mouse button once, quickly. Clicking is used for making selections. For example, to select an item in a menu bar or in a menu displayed by a menu bar's item, click it. In this book, when the text mentions selecting a menu item or command, click the menu item's text to select it with the mouse. Often, when you click an object once, the selected object is highlighted. Double-clicking tends to execute commands, such as a menu option or a command button. When you double-click an object, click the object twice quickly.

Using the Keyboard to Select

You can duplicate most mouse actions with the keyboard. Windows is designed to let you make most selections with the mouse or the keyboard. You can use whichever is more convenient. When you are using the keyboard to enter data, you may find using the keyboard easier since your hands are already on the keyboard.

The menus in Windows are activated with the ALT key. You can activate one of the menus for an item in the current menu bar by pressing ALT and the underlined letter at the same time. All items on a menu have an underlined letter as shown in Figure B.2, as do menu options and dialog box items. This underlined letter is the letter that you can type to select an item with the keyboard. If you press the ALT key without an underlined letter key within an application, it normally makes the menu bar active. Once the menu bar is active, you can type the underlined letter to select the menu option. You can also press the RIGHT and LEFT ARROW keys to move to the menu item or control menu box. You can open these menus by pressing ENTER or the DOWN ARROW. From the menu now displayed, you can type the underlined letter of the option you want, or press the arrow keys to move through the menu options until you have highlighted the one you want to select and press ENTER. In this appendix, when the text mentions selecting a menu item or command, use the ALT key to activate the menu and type the underlined letter to select menu selections with the keyboard. For the control menu boxes, you can press ALT-SPACEBAR to select the active application window's control menu box, and press ALT-HYPHEN to select the active document window's control menu box.

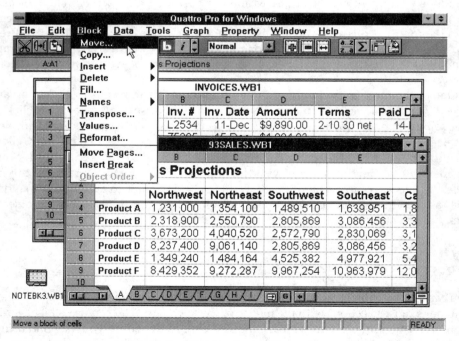

Figure B.2   Menu Options with Underlined Letters to Make Selection Easier

USING WINDOWS

Now that you know the screen components of Windows and how to select objects and commands, you are ready to start using Windows and Windows applications. In this section, you will learn how to start an application, and how to switch between applications or document windows.

When you first start Windows, you see a screen with the application window for the Program Manager as in Figure B.3. The screen will appear differently depending on the settings from the last time you used Windows. The Program Manager is the central application for Windows. It controls the applications that you are using. From this application, you can start and run other applications. You can also end the Program Manager when you are finished with Windows.

Using the Program Manager

When you start Windows, you probably see the Program Manager. The Program Manager contains the programs you have installed for Windows. From this window, you can select the Windows applications you want to use. The document windows in the Program Manager are called group windows. When you start Windows, some group windows may be minimized as in Figure B.3 so they appear as icons. The group windows contain program groups that are groups of applications you can use with Windows. When these program group windows are expanded, you will see other icons inside of them. These icons are called program items. Program items symbolize applications or documents. The program items are arranged into program groups so that related items are all stored in the same group. By selecting a program item, you start or open the application or document that it symbolizes.

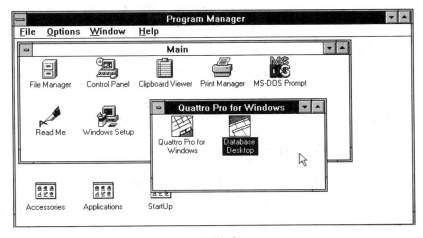

Figure B.3   Program Manager Window

STARTING APPLICATIONS   To start an application, you must select its group window and then select the application from the group window. After you have installed Quattro Pro for Windows, one of the Program Manager's groups is the Quattro Pro for Windows program group. In that program group is the Quattro Pro for Windows program item. Selecting this program item starts Quattro Pro for Windows.

The first step of starting an application is displaying the group window for the program group containing the application you want. You have several methods to select a program group to restore it to a window. You can double-click the program group's icon. You can press CTRL-TAB until the group you want is highlighted, and then press ENTER. The third is to activate the Window menu in the Program Manager menu bar (by clicking Window or by pressing ALT and typing **W**). At the bottom of this menu is a listing of all the program groups. You can click the window you want, type the number that appears before that group, or use the arrow keys to highlight the group name and press ENTER.

Now that you have opened the program group window, you can see the program items which appear inside the program group, as in Figure B.3. Select the icon for the application you want to start. You can do this by double-clicking the item, or by pressing the arrow keys until the item is highlighted and then ENTER. If the program item is a document rather than an application, selecting it to open it also starts the application which created it. If Windows is not sure what application was used to create it, it displays a dialog box telling you that there is not an associated program. In this case, refer to your Windows' documentation to find out how to associate a file type with an application so that opening the document starts the application. This is done using the File Manager and described in Chapter 7.

CREATING PROGRAM ITEMS   Program items, as mentioned above, can be either applications or documents. When you install a Windows applications such as Quattro Pro on your machine, it is automatically set up in Windows, and a program item is created for it. However, you may find that you want to create program items for various applications and documents you have, such as Quattro Pro notebooks. This is convenient, because it makes it easy for you to find documents. Instead of having to start your application, and then find the correct file, you create the program item once. Then just double-click on the Program Item, and you have started the program with the correct document already open.

The process of creating a program item is very simple. First, select the program group that you want to add the program item. The program group can still be minimized as an icon or displayed as a window. Then select New from the File menu of the Program Manager to open the New Program Object dialog box. Select the Program Item radio button and OK, opening the Program Item Properties dialog box shown in Figure B.4 (shown for Windows 3.1). Enter the label that you want to appear below the icon in the Description text box. You will want to keep this label short, but clear enough that you know what the icon is. In the Command Line text box, type the drive, path, and file name you want executed when you select

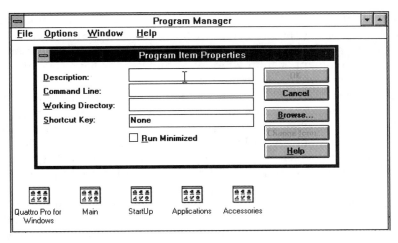

Figure B.4   Program Item Properties Dialog Box

the icon. You can also select the Browse button to search for the file to add. While there are other options available in the Program Item Properties dialog box, you will not need them when creating a program item for a document. Now that you have supplied all the necessary information, select OK. The program item that you just created using the default icon appears in the program group.

EXITING THE PROGRAM MANAGER AND WINDOWS   When you exit the Program Manager, you exit Windows. Exiting the Program Manager is just like exiting any other application in Windows. Activate the File menu then select Exit. Before you can leave Windows, you see a dialog box asking you to confirm that you really want to leave Windows. If there were any open applications when you chose to leave Windows, Windows will close them. Windows will also ask you if you want to save any open documents that have been changed since the last time they were saved. You can also close Windows applications using the Active Task Manager. Simply select the application in the list box, and then select the End Task command button.

   If you have been running any DOS-based programs in a window, you must exit those programs individually before you can exit Windows. While you can close a Windows program simply by closing the window itself, this does not work for windows containing DOS-based programs. These programs must be exited in the same fashion that you would exit them if running them without Windows.

Switching Between Applications

One of the greatest advantages to Windows is that you can run several applications at the same time, each in its own window. As you switch from one application to another, you simply change the active application, just as you might change which file folder on your desk is on top on the stack. The easiest method of switching to another window is to click on the desired window with your mouse. However, if you have an application window maximized, or have several windows open at once, you may find another method easier.

The Task List is a list of all open Windows and non-Windows applications that you can switch to by selecting the application name in the list. To display the Task List, press CTRL-ESC or double-click an empty area of the Windows desktop. This opens the Task List dialog box as in Figure B.5. You can either double-click the application you want to switch to, or highlight it and press ENTER (pressing ENTER selects the Switch To command button). Selecting the application in the task list makes that application the active application.

You can also switch between applications using simple key combinations. Simply press ALT-TAB. In Windows 3.0, pressing ALT-TAB switches between the current application and the last one you used. In Windows 3.1, you can hold down ALT and each time you press TAB, the previous application used becomes the next used application. You can also cycle between the open applications in both Windows 3.0 and 3.1 by pressing ALT-ESC.

Sizing and Moving Windows

As you open many applications and document windows, you will quickly discover that you want to be able to change the size or position of windows. You may want to display two application windows side-by-side to facilitate editing, or you may want to enlarge a single window so that it covers the entire screen to make it easier to edit its contents. You can also tile and cascade windows which are two options that quickly arrange the open windows in Windows or within an application window. The steps for sizing and positioning windows apply to sizing and positioning document windows as well as application windows.

SIZING WINDOWS   Most windows can be resized to fit any area you want. You can size any window that has a border of a line without any thickness. To size a window with a mouse, move the mouse so that it is pointing at the window's border, the thin strip of color around the edge of the window. You will notice that

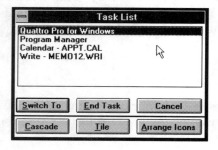

Figure B.5   Task List to Switch and Organize Applications

the arrow changes shape when it points to the window border, becoming a double-headed arrow. Drag the arrow and the window border to the new position. When you release the mouse button, the window changes size to fill the space you have now marked for it.

To size a window using the keyboard alone, you must first press ALT-SPACEBAR or ALT-HYPHEN to select the application or the document window's control menu box. Select S̲ize. The first arrow key you press selects the side of the window you want to change. For example, pressing the UP ARROW moves the mouse to the top border since when you subsequently press the UP ARROW or DOWN ARROW, you are changing the top of the window while you leave the bottom of the window in its current location. You can only change the top or the bottom or the left and the right when you change the window's size. When the window is the size you want, press ENTER. This freezes the window at this size.

Two preset sizes for windows are available to you. You can maximize a window, or minimize it. When you minimize a window, you reduce the window to an icon . When you maximize a window, the window becomes as large as the screen, if it is an application window, or as large as the application window, if it is a document window. To minimize or maximize a window with a mouse, click on the minimize or maximize button in the upper right corner of the title bar. To do this with the keyboard, press ALT-SPACEBAR or ALT-HYPHEN to select the application or the document window's control menu box and select either Ma̲ximize or Mi̲nimize. If your window is either maximized or minimized, you can also select R̲estore to restore the window to its previous size. To access the control menu of a minimized window, double-click on it with the mouse, or highlight it and press ENTER. The control menu for a window's icon appears when you select the application or when you select the document window.

MOVING WINDOWS   You may find that you want to move a window on the screen. If you are trying to arrange the windows so that you can see into more than one window at a time, you may want to arrange the windows to your satisfaction. Moving a window with the mouse is intuitive. Point the mouse at the title bar of the window and drag the window by the title bar to a new location. When the window is where you want it on the screen, release the mouse button.

Moving with the keyboard is much like sizing a window. Press ALT-SPACEBAR or ALT-HYPHEN to select the application or the document window's control menu box. Select M̲ove. Once again, use the arrow keys to move the window in the direction of the arrow key. When the window is in the position you want it, press ENTER.

TILING AND CASCADING WINDOWS   Windows and Windows applications have two choices for quickly sizing and positioning the open windows: tiling and cascading. The steps you perform depend on whether you are tiling or cascading application or document windows.

When you tile windows, all of the non-minimized open windows are resized and moved so the available area is divided between the open windows. Figure B.6 shows several application windows tiled. To tile application windows, first, dis-

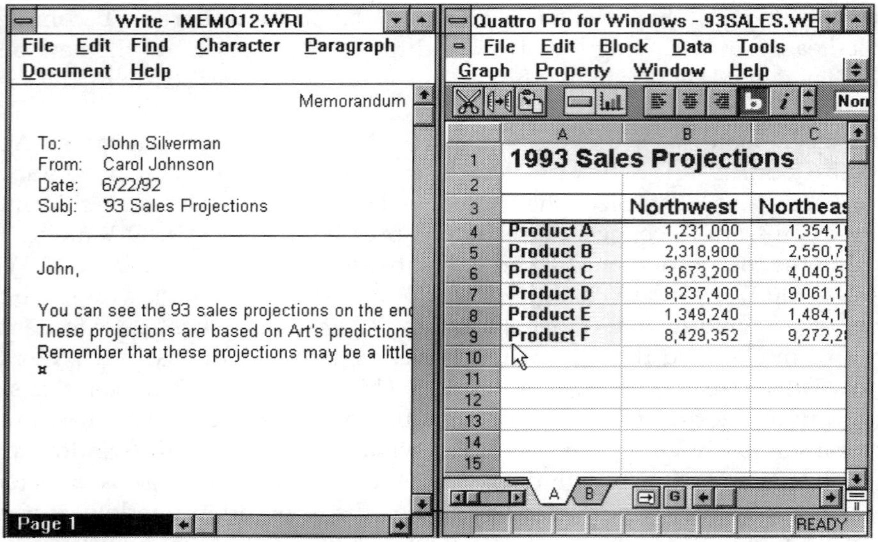

```
┌─ Write - MEMO12.WRI ─────▼▲│┌─Quattro Pro for Windows - 93SALES.WE ▼▲│
 File  Edit  Find  Character  Paragraph  │ File   Edit   Block   Data   Tools
 Document  Help                           │ Graph   Property   Window   Help
                          Memorandum      │  [icons]                    Nor
                                          │         A          B          C
 To:    John Silverman                    │ 1  1993 Sales Projections
 From:  Carol Johnson                     │ 2
 Date:  6/22/92                           │ 3            Northwest   Northeas
 Subj:  '93 Sales Projections             │ 4  Product A    1,231,000    1,354,1
                                          │ 5  Product B    2,318,900    2,550,7
 John,                                    │ 6  Product C    3,673,200    4,040,5
                                          │ 7  Product D    8,237,400    9,061,1
 You can see the 93 sales projections on the en│ 8  Product E    1,349,240    1,484,1
 These projections are based on Art's prediction│ 9  Product F    8,429,352    9,272,2
 Remember that these projections may be a little│ 10
 ▓                                        │ 11
                                          │ 12
                                          │ 13
                                          │ 14
                                          │ 15
                                          │   A B
 Page 1                                   │                           READY
```

Figure B.6 Tiling Makes All Windows Easier to See

play the Task List window by double-clicking an empty desktop area or pressing CTRL-ESC. Next, select the Tile button by clicking it or pressing ALT-T. To tile document windows, select the Window menu from the menu bar and select Tile. The Program Manager and many Windows applications have this command, including Quattro Pro for Windows. When you tile document windows, you tile them within the size of the application window.

When you cascade windows, all of the open windows become the same size and are arranged so the title bar for each window is visible. Figure B.7 shows two

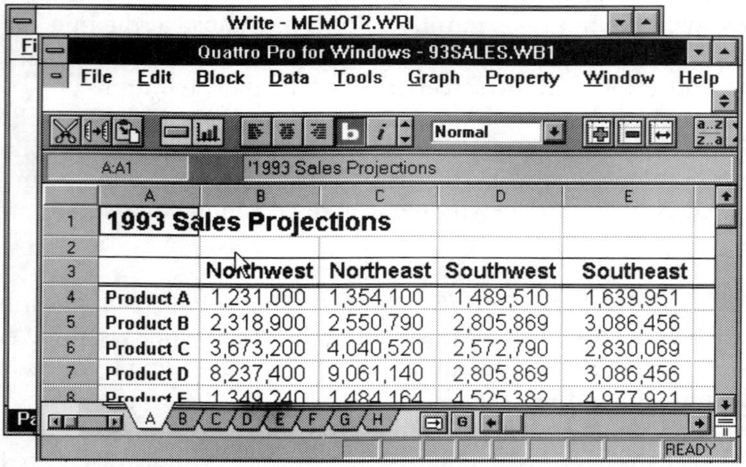

```
┌─ Write - MEMO12.WRI ────────────────▼▲│
 F┌─ Quattro Pro for Windows - 93SALES.WB1 ──▼▲│
   File   Edit   Block   Data   Tools   Graph   Property   Window   Help
   [icons]                      Normal
     A:A1              '1993 Sales Projections
         A        B        C         D          E
   1  1993 Sales Projections
   2
   3         Northwest   Northeast   Southwest    Southeast
   4  Product A  1,231,000   1,354,100   1,489,510   1,639,951
   5  Product B  2,318,900   2,550,790   2,805,869   3,086,456
   6  Product C  3,673,200   4,040,520   2,572,790   2,830,069
   7  Product D  8,237,400   9,061,140   2,805,869   3,086,456
   8  Product E  1,349,240   1,484,164   4,525,382   4,977,921
    A B C D E F G H                              READY
```

Figure B.7 Cascading Makes It Easier to See One Window

application windows cascaded. To cascade application windows, first, display the Task List window by double-clicking an empty desktop area or pressing CTRL-ESC. Next, select the Cascade button by clicking it or pressing ALT-C. To cascade document windows, select the Window menu from the menu bar and select Cascade. The Program Manager and many Windows applications have this command, including Quattro Pro for Windows.

Using the File Manager

The File Manager is one of the component programs of Windows. It is used to carry out the file management tasks that you made previously using DOS commands. These file management tasks are much easier in the File Manager's graphical interface. To start the File Manager, select its icon in the Main program group in the Program Manager.

The File Manager application window displays document windows called directory windows as in Figure B.8. These directory windows show you the information about the files. The default setting for directory windows shows a graphical tree listing the directories on the current disk on the left, a listing of the file and subdirectory names in the current directory on the right, and the available drives on the top. Each drive, directory, and file has a different icon. You can select a drive listed by clicking the drive icon at the top of the window or by pressing CTRL and the drive letter. You can also switch between the three parts of the directory window by pressing TAB. To change the directory listed, move to the directory name in the tree and press ENTER or click it. To use the File Manager to work with a file, move to the file you want to change in the right side of the directory window.

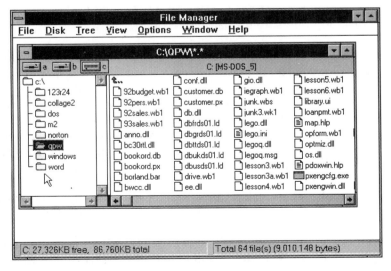

Figure B.8   File Manager Window

When you are starting to use Quattro Pro, you will want to use the File Manager to format disks and copy files. Formatting disks prepares floppy disks to accept information. Copying files lets you make extra copies of your Quattro Pro files as backups in case anything happens to your originals.

FORMATTING DISKS   You can use the File Manager to format of floppy disks. All floppy disks must be formatted before they can store files. When you format a floppy disk, you are organizing how the disk is arranged so other commands can store the data on the disk. The steps for formatting a disk are different in Windows 3.0 and Windows 3.1.

In Windows 3.0, select Format Diskette from the Disk menu. If you have more than one floppy disk drive, you have a dialog box to select the drive to format from the Disk drop-down list box. Then select OK. Next, when the File Manager knows the drive to format, the File Manager displays a dialog box warning about losing data. Select Format. Next, you can select the disk's format (if the drive supports more than one), and whether the disk will contain system files used to boot computers. If the selected drive can format a disk to more than one capacity, you can select the High Capacity check box to format the disk using the higher format capacity. Select OK. After the disk is formatted, you can select Yes to return to the Format Disk dialog box to format another disk, or No to stop formatting disks.

In Windows 3.1, select Format Disk from the Disk menu, opening the Format Disk dialog box. In the Disk In drop-down list box, select the disk drive containing the floppy disk you wish to format. In the Capacity drop-down list box, select which of the available formats you want to use to format the disk. The File Manager knows the choices for capacity the drive can format the disk. If you want a volume label, which is a title for your floppy disk, type the label into the Label text box. At this point, select OK. From the Confirm Format Disk dialog box, select Yes as confirmation that you are formatting the disk (this removes previous data). After the disk is formatted, you can select Yes to return to the Format Disk dialog box to format another disk or No to stop formatting disks.

COPYING FILES   You can also use the File Manager as an easy method to copy files from one disk to another. You may want to copy a file from your hard drive to a disk to give to someone else, or to create a back-up of files you do not want to lose. To copy a file with the mouse, simply point at the file with your mouse, and then drag the file icon to a directory or drive icon. Assuming you are dragging the files to another disk, they are copied. If you want to copy a file to a new location on the same disk, you must hold down CTRL as you drag the file. You can tell the File Manager is copying them because the icon you are dragging will have a plus sign in it. When you release the mouse, you are prompted about copying the files. To copy a file without a mouse, select Copy from the File menu, type the drive and directory information where you want the file copied, and select OK.

DELETING FILES   You can use the File Manager to delete the files you no longer need. To delete a file, select the file to delete and either press DEL or select Delete from the File menu. You must respond to the prompt about deleting the file since the File Manager wants to double-check that you are deleting the correct file. Since you cannot see the contents of the your files in the File Manager, before you delete any file, double-check that it is either backed up on another disk, or that you have looked at it and made sure that it is no longer needed. If you later realize you have deleted a file you want, you probably will not be able to restore it.

Using the Control Panel

The Control Panel is an application that changes many of the settings that run Windows and Windows applications. To start the Control Panel, select the Control Panel icon in the Main program group. When you start the Control Panel, you will see that it looks like another program group because it is filled with icons as shown in Figure B.9. Selecting one of these icons each open a dialog box. You can also open these dialog boxes by selecting the name of the icon from the Settings menu. In the dialog boxes, you can alter different settings used to run Windows and Windows applications. Not all icons may be available depending on your system. The icons and the settings you can change include:

Icon	Purpose
Color	Changes the colors used.
Fonts	Selects the fonts available.
Ports	Sets the communication settings for serial ports.
Mouse	Changes settings for your mouse, such as switching the buttons.
Desktop	Sets the appearance of the desktop (the background).
Keyboard	Sets the keyboard repeat rate and delay.
Printers	Selects the printers.
International	Sets various international settings, such as currency formatting and date styles.
Date/Time	Changes your computer's internal clock settings.

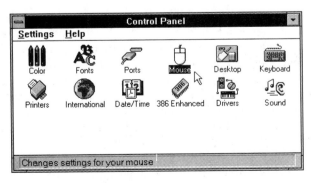

Figure B.9 Control Panel

386 Enhanced	Controls the settings that optimizes Windows in 386 Enhanced mode.
Drivers	Installs various device drivers.
Sound	Assigns certain sounds to different system events.
Network	Changes settings used to connect to a network.

CHANGING THE MOUSE BUTTONS   Many left-handed people prefer to switch the mouse buttons so that the mouse is more convenient for the left hand. By switching the mouse buttons in the Control Panel, you are switching them for all Windows applications. In Windows 3.1, you also switch the mouse buttons for non-Windows applications that you run from a window. When the mouse buttons are switched, the left mouse button does the same things the left mouse button is described as doing in this book, and vice versa. For example, you make most selections using the left mouse button. In this book, you will learn about right-clicking objects to inspect properties in Quattro Pro. If you switch the mouse buttons, you will press the right mouse button to make selections and the left mouse button to inspect properties.

To switch the mouse button, first open the Control Panel, and then select the Mouse icon or Mouse from the Settings menu, opening the Mouse dialog box. Select the Swap Left/Right Buttons check box. When you do so you will notice that the R and L in the mouse above the check box switch places. As you click the mouse buttons, you will see each of these boxes highlighted, to show you graphically which button is which. Select OK. The other settings in the dialog box let you change how fast the mouse pointer moves as you move the external mouse, how fast you need to double-click the mouse buttons to register a double-click, and add mouse trails (Windows 3.1 only).

INSTALLING PRINTERS   In Windows and Windows applications, you install the printers once in Windows and all of the Windows application use the printer information you have installed in Windows. You must install a printer in Windows before you can print with Quattro Pro for Windows. Installing a printer loads a printer driver file which provides the information Windows needs to use a physically installed printer.

The first step in installing a printer driver is to activate the Printers dialog box, by selecting the Printers icon or selecting Printers from the Settings menu in the Control Panel. If the printer you want to use appears in the Installed Printers list box, then you do not need to install it. You may want to make it the default printer, by highlighting it in this list box, and selecting the Set as the Default Printer button. If you are using Windows 3.0, you will want to click the Active radio button under Status to make the highlighted printer the default.

If the printer does not appear in this list box, click the Add button. This extends the dialog box, as show in Figure B.10. In the List of Printers list box, find your printer name in the list then select the Install button. You will need to put the Windows Setup disk with the printer driver files in a drive so the Control Panel can copy the printer driver file from the disk. Select OK when you are finished

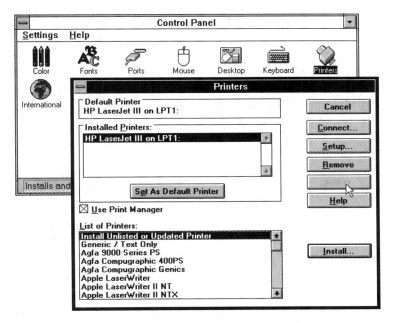

Figure B.10   Printers Dialog Box to Install Printers

installing the printer. Select Close or Cancel when you want to close the Printers dialog box.

Printing with Windows

With DOS-based programs, when you print a document, your program has to send the information to your printer. Since the printer cannot print the page as fast as the computer can read it, your computer must wait for the printer to print information it has sent before it can continue sending more information to print. Often, you must wait until all of the information is sent to the printer until you can do another task with the computer. Windows has a print queue built in. With a print queue, your application sends the information to print to a temporary file. While you continue working with your application or another application, the queue works in the background to send the information to the printer at the printer's speed. This print queue is handled by Windows' Print Manager. The Windows' Print Manager only affects printing from Windows applications so non-Windows applications are not affected.

Normally, you never need to look at the Print Manager when you are printing. You will only see the Print Manager icon in the Windows desktop. It disappears when it has finished sending all of the information to the printer. Sometimes, you may find that you want to change the order you print different requests or cancel a printing request. When you need to do either task, you can open the Print

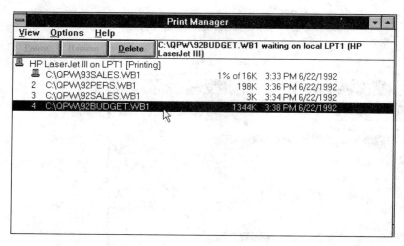

Figure B.11   Print Manager Listing Order of Print Jobs

Manager to change the order of the print jobs or cancel a print job. To display the Print Manager in a window, double-click the Print Manager icon in the Windows desktop, display the Task List and select Print Manager, or select the Print Manager from the Program Manager's Main group window. This opens a Print Manager window like the one shown in Figure B.11. Each installed printer has a separate section in the Print Manager window. Each print request is stored as a print job in the Print Manager.

CHANGING THE PRINT QUEUE ORDER   Rearranging the order print jobs are run lets you rush one of the print jobs. For example, suppose you discover that you needed the fourth print job in Figure B.11, 92BUDGET.WB1, printed before the other print jobs. You can change where a specific print job is in the print queue, which is the list of files waiting to be printed. When you change a print job's location in the print queue, you change the order that the jobs are printed. To move a file up in the print order, simply drag the print job to the position you want it to have in the queue. While you drag the print job, the pointer changes to a vertical thicker arrow. With the keyboard, you can highlight that job, and then press CTRL-UP ARROW or CTRL-DOWN ARROW, to change the print order.

CANCELING A PRINT JOB   Another chore you might want to do with the Print Manager is to cancel a print job. For example, you may find you have printed a report with the wrong heading, or your report has some errors you want to fix. To cancel a print job, highlight the print job in the queue. Then select the Delete button by clicking it or pressing ALT-D. After selecting OK to the confirmation prompt, the Print Manager deletes the temporary file and removes the print job from the list of jobs to print. You must reprint your report from the Windows application to print that report.

Appendix C

Command Reference

This appendix defines all the Quattro Pro commands available in a notebook window. This appendix also includes major notebook and graph properties. While the description of each command and property is brief, the major points are covered, including the options available.

MENU COMMANDS

The menu commands in Quattro Pro provide you with a wealth of features. These commands are listed in alphabetical order, for example, File | Save As is listed after File | Save All. Most of the commands display dialog boxes that have OK, Cancel, and Help buttons. OK finishes the command and usually performs the commands according to the selections you have made in the dialog box. Cancel aborts the command. Help displays the help application window with the current information displayed matching the command you have selected before selecting the Help button. Most of the commands that use blocks pick up any block you have selected before selecting the command. Some commands require that you select a block or position the selector before you use the command. For the commands that prompt for a file, the dialog box selections all of these commands used are described under File | Open. Notes point out unusual features, shortcuts, or special uses for some commands. The Draw commands are only available when a graph window is an active window and the Dialog commands are only available when you are editing a dialog box or SpeedBar.

Block | Copy

The Block | Copy command copies numbers, labels, and formulas to other cells in a notebook. You need to tell Quattro Pro which cells to copy and where to copy them to. The From block can consist of one cell, a block of cells, or a noncontiguous block of cells. The To block can be a single cell or a block of cells. The size of the From block determines whether Quattro Pro makes one or several copies of the source block. You can supply either block as a cell address, a block name, or an address. You can point to the blocks using the arrow keys or mouse. To specify the To block, you only need to include the top left cell address of the desired location in the notebook for each copy that Quattro Pro makes. For example, if you want to copy the contents of A:A1..A5 to A:C1..E5, the To block is specified as A:C1..E1.

You can copy cells to another location in the same page, to a different page of the same notebook or to a different open notebooks. If you are copying between notebooks, you must include the file name enclosed in brackets ([ ]) when you reference an open but inactive notebook, or use the pointing method. The From block does not have to be in an open notebook but the To one does. Quattro Pro automatically adds the file name for you if you point to a block in another notebook.

You can also use the Block | Copy command to copy a block containing formulas with absolute cell references, and adjust the addresses cells in the formulas, as if the absolute cell references are temporarily relative cell references. After using this Model copy feature, the new copy of the formulas have the same absolute references, but the references have been adjusted.

The Block | Copy command can copy in four different situations:

1. One cell to one cell.
2. One cell to many cells.
3. A block of cells to another block of cells whose block size and shape is the same as the original block.
4. A block of cells to another block in the same basic as the original block. For example, Quattro Pro can copy a row of 10 cells to several rows of 10 cells.

Options

To—Specify the block you want to copy in this text box. If you selected a block before invoking this command, that block is supplied in this text box.

From—Specify where you want to copy the contents of the To block. You only need specify the upper left corner of the From block for each copy.

Model copy—Selecting this check box lets you temporarily treat absolute references as relative while they are copied to the new location.

Note

You can copy cells to only one notebook at a time. You can also use the Edit | Copy and Edit | Paste commands to copy blocks of data. You can use the drag and drop method to duplicate the Block | Copy command, by selecting the block to copy, and dragging the block while pressing CTRL.

Block | Delete | Columns

This command deletes entire or partial columns of a notebook. If you want to delete entire columns, you must select a block containing at least one cell from each column you want to delete. If you want to delete partial columns, the block you select must contain at least one cell from each column you want to delete as well as the pages and rows where you want the columns deleted. When you delete entire or partial columns, the contents of the columns to the right of the deleted columns shift to the left fill in the deleted columns.

Options

Block—Select the block containing the columns to delete in this text box. If you have selected a block before entering this command, the selected block is entered in this text box.

Entire—Select this radio button to delete complete columns.

Partial—Select this radio button to delete the selected columns for only the selected pages and rows.

Note

You can also delete columns by selecting the columns to delete and selecting the Delete button in the SpeedBar which has a minus sign in it, and then selecting the Columns radio button and the Entire or Partial radio button to delete entire or partial columns.

Block | Delete | Pages

This command deletes either entire or partial pages from your notebook. If you want to delete entire pages, you must select a block containing at least one cell on each page you want to delete. If you want to delete partial pages, you must select a block containing the pages you want to delete as well as the rows and columns where you want the pages deleted. When you delete an entire or partial page, the contents of the corresponding cells on the next page move up into the deleted cells.

Options

Block—Select the block containing the pages to delete in this text box. If you select a block before entering this command, the selected block is entered in this text box.

Entire—Select this radio button to delete entire pages.

Partial—Select this radio button to delete the selected pages for only the selected rows and columns.

Note

You can also delete pages by selecting the pages to delete and the Delete button in the SpeedBar which has a minus sign in it, and then selecting the Pages radio button and the Entire or Partial radio button to delete entire or partial pages.

Block | Delete | Rows

This command deletes either entire or partial rows from the notebook. If you want to delete entire rows, you must select a block containing at least one cell in each row you want to delete. If you want delete partial rows, you must select a block containing the rows you want to delete as well as the columns and pages where you want the rows deleted. When you delete an entire or partial row, the contents of the cells directly beneath the deleted rows move up replacing the deleted rows.

Options

Block—Select the block containing the rows to delete in this text box. If you select a block before entering this command, the selected block is entered in this text box.
Entire—Select this radio button to delete entire rows.
Partial—Select this radio button to delete the selected rows for only the selected pages and columns.

Note

You can also delete rows by selecting the rows to delete and the Delete button in the SpeedBar which has a minus sign in it, and then selecting the Rows radio button and the Entire or Partial radio button to delete entire or partial columns.

Block | Fill

This command directs Quattro Pro to enter a series of evenly spaced values in a block of cells with either a row or column orientation. The choices for the series lets you select how the values in the block are incremented.

Options

Block—Select the blocks that you want to fill with values in this text box.
Start—Type the value, date, or formula for the first value in the series in this text box.
Step—Type the value, date, or formula for the step by which you want to increment the series of numbers in this text box.
Stop—Type the value, date, or formula for the last value in the series. This value will not be reached if there are insufficient cells in the block to contain all the numbers.
Column—Select this radio button if you want the block filled with values one column at a time.
Row—Select this radio button if you want the block filled with values one row at a time.
Linear—Select this radio button to generate the next value in the series by adding the step value to the last value.
Growth—Select this radio button to generate the next value in the series by multiplying the last value by the step value.
Power—Select this radio button to generate the next value in the series by raising the last value by the step value.

Year—Select this radio button to generate the next value in the series by adding years to the last value.

Month—Select this radio button to generate the next value in the series by adding months to the last value.

Week—Select this radio button to generate the next value in the series by adding weeks to the last value.

Weekday—Select this radio button to generate the next value in the series by adding days to the last value so the next value is not on a weekend.

Day—Select this radio button to generate the next value in the series by adding days to the last value.

Hour—Select this radio button to generate the next value in the series by adding hours to the last value.

Minute—Select this radio button to generate the next value in the series by adding minutes to the last value.

Second—Select this radio button to generate the next value in the series by adding seconds to the last value.

Note

You can also quickly fill a series using the SpeedFill button in the SpeedBar which is the second one from the end. To use this button, enter the start value in the first cell of a block and then fill in the next one or two cells to develop a pattern. To generate the values, select the block to fill and select the SpeedFill button in the SpeedBar.

Block I Insert I Columns

This command inserts entire or partial columns in a notebook. If you want to insert entire columns, you must select a block containing at least one cell from each column you want to insert. If you want to insert partial columns, then you must select a block containing at least one cell from each column you want to insert as well as the pages and rows where you want the columns inserted. When you insert entire or partial columns, the contents of the cells to the right of the inserted columns shift further right to make room for the new columns.

Options

Block—Select the block containing the columns to insert in this text box. If you have selected a block before entering this command, the selected block is entered in this text box.

Entire—Select this radio button to insert entire columns.

Partial—Select this radio button to insert the selected number of columns for only the selected pages and rows.

Note

You can also insert columns by selecting the columns to insert and the Insert button in the SpeedBar which has a plus sign, and then selecting the Columns radio button and the Entire or Partial radio button to insert entire or partial columns.

Block | Insert | File

This command inserts files into your current notebook. You can use it to insert any of the file types that Quattro Pro can translate from directly. The file starts being inserted at the selector's position. If the file is in a format that does not support pages, it is inserted as a single page, and the page has the name of the file. If the file is in a format that does support multiple pages, the inserted pages have the name of the first six characters of the file they came from followed by their page name. If the file has more pages then exist between your selector and the end of the notebook, you will be unable to insert the file.

Options

The only options for this command is to select the file that you want to insert. The options for selecting the file are the same File Name text box and list box, the Directories list box, the File Types drop-down list box, and the Drives drop-down list box as you use for other commands that let you select files.

Block | Insert | Pages

This command inserts either entire or partial pages into your notebook. If you want to insert entire pages, you must select a block containing at least one cell on each page you want to insert. If you want to insert partial pages, you must select a block containing the pages you want to insert as well as the rows and columns where you want the pages inserted. When you insert a partial page, the previous contents of the current page shift backward to make room for the inserted pages. This continues for all 256 pages.

Options

Block—Specify the block containing the pages to insert in this text box. If you select a block before entering this command, the selected block is entered in this text box.
Entire—Select this radio button if you want to insert entire pages.
Partial—Select this radio button to insert the selected pages for only the selected columns and rows.

Note

You can also insert pages by selecting the pages and the Insert button in the SpeedBar which has a plus sign, and then selecting the Pages radio button and the Entire or Partial radio button to insert entire or partial pages.

Block | Insert | Rows

This command inserts entire or partial rows in a notebook. If you want to insert entire rows, you must select a block containing at least one cell on each row you want to insert. If you want to insert partial rows, you must select a block containing the rows you want to insert as well as the columns and pages where you want the rows inserted. When you insert entire or partial rows, the contents of the cells below the inserted rows shift down to make room for the new rows.

Options

Block—Specify the block containing the pages to insert in this text box. If you select a block before entering this command, the selected block is entered in this text box.
Entire—Select this radio button to insert entire rows.
Partial—Select this radio button to insert the selected rows for only the selected columns and pages.

Note

You can also insert rows by selecting the rows to insert and the Insert button in the SpeedBar which has a plus sign, and then selecting the Rows radio button and the Entire or Partial radio button to insert entire or partial rows.

Block | Insert Break

This command inserts a row and a page break at the selector's position. This command directs where Quattro Pro should insert page breaks. It inserts a row and puts a vertical bar and two colons (| ::) into the current column. When you print a block, Quattro Pro checks the first column of the block for inserted page breaks. When Quattro Pro finds an inserted page break, Quattro Pro breaks pages at that location and does not print any cell contents that appear in this row. You can also add page breaks by putting the page break indicator (| ::) into the first column of a blank row.

Options

None.

Note

The page break indicator must be in the first column of the print block. If the print block does not include the column with the page break, you will want to copy the page break symbol to the appropriate column before printing the block.

Block | Move Pages

This command moves the pages of your notebook from one position to another.

Options

Move page—Specify the page or pages that you want to move in this text box.
To before page—Specify the page where you want the moved pages to appear immediately in front of in this text box.

Note

You can also move pages by dragging and dropping their page tabs. To drag and drop page tabs and the pages attached to the page tabs, point to the page tab to move and drag it down and then to the right or left to position the page tab between the pages where you want the page inserted.

Block | Move

This command moves a block of cell entries to any desired location on the current notebook, or in another open notebook. This command adjusts formulas within the block being moved to correspond to the new location. The adjustment occurs whether the formula in the cell contains relative (A1), mixed ($A1,A$1), or absolute ($A$1) addresses. Also, Quattro Pro adjusts formulas, not in the block you are moving, that refer to cells in the moved block regardless of the type of cell references these formulas contain. To execute this command, Quattro Pro needs to know the From block containing the data to move and the To block that tells Quattro Pro the new location.

Options

From—Specify the block of cells which you want to move in this text box.
To—Specify the location to which you want to move the block of cells in this text box.

Note

You can duplicate this command by using the drag and drop method of moving data. To drag and drop cells to move their contents, select the cells you want to move, and then drag them with the mouse to the desired location. You can also use the Edit | Cut and the Edit | Paste commands to use the Windows Clipboard to move text entries.

Block | Names | Create

This command assigns names to blocks of cells so you can refer to the cells with the assigned names rather than cell or block addresses. Formulas are easier to understand when they use the block names rather than the cell addresses. These assigned names can replace cell or block addresses in any of Quattro Pro's commands. Once you name a block, Quattro Pro changes any formulas that refer to that block so that they use the name. You can select block names where Quattro Pro expects you to enter a cell address or block name by pressing F3 (CHOICES). You can use more than one name for the same block or create an overlapping block.

Options

Name—Enter the name that you want to use in this text box. A name can be up to 15 characters long without spaces.

Block(s)—Specify the block that you want the name assigned to in this text box. The block can be contiguous, non-contiguous, and three-dimensional (encompassing multiple pages). Initially this text box contains the current cell or the block you selected before the command.

Names—Select a block name from this list box if you want to assign a new name to a previously created block address or a new block address to a previously created block name. When you select a block name, the entries in the *Name* and the *Block(s)* text boxes change to the block name and address that belongs to the selected name.

Note

You can also perform this command by pressing CTRL-F3 (NAME BLOCK).

Block I Names I Delete

This command removes block names that you no longer need. Each time you use this command you can delete one block name. Formulas that use references to these block names are adjusted by Quattro Pro to use the cell addresses or block addresses instead.

Options

Name—You can type the block name you want to delete in this text box.

Block(s)—This text box displays the cell addresses referred to by the selected name, allowing you to double-check that you are deleting the correct name.

Names—Select the block name which you want to delete from this list box. Quattro Pro puts the selected block name in the *Name* text box and the block name's address in the *Block(s)* text box.

Block I Names I Labels

This command uses labels to assign block names to adjacent cells. Each label is assigned to a single cell. The cell that is assigned the block name must be adjacent to the cell that contains the label. Quattro Pro limits block names to 15 characters and will truncate longer labels.

Options

Blocks—Specify the block containing the labels to use as block names in this text box.

Right—Select this radio button to assign the selected labels as block names to the cells immediately to the right.

Left—Select this radio button to assign the selected labels as block names to the cells immediately to the left.

Up—Select this radio button to assign the selected labels as block names to the cells directly above.

Down—Select this radio button to assign the selected labels as block names to the cells directly below.

Block I Names I Make Table

This command creates a table of the block names in the current notebook and the addresses that these names are assigned. Quattro Pro uses the upper-left cell of the address you provide as the upper-left corner of the table. The table uses two columns and as many rows as the notebook has block names. The first column of the table contains the block names, and the second column contains the block addresses.

Options
Block—Specify the cell to be the upper-left corner of the table in this text box.

Block I Names I Reset

This command removes all the assigned block names in the current notebook at once. You can select this command instead of deleting each assigned block name individually with the Block I Names I Delete command.

Options
Select Yes to remove all the block names or No to cancel the command.

Block I Object Order I Bring Forward

This command is used to change the order of floating objects that overlap, such as graphs, SpeedButtons, and OLE objects, by bringing the selected object forward one layer. If the selected object is already at the top of the group of floating objects, this command has no effect. You must select the floating graph, SpeedButton, or OLE object you want in front before using this command.

Options
None.

Block I Object Order I Bring to Front

This command is used with floating objects that overlap, such as graphs, SpeedButtons and OLE objects, to layer them correctly. This command brings the selected object to top of the other floating objects. You must select the floating graphs, SpeedButtons, or OLE objects you want on top before using this command.

Options
None.

Block I Object Order I Send Back

This command is used with floating objects that overlap, such as graphs, SpeedButtons and OLE objects, to layer them correctly. This command puts the selected object underneath all the other floating objects. You must select the floating graph, SpeedButton, or OLE object you want below the other objects before using this command.

Options
None.

Block I Object Order I Send to Back

This command is used with overlapping floating objects, such as graphs, SpeedButtons and OLE objects. It puts the selected object underneath all the other objects. You must select the floating graph, SpeedButton, or OLE object you want on the bottom before using this command.

Options
None.

Block I Reformat

This command rearranges text entries in a column, so that they appear within a block. It rearranges the text in each cell in the block so that the modified entries are as wide as the block you select for this command. The text is still stored as labels in the first column, but has the appearance of being word-wrapped like word processing text. When a label entry reaches the width of the selected block, the remainder of the entry is transferred to the next cell below. This continues for all of the labels. Quattro Pro continues rearranging the labels until it finds a nonlabel cell in the first column of the block you select, or, if the block you select has more than one row, Quattro Pro has rearranged all of the labels in the block.

Options
Block—Specify the block where you want the reformatted labels to appear in this text box. The block should contain the columns that you want the long labels to appear across. You can select a block containing one row or many to control whether contents below the rearranged labels are vertically shifted. If you do not want to limit the number of rows the labels can use, specify only one row in the selected block. Any entries in the first column below the rearranged labels may be shifted up or down. You can also select a block containing only the rows you want

the labels rearranged for. When the block contains more than one row, any entries below the rearranged labels do not change their position.

Block | Transpose

This command copies entries stored in a row or column to the reverse orientation. When you select this command, you need to specify the From block you are copying and the block where you are copying these transposed entries. These blocks do not have to be in the same notebook, but both notebooks must be open.

Options

From—Specify the block which you want to transpose in this text box.
To—Specify the first cell in the block where the transposed entries are to appear in this text box.

Note

Quattro Pro does not correctly adjust relative cell references in formulas that you transpose, even if the referenced cells are also transposed. You can edit the formulas and change all the relative address references to absolute references before invoking the command. You can also transpose entries copied onto the Clipboard using the Edit | Paste Special command.

Block | Values

This command copies the values of a block containing formulas to the same block of cells or to a different block of cells. The converted entries contain values rather than formulas.

Options

From—Specify the cell or block of cells containing formulas that you want to convert to values in this text box.
To—Specify the cell or block of cells where you want the values created from the formulas specified in the From text box to appear.

Note

If you want to convert a formula to a value for a single cell, press F2 (EDIT) or click the input line to enter EDIT mode, press F9 (CALC) to calculate the results, and press ENTER or click ✓ to finalize the value. You can also copy the values of the entries copied on the Clipboard using the Edit | Paste Special command.

Data | Database Desktop

This command opens the Database Desktop which provides advanced database management features to different types of databases. From the database desktop, you can create related groups of tables and queries.

Options

This command opens the Database Desktop application window. This application window has its own commands. Since the Database Desktop is a separate application window, you can return to Quattro Pro the same way you switch to other applications. When you are finished with the Database Desktop, you can select the File I Exit command or close the application window.

Data I Frequency

This command constructs a frequency distribution table for values in a block. It tells you the number of times values fall within specified established intervals. Before you use this command, you must create a column of value entries recording the specified frequency intervals (bins). These entries in the column must be in ascending order. The column next to the frequency intervals must be empty. The cell below the last frequency interval must be empty as well as the cell to its right. Quattro Pro analyzes your data against these bins, and enters the number of the values which fit into each bin in the column to the left of the bin values. The first value in the frequency distribution includes all values below the first bin number, and the last value is for all the value over the last bin value.

Options

Value Block(s)—Select the blocks containing the values for which you want a frequency distribution table created.

Bin Block—Select the block containing the series of values to use to create the bins for the frequency distribution.

Reset—Select this button to remove the blocks from the Value Block(s) and Bin Block text boxes.

Data I Parse

This command divides long labels into smaller entries. It is primarily used on data imported as a text file. This command can divide the long labels into labels, numeric values, date, and time serial numbers. It assumes that the data it is parsing is in a consistent format. To use this command, place your selector in the top row of the data to be parsed and create a format line. Creating a format line adds a blank row above the data and inserts the format line indicating how the long labels will be divided. A format line uses these characters to indicate the data type:

L—Character below this letter is the first character of a label entry.

V—Character below this letter is the first character of a value entry.

D—Character below this letter is the first character of a date serial number.

T—Character below this letter is the first character of a time serial number.

>—Character below this letter is a continuation of a label, value, date, or time entry.

*—Character below this letter is blank but may be used by the other data that will be parsed as a continuation of an entry.

S—Characters in the column below this letter are ignored in the parsing process.

Options

Input—Select the block of cells to parse in this text box. The format line must be the first line of this block.

Output—Select where this command will put the parsed data in this text box. Quattro Pro only needs to know the upper-left corner of the output block. Since Quattro Pro writes over any existing information in the output area, the output area should be blank.

Create—This button inserts a row above the selector, places a format line in the cell above the selector, and moves the selector to the format line. The format line is Quattro Pro's description of how it thinks the labels below should be broken into cells.

Edit—This button edits the format line by opening a dialog box displaying the format line over the data that is being parsed. This is displayed in a monospaced font, in which each letter takes the same amount of room, making it easier to edit the format line. Select OK to return to the Data Parse dialog box.

Reset—This option removes the setting from the input and output text boxes.

Data I Query

This command searches through a notebook database and locates records that meet specified criteria. To use it, you must specify the block of cells that contains the data entries you wish to search, and the criteria it is to use. The database and the criteria must be entered into a notebook before you select this command. If the data that fits the criteria is to be written to a separate area, you must enter the field names in this output area first.

Options

Database Block—Select the location of the database in this text box. If the block is in another notebook, you must precede the block address or name with the file name enclosed in brackets. The block does not have to contain all the database's fields, but the block must contain all the fields used by the criteria and the output block (if any) as well as the field names.

Criteria Table—Select the location of your criteria in this text box. You must enter your criteria on the notebook in an acceptable tabular form before selecting the Data I Query command.

Output Block—Before you use the Extract and Extract Unique options, you must select the block where Quattro Pro stores the selected records in this text box. If the output block contains only one row, Quattro Pro erases all rows between the selected one and the end of the notebook page and uses as many rows it needs to copy the extracted records. If the output block contains more than one row, Quattro Pro only uses the output block. When Quattro Pro fills the output block and more room is needed for extracted records, Quattro Pro displays an error message.

Locate—Select this button to highlight the records that meet your specified criteria. You can use the arrow keys and the mouse to switch to other records and fields that meet the specified criteria. You can also edit highlighted records.

Extract—Select this button to copy the database records that match the criteria to the specified output block. In addition to the database and criteria table, you need to specify an output block for this option.

Extract Unique—Select this button to copy the database records that match the criteria that are unique to the specified output area. Quattro Pro determines uniqueness using only the fields appearing in the output block. You need to specify a database block, criteria, and the output block before you use this option.

Delete—This option deletes records that meet specified criteria. Quattro Pro prompts for confirmation that you want to delete the records. Select No to keep the records or Yes to remove the records from the database.

Field Names—Select this button to assign the field names in the top row of each field in the database. This option allows you to use field names when specifying your criteria instead of cell addresses.

Reset—Select this button to remove the block addresses selected for the Database Block, Criteria Table, and Output Block text boxes.

Note

You can execute the last Data | Query command again using the same settings by pressing F7 (QUERY). Use this shortcut when you are changing the entries in the criteria table and want to see the effect.

Data | Restrict Input

This command restricts data entry to a specific block, as if you are entering data in an entry form. After you execute this command, the selector moves only to unprotected cells in the block. Even though the other cells are visible, they are inaccessible. When you are in this mode, Quattro Pro does not allow you to use the menu. Before you use this command, you first need to unprotect the cells where you want to make entries by setting the Protection property for those cells to Unprotect. To end this mode, simply press the ESC key or press ENTER without typing an entry.

Options

Input Range—Enter the block which you want to be able to make entries in unprotected cells.

Data | Sort

The Data | Sort command sorts your database records in a sequence you specify. The data to sort must be in the notebook before you invoke this command. You can sort your records using up to five keys. The first key is the primary key. Quattro Pro allows four additional keys as tie-breakers for duplicate entries in keys with a higher priority. Quattro Pro does not adjust formulas when it sorts data. If you have formulas in the sort block, change them to use absolute addresses or convert them to values before sorting. If you have formulas outside the sort block that refer to values in the sort block, change them to values or reenter them after sorting.

Options

Block—Select the block of cells you wish to sort in this text box. Do not include any database field names when using this option, since Quattro Pro will sort these entries as well. You must include all the fields of the database or the database will lose its integrity after sorting, since only some fields in the database were sorted.

1st Key—Select a cell in the column containing the field used as the primary key or controlling sequence for the sort in this text box. You specify whether you want to sort the data in ascending or descending order by selecting or clearing the check box after the text box. When that check box is selected, the sort is done in ascending order.

2nd, 3rd, 4th, 5th—Select a cell in the column that contains the field to use as additional sort keys. Enter the column that contains the field to use as a sort key in the text box, and select the check box to sort in an ascending order, or clear it to sort in a descending order.

Reset—Select this button to remove the specifications made by the other options.

Numbers First—Select this radio button to place numbers before letters when sorting labels in ascending order, or after the letters when sorting in descending order.

Labels First—Select this radio button to place letters before numbers when sorting labels in ascending order, or after the numbers when sorting in descending order.

Character Code—Select this radio button to sort lower- and uppercase letters separately. With this option, the sort is done according to the character code of each letter.

Dictionary—Select this radio button to sort lower- and uppercase letters together. With this option, the sort is done according to the language set with the International application property.

Note

You can also use the Upper and Lower SpeedSort buttons to sort a block. These are on the button labeled a..z and z..a. After selecting a block, hold down CTRL and SHIFT then click cells in the columns in the order you want them used as sort keys. If you do not select sort keys, Quattro Pro uses the first column's entries as the first sort key. Then select the Upper SpeedSort button (the half labeled a..z) to sort the block in ascending order or select the Lower SpeedSort button (the half labeled a..z) to sort the block in descending order.

Data | Table Query

This command lets you query external databases using predefined queries. The queries can be defined in a block in a notebook or in an external query-by-example file. When you select OK, the query is performed. This command is for querying databases that are not stored in a spreadsheet format such as Quattro Pro for Windows.

Options

Query in File—Select this radio button to perform the query using a query stored in a query-by-example file. When you select this radio button, you can enter the query-by-example file in the QBE file text box or use the Browse button to select the query-by-example file.

Query in Block—Select this radio button to perform the query using a query stored in a block of cells. When you select this radio button, you can enter the block address in the QBE block.

Browse—Select this button to select a query-by-example file that contains the query. Query-by-example files have a .QBE extension. Once you select Browse, you can select a file from the Table Query dialog box using the same File Name text box and list box, Directories list box, File Types drop-down list box, and Drives drop-down list box you use for other commands that let you select files.

QBE file/block—Select the query-by-example file or the block containing the query in this text box. If you select a file using the Browse button, the file is entered into this text box for you.

Destination—Select the block for the location where you want the output for the query placed. The output block contains the field names from the database you want placed in the output. If the output block contains only one row, Quattro Pro erases all rows between the selected one and the end of the notebook page and uses as many rows it needs to copy the extracted records. If the output block contains more than one row, Quattro Pro only uses the output block. When Quattro Pro fills the output block and more room is needed for extracted records, Quattro Pro displays an error message.

Data I What-If

This command performs a what-if analysis. You can substitute alternative values in your formulas and record the results of the substitutions in a table. You can create a table showing the results of varying one cell or two cells. In either case, you must create a table for the calculated values to appear in before invoking this command.

A one-way what-if table is created by selecting a blank area and placing input values for one variable in a column. Next, enter formulas or the references to other formulas you wish computed with the input values in the row above the column of input values starting with the cell to the right. These entries create a structure for the what-if table with the input values forming the left edge of the table and the formulas forming the top edge of the table.

A two-way table records two values for two different input variables. Quattro Pro puts one row and one column value in the two input cells at a time and records the resulting value of a formula in the table. When setting up the table, put the input values of the first variable in a column in a blank area of the notebook. Move to the cell one row above the first input value and one column to the right. Enter the values for the second input variable across the row. Place the formula or cell reference which you want evaluated in the cell above the first column variable value.

Options

One free variable—Select this radio button to construct a one-way table.

Two free variables—Select this radio button to construct a two-way table.

Data table—Select the location of the table in this text box. If you have selected a block before selecting the Data | What-If command, this block is already selected.

Input cell—Select the cell to systematically replace each of the values in the column while the values for the one-way table are generated. This text box only appears when the One free variable radio button is selected.

Column input cell—Select the cell to systematically replace each of the values in the left most column of the table while the values for the two-way table are generated. This text box only appears when the Two free variables radio button is selected.

Row input cell—Select the cell to systematically replace each of the values in the top row of the table while the values for the two-way table are generated. This text box only appears when the Two free variables radio button is selected.

Reset—Select this button to remove the block and cell addresses selected in the Data table, Input cell, Column input cell, or Row input cell text boxes.

Generate—Select this button to generate the values for the what-if table, based on the other options you have set. For a one-way table, the table is filled in with the values of the formula in the top of the table after the values from the first column are substituted in the input cell. This two-way table is similar to the one-way table; however, the two-way table uses two input values and evaluates only one formula.

Note

You can execute the last Data | What-If command using the same settings by pressing F8 (TABLE).

Dialog | Align | Bottom

This command aligns the selected controls so that the bottom edge of each control has the same vertical position. Select the controls to align before selecting this command.

Options

None.

Dialog | Align | Horizontal Center

This command aligns the selected controls so that their horizontal centers have the same horizontal location as the dialog box. This means that if you created a horizontal line passing through the center of the dialog box, the centers of all the selected controls are also along that line.

Options

None.

Dialog | Align | Horizontal Space

This command adds the same amount of horizontal space between the selected controls. This command is for evenly spacing selected controls horizontally. You must select the controls to space before you select this command.

Options

Space between objects—Type the number of pixels you want set horizontally between each of the selected controls.

Dialog | Align | Left

This command aligns the selected controls so that the left edge of each control has the same horizontal position. Select the controls to align before selecting this command.

Options

None.

Dialog | Align | Resize to Same

This command adjusts the height and width of the selected controls so they are all the same size. Before you use this command, select the control you want the other controls to be resized to and then add the other controls you want in the same size to the selection.

Options

None.

Dialog | Align | Right

This command aligns the selected controls so that the right edge of each control has the same horizontal position. Select the controls to align before selecting this command.

Options

None.

Dialog | Align | Top

This command aligns the selected controls so that the top edge of each control has the same vertical position. Select the controls to align before selecting this command.

Options
None.

Dialog | Align | Vertical Center

This command aligns the selected controls at the vertical center of the dialog box. This means that if you created a vertical line passing through the center of the dialog box, the centers of all the selected controls fall along that line.

Options
None.

Dialog | Align | Vertical Space

This command adds the same amount of vertical space between the selected controls. This command is for evenly spacing selected controls vertically. You must select the controls to space before you select this command.

Options
Space between objects—Type the number of pixels you want set vertically between each of the selected controls.

Dialog | Close SpeedBar

This command closes the current SpeedBar. If the SpeedBar that is closed contains changes that you have not saved, Quattro Pro prompts you to save the SpeedBar.

Options
Yes—Select this button to save the contents of the SpeedBar just as if you selected the Dialog | Save SpeedBar command.
No—Select this button to omit saving the contents of the indicated SpeedBar.
Cancel—Select this button to cancel the Dialog | Close SpeedBar command.

Note
You can also close the SpeedBar by selecting Close from the SpeedBar's control menu or double-clicking it.

Dialog | Connect

This command creates a link between a control and a cell in a notebook. It is for creating links to dialog box controls that receive their initial values and store the control's result in a cell.

Options

> *Source*—Select the dialog box control name in this text box that you want for the connection. Usually, you select the dialog box control you want for the connection before selecting this command so that you do not have to change the entry in this text box.
>
> *Target*—Select the notebook cell, block, or the name of another control where you want the contents of the dialog box control placed.
>
> *Dynamic Connection*—Select this check box to have the contents of the target cell updated while you change the value of the dialog box control (when you are using the dialog box as a dialog box). Clear this check box to have the contents of the target cell updated only when you complete the dialog box.

Note

> This command creates the link commands that perform the connection. When you use this command again on the same control, the Target text box is empty. If you want to modify the connection, use the Dialog | Links command.

Dialog | Links

> This command assigns link commands to a control in a dialog box or SpeedBar. After you select this command you can create, modify, and delete the link commands that the control performs. Link commands are how you make the dialog box and SpeedBar controls you have created perform a function.

Options

> The primary part of the Object Link dialog box are the link commands that are listed in the top half of the dialog box. For each part of the link command, you can select a different entry by clicking the part to change and then dragging the mouse to the replacement you want for that part of the link command. Some parts let you type an entry, such as when you have a control perform macro instructions. Besides changing the link commands in the top half, you also have the following buttons:
>
> *Add*—Select this button to add a new link command at the bottom of the list that you can subsequently modify.
>
> *Insert*—Select this button to add a new link command above the currently selected one in the list that you can subsequently modify.
>
> *Delete*—Select this button to remove the currently selected link command in the list.
>
> *Delete All*—Select this button to remove all of the listed link commands.

Dialog | New SpeedBar

> This command opens a new empty SpeedBar. The new SpeedBar is initially named SpBar#.BAR where # is the next highest unused number.

Options
None.

Dialog | Open SpeedBar

This command opens the SpeedBar for editing. Editing a SpeedBar lets you create a secondary SpeedBar. Creating and editing SpeedBars are described further in Chapter 12.

Options
The File Name text and list box, Directories list box, File Types drop-down list box, and Drives drop-down list box options for this command are identical to the other commands that let you select files. They are described under File | Open.

Dialog | Order | Order Controls

This command orders the controls to match the initial values provided by the arguments of the {DODIALOG} macro command that invokes the dialog box. Before you select this command, select the controls in the order that their initial values appear in the {DODIALOG} macro command's argument block. You can add controls to the selected controls by holding down SHIFT while you click each one.

Options
None.

Dialog | Order | Order From

This command inserts controls into the control order that matches the initial values provided by the arguments of the {DODIALOG} macro command that invokes the dialog box. Before you select this command, select the control that you will want the inserted controls to follow. Then select each of the controls you want inserted in the control order. You can add controls to the selected controls by holding down SHIFT while you click each one.

Options
None.

Dialog | Order | Order Tab Controls

This command orders the controls for the tab order. The tab order is the order you move from one control in a dialog box to another as you press TAB. Before you select this command, select the controls in the order you want to move to them with the TAB key. You can add controls to the selected controls by holding down SHIFT while you click each one.

Options
None.

Dialog | Order | Order Tab From

This command inserts controls into the tab order. The tab order is the order you move from one control in a dialog box to another as you press TAB. Before you select this command, select the control that you want the inserted controls to follow. Then select each of the controls you want inserted in the tab order. You can add controls to the selected controls by holding down SHIFT while you click each one.

Options
None.

Dialog | Order | Send Backward

This command sends the selected control one layer back when a dialog box or SpeedBar has several overlapping controls. This is similar, in visual terms, to moving a card, further down in the deck. You must select the control you want to move backward before you select this command.

Options
None.

Dialog | Order | Send to Back

This command moves the selected control, when the dialog box or SpeedBar has overlapping controls, to the very back of the stack. This is similar, in visual terms, to moving a card to the bottom of the deck. You must select the control you want to move backward before you select this command.

Options
None.

Dialog | Order | Bring Forward

This command brings the selected control one layer forward when a dialog box or SpeedBar has several overlapping controls. This is similar, in visual terms, to moving a card, higher in the deck. You must select the control you want to move forward before you select this command.

Options
None.

Dialog | Order | Bring to Front

This command moves the selected control, when the dialog box or SpeedBar has overlapping controls, to the very front of the stack. This is similar, in visual terms, to moving a card to the top of the deck. You must select the control you want to move forward before you select this command.

Options
None.

Dialog | Save SpeedBar

This command saves a SpeedBar in a file. Saving the SpeedBar you have created puts it on disk so you can select it later to include it as a secondary SpeedBar. Saving does not close the SpeedBar window, so you can continue editing it. The SpeedBar is saved with the default filename, unless you assign a new name by inspecting the SpeedBar's properties. SpeedBars are usually saved in the same directory as the Quattro Pro for Windows program files.

Options
None.

Dialog | Save SpeedBar As

This command lets you alter the file name and other file options while saving a SpeedBar. Using this command, you can save a file to another location or with a different name. To prevent you from accidentally replacing the wrong SpeedBar, Quattro Pro will prompt you to cancel, replace, or backup when you save a SpeedBar.

Options
The options are identical to those for the File | Save command described below. The following options appear if you are saving a file to an already existing SpeedBar:
Replace—Select this button to replace the selected SpeedBar file with the current SpeedBar you are using.
Backup—Select this button to rename the currently saved SpeedBar file with the

same file name and the extension .BAK, and then save the current SpeedBar notebook to the original file name.
Cancel—Select this option to cancel the command.

Draw | Align | Bottom

This command aligns a group of objects so that the bottom edge of each object is on a line with the bottom edge of every other object.

Options
None.

Draw | Align | Horizontal Center

This command aligns a group of objects so that their horizontal centers are all in line with the horizontal centers of the graph. This means that if you created a horizontal line passing through the center of the graph, the centers of all the other objects are also along that line.

Options
None.

Draw | Align | Left

This command aligns a group of objects so the left edge of each object is in line with the left edge of every other object.

Options
None.

Draw | Align | Right

This command aligns a group of objects so that the right edge of each object is on a line with the right edge of every other object.

Options
None.

Draw | Align | Top

This command aligns a group of objects so that the top edge of each object is on a line with the top edge of every other object.

Options
None.

Draw | Align | Vertical Center

This command aligns a group of objects so that their vertical centers are all in line with the vertical centers of the graph. This means that if you created a vertical line passing through the center of the graph, the centers of all the other objects are also along that line.

Options
None.

Draw | Bring Forward

This command brings the selected object one layer forward when a graph has several overlapping objects. This is similar, in visual terms, to moving a card higher in the deck. You must select the object you want to move forward before you select this command.

Options
None.

Draw | Bring to Front

This command moves the selected object, when the graph has overlapping objects, to the very front of the stack. This is similar, in visual terms, to moving a card to the top of the deck. You must select the object you want to move forward before you select this command.

Options
None.

Draw | Export

This command saves a graph in a graphics format file. You can do this to make slides at a service bureau, or to use the graph in another application or program. You can select the format in which Quattro Pro saves the graph. Quattro Pro can save graphs in the .BMP, .CGM, .EPS, .GIF, .PCX, .and .TIF formats.

Options
File Name—Type the file name you want to assign to the graphics file in this text box. You can also select a file name from the list box. The files shown in this list

box have the extension set in the File Types drop-down list box and are in the directory chosen in the Directories list box on the Drives drop-down list box.

File Types—Select the format you want the graphics file saved from the drop-down list box. The extension you select determines the format in which the file is saved.

Directories—Select the directory from the list box where you want the graphics file saved. The directories are those in the drive selected in the Drives drop-down list box.

Drives—Select the drive to save the graphics file.

None—Select this radio button to save a TIFF file without any compression. The file takes up a great deal of space on the disk, but can be read by most applications which support graphics.

PackBits—Select this radio button to save a TIFF file with the PackBits method of compression. The file takes up less space, but some applications cannot read this form of compression.

Bitmap gray scale—Select this check box to save a bitmap or TIFF file with all the colors converted to various shades of gray. Some applications cannot support color, but can support a gray scale file.

Draw I Group

This command marks the selected objects as a group. After a group of objects are marked as a group, you can move them as a unit, alter the properties for all of them at once, and change the color of all the objects in the group. All actions you carry out on the group act on every object within the group. You must select the objects to be part of the group before you select this command. You can hold down SHIFT to add the objects you click to the current selection. After you mark objects as a group, they have a single set of handles instead of each of the objects in the group having separate handles.

Options
None.

Draw I Import

This command opens a graphics file and places it in the current graph. Quattro Pro can translate several graphic formats, including .BMP, .CGM, .CLP, .EPS, .GIF, .PCX, .PIC, and .TIF. A graphics file is imported in three ways. One method is to add a large rectangle that is filled with the contents of the file (.BMP, .GIF, .EPS, PCX, and .TIF files). A second way, used by .CGM and .CLP files, is to add the imported graphics as drawn objects which can be modified as if you added them by copying the drawn objects from one Quattro Pro graph to another. A third way, used by .PIC files, is importing the graphic as an unmodifiable object which can only be moved and sized.

Options

The only option for this command is to select the file that you want to import. The options for selecting the file are the same File Name text box and list box, Directories list box, File Types drop-down list box, and Drives drop-down list box as you use for other commands that let you select files. The default selections for the file types are different to match the different formats graphics files use. The available file types include .BMP, .CGM, .CLP, .EPS, .GIF, .PCX, .PIC, and .TIF.

Draw | Send Backward

This command sends the selected object one layer back when a graph has several overlapping objects. This is similar, in visual terms, to moving a card further down in the pile. You must select the object you want to move backward before you select this command.

Options

None.

Draw | Send to Back

This command moves the selected object, when the graph has overlapping objects, to the very back of the stack. This is similar, in visual terms, to moving a card to the bottom of the deck. You must select the object you want to move backward before you select this command.

Options

None.

Draw | Ungroup

This command ungroups the objects in the selected group, so that they can be edited and moved separately. After you ungroup objects, each of the objects now have separate handles.

Options

None.

Edit | Clear

This command deletes entries in one or more cells and restores the formatting of those cells back to the Normal style. You must select the cell or block of cells which you want to clear before invoking this command. You cannot clear the contents or formatting of a protected cell while protection is enabled.

Options
>   None.

Edit I Clear Contents

This command clears the contents of a cell, but does not affect the cell's properties. Therefore, a cell with a currency format and a 16-point font retains the numeric format and font selection after you use this command. You cannot clear protected cells while protection is enabled. You must select the cell or block of cells you wish to clear before you select this command.

Options
>   None.

Note
>   You can also clear the contents of a block of cells by selecting the block of cells and pressing the DEL key.

Edit I Copy

This command transfers a copy of the selected block or object to the Windows Clipboard without affecting the original copy in the notebook. The copy of the information in the Clipboard can be copied back into the notebook, into another notebook, or into a document in another application. You must select the block or object you want to copy to the Clipboard before invoking this command. You can use this command to copy cell contents, graphs, and graph objects.

Options
>   None.

Note
>   You can also copy the selected data to the Clipboard by clicking the Copy button on the SpeedBar (second one from the left) or by pressing CTRL-INS.

Edit I Cut

This command transfers the currently selected block, graph, or graph object to the Windows Clipboard and removes the information from the notebook while doing so. The copy of the information in the Clipboard can be copied into the same notebook, into another notebook, or into a document in some other application. You must select the block which you want to cut to the Clipboard before invoking this command.

Options
>   None.

Note

You can also cut the selected data to the Clipboard by clicking the Cut button on the SpeedBar (first one from the left) or by pressing SHIFT-DEL.

Edit | Define Style

This command creates and revises the named styles that you use in a notebook. A named style is a group of block properties including alignment, numeric format, protection, line drawing, shading, font, and text color. The style named Normal is the default style for the entire notebook, and is used by a cell until you assign another named style to it. Changing the Normal style, then, changes your default formatting. If you revise a named style, all cells in the notebook formatted with that style are immediately updated to the new style properties. You can also override the style for individual cells by changing their block's properties. You can assign a named style to a block by clicking the Style List drop-down list box in the SpeedBar or pressing CTRL-SHIFT-S and then selecting one of the named styles from the list.

Options

Define Style For—Select the name of a style from this drop-down list box if you want to revise a style, or type a new name if you are creating a new style.

Delete—Select this button to delete the style currently displayed in the Define Style For text box. You cannot delete the Normal style.

Merge—Select this button to set the style named in the Define Style For drop-down list box to adopt the properties of a cell, or another named style. Merging styles is used to assign properties quickly to a new named style. From the displayed Merge Style dialog box, select Style to use the properties of an existing style, or Cell to use the properties of a selected cell. Select an existing style name from the Select Style drop-down list box, or select a cell from the Select Cell text box.

Alignment—Select this button to set the alignment of cells using the named style. Select from General, Left, Right, or Center.

Format—Select this button to set the numeric format of the cells using the named style. You have all the formatting options that are available through the Numeric Format block property.

Protection—Select this button to set whether the cells using the named style are protected or unprotected when page protection is enabled. Select either Protect or Unprotect.

Line Drawing—Select this button to set the lines drawn around the cells that use the selected named style. You can select from no line, a single line, a double line, or thick line. These lines can appear on the top, bottom, right, or left of the cell. The selections are made in the same fashion as setting lines for the Line Drawing block property.

Shading—Select this button to set the shading for the cells using the named style. The options that appear are identical to those that appear with the Shading block property.

Font—Select this button to set the font of the cells that use the selected named style. The options are identical to the options for the Font block property.
Text Color—Select this button to set the color of the text. You can select a color from the default color palette.

Note

You can also quickly assign a group of block properties using the SpeedFormat button in the SpeedBar, which is the last button on the default SpeedBar. When you select a format name from the Formats list box, you are setting the block properties for the borders of the selected block and the cells in the middle of the block. The dialog box includes a sample of how the selected format will make the block appear. You can also remove parts of the quick format that this SpeedBar adds by clearing the property buttons in the bottom half of the SpeedFormat dialog box.

Edit | Goto

This command moves the selector to a different point in the notebook, or another open notebook. It can be used to select noncontiguous blocks, access frozen titles, and move to specific points on another page.

Options

Reference—Type the cell address, block address, or block name where you want the selector moved, or use Block Names to select the location.
Block Names—Select a block name from this list box to enter into the Reference text box.

Note

You can also perform this command by pressing F5 (GOTO).

Edit | Paste

This command copies the current contents of the Windows Clipboard to the notebook, starting at the location selected when you invoke this command. If you select more than one cell, the contents of the Clipboard may be pasted into each cell, depending on the format of the source application.

When you paste data that was created in Quattro Pro and transferred to the Clipboard with either the Edit | Copy or the Edit | Cut command, the information appears as if it were copied with the Block | Copy command. Unlike the Block | Copy command, the contents are still in the Clipboard, so you can continue pasting the contents to other locations. However, when you use the Edit | Paste command to paste information from another application into Quattro Pro, Quattro Pro selects one of several acceptable formats that are most compatible with it. If you are pasting information created with an application that acts as a server for DDE links

(Windows 3.0) or a server for OLE links (Windows 3.1), the information may be pasted into your Quattro Pro notebook as a linked object.

Options
None.

Note
You can also paste Clipboard data by clicking the Paste button on the SpeedBar (third one from the left) or by pressing SHIFT-INS.

Edit I Paste Format

This command allows you to select the format with which information is pasted in a Quattro Pro notebook. The options consist of the different format types which the data can be formatted in, given its source application. For example, with Windows 3.1, this command can be used to decide whether a drawing created with the Paintbrush Windows accessory is pasted in as an OLE object or a bitmapped graphic.

Options
Select a format from the Paste special format dialog box.

Edit I Paste Link

This command is used to create DDE links between a DDE server application and Quattro Pro. DDE links connect directly to a document created by another application. Each time that data in the other application is updated, the contents of the DDE link are also updated. Before you use this command, you must first copy the information you want to link to the Clipboard in that other application. Make sure you have saved the document in the other application first so the DDE link has a file name to work with. Once the information is on the Clipboard, you can use this command to create a DDE link. The link occurs at the cell the selector is in when you choose this command. This command can also copy information within Quattro Pro itself. If you use the Edit I Paste Link command with Quattro Pro data in the Clipboard, the cells where the Clipboard contents are copied include the link formulas to references the cells in the notebooks the information was copied from.

Options
None.

Edit I Paste Special

This command performs several special copying features that are similar to Block menu commands, except that the data is copied from the Clipboard. This command copies properties and/or entries from one location to another. Use this command to copy entries without copying the properties of the entries. You can also use this command to copy the properties and styles from one location to another and have the properties and styles applied to a different set of entries. This command can also copy formulas, or only the values the formulas currently equal. This command can transpose the columns and rows of the copied entries or properties. It can omit copying blank cells that will otherwise erase existing entries. Before you use this command you must move the selector to where you want the copies placed.

Options

Properties—Select this check box to copy the properties of the original entries.

Contents—Select this check box to copy the cell contents without necessarily copying the properties.

Formulas—Select this radio button to copy any formulas in the Clipboard's contents as their formulas. This radio button is only available when the Contents check box is selected.

Values Only—Select this radio button to copy the values of any formulas in the Clipboard's contents instead of their formulas. This radio button is only available when the Contents check box is selected.

Transpose rows and columns—Select this check box to transpose the Clipboard's contents as it copies the rows and columns of information from the Clipboard.

Avoid pasting blanks—Select this check box to prevent overwriting cells that have entries with empty cells that are part of the Clipboard's contents.

Edit I Search and Replace

This command searches for and replaces entries containing certain characters. You can also use this command to search for values which meet conditional criteria. To begin the search and replace operation, select either Next or Previous as described below.

Options

Block(s)—Select the block of cells you want to search. If you leave this blank, Quattro Pro searches the entire page. If you have selected a block before selecting this command, the block is already entered in the text box.

Find—Enter the string to find, such as Sales, or the condition, such as ? >100000. If you enter a condition, you must select the Condition radio button.

Replace—Enter the characters or data that replaces the searched for entry when it is found.

Formula—Select this radio button so Quattro Pro looks for the character string in the entered text of formulas rather than the computed values of formulas. Quattro Pro always searches labels and value entries.

Value—Select this radio button for Quattro Pro to look for the character string in the calculated results of formulas, as well as labels and value entries.

Condition—Select this radio button for Quattro Pro to search for cell entries using the condition entered as the find string.

Columns first—Select this check box to search the block on a column-by-column basis. Clear this check box to search the block on a row-by-row.

Match whole—Select this check box if you want Quattro Pro to find matching entries when the cell only contains the string entered in the Find text box. Clear this check box if you want Quattro Pro to find cells that contain the find string when the cell contains additional characters before or after the find string.

Case Sensitive—Select this check box if you want the string in the block to have the same case as the find string. Clear this check box if the string in the block can have the same letters as the find string but may be in a different case.

Next—Select this button to locate the find string using the options specified with the other selections. The selector is moved to the cell containing the find string which you see in the input line. The dialog box remains displayed so you can select other buttons. To leave the dialog box, select the Close button.

Previous—Select this button to find the locate string by using the options specified with the other selections, but proceed backward through the block.

Replace—Select this button to replace the find string with the replacement string, then move to the next instance of the find string.

Replace All—Select this button to locate all instances of the find string and replace all of them with the replacement string.

Reset—Select this button to remove the find and replace string and reset the other options to the defaults.

Note

When your find string is a label, and Match whole is selected, you must include a label indicator in the find string, or select Value. Otherwise Quattro Pro will look at your entry, which includes a label indicator, and assume that your find string does not match.

Edit I Undo

This command removes the effect of the last "undo-able" command that you performed. This command only works when the Undo enabled check box for the Startup application property is selected. The Edit I Undo command cannot undo all of the actions you perform with Quattro Pro. This command acts as a toggle switch. The first time you execute the command, Quattro Pro shows the notebook without the effect of the last undo-able command. When you execute this command again, Quattro Pro shows the notebook with the effect of the last undo-able command. After undoing the last undoable command, Undo in the Edit menu changes to Redo. To the right of Undo or Redo in the Edit menu is a brief description of the action Quattro Pro will undo or redo.

Options

None.

File | Close

This command closes the current window and moves to another window. If the window that is closed contains changes that you have not saved, Quattro Pro prompts you to save the notebook. Closing a window does not affect the size or position of the remaining windows. If you are closing a notebook that has any graph windows or dialog boxes open, the graph windows and dialog boxes are also closed. If you are closing a copy of a notebook when more than one copy is open with the Window | New View command, you will close all copies of that notebook as well as any open graph windows or dialog boxes.

Options
Yes—Select this button to save the contents of the current notebook just as if you selected the File | Save command.
No—Select this button to omit saving the contents of the indicated notebook.
Cancel—Select this button to cancel the File | Close command.

Note
If you want to close only one copy of a notebook with the Window | New View command and more than one copy is open , select Close from that copy's control menu.

File | Close All

This command closes all open windows. If any open notebooks contain unsaved changes, Quattro Pro prompts you to save the notebooks.

Options
Yes—Select this button to save the contents of the current notebook just as if you selected the File | Save command.
No—Select this button to omit saving the contents of the indicated notebook.
Cancel—Select this button to cancel the File | Close All command.

File | Exit

This command closes the open windows and then exits from Quattro Pro. As Quattro Pro closes each notebook window, Quattro Pro will prompt you to save the notebook if the current notebook contains unsaved changes.

Options
Yes—Select this button to save the contents of the current notebook just as if you selected the File | Save command.
No—Select this button to omit saving the contents of the indicated notebook.
Cancel—Select this button to cancel the File | Exit command.

Note

You can also perform this command by pressing ALT-F4 (QUIT QUATTRO PRO) to close Quattro Pro's application window, double-clicking the application control menu box, or selecting C̲lose from the application control menu.

File I Named Settings

This command creates named settings which are a set of print settings that you use in a notebook. Instead of setting the F̲ile I P̲rint and F̲ile I Page Se̲tup commands each time you want to print, you can create named settings. Each named setting contains a different set of print settings set with those commands. When you choose to use a new named settings, all of the print settings are reset to correspond to the named settings.

Options

N̲amed Settings—Select the previously created named settings from this list box to make the print settings assigned to the name the current print settings.

C̲reate—Select this button to create new named settings using the current print settings. Quattro Pro prompts you for the name of the new named settings. Type the name for the print settings, which follows the same rules as block names and select OK.

U̲pdate—Select this button to update the name selected in the N̲amed Settings list box with the current print settings.

D̲elete—Select this button to delete the named settings currently selected in the N̲amed Settings list box.

Note

Since named settings are saved with the notebook, after you create or update a named setting, be sure to save the notebook again.

File I New

This command opens a new window with an empty unnamed notebook. The new file is named NOTEBK followed by the next highest unused notebook number until you save or erase the file. Quattro Pro can open as many notebooks as your computer's memory will allow.

Options

None.

Note

Be sure to save any unnamed notebooks before you save notebooks containing formulas that reference the unnamed notebook so that Quattro Pro can replace the NOTEBK# references with the correct file name.

File I Open

This command opens a file in a new notebook window. It is different from File I Retrieve, since it opens a new window instead of replacing the contents of a current window. Your computer's memory limits the number of Quattro Pro notebooks you can have open. When you select this command, you must select the file that you want to open. The file can be on your hard disk or on a floppy disk in the drive. By selecting a file that does not have the default extension of .WB1, Quattro Pro will convert the file from another format to its own. Using a different file format lets you use Quattro Pro with files created by other applications such as Paradox, Reflex, dBASE, Excel and 1-2-3.

Options

The options for this command select the file you want to open. They are also the same file selection options for all commands that let you select files. Once you select a file, if the file is password protected, you are prompted for the password which you must correctly enter before the file is opened.

File Name—Either type the name of the file that you want to open in this text box or select the file from the list box below. The files shown in this list box have the extension set in the File Types drop-down list box, in the directory chosen in the Directories list box, on the drive selected by the Drives drop-down list box. You can enter a file name template in this text box to find a file name that fits, using the DOS wild card characters, ? and *. For example, QPW*.W?? finds any files starting with QPW and having an extension starting with W.

File Types—Select from this drop-down list box the file extensions for the file types you want to see listed in the File Names list box. The default extension is *.W?? to list all worksheet files. Select the appropriate extension from this drop-down list box, and only the files which have that extension are shown. You can also set the extension of the listed files by typing *. and the extension in the File Name text box.

Directories—Select from this list box the directory of the file you want to open. The files in the directory are displayed in the File Name list box. The directories are those in the drive selected in the Drives drop-down list box.

Drives—Select the drive from this drop-down list box that contains the file you want to open.

File I Page Setup

This command sets up the pages when you print from pages or graphs. You have access to the same options whether you are printing spreadsheet data or graphs, but the settings for each are stored separately, so that you can use one group of settings to print notebook pages and another to print graphs. With this command, you can set headers and footers to print on each page, margins, paper size, scaling, and paper orientation. You can choose to center blocks as they print, to print the block to fit on the page, or to print the block as if it were one large block without page breaks. You can also restore the default settings. With the File I Named Settings command, you can save sets of print settings so that you can change them quickly as you print different reports.

Options

Header—Enter the text header, which is text that appears at the top of every page, in this text box. Headers normally include information that do not appear in the print block, such as report titles and dates. Headers can be divided into three parts by separating each part with a vertical bar (I). The first is left aligned, the second center aligned, and the third right aligned., You can use up to 256 characters, using the following special codes to insert specific information in the header:

Code Meaning
#d   Current date in Windows' Short International format
#D   Current date in Window's Long International format
#ds   Current date in Quattro Pro's Short Date format
#Ds   Current date in Quattro Pro's Long Date format
#t   Current time in Windows' Short International format
#T   Current time in Windows' Long International format
#ts   Current time in Quattro Pro's Short Time format
#Ts   Current time in Quattro Pro's Long Time format
#p   Current page number
#p+n Current page number plus *n*
#P   Number of pages in printout
#P+n Number of pages in printout plus *n*
#f   Name of notebook file, without path
#F   Name of notebook file, with path
#n   Puts the rest of the entry on the second line
Current page number (Quattro Pro for DOS compatibility)
@   Current date (Quattro Pro for DOS compatibility)

Footer—Enter the text of the footer, which is text that appears at the bottom of every page, in this text box. Footers normally include information that does not appear in the print block, such as page numbers, and authors' names. Footers follow the same pattern as headers and can use all of the special characters described above for headers.

Header Font—Select this button to change the font used by both the header and the footer. Once you select this button to open the Font dialog box, you have the same options for the Font block property.

Top—Type the distance between the top of the page and the header.

Header—Type the distance between the header and the beginning of the block or graphic.

Left—Type the distance between the left edge of the page and the block or graphic.

Right—Type the distance between the right edge of the page and block or graphic.

Footer—Type the distance between the bottom of the print block or graphic and the footer.

Bottom—Type the distance between the footer and the bottom of the paper.

Break pages—Select this check box to have the output separated into pages depending on the selected margins and page size. Clear this check box to print the print block as if it were one large page. When page breaks are not printed, this feature disables headers and footers and ignores the page breaks.

Print to fit—When this option is selected the print block is reduced to fit on one page.

Center blocks—When this option is selected, the blocks that are printed are centered in the page, rather than simply starting at the upper left corner.

Paper type—This option sets the paper size. Select one of the defined paper sizes from this list box. The page sizes are set through the printer driver for the selected printer.

Scaling—This option sets the scaling for the print block. Enter a number between 1 and 1000 to size the print block when it prints. 100 percent is full size printout. Smaller numbers shrink the print block, larger ones expand it.

Portrait—Select this radio button to set the orientation of the paper during printing so that the print block occurs vertically on the page.

Landscape—Select this radio button to set the orientation of the paper during printing so that the print block is printed sideways.

Note

The margin options are entered in the default measurement, which follows the word Margin above this section. If you wish to enter these measurements in another system, simply add **in** for inches or **cm** for centimeters after the value. Quattro Pro will convert your measurement into the standard measurement system.

File | Print

This command prints a block of data or a graph from the current notebook. The block can be a single cell, a contiguous block, a noncontiguous block, or a three-dimensional block. Using this command, you can set the data to print, the pages to print, and how many copies you want printed. You can also preview the printed block. You can set spreadsheet printing options, such as row and column headings, the number of lines of printout between contiguous blocks or pages, and to print borders, gridlines, and cell formulas. Printing also uses the print settings set by the File | Page Setup and File | Printer Setup commands. When you are finished making changes to the print settings and you are ready to print the selected block or graph, select the Print button.

Options

Print block(s)—Select the block or blocks which you want to print in this text box. The block can be contiguous, noncontiguous, or three-dimensional. Contiguous blocks that are part of noncontiguous blocks print as if they were selected separately, as do multiple pages in 3-D blocks.

All pages—Select this radio button to print the entire print block.

From...to...—Select this radio button to print selected pages of the print block. Enter the first page in the first text box and the final page in the second.

Copies—Type the number of copies of the printout you want in this text box. The default is to print only one copy.

Preview—Select this button to preview the printout. For more details, see the command File | Print Preview.

Options—Select this button to open the Spreadsheet Print Options dialog box, which provides further printing options that apply specifically to notebooks. In this dialog box, you can set rows to print at the top of every page by entering the block containing the cells in the Top heading text box. To have columns printed at the right of every page, enter the block containing the cells in the Left heading text box. Select Cell formulas to print a list of cells and their contents. Clear Cell formulas to print the cells as they appear in the notebook. Select Gridlines to print the block with the gridlines that separate cells. Clear Gridlines to omit printing any gridlines. Select Row/Column borders to print the print block with the row and column identifiers that you see in the window. Clear Row/Column borders to print the print block without the row and column identifiers. Underneath Print between blocks and Print between 3D pages, you can select how different contiguous blocks or pages within the print block are separated. When you select the Page advance radio button, each contiguous block or page is printed on a separate page. When you select the Lines radio button and specify how many lines, each contiguous block or page is separated by the number of lines you selected. The default is zero lines so the contiguous blocks and pages are printed continuously.

Note

When you print a graph, the Graph Print dialog box that this command displays contains the Copies text box and the Preview button, as well as the Print, Close, and Help buttons.

File | Print Preview

This command previews the printout block as it appears on the page. Previewing the printout gives you a chance to see that all the settings are correct. You can also preview the output by selecting the Preview button after selecting the File | Print command. The SpeedBar provides options for controlling the preview or setting page and print options. When you preview a printout, the page is first shown at a size so that the entire page appears in the window. Click the left mouse button to zoom into the page. Clicking the right mouse button zooms back from the page.

Options

Previous—Select this button to move to the previous page in the printout. You can also press PGUP. A third option is to type the page number you want to see in the adjacent text box.

Next—This button moves to the next page in the printout. You can also press

PGDN. A third option is to type the page number you want to see in the adjacent text box.

Color—Select this button to toggle between showing the page in color and black and white palettes. This button allows you to view the page as it is formatted, or as it will print using a black and white printer.

Margin—Select this button to add gray dashed lines on the page, which indicate the margins. You can drag these lines with the mouse to move the margins.

Setup—This button opens the same dialog box as the File I Page Setup command, but returns to the preview after you close it. See the File I Page Setup to learn about these options.

Options—This button is like choosing Options after selecting the File I Print command, except that you return to the preview when you are done.

Print—This button prints the print block as it appears in the preview.

End—Select this button to end the preview.

File I Printer Setup

This command selects the destination of your data, either to a printer or a file. It also sets certain options for your printer. This command can access the Printer Setup dialog box which you can also reach by selecting Printers from Windows' Control Panel. The changes that you make in this dialog box become Windows default options, and are used by other Windows applications. Many of these options, such as paper size and orientation, can also be set with the File I Page Setup.

Options

Printer and Port—Select the printer that you plan to use from this list box. The printers available are those which are installed for Windows.

Redirect to File—Select this check box to print your print block to a binary file, which includes all the printer codes needed to print the print block with the selected printer. You can use this command to print to a file, move to a system with a better printer, and copy the file to the printer, so that you can get the superior quality output. Enter the file name you wish to use in the text box, or select the Browse button to select a file name.

Browse—Select this button to browse through the directory structure of your disk to select a file you wish to replace with the coded print output.

Setup—This button accesses the Windows printer definition for the selected printer. The changes you make in these settings become the new Windows defaults, and will affect the printing of all Windows applications. The options that appear in this dialog box vary depending on the printer you have selected.

File I Retrieve

This command retrieves a notebook that you have saved before and places the notebook in the current window. It is just like the File I Open command except that the contents of the current notebook window are replaced by the file you select. The notebooks in the other windows are left intact.

Options

If the file in the current window contains unsaved changes, you are prompted to confirm that you want to lose the changes. Select Yes to retrieve a notebook file without saving the contents of the notebook window, or No to cancel the File | Retrieve command. Next, you must select the file to retrieve. The options for this command, at this point, include using the same File Name text box and list box, Directories list box, File Types drop-down list box, and Drives drop-down list box that you use for other commands that let you select files. Once you select a file, if the file is password protected, you are prompted for the password which you must correctly enter before the file is retrieved.

File | Save

This command saves a file. Saving a file puts it permanently on disk so that you can open it at a later time. Saving does not close the notebook window, so you can continue working on the data. You want to save the file frequently to insure you do not lose important data. By saving a file with a different extension from .WB1, you can save the file in another format which other applications can use. You can save the file with a password, which must be entered before anyone can open the file. If you have not saved the file before, you can enter a file name. If the file has been saved before, Quattro Pro uses the same file name to save the file again without any prompts. You can save the file to any drive or directory. If you want to make changes to how a file is saved for a file you have saved already, use the File | Save As command.

Options

These are the options presented if you are saving a file for the first time.

File Name—Type the file name you want for the file in this text box. You can also select a file name from the list box. The files that are shown in this list box have the extension set in the File Types drop-down list box and are in the directory chosen in the Directories list box and the Drives drop-down list box.

File Types—Select the extension of the files you want to see in the File Names list box from this drop-down list box. The extension you select determines the format in which the file is saved, unless you type a file extension in the File Name text box. By specifying an extension other than .WB1, Quattro Pro saves the file in another format. This feature allows Quattro Pro to save files for Quattro Pro for DOS, 1-2-3, dBASE, Multiplan, Paradox, Reflex, Surpass, Excel and Symphony. If you use a .DB, .DB2, .DBF, .R2D, or .RXD extension, Quattro Pro prompts you for the information it needs to convert the notebook into a database file.

Directories—Select the directory of the files you want displayed in the File Name text box. The directories are those in the drive selected in the Drives drop-down list box.

Drives—Select the drive to search for the file to save.
Protection Password—Enter up to fifteen characters to use as a password in this text box, if you want to use one. Quattro Pro distinguishes between upper- and lowercase characters in the password. As you type the password, the character spaces are indicated by pound signs (#) rather than the characters themselves. After you select OK to save the file, you must enter the password again in a Verify Password text box. To password protect a file you have saved before, use the File | Save As command.

File | Save All

This command saves all open files as if you selected the File | Save command for each open notebook.

Options

This command has the same options as the File | Save command described above, except they are repeated for each open notebook.

File | Save As

This command lets you alter the file name and other file options while saving a file. The command is the same as File | Save except that when the file has been previously saved, you will still see the Save File dialog box and can select the file name, location, and optional password. Using this command, you can save a file in a new format, with a different name, or with a password. Saving a notebook with a new file name, an extension, or in a different directory or drive does not alter the original file. To prevent you from accidentally using a name already assigned to another file, when you use this command, Quattro Pro will prompt you to cancel, replace, or backup a file that you are replacing with new information.

Options

The options are identical to those for the File | Save command described above. The following options appear if you are saving a file to an already existing file name:
Replace—Select this button to replace the selected file with current file you are using.
Backup—Select this button to rename the currently saved file with the same file name and the extension .BAK, and then save the current notebook to the original file name.
Cancel—Select this option to cancel the command.

File | Workspace | Restore

This command restores a workspace you have saved as a workspace file. A workspace file opens files and arranges their windows in the position and size you have saved them.

Options

The options for selecting the workspace file are the same File Name text box and list box, the Directories list box, the File Types drop-down list box, and the Drives drop-down list box as you use for other commands that let you select files. Workspace files have a .WBS extension.

File I Workspace I Save

This command saves the size and position of all open windows as well as the file names of the open notebooks. This lets you treat a set of notebook windows as a group so that you do not have to open each notebook and arrange each window separately each time you want to work with the same group of files. Saving a workspace only saves the names of the open windows and their size and position rather than saving the data files.

Options

The options for saving the workspace file are the same File Name text box and list box, the Directories list box, the File Types drop-down list box, and the Drives drop-down list box as you use for other commands that let you save files. Workspace files have a .WBS extension.

Graph I Copy

This command copies a graph. You can create a new graph by copying a graph to a new graph name. You can also transfer part of a graph to an existing graph. When you copy the graph, you can copy the entire graph, the graph properties only, the data references only, or the drawn objects only.

Options

From—Select the graph which you want to copy in this list box, which lists all the graphics in the notebook.
To—Select the graph to which you want to copy in this drop-down list box, or type a new graph name to create a new graph.
Style—Select this check box to copy the style of the From graph to the To graph. Style includes font and color changes, and the type of graph. Clear this check box when you do not want the graph's properties copied to the To graph.
Data—Select this check box to copy the data of the From graph to the To graph. This copies to the To graph all references to cells, either in the data ranges or in the titles. You are copying the block addresses the graph uses rather than the data itself. Clear this check box when you do not want the To graph to use the same data as the From graph.
Annotate objects—Select this option to copy all drawn objects to the To graph. Clear this check box when you do not want drawn objects copied to the To graph.

Note

You can copy graphs to another notebook or application by copying the graph to the Clipboard then pasting the graph onto the Graphs page in the other notebook or in the application where you want the graph to appear.

Graph | Delete

This command deletes a graph entirely from your notebook. Both the inserted floating objects that contain the graph and the icon appearing on the Graphs page are deleted. You will need to recreate the graph from scratch if you later decide to use it.

Options

The only option is to select the name of the graph which you want to delete from the Select Graph list box.

Note

Deleting a floating graph that contains a graph name does not delete the graph, since you only are deleting where the graph displays. You can delete a graph by going to the Graphs page, selecting the graph to delete, and pressing DEL.

Graph | Edit

This command opens a graph window so that you can edit the graph features. Most graph properties cannot be changed without working in a graph window. Once the graph to edit is selected, the graph appears in a graph window. A graph window is a separate window from the notebook. You can also edit a graph by double-clicking where it appears as a floating graph or on the Graphs page.

Options

The only option is to select the name of the graph which you want to delete from the Select Graph list box.

Graph | Insert

This command inserts a graph as a floating object on a notebook page. By inserting a graph onto a page, you are placing the graph next to your spreadsheet data. When the print block contains an inserted graph, Quattro Pro prints the graph. Quattro Pro rescales the text in the graph to fit the dimensions of the graph on the notebook page. Once a graph is inserted, you can move it by dragging the graph to a new location or size it by dragging one of the corners to a new location.

Options

The only option for this command is to select the name of the graph from the Select Graph list box and to indicate the location of the graph using the mouse. For the location, you can either select the starting position to use the default graph size or you can drag the mouse to cover the area you want the graph to fill. The location does not have to be precisely the size of a block on the page, since the graphic floats over the page.

Note

You can also insert a graph onto a page by copying a graph to the Clipboard and then pasting it onto the page where you want it to appear. You can also insert a graph by clicking the Graph button on the SpeedBar then clicking where you want the graph to appear, or by dragging the mouse to cover the section where you want the graph to appear. Once an empty text graph is inserted on the page, you can change the graph to another graph by changing the floating graph's Source Graph property.

Graph I New

This command creates a new graph. You can choose the graph name and select the series to use in the new graph. If you want to create a text graph, simply do not specify any data series. If a block is selected before you select this command, Quattro Pro divides the block into rows or columns and enters the individual block addresses in the text boxes. Quattro Pro assumes you would rather have more data points with fewer series. Quattro Pro counts the number of columns and rows in the block to decide whether to divide the block by columns or rows. If you have more columns than rows, Quattro Pro divides the block by rows. If you have more rows than columns, Quattro Pro divides the block by columns. When the block has the same number of columns and rows, Quattro Pro also divides the block by columns. If you select a noncontiguous block before selecting the command, Quattro Pro looks at the first contiguous block to decide whether to divide the block by rows or columns. If the first row or column contains labels, that row or column is used for the x-axis. If the first row or column contains values, Quattro Pro starts using the first row or column as the first series. When the first entry in every row or column is a label, Quattro Pro uses the block containing the first entries for the legend. You can override the default settings by making entries into the Graph New dialog box.

Options

Graph Name—Type the name you want to use for the graph in this text box. The name can be up to 15 characters long with no spaces.
X-Axis—Specify the block containing the data that can be used to identify the points on the x-axis in this text box.
Legend—Specify the block containing the labels for the data series in this text box.
1st, 2nd, etc.—Select the blocks containing each data series in these text boxes. You

can create as many data series as your computer's memory will allow. The data series can consist of contiguous or noncontiguous blocks.

Reverse series—Select this check box to reverse the order of the data series. Clearing the check box uses the data series in the order that the rows or columns appear in the preselected block.

Row/column swap—Select this check box to switch the division of the preselected block into rows or columns. Clear this check box to use the default division.

Add—Select this button to add a new data series to the list of data series.

Delete—Select this button to delete the current selected data series from the list of data series.

Note

You can create a graph and insert on a page at the same time. Select the block to use for the graph just as if you will use the Graph | New command. Click the Graph button on the SpeedBar then click where you want the graph to appear, or drag the mouse to cover the section where you want the graph to appear. Quattro Pro creates a graph using the data from the selected spreadsheet block and the default graph settings.

Graph | Series

This command changes or adds to the data series used to create the graph.

Options

X-Axis—Select the block containing the data to identify the points on the x-axis in this text box.

Legend—Select the block containing the labels for each data series in this text box.

1st, 2nd, etc.—Select the blocks containing each data series in these text boxes. You can create as many data series as your computer's memory will allow. The data series can consist of contiguous or noncontiguous blocks.

Reverse series—Select this check box to reverse the order of the data series. Clear this check box to use the default order.

Row/column swap—Select this check box to alter the orientation of the data series from rows to columns and back. Clear this check box to use the original division for whether a block is divided by rows or columns.

Add—Select this button to add a new data series to the list of data series.

Delete—Select this button to delete the current selected data series from the list of data series.

Graph | Slide Show

This command runs a slide show that you created using several graphs as slides. Slide shows are created using the Create Slide Show tool on the Graphs page's SpeedBar.

Options

The only option is to select which of the slide shows you want to run. Select the slide show from the list and OK to start the slide show. If you select this command on the Graphs page with a slide show selected, you do not have to select a slide show or OK.

Note

You can also run a slide show from the Graphs pages by clicking the Run Slide Show button on the SpeedBar which is the last button on the SpeedBar.

Graph I Titles

This command allows you to enter titles for the entire graph or each axis. These can contain information explaining the graph as a whole or the data displayed on an axis.

Options

Main Title—Type the text of the main title in this text box.
Subtitle—Type the text of the title to appear immediately under the main title in this text box.
X-Axis Title—Type the text of the title describing the x-axis in this text box.
Y1-Axis Title—Type the text of the title describing the first y-axis in this text box.
Y2-Axis Title—Type the text of the title describing the second y-axis in this text box.

Note

You can also enter **\cell address** to use a cell entry as a title. Remember to include the page name otherwise the graph uses the entries from page A.

Graph I Type

This command selects the type of graph Quattro Pro uses to display your data. Quattro Pro has 33 graph types. The default is a vertical stacked bar graph. Quattro Pro lets you change from one type of graph to another.

Options

2-D—Select this radio button to choose from nine types of two-dimensional graphs: Bar, Variance, Stacked Bar, High Low, Line, XY, Area, Column, and Pie graphs.
3-D—Select this radio button to choose from twelve types of three-dimensional graphs: 3-D Bar, 3-D Stacked Bar, 2.5-D Bar, 3-D Step, 3-D Unstacked Area, 3-D Ribbon, 3-D Area, 3-D Column, 3-D Pie, 3-D Surface, 3-D Contour, and 3-D Shaded Surface graphs.
Rotate—Select this radio button to choose from five types of rotated graphs: Rotated 2-D Bar, Rotated 3-D Bar, Rotated 2.5-D Bar, Rotated Area, and Rotated Line graphs.

Combo—Select this radio button to choose from eight types of combination graphs: Line-Bar, Multiple Columns, Area-Bar, Multiple 3-D Columns, High Low-Bar, Multiple Pies, Multiple Bar, and Multiple 3-D Pie graphs.

Text—Select this radio button to make the graph a text graph. A text graph is a blank graph primarily for creating custom drawings or text graphs.

Graph | View

This command displays a full-screen graph. Pressing any key returns you to the previous display.

Options

Select the graph you want to see from the Selected Graph list box and select OK. If you select a graph on the Graphs page before using this command, you do not have to select which graph to display.

Note

This command's shortcut is to press F11 (GRAPH).

Help | About Quattro Pro

This command displays a dialog box giving information about Quattro Pro's copyright date and release number, as well as the available memory.

Options

None.

Help | Contents

This command starts the Help application window showing the Help Contents page. This page serves as a starting point which allows you to access any information on Quattro Pro.

Options

Selecting a hotspot to move to a new help topic.

Help | Functions

This command starts the Help application showing information about the different @functions that Quattro Pro supports.

Options

Select one of the hotspots to move to a help topic that details the category of functions.

Help | Keyboard

This command starts the Help application showing information about using the keyboard in Quattro Pro.

Options

You can select a hotspot to proceed to another help topic detailing specific uses of the keyboard.

Help | Macros

This command starts the Help application showing information about the macro commands.

Options

Select one of the hotspots to move to a help topic explaining the details about a category of macro commands.

Help | Screen Areas

This command starts the Help application showing the Screen Areas help topic.

Options

From the sample screen in the help window, click on any part of the sample window to learn about the name and uses of that part of the window.

Help | Support Info

This command displays information on how you can contact Borland for Quattro Pro assistance.

Options

Select a button to change the help information displayed.

Property | Active Notebook

This command lets you select the properties the notebook uses. These properties include recalculation settings, notebook magnification, the colors in the notebook palette, information at the sides of a notebook window, and whether a notebook is a macro library.

Options

Quattro Pro has many notebook properties. They are listed separately later in the appendix.

Note

You can also inspect notebook properties by right-clicking the notebook title bar.

Property | Active Page

This command lets you select the properties the page uses. These properties include the page name, whether protection is enabled, the color of lines, whether values that meet a condition are displayed in a different color, default label alignment, whether zeros appear on the page, default column width, and whether the page displays grid lines or the row and column borders.

Options

Quattro Pro has many page properties. They are listed separately later in the appendix.

Note

You can also inspect page properties by right-clicking the page tab.

Property | Application

This command lets you select the properties that the application uses. These properties include which parts of the window are displayed; how dates, currency values, and times are formatted; the location where Quattro Pro looks for files; how Quattro Pro runs macros; and whether you are using a secondary SpeedBar.

Options

Quattro Pro has many application properties. These are listed separately later in the appendix.

Note

You can also inspect application properties by right-clicking the application title bar.

Property | Current Object

This command lets you select the properties of the currently selected object. The types of properties you can select depend on the object selected. For example, a block, an object in a graph, or an object in a dialog box may be the currently selected object.

Options

The properties you can select depend on the object selected. The properties for blocks and graph objects which you can change with this command are listed separately later in the appendix. Properties for dialog box objects are described in Chapter 12.

Note

You can also inspect application properties by right-clicking the object.

Property | Dialog

This command lets you select the properties of the dialog box or SpeedBar you are editing. This is available only when the current window is a dialog box or SpeedBar you are editing.

Options

The properties for a dialog box are described with the other dialog box features in Chapter 12.

Note

You can also inspect a dialog box's or SpeedBar's properties by right-clicking the dialog box or SpeedBar title bar.

Property | Graph Pane

This command lets you select the properties of the graph pane which is the area where the graphed data appears within the graph. These properties include the parts of the graph pane that appears and how the graph pane is filled. This command is only available when a graph is the current window.

Options

Quattro Pro has many graph pane properties. These are listed separately later in the appendix.

Note

You can also inspect graph pane by right-clicking the graph pane in a location where the graph's data does not appear.

Property | Graph Setup

This command lets you select some of the basic settings a graph displayed in a graph window uses. These properties include the graph type, legend position, three-dimensional enhancements, the box's appearance around the graph, how the graph background is filled, and whether the overall graph is a graph button. This command is only available when a graph is the current window.

Options

Quattro Pro has many graph setup properties. These are listed separately later in the appendix.

Note

You can also inspect graph setup properties by right-clicking the graph in a window in any location where another part of the graph does not appear.

Property | Graph Window

This command lets you select the properties of a graph window. These properties include the aspect ratio and grid. This command is only available when a graph is the current window.

Options

Quattro Pro has many graph properties. These are listed separately later in the appendix.

Note

You can also inspect graph window properties by right-clicking the graph window title bar or the empty area between the graph window border and the graph.

Property | Legend

This command lets you select the properties a graph's legend uses. These properties include setting the appearance of the text in the legend and how the box that indicates the legend appears. This command is only available when a graph is the current window.

Options

Quattro Pro has many legend properties. They are listed separately later in the appendix.

Note

You can also inspect legend properties by right-clicking the legend.

Property | X Axis

This command lets you select the properties of the X axis of a graph. These properties include the series, scaling, tick marks, and the font of the labels or values along the X axis. This command is only available when a graph is the current window.

Options

Quattro Pro has many X axis properties. These are listed separately later in the appendix.

Note

You can also inspect X axis properties by right-clicking the labels or values that appear along the X axis.

Property I Y Axis

This command lets you select the properties of the Y axis of a graph. These properties include the scaling, tick marks, and the font of the values along the Y axis. This command is only available when a graph is the current window.

Options

Quattro Pro has many Y axis properties. They are listed separately later in the appendix.

Note

You can also inspect Y axis properties by right-clicking the values that appear along the Y axis.

Tools I Advanced Math I Invert

This command computes an inverted matrix. An inverted matrix is a matrix which, when multiplied by its original matrix, creates an identity matrix. Matrix inversion is used in solving simultaneous equations. A matrix is a group of numbers arranged in tabular form. For example, a matrix consisting of eight rows and four columns of numbers is an eight by four matrix. To invert a matrix, the matrix must have the same number of rows and columns.

Options

Source—Select the block containing the matrix to invert in this text box. If you have selected a block before selecting this command, the block is entered in this text box.

Destination—Select where the inverted matrix is to appear in this text box. You only need to select the upper left corner of the destination area.

Tools I Advanced Math I Multiply

This command multiplies two matrices. A matrix is a group of numbers arranged in tabular form. For example, a matrix consisting of eight rows and four columns of numbers is an eight by four matrix. The order of the matrices is important, since the first matrix must have the same number of columns as the number of rows in the second matrix.

Options

Matrix 1—Select the block containing the first matrix in this text box. If you have selected a block before selecting this command, the block is entered in this text box.

Matrix 2—Select the block containing the second matrix in this text box.

Destination—Select the upper left corner of the destination area where you want the product of the matrix multiplication written.

Tools I Advanced Math I Regression

This command performs regression analysis to estimate the relationship between two or more variables. It estimates the correlation between one or more sets of independent variables and a dependent variable. The command calculates the estimated coefficients of the independent variables and evaluates how well the independent variables predict the value of the dependent variable. Before you use this command, you must perform a few preliminary steps. Enter your dependent and independent data into their respective columns. Each column used in the regression analysis should contain only numeric values and should have the same number of entries.

Options

Independent—Select the block containing the independent variables used in the regression analysis in this text box. You specify up to 150 columns for 150 independent variables. Each variables must be in its own column, but the columns do not have to be contiguous.

Dependent—Select the block containing the column containing the dependent variables' values.

Output—Select the block for the output location. You only need to specify the upper left corner of the output area. The output overwrites any existing data.

Reset—Select this button to remove the settings in the text box and select the Compute radio button.

Compute—Select this radio button to have Quattro Pro compute the Y-intercept.

Zero—Select this radio button to have Quattro Pro set the Y-intercept to zero.

Tools I Combine

This command combines some or all of the entries from a notebook file into the current notebook. When you use this command, Quattro Pro uses the current cell in the current notebook as the left uppermost cell that is combined with data from disk. You can combine the entire notebook on disk, or only blocks from it. You can simply replace the current notebook's cell contents with the contents of the cells from notebook in the disk file. Or, you can use the values from the disk file to perform mathematical operations with the data in your current notebook, such as addition and division. You can use this feature to create notebooks detailing yearly totals from quarterly report notebooks.

Options

File Name—Select the name of the file you want to combine data from in this text box, or select the file name from this list box.

File Types—Select the extension of the file you want to combine in this drop-down list box, which also controls which files are displayed in the File Name list box.

Directories—Select the directory to search for the file on disk in this list box.

Drives—Select the drive on which the file on the disk is to be found from this drop-down list box.

Copy—Select this radio button to copy the data from the disk file into the current notebook.

Add—Select this radio button to add the values from the disk file into the values in the current notebook.

Subtract—Select this radio button to subtract the values from the disk file from the values in the current notebook.

Multiply—Select this radio button to multiply the values from the disk file by the values in the current notebook.

Divide—Select this radio button to divide the values in the current notebook by the values from the disk file.

Entire File—Select this radio button to combine the entire disk file into the current notebook.

Block(s)—Select this radio button to combine blocks of data from the disk file into the current notebook. Specify the block addresses and names in the adjoining text box.

Tools | Define Group

This command defines a set of pages into a group. By treating them as a group, you can make changes to all these pages at once by making a change to a single page. You can use the group name in commands or formulas. Each page can be a member of only one group at a time. Groups must consist of contiguous pages.

Options

Group Name—Enter the name for the group in this text box. The name may be up to 15 characters long and may not contain spaces.

First Page—Select the first page in the group in this text box. If you select a multipage block before selecting this command, the first page of the group is entered in this text box already.

Last Page—Specify the last page in the group in this text box. If you select a multipage block before selecting this command, the first page of the group is entered in this text box already.

Defined Groups—This list box displays the other group names in the current notebook.

Delete—Select this button to delete the group name selected in the Defined Group list box.

Note

Once a group is created, you can enable Group mode by pressing ALT-F5 (GROUP) or clicking the Group button which is the button containing a G to the right of the page tabs. While Group mode is enabled, commands that use a block use all pages in the group even when you select a block that includes only one page. You can also repeat an entry in all of the pages of a group (called drilling) by pressing SHIFT-ENTER instead of ENTER to finish an entry. Pressing ALT-F5 (GROUP) or clicking the Group button again turns off the Group mode.

Tools | Extract

This command saves a section of a notebook to another notebook file. You can save formulas or values from a block of the notebook. The new file has all of the column and row settings as well as the same page and notebook settings as the original.

Options

The File Name text and list box, the Directories list box, the File Types drop-down list box, the Drives drop-down list box, and Password Protection text box options for this command are identical to the other commands, described under File | Save, that let you select files. The Tools | Extract also has the following options which are specific for extracting files:

Block(s)—Specify the blocks of the current notebook which you want saved into the new file in this text box.

Formulas—Select this radio button to save formulas in the current notebook as formulas in the new file.

Values—Select this radio button to convert formulas to values before saving them in the new file.

Note

You can obtain the same results produced with this command by copying the data you want to an empty notebook and saving it. This method, however, does not copy all of the column and row settings or page and notebook properties.

Tools | Import

This command imports data from a text file and places it in the current notebook. It can import text files and delimited files, and is often used to import data from sources that Quattro Pro cannot automatically import. In some DOS programs, printing the information to a file puts the information in a format that Quattro Pro can import with this command.

Options

The File Name text and list box, the Directories list box, the File Types drop-down list box, and the Drives drop-down list box, options for this command are identical to the other commands, that are described under File I Open, that let you select files. The Tools I Import also has the following options which are specific for importing text files:

ASCII Text File—Select this radio button when the sections information in the file you want to import is not separated by commas or quotes. When Quattro Pro imports this type of file, each line in the import file is stored in a notebook cell, starting with the current cell and working down. Once Quattro Pro imports the data, you can divide it into smaller sections using the Data I Parse command.

Comma & " Delimited File—Select this option when the different pieces of information in each file are separated by commas and the nonnumeric data are encased in quotes. When Quattro Pro imports this type of file, each record is stored in a row. Each piece of data separated by commas is stored in a different column.

Only Commas—Select this option when the different pieces of information in each file are separated by commas. Unlike the comma-and-quote delimited files, the text data is not enclosed in quotes. When Quattro Pro imports this type of file, each record is stored in a row. Each piece of data separated by commas is stored in a different column.

Tools I Macro I Debugger

This command invokes the DEBUG mode. When you run a macro during DEBUG mode, the Macro Debugger Window opens, which allows you to monitor the progress of a macro as it runs and correct any errors. In the Macro Debugger window, the macro runs one step at a time when you press the SPACEBAR or click the mouse. You can have it run at full speed by pressing ENTER. The Macro Debugger Window displays the macro instruction it is performing, the macro instruction before that, and the cell containing the next macro instruction it will perform. The Macro Debugger window has commands that offer several options for you to monitor the progress of a macro as it executes. You can display the menu by typing a /. Quattro Pro displays the macro instructions it is performing in the Macro Debugger window.

Options

Breakpoints—Select this command to instruct Quattro Pro to start executing macro instructions one step at a time when it reaches a specific cell. When you select this option, you must select which of four breakpoints you want to set. Then specify the cell containing the breakpoint in the Location text box. If the cell for the breakpoint is part of a loop, you may want to specify the number of times the loop performs until the cell becomes a breakpoint in the Pass count text box.

Conditional—Select this command to instruct Quattro Pro to start executing macro instructions one step at a time when a condition becomes true. You must select which of four conditional breakpoints you want to set. Then specify the cell containing the logical formula for the conditional breakpoint in the Location text box.

Trace—Select this command to display the value of one to four cells in the lower half of the Debug Window. Select which of the four trace cells you want to set. Then specify the cell you want to display in the Location text box.

Edit—Select this command to edit a cell. Specify the cell you want to edit in the Cell text box. Enter the cell's new contents in the Content text box. Use this option for editing a cell during macro execution.

Go—Select this command to run the remainder of the macro at normal speed. You can also run the macro at normal speed by pressing ENTER.

Terminate—Select this command to halt a macro's execution. This is the same as pressing CTRL-BREAK.

Reset—Select this command to remove the settings for the standard breakpoints, conditional breakpoints, and trace cells.

Tools | Macro | Execute

This command starts running a macro that you select. The macro can come from the current notebook or an open notebook.

Options

Location—Specify the first cell in the macro in this text box.

Macro Library—Select an open notebook from this drop-down list box that is a macro library which contains the macro you want to run.

Macros/Namedblocks—Select the macro that you want to run from this list box. This list box lists all the macros in the notebook selected in the Macro Library drop-down list box.

Note

You can also perform this command by pressing ALT-F2 (MACRO). If it is an instant macro you can press CTRL and type the letter to execute the macro.

Tools | Macro | Options

This command selects options for how the macro is recorded. You can record the macro so that it records strictly your keystrokes, or so that it records the effect of your keystrokes. You can also select whether the selected cell in the macro are recorded as their cell addresses or relative distances.

Options

Logical—Select this radio button to record the macro instructions using command equivalents and macro commands instead of the keys you are pressing to select commands and make choices.

Keystroke—Select this radio button to record the actual keystrokes that you press as you record the actions you want stored in the macro. You can use this radio button to create a macro that you can use in another program, such as 1-2-3.

Absolute—Select this radio button to have all cell references recorded absolutely. This means that the selected cells are recorded as their cell addresses rather than their relative position from the selector's position when you record the macro.

Relative—Select this radio button to have all cell references recorded relatively. This means that cell selection is indicated by the direction and the number from the starting cell. Macros are recorded this way to be adjustable depending on where you start the macro.

Tools | Macro | Record

This command turns the macro recorder on. Once you execute this command, Quattro Pro records the commands and keystrokes you perform until you select this command again. When you select it while recording a macro, Record reads Stop Record. The commands are recorded in the notebook or in an open macro library notebook. Your only options for this command are to select where the commands are recorded.

Options

Location—Specify the first cell where the macro instructions are recorded in this text box.

Macro Library—Select the current notebook or an open notebook that is a macro library from this drop-down list box to determine where the macro instructions are recorded.

Macros/Namedblocks—You can select a macro name from this list box to have macro instructions recorded at that macro's location. You will replace the named macro with the macro you are now recording.

Tools | Optimizer

This command starts the Optimizer to find the best values for selected notebook cells that produce the results you want in other cells. You can use this command for solving linear and nonlinear problems. You use this command when you want to find the values you can use in one set of cells that, through the calculations in the notebook, produces other results. The options for this command describe the cells you want to change, how you want them changed, and the limits that you place on the cells used by the model. Before you use this command, you must create the model that the Optimizer will try to find the best solution for. In the initial cells that you want the Optimizer to find the best values for, put values in these cells that are the best estimate of what you expect the results to be. Since it reduces the time the Optimizer needs to find a solution, and, because in nonlinear problems there may be more than one solution, the initial values determine which of the solutions it finds will be put into the notebook cells.

Options

Solution Cell—Select the cell in this text box that contains the final result or the formula you want to minimize, maximize, or solve.

Max—Select this radio button when you want the solution to be as large as possible.

Min—Select this radio button when you want the solution to be as small as possible.

None—Select this radio button when the problem does not have a solution cell.

Target Value—Select this radio button when you want the solution to be equal to the value that you enter in the adjoining text box.

Variable Cell(s)—Select the blocks that the Optimizer can change to make the solution cell equal its solution while staying within the limits set by the constraints. If protection is enabled, these cells must be unprotected. These cells must contain numbers and cannot contain dates, formulas, or labels. If the cell you select with Solution Cell is a value, it must be included in the block you select with this option so that the Optimizer can change it.

Constraints—Select a constraint from this list box when you want to change or delete one of the existing constraints. This list box displays the limits that are placed on cells in the model when the Optimizer searches for the best solution. The limits you can put on cell formulas and numbers include having a cell less than or equal to, greater than or equal to, or equal to another value.

Add—This option adds a constraint to the Constraints list box. To create a constraint, you select this push button, opening the Add Constraints dialog box. Specify the cell containing a formula result or value on which you want to place a limit in the Cell text box. Then choose an operator from the Operator drop-down list box to set the relationship you want between the constrained cell and its constraint value. Finally, specify the value or cell you want the constraint cell to equal in the Constant text box and select OK.

Change—Select this button to change the selected constraint in the Constraints list box. Select the constraint and then this option to alter it. Then change the entries in the Cell text box, Operator drop-down list box, and Constant text box to match what you want for the constraint. Select OK to return to the Optimizer dialog box.

Delete—Select this button to delete the selected constraint in the Constraints list box.

Options—This option lets you change the settings the Optimizer uses to find the values for the variable cells. You do not have to change any of the Optimizer options to use the Optimizer—only the ones you want. Once you select Options, you have another dialog box. Choose Max. Time and specify how many seconds between 1 and 1000 the Optimizer may spend looking for a solution. Choose Max. Iterations and set the maximum number of iterations (between 1 and 1000) or cycles through potential values for the variable cells that the Optimizer can try. Choose Precision and enter a number between 0 and 1 to set the decimal precision a constraint cell must equal to or be relative to in its constraint value. Choose either Tangent or Quadratic to set how the Optimizer finds the initial estimates of the variable cells. Tangent works better in linear problems and Quadratic works better in highly nonlinear ones. If you see the message "All remedies failed to find better solution," choose Central, which sets how the Optimizer finds the estimates of partial derivatives. You can select Forward to return to the default, which requires fewer calculations. If you see the message "Objective function changing too slowly," choose Conjugate, which sets the search direction. You can select Newton to return to the default, which is faster. Choose Assume Linear to have Optimizer solve the model using linear methods because it can solve linear problems quicker than nonlinear ones. If your problem is nonlinear, clear this check box for the Optimizer to find the best results. Choose Show Iteration Results to have Quattro Pro pause after each Optimizer iteration and prompt you to stop or continue the process. Clear this check box to omit this pause. Select Reporting to specify where Optimizer places an answer report in the notebook listing the variable cells with their original and final values, the solution cell, the constraints, the variable dual values, and the constraint dual values or a detailed report listing the values of the variable cells and the solution cell for each iteration the Optimizer performs. You can also save the model for future use by selecting Save Model and specifying the block containing the model, which must be at least three columns wide. The model is saved with the notebook. You can reuse the model by selecting Load Model and selecting the upper-left corner of the model's block.

Reset—Select this button to reset all the Optimizer settings to their default settings.

Solve—Select this button to start the Optimizer solving the model you have set, using the specified settings.

Tools | Solve For

This command alters the number stored in a cell so that another cell that contains a formula equals a predefined value. This command lets you work backward through calculations to find the initial value that will produce the desired result.

Options

Formula Cell—Select the cell or block name of a cell containing a formula that afterward will equal the value set entered in the Target Value text box.

Target Value—Type the value that the cell selected with the Formula Cell option will equal after you select OK in this text box.

Variable Cell—Select the cell or block name to which Quattro Pro can change the value stored in the cell so that the cell selected with Formula Cell will equal the number entered in the Target Value text box. It can contain any entry, although after you select OK it will contain a number.

Max Iterations—Specify a number between 1 and 100 for the number of attempts Quattro Pro performs to find the answer.

Accuracy—Specify a number that the result of the cell selected with Formula Cell must be within for the value selected with Target Value for Quattro Pro to consider the answer of the current iteration to be a solution.

For example, entering .5 for this option and 100 for the target value means that an answer between 99.5 and 100.5 is acceptable.

Tools | UI Builder

This command opens a dialog box that you can manipulate to create your own custom dialog boxes. After you select this command, you have added a dialog box. You can also create and modify SpeedBars that you can use in addition to the SpeedBar provided as a Quattro Pro default. You can also perform this command by clicking the New Dialog button or the New SpeedBar button in the SpeedBar on the Graphs page or by double-clicking a dialog box you have created that is displayed as an icon on the Graphs page.

Options

Once you have used this command, you can customize dialog boxes and SpeedBars. While you are working on dialog boxes and SpeedBars, the default SpeedBar is different and the menu bar includes Dialog. You can switch between editing dialog boxes and SpeedBars and the other windows you are using. Chapter 12 contains additional information about creating dialog boxes and SpeedBars.

Tools | Update Links | Change Link

Select this command when you want to move links to one file so that the data is retrieved from another file.

Options

Change Link From—Select the file which you want break links to from this list box.
To—Specify the file which you want the links connecting to in this text box.

Tools | Update Links | Delete Links

This command deletes the links to one file. The information is removed from the current worksheet and ERR is returned any place there was a link to that file.

Options

Hotlinks—Select the file from this list box with links to the current notebook which you want to delete. The list box contains a list of the files to which the current notebook has links.

Tools | Update Link | Open Links

This command opens one of the files to which the current notebook has links.

Options

Hotlinks—Select the file that you want to open from this list box. The list box contains a list of the files to which the current notebook has links.

Tools I Update Links I Refresh Links

This command rechecks all of the values used by link formulas from the files currently stored on disk. You may need to use this command if you are working on a network and someone may be updating the referenced file while you are working.

Options

Hotlinks—Select the file from which you want to update the values from this list box. The list box contains a list of the files to which the current notebook has links.

Window I 1-9

Selecting a number between 1 and 9 from the Window menu selects which of the open windows is the active window. The active window is indicated in the Window menu with a check mark. After each of the numbers there is the notebook, graph, dialog box, or SpeedBar name that each number represents.

Options

Once you select a number between 1 and 9 from the Window menu, the notebook, graph, dialog box, or SpeedBar becomes active.

Window I Arrange Icons

This command only affects minimized notebook windows. It arranges the icons for these windows in neat rows, starting at the lower left corner of the application window.

Options

None.

Window I Cascade

This command sizes and arranges all the currently open notebook windows so that the title bar of each window shows, but each notebook is covered by the notebook window on top.

Options

None.

Window I Hide

This command hides the current notebook. To display it later, use the Window I Show command. The hidden window is only closed when you display the window again then close the window, or you exit Quattro Pro. You may want to hide a macro library notebook window so that you do not accidentally change it.

Options
None.

Window | Locked Titles

This command marks certain rows or columns as locked titles on a page. Locked titles do not scroll off the window as you scroll through your notebook; but they remain at the top and/or left side of the notebook window so you can use them as reference points while looking at the data. Before you use this command, you must position the selector so that the rows you want frozen are above the selector's position and the columns you want frozen are to the left of the selector's position. When you lock titles in a notebook, you cannot move to the cells that appear in the title. The mouse pointer also looks different to indicate that you cannot click a cell in the area to select it. If you need to move to a cell in the title area, use the Edit | Goto command. Each page can have its titles set separately.

Options
Horizontal—Select this radio button to mark the rows above the selector as locked horizontal titles.
Vertical—Select this radio button to mark the columns to the left of the selector as locked vertical titles.
Both—Select this radio button to mark the rows above the selector and the columns to its left as locked titles.
Clear—Select this radio button to clear locked titles from the window.

Window | More Windows

This command selects which window is the active window. This command only appears when you have more than nine windows open in Quattro Pro.

Options
Select the name of the window you want to open from the list box to make the selected window the one on top.

Window | New View

This command opens a new window showing the current notebook. Any changes made in one window affect the notebook shown in the other windows in the same notebook. When you want to close one copy of the notebook without closing the other copies, select Close in the window's control menu rather than using the File | Close command.

Options
   None.

Window | Panes

This command separates a single window so that there are two panes within it, showing different portions of the notebook. You can use this command to view widely separated data without having to open a new view. The panes can be broken horizontally, vertically, and can be synchronized in their scrolling or not.

Options

Horizontal—Select this radio button to break the window into panes horizontally. When horizontal panes are scrolled in synchronization, they show the same columns but different rows of the notebook.

Vertical—Select this radio button to break the window vertically. When vertical panes are scrolled in synchronization, they show the same rows, but different columns of the notebook.

Clear—Select this radio button to remove the break between panes and return to a normal display.

Synchronize—Selecting this check box synchronizes the panes when they scroll. When this check box is cleared, the panes scroll independently.

Note

You can also divide a window into panes by dragging the pane splitter, which is in the window's lower right corner, up or to the right. The window is split into panes where you release the mouse. You can readjust the pane size with the pane splitter by dragging it to a new location.

Window | Show

This command displays a hidden notebook.

Options

Select the hidden window that you want to display again from the Hidden Window list box.

Window | Tile

This command tiles all the currently open notebook windows. When the windows are tiled, they are each sized and placed so that none of them are overlapping. If there are several notebooks, each single notebook is very small. Minimized notebooks are not opened and sized.

Options
   None.

PROPERTIES

Quattro Pro has many properties that you can change for the different parts of Quattro Pro. The properties are presented as the object that uses them followed by the property name.

Active Block | Alignment

This property aligns entries in a block of cells according to your specification. This setting affects both numbers and labels entered in the block. However, this property affects the blank cells within the block into which you subsequently enter numbers. Blank cells use the page's default label alignment setting when you make label entries in them.

Options
General—Select this radio button to align label entries according to the setting of the Label Alignment page property and right-align numeric entries.
Left—Select this radio button to align entries at the left of the cell.
Right—Select this radio button to align entries at the right of a cell.
Center—Select this radio button to center entries within a cell.

Note
You can also change this property of a block by clicking the Align Left, Align Center, or Align Right buttons on the SpeedBar.

Active Block | Column Width

This property sets the column widths in the selected block. The options for this property let you set the column widths to a new value, select different measuring systems to use for that value, reset the widths to the default, or set the widths to be as wide as the data contained in the block.

Options
Column Width—Enter the width you want the selected columns to be in this text box when you select the Set Width radio button.
Extra Characters (0-40)—Enter the number of characters, wider than the longest entry you want the selected columns to be in, when you select the Auto Width radio button.
Set Width—Select this radio button to set the widths of the columns in the block to the value entered in the Column Width text box. You only need to select one cell in each column to change.
Reset Width—Select this radio button to change the column widths of a block to the default column width set with the Default Width page property. You only need to select one cell in each column to change.

Auto Width—Select this radio button to set each column width in the block to a width sufficient to display the longest entry in each column of the block plus the number of extra characters specified in the Extra Characters text box. The block you select before selecting this radio button should either include one row from the columns you want to affect to have Quattro Pro adjust the column's width for all of the column's entries or should only include the cell entries you want Quattro Pro to use to decide the new columns' width.

Characters—Select this radio button to measure the column width in terms of the character width using the font set by the Normal named style.

Inches—Select this radio button to measure the column width in inches.

Centimeters—Select this radio button to measure the column width in centimeters.

Note

You can use the Fit button from the SpeedBar to adjust the width of selected columns to fit the widest entry in the column. You can also adjust the width of a single column by dragging the right column border to a new location.

Active Block | Data Entry Input

This property limits the type of entries accepted in a block.

Options

General—Select this radio button to remove the data entry restrictions placed by the other two choices.

Labels Only—Select this radio button to limit entries in the block to labels. Quattro Pro treats any entry as a label, allowing you to type Social Security numbers and phone numbers without preceding the entry with a label-prefix character.

Dates Only—Select this radio button to limit entries in the block to only dates or times. When you make an entry in one of these cells, Quattro Pro interprets the entry as a date or time. If the entry is not a valid date or time, Quattro Pro displays an error message and does not accept the entry.

Active Block | Font

This property sets the font of the spreadsheet cells. Quattro Pro uses all the fonts that Windows provides, including printer fonts.

Options

Typeface—Select one of the fonts listed in this text box to choose the typeface of the font. The displayed fonts include all the fonts installed in Windows, including TrueType and printer fonts.

Point Size—Select the size of the font from one of the sizes listed in this drop-down list box or type the font size to set the size for the block. For scalable fonts, you can type a point size that is not one of the ones listed.

Bold—Select this check box to add boldfacing or clear this check box to remove it.

Italics—Select this check box to add italics or clear this check box to remove it.

Underline—Select this check box to add underlining or clear this check box to remove it.

Strikeout—Select this check box to use strikeout characters (a line through the middle of it) or clear this check box to remove it.

Note

You can duplicate some of these options using the SpeedBar. Click the up or down arrows to the right of the *i* SpeedBar button to change the size of the font in the selected block. Click the **b** SpeedBar button to boldface the selected cells, or the *i* SpeedBar button to italicize the selected cells.

Active Block | Line Drawing

This property draws lines at the edges of cells on a notebook page.

Options

Line Segments—Click on the line segments in this diagram to select the line segments you want to draw in the block.

All—Select this button to draw a line around the four sides of each cell in the block.

Outline—Select this button to draw a line around the four sides of the block.

Inside—Select this button to draw horizontal and vertical lines between the cells in the block.

Line Types—Select one of the five buttons of the pictured line types before selecting which line segments to draw. You can select No Change, so you can select line segments that you do not want to change from its current setting; No Line to remove any lines from the selected side of the cell; and three line types, single, double and wide.

Active Block | Numeric Format

This property changes the appearance of numeric entries. Quattro Pro provides a wide variety of numeric formats. This property only changes the cell's appearance, never the value of the entry. For some of the format types, you can select how many decimal places are displayed, overriding the default of two.

Options

Fixed—Select this radio button to display a fixed number of decimal places for all the values in a block, for example, 1000.11. Enter the number of decimal places to display in the text box.

Scientific—Select this radio button to display values in scientific exponential notation, for example, 1.00011E+03. Enter the number of decimal places in the text box.

Currency—Select this radio button to display values as currency. Quattro Pro displays the currency symbol next to the number, for example, $1,000.11. Quattro Pro adds commas as thousand separators and shows negative values in parentheses. Enter the number of decimal places to display in the text box.

Comma—Select this radio button to display values with commas for thousand separators, for example, 1,000.11, and to enclose negative values in parentheses. Enter the number of decimal places in the text box.

General—Select this radio button to display the values in the default display format. This numeric format displays whole numbers, decimal fractions, and scientific notation depending on the magnitude of the value.

+/— —Select this radio button to create simple horizontal bar charts. This numeric format transforms positive values into + signs with one + for each positive integer in the cell value. Quattro Pro displays negative values as — signs with one minus sign generated for each negative integer. 0 displays as a period.

Percent—Select this radio button to multiply the cell entry by 100 and place a percent symbol after the entry. For example, Quattro Pro displays 0.95 as 95.00% and 1.2 as 120.00%. You can set the number of decimal places shown in the text box.

Date—Select this radio button to display your values as dates. With a display format of Date, you can display date entries in the form of DD-MMM-YY, DD-MMM, MMM-YY, Long Date Intl., and Short Date Intl.

Time—Select this radio button to display your values as times. With a display format of Time, you can display time entries in the form of HH:MM:SS AM/PM, HH:MM AM/PM, Short Time Intl., or Long Time Intl.

Text—Select this radio button to display the formulas in the cells rather than their values. Numeric values appear in the General format.

Hidden—Select this radio button to hide the cell contents in the notebook. The content of cells formatted as hidden show up only on the input line.

User defined—Select this radio button to display the values using one of the user-defined formats. Select one of the format definitions from the Formats defined drop-down list box or type one of your own.

Active Block | Protection

This property protects or unprotects cells within the selected block. Once you enable page protection, protected cells do not accept entries of any type. Cell protection has no effect unless you enable page protection using the Protection page property. The default is for cells to be protected, but for page protection to be disabled.

Options

Protect—Select this radio button to make the selected block protected so that when page protection is enabled, you cannot make entries in these cells.

Unprotect—Select this radio button to make the selected block unprotected so that when page protection is enabled, you can make entries in these cells.

Active Block | Reveal/Hide

This property hides and displays columns and rows. You can hide columns and rows to temporarily remove them from display. When columns and rows are hidden, Quattro Pro constructs the display from the remaining columns and rows, effectively moving columns from the right to the left, and rows below the hidden rows up to fill in the space vacated by the hidden columns and rows. Quattro Pro does not reletter the exposed columns and rows as it would if you deleted columns and rows. The information in the hidden columns and rows are still in memory. This information can be referenced in formulas. To change this property of a column or row, you only need to select one cell from each column or row. When you want to display hidden columns or rows, select a block containing the columns or rows on either side of the hidden columns or rows. In POINT mode the hidden columns and rows are displayed with an asterisk next to the row or column label.

Options

Columns—Select this radio button to hide or display columns.

Rows—Select this radio button to hide or display rows.

Reveal—Select this radio button to display columns or rows that you have previously hidden.

Hide—Select this radio button to hide the selected columns or rows.

No Change—Select this button, the default, in order not to change the status of any rows or columns in a block. This setting is the default so that when you select a block containing both revealed and hidden rows or columns, you do not accidentally change their status.

Active Block | Row Height

This property specifies the height of the rows in your selected block. You can also choose the measuring system that you want to use to specify a height for the row. The default row height is based on the height of the largest characters in the row. You only need to select one cell from each row that you want to change the height.

Options

Row Height—Enter the height of the row in terms of the measuring system specified in this text box when you have selected the Set Height radio button.

Set Height—Select this radio button to set the height to the height entered in the Row Height text box.

Reset Height—Select this radio button to set the row to the default height.

Points—Select this radio button to use points to measure row height.

Inches—Select this radio button to use inches to measure row height.

Centimeter—Select this radio button to use centimeters to measure row height.

Active Block | Shading

This property adds shading to cells. The options for this property select the shading that Quattro Pro adds. You can either select one of the standard colors, or a blending of two of the standard colors. How the colors print depends on the printer you are using, and its color settings. A black and white printer will attempt to translate the colors into various shades of gray when you print it.

Options
Color 1—Select one of these blocks of color for the first color in the blend.
Color 2—Select one of these blocks of color for the second color in the blend.
Blend—Select one of the seven blocks of color to shade the selected block. The left block is the color selected with Color 1 and the right block is the color selected with Color 2. The five intermediate blocks are shades made by combining those two colors.

Active Block | Text Color

This property sets the color of the text in the block. How the colors print depends on your printers and their color settings. A black and white printer will attempt to translate the colors into shades of gray when you print a selection with color changes in it.

Options
The only option is to select the color that the text will appear. You cannot create blended colors.

Active Page | Borders

This property lets you hide or display the row and column borders that appear at the top and left of notebook page. When the row and column borders do not appear, Quattro Pro uses the additional space to display more of the page. This property is often used in macros to create custom displays for user input.

Options
Row Borders—Select this check box to display the row borders. When it is cleared, the row borders do not appear.
Column Borders—Select this check box to display the column borders. When it is cleared, the column borders do not appear.

Active Page | Conditional Color

This property sets the colors Quattro Pro uses on the current page to display cells if the cells' contents meet certain conditions. The conditions affect value entries only, not labels. When you use conditional colors, it overrides the text color set with the Text Color block property.

Options

Enable—Select this check box to enable Quattro Pro's use of conditional colors. Clear this check box (the default) to disable the conditional color property. When you enable conditional colors, the colors of the value entries on the page are set by the conditional colors specified by this property.

Smallest Normal Value—Enter the lowest value of the normal range in this text box. All cells with values below this value display in the color chosen by Below Normal Color.

Greatest Normal Value—Enter the highest value in the normal range in this text box. All cells with values above this value display in the color chosen by Above Normal Color.

Below Normal Color—Select this radio button to set the color for cell values that are less than the value entered in the Smallest Normal Value text box. After selecting this radio button, select a color from the color palette.

Normal Cell Color—Select this radio button to set the color for cell values that are between the value entered in the Smallest Normal Value text box and the value entered in the Greatest Normal Value text box. After selecting this radio button, select a color from the color palette.

Above Normal Color—Select this radio button to set the color for cell values that are greater than the value in the Greatest Normal Value text box. After selecting this radio button, select a color from the color palette.

ERR Color—Select this radio button to set the color for cells equaling ERR. After selecting it, select a color from the color palette.

Active Page | Default Width

This property changes the width of all the columns on the notebook page that have not had their column widths set with the Column Width block property.

Options

Column Width—Enter the width of the column in this text box to set the default column width for this page, in the measurement chosen.

Characters—Select this radio button to specify the default column width in characters.

Inches—Select this radio button to specify the default column width in inches.

Centimeters—Select this radio button to specify the default column width in centimeters.

Active Page | Display Zeros

This property either hides or displays the zeros in cells that equal zero. Cells that equal zero will appear blank, but their content will appear on the input line when selected.

Options

> *Yes*—Select this radio button to hide all zeros on the page, which lets all cells equaling zero look empty.
>
> *No*—Select this radio button to display all zeros on the page.

Active Page | Grid Lines

This property adds or removes the grid lines that mark the edges of cells.

Options

> *Horizontal*—Select this check box to display the horizontal grid lines. When the check box is cleared, horizontal grid lines do not appear.
>
> *Vertical*—Select this check box to display the vertical grid lines. When the check box is cleared, vertical grid lines do not appear.

Active Page | Label Alignment

This property sets the alignment for all new label entries on the current notebook page. This property does not affect value entries or existing label entries on the page. You can override this property for a block by changing the Alignment block property.

Options

> *Left*—Select this radio button to align labels subsequently entered at the left side of the cell.
>
> *Right*—Select this radio button to align labels subsequently entered at the right side of the cell.
>
> *Center*—Select this radio button to center labels subsequently entered within the cell.

Active Page | Line Color

This property sets the color for the lines added on the current page with the Line Drawing block property. All lines on a single page must be the same color, but you can set different colors for each page of a notebook.

Options

> Select one of the colors from the color palette.

Active Page | Name

This property assigns a name to a page of a notebook. The default name for the pages are A through IV. The name may be up to fifteen characters long, and can consist of a combination of letters and numbers. You cannot use special characters or spaces in a page name.

Options

Page Name—Enter the name you want to assign to the page in this text box.
Reset—Select this button if you want to return to the original name of the page. The pages are originally named A through IV.

Active Page | Protection

This property turns page protection on and off. Page protection prevents the data on a page from being accidentally overwritten. When you use this property to enable page protection, you cannot delete, edit, or replace the entries in cells which have the protected property. Even though blocks of cells have a protection property, disabling the page protection property causes Quattro Pro to ignore this property.

Options

Enable—Select this radio button to enable protection for the protected cells on your notebook page.
Disable—Select this radio button to disable protection for all the cells on your notebook page.

Active Notebook | Display

This property chooses to display or hide the vertical or horizontal scroll bar or the page tabs.

Options

Vertical Scroll Bar—Select this check box to display the vertical scroll bar. When the check box is cleared, the vertical scroll bar does not appear.
Horizontal Scroll Bar—Select this check box to display the horizontal scroll bar, and clear it to not display the horizontal scroll bar.
Page Tabs—Select this check box to display the page tabs. The page tabs do not appear when the check box is cleared. Hiding the page tabs also hides the page scroll bar, the SpeedTab button, and the Group mode button. Also, you cannot rearrange pages using the page tabs when they do not appear.

Active Notebook | Macro Library

This property makes the current notebook a macro library file or removes the macro library setting from an existing macro library. Quattro Pro searches open macro libraries when you try to execute a macro that is not in the current notebook. A macro library lets you gather your most frequently used macros into one notebook.

Options
> *Yes*—Selecting this radio button makes the notebook a macro library.
> *No*—Selecting this radio button removes the macro library setting from the notebook.

Active Notebook I Palette

This property changes the colors used in the notebook. These are the colors that are used in the Shading block property, the Text Color block property, and the Line Color page property.

Options
> *Edit Color*—Select this button after selecting one of the colors from the Notebook Palette to change that color. Selecting this button opens the Edit Palette Color dialog box in which you can select a color, or create one using one of three systems for specifying colors.
> *Reset Defaults*—Select this button to restore the palette to the default colors.

Active Notebook I Recalc Settings

This property sets how Quattro Pro recalculates the notebook. These settings include the order in which Quattro Pro recalculates the formulas, the number of times Quattro Pro recalculates the formulas, and the timing of formula recalculation.

Options
> *Automatic*—Select this radio button to recalculate formulas as the values that they depend on change.
> *Manual*—Select this radio button to recalculate formulas in the notebook when you press F9 (CALC).
> *Background*—Select this radio button to recalculate formulas as the values that depend on change but only when you are not using the notebook for other operations.
> *Natural*—Select this radio button to recalculate the cells referenced by a formula before the formula is recalculated.
> *Column-wise*—Select this radio button to recalculate the notebook one column at a time.
> *Row-wise*—Select this radio button to recalculate the notebook one row at a time.
> *# of Iterations*—Specify the number of times Quattro Pro recalculates a circular reference before completing the recalculation process by entering it in this text box. Quattro Pro's default is 1 but you should enter a higher number if the notebook contains intentional circular references.
> *Circular Cell*—You cannot select this because below Circular Cell is the address of the first cell that is part of a circular reference. This option only appears when one of the open notebooks has a circular reference.

Active Notebook I Zoom Factor

This property enlarges or reduces the notebook display to be larger or smaller in the notebook window. This command does not affect the size of the data when you print it. You can use this option to quickly see more or less of the notebook's data.

Options

Zoom Percentage (25–200)—Enter the percentage of the original size that you want the notebook to appear in this drop-down list box. Numbers less than 100 reduce the notebook size, so you see more of it in the window; numbers more than 100 expand the notebook size so you can see less of it in the window. You can also select the zoom percentage by selecting one of the numbers from the drop-down list box.

Application I Display

This property sets certain application display options. You can choose whether to display a clock in the status line and its format; to show or hide the SpeedBar, the input line, or the status line; and the syntax to be used for specifying blocks that include multiple pages.

Options

None—Select this radio button to remove any display of a clock in the status line. This is the default option.

Standard—Select this radio button to display the date and time using the MM-DDD-YY and HH:MM AM/PM format on the status line.

International—Select this radio button to display the date and time with the current international date and time formats on the status line.

Show SpeedBar—Select this check box to display the SpeedBar or clear it to remove it from the Quattro Pro window. Hiding this SpeedBar hides the primary SpeedBar only.

Show Input Line—Select this check box to display the input line and clear it to remove it from the Quattro Pro window.

Show Status Line—Select this check box to display the status line or clear it to remove it from the Quattro Pro window.

A..B:A1..B2—Select this radio button to display references to multipage blocks with all of the pages including first, separated from the cell references by a colon.

A:A1..B:B2—Select this radio button to display references to multipage blocks with the first cell on the first page together, separated with two periods from the last cell on the last page.

Application I International

This property specifies several different settings that customize your notebook to different international styles. You can select how to show currency values and how to indicate negative values. You can also set punctuation settings that control what character separates thousands and the decimal point. You can also select the format for the international date format and format for the international time format. You can select a language setting for Quattro Pro. You can also choose to convert LICS characters, used in 1-2-3 files, to ANSI characters as you open a 1-2-3 spreadsheet.

Options

Currency—Select this radio button to control how currency is formatted. First select either Windows Default, if you want to use the Windows settings set from the Control Panel, or Quattro Pro/Windows, to set the currency formatting using the remaining dialog box elements. If you select the Quattro Pro/Windows radio button, enter the currency symbol you want to use in the Currency Symbox text box. Select Prefix to place the symbol before the number or Suffix to place it after the number. Select Signed to use a negative sign or Parentheses to use parentheses to indicate negative numbers.

Punctuation—Select this radio button to select the characters to use as decimal points, thousands separators, and list separators. You can select Windows Default to use the Windows settings from the Control Panel, or select one of eight different combinations which use semicolons, colons, commas, periods, and spaces.

Date Format—Select this radio button to choose the format used for the Long International Date and Short International Date formats used by the Numeric Format property for blocks and named styles. You can select the Windows Default to use the settings set by the Control Panel or select one of four other formats.

Time Format—Select this radio button to choose the format used for the Long International Time and Short International Time formats used by the Numeric Format property for blocks and named styles. You can select the Windows Default to use the settings set by the Control Panel or select one of four other formats.

Language—Select this radio button to choose the language Quattro Pro uses to decide an alphabet's order when you sort data. You can select the Windows Default to use the settings set by the Control Panel or select a language from the list box after selecting the Quattro Pro/Windows radio button.

LICS—Select this check box to allow Quattro Pro to translate LICS characters, used in 1-2-3 spreadsheets, into standard ANSI characters. ANSI and LICS characters are the same except for the extended character range, which is codes 128 through 255, which normally defines international and other extended characters. With this selected, you can both retrieve 1-2-3 styles and see the codes correctly, or save Quattro Pro notebooks in a 1-2-3 format, and have the ANSI extended characters translated into LICS characters in the file.

Application | Macro

This property selects which parts of the Quattro Pro window are redrawn as a macro is executed. This property also has options to make it possible to run

1-2-3 macro within Quattro Pro for Windows, and to set which menu appears when you type a / from READY mode.

Options

Both—Select this radio button to suppress the redrawing of both the panel and the window as a macro is running, making the macro run faster.

Panel—Select this radio button to suppress the redrawing of the panel only, which includes the input line, the menus, the status line, and dialog boxes.

Window—Select this radio button to suppress the redrawing of the notebook windows only, allowing the panel to be redrawn.

None—Select this radio button to omit suppressing redrawing the windows and panel when you run a macro. This is the slowest way to run a macro.

Key Reader—Select this check box to have Quattro Pro assume that macro instructions, such as /FR, are designed to execute menu commands. Clear this check box when you are running macros that do not use keystrokes to perform menu commands.

Slash Key—Select the menu from this drop-down list box you want to appear when you type a /. You can select Menu Bar so the Quattro Pro menu bar is selected when you type a /. You can also select Quattro Pro–DOS to display a menu compatible with Quattro Pro for DOS.

Application I SpeedBar

This property lets you add a secondary SpeedBar to use in addition to the default SpeedBar. When you hide the primary SpeedBar with the Display application property, the secondary SpeedBar will still appear.

Options

Secondary SpeedBar—Enter the file name of the secondary SpeedBar that you want to use in this text box, including all path information.

Browse—Select this button to search for the correct file name of the SpeedBar that you want to use. The file name that you select in the SpeedBar dialog box appears in the Secondary SpeedBar text box.

Reset—Select this push button to reset the Secondary SpeedBar to its default contents, which is blank.

Application I Startup

This property sets the initial settings that Quattro Pro uses to start every session. You can use this property to specify the directory Quattro Pro uses in opening and saving files, the file that is opened each time you start Quattro Pro, the macro that automatically starts running when you open a notebook, and the default file extension. You can also choose to use or disable the Beep, to enable or disable Undo and make the keyboard compatible with Quattro Pro for DOS or Windows.

Options

Directory—Enter the drive and directory where Quattro Pro automatically looks when you open and save files, or execute any other command that works with files.

Autoload File—Enter the notebook name you want Quattro Pro to automatically open each time you start Quattro Pro. If Quattro Pro cannot open this file, Quattro Pro opens an empty notebook.

Startup Macro—Enter the macro name you want Quattro Pro to attempt to execute each time a file is opened. You can change the macro name from the default of \0 to another valid macro name by entering the name in this text box.

File Extension—Enter the default file extension Quattro assigns when you save files. The default is .WB1, but you can use any valid extension. If you select an extension that indicates another format, such as .WK1, the files will be saved in that format.

Use Beep—Select this check box to turn on sounds, such as when you make an error in Quattro Pro. If this check box is cleared, Quattro Pro will not makes sounds. You can also turn your system's sounds on and off using the Control Panel.

Undo Enabled—Select this check box to enable the undo function. Once this check box is selected, you can use Edit | Undo to remove the effect of an undoable action. Clear this check box to disable the undo function.

Compatible Keys—Select this check box to leave the a selection of keys compatible with Quattro Pro for DOS. Clear this check box to have those keys operate in greater compatibility with Windows. When this check box is selected, the default, the UP ARROW and DOWN ARROW keys move from one entry to another, CTRL-LEFT ARROW and CTRL-RIGHT ARROW move five characters at a time in either direction, and, after pressing ALT-F3 (FUNCTIONS) to add a function, typing a letter adds the first function that starts with the letter you have typed. When the check box is cleared, the UP ARROW and DOWN ARROW keys move between lines when you are editing a long entry in EDIT mode, CTRL-LEFT ARROW and CTRL-RIGHT ARROW move one word at a time, and, after pressing ALT-F3 (FUNCTIONS) to add a function, typing a letter highlights the first function with that starts with the letter you have typed without selecting it.

GRAPH PROPERTIES

Graph properties overlap extensively, so that many different objects have identical properties. Therefore, the Graph properties are listed alphabetically by property, not by the object the property affects. The objects affected by each property are listed under the property. Some of these properties may have a slightly different effect, depending on which object they are formatting. Properties that affect series, pie slices, and column segments can be set separately for each series, pie slice, and column segment.

3D Options

This property affects the appearance of three-dimensional graphs. You can choose which parts of the walls appear and whether or not the walls are thick, which looks more three-dimensional, or thin, which looks flatter.

This is a property for Graph Setup and Background.

Options

Show left wall—Select this check box to show the left wall of the 3D graph. When you clear the check box, the graph does not have a left wall.

Show back wall—Show the back wall of the 3D graph by selecting this check box. When it is cleared, there is no back wall.

Show base—Select this check box to show the base of the 3D graph. When you clear the check box, the graph does not have a base.

Thick walls—Select this check box to display the walls and base as being three-dimensional. Clear this check box to display the walls as a flat plane with no depth.

3D View

This property allows you to rotate a 3D graph so that you change the angle at which you are looking at it, the way that you might rotate and move a small model in your hand in order to see it better.

This is a property for Graph Setup and Background.

Options

Rotation—Rotate the graph horizontally, as if a model is sitting on a desk and you were turning it left and right, by moving the scroll box, or entering a new number for the rotation.

Elevation—Rotate the graph vertically, as if a model is sitting on a desk and you were moving from looking at it level with its base to straight down from above, by moving the scroll box, or entering a new number for the elevation.

Perspective—Select this check box to use perspective to visually indicate the depth. When it is selected you can select the degree of perspective used from the scroll bar beneath the check box.

Depth—You can give the graph more depth, the distance from front to back, by changing the value of this scroll bar.

Height—You can give the graph more height from the base to the top of the highest column or data point by changing the value of this scroll bar.

Apply—Select this button to apply the changes you have made to the 3-D View property, so that you can view the graph before closing the dialog box.

Reset—Select this button to restore the 3-D View settings to their default settings.

Alignment

This property selects the alignment of text, applies word-wrap to text, and sets the distance between tab stops in a text box.

This is a property for text boxes.

Options

Text Alignment—Select one of three buttons to left-align, right-align, or center the text in the text box.

Wordwrap—Select this check box to have the text wrap when it reaches the edge of the text box. The text box grows downward to make room for the additional lines. When you clear this check box, the text stays on one line until you press ENTER, at which point the text box enlarges to make room for the full line of text.

Tab stops every ... inches—Set how far apart, in inches, the tab stops occur, by entering a value in inches in the text box.

Aspect Ratio

The aspect ratio controls the proportion between height and width of the graph. You select different aspect ratios depending on what you plan to do with the graph you have created.

This is a property for Graph Window.

Options

Floating Graph—Select this radio button to set the graph's proportion as a floating object in a notebook. This option is not available if the graph does not appear in a floating graph.

Screen Slide—Select this radio button to set the graph's proportions for slide shows.

35mm Slide—Select this radio button to set the graph's proportions for sending the graph to a service bureau to create 35-millimeter slides.

Printer Preview—Select this radio button to set the graph's proportions to match its size if you printed it from the graph window.

Full Extent—Select this radio button to set the graph's proportions to take full advantage of the space in the graph window.

Bar Options

This property controls the way that bars appear in a bar graph. You can control the width of the bars, measured as a percentage of the distance between the tick marks; the width of the margins, the distance between the edges of the graph and the first and last bar; and how the bars overlap.

This is a property for a series when the graph type is one that uses bars.

Options

Bar width percentage—Change the scroll box position or enter a number in the adjoining text box to change the percentage of space between the tick marks which the bars use, controlling the width of the bars. When Quattro first creates a bar graph, it allows the bars to use some percentage of the space between tick marks on the x-axis, and divides that space evenly between the bars.

Bar margins percentage—Change the scroll box position or enter a number in the adjoining text box to set the width of the margin, the distance between the right edge of the graph and the last bar, and the left edge and the first bar. This is also indicated as a percentage of the full margin, which is one inch on either side.

No—Select this radio button to put the bars side by side without overlapping.

Partial—Select this radio button to partially overlap the bars at each point on the x-axis.

Full—Select this radio button to fully overlap the bars at each point on the x-axis.

Bkg Color

This property sets the background color of the selected object. The background color is not displayed if the fill style is solid, because the fill color will overlay it. However, it will appear if a pattern or wash is selected as the fill style.

This is a property for the following objects: Arrow, Box, Ellipse, Freehand Polygon, Polygon, Rectangle, Rounded Rectangle, Text Box, Area Fill, Bar Series, Line Series, Column Graph, Graph Pane, Pie Graph, Graph Title Box, Legend Box, Graph Series, and Graph Setup and Background.

Options

Select one of the available colors in the palette. You can also create a custom color by selecting one of three models for defining colors and changing the sliding scales. You select the radio button for the models you want to use. HSB combines hue, saturation, and brightness to create colors; RBG combines red, blue, and green; and CMY combines cyan, magenta, and yellow.

Border Color

This property defines the color of the line which is the border of the selected object.

This is a property for the following objects: Arrow, Box, Ellipse, Freehand Polygon, Polygon, Rectangle, Rounded Rectangle, Text Box, Area Fill, Bar Series, Line Series, Column Graph, Graph Pane, Pie Graph, Graph Title Box, Legend Box, Graph Series and Setup.

Options

Select one of the available colors in the palette. You can also create a custom color by selecting one of three models for defining colors and changing the sliding scales. You select the radio button for the model you want to use. HSB combines hue, saturation, and brightness to create colors; RBG combines red, blue, and green; and CMY combines cyan, magenta, and yellow.

Border Options

This property only affects the graph panes—the rectangle on two dimensional graphs created by the x and y axes where the data in the graph is displayed. This property selects the sides a border around the graph pane will be visible.

This is a property for Graph Panes.

Options

Left border—Select this check box to display the left border. Clear this check box to remove it.

Top border—Select this check box to display the top border. Clear this check box to remove it.

Right border—Select this check box to display the right border. Clear this check box to remove it.

Bottom border—Select this check box to display the bottom border. Clear this check box to remove it.

Border Style

This property selects the style of the line that makes up the border of an object.

This is a property for the following objects: Arrow, Box, Ellipse, Freehand Polygon, Polygon, Rectangle, Rounded Rectangle, Area Fill, Bar Series, Line Series, Column Graph, Graph Pane, Pie Graph, Graph Title Box, Legend, and Graph Series.

Options

Select one of the nine buttons for the different styles of lines, including different thicknesses, and different types of dotted and dashed lines.

Box Type

This property selects the type of box that borders the selected object.

This is a property for Graph Setup and Background, Graph Title, Legend, and the box around drawn text objects.

Options

Select a button for one of the twelve different types of boxes, that vary by the type of border, three-dimensional appearance, or beveled edges.

Explode Slice

This property only affects pie graphs; it allows you to explode a pie slice out of a pie graph, like a slice of pie pulled part way out of a pie.

This is a property for Pie Graphs.

Options

Explode distance—Use this scroll bar to control how far from the pie the exploded pie slice is moved. 100 percent would move the tip of the slice to the outside edge of the pie.

Explode—Select this check box to explode the pie slice. Clear the check box when you do not want the pie slice exploded.

Fill Color

This property controls the fill color of an object. If the object has a fill style with a pattern or a wash, the fill color is the pattern color in the pattern, or the darker color in the wash. (The fill color need not actually be darker, but the buttons indicating how the wash is done will show the fill color as the darker of the two.) To set the other color used in patterns and washes, change the Bkg Color property.

This is a property for the following objects: Arrow, Box, Ellipse, Freehand Polygon, Polygon, Rectangle, Rounded Rectangle, Text Box, Area Fill, Bar Series, Line Series, Column Graph, Graph Pane, Pie Graph, Graph Title Box, Legend Box, Graph Series, and Graph Setup and Background.

Options

Select one of the available colors in the palette. You can also create a custom color by selecting one of three models for defining colors and changing the sliding scales. You select the radio button for the models you want to use. HSB combines hue, saturation, and brightness to create colors; RBG combines red, blue, and green; and CMY combines cyan, magenta, and yellow.

Fill Style

This property selects a fill style for various objects. The fill style controls how the background and fill colors are used in filling that object. You can use no fill style, a solid fill style, a patterned fill, a wash, or select a bitmap file to use to fill the object.

This is a property for the following objects: Arrow, Box, Ellipse, Freehand Polygon, Polygon, Rectangle, Rounded Rectangle, Text, Text Box, Area Fill, Bar Series, Line Series, Column Graph, Graph Pane, Pie Graph, Graph Title Box, Legend Box, Graph Series, and Graph Setup and Background.

Options

None—Select this radio button to not fill the selected object. This fill style creates a transparent object. If you place it over another object, the other object shows through.

Solid—Select this radio button to use a solid fill. The object will use the fill color only.

Pattern—Select this radio button to use a pattern that combines the colors selected by Fill Color and Bkg Color. Choose from 24 different fill patterns when you select this radio button.

Wash—Select this radio button to use a wash fill style which makes a transition fading between the colors selected by Fill Color and Bkg Color. Choose from six types of washes. The six buttons change the location of the pure colors within the object.

Bitmap—Select this radio button to fill the object with a bitmap stored on disk. You can enter the file name of the bitmapped file in the File name text box. You can use the Browse button to browse through your directory structure to locate the correct file. You can select either Crop to fit or Shrink to fit to control how the bitmapped object fits inside the object.

Format

This property selects the numeric format for a series of values.
This is a property for Series Labels.

Options

The options for this property are the same as the Numeric Format property for blocks in a notebook page.

Graph Button

This property creates a graph button. When the graph is displayed on the full screen, the viewer can select this graph button by clicking it or typing the first character. The graph button then shows another graph, executes a macro, or executes the macro and shows another graph. You can also create a background graph button by inspecting the graph setup and background which executes when someone clicks the mouse somewhere other than a text box's graph button or types a key that does not match the first letter of the text in any other graph buttons.
This is a property for Graph Setup and Background, and Text Box.

Options

Select Graph—Select this check box to have Quattro Pro show a graph when this graph button is selected. Then select a graph from the list box.

Effect—Select an effect which removes the old graph and displays the new one from this drop-down list box.

Slow, Med, Fast—Select one of these radio buttons to set the speed of the transfer from the old to the new graph.

Overlay—Select this check box when you want the second graph to appear on top of the first graph, rather than removing the first from the screen. Usually, you want this check box cleared so that the first graph does not appear combined with the second.

Display time ...secs—Type the number of seconds you want the graph to appear. If you use the default of 0, the graph appears until the view presses a key or clicks the mouse.

Execute Macro—Select this check box when you want macro instructions performed when the view selects this graph button. In the adjoining text box, type the macro instructions you want Quattro Pro to perform.

Graph Type

This property changes the type of graph displayed.

This is a property for Graph Setup and Background.

Options

The options for this property are the same as the Graph | Type command, and have the same effect on the graph..

Grid

This property displays or uses a grid to position graph objects. You can display the grid, have objects snap to the grid when you position them, and change the grid size which is measured as a percentage of the graph window size. The grid does not print, nor does it appear in slide shows.

This is a property for the Graph Window.

Options

Display Grid—Select this check box to display the grid in the graph window. Clear the check box to remove the grid. As a default, the grid does not display.

Snap to Grid—Select this check box to have all objects you add and position start at a grid point. You can clear this box when you want objects to start at positions between grid points.

Grid Size—Select the distance between the grid points. This distance is measured as a percentage of the length of the edge of the graph window. Therefore, 10 would create grid points every tenth of the graph's width. The default grid size is 4 percent.

Label Alignment

Data point labels display the numeric value of a data point near the data point on the graph. These are especially useful with bar and line graphs where the trend of the data is easily seen, but precise numbers may also be wanted. This property aligns the label at different places around the data point. The options you have for this property depend on whether the y-axis appears horizontally or vertically.

This is a property for Series Labels.

Options

Above—Select this radio button to place the labels above the data point. On a bar graph, this is above the top of the bar, and in a line graph, above the data point.
Top—Select this radio button to place the labels at the top of the bar, but not above it. This radio button does not appear with line type graphs.
Center (Middle)—Select this radio button to place the labels at the vertical center of the bar, or in line graphs, directly over the data point.
Below (Bottom)—Select this radio button to place the labels below the data point in line graphs, and at the bottom of the bar in bar graphs.
Left—Select this radio button to place the labels to the left of the data point in a line graph.
Right—Select this radio button to place the labels to the left of the data point in a line graph.

Label Options

This property sets certain features for the labels of a pie or column graph. Label series used with other types of graphs can have their properties inspected independently.

This is a property for Pie Graphs and Column Graphs.

Options

Label series—Select the block containing the label data to use with each pie slice in this text box.
Currency—Select this radio button to display the labels as currency, with two decimal places.
Percent—Select this radio button to display the labels as a percentage of the whole, with two decimal places.
Value—Select this radio button to display the labels as values, with general formatting.
None—Select this radio button to not display the labels.
Show Tick—Select this check box to show the tick mark connecting the label and the pie slice it represents. Clear the check box when you do not want to connect a pie slice with its label.

Legend Position

This property selects where the graph's legend appears.
This is a property for Graph Setup and Background and Legends.

Options

Select one of the three buttons: The first removes the legend from your graph, the second places the legend underneath the graph pane, and the third places it on the right side of the graph pane.

Line Color

This property sets the color of the selected line.
This is a property for Polylines, Freehand Polylines, Lines, and Line Series.

Options

Select one of the available colors in the palette. You can also create a custom color by selecting one of three models for defining colors and changing the sliding scales. You select the radio button for the model you want to use. HSB combines hue, saturation, and brightness to create colors; RBG combines red, blue, and green; and CMY combines cyan, magenta, and yellow.

Line Style

This property sets the style of line for the line in the selected object.
This is a property for Polylines, Freehand Polylines, Lines, and Line Series.

Options

You can select one of nine styles of lines, including different thicknesses and different types of dotted and dashed lines.

Major Grid Style

This property sets the color and style of the lines that stretch from a major tick mark to the opposite side of the graph pane. These grid lines are a part of the graph; they appear when the graph is printed or in slide shows.
This is a property for X-Axis, Y-Axis, and Secondary Y-Axis.

Options

Line style—Select one of nine styles of lines, including different thicknesses and different types of dotted and dashed lines.

Color—Select a color for the gridlines. Select one of the available colors in the palette. You can also create a custom color by selecting one of three models for defining colors and changing the sliding scales. You select the radio button for the model you want to use. HSB combines hue, saturation, and brightness to create colors; RBG combines red, blue, and green; and CMY combines cyan, magenta, and yellow.

Marker Style

This property selects the style of marker to indicate the data points in the various types of line graphs.

This is a property for a series in a line graph.

Options

Select from 16 types of markers. The color and line style of these markers are set by the Line Style and Line Color properties. The ones that are filled have their interior colors and styles set by the Fill Color, Bkg Color, and Fill Style properties. *Weight*—Use this scroll bar and adjoining text box to select the weight or size of the marker.

Minor Grid Style

This property sets the style for the lines that stretch from a minor tick point to the opposite side of the graph pane. These grid lines are a part of the graph; they appear when the graph is printed or in slide shows.

This is a property for X-Axis when the graph type is an XY graph, Y-Axis, and Secondary Y-Axis.

Options

Line style—Select one of nine styles of lines, including different thicknesses and different types of dotted and dashed lines.

Color—Select a color for the gridlines. Select one of the available colors in the palette. You can also create a custom color by selecting one of three models for defining colors and changing the sliding scales. You select the radio button for the model you want to use. HSB combines hue, saturation, and brightness to create colors; RBG combines red, blue, and green; and CMY combines cyan, magenta, and yellow.

Numeric Format

This property selects the numeric format for a series of values.

This is a property for X-Axis (XY graph), Y-Axis, and Secondary Y-Axis.

Options

The options for this property are the same as the Numeric Format property for blocks in a notebook page.

Scale

This property sets the scaling that an axis uses.

This is a property for X-Axis (XY graph), Y-Axis, and Secondary Y-Axis.

Options

Normal—Select this radio button so that the values between major tick marks on the axis are the same amount.

Log—Select this radio button so that the values between two major tick marks are ten times the value between the preceding major tick marks.

Show units—Select this check box to display only the first few numbers along the axis, and put a label along the margin indicating how the values have been truncated. Clear this check box to omit showing the values in the thousands or millions.

Automatic—Select this check box to have Quattro Pro automatically select the values for the highest and lowest value to appear along the axes and the increment between them. Clear this box when you want to use the values you enter in the High, Low, and Increment text boxes. This check box is also cleared when you make an entry into the High, Low, and Increment text boxes.

High—Enter the highest value to appear along the axis in this text box. If you enter a number lower than that in the Low text box, the scale is a decreasing scale.

Low—Enter the lowest value to appear along the axis in this text box. If you enter a number higher than that in the High text box, the scale is a decreasing scale.

Increment—Enter the increment, the value between each major tick mark, in this text box.

No. of minors—Enter the number of minor tick marks to appear between major tick marks in this text box. The default line style for minor tick marks is 1.

Series Options

This property changes many of the settings for a data series in a graph. You can change the block from a notebook the data series represents, the label series that provides interior labels for each data point, or the entry used for the data series' legend. You can also choose to override the graph type to make this one data series display in a different type of graph. You can select to use the primary or the secondary y-axis for the display of the data series in the graph.

This is a property for data series when the graph is a type that displays bars or lines.

Options

    Data series—Select the block from a notebook that the line, area, or bar represents in this text box.

    Label series—Select the block from a notebook of data to provide labels for the data series in this text box.

    Legend—Enter the legend text or cell reference used to describe this data series in the legend in this text box.

    Bar—Select this radio button to display the selected data series as a bar, regardless of the selected graph type.

    Line—Select this radio button to display the selected data a series as a line, regardless of the selected graph type.

    Area—Select this radio button to display the selected data series as an area, regardless of the selected graph type.

    Default—Select this radio button to display the selected data series as the selected graph type. This radio button is the default.

    Primary—Select this radio button to use the primary y-axis to display the selected data series.

    Secondary—Select this radio button to use the secondary y-axis to display the selected data series. Using a secondary y-axis allows you to graph two sets of data using different scales along the y-axis.

Text Bkg Color

This property selects a background color for text in your graph. As with background colors for other objects, this color is only seen when you select a style other than solid for your text. For example, this color would be used in a wash.

    This is a property for Text, Axis Title, Graph Subtitle, Graph Title, Legend Box, Pie Graph Series Label, X-Axis, and Y-Axis.

Options

Select one of the available colors in the palette. You can also create a custom color by selecting one of three models for defining colors and changing the sliding scales. You select the radio button for the model you want to use. HSB combines hue, saturation, and brightness to create colors; RBG combines red, blue, and green; and CMY combines cyan, magenta, and yellow.

Text Color

This property sets the color for your text. If you use a text style, this color may be overlaid or used to create a wash to color your text with.

    This is a property for Text, Axis Title, Graph Subtitle, Graph Title, Legend Box, Pie Graph Series Label, X-Axis, and Y-Axis.

Options

Select one of the available colors in the palette. You can also create a custom color by selecting one of three models for defining colors and changing the sliding scales. You select the radio button for the model you want to use. HSB combines hue, saturation, and brightness to create colors; RBG combines red, blue, and green; and CMY combines cyan, magenta, and yellow.

Text Font

This property allows you to select a font for use with your graph.

This is a property for Text, Axis Title, Graph Subtitle, Graph Title, Legend Box, Pie Graph Series Label, X-Axis, and Y-Axis.

Options

Typeface—Select one of the fonts listed in this text box to choose the typeface of the font. The displayed fonts include all the fonts installed in Windows, including TrueType and printer fonts.

Point Size—Select the size of the font from one of the sizes listed in the drop-down list box, or type the font size to set the size for the block. For scalable fonts, you can type a point size that is not one of the ones listed.

Bold—Select this check box to add boldfacing, or clear this check box to remove it.

Italics—Select this check box to add italics, or clear this check box to remove it.

Underline—Select this check box to add underlining, or clear this check box to remove it.

Strikeout—Select this check box to strikeout a character (a line through the middle of it), or clear this check box to remove it.

Text Style

This property applies a style to text in your graph. You can choose a solid color, a wash, or a bitmapped image. You can also choose to create a shadow of your text in the background color.

This is a property for Text, Axis Title, Graph Subtitle, Graph Title, Legend Box, Pie Graph, Series Label, X-Axis, and Y-Axis.

Options

Solid—Select this radio button to fill the text solidly with the color selected by Text Color.

Wash—Select this radio button to fill the text with a wash fill style that makes a transition that fades between the colors selected by Text Color and Text Bkg Color. Choose from six types of washes. The six buttons change the location of the pure colors within the object.

Bitmap—Select this radio button to fill the text with a bitmap stored on disk. You can enter the file name of the bitmapped file in the File name text box. You can use the Browse button to browse through your directory structure to locate the correct file. You can select either Crop to fit or Shrink to fit to control how the bitmapped object fits inside the object.

Shadow—Select this check box to display the text with a shadow. The shadow is the Text Bkg Color, if Solid is the selected text style, or black if anything else is selected.

Tick Options

This property sets the appearance of the tick marks along the axes of a two-dimensional graph. The options you have for this property depend on whether you are setting this property for an axis that is horizontal or vertical.

This is a property for X-Axis, Y-Axis and second Y-Axis.

Options

None—Select this radio button to remove any tick mark from the selected axis.

Left—Select this radio button to put the tick mark only on the left side of a vertical axis.

Right—Select this radio button to put the tick mark only on the right side of a vertical axis.

Below—Select this radio button to put the tick mark below a horizontal axis.

Above—Select this radio button to put the tick mark above a horizontal axis.

Across—Select this radio button to put the tick mark across the axis, so that it appears on both sides.

Display labels—Select this check box to display the axis labels along the selected axis. Clear this check box to remove the axis labels along the selected axis.

1, 2, 3—Select one of these radio buttons for the number of rows you want the axis labels distributed over. These radio buttons are only available for the x-axis when the graph type is not an XY graph.

No overlapping labels—Select this check box when you want Quattro Pro to truncate long labels that overlap one another. Clear this check box when you do not want the long axis labels truncated. These radio buttons are only available for the x-axis when the graph type is not an XY graph.

Skip—Enter the number or click the arrows to set how many labels along the axis you want skipped. The default is 0, so all axis labels appear, but by increasing the number, you skip axis labels to make the axis less congested. These radio buttons are only available for the x-axis when the graph type is not an XY graph.

Length limit—Select this check box if you want to limit the number of characters in the axis labels.

Characters—Enter the maximum number of characters that each axis label can display in this text box after you have selected the Length limit check box.

Title

This property sets the text of the title describing the axis.
This is a property for the Axis Title.

Options

The only option is the text of the title. You can use the contents of the cell by typing \ followed by the cell address or block name (remember the page name).

X-Axis Series

This property selects the block containing the labels for the X-Axis in a graph. This can include dates, labels, or values.
This option only affects the X-Axis series of a graph that is not an XY graph.

Options

The only option is to select the block containing the labels for the X-Axis.

Appendix D

Quattro Pro Command Equivalents

Command equivalents tell Quattro Pro a menu command to perform within a macro. Menu equivalent commands are used to build macros in graph buttons in a graph, or slide show, and as macro commands in SpeedBar buttons. Table D.1 lists each default Quattro Pro for Windows menu tree commands and the command equivalent that performs the same task. The information in the third column is the information you must provide for the command equivalent to function properly. This is usually the same information you provide in the dialog box of the command. The argument information that is in quotes is entered directly as it appears and when several are presented for an argument, use only one. Usually, you have one of several choices to select from. The arguments enclosed by < > are optional. The information in italics must be replaced with the information they describe. The arguments that end with a ? should be replaced by "Yes" or "No". You can also put a ? or ! immediately after the command equivalent. The ? lets the macro user control the dialog box for the menu command until the user leaves the dialog box and the ! lets the macro control the dialog box.

Table D.1   Menu Commands and Command Equivalents

Menu Command	Command Equivalent	Arguments
Block | Copy	{BlockCopy	*SourceBlock, DestBlock,* <ModelCopy?>}
Block | Delete | Columns	{BlockDelete.Columns	*Block,* "Partial" or "Entire"}
Block | Delete | Pages	{BlockDelete.Pages	*Block,* "Partial" or "Entire"}
Block | Delete | Rows	{BlockDelete.Rows	*Block,* "Partial" or "Entire"}
Block | Fill | Blocks	{BlockFill.Block	*Block*}
Block | Fill | OK	{BlockFill.Go}	
Block | Fill | Order	{BlockFill.Order	"Column" or "Row"}
Block | Fill | Series	{BlockFill.Series	"Linear" "Growth" "Power" "Year" "Month" "Week" "Weekday" "Day" "Hour" "Minute" or "Second"}
Block | Fill | Start	{BlockFill.Start	*Value*}
Block | Fill | Step	{BlockFill.Step	*Value*}
Block | Fill | Stop	{BlockFill.Stop	*Value*}
Block | Insert | Columns	{BlockInsert.Columns	*Block,* "Partial" or "Entire"}
Block | Insert | File	{BlockInsert.File	*Filename, BeforeBlock*}
Block | Insert | Pages	{BlockInsert.Pages	*Block,* "Partial" or "Entire"}
Block | Insert | Rows	{BlockInsert.Rows	*Block,* "Partial" or "Entire"}
Block | Insert Break	{InsertBreak}	
Block | Move	{BlockMove	*SourceBlock, DestBlock*}
Block | Move Pages	{BlockMovePages	*SourcePages, BeforePage*}
Block | Names | Create	{BlockName.Create	*BlockName,* Block}
Block | Names | Delete	{BlockName.Delete	*BlockName*}
Block | Names | Labels	{BlockName.Labels	*Block,* "Left" "Right" "Up" or "Down"}
Block | Names | Make Table	{BlockName.MakeTable	*Block*}
Block | Names | Reset	{BlockName.Reset}	
Block | Object Order | Bring Forward	{FloatOrder.Up}	
Block | Object Order | Bring to Front	{FloatOrder.Down}	
Block | Object Order | Send Back	{FloatOrder.Top}	
Block | Object Order | Send to Back	{FloatOrder.Bottom}	
Block | Reformat	{BlockReformat	*Block*}
Block | Transpose	{BlockTranspose	*SourceBlock, DestBlock*}
Block | Values	{BlockValues	*SourceBlock, DestBlock*}
Data | Database Desktop	{TableView}	
Data | Frequency | Bin Block	{Frequency.Bin_Block	*Block*}

(continued)

Table D.1 Menu Commands and Command Equivalents *(continued)*

Menu Command	Command Equivalent	Arguments
Data | Frequency | OK	{Frequency.Go}	
Data | Frequency | Reset	{Frequency.Reset}	
Data | Frequency | Value Blocks	{Frequency.Value_Block	*Block}*
Data | Parse | Create	{Parse.Create}	
Data | Parse | Edit	{Parse.EditLine	*NewEditLine}*
Data | Parse | Input	{Parse.Input	*Block}*
Data | Parse | OK	{Parse.Go}	
Data | Parse | Output	{Parse.Output	*Block}*
Data | Parse | Reset	{Parse.Reset}	
Data | Query | Criteria Table	{Query.Criteria_Table	*Block}*
Data | Query | Database Block	{Query.Database_Block	*Block}*
Data | Query | Delete	{Query.Delete}	
Data | Query | Extract	{Query.Extract}	
Data | Query | Extract Unique	{Query.Unique}	
Data | Query | Field Names	{Query.Assign_Names}	
Data | Query | Locate	{Query.Locate}	
Data | Query | Locate	{Query.EndLocate}	
Data | Query | Output Block	{Query.Output_Block	*Block}*
Data | Query | Reset	{Query.Reset}	
Data | Restrict Input	{RestrictInput.Enter	*Block}*
Data | Restrict Input	{RestrictInput.Exit}	
Data | Sort | Block	{Sort.Block	*Block}*
Data | Sort | Column 1st	{Sort.Key_1	*Block}*
Data | Sort | Column 2nd	{Sort.Key_2	*Block}*
Data | Sort | Column 3rd	{Sort.Key_3	*Block}*
Data | Sort | Column 4th	{Sort.Key_4	*Block}*
Data | Sort | Column 5th	{Sort.Key_5	*Block}*
Data | Sort | Ascending 1st	{Sort.Order_1	"Ascending" or "Descending"}
Data | Sort | Ascending 2nd	{Sort.Order_2	"Ascending" or "Descending"}
Data | Sort | Ascending 3rd	{Sort.Order_3	"Ascending" or "Descending"}
Data | Sort | Ascending 4th	{Sort.Order_4	"Ascending" or "Descending"}
Data | Sort | Ascending 5th	{Sort.Order_5	"Ascending" or "Descending"}
Data | Table Query | Destination	{TableQuery.Destination _Block	*Block}*

(continued)

Table D.1   Menu Commands and Command Equivalents *(continued)*

Menu Command	Command Equivalent	Arguments
Data l Table Query l OK	{TableQuery.Go}	
Data l Table Query l QBE block	{TableQuery.QueryBlock	*Block*}
Data l Table Query l QBE file	{TableQuery.QueryFile	*Filename*}
Data l Table Query l Query in Block	{TableQuery.QueryInFile	No}
Data l Table Query l Query in File	{TableQuery.QueryInFile	Yes}
Data l What-If l One free variable	{WhatIf.One_Way}	
Data l What-If l Two Free Variables	{WhatIf.Two_Way}	
Data l What-If l Data Table	{WhatIf.Block	*Block*}
Data l What-If l Input Cell	{WhatIf.Input_Cell_1	Cell}
Data l What-If l Column Input Cell	{WhatIf.Input_Cell_1	Cell}
Data l What-If l Row Input Cell	{WhatIf.Input_Cell_2	Cell}
Data l What-If l Reset	{WhatIf.Reset}	
Dialog l Align l Bottom	{Align.Bottom}	
Dialog l Align l Horizontal Center	{Align.Horizontal_Center}	*Value}*
Dialog l Align l Horizontal Space	{Align.Horizontal_Space	
Dialog l Align l Left	{Align.Left}	
Dialog l Align l Resize to Same	{ResizeToSame}	
Dialog l Align l Right	{Align.Right}	
Dialog l Align l Top	{Align.Top}	
Dialog l Align l Vertical Center	{Align.Vertical_Center}	
Dialog l Align l Vertical Space	{Align.Vertical_Space	*Value}*
Dialog l Order l Bring Forward	{Order.Forward}	
Dialog l Order l Bring to Front	{Order.ToFront}	
Dialog l Order l Order Tab Controls	{Controls.Order}	
Dialog l Order l Order Tab From	{Controls.OrderFrom}	

(continued)

Table D.1   Menu Commands and Command Equivalents *(continued)*

Menu Command	Command Equivalent	Arguments
Dialog | Order | Send Backward	{Order.Backward}	
Dialog | Order | Send to Back	{Order.ToBack}	
Dialog | Order | Tab Controls	{Controls.OrderTab}	
Dialog | Order | Tab From	{Controls.OrderTabFrom}	
Draw | Align | Bottom	{Align.Bottom}	
Draw | Align | Horizontal Center	{Align.Horizontal_Center}	
Draw | Align | Left	{Align.Left}	
Draw | Align | Right	{Align.Right}	
Draw | Align | Top	{Align.Top}	
Draw | Align | Vertical Center	{Align.Vertical_Center}	
Draw | Bring Forward	{Order.Forward}	
Draw | Bring to Front	{Order.ToFront}	
Draw | Export	{ExportGraphic	*Filename, <Grayscale?>,* *<Compression?>}*
Draw | Group	{GroupObjects}	
Draw | Import	{ImportGraphic	*Filename, <DontSave?>}*
Draw | Send Backward	{Order.Backward}	
Draw | Send to Back	{Order.ToBack}	
Draw | Ungroup	{UngroupObjects}	
Edit | Clear	{EditClear}	
Edit | Clear Contents	{ClearContents	<PageOnly?>}
Edit | Copy	{EditCopy}	
Edit | Cut	{EditCut}	
Edit | Define Style | Alignment	{NamedStyle.Alignment	"General" "Left" "Right" or "Center"}
Edit | Define Style | Define Style For	{NamedStyle.Define	*StyleName, Align?,* NumericFormat?, Protection?, Lines?, Shading?, Font?, TextColor?}
Edit | Define Style | Delete	{NamedStyle.Delete	*StyleName}*
Edit | Define Style | Font	{NamedStyle.Font	*"Fontname, Pointsize,* Bold?, Italic?, Underline?, Strikethough?"}
Edit | Define Style | Format	{NamedStyle.Numeric_ Format	*"NumericFormat"}*

(continued)

Table D.1   Menu Commands and Command Equivalents *(continued)*

Menu Command	Command Equivalent	Arguments
Edit | Define Style | Line Drawing	{NamedStyle.Line_Drawing	*"LeftLine, TopLine, RightLine, BottomLine"*}
Edit | Define Style | Protection	{NamedStyle.Protection	"Protected" or "Unprotected"}
Edit | Define Style | Shading	{NamedStyle.Shading	*Color1, Color2, Blend*}
Edit | Define Style | Text Color	{NamedStyle.Text_Color	*ColorNumber*}
Edit | Goto	{EditGoto	*Block*}
Edit | Paste	{EditPaste}	
Edit | Paste Format	{PasteFormat	*LinkType*}
Edit | Paste Link	{PasteLink}	
Edit | Paste Special	{PasteSpecial	Properties or "",Values or "", Transpose or "", NoBlanks or ""}
Edit | Search and Replace | Blocks	{Search._Block	*Block*}
Edit | Search and Replace | Case	{Search.Case	"Any" or "Exact"}
Edit | Search and Replace | Direction	{Search.Direction	"Row" or "Column"}
Edit | Search and Replace | Look In	{Search.Look_In	"Formula" "Value" or "Condition"}
Edit | Search and Replace | Match	{Search.Match	"Part" or "Whole"}
Edit | Search and Replace | Next	{Search.Next}	
Edit | Search and Replace | Replace	{Search.Replace}	
Edit | Search and Replace | Replace All	{Search.Replace All}	
Edit | Search and Replace | Replaced With	{Search.Find	*String}*
Edit | Search and Replace | Reset	{Search.Reset}	
Edit | Undo	{Undo}	
File | Close	{WindowClose}	
File | Close All	{FileCloseAll}	
File | Exit	{FileExit}	
File | Named Settings | Create	{Print.Create	*NamedSetting*}
File | Named Settings | Delete	{Print.Delete	*NamedSetting*}

(continued)

Table D.1   Menu Commands and Command Equivalents *(continued)*

Menu Command	Command Equivalent	Arguments
File | Named Settings | Named Settings	{Print.Use	*NamedSetting*}
File | Named Settings | Update	{Print.Create	*NamedSetting*}
File | New	{FileNew}	
File | Open	{FileOpen	*Filename*}
File | Page Setup | Bottom	{Print.Bottom_Margin	*Value*}
File | Page Setup | Break pages	{Print.Page_Breaks	"Yes" or "No"}
File | Page Setup | Center blocks	{Print.CenterBlock	"Yes" or "No"}
File | Page Setup | Footer	{Print.Footer	*FooterString*}
File | Page Setup | Footer (margin)	{Print.Footer_Margin	*Value*}
File | Page Setup | Header	{Printer.Header	*HeaderString*}
File | Page Setup | Header (margin)	{Print.Header_Margin	*Value*}
File | Page Setup | Header Font	{Print.Headers_Font	*"Typeface*, *PointSize*, Bold?, Italic?, Underline?, Strikeout?"}
File | Page Setup | Left	{Print.Left_Margin	*Value*}
File | Page Setup | Paper type	{Print.Paper_Type	*PaperSize*}
File | Page Setup | Print orientation	{Print.Orientation	"Landscape" or "Portrait"}
File | Page Setup | Print to fit	{Print.Print_To_Fit	"Yes" or "No"}
File | Page Setup | Reset Defaults	{Print.PageSetupReset} or {Print.PrintReset}	
File | Page Setup | Right	{Print.Right_Margin	*Value*}
File | Page Setup | Scaling	{Print.Scaling	*PercentageValue*}
File | Page Setup | Top	{Print.Top_Margin	*Value*}
File | Print | All pages	{Print.AllPages	"Yes" or "No"}
File | Print | Options | Borders	{Print.Borders	"Yes" or "No"}
File | Print | Options | Cell formulas	{Print.Cell_Formulas	"Yes" or "No"}
File | Print | Copies	{Print.Copies	*Value*}
File | Print | From	{Print.Start_Page_Number	Value}
File | Print | Options | Gridlines	{Print.Gridlines	"Yes" or "No"}
File | Print | Left heading	{Print.Left_Heading	*Block*}
File | Print | Options	{Print!}{Alt+O}	

(continued)

Table D.1   Menu Commands and Command Equivalents *(continued)*

Menu Command	Command Equivalent	Arguments
File I Print I Preview	{Preview}	
File I Print I Print	{Print.DoPrint}	
File I Print I Option I Print between 3D pages I Lines	{Print.Between_Page _Formatting	"Lines"}
File I Print I Options I Print between 3D pages I Lines	{Print.Lines_Between_Pages	*Value}*
File I Print I Options I Print between 3D pages I Page advance	{Print.Between_Page_ Formatting	"Page Advance"}
File I Print I Options I Print between blocks I Line	{Print.Between_Block _Formatting	"Lines"}
File I Print I Options I Print between blocks I Line	{Print.Lines_Between _Blocks	*Value}*
File I Print I Options I Print between blocks I Page advance	{Print.Between_Block_ Formatting	"Page Advance"}
File I Print I Print blocks	{Print.Print_Block	Blocks}
File I Print I Options I Reset Defaults	{Print.PrintOptionsReset}	
File I Print I Reset Defaults	{Print.PrintReset}	
File I Print I To	{Print.End_Page_Number	*Value}*
File I Print I Options I Top heading	{Print.Col_Borders	*Block}*
File I Print Preview	{Preview}	
File I Printer Setup	{PrinterSetup	*Printer*, *Port*, PrintToFile?, *Filename}*
File I Printer Setup I Set Up	{PrinterSetup!}{TAB 5} {PAUSEMACRO}	
File I Retrieve	{FileRetrieve	*Filename}*
File I Save	{FileSave}	
File I Save All	{FileSaveAll}	
File I Save As	{FileSaveAs	*Filename}*
File I Workspace I Restore	{Workspace.Restore	*Filename}*
File I Workspace I Save	{Workspace.Save	*Filename}*
Graph I Copy	{GraphCopy	*GraphName*, *DestFile*, Style?, Data?, Annotations?}
Graph I Delete	{GraphDelete	*Name}*
Graph I Edit	{GraphEdit	*Name}*
Graph I Insert	{FLOATCREATE}	
Graph I New	{GraphNew	*Name}*
Graph I Series I Add	{Series.Insert	*SeriesNumber*, *Block}*

(continued)

Table D.1   Menu Commands and Command Equivalents *(continued)*

Menu Command	Command Equivalent	Arguments
Graph | Series | Add	{Series.Data_Range	*SeriesNumber, Block,* <CreateIfNonexistent?>}
Graph | Series | Add	{Series.Label_Range	*SeriesNumber, Block,* <CreateIfNonexistent?>}
Graph | Series | Add	{Series.Legend	*SeriesNumber, LegendText}*
Graph | Series | Delete	{Series.Delete	*SeriesNumber,* AllSeries?}
Graph | Series | OK	{Series.Go}	
Graph | Series | Reverse Series	{Series.Reverse_Series	"Yes" or "No"}
Graph | Series | Row/ column swap	{Series.Swap_Row_Col	"Yes" or "No"}
Graph | Slide Show	{Slide.Run	*SlideShowName}*
Graph | Titles	{GraphSettings.Title	*Main, Sub, X-Axis, Y-Axis, Y2-Axis}*
Graph | Type	{GraphSetting.Type	"Bar,2-D" "Variance,2-D" "Stacked Bar,2-D" "HiLo, 2-D" "Line,2-D" "XY,2-D" "Area,2-D" "Area,2-D" "Column,2-D" "Pie,2-D" "3D Bar,3-D" "3D Stacked Bar,3-D" "Half-D Bar" "3D Step,3-D" "3D Unstacked Area,3-D" "3D Ribbon,3-D" "3D Area,3-D" "3D Column,3-D" "3D Pie, 3-D" "3D Contour,3-D" "3D Surface,3-D" "3D Shaded Surface,3-D" "R3D Bar,Rotate" "RHalfD Bar,Rotate" "R2D Bar,Rotate" "Rotated Area,Rotate" "Rotated Line,Rotate" "Area_bar,Combo" "Hilo_bar,Combo" "Line_bar,Combo" "Multiple 3D columns,Combo" "Multiple 3D Pies,Combo" "Multiple

(continued)

Table D.1   Menu Commands and Command Equivalents *(continued)*

Menu Command	Command Equivalent	Arguments
		Bar,Combo" "Multiple Columns,Combo" "Multiple Pies,Combo" or "Text,Text"}
Graph I View	{Graph.View}	*GraphName}*
Property I Application I Display I 3-D Syntax	{Application.Display. Range_Syntax	"A..B:A1..B2" or "A:A1..B:B2"}
Property I Application I Display I Clock Display	{Application.Display. Clock _Display	"None" "Standard" or "International"}
Property I Application I Display I Show Input Line	{Application.Display. Show _InputLine	"Yes" or "No"}
Property I Application I Display I Show SpeedBar	{Application.Display. Show_Toolbar	"Yes" or "No"}
Property I Application I Display I Show Status Line	{Application.Display. Show_StatusLine	"Yes" or "No"}
Property I Application I International I Currency	{Application.International. Currency	"Windows Default" or "Quattro Pro/Windows"}
Property I Application I International I Currency Symbol	{Application.International. Currency_Symbol	*Symbol}*
Property I Application I International I Dateformat	{Application.Date_Format	*String}*
Property I Application I International I LICS	{Application.International. LICS_Conversion	"Yes" or "No"}
Property I Application I International I Negative	{Application.International. Negative	"Signed" or "Parenthesis"}
Property I Application I International I Placement	{Application.International. Placement	"Prefix" or "Suffix"}
Property I Application I International I Punctuation	{Application.International. Punctuation	*String}*
Property I Application I International I Time Format	{Application.Time_Format	*String}*
Property I Application I International I Language	{Application.International. Sort_Table	*String}*
Property I Application I Macro I KeyReader	{Application.Macro.Key Reader	"Yes" or "No"}

(continued)

Table D.1   Menu Commands and Command Equivalents *(continued)*

Menu Command	Command Equivalent	Arguments
Property l Application l Macro l Macro Suppress-Redraw	{Application.Macro. Macro_Redraw	"Both" "Panel" "Window" or "None"}
Property l Application l Macro l Slash Key	{Application.Macro. Slash_Key	*MenuName*}
Property l Application l SpeedBar l Enable Inspection	{Application.Enable _Inspection	"Yes" or "No"}
Property l Application l SpeedBar l Secondary SpeedBar	{Application.SpeedBar	*SpeedBarName*}
Property l Application l Startup l Autoload File	{Application.Startup. Autoload_File	*String*}
Property l Application l Startup l Directory	{Application.Startup. Startup _Directory	*String*}
Property l Application l Startup l File Extension	{Application.Startup. File_Extension	*String*}
Property l Application l Startup l Startup Macro	{Application.Startup. Startup_Macro	*String*}
Property l Application l Startup l Undo enabled	{Application.Startup.Undo	"Yes" or "No"}
Property l Application l Startup l Use Beep	{Application.Startup.Beep	"Yes" or "No"}
Property l Application l Title	{Application.Title	*Title*}
Property l Current Object	{SETPROPERTY	*Property,Setting*}
Property l Graph Window l Aspect Ratio	{GraphWindow. Aspect _Ratio	"Floating Graph" "Screen Slide" "35mm Slide" "Printer Preview" or "Full Extent"}
Property l Graph Window l Grid Options	{GraphWindow.Grid_Options	*GridSize*, DisplayGrid?, SnapToGrid?}
Property l Graph Window l Name	{GraphWindow.Name	*GraphName*}
Property l Active Notebook l Display l Horizontal Scroll Bar	{Notebook.Display.Show _HorizontalScroller	"Yes" or "No"}
Property l Active Notebook l Display l Page Tabs	{Notebook.Display. Show_Tabs	"Yes" or "No"}
Property l Active Notebook l Display l Vertical Scroll Bar	{Notebook.Display.Show _VerticalScroller	"Yes" or "No"}

(continued)

Table D.1   Menu Commands and Command Equivalents *(continued)*

Menu Command	Command Equivalent	Arguments
Property I Active Notebook I Macro Library	{Notebook.Macro_Library	"Yes" or "No"}
Property I Active Notebook I Palette	{Notebook.Palette.Color_ 1-16	*Red-Green-Blue*"}
Property I Active Notebook I Recalc Settings	{Notebook.Recalc_Settings	"Automatic" "Manual" "Background" or "Natural", "Column-wise" or "Row-wise", *Iterations*}
Property I Active Notebook I Zoom Factor	{Notebook.Zoom_Factor	25-200}
Property I Active Page I Borders I Column Borders	{Page.Borders.Column_ Borders	"Yes" or "No"}
Property I Active Page I Borders I Row Borders	{Page.Borders.Row_ Borders	"Yes" or "No"}
Property I Active Page I Conditional Color I Above Normal Color	{Page.Conditional_Color. Above_Normal_Color	0-15}
Property I Active Page I Conditional Color I Below Normal Color	{Page.Conditional_Color. Below_Normal_Color	0-15}
Property I Active Page I Conditional Color I Enable	{Page.Conditional_Color. Eanble	"Yes" or "No"}
Property I Active Page I Conditional Color I ERR Color	{Page.Conditional_Color. ERR_Color	0-15}
Property I Active Page I Conditional Color I Greatest Normal Value	{Page.Conditional_Color. Greatest_Normal_Value	*Value*}
Property I Active Page I Conditional Color I Normal Color	{Page.Conditional_Color. Normal_Color	0-15}
Property I Active Page I Conditional Color I Smallest Normal Value	{Page.Conditional_Color. Smallest_Normal_Value	*Value*}
Property I Active Page I Default Width	{Page.Default_Width}	
Property I Active Page I Display Zeros	{Page.Display_Zeros	"Yes" or "No"}

(continued)

Table D.1   Menu Commands and Command Equivalents *(continued)*

Menu Command	Command Equivalent	Arguments
Property I Active Page I Grid Lines I Horizontal	{Page.Grid_Lines. Horizontal	"Yes" or "No"}
Property I Active Page I Grid Lines I Vertical	{Page.Grid_Lines.Vertical	"Yes" or "No"}
Property I Active Page I Label Alignment	{Page.Label_Alignment	"Left" "Right" or "Center"}
Property I Active Page I Line Color	{Page.Line_Color	0-15}
Property I Active Page I Name	{Page.Name	*NewName*}
Tools I Advanced Math I Invert I Destination	{Invert.Destination_Block	*Block*}
Tools I Advanced Math I Invert I Source	{Invert.Source_Block	*Block*}
Tools I Advanced Math I Multiply I Destination	{Multiply.Destination_ Block	*Block*}
Tools I Advanced Math I Multiply I Matrix 1	{Multiply.Matrix_1	*Block*}
Tools I Advanced Math I Multiply I Matrix 2	{Multiply.Matrix_2	*Block*}
Tools I Advanced Math I Multiply I OK	{Multiply.Go}	
Tools I Advanced Math I Regression I Dependent	{Regression.Dependent_ Block	*Block*}
Tools I Advanced Math I Regression I Independent	{Regression.Indpendent_ Block	*Block*}
Tools I Advanced Math I Regression I OK	{Regression.Go}	
Tools I Advanced Math I Regression I Output	{Regression.Output	*Block*}
Tools I Advanced Math I Regression I Reset	{Regression.Reset}	
Tools I Advanced Math I Regression I Y-Intercept	{Regression.Y_Intercept	"Compute" or "Zero"}
Tools I Combine	{FileCombine	*Filename, <Blocks>,* "Copy" "Add" "Divide" "Multiply" or "Subtract"}
Tools I Define Group I OK	{Group.Define	*GroupName, StartPage, EndPage*}
Tools I Define Group I Delete	{Group.Delete	*GroupName*}

(continued)

Table D.1   Menu Commands and Command Equivalents *(continued)*

Menu Command	Command Equivalent	Arguments
Tools I Define Group I Delete	{Group.ResetNames}	
Tools I Extract	{FileExtract	"Formulas" or "Values", *Blocks, Filename*}
Tools I Import	{FileImport	*Filename*, "ASCII" "Comma and """ or "Only Commas"}
Tools I Macro I Debugger	{STEPON} or {STEPOFF}	
Tools I Macro I Execute	{BRANCH	*MacroName*}
Tools I Macro I Execute	{MacroName}	
Tools I Optimizer I Solution Cell	{Optimizer	*ObjectiveCell*, "Max" "Min" or "None"}
Tools I Optimizer I Variable Cells	{Optimizer.Variable_Cells	*Blocks*}
Tools I Optimizer I Constraints I Add	{Optimizer.AddConstraint	*Constraint,cell,relation,<value or cell*}
Tools I Optimizer I Constraints I Change	{Optimizer.Change Constraint	*Constraint,cell,relation,<value or cell*}
Tools I Optimizer I Constraints I Delete	{Optimizer.Delete Constraint	*Constraint_*}
Tools I Optimizer I Options I Derivatives	{Optimizer.Derivatives	"Forward" or "Central"}
Tools I Optimizer I Options I Estimates	{Optimizer.Estimates	"Tangent" or "Quadratic"}
Tools I Optimizer I Options I Linear or NonLinear	{Optimizer.Linear	"Yes" or "No"}
Tools I Optimizer I Options I Load Model	{Optimizer.Load_Model	*Block*}
Tools I Optimizer I Options I Max Iterations	{Optimizer.Max_Iters	*Value*}
Tools I Optimizer I Options I Max Time	{Optimizer.Max_Time	*Value*}
Tools I Optimizer I Options I Precision	{Optimizer.Precision	*Value*}
Tools I Optimizer I Options I Reporting I Answer Report Block	{Optimizer.Answer_ Reporting	*Cell*}
Tools I Optimizer I Options I Reporting I Detail Answer Block	{Optimizer.Detail_Reporting	*Cell*}
Tools I Optimizer I Options I Save Model	{Optimizer.Save_Model	*Block*}

(continued)

Table D.1   Menu Commands and Command Equivalents *(continued)*

Menu Command	Command Equivalent	Arguments
Tools I Optimizer I Options I Search	{Optimizer.Search	"Newton" or "Conjugate"}
Tools I Optimizer I Options I Show Iteration Results	{Optimizer.Show_ Iters	"Yes" or "No"}
Tools I Optimizer I Reset	{Optimizer.Reset}	
Tools I Optimizer I Solve	{Optimizer.Solve}	
Tools I Solve For I Formula Cell	{SolveFor.Formula_Cell	*Cell*}
Tools I Solve For I Max Iterations	{SolveFor.Max_Iters	*Value*}
Tools I Solve For I OK	{SolveFor.Go}	
Tools I Solve For I Accuracy	{SolveFor.Accuracy	*Value*}
Tools I Solve For I Target Value	{SolveFor.Value	*Cell*}
Tools I Solve For I Variable Cell	{SolveFor.Variable_Cell	*Cell*}
Tools I Update Links I Change Link	{Links.Change	*OldName, NewName*}
Tools I Update Links I Delete Links	{Links.Delete	*LinkName*}
Tools I Update Links I Open Links	{Links.Open	*LinkName*}
Tools I Update Links I Refresh Links	{Links.Refresh	*LinkName*}
Window I 1-9 or More Windows	{Activate	*WindowName*}
Window I 1-9 or More Windows	{Window	*n*}
Window I Arrange Icons	{WindowArrIcon}	
Window I Cascade	{WindowCascade}	
Window I Hide	{WindowHide}	
Window I Locked Titles	{WindowTitles	"Clear" "Horizontal" "Vertical" or "Both"}
Window I New View	{WindowNewView}	
Window I Panes	{WindowPanes	"Horizontal" "Vertical" or "Clear", "Synch" or "Unsynch", Width, Height}
Window I Show	{WindowShow	*Name*}
Window I Tile	{WindowTile}	

Appendix E

Menu Equivalent Commands

If you are creating macros that will be used in Quattro Pro for DOS, use menu-equivalent commands. Menu equivalent commands tell Quattro a menu command to perform regardless of the menu command tree used. You can use menu equivalent commands anywhere you would use macro instructions. If you are creating macros for both Quattro Pro for DOS and Quattro Pro for Windows, use the {IF @VERSION<100} macro command. When you use this command include the {BRANCH} or {subroutine} command that switches macro execution to Quattro Pro for DOS commands. Table E.1 lists each default Quattro Pro 4.0 menu tree command and the menu equivalent command that performs the same task. For menu equivalent commands you must select from a list of options; you can make these selections by using {EDIT} and the text of the entry you want to select, as in using {EDIT}Dutch-SC~ to select the Dutch-SC from a font list.

Table E.1   Quattro Pro Commands and Menu Equivalent Commands

Quattro Commands	Menu Equivalent
/Database Data Entry Dates Only	{/ Publish;DataEntryDate}
/Database Data Entry General	{/ Publish;DataEntryFormula}
/Database Data Entry Labels Only	{/ Publish;DataEntryLabel}
/Database Paradox Access Go	{/ Paradox;SwitchGo}
/Database Paradox Access Load File	{/ Paradox;SwitchFile}
/Database Paradox Access Autoload	{/ Paradox;SwitchAutoLoad}
/Database Query Assign Names	{/ Query;AssignNames}
/Database Query Block	{/ Query;Block}
/Database Query Criteria Table	{/ Query;CriteriaBlock}
/Database Query Delete	{/ Query;Delete}
/Database Query Extract	{/ Query;Extract}
/Database Query Locate	{/ Query;Locate}
/Database Query Output Block	{/ Query;Output}
/Database Query Reset	{/ Query;Reset}
/Database Query Unique	{/ Query;Unique}
/Database Restrict Input	{/ Block;Input}
/Database Sort 1st Key	{/ Sort;Key1}
/Database Sort 2nd Key	{/ Sort;Key2}
/Database Sort 3rd Key	{/ Sort;Key3}
/Database Sort 4th Key	{/ Sort;Key4}
/Database Sort 5th Key	{/ Sort;Key5}
/Database Sort Block	{/ Sort;Block}
/Database Sort Go	{/ Sort;Go}
/Database Sort Reset	{/ Sort;Reset}
/Database Sort Sort Rules Label Order	{/ Startup;LabelOrder}
/Database Sort Sort Rules Numbers Before Labels	{/ Startup;CellOrder}

Table E.1 Quattro Pro Commands and Menu Equivalent Commands *(continued)*

Quattro Commands	Menu Equivalent
/Database Sort Sort Rules Sort Rows/Columns	{/ Startup;SortOrder}
/Edit Copy	{/ Block;Copy}
/Edit Copy Special Contents	{/ Block;CopyContents}
/Edit Copy Special Format	{/ Block;CopyFormat}
/Edit Delete Column Block	{/ Column;Delete Block}
/Edit Delete Columns	{/ Column;Delete}
/Edit Delete Row Block	{/ Row;DeleteBlock}
/Edit Delete Rows	{/ Row;Delete}
/Edit Erase Block	{/ Block;Erase}
/Edit Fill	{/ Math;Fill}
/Edit Insert Column Block	{/ Column;Insert Block}
/Edit Insert Columns	{/ Column;Insert}
/Edit Insert Row Block	{/ Row;InsertBlock}
/Edit Insert Rows	{/ Row;Insert}
/Edit Move	{/ Block;Move}
/Edit Names Create	{/ Name;Create}
/Edit Names Delete	{/ Name;Delete}
/Edit Names Labels Down	{/ Name;UnderCreate}
/Edit Names Labels Left	{/ Name;LeftCreate}
/Edit Names Labels Right	{/ Name;RightCreate}
/Edit Names Labels Up	{/ Name;AboveCreate}
/Edit Names Make Table	{/ Name;Table}
/Edit Names Reset	{/ Name;Reset}
/Edit Search & Replace Block	{/ Audit;ReplaceRange}
/Edit Search & Replace Case Sensitive	{/ Audit;SearchCase}
/Edit Search & Replace Case Sensitive Any Case	{/ Audit;SearchAnyCase}

Table E.1 Quattro Pro Commands and Menu Equivalent Commands *(continued)*

Quattro Commands	Menu Equivalent
/Edit Search & Replace Case Sensitive Exact Case	{/ Audit;SearchExactCase}
/Edit Search & Replace Direction	{/ Audit;SearchDirection}
/Edit Search & Replace Direction Column	{/ Audit;SearchByCol}
/Edit Search & Replace Direction Row	{/ Audit;SearchByRow}
/Edit Search & Replace Look In	{/ Audit;SearchLookIn}
/Edit Search & Replace Look In Condition	{/ Audit;SearchCondition}
/Edit Search & Replace Look In Formula	{/ Audit;SearchFormula}
/Edit Search & Replace Look In Value	{/ Audit;SearchValue}
/Edit Search & Replace Match	{/ Audit;SearchMatch}
/Edit Search & Replace Match Part	{/ Audit;SearchForPart}
/Edit Search & Replace Match Whole	{/ Audit;SearchForWhole}
/Edit Search & Replace Next	{/ Audit;Replace}
/Edit Search & Replace Options Reset	{/ Audit;SearchReset}
/Edit Search & Replace Previous	{/ Audit;SearchPrev}
/Edit Search & Replace Replace String	{/ Audit;ReplaceString}
/Edit Search & Replace Search String	{/ Audit;SearchString}
/Edit Transpose	{/ Block;Transpose}
/Edit Undo	{/ Basics;Undo} or {UNDO}
/Edit Values	{/ Block;Values}
/File Close	{/ Basics;Close}
/File Close All	{/ System;TidyUp}
/File Directory	{/ File;Directory}
/File Erase	{/ Basics;Erase}
/File Exit	{/ System;Exit}
/File New	{/ View;NewWindow}
/File Open	{/ View;OpenWindow}
/File Retrieve	{/ File;Retrieve}

Table E.1   Quattro Pro Commands and Menu Equivalent Commands *(continued)*

Quattro Commands	Menu Equivalent
/File Save	{/ File;SaveNow}
/File Save All	{/ File:SaveAll}
/File Save As	{/ File;Save}
/File Utilities DOS Shell	{/ Basics;OS} or {/Basics;Shell}
/File Utilities File Manager	{/ View;NewFileMgr}
/File Utilities SQZ! Remove Blanks	{/ SQZ;Blanks}
/File Utilities SQZ! Storage of Values	{/ SQZ;Values}
/File Utilities SQZ! Version	{/ SQZ;Version}
/File Workspace Restore	{/ System;RestoreWorkspace}
/File Workspace Save	{/ System;SaveWorkspace}
/Graph Annotate	{/ Graph;Annotate}
/Graph Customize Series	{/ Dialog;GraphCustomize} when Quattro Pro displays dialog boxes
/Graph Customize Series Bar Width	{/ Graph;BarWidth}
/Graph Customize Series Bubbles Colors 1st Bubble through 9th Bubble	{/ BubbleColor;1} through {/ BubbleColor;9}
/Graph Customize Series Bubbles Max Bubble Size	{/ Bubble Size}
/Graph Customize Series Bubbles Patterns 1st Bubble through 9th Bubble	{/ BubblePattern;1} through {/ BubblePattern;9}
/Graph Customize Series Colors 1st Series through 6th Series	{/ 1Series;Color} through {/ 6Series;Color}
/Graph Customize Series Fill Patterns 1st Series through 6th Series	{/ 1Series;Pattern} through {/ 6Series;Pattern}
/Graph Customize Series Interior Label 1st Series through 6th Series	{/ CompGraph;ALabels} through {/ CompGraph;FLabels}
/Graph Customize Series Markers & Lines Formats 1st Series through 6th Series	{/ CompGraph;AFormat} through {/ CompGraph;FFormat}
/Graph Customize Series Markers & Lines Formats Graph	{/ CompGraph;GraphFormat}

Table E.1   Quattro Commands and Menu Equivalent Commands *(continued)*

Quattro Commands	Menu Equivalent
/Graph Customize Series Markers & Lines Line Styles 1st Series through 6th Series	{/ 1Series;LineStyle} through {/ 6Series;LineStyle}
/Graph Customize Series Markers & Lines Markers 1st Series through 6th Series	{/ 1Series;Markers} through {/ 6Series;Markers}
/Graph Customize Series Override Type 1st Series through 6th Series	{/ 1Series;Type} through {/ 6Series;Type}
/Graph Customize Series Pies Colors 1st Slice through 9th Slice	{/ PieColor;1} through {/ PieColor;9}
/Graph Customize Series Pies Explode 1st Slice through 9th Slice	{/ PieExploded;1} through {/ PieExploded;9}
/Graph Customize Series Pies Label Format	{/ Pie;ValueFormat}
/Graph Customize Series Pies Patterns 1st Slice through 9th Slice	{/ PiePattern;1} through {/ PiePattern;9}
/Graph Customize Series Pies Tick Marks	{/ Pie;TickMarks}
/Graph Customize Series Reset 1st Series through 6th Series	{/ Graph;Reset1} through {/ Graph;Reset6}
/Graph Customize Series Reset Graph	{/ Graph;ResetAll}
/Graph Customize Series Reset X-Axis Series	{/ XAxis;Reset}
/Graph Customize Series Update	{/ Graph;UpdateGraph}
/Graph Customize Series Y-Axis 1st Series through 6th Series	{/ 1Series;YAxis} through {/ 6Series;YAxis}
/Graph Fast Graph	{/ Graph;FastGraph}
/Graph Graph Type	{/ Graph;Type}
/Graph Hide	{/ Graph;NameHide}
/Graph Insert	{/ Graph;NameInsert}
/Graph Name Autosave Edits	{/ Graph;NameAutosave}
/Graph Name Create	{/ Graph;NameCreate}
/Graph Name Display	{/ Graph;NameUse}
/Graph Name Erase	{/ Graph;NameDelete}

Table E.1   Quattro Pro Commands and Menu Equivalent Commands *(continued)*

Quattro Commands	Menu Equivalent
/Graph Name Graph Copy	{/ Graph;NameCopy}
/Graph Name Reset	{/ Graph;NameReset}
/Graph Name Slide	{/ Graph;NameSlide}
/Graph Overall Background Color	{/ Graph;BackColor}
/Graph Overall Color/B&W B&W	{/ Graph;BW}
/Graph Overall Color/B&W Color	{/ Graph;Color}
/Graph Overall Drop Shadow Color	{/ Graph;DS*color*}
/Graph Overall Grid Both	{/ CompGraph;GridBoth}
/Graph Overall Grid Clear	{/ CompGraph;GridClear}
/Graph Overall Grid Fill Color	{/ Graph;GridFill}
/Graph Overall Grid Grid Color	{/ Graph;GridColor}
/Graph Overall Grid Horizontal	{/ CompGraph;GridHorz}
/Graph Overall Grid Line Style	{/ Graph;GridLines}
/Graph Overall Grid Vertical	{/ CompGraph;GridVert}
/Graph Overall Outlines Graph	{/ Graph;GraphOtl}
/Graph Overall Outlines Legend	{/ Graph;LegendOtl}
/Graph Overall Outlines Titles	{/ Graph;TitleOtl}
/Graph Overall Three-D	{/ Graph;3D}
/Graph Series 1st Series through 6th Series	{/ 1Series;Block} through { / 6Series;Block}
/Graph Series Analyze 1st Series through 6th Series	{/ GraphAnalyze1;ShowKind} through {/ GraphAnalyze6;ShowKind}
/Graph Series Analyze 1st Series through 6th Series Aggregation	{/ GraphAnalyze1;Aggregation} through {/ GraphAnalyze6;Aggregation}
/Graph Series Analyze 1st Series through 6th Series Aggregation Aggregation Period	{/ GraphAnalyze1;AgPeriod} through {/ GraphAnalyze6;AgPeriod}

Table E.1   Quattro Pro Commands and Menu Equivalent Commands *(continued)*

Quattro Commands	Menu Equivalent
/Graph Series Analyze 1st Series through 6th Series Aggregation Aggregation Period Weeks	{/ GraphAnalyze1;AgWeeks} through {/ GraphAnalyze6;AgWeeks}
/Graph Series Analyze 1st Series through 6th Series Aggregation Aggregation Period Months	{/ GraphAnalyze1;AgMonths} through {/ GraphAnalyze6;AgMonths}
/Graph Series Analyze 1st Series through 6th Series Aggregation Aggregation Period Quarters	{/ GraphAnalyze1;AgQuarters} through {/ GraphAnalyze6;AgQuarters}
/Graph Series Analyze 1st Series through 6th Series Aggregation Period Years	{/ GraphAnalyze1;AgYears} through {/ GraphAnalyze6;AgYears)
/Graph Series Analyze 1st Series through 6th Series Aggregation Aggregation Period Arbitrary	{/ GraphAnalyze1;AgArbitrary} through {/ GraphAnalyze6;AgArbitrary}
/Graph Series Analyze 1st Series through 6th Series Aggregation Function	{/ GraphAnalyze1;Function} through {/ GraphAnalyze6;Function}
/Graph Series Analyze 1st Series through 6th Series Aggregation Series Period	{/ GraphAnalyze1;AgSeriesPeriod} through {/ GraphAnalyze6;AgSeriesPeriod}
/Graph Series Analyze 1st Series through 6th Series Aggregation Series Period Days	{/ GraphAnalyze1;AgSeriesDays} through {/ GraphAnalyze6;AgSeriesDays}
/Graph Series Analyze 1st Series through 6th Series Aggregation Series Period Weeks	{/ GraphAnalyze1;AgSeriesWeeks} through {/ GraphAnalyze6;AgSeriesWeeks}
/Graph Series Analyze 1st Series through 6th Series Aggregation Series Period Months	{/ GraphAnalyze1;AgSeries Months} through {/ GraphAnalyze6;AgSeriesMonths}
/Graph Series Analyze 1st Series through 6th Series Aggregation Series Period Quarters	{/ GraphAnalyze1;AgSeries Quarters} through {/ GraphAnalyze6; AgSeriesQuarters}

Table E.1   Quattro Pro Commands and Menu Equivalent Commands *(continued)*

Quattro Commands	Menu Equivalent
/Graph Series Analyze 1st Series through 6th Series Aggregation Series Period Years	{/ GraphAnalyze1;AgSeriesYears} through {/ GraphAnalyze6;AgSeriesYears}
/Graph Series Analyze 1st Series through 6th Series Exponential Fit	{/ GraphAnalyze1;ExponFit} through {/ GraphAnalyze6;ExponFit}
/Graph Series Analyze 1st Series through 6th Series Linear Fit	{/ GraphAnalyze1;LinearFit} through {/ GraphAnalyze6;LinearFit}
/Graph Series Analyze 1st Series through 6th Series Moving Average	{/ GraphAnalyze1;MovingAvg} through {/ GraphAnalyze6;MovingAvg}
/Graph Series Analyze 1st Series through 6th Series Moving Average Period	{/ GraphAnalyze1;MovingAvg Periods} through {/ GraphAnalyze6; MovingAvgPeriods}
/Graph Series Analyze 1st Series through 6th Series Moving Average Weighted	{/ GraphAnalyze1;MovingAvg Weighted} through {/ GraphAnalyze6; MovingAvgWeighted}
/Graph Series Analyze 1st Series through 6th Series Reset	{/ GraphAnalyze1;Reset} through {/ GraphAnalyze6;Reset}
/Graph Series Analyze 1st Series through 6th Series Table	{/ GraphAnalyze1;Table} through {/ GraphAnalyze6;Table}
/Graph Series Analyze All	Same as /Graph Series Analyze 1st Series except the general category is GraphAnalyzeAll
/Graph Series Analyze X-Axis Series	Same as /Graph Series Analyze 1st Series except the general category is GraphAnalyzeX
/Graph Series Group Columns	{/ Graph;ColumnSeries}
/Graph Series Group Rows	{/ Graph;Row Series}
/Graph Series X-Axis Series	{/ X-Axis;Labels}

Table E.1   Quattro Pro Commands and Menu Equivalent Commands *(continued)*

Quattro Commands	Menu Equivalent
/Graph Text 1st Line	{/ Graph;Main Title}
/Graph Text 2nd Line	{/ Graph;SubTitle}
/Graph Text Font	{/ GraphPrint;Fonts}
/Graph Text Legends 1st Series through 6th Series	{/ 1Series;Legend} through {/ 6Series;Legend}
/Graph Text Legends Position	{/ Graph;LegendPos}
/Graph Text Secondary Y-Axis	{/ Y2Axis;Title}
/Graph Text X-Title	{/ XAxis;Title}
/Graph Text Y-Title	{/ YAxis;Title}
/Graph View	{/ Graph;View} or {GRAPH}
/Graph X-Axis	{/ Dialog;GraphXAxis} when Quattro Pro displays dialog boxes
/Graph X-Axis Alternate Ticks	{/ XAxis;Alternate}
/Graph X-Axis Display Scaling	{/ XAxis;ShowScale}
/Graph X-Axis Format of Ticks	{/ XAxis;Format}
/Graph X-Axis High	{/ XAxis;Max}
/Graph X-Axis Increment	{/ XAxis;Step}
/Graph X-Axis Low	{/ XAxis;Min}
/Graph X-Axis Mode	{/ XAxis;ScaleType}
/Graph X-Axis No. of Minor Ticks	{/ XAxis;Skip}
/Graph X-Axis Scale	{/ XAxis;ScaleMode}
/Graph Y-Axis	{/ Dialog;GraphYAxis} when Quattro Pro displays dialog boxes
/Graph Y-Axis 2nd Y-Axis	{/ Dialog;Graph2YAxis} when Quattro Pro displays dialog boxes
/Graph Y-Axis 2nd Y-Axis Display Scaling	{/ Y2Axis;ShowScale}
/Graph Y-Axis 2nd Y-Axis Format of Ticks	{/ Y2Axis;Format}
/Graph Y-Axis 2nd Y-Axis High	{/ Y2Axis;Max}

Table E.1   Quattro Pro Commands and Menu Equivalent Commands *(continued)*

Quattro Commands	Menu Equivalent
/Graph Y-Axis 2nd Y-Axis Increment	{/ Y2Axis,Step}
/Graph Y-Axis 2nd Y-Axis Low	{/ Y2Axis;Min}
/Graph Y-Axis 2nd Y-Axis Mode	{/ Y2Axis;ScaleType}
/Graph Y-Axis 2nd Y-Axis No. of Minor Ticks	{/ Y2Axis;Skip}
/Graph Y-Axis 2nd Y-Axis Scale	{/ Y2Axis;ScaleMode}
/Graph Y-Axis Display Scaling	{/ YAxis;ShowScale}
/Graph Y-Axis Format of Ticks	{/ YAxis;Format}
/Graph Y-Axis High	{/ YAxis;Max}
/Graph Y-Axis Increment	{/ YAxis;Step}
/Graph Y-Axis Low	{/ YAxis;Min}
/Graph Y-Axis Mode	{/ YAxis;ScaleType}
/Graph Y-Axis No. of Minor Ticks	{/ YAxis;Skip}
/Graph Y-Axis Scale	{/ YAxis;ScaleMode}
/Options Colors Conditional Above Normal Color	{/ ValueColors;High}
/Options Colors Conditional Below Normal Color	{/ ValueColors;Low}
/Options Colors Conditional ERR	{/ ValueColors;Err}
/Options Colors Conditional Greatest Normal Value	{/ ValueColors;Max}
/Options Colors Conditional Normal Cell Color	{/ ValueColors;Normal}
/Options Colors Conditional On/Off	{/ ValueColors;Enable}
/Options Colors Conditional Smallest Normal Value	{/ ValueColors;Min}
/Options Colors Desktop Background	{/ Startup;DesktopColor}
/Options Colors Desktop Desktop	{/ Startup;DesktopChar}
/Options Colors Desktop Errors	{/ ErrorColor;SetErrorColor}
/Options Colors Desktop Highlight-Status	{/ Color;Indicators}
/Options Colors Desktop Status	{/ Color;Status}

Table E.1 Quattro Pro Commands and Menu Equivalent Commands *(continued)*

Quattro Commands	Menu Equivalent
/Options Colors File Manager Active Cursor	{/ FileMgrColors;ActiveCursor}
/Options Colors File Manager Banner	{/ FileMgrColors;Banner}
/Options Colors File Manager Copy	{/ FileMgrColors;Copy}
/Options Colors File Manager Cut	{/ FileMgrColors;Cut}
/Options Colors File Manager Frame	{/ FileMgrColors;Frame}
/Options Colors File Manager Inactive cursor	{/ FileMgrColors;InactiveCursor}
/Options Colors File Manager Marked	{/ FileMgrColors;Marked}
/Options Colors File Manager Text	{/ FileMgrColors;Text}
/Options Colors Help Banner	{/ HelpColors;Banner}
/Options Colors Help Frame	{/ HelpColors;Frame}
/Options Colors Help Highlight	{/ HelpColors;Highlight}
/Options Colors Help Keywords	{/ HelpColors;Keyword}
/Options Colors Help Text	{/ HelpColors;Text}
/Options Colors Menu Banner	{/ MenuColors;Banner}
/Options Colors Menu Drop Shadow	{/ Startup;Shadow}
/Options Colors Menu Explanation	{/ MenuColors;Explanation}
/Options Colors Menu Frame	{/ MenuColors;Frame}
/Options Colors Menu Highlight	{/ MenuColors;MenuBar}
/Options Colors Menu Key Letter	{/ MenuColors;FirstLetter}
/Options Colors Menu Settings	{/ MenuColors;Settings}
/Options Colors Menu Shadow	{/ Startup;ShadowChar}
/Options Colors Menu SpeedBar	{/ Startup;PaletteCol}
/Options Colors Menu Text	{/ MenuColors;Text}
/Options Colors Palettes Black & White	{/ Color;BWCGAPalette}
/Options Colors Palettes Color	{/ Color;ColorPalette}
/Options Colors Palettes Gray Scale	{/ Color;GSPalette}
/Options Colors Palettes Monochrome	{/ Color;BWPalette}

Table E.1   Quattro Pro Commands and Menu Equivalent Commands *(continued)*

Quattro Commands	Menu Equivalent
/Options Colors Palettes Version 3 Color	{/ Color;Ver3Palette}
/Options Colors Spreadsheet Banner	{/ Color;Banner}
/Options Colors Spreadsheet Borders	{/ Color;Border}
/Options Colors Spreadsheet Cells	{/ Color;Cells}
/Options Colors Spreadsheet Drawn Lines	{/ Color;LineDrawing}
/Options Colors Spreadsheet Frame	{/ Color;Frame}
/Options Colors Spreadsheet Graph Frames	{/ Color;GraphFrame}
/Options Colors Spreadsheet Highlight	{/ Color;Cursor}
/Options Colors Spreadsheet Input Line	{/ Color;Edit}
/Options Colors Spreadsheet Labels	{/ ValueColors;Labels}
/Options Colors Spreadsheet Shading	{/ Color;Shading}
/Options Colors Spreadsheet Titles	{/ Color;Titles}
/Options Colors Spreadsheet Unprotected	{/ Color;Unprotect}
/Options Colors Spreadsheet WYSIWYG Colors Background	{/ WYSIWYG;Cells}
/Options Colors Spreadsheet WYSIWYG Colors Cursor	{/ WYSIWYG;Cursor}
/Options Colors Spreadsheet WYSIWYG Colors Drawn Lines	{/ WYSIWYG;Lines}
/Options Colors Spreadsheet WYSIWYG Colors Grid Lines	{/ WYSIWYG;Grid}
/Options Colors Spreadsheet WYSIWYG Colors Locked Titles Text	{/ WYSIWYG;TitlesF}
/Options Colors Spreadsheet WYSIWYG Colors Row and Column Labels Face	{/ WYSIWYG;BezelFront}
/Options Colors Spreadsheet WYSIWYG Colors Row and Column Labels Highlight	{/ WYSIWYG;BezelTop}
/Options Colors Spreadsheet WYSIWYG Colors Row and Column Labels Shadow	{/ WYSIWYG;BezelBottom}
/Options Colors Spreadsheet WYSIWYG Colors Row and Column Labels Text	{/ WYSIWYG;BezelText}

Table E.1   Quattro Pro Commands and Menu Equivalent Commands *(continued)*

Quattro Commands	Menu Equivalent
/Options Colors Spreadsheet WYSIWYG Colors Shaded Cells	{/ WYSIWYG;Shading}
/Options Colors Spreadsheet WYSIWYG Colors Titles Background	{/ WYSIWYG;TitlesB}
/Options Colors Spreadsheet WYSIWYG Colors Unprotected	{/ WYSIWYG;Unprotected}
/Options Display Mode	{/ ScreenHardware;TextScreenMode}
/Options Formats Align Labels	{/ Defaults;Alignment}
/Options Formats Global width	{/ Defaults;ColWidth}
/Options Formats Hide Zeros	{/ Defaults;Zero}
/Options Formats Numeric Format	{/ Defaults;Format}
/Options Graphics Quality	{/ Defaults;GraphicsQuality}
/Options Hardware Coprocessor	{/ Basics;ShowCoProc}
/Options Hardware EMS Memory Bytes Available	{/ Basics;ShowEMS}
/Options Hardware EMS Memory Bytes Total	{/ Basics;ShowEMSTotal}
/Options Hardware EMS Memory % Available	{/ Basics;ShowEMSPct}
/Options Hardware Mouse Button	{/ Hardware;MouseButton}
/Options Hardware Normal Memory Bytes Available	{/ Basics;ShowMem}
/Options Hardware Normal Memory Bytes Total	{/ Basics;ShowMemTotal}
/Options Hardware Normal Memory % Available	{/ Basics;ShowMemPct}
/Options Hardware Printers 1st Printer Baud rate	{/ GPrinter1;Baud}
/Options Hardware Printers 1st Printer Device	{/ GPrinter1;Device}
/Options Hardware Printers 1st Printer Make	{/ GPrinter1;ShowMake}
/Options Hardware Printers 1st Printer Mode	{/ GPrinter1;ShowMode}
/Options Hardware Printers 1st Printer Model	{/ GPrinter1;ShowModel}

Table E.1 **Quattro Pro Commands and Menu Equivalent Commands** (*continued*)

Quattro Commands	Menu Equivalent
/Options Hardware Printers 1st Printer Parity	{/ GPrinter1;Parity}
/Options Hardware Printers 1st Printer Stop bits	{/ GPrinter1;Stop}
/Options Hardware Printers 1st Printer Type of printer	{/ GPrinter1;Type}
/Options Hardware Printers 2nd Printer Baud rate	{/ GPrinter2;Baud}
/Options Hardware Printers 2nd Printer Device	{/ GPrinter2;Device}
/Options Hardware Printers 2nd Printer Make	{/ GPrinter2;ShowMake}
/Options Hardware Printers 2nd Printer Mode	{/ GPrinter2;ShowMode}
/Options Hardware Printers 2nd Printer Model	{/ GPrinter2;ShowModel}
/Options Hardware Printers 2nd Printer Parity	{/ GPrinter2;Parity}
/Options Hardware Printers 2nd Printer Stop bits	{/ GPrinter2;Stop}
/Options Hardware Printers 2nd Printer Type of printer	{/ GPrinter2;Type}
/Options Hardware Printers Auto LF	{/ Hardware;AutoLf}
/Options Hardware Printers Background	{/ Hardware;BackgroundPrint}
/Options Hardware Printers' Default Printer	{/ Defaults;PrinterName}
/Options Hardware Printers Fonts Autoscale Fonts	{/ Hardware;AutoFonts}
/Options Hardware Printers Fonts Cartridge Fonts Left Cartridge	{/ Hardware;LJetLeft}
/Options Hardware Printers Fonts Cartridge Fonts Right Cartridge	{/ Hardware;LJetRight}
/Options Hardware Printers Fonts Cartridge Fonts Shading Level	{/ Hardware;LJShadeLevel}
/Options Hardware Printers Plotter Speed	{/ GraphPrint;PlotSpeed}
/Options Hardware Printers Single Sheet	{/ Hardware;SingleSheet}
/Options Hardware Screen Aspect Ratio	{/ ScreenHardware;AspectRatio}
/Options Hardware Screen CGA Snow Suppression	{/ ScreenHardware;Retrace}

Table E.1 Quattro Pro Commands and Menu Equivalent Commands *(continued)*

Quattro Commands	Menu Equivalent
/Options Hardware Screen Resolution	{/ Graph;ScreenMode}
/Options Hardware Screen Screen Type	{/ScreenHardware;GraphScreenType}
/Options International Currency	{/ Intnl;Currency}
/Options International Date	{/ FormatChanges;IntlDate}
/Options International LICS/LMBCS Conversion	{/ Intnl;LICS}
/Options International Negative	{/ Intnl;Negative}
/Options International Overstrike Print	{/ Intnl;PrintComposed}
/Options International Punctuation	{/ Intnl;Punctuation}
/Options International Time	{/ FormatChanges;IntnlTime}
/Options International Use Sort Table	{/ Intnl;UseSortTable}
/Options Network Banner	{/ Network;Banner}
/Options Network Drive mappings	{/ Network;DriveMaps}
/Options Network Queue Monitor	{/ Network:MonitorQueue}
/Options Network Refresh Interval	{/ Network;Interval}
/Options Network User Name	{/ Network;UserName}
/Options Other Clock	{/ Defaults;ClockFormat}
/Options Other Expanded Memory	{/ Defaults;ExpMem}
/Options Other Macro	{/ Defaults;Suppress}
/Options Other Paradox Network Type	{/ Paradox;NetType}
/Options Other Paradox Directory	{/ Paradox;NetDir}
/Options Other Paradox Retries	{/ Paradox;NetRetries}
/Options Other Undo	{/ Defaults;Undo}
/Options Protection	{/ Protection;Status}
/Options Protection Disable	{/ Protection;Disable}
/Options Protection Enable	{/ Protection;Enable}
/Options Protection Formulas	{/ Protection;FormStatus}
/Options Protection Formulas Protect	{/ Protection;FormProtect}

Table E.1 Quattro Pro Commands and Menu Equivalent Commands *(continued)*

Quattro Commands	Menu Equivalent
/Options Protection Formulas Unprotect	{/ Protection;FormUnprotect}
/Options Recalculation Circular Cell	{/ Audit;ShowCirc}
/Options Recalculation Iteration	{/ Defaults;RecalcIteration}
/Options Recalculation Mode	{/ Defaults;RecalcMode}
/Options Recalculation Order	{/ Defaults;RecalcOrder}
/Options SpeedBar EDIT mode SpeedBar A Button through O Button Long name	{/ Buttons2;LrgText1} through {/ Buttons2;LgrText15}
/Options SpeedBar EDIT mode SpeedBar A Button through O Button Macro	{/ Buttons2;Macro1} through {/ Buttons2;Macro15}
/Options SpeedBar EDIT mode SpeedBar A Button through O Button Short name	{/ Buttons2;SmlText1} through {/ Buttons2:SmlText15}
/Options SpeedBar READY mode SpeedBar A Button through O Button Long name	{/ Buttons1;LrgText1} through {/ Buttons1;LrgText15}
/Options SpeedBar READY mode SpeedBar A Button throughO Button Macro	{/ Buttons1;Macro1} through {/ Buttons1;Macro15}
/Options SpeedBar READY mode SpeedBar A Button through O Button Short name	{/ Buttons1;SmlText1} through {/ Buttons1;SmlText15}
/Options Startup Autoload File	{/ Startup;File}
/Options Startup Beep	{/ Startup;Beep}
/Options Startup Directory	{/ Defaults;Directory}
/Options Startup Edit Menus	{/ MenuBuilder;Run}
/Options Startup File Extension	{/ Startup;Extension}
/Options Startup Menu Tree	{/ Startup;Menus}
/Options Startup Startup Macro	{/ Startup;Macro}
/Options Startup Use Dialogs	{/ Dialog;Enable}
/Options Update	{/ Defaults;Update}
/Options WYSIWYG Zoom %	{/ WYSIWYG;Zoom}
/Print Adjust Printer Align	{/ Print;Align}
/Print Adjust Printer Form Feed	{/ Print;FormFeed}

Table E.1 Quattro Pro Commands and Menu Equivalent Commands *(continued)*

Quattro Commands	Menu Equivalent
/Print Adjust Printer Skip Line	{/ Print;SkipLine}
/Print Block	{/ Print;Block}
/Print Copies	{/ Print;Copies}
/Print Destination Binary File	{/ Print;OutputHQFile}
/Print Destination File	{/ Print;OutputFile}
/Print Destination Graphics Printer	{/ Print;OutputHQ}
/Print Destination Printer	{/ Print;OutputPrinter}
/Print Destination Screen Preview	{/ Print;OutputPreview}
/Print Format	{/ Print;Format}
/Print Graph Print Destination File	{/ GraphPrint;DestIsFile}
/Print Graph Print Destination Graph Printer	{/ GraphPrint;DestIsPtr}
/Print Graph Print Destination Screen Preview	{/ GraphPrint;DestIsPreview}
/Print Graph Print Go	{/ GraphPrint;Go}
/Print Graph Print Layout 4:3 Aspect	{/ Hardware;Aspect43}
/Print Graph Print Layout Dimensions	{/ GraphPrint;Dimensions}
/Print Graph Print Layout Height	{/ GraphPrint;Height}
/Print Graph Print Layout Left Edge	{/ GraphPrint;Left}
/Print Graph Print Layout Orientation	{/ GraphPrint;Rotated}
/Print Graph Print Layout Reset	{/ Print;ResetAll}
/Print Graph Print Layout Top Edge	{/ GraphPrint;Top}
/Print Graph Print Layout Update	{/ Print;Update}
/Print Graph Print Layout Width	{/ GraphPrint;Width}
/Print Graph Print Name	{/ GraphPrint;Use}
/Print Graph Print Write Graph File EPS File	{/ GraphFile;Postscript}
/Print Graph Print Write Graph File PCX File	{/ GraphFile;PCX}
/Print Graph Print Write Graph File PIC File	{/ GraphFile;PIC}
/Print Graph Print Write Graph File Slide EPS	{/ GraphFile;SlideEPS}

Table E.1   Quattro Pro Commands and Menu Equivalent Commands *(continued)*

Quattro Commands	Menu Equivalent
/Print Headings Left Heading	{/ Print;LeftBorder}
/Print Headings Top Heading	{/ Print;TopBorder}
/Print Layout	{/ Dialog;PrintLayout} when Quattro Pro displays dialog boxes
/Print Layout Break Pages	{/ Print;Breaks}
/Print Layout Dimensions	{/ Print;Dimensions}
/Print Layout Footer	{/ Print;Footer}
/Print Layout Header	{/ Print;Header}
/Print Layout Margins Bottom	{/ Print;BottomMargin}
/Print Layout Margins Left	{/ Print;LeftMargin}
/Print Layout Margins Page Length	{/ Print;PageLength}
/Print Layout Margins Right	{/ Print;RightMargin}
/Print Layout Margins Top	{/ Print;TopMargin}
/Print Layout Orientation	{/ Print;Rotated}
/Print Layout Percent Scaling	{/ Print;PercentScaling}
/Print Layout Reset All	{/ Print;ResetAll}
/Print Layout Reset Headings	{/ Print;ResetBorders}
/Print Layout Reset Layout	{/ Print;ResetDefaults}
/Print Layout Reset Print Block	{/ Print;ResetBlock}
/Print Layout Setup String	{/ Print;Setup}
/Print Layout Update	{/ Print;Update}
/Print Print Manager	{/ View;NewPrintMgr}
/Print Print-To-Fit	{/ Print;PrintToFit}
/Print Spreadsheet Print	{/ Print;Go}
/Style Alignment Center	{/ Publish;AlignCenter}
/Style Alignment General	{/ Publish;AlignDefault}
/Style Alignment Left	{/ Publish;AlignLeft}

Table E.1 Quattro Pro Commands and Menu Equivalent Commands *(continued)*

Quattro Commands	Menu Equivalent
/Style Alignment Right	{/ Publish;AlignRight}
/Style Block Size Auto Width	{/ Block;AdjustWidth}
/Style Block Size Height Set Row Height	{/ Block;SetHeight}
/Style Block Size Height Reset Row Height	{/ Block;ResetHeight}
/Style Block Size Reset Width	{/ Block;ResetWidth}
/Style Block Size Set Width	{/ Block;SetWidth}
/Style Column Width	{/ Column;Width}
/Style Define Style Create	{/ Publish;EditNamedStyle}
/Style Define Style Erase	{/ Publish;EraseNamedStyle}
/Style Define Style File Retrieve	{/ Publish;LoadStyleSheet}
/Style Define Style File Save	{/ Publish;SaveStyleSheet}
/Style Define Style Remove	{/ Publish;DeleteNamedStyle}
/Style Font	{/ Publish;ApplyAnonymousStyle}
/Style FontTable	{/ Publish;Font}
/Style Hide Column Expose	{/ Column;Display}
/Style Hide Column Hide	{/ Column;Hide}
/Style Insert Break	{/ Print;CreatePageBreak}
/Style Line Drawing	{/ Publish;LineDrawing}
/Style Numeric Format	{/ Block;Format}
/Style Protection Protect	{/ Block;Protect}
/Style Protection Unprotect	{/ Block;Unprotect}
/Style Reset Width	{/ Column;Reset}
/Style Shading Black	{/ Publish;ShadingBlack}
/Style Shading Grey	{/ Publish;ShadingGrey}
/Style Shading None	{/ Publish;ShadingNone}
/Style Use Style	{/ Publish;UseNamedStyle}
/Tools Advanced Math Invert	{/ Math;InvertMatrix}

Table E.1 Quattro Pro Commands and Menu Equivalent Commands *(continued)*

Quattro Commands	Menu Equivalent
/Tools Advanced Math Multiply	{/ Math;MultiplyMatrix}
/Tools Advanced Math Regression Dependent	{/ Regression;Dependent}
/Tools Advanced Math Regression Go	{/ Regression;Go}
/Tools Advanced Math Regression Independent	{/ Regression;Independent}
/Tools Advanced Math Regression Output	{/ Regression;Output}
/Tools Advanced Math Regression Reset	{/ Regression;Reset}
/Tools Advanced Math Regression Y Intercept	{/ Regression;Intercept}
/Tools Audit Blank References	{/ Auditor;BlankReference}
/Tools Audit Circular	{/ Auditor;TypeCIRC}
/Tools Audit Dependency	{/ Auditor;TypeDependency}
/Tools Audit Destination	{/ Auditor;Destination}
/Tools Audit ERR	{/ Auditor;TypeERR}
/Tools Audit External Links	{/ Auditor;TypeExternalReference}
/Tools Audit Label References	{/ Auditor;TypeLabelReference}
/Tools Combine Add Block	{/ File;AddRange}
/Tools Combine Add File	{/ File;AddFile}
/Tools Combine Copy Block	{/ File;CopyRange}
/Tools Combine Copy File	{/ File;CopyFile}
/Tools Combine Subtract Block	{/ File;SubtractRange}
/Tools Combine Subtract File	{/ File;SubtractFile}
/Tools Frequency	{/ Math;Distribution}
/Tools Import ASCII Text File	{/ File;ImportText}
/Tools Import Comma & "" Delimited File	{/ File;ImportNumbers}
/Tools Import Only Commas	{/ File;ImportComma}
/Tools Library Load	{/ Library;Load}
/Tools Library Unload	{/ Library;Unload}
/Tools Macro	{/ Macro;Menu}

Table E.1   Quattro Pro Commands and Menu Equivalent Commands *(continued)*

Quattro Commands	Menu Equivalent
/Tools Macro Clear Breakpoints or ALT-F2 Clear Breakpoints	{/ Name;BkptReset}
/Tools Macro Debugger or ALT-F2 Debugger	{/ Macro;Debug}
/Tools Macro Execute or ALT-F2 Execute	{/ Name;Execute}
/Tools Macro Instant Replay or ALT-F2 Instant Replay	{/ Macro;Replay}
/Tools Macro Key Reader or ALT-F2 Key Reader	{/ Macro;Reader}
/Tools Macro Library or ALT-F2 Library	{/ Macro;Library}
/Tools Macro Macro Recording or ALT-F2 Macro Recording	{/ Startup;Record}
/Tools Macro Name Create or ALT-F2 Name Create	{/ Name;Create}
/Tools Macro Name Delete or ALT-F2 Name Delete	{/ Name;Delete}
/Tools Macro Paste or ALT-F2 Paste	{/ Macro;Paste}
/Tools Macro Record or ALT-F2 Record	{/ Macro;Record}
/Tools Macro Transcript or ALT-F2 Transcript	{/ Macro;Transcript}
/Tools Optimizer Answer Report	{/ Solution;Answer}
/Tools Optimizer Constraints	{/ Solution;Constraints}
/Tools Optimizer Detail Report	{/ Solution;Detail}
/Tools Optimizer Go	{/ Solution;Go}
/Tools Optimizer Model	{/ Solution;LoadSave}
/Tools Optimizer Model Load	{/ Solution;Load}
/Tools Optimizer Model Save	{/ Solution;Save}
/Tools Optimizer Options Derivatives	{/ Solution;Derivatives}
/Tools Optimizer Options Derivatives Central	{/ Solution;Central}
/Tools Optimizer Options Derivatives Forward	{/ Solution;Forward}
/Tools Optimizer Options Estimates	{/ Solution;Estimates}
/Tools Optimizer Options Estimates Quadratic	{/ Solution;Quad}

Table E.1 Quattro Pro Commands and Menu Equivalent Commands *(continued)*

Quattro Commands	Menu Equivalent
/Tools Optimizer Options Estimates Tangent	{/ Solution;Tangent}
/Tools Optimizer Options Linear or Nonlinear	{/ Solution;Linear}
/Tools Optimizer Options Linear or Nonlinear Linear	{/ Solution;SetLinear}
/Tools Optimizer Options Linear or Nonlinear Nonlinear	{/ Solution;SetNonLinear}
/Tools Optimizer Options Max Iterations	{/ Solution;MaxIterations}
/Tools Optimizer Options Max Time	{/ Solution;MaxTime}
/Tools Optimizer Options Precision	{/ Solution;Precision}
/Tools Optimizer Options Search	{/ Solution;Search}
/Tools Optimizer Options Search Conjugate	{/ Solution;Conjugate}
/Tools Optimizer Options Search Newton	{/ Solution;Newton}
/Tools Optimizer Options Show Iteration Results	{/ Solution;Show}
/Tools Optimizer Reset All	{/ Solution;Reset}
/Tools Optimizer Reset Answer Report	{/ Solution;ResetAns}
/Tools Optimizer Reset Constraints	{/ Solution;ResetCon}
/Tools Optimizer Reset Detail Report	{/ Solution;ResetDet}
/Tools Optimizer Reset Options	{/ Solution;ResetOpt}
/Tools Optimizer Reset Solution Cell	{/ Solution;ResetSol}
/Tools Optimizer Reset Variable Cell(s)	{/ Solution;ResetVar}
/Tools Optimizer Restore	{/ Solution;Restore}
/Tools Optimizer Solution	{/ Solution;Solution}
/Tools Optimizer Solution Cell	{/ Solution;GoalCell}
/Tools Optimizer Solution Max, Min, Equal	{/ Solution;MinMax}
/Tools Optimizer Solution Max, Min, Equal Maximize	{/ Solution;Maximum}
/Tools Optimizer Solution Max, Min, Equal Minimize	{/ Solution;Minimum}

Table E.1   Quattro Pro Commands and Menu Equivalent Commands *(continued)*

Quattro Commands	Menu Equivalent
/Tools Optimizer Solution Max, Min, Equal Equal	{/ Solution;Equal}
/Tools Optimizer Solution Max, Min, Equal None	{/ Solution;NoGoal}
/Tools Optimizer Variable Cells	{/ Solution;Variable}
/Tools Parse Create	{/ Parse;CreateLine}
/Tools Parse Edit	{/ Parse;EditLine}
/Tools Parse Go	{/ Parse;Go}
/Tools Parse Input	{/ Parse;Input}
/Tools Parse Output	{/ Parse;Output}
/Tools Parse Reset	{/ Parse;Reset}
/Tools Reformat	{/ Block;Justify}
/Tools Solve For Formula Cell	{/ Math;SolveFormula}
/Tools Solve For Go	{/ Math;SolveGo}
/Tools Solve For Parameters Accuracy	{/ Math;SolveAccuracy}
/Tools Solve For Parameters Max Iterations	{/ Math;SolveMaxIt}
/Tools Solve For Reset	{/ Math;SolveReset}
/Tools Solve For Target Value	{/ Math;SolveTarget}
/Tools Solve For Variable Cell	{/ Math;SolveVariable}
/Tools Update Links Change	{/ HotLink;Change}
/Tools Update Links Delete	{/ HotLink;Delete}
/Tools Update Links Open	{/ HotLink;Open}
/Tools Update Links Refresh	{/ HotLink;Update}
/Tools What-If 1 Variable	{/ Math;1CellWhat-If}
/Tools What-If 2 Variables	{/ Math;2CellWhat-If}
/Tools What-If Reset	{/ Math;ResetWhat-If}
/Tools Xtract Formulas	{/ File;ExtractFormulas}
/Tools Xtract Values	{/ File;ExtractValues}

Table E.1   Quattro Pro Commands and Menu Equivalent Commands *(continued)*

Quattro Commands	Menu Equivalent
/Window Move/Size	{/ View;Size}
/Window Options Clear	{/ Windows;Clear}
/Window Options Grid Lines	{/ Windows;GridLines}
/Window Options Horizontal	{/ Windows;Horizontal}
/Window Options Locked Titles Both	{/ Titles;Both}
/Window Options Locked Titles Clear	{/ Titles;Clear}
/Window Options Locked Titles Horizontal	{/ Titles;Horizontal}
/Window Options Locked Titles Vertical	{/ Titles;Vertical}
/Window Options Map View	{/ Windows;MapView}
/Window Options Print Block	{/ Windows;PrintBlock}
/Window Options Row & Col Borders Display	{/ Windows;RowColDisplay}
/Window Options Row & Col Borders Hide	{/ Windows;RowColHide}
/Window Options Sync	{/ Windows;Synch}
/Window Options Unsync	{/ Windows;Unsynch}
/Window Options Vertical	{/ Windows;Vertical}
/Window Pick	{/ View;Choose}
/Window Stack	{/ View;Cascade}
/Window Tile	{/ View;Arrange}
/Window Zoom	{/ View;Zoom}
Gray + key when using the file options	{/ File;List}

File Manager Menu Equivalent Commands

/Edit All Select	{/ FileMgr;AllMark}
/Edit Copy	{/ FileMgr;Copy}
/Edit Duplicate	{/ FileMgr;Duplicate}
/Edit Erase	{/ FileMgr;Erase}
/Edit Move	{/ FileMgr;Cut}
/Edit Paste	{/ FileMgr;Paste}

Table E.1   Quattro Pro Commands and Menu Equivalent Commands *(continued)*

Quattro Commands	Menu Equivalent
/Edit Rename	{/ FileMgr;Rename}
/Edit Select File	{/ File Mgr;Mark}
/File Close	{/ Basics;Close}
/File Close All	{/ System;TidyUp}
/File Exit	{/ System;Exit}
/File Make Dir	{/ FileMgr;MakeDir}
/File New	{/ View;NewWindow}
/File Open	{/ View;OpenWindow}
/File Read Dir	{/ FileMgr;ReadDir}
/File Utilities DOS Shell	{/ Basics;OS} or {/ Basics;Shell}
/File Utilities File Manager	{/ View;NewFileMgr}
/File Utilities SQZ! Remove Blanks	{/ SQZ;Blanks}
/File Utilities SQZ! Storage of Values	{/ SQZ;Values}
/File Utilities SQZ! Version	{/ SQZ;Version}
/File Workspace Restore	{/ System;RestoreWorkspace}
/File Workspace Save	{/ System;SaveWorkspace}
/Options Beep	{/ Startup;Beep}
/Options Colors: Same as /Options Colors for spreadsheets	
/Options Display Mode	{/ ScreenHardware;TextScreenMode}
/Options File List Full View	{/ FileMgr;Narrow}
/Options File List Wide View	{/ FileMgr;Wide}
/Options Hardware: Same as /Option Hardware for spreadsheets	
/Options Startup Directory Current	{/ FileMgr;CurrDir}
/Options Startup Directory Previous	{/ FileMgr;SameDir}
/Options Startup Edit Menus	{/ MenuBuilder;Run}
/Options Startup Menu Tree	{/ Startup;Menus}
/Options Update	{/ Defaults;Update}

Table E.1   Quattro Pro Commands and Menu Equivalent Commands *(continued)*

Quattro Commands	Menu Equivalent
/Print Adjust Printer Align	{/ FileMgrPrint;Align}
/Print Adjust Printer Form Feed	{/ FileMgrPrint;FormFeed}
/Print Adjust Printer Skip Line	{/ FileMgrPrint;SkipLine}
/Print Block	{/ FileMgrPrint;Block}
/Print Destination File	{/ FileMgrPrint;OutputFile}
/Print Destination Printer	{/ FileMgrPrint;OutputPrinter}
/Print Go	{/ FileMgrPrint;Go}
/Print Page Layout Break Pages	{/ FileMgrPrint;Breaks}
/Print Page Layout Footer	{/ FileMgrPrint;Footer}
/Print Page Layout Header	{/ FileMgrPrint;Header}
/Print Page Layout Margins & Length Bottom	{/ FileMgrPrint;BottomMargin}
/Print Page Layout Margins & Length Left	{/ FileMgrPrint;Left Margin}
/Print Page Layout Margins & Length Page Length	{/ FileMgrPrint;PageLength}
/Print Page Layout Margins & Length Right	{/ FileMgrPrint;RightMargin}
/Print Page Layout Margins & Length Top	{/ FileMgrPrint;TopMargin}
/Print Page Layout Setup String	{/ FileMgrPrint;Setup}
/Print Reset All	{/ FileMgrPrint;ResetAll}
/Print Reset Layout	{/ FileMgrPrint;ResetDefaults}
/Print Reset Print Block	{/ FileMgrPrint;ResetBlock}
/Sort DOS Order	{/ FileMgr;SortNone}
/Sort Extension	{/ FileMgr;SortExt}
/Sort Name	{/ FileMgr;SortName}
/Sort Size	{/ FileMgr;SortSize}
/Sort Timestamp	{/ FileMgr;SortDate}
/Tree Close	{/ FileMgr;TreeClear}
/Tree Open	{/ FileMgr;TreeShow}

Table E.1 Quattro Pro Commands and Menu Equivalent Commands *(continued)*

Quattro Commands	Menu Equivalent
/Tree Resize	{/ FileMgr;TreeSize}
/Window Move/Size	{/ View;Size}
/Window Pick	{/ View;Choose}
/Window Stack	{/ View;Cascade}
/Window Tile	{/ View;Arrange}
/Window Zoom	{/ View;Zoom}

Appendix F

Quattro Pro for Windows Menus

This appendix shows the Quattro Pro menus for each menu item in the menu bar. Next to each command is the chapter number that covers the command in more detail. You can also check Appendix C for a synopsis of the command. This appendix also includes a sample notebook and a sample graph window with the parts of the screen where you can right-click objects to display their Object Inspectors. Use this appendix to find a command you want to use or as a checklist of Quattro Pro's commands that you want to add to your skills.

Notebook Window Commands

File	Edit	Block	Data	Tools	Graph	Property	Window	Help

File Menu	
New	7
Open...	7
Close	7
Save	7
Save As...	7
Retrieve...	7
Save All	7
Close All	7
Print Preview	6
Page Setup...	6
Print...	6
Printer Setup...	6
Named Settings...	6
Workspace	7
Exit	1

Workspace	
Save...	7
Restore...	7

Edit Menu		
Undo		4
Cut	Shift+Del	4
Copy	Ctrl+Ins	4
Paste	Shift+Ins	4
Clear		4
Clear Contents	Del	4
Paste Link		7
Paste Special...		4
Paste Format...		7
Goto...	F5	1
Search and Replace...		5
Define Style...		3
Insert Object...		9

Block Menu	
Move...	4
Copy...	4
Insert	4
Delete	4
Fill...	5
Names	4
Transpose...	4
Values...	4
Reformat...	4
Move Pages...	4
Insert Break	6
Object Order	7

Insert/Delete	
Rows...	4
Columns...	4
Pages...	4
File... *(Insert only)*	4

Names		
Create...	Ctrl+F3	4
Delete...		4
Labels...		4
Reset		4
Make Table...		4

Object Order	
Bring Forward	7
Send Backward	7
Bring to Front	7
Send to Back	7

Data Menu	
Sort...	11
Query...	11
Restrict Input...	11
Parse...	7
What−If...	7
Frequency...	7
Database Desktop...	11
Table Query...	11

Tools Menu	
Macro	13
Define Group...	3
Combine...	7
Extract...	7
Import...	7
Update Links	7
Advanced Math	5
Optimizer...	5
Solve For...	5
UI Builder	12

Macro		
Execute...	Alt+F2	13
Record...		13
Options...		13
Debugger		13

Update Links	
Open Links...	7
Refresh Links...	7
Delete Links...	7
Change Link...	7

Advanced Math	
Regression...	5
Invert...	5
Multiply...	5

Graph Menu		
Type...		9
Series...		9
Titles...		9
New...		9
Edit...		9
Insert...		9
Delete...		10
Copy...		10
View	F11	9
Slide Show...		10

Properties Menu		
Current Object...	F12	3
Application...	ALT+F12	12
Active Notebook	SHIFT+F12	12
Active Page...		3

Windows Menu	
New View	4
Tile	1
Cascade	1
Arrange Icons	1
Hide	4
Show...	4
Panes...	4
Locked Titles...	4
1 NOTEBK1.WB1	1
More Windows...	4

Help		
Contents	F1	1
Screen Areas		1
Keyboard		1
Functions		1
Macros		1
About Quattro Pro...		1

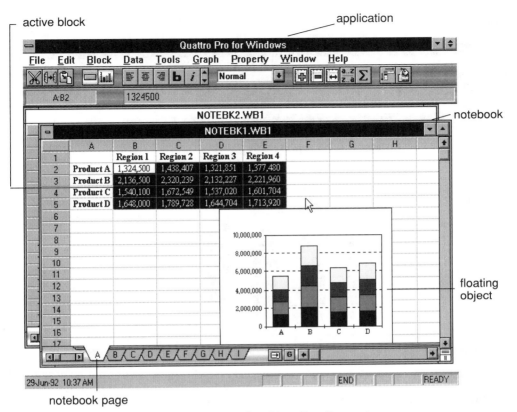

Figure F.1 **Parts of the Notebook That You Can Inspect**

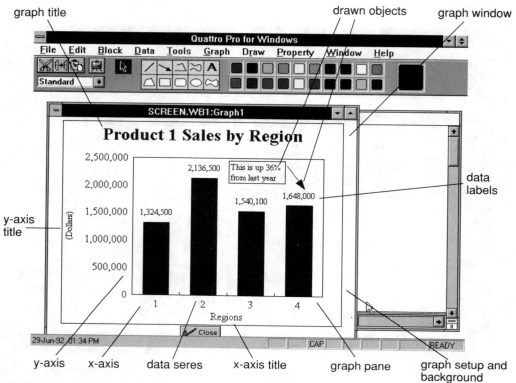

Figure F.2   **Part of the Graph Window That You Can Inspect**

Index